# CRIMINAL PROCEDURE

*Seventh Edition*

JOEL SAMAHA
*University of Minnesota*

WADSWORTH
CENGAGE Learning

Australia • Brazil • Japan • Korea • Mexico • Singapore • Spain • United Kingdom • United States

**Criminal Procedure, Seventh Edition**
**Joel Samaha**

Senior Acquisitions Editor, Criminal Justice:
Carolyn Henderson Meier

Assistant Editor: Meaghan Banks

Marketing Manager: Terra Schultz

Marketing Assistant: Emily Elrod

Marketing Communications Manager:
Tami Strang

Project Manager, Editorial Production:
Jennie Redwitz

Creative Director: Rob Hugel

Art Director: Vernon Boes

Print Buyer: Linda Hsu

Permissions Editor: Bobbie Broyer

Production Service: Ruth Cottrell

Text Designer: Adriane Bosworth

Copy Editor: Lura Harrison

Illustrator: Judith Ogus

Cover Designer: Bill Stanton

Cover Image: Center: iStockphoto. Right:
© Bruce Forster/Getty Images

Compositor: International Typesetting
and Composition

Photos on pages i, 2–3, 20–21, 46–47,
80–81, 148–149, 188–189, 242–243,
272–273, 316–317, 338–339, 372–373,
400–401, 444–445, 468–469, 498–499:
© Adam Mandoki/iStockphoto®.

For product information and technology assistance, contact us at
**Cengage Learning Customer & Sales Support, 1-800-354-9706**

For permission to use material from this text or product,
submit all requests online at **cengage.com/permissions**
Further permissions questions can be e-mailed to
**permissionrequest@cengage.com**

*ExamView*® and *ExamView Pro*® are registered trademarks of FSCreations, Inc. Windows is a registered trademark of the Microsoft Corporation used herein under license. Macintosh and Power Macintosh are registered trademarks of Apple Computer, Inc. Used herein under license.

© 2008 Cengage Learning, Inc. All Rights Reserved. Cengage Learning WebTutor™ is a trademark of Cengage Learning, Inc.

Library of Congress Control Number: 2007929669

ISBN-13: 978-0-495-09546-0

ISBN-10: 0-495-09546-X

**Wadsworth**
10 Davis Drive
Belmont, CA 94002-3098
USA

Cengage Learning is a leading provider of customized learning solutions with office locations around the globe, including Singapore, the United Kingdom, Australia, Mexico, Brazil, and Japan. Locate your local office at: **international.cengage.com/region**

Cengage Learning products are represented in Canada by Nelson Education, Ltd.

For your course and learning solutions, visit **academic.cengage.com**

Purchase any of our products at your local college store or at our-preferred online store **www.ichapters.com**

Printed in the United States of America
2  3  4  5  6  7  11  10  09  08

*For my students, my sons Adam and Luke, and my dear friends Steve and Doug*

# About the Author

Professor **Joel Samaha** teaches Criminal Law, Criminal Procedure, Introduction to Criminal Justice, and The Constitution in Crisis Times at the University of Minnesota. He is both a lawyer and an historian whose primary interest is crime control in a constitutional democracy. He received his B.A., J.D., and Ph.D. from Northwestern University. Professor Samaha also studied under the late Sir Geoffrey Elton at Cambridge University, England.

Professor Samaha was admitted to the Illinois Bar in 1962 and practiced law briefly in Chicago. He taught at UCLA before going to the University of Minnesota in 1971. At the University of Minnesota, he served as Chair of the Department of Criminal Justice Studies from 1974 to 1978. He now teaches and writes full time. He has taught both television and radio courses in criminal justice and has co-taught a National Endowment for the Humanities seminar in legal and constitutional history. He was named the College of Liberal Arts Distinguished Teacher in 1974. In 2007 he was awarded the title of University of Minnesota Morse Alumni Distinguished Teaching Professor and inducted into the Academy of Distinguished Teachers.

In addition to *Law and Order in Historical Perspective* (1974), an analysis of law enforcement in pre-industrial English society, Professor Samaha has transcribed and written a scholarly introduction to a set of local criminal justice records from the reign of Elizabeth I. He has also written several articles on the history of criminal justice, published in the *Historical Journal, The American Journal of Legal History, Minnesota Law Review, William Mitchell Law Review*, and *Journal of Social History*. In addition to *Criminal Procedure*, he has written two other textbooks, *Criminal Law* in its ninth edition, and *Criminal Justice* in its seventh edition.

# Brief Contents

# Contents

# 15 Criminal Procedure in Crisis Times    498

# APPENDIX: Selected Amendments of the Constitution of the United States    527

# Glossary    529

# Bibliography    541

# Case Index    549

# Index    555

# Preface

Balancing the power of government to enforce the criminal law against the rights of individuals to come and go as they please without government interference is the central problem in the law of criminal procedure in a constitutional democracy. It's also the heart of *Criminal Procedure 7*. It's a problem that always fascinates my students, stimulates them to think, and provokes them to discuss it not only in class but also with their friends and family outside class. (Of course, it's also a topic that's of special concern since September 11, 2001.) I'm not surprised.

The balance between government power and individual rights has fascinated me since 1958 when I was lucky enough to study criminal procedure at Northwestern University Law School under the sparkling Claude R. Sowle and the legendary Fred E. Inbau. Professor Sowle, a brilliant advocate and a distinguished teacher, emphasized the philosophical underpinnings of the law of criminal procedure. Professor Inbau, a famous interrogator and a highly respected student of the law of interrogation, spoke from the 1930s right up to his death in the late 1990s with the authority of one who has actually applied abstract principles to everyday police practices.

In 1968, I began work on what would eventually become my *Law and Order in Historical Perspective*, a reconstruction of the criminal process in 16th-century England. In 1971, I taught criminal procedure for the first time. I've done so ever since. My students have included undergraduates, graduate students, and law students. That many of these students are now police officers and administrators; corrections officers and administrators; criminal defense attorneys, prosecutors, and judges; and legislators testifies to their enduring interest in the law of criminal procedure and to their commitment to the application of formal law to informal real-life decision making.

*Criminal Procedure 7*, like its predecessors, reflects my conviction that the best way to learn the law of criminal procedure is to understand general principles and critically examine the application of these principles to real problems. By "critically," I don't mean "negatively"; *Criminal Procedure* doesn't "bash the system." Rather, it examines and weighs the principles that govern the balance between government power and individual life, liberty, privacy, and property. It tests the weight of strong, honest feelings about this balance in the bright light of reason, logic, and facts. *Criminal Procedure* proceeds on the assumptions that the general principles governing the balance between government power and individual rights have real meaning only in the context of a specific reality, and that reality makes sense only when seen in the light of general principles applied to specific facts in particular circumstances.

# BALANCING CONFLICTING INTERESTS

*Criminal Procedure* is organized according to the central theme of balancing conflicting interests. First, the law of criminal procedure balances the interest in obtaining the correct result in particular cases against the interest in upholding a fair process in all cases. This balancing of result and process reflects the struggle to answer the timeless question of whether the ends justify the means. In criminal procedure, the ends refer to the correct result in the case at hand; the means refer to the process by which to obtain the correct result. The law of criminal procedure recognizes the importance of obtaining the correct result—namely, the ends of both convicting the guilty and freeing the innocent. But the law of criminal procedure also promotes the value of enforcing the law according to fair procedures. In other words, in the law of criminal procedure the ends don't justify the means. In fact, when forced to choose, the framers of our constitutional system decided that the means of fair procedures trump the ends of correct results. Or, to put it another way, ensuring fair proceedings for all people is more important than convicting even one guilty person by unfair means.

This balance depends on two requirements: (1) facts, not hunches, to back up official decisions affecting the rights of individuals caught up in the criminal justice system and (2) hearing before condemnation.

## Facts, Not Hunches

Hunches or whims aren't enough to back up government invasions and deprivations of liberty, privacy, and property. The U.S. Constitution and the constitutions of the states demand that the government back up all invasions of liberty, privacy, and property with facts in the light of the totality of the circumstances surrounding the particular invasion and/or deprivation.

No police officer can justify detaining a person merely by claiming that she had a "hunch" that something was wrong. The greater the invasion, the more facts and circumstances government officers have to produce to back up their invasions. So to detain a person briefly on the street, police officers need only a few facts and circumstances that create a "reasonable suspicion" that a crime may be afoot. But to convict defendants and send them to prison, the government has to prove they're guilty "beyond a reasonable doubt." This reliance on facts in the light of the totality of the surrounding circumstances (objective basis or quantum of proof) to back up government action lies at the heart of our constitutional democracy.

## Hearing Before Condemnation

"A law that hears before it condemns" is the foundation of our constitutional system, said the great 19th-century lawyer Daniel Webster. A law that "hears before it condemns" is a law that deprives persons of life, liberty, privacy, and property only according to fair procedures. In the case of invasions before conviction, courts review street stops and frisks, arrests, searches, interrogations, and the conduct of identification procedures. In the case of conviction, courts are required to "hear" cases, either by trials or by approving guilty pleas, before defendants are "condemned." This review by courts, known as *judicial review,* is an essential element of our legal system.

# TEXT AND CASES

*Criminal Procedure* is and has always been a text-case book, meaning that it contains both text and excerpts of actual court opinions that apply the general principles discussed in the text to concrete cases. The text and case excerpts complement each other. The text enriches the understanding of the cases, while the cases enhance the understanding of the text. The cases aren't just examples, illustrations, or attention grabbers; they explain, clarify, elaborate, and apply the general principles and constitutional provisions to real-life situations. Moreover, the cases are excellent tools for developing the critical thinking skills of students of all levels.

The cases and the text are independent enough of each other that they can stand alone. They are set off clearly from each other in design (the text appears in a one-column format; edited cases appear in shaded two columns). This separation of text from cases allows instructors who favor the case analysis approach to emphasize cases over text, leaving the text for students to read if they need to in order to understand the cases. Instructors who favor the text approach can focus on the text, allowing students to read the cases as enrichment or as examples of the principles, constitutional provisions, and rules discussed in the text.

The case excerpts are edited for nonlawyers to supply students with a full statement of the facts of the case; the court's application of the law to the facts of the case; key portions of the reasoning of the court; and its decision. Excerpts also contain portions of the dissenting opinions and, when appropriate, parts of the concurring opinions.

A case question at the beginning of the case focuses on the main principle of the case. The case history gives a brief procedural history of the case. And the questions at the end of the case excerpts test whether students know the facts of the case, whether they understand the law of the case, and whether they comprehend the application of the law to the facts of the case. The questions also supply the basis for developing critical thinking skills, not to mention provoking exciting class discussions on the legal, ethical, and policy issues raised by the edited case.

## The "Exploring Further" Feature

This feature provides examples of how the interpretation and application of the principle of the main case excerpt can vary, depending on the facts of each case and the interpretation by courts. By exploring such variations, this feature reinforces and deepens students' understanding of the law of criminal procedure while also prompting them to think critically about the practical application of these procedures to real life.

# NEW AND ENHANCED FEATURES IN *CRIMINAL PROCEDURE 7*

*New Cases* A number of new cases and many re-edited existing cases appear in *Criminal Procedure 7*. I added, replaced, and re-edited cases for three reasons. First, I wanted to reflect new developments in the law since the last edition. Second, I included cases I've found since the last edition that explain the law better and apply the law to the facts in clearer and more interesting ways for students. Third, experiences through actual use in the classroom led me to re-edit some cases.

*Streamlining* I've worked especially hard to streamline the case excerpts and the text throughout. The result is a shift from excerpts making up the largest proportion of the book to more text. The result is that descriptions, explanations, and analyses of the law have expanded.

*Empirical Research* Recent editions of *Criminal Procedure* have included some of the rich social science research explaining and evaluating criminal procedures. This edition has included more of this research, sometimes highlighting it in special sections.

*Criminal Procedure in Crisis Times* The coverage in Chapter 15 of the procedural changes enacted in the revisions to the USA Patriot Act, other legislation, military tribunals, and the latest U.S. Supreme Court cases applying these laws builds on the broad and enduring theme of criminal procedure stressed in the previous chapters—the problem of balancing the power of government and the rights of individuals in a constitutional democracy. The chapter stresses the need for recalibration of the balance during emergencies and then applies this general recalibration to the specific readjustments made (and still being made) since September 11, 2001, to provide for national security.

# ORGANIZATION AND CHAPTER-BY-CHAPTER REVISIONS

*Criminal Procedure 7*, like its predecessors, is based on the assumption that thinking critically about criminal procedure requires an understanding of the structure and process of the law and the practice of criminal procedure in a constitutional democracy.

## Chapter 1, Crime Control in a Constitutional Democracy

Chapter 1 is a road map for students' journeys through the criminal process in our U.S. version of constitutional democracy.

> *New Section* Equality as a basic value and a constitutional requirement in the law of criminal procedure

## Chapter 2, Criminal Procedure and the Constitution

Chapter 2 covers the basic constitutional principles that govern the whole of the criminal process, mainly due process and equal protection of the law. An understanding of these principles is a necessary prerequisite to understanding and thinking critically about the content in the rest of the book.

> *Expanded Coverage* The role and importance of the U.S. Supreme Court in making and interpreting criminal procedure law

## Chapters 3 through 7

Chapters 3 through 7 describe and critically examine searches and seizures. Government searches and seizures affect far more people than any other criminal procedure. Probably as a result of both this disproportionate effect and the complicated business of applying it in real life, there are more search and seizure cases than any other type in the law of criminal procedure and in *Criminal Procedure*.

## Chapter 3, The Definition of Searches and Seizures

Chapter 3 describes and analyzes two questions: When is a government action a search? When is a government action a seizure?

*New Section* Empirical findings on Fourth Amendment seizures

*Expanded Coverage*

- The privacy doctrine
- The plain view doctrine
- The importance of *U.S. v. Mendenhall, Florida v. Royer,* and *Florida v. Bostick* on the constitutional meaning of seizures in the context of airports and bus stations

*New Case Excerpt Illinois v. Caballes* (2005). The use of drug-sniffing dogs

## Chapter 4, Stop and Frisk

Chapter 4 describes and critically examines the myriad brief encounters between police and individuals that take place on the street.

*New Sections*

- Stops and "high crime"; "known for drug trafficking" neighborhoods
- Seizure of contraband during frisks

*Expanded Coverage* When stops empower officers to frisk automatically

*New Case Excerpts*

- *Adams v. Williams* (1972). Expansion of the power to stop and frisk
- *U.S. v. Cortez* (1981). Definition of reasonable suspicion to stop
- *U.S. v. Brignoni-Ponce* (1975). Race and ethnicity as building blocks for reasonable suspicion
- *Minnesota v. Dickerson* (1993). Discovery of drugs during frisk for weapons

## Chapter 5, Seizure of Persons: Arrest

Chapter 5 examines arrest, the Fourth Amendment seizure that consists of taking suspects into custody, usually by taking them to the police station. When is a detention an arrest? What amounts to probable cause? What is the proper manner of arrest?

*Expanded Coverage* Use of new technologies to arrest suspects and more discussion of traditional methods, such as tight handcuffing behind the back

*New Case Excerpts*

- *U.S. v. Watson* (1976). Landmark case authorizing an arrest without a warrant
- *Kuha v. Minnetonka* (2003). Police dog "bite and hold" as reasonable force to arrest DWI suspect
- *Hedgepeth v. Washington Metropolitan Transit Authority* (2003). Full-custody arrest for eating a french fry in a subway station (Exploring Further excerpt)

*New Graphic* Use of force cases, for example, dog "bite and hold," pepper spray, lead-filled "bean bag rounds," Taser (stun gun)

# Chapter 6, Searches for Evidence

Chapter 6 covers searches for evidence, both with and without warrants. It examines when warrants are required, the exceptions to the warrant requirement, and the manner in which searches are conducted.

*New Sections*

- Exceptions to the knock-and-announce rule
- Occupants' failure to respond to officers' announcement
- Empirical research on consent searches
- Searches of containers in vehicles

*New Case Excerpts*

- *U.S. v. Banks* (2003). Ten-second wait after officers' knock and announce found reasonable by U.S. Supreme Court
- *U.S. v. Gray* (2004). Withdrawing consent to search part way through the search was valid—officer should have stopped the search
- *Georgia v. Randolph* (2006). Third-party consent. Spouse can overrule other spouse's consent to search their house (Exploring Further excerpt)

# Chapter 7, Special-Needs Searches

Chapter 7 describes special-needs searches that go beyond ordinary law enforcement, including inventory searches, student searches, employee drug testing, searches of prison visitors, and searching college students' dorm rooms.

*New Sections*

- DNA testing and storing of prisoners' DNA
- High school student drug testing

*New Case Excerpts*

- *Colorado v. Bertine* (1987). Landmark U.S. Supreme Court inventory search case
- *Samson v. California* (2006). U.S. Supreme Court held that parolee serving time in community can be searched by police officer without probable cause or warrant
- *Board of Education v. Earls* (2002). U.S. Supreme Court upheld "suspicionless urinalysis" for "all students who participate in competitive extracurricular activities"

# Chapter 8, Self-Incrimination

Chapter 8 covers police interrogation and confessions and the right to remain silent.

*New Sections*

- Nature and role of confessions
- False confessions and recording interrogations
- The meaning of interrogation

*New Case Excerpts*

- *Brewer v. Williams* (1977). Famous "Christian burial speech" that elicited confession used to convict defendant upheld by landmark U.S. Supreme Court interrogation and confession case
- *Moran v. Burbine* (1986). Landmark U.S. Supreme Court case regarding waiver of right to remain silent

## Chapter 9, Identification Procedures

Chapter 9 describes police identification procedures, including lineups, "mug shots," and DNA testing and discusses the need for, the fairness of, and the reliability of interrogation and identification procedures to obtain the truth.

> *Restructured Section* "Memory and Mistaken Identification" is now divided into the three subsections acquisition, retention, and retrieval, rather than type of procedure (namely, lineup, show-up, and photograph)

> *New Graphic* Empirical support for Supreme Court's five-factor test of lineup, show-up, and "mug shot" identification procedures

## Chapter 10, Remedies for Constitutional Violations I: The Exclusionary Rule and Entrapment and Chapter 11, Constitutional Violations II: Other Remedies against Official Misconduct

These two chapters critically examine the remedies against the government when officials violate the constitutional rights discussed in Chapters 3 through 9. Chapter 10 focuses on process remedies, examining the main process remedy, the exclusionary rule, as well as entrapment.

Chapter 11 concentrates on the right to sue the government for the injuries that result from constitutional violations and other illegal official actions. Both chapters invite students to think critically about the nature, value, and purposes of the various remedies against mistakes and misconduct by government officials in the enforcement, prosecution, and disposition of criminal laws.

> *Streamlining* Case excerpts edited to rebalance the edition toward more text and fewer excerpts

## Chapter 12, Court Proceedings I: Before Trial and Chapter 13, Court Proceedings II: Trial and Conviction

These two chapters cover court proceedings before trial (the decision to charge, bail, and the right to counsel) and disposition by trial and by guilty plea.

> *Reorganization* Court proceedings are divided into two parts: Chapter 12, court proceedings before trial, and Chapter 13, court proceedings during case dispositions by trial or guilty plea

## Chapter 14, After Conviction

Chapter 14 examines proceedings following conviction (sentencing, appeal, and habeas corpus).

> *Major New Section* "Trial Rights at Sentencing"—the highly controversial Supreme Court decisions that might end federal and state sentencing guidelines laws

> *Major Revised Section* Proportionality requirement in cruel and unusual punishment

> *New Cases*

> - *Ewing v. California* (2003). Three-strikes law: Gary Ewing sentenced to 25 years to life for stealing three golf clubs—"cruel and unusual punishment"?

- *Blakely v. Washington* (2004). Struck down part of Washington State's sentencing guidelines statute and sent shock waves throughout the states with sentencing guidelines statutes

*New Graphic* "Major Supreme Court Sentencing Rights Cases" summarizes the major cases behind all the sentencing rights hullabaloo: *Apprendi v. New Jersey* (2000); *Harris v. U.S.* (2002); *Blakely v. Washington* (2004); *U.S. v. Booker* (2005)

## Chapter 15, Criminal Procedure in Crisis Times

Chapter 15 examines the effects of 9/11 on criminal procedure.

*Major Updates*

- Detention of terrorist suspects
- Trial of terrorist suspects in military courts
- Stripping regular courts of jurisdiction in terrorist cases until final decisions by military courts; includes analysis of the Detainee Treatment Act of 2005

*New Sections*

- "USA Patriot Act 'Libraries Provision,'" discussing the reenactment of the controversial § 215, the so-called libraries provision, which doesn't mention libraries and involves only a handful of cases dealing with libraries
- "National Security Agency 'Terrorist Surveillance Program (TSP),'" focusing on the use of warrantless eavesdropping of U.S. citizens' phone calls and e-mails for the purpose of gathering intelligence if one party might be communicating with al Qaeda or groups associated with al Qaeda. Describes the details behind the hullabaloo over not going to the secret court established by the Foreign Intelligence Surveillance Act to review spying for the purpose of gathering intelligence. Also covers the abrupt elimination of the TSP on January 18, 2007
- "Torture during Detention" includes discussion contrasting the constitutionality of admitting evidence of coerced confessions for criminal conviction with coercion not intended for prosecution but used instead to obtain information to prevent a terrorist attack

*New Statute* Military Commissions Act (MCA) of 2006, in which Congress accepted the Court's invitation to overrule *Hamdan v. Rumsfeld*. Highlights the main provisions of the act, including trial rights of terrorist suspects, sentencing, punishment, and review of military courts. Gives the president most of what he asked for in controlling alien terrorist suspects

*New Case Excerpt Hamdan v. Rumsfeld* (2006). Challenge by Osama bin Laden's driver of the constitutionality of having a military commission try him for war crimes. Supreme Court upheld the challenge but invited Congress to change the law on habeas corpus review of military trials before they're heard

# PEDAGOGICAL AIDS

However it's organized and presented, the law of criminal procedure is a complicated subject that embraces a lot of technical concepts. I've tried to help students work through these complexities, primarily by writing clear, direct prose. But there are special features as well. Each chapter contains an **Outline** and a list of the **Main Points**. I've also boldfaced **key terms** in the text, which appear in a list at the end of each chapter as well as in the **Glossary** at the end of the book. The **Summary** in each chapter includes the chapter's content in detailed outline form. **Review Questions** at the end of each chapter provide a good test of whether students have identified and understood the main points in the chapter.

Students frequently comment that the combination of the Outline and the Main Points at the beginning of the chapter tell them what they should look for as they read and that the Summary, Key Terms, and Review Questions at the end of each chapter tell them whether they have found and understood what they looked for.

# MEETING THE NEEDS OF A VARIETY OF CLASS DESIGNS

Some criminal procedure courses and many criminal procedure texts (particularly those designed for undergraduates) cover only the law of arrest, search and seizure, interrogation, and identification procedures. In other words, these courses and texts focus on police practices during the contacts between individuals and the police on the street and at the police station. They usually cover the constitutional framework of criminal procedure, and they sometimes include discussions of the exclusionary rule. *Criminal Procedure 7* lends itself to this type of course because instructors can use Chapters 3 through 9, which can stand alone, without covering either Chapters 1 and 2, on the general principles and constitutional provisions, or Chapters 10 and 11, on remedies for illegal official conduct. Instructors who want to teach the exclusionary rule and the constitutional provisions can add Chapter 2, on criminal procedure and the Constitution, and Chapter 10, which covers the exclusionary rule.

*Criminal Procedure 7* is also suitable for courses that cover the entire criminal process, from the early encounters between individuals and the police on the street to procedures following conviction. And, for students in courses covering only police practices, Chapters 1, 2, and 10 through 15 should fill the gap if they want to read about the other subjects covered in the study of the law of criminal procedure.

# SUPPLEMENTS

An extensive package of supplemental aids accompanies this edition of *Criminal Procedure*. Supplements are available to qualified adopters. Please consult your local sales representative for details.

## For the Instructor

*Instructor's Resource Manual* The fully updated and revised *Instructor's Resource Manual* for this edition includes learning objectives, key terms with definitions, chapter outlines, chapter summaries, discussion topics, lecture suggestions, and recommended readings, as well as a complete test bank. Each chapter's test bank contains approximately seventy multiple-choice, true-false, fill-in-the-blank, and essay questions, which are coded according to difficulty level; a full answer key is included. Each question in the test bank has been carefully reviewed by experienced criminal justice instructors for quality, accuracy, and content coverage. Our Instructor Approved seal, which appears on the front cover, is our assurance that you're working with an assessment and grading resource of the highest caliber.

*ExamView® Computerized Testing* The comprehensive *Instructor's Resource Manual* described above is backed up by ExamView, a computerized test bank available for PC and Mac computers. With this easy-to-use assessment and tutorial system, you can create, deliver, and customize tests and study guides (both print and online) in minutes. You can easily edit and import your own questions and graphics, change test layouts, and reorganize questions. And using ExamView's complete word-processing capabilities, you can enter an unlimited number of new questions or edit existing questions.

*WebTutor™ ToolBox on Blackboard® and WebCT®* A powerful combination: ToolBox is an easy-to-use course management tool for whichever program you use—WebCT or Blackboard—with content from this text's rich companion website, all in one place. You can use ToolBox as is, from the moment you log on—or, if you prefer, customize the program with web links, images, and other resources.

*The Wadsworth Criminal Justice Video Library* So many exciting new videos—so many great ways to enrich your lectures and spark discussion of the material in this text! A list of our unique and expansive video program follows. Or visit www.thomsonedu.com/ criminaljustice/media_center for a complete, up-to-the-minute list of all of Wadsworth's video offerings (many of which are also available in DVD format), as well as clip lists and running times.

The library includes these selections and many others:

- *ABC® Videos.* Featuring short, high-interest clips from current news events specially developed for courses, including "Introduction to Criminal Justice," "Criminology," "Corrections," "Terrorism," and "White-Collar Crime," these videos are perfect for use as discussion starters, lecture launchers, or to spark student interest. The brief video clips provide students with a new lens through which to view the past and present, one that will greatly enhance their knowledge and understanding of significant events and open up to them new dimensions in learning. Clips are drawn from such programs as *World News Tonight, Good Morning America, This Week, PrimeTime Live, 20/20,* and *Nightline,* as well as numerous ABC News specials and material from the Associated Press Television News and British Movietone News collections.

- *The Wadsworth Custom Videos for Criminal Justice.* Produced by Wadsworth and Films for the Humanities, these videos include short (5- to 10-minute) segments that encourage classroom discussion. Topics include white-collar crime, domestic violence, forensics, suicide and the police officer, the court process, the history of corrections, prison society, and juvenile justice.

- *Court TV Videos.* These one-hour videos present seminal and high-profile cases, such as the interrogation of Michael Crowe and serial killer Ted Bundy, as well as crucial and current issues, such as cybercrime, double jeopardy, and the management of the prison on Riker's Island.

- *A&E American Justice.* With 40 videos to choose from, select among topics such as deadly force, women on death row, juvenile justice, strange defenses, and Alcatraz.

- *Films for the Humanities.* With nearly two hundred videos, choose from a variety of topics, such as elder abuse, supermax prisons, suicide and the police officer, the making of an FBI agent, domestic violence, and more.

- *Oral History Project.* Developed in association with the American Society of Criminology, the Academy of Criminal Justice Society, and the National Institute of

Justice, these videos will help you introduce your students to the scholars who have developed the criminal justice discipline. Compiled over the last several years, each video features a set of guest lecturers: scholars whose thinking has helped to build the foundation of present ideas in the discipline.

## The Wadsworth Criminal Justice Resource Center

*academic.cengage.com/criminaljustice* Designed with the instructor in mind, this website features information about the technology and teaching solutions of Wadsworth, a part of Cengage Learning, as well as several features created specifically for today's criminal justice student. Supreme Court updates, timelines, and hot-topic polling can all be used to supplement in-class assignments and discussions. You'll also find a wealth of links to careers and news in criminal justice, book-specific sites, and much more.

## For the Student

*Companion Website* Based on the author's own use, comments from students at the University of Minnesota, and feedback from adopters of *Criminal Procedure*'s previous editions, the website contains the following components for each chapter:

- *Chapter Summaries in Detailed Outline Form.* The outlined chapter summaries have been included, so students can expand them by adding their own notes from class, their reading assignments, and so on. Encouraging students to build their own outline can help them study and review.

- *Assignments.* Instructors may use a variety of assignments either as required work or for extra credit enrichment. The assignments allow for more in-depth learning and critical thinking about balances in the law of criminal procedure as it operates in a constitutional democracy. Each assignment asks specific questions about the statutes, cases, and other sources and includes specific instructions on how to find the materials included in the assignments.

- *Exploring Further Cases.* Full case reports of all case excerpts in the Exploring Further features are included.

- *Review Questions.* All end-of-chapter Review Questions are included.

- *The U.S. Constitution.* A complete version of the U.S. Constitution is provided. Complete versions of the Fourth, Fifth, Sixth, Eighth, and Fourteenth Amendments are included in the Appendix for easy access.

- *Rest of the Story.* Putting the people back in "We the People"—this is how Professor Michael Dorf introduces *Constitutional Law Stories* (2004). The "Rest of the Story" feature is my effort to put the people back into a few of the leading criminal procedure cases. The feature demonstrates that the cases involve real people; they don't just decide an impersonal legal principle. Students frequently want to get beyond the confines of the case excerpt; they wonder what happened to criminals and their victims before, during, and after the crime, and they even want to know what they looked like.

  It's impossible to present this information in most cases, but I've been able to do it for five case excerpts: the historic forced confession case of *Brown v. Mississippi* (Chapter 2); the landmark U.S. Supreme Court stop-and-frisk case *Terry v. Ohio* (Chapter 4); the famous *Miranda v. Arizona* (Chapter 8); the landmark case of

*Mapp v. Ohio* on the exclusionary rule (Chapter 10); and another landmark case, *Gideon v. Wainwright* (Chapter 12).

- *State Constitutional Law.* This includes cases where states have interpreted their own constitution's criminal procedure rights to raise the minimum required by the U.S. Bill of Rights.

***Handbook of Selected Supreme Court Cases, Third Edition*** This supplementary handbook covers almost forty landmark cases, each of which includes a full case citation, an introduction, a summary from WestLaw, excerpts from the case, and the decision. The updated edition includes *Hamdi v. Rumsfeld, Roper v. Simmons, Ring v. Arizona, Atkins v. Virginia, Illinois v. Caballes,* and much more.

# ACKNOWLEDGMENTS

*Criminal Procedure 7* didn't get here by my efforts alone; I had a lot of help. I am grateful for all those who have provided feedback over the years and as always, I'm particularly indebted to the reviewers of this edition:

Robert Edwards, Champlain College

Steven Gilbert, SUNY Canton

Ronald Server, Prairie View A&M University

Don Wallace, Central Missouri State University

Criminal Justice Editor Carolyn Henderson Meier has helped me at every stage of the book. Jennie Redwitz ironed out all kinds of rough spots along the way. The book also benefited yet one more time from Lura Harrison's painstaking copy editing. Ruth Cottrell's calm efficiency, warm kindnesses, careful editing, and extraordinary patience were as welcome and necessary as they have been in earlier editions.

What would I do without Doug and Steve? Doug takes me there and gets me here and everywhere, day in and day out, days that now have stretched into years. And my old and dear friend Steve, who from the days when he watched over my kids to now decades later when he keeps the Irish Wolfhounds, the Siamese cat, the Standard Poodle, me, and a lot more around here in order. And they do it all while putting up with what my beloved mentor at Cambridge, Sir Geoffrey Elton, called "Joel's mercurial temperament." Only those who really know me can understand how I can try the patience of Job! Friends and associates like these have made *Criminal Procedure 7* whatever success it enjoys. As for its faults, I claim total ownership.

JOEL SAMAHA
*Minneapolis*

# CRIMINAL PROCEDURE

# Crime Control in a Constitutional Democracy

## MAIN POINTS

- Our constitutional democracy balances the need to provide for the public's safety against other equally important values—individual liberty, privacy, and dignity.
- In a constitutional democracy, neither a single dictator nor an overwhelming majority of the people has total power over us as individuals.
- Criminal procedure balances the aim of getting the right result (catch the guilty and free the innocent) in each case with guaranteeing a fair process in all cases.
- The decisions of the Warren Court during the 1960s, dubbed as the "due process revolution," sought to expand defendants' rights and impose the expansion on state criminal justice.
- Balancing values in emergencies, especially during the "war" on drugs and the war on "terror," has tested the right amount of community security and individual autonomy.
- Equal justice has been a major theme in the law of criminal procedure since the adoption, after the Civil War, of the Fourteenth Amendment, guaranteeing "equal protection of the law."
- Criminal procedure in practice blends the formal law of criminal procedure and informal influences that enter the process by way of discretion.
- The agents of crime control aren't free to do whatever they please. They need an objective basis for their actions; subjective "hunches" and "mere suspicion" aren't enough.
- The trump card of fair procedures is the power to ban the use of illegally obtained evidence to prove the guilt of defendants.
- The ancient ideas of precedent and stare decisis contribute to stable and predictable decision making.

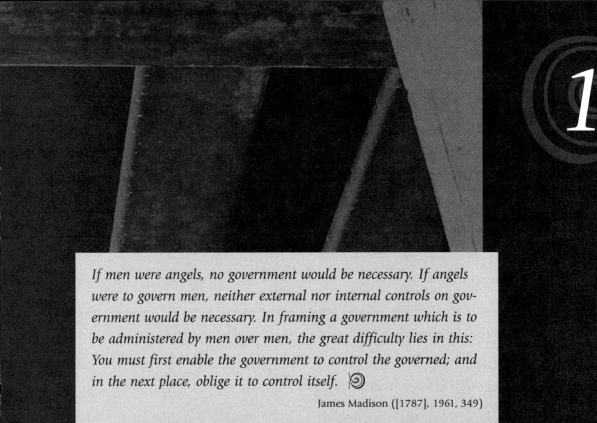

*If men were angels, no government would be necessary. If angels were to govern men, neither external nor internal controls on government would be necessary. In framing a government which is to be administered by men over men, the great difficulty lies in this: You must first enable the government to control the governed; and in the next place, oblige it to control itself.*

James Madison ([1787], 1961, 349)

I f we lived in a police state, officials could break into our houses in the dead of night and shoot us in our beds based on nothing more than the whim of the current dictator. If we lived in a *pure* democracy, the majority who won the last election could authorize the police to shoot anyone who they had a hunch was a street gang member. But we live in a **constitutional democracy**, where neither a single dictator nor an overwhelming majority of the people has total power over us as individuals. Our constitutional democracy balances the need to provide for the public's safety and security against other equally important values—individual liberty, privacy, and dignity.

In the U.S. version of constitutional democracy, a majority of the people's elected representatives have wide latitude to *create* criminal laws that define criminal behavior and punishment. But in *enforcing* the criminal law, officials are much more restricted by the law of criminal procedure. *Criminal Procedure 7* takes you on a journey through the law of criminal procedure (Figure 1.1 on page 6): from police investigation of suspicious behavior on the streets and other public places; then to detention and further investigation at not-so-public police stations; next to trials and sentencing in trial courts; and finally to review of convictions in courts of appeals.

In our *federal* form of constitutional democracy, local and state officials have a monopoly on these day-to-day operations. The law of criminal procedure that controls their monopoly is mostly *constitutional* law. Most constitutional law in the United States is made by judges, and published in the reports of their decisions. Specifically, we're referring here to U.S. Supreme Court cases, which you're going to be reading a lot of in this book. According to respected experts, Supreme Court justices are the "primary generators of rules for regulating the behavior of police, prosecutors, and the other actors who administer the criminal process" (Allen, Hoffman, Livingston, and Stuntz 2005, 77). One distinguished federal judge called the Supreme Court's opinions interpreting the Bill of Rights—the part of the Constitution where most of these rules originate—a national "code of criminal procedure" (Friendly 1965, 929).

This code of criminal procedure gives government officials the power to protect public safety by enforcing the criminal law. But, at the same time, it also limits that power by guaranteeing the fair and equal administration of criminal justice to everybody, including criminal suspects, defendants, and convicted offenders. All the specific rules made by the Supreme Court spring from two clauses in the Fourteenth Amendment to the U.S. Constitution: "Due process of law" guarantees fairness, and "equal protection of the laws" guarantees equality.

U.S. Supreme Court justices don't make all criminal procedure law. States are free to rely on their own state constitutions to raise minimum operating procedures established by the U.S. Supreme Court. (You'll learn about some other sources later in this chapter and scattered throughout the remaining chapters.) Finally, and this is very important, judge-made law leaves plenty of "play in the joints" for criminal justice professionals to exercise discretionary decision making. This, too, we'll discuss later in this chapter, and throughout the remainder of the book, where you'll discover just how important discretion is in the day-to-day operation of the criminal process.

 Go to Exercise 1.1 on the Samaha Criminal Procedure 7e website to learn more about the Bill of Rights as a code of criminal procedure and to Exercise 1.2 on the Samaha Criminal Procedure 7e website to learn more about your state's code of criminal procedure: academic.cengage.com/criminaljustice/samaha.

# BALANCING VALUES IN CRIMINAL PROCEDURE

At the heart of our constitutional democracy is the idea of balancing values, balances between values we believe essential to the quality of life. Let's look at two sets of these values: first, balances between community security and individual autonomy and then between ends and means. Next, we'll look at the history of balancing values in our society and at what happens to that balance during national emergencies.

## Community Security and Individual Autonomy

The objective of community security is a community where we're safe, or at least where we *feel* safe. Our lives are safe from murder; our bodies are safe from rape and other assaults; our homes are safe from burglars, arsonists, and trespassers; our secrets are safe from exposure; and our "stuff" is safe from thieves and vandals.

Individual autonomy means individuals control their own lives. They can come and go as they please; develop their body and mind as they wish to do; believe whatever or whomever they want to believe; worship any god they like; associate with anybody they choose to be with; and do whatever else they wish to do in the privacy of their own homes (assuming that they're competent adults and what they want to do doesn't include committing crimes that violate the community's or other persons' safety against their will). In other words, they can't tip the balance between community security and individual autonomy in their favor whenever and however they want.

Weighed on one side of the balance is the amount of government power needed to control crime for everybody's safety and security. Weighed on the other side is the amount of control individuals have over their own lives. James Madison (see the passage quoted in the chapter opener) and others who wrote and adopted the U.S. Constitution in the 1700s were realists. They accepted human nature for what it is: People aren't angels. Left to do as they please, ordinary individuals will break the law. And, because they're people, too, government officials left to do as they please will abuse their power. So the Founders expected excesses from both ordinary people and government officials who live in a real world inhabited by imperfect people. Let me be clear right at the beginning of our journey through the criminal process: I subscribe to Madison's view of human nature and the world.

A few words of caution: Because both community security and individual autonomy are equally important, striking the balance between them is difficult, and where it's

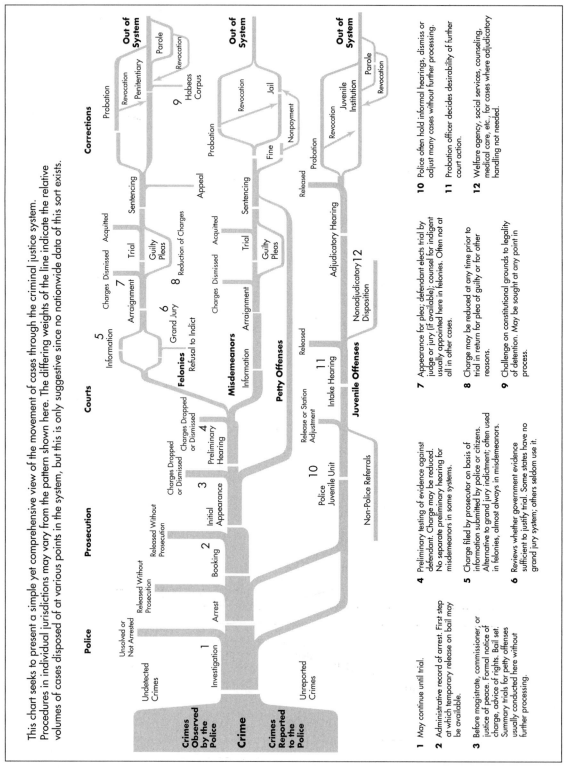

**FIGURE 1.1** A General View of the Criminal Justice System

struck never satisfies anyone completely. The late U.S. Supreme Court Chief Justice William Rehnquist (1974) expressed the challenge this way:

> Throughout the long history of political theory and the development of constitutional law in our country, the most difficult cases to decide have been those in which two competing values, each able to marshal respectable claims on its behalf, meet in a contest in which one must prevail over the other. (1)

Another important point: The balance between crime control and individual rights is flexible. Where exactly the balance is struck shifts, depending on the circumstances. Put another way, the right balance falls within a zone; it's not a point on the spectrum between total control and total freedom (*Llaguno v. Mingey* 1985, 1565). The most extreme examples are emergencies, especially wartime. As one lawyer prosecuting suspected disloyalists during the Civil War put it (I'm paraphrasing here), "During wartime the Bill of Rights is put to sleep. We'll wake it up when the emergency passes" (Gayarré 1903, 601). But it's not just during emergencies such as wars that we'll see the balance struck in various places in the zone. We'll see many examples where courts move around in the zone between order and liberty.

## Ends and Means

The quality of life also depends on a second balance of values—between ends and means. Or, to be more precise, the balance between result and process. In criminal procedure, the "ends" side of the balance consists of the search for the truth to obtain the correct result in individual cases. The correct result has two dimensions: (1) catching, convicting, and punishing guilty people and (2) freeing as soon as possible, innocent people caught up in government efforts to control crime. Keep in mind these words of the late Professor Jerome Hall (1942) as we make our journey through the law of criminal procedure:

> [Criminal law's] ultimate ends are dual and conflicting. It must be designed from inception to end to acquit the innocent as readily as to convict the guilty. This presents the inescapable dilemma of criminal procedure . . . that the easier it is made to prove guilt, the more difficult it becomes to establish innocence. (728)

At the "means" end of the end-means balance is the commitment to fairness in dealing with suspects, defendants, and offenders. In our constitutional democracy, we don't believe in catching, convicting, and punishing criminals *at any price.* According to one court, "Truth, like all other good things, may be loved unwisely, may be pursued too keenly, may cost too much" (*Pearce v. Pearce* 1846, 63 ER 950, 957). The U.S. Constitution and provisions in every state constitution limit public officials' power to control crime (see Chapter 2, "Due Process of Law" and "Equal Protection of the Law").

Balancing ends and means creates an uncomfortable tension. The rules that protect everybody against government abuses of power also can get in the way of the search for truth in individual cases. This interference can, and probably does, reduce the security of all people. Some guilty individual will go free in one case today to make sure the government will play by the rules in all cases tomorrow!

It might help you to understand and accept the importance of this balance between ends and means if you frequently remind yourself that the rules we make to control crime apply to all government officials and all suspects, defendants, and offenders. In other words, the rules don't just apply to good cops and prosecutors who follow the rules for catching and convicting bad (guilty) people. They also apply to bad cops and prosecutors who abuse their power when they apprehend and prosecute innocent people.

The balance between result and process never rests easily at a point that satisfies everyone. Throughout our history, the particular balance struck has caused great frustration, even anger. Those who fear criminals more than they fear government abuses of power stress the importance of the value of the correct result in the case at hand. They complain of rules or "technicalities" that "handcuff the police" and allow criminals to go free. Those who fear government abuses of power more than they fear criminals complain that we haven't obliged the government to "control itself," as Madison warned us to do.

The great U.S. Court of Appeals Judge Learned Hand clearly took the side of government power in this debate. According to Judge Hand (1922):

> Under our criminal procedure the accused has every advantage. While the prosecution is held rigidly to the charge, he need not disclose the barest outline of his defense. He is immune from question or comment on his silence; he cannot be convicted when there is the least fair doubt in the minds of any one of the twelve. . . . Our dangers do not lie in too little tenderness to the accused. Our procedure has been always haunted by the ghost of the innocent man convicted. It is an unreal dream. What we need to fear is the archaic formalism and the watery sentiment that obstructs, delays, and defeats the prosecution of crime. (659)

Professor Joseph Goldstein (1960), weighing in on the side of controlling government, strongly disagrees with Judge Hand's position. Goldstein believes the process favors the government, not criminal suspects and defendants:

> The fact is that . . . [Judge Hand's] view does not accurately represent the process. . . . Criminal procedure . . . does not give the accused "every advantage" but, instead, gives overwhelming advantage to the prosecution. The real effect of the "modern" approach has been to aggravate this condition by loosening standards of . . . proof without introducing compensatory safeguards earlier in the process. Underlying this development has been a . . . rejection of the presumption of innocence in favor of a presumption of guilt. (1152)

## The History of Balancing Values

Some have argued that the history of criminal justice in the Western world, from the Roman Republic to today, has been a pendulum swing between periods of result and process alternately holding the upper hand. When there was an excess of one, then the pendulum swung back to the other, and so on throughout Western history (Pound 1921).

Let's enter the story in the 1960s, when evidence of excessive police power spawned a reaction called the **due process revolution**. Led by the U.S. Supreme Court (called the "Warren Court" after its chief justice, Earl Warren), this revolution tilted the balance of power toward process and individual rights. According to its critics, it tilted the balance too far—so far that it created a criminal procedure soft on criminals and hard on victims (Cronin and others 1981).

From the late 1960s to 2007, as I write this book, there has been a definite pendulum swing from process back to result. In 1968, presidential candidate Richard Nixon promised to appoint "law and order" judges. And President Nixon did what Candidate Nixon promised. He started in 1969 by nominating a "tough on crime" U.S. Court of Appeals judge, Warren Burger, to succeed the retiring Earl Warren as chief justice of the United States.

All the presidents since President Nixon have appointed justices who've voted to "curb" the process precedents created by the Warren Court. *Curbed* but not *obliterated*—most of the rest of this book is about how the Court has limited the Warren Court precedents. As you read the book and study the cases in your class, you decide for yourself how to characterize this now 40-year history. You'll be better equipped to answer these and other questions: How much has changed? Is the trend only rebalancing result and process to where it was before 1960? Is the post-1960 trend good or bad? Is it right or wrong?

One thing isn't in question: With some significant exceptions, which we'll cover where appropriate, the trend is away from process, intended to protect defendants, toward result, intended to get at the truth to convict criminals and release innocent suspects and defendants.

## Balancing Values in Emergencies

Nothing in recent history has tested the balances between community security and individual autonomy and between ends and means more than two "wars," first on drugs and now on terror. Putting aside ordinary rules during extraordinary emergencies is a fact of life in every society under every form of government (Rossiter 1948).

Even during ordinary times, individuals demand extraordinary measures when they're victims or *feel* like victims. During the 1970s, a Minneapolis police chief told me the story of a woman who came into a Minneapolis Police Department precinct office and demanded the officer in charge go into her neighbor's house and get a television set she was sure the neighbor had taken. "We can't just go in there because you tell us to," said the officer. "Why not?" the woman asked. "Because you need a warrant," the officer explained. "And you can't get a warrant without probable cause, and you don't have probable cause. That's the law." Without pausing for a second, the woman asked, "How do we get this law changed?" (As you'll learn in Chapter 6, the "law" she was talking about is the Fourth Amendment right against "unreasonable searches and seizure," an essential part of the Bill of Rights.)

# EQUALITY

Most of the history of criminal procedure, especially state criminal procedure since the Civil War, developed in response to racial discrimination (Chapter 2). You can't understand the law of criminal procedure unless you put it into this sociohistorical context. Racial discrimination has definitely lessened, but it hasn't disappeared. At all stages in the criminal process, race can infect decision making, especially at the early stages of the process, such as street stops and frisks (Chapter 4).

Racial discrimination is only one dimension of a threat to our deep commitment to the ideal of equal justice for all. This ideal reaches beyond the need to root out racial discrimination; it includes class, gender, ethnic, and religious discrimination. Gender can affect who's excused from jury duty or excluded from jury service (Chapter 13). Ethnicity affects the same types of decisions as race (noted above; discussed further in Chapter 4). Religion combined with ethnicity affects decisions involving terrorist crimes (Chapter 15).

Further, money too often determines who gets the best lawyer, how early in the criminal process she gets one, and who can pay for expensive appeals. Despite the U.S. Supreme Court's command that the Sixth Amendment's right to counsel guarantees the right to "effective" counsel, even when you're too poor to afford a lawyer, the reality falls far short of the constitutional command (Chapter 12).

# DISCRETION

You can't really understand how the ideal of equality and balancing of values works in practice—or, for that matter, most of what else is happening in your journey through the law of criminal procedure—unless you understand the importance of *discretion*. And you can't understand the importance of discretion until you understand the difference between decisions made according to the formal law of criminal procedure and the leeway within the formal law given to informal official discretionary decision making. So let's look briefly at these differences.

Formal decision making consists of decisions made according to the law of criminal procedure—namely, the rules spelled out in the Constitution, judicial opinions, laws, other written sources you'll learn about throughout the text and cases. **Discretionary decision making**—informal decision making, or judgments, by professionals based on their training and experience and unwritten rules—is how the process works on a day-to-day basis.

Think of each step in the criminal process from investigation to appeals from convictions as a decision point. Each step presents a criminal justice professional with the opportunity to decide whether or not to start, continue, or end the criminal process. The police can investigate suspects, or not, and arrest them, or not—initiating the formal criminal process, or stopping it. Prosecutors can charge suspects and continue the criminal process, divert suspects to some social service agency, or take no further action—effectively terminating the criminal process.

Defendants can plead guilty (usually on their lawyers' advice) and avoid trial. Judges can suspend sentences or sentence convicted offenders to the maximum allowable penalty—hence, either minimizing or maximizing the punishment the criminal law prescribes.

Justice, fairness, and predictability all require the certainty and the protection against abuses assured by written rules. These same goals also require discretion to soften the rigidity of written rules. The tension between formal law and informal discretion—a recurring theme in criminal procedure—is as old as law; arguments raged over it in Western civilization as early as the Middle Ages.

In the end, the criminal process in practice is a blend of the formal law of criminal procedure and informal influences that enter the process by way of discretion. Discretion and law complement each other in promoting and balancing the interests in criminal procedure.

# THE OBJECTIVE BASIS REQUIREMENT

However much "play in the joints" discretion creates in the formal rules of law, one thing is certain: The agents of crime control aren't free to do whatever they please. That's because of another principle of criminal procedure you need to carry with you in your journey through the law of criminal procedure, the **objective basis requirement**. The requirement is that the government has to back up with facts every officially triggered restraint on the rights of individuals to come and go as they please and be let alone by the government. Hunches are never enough.

There's also a related requirement (there's no official name for it; we'll call it the **graduated objective basis requirement**) that goes like this: The greater the limit, the __more facts required to back it up.__ So to arrest a person, police have to have enough facts to add up to probable cause (Chapter 4), but to convict a defendant, the government has to marshal enough evidence to prove guilt beyond a reasonable doubt (Chapter 13).

# "GOOD" EVIDENCE AND "BAD" METHODS

Most of the cases you're going to read in this book are in court because defendants want to take advantage of the trump card of fair procedures—the **exclusionary rule** (Chapter 10). This rule requires courts to throw out "good" evidence (evidence that proves defendants are guilty) if the government got it by "bad" methods (methods that violate the U.S. or state constitutions). Referring to the exclusionary rule, the great judge Benjamin Cardozo once asked, "Should the culprit go free because the constable blundered?" The answer by supporters of the rule, "Well, if the culprit goes free, it's the Constitution that set him free."

# THE TEXT-CASE METHOD

You won't be ready to begin your journey through the criminal process until you understand the method of *Criminal Procedure 7*. Your book is what I call a text-case book; it's part text and part excerpts from real-life criminal procedure cases, edited for nonlawyers. The text part of the book explains the general principles, practices, and issues related to the law of criminal procedure.

The case excerpts provide you with real-life encounters between criminal suspects, defendants, and offenders on one side and law enforcement officers, prosecutors, defense lawyers, and judges on the other. The excerpts let you see how the general principles apply to the specifics of real-life situations, allowing you to think critically about the principles and the issues they raise. I believe the best way to test whether you understand the principles and issues is to apply them to concrete situations. So although you can learn a lot from the text alone, you won't get the full benefit of what you've learned without applying and thinking about it by reading the case excerpts.

Most of the case excerpts are U.S. Supreme Court cases because, as pointed out earlier, Supreme Court justices are the "primary generators of rules for regulating the behavior of police, prosecutors, and the other actors who administer the criminal process" (page 4). Sometimes, you'll also read U.S. Courts of Appeals cases. These cases are included when they deal with issues not yet decided by the U.S. Supreme Court or when they interpret rules already established by the Supreme Court (see Figure 1.2). Occasionally, you'll also read cases from state courts. State cases are important for at least two reasons. First, every state has a bill of rights that contains provisions similar or identical to those in the U.S. Bill of Rights. State courts decide for themselves how to interpret and apply their own state constitutional provisions.

Let's take a closer look at what you'll be reading in excerpts from these cases throughout the book. We'll begin with a look at the parts of the case excerpts, then examine the importance of precedent and stare decisis, appellate cases, and, finally, outline an approach to briefing the cases.

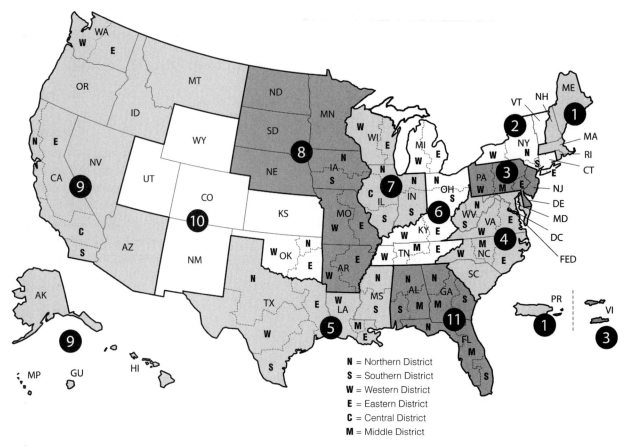

**FIGURE 1.2** The Structure of the U.S. Federal Court System

## The Parts of Case Excerpts

Don't worry if reading cases intimidates you at first. Like so many students before you, you'll get the hang of it before long. To help you get the most out of the case excerpts, in this section I've included a set of detailed instructions for reading and analyzing the excerpts. (Because they're excerpts, I've also included instructions for finding cases, so you can read the whole case if your instructor assigns it or if you'd like to read it unedited.)

Next, I've outlined the main parts of each case, the (1) title, (2) citation, (3) procedural history, (4) judge, (5) facts, (6) decision, and (7) opinion. Learn and become familiar with them right at the beginning, and I'm sure you'll catch on to how to read cases sooner.

1. *Title.* The title in criminal cases consists of two names, one on either side of "v." (the abbreviation for "versus" or "against"). The government (U.S. or the state, called variously "State," "People," or "Commonwealth," depending on what the state calls itself) is always the first party in the trial court because the government starts all criminal cases. The name on the right in the trial court is always the defendant's. There are no trial court cases in this book because, unfortunately, trial records aren't published. We enter the case after the trial court has decided an issue in the case, a higher court

has reviewed the trial court's decision, *and* it has decided to publish its opinion. (Reviewing courts don't have to publish their opinions; the decision to publish is discretionary.)

The placement of names to the left or right of the "v." in cases of appeal varies. In federal cases, the party appealing the decision of the court below is placed to the left of the "v." Some states follow the federal practice. The others keep the order of the original case; that is, the name of the state is always to the left, and the defendant's is always to its right.

Keep in mind that the government can't appeal a verdict of "not guilty." Why? Because the double jeopardy clause of the U.S. Constitution forbids it (Chapter 12). The government can appeal some trial court decisions (which, occasionally, we'll encounter) but never an acquittal.

2. *Citation.* After the title of the case, you'll see a string of letters and numbers. These are called the case **citation**. The case citation (like a footnote, endnote, or other reference in articles and books) tells you the source of the material quoted or relied upon. So the citation tells you where you can find the published report of the case. The information in the citation tells you: (a) the court that's reporting the case, (b) the date the court decided the case, and (c) the book, volume, and page where the case report begins.

For example, in *Rochin v. California*, the citation reads "342 U.S. 165 (1952)". This means that you'll find the case reported in Volume 342 of the *United States Reports*, beginning on page 165; the volume includes cases decided by the Court in the year 1952. "U.S." is the abbreviation for *United States Reports*, the official U.S. government publication of U.S. Supreme Court cases. Two other widely used nongovernment publications, *Supreme Court Reporter*, abbreviated "S.Ct.," and the *Lawyer's Edition*, abbreviated "L.Ed.," also report U.S. Supreme Court cases. The U.S. Court of Appeals decisions are reported in *The Federal Reporter*, abbreviated "F.," "F.2d." (second series), and "F.3d." (third series).

3. *Procedural history.* The case **procedural history** is a brief description of the procedural steps and judgments (decisions) made by each court that has heard the case.

4. *Judge.* This is the name of the judge who wrote the opinion and issued the court's judgment in the case. Supreme Court judges and most state supreme court judges have the title "Justice"; intermediate appeals court judges have the title "Judge."

5. *Facts.* The facts of the case are the critical starting point in reading and analyzing cases. If you don't know the facts, you can't understand the principle the case is teaching. One of my favorite law professors used to tell us again and again: "Remember cases are stories with a point. You can't get the point if you don't know the story." He also told us something else I think will help you: "Forget you're lawyers. Tell me the story as if you were telling it to your grandmother who doesn't know anything about the law." Take Professor Hill's advice. I do, because it's still good advice.

6. *Court judgment (decision).* The **court's judgment** (sometimes called the court's **decision**) is how the court disposes of the case. In the trial court, the judgments are almost always guilty or not guilty. In appeals courts, the judgments are affirmed,

reversed, or reversed and remanded. This is the most important legal action of the court, because it decides what happens to the defendant and the government.

7. *Court opinion.* **Court opinions** explain why courts decided and entered the judgment in the case. The opinion contains two essential ingredients:
   a. The court's holding—the legal rule the court applied to the facts of the cases.
   b. The court's reasoning—the reasons and arguments the court gives to support its holding.

Appellate courts, whether federal or state, can issue four types of opinions:
   a. *Majority opinion.* The U.S. Supreme Court consists of nine justices, each of whom has a vote and the right to submit an opinion. The **majority opinion** is the law. In most cases, five justices make up the majority. Sometimes, less than nine justices participate; in these cases, the majority can be less than five.
   b. *Concurring opinion.* Sometimes, justices agree with the decision reached in another opinion but write separate opinions giving their own reasons for reaching the decision. Opinions that agree with the result of another opinion whether majority or dissent are called **concurring opinions**.
   c. *Plurality opinions.* If a majority of the justices agree with the decision in a case but they can't agree on the reasons, the opinion with the reasoning agreed to by the largest number of justices is called a **plurality opinion**. For example, suppose that seven justices agree with the result and four give one set of reasons, three give another set of reasons, and two dissent. The opinion to which the four subscribe is the plurality opinion. A plurality opinion is a very weak precedent.
   d. *Dissenting opinion.* If justices don't agree with the court's decision and/or its reasoning, they can write their own **dissenting opinions** explaining why they don't agree with the reasoning, the decision, or both. Often, the dissenting opinions point to the future; many majority opinions of today are based on dissents from the past. The late Chief Justice Charles Evans Hughes once said a dissent should be "an appeal to the brooding spirit of the law, to the intelligence of a future day" (Lewis 1994, A13).

The conflicting arguments and reasoning in the majority, plurality, concurring, and dissenting opinions challenge you to think about the issues in the cases, because, most of the time, all the justices argue their views of the case convincingly. First, the majority opinion, then the concurring opinion(s), and finally the dissenting opinion(s) present arguments that will sway your opinion one way and then another. This is good. It teaches you that there's more than one reasonable position on all the important issues in the law of criminal procedure. Reasonable people do disagree!

## Precedent and Stare Decisis

You'll notice that court opinions refer to past cases to back up their reasons and their decision in the present case. These prior decisions are called **precedent**. The ancient and firmly entrenched doctrine called **stare decisis** binds judges to follow precedent.

But stare decisis only binds judges to the prior decisions of either their own court or of courts superior to theirs in their own jurisdiction. **Jurisdiction** means the power to hear and decide cases in a specific geographical area (such as a county, a state, or a federal district) or the subject matter (for example, criminal appeals) the court controls.

Supreme Court Justice and respected judicial philosopher Benjamin Cardozo (1921) once said this about precedent and the doctrine of stare decisis:

> It is easier to follow the beaten track than it is to clear another. In doing this, I shall be treading in the footsteps of my predecessors, and illustrating the process that I am seeking to describe, since the power of precedent, when analyzed, is the power of the beaten path. (62)

The idea of precedent isn't special to the law of criminal procedure, nor is it the basis only of legal reasoning (Schauer 1987, 571). We're accustomed to the basic notion of precedent in ordinary life. We like to do things the way we've done them in the past. For example, if a professor asks multiple-choice questions covering only material in the text on three exams, you expect multiple-choice questions on the fourth exam. If you get an essay exam instead, you won't like it. Not only won't you like it; you'll probably think it's "unfair." Why? Because precedent—the way we've done things before—makes life stable and predictable.

Knowing what to expect, and counting on it, guides our actions in the future so we can plan for and meet challenges and solve problems. Changing this without warning is unfair. In ordinary life, then, as in criminal procedure, following past practice gives stability, predictability, and a sense of fairness and justice to decisions.

Of course, doing things the way we've always done them isn't always right or good. When we need to, we change (usually reluctantly) and do things differently. These changes themselves become guides to future action—so, too, with legal precedent. Courts occasionally change precedent but not often and then only reluctantly.

Courts, like individuals in ordinary life, don't like to change, particularly when they have to admit they were wrong. That's why, as you read the case excerpts, you'll rarely find one that comes right out and says, "We were wrong, so we overrule our prior decision." Instead, when courts decide to get off the beaten path, they do it by **distinguishing cases**. This means that a court decides that a prior decision doesn't apply to the current case because the facts are different. For example, the rule that controls the right to a lawyer in death penalty cases doesn't have to apply to a case punishable by a fine. As the Court has noted, "Death is different" (Schauer 1987, 571).

## Appellate Cases

Most of the cases in this textbook are **appellate court cases**. This means that a lower court has already taken some action in the case and that one of the parties has asked a higher court to review the lower court's action. Parties seek appellate review of what they claim were errors by the trial court or unlawful actions by police, judges, prosecutors, or defense lawyers.

Only defendants can appeal convictions; the government can never appeal acquittals. However, many appellate reviews arise out of proceedings before trial and convictions. Both the government and the defendant can appeal pretrial proceedings. Most appellate cases in this book arise out of defendants' motions to throw out evidence obtained by law enforcement officers during searches and seizures, interrogation, and identification procedures, such as lineups. These motions are heard in a proceeding called a "suppression hearing."

Courts call parties in appellate courts by different names. The most common parties in the appellate courts are the **appellant** (the party appealing) and the **appellee** (the party appealed against). Both of these terms originate from the word *appeal*. In the excerpts of older cases, you'll find other names for the parties. The older cases refer to the "plaintiff in error," the party that claims the lower courts erred in their rulings, and to the "defendant in error," the party who won in the lower court. These names stem from an old and no longer used writ called the "writ of error."

A **petitioner** is a defendant in a noncriminal case. The petitioner asks the higher court to review a decision made by either a lower court or some other official. The two main petitions you'll encounter in case excerpts are **habeas corpus**, Latin for "you have the body," and **certiorari**, Latin for "to be certified":

1. *Habeas corpus.* Called a **collateral attack** because it's a separate proceeding from the criminal case, habeas corpus is a *civil action* (a noncriminal proceeding) that reviews the constitutionality of the petitioner's detention or imprisonment. You can recognize these proceedings by their title. Instead of the name of a state or the United States, you'll see two individuals' names, such as in *Adams v. Williams* (excerpted in Chapter 4). Williams, a state prisoner, sued Adams, the warden of the prison where Williams was held. The suit petitioned the court to order Adams to prove that Williams was being imprisoned lawfully.

2. *Certiorari.* Most appeals to the U.S. Supreme Court are based on writs of certiorari. *Certiorari* is a proceeding in the U.S. Supreme Court to review decisions of lower courts. These proceedings begin when petitioners ask for reviews of court decisions.

    It's important to understand right away that the Court doesn't grant certiorari to prevent the punishment of innocent defendants. Petitioners would get nowhere if their petitions read, "I'm innocent; they convicted the wrong person." As a legal matter, the Court isn't interested in whether individual defendants are innocent or guilty; that's the job of the lower courts. The Supreme Court grants certiorari because a case raises an important constitutional issue that affects large numbers of individuals; in a sense, the defendant in the case reviewed represents these other individuals.

    Granting certiorari is wholly discretionary, and the Court grants it—that is, it issues a **writ of certiorari** (an order to the court that decided the case to send up the record of its proceedings to the U.S. Supreme Court for review)—in only a tiny percentage of petitions. Four of the nine Supreme Court justices have to vote to review a case, a requirement known as the **rule of four,** before the Court will hear an appeal by issuing a writ of certiorari.

## Briefing the Cases

To guide your reading, and to help you get the most out of the case excerpts, you should summarize the main parts of the case. In law school, we called this "briefing" a case. Whether you call it a brief, a summary, or a study guide, you should sort out the parts of the opinion and write out short summaries of each part. I recommend using a separate card or sheet of paper for each case. At the top of each card or sheet, put the name and the citation of the case. Then, summarize briefly and accurately the (1) history, (2) facts, (3) issue, (4) decision, (5) opinions, and (6) disposition of the case.

1. *History.* The history of the case refers to the formal procedural steps the case has taken and the decisions at each of these steps, beginning usually with the indictment and moving through the trial court and appellate courts to the court whose excerpt you're briefing. This part of your brief puts the excerpt in its correct

procedural place so that you'll know where the case has been, what decisions were made before it got to the appellate court, and the decision of the appellate court in the case whose excerpted facts and opinion you're about to read.

2. *Facts.* There are two types of relevant facts in criminal procedure cases: acts by government officials, and the objective basis for the actions.

   a. *Acts by government officials.* List the specific acts by government officials that the defendant claims violated the Constitution. List each act by the government accurately and in chronological order. Also, include circumstances surrounding the acts. I recommend that you put each act and circumstance on a separate line of your brief. Think of these facts as notes for a story you're going to tell someone who isn't familiar at all with what government officials did and the circumstances surrounding the acts.

   b. *Objective basis (quantum of proof).* **Objective basis** (also called the **quantum of proof**) means the facts and circumstances that back up the act by government officials. As you'll learn over and over in your study of criminal procedure, government officials can't restrict your freedom of movement or your privacy on a hunch (also known as "mere suspicion"; they have to justify their actions by facts and circumstances that backed up their actions. For example, a law enforcement officer can't back up patting you down by claiming she had a "hunch" you were carrying a gun. But she can back it up by saying there was a bulge at your waist inside your shirt that resembled the shape of a gun.

3. *Constitutional (legal) question.* The point of the case stories is the constitutional question they raise. For example, "Was ordering the passenger Jimmy Lee Wilson out of the car stopped for speeding a 'reasonable' Fourth Amendment seizure?" (*Maryland v. Wilson*, Chapter 4).

4. *Decision or holding.* The decision of the court part of your brief should state the court's answer to the question—for example, a law enforcement officer feeling the suspect's outer clothing backed up by seeing a bulge at the suspect's waist was a reasonable Fourth Amendment search.

5. *Opinions.* State in simple English the arguments and reasons included in the majority, plurality, concurring, and dissenting opinions.

6. *Judgment (disposition).* Courts don't have to write opinions. Many times (and in trial courts in almost every case) they don't, which as students is our loss (or maybe to you it's a blessing). The judgment of the case is the only binding action of the court. It states what's going to happen to the judgment of the court below and, ultimately, to the defendant or convicted offender. Common judgments in criminal cases include affirmed, reversed, or reversed and remanded.

   a. *Affirmed.* **Affirmed** means the appellate court upheld a lower court's judgment.

   b. *Reversed and/or remanded.* **Reversed** means the appellate court set aside, or nullified, the lower court's judgment. **Remanded** means that the appellate court sent the case back to the lower court for further action.

Notice that neither reversed nor remanded means that the defendant automatically goes free. Fewer than half the defendants who win their cases in the Supreme Court ultimately triumph when their cases are reversed and/or remanded to lower courts, particularly to state courts. For example, in the famous *Miranda v. Arizona* case (Chapter 8), the prison gates didn't open for Ernesto Miranda. He was detained in jail while he was retried without the confession he made, promptly convicted, and sent from jail to prison.

# SUMMARY

### I. Balancing Values in Criminal Procedure
A. Balance between government power and personal choice is the "big picture."
B. The balance is between two sets of values:
1. Community security vs. individual autonomy
2. Ends vs. means
C. Community security is weighed against individual autonomy.
1. The objective of community security is we are (or believe we are) safe in our community.
2. Individual autonomy allows us to have control over our lives.
3. Striking this balance is often difficult, and it never satisfies anyone completely.
4. The balance between crime control and individual rights is flexible, meaning the balance falls within a zone.
D. The ends are weighed against the means.
1. "Ends" consists of the search for truth to obtain correct results in individual cases.
2. Two phases of "ends" are catching, convicting, and punishing guilty people and freeing as soon as possible innocent people.
3. "Means" is the commitment to fairness in dealing with those caught up in the criminal process.
4. Balancing ends and means creates an uncomfortable tension for those that enforce the law; it hampers the search for truth while protecting citizens from police abuses.
E. The due process revolution came about in the 1960s when evidence of excess police power spawned a reaction to change. The Warren Court tilted the balance of power toward process and individual rights.
F. The balances between community security and individual autonomy and between ends and means have been tested during emergencies, especially the "wars" on drugs and terror.

### II. Equality
A. Most of the history of criminal procedure, especially state criminal procedure since the Civil War, developed in response to racial discrimination.
B. Not only does the search for equal justice for all look to root out racial discrimination but also class, gender, ethnic, and religious discrimination.

### III. Discretion
A. Understanding the importance of discretion is key to understanding the balancing of values in our society along with equality.
B. There are two types of decision making:
1. Formal decision making according to the law of criminal procedure
2. Informal decision making, or judgments, by professionals based on their training and experience and unwritten rules

### IV. The Objective Basis Requirement
A. The agents of crime control aren't free to do whatever they please.
B. The objective basis requirement is that the government back up with facts every officially triggered restraint on the right of locomotion.

C. Hunches are never enough.

D. The graduated objective basis requirement demands that the further restraints on locomotion go, the more evidence is required to back it up.

### V. "Good" Evidence and "Bad" Methods

A. Most cases that end up in the higher appellate courts are there because individuals want to take advantage of the abuses of power by the government.

A. The exclusionary rule forces courts to throw out "good" evidence if the government got it by "bad" methods.

## REVIEW QUESTIONS

1. Describe what James Madison meant by the passage beginning with, "If men were angels . . ."

2. Identify and describe the difference between crime control for a police state, a pure democracy, and a constitutional democracy.

3. Identify and describe the two elements in balancing community security and individual autonomy.

4. Describe the two elements in balancing ends and means in a constitutional democracy.

5. How does balancing ends and means create an uncomfortable tension for those trying to enforce the law?

6. Describe the attitude toward personal liberties from the 1960s to the 1990s.

7. Identify and describe two emergencies that have tested the balance between community security and individual autonomy.

8. Identify and describe two types of decision making in criminal procedure.

9. Identify and describe two elements of the objective basis requirement.

10. What is meant by the phrase, "Hunches are never enough"?

11. Describe "good" evidence and "bad" methods in terms of criminal procedure.

## KEY TERMS

constitutional democracy, p. 4
due process revolution, p. 8
discretionary decision making, p. 10
objective basis requirement, p. 10
graduated objective basis
    requirement, p. 10
exclusionary rule, p. 11
citation, p. 13
procedural history, p. 13
court judgment (decision), p. 13
court opinion, p. 14

majority opinion, p. 14
concurring opinion, p. 14
plurality opinion, p. 14
dissenting opinion, p. 14
precedent, p. 14
stare decisis, p. 14
jurisdiction, p. 14
distinguishing cases, p. 15
appellate court case, p. 15
appellant, p. 16
appellee, p. 16

petitioner, p. 16
habeas corpus, p. 16
collateral attack, p. 16
certiorari, p. 16
writ of certiorari, p. 16
rule of four, p. 16
objective basis, p. 17
quantum of proof, p. 17
affirmed, p. 17
reversed, p. 17
remanded, p. 17

# Criminal Procedure and the Constitution

## MAIN POINTS

- Ordinary laws are detailed, constantly changing rules passed by legislatures; constitutions are a set of permanent, general principles.
- The law of criminal procedure consists of rules the government has to follow to detect and investigate crimes, apprehend suspects, prosecute and convict defendants, and punish criminals.
- The U.S. Constitution is the highest authority in all criminal proceedings.
- The U.S. Supreme Court has the final word in saying what the Constitution means.
- In cases involving the U.S. Constitution, state court decisions aren't final.
- From the 1930s through the 1950s, a majority of the U.S. Supreme Court rejected the claim that the Bill of Rights applied to state criminal proceedings.
- The 1960s were a time of expanding individual rights, especially of the most vulnerable classes and of "outsiders," and imposing them on state criminal justice.
- Constitutional democracy can't survive without protecting the right to fair procedures guaranteed by due process of law.

*The state is free to regulate the procedure of its courts in accordance
with its own conceptions of policy, unless in so doing it offends some
principle of justice so rooted in the traditions and conscience of our
people as to be ranked as fundamental. . . . The rack and torture
chamber may not be substituted for the witness stand. The state
may not permit an accused to be hurried to conviction under mob
domination—where the whole proceeding is but a mask—without
supplying corrective process.*

*The state may not deny to the accused the aid of counsel. Nor
may a state, through the action of its officers, contrive a conviction
through the pretense of a trial which in truth is "but used as a means
of depriving a defendant of liberty through a deliberate deception
of court and jury by the presentation of testimony known to be
perjured."*

*And the trial equally is a mere pretense where the state authori-
ties have contrived a conviction resting solely upon confessions
obtained by violence. The due process clause requires "that state
action, whether through one agency or another, shall be consistent
with the fundamental principles of liberty and justice which lie at
the base of all our civil and political institutions."*

*It would be difficult to conceive of methods more revolting to the
sense of justice than those taken to procure the confessions of these
petitioners, and the use of the confessions thus obtained as the basis
for conviction and sentence was a clear denial of due process.*

Chief Justice Charles Evans Hughes (*Brown v. Mississippi*, 1936)

"We must never forget that it is a *constitution* we are expounding," Chief Justice John Marshall wrote in the great case of *McCulloch v. Maryland* (1819). The chief justice was referring to a deeply embedded idea in our constitutional democracy—the idea of **constitutionalism**. The core of the idea is that constitutions adopted by the whole people are a higher form of law than ordinary laws passed by legislatures. Constitutions are forever; ordinary laws are for now. Laws are detailed, constantly changing rules passed by legislatures; constitutions are a set of permanent (or at least very hard to change), general principles. We can boil down the difference between laws and constitutions into six contrasting characteristics (Gardner 1991, 814):

1. Constitutions are a higher form of law that speak with a political authority that no ordinary law or other government action can ever match.
2. Constitutions express the will of the whole people.
3. Constitutions always bind the government.
4. Constitutions can't be changed by the government.
5. Only the direct action of the whole people can change constitutions.
6. Constitutions embody the fundamental values of the people.

The **law of criminal procedure** consists of the rules government has to follow to detect and investigate crimes, apprehend suspects, prosecute and convict defendants, and punish criminals. The dominant source, and the one you'll learn the most about, is the U.S. Constitution, particularly the criminal procedure clauses in the Bill of Rights. Equally important are the rules generated by the U.S. Supreme Court cases based on the Bill of Rights. From time to time, you'll also learn about criminal procedure law included in the lower federal court cases—namely, those of the U.S. Courts of Appeals and the U.S. District Courts; state and federal statutes; state constitutions and state cases; the rules of courts and law enforcement agencies; and the American Law Institute's (hereafter ALI) remarkable *Model Code of Pre-Arraignment Procedure* (1975).

The U.S. Constitution is the highest authority in criminal procedure; it trumps all other sources. There are two criminal procedure provisions in the body of the Constitution: Article I, § 9, recognizes habeas corpus (the right of individuals to challenge any government detention) (Chapter 14), and Article III, § 2, guarantees trial by jury in the community where the crimes were committed (Chapter 13).

Most criminal procedure provisions are in the Fourth, Fifth, Sixth, Eighth, and Fourteenth Amendments to the Constitution, the part known as the Bill of Rights. These amendments contain 18 guarantees to persons suspected of, charged with, and convicted of crimes (Table 2.1). At first, the guarantees listed in Table 2.1 applied only to the federal government, but since the 1960s, they've applied to state and local governments, too.

| TABLE 2.1 | Criminal Procedure Protections in the Bill of Rights* |
|---|---|
| **Amendment** | **Protection Offered** |
| Fourth Amendment | 1. The right to be free from unreasonable searches |
| | 2. The right to be free from unreasonable seizures |
| | 3. The right to probable cause to back up searches and seizures |
| Fifth Amendment | 4. The right to grand jury indictment in federal cases |
| | 5. The right against double jeopardy |
| | 6. The right to due process in federal cases |
| | 7. The right against self-incrimination |
| Sixth Amendment | 8. The right to a speedy trial |
| | 9. The right to a public trial |
| | 10. The right to an impartial jury |
| | 11. The right to have a jury made up of persons from the state and district where the crime was committed |
| | 12. The right to be informed of the charges against the accused |
| | 13. The right to confront witnesses against the accused |
| | 14. The right to a compulsory process to obtain witnesses in favor of the accused |
| | 15. The right of the accused to defense counsel |
| Eighth Amendment | 16. The right against excessive bail |
| | 17. The right against excessive fines |
| | 18. The right against cruel and unusual punishment |
| Fourteenth Amendment | 19. The right to due process of law in state criminal proceedings |
| | 20. The right to equal protection of the law in state criminal proceedings |

*See the Appendix for the full text of these amendments.

# THE U.S. CONSTITUTION AND THE COURTS

According to the U.S. Constitution, Article VI (the **supremacy clause**):

> This constitution, and the laws of the United States which shall be made in pursuance thereof . . . shall be the supreme law of the land; and the judges in every state shall be bound thereby, anything in the constitution or laws of any state to the contrary notwithstanding.

In other words, the U.S. Constitution is the last word in criminal procedure. True as this may be, the Constitution doesn't come with an instruction manual. It requires—and gets—a lot of interpretation. Who tells officials (and us, too, of course) what the Constitution means? Chief Justice John Marshall answered the question in the great case of *Marbury v. Madison* (1803). Writing for the Court, Marshall established what later courts would call the principle of **judicial review**. According to that principle, courts and, ultimately, the U.S. Supreme Court, *not* the Congress and *not* the president, have the final word in saying what the Constitution means.

Alexander Hamilton defended this startlingly vast power of judicial review in the *Federalist Papers* ([1788]; 1961):

> The interpretation of the laws is the proper and peculiar province of the courts. A constitution is, in fact, and must be regarded by the judges as, a fundamental law. It therefore belongs to them to ascertain its meaning, as well as the meaning of any particular act proceeding from the legislative body. If there should happen to be an irreconcilable variance between the two, that which has the superior obligation and validity ought, of course, to be preferred; or, in other words, the Constitution ought to be preferred to the statute, the intention of the people to the intention of their agents. (485–86)

The supremacy clause and judicial review together establish that criminal procedure has to answer to the U.S. Constitution, and courts determine which procedures are in line with the Constitution. All courts can interpret the Constitution, but the U.S. Supreme Court has the last word; its decisions bind all other courts, legislatures, executives, and criminal justice officials.

Despite this enormous power, it's important to keep in mind two important limits on the Court's power. First, the U.S. Constitution and Supreme Court are at the top of a pyramid with a very wide state and local base of criminal justice administration. So the Supreme Court has to depend on local courts, prosecutors, and police officers to apply its decisions to day-to-day operations. Second, and just as important, U.S. Courts of Appeals, U.S. District Courts, and state courts answer constitutional questions the Supreme Court hasn't answered yet—and often never will (Amsterdam 1970, 785).

One final point: The U.S. Supreme Court has more power over criminal procedure in lower federal courts than it does over state courts. Why? Because of its **supervisory power**—the power to make rules to manage how lower federal courts conduct their business. The Court can only control the law of criminal procedure in state courts if the states' rules violate the U.S. Constitution. Many procedures (some of them very important for defendants and the state) don't violate the Constitution.

# STATE CONSTITUTIONS AND STATE COURTS

Every state constitution guarantees its citizens **parallel rights**—rights similar to those in the U.S. Constitution and the Bill of Rights. For example, every state constitution guarantees rights against self-incrimination and unreasonable searches and seizures, as well as the right to counsel and to jury trial. In addition to parallel rights, some state constitutions provide rights not specifically mentioned in the U.S. Constitution, such as the right to privacy.

State courts are a source of criminal procedure law in two types of cases: (1) those involving the U.S. Constitution that the U.S. Supreme Court hasn't decided yet and (2) those involving their own state constitutions. In cases involving the U.S. Constitution, state court decisions aren't final. They can always be appealed to federal courts. Many cases excerpted in this book started in state courts and ended in the U.S. Supreme Court. But, in practice, most criminal cases never get past state courts.

State courts are the final authority in cases based on their own state constitutions and statutes. The federal courts—even the U.S. Supreme Court—can't interpret state constitutions and statutes unless the state provisions and state courts interpreting them fail to meet the minimum standards set by the U.S. Constitution. In referring to this federal rights floor, a Supreme Court justice once said, "It doesn't pay a law much of a compliment to declare it constitutional." States are free to *raise* the minimum, and sometimes they do, but they can never *lower* the floor.

# DUE PROCESS OF LAW

The application of the Bill of Rights to state proceedings in the 1960s "due process revolution" resulted in an enormous expansion of the rights of individuals. How was this expansion accomplished? First, more classes of people (the vulnerable as well as the powerful, including criminal suspects, defendants, and offenders) were included within the scope of constitutional protection. Second, states as well as the federal government were compelled to guarantee those rights to these vulnerable classes. The bases for this two-pronged expansion were two guarantees states have to provide according to the Fourteenth Amendment: due process and equal protection of the law. The Fourteenth Amendment commands that

> No state shall . . . deprive any citizen of life, liberty, or property without due process of law; nor deny to any person within its jurisdiction the equal protection of the laws.

From colonial times until the Civil War, criminal justice was a local affair. In view of this history, it's not surprising that the Bill of Rights wasn't applied to the states. As early as 1833, Chief Justice John Marshall noted that the question of whether the Bill of Rights extended to the states was "of great importance, but not of much difficulty" (*Barron v. Baltimore* 1833, 247). If the Congress that created the Bill of Rights had meant to take the highly unusual step of applying them to the states, it would have said so, "in plain and intelligible language" (250).

The Fourteenth Amendment, adopted in the aftermath of the Civil War, changed all that (Nelson 1988, Chapter 2). A main goal of the Civil War was to establish federal supremacy over states' rights (vindicated by the crushing defeat of the Confederacy). A second principle, that everyone was entitled to equal rights, triumphed at least on paper in the abolition of slavery.

The drafters of the amendment left the definitions of due process and equal protection general (and not by accident, vague). You should already know one reason why they did: They were *constitutional* provisions, not ordinary laws. The other reason is rooted in the history of the time: States' rights and equality were enormously controversial issues. No matter how decisive in military terms the victory of the Union and the defeat of the secessionists were, the outcome couldn't guarantee the triumph of the great principles for which millions had fought and died. Don't forget this history. It will help you to appreciate the struggle to define the due process and equal protection guarantees.

Let's look next at the meaning of due process, some famous cases that led to U.S. Supreme Court rulings on due process, and two contrasting views on how the Fourteenth Amendment should be applied to state criminal proceedings: the fundamental fairness doctrine and the incorporation doctrine.

## The Meaning of *Due Process*

How do the courts, particularly the U.S. Supreme Court, define **due process**, this broad and vague idea that lends itself to many interpretations? Some emphasize the "process" part, contending that due process guarantees fair procedures for deciding cases. (A piece of advice: Whenever you see "due process" think *"fair process."*) We call this definition **procedural due process**. This is the meaning we'll discuss in this book. (We leave aside substantive due process, the other meaning of due process, which is a topic for courses in constitutional and criminal *law*, not criminal procedure.)

What fair procedures does due process guarantee? The Bill of Rights lists several. Are these the specific ones due process guarantees? Yes, say some experts. According to these experts, the authors of the Bill of Rights were codifying a specific list of hard-fought and proudly won procedures to protect private persons against government excesses.

Other experts disagree. They maintain that if due process is just shorthand for the Bill of Rights, then the Fourteenth Amendment due process clause is wasted language, because the Fifth Amendment already includes a due process clause, "No person shall be denied life, liberty, or property without due process of law" (*Adamson v. California* 1947).

Besides, they say, the framers wouldn't have frozen criminal procedure at a particular 18th-century moment. The authors of the Constitution looked forward; they hoped the meaning of due process would evolve and expand to meet the needs and wants of an ever-advancing society. Until the 1930s, the U.S. Supreme Court time and again—sometimes exasperated that lawyers didn't get the message—stubbornly refused to apply the Fourteenth Amendment due process clause to state criminal proceedings.

## *Hurtado* and Charging by Information

*Hurtado v. California*, decided in 1884, began a line of cases that rejected the idea that due process was shorthand for the application of the specific provisions in the Bill of Rights to state criminal proceedings. The case involved Joseph Hurtado and José Estuardo, who'd been close friends for several years. Then Hurtado discovered Estuardo was having an affair with his wife. When confronted, Estuardo admitted it and said, "I'm the meat and you're the knife; kill me if you like." Instead, Hurtado demanded that Estuardo leave Sacramento. Estuardo promised to leave but then reneged and renewed his pursuit of Hurtado's wife. The case began with a brawl in a Sacramento tavern. Hurtado assaulted Estuardo. A few days later, Hurtado shot Estuardo in the chest. When Estuardo turned to flee, Hurtado shot him in the back. Estuardo fell to the ground; Hurtado shot him again and then bludgeoned him with the pistol (Cortner 1981, 18–19).

In the federal courts, and in most state courts of the time, a grand jury would have decided whether to indict Hurtado. But California didn't follow the practice of indictment by grand jury review. California was one of a number of states that during the 1800s replaced the grand jury with a procedure known as charging by **information**.

In proceeding by information, prosecutors charged criminal defendants directly; they didn't have to rely on grand juries. But there was a problem: the Fifth Amendment requires indictment by a grand jury in capital or otherwise "infamous" crimes. Following Hurtado's conviction, the judge sentenced him to "be hung by the neck until he is dead." After losing an appeal based on trial errors, Hurtado appealed to the U.S. Supreme Court. The basis of his appeal was that failure to indict him by grand jury review violated his Fifth Amendment right to grand jury indictment in a capital case. Hurtado's lawyer made the then novel argument that Fourteenth Amendment due process commanded states to provide Fifth Amendment grand jury indictment in capital cases.

Hurtado's lawyer relied on an earlier U.S. Supreme Court case that decided due process required "a fair trial in a court of justice, according to the modes of proceeding applicable to such case." Hurtado's lawyer argued that due process meant more than that; namely, it included all the ancient common-law rights inherited from England and recognized as fundamental to free people. Grand jury indictment, he maintained, was one of these fundamental rights. The Court rejected this argument, affirming Hurtado's conviction. According to Justice Stanley Matthews:

[I]ncluding only procedures adopted in the past would be to deny every quality of the law but its age, and to render it incapable of progress or improvement. It would be to stamp on our jurisprudence the unchangeableness attributed to the laws of the Medes and Persians. [The Constitution and due process were made] for an undefined and expanding future, and for a people gathered from many nations and of many tongues. . . . [Because the common law drew] its inspiration from every fountain of justice, we are not to assume that the sources of its supply have been exhausted. On the contrary, we should expect that the new and various experiences of our own situation and system will mold and shape it into new and not less useful forms. (530)

Justice John Marshall Harlan, the lone dissenter, argued that the Fourteenth Amendment due process clause "imposed upon the states the same restrictions, in respect of proceedings involving life, liberty, and property, which had been imposed upon the general government" (541). Lawyers tried more than once to get the Court to see things the way Justice Harlan did. In the 1960s, the Court would adopt Justice Harlan's position when it subscribed to the incorporation doctrine (discussed later). But for the time being, the Court stuck steadfastly to its position that state criminal procedure was a local matter and none of the federal government's business.

## The "Scottsboro Boys" and Due Process of Law

Then came the German war machine of the First World War and the rise of fascism and other totalitarian governments of the 1920s and 1930s. These developments revived old American suspicions of arbitrary government. It was probably no coincidence that the U.S. Supreme Court first applied the Fourteenth Amendment due process clause to state criminal procedures in a case it decided just as Hitler was rising to power in Nazi Germany (Allen 1978, 157–58).

That first case began in northern Alabama one morning in March 1931 when seven scruffy White boys came into a railway station in northern Alabama and told the stationmaster that a "bunch of Negroes" had picked a fight with them and thrown them off a freight train. The stationmaster phoned ahead to Scottsboro, where a deputy sheriff deputized every man who owned a gun. When the train got to Scottsboro, the posse rounded up nine Black boys and two White girls. The girls were dressed in men's caps and overalls. Five of the boys were from Georgia and four from Tennessee. They ranged in age from 12 to 20. One was blind in one eye and had only 10 percent vision in the other; one walked with a cane; all were poor and illiterate.

After the deputy sheriff had tied the boys together and was loading them into his truck, Ruby Bates told the sheriff that the boys had raped her and her friend, Victoria Price. By nightfall, a mob of several hundred people had surrounded the little Scottsboro jail, vowing to avenge the rape by lynching the boys.

When the trial began on Monday morning April 6, 1931, 102 National Guardsmen struggled to keep several thousand people at least 100 feet away from the courthouse. Inside the courtroom, Judge Alfred E. Hawkins offered the job of defense attorney to anyone who would take it. Only Chattanooga lawyer Stephen Roddy—an alcoholic already drunk at 9:00 A.M.—who admitted he didn't know anything about Alabama law, accepted. Judge Hawkins then appointed as defense counsel "all members" of the local bar present in the courtroom.

By Thursday, eight of the boys had been tried, convicted, and sentenced to death. Only 12-year-old Roy Wright remained because the jury hung, with seven demanding death and five holding out for life imprisonment. Judge Hawkins declared a mistrial in Roy Wright's trial and sentenced the others to death by electrocution.

Liberals, radicals, and Communists around the country rallied to the defense of the "Scottsboro boys," as the defendants became popularly known. In March 1932, the Alabama Supreme Court upheld all of the convictions except for Eugene Williams, who was granted a new trial as a juvenile. In November, the U.S. Supreme Court ruled in _Powell v. Alabama_ (1932) that Alabama had denied the boys due process of law. According to Justice Sutherland:

> Notwithstanding the sweeping character of the language in the _Hurtado_ Case [that the criminal procedure amendments in the Bill of Rights do not apply to the states], the rule laid down is not without exceptions. The rule . . . in some instances may be conclusive; but it must yield to more compelling considerations whenever such considerations exist.
>
> The fact that the right involved is of such a character that it cannot be denied without violating those fundamental principles of liberty and justice which lie at the base of all our civil and political institutions is obviously one of those compelling considerations which must prevail in determining whether it is embraced within the due process clause of the Fourteenth Amendment, although it be specifically dealt with in another part of the Federal Constitution. . . . If this is so, it is not because those rights are enumerated in the first eight Amendments, but because they are of such a nature that they are included in the conception of due process of law.
>
> While the question has never been categorically determined by this court, a consideration of the nature of the right and a review of the expressions of this and other courts makes it clear that the right to the aid of counsel is of this fundamental character. . . .
>
> In the light of the facts, . . . the ignorance and illiteracy of the defendants, their youth, the circumstances of public hostility, the imprisonment and the close surveillance of the defendants by the military forces, the fact that their friends and families were all in other states and communication with them necessarily difficult, and above all that they stood in deadly peril of their lives—we think the failure of the trial court to give them reasonable time and opportunity to secure counsel was a clear denial of due process.
>
> But passing that, and assuming their inability, even if opportunity had been given, to employ counsel, as the trial court evidently did assume, we are of opinion that, under the circumstances just stated, the necessity of counsel was so vital and imperative that the failure of the trial court to make an effective appointment of counsel was likewise a denial of due process within the meaning of the Fourteenth Amendment. . . . (64–71)

Two members of the Court dissented because they objected to imposing the Bill of Rights on state criminal justice. Writing for himself and Justice McReynolds, Justice Pierce Butler wrote:

> The Court . . . declares that "the failure of the trial court to make an effective appointment of counsel was . . . a denial of due process within the meaning of the Fourteenth Amendment." This is an extension of federal authority into a field hitherto occupied exclusively by the several States. . . . The record wholly fails to reveal that petitioners have been deprived of any right guaranteed by the Federal Constitution, and I am of opinion that the judgment should be affirmed. (76–77)

## _Brown v. Mississippi_ and Coerced Confessions

With monsters like Hitler, Stalin, Mussolini, and Franco in the background providing hideous examples of what governments can do to individuals not protected by rights, the Court soon revisited the problem of state criminal justice. In 1936, the Court inched ahead the process of applying the due process clause to state criminal proceedings in _Brown v. Mississippi._

On the night of March 30, 1934, a deputy sheriff named Dial and other White men came to Yank Ellington's house and took him to a dead White man's house. There, they accused Ellington, a Black man, of murdering Raymond Stewart, the dead White man. When he denied it, they

> seized him, and with the participation of the deputy they hanged him by a rope to the limb of a tree, and, having let him down, they hung him again, and when he was let down the second time, and he still protested his innocence, he was tied to a tree and whipped, and, still declining to accede to the demands that he confess, he was finally released, and he returned with some difficulty to his home, suffering intense pain and agony. (281)

A day or two later, the deputy and another man returned to Ellington's house and arrested him. While on the way to jail,

> the deputy stopped and again severely whipped the defendant, declaring that he would continue the whipping until he confessed, and the defendant then agreed to confess to such a statement as the deputy would dictate, and he did so, after which he was delivered to jail.
>
> Two other ignorant negroes, Ed Brown and Henry Shields, were also arrested and taken to the same jail. On Sunday night, April 1, 1934, the same deputy, accompanied by a number of white men, one of whom was also an officer, and by the jailer, came to the jail, and the two last named defendants were made to strip and they were laid over chairs and their backs were cut to pieces with a leather strap with buckles on it, and they were likewise made by the said deputy definitely to understand that the whipping would be continued unless and until they confessed, and not only confessed, but confessed in every matter of detail as demanded by those present; and in this manner the defendants confessed the crime, and, as the whippings progressed and were repeated, they changed or adjusted their confession in all particulars of detail so as to conform to the demands of their torturers.
>
> When the confessions had been obtained in the exact form and contents as desired by the mob, they left with the parting admonition and warning that, if the defendants changed their story at any time in any respect from that last stated, the perpetrators of the outrage would administer the same or equally effective treatment. (281–82)

U.S. Supreme Court Chief Justice Charles Evans Hughes wrote that the trial "transcript reads more like pages torn from some medieval account than a record made within the confines of a modern civilization which aspires to an enlightened constitutional government" (282).

The chief justice continued:

> On the next day, that is, on Monday, April 2, when the defendants had been given time to recuperate somewhat from the tortures to which they had been subjected, the [sheriff and others] . . . came to the jail, accompanied by eight other persons, some of them deputies, there to hear the free and voluntary confession of these miserable and abject defendants.
>
> The sheriff . . . admitted that one of the defendants, when brought before him to confess, was limping and did not sit down, and that this particular defendant then and there stated that he had been strapped so severely that he could not sit down, and, as already stated, the signs of the rope on the neck of another of the defendants were plainly visible to all.
>
> Nevertheless the solemn farce of hearing the free and voluntary confessions was gone through with. . . . There was . . . enough before the court when these confessions were first offered to make known to the court that they were not, beyond all reasonable doubt, free and voluntary; and the failure of the court then to exclude the confessions is sufficient to reverse the judgment, under every rule of procedure that has heretofore been prescribed, and hence it was not necessary subsequently to renew the objections by motion or otherwise. (282–83)

On April 5, in the words of Chief Justice Hughes, the defendants' so-called trial was opened, and was concluded on the next day, April 6, 1934, and resulted in a pretended conviction with death sentences. The evidence upon which the conviction was obtained was the so-called confessions. . . . The defendants were put on the stand, and by their testimony the facts and the details thereof as to the manner by which the confessions were extorted from them were fully developed, and it is further disclosed by the record that the same deputy, Dial, under whose guiding hand and active participation the tortures to coerce the confessions were administered, was actively in the performance of the supposed duties of a court deputy in the courthouse and in the presence of the prisoners during what is denominated, in complimentary terms, the trial of these defendants. This deputy was put on the stand by the state in rebuttal, and admitted the whippings.

It is interesting to note that in his testimony with reference to the whipping of the defendant Ellington, and in response to the inquiry as to how severely he was whipped, the deputy stated, "Not too much for a negro; not as much as I would have done if it were left to me."

Two others who had participated in these whippings were introduced and admitted it—not a single witness was introduced who denied it. The facts are not only undisputed, they are admitted, and admitted to have been done by officers of the state, in conjunction with other participants, and all this was definitely well known to everybody connected with the trial, and during the trial, including the state's prosecuting attorney and the trial judge presiding. (284–85)

After a one-day trial, all three defendants were convicted and sentenced to death. The Mississippi Supreme Court affirmed the convictions. In the opinion reversing the convictions, Chief Justice Hughes wrote:

The state is free to regulate the procedure of its courts in accordance with its own conceptions of policy, unless in so doing it "offends some principle of justice so rooted in the traditions and conscience of our people as to be ranked as fundamental." . . .

The rack and torture chamber may not be substituted for the witness stand. The state may not permit an accused to be hurried to conviction under mob domination—where the whole proceeding is but a mask—without supplying corrective process.

The state may not deny to the accused the aid of counsel. Nor may a state, through the action of its officers, contrive a conviction through the pretense of a trial which in truth is "but used as a means of depriving a defendant of liberty through a deliberate deception of court and jury by the presentation of testimony known to be perjured."

And the trial equally is a mere pretense where the state authorities have contrived a conviction resting solely upon confessions obtained by violence. The due process clause requires "that state action, whether through one agency or another, shall be consistent with the fundamental principles of liberty and justice which lie at the base of all our civil and political institutions."

It would be difficult to conceive of methods more revolting to the sense of justice than those taken to procure the confessions of these petitioners, and the use of the confessions thus obtained as the basis for conviction and sentence was a clear denial of due process. (285–86)

 To learn more about the trial in *Brown v. Mississippi*, read the "Rest of the Story" on the Samaha Criminal Procedure 7e website: academic.cengage.com/criminaljustice/samaha.

## The Fundamental Fairness Doctrine

The two great cases *Powell v. Alabama* and *Brown v. Mississippi* established what came to be called the **fundamental fairness doctrine** of due process. According to the fundamental fairness doctrine, due process is a command to the states to provide two basics of a fair trial:

1. *Notice* to defendants of the charges against them

2. A *hearing* on the facts before convicting and punishing defendants

The specifics of notice and hearing facts are left to the individual states *and* to the developing notions of natural law.

From the 1930s through the 1950s, except for cases of extreme physical brutality like *Brown* and *Powell*, where Mississippi and Alabama provided no real hearing at all, a majority of the Court continued to reject the claim that the Bill of Rights applied to state criminal justice.

In <u>*Palko v. Connecticut* (1937)</u>, "one of the most influential [opinions] in the history of the court," Justice Cardozo conceded that some rights are "implicit in the concept of ordered liberty and thus, through the Fourteenth Amendment, became valid as against the states" (325). But, according to the Court, the Fourteenth Amendment imposes on the states only the rights that are "of the very essence of a scheme of ordered liberty" (325).

The Bill of Rights might include *some* of these fundamental rights. In *Palko*, the question was whether double jeopardy was one of them. Justice Cardozo put it this way: Did exposing Frank Palko to double jeopardy subject him to

> a hardship so shocking that our polity will not endure it? Does it violate those "fundamental principles of liberty and justice which lie at the base of all our civil and political institutions"? [No.] . . . The edifice of justice stands, in its symmetry, to many, greater than before. (328)

Justice Felix Frankfurter, the greatest defender of fundamental fairness, tried to capture its essence in two phrases: procedures that "offend the community's sense of fair play and decency" (*Rochin v. California* 1952, 173; excerpted later in the chapter, p. 33), and "conduct that shocks the conscience" (172).

## The Incorporation Doctrine

During the 1940s and 1950s, all the justices came to accept the idea that the Bill of Rights does impose limits on state criminal procedure. But they disagreed hotly over exactly why and what those limits are. The *fundamental fairness doctrine*, the idea that some higher law than the Bill of Rights defined due process, fueled a great debate on and off the Court.

A growing minority on the Court came to reject the fundamental fairness doctrine. In its place, they argued for the **incorporation doctrine**, which defined Fourteenth Amendment due process as applying the specific provisions of the Bill of Rights to state criminal procedure. By the 1960s, incorporation had claimed a majority of the Court as advocates. Part of the explanation was the Court's membership changed. The leaders of fundamental fairness, Justices Felix Frankfurter and Charles Whittaker, an ally of Justice Frankfurter, retired in 1962. President John F. Kennedy replaced them with two incorporationists, Justices Byron R. White and Arthur J. Goldberg.

The fundamental fairness doctrine and the incorporation doctrine differed significantly. First, the fundamental fairness doctrine focused on general fairness, whereas the incorporation doctrine focused on specific procedures. According to Professor Jerold Israel (1982):

> The concept of due process dated back to the Magna Carta, and English and American commentators had discussed it at length. The proponents of fundamental fairness viewed those authorities as having established a flexible standard of justice that focused on the

essence of fairness rather than the familiarity of form. Due process, under this view, was "a concept less rigid and more fluid than those envisaged in other specific and particular provisions of the Bill of Rights." Indeed, Justice Frankfurter described it as "perhaps, the least frozen concept of our law—the least confined to history and the most absorptive of powerful social standards of a progressive society."

Its basic objective was to provide "respect enforced by law" for that feeling of just treatment which has evolved through centuries of Anglo American constitutional history and civilization. Thus, it had a "natural law" background, which extended beyond procedural fairness and imposed limits as well on the substance of state regulation. (274)

According to proponents of the fundamental fairness doctrine, due process *might* include *some* of the specific procedural rights in the Bill of Rights, but, if it does, it's purely by chance.

On the other hand, the incorporation doctrine says that due process is shorthand for the specific procedural guarantees in the Bill of Rights. Justice Hugo L. Black, the incorporation doctrine's strongest advocate, maintained that due process grants only a "right to be tried by an independent and unprejudiced court using established procedures and applying valid pre-existing laws" (*Duncan v. Louisiana* 1968, 145). According to Justice Black, due process absorbs every specific right listed in the Bill of Rights (169).

Second, fundamental fairness and incorporation differ over the degree of uniformity of procedures required in state and local systems of criminal justice. According to the fundamental fairness doctrine, states could define most of their own criminal procedure law. The incorporation doctrine says that the states have to apply the procedures outlined in the Bill of Rights.

When the Court finally adopted the incorporation doctrine, justices continued to disagree strongly over which provisions the Fourteenth Amendment incorporated. A few justices, such as Justice Black, called for total incorporation, meaning that all the provisions were incorporated under the due process clause. Most supported the more moderate selective incorporation, meaning that some rights were incorporated and others weren't (Table 2.2).

The conflict over the fundamental fairness and incorporation doctrines is clear in our first case excerpt, *Rochin v. California* (1952). Although the case was decided before the Court's shift to selective incorporation, it's an excellent example of the two doctrines and how they apply to police actions. Writing for the Court majority, Justice Frankfurter applied the fundamental fairness doctrine but not without spirited dissenting opinions from Justices Black and Douglas, who favored the incorporation doctrine. Before you read the excerpt, study carefully "Briefing the Cases," in Chapter 1.

**TABLE 2.2**   **Fundamental Fairness and Total and Selective Incorporation**

| Fundamental Fairness | Total Incorporation | Selective Incorporation |
|---|---|---|
| General fairness | Entire Bill of Rights incorporated | Some of Bill of Rights incorporated |
| States define their own provisions | States have to follow procedures exactly as defined by U.S. Supreme Court | States have to follow procedures exactly as defined by U.S. Supreme Court |

## *Rochin v. California*
### 342 U.S. 165 (1952)

## HISTORY

Antonio Rochin was convicted of illegally possessing two capsules of morphine. He challenged the use of the two capsules as evidence against him. The trial court admitted the morphine capsules. Rochin appealed. The California District Court of Appeal affirmed the conviction. The California Supreme Court denied Rochin's petition to rehear the case without writing an opinion. The U.S. Supreme Court reversed.

FRANKFURTER, J.

## FACTS

Having "some information that Rochin was selling narcotics," three deputy sheriffs of the County of Los Angeles, on the morning of July 1, 1949, made for the two-story dwelling house in which Rochin lived with his mother, common-law wife, brothers and sisters. Finding the outside door open, they entered and then forced open the door to Rochin's room on the second floor. Inside they found petitioner sitting partly dressed on the side of his bed, upon which his wife was lying. On a "night stand" beside the bed the deputies spied two capsules. When asked, "Whose stuff is this?" Rochin seized the capsules and put them in his mouth. A struggle ensued, in the course of which the three officers "jumped upon him" and attempted to extract the capsules. The force they applied proved unavailing against Rochin's resistance.

He was handcuffed and taken to a hospital. At the direction of one of the officers a doctor forced an emetic solution through a tube into Rochin's stomach against his will. This "stomach pumping" produced vomiting. In the vomited matter were found two capsules which proved to contain morphine.

Rochin was brought to trial before a California Superior Court, sitting without a jury, on the charge of possessing "a preparation of morphine" in violation of the California Health and Safety Code 1947, § 11500. Rochin was convicted and sentenced to sixty days' imprisonment. The chief evidence against him was the two capsules. They were admitted over petitioner's objection, although the means of obtaining them was frankly set forth in the testimony by one of the deputies, substantially as here narrated.

On appeal, the District Court of Appeal affirmed the conviction, despite the finding that the officers "were guilty of unlawfully breaking into and entering defendant's room and were guilty of unlawfully assaulting and battering defendant while in the room," and "were guilty

of unlawfully assaulting, battering, torturing and falsely imprisoning the defendant at the alleged hospital."

One of the three judges, while finding that "the record in this case reveals a shocking series of violations of constitutional rights," concurred only because he felt bound by decisions of his Supreme Court. These, he asserted, "have been looked upon by law enforcement officers as an encouragement, if not an invitation, to the commission of such lawless acts."

The Supreme Court of California denied without opinion Rochin's petition for a hearing. This Court granted certiorari, because a serious question is raised as to the limitations which the Due Process Clause of the Fourteenth Amendment imposes on the conduct of criminal proceedings by the States.

## OPINION

In our federal system the administration of criminal justice is predominantly committed to the care of the States. . . . Broadly speaking, crimes in the United States are what the laws of the individual States make them. . . . Accordingly, in reviewing a State criminal conviction under a claim of right guaranteed by the Due Process Clause of the Fourteenth Amendment . . . we must be deeply mindful of the responsibilities of the States for the enforcement of criminal laws, and exercise with due humility our merely negative function in subjecting convictions from state courts to the very narrow scrutiny which the Due Process Clause of the Fourteenth Amendment authorizes. Due process of law, itself a historical product, is not to be turned into a destructive dogma against the States in the administration of their systems of criminal justice.

However, this Court too has its responsibility. Regard for the requirements of the Due Process Clause inescapably imposes upon this court an exercise of judgment upon the whole course of the proceedings . . . in order to ascertain whether they offend those canons of decency and fairness which express the notions of justice of English speaking peoples even toward those charged with the most heinous offenses. These standards of justice are not authoritatively formulated anywhere as though they were specifics. Due process of law is a summarized constitutional guarantee of respect for those personal immunities which, as Mr. Justice Cardozo twice wrote for the Court, are "so rooted in the traditions and conscience of our people as to be ranked as fundamental," or are "implicit in the concept of ordered liberty."

The Court's function in the observance of this settled conception of the Due Process Clause does not leave us without adequate guides in subjecting State criminal procedures to constitutional judgment. In dealing not with the machinery of government but with human rights, the absence of formal exactitude, or want of fixity of meaning, is not an unusual or even regrettable attribute of constitutional provisions. Words being symbols do not speak without a gloss explanation. . . .

When the gloss . . . is a function of the process of judgment, the judgment is bound to fall differently at different times and differently at the same time through different judges. Even more specific provisions, such as the guaranty of freedom of speech and the detailed protection against unreasonable searches and seizures, have inevitably evoked as sharp divisions in this Court as the least specific and most comprehensive protection of liberties, the Due Process Clause.

The vague contours of the Due Process Clause do not leave judges at large. We may not draw on our merely personal and private notions and disregard the limits that bind judges in their judicial function. Even though the concept of due process of law is not final and fixed, these limits are derived from considerations that are fused in the whole nature of our judicial process. These are considerations deeply rooted in reason and in the compelling traditions of the legal profession. The Due Process Clause places upon this Court the duty of exercising a judgment . . . upon interests of society pushing in opposite directions.

. . . In each case "due process of law" requires an evaluation based on a . . . detached consideration of conflicting claims, on a judgment . . . duly mindful of reconciling the needs both of continuity and of change in a progressive society.

Applying these general considerations to the circumstances of the present case, we are compelled to conclude that the proceedings by which this conviction was obtained do more than offend some fastidious squeamishness or private sentimentalism about combating crime too energetically. This is conduct that shocks the conscience. Illegally breaking into the privacy of Rochin, the struggle to open his mouth and remove what was there, the forcible extraction of his stomach's contents—this course of proceeding by agents of government to obtain evidence is bound to offend even hardened sensibilities. They are methods too close to the rack and the screw to permit of constitutional differentiation. . . .

On the facts of this case the conviction of Rochin has been obtained by methods that offend the Due Process Clause. The judgment below must be reversed.

## CONCURRING OPINION

BLACK, J.

. . . I believe that faithful adherence to the specific guarantees in the Bill of Rights insures a more permanent protection of individual liberty than that which can be afforded by the nebulous standards stated by the majority. What the majority hold is that the Due Process Clause empowers this Court to nullify any state law if its application "shocks the conscience," offends "a sense of justice" or runs counter to the "decencies of civilized conduct."

The majority emphasize that these statements do not refer to their own consciences or to their senses of justice and decency. For we are told that "we may not draw on our merely personal and private notions"; our judgment must be grounded on "considerations deeply rooted in reason and in the compelling traditions of the legal profession."

We are further admonished to measure the validity of state practices, not by our reason, or by the traditions of the legal profession, but by "the community's sense of fair play and decency"; by the "traditions and conscience of our people"; or by "those canons of decency and fairness which express the notions of justice of English speaking peoples." These canons are made necessary, it is said, because of "interests of society pushing in opposite directions."

If the Due Process Clause does vest this Court with such unlimited power to invalidate laws, I am still in doubt as to why we should consider only the notions of English speaking peoples to determine what are immutable and fundamental principles of justice.

Moreover, one may well ask what avenues of investigation are open to discover "canons" of conduct so universally favored that this Court should write them into the Constitution? All we are told is that the discovery must be made by an "evaluation based on a disinterested inquiry pursued in the spirit of science, on a balanced order of facts." . . .

Of even graver concern, however, is the use of philosophy to nullify the Bill of Rights. I long ago concluded that the accordion-like qualities of this philosophy must inevitably imperil all the individual liberty safeguards specifically enumerated in the Bill of Rights. . . .

## Questions

1. Why did the police actions violate Rochin's due process?

2. Does the police conduct in this case "shock your conscience"? Why or why not?

3. Are "shocks the conscience," offending the "community's sense of fair play and decency," "traditions and conscience of our people," and "those canons of decency and fairness which express the notions of justice of English speaking peoples" purely a matter of personal opinion, or are they objective tests? Explain.

4. Summarize how Justice Frankfurter defines and defends the fundamental fairness doctrine.

5. Summarize how Justice Black defines and defends the incorporation doctrine.

6. In your opinion, which doctrine is better? Back up your answer with the facts of the case and the arguments of the majority and concurring opinions.

| TABLE 2.3 | Bill of Rights Provisions Incorporated (as of 2007) |
|---|---|
| **Bill of Rights Provision** | **Case** |
| Unreasonable searches and seizures | *Wolf v. Colorado* (1949) |
| Exclusionary rule applied to state searches and seizures | *Mapp v. Ohio* (1961) |
| Self-incrimination | *Malloy v. Hogan* (1964) |
| Assistance of counsel | *Gideon v. Wainwright* (1963) |
| Confront witnesses against the accused | *Pointer v. Texas* (1965) |
| Compulsory process to obtain witnesses | *Washington v. Texas* (1967) |
| Speedy trial | *Klopfer v. North Carolina* (1967) |
| Cruel and unusual punishment | *Robinson v. California* (1962) |

During the 1960s, the majority of the Supreme Court opted for the selective incorporation doctrine. By 1970, Justice William Brennan (1977) wrote, the incorporation doctrine had changed the "face of the law" (493).

Cases decided in the 1960s specifically incorporated all but four of the Bill of Rights guarantees relating to criminal justice: public trial, notice of charges, prohibition of excessive bail, and prosecution by indictment (Table 2.3). In cases decided since the 1960s, the Court has implied that the Fourteenth Amendment due process absorbs all but indictment by grand jury.

Incorporated rights apply to the states exactly as the U.S. Supreme Court mandates the federal courts to practice them. States have to apply the rights "jot-for-jot and case for case," as one of the doctrine's severest critics, Justice John Harlan, put it. Justice Brennan defended the jot-for-jot standard: "Only impermissible subjective judgments can explain stopping short of the incorporation of the full sweep of the specific being absorbed" (Friendly 1965, 936).

The Court didn't just shift its reason for intervening in state criminal procedure, it did something far more consequential and controversial for day-to-day criminal procedure. It also expanded its intervention from the courtroom to the police station in interrogation and right to counsel (Chapter 8); search and seizure (Chapters 3–7); identification procedures (Chapter 9); and even onto the street and other public places (stop and frisk, Chapter 4).

The labels used to describe this enormous expansion of federal intervention in local law enforcement ("handcuffing the police," "constitutionalizing criminal procedure," "policing the police," "judicial lawmaking") only hint at the firestorm of controversy set off by the highest court in the land (and the least democratic branch of the government) when the U.S. Supreme Court got involved in reviewing the day-to-day activities of police officers in every city, town, and village in the country (Graham 1970).

The critics of incorporation—it had and still has many—charged that incorporation destroys federalism, interferes with local criminal justice, and guts the need for both local variety and experiments with different solutions to problems in criminal justice administration. They maintain that the great differences among the states and among federal, state, and local systems of criminal justice demand local control and variation.

Critics rightly observe that federal criminal justice consists mainly of cases involving fraud, tax evasion, and other complex crimes. Investigation takes place largely in offices, not in the field. Local law enforcement deals mainly with the hurly-burly street crimes that bring local police into contact with violent individuals and strangers who are difficult to identify, apprehend, and bring to trial. As a result, the critics say, the Bill of Rights works well for federal but not state and local criminal justice. Furthermore, most local police aren't highly trained college graduates, as are the federal police, particularly FBI agents. So, according to the critics, the incorporation doctrine works effectively for the 0.6 percent of federal criminal cases but not for the remaining 99.4 percent of state cases (Graham 1970).

The criticisms target all criminal justice agencies, but perhaps nothing generates more controversy than whether or not uniform standards ought to apply to local police departments. Cries that the U.S. Supreme Court was "running local police departments" from Washington and "handcuffing" local police by doing so were common during the late 1960s, following the decision in the famous *Miranda* case (Chapter 8). So damaging to the Court's prestige was *Miranda v. Arizona* (1966) that the decision was labeled one of three times in its history that the Court was the object of a "self-inflicted wound" (Graham 1970).

The Court may have wounded itself, but, by most accounts, contrary to its opponents' fears, the incorporation doctrine hasn't wounded criminal justice. The Supreme Court's flexible interpretations of the constitutional protections permit plenty of local diversity and experimentation. A good example is *Chandler v. Florida* (1981). Noel Chandler argued that Florida's practice of televising trials violated his right to a fair trial. The Court rejected Chandler's claim. Chief Justice Warren Burger, no fan of television in the courts, supported the right of local jurisdictions to follow their own practices:

> Dangers lurk in this, as in most experiments, but unless we were to conclude that television coverage under all conditions is prohibited by the Constitution, the state must be free to experiment. We are not empowered by the Constitution to oversee or harness state procedural experimentation; only when the state action infringes fundamental guarantees are we authorized to intervene. We must assume state courts will be alert to any factors that impair the fundamental rights of the accused. Absent a showing of prejudice of constitutional dimensions to these defendants, there is no reason for this Court either to endorse or to invalidate Florida's experiment. (582)

# EQUAL PROTECTION OF THE LAW

Constitutional democracy couldn't survive without protecting our right to fair procedures guaranteed by due process of law. But neither could it survive without the equal protection of those procedures for everybody. Equality is deeply embedded in the concept of U.S. constitutionalism. In the years just prior to the Revolution, one commentator wrote, "The least considerable man among us has an interest equal to the proudest nobleman, in the laws and constitution of his country" (Inbau and others 1984, 209). In the 1960s, we used to state this value on equality in blunter terms: "If the rich can beat the rap, then everyone should beat the rap."

Equality before the law is more than a slogan in criminal justice; since 1868, it's been a constitutional command. According to the Fourteenth Amendment to the U.S. Constitution:

> No state shall . . . deny to any person within its jurisdiction the equal protection of the laws.

Be aware that **equal protection** of the law doesn't mean state officials have to treat everybody exactly alike. It means they can't investigate, apprehend, convict, and punish people *unreasonably*. So courts look very suspiciously at the reasonableness of certain classifications, particularly those based on race or ethnicity. In practice, it's very difficult to prove claims that officials denied equal protection. Claimants have to prove two facts: first, that the official action had a **discriminatory effect**. Specifically, this means proving that race or some other illegal group characteristic (not a legitimate criterion, such as seriousness of the offense or criminal record) accounts for the official decision.

Second, and much more difficult, claimants have to prove **discriminatory purpose**—that in the case at hand, the specific officer intended to discriminate against the complainant because of her race or other illegal criteria. For example, proving an official said (and meant) "I hate Hispanics" isn't good enough to win an equal protection case. The claimant has to prove, for example, that the prosecutor decided to charge a specific Hispanic because of her Hispanic ethnicity. So proving the prosecutor said (and meant), "I charged her because she was Hispanic" would be good enough. Of course, in this day and age of political correctness, it's unlikely any prosecutor would say that. Without such an admission, the claimant probably couldn't prove discriminatory intent.

In addition to the difficulty of proving discriminatory effect and discriminatory purpose, there's another hurdle: the **presumption of regularity**. Government actions are presumed lawful unless there's "clear evidence to the contrary." Claimants have the burden to *disprove* they were denied equal protection. In our next case excerpt, *U.S. v. Armstrong* (1996), the U.S. Supreme Court ruled that Christopher Lee Armstrong and four other Black men didn't overcome the presumption of regularity.

C A S E    *Was the Race-Based Drug Prosecution Provable?*

### *U.S. v. Armstrong*
517 U.S. 456 (1996)

### HISTORY

Christopher Lee Armstrong, Aaron Hampton, Freddie Mack, Shelton Martin, and Robert Rozelle (respondents) were indicted on charges of conspiring to possess with intent to distribute more than 50 grams of cocaine base (crack) and conspiring to distribute the same, in violation of 21 U.S.C. §§ 841 and 846, and federal firearms offenses.

They entered a **motion for discovery** on a claim of selective prosecution. (*Discovery* is a legal action asking for a court order to compel one side—the U.S. Attorney's office in this case—to turn over information that may help the other side—in this case, the respondents.)

The U.S. District Court for the Central District of California granted the motion. The Government appealed. A three-judge panel of the 9th Circuit Court of Appeals reversed. Rehearing **en banc** (hearing by all the judges on the Court) was granted. The full Court of Appeals affirmed

the District Court. The U.S. Supreme Court granted certiorari, and reversed and remanded the case.

REHNQUIST, C.J., JOINED BY O'CONNOR, SCALIA, KENNEDY, SOUTER, THOMAS, AND GINSBURG, JJ.

In this case, we consider the showing necessary for a defendant to be entitled to discovery on a claim that the prosecuting attorney singled him out for prosecution on the basis of his race. We conclude that respondents failed to satisfy the threshold showing: They failed to show that the Government declined to prosecute similarly situated suspects of other races.

### FACTS

For three months prior to the indictment, agents of the Federal Bureau of Alcohol, Tobacco, and Firearms and the Narcotics Division of the Inglewood, California, Police Department had infiltrated a suspected crack distribution ring by using three confidential informants. On seven separate occasions during this period, the informants had bought a total of 124.3 grams of crack from respondents and witnessed respondents carrying firearms during the sales.

The agents searched the hotel room in which the sales were transacted, arrested respondents Armstrong and Hampton in the room, and found more crack and a loaded gun. The agents later arrested the other respondents as part of the ring.

In response to the indictment, respondents filed a motion for discovery or for dismissal of the indictment, alleging they were selected for federal prosecution because they are black. In support of their motion, they offered only an affidavit by a "Paralegal Specialist," employed by the Office of the Federal Public Defender representing one of the respondents.

The only allegation in the affidavit was that, in every one of the 24 § 841 or § 846 cases closed by the office during 1991, the defendant was black. Accompanying the affidavit was a "study" listing the 24 defendants, their race, whether they were prosecuted for dealing cocaine as well as crack, and the status of each case.

The Government opposed the discovery motion, arguing . . . that there was no evidence or allegation "that the Government has acted unfairly or has prosecuted nonblack defendants or failed to prosecute them."

The District Court granted the motion. It ordered the Government

1. to provide a list of all cases from the last three years in which the Government charged both cocaine and firearms offenses,

2. to identify the race of the defendants in those cases,

3. to identify what levels of law enforcement were involved in the investigations of those cases, and

4. to explain its criteria for deciding to prosecute those defendants for federal cocaine offenses.

The Government moved for reconsideration of the District Court's discovery order. With this motion it submitted affidavits and other evidence to explain why it had chosen to prosecute respondents and why respondents' study did not support the inference that the Government was singling out blacks for cocaine prosecution.

The federal and local agents participating in the case alleged in affidavits that race played no role in their investigation. An Assistant United States Attorney explained in an affidavit that the decision to prosecute met the general criteria for prosecution, because

there was over 100 grams of cocaine base involved, over twice the threshold necessary for a ten year mandatory minimum sentence; there were multiple sales involving multiple defendants, thereby indicating a fairly substantial crack cocaine ring; . . . there were multiple federal firearms violations intertwined with the narcotics trafficking; the overall evidence in the case was extremely strong, including audio and videotapes of defendants; . . . and several of the defendants had criminal histories including narcotics and firearms violations.

The Government also submitted sections of a published 1989 Drug Enforcement Administration report which concluded that "large-scale, interstate trafficking networks controlled by Jamaicans, Haitians and Black street gangs dominate the manufacture and distribution of crack."

In response, one of respondents' attorneys submitted an affidavit alleging that an intake coordinator at a drug treatment center had told her that there are "an equal number of Caucasian users and dealers to minority users and dealers."

Respondents also submitted an affidavit from a criminal defense attorney alleging that in his experience many non blacks are prosecuted in state court for crack offenses, and a newspaper article reporting that federal "crack criminals . . . are being punished far more severely than if they had been caught with powder cocaine, and almost every single one of them is black."

The District Court denied the motion for reconsideration. When the Government indicated it would not comply with the court's discovery order, the court dismissed the case. . . .

A divided three-judge panel of the Court of Appeals for the Ninth Circuit reversed, holding that, because of the proof requirements for a selective-prosecution claim, defendants must "provide a colorable basis for believing that 'others similarly situated have not been prosecuted'" to obtain discovery.

The Court of Appeals voted to rehear the case *en banc*, and the *en banc* panel affirmed the District Court's order of dismissal, holding that "a defendant is not required to demonstrate that the government has failed to prosecute others who are similarly situated." We granted certiorari to determine the appropriate standard for discovery for a selective-prosecution claim.

## OPINION

The presumption of regularity supports prosecutorial decisions and, in the absence of clear evidence to the contrary, courts presume that they have properly discharged their official duties. In the ordinary case, so long as the prosecutor has probable cause to believe that the accused committed an offense defined by statute, the decision whether or not to prosecute, and what charge to file or bring before a grand jury, generally rests entirely in his discretion.

Of course, a prosecutor's discretion is "subject to constitutional constraints." . . . The decision whether to prosecute may not be based on "an unjustifiable standard such as race, religion, or other arbitrary classification." A defendant may demonstrate that the administration of a criminal law is "directed so exclusively against a particular class of persons . . . with a mind so unequal and oppressive" that the system of prosecution amounts to "a practical denial" of equal protection of the law.

In order to dispel the presumption that a prosecutor has not violated equal protection, a criminal defendant must present "clear evidence to the contrary." . . . Judicial deference to the decisions of these executive officers rests in part on an assessment of the relative competence of prosecutors and courts. "Such factors as the strength of the case, the prosecution's general deterrence value, the Government's enforcement priorities, and the case's relationship to the Government's overall enforcement plan are not readily susceptible to the kind of analysis the courts are competent to undertake."

It also stems from a concern not to unnecessarily impair the performance of a core executive constitutional function. "Examining the basis of a prosecution delays the criminal proceeding, threatens to chill law enforcement by subjecting the prosecutor's motives and decision making to outside inquiry, and may undermine prosecutorial effectiveness by revealing the Government's enforcement policy."

The requirements for a selective-prosecution claim draw on "ordinary equal protection standards." The claimant must demonstrate that the federal prosecutorial policy "had a discriminatory effect and that it was motivated by a discriminatory purpose." To establish a discriminatory effect in a race case, the claimant must show that similarly situated individuals of a different race were not prosecuted. . . .

Having reviewed the requirements to prove a selective prosecution claim [itself], we turn to the showing necessary to obtain discovery in support of such a claim. If discovery is ordered, the Government must assemble from its own files documents which might corroborate or refute the defendant's claim. Discovery . . . will divert prosecutors' resources and may disclose the Government's prosecutorial strategy. The justifications for a rigorous standard for the elements of a selective-prosecution claim thus require a correspondingly rigorous standard for discovery in aid of such a claim. . . .

In this case we consider what evidence constitutes "some evidence tending to show the existence" of the discriminatory effect element. The Court of Appeals held that a defendant may establish a colorable basis for discriminatory effect without evidence that the Government has failed to prosecute others who are similarly situated to the defendant. We think it was mistaken in this view. . . .

In the case before us, respondents' "study" did not constitute "some evidence tending to show the existence of the essential elements of" a selective-prosecution claim. The study failed to identify individuals who were not black and could have been prosecuted for the offenses for which respondents were charged, but were not so prosecuted. This omission was not remedied by respondents' evidence in opposition to the Government's motion for reconsideration.

The newspaper article, which discussed the discriminatory effect of federal drug sentencing laws, was not relevant to an allegation of discrimination in decisions to prosecute. Respondents' affidavits, which recounted one attorney's conversation with a drug treatment center employee and the experience of another attorney defending drug prosecutions in state court, recounted hearsay and reported personal conclusions based on anecdotal evidence.

The judgment of the Court of Appeals is therefore reversed, and the case is remanded for proceedings consistent with this opinion.

# DISSENT

STEVENS, J.

. . . The Court correctly concludes that in this case the facts presented to the District Court in support of respondents' claim that they had been singled out for prosecution because of their race were not sufficient to prove that defense. Moreover, I agree with the Court that their showing was not strong enough to give them a right to discovery. . . .

Like Chief Judge Wallace of the Court of Appeals, however, I am persuaded that the District Judge did not abuse her discretion when she concluded that the factual showing was sufficiently disturbing to require some response from the United States Attorney's Office. Perhaps the discovery order was broader than necessary, but I cannot agree with the Court's apparent conclusion that no inquiry was permissible.

The District Judge's order should be evaluated in light of three circumstances that underscore the need for judicial vigilance over certain types of drug prosecutions. First, the Anti-Drug Abuse Act of 1986 and subsequent legislation established a regime of extremely high penalties for the possession and distribution of so-called "crack" cocaine.

Those provisions treat one gram of crack as the equivalent of 100 grams of powder cocaine. The distribution of 50 grams of crack is thus punishable by the same mandatory minimum sentence of 10 years in prison that applies to the distribution of 5,000 grams of powder cocaine.

The Sentencing Guidelines extend this ratio to penalty levels above the mandatory minimums: For any given quantity of crack, the guideline range is the same as if the offense had involved 100 times that amount in powder cocaine. These penalties result in sentences for crack offenders that average three to eight times longer than sentences for comparable powder offenders.

Second, the disparity between the treatment of crack cocaine and powder cocaine is matched by the disparity between the severity of the punishment imposed by federal law and that imposed by state law for the same conduct.

For a variety of reasons, often including the absence of mandatory minimums, the existence of parole, and lower baseline penalties, terms of imprisonment for drug offenses tend to be substantially lower in state systems than in the federal system. The difference is especially marked in the case of crack offenses. The majority of States draw no distinction between types of cocaine in their penalty schemes; of those that do, none has established as stark a differential as the Federal Government. For example, if respondent Hampton is found guilty, his federal sentence might be as long as a mandatory life term. Had he been tried in state court, his sentence could have been as short as 12 years, less worktime credits of half that amount.

Under California law at the time of the offenses, possession for sale of cocaine base involving 50 grams carried a penalty of imprisonment for either three, four, or five years. If the defendant had no prior convictions, he could be granted probation. § 11370. For each prior felony drug conviction, the defendant received an additional 3-year sentence. § 11370.2.

Thus, with three priors and the possibility of work time reductions, Hampton could have served as little as six years under California law. Since the time of the offenses, California has raised several of these penalties, but the new punishments could not be applied to respondents.

Finally, it is undisputed that the brunt of the elevated federal penalties falls heavily on blacks. While 65% of the persons who have used crack are white, in 1993 they represented only 4% of the federal offenders convicted of trafficking in crack. Eighty-eight percent of such defendants were black. During the first 18 months of full guideline implementation, the sentencing disparity between black and white defendants grew from preguideline levels: Blacks on average received sentences over 40% longer than whites.

Those figures represent a major threat to the integrity of federal sentencing reform, whose main purpose was the elimination of disparity (especially racial) in sentencing. . . .

The extraordinary severity of the imposed penalties and the troubling racial patterns of enforcement give rise to a special concern about the fairness of charging practices for crack offenses. Evidence tending to prove that black defendants charged with distribution of crack in the Central District of California are prosecuted in federal court, whereas members of other races charged with similar offenses are prosecuted in state court, warrants close scrutiny by the federal judges in that district.

In my view, the District Judge, who has sat on both the federal and the state benches in Los Angeles, acted well within her discretion to call for the development of facts that would demonstrate what standards, if any, governed the choice of forum where similarly situated offenders are prosecuted.

Respondents submitted a study showing that of all cases involving crack offenses that were closed by the Federal Public Defender's Office in 1991, 24 out of 24 involved black defendants. To supplement this evidence, they submitted affidavits from two of the attorneys in the defense team. The first reported a statement from an intake coordinator at a local drug treatment center that, in his experience, an equal number of crack users and dealers were Caucasian as belonged to minorities.

The second was from David R. Reed, counsel for respondent Armstrong. Reed was both an active court-appointed attorney in the Central District of California and one of the directors of the leading association of criminal defense lawyers who practice before the Los Angeles County courts. Reed stated that he did not recall "ever handling a [crack] cocaine case involving non-black defendants" in federal court, nor had he even heard of one. He further stated that "there are many crack cocaine sales cases prosecuted in state court that do involve racial groups other than blacks."

The majority discounts the probative value of the affidavits, claiming they recounted "hearsay" and reported "personal conclusions based on anecdotal evidence." But the Reed affidavit plainly contained more than mere hearsay; Reed offered information based on his own extensive experience in both federal and state courts. Given the breadth of his background, he was well qualified to compare the practices of federal and state prosecutors.

In any event, the Government never objected to the admission of either affidavit on hearsay or any other grounds. It was certainly within the District Court's discretion to credit the affidavits of two members of the bar of that Court, at least one of whom had presumably acquired a reputation by his frequent appearances there, and both of whose statements were made on pains of perjury.

The criticism that the affidavits were based on "anecdotal evidence" is also unpersuasive. I thought it was agreed that defendants do not need to prepare sophisticated statistical studies in order to receive mere discovery in cases like this one. Certainly evidence based on a drug counselor's personal observations or on an attorney's practice in two sets of courts, state and federal, can "'tend to show the existence'" of a selective prosecution.

Even if respondents failed to carry their burden of showing that there were individuals who were not black but who could have been prosecuted in federal court for the same offenses, it does not follow that the District Court abused its discretion in ordering discovery. There can be no doubt that such individuals exist, and indeed the Government has never denied the same. In those circumstances, I fail to see why the District Court was unable to take judicial notice of this obvious fact and demand information from the Government's files to support or refute respondents' evidence.

The presumption that some whites are prosecuted in state court is not "contradicted" by the statistics the majority cites, which show only that high percentages of blacks are convicted of certain federal crimes, while high percentages of whites are convicted of other federal crimes. Those figures are entirely consistent with the allegation of selective prosecution.

The relevant comparison, rather, would be with the percentages of blacks and whites who commit those crimes. But, as discussed above, in the case of crack far greater numbers of whites are believed guilty of using the substance. The District Court, therefore, was entitled to find the evidence before it significant and to require some explanation from the Government.

Also telling was the Government's response to respondents' evidentiary showing. It submitted a list of more than 3,500 defendants who had been charged with federal narcotics violations over the previous three years. It also offered the names of 11 nonblack defendants whom it had prosecuted for crack offenses. All 11, however, were members of other racial or ethnic minorities. The District Court was authorized to draw adverse inferences from the Government's inability to produce a single example of a white defendant, especially when the very purpose of its exercise was to allay the court's concerns about the evidence of racially selective prosecutions. As another court has said: "Statistics are not, of course, the whole answer, but nothing is as emphatic as zero. . . ."

In sum, . . . "while the exercise of discretion by prosecutors and investigators has an impact on sentences in almost all cases to some extent, because of the 100-to-1 quantity ratio and federal mandatory minimum penalties, discretionary decisions in cocaine cases often have dramatic effects."

The severity of the penalty heightens both the danger of arbitrary enforcement and the need for careful scrutiny of any colorable claim of discriminatory enforcement. In this case, the evidence was sufficiently disturbing to persuade the District Judge to order discovery that might help explain the conspicuous racial pattern of cases before her court. I cannot accept the majority's conclusion that the District Judge either exceeded her power or abused her discretion when she did so. I therefore respectfully dissent.

## Questions

1. Summarize the facts presented by the defendants in favor of the discovery of information to support a claim of selective enforcement of the drug laws.

2. Summarize the facts presented by the government against the discovery of information to support a claim of selective enforcement of the drug laws.

3. Assume that you're the defendants' lawyer. Argue the case in favor of discovery.

4. Assume that you're the prosecutor. Argue the case against discovery.

5. Now, assume that you're the judge. Rule on the motion to discover. State your reasons for your ruling on the motion.

 Go to Exercise 2.1 on the Samaha Criminal Procedure 7e website to learn more about the statistics relied on by the majority and the dissent in *U.S. v. Armstrong:* academic.cengage.com/criminaljustice/samaha.

## SUMMARY

### I. Constitutions
A. Constitutions last forever and are a set of permanent, general principles.
B. Constitutions have six characteristics:
   1. They are the highest form of law.
   2. They express the will of the whole people.
   3. They always bind the government.
   4. They cannot be changed by the government.
   5. They can only be changed by direct action by the whole people.
   6. They embody the fundamental values of the people.
C. The law of criminal procedure is based on the Bill of Rights.
D. The highest authority in criminal procedure is the U.S. Constitution.

### II. Criminal Procedure Provisions and the Constitution
A. Most criminal procedure provisions are found in the following amendments to the Constitution:
   1. Fourth
   2. Fifth
   3. Sixth
   4. Eighth
   5. Fourteenth

### III. The U.S. Constitution and the Courts
A. The U.S. Constitution is the last word in criminal procedure.
B. The supremacy clause and judicial review together establish that criminal procedure has to answer to the U.S. Constitution.

C. All courts can interpret the Constitution, but the U.S. Supreme Court has the final word.

D. The decisions of the high court bind all other courts.

E. There are two limits on the Supreme Court's enormous power:
1. The dependence on local courts, prosecutors, and police to apply its decisions to day-to-day operations
2. The power of other courts to answer constitutional questions the Supreme Court has yet to answer

F. The U.S. Supreme Court can only control the law of criminal procedure in state courts if the states' rules violate the U.S. Constitution.

## IV. State Constitutions and State Courts

A. All state constitutions guarantee state citizens basic equal rights.

B. State courts are a source of criminal procedure in two types of cases:
1. Those involving the U.S. Constitution that the U.S. Supreme Court hasn't made a decision on yet
2. Those involving their own state constitution

C. States are allowed to raise the minimum standards of rights set by the U.S. Supreme Court but can't reduce rights below that standard.

## V. Due Process of Law

A. According to the Fourteenth Amendment, due process and equal protection of the law are two guarantees that states have to provide.

B. The "due process revolution" expanded the protection of rights to all people, from the powerful to the vulnerable classes.

C. States and the federal government were compelled to guarantee these rights to vulnerable classes.

D. Due process guarantees fair procedures for deciding cases.
1. In *Hurtado v. California* (1884), defendant Joseph Hurtado was indicted in a murder case without being charged by a grand jury.
   a. He argued that charging by information was unconstitutional under the Fourteenth Amendment due process command, in which states provide a grand jury indictment under the Fifth Amendment.
   b. The court rejected his argument but would later adopt this view in the 1960s.
2. The famous Scottsboro case (1932), *Powell v. Alabama*, set the stage for incorporation doctrine in the 1960s.
   a. Nine Black defendants were rounded up and charged with raping two White girls.
   b. With an alcoholic defense attorney, eight of the boys were tried, convicted, and sentenced to death within four days.
   c. The Alabama Supreme Court upheld the convictions.
   d. The U.S. Supreme Court overturned the convictions, citing that the boys were denied due process of law.
3. *Brown v. Mississippi* (1936) helped the court inch forward the idea of due process in state criminal proceedings.
   a. Yank Ellington, Ed Brown, and Henry Shields, all Black men, were accused of killing a White man.
   b. They were severely and repeatedly beaten until they confessed, agreeing to exactly the terms their accusers demanded.

c. After a one-day trial, all three were convicted and sentenced to death.
d. The Mississippi Supreme Court affirmed the convictions.
e. The U.S. Supreme Court reversed the convictions on the ground that the confessions were anything but voluntary.

E. The fundamental fairness doctrine commands states to provide two basics of a fair trial:
1. Notice to defendants of the charges against them
2. A hearing on the facts before convicting and punishing defendants

F. From the 1930s through the 1950s, a majority of the Court rejected the notion that the Bill of Rights applied to state criminal proceedings.
1. During the 1940s and 1950s, all the justices came to believe that the Bill of Rights does impose limits on state criminal proceedings.
2. Finally, in the 1960s, a majority of the court defined Fourteenth Amendment due process as applying the specific provisions of the Bill of Rights to state criminal procedure.

## VI. Equal Protection of the Law

A. Equal protection of the law is more than a slogan in criminal justice; it has been a constitutional command since 1868.
B. Equal protection protects people from being investigated, apprehended, convicted, and punished unreasonably.
C. In claiming violation of equal protection of the law, defendants have to prove two very high burden of proof elements, and they rarely succeed:
1. The official action was based on race or some other group identity.
2. The named official in the case intended to discriminate against the named individual because of race or some other group identity.

## REVIEW QUESTIONS

1. What is the difference between constitutions and laws?

2. Identify six characteristics of constitutionalism.

3. Identify and summarize the five amendments to the U.S. Constitution that most concern criminal procedure.

4. What is the meaning of the supremacy clause?

5. Identify and describe two limits imposed on the U.S. Supreme Court.

6. Explain the meaning and significance of the phrase, "It doesn't pay a law much of a compliment to declare it constitutional."

7. How did the expansion of the Bill of Rights to state proceedings change the due process and equal protection of law clauses?

8. Explain how the Bill of Rights has been applied to criminal procedure from colonial times until the Civil War.

9. Identify the major aspects of the 1960s "due process revolution."

10. Identify the circumstances surrounding *Hurtado v. California*. What significance to the Fourteenth Amendment does this case have?

11. What did political movements in Europe have to do with the decision in *Powell v. Alabama?*

12. What was the main argument in *Powell v. Alabama,* and what was the decision?

13. Describe the proceedings of the *Brown v. Mississippi* case. What impact did it have in terms of the Fourteenth Amendment?

14. Identify and explain two elements of the fundamental fairness doctrine.

15. Explain the differences between the fundamental fairness doctrine and the incorporation doctrine.

16. Identify the arguments for and against the fundamental fairness doctrine and the incorporation doctrine.

17. Identify and describe the two elements claimants have to prove violated their right to equal protection of the law.

18. Explain why it's difficult to win claims that the government denied a person equal protection of the law.

## KEY TERMS

constitutionalism, p. 22
law of criminal procedure, p. 22
*Model Code of Pre-Arraignment*
    *Procedure,* p. 22
supremacy clause, p. 23
judicial review, p. 23
supervisory power, p. 24

parallel rights, p. 24
due process, p. 25
procedural due process, p. 25
information, p. 26
fundamental fairness doctrine,
    p. 30
incorporation doctrine, p. 31

equal protection, p. 36
discriminatory effect, p. 37
discriminatory purpose, p. 37
presumption of regularity, p. 37
motion for discovery, p. 37
en banc, p. 37

# The Definition
# of Searches and Seizures

## MAIN POINTS

- Crime control depends on information, but that information usually comes from reluctant sources.
- Originally, search and seizure were government operations used to enforce sedition and customs laws.
- The Fourth Amendment balances government power to control crime and the right of people to be let alone by the government; so it doesn't ban all searches and seizures, only "unreasonable" ones.
- Government actions aren't searches unless they invade a person's reasonable expectation of privacy.
- Discoveries of evidence in plain view, in public places, in open fields, or on abandoned property aren't searches, and so the Fourth Amendment doesn't apply to them.
- Searches aren't unreasonable if they're backed up by an objective basis (facts and circumstances); the more invasive the search, the greater the objective basis required.
- People aren't "seized" whenever officers approach them and ask questions; they're seized only when they're either physically detained or submit to an officer's display of authority.

*The right of the people to be secure in their houses, persons, papers, and effects against unreasonable searches and seizure, shall not be violated; and no warrants shall be issued but upon probable cause, supported by oath or affirmation, and particularly describing the place to be searched, and the persons or things to be seized.*

Fourth Amendment, U.S. Constitution

*For clarity and consistency, the law of the fourth amendment is not the Supreme Court's most successful product. In Mr. Justice Frankfurter's graceful phrase, " . . . the course of the true law pertaining to searches and seizures . . . has not . . . run smooth." Professor LaFave, who borrowed that phrase to title an article, observed that "[no] area of the law has more bedeviled the judiciary, from the Justices of the Supreme Court down to the magistrate. . . ." In a badly fractured recent decision, one of the few passages that commanded a majority of the Court, conceded that "it would be nonsense to pretend that our decision reduces Fourth Amendment law to complete order and harmony." A subsequent article concluded that "[t]he fourth amendment cases are a mess."*

Anthony Amsterdam (1974, 349)

## CASES COVERED

*Katz v. U.S.*, 389 U.S. 347 (1967)

*U.S. v. White*, 401 U.S. 745 (1971)

*Kyllo v. U.S.*, 533 U.S. 27 (2001)

*Illinois v. Caballes*, 543 U 405 (2005)

*California v. Hodari D.*, 499 U.S. 621 (1991)

C rime control in a constitutional democracy depends on information. Almost all information the police need comes from what they see and hear. As long as what they see and hear by watching and listening is available to the general public, they're "free to use that tactic [surveillance] when and on whom they wish, free of legal constraint" (Stuntz 2002, 1387).

Unfortunately, information isn't always accessible to the naked eye and ear (or nose or fingers) in public. It comes from reluctant, sometimes stubborn, fearful, and even hostile, sources—criminals, suspects, victims, and witnesses. Criminals don't want to incriminate themselves. Potential criminals don't want to give away their criminal schemes. Victims and other witnesses often are afraid to talk, or they don't want to give up their friends and family. So law enforcement officers, sometimes, have to rely on four involuntary methods to get information—searches and seizures (Chapters 3–7), interrogation (Chapter 8), and identification procedures (Chapter 9).

All four of these methods of obtaining evidence not available to the general public are limited by the Fourth Amendment ban on "unreasonable searches and seizure" (discussed in this and the next four chapters), the Fifth Amendment ban on self-incrimination, and the right to due process (discussed in Chapters 8 and 9). In practice, when law enforcement officers use these methods, they have to follow rules generated by the U.S. Supreme Court in cases, many of which you'll read in excerpts in this chapter and in Chapters 4 through 9. Incidentally, all the federal and state courts, the U.S. Congress and state legislatures, and city councils and all other governing and administrative bodies are also bound by the Supreme Court's rules.

Although getting information to control crime is the main purpose of searches and seizures, there are also some special needs for searches and seizures that go beyond law enforcement purposes. These special-needs searches include searches and seizures to:

1. Protect officers from armed suspects (Chapters 4, 6)
2. Protect the property of detained suspects from loss or damage (Chapter 7)
3. Protect officials from lawsuits (Chapter 7)
4. Detect drug use among students and public employees (Chapter 7)
5. Prevent drunk driving (Chapter 7)

In this chapter, we'll first examine the history and purposes of the Fourth Amendment. Then, we'll turn to the three main steps in Fourth Amendment analyses, phrased here in the form of three questions:

1. *Was the law enforcement action a "search" or a "seizure"?* (the subject of this chapter). If it wasn't, the Fourth Amendment isn't involved and the analysis ends.
2. *If the action was a search or a seizure, was it reasonable?* (Chapters 4–7). If it was, the inquiry ends because the Fourth Amendment bans only *unreasonable* searches and seizures.

3. *If the action was an unreasonable search, does the Fourth Amendment ban its use as evidence?* (Chapter 10). If it does, the case isn't necessarily over because there may be enough other evidence to convict the defendant, either now or sometime in the future.

The first question may be the most important of the three. Why? Because if a law enforcement action isn't a search or a seizure, then it's beyond the reach of the limits mandated by the Fourth Amendment. Taking the action outside the Fourth Amendment means that appropriate law enforcement action depends on the good judgment, or discretion, of individual officers. In Judge Charles E. Moylan's blunt language, if there's no search, "the law does not give a constitutional damn about noncompliance" (1977, 76).

Be careful that you don't carry the "constitutional damn" idea too far. Judge Moylan is referring specifically to the Fourth Amendment. Other constitutional provisions, such as the due process and equal protection clauses (Chapter 2), may apply. Also, officers' actions might be federal and/or state crimes (Chapter 11). Furthermore, the actions might give rise to private lawsuits in which plaintiffs can recover money awards for wrongdoing by law enforcement officials (Chapter 11). Finally, the actions may violate law enforcement agency rules that can result in agency disciplinary actions, such as demotions or termination (Chapter 11).

## THE HISTORY AND THE PURPOSES OF THE FOURTH AMENDMENT

The Fourth Amendment was created to make sure the government doesn't use illegal methods to get evidence. To understand why, let's look at a little history. Search and seizure law began long before the adoption of the Fourth Amendment. It started with the invention of the printing press and had nothing to do with the crimes law enforcement is concerned with today—murder, rape, robbery, burglary, theft, and crimes against public order and morals, such as prostitution, pornography, and especially illegal drug crimes.

Let's enter the story in the 1700s, when English monarchs had for two centuries been sending out their agents to conduct search and destroy missions against *seditious libels* (printed criticism of the government) and libelers. The practice reached a high point in the 1700s. The low respect the English had for their imported German kings (the four Georges of the House of Hanover) raised the number of seditious libels to epidemic proportions.

To fight this epidemic, the Crown relied on writs of assistance, granting royal agents two enormous powers. The first part, called the "general warrant," empowered royal agents to search anyone, anywhere, anytime. The second part, the writ of assistance, empowered the agents to order anyone who happened to be nearby to help execute the warrant. Writs of assistance were issued at the beginning of a new monarch's reign and were good for the life of the monarch. Like the holder of a blank check who can fill in the amount, the writ permitted the officer to fill in names of persons, homes, shops, offices, private papers, and other items the officer wanted to search. So for the life of the monarch, officers of the Crown had total discretion as to whom, where, and what to search and seize. In the case of George III, that meant the authority was good from 1760 to 1820!

Writs of assistance weren't used just to search for and destroy seditious libels. They were used to collect taxes on a long list of commonly used items, including cider, beer, and paper. The British hated paying these taxes, and the American colonists hated paying customs duties on them; both were notorious for not paying any of them.

Smuggling goods into and out of the American colonies was rampant. The writs of assistance became the main weapon used to collect the hated customs in the American colonies. Notice what these original searches and seizures were not directed at: looking for and gathering evidence of common felonies against individuals and their property and arresting suspects involved in these activities. So their purposes were very different from what they're used for today (Taylor 1969, Part I).

It was the use of the hated writs of assistance in these political and tax collection cases that prompted William Pitt to speak in the House of Commons the most famous words ever uttered against the power of government to search:

> The poorest man may in his cottage bid defiance to all the forces of the Crown. It may be frail—its roof may shake—the wind may blow through it—the storm may enter—but the King of England cannot enter—all his force dares not cross the threshold of the ruined tenement. (quoted in Hall 1993, 2:4)

In the United States, it was in a customs case that the young lawyer and future president John Adams watched the great colonial trial lawyer James Otis attack the writs of assistance in a Boston courtroom. Otis argued that writs of assistance were illegal. According to Otis, only searches with specific dates, naming the places or persons to be searched and seized, and based on probable cause, were lawful where free people lived. Otis's argument moved John Adams to write years later: "There was the Child Independence born" (Smith 1962, 56). But the powerful oratory hurled against the writs of assistance didn't stop either the English Crown or American governors from using them.

The authors of the Bill of Rights didn't forget their hatred for the general warrant, and they wrote their opposition to it into the Fourth Amendment to the U.S. Constitution (see p. 47). But the Fourth Amendment wasn't aimed at *crippling* law enforcement's power to protect the value of property and personal security. It was aimed only at limiting that power enough so as not to infringe "unreasonably" on two other values at the heart of a free society: (1) **liberty**, the right to come and go as we please, sometimes called the "right of locomotion," and (2) **privacy**, the right to be let alone by the government.

The Fourth Amendment is supposed to make sure the government has enough power to make us safe and secure by looking for, getting, and using the evidence it needs to control crime, protect officers, seize suspects, and meet special needs beyond criminal law enforcement. It just can't do any of these by *unreasonable* searches and seizures.

In all of what follows in this chapter, and in Chapters 4 through 7, keep in mind that the Fourth Amendment protects us only from invasions by *law enforcement officers;* it doesn't protect us from invasions by *private persons.* Protections against invasions of our liberty and privacy—for example, false imprisonment, trespass, and invasions of privacy (Chapter 11)—by private persons depend on federal and state laws.

Now, let's turn to the topics in the rest of the chapter: When are law enforcement actions searches and seizures?

# SEARCHES

Until 1967, the U.S. Supreme Court defined searches according to the **trespass doctrine**. According to the Court's definition of the trespass doctrine, to amount to a "search," officers had to invade physically a "constitutionally protected area." Constitutionally protected areas were the places named in the Fourth Amendment—persons, houses, papers, and effects (personal stuff). According to the Supreme Court, searching of persons that amounted to trespassing included touching their bodies, rummaging through their pockets, taking blood tests, and performing surgery to remove bullets. On the other hand, the Court ruled that ordering suspects to give handwriting samples, voice samples, or hair specimens aren't searches of their person because they're less invasive. Houses include apartments, hotel rooms, garages, business offices, stores, and even warehouses. Papers include a broad range of personal writings, including diaries and letters. Effects include many items of personal property: cars, purses, briefcases, and packages.

In our study of searches, we'll look at the privacy doctrine, the impact of electronic surveillance on privacy, the differences between the plain view and the open fields doctrines and how they affect our privacy rights, and the issue of whether we have any right to privacy with regard to property we abandon.

## The Privacy Doctrine

The privacy doctrine was first suggested in a famous dissent in a Prohibition Era case, _Olmstead v. U.S. (1928)_. In Olmstead, the defendants' telephones were tapped without a warrant to find evidence of violations of alcohol laws. The government collected more than 775 pages of notes from the wiretaps and, based on this information, indicted more than seventy people. The Supreme Court applied the trespass doctrine to the case, holding that the government wiretaps were not Fourth Amendment searches of the defendants' houses, papers, or effects, because no officers physically entered the defendants' buildings. Disagreeing with the majority, Justice Louis Brandeis wrote one of the most famous dissents in the history of the Court. He conceded that wiretaps were not physical trespasses. He argued that, nevertheless,

> The makers of the Constitution . . . recognized the significance of man's spiritual nature, of his feelings and of his intellect. They knew that only a part of the pain, pleasure and satisfactions of life are to be found in material things. They sought to protect Americans in their beliefs, their thoughts, their emotions and their sensations. They conferred, as against the Government, the right to be let alone—the most comprehensive of rights and the right most valued by civilized men. (478)

In 1983, the late senator and constitutional scholar Sam Ervin (1983) reaffirmed Brandeis's notion of the right to privacy:

> The oldest and deepest hunger in the human heart is for a place where one may dwell in peace and security and keep inviolate from public scrutiny one's innermost aspirations and thoughts, one's most intimate associations and communications, and one's most private

## TABLE 3.1 The Expectation of Privacy and Places Where We Expect It

| Search | No Search |
| --- | --- |
| Eavesdropping on telephone conversations | Overhearing a conversation on the street |
| Climbing over a backyard fence | Observing a backyard from the window of an airplane |
| Hiding in the bushes outside a house looking inside | Standing on the street and looking into the living room through open curtains |
| Opening a briefcase and looking inside | Observing someone carrying a briefcase |

Stuntz 2002, 1387.

activities. This truth was documented by Micah, the prophet, 2,700 years ago when he described the Mountain of the Lord as a place where "they shall sit every man under his own vine and fig tree and none shall make them afraid." (283)

In 1967, Justice Brandeis's dissent became the law of the land when, in the landmark case *Katz v. U.S.*, the Supreme Court replaced the trespass doctrine with the privacy doctrine. Justice Potter Stewart, a leading expert on Fourth Amendment law, wrote the majority opinion in the case. Justice Stewart was not only an expert on the law, he was one of the Court's masters at turning phrases. One of his most memorable was the one he wrote about the privacy doctrine—"The Fourth Amendment protects people, not places" (351).

Before we go on, let's clarify a point about Justice Stewart's wonderful phrase. In applying the privacy doctrine, the expectation of privacy depends almost always on *where* people expect privacy. So places are still important. (See examples in Table 3.1.)

Justice Stewart surely wrote the most memorable phrase in *Katz v. U.S.* But Justice John Marshall Harlan's concurring opinion established the two-pronged expectation-of-privacy test that the Supreme Court has followed ever since. The two prongs are:

1. *Subjective privacy.* Whether the "person exhibited an actual [personal] expectation of privacy"

2. *Objective privacy.* Whether the subjective expectation of privacy is reasonable— that is, an expectation "that society is prepared to recognize as 'reasonable'"

Before you read *Katz*, you should be aware of an important point. Courts consider the expectation of privacy at the moment law enforcement officers observe an action. "The duration and intensity" of the observation don't matter. For example, it's not a search if police officers stake out a private home, move into a house across the street, and watch who and what's coming and going for weeks. Similarly, it's not a search if officers follow someone down the street, into a restaurant, watch her while she eats, follow her when she leaves and into several stores to watch her shop, and any other public place. Why aren't they searches? Because any member of the public could've done the same thing. Of course, the actions might be something else—for example, stalking, which is a crime in many states today (Stuntz 2002, 1387).

In theory, the privacy doctrine is a fine example of balancing the government's power to control crime and the individual's right to be let alone by the government. In practice, as you learned in the last paragraph, it allows the police a lot of leeway. You'll learn later in this chapter that courts often weigh the balance in favor of the government.

According to former prosecutor, defense attorney, and Fourth Amendment specialist John Wesley Hall, Jr. (1993):

> When [society's need for security and the individual's need for privacy] are balanced, the former usually weighs heavily. . . . While this is perhaps a valid purpose in the administration of criminal justice, we must not lose sight of the fundamental precepts of the Fourth Amendment that the individual is to be free from arbitrary and oppressive governmental intrusions. (6)

Professor William Stuntz (2002) refers to the leeway officers have under the Court's application of the "reasonable expectation of privacy" test.

> A reasonable expectation of privacy is the kind of expectation any citizen might have with respect to any other citizen. A fair translation of that standard might go as follows: Police can see and hear the things that any member of the public might see and hear, without fear of Fourth Amendment regulation. Only when they see and hear things that members of the public would not be allowed to see and hear, has a "search" taken place. (1387)

In *Katz v. U.S.*, Charles Katz went into a public telephone booth, closed the door, put his money in the slot, and took bets on the upcoming week's college basketball games. Katz was a bookie and his customers were from around the country. It was from these very unremarkable facts that the privacy test was created and that the majority of the Court decided that Katz had a reasonable expectation of privacy in his end of the betting conversations. You'll also learn, in Justice Harlan's concurring opinion, the exact statement of the privacy test currently used by the Court. Finally, you'll learn that Justice Black flatly rejected the new test because it created law based on the justice's personal opinions instead of on the original intent of those who wrote the Fourth Amendment.

## CASE — *Did He Have a Right to Privacy That Society Recognizes?*

### *Katz v. U.S.*
389 U.S. 347 (1967)

### HISTORY

Charles Katz was convicted under a federal statute of transmitting wagering information by telephone across state lines. The court of appeals affirmed the conviction. The Supreme Court granted certiorari and reversed.

STEWART, J.

### FACTS

[The facts are taken from *Katz v. U.S.*, 369 F.2d 130 [9th Cir. 1966].] In February of 1965 Charles Katz was seen placing calls from a bank of three public telephone booths during certain hours and on an almost daily basis. He was never observed in any other telephone booth. In the period of February 19 to February 25, 1965, at set hours, Special Agents of the Federal Bureau of Investigation placed microphones on the tops of two of the public telephone booths normally used by Katz. The other phone was placed out of order by the telephone company.

The microphones were attached to the outside of the telephone booths with tape. There was no physical penetration inside of the booths. The microphones were activated only while Katz was approaching and actually in the booth. Wires led from microphones to a wire recorder on top of one of the booths. Thus the F.B.I. obtained a record of Katz's end of a series of telephone calls. A study of the transcripts of the recordings made of Katz's end of the conversations revealed that the conversations had to do with the placing of bets and the obtaining of gambling information by Katz.

At the trial evidence was introduced to show that from February 19 to February 25, 1965, inclusive, the appellant placed calls from two telephone booths located in the 8200 block of Sunset Boulevard in Los Angeles. The conversations were overheard and recorded every day except February 22. The transcripts of the recordings and the normal business records of the telephone company were used to determine that the calls went to Boston, Massachusetts, and Miami, Florida.

The testimony of Joseph Gunn of the Administrative Vice Division of the Los Angeles Police Department, who was the expert called by the government in the area of bookmaking, was that the transcripts of the conversations showed that bets were made and information assisting in the placing of bets was transmitted on the dates and at the times alleged in the indictment. Bets were recorded like "Give me Duquesne minus 7 for a nickel." Information relating to the line and the acquiring of credit was also transmitted.

From all of the evidence in the case the court found the volume of business being done by Katz indicated that it was not a casual incidental occupation of Katz. The court found that he was engaged in the business of betting or wagering at the time of the telephone conversations, which were transmitted and recorded. . . . Katz was convicted of transmitting wagering information by telephone from Los Angeles to Miami and Boston, in violation of a federal statute. We granted certiorari to consider the constitutional questions thus presented.

## OPINION

Katz has phrased those questions as follows:

A. Whether a public telephone booth is a constitutionally protected area so that evidence obtained by attaching an electronic listening recording device to the top of such a booth is obtained in violation of the right to privacy of the user of the booth.

B. Whether physical penetration of a constitutionally protected area is necessary before a search and seizure can be said to be violative of the Fourth Amendment to the United States Constitution.

We decline to adopt this formulation of the issues. . . . The Fourth Amendment cannot be translated into a general constitutional "right to privacy." That Amendment protects individual privacy against certain kinds of governmental intrusion, but its protections go further, and often have nothing to do with privacy at all. . . . The protection of a person's general right to privacy—his right to be let alone by other people—is, like the protection of his property and of his very life, left largely to the law of the individual States.

Because of the misleading way the issues have been formulated, the parties have attached great significance to the characterization of the telephone booth from which the petitioner placed his calls. The petitioner has strenuously argued that the booth was a "constitutionally protected area." The Government has maintained with equal vigor that it was not.

But this effort to decide whether or not a given "area," viewed in the abstract, is "constitutionally protected" deflects attention from the problem presented by this case. For the Fourth Amendment protects people, not places. What a person knowingly exposes to the public, even in his own home or office, is not a subject of Fourth Amendment protection. But what he seeks to preserve as private, even in an area accessible to the public, may be constitutionally protected.

The Government stresses the fact that the telephone booth from which the petitioner made his calls was constructed partly of glass, so that he was as visible after he entered it as he would have been if he had remained outside. But what he sought to exclude when he entered the booth was not the intruding eye—it was the uninvited ear. He did not shed his right to do so simply because he made his calls from a place where he might be seen. No less than an individual in a business office, in a friend's apartment, or in a taxicab, a person in a telephone booth may rely upon the protection of the Fourth Amendment. One who occupies it, shuts the door behind him, and pays the toll that permits him to place a call is surely entitled to assume that the words he utters into the mouthpiece will not be broadcast to the world. To read the Constitution more narrowly is to ignore the vital role that the public telephone has come to play in private communication.

The Government contends, however, that the activities of its agents in this case should not be tested by Fourth Amendment requirements, for the surveillance technique they employed involved no physical penetration of the telephone booth from which the petitioner placed his calls. . . . [But,] we have expressly held that the Fourth Amendment governs not only the seizure of tangible items, but extends as well to the recording of oral statements overheard without any "technical trespass under . . . local property law. Once this much is acknowledged, and once it is recognized that the Fourth Amendment protects people—and not simply "areas"—against unreasonable searches and seizures it becomes clear that the reach of that Amendment cannot turn upon the presence or absence of a physical intrusion into any given enclosure.

We conclude that the . . . "trespass" doctrine . . . can no longer be regarded as controlling. The Government's activities in electronically listening to and recording the petitioner's words violated the privacy upon which he justifiably relied while using the telephone booth and thus constituted a "search and seizure" within the meaning of the Fourth Amendment. The fact that the electronic device employed to achieve that end did not happen to penetrate the wall of the booth can have no constitutional significance. . . .

JUDGMENT REVERSED.

## CONCURRING OPINION

### HARLAN, J.

. . . As the Court's opinion states, "the Fourth Amendment protects people, not places." The question, however, is what protection it affords to those people. Generally, as here, the answer to that question requires reference to a "place."

My understanding of the rule that has emerged from prior decisions is that there is a twofold requirement, first that a person have exhibited an actual (subjective) expectation of privacy and, second, that the expectation be one that society is prepared to recognize as "reasonable."

Thus a man's home is, for most purposes, a place where he expects privacy, but objects, activities, or statements that he exposes to the "plain view" of outsiders are not "protected" because no intention to keep them to himself has been exhibited. On the other hand, conversations in the open would not be protected against being overheard, for the expectation of privacy under the circumstances would be unreasonable.

The critical fact in this case is that "one who occupies it (a telephone booth) shuts the door behind him, and pays the toll that permits him to place a call is surely entitled to assume" that his conversation is not being intercepted. The point is not that the booth is "accessible to the public" at other times, but that it is a temporarily private place whose momentary occupants' expectations of freedom from intrusion are recognized as reasonable. . . .

## DISSENT

### BLACK, J.

If I could agree with the Court that eavesdropping carried on by electronic means (equivalent to wiretapping) constitutes a "search" or "seizure," I would be happy to join the Court's opinion. . . . My basic objection is twofold: (1) I do not believe that the words of the Amendment will bear the meaning given them by today's decision, and (2) I do not believe that it is the proper role of this Court to rewrite the Amendment in order "to bring it into harmony with the times" and thus reach a result that many people believe to be desirable.

While I realize that an argument based on the meaning of words lacks the scope, and no doubt the appeal, of broad policy discussions and philosophical discourses on such nebulous subjects as privacy, for me the language of the Amendment is the crucial place to look in construing a written document such as our Constitution. . . .

The first clause protects "persons, houses, papers, and effects, against unreasonable searches and seizures. . . ." These words connote the idea of tangible things with size, form, and weight, things capable of being searched, seized, or both. The second clause of the Amendment still further establishes its Framers' purpose to limit its protection to tangible things by providing that no warrants shall issue but those "particularly describing the place to be searched, and the persons or things to be seized." . . .

Tapping telephone wires, of course, was an unknown possibility at the time the Fourth Amendment was adopted. But eavesdropping (and wiretapping is nothing more than eavesdropping by telephone) was . . . an ancient practice which at common law was condemned as a nuisance. In those days the eavesdropper listened by naked ear under the eaves of houses or their windows, or beyond their walls seeking out private discourse.

There can be no doubt that the Framers were aware of this practice, and if they had desired to outlaw or restrict the use of evidence obtained by eavesdropping, I believe that they would have used the appropriate language to do so in the Fourth Amendment. They certainly would not have left such a task to the ingenuity of language-stretching judges.

No one, it seems to me, can read the debates on the Bill of Rights without reaching the conclusion that its Framers and critics well knew the meaning of the words they used, what they would be understood to mean by others, their scope and their limitations. Under these circumstances it strikes me as a charge against their scholarship, their common sense and their candor to give to the Fourth Amendment's language the eavesdropping meaning the Court imputes to it today.

I do not deny that common sense requires and that this Court often has said that the Bill of Rights' safeguards should be given a liberal construction. This principle, however, does not justify construing the search and seizure amendment as applying to eavesdropping or the "seizure" of conversations. The Fourth Amendment was aimed directly at the abhorred practice of breaking in, ransacking and searching homes and other buildings and seizing people's personal belongings without warrants issued by magistrates. . . .

Since I see no way in which the words of the Fourth Amendment can be construed to apply to eavesdropping, that closes the matter for me. In interpreting the Bill of Rights, I willingly go as far as a liberal construction of the language takes me, but I simply cannot in good conscience give a meaning to words which they have never before been thought to have and which they certainly do not have in common ordinary usage. I will not distort the words of the Amendment in order to "keep the Constitution up to date" or "to bring it into harmony with the times." It was never meant that this Court have such power, which in effect would make us a continuously functioning constitutional convention.

With this decision the Court has completed, I hope, its rewriting of the Fourth Amendment, which started only recently when the Court began referring incessantly to the Fourth Amendment not so much as a law against unreasonable searches and seizures as one to protect an individual's privacy.

By clever word juggling the Court finds it plausible to argue that language aimed specifically at searches and seizures of things that can be searched and seized may, to protect privacy, be applied to eavesdropped evidence of conversations that can neither be searched nor seized. Few things happen to an individual that do not affect his privacy in one way or another. Thus, by arbitrarily substituting the Court's language, designed to protect privacy, for the Constitution's language, designed to protect against unreasonable searches and seizures, the Court has made the Fourth Amendment its vehicle for holding all laws violative of the Constitution which offend the Court's broadest concept of privacy.

. . . The Court talks about a constitutional "right of privacy" as though there is some constitutional provision or provisions forbidding any law ever to be passed which might abridge the "privacy" of individuals. But there is not. I [have] made clear [dissenting in *Griswold v. Connecticut*] . . . my fear of the dangers involved when this Court uses the "broad, abstract and ambiguous concept" of "privacy" as a "comprehensive substitute for the Fourth Amendment's guarantee against 'unreasonable searches and seizures.'"

The Fourth Amendment protects privacy only to the extent that it prohibits unreasonable searches and seizures of "persons, houses, papers, and effects." No general right is created by the Amendment so as to give this Court the unlimited power to hold unconstitutional everything which affects privacy. Certainly the Framers, well acquainted as they were with the excesses of governmental power, did not intend to grant this Court such omnipotent lawmaking authority as that. The history of governments proves that it is dangerous to freedom to repose such powers in courts.

For these reasons I respectfully dissent.

## Questions

1. List the specific government invasions in the case.

2. State the privacy and trespass doctrines.

3. Why did the majority of the Court reject the trespass doctrine?

4. State Justice Harlan's formulation of the privacy test.

5. Using Justice Harlan's formulation of the test, in your opinion, did Katz have a subjective and objective expectation of privacy in his conversations?

6. On the basis of the facts, is Justice Stewart correct that the Fourth Amendment protects people, not places?

7. Is Justice Black right in his dissent that there is no right to privacy in the Fourth Amendment? Explain your answer.

8. What if it's true that the framers of the Fourth Amendment didn't intend to protect us from government eavesdropping? Should something written over two hundred years ago bind the Court (and us) today? Explain your answer.

9. Do you agree that the Supreme Court doesn't have the authority to keep the Constitution "up to date"? Explain your answer.

### EXPLORING FURTHER

# The Expectation of Privacy

## 1. Did He Have a Reasonable Expectation of Privacy in His Bank Records?

### U.S. v. Miller, 425 U.S. 435 1976

FACTS In response to an informant's tip, a deputy sheriff from Houston County, Georgia, stopped a van-type truck occupied by two of Mitch Miller's alleged co-conspirators.

The truck contained distillery apparatus and raw material. A few weeks later, a fire broke out in a Kathleen, Georgia, warehouse rented to Miller. During the blaze, firefighters and sheriff's department officials discovered a 7,500-gallon-capacity distillery, 175 gallons of non-tax-paid whiskey, and related paraphernalia.

Two weeks later agents from the Treasury Department's Alcohol, Tobacco, and Firearms Bureau presented grand jury subpoenas to the presidents of the Citizens & Southern National Bank of Warner Robins and the Bank of Byron, where Miller maintained accounts. The subpoenas required the two presidents to appear in court and to produce all records of accounts—savings, checking, loan or otherwise, in the name of Mr. Mitch Miller.

The banks didn't tell Miller about the subpoenas but ordered their employees to make the records available and to provide copies of any documents the agents desired.

At the Bank of Byron, an agent was shown microfilm records of the relevant account and provided with copies of one deposit slip and one or two checks. At the Citizens & Southern National Bank microfilm records also were shown to the agent, and he was given copies of the records of the respondent's account during the applicable period.

These included all checks, deposit slips, two financial statements, and three monthly statements. The bank presidents were then told that it wouldn't be necessary to appear in person before the grand jury.

In a motion to suppress the bank records, Miller contended that the bank records were illegally seized. Did Miller have a reasonable expectation of privacy in his bank records?

DECISION The trial court overruled the motion, and the U.S. Supreme Court agreed. According to the Court:

Miller urges that he has a Fourth Amendment interest in the records kept by the banks because . . . he has a reasonable expectation of privacy [in the records]. . . . We . . . perceive no legitimate "expectation of privacy" in their contents. The checks are not confidential communications but negotiable instruments to be used in commercial transactions. All of the documents obtained, including financial statements and deposit slips, contain only information voluntarily conveyed to the banks and exposed to their employees in the ordinary course of business. . . .

The depositor takes the risk, in revealing his affairs to another, that the information will be conveyed by that person to the Government. This Court has held repeatedly that the Fourth Amendment does not prohibit the obtaining of information revealed to a third party and conveyed by him to Government authorities, even if the information is revealed on the assumption that it will be used only for a limited purpose and the confidence placed in the third party will not be betrayed.

Justice Brennan dissented. According to Justice Brennan:

The customer of a bank expects that the documents, such as checks, which he transmits to the bank in the course of his business operations, will remain private, and that such an expectation is reasonable. The prosecution concedes as much, although it asserts that this expectation is not constitutionally cognizable. Representatives of several banks testified at the suppression hearing that information in their possession regarding a customer's account is deemed by them to be confidential.

## 2. Did He Have a Reasonable Expectation of Privacy in Numbers Dialed from His Home Telephone?

*Smith v. Maryland*, 442 U.S. 745 (1979)

*FACTS* In Baltimore, Maryland, Patricia McDonough was robbed. She gave the police a description of the robber and of a 1975 Monte Carlo automobile she had observed near the scene of the crime. After the robbery, McDonough began receiving threatening and obscene phone calls from a man identifying himself as the robber. On one occasion, the caller asked that she step out on her front porch; she did so, and saw the 1975 Monte Carlo she had earlier described to police moving slowly past her home. On March 16, police spotted a man who met McDonough's description driving a 1975 Monte Carlo in her neighborhood. By tracing the license plate number, police learned that the car was registered in the name of Michael Lee Smith.

The next day, the telephone company, at police request, installed a pen register at its central offices to record the numbers dialed from the telephone at Smith's home. The police didn't get a warrant or court order before having the pen register installed. The register revealed that on March 17 a call was placed from Smith's [the defendant's] home to McDonough's phone.

On the basis of this and other evidence, the police obtained a warrant to search the petitioner's residence. The search revealed that a page in Smith's phone book was turned down to the name and number of Patricia McDonough; the phone book was seized. Smith was arrested, and a six-man lineup was held on March 19. McDonough identified the petitioner as the man who had robbed her.

Smith was indicted in the Criminal Court of Baltimore for robbery. He moved to suppress "all fruits derived from the pen register" on the ground that the police had failed to secure a warrant prior to its installation. Did he have a reasonable expectation of privacy in the numbers he dialed from his home telephone?

*DECISION* No, said the U.S. Supreme Court. According to the majority:

We doubt that people in general entertain any actual expectation of privacy in the numbers they dial. . . . Smith can claim no legitimate expectation of privacy here. When he used his phone, Smith voluntarily conveyed numerical information to the telephone company and "exposed" that information to its equipment in the ordinary course of business. In so doing, he assumed the risk that the company would reveal to police the numbers he dialed. The switching equipment that processed those numbers is merely the modern counterpart of the operator who, in an earlier day, personally completed calls for the subscriber.

Justice Stewart disagreed. (Recall that Justice Stewart wrote the opinion in *Katz v. U.S.*) According to his dissent:

I think that the numbers dialed from a private telephone—like the conversations that occur during a call—are within the constitutional protection recognized in *Katz*. It seems clear to me that information obtained by pen register surveillance of a private telephone is information in which the telephone subscriber has a legitimate expectation of privacy. The information captured by such surveillance emanates from private conduct within a person's home or office—locations that without question are entitled to Fourth and Fourteenth Amendment protection. . . .

The numbers dialed from a private telephone—although certainly more prosaic than the conversation itself—are not without "content." Most private telephone subscribers may have their own numbers listed in a publicly distributed directory, but I doubt there are any who would be happy to have broadcast to the world a list of the local or long distance numbers they have called. This is not because such a list might in some sense be incriminating, but because it easily could reveal the identities of the persons and the places called, and thus reveal the most intimate details of a person's life.

Justice Marshall also dissented:

Just as one who enters a public telephone booth is "entitled to assume that the words he utters into the mouthpiece will not be broadcast to the world," so too, he should be entitled to assume that the numbers he dials in the privacy of his home will be recorded, if at all, solely for the phone company's business purposes. Accordingly, I would require law enforcement officials to obtain a warrant before they enlist telephone companies to secure information otherwise beyond the government's reach.

## 3. Did They Have a Reasonable Expectation of Privacy in Their Trash?

*California v. Greenwood* (1988)

*FACTS* Investigator Jenny Stracner of the Laguna Beach Police Department received information indicating that Billy Greenwood might be engaged in narcotics trafficking. Stracner asked the neighborhood's regular trash collector to pick up the plastic garbage bags that Greenwood had left on the curb in front of his house and to turn the bags over to her without mixing their contents with garbage from other houses. The trash collector cleaned his truck bin of other refuse, collected the garbage bags from the street in front of Greenwood's house, and turned the bags over to Stracner. The officer searched through the rubbish and found items indicative of narcotics use.

Stracner recited the information that she had gleaned from the trash search in an affidavit in support of a warrant to search Greenwood's home. Police officers encountered both Greenwood and Dyanne Van Houten at the house later that day when they arrived to execute the warrant. The police discovered quantities of cocaine and hashish during their search of the house. Did Greenwood and Van Houten have a reasonable expectation of privacy in the trash?

DECISION No, said the U.S. Supreme Court. According to Justice White, writing for the majority:

It may well be that respondents did not expect that the contents of their garbage bags would become known to the police or other members of the public. An expectation of privacy does not give rise to Fourth Amendment protection, however, unless society is prepared to accept that expectation as objectively reasonable. Here, we conclude that respondents exposed their garbage to the public sufficiently to defeat their claim to Fourth Amendment protection.

It is common knowledge that plastic garbage bags left on or at the side of a public street are readily accessible to animals, children, scavengers, snoops, and other members of the public. Moreover, respondents placed their refuse at the curb for the express purpose of conveying it to a third party, the trash collector, who might himself have sorted through respondents' trash or permitted others, such as the police, to do so. Accordingly, having deposited their garbage "in an area particularly suited for public inspection and, in a manner of speaking, public consumption, for the express purpose of having strangers take it," respondents could have had no reasonable expectation of privacy in the inculpatory items that they discarded.

Furthermore, as we have held, the police cannot reasonably be expected to avert their eyes from evidence of criminal activity that could have been observed by any member of the public. Hence, "what a person knowingly exposes to the public, even in his own home or office, is not a subject of Fourth Amendment protection."

Justices Brennan and Marshall disagreed. Justice Brennan wrote in his dissent:

Every week for two months, and at least once more a month later, the Laguna Beach police clawed through the trash that Greenwood left in opaque, sealed bags on the curb outside his home. Complete strangers minutely scrutinized their bounty, undoubtedly dredging up intimate details of Greenwood's private life and habits. . . .

The Framers of the Fourth Amendment understood that "unreasonable searches" of "papers and effects"—no less than "unreasonable searches" of "persons and houses"—infringe privacy. . . . So long as a package is closed against inspection, the Fourth Amendment protects its contents, wherever they may be, and the police must obtain a warrant to search it just as is required when papers are subjected to search in one's own household. . . .

A trash bag . . . is a common repository for one's personal effects and . . . is therefore . . . inevitably associated with the expectation of privacy. Almost every human activity ultimately manifests itself in waste products. . . . If you want to know what is really going on in a community, look at its garbage. A single bag of trash testifies eloquently to the eating, reading, and recreational habits of the person who produced it. A search of trash, like a search of the bedroom, can relate intimate details about sexual practices, health, and personal hygiene. . . .

Beyond a generalized expectation of privacy, many municipalities, whether for reasons of privacy, sanitation, or both, reinforce confidence in the integrity of sealed trash containers by prohibiting anyone, except authorized employees of the Town . . . to rummage into, pick up, collect, move or otherwise interfere with articles or materials placed on . . . any public street for collection. . . .

Had Greenwood flaunted his intimate activity by strewing his trash all over the curb for all to see, or had some nongovernmental intruder invaded his privacy and done the same, I could accept the Court's conclusion that an expectation of privacy would have been unreasonable. Similarly, had police searching the city dump run across incriminating evidence that, despite commingling with the trash of others, still retained its identity as Greenwood's, we would have a different case. But all that Greenwood "exposed . . . to the public" were the exteriors of several opaque, sealed containers. Until the bags were opened by police, they hid their contents from the public's view. . . .

In holding that the warrantless search of Greenwood's trash was consistent with the Fourth Amendment, the Court paints a grim picture of our society. It depicts a society in which local authorities may command their citizens to dispose of their personal effects in the manner least protective of the sanctity of the home and the privacies of life, and then monitor them arbitrarily and without judicial oversight—a society that is not prepared to recognize as reasonable an individual's expectation of privacy in the most private of personal effects sealed in an opaque container and disposed of in a manner designed to commingle it imminently and inextricably with the trash of others.

The American society with which I am familiar chooses to dwell in reasonable security and freedom from surveillance, and is more dedicated to individuals' liberty and more sensitive to intrusions on the sanctity of the home than the Court is willing to acknowledge.

Go to Exercise 3.1 on the Samaha Criminal Procedure 7e website to learn more about *California v. Greenwood* and state constitutional law: academic.cengage.com/criminaljustice/samaha. You will also find the full text of the Exploring Further excerpts on this website.

## Electronic Surveillance

*Katz v. U.S.* involved the government's listening to private conversations where none of the parties consented to the eavesdropping. What if one of the participants in a private conversation consents to the government's listening? Do parties who don't consent—and don't know—that one of the people in the conversation is a "false friend" or an undercover agent have a reasonable expectation of privacy in the conversation? No, said the U.S. Supreme Court in our next case excerpt, *U.S. v. White*.

## CASE | *Were Statements Made to an Informant Wired for Sound "Searches" to the Police?*

### U.S. v. White
401 U.S. 745 (1971)

### HISTORY

James A. White, Defendant, was convicted in the U.S. District Court for the Northern District of Illinois, Eastern Division, of two narcotics violations. He was fined, and sentenced as a second offender to 25-year concurrent sentences. He appealed. The U.S. Court of Appeals for the Seventh Circuit, reversed and remanded. The U.S. Supreme Court granted certiorari, and reversed the judgment of the Court of Appeals.

WHITE, J. (PLURALITY OF 4)

### FACTS

The issue before us is whether the Fourth Amendment bars from evidence the testimony of governmental agents who related certain conversations which had occurred between defendant White and a government informant, Harvey Jackson, and which the agents overheard by monitoring the frequency of a radio transmitter carried by Jackson and concealed on his person. On four occasions the conversations took place in Jackson's home; each of these conversations was overheard by an agent concealed in a kitchen closet with Jackson's consent and by a second agent outside the house using a radio receiver. Four other conversations—one in White's home, one in a restaurant, and two in Jackson's car—were overheard by the use of

radio equipment. The prosecution was unable to locate and produce Jackson at the trial and the trial court overruled objections to the testimony of the agents who conducted the electronic surveillance. The jury returned a guilty verdict and defendant appealed.

### OPINION

. . . The Fourth Amendment . . . affords no protection to a wrongdoer's misplaced belief that a person to whom he voluntarily confides his wrongdoing will not reveal it. . . . A police agent who conceals his police connections may write down for official use his conversations with a defendant and testify concerning them, without a warrant authorizing his encounters with the defendant and without otherwise violating the latter's Fourth Amendment rights.

For constitutional purposes, no different result is required if the agent instead of immediately reporting and transcribing his conversations with defendant, either simultaneously records them with electronic equipment which he is carrying on his person or carries radio equipment which simultaneously transmits the conversations either to recording equipment located elsewhere or to other agents monitoring the transmitting frequency. If the conduct and revelations of an agent operating without electronic equipment do not invade the defendant's constitutionally justifiable expectations of privacy, neither does a simultaneous recording of the same conversations made by the agent or by others from transmissions received from the agent to whom the defendant is talking and whose trustworthiness the defendant necessarily risks.

Our problem is not what the privacy expectations of particular defendants in particular situations may be or the extent to which they may in fact have relied on the discretion of their companions. Very probably, individual defendants neither know nor suspect that their colleagues have gone or will go to the police or are carrying recorders or transmitters. Otherwise, conversation would cease and our problem with these encounters would be nonexistent or far different from those now before us.

Our problem, in terms of the principles announced in *Katz*, is what expectations of privacy are constitutionally "justifiable"—what expectations the Fourth Amendment will protect in the absence of a warrant. So far, the law permits the frustration of actual expectations of privacy by permitting authorities to use the testimony of those associates who for one reason or another have determined to turn to the police, as well as by authorizing the use of informants. . . . If the law gives no protection to the wrongdoer whose trusted accomplice is or becomes a police agent, neither should it protect him when that same agent has recorded or transmitted the conversations which are later offered in evidence to prove the State's case.

Inescapably, one contemplating illegal activities must realize and risk that his companions may be reporting to the police. If he sufficiently doubts their trustworthiness, the association will very probably end or never materialize. But if he has no doubts, or allays them, or risks what doubt he has, the risk is his. In terms of what his course will be, what he will or will not do or say, we are unpersuaded that he would distinguish between probable informers on the one hand and probable informers with transmitters on the other.

Given the possibility or probability that one of his colleagues is cooperating with the police, it is only speculation to assert that the defendant's utterances would be substantially different or his sense of security any less if he also thought it possible that the suspected colleague is wired for sound. At least there is no persuasive evidence that the difference in this respect between the electronically equipped and the unequipped agent is substantial enough to require discrete constitutional recognition, particularly under the Fourth Amendment which is ruled by fluid concepts of "reasonableness."

Nor should we be too ready to erect constitutional barriers to relevant and probative evidence which is also accurate and reliable. An electronic recording will many times produce a more reliable rendition of what a defendant has said than will the unaided memory of a police agent. It may also be that with the recording in existence it is less likely that the informant will change his mind, less chance that threat or injury will suppress unfavorable evidence and less chance that cross-examination will confound the testimony. Considerations like these obviously do not favor the defendant, but we are not prepared to hold that a defendant who has no constitutional right to exclude the informer's unaided testimony nevertheless has a Fourth Amendment privilege against a more accurate version of the events in question. . . .

The judgment of the Court of Appeals is reversed. It is so ordered.

## DISSENT

### DOUGLAS, J.

The issue in this case is clouded and concealed by the very discussion of it in legalistic terms. What the ancients knew as "eavesdropping," we now call "electronic surveillance"; but to equate the two is to treat man's first gunpowder on the same level as the nuclear bomb. Electronic surveillance is the greatest leveler of human privacy ever known. How most forms of it can be held "reasonable" within the meaning of the Fourth Amendment is a mystery.

To be sure, the Constitution and Bill of Rights are not to be read as covering only the technology known in the 18th century. Otherwise its concept of "commerce" would be hopeless when it comes to the management of modern affairs. At the same time the concepts of privacy which the Founders enshrined in the Fourth Amendment vanish completely when we slavishly allow an all-powerful government, proclaiming law and order, efficiency, and other benign purposes, to penetrate all the walls and doors which men need to shield them from the pressures of a turbulent life around them and give them the health and strength to carry on. . . .

We have become a fearful people. There was a time when we feared only our enemies abroad. Now we seem to be as fearful of our enemies at home, and depending on whom you talk to, those enemies can include people under thirty, people with foreign names, people of different races, people in the big cities. We have become a suspicious nation, as afraid of being destroyed from within as from without. Unfortunately, the manifestations of that kind of fear and suspicion are police state measures. . . .

Must everyone live in fear that every word he speaks may be transmitted or recorded and later repeated to the entire world? I can imagine nothing that has a more chilling effect on people speaking their minds and expressing their views on important matters. The advocates of that regime should spend some time in totalitarian countries and learn firsthand the kind of regime they are creating here.

A technological breakthrough in techniques of physical surveillance now makes it possible for government agents and private persons to penetrate the privacy of homes, offices, and vehicles; to survey individuals moving about in public places; and to monitor the basic channels of communication by telephone, telegraph, radio, television, and data line. Most of the "hardware" for this physical surveillance is cheap, readily available to the general public, relatively easy to install, and not presently illegal to own. As of the 1960s, the new surveillance technology is being used widely by government agencies of all types and at every level of government, as well as by private agents for a rapidly growing number of businesses, unions, private organizations, and individuals in every section of the United States. . . . The scientific prospects for the next decade indicate a continuing increase in the range and versatility of the listening and watching devices, as well as the possibility of computer processing of recordings to identify automatically the speakers or topics under surveillance. These advances will come just at the time when personal contacts, business affairs, and government operations are being channeled more and more into electronic systems such as data-phone lines and computer communications.

## DISSENT

### HARLAN, J.

We deal here with the constitutional validity of instantaneous third-party electronic eavesdropping, conducted by federal law enforcement officers, without any prior judicial approval of the technique utilized, but with the consent and cooperation of a participant in the conversation, and where the substance of the matter electronically overheard is related in a federal criminal trial by those who eavesdropped as direct, not merely corroborative, evidence of the guilt of the nonconsenting party. . . .

Since it is the task of the law to form and project, as well as mirror and reflect, we should not, as judges, merely recite the expectations and risks without examining the desirability of saddling them upon society. The critical question, therefore, is whether under our system of government, as reflected in the Constitution, we should impose on our citizens the risks of the electronic listener or observer without at least the protection of a warrant requirement.

This question must, in my view, be answered by assessing the nature of a particular practice and the likely extent of its impact on the individual's sense of security balanced against the utility of the conduct as a technique of law enforcement. For those more extensive intrusions that significantly jeopardize the sense of security which is the paramount concern of Fourth Amendment liberties, I am of the view that more than self-restraint by law enforcement officials is required and at the least warrants should be necessary.

The impact of the practice of third-party bugging, must, I think, be considered such as to undermine that confidence and sense of security in dealing with one another that is characteristic of individual relationships between citizens in a free society. It goes beyond the impact on privacy occasioned by the ordinary type of "informer" investigation. . . . The argument of the plurality opinion, to the effect that it is irrelevant whether secrets are revealed by the mere tattletale or the transistor, ignores the differences occasioned by third-party monitoring and recording which insures full and accurate disclosure of all that is said, free of the possibility of error and oversight that inheres in human reporting.

Authority is hardly required to support the proposition that words would be measured a good deal more carefully and communication inhibited if one suspected his conversations were being transmitted and transcribed. Were third-party bugging a prevalent practice, it might well smother that spontaneity—reflected in frivolous, impetuous, sacrilegious, and defiant discourse—that liberates daily life. Much offhand exchange is easily forgotten and one may count on the obscurity of his remarks, protected by the very fact of a limited audience, and the likelihood that the listener will either overlook or forget what is said, as well as the listener's inability to reformulate a conversation without having to contend with a documented record. All these values are sacrificed by a rule of law that permits official monitoring of private discourse limited only by the need to locate a willing assistant. . . .

Finally, it is too easy to forget—and, hence, too often forgotten—that the issue here is whether to interpose a search warrant procedure between law enforcement agencies engaging in electronic eavesdropping and the public generally. By casting its "risk analysis" solely in terms of the expectations and risks that "wrongdoers" or "one contemplating illegal activities" ought to bear, the plurality opinion, I think, misses the mark entirely. [*On Lee*, omitted here] . . . does not simply mandate that criminals must daily run the risk of unknown eavesdroppers prying into their private affairs; it subjects each and every law-abiding member of society to that risk. The very purpose of interposing the Fourth Amendment warrant requirement is to redistribute the privacy risks throughout society. . . .

The interest *On Lee* fails to protect is the expectation of the ordinary citizen, who has never engaged in illegal conduct in his life, that he may carry on his private discourse freely, openly, and spontaneously without measuring his every word against the connotations it might carry when instantaneously heard by others unknown to him and unfamiliar with his situation or analyzed in a cold, formal record played days, months, or years after the conversation. Interposition of a warrant requirement is designed not to shield "wrongdoers," but to secure a measure of privacy and a sense of personal security throughout our society.

The Fourth Amendment does, of course, leave room for the employment of modern technology in criminal law enforcement, but in the stream of current developments in Fourth Amendment law I think it must be held that third-party electronic monitoring, subject only to the self-restraint of law enforcement officials, has no place in our society.

## Questions

1. Is the court saying it's reasonable to expect people we confide in may be wired for sound to the police? Do you expect this?

2. Which is most intrusive: listening to James White in his home, in Harvey Jackson's home, in a restaurant,

on the street, or in a car? Or are they all about the same? Why? Why not?

3. Does Justice Douglas in his dissent that everyone will live in fear that what she or he says will be reported, or transmitted by radio, to the police have a point? Explain.

4. Should the police have been required to get a warrant here? Explain your answer.

 Go to Exercise 3.2 on the Samaha Criminal Procedure 7e website to learn more about *U.S. v. White*: academic.cengage.com/criminaljustice/samaha.

Technology that allows officers to get information about possible suspects has advanced significantly since 1971 when the Court decided *U.S. v. White*. One of those advances is the development of **thermal imagers**, devices that detect, measure, and record infrared radiation invisible to the naked eye. The imagers convert radiation into images based on the amount of heat (black is cool, white is hot, shades of gray are in between). What if unknown to you, police officers parked on the street outside your house, aimed a thermal imager at your house and measured and recorded the amount of heat coming out of various parts of your house? Do you have an expectation of privacy in these heat waves? If you do, is it an expectation society is prepared to recognize? The U.S. Supreme Court held that the discovery and measurement of heat—something invisible to the naked eye—escaping from your home is a Fourth Amendment search in *Kyllo v. U.S.* (2001).

# CASE   *Was the Thermal Imaging of a Private Home a Search?*

## Kyllo v. U.S.
### 533 U.S. 27 (2001)

### HISTORY

After unsuccessfully moving to suppress evidence, Danny Kyllo entered a conditional guilty plea to manufacturing marijuana, and then appealed. Following remand, the U.S. District Court for the District of Oregon again denied Kyllo's suppression motion; Kyllo appealed again. The Ninth Circuit Court of Appeals affirmed. Certiorari was granted. The U.S. Supreme Court (5 to 4) reversed and remanded.

SCALIA, J.

### FACTS

In 1991 Agent William Elliott of the United States Department of the Interior came to suspect that marijuana was being grown in the home belonging to petitioner Danny Kyllo, part of a triplex on Rhododendron Drive in Florence, Oregon. Indoor marijuana growth typically requires high-intensity lamps.

In order to determine whether an amount of heat was emanating from Kyllo's home consistent with the use of such lamps, at 3:20 A.M. on January 16, 1992, Agent Elliott and Dan Haas used an Agema Thermovision 210 thermal imager to scan the triplex. Thermal imagers detect infrared radiation, which virtually all objects emit but which is not visible to the naked eye. The imager converts radiation into images based on relative warmth—black is cool, white is hot, shades of gray connote relative differences; in that respect, it operates somewhat like a video camera showing heat images.

The scan of Kyllo's home took only a few minutes and was performed from the passenger seat of Agent Elliott's vehicle across the street from the front of the house and also from the street in back of the house. The scan showed that the roof over the garage and a side wall of Kyllo's home were relatively hot compared to the rest of the home and substantially warmer than neighboring homes in the triplex. Agent Elliott concluded that Kyllo was using halide lights to grow marijuana in his house, which indeed he was.

Based on tips from informants, utility bills, and the thermal imaging, a Federal Magistrate Judge issued a warrant authorizing a search of Kyllo's home, and the agents found an indoor growing operation involving more than 100 plants.

Kyllo was indicted on one count of manufacturing marijuana, in violation of 21 U.S.C. § 841(a)(1). He unsuccessfully moved to suppress the evidence seized from his home and then entered a conditional guilty plea. The Court of Appeals for the Ninth Circuit remanded the case for an evidentiary hearing regarding the intrusiveness of thermal imaging. On remand the District Court found that the Agema 210 "is a non-intrusive device which emits no rays or beams and shows a crude visual image of the heat being radiated from the outside of the house"; it "did not show any people or activity within the walls of the structure"; "the device used cannot penetrate walls or windows to reveal conversations or human activities"; and "no intimate details of the home were observed."

Based on these findings, the District Court upheld the validity of the warrant that relied in part upon the thermal imaging, and reaffirmed its denial of the motion to suppress. A divided Court of Appeals initially reversed, but that opinion was withdrawn and the panel (after a change in composition) affirmed, with Judge Noonan dissenting. The court held that Kyllo had shown no subjective expectation of privacy because he had made no attempt to conceal the heat escaping from his home, and even if he had, there was no objectively reasonable expectation of privacy because the imager "did not expose any intimate details of Kyllo's life," only "amorphous 'hot spots' on the roof and exterior wall." We granted certiorari.

## OPINION

. . . At the very core of the Fourth Amendment stands the right of a man to retreat into his own home and there be free from unreasonable governmental intrusion. With few exceptions, the question whether a warrantless search of a home is reasonable and hence constitutional must be answered no. On the other hand, the antecedent question whether or not a Fourth Amendment "search" has occurred is not so simple. . . . As Justice Harlan's oft-quoted concurrence described it, a Fourth Amendment search occurs when the government violates a subjective expectation of privacy that society recognizes as reasonable. . . .

The present case involves officers on a public street engaged in more than naked-eye surveillance of a home. We have previously reserved judgment as to how much technological enhancement of ordinary perception from such a vantage point, if any, is too much. . . . It would be foolish to contend that the degree of privacy secured to citizens by the Fourth Amendment has been entirely unaffected by the advance of technology. For example, as the cases discussed above make clear, the technology enabling human flight has exposed to public view (and hence, we have said, to official observation) uncovered portions of the house and its curtilage [area immediately surrounding a home] that once were private. The question we confront today is what limits there are upon this power of technology to shrink the realm of guaranteed privacy.

The *Katz* test—whether the individual has an expectation of privacy that society is prepared to recognize as reasonable—has often been criticized as circular, and hence subjective and unpredictable. While it may be difficult to refine *Katz* when the search of areas such as telephone booths, automobiles, or even the curtilage and uncovered portions of residences is at issue, in the case of the search of the interior of homes . . . there is a ready criterion, with roots deep in the common law, of the minimal expectation of privacy that exists, and that is acknowledged to be reasonable.

To withdraw protection of this minimum expectation would be to permit police technology to erode the privacy guaranteed by the Fourth Amendment. We think that obtaining by sense-enhancing technology any information regarding the interior of the home that could not otherwise have been obtained without physical "intrusion into a constitutionally protected area," constitutes a search—at least where (as here) the technology in question is not in general public use. This assures preservation of that degree of privacy against government that existed when the Fourth Amendment was adopted. On the basis of this criterion, the information obtained by the thermal imager in this case was the product of a search.

The Government maintains, however, that the thermal imaging must be upheld because it detected "only heat radiating from the external surface of the house." . . . We rejected such a mechanical interpretation of the Fourth Amendment in *Katz*, where the eavesdropping device picked up only sound waves that reached the exterior of the phone booth. Reversing that approach would leave the homeowner at the mercy of advancing technology—including imaging technology that could discern all human activity in the home. While the technology used in the present case was relatively crude, the rule we adopt must take account of more sophisticated systems that are already in use or in development. . . .

The Government also contends that the thermal imaging was constitutional because it did not "detect private activities occurring in private areas." . . . The Fourth Amendment's protection of the home has never been tied to measurement of the quality or quantity of information obtained.

In *Silverman*, for example, we made clear that any physical invasion of the structure of the home, "by even a fraction of an inch," was too much, and there is certainly no exception to the warrant requirement for the officer who barely cracks open the front door and sees nothing but the nonintimate rug on the vestibule floor. In the home, our cases show, all details are intimate details, because the entire area is held safe from prying government eyes.

Thus, in *Karo*, the only thing detected was a can of ether in the home; and in *Arizona v. Hicks*, the only thing detected by a physical search that went beyond what officers lawfully present could observe in "plain view" was the registration number of a phonograph turntable. These were intimate details because they were details of the home, just as was the detail of how warm—or even how relatively warm—Kyllo was heating his residence. . . .

We have said that the Fourth Amendment draws "a firm line at the entrance to the house." That line, we think, must be not only firm but also bright—which requires clear specification of those methods of surveillance that require a warrant. While it is certainly possible to conclude from the videotape of the thermal imaging that occurred in this case that no "significant" compromise of the homeowner's privacy has occurred, we must take the long view, from the original meaning of the Fourth Amendment forward. . . .

Where, as here, the Government uses a device that is not in general public use, to explore details of the home that would previously have been unknowable without physical intrusion, the surveillance is a "search" and is presumptively unreasonable without a warrant.

Since we hold the Thermovision imaging to have been an unlawful search, it will remain for the District Court to determine whether, without the evidence it provided, the search warrant issued in this case was supported by probable cause—and if not, whether there is any other basis for supporting admission of the evidence that the search pursuant to the warrant produced.

The judgment of the Court of Appeals is reversed; the case is remanded for further proceedings consistent with this opinion.

## DISSENT

STEVENS, J.

There is, in my judgment, a distinction of constitutional magnitude between "through-the-wall surveillance" that gives the observer or listener direct access to information in a private area, on the one hand, and the thought processes used to draw inferences from information in the public domain, on the other hand. The Court has crafted a rule that purports to deal with direct observations of the inside of the home, but the case before us merely involves indirect deductions from "off-the-wall" surveillance, that is, observations of the exterior of the home. Those observations were made with a fairly primitive thermal imager that gathered data exposed on the outside of Kyllo's home but did not invade any constitutionally protected interest in privacy. . . .

. . . This case . . . is controlled by established principles from our Fourth Amendment jurisprudence. One of those core principles, of course, is that *"searches and seizures inside a home without a warrant are presumptively unreasonable"* [italics added]. But it is equally well settled that searches and seizures of property in plain view are presumptively reasonable. Whether that property is residential or commercial, the basic principle is the same: What a person knowingly exposes to the public, even in his own home or office, is not a subject of Fourth Amendment protection. That is the principle implicated here. . . .

The notion that heat emissions from the outside of a dwelling are a private matter implicating the protections of the Fourth Amendment . . . is . . . quite difficult to take seriously. Heat waves, like aromas that are generated in a kitchen, or in a laboratory or opium den, enter the public domain if and when they leave a building. A subjective expectation that they would remain private is not only implausible but also surely not "one that society is prepared to recognize as 'reasonable.' " . . .

There is a strong public interest in avoiding constitutional litigation over the monitoring of emissions from homes, and over the inferences drawn from such monitoring. Just as "the police cannot reasonably be expected to avert their eyes from evidence of criminal activity that could have been observed by any member of the public," so too public officials should not have to avert their senses or their equipment from detecting emissions in the public domain such as excessive heat, traces of smoke, suspicious odors, odorless gases, airborne particulates, or radioactive emissions, any of which could identify hazards to the community.

In my judgment, monitoring such emissions with "sense-enhancing technology," and drawing useful conclusions from such monitoring, is an entirely reasonable public service.

On the other hand, the countervailing privacy interest is at best trivial. After all, homes generally are insulated to keep heat in, rather than to prevent the detection of heat going out, and it does not seem to me that society will suffer from a rule requiring the rare homeowner who both intends to engage in uncommon activities that produce extraordinary amounts of heat, and wishes to conceal that production from outsiders, to make sure that the surrounding area is well insulated. The interest in concealing the heat escaping from one's house pales in significance to "the chief evil against which the wording of the Fourth Amendment is directed," the "physical entry of the home," and it is hard to believe that it is an interest the Framers sought to protect in our Constitution.

Since what was involved in this case was nothing more than drawing inferences from off-the-wall surveillance, rather than any "through-the-wall" surveillance, the officers' conduct did not amount to a search and was perfectly reasonable. . . .

I respectfully DISSENT.

## Questions

1. Describe specifically the information officers Elliott and Haas got from Kyllo's house.

2. Describe exactly how the officers got the information.

3. Summarize the arguments the majority makes to support its conclusion that getting and recording thermal images are searches and seizures.

4. Summarize the arguments the dissent makes to support its conclusions that they aren't searches and seizures.

# The Plain View Doctrine

According to the *plain view doctrine*, individuals have no reasonable expectation of privacy in what officers discover by their ordinary senses. Although the doctrine takes its name from the sense of sight, it applies to discovery by the other senses, too—namely, hearing, smell, and sometimes even touch. (Unless otherwise noted, we'll use "plain view" to include all the ordinary senses.) There are two kinds of plain view. In both kinds, the issue is rarely whether there's a *search*; it's whether officers can *seize* the items in plain view.

The first type is **search-related plain view**. It refers to items in plain view that officers discover while they're searching for items for which they're specifically authorized to search. For example, in one leading Supreme Court case, an officer had a warrant to search for jewelry taken during a robbery. During the search, he saw an Uzi machine gun and other weapons in plain view (*Horton v. California* 1990). This kind of plain view we'll discuss in relation to seizures during frisks in Chapter 4; during arrests in Chapter 5; during searches for evidence in Chapter 6; and during inventory searches in Chapter 7.

The second type, **nonsearch-related plain view**, refers to plain view that doesn't involve a Fourth Amendment intrusion at all. This can occur in several settings. Here are a few examples: An officer sees a diner in a restaurant take a "joint" out of her pocket; an officer sees a passenger in a car stopped at a stoplight hand a joint to the driver; or an officer walking down the street sees a resident smoking pot in her living room in front of her ground-level apartment window that is clearly visible from the public sidewalk.

All three of our examples satisfy the two conditions of the **plain-view doctrine**, which says that discoveries made under two conditions aren't searches:

1. Officers are where they have a legal right to be—namely, any place where you or I could lawfully be.

2. Officers haven't beefed up their ordinary senses with advanced technology that's not readily available to you or me.

Condition 2 requires that courts distinguish between technological enhancements that many people use and anyone can get easily—flashlights, bifocals, and magnifying glasses—and high-powered devices that only a few people have or can get easily. So eyesight enhanced by a flashlight is treated like ordinary eyesight; eyesight enhanced by X-ray isn't. In *U.S. v. Kim* (1976), for example, FBI agents used an 800-millimeter telescope with a 60-millimeter opening to observe activities in Earl "The Old Man" Kim's apartment. The surveillance took place nearly a quarter mile from the apartment. The telescope was so powerful the agents could even see what Kim was reading. According to the U.S. District Court for the District of Hawaii, "It is inconceivable that the government can intrude so far into an individual's home that it can detect the material he is reading and still not have engaged in a search" (1255).

The U.S. Supreme Court came to a different result when it applied the plain view doctrine in *California v. Ciraolo* (1986). The police saw marijuana growing in Dante Ciraolo's yard from a plane 1,000 feet in the air. The police had hired the plane because two privacy fences blocked their view from the ground. According to the Court, the use of the plane didn't enhance the officers' naked eye such that it turned the observation into a Fourth Amendment search.

In a similar case, *Dow Chemical Corporation v. U.S.* (1986), Dow maintained elaborate security around a 2,000-acre chemical plant that bars ground-level observation.

When Dow refused the Environmental Protection Agency's (EPA's) request for an onsite inspection, the EPA employed a commercial air photographer to fly over the plant and take photographs to determine whether Dow was complying with EPA standards. The U.S. Supreme Court ruled that such aerial observation and photography weren't Fourth Amendment searches.

We've discussed so far only the application of the doctrine to what officers *see* (1) when they're where they have a legal right to be and (2) without the aid of technology not available to the general public. But, as we mentioned earlier, the doctrine also applies to what officers hear, smell, and even, sometimes, what they feel. In our next case excerpt, the U.S. Supreme Court held that the Fourth Amendment didn't apply to a drug-sniffing dog who, as he circled Roy Caballes's car, alerted officers at the trunk to what turned out to be marijuana inside.

## CASE    *Was the Dog Sniff a Search?*

### Illinois v. Caballes (2005)
#### 543 U.S. 405 (2005)

### HISTORY

Roy I. Caballes, Defendant, was convicted of cannabis trafficking, following a bench trial in the Circuit Court, La Salle County, and sentenced to 12 years' imprisonment and a $256,136 fine. He appealed. The Illinois Appellate Court affirmed. Granting petition for leave to appeal, the Illinois Supreme Court, reversed. The U.S. Supreme Court granted certiorari, vacated the judgment and remanded the case.

STEVENS, J.

### FACTS

Illinois State Trooper Daniel Gillette stopped Roy Caballes for speeding on an interstate highway. When Gillette radioed the police dispatcher to report the stop, a second trooper, Craig Graham, a member of the Illinois State Police Drug Interdiction Team, overheard the transmission and immediately headed for the scene with his narcotics-detection dog. When they arrived, Caballes's car was on the shoulder of the road and Caballes was in Gillette's vehicle. While Gillette was in the process of writing a warning ticket, Graham walked his dog around Caballes's car. The dog alerted at the trunk. Based on that alert, the officers searched the trunk, found marijuana, and arrested Caballes. The entire incident lasted less than 10 minutes.

### OPINION

. . . Official conduct that does not "compromise any legitimate interest in privacy" is not a search subject to the Fourth Amendment. . . . Any interest in possessing contraband cannot be deemed "legitimate," and thus, governmental conduct that *only* reveals the possession of contraband compromises no legitimate privacy interest. This is because the expectation that certain facts will not come to the attention of the authorities" is not the same as an interest in "privacy that society is prepared to consider reasonable.

In *U.S. v. Place* (1983), we treated a canine sniff by a well-trained narcotics-detection dog as "*sui generis*" [unique] because it "discloses only the presence or absence of narcotics, a contraband item." Caballes likewise concedes that "drug sniffs are designed, and if properly conducted are generally likely, to reveal only the presence of contraband." Although Caballes argues that the error rates, particularly the existence of false positives, call into question the premise that drug-detection dogs alert only to contraband, the record contains no evidence or findings that support his argument. Moreover, Caballes does not suggest that an erroneous alert, in and of itself, reveals any legitimate private information, and, in this case, the trial judge found that the dog sniff was sufficiently reliable to establish probable cause to conduct a full-blown search of the trunk.

Accordingly, the use of a well-trained narcotics-detection dog—one that does not expose noncontraband items that otherwise would remain hidden from public view during a lawful traffic stop, generally does not implicate legitimate privacy interests. In this case, the dog sniff was performed on the exterior of Caballes's car while he was lawfully seized for a traffic violation. Any intrusion on Caballes's privacy expectations does not rise to the level of a constitutionally cognizable infringement.

This conclusion is entirely consistent with our recent decision that the use of a thermal-imaging device to detect the growth of marijuana in a home constituted an unlawful search. *Kyllo v. U.S.* (2001) [excerpted in the last section]. Critical to that decision was the fact that the device was capable of detecting lawful activity—in that case, intimate details in a home, such as "at what hour each night the lady of the house takes her daily sauna and bath."

The legitimate expectation that information about perfectly lawful activity will remain private is categorically distinguishable from Caballes's hopes or expectations concerning the nondetection of contraband in the trunk of his car. A dog sniff conducted during a concededly lawful traffic stop that reveals no information other than the location of a substance that no individual has any right to possess does not violate the Fourth Amendment.

The judgment of the Illinois Supreme Court is vacated, and the case is remanded for further proceedings not inconsistent with this opinion.

*It is so ordered.*

## DISSENT

### SOUTER, J.

. . . The infallible dog . . . is a creature of legal fiction. Although the Supreme Court of Illinois did not get into the sniffing averages of drug dogs, their supposed infallibility is belied by judicial opinions describing well-trained animals sniffing and alerting with less than perfect accuracy, whether owing to errors by their handlers, the limitations of the dogs themselves, or even the pervasive contamination of currency by cocaine. See, *e.g.*, *U.S. v. Kennedy* (C.A.10 1997) (describing a dog that had a 71% accuracy rate); *U.S. v. Scarborough* (C.A.10 1997) (describing a dog that erroneously alerted 4 times out of 19 while working for the postal service and 8% of the time over its entire career); *U.S. v. Limares* (C.A.7 2001) (accepting as reliable a dog that gave false positives between 7% and 38% of the time); *Laime v. State* (Ark 2001) (speaking of a dog that made between 10 and 50 errors); *U.S. v. $242, 484.00* (C.A.11 2003) (noting that because as much as 80% of all currency in circulation contains drug residue, a dog alert "is of little value"); *U.S. v. Carr* (C.A.3 1994) ("[A] substantial portion of United States currency . . . is tainted with sufficient traces of controlled substances to cause a trained canine to alert to their presence"). Indeed, a study cited by Illinois in this case for the proposition that dog sniffs are "generally reliable" shows that dogs in artificial testing situations return false positives anywhere from 12.5% to 60% of the time, depending on the length of the search. K. Garner et al., Duty Cycle of the Detector Dog: A Baseline Study 12 (Apr. 2001) (prepared by Auburn U. Inst. for Biological Detection Systems). In practical terms, the evidence is clear that the dog that alerts hundreds of times will be wrong dozens of times.

Once the dog's fallibility is recognized, however, that ends the justification . . . for treating the sniff as *sui generis* under the Fourth Amendment: the sniff alert does not necessarily signal hidden contraband, and opening the container or enclosed space whose emanations the dog has sensed will not necessarily reveal contraband or any other evidence of crime. . . .

The . . . sniff and alert cannot claim the certainty that *Place* assumed, both in treating the deliberate use of sniffing dogs as *sui generis* and then taking that characterization as a reason to say they are not searches subject to Fourth Amendment scrutiny. And when that aura of uniqueness disappears, there is . . . no good reason . . . to ignore the actual function that dog sniffs perform. They are conducted to obtain information about the contents of private spaces beyond anything that human senses could perceive, even when conventionally enhanced. . . .

Thus in practice the government's use of a trained narcotics dog functions as a limited search to reveal undisclosed facts about private enclosures, to be used to justify a further and complete search of the enclosed area. And given the fallibility of the dog, the sniff is the first step in a process that may disclose "intimate details" without revealing contraband, just as a thermal-imaging device might do, as described in *Kyllo v. U.S.* (2001).

### GINSBURG, J., JOINED BY SOUTER J.

. . . In my view, the Court diminishes the Fourth Amendment's force. . . . A drug-detection dog is an intimidating animal. Injecting such an animal into a routine traffic stop changes the character of the encounter between the police and the motorist. The stop becomes broader, more adversarial, and (in at least some cases) longer. Caballes—who, as far as Troopers Gillette and Graham knew, was guilty solely of driving six miles per hour over the speed limit— was exposed to the embarrassment and intimidation of being investigated, on a public thoroughfare, for drugs. Even if the drug sniff is not characterized as a Fourth Amendment "search," the sniff surely broadened the scope of the traffic-violation-related seizure.

The Court has never removed police action from Fourth Amendment control on the ground that the action is well calculated to apprehend the guilty. Under today's decision, every traffic stop could become an occasion to call in the dogs, to the distress and embarrassment of the law-abiding population. . . .

## Questions

1. List all the officers' acts that *might* qualify as ones in which there's a reasonable expectation of privacy.
2. Summarize the arguments in the majority and dissenting opinions regarding whether the dog sniff was (or wasn't) a search.
3. In your opinion, was the drug-sniffing dog circling Roy Caballes's car an enhancement of Officer Graham's sense of smell? Explain your answer.
4. In your opinion, what's the significance of the numbers Justice Souter cites in support of his argument?

# The Open Fields Doctrine

The Fourth Amendment protects our right to be secure in our persons, houses, papers, and effects, but through its decisions, the Supreme Court has made it clear that this protection doesn't extend to all places—namely, to open fields, public places, and abandoned property.

According to the **open fields doctrine**, "the special protection accorded by the Fourth Amendment to the people in their 'persons, houses, papers, and effects' is not extended to the open fields" (*Hester v. U.S.* 1924, 28). In *Oliver v. U.S.* (1984), the U.S. Supreme Court concluded that society isn't prepared to recognize any reasonable expectation of privacy in open fields because:

> Open fields do not provide the setting for those intimate activities that the Amendment is intended to shelter from government interference or surveillance. There is no societal interest in protecting the privacy of those activities, such as the cultivation of crops, that occur in open fields. (178)

What if owners give notice they expect privacy—for example, by building fences or putting up "No Trespassing" signs? Does the doctrine still apply? Yes, says the Supreme Court. Why? Because of the practical difficulties officers would face in administering the policy with those kinds of exceptions:

> Police officers would have to guess before every search whether landowners had erected fences sufficiently high, posted a sufficient number of warning signs, or located contraband in an area sufficiently secluded to establish a right of privacy. (181)

On the other hand, the ground and buildings immediately surrounding a home (the **curtilage**), such as garages, patios, and pools, aren't open fields. Why? Because this is where family and other private activities take place. The Supreme Court has identified the following criteria to determine whether an area falls within the curtilage:

- The distance from the house
- The presence or absence of a fence around the area
- The use or purpose of the area
- The measures taken to prevent public view

In applying these criteria in *U.S. v. Dunn* (1987), the Court concluded that Ronald Dunn's barn wasn't part of the curtilage because it was 60 yards from the house; it was 50 yards beyond a fence surrounding the house; it wasn't used for family purposes; and Dunn took no measures to hide it from public view. So the crystal meth lab the officers discovered by shining a flashlight through a window in the barn wasn't a search.

The Fourth Amendment doesn't protect what officers can discover through their ordinary senses in public places, including streets, parks, and other publicly owned areas. Public places also include privately owned businesses that are open to the public. But "employees only" areas, such as offices, restrooms, basements, and other places not open to the public, aren't public places. Public restrooms are public places, too, even enclosed stalls—at least as much as officers can see over and under partitions or through cracks or other gaps in partitions (Hall 1993, 543–48).

## Abandoned Property

According to the U.S. Supreme Court, there's no "reasonable expectation of privacy" in abandoned property. But what does "abandoned" mean? There's a physical and a mental element to abandonment:

1. Physically giving up possession of something

2. Intending to give up the expectation of privacy

So I legally abandon an apple core when I throw it away after I've eaten what I want of the apple. But I don't abandon my car when I park it in the University of Minnesota parking ramp while I teach my "Criminal Procedure in U.S. Society" class. I've given it up only for the purpose of safekeeping until I'm ready to go home. How does this relate to the law of searches? An officer's actions don't amount to a search if there's proof that the person gave up physical possession of something and that person also intended to give up a reasonable expectation of privacy in that something.

The U.S. Supreme Court has adopted a **totality-of-circumstances test** (a test you'll encounter frequently in the text and case excerpts) to determine whether throwing away property proves the intent to give up the reasonable expectation of privacy protected by the Fourth Amendment. The Court looks at all the facts in each case to determine the intent to abandon, the actions indicating abandonment, and therefore the termination of a reasonable expectation of privacy in the items seized by the government.

In the leading abandonment case decided during the Prohibition era, *Hester v. U.S.* (1924), revenue agents chased Hester through open fields. When the agents fired a shot, Hester dropped the illegal liquor he was carrying. The Supreme Court held that the facts indicated that Hester intended to abandon the alcohol. Later, in a famous Cold War case, immigration officials arrested suspected Communist spy Rudolf Abel. After Abel checked out of the hotel where FBI agents had arrested him, the agents searched his hotel room. They seized several items Abel had left behind in a wastepaper basket. The U.S. Supreme Court held that Abel had abandoned the room and, therefore, intended to give up his reasonable expectation of privacy in what he left behind in the wastepaper basket (*Abel v. U.S.* 1960).

# SEIZURES

When are individuals "seized" in the Fourth Amendment sense? According to the U.S. Supreme Court in the landmark "stop and frisk" case, *Terry v. Ohio* (1968), which we'll discuss in Chapter 4:

> Only when the officer, by means of physical force or show of authority, has in some way restrained the liberty of a citizen may we conclude that a "seizure" has occurred. (21)

*Terry* was the first case in which the Court took up the question of when contacts between individuals and law enforcement officers trigger the Fourth Amendment's protection against an officer's interference with our right to come and go as we please. We learned very little about when a contact becomes a seizure, because the case focused mainly on the officer's frisk of the defendant. Unfortunately, what we didn't learn until later cases fleshed it out is that there are two kinds of Fourth Amendment seizures (also known as "stops")—actual seizures and show-of-authority seizures. **Actual seizures** occur when officers physically grab individuals with the intent to keep them from leaving. **Show-of-authority seizures** take place when officers display their authority by ordering suspects to stop, drawing their weapons, or otherwise acting such that a reasonable person wouldn't feel free to leave or "otherwise terminate the encounter, *and* individuals submit to the authority." (See Table 3.2 for examples.)

| TABLE 3.2 | Show-of-Authority Seizures |
|---|---|
| **Show of Authority** | **No Show of Authority** |
| Setting up a roadblock | Approaching an individual on the sidewalk |
| Flashing an emergency light | Identifying oneself as a law enforcement officer |
| Ordering a person to leave a vehicle | Asking questions |
| Surrounding a car | Requesting to search |
| Drawing a weapon | Following a pedestrian in a police car |
| Several officers present | |
| Using a commanding tone of voice | |

The Court revisited the problem of defining seizure 12 years later in *U.S. v. Mendenhall* (1980). Federal DEA agents approached Sylvia Mendenhall as she was walking through a concourse in the Detroit airport, identified themselves, and asked to see her ID and ticket, which she handed to them. Justice Potter Stewart, in a part of his opinion joined only by Justice William Rehnquist, concluded the agents hadn't seized Mendenhall. Here's how Justice Stewart defined a seizure:

> [A] person has been "seized" within the meaning of the Fourth Amendment only if, in view of all of the circumstances surrounding the incident, a reasonable person would have believed that he was not free to leave. (555)

Justice Stewart explained why:

> On the facts of this case, no "seizure" of the respondent occurred. The events took place in the public concourse. The agents wore no uniforms and displayed no weapons. They did not summon the respondent to their presence, but instead approached her and identified themselves as federal agents. They requested, but did not demand to see the respondent's identification and ticket. Such conduct without more, did not amount to an intrusion upon any constitutionally protected interest. The respondent was not seized simply by reason of the fact that the agents approached her, asked her if she would show them her ticket and identification, and posed to her a few questions. Nor was it enough to establish a seizure that the person asking the questions was a law enforcement official. In short, nothing in the record suggests that the respondent had any objective reason to believe that she was not free to end the conversation in the concourse and proceed on her way, and for that reason we conclude that the agents' initial approach to her was not a seizure. (555)

A majority of the Court adopted Justice Stewart's **"reasonable person would not feel free to leave" definition of seizure** in *Florida v. Royer* (1983). Justice Byron White added this important passage to his opinion regarding officers who approach individuals and ask them questions:

> Law enforcement officers do not violate the Fourth Amendment by merely approaching an individual on the street or in another public place, by asking him if he is willing to answer some questions, [or] by putting questions to him if the person is willing to listen. . . . Nor would the fact that the officer identifies himself as a police officer without more, convert the encounter into a seizure. (*Florida v. Royer* 1983, 497)

Because they're not "seized," individuals approached can walk away and ignore the officer's request. And walking away doesn't *by itself* provide the objective basis required to "seize" persons. Again, in Justice White's words:

The person approached, however, need not answer any question put to him; indeed, he may decline to listen to the questions at all and may go on his way. He may not be detained, even momentarily without reasonable, objective grounds for doing so; and his refusal to listen or answer does not, without more, furnish such grounds. (497–98)

The U.S. Supreme Court modified the "free to leave" definition when officers approach passengers in a bus who are physically able to leave, distinguishing it from when officers approach individuals in airports. *Florida v. Bostick* (1991) involved the boarding of a Greyhound bus by officers during a brief stop at Fort Lauderdale on its 19-hour trip from Miami to Atlanta. Most of the passengers couldn't afford to fly. One of the passengers, Terrence Bostick, a 28-year-old Black man, was asleep on the back seat (Cole 1999, 16) when two officers woke him up. They were wearing their bright green "raid" jackets with the Broward County Sheriff's Office insignia and displaying their badges; one carried a gun in a plastic gun pouch. They were "working the bus," looking for passengers who might be carrying illegal drugs.

The officers asked for Bostick's identification; he gave it to them. Then, they asked him if they could search his bag; he said yes. They found a pound of cocaine. The officers admitted that until they found the cocaine they had no basis for suspecting Bostick was guilty of any crime. "Working" buses is a common tactic in drug law investigation. And it works. One officer testified that he had searched 3,000 bags without once being refused consent (Cole 1999, 16); one 13-month period produced 300 pounds of cocaine, 800 pounds of marijuana, 24 handguns, and 75 suspected drug "mules" (16).

The Court in *Bostick* acknowledged that a reasonable person wouldn't feel free to leave the bus. Nonetheless, the Court concluded that no Fourth Amendment seizure took place. According to the Court:

> Bostick's freedom of movement was restricted by a factor independent of police conduct, i.e., by his being a passenger on a bus. Accordingly, the "free to leave" analysis on which Bostick relies is inapplicable. In such a situation, the appropriate inquiry is whether a reasonable person would feel free to decline the officers' requests or otherwise terminate the encounter. (436)

The Court applied the *Bostick* standard in *U.S. v. Drayton* (2002). During a bus stop, the driver left the bus, leaving three police officers in charge of the bus. One stood guard at the front of the bus, another at the rear, while the third questioned every passenger without telling them their right not to cooperate. The Court held that there was no seizure because reasonable people would have felt free to get up and leave the bus. But, would they? Let's look at the answer provided by the empirical evidence.

## Empirical Findings

It's clear from the discussion of *Mendenhall*, *Royer*, *Bostick*, and *Drayton* that the Supreme Court has firmly, and repeatedly, taken the position that police encounters with citizens are not usually coercive. Scientific findings, as you'll also learn in consent searches (Chapter 6), police interrogation (Chapter 8), and identification procedures (Chapter 9), don't support the Court's position. Professor Janice Nadler (2002), in her survey of Fourth Amendment empirical research on encounters with law enforcement, has demonstrated an "ever-widening gap between Fourth Amendment . . . jurisprudence on the one hand, and scientific findings about the psychology of compliance . . . on the other" (155).

The question of whether a citizen feels free to terminate a police encounter depends crucially on certain empirical claims. . . . These questions cannot reliably be answered solely from the comforts of one's armchair, while reflecting only on one's own experience. An examination of the existing empirical evidence on the psychology of coercion suggests that in many situations where citizens find themselves in an encounter with the police, the encounter is not consensual because a reasonable person would not feel free to terminate the encounter. . . .

Even worse, the existing empirical evidence also suggests that observers outside of the situation systematically overestimate the extent to which citizens in police encounters feel free to refuse. Members of the Court are themselves such outside observers, and this partly explains why the Court has repeatedly held that citizen encounters are consensual. (155–56)

## Fleeing Suspects

When are you seized when you run away from the police? According to the U.S. Supreme Court in our next excerpt, *California v. Hodari D.* (1991), you're seized when you're either grabbed by the chasing officer or when you submit to a display of police authority.

C A S E     *When Did the Police Seize Him?*

### *California v. Hodari D.*
499 U.S. 621 (1991)

### HISTORY

Hodari D., a juvenile, appealed from an order of the Superior Court, Alameda County, denying his motion to suppress and finding that he was in possession of cocaine. The California Court of Appeal reversed. The California Supreme Court denied the state's application for review. Certiorari was granted. The Supreme Court reversed and remanded.

SCALIA, J., JOINED BY REHNQUIST, CJ., AND BLACKMUN, O'CONNOR, KENNEDY, AND SOUTER, JJ.

### FACTS

Late one evening in April 1988, Officers Brian McColgin and Jerry Pertoso were on patrol in a high-crime area of Oakland, California. They were dressed in street clothes but wearing jackets with "Police" embossed on both front and back. Their unmarked car proceeded west on Foothill Boulevard, and turned south onto 63rd Avenue. As they rounded the corner, they saw four or five youths huddled around a small red car parked at the curb. When the youths saw the officers' car approaching they apparently panicked, and took flight. The respondent here, Hodari D., and one companion ran west through an alley; the others fled south. The red car also headed south, at a high rate of speed. The officers were suspicious and gave chase. McColgin remained in the car and continued south on 63rd Avenue. Pertoso left the car, ran back north along

63rd, then west on Foothill Boulevard, and turned south on 62nd Avenue.

Hodari, meanwhile, emerged from the alley onto 62nd and ran north. Looking behind as he ran, he did not turn and see Pertoso until the officer was almost upon him, whereupon he tossed away what appeared to be a small rock. A moment later, Pertoso tackled Hodari, handcuffed him, and radioed for assistance. Hodari was found to be carrying $130 in cash and a pager; and the rock he had discarded was found to be crack cocaine.

In the juvenile proceeding brought against him, Hodari moved to suppress the evidence relating to the cocaine.

The court denied the motion without opinion. The California Court of Appeal reversed, holding that Hodari had been "seized" when he saw Officer Pertoso running toward him, that this seizure was unreasonable under the Fourth Amendment, and that the evidence of cocaine had to be suppressed as the fruit of that illegal seizure. The California Supreme Court denied the state's application for review.

We granted certiorari.

### OPINION

[The only question the Court decided was] "whether, at the time he dropped the drugs, Hodari had been seized within the meaning of the Fourth Amendment." [The reason this was the only question is because] California conceded below that Officer Pertoso did not have the "reasonable suspicion" required to justify stopping Hodari. That it would be unreasonable to stop, for brief inquiry, young men who scatter in panic upon the mere sighting of the police is not self-evident, and arguably contradicts proverbial common sense. See Proverbs 28:1 ("The wicked flee when no man pursueth"). We do not decide that point here, but rely entirely upon the state's concession.

[If Pertoso had seized him at the time he dropped the drugs], Hodari argues, the drugs were the fruit of that seizure and the evidence concerning them was properly excluded. If not, the drugs were abandoned by Hodari and lawfully recovered by the police, and the evidence should have been admitted. (In addition, of course, Pertoso's seeing the rock of cocaine, at least if he recognized it as such, would provide reasonable suspicion for the unquestioned seizure that occurred when he tackled Hodari.)

We have long understood that the Fourth Amendment's protection against "unreasonable . . . seizures" includes seizure of the person. From the time of the founding to the present, the word "seizure" has meant a "taking possession." . . . Hodari contends (and we accept as true for purposes of this decision) that Pertoso's pursuit qualified as a "show of authority" calling upon Hodari to halt. The narrow question before us is whether, with respect to a show of authority as with respect to application of physical force, a seizure occurs even though the subject does not yield. We hold that it does not. . . .

Respondent contends that his position is sustained by the so-called *Mendenhall* test, formulated by Justice Stewart's opinion in *U.S. v. Mendenhall* (1980): A person has been "seized" within the meaning of the Fourth Amendment only if, in view of all the circumstances surrounding the incident, a reasonable person would have believed that he was not free to leave. In seeking to rely upon that test here, Hodari fails to read it carefully. It says that a person has been seized "only if," not that he has been seized "whenever"; it states a necessary, but not a sufficient, condition for seizure—or, more precisely, for seizure effected through a "show of authority."

*Mendenhall* establishes that the test for existence of a "show of authority" is an objective one: not whether the citizen perceived that he was being ordered to restrict his movement, but whether the officer's words and actions would have conveyed that to a reasonable person. Application of this objective test was the basis for our decision in the other case principally relied upon by respondent, where we concluded that the police cruiser's slow following of the defendant did not convey the message that he was not free to disregard the police and go about his business. We did not address in *Michigan v. Chesternut*, however, the question whether, if the Mendenhall test was met—if the message that the defendant was not free to leave had been conveyed—a Fourth Amendment seizure would have occurred.

Quite relevant to the present case, however, was our decision in *Brower v. Inyo County* (1989). In that case, police cars with flashing lights had chased the decedent for 20 miles—surely an adequate "show of authority"—but he did not stop until his fatal crash into a police-erected blockade. The issue was whether his death could be held to be the consequence of an unreasonable seizure

in violation of the Fourth Amendment. We did not even consider the possibility that a seizure could have occurred during the course of the chase because, as we explained, that "show of authority" did not produce his stop. . . .

In sum, assuming that Pertoso's pursuit in the present case constituted a "show of authority" enjoining Hodari to halt, since Hodari did not comply with that injunction he was not seized until he was tackled. The cocaine abandoned while he was running was in this case not the fruit of a seizure, and his motion to exclude evidence of it was properly denied. We reverse the decision of the California Court of Appeal, and remand for further proceedings not inconsistent with his opinion.

It is so ordered.

## DISSENT

### STEVENS, J., JOINED BY MARSHALL, J.

The court's narrow construction of the word "seizure" represents a significant, and in my view, unfortunate, departure from prior case law construing the Fourth Amendment.

Almost a quarter of a century ago, in two landmark cases—one broadening the protection of individual privacy [*Katz v. U.S.*] and the other broadening the powers of law enforcement officers [*Terry v. Ohio*]—we rejected the method of Fourth Amendment analysis that today's majority endorses. In particular, the Court now adopts a definition of "seizure" that is unfaithful to a long line of Fourth Amendment cases. Even if the Court were defining seizure for the first time, which it is not, the definition that it chooses today is profoundly unwise. In its decision, the Court assumes, without acknowledging, that a police officer may now fire his weapon at an innocent citizen and not implicate the Fourth Amendment—as long as he misses his target. . . .

The Court's gratuitous quotation from Proverbs 28:1, mistakenly assumes that innocent residents have no reason to fear the sudden approach of strangers. We have previously considered, and rejected, this ivory-towered analysis of the real world for it fails to describe the experience of many residents, particularly if they are members of a minority. It has long been "a matter of common knowledge" that men who are entirely innocent do sometimes fly from the scene of a crime through fear of being apprehended as the guilty parties, or from an unwillingness to appear as witnesses. Nor is it true as an accepted axiom of criminal law that "the wicked flee when no man pursueth, but the righteous are as bold as a lion." . . .

Whatever else one may think of today's decision, it unquestionably represents a departure from earlier Fourth Amendment case law. The notion that our prior cases contemplated a distinction between seizures effected by a touching on the one hand, and those effected by a show of force on the other hand, and that all of our repeated descriptions of the Mendenhall test stated only a necessary, but not a sufficient, condition for finding seizures in the latter category, is nothing if not creative lawmaking. Moreover, by narrowing the definition of the term seizure, instead of enlarging the scope of reasonable justifications for seizures, the Court has significantly limited the protection provided to the ordinary citizen by the Fourth Amendment. . . .

In this case the officer's show of force—taking the form of a head-on chase—adequately conveyed the message that respondent was not free to leave. . . . There was an interval of time between the moment that respondent saw the officer fast approaching and the moment when he was tackled, and thus brought under the control of the officer.

The question is whether the Fourth Amendment was implicated at the earlier or the later moment. Because the facts of this case are somewhat unusual, it is appropriate to note that the same issue would arise if the show of force took the form of a command to "freeze," a warning shot, or the sound of sirens accompanied by a patrol car's flashing lights. In any of these situations, there may be a significant time interval between the initiation of the officer's show of force and the complete submission by the citizen. At least on the facts of this case, the Court concludes that the timing of the seizure is governed by the citizen's reaction, rather than by the officer's conduct. One consequence of this conclusion is that the point at which the interaction between citizen and police officer becomes a seizure occurs, not when a reasonable citizen believes he or she is no longer free to go, but rather, only after the officer exercises control over the citizen. . . .

It is too early to know the consequences of the Court's holding. If carried to its logical conclusion, it will encourage unlawful displays of force that will frighten countless innocent citizens into surrendering whatever privacy rights they may still have. . . . The Court today defines a seizure as commencing, not with egregious police conduct, but rather, with submission by the citizen. Thus, it both delays the point at which "the Fourth Amendment becomes relevant" to an encounter and limits the range of encounters that will come under the heading of "seizure." Today's qualification of the Fourth Amendment means that innocent citizens may remain "secure in their persons . . . against unreasonable searches and seizures" only at the discretion of the police.

Some sacrifice of freedom always accompanies an expansion in the executive's unreviewable law enforcement powers. A court more sensitive to the purposes of the Fourth Amendment would insist on greater rewards to society before decreeing the sacrifice it makes today. Alexander Bickel presciently wrote that "many actions of government have two aspects: their immediate, necessarily intended, practical effects, and their perhaps unintended or unappreciated bearing on values we hold to have more general and permanent interest." The Court's immediate concern with containing criminal activity poses a substantial, though unintended, threat to values that are fundamental and enduring.

I respectfully DISSENT.

## Questions

1. What are the relevant facts in determining when the officer seized Hodari D.?

2. What criteria does the Court use in determining when seizures occur?

3. Why does the dissent see a danger in distinguishing between show-of-authority stops and actual-seizure stops? Do you agree that this poses a danger?

4. When do you think the officer stopped Hodari D.? Why is it important in this case?

5. Why is it important generally?

6. Consider the following remarks of Professor Richard Uviller, who observed the police in New York City for a period of a year:

> [T]he manifest confidence [exuded by the police] begets submission. And the cops learn the firm tone and hand that informs even the normally aggressive customer of the futility of resistance. It's effective. In virtually every encounter I have witnessed, the response of the person approached was docile, compliant, and respectful.

Do you think Professor Uviller's observations support the argument that no reasonable person feels free to leave the presence of a police officer? Do you believe that it supports the argument that a request by a police officer is really a command that citizens aren't free to deny? Defend your answer.

 Go to Exercise 3.3 on the Samaha Criminal Procedure 7e website to learn more about *California v. Hodari D.*: academic.cengage.com/criminaljustice/samaha.

 Go to the State Constitutional Law feature on the Criminal Procedure 7e website to learn more about how some states haven't followed *California v. Hodari D.*: academic.cengage.com/criminaljustice/samaha.

It's important to note two kinds of restraints on freedom of movement that have no Fourth Amendment significance: psychological pressure and a sense of moral duty. You may feel a psychological pressure—and, as responsible members of your community, you *should* also feel a *moral* duty—to cooperate with police officers. But neither psychological pressure nor your sense of moral duty, by themselves, can turn a police encounter into a Fourth Amendment seizure (*INS v. Delgado* 1984). Why? Because these are self-imposed restraints; law enforcement officers didn't impose them on you.

The American Law Institute (ALI) (1975) also takes the position that simple questioning by law enforcement officers isn't a seizure. According to its respected *Model Code of Pre-Arraignment Procedure:*

§110.1 REQUESTS FOR COOPERATION BY LAW ENFORCEMENT OFFICERS

(1) Authority to Request Cooperation.

A law enforcement officer may . . . request any person to furnish information or otherwise cooperate in the investigation or prevention of crime. The officer may request the person to respond to questions, to appear at a police station, or to comply with any other reasonable request. In making requests . . . no officer shall indicate that a person is legally obliged to furnish information or otherwise to cooperate if no such legal obligation exists.

Compliance with a request for information or other cooperation . . . shall not be regarded as involuntary or coerced solely on the ground that such request was made by one known to be a law enforcement officer. (3)

# SUMMARY

**I. Searches and Seizures**
   A. Crime control in a constitutional democracy depends on information, most of which comes from what police see and hear.
   B. Not all information can be gathered from ordinary senses; it comes from reluctant sources, including:
      1. Criminals
      2. Suspects
      3. Victims
      4. Witnesses
   C. Law enforcement officers have to rely on four involuntary methods to get information:
      1. Searches
      2. Seizures
      3. Interrogation
      4. Identification Procedures
   D. Some searches and seizures go beyond the purpose of crime control: they were implemented to:
      1. Protect officers from armed suspects
      2. Protect the property of detained suspects from loss or damage
      3. Protect officials from lawsuits
      4. Detect drug use among students and public employees
      5. Prevent drunk driving

**II. The History and Purposes of the Fourth Amendment**
   A. Searches and seizures originally were aimed at sedition (criticism of English monarchs) and tax evasions, not looking for and taking evidence of common felonies against individuals and their property and arresting suspects involved in such activities.

B. The Fourth Amendment bans all unreasonable searches and seizures.
   1. However, it wasn't aimed at crippling law enforcement's power.
   2. Instead, it was aimed at limiting police power enough so as not to infringe "unreasonably" on two other values at the heart of a free society:
      a. Liberty
      b. Privacy
C. The Fourth Amendment ensures that all searches and seizures are done reasonably.
D. The Fourth Amendment only protects us from invasions by law enforcement officers, not private individuals.
E. There are three main steps in Fourth Amendment analyses:
   1. Was the law enforcement action a search or a seizure?
   2. If the action was a search or a seizure, was it reasonable?
   3. If the action was an unreasonable search, does the Fourth Amendment ban its use as evidence?

**III. Searches**
A. Until 1967, the U.S. Supreme Court defined searches according to what was then the trespass doctrine.
   1. It meant that officers had to invade physically a "constitutionally protected area."
   2. Such areas include:
      a. Persons
      b. Houses
      c. Papers
      d. Effects
B. In 1967, the Supreme Court replaced the trespass doctrine with the two-pronged expectation-of-privacy test:
   1. Subjective privacy. Did the person exhibit an actual personal expectation of privacy?
   2. Objective privacy. Is society prepared to recognize the privacy as reasonable?

**IV. Electronic Surveillance**. There's no reasonable expectation of privacy in statements that include the following elements:
A. Statements are made by private individuals.
B. Statements are made to and recorded by undercover government agents.
C. Individuals who made the statements don't know they revealed them to undercover agents and that agents were recording the statements.

**V. The Plain View Doctrine**
A. There is no reasonable expectation of privacy in what officers discover by their ordinary senses—or in plain view.
B. Plain view "searches" are really nonsearches, and they fall into two categories:
   1. Search-related plain view refers to items in plain view that officers find during an authorized search.
   2. Nonsearch-related plain view refers to items that officers discover where no Fourth Amendment intrusion exists.
C. According to the plain view doctrine, plain view searches need to satisfy two conditions:
   1. Officers are where they have a legal right to be.
   2. Officers haven't beefed up their ordinary senses with advanced technology.

## VI. Unprotected Places

A. The Fourth Amendment protects our right to be secure in our persons, houses, papers, and effects but not in:

    1. Open Fields

        a. Open fields don't provide the setting for intimate activities that the amendment is intended to shelter people from.

        b. The grounds immediately surrounding a home, curtilage, aren't considered "open fields."

        c. Garages, patios, and pools are considered curtilage.

        d. The Supreme Court defines curtilage by:

    (1) The distance from the home

    (2) The presence or absence of a fence around the area

    (3) The use or purpose of the area

    (4) The measures taken to prevent public view

    2. Public Places

        a. Items and actions officers discover through their ordinary senses in public places aren't protected by the Fourth Amendment.

        b. Public places include privately owned businesses open for the public.

    3. Abandoned Property

        a. According to the U.S. Supreme Court, there's no reasonable expectation of privacy in abandoned property.

        b. Abandonment consists of both a physical and a mental element:

    (1) Physically giving up the possession of something

    (2) Intending to give up the expectation of privacy

        c. The U.S. Supreme Court has adopted a totality-of-circumstances test to determine whether throwing away property proves the intent to give up the reasonable expectation of privacy protected by the Fourth Amendment.

## VII. Seizures

A. You have been "seized" when an officer takes away your right to leave or stay in a place you want to be.

B. There are two kinds of Fourth Amendment seizures known as "stops":

    1. Actual-seizure stops. An officer physically grabs a suspect with the intent to keep him from leaving.

    2. Show-of-authority stops. An officer displays her authority by ordering suspects to stop, and the suspect submits to the show of authority.

C. Two kinds of restraints on your freedom of movement have no Fourth Amendment significance:

    1. Psychological pressure

    2. A sense of moral duty

# REVIEW QUESTIONS

1. What does crime control depend on?

2. Identify four sources law enforcement officers depend on to obtain information. Why is each one reluctant to divulge information?

3. Identify four involuntary methods law enforcement officials rely on for information.

4. Crime control is the main purpose of searches and seizures. Identify five special needs for searches and seizures that go beyond law enforcement purposes.

5. Identify and describe each element of the three main steps in Fourth Amendment analyses.

6. Describe the origins and original purposes of searches and seizures.

7. Identify and describe the two values at the heart of a free society.

8. Identify and describe the balance of interests the Fourth Amendment is supposed to protect.

9. Compare the trespass doctrine with the privacy doctrine in defining Fourth Amendment searches.

10. Compare the privacy doctrine in theory and in practice.

11. Identify the two-pronged expectation-of-privacy test the U.S. Supreme Court adopted in *Katz v. U.S.*

12. Why can plain view searches be called nonsearches?

13. Identify and give an example of the two types of plain view searches.

14. What two elements need to happen to satisfy a plain view search?

15. Identify three unprotected areas that aren't protected from the Fourth Amendment. Explain why each place isn't protected.

16. Identify the four elements the court uses to define curtilage.

17. Identify the mental and physical element to abandonment.

18. Identify and describe two types of seizure "stops." Give an example of each.

19. What two restraints on your freedom of movement have no Fourth Amendment significance?

## KEY TERMS

liberty, p. 50
privacy, p. 50
trespass doctrine, p. 51
privacy doctrine, p. 52
subjective privacy, p. 52
objective privacy, p. 52

thermal imagers, p. 62
search-related plain view, p. 65
nonsearch-related plain view, p. 65
plain-view doctrine, p. 65
open fields doctrine, p. 68
curtilage, p. 68

totality-of-circumstances test, p. 69
actual seizures, p. 69
show-of-authority seizures, p. 69
"reasonable person would not feel free to leave" definition of seizure, p. 70

# Stop and Frisk

## MAIN POINTS

- The power to stop and question suspicious persons is ancient.
- Modern stop-and-frisk law grew out of the practical problems of investigating suspicious people and circumstances in large cities.
- Stops balance society's need to investigate crime against the rights of individuals to come and go as they please.
- Officers can't stop people on a hunch or a whim.
- Race and ethnicity can be *part* of a reasonable suspicion to stop.
- Frisks balance the government's interest in criminal law enforcement against the individual's privacy right not to be touched by an officer.
- Lawful frisks require a lawful stop plus reason to *suspect* that a suspect *may* be armed.
- Officers can *always* remove passengers from vehicles they've stopped lawfully.
- The need to control who and what comes into the United States justifies severe reductions in individual liberty and privacy at international borders.
- Searches directed at groups can be reasonable without *individualized* suspicion.

*A customs inspector told Elvira Montoya de Hernandez, a passenger arriving at Los Angeles International Airport on a flight from Bogotá, Colombia, that he suspected she was smuggling drugs in her alimentary canal. The officer placed her in a customs office under observation and told her that if she went to the toilet she would have to use a wastebasket in the women's restroom so that female inspectors could inspect her stool for balloons or capsules carrying narcotics. The inspector refused Montoya de Hernandez's request to call her husband in Colombia. Montoya de Hernandez remained detained under watch in the customs office, for most of the time curled up in a chair leaning to one side. She refused all offers of food and drink, and refused to use the toilet facilities. She exhibited symptoms of discomfort with "heroic efforts to resist the usual calls of nature." At the shift change at 4:00 P.M. the next afternoon, almost 16 hours after her flight had landed, Montoya de Hernandez still had not defecated or urinated or partaken of food or drink.*

U.S. v. Montoya de Hernandez (1985), U.S. Supreme Court

The power to stop and question suspicious persons is ancient. From at least the Middle Ages, English constables were bound by their office to detain suspicious people, especially the dreaded "nightwalkers." (Anyone walking around between dusk and dawn was automatically suspected of being up to no good [Stern 1967, 532].) The English brought "stop and frisk" to their American colonies, and nobody challenged it until the 1960s.

Then, during the due process revolution of that decade (Chapter 2), civil libertarians did challenge the power of police to detain suspicious people on a hunch. On what basis? Private individuals, they argued, especially "outsiders," need the courts to protect their rights whenever they're out on the streets and other public places. Not surprisingly, law enforcement officers didn't see it that way. They argued that until they made an **arrest** (Chapter 5)—took suspects to the police station and kept them there against their will—their good judgment, based on their professional expertise gained from training and experience, was enough. Formal rules written by judges who had no knowledge and experience of the "street" and "street people" would only interfere with crime control (Remington 1960, 390).

**Fourth Amendment stops** are brief detentions that allow law enforcement officers to freeze suspicious situations briefly so they can investigate them. Fourth Amendment seizures of persons include everything from these brief street stops to lengthy jail detentions (Figure 4.1 on page 85). **Fourth Amendment frisks** are once-over-lightly pat downs of outer clothing by officers to protect themselves by taking away suspects' weapons. (We don't expect officers to risk their lives when they approach a person to check out possible danger.)

Fourth Amendment searches of persons include everything from these protective pat downs for weapons to strip and body-cavity searches. Chapters 5 and 6 analyze the greater invasions of arrests and full-blown searches in the unfamiliar and isolated surroundings of police stations and jails. This chapter examines stops and frisks, the least invasive seizures and searches of persons in familiar and more comfortable public places, such as streets, parks, and malls.

We've already touched on how the U.S. Constitution requires government officers to have an objective basis (suspicious facts and circumstances), not just hunches, to back up official unwanted interferences with individuals' rights (Chapters 2–3). We further noted that the greater the invasion, the greater the objective basis required by the Constitution to back it up. With specific reference to Fourth Amendment searches and seizures, this means officers need to prove fewer suspicious facts and circumstances to back up stops and frisks than they do for arrests (Chapter 5) and full-blown searches (Chapter 6).

Stops and frisks represent the beginning of a chronological path through the investigative process, beginning with the more frequent and more-visible (but less intrusive) searches and seizures in public to the more-intrusive (but less visible) searches and seizures out of sight in police stations.

Stops and frisks aren't just fine points for constitutional lawyers and courts to debate. They also reflect broad public policies aimed at balancing the values of crime control and individual liberty and privacy. As we've just seen, although they may take place in the less-intimidating atmosphere of public places and invade liberty and privacy less than arrests and searches, stops and frisks affect a lot more people. The ratio of stops to arrests is about one arrest to every nine stops (Spitzer 1999, Table I.B.1). In fact, for most people, stops and frisks are the only uninvited (and unwanted) contact with the police they'll ever have.

Just as important, because stops and frisks take place in public, the display of police power is there for everybody to see. This visibility of stops and frisks probably shapes public opinion of police power more than the greater invasions of arrest and searches that we never see. Deciding which is more important—crime control by means of less-intrusive public stops and frisks affecting more people or often invisible arrests and searches affecting fewer people—is both a constitutional and public policy question of great importance.

The importance of the constitutional and policy dimensions of stops and frisks isn't due solely to their numbers but to their geographic and demographic distribution. Black and Latino young men living in poor urban neighborhoods, or who happen to be in White neighborhoods, experience stops and frisks far more frequently than Whites, even poor Whites living in the same poor neighborhoods as Blacks and Latinos (Spitzer 1999).

According to police scholar Jerome Skolnick (1998):

> One of the problems with stop and frisk . . . is that any review of police-community relations finds that there is hostility between the police and the minority communities. A lot of that problem has to do with stop and frisk. Field interrogations that are excessive, that are discourteous, and that push people around, generate friction. (1267)

The tough policy question in light of these facts is how to "prevent crime without losing control of the police who may use these powers unfairly to harass Black and Latino kids on the streets" (Katz 2004, 458).

As we examine the realities of stop and frisk, keep in mind these very important facts:

- Officers are going to stop many people who haven't done anything wrong, and they'll frisk lots of people who aren't armed.
- Most of these same people want police protection and (at least in high-crime neighborhoods) need it more than people who live in safe neighborhoods.

- Both lawbreakers and law abiders in high-street-crime neighborhoods form lasting opinions about the police from street encounters they've either watched or experienced.
- Stops and frisks aren't distributed evenly; they fall most heavily on Black and Latino young men in poor urban neighborhoods.

# STOP-AND-FRISK LAW

Stop-and-frisk law follows the three-step analysis we used to decide whether an officer's action was a search or a seizure at all in Chapter 3:

1. Was the officer's action a stop or a frisk?

2. If the officer's action was a stop or a frisk, was it unreasonable?

3. If the stop or frisk was unreasonable, should evidence obtained during the stop and/or frisk be excluded from legal proceedings against the defendants (Chapter 10)?

If the action *wasn't* a stop or a frisk (step 1, Chapter 3), then the Fourth Amendment doesn't apply at all, and the analysis stops. This means the courts don't have the authority to review what officers do in such situations; it's left to officers' discretion. If the action *was* a stop or a frisk, then the analysis proceeds to the next step—namely, whether it was reasonable (step 2, this chapter). If it was reasonable, the analysis is over. If it was unreasonable, the analysis proceeds to decide whether the evidence has to be excluded (step 3, Chapter 10).

## Two Approaches to Fourth Amendment Analyses

Before we analyze stops and frisks, we need to break down the two parts of the Fourth Amendment:

1. *Reasonableness clause.* "The right of the people to be secure in their persons, houses, papers, and effects against unreasonable searches and seizures shall not be violated."

2. *Warrant clause.* ". . . and no warrants shall issue but upon probable cause, supported by oath or affirmation, and particularly describing the place to be searched, and the persons or things to be seized."

Until the 1960s, the U.S. Supreme Court followed the **conventional Fourth Amendment approach**, which says the warrant and reasonableness clauses are firmly connected. Specifically, the reasonableness clause is just a stirring introduction to the heart of the people's right against unreasonable searches and seizures—the warrant clause. The warrant clause guarantees that only searches and seizures based on warrants and probable cause are reasonable.

In the 1960s, the Supreme Court shifted from this conventional approach to the **reasonableness Fourth Amendment approach**. It says the two clauses are separate, and they address separate problems. The warrant clause tells us what the Fourth Amendment requires only when law enforcement officers obtain warrants (Chapter 6).

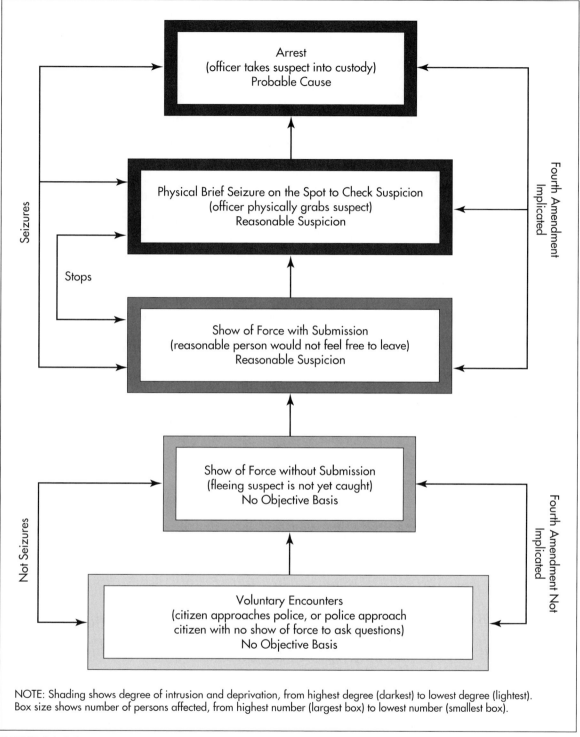

NOTE: Shading shows degree of intrusion and deprivation, from highest degree (darkest) to lowest degree (lightest). Box size shows number of persons affected, from highest number (largest box) to lowest number (smallest box).

**FIGURE 4.1** Seizures

But only a tiny fraction of searches and seizures are made with warrants, and some searches and seizures don't require probable cause either. That means the warrant clause doesn't come into play very often.

So, according to the Court, we can't read the Fourth Amendment to mean searches and seizures without warrants and probable cause are *always* unreasonable. Since the 1960s, the Court has spent a lot of its time reviewing, case by case, the circumstances that make a search or seizure unreasonable. By now it should be clear to you that the Court's decisions aren't always clear. But don't blame the Court; after all, "unreasonable" is probably the vaguest, and therefore also one of the toughest to define, words in the Constitution.

The Fourth Amendment has generated more cases, and takes up more pages in criminal procedure books, including this one, than any other subject in the law of criminal procedure. Why? All lower courts have to follow these decisions. State legislatures also consult them when they write criminal procedure rules. And, most important, local police departments and police officers know their stop-and-frisk rules and actions might be reviewed by at least some court and could go all the way to the Supreme Court.

Reasonableness is a broad—and some say too subjective—standard. According to Professor John M. Copacino (1994), in balancing the interest of the government in crime control and special needs against the invasions of individual liberty and privacy:

> [T]he Supreme Court has been satisfied by broad characterization of the government's interest, usually unaccompanied by any hard evidence. Similarly, in assessing the harm caused to the individual by the intrusion, the Court does not cite any empirical evidence, expert testimony, or individual testimony from those who have been affected by the search or seizure. It simply proclaims its subjective judgment of the citizen's likely reactions. (236)

When the U.S. Supreme Court decided there were more reasonable searches and seizures without than with warrants, it created two major challenges:

1. When does the Fourth Amendment require warrants?

2. What does "unreasonable" mean?

The Court has formulated a method for meeting these challenges. One type of reasonable search and seizure is based on warrants and probable cause. The other type—which, in practice, includes the vast majority of searches and seizures—has to pass the **reasonableness test**.

The reasonableness test consists of two elements that it's the government's burden to prove:

1. *Balancing element.* The need to search and/or seize outweighs the invasion of liberty and privacy rights of the individuals.

2. *Objective basis.* There are enough facts and circumstances to back up the search and/or seizure.

There's no "bright line" (clear) rule to tell officers, courts, or us what's reasonable. According to the U.S. Supreme Court, courts have to decide whether searches and seizures are reasonable on a **case-by-case basis**. How do they do it? They look at the totality of circumstances surrounding the specific searches and seizures in individual cases. Officers make a preliminary (usually on the spur of the moment under pressure) reasonableness decision on the street and in police stations.

In making their decision, officers are allowed to view the totality of circumstances through the lens of their professional training and experience. But officers' decisions aren't final. That's left to judges. Judges review the totality of the circumstances the officers acted on and decide whether they meet the constitutional standard of reasonableness.

The test of reasonableness also requires a case-by-case evaluation of whether there was enough objective basis to back up the searches and seizures. The objective basis ranges from the probable cause required to back up full-blown searches (Chapter 6) and seizures (arrests, Chapter 5) to the lesser reasonable suspicion required to back up stops and frisks. Both probable cause (always) and reasonable suspicion (usually) require **individualized suspicion**, meaning suspicion that points to specific individuals. However, DWI roadblocks (discussed later in this chapter) and some noncriminal law enforcement searches (Chapter 7) don't require individualized suspicion. In these cases, the objective basis consists of standard procedures such as random stops.

Today's stop-and-frisk law grew out of the Supreme Court's ruling in one case. Let's look at the Fourth Amendment issues surrounding that case, *Terry v. Ohio*, and at stop-and-frisk law after *Terry*.

## *Terry v. Ohio* and Stop and Frisk

Today's stop-and-frisk law grew out of the practical problems police officers face in preventing and investigating crime on the streets and other public places in our largest cities. In these investigations, officers are usually dealing with people they don't know and probably won't ever see again. Usually, these strangers' suspicious behavior doesn't add up to the probable cause needed to arrest them (Chapter 5).

For example, suppose an officer doesn't have enough facts and circumstances viewed through the lens of her professional experience and training to arrest two men who peer into a store window, look around as if to see if anyone was watching them, and pace up and down repeating this pattern for several minutes. What should the officer do? Nothing? Keep watching them? Briefly detain them and pat them down for weapons? Take them to the police station? These were the issues raised in the famous *Terry v. Ohio* case.

The answer depends on three possible interpretations of the Fourth Amendment (Dix 1985, 853–55):

1. The Fourth Amendment applies only to full searches and arrests; so short of full arrests and searches, officers' discretion controls their contacts with individuals in public places.

2. Even brief street detentions are arrests, and pat downs are searches, so the police can't do anything unless they've got probable cause.

3. Stops and frisks are searches and seizures, but they're "minor" ones, so officers have to back them up with facts. But they need fewer facts than they'd need to arrest and search.

If officers can't take any action until they've got probable cause (alternative 2), crime control suffers because they'll probably never see the suspects again. But if the Fourth Amendment doesn't apply at all to these street encounters (alternative 1), then people on the street are subject to the whims of every officer. So both alternatives 1 and 2 are unacceptable; the U.S. Supreme Court chose alternative 3.

According to the Court, the Fourth Amendment gives the police enough power to "freeze" suspicious events and people briefly to find out if criminal activity "may be afoot." The Fourth Amendment also gives officers the power to protect themselves by frisking the people they stop. But officers can't freeze all the events and lay hands on all the people they've got a hunch may be up to no good; their stops and frisks have to be "reasonable." Courts can later review their stops and frisks to make sure they were reasonable.

What's "reasonable"? First, in the balance between crime control and individual freedom and privacy, in each case, the need to control crime has to outweigh the invasions against the individuals' rights. Second, officers can't stop and frisk people on a hunch, whim, or "mere suspicion." They need facts—not as many as would add up to probable cause (Chapters 5–6) but enough so that later a neutral judge can decide if there was enough objective basis to back up both the stop and the frisk.

In our next case excerpt, the landmark case *Terry v. Ohio* (1968), the U.S. Supreme Court applied alternative 3, holding that the stop and frisk of John Terry satisfied the reasonableness requirement of the Fourth Amendment.

# CASE    *Was He Seized and Searched?*

## Terry v. Ohio

392 U.S. 1 (1968)

### HISTORY

John W. Terry, petitioner, was prosecuted for carrying a concealed weapon. The Court of Common Pleas of Cuyahoga County, Ohio, overruled a pretrial motion to suppress. Terry was convicted and sentenced to one to three years in the Ohio Penitentiary. Terry appealed. The defendant appealed. The Court of Appeals for the Eighth Judicial District, of Ohio affirmed. The Ohio Supreme Court dismissed an appeal on the ground that no substantial constitutional question was involved. The U.S. Supreme Court granted certiorari, and affirmed.

WARREN, J.

This case presents serious questions concerning the role of the Fourth Amendment in the confrontation on the street between the citizen and the policeman investigating suspicious circumstances. Petitioner Terry was convicted of carrying a concealed weapon and sentenced to the statutorily prescribed term of one to three years in the penitentiary. Following the denial of a pretrial motion to suppress, the prosecution introduced in evidence two revolvers and a number of bullets seized from Terry and a codefendant, Richard Chilton, by Cleveland Police Detective Martin McFadden.

### FACTS

Officer Martin McFadden testified that while he was patrolling in plain clothes in downtown Cleveland at approximately 2:30 in the afternoon of October 31, 1963, his attention was attracted by two men, Chilton and Terry, standing on the corner of Huron Road and Euclid Avenue.

He had never seen the two men before, and he was unable to say precisely what first drew his eye to them. However, he testified that he had been a policeman for 39 years and a detective for 35 and that he had been assigned to patrol this vicinity of downtown Cleveland for shoplifters and pickpockets for 30 years. He explained that he had developed routine habits of observation over the years and that he would "stand and watch people or walk and watch people at many intervals of the day." He added: "Now, in this case when I looked over they didn't look right to me at the time."

His interest aroused, Officer McFadden took up a post of observation in the entrance to a store 300 to 400 feet away from the two men. "I get more purpose to watch them when I seen their movements," he testified.

He saw one of the men leave the other one and walk southwest on Huron Road, past some stores. The man paused for a moment and looked in a store window, then walked on a short distance, turned around and walked back toward the corner, pausing once again to look in the same store window. He rejoined his companion at the corner, and the two conferred briefly.

Then the second man went through the same series of motions, strolling down Huron Road, looking in the same window, walking on a short distance, turning back, peering in the store window again, and returning to confer with the first man at the corner.

The two men repeated this ritual alternately between five and six times apiece—in all, roughly a dozen trips. At one point, while the two were standing together on the corner, a third man approached them and engaged them briefly in conversation. This man then left the two others and walked west on Euclid Avenue.

Chilton and Terry resumed their measured pacing, peering and conferring. After this had gone on for 10 to 12 minutes, the two men walked off together, heading west on Euclid Avenue, following the path taken earlier by the third man.

By this time Officer McFadden had become thoroughly suspicious. He testified that after observing their elaborately casual and oft-repeated reconnaissance of the store window on Huron Road, he suspected the two men of "casing a job, a stick-up," and that he considered it his duty as a police officer to investigate further. He added that he feared "they may have a gun."

Thus, Officer McFadden followed Chilton and Terry and saw them stop in front of Zucker's store to talk to the same man who had conferred with them earlier on the street corner. Deciding that the situation was ripe for direct action, Officer McFadden approached the three men, identified himself as a police officer and asked for their names. At this point his knowledge was confined to what he had observed. He was not acquainted with any of the three men by name or by sight, and he had received no information concerning them from any other source.

When the men "mumbled something" in response to his inquiries, Officer McFadden grabbed petitioner Terry, spun him around so that they were facing the other two, with Terry between McFadden and the others, and patted down the outside of his clothing. In the left breast pocket of Terry's overcoat Officer McFadden felt a pistol. He reached inside the overcoat pocket, but was unable to remove the gun.

At this point, keeping Terry between himself and the others, the officer ordered all three men to enter Zucker's store. As they went in, he removed Terry's overcoat completely, removed a .38-caliber revolver from the pocket and ordered all three men to face the wall with their hands raised. Officer McFadden proceeded to pat down the outer clothing of Chilton and the third man, Katz. He discovered another revolver in the outer pocket of Chilton's overcoat, but no weapons were found on Katz.

The officer testified that he only patted the men down to see whether they had weapons, and that he did not put his hands beneath the outer garments of either Terry or Chilton until he felt their guns. So far as appears from the record, he never placed his hands beneath Katz' outer garments. Officer McFadden seized Chilton's gun, asked the proprietor of the store to call a police wagon, and took all three men to the station, where Chilton and Terry were formally charged with carrying concealed weapons.

## OPINION

The Fourth Amendment . . . right . . . against unreasonable searches and seizures . . . belongs as much to the citizen on the streets of our cities as to the homeowner closeted in his study to dispose of his secret affairs. . . . Unquestionably Terry was entitled to the protection of the Fourth Amendment as he walked down the street in Cleveland. The question is whether in all the circumstances of this on-the-street encounter, his right to personal security was violated by an unreasonable search and seizure. . . .

We would be less than candid if we did not acknowledge that this question thrusts to the fore difficult and troublesome issues regarding a sensitive area of police activity—issues which have never before been squarely presented to this Court. . . . In this context we approach the issues in this case mindful of the limitations of the judicial function in controlling the myriad daily situations in which policemen and citizens confront each other on the street. The State has characterized the issue here as "the right of a police officer . . . to make an on-the-street stop, interrogate and pat down for weapons (known in street vernacular as 'stop and frisk')." But this is only partly accurate. For the issue is not the abstract propriety of the police conduct, but the admissibility against petitioner of the evidence uncovered by the search and seizure. Ever since its inception, the rule excluding evidence seized in violation of the Fourth Amendment has been recognized as a principal mode of discouraging lawless police conduct.

The exclusionary rule has its limitations, however, as a tool of judicial control. . . . Doubtless some police "field interrogation" conduct violates the Fourth Amendment. But a stern refusal by this Court to condone such activity does not necessarily render it responsive to the exclusionary rule. Regardless of how effective the rule may be where obtaining convictions is an important objective of the police, it is powerless to deter invasions of constitutionally guaranteed rights where the police either have no interest in prosecuting or are willing to forgo successful prosecution in the interest of serving some other goal. . . .

Proper adjudication of cases in which the exclusionary rule is invoked demands a constant awareness of these limitations. The wholesale harassment by certain elements of the police community, of which minority groups, particularly Negroes, frequently complain, will not be stopped by the exclusion of any evidence from any criminal trial. Yet a rigid and unthinking application of the exclusionary rule, in futile protest against practices which it can never be used effectively to control, may exact a high toll in human injury and frustration of efforts to prevent crime. . . .

Having thus roughly sketched the perimeters of the constitutional debate over the limits on police investigative conduct in general and the background against which this case presents itself, we turn our attention to the quite narrow question posed by the facts before us: whether it is always unreasonable for a policeman to seize a person and subject him to a limited search for weapons unless there is probable cause for an arrest . . .

Our first task is to establish at what point in this encounter . . . Officer McFadden "seized" Terry and whether and when he conducted a "search." There is some suggestion in the use of such terms as "stop" and "frisk" that such police conduct is outside the purview of the Fourth Amendment because neither action rises to the level of a "search" or "seizure" within the meaning of the Constitution.

We emphatically reject this notion. It is quite plain that the Fourth Amendment governs "seizures" of the person which do not eventuate in a trip to the station house and prosecution for crime—"arrests" in traditional terminology. It must be recognized that whenever a police officer accosts an individual and restrains his freedom to walk away, he has "seized" that person. And it is nothing less than sheer torture of the English language to suggest that a careful exploration of the outer surfaces of a person's clothing all over his or her body in an attempt to find weapons is not a "search." Moreover, it is simply fantastic to urge that such a procedure performed in public by a policeman while the citizen stands helpless, perhaps facing a wall with his hands raised, is a "petty indignity." It is a serious intrusion upon the sanctity of the person, which may inflict great indignity and arouse strong resentment, and it is not to be undertaken lightly. . . .

The . . . central inquiry under the Fourth Amendment [is]—the reasonableness in all the circumstances of the particular governmental invasion of a citizen's personal security. . . . In this case there can be no question that Officer McFadden "seized" Terry and subjected him to a "search" when he took hold of him and patted down the outer surfaces of his clothing. We must decide whether at that point it was reasonable for Officer McFadden to have interfered with petitioner's personal security as he did.

. . . [I]n determining whether the seizure and search were "unreasonable" our inquiry is a dual one—whether the officer's action was justified at its inception, and whether it was reasonably related in scope to the circumstances which justified the interference in the first place. . . .

. . . [I]n justifying the particular intrusion the police officer must be able to point to specific and articulable facts which, taken together with rational inferences from those facts, reasonably warrant that intrusion. . . . [T]he Fourth Amendment is meaningful only if at some point the conduct of those charged with enforcing the laws can be subjected to the more detached, neutral scrutiny of a judge who must evaluate the reasonableness of a particular search or seizure. . . . [I]n making that assessment it is imperative that the facts be judged against an objective standard: would the facts available to the officer at the moment of the seizure or the search "warrant a man of reasonable caution in the belief" that the action taken was appropriate?

Anything less would invite intrusions upon constitutionally guaranteed rights based on nothing more substantial than inarticulate hunches. . . . And simple "good faith on the part of the arresting officer is not enough." . . . If subjective good faith alone were the test, the protections of the Fourth Amendment would evaporate, and the people would be "secure in their persons, houses, papers, and effects" only in the discretion of the police.

Applying these principles to this case, we consider first the nature and extent of the government interests involved. One general interest is of course that of effective crime prevention and detection; it is this interest which underlies the recognition that a police officer may in appropriate circumstances and in an appropriate manner approach a person for purposes of investigating possibly criminal behavior even though there is no probable cause to make an arrest. It was this legitimate investigative function Officer McFadden was discharging when he decided to approach Terry and his companions. He had observed Terry, Chilton, and Katz go through a series of acts, each of them perhaps innocent in itself, but which taken together warranted further investigation.

There is nothing unusual in two men standing together on a street corner, perhaps waiting for someone. Nor is there anything suspicious about people in such circumstances strolling up and down the street, singly or in pairs. Store windows, moreover, are made to be looked in.

But the story is quite different where, as here, two men hover about a street corner for an extended period of time, at the end of which it becomes apparent that they are not waiting for anyone or anything; where these men pace alternately along an identical route, pausing to stare in the same store window roughly 24 times; where each completion of this route is followed immediately by a conference between the two men on the corner; where they are joined in one of these conferences by a third man who leaves swiftly; and where the two men finally follow the third and rejoin him a couple of blocks away. It would have been poor police work indeed for an officer of 30 years' experience in the detection of thievery from stores in this same neighborhood to have failed to investigate this behavior further.

The crux of this case, however, is not the propriety of Officer McFadden's taking steps to investigate Terry's suspicious behavior, but rather, whether there was justification for McFadden's invasion of Terry's personal security by searching him for weapons in the course of that investigation. We are now concerned with more than the governmental interest in investigating crime; in addition, there is the more immediate interest of the police officer in taking steps to assure himself that the person with whom he is dealing is not armed with a weapon that could unexpectedly and fatally be used against him. Certainly it would be unreasonable to require that police officers take unnecessary risks in the performance of their duties. . . .

We must still consider, however, the nature and quality of the intrusion on individual rights which must be accepted if police officers are to be conceded the right to search for weapons in situations where probable cause to arrest for crime is lacking. Even a limited search of the outer clothing for weapons constitutes a severe, though brief, intrusion upon cherished personal security, and it must surely be an annoying, frightening, and perhaps humiliating experience. . . .

Our evaluation of the proper balance that has to be struck in this type of case leads us to conclude that there must be a narrowly drawn authority to permit a reasonable search for weapons for the protection of the police officer, where he has reason to believe that he is dealing with an armed and dangerous individual. . . . [I]n determining whether the officer acted reasonably in such circumstances, due weight must be given, not to his inchoate and unparticularized suspicion or "hunch," but to the specific reasonable inferences which he is entitled to draw from the facts in light of his experience.

We must now examine the conduct of Officer McFadden in this case to determine whether his search and seizure of petitioner were reasonable, both at their inception and as conducted. He had observed Terry, together with Chilton and another man, acting in a manner he took to be preface to a "stick-up." We think on the facts and circumstances Officer McFadden detailed before the trial judge a reasonably prudent man would have been warranted in believing petitioner was armed and thus presented a threat to the officer's safety while he was investigating his suspicious behavior.

The actions of Terry and Chilton were consistent with McFadden's hypothesis that these men were contemplating a daylight robbery—which, it is reasonable to assume, would be likely to involve the use of weapons—and nothing in their conduct from the time he first noticed them until the time he confronted them and identified himself as a police officer gave him sufficient reason to negate that hypothesis. Although the trio had departed the original scene, there was nothing to indicate abandonment of an intent to commit a robbery at some point.

The manner in which the seizure and search were conducted is, of course, as vital a part of the inquiry as whether they were warranted at all. The Fourth Amendment proceeds as much by limitations upon the scope of governmental action as by imposing preconditions upon its initiation.

. . . [S]uch a search . . . is not justified by any need to prevent the disappearance or destruction of evidence of crime. The sole justification of the search in the present situation is the protection of the police officer and others nearby, and it must therefore be confined in scope to an intrusion reasonably designed to discover guns, knives, clubs, or other hidden instruments for the assault of the police officer.

The scope of the search in this case presents no serious problem in light of these standards. Officer McFadden patted down the outer clothing of petitioner and his two companions. He did not place his hands in their pockets or under the outer surface of their garments until he had felt weapons, and then he merely reached for and removed the guns. . . . Officer McFadden confined his search strictly to what was minimally necessary to learn whether the men were armed and to disarm them once he discovered the weapons. He did not conduct a general exploratory search for whatever evidence of criminal activity he might find.

We conclude that the revolver seized from Terry was properly admitted in evidence against him. . . . Each case of this sort will, of course, have to be decided on its own facts.

We merely hold today that where a police officer observes unusual conduct which leads him reasonably to conclude in light of his experience that criminal activity may be afoot and that the persons with whom he is dealing may be armed and presently dangerous, where in the course of investigating this behavior he identifies himself as a policeman and makes reasonable inquiries, and where

nothing in the initial stages of the encounter serves to dispel his reasonable fear for his own or others' safety, he is entitled for the protection of himself and others in the area to conduct a carefully limited search of the outer clothing of such persons in an attempt to discover weapons which might be used to assault him. Such a search is a reasonable search under the Fourth Amendment, and any weapons seized may properly be introduced in evidence against the person from whom they were taken.

## CONCURRING OPINIONS

### HARLAN, J.

. . . A police officer's right to make an on-the-street "stop" and an accompanying "frisk" for weapons is of course bounded by the protections afforded by the Fourth and Fourteenth Amendments. The Court holds, and I agree, that while the right does not depend upon possession by the officer of a valid warrant, nor upon the existence of probable cause, such activities must be reasonable under the circumstances as the officer credibly relates them in court. Since the question in this and most cases is whether evidence produced by a frisk is admissible, the problem is to determine what makes a frisk reasonable. . . .

The state courts held . . . that when an officer is lawfully confronting a possibly hostile person in the line of duty he has a right, springing . . . from the necessity of the situation . . . to frisk for his own protection. . . . The holding has, however, two logical corollaries that I do not think the Court has fully expressed.

In the first place, if the frisk is justified in order to protect the officer during an encounter with a citizen, the officer must first have constitutional grounds to insist on an encounter, to make a forcible stop. . . . I would make it perfectly clear that the right to frisk in this case depends upon the reasonableness of a forcible stop to investigate a suspected crime.

Where such a stop is reasonable, however, the right to frisk must be immediate and automatic if the reason for the stop is, as here, an articulable suspicion of a crime of violence. . . . A limited frisk incident to a lawful stop must often be rapid and routine. There is no reason why an officer, rightfully but forcibly confronting a person suspected of a serious crime, should have to ask one question and take the risk that the answer might be a bullet.

The facts of this case are illustrative of a proper stop and an incident frisk. Officer McFadden had no probable cause to arrest Terry for anything, but he had observed circumstances that would reasonably lead an experienced, prudent policeman to suspect that Terry was about to engage in burglary or robbery. His justifiable suspicion afforded a proper constitutional basis for accosting Terry, restraining his liberty of movement briefly, and addressing questions to him, and Officer McFadden did so. When he did, he had no reason whatever to suppose that Terry might be armed, apart from the fact that he suspected him of planning a violent crime. McFadden asked Terry his name, to which Terry "mumbled something." Whereupon McFadden, without asking Terry to speak louder and without giving him any chance to explain his presence or his actions, forcibly frisked him.

I would affirm this conviction for what I believe to be the same reasons the Court relies on. I would, however, make explicit what I think is implicit in affirmance on the present facts. Officer McFadden's right to interrupt Terry's freedom of movement and invade his privacy arose only because circumstances warranted forcing an encounter with Terry in an effort to prevent or investigate a crime. Once that forced encounter was justified, however, the officer's right to take suitable measures for his own safely followed automatically. Upon the foregoing premises, I join the opinion of the Court.

### WHITE, J.

. . . I think an additional word is in order concerning the matter of interrogation during an investigative stop. There is nothing in the Constitution which prevents a policeman from addressing questions to anyone on the streets. Absent special circumstances, the person approached may not be detained or frisked but may refuse to cooperate and go on his way. However, given the proper circumstances, such as those in this case, it seems to me the person may be briefly detained against his will while pertinent questions are directed to him. Of course, the person stopped is not obliged to answer, answers may not be compelled, and refusal to answer furnishes no basis for an arrest, although it may alert the officer to the need for continued observation. In my view, it is temporary detention, warranted by the circumstances, which chiefly justifies the protective frisk for weapons. Perhaps the frisk itself, where proper, will have beneficial results whether questions are asked or not. If weapons are found, an arrest will follow. If none are found, the frisk may nevertheless serve preventive ends because of its unmistakable message that suspicion has been aroused. But if the investigative stop is sustainable at all, constitutional rights are not necessarily violated if pertinent questions are asked and the person is restrained briefly in the process.

## DISSENT

### DOUGLAS, J.

. . . The requirement of probable cause has roots that are deep in our history. The general warrant, in which the name of the person to be arrested was left blank, and the writs of assistance, against which James Otis inveighed, both perpetuated the oppressive practice of allowing the police to arrest and search on suspicion. Police control took the place of judicial control, since no showing of "probable cause" before a magistrate was required. . . .

The infringement on personal liberty of any "seizure" of a person can only be "reasonable" under the Fourth Amendment if we require the police to possess "probable cause" before they seize him. Only that line draws a meaningful distinction between an officer's mere inkling and the presence of facts within the officer's personal knowledge which would convince a reasonable man that the person seized has committed, is committing, or is about to commit a particular crime. . . .

To give the police greater power than a magistrate is to take a long step down the totalitarian path. Perhaps such a step is desirable to cope with modern forms of lawlessness. But if it is taken, it should be the deliberate choice of the people through a constitutional amendment. Until the Fourth Amendment . . . is rewritten, the person and the effects of the individual are beyond the reach of all government agencies until there are reasonable grounds to believe (probable cause) that a criminal venture has been launched or is about to be launched.

There have been powerful hydraulic pressures throughout our history that bear heavily on the Court to water down constitutional guarantees and give the police the upper hand. That hydraulic pressure has probably never been greater than it is today.

Yet if the individual is no longer to be sovereign, if the police can pick him up whenever they do not like the cut of his jib, if they can "seize" and "search" him in their discretion, we enter a new regime. The decision to enter it should be made only after a full debate by the people of this country.

## Questions

1. List in chronological order all of McFadden's actions from the time he started watching Terry until he arrested him.

2. According to Professor Lewis Katz (2004), who worked on one of the briefs in the case:

   . . . The Court played fast and loose with the most important fact in the case: the number of trips Terry and Chilton made up the street and how many times they looked into the store window. [Chief Justice] Warren reported that the two men looked into the window twenty-four times. That figure is reported with a certainty that the evidence does not support. McFadden was confused about how many times this occurred; a fair reading of the many times he stated what happened leads to the conclusion that they looked into the window between four and twenty-four times. His police report written immediately after the arrests stated that each man made three trips. This fact is critical because it is unclear as to whether the seizure would have been reasonable based on fewer observations of the store window. (454)

   Do you agree that Chief Justice Warren "played fast and loose with the most important fact in the case"? Does this added information affect your opinion? Does it bother you that the chief justice isn't clear on the facts? Explain your answers.

3. According to the Court, at what point did McFadden seize Terry? Summarize the Court's reasons for picking that point.

4. According to the Court, at what point did McFadden search Terry? Summarize the Court's reasons for picking that point.

5. What was the objective basis (facts and circumstances) for McFadden's "stop" of Terry?

6. What was the objective basis (facts and circumstances) for McFadden's "frisk" of Terry?

7. Summarize the main points of Justice Harlan's concurring opinion. What do they add to your understanding of Chief Justice Warren's opinion?

8. During the oral argument before the Supreme Court, it came out that in all of Officer McFadden's experience, he'd never investigated a robbery; his experience was limited to spotting and investigating shoplifters and pickpockets. Does this matter? Explain your answer.

9. It was also learned during the oral argument that Terry, Chilton, and Katz were a lot bigger than Officer McFadden. Does this matter? Why?

10. Consider the following excerpt from an amicus curiae brief filed in *Terry v. Ohio:*

    In the litigation now before the Court—as is usual in cases where police practices are challenged—two parties essentially are represented. Law enforcement officers, legal representatives of their respective States, ask the Court to broaden police powers, and thereby to sustain what has proved to be a "good pinch."

    Criminal defendants caught with the goods through what in retrospect appears to be at least shrewd and successful (albeit constitutionally questionable) police work ask the Court to declare that work illegal and to reverse their convictions.

    Other parties intimately affected by the issues before the Court are not represented. The many thousands of our citizens who have been or may be stopped and frisked yearly, only to be released when the police find them innocent of any crime, are not represented. The records of their cases are not before the Court and cannot be brought here. Yet it is they, far more than those charged with crime, who will bear the consequences of the rules of constitutional law which this Court establishes.

    The determination of the quantum of "belief" or "suspicion" required to justify the exercise of intrusive police authority is precisely the determination of how far afield from instances of obvious guilt the authority stretches. To lower that quantum is to broaden the police net and, concomitantly, to increase the number (and probably the proportion) of innocent people caught up in it.

    The innocent are those this Court will never see. (Kurland and Casper 1975)

    What's the point the brief makes? What's the importance of the point?

11. During oral arguments of the case before the Supreme Court, Louis Stokes, Terry's lawyer, revealed some of what happened at the suppression hearing. Stokes said, among other things, that Officer McFadden testified that he didn't know the men, that they walked normally, that they were standing in front of a store talking normally, and that they were facing away from the store windows. When asked why he approached Terry, Chilton, and Katz, Officer McFadden replied, "Because . . . I didn't like them." Is this testimony important? Also, McFadden was White and Terry and Chilton were Black. Is this important?

 Go to Exercise 4.1 on the Samaha Criminal Procedure 7e website to learn more about *Terry v. Ohio.* Then, read the "Rest of the Story": academic.cengage.com/criminaljustice/samaha.

## Stop and Frisk after *Terry*

Judge Michael R. Juviler was a prosecutor in 1968. On the same day that *Terry v. Ohio* was argued, he argued in favor of the power to stop and frisk in a New York case before the U.S. Supreme Court. On the 30th anniversary of the decision, he recalled:

> After the *Terry* opinions were filed, we felt perhaps like the makers of the hydrogen bomb. What had we created? What had we contributed to? Would this lead to further racial divisions, police abuse, police "testilying [police perjury]"? (Juviler 1998, 743–44)

At the time *Terry* was decided, many commentators, and some judges, interpreted the decision as a *grudging* watering down of the protections of the right against unreasonable search and seizure. This watering down seemed necessary in the climate of the times. The case was decided at a time when race riots, mass antiwar protests that sometimes turned violent and even lethal, and skyrocketing crime rates plagued our largest cities. Law enforcement had to have tools to respond to this violence, crime, and disorder. The decision was praised for balancing the need for safety and the rights of individuals.

As you read the remaining sections in the chapter, think about Judge Juviler's comment, and ask yourself whether his worries have come to pass. Certainly, it's true that the cases that followed *Terry*, some of which you'll read in the sections that follow, expanded the power of the police in several ways. First, it expanded the scope of the power beyond serious crimes against the person to possessory crimes, especially illegal drug possession. Second, it expanded the time and location where the powers can be exercised. Third, it expanded the objective basis for stops and frisks from firsthand observation by officers to include informants, anonymous tips, and even to profiles. Think seriously about whether these changes are good or bad or right or wrong.

Four years after the Court decided *Terry v. Ohio*, it began to flesh out what the balancing and objective basis of the reasonableness approach to Fourth Amendment stops meant. That fleshing out signaled a trend, broken only rarely, that the Court has followed up to 2007—tipping reasonableness in favor of law enforcement. The case was our next case excerpt, *Adams v. Williams* (1971), where the Court decided that *Terry v. Ohio* wasn't limited to serious crimes against persons backed up by reasonable suspicion, consisting only of direct observation by officers who stopped and frisked a suspect. It also applied to drug possession backed up by the secondhand hearsay of an informant.

## CASE    *Was the Stop and Frisk Reasonable?*

### Adams v. Williams
407 U.S. 143 (1972)

### HISTORY

Robert Williams, Respondent, was convicted in a Connecticut state court of illegal possession of a handgun found during a "stop and frisk," as well as of possession of heroin that was found during a full search incident to his weapons arrest. After respondent's conviction was affirmed by the Supreme Court of Connecticut, this Court denied certiorari. Williams' petition for federal habeas corpus relief was denied by the District Court and by a divided panel of the Second Circuit, but on rehearing en banc the Court of Appeals granted relief. That court held that evidence introduced at Williams' trial had been obtained by an unlawful search of his person and car, and thus the state court judgments of conviction should be set aside. Since we conclude that the policeman's actions here conformed to the standards this Court laid down in *Terry v. Ohio*, we reverse.

REHNQUIST, J.

### FACTS

Police Sgt. John Connolly was alone early in the morning on car patrol duty in a high-crime area of Bridgeport, Connecticut. At approximately 2:15 A.M. a person known to Sgt. Connolly approached his cruiser and informed him that an individual seated in a nearby vehicle was carrying narcotics and had a gun at his waist.

After calling for assistance on his car radio, Sgt. Connolly approached the vehicle to investigate the informant's report. Connolly tapped on the car window and asked the occupant, Robert Williams, to open the door. When Williams rolled down the window instead, the sergeant reached into the car and removed a fully loaded revolver from Williams' waistband. The gun had not been visible to Connolly from outside the car, but it was in precisely the place indicated by the informant.

Williams was then arrested by Connolly for unlawful possession of the pistol. A search incident to that arrest was conducted after other officers arrived. They found substantial quantities of heroin on Williams' person and in the car, and they found a machete and a second revolver hidden in the automobile.

### OPINION

Respondent contends that the initial seizure of his pistol, upon which rested the later search and seizure of other weapons and narcotics, was not justified by the informant's tip to Sgt. Connolly. He claims that absent a more reliable informant, or some corroboration of the tip, the policeman's actions were unreasonable under the standards set forth in *Terry v. Ohio.*

In *Terry* this Court recognized that "a police officer may in appropriate circumstances and in an appropriate manner approach a person for purposes of investigating possibly criminal behavior even though there is no probable cause to make an arrest." The Fourth Amendment does not require a policeman who lacks the precise level of information necessary for probable cause to arrest to simply shrug his shoulders and allow a crime to occur or a criminal to escape.

On the contrary, *Terry* recognizes that it may be the essence of good police work to adopt an intermediate response. A brief stop of a suspicious individual, in order to determine his identity or to maintain the status quo momentarily while obtaining more information, may be most reasonable in light of the facts known to the officer at the time.

The Court recognized in *Terry* that the policeman making a reasonable investigatory stop should not be denied the opportunity to protect himself from attack by a hostile suspect. "When an officer is justified in believing that the individual whose suspicious behavior he is investigating at close range is armed and presently dangerous to the officer or to others," he may conduct a limited protective search for concealed weapons. The purpose of this limited search is not to discover evidence of crime, but to allow the officer to pursue his investigation without fear of violence, and thus the frisk for weapons might be equally necessary and reasonable, whether or not carrying a concealed weapon violated any applicable state law. So long as the officer is entitled to make a forcible stop, and has reason to believe that the suspect is armed and dangerous, he may conduct a weapons search limited in scope to this protective purpose.

Applying these principles to the present case, we believe that Sgt. Connolly acted justifiably in responding to his informant's tip. The informant was known to him personally and had provided him with information in the past. This is a stronger case than obtains in the case of an anonymous telephone tip. The informant here came forward personally to give information that was immediately verifiable at the scene. Indeed, under Connecticut law, the informant might have been subject to immediate arrest for making a false complaint had Sgt. Connolly's investigation proved the tip incorrect. Thus, while the Court's decisions indicate that this informant's unverified tip may have been insufficient for a narcotics arrest or search warrant, the information carried enough indicia of reliability to justify the officer's forcible stop of Williams.

In reaching this conclusion, we reject respondent's argument that reasonable cause for a stop and frisk can only be based on the officer's personal observation, rather than on information supplied by another person. Informants' tips, like all other clues and evidence coming to a policeman on the scene, may vary greatly in their value and reliability. One simple rule will not cover every situation. Some tips, completely lacking in indicia of reliability, would either warrant no police response or require further investigation before a forcible stop of a suspect would be authorized. But in some situations—for example, when the victim of a street crime seeks immediate police aid and gives a description of his assailant, or when a credible informant warns of a specific impending crime—the subtleties of the hearsay rule should not thwart an appropriate police response.

While properly investigating the activity of a person who was reported to be carrying narcotics and a concealed weapon and who was sitting alone in a car in a high-crime area at 2:15 in the morning, Sgt. Connolly had ample reason to fear for his safety. When Williams rolled down his window, rather than complying with the policeman's request to step out of the car so that his movements could more easily be seen, the revolver allegedly at Williams' waist became an even greater threat. Under these circumstances the policeman's action in reaching to the spot where the gun was thought to be hidden constituted a limited intrusion designed to insure his safety, and we conclude that it was reasonable. The loaded gun seized as a result of this intrusion was therefore admissible at Williams' trial. . . .

Under the circumstances surrounding Williams' possession of the gun seized by Sgt. Connolly, the arrest on the weapons charge was supported by probable cause, and the search of his person and of the car incident to that arrest was lawful [Chapter 5]. The fruits of the search were therefore properly admitted at Williams' trial, and the Court of Appeals erred in reaching a contrary conclusion.

REVERSED.

## DISSENT

DOUGLAS, J., JOINED BY MARSHALL, J.

. . . The easy extension of *Terry v. Ohio*, to "possessory offenses" is a serious intrusion on Fourth Amendment safeguards. If it is to be extended to the latter at all, this should be only where observation by the officer himself or well authenticated information shows that criminal activity may be afoot.

BRENNAN, J.

The crucial question on which this case turns, as the Court concedes, is whether, there being no contention that Williams acted voluntarily in rolling down the window of his car, the State had shown sufficient cause to justify Sgt. Connolly's "forcible" stop. I would affirm, believing, for the following reasons stated by Judge, now Chief Judge, Friendly, dissenting, that the State did not make that showing:

To begin, I have the gravest hesitancy in extending *Terry v. Ohio*, to crimes like the possession of narcotics. . . . There is too much danger that, instead of the stop being the object and the protective frisk an incident thereto, the reverse will be true. Against that we have here the added fact of the report that Williams had a gun on his person. . . . But Connecticut allows its citizens to carry weapons, concealed or other-wise, at will, provided only they have a permit, and gives its police officers no special authority to stop for the purpose of determining whether the citizen has one. . . .

If I am wrong in thinking that *Terry* should not be applied at all to mere possessory offenses, . . . I would not find the combination of Officer Connolly's almost meaningless observation and the tip in this case to be sufficient justification for the intrusion. The tip suffered from a threefold defect, with each fold compounding the others. The informer was unnamed, he was not shown to have been reliable with respect to guns or narcotics, and he gave no information which demonstrated personal knowledge or—what is worse—could not readily have been manufactured by the officer after the event. . . .

"*Terry v. Ohio* was intended to free a police officer from the rigidity of a rule that would prevent his doing anything to a man reasonably suspected of being about to commit or having just committed a crime of violence, no matter how grave the problem or impelling the need for swift action, unless the officer had what a court would later determine to be probable cause for arrest. It was meant for the serious cases of imminent danger or of harm recently perpetrated to persons or property, not the conventional ones of possessory offenses. If it is to be extended to the latter at all, this should be only where observation by the officer himself or well authenticated information shows 'that criminal activity may be afoot.' 392 U.S., at 30, 88 S.Ct., at 1868, 20 L.Ed.2d 889. I greatly fear that if the (contrary view) should be followed, *Terry* will have opened the sluicegates for serious and unintended erosion of the protection of the Fourth Amendment."

MARSHALL, J. JOINED BY DOUGLAS, J.

Four years have passed since we decided *Terry v. Ohio*, and its companion cases, *Sibron v. New York* and *Peters v. New York*. . . . This case marks our first opportunity to give some flesh to the bones of *Terry*. Unfortunately, the flesh provided by today's decision cannot possibly be made to fit on *Terry*'s skeletal framework.

. . . We upheld the stop and frisk in *Terry* because we recognized that the realities of on-the-street law enforcement require an officer to act at times on the basis of strong evidence, short of probable cause, that criminal activity is taking place and that the criminal is armed and dangerous. Hence, *Terry* stands only for the proposition that police officers have a "narrowly drawn authority to . . . search for weapons" without a warrant.

In today's decision the Court ignores the fact that *Terry* begrudgingly accepted the necessity for creating an exception from the warrant requirement of the Fourth Amendment and treats this case as if warrantless searches were the rule rather than the "narrowly drawn" exception. This decision betrays the careful balance that *Terry* sought to strike between a citizen's right to privacy and his government's responsibility for effective law enforcement and expands the concept of warrantless searches far beyond anything heretofore recognized as legitimate. I dissent. . . .

Mr. Justice Douglas was the sole dissenter in *Terry*. He warned of the "powerful hydraulic pressures throughout our history that bear heavily on the Court to water down constitutional guarantees. . . ." While I took the position then that we were not watering down rights, but were hesitantly and cautiously striking a necessary balance between the rights of American citizens to be free from government intrusion into their privacy and their government's urgent need for a narrow exception to the warrant requirement of the Fourth Amendment, today's decision demonstrates just how prescient Mr. Justice Douglas was.

It seems that the delicate balance that *Terry* struck was simply too delicate, too susceptible to the "hydraulic pressures" of the day. As a result of today's decision, the balance struck in *Terry* is now heavily weighted in favor of the government. And the Fourth Amendment, which was included in the Bill of Rights to prevent the kind of arbitrary and oppressive police action involved herein, is dealt a serious blow. Today's decision invokes the specter of a society in which innocent citizens may be stopped, searched, and arrested at the whim of police officers who have only the slightest suspicion of improper conduct.

## Questions

1. List all of Officer Connolly's actions that infringed on Robert Williams's privacy and/or liberty.

2. List the facts that Connolly relied on to back up his actions.

3. Compare the facts in *Williams* with those in *Terry* in three respects: the crimes involved, the degree of the intrusions involved, and the objective basis for the officers' actions.

4. Summarize the majority opinion's reasons for ruling that the stop and frisk of Williams were reasonable.

5. Summarize the dissents' arguments for disagreeing with the majority opinion.

6. Do you agree more with the majority or the dissent? Explain your answer.

Now that you've got an overview of stops and frisks in the early cases, let's turn to a closer examination of each of these law enforcement actions. First, we'll look at stops, then at frisks, and finally at some special situations involving one or both—namely, vehicles, borders, and roadblocks.

# STOPS AND THE FOURTH AMENDMENT

Beginning with *Terry v. Ohio*, we can divide the framework for analyzing police encounters with individuals into the three categories shown in Table 4.1.

We've already examined the difference between voluntary encounters with the police (which are left to police discretion) and the two kinds of stops to investigate suspicious persons and circumstances that qualify as Fourth Amendment seizures (see Chapter 3, actual-seizure and show-of-authority stops).

Remember, the first question in the three-step analysis of Fourth Amendment seizures is, "Was the police action a stop?" If it wasn't, then the Fourth Amendment doesn't apply at all, and the analysis stops. But if the action was a stop, then the analysis proceeds to answering the question in step 2, "Was the stop reasonable?" What's a "reasonable" stop?

Reasonableness depends on two elements:

1. Does the objective basis for the stop add up to reasonable suspicion? Reasonable suspicion, discussed later, consists of something more than a hunch but less than probable cause, the objective basis required to arrest a suspect (Chapter 5).

2. Are the requirements of the "scope of the stop" met?
   a. The *duration* is short.
   b. The *location* of the investigation is at or near the scene of the stop.

According to *Terry*, as long as officers can point to facts and circumstances amounting to reasonable suspicion, officers can "freeze" suspicious people and situations in time and space. But the freeze can last only long enough (duration) to let officers get enough information to arrest suspects; if they don't, they have to let them go. And the freeze has to take place (location) on the spot or very near the place where the stop took place.

How many facts are enough to add up to reasonable suspicion? How long is "only long enough," or, in Fourth Amendment terms, how long is reasonable? And exactly what is "on the spot"? Or how far, if any distance at all, is it reasonable for officers to

| **TABLE 4.1** | **Three Kinds of Police-Individual Contacts** | |
| --- | --- | --- |
| *Voluntary Encounters* | Willing contacts without physical force or intimidation | Fourth Amendment doesn't apply |
| *Stops* | Brief (usually minutes), on-the-spot detentions that require reasonable suspicion to back them up | Fourth Amendment applies |
| *Arrests* | Longer detentions (hours or a few days) in police stations that require probable cause to back them up (Chapter 5) | Fourth Amendment applies |

move suspects from the spot? Let's try to answer these questions. First, we'll look at the objective basis for reasonable suspicion and then examine the scope of the stop allowed under the reasonableness test.

## Reasonable Suspicion to Back Up Stops

According to the U.S. Supreme Court in *Terry v. Ohio*, hunches aren't enough to back up even brief stops on the street or other public places. Officers have to point to *articulable facts* that show "criminal activity may be afoot." Simply put, **articulable facts** are facts officers can name to back up their stops of citizens, and, by definition, "hunches" aren't enough. In *Terry*, the nameable facts included Officer McFadden's direct observation of Terry and Chilton pacing up and down and peering into a store window in downtown Cleveland. Seeing this aroused his suspicion that the three men were "casing" the store and were about to rob it.

Chief Justice Warren never used the words "reasonable suspicion." But Justice Harlan did. In his concurring opinion, Justice Harlan defined the standard the Court has followed right up to 2007:

> Officer McFadden had no probable cause to arrest Terry for anything, but he had observed circumstances that would reasonably lead an experienced, prudent policeman to suspect that Terry was about to engage in burglary or robbery. His justifiable suspicion afforded a proper constitutional basis for accosting Terry, restraining his liberty of movement briefly, and addressing questions to him, and Officer McFadden did so. (*Terry v. Ohio* 1968, 32)

In this book, we'll refer to **reasonable suspicion** as the totality of articulable facts and circumstances that would lead an officer, in the light of her training and experience, to *suspect* that crime *may* be afoot. (Notice the emphasis on "suspect" and "may" in contrast to the definition of arrest, which requires enough facts and circumstances to justify officers' *belief* that crime *is* afoot [Chapter 5].) The **totality-of-facts-and-circumstances test**—usually called just the "totality-of-circumstances test"—is a favorite standard the Court applies to decide whether official actions are constitutional. (You'll notice this as we work our way through the rest of the book.)

It might help you to call the test the **whole picture test**, an idea of Chief Justice Warren Burger's, who wrote that the "essence" of reasonable suspicion is "that the totality of circumstances—the whole picture—must be taken into account." Based upon that whole picture, "the detaining officers must have a particularized and objective basis for suspecting the particular person stopped of criminal activity" (*U.S. v. Cortez* 1981, 417–18).

According to the chief justice:

> When used by trained law enforcement officers, objective facts, meaningless to the untrained, can be combined with permissible deductions from such facts to form a legitimate basis for suspicion of a particular person and for action on that suspicion. (419)

The chief justice referred to the border patrol officers' work in our next case excerpt, *U.S. v. Cortez*, as,

> the kind of work often suggested by judges and scholars as examples of appropriate and reasonable means of law enforcement. Here, fact on fact and clue on clue afforded a basis for the deductions and inferences that brought the officers to focus on "Chevron" [the defendant, who was a smuggler of Mexican illegal aliens across the Arizona border]. (419)

## U.S. v. Cortez
449 U.S. 411 (1981)

### HISTORY

Jesus Cortez and Pedro Hernandez-Loera, Respondents, were convicted before the U.S. District Court for the District of Arizona, of transporting illegal aliens, and were sentenced to concurrent prison terms of five years on each of six counts. In addition, Hernandez-Loera was fined $12,000. They appealed. A divided panel (3–2) of the Court of Appeals for the 9th Circuit reversed the judgment of the District Court. The U.S. Supreme Court granted Certiorari, and reversed the Court of Appeals.

BURGER, C.J.

### FACTS

Late in 1976, Border Patrol officers patrolling a sparsely populated section of southern central Arizona found human footprints in the desert. In time, other sets of similar footprints were discovered in the same area. From these sets of footprints, it was deduced that, on a number of occasions, groups of from 8 to 20 persons had walked north from the Mexican border, across 30 miles of desert and mountains, over a fairly well-defined path, to an isolated point on Highway 86, an east-west road running roughly parallel to the Mexican border.

Officers observed that one recurring shoeprint bore a distinctive and repetitive V-shaped or chevron design. Because the officers knew from recorded experience that the area through which the groups passed was heavily trafficked by aliens illegally entering the country from Mexico, they surmised that a person, to whom they gave the case-name "Chevron," was guiding aliens illegally into the United States over the path marked by the tracks to a point where they could be picked up by a vehicle.

The tracks led into or over obstacles that would have been avoided in daylight. From this, the officers deduced that "Chevron" probably led his groups across the border and to the pickup point at night. Moreover, based upon the times when they had discovered the distinctive sets of tracks, they concluded that "Chevron" generally traveled during or near weekends and on nights when the weather was clear.

Their tracking disclosed that when "Chevron's" groups came within 50 to 75 yards of Highway 86, they turned right and walked eastward, parallel to the road. Then, approximately at highway milepost 122, the tracks would turn north and disappear at the road. From this pattern, the officers concluded that the aliens very likely were picked up by a vehicle, probably one approaching from the east, for after a long overland march the group was most likely to walk parallel to the highway *toward* the approaching vehicle. The officers also concluded that, after the pickup, the vehicle probably returned to the east, because it was unlikely that the group would be walking away from its ultimate destination.

On the Sunday night of January 30–31, 1977, Officers Gray and Evans, two Border Patrolmen who had been pursuing the investigation of "Chevron," were on duty in the Casa Grande area. The latest set of observed "Chevron" tracks had been made on Saturday night, January 15–16. January 30–31 was the first clear night after three days of rain. For these reasons, Gray and Evans decided there was a strong possibility that "Chevron" would lead aliens from the border to the highway that night.

The officers assumed that, if "Chevron" did conduct a group that night, he would not leave Mexico until after dark, that is, about 6 P.M. They knew from their experience that groups of this sort, traveling on foot, cover about two and a half to three miles an hour. Thus, the 30-mile journey would take from 8 to 12 hours. From this, the officers calculated that "Chevron" and his group would arrive at Highway 86 somewhere between 2 A.M. and 6 A.M. on January 31.

About 1 A.M., Gray and Evans parked their patrol car on an elevated location about 100 feet off Highway 86 at milepost 149, a point some 27 miles east of milepost 122. From their vantage point, the officers could observe the Altar Valley, an adjoining territory they had been assigned to watch that night, and they also could see vehicles passing on Highway 86. They estimated that it would take approximately one hour and a half for a vehicle to make a round trip from their vantage point to milepost 122. Working on the hypothesis that the pickup vehicle approached milepost 122 from the east and thereafter returned to its starting point, they focused upon vehicles that passed them from the east and, after about one hour and a half, passed them returning to the east.

Because "Chevron" appeared to lead groups of between 8 and 20 aliens at a time, the officers deduced that the pickup vehicle would be one that was capable of carrying that large a group without arousing suspicion. For this reason, and because they knew that certain types of vehicles were commonly used for smuggling sizable groups of aliens, they decided to limit their attention to vans, pickup trucks, other small trucks, campers, motor homes, and similar vehicles.

Traffic on Highway 86 at milepost 149 was normal on the night of the officers' surveillance. In the 5-hour period between 1 A.M. and 6 A.M., 15 to 20 vehicles passed the officers heading west, toward milepost 122. Only two of them—both pickup trucks with camper shells—were of the kind that the officers had concluded "Chevron" would likely use if he was to carry aliens that night. One, a distinctively colored pickup truck with a camper shell, passed for the first time at 4:30 A.M. Officer Gray was able to see and record only a partial license number, "GN 88-." The second camper passed them 15 or 20 minutes later. As far as the record shows, it did not return. At 6:12 A.M., almost exactly the estimated one hour and a half later, a vehicle looking like this same pickup passed them again, this time heading east.

The officers followed the pickup and were satisfied from its license plate, "GN 8804" that it was the same vehicle that had passed at 4:30 A.M. At that point, they flashed their police lights and intercepted the vehicle. Respondent Jesus Cortez was the driver and owner of the pickup; respondent Pedro Hernandez-Loera was sitting in the passenger's seat. Hernandez-Loera was wearing shoes with soles matching the distinctive "chevron" shoeprint.

The officers identified themselves and told Cortez they were conducting an immigration check. They asked if he was carrying any passengers in the camper. Cortez told them he had picked up some hitchhikers, and he proceeded to open the back of the camper. In the camper, there were six illegal aliens. The officers then arrested the respondents.

Cortez and Hernandez-Loera were charged with six counts of transporting illegal aliens in violation of 8 U.S.C. § 1324(a). By pretrial motion, they sought to suppress the evidence obtained by Officers Gray and Evans as a result of stopping their vehicle. They argued that the officers did not have adequate cause to make the investigative stop.

## OPINION

The Fourth Amendment applies to seizures of the person, including brief investigatory stops such as the stop of the vehicle here. An investigatory stop must be justified by some objective manifestation that the person stopped is, or is about to be, engaged in criminal activity. Courts have used a variety of terms to capture the elusive concept of what cause is sufficient to authorize police to stop a person. . . . But the essence of all that has been written is that the totality of the circumstances—the whole picture—must be taken into account. Based upon that whole picture the detaining officers must have a particularized and objective basis for suspecting the particular person stopped of criminal activity.

. . . The evidence collected [by officers] must be seen and weighed [by courts] not in terms of library analysis by scholars, but as understood by those versed in the field of law enforcement.

This case portrays at once both the enormous difficulties of patrolling a 2,000-mile open border and the patient skills needed by those charged with halting illegal entry into this country. It implicates . . . the imperative of recognizing that, when used by trained law enforcement officers, objective facts, meaningless to the untrained, can be combined with permissible deductions from such

facts to form a legitimate basis for suspicion of a particular person and for action on that suspicion. We see here the kind of police work often suggested by judges and scholars as examples of appropriate and reasonable means of law enforcement. Here, fact on fact and clue on clue afforded a basis for the deductions and inferences that brought the officers to focus on "Chevron."

Of critical importance, the officers knew that the area was a crossing point for illegal aliens. They knew that it was common practice for persons to lead aliens through the desert from the border to Highway 86, where they could—by prearrangement—be picked up by a vehicle. Moreover, based upon clues they had discovered in the 2-month period prior to the events at issue here, they believed that one such guide, whom they designated "Chevron," had a particular pattern of operations.

By piecing together the information at their disposal, the officers tentatively concluded that there was a reasonable likelihood that "Chevron" would attempt to lead a group of aliens on the night of Sunday, January 30–31. Someone with chevron-soled shoes had led several groups of aliens in the previous two months, yet it had been two weeks since the latest crossing. "Chevron," they deduced, was therefore due reasonably soon. "Chevron" tended to travel on clear weekend nights. Because it had rained on the Friday and Saturday nights of the weekend involved here, Sunday was the only clear night of that weekend; the officers surmised it was therefore a likely night for a trip.

Once they had focused on that night, the officers drew upon other objective facts known to them to deduce a time frame within which "Chevron" and the aliens were likely to arrive. From what they knew of the practice of those who smuggle aliens, including what they knew of "Chevron's" previous activities, they deduced that the border crossing and journey through the desert would probably be at night. They knew the time when sunset would occur at the point of the border crossing; they knew about how long the trip would take. They were thus able to deduce that "Chevron" would likely arrive at the pickup point on Highway 86 in the time frame between 2 A.M. and 6 A.M.

From objective facts, the officers also deduced the probable point on the highway—milepost 122—at which "Chevron" would likely rendezvous with a pickup vehicle. They deduced from the direction taken by the sets of "Chevron" footprints they had earlier discovered that the pickup vehicle would approach the aliens from, and return with them to, a point east of milepost 122. They therefore staked out a position east of milepost 122 (at milepost 149) and watched for vehicles that passed them going west and then, approximately one and a half hours later, passed them again, this time going east.

From what they had observed about the previous groups guided by the person with "chevron" shoes, they deduced that "Chevron" would lead a group of 8 to 20 aliens. They therefore focused their attention on enclosed vehicles of that passenger capacity.

The analysis produced by Officers Gray and Evans can be summarized as follows: if, on the night upon which they believed "Chevron" was likely to travel, sometime between 2 A.M. and 6 A.M., a large enclosed vehicle was seen to make an east-west-east round trip to and from a deserted point (milepost 122) on a deserted road (Highway 86), the officers would stop the vehicle on the return trip. In a 4-hour period the officers observed only one vehicle meeting that description. And it is not surprising that when they stopped the vehicle on its return trip it contained "Chevron" and several illegal aliens.

The limited purpose of the stop in this case was to question the occupants of the vehicle about their citizenship and immigration status and the reasons for the round trip in a short timespan in a virtually deserted area. No search of the camper or any of its occupants occurred until after respondent Cortez voluntarily opened the back door of the camper; thus, only the stop, not the search is at issue here. The intrusion upon privacy associated with this stop was limited and was "reasonably related in scope to the justification for [its] initiation."

. . . Stops by the Border Patrol may be justified under circumstances less than those constituting probable cause for arrest or search. (The wide public interest in effective measures to prevent the entry of illegal aliens at the Mexican border has been cataloged by this Court.) Thus, the test is not whether Officers Gray and Evans had probable cause to conclude that the vehicle they stopped would contain "Chevron" and a group of illegal aliens. Rather the question is whether, based upon the whole picture, they, as experienced Border Patrol officers, could reasonably surmise that the particular vehicle they stopped was engaged in criminal activity. On this record, they could so conclude.

REVERSED.

## Questions

1. List the facts and circumstances the officers based their stop of Cortez and Hernandez-Loera on.

2. Summarize the Court's reasons for concluding the facts added up to reasonable suspicion.

3. In the Court of Appeals (*U.S. v. Cortez* 1979), two members of the three-judge panel concluded the officers lacked reasonable suspicion to stop Cortez and Hernandez-Loera. According to Judge Hug:

   > The officers did not have a valid basis for singling out the Cortez vehicle. They saw no one in the camper. They saw nothing suspicious about the vehicle itself. They had no specific information about illegal movement of aliens in the area that night. They observed no mechanical or equipment defects in connection with the vehicle. They observed no violation of the traffic laws. . . .
   >
   > The sole suspicious fact connected with this specific vehicle was that it passed the officers' post headed west and returned headed east, both times in the pre-dawn hours. The passage of nearly two hours' time and the fact that the vehicle could have traveled to a small town and returned within that time, both furnish far too many innocent inferences to make the officers' suspicions reasonably warranted. (508)

   Do you agree? Explain your answer.

Information that officers can rely on to build reasonable suspicion comprises two types:

1. *Direct information.* Facts and circumstances officers learn firsthand from what they themselves see, hear, smell, and touch

2. *Hearsay information.* Facts and circumstances officers learn secondhand from victims, witnesses, other police officers, and anonymous, professional, or paid informants

Table 4.2 elaborates on direct and hearsay bases for reasonable suspicion.

Recall that in 1968, when *Terry v. Ohio* was decided, reasonable suspicion was based on Officer McFadden's firsthand observations. Recall also, that four years later, in *Adams v. Williams*, the Court decided that an informant's tip plus the time (2:00 A.M.) and the location (a high-crime neighborhood) added up to reasonable suspicion to stop Williams. So officers can rely on secondhand information, or hearsay, either partly or completely.

## TABLE 4.2    Direct and Hearsay Bases for Reasonable Suspicion

| Direct Information | Hearsay |
| --- | --- |
| Flight | Victim statement |
| Furtive movement | Eyewitness statement |
| Hiding | Statements by fellow officers |
| Resisting an officer | Statements by informants |
| Attempting to destroy evidence | Anonymous tip |
| Evasive answers | |
| Contradictory answers | |
| Weapons or contraband in plain view | |

Officers usually get information secondhand through victims, witnesses, other police officers, and professional informants. In *Williams*, Officer Connolly knew the informant (even though he never named him). But what about anonymous tips? Are they enough to add up to reasonable suspicion? In *Alabama v. White* (1990), the police received an anonymous telephone tip

> stating that Vanessa White would be leaving 235-C Lynwood Terrace Apartments at a particular time in a brown Plymouth station wagon with the right taillight lens broken, that she would be going to Dobey's Motel, and that she would be in possession of about an ounce of cocaine inside a brown attaché case. (327)

By itself, the Court ruled, the tip wouldn't have justified a *Terry* stop. But when the officer's later direct observation confirmed the informant's prediction about White's movements, it was reasonable to suspect that the tipster had inside knowledge about the suspect and to credit his assertion about the cocaine. The Court still regarded the case as borderline. Although the Court held that the suspicion in *White* became reasonable after police surveillance, it classified *White* as a "close case."

Then, in 2000, came our next case excerpt, when the Court held that the anonymous tip that a "young Black male standing at a particular bus stop and wearing a plaid shirt was carrying a gun" *didn't* amount to reasonable suspicion (*Florida v. J. L.* 2000, 268).

## CASE    *Did the Anonymous Tip Add Up to Reasonable Suspicion?*

### *Florida v. J. L.*
529 U.S. 266 (2000)

### HISTORY

J. L., Juvenile, being tried on an illegal possession of weapons charge, moved to suppress evidence. The Circuit Court of Dade County granted the motion, and the state appealed. The District Court of Appeal reversed the trial court. The Juvenile petitioned for review, and the Florida Supreme Court reversed the Court of Appeal. After granting the state's petition for certiorari, the U.S. Supreme Court affirmed the Florida Supreme Court.

GINSBURG, J., FOR A UNANIMOUS COURT.

### FACTS

On October 13, 1995, an anonymous caller reported to the Miami-Dade Police that a young black male standing at a particular bus stop and wearing a plaid shirt was carrying a gun. So far as the record reveals, there is no audio recording of the tip, and nothing is known about the informant.

Sometime after the police received the tip—the record does not say how long—two officers were instructed to respond. They arrived at the bus stop about six minutes later and saw three black males "just hanging out [there]." One of the three, respondent J. L., was wearing a plaid shirt. Apart from the tip, the officers had no reason to suspect any of the three of illegal conduct. The officers did not see a firearm, and J. L. made no threatening or otherwise unusual movements. One of the officers approached J. L., told him to put his hands up on the bus stop, frisked him, and seized a gun from J. L.'s pocket. The second officer frisked the other two individuals, against whom no allegations had been made, and found nothing.

J. L., who was at the time of the frisk "10 days shy of his 16th birthday," was charged under state law with carrying a concealed firearm without a license and possessing a firearm while under the age of 18. He moved to suppress the gun as the fruit of an unlawful search, and the trial court granted his motion. The intermediate appellate court reversed, but the Supreme Court of Florida quashed that decision and held the search invalid under the Fourth Amendment.

Anonymous tips, the Florida Supreme Court stated, are generally less reliable than tips from known informants and can form the basis for reasonable suspicion only if accompanied by specific indicia of reliability, for example, the correct forecast of a subject's "not easily predicted" movements. The tip leading to the frisk of J. L., the court observed, provided no such predictions, nor did it contain any other qualifying indicia of reliability.

Two justices dissented. The safety of the police and the public, they maintained, justifies a "firearm exception" to the general rule barring investigatory stops and frisks on the basis of bare-boned anonymous tips.

Seeking review in this Court, the State of Florida noted that the decision of the State's Supreme Court conflicts with decisions of other courts declaring similar searches compatible with the Fourth Amendment. We granted certiorari, and now affirm the judgment of the Florida Supreme Court.

## OPINION

. . . Officers' suspicion that J. L. was carrying a weapon arose not from any observations of their own but solely from a call made from an unknown location by an unknown caller. Unlike a tip from a known informant whose reputation can be assessed and who can be held responsible if her allegations turn out to be fabricated, an anonymous tip alone seldom demonstrates the informant's basis of knowledge or veracity.

As we have recognized, however, there are situations in which an anonymous tip, suitably corroborated, exhibits "sufficient indicia of reliability to provide reasonable suspicion to make the investigatory stop." The question we here confront is whether the tip pointing to J. L. had those indicia of reliability.

In *Alabama v. White* (1990), the police received an anonymous tip asserting that a woman was carrying cocaine and predicting that she would leave an apartment building

at a specified time, get into a car matching a particular description, and drive to a named motel. Standing alone, the tip would not have justified a *Terry* stop. Only after police observation showed that the informant had accurately predicted the woman's movements, we explained, did it become reasonable to think the tipster had inside knowledge about the suspect and therefore to credit his assertion about the cocaine.

Although the Court held that the suspicion in *White* became reasonable after police surveillance, we regarded the case as borderline. Knowledge about a person's future movements indicates some familiarity with that person's affairs, but having such knowledge does not necessarily imply that the informant knows, in particular, whether that person is carrying hidden contraband. We accordingly classified *White* as a "close case."

The tip in the instant case lacked the moderate indicia of reliability present in White and essential to the Court's decision in that case. The anonymous call concerning J. L. provided no predictive information and therefore left the police without means to test the informant's knowledge or credibility. That the allegation about the gun turned out to be correct does not suggest that the officers, prior to the frisks, had a reasonable basis for suspecting J. L. of engaging in unlawful conduct:

> The reasonableness of official suspicion must be measured by what the officers knew before they conducted their search. All the police had to go on in this case was the bare report of an unknown, unaccountable informant who neither explained how he knew about the gun nor supplied any basis for believing he had inside information about J. L.

If *White* was a close case on the reliability of anonymous tips, this one surely falls on the other side of the line.

Florida contends that the tip was reliable because its description of the suspect's visible attributes proved accurate: There really was a young black male wearing a plaid shirt at the bus stop. The United States as amicus curiae makes a similar argument, proposing that a stop and frisk should be permitted "when (1) an anonymous tip provides a description of a particular person at a particular location illegally carrying a concealed firearm, (2) police promptly verify the pertinent details of the tip except the existence of the firearm, and (3) there are no factors that cast doubt on the reliability of the tip. . . ." These contentions misapprehend the reliability needed for a tip to justify a *Terry* stop.

An accurate description of a subject's readily observable location and appearance is of course reliable in this limited sense: It will help the police correctly identify the person whom the tipster means to accuse. Such a tip, however, does not show that the tipster has knowledge of concealed criminal activity. The reasonable suspicion here at issue requires that a tip be reliable in its assertion of illegality, not just in its tendency to identify a determinate person.

A second major argument advanced by Florida . . . is, in essence, that the standard *Terry* analysis should be modified to license a "firearm exception." Under such an exception, a tip alleging an illegal gun would justify a stop and frisk even if the accusation would fail standard pre-search reliability testing. We decline to adopt this position.

Firearms are dangerous, and extraordinary dangers sometimes justify unusual precautions. Our decisions recognize the serious threat that armed criminals pose to public safety; *Terry's* rule, which permits protective police searches on the basis of reasonable suspicion rather than demanding that officers meet the higher standard of probable cause, responds to this very concern.

But an automatic firearm exception to our established reliability analysis would rove too far. Such an exception would enable any person seeking to harass another to set in motion an intrusive, embarrassing police search of the targeted person simply by placing an anonymous call falsely reporting the target's unlawful carriage of a gun. Nor could one securely confine such an exception to allegations involving firearms.

Several Courts of Appeals have held it *per se* foreseeable for people carrying significant amounts of illegal drugs to be carrying guns as well. If police officers may properly conduct *Terry* frisks on the basis of bare-boned tips about guns, it would be reasonable to maintain under the above-cited decisions that the police should similarly have discretion to frisk based on bare-boned tips about narcotics. As we clarified when we made indicia of reliability critical in *Adams and White*, the Fourth Amendment is not so easily satisfied.

The facts of this case do not require us to speculate about the circumstances under which the danger alleged in an anonymous tip might be so great as to justify a search even without a showing of reliability. We do not say, for example, that a report of a person carrying a bomb need bear the indicia of reliability we demand for a report of a person carrying a firearm before the police can constitutionally conduct a frisk. Nor do we hold that public safety officials in quarters where the reasonable expectation of Fourth Amendment privacy is diminished, such as airports, and schools, cannot conduct protective searches on the basis of information insufficient to justify searches elsewhere.

Finally, the requirement that an anonymous tip bear standard indicia of reliability in order to justify a stop in no way diminishes a police officer's prerogative, in accord with *Terry*, to conduct a protective search of a person who has already been legitimately stopped.

We speak in today's decision only of cases in which the officer's authority to make the initial stop is at issue. In that context, we hold that an anonymous tip lacking indicia of reliability of the kind contemplated in *Adams* and does not justify a stop and frisk whenever and however it alleges the illegal possession of a firearm.

The judgment of the Florida Supreme Court is AFFIRMED.

## Questions

1. Describe the details of the tip that led the officers to stop J. L.

2. Summarize the reasons the Court rejected the tip that led to the stop of J. L.

3. Under what circumstances might an anonymous tip amount to reasonable suspicion?

4. Why did the Court reject the argument that anonymous tips about weapons should be enough to add up to reasonable suspicion? Do you agree? Defend your answer.

5. In an article criticizing the use of anonymous tips, Professor David S. Rudstein (1990/91) wrote:

   > Any person with a bit of knowledge of another individual can make that individual the target of a prank, or if he harbors a grudge against the individual, can maliciously attempt to inconvenience and embarrass him, by formulating a tip about the individual similar to the one in *White* and then anonymously passing it on to the police. (679)

   Do you agree? Explain your answer.

Table 4.3 lists other reasons that, according to the courts, are insufficient for reasonable suspicion unless they're backed up by other evidence.

The examples in Table 4.3 point to two other kinds of information officers use to back up reasonable stops: individualized suspicion and categorical suspicion (Harris 1998). *Individualized suspicion* consists of "facts that would tell both the officer on the street and a court ruling on a suppression motion whether or not there was reasonable suspicion) . . ." (987). Terry and Chilton's casing Zucker's clothing

| TABLE 4.3 | Reasons Insufficient by Themselves for Reasonable Suspicion |
|---|---|

1. General suspicion that drug dealing went on in a tavern (*Ybarra v. Illinois,* 444 U.S. 85 [1979])

2. Driver double-parked within 10 feet of a pedestrian in a drug-trafficking location (*Rivera v. Murphy,* 979 F.2d 259 [1st Cir. 1992])

3. Other bar patrons, not the one detained, possessed weapons and contraband (*U.S. v. Jaramillo,* 25 F.3d 1146 [2nd Cir. 1994])

4. Passenger leaving airplane appeared nervous in the presence of officers (*U.S. v. Caicedo,* 85 F.3d 1184 [6th Cir. 1996])

5. Driver of a car with out-of-state license plates and no noticeable luggage avoided eye contact with a police car (*U.S. v. Halls,* 40 F.3d 275 [8th Cir. 1995])

6. "Hispanic-looking" males in a heavy truck near the border looked nervous, did not acknowledge police presence, and drove faster than the flow of traffic (*U.S. v. Garcia-Camacho,* 53 F.3d 244 [9th Cir. 1995])

7. Generalized suspicion of criminal activity in a high-crime neighborhood (*Brown v. Texas,* 443 U.S. 47 [1979])

8. Nervous man traveling alone who left an airline terminal quickly after picking up one suitcase and had a one-way ticket that he had bought with cash from a drug-source city (*U.S. v. Lambert,* 46 F.3d 1064 [10th Cir. 1995])

9. Driver failed to look at patrol car late at night (*U.S. v. Smith,* 799 F.2d 704 [11th Cir. 1986])

10. "Mexican-appearing" person, driving a car with out-of-state license plates and no suitcases, appeared nervous in talking with officers during discussion of a speeding ticket (*U.S. v. Tapia,* 912 F.2d 1367 [11th Cir. 1990])

store before Officer McFadden approached them is an excellent example of individualized suspicion. Individualized suspicion is necessary in all cases, but it may not be enough to amount to reasonable suspicion. Categorical suspicion can help meet that threshold.

**Categorical suspicion** refers to suspicion that falls on suspects because they fit into a broad category of people, such as being in a particular location, being members of a particular race or ethnicity, or fitting a profile. Categorical suspicion is never enough by itself to amount to reasonable suspicion. But taken together with individualized suspicion, it can be one of the building blocks in the whole picture of reasonable suspicion. The next three sections examine how location, race and ethnicity, and profiles can support individualized suspicion when it's not enough to amount to reasonable suspicion.

***"High Crime" and "Known for Drug Trafficking" Neighborhoods*** Whether you're stopped often depends on *where* you're stopped. The character of a neighborhood is a frequently used building block for establishing reasonable suspicion. According to Professor Margaret Raymond (1999):

> Characterization of that neighborhood as a "high crime area" or one "known for trafficking" is often critical to the finding of reasonable suspicion. This factor has become a significant and frequently invoked basis on which to argue that highly ambiguous conduct is sufficiently suspicious to justify a stop. (100)

In *Illinois v. Wardlow*, the U.S. Supreme Court found that Sam Wardlow's unprovoked flight from the police, in a neighborhood known for high amounts of drug trafficking, added up to reasonable suspicion to stop him.

# Does Sudden Unprovoked Flight in a High-Drug Area Amount to Reasonable Suspicion?

## Illinois v. Wardlow

528 U.S. 119 (2000)

### HISTORY

William "Sam" Wardlow (respondent) was arrested and charged with unlawful use of a weapon by a felon. The Illinois trial court denied his motion to suppress. Wardlow was convicted. The Illinois Appellate Court reversed the conviction. The Illinois Supreme Court affirmed the Appellate Court. The U.S. Supreme Court (5–4) granted certiorari and reversed the Illinois Supreme Court.

REHNQUIST, C.J.

### FACTS

On September 9, 1995, Officers Nolan and Harvey were working as uniformed officers in the special operations section of the Chicago Police Department. The officers were driving the last car of a four-car caravan converging on an area known for heavy narcotics trafficking in order to investigate drug transactions. The officers were traveling together because they expected to find a crowd of people in the area, including lookouts and customers.

As the caravan passed 4035 West Van Buren, Officer Nolan observed Wardlow standing next to the building holding an opaque bag. Wardlow looked in the direction of the officers and fled. Nolan and Harvey turned their car southbound, watched him as he ran through the gangway and an alley, and eventually cornered him on the street. Nolan then exited his car and stopped Wardlow. He immediately conducted a protective pat-down search for weapons because in his experience it was common for there to be weapons in the near vicinity of narcotics transactions.

During the frisk, Officer Nolan squeezed the bag Wardlow was carrying and felt a heavy, hard object similar to the shape of a gun. The officer then opened the bag and discovered a .38-caliber handgun with five live rounds of ammunition. The officers arrested Wardlow.

The Illinois trial court denied Wardlow's motion to suppress, finding the gun was recovered during a lawful stop and frisk. Following a stipulated bench trial, Wardlow was convicted of unlawful use of a weapon by a felon. The Illinois Appellate Court reversed Wardlow's conviction, concluding that the gun should have been suppressed because Officer Nolan did not have reasonable suspicion sufficient to justify an investigative stop pursuant to *Terry v. Ohio*.

The Illinois Supreme Court agreed. While rejecting the Appellate Court's conclusion that Wardlow was not in a high crime area, the Illinois Supreme Court determined that sudden flight in such an area does not create a reasonable suspicion justifying a *Terry* stop.... The court explained that although police have the right to approach individuals and ask questions, the individual has no obligation to respond.

The person may decline to answer and simply go on his or her way, and the refusal to respond, alone, does not provide a legitimate basis for an investigative stop. The court then determined that flight may simply be an exercise of this right to "go on one's way," and, thus, could not constitute reasonable suspicion justifying a *Terry* stop.

The Illinois Supreme Court also rejected the argument that flight combined with the fact that it occurred in a high crime area supported a finding of reasonable suspicion because the "high crime area" factor was not sufficient standing alone to justify a *Terry* stop. Finding no independently suspicious circumstances to support an investigatory detention, the court held that the stop and subsequent arrest violated the Fourth Amendment. We granted certiorari, and now reverse.

### OPINION

Nolan and Harvey were among eight officers in a four-car caravan that was converging on an area known for heavy narcotics trafficking, and the officers anticipated encountering a large number of people in the area, including drug customers and individuals serving as lookouts. It was in this context that Officer Nolan decided to investigate Wardlow after observing him flee.

An individual's presence in an area of expected criminal activity, standing alone, is not enough to support a reasonable, particularized suspicion that the person is committing a crime. But officers are not required to ignore the relevant characteristics of a location in determining whether the circumstances are sufficiently suspicious to warrant further investigation. Accordingly, we have previously noted the stop occurred in a "high crime area" among the relevant contextual considerations in a *Terry* analysis. *Adams v. Williams* (1972) [excerpted earlier on p. 94].

In this case, moreover, it was not merely Wardlow's presence in an area of heavy narcotics trafficking that aroused the officers' suspicion but his unprovoked flight upon noticing the police. Our cases have also recognized that nervous, evasive behavior is a pertinent factor in determining reasonable suspicion. Headlong flight—wherever it occurs—is the consummate act of evasion: it is not necessarily indicative of wrongdoing, but it is certainly suggestive of such.

In reviewing the propriety of an officer's conduct, courts do not have available empirical studies dealing with inferences drawn from suspicious behavior, and we cannot reasonably demand scientific certainty from judges or law enforcement officers where none exists. Thus, the determination of reasonable suspicion must be based on commonsense judgments and inferences about human behavior. We conclude Officer Nolan was justified in suspecting that Wardlow was involved in criminal activity, and, therefore, in investigating further.

. . . [When] an officer, without reasonable suspicion or probable cause, approaches an individual, the individual has a right to ignore the police and go about his business. And any "refusal to cooperate, without more, does not furnish the minimal level of objective justification needed for a detention or seizure." But unprovoked flight is simply not a mere refusal to cooperate. Flight, by its very nature, is not "going about one's business"; in fact, it is just the opposite. Allowing officers confronted with such flight to stop the fugitive and investigate further is quite consistent with the individual's right to go about his business or to stay put and remain silent in the face of police questioning.

Wardlow also argues that there are innocent reasons for flight from police and that, therefore, flight is not necessarily indicative of ongoing criminal activity. This fact is undoubtedly true, but does not establish a violation of the Fourth Amendment. Even in *Terry*, the conduct justifying the stop was ambiguous and susceptible of an innocent explanation. The officer observed two individuals pacing back and forth in front of a store, peering into the window and periodically conferring. All of this conduct was by itself lawful, but it also suggested that the individuals were casing the store for a planned robbery. *Terry* recognized that the officers could detain the individuals to resolve the ambiguity.

In allowing such detentions, *Terry* accepts the risk that officers may stop innocent people. Indeed, the Fourth Amendment accepts that risk in connection with more drastic police action; persons arrested and detained on probable cause to believe they have committed a crime may turn out to be innocent.

The *Terry* stop is a far more minimal intrusion, simply allowing the officer to briefly investigate further. If the officer does not learn facts rising to the level of probable cause, the individual must be allowed to go on his way. But in this case the officers found Wardlow in possession of a handgun, and arrested him for violation of an Illinois firearms statute. . . .

The judgment of the Supreme Court of Illinois is reversed, and the cause is remanded for further proceedings not inconsistent with this opinion. It is so ordered.

## CONCURRING AND DISSENTING OPINIONS

STEVENS, J., JOINED BY SOUTER, GINSBURG, AND BREYER, JJ., CONCURRING IN PART AND DISSENTING IN PART.

The State of Illinois asks this Court to announce a "bright line rule" authorizing the temporary detention of anyone who flees at the mere sight of a police officer. Wardlow counters by asking us to adopt the opposite *per se* rule—that the fact that a person flees upon seeing the police can never, by itself, be sufficient to justify a temporary investigative stop. . . .

The Court today wisely endorses neither *per se* rule. Instead, it rejects the proposition that "flight is . . . necessarily indicative of ongoing criminal activity," adhering to the view that "the concept of reasonable suspicion . . . is not readily, or even usefully, reduced to a neat set of legal rules," but must be determined by looking to "the totality of the circumstances—the whole picture."

Abiding by this framework, the Court concludes that "Officer Nolan was justified in suspecting that Wardlow was involved in criminal activity." Although I agree with the Court's rejection of the per se rules proffered by the parties, unlike the Court, I am persuaded that in this case the brief testimony of the officer who seized Wardlow does not justify the conclusion that he had reasonable suspicion to make the stop. . . .

The question in this case concerns "the degree of suspicion that attaches to" a person's flight—or, more precisely, what "commonsense conclusions" can be drawn respecting the motives behind that flight. . . .*

Given the diversity and frequency of possible motivations for flight, it would be profoundly unwise to endorse either per se rule. The inference we can reasonably draw about the motivation for a person's flight, rather, will depend on a number of different circumstances. Factors such as the time of day, the number of people in the area, the character of the neighborhood, whether the officer was in uniform, the way the runner was dressed, the direction and speed of the flight, and whether the person's behavior was otherwise unusual might be relevant in specific cases.

This number of variables is surely sufficient to preclude either a bright-line rule that always justifies, or that never justifies, an investigative stop based on the sole fact that flight began after a police officer appeared nearby.

Still, Illinois presses for a *per se* rule regarding "unprovoked flight upon seeing a clearly identifiable police officer." The phrase "upon seeing," as used by Illinois, apparently assumes that the flight is motivated by the presence of the police officer.†

---

*Compare, Proverbs 28:1: "The wicked flee when no man pursueth: but the righteous are as bold as a lion" with Proverbs 22:3: "A shrewd man sees trouble coming and lies low; the simple walk into it and pay the penalty." I have rejected reliance on the former proverb in the past, because its "ivory-towered analysis of the real world" fails to account for the experiences of many citizens in this country, particularly those who are minorities. That this pithy expression fails to capture the total reality of our world, however, does not mean it is inaccurate in all instances.

†[*Note:* Nowhere in Illinois' briefs does it specify what it means by "unprovoked." At oral argument, Illinois explained that if officers precipitate a flight by threats of violence, that flight is "provoked." But if police officers in a patrol car—with lights flashing and siren sounding—descend upon an individual for the sole purpose of seeing if he or she will run, the ensuing flight is "unprovoked."] Illinois contends that unprovoked flight is "an extreme reaction," because innocent people simply do not "flee at the mere sight of the police." To be sure, Illinois concedes, an innocent person—even one distrustful of the police—might "avoid eye contact or even sneer at the sight of an officer," and that would not justify a *Terry* stop or any sort of per se inference. But, Illinois insists, unprovoked flight is altogether different. Such behavior is so "aberrant" and "abnormal" that a per se inference is justified.

Even assuming we know that a person runs because he sees the police, the inference to be drawn may still vary from case to case. Flight to escape police detection . . . may have an entirely innocent motivation:

It is a matter of common knowledge that men who are entirely innocent do sometimes fly from the scene of a crime through fear of being apprehended as the guilty parties, or from an unwillingness to appear as witnesses. Nor is it true as an accepted axiom of criminal law that "the wicked flee when no man pursueth, but the righteous are as bold as a lion." Innocent men sometimes hesitate to confront a jury—not necessarily because they fear that the jury will not protect them, but because they do not wish their names to appear in connection with criminal acts, are humiliated at being obliged to incur the popular odium of an arrest and trial, or because they do not wish to be put to the annoyance or expense of defending themselves.
*Alberty v. U.S.,* 162 U.S. 499, 511 (1896).

In addition to these concerns, a reasonable person may conclude that an officer's sudden appearance indicates nearby criminal activity. And where there is criminal activity there is also a substantial element of danger—either from the criminal or from a confrontation between the criminal and the police. These considerations can lead to an innocent and understandable desire to quit the vicinity with all speed.

Among some citizens, particularly minorities and those residing in high crime areas, there is also the possibility that the fleeing person is entirely innocent, but, with or without justification, believes that contact with the police can itself be dangerous, apart from any criminal activity associated with the officer's sudden presence. . . . * For such a person, unprovoked flight is neither "aberrant" nor "abnormal." . . . †

Many stops never lead to an arrest, which further exacerbates the perceptions of discrimination felt by racial minorities and people living in high crime areas. . . . ‡

---

*See Casimir, Minority Men: We Are Frisk Targets, *N.Y. Daily News,* Mar. 26, 1999, p. 34 (informal survey of 100 young black and Hispanic men living in New York City; 81 reported having been stopped and frisked by police at least once; none of the 81 stops resulted in arrests); Brief for NAACP Legal Defense & Educational Fund as Amicus Curiae 17–19 (reporting figures on disproportionate street stops of minority residents in Pittsburgh and Philadelphia, Pennsylvania, and St. Petersburg, Florida); U.S. Dept. of Justice, Bureau of Justice Statistics, S. Smith, Criminal Victimization and Perceptions of Community Safety in 12 Cities (25 June 1998) (African-American residents in 12 cities are more than twice as likely to be dissatisfied with police practices than white residents in same community).

†See, e.g., Kotlowitz, Hidden Casualties: Drug War's Emphasis on Law Enforcement Takes a Toll on Police, *Wall Street Journal,* Jan. 11, 1991 ("Black leaders complained that innocent people were picked up in the drug sweeps. . . . Some teen-agers were so scared of the task force they ran even if they weren't selling drugs.")

‡See Goldberg, "The Color of Suspicion," *N.Y. Times Magazine,* June 20, 1999, (reporting that in a 2-year period, New York City Police Department Street Crimes Unit made 45,000 stops, only 9,500, or 20%, of which resulted in arrest); Casimir (reporting that in 1997, New York City's Street Crimes Unit conducted 27,061 stop-and-frisks, only 4,647 of which, 17%, resulted in arrest).

Even if these data were race neutral, they would still indicate that society as a whole is paying a significant cost in infringement on liberty by these virtually random stops. Moreover, these concerns and fears are known to the police officers themselves, and are validated by law enforcement investigations into their own practices . . .

. . . The Massachusetts Attorney General investigated . . . allegations of egregious police conduct toward minorities. The report stated:

Perhaps the most disturbing evidence was that the scope of a number of *Terry* searches went far beyond anything authorized by that case and indeed, beyond anything that we believe would be acceptable under the federal and state constitutions even where probable cause existed to conduct a full search incident to an arrest.

Forcing young men to lower their trousers, or otherwise searching inside their underwear, on public streets or in public hallways, is so demeaning and invasive of fundamental precepts of privacy that it can only be condemned in the strongest terms. The fact that not only the young men themselves, but independent witnesses complained of strip searches, should be deeply alarming to all members of this community.

Accordingly, the evidence supporting the reasonableness of these beliefs is too pervasive to be dismissed as random or rare, and too persuasive to be disparaged as inconclusive or insufficient. In any event, just as we do not require "scientific certainty" for our commonsense conclusion that unprovoked flight can sometimes indicate suspicious motives, neither do we require scientific certainty to conclude that unprovoked flight can occur for other, innocent reasons. . . .

"Unprovoked flight," in short, describes a category of activity too broad and varied to permit a per se reasonable inference regarding the motivation for the activity. While the innocent explanations surely do not establish that the Fourth Amendment is always violated whenever someone is stopped solely on the basis of an unprovoked flight, neither do the suspicious motivations establish that the Fourth Amendment is never violated when a *Terry* stop is predicated on that fact alone. . . .

Guided by that totality-of-the-circumstances test, the Court concludes that Officer Nolan had reasonable suspicion to stop respondent. In this respect, my view differs from the Court's. The entire justification for the stop is articulated in the brief testimony of Officer Nolan. Some facts are perfectly clear; others are not. This factual insufficiency leads me to conclude that the Court's judgment is mistaken.

Wardlow was arrested a few minutes after noon on September 9, 1995. Nolan was part of an eight-officer, four-car caravan patrol team. The officers were headed for "one of the areas in the 11th District [of Chicago] that's high [in] narcotics traffic." The reason why four cars were in the caravan was that "normally in these different areas there's an enormous amount of people, sometimes look-outs, customers." Officer Nolan testified that he was in uniform on that day, but he did not recall whether he was driving a marked or an unmarked car.

Officer Nolan and his partner were in the last of the four patrol cars that "were all caravaning eastbound down Van Buren." Nolan first observed respondent "in front of 4035 West Van Buren." Wardlow "looked in our direction and began fleeing." Nolan then "began driving southbound down the street observing [respondent] running through the gangway and the alley southbound," and observed that Wardlow was carrying a white, opaque bag under his arm.

After the car turned south and intercepted respondent as he "ran right towards us," Officer Nolan stopped him and conducted a "protective search," which revealed that the bag under respondent's arm contained a loaded handgun.

This terse testimony is most noticeable for what it fails to reveal. Though asked whether he was in a marked or unmarked car, Officer Nolan could not recall the answer. He was not asked whether any of the other three cars in the caravan were marked, or whether any of the other seven officers were in uniform. Though he explained that the size of the caravan was because "normally in these different areas there's an enormous amount of people, sometimes lookouts, customers," Officer Nolan did not testify as to whether anyone besides Wardlow was nearby 4035 West Van Buren. Nor is it clear that that address was the intended destination of the caravan.

As the Appellate Court of Illinois interpreted the record, "it appears that the officers were simply driving by, on their way to some unidentified location, when they noticed defendant standing at 4035 West Van Buren." Officer Nolan's testimony also does not reveal how fast the officers were driving. It does not indicate whether he saw respondent notice the other patrol cars. And it does not say whether the caravan, or any part of it, had already passed Wardlow by before he began to run. Indeed, the Appellate Court thought the record was even "too vague to support the inference that . . . defendant's flight was related to his expectation of police focus on him."

Presumably, respondent did not react to the first three cars, and we cannot even be sure that he recognized the occupants of the fourth as police officers. The adverse inference is based entirely on the officer's statement: "He looked in our direction and began fleeing." No other factors sufficiently support a finding of reasonable suspicion.

Though respondent was carrying a white, opaque bag under his arm, there is nothing at all suspicious about that. Certainly the time of day—shortly after noon—does not support Illinois' argument. Nor were the officers "responding to any call or report of suspicious activity in the area."

Officer Nolan did testify that he expected to find "an enormous amount of people," including drug customers or lookouts, and the Court points out that "[i]t was in this context that Officer Nolan decided to investigate Wardlow after observing him flee." This observation, in my view, lends insufficient weight to the reasonable suspicion analysis; indeed, in light of the absence of testimony that anyone else was nearby when respondent began to run, this observation points in the opposite direction.

The State, along with the majority of the Court, relies as well on the assumption that this flight occurred in a high crime area. Even if that assumption is accurate, it is insufficient because even in a high crime neighborhood unprovoked flight does not invariably lead to reasonable suspicion.

On the contrary, because many factors providing innocent motivations for unprovoked flight are concentrated in high crime areas, the character of the neighborhood arguably makes an inference of guilt less appropriate, rather than more so. Like unprovoked flight itself, presence in a high crime neighborhood is a fact too generic and susceptible to innocent explanation to satisfy the reasonable suspicion inquiry.

It is the State's burden to articulate facts sufficient to support reasonable suspicion. In my judgment, Illinois has failed to discharge that burden. I am not persuaded that the mere fact that someone standing on a sidewalk looked in the direction of a passing car before starting to run is sufficient to justify a forcible stop and frisk.

I therefore respectfully DISSENT from the Court's judgment to reverse the court below.

## Questions

1. Identify the "articulable" facts Officer Nolan relied on to stop Wardlow.

2. List the Court's reasons for concluding these facts added up to reasonable suspicion.

3. Compare the facts Nolan possessed with those possessed by Officer McFadden in *Terry v. Ohio*. In your opinion, which officer had more articulable facts?

4. Even if one had more than the other, did they both have reasonable suspicion? Defend your answer.

5. Is reasonable suspicion enough of a safeguard to the right of all people, innocent and guilty, to come and go as they please? Defend your answer.

6. List and summarize the empirical evidence Justice Stevens includes in his dissenting opinion. Is the evidence reliable? Assuming the evidence is reliable, does it have anything to do with whether Nolan's stop and frisk of Wardlow was reasonable? Defend your answer.

 Go to Exercise 4.2 on the Samaha Criminal Procedure 7e website to learn more about reasonable suspicion: academic.cengage.com/criminaljustice/samaha.

*Race and Ethnicity* Should officers be allowed to view race and ethnicity through the lens of their training and experience as part of the totality of circumstances adding up to reasonable suspicion? Or must reasonable suspicion be color and ethnicity blind? Even asking this question generates explosive controversy (Kennedy 1997, Chapter 4).

The U.S. Supreme Court has made it clear that race and ethnicity by themselves can never amount to reasonable suspicion. But the Supreme Court and almost all lower courts have made it equally clear that when it comes to reasonable suspicion, color and ethnicity are *part* of reality, however uncomfortable that reality may be. "Facts are not to be ignored simply because they may be unpleasant," wrote U.S. Eighth Circuit Court of Appeals Judge Wollman in *U.S. v. Weaver* (1992, 394).

We need to distinguish between two uses of race and ethnicity as building blocks in reasonable suspicion. First, and usually not problematic, race or ethnicity is a building block when it's part of individualized suspicion, as when a witness identifies her attacker as White, or Black, or Hispanic. Second, it's a building block when it's a categorical circumstance, such as it was in *U.S. v. Weaver*, where the U.S. Eighth Circuit Court of Appeals held that law enforcement officers could use Weaver's race as *part* of reasonable suspicion.

Arthur Weaver caught the attention of Drug Enforcement Administration (DEA) agents and Kansas City detectives when he got off an early morning direct flight from Los Angeles. The DEA agent testified that several factors caused him to suspect that Weaver might be carrying drugs:

> Number one, we have intelligence information and also past arrest history on two black— all black street gangs from Los Angeles called the Crips and the Bloods. They are notorious for transporting cocaine into the Kansas City area from Los Angeles for sale. Most of them are young, roughly dressed male blacks. (394, n. 2)

According to Judge Wollman:

> We agree with the dissent that large groups of our citizens should not be regarded by law enforcement officers as presumptively criminal based upon their race. We would not hesitate to hold that a solely race-based suspicion of drug courier status would not pass constitutional muster. Accordingly, had Hicks relied solely upon the fact of Weaver's race as a basis for his suspicions, we would have a different case before us. As it is, however, facts are not to be ignored simply because they may be unpleasant—and the unpleasant fact in this case is that Hicks had knowledge, based upon his own experience and upon the intelligence reports he had received from the Los Angeles authorities, that young male members of black Los Angeles gangs were flooding the Kansas City area with cocaine. To that extent, then, race, when coupled with the other factors Hicks relied upon, was a factor in the decision to approach and ultimately detain Weaver. We wish it were otherwise, but we take the facts as they are presented to us, not as we would like them to be. (394)

Chief Judge Arnold dissented:

> One of the most disturbing aspects of this case is the agents' reference to Weaver as "a roughly dressed young black male." Most young people on airplanes are roughly dressed, or at least they look that way to one of my age and stage. (This could be said of older people, too, I suspect.) . . .
>
> When public officials begin to regard large groups of citizens as presumptively criminal, this country is in a perilous situation indeed. Airports are on the verge of becoming war zones, where anyone is liable to be stopped, questioned, and even searched merely on the basis of the on-the-spot exercise of discretion by police officers. The liberty of the citizen, in my view, is seriously threatened by this practice. The sanctity of private property, a precious human right, is endangered.

It's hard to work up much sympathy for Weaver. He's getting what he deserves, in a sense. What is missing here, though, is an awareness that law enforcement is a broad concept. It includes enforcement of the Bill of Rights, as well as enforcement of criminal statutes. Cases in which innocent travelers are stopped and impeded in their lawful activities don't come to court. They go on their way, too busy to bring a lawsuit against the officious agents who have detained them. (397)

In our next case excerpt, *U.S. v. Brignoni-Ponce* (1975), the U.S. Supreme Court rejected the claim that Felix Humbarto Brignoni-Ponce's ethnicity could be the *only* building block in reasonably suspecting he was transporting illegal Mexican immigrants across the Mexican border.

---

## CASE | *Can Ethnicity Be the Only Building Block for Reasonable Suspicion?*

### U.S. v. Brignoni-Ponce
422 U.S. 873 (1975)

### HISTORY

Felix Humberto Brignoni-Ponce, Respondent, was convicted before the United States District Court for the Southern District of California of transporting aliens and he appealed. The Court of Appeals, reversed and remanded, and the United States brought certiorari. The Supreme Court, affirmed.

POWELL, J.

### FACTS

As a part of its regular traffic-checking operations in southern California, the Border Patrol operates a fixed checkpoint on Interstate Highway 5 south of San Clemente. On the evening of March 11, 1973, the checkpoint was closed because of inclement weather, but two officers were observing northbound traffic from a patrol car parked at the side of the highway. The road was dark, and they were using the patrol car's headlights to illuminate passing cars.

They pursued respondent's car and stopped it, saying later that their only reason for doing so was that its three occupants appeared to be of Mexican descent. The officers questioned respondent and his two passengers about their citizenship and learned that the passengers were aliens who had entered the country illegally. All three were then arrested, and respondent was charged with two counts of knowingly transporting illegal immigrants, a violation of § 274(a)(2) of the Immigration and Nationality Act.

At trial respondent moved to suppress the testimony of and about the two passengers, claiming that this evidence was the fruit of an illegal seizure. The trial court denied the motion, the aliens testified at trial, and respondent was convicted on both counts.

### OPINION

The only issue presented for decision is whether a roving patrol may stop a vehicle in an area near the border and question its occupants when the only ground for suspicion is that the occupants appear to be of Mexican ancestry. For the reasons that follow, we affirm the decision of the Court of Appeals. . . .

The Fourth Amendment applies to all seizures of the person, including seizures that involve only a brief detention short of traditional arrest. . . . As with other categories of police action subject to Fourth Amendment constraints, the reasonableness of such seizures depends on a balance between the public interest and the individual's right to personal security free from arbitrary interference by law officers.

The Government makes a convincing demonstration that the public interest demands effective measures to prevent the illegal entry of aliens at the Mexican border. Estimates of the number of illegal immigrants in the United States vary widely. A conservative estimate in 1972 produced a figure of about one million, but the INS now suggests there may be as many as 10 or 12 million aliens illegally in the country.

Whatever the number, these aliens create significant economic and social problems, competing with citizens and legal resident aliens for jobs, and generating extra demand for social services. The aliens themselves are vulnerable to exploitation because they cannot complain of substandard working conditions without risking deportation.

The Mexican border is almost 2,000 miles long, and even a vastly reinforced Border Patrol would find it impossible to prevent illegal border crossings. Many aliens cross the Mexican border on foot, miles away from patrolled areas, and then purchase transportation from the border area to inland cities, where they find jobs and elude the immigration authorities.

Others gain entry on valid temporary border-crossing permits, but then violate the conditions of their entry.

Most of these aliens leave the border area in private vehicles, often assisted by professional "alien smugglers." The Border Patrol's traffic-checking operations are designed to prevent this inland movement. They succeed in apprehending some illegal entrants and smugglers, and they deter the movement of others by threatening apprehension and increasing the cost of illegal transportation.

Against this valid public interest we must weigh the interference with individual liberty that results when an officer stops an automobile and questions its occupants. The intrusion is modest. The Government tells us that a stop by a roving patrol "usually consumes no more than a minute." There is no search of the vehicle or its occupants, and the visual inspection is limited to those parts of the vehicle that can be seen by anyone standing alongside. According to the Government, "all that is required of the vehicle's occupants is a response to a brief question or two and possibly the production of a document evidencing a right to be in the United States."

Because of the limited nature of the intrusion, stops of this sort may be justified on facts that do not amount to the probable cause required for an arrest. . . . Because of the importance of the governmental interest at stake, the minimal intrusion of a brief stop, and the absence of practical alternatives for policing the border, we hold that when an officer's observations lead him reasonably to suspect that a particular vehicle may contain aliens who are illegally in the country, he may stop the car briefly and investigate the circumstances that provoke suspicion.

As in *Terry*, the stop and inquiry must be "reasonably related in scope to the justification for their initiation." The officer may question the driver and passengers about their citizenship and immigration status, and he may ask them to explain suspicious circumstances, but any further detention or search must be based on consent or probable cause.

We are unwilling to let the Border Patrol dispense entirely with the requirement that officers must have a reasonable suspicion to justify roving-patrol stops. In the context of border area stops, the reasonableness requirement of the Fourth Amendment demands something more than the broad and unlimited discretion sought by the Government.

Roads near the border carry not only aliens seeking to enter the country illegally, but a large volume of legitimate traffic as well. San Diego, with a metropolitan population of 1.4 million, is located on the border. Texas has two fairly large metropolitan areas directly on the border: El Paso, with a population of 360,000, and the Brownsville-McAllen area, with a combined population of 320,000.

We are confident that substantially all of the traffic in these cities is lawful and that relatively few of their residents have any connection with the illegal entry and transportation of aliens. To approve roving-patrol stops of all vehicles in the border area, without any suspicion that a particular vehicle is carrying illegal immigrants, would subject the residents of these and other areas to potentially unlimited interference with their use of the highways, solely at the discretion of Border Patrol officers.

The only formal limitation on that discretion appears to be the administrative regulation defining the term "reasonable distance" . . . to mean within 100 air miles from the border. Thus, if we approved the Government's position in this case, Border Patrol officers could stop motorists at random for questioning, day or night, anywhere within 100 air miles of the 2,000-mile border, on a city street, a busy highway, or a desert road, without any reason to suspect that they have violated any law.

We are not convinced that the legitimate needs of law enforcement require this degree of interference with lawful traffic. . . . The nature of illegal alien traffic and the characteristics of smuggling operations tend to generate articulable grounds for identifying violators. Consequently, a requirement of reasonable suspicion for stops allows the Government adequate means of guarding the public interest and also protects residents of the border areas from indiscriminate official interference. Under the circumstances, and even though the intrusion incident to a stop is modest, we conclude that it is not "reasonable" under the Fourth Amendment to make such stops on a random basis.*

The Government also contends that the public interest in enforcing conditions on legal alien entry justifies stopping persons who may be aliens for questioning about their citizenship and immigration status. Although we may assume for purposes of this case that the broad congressional power over immigration authorizes Congress to admit aliens on condition that they will submit to reasonable questioning about their right to be and remain in the country, this power cannot diminish the Fourth Amendment rights of citizens who may be mistaken for aliens. For the same reasons that the Fourth Amendment forbids stopping vehicles at random to inquire if they are carrying aliens who are illegally in the country, it also forbids stopping or detaining persons for questioning about their citizenship on less than a reasonable suspicion that they may be aliens.

. . . Except at the border and its functional equivalents, officers on roving patrol may stop vehicles only if they are aware of specific articulable facts, together with rational inferences from those facts, that reasonably warrant suspicion that the vehicles contain aliens who may be illegally in the country.

Any number of factors may be taken into account in deciding whether there is reasonable suspicion to stop a car

---

*Our decision in this case takes into account the special function of the Border Patrol, the importance of the governmental interests in policing the border area, the character of roving-patrol stops, and the availability of alternatives to random stops unsupported by reasonable suspicion. Border Patrol agents have no part in enforcing laws that regulate highway use, and their activities have nothing to do with an inquiry whether motorists and their vehicles are entitled, by virtue of compliance with laws governing highway usage, to be upon the public highways. Our decision thus does not imply that state and local enforcement agencies are without power to conduct such limited stops as are necessary to enforce laws regarding drivers' licenses, vehicle registration, truck weights, and similar matters.

in the border area. Officers may consider the characteristics of the area in which they encounter a vehicle. Its proximity to the border, the usual patterns of traffic on the particular road, and previous experience with alien traffic are all relevant. They also may consider information about recent illegal border crossings in the area. The driver's behavior may be relevant, as erratic driving or obvious attempts to evade officers can support a reasonable suspicion.

Aspects of the vehicle itself may justify suspicion. For instance, officers say that certain station wagons, with large compartments for fold-down seats or spare tires, are frequently used for transporting concealed aliens. The vehicle may appear to be heavily loaded, it may have an extraordinary number of passengers, or the officers may observe persons trying to hide.

The Government also points out that trained officers can recognize the characteristic appearance of persons who live in Mexico, relying on such factors as the mode of dress and haircut. In all situations the officer is entitled to assess the facts in light of his experience in detecting illegal entry and smuggling.

In this case the officers relied on a single factor to justify stopping respondent's car: the apparent Mexican ancestry of the occupants. We cannot conclude that this furnished reasonable grounds to believe that the three occupants were aliens. At best the officers had only a fleeting glimpse of the persons in the moving car, illuminated by headlights. Even if they saw enough to think that the occupants were of Mexican descent, this factor alone would justify neither a reasonable belief that they were aliens, nor a reasonable belief that the car concealed other aliens who were illegally in the country.

Large numbers of native-born and naturalized citizens have the physical characteristics identified with Mexican ancestry, and even in the border area a relatively small proportion of them are aliens. The likelihood that any given person of Mexican ancestry is an alien is high enough to make Mexican appearance a relevant factor, but standing alone it does not justify stopping all Mexican-Americans to ask if they are aliens.

The judgment of the Court of Appeals is AFFIRMED.

## CONCURRING OPINION

### DOUGLAS, J.

. . . The stopping of respondent's automobile solely because its occupants appeared to be of Mexican ancestry was a patent violation of the Fourth Amendment. I cannot agree, however, with the standard the Court adopts to measure the lawfulness of the officers' action.

The fears I voiced in *Terry* about the weakening of the Fourth Amendment have regrettably been borne out by subsequent events. Hopes that the suspicion test might be employed only in the pursuit of violent crime—a limitation endorsed by some of its proponents—have now been dashed, as it has been applied in narcotics investigations, in apprehension of "illegal" aliens, and indeed has come to be viewed as a legal construct for the regulation of a general investigatory police power.

The suspicion test has been warmly embraced by law enforcement forces and vigorously employed in the cause of crime detection. In criminal cases we see those for whom the initial intrusion led to the discovery of some wrongdoing. But the nature of the test permits the police to interfere as well with a multitude of law-abiding citizens, whose only transgression may be a nonconformist appearance or attitude. As one commentator has remarked:

"Police power exercised without probable cause is arbitrary. To say that the police may accost citizens at their whim and may detain them upon reasonable suspicion is to say, in reality, that the police may both accost and detain citizens at their whim." Amsterdam, Perspectives on the Fourth Amendment, 58 Minn.L.Rev. 349, 395 (1974).

. . . Ultimately the degree to which the suspicion test actually restrains the police will depend more upon what the Court does henceforth than upon what it says today. If my Brethren mean to give the suspicion test a new bite, I applaud the intention. But in view of the developments since the test was launched in *Terry*, I am not optimistic. This is the first decision to invalidate a stop on the basis of the suspicion standard. In fact, since *Terry* we have granted review of a case applying the test only once, in *Adams v. Williams* (1972), where the Court found the standard satisfied by the tip from an informant whose credibility was not established and whose information was not shown to be based upon personal knowledge.

If in the future the suspicion test is to provide any meaningful restraint of the police, its force must come from vigorous review of its applications, and not alone from the qualifying language of today's opinion. For now, I remain unconvinced that the suspicion test offers significant protection of the "comprehensive right of personal liberty in the face of governmental intrusion" . . . that is embodied in the Fourth Amendment.

## Questions

1. Identify and summarize the balance between the government's interest and individuals' rights according to the Court.

2. State the Court's definition of *reasonable suspicion*.

3. List the facts officers can take into account in forming a reasonable suspicion in a case.

4. Summarize the Court's position on Brignoni-Ponce's ethnicity in building reasonable suspicion.

5. Summarize Justice Douglas's concurring opinion. To what extent, if at all, do you agree with Justice Douglas? Explain your answer.

| TABLE 4.4 | Primary and Secondary Characteristics of Drug Couriers |
| --- | --- |
| **Primary Characteristics** | **Secondary Characteristics** |
| • Arriving or departing from "source" cities | • Using public transportation when leaving airports |
| • Carrying little or no luggage, or empty suitcases | • Making telephone calls immediately after getting off the plane |
| • Traveling by an unusual itinerary | • Leaving false or fictitious callback numbers when leaving the plane |
| • Using an alias | • Making excessively frequent trips to source or distribution cities |
| • Carrying unusually large amounts of cash | |
| • Purchasing tickets with large numbers of small bills | |
| • Appearing unusually nervous | |

*Profiles* Profiles consist of lists of circumstances that might, or might not, be linked to particular kinds of behavior. Profiles have been popular law enforcement tools since the 1970s when the government introduced an airline hijacker profile.

In this section, we'll focus on **drug courier profiles**, lists of characteristics that drug traffickers are supposed to possess. Drug Enforcement Agent Paul Markonni developed the drug courier profile in 1974 while he was assigned to the Detroit DEA office and trained other agents in its use. Since then, it's become a "nationwide law enforcement tool." Officers stationed at airports observe travelers, looking for seven primary and four secondary characteristics (Table 4.4; *U.S. v. Elmore* 1979, 1039, n. 3).

If their suspicions are aroused, agents approach travelers, identify themselves, seek their consent to be questioned, and ask to see their identification and ticket. If this doesn't remove their suspicion, the agents ask travelers to come with them to another location, usually a room used by law enforcement officers. Once inside the room, agents ask travelers to consent to searches of their persons and luggage. If travelers refuse, agents either have to let them go or "seize" them (Cloud 1985, 848–49).

Since the introduction of the airport drug courier profile, law enforcement has introduced a number of other profiles: for illegal aliens entering the United States, international drug smugglers, customers of suspected domestic drug dealers, and high-way drug couriers.

The Supreme Court, in *Reid v. Georgia* (1980), ruled that the drug courier profile *by itself* can't amount to reasonable suspicion. A DEA agent suspected that Tommy Reid, Jr., possessed cocaine, based on the DEA drug courier profile, "a somewhat informal compilation of characteristics typical of persons unlawfully carrying narcotics" (440). The Georgia Court of Appeals held that the profile was enough to satisfy the reasonable suspicion requirement.

> Specifically, the [lower] court thought it relevant that (1) the petitioner had arrived from Fort Lauderdale, which the agent testified is a principal place of origin of cocaine sold elsewhere in the country, (2) the petitioner arrived in the early morning, when law enforcement activity is diminished, (3) he and his companion appeared to the agent to be trying to conceal the fact that they were traveling together, and (4) they apparently had no luggage other than their shoulder bags. (441–42)

The U.S. Supreme Court disagreed:

We conclude that the agent could not as a matter of law, have reasonably suspected the petitioner of criminal activity on the basis of these observed circumstances. Of the evidence relied on, only the fact that the petitioner preceded another person and occasionally looked backward at him as they proceeded through the concourse relates to their particular conduct. The other circumstances describe a very large category of presumably innocent travelers, who would be subject to virtually random seizures were the Court to conclude that as little foundation as there was in this case could justify a seizure. Nor can we agree, on this record, that the manner in which the petitioner and his companion walked through the airport reasonably could have led the agent to suspect them of wrongdoing. Although there could, of course, be circumstances in which wholly lawful conduct might justify the suspicion that criminal activity was afoot, this is not such a case. The agent's belief that the petitioner and his companion were attempting to conceal the fact that they were traveling together, a belief that was more an inchoate and unparticularized suspicion or hunch, than a fair inference in the light of his experience, is simply too slender a reed to support the seizure in this case. (442)

What about the *characteristics* in the profiles that fit the individual defendant? Can officers use them as part of the totality of circumstance amounting to reasonable suspicion? Yes, ruled the Supreme Court in the frequently cited *U.S. v. Sokolow* (1989), our next case excerpt.

CASE    *Does Fitting a Drug Courier Profile Amount to Reasonable Suspicion?*

### U.S. v. Sokolow
490 U.S. 1 (1989)

### HISTORY

Andrew Sokolow, Respondent, was convicted in the United States District Court for the District of Hawaii of possessing cocaine with intent to distribute. Defendant appealed. The Court of Appeals for the Ninth Circuit reversed and remanded. The U.S. Supreme Court granted certiorari, and reversed the Circuit Court, and remanded the case.

REHNQUIST, C.J., JOINED BY WHITE, BLACKMUN, STEVENS, O'CONNOR, SCALIA, AND KENNEDY, JJ.

Respondent Andrew Sokolow was stopped by Drug Enforcement Administration (DEA) agents upon his arrival at Honolulu International Airport. The agents found 1,063 grams of cocaine in his carry-on luggage. When respondent was stopped, the agents knew, among other things, (1) he paid $2,100 for two airplane tickets from a roll of $20 bills; (2) he traveled under a name that did not match the name under which his telephone number was listed; (3) his original destination was Miami, a source city for illicit drugs; (4) he stayed in Miami for only 48 hours, even though a round-trip flight from Honolulu to Miami takes 20 hours; (5) he appeared nervous during his trip; and (6) he checked none of his luggage. A divided panel

of the United States Court of Appeals for the Ninth Circuit held that the DEA agents did not have a reasonable suspicion to stop respondent, as required by the Fourth Amendment. We take the contrary view.

### FACTS

This case involves a typical attempt to smuggle drugs through one of the Nation's airports. On a Sunday in July 1984, respondent went to the United Airlines ticket counter at Honolulu Airport, where he purchased two round-trip tickets for a flight to Miami leaving later that day. The tickets were purchased in the names of "Andrew Kray" and "Janet Norian" and had open return dates. Respondent paid $2,100 for the tickets from a large roll of $20 bills, which appeared to contain a total of $4,000. He also gave the ticket agent his home telephone number. The ticket agent noticed that respondent seemed nervous; he was about 25 years old; he was dressed in a black jumpsuit and wore gold jewelry; and he was accompanied by a woman, who turned out to be Janet Norian. Neither respondent nor his companion checked any of their four pieces of luggage.

After the couple left for their flight, the ticket agent informed Officer John McCarthy of the Honolulu Police Department of respondent's cash purchase of tickets to Miami. Officer McCarthy determined that the telephone number respondent gave to the ticket agent was subscribed to a "Karl Herman," who resided at 348-A Royal Hawaiian Avenue in Honolulu. Unbeknownst to McCarthy (and later to the DEA agents), respondent was Herman's roommate. The ticket agent identified respondent's voice on the answering machine at Herman's number. Officer McCarthy was unable to find any listing under the name "Andrew Kray" in Hawaii. McCarthy subsequently learned that return reservations from Miami to Honolulu had been made in the names of Kray and Norian, with their arrival scheduled for July 25, three days after respondent and his companion had left. He also learned that Kray and Norian were scheduled to make stopovers in Denver and Los Angeles.

On July 25, during the stopover in Los Angeles, DEA agents identified respondent. He "appeared to be very nervous and was looking all around the waiting area." Later that day, at 6:30 P.M., respondent and Norian arrived in Honolulu. As before, they had not checked their luggage. Respondent was still wearing a black jumpsuit and gold jewelry. The couple proceeded directly to the street and tried to hail a cab, where Agent Richard Kempshall and three other DEA agents approached them. Kempshall displayed his credentials, grabbed respondent by the arm, and moved him back onto the sidewalk. Kempshall asked respondent for his airline ticket and identification; respondent said that he had neither. He told the agents that his name was "Sokolow," but that he was traveling under his mother's maiden name, "Kray."

Respondent and Norian were escorted to the DEA office at the airport. There, the couple's luggage was examined by "Donker," a narcotics detector dog, which alerted on respondent's brown shoulder bag. The agents arrested respondent. He was advised of his constitutional rights and declined to make any statements. The agents obtained a warrant to search the shoulder bag. They found no illicit drugs, but the bag did contain several suspicious documents indicating respondent's involvement in drug trafficking. The agents had Donker reexamine the remaining luggage, and this time the dog alerted on a medium-sized Louis Vuitton bag. By now, it was 9:30 P.M., too late for the agents to obtain a second warrant. They allowed respondent to leave for the night, but kept his luggage. The next morning, after a second dog confirmed Donker's alert, the agents obtained a warrant and found 1,063 grams of cocaine inside the bag.

Respondent was indicted for possession with the intent to distribute cocaine in violation of 21 U.S.C. § 841(a)(1). The United States District Court for Hawaii denied his motion to suppress the cocaine and other evidence seized from his luggage, finding that the DEA agents had a reasonable suspicion that he was involved in drug trafficking when they stopped him at the airport. Respondent then entered a conditional plea of guilty to the offense charged.

The United States Court of Appeals for the Ninth Circuit reversed respondent's conviction by a divided vote, holding that the DEA agents did not have a reasonable suspicion to justify the stop. The majority divided the facts bearing on reasonable suspicion into two categories. In the first category, the majority placed facts describing "ongoing criminal activity," such as the use of an alias or evasive movement through an airport; the majority believed that at least one such factor was always needed to support a finding of reasonable suspicion.

In the second category, it placed facts describing "personal characteristics" of drug couriers, such as the cash payment for tickets, a short trip to a major source city for drugs, nervousness, type of attire, and unchecked luggage. The majority believed that such characteristics, "shared by drug couriers and the public at large," were only relevant if there was evidence of ongoing criminal behavior and the Government offered "empirical documentation" that the combination of facts at issue did not describe the behavior of "significant numbers of innocent persons."

Applying this two-part test to the facts of this case, the majority found that there was no evidence of ongoing criminal behavior, and thus that the agents' stop was impermissible. The dissenting judge took the view that the majority's approach was "overly mechanistic" and "contrary to the case-by-case determination of reasonable articulable suspicion based on *all* the facts."

We granted certiorari to review the decision of the Court of Appeals because of its serious implications for the enforcement of the federal narcotics laws. We now REVERSE.

## OPINION

The Court of Appeals held that the DEA agents seized respondent when they grabbed him by the arm and moved him back onto the sidewalk. The Government does not challenge that conclusion, and we assume—without deciding—that a stop occurred here. Our decision, then, turns on whether the agents had a reasonable suspicion that respondent was engaged in wrongdoing when they encountered him on the sidewalk. In *Terry v. Ohio,* we held that the police can stop and briefly detain a person for investigative purposes if the officer has a reasonable suspicion supported by articulable facts that criminal activity "may be afoot," even if the officer lacks probable cause.

The officer, of course, must be able to articulate something more than an "inchoate and unparticularized suspicion or 'hunch.'" . . . The concept of reasonable suspicion . . . is not "readily, or even usefully, reduced to a neat set of legal rules." We think the Court of Appeals' effort to refine and elaborate the requirements of "reasonable suspicion" in this case creates unnecessary difficulty in dealing with one of the relatively simple concepts embodied in the Fourth Amendment. In evaluating the validity of a stop such as this, we must consider the totality of the circumstances—the whole picture.

The rule enunciated by the Court of Appeals, in which evidence available to an officer is divided into evidence of "ongoing criminal behavior," on the one hand, and "probabilistic" evidence, on the other, is not in keeping with . . . our decisions. It also seems to us to draw a sharp line between types of evidence, the probative value of which varies only in degree. The Court of Appeals classified evidence of traveling under an alias, or evidence that the suspect took an evasive or erratic path through an airport, as meeting the test for showing "ongoing criminal activity." But certainly instances are conceivable in which traveling under an alias would not reflect ongoing criminal activity: for example, a person who wished to travel to a hospital or clinic for an operation and wished to conceal that fact. One taking an evasive path through an airport might be seeking to avoid a confrontation with an angry acquaintance or with a creditor. This is not to say that each of these types of evidence is not highly probative, but they do not have the sort of ironclad significance attributed to them by the Court of Appeals.

On the other hand, the factors in this case that the Court of Appeals treated as merely "probabilistic" also have probative significance. Paying $2,100 in cash for two airplane tickets is out of the ordinary, and it is even more out of the ordinary to pay that sum from a roll of $20 bills containing nearly twice that amount of cash. Most business travelers, we feel confident, purchase airline tickets by credit card or check so as to have a record for tax or business purposes, and few vacationers carry with them thousands of dollars in $20 bills.

We also think the agents had a reasonable ground to believe that respondent was traveling under an alias; the evidence was by no means conclusive, but it was sufficient to warrant consideration. While a trip from Honolulu to Miami, standing alone, is not a cause for any sort of suspicion, here there was more: surely few residents of Honolulu travel from that city for 20 hours to spend 48 hours in Miami during the month of July.

Any one of these factors is not by itself proof of any illegal conduct and is quite consistent with innocent travel. But we think taken together they amount to reasonable suspicion. . . . There could, of course, be circumstances in which wholly lawful conduct might justify the suspicion that criminal activity was afoot. Indeed, *Terry* itself involved "a series of acts, each of them perhaps innocent" if viewed separately, "but which taken together warranted further investigation." . . .

We do not agree with respondent that our analysis is somehow changed by the agents' belief that his behavior was consistent with one of the DEA's "drug courier profiles."* A court sitting to determine the existence of reasonable suspicion must require the agent to articulate the factors leading to that conclusion, but the fact that these factors may be set forth in a "profile" does not somehow detract from their evidentiary significance as seen by a trained agent. . . .

---

*Agent Kempshall testified that Sokolow's behavior "had all the classic aspects of a drug courier." Since 1974, the DEA has trained narcotics officers to identify drug smugglers on the basis of the sort of circumstantial evidence at issue here.

We hold that the agents had a reasonable basis to suspect that respondent was transporting illegal drugs on these facts. The judgment of the Court of Appeals is therefore reversed, and the case is remanded for further proceedings consistent with our decision. *It is so ordered.*

## DISSENT

### MARSHALL, J., JOINED BY BRENNAN, J.

Because the strongest advocates of Fourth Amendment rights are frequently criminals, it is easy to forget that our interpretations of such rights apply to the innocent and the guilty alike. In the present case, the chain of events set in motion when respondent Andrew Sokolow was stopped by Drug Enforcement Administration (DEA) agents at Honolulu International Airport led to the discovery of cocaine and, ultimately, to Sokolow's conviction for drug trafficking. But in sustaining this conviction on the ground that the agents reasonably suspected Sokolow of ongoing criminal activity, the Court diminishes the rights of *all* citizens "to be secure in their persons." Finding this result constitutionally impermissible, I dissent.

. . . By requiring reasonable suspicion . . . , the Fourth Amendment protects innocent persons from being subjected to "overbearing or harassing" police conduct carried out solely on the basis of imprecise stereotypes of what criminals look like, or on the basis of irrelevant personal characteristics such as race. To deter such egregious police behavior, we have held that a suspicion is not reasonable unless officers have based it on "specific and articulable facts." . . . Before detaining an individual, law enforcement officers must reasonably suspect that he is engaged in, or poised to commit, a criminal act *at that moment.* . . .

Evaluated against this standard, the facts about Andrew Sokolow known to the DEA agents at the time they stopped him fall short of reasonably indicating that he was engaged at the time in criminal activity. It is highly significant that the DEA agents stopped Sokolow because he matched one of the DEA's "profiles" of a paradigmatic drug courier. In my view, a law enforcement officer's mechanistic application of a formula of personal and behavioral traits in deciding whom to detain can only dull the officer's ability and determination to make sensitive and fact-specific inferences "in light of his experience," particularly in ambiguous or borderline cases.

Reflexive reliance on a profile of drug courier characteristics runs a far greater risk than does ordinary, case-by-case police work of subjecting innocent individuals to unwarranted police harassment and detention. This risk is enhanced by the profile's chameleon-like way of adapting to any particular set of observations. . . .

The facts known to the DEA agents at the time they detained the traveler in this case . . . [include:] Sokolow gave no indications of evasive activity. On the contrary, the sole behavioral detail about Sokolow noted by the DEA agents was that he was nervous. With news accounts proliferating of plane crashes, near collisions, and air terrorism, there are manifold and good reasons for being agitated while awaiting a flight, reasons that have nothing to do with one's involvement in a criminal endeavor. The remaining circumstantial facts known about Sokolow, considered either singly or together, are scarcely indicative of criminal activity. Like the information disavowed . . .

The fact that Sokolow took a brief trip to a resort city for which he brought only carry-on luggage also describes a very large category of presumably innocent travelers.

That Sokolow embarked from Miami, a source city for illicit drugs, is no more suggestive of illegality; thousands of innocent persons travel from "source cities" every day and, judging from the DEA's testimony in past cases, nearly every major city in the country may be characterized as a source or distribution city.

That Sokolow had his phone listed in another person's name also does not support the majority's assertion that the DEA agents reasonably believed Sokolow was using an alias; it is commonplace to have one's phone registered in the name of a roommate, which, it later turned out, was precisely what Sokolow had done.

That Sokolow was dressed in a black jumpsuit and wore gold jewelry also provides no grounds for suspecting wrongdoing, the majority's repeated and unexplained allusions to Sokolow's style of dress notwithstanding. For law enforcement officers to base a search, even in part, on a "pop" guess that persons dressed in a particular fashion are likely to commit crimes not only stretches the concept of reasonable suspicion beyond recognition, but also is inimical to the self-expression which the choice of wardrobe may provide.

Finally, that Sokolow paid for his tickets in cash indicates no imminent or ongoing criminal activity. The majority "feel[s] confident" that "[m]ost business travelers . . . purchase airline tickets by credit card or check." Why the majority confines its focus only to "business travelers" I do not know, but I would not so lightly infer ongoing crime from the use of legal tender. Making major cash purchases, while surely less common today, may simply reflect the traveler's aversion to, or inability to obtain, plastic money. . . .

Moreover, it is unreasonable to suggest that, had Sokolow left the airport, he would have been gone forever and thus immune from subsequent investigation. *Ante,* at 1587. Sokolow, after all, had given the airline his phone number, and the DEA, having ascertained that it was indeed Sokolow's voice on the answering machine at that number, could have learned from that information where Sokolow resided.

. . . Nothing about the characteristics shown by airport traveler Sokolow reasonably suggests that criminal activity is afoot. The majority's hasty conclusion to the contrary serves only to indicate its willingness, when drug crimes or antidrug policies are at issue, to give short shrift to constitutional rights. . . .

## Questions

1. What were the facts upon which DEA agents based the "stop"?

2. Which of the facts point to Sokolow specifically, and which are facts that make him fit the drug courier profile?

3. If you don't count the profile facts, was there reasonable suspicion to suspect Sokolow possessed cocaine with the intent to distribute it? Defend your answer.

4. Under what conditions, if any, should "circumstantial" evidence like the drug courier profile provide the basis for stops?

## The Scope of Reasonable Stops

A brief freeze in time and space—the scope of a reasonable stop has to include these two things. So there are two elements to the scope of a reasonable stop: short duration and on-the-spot location of the investigation. Let's look at each.

***Short Duration*** According to the American Law Institute's (a group of distinguished prosecutors, defense lawyers, law enforcement officers, and academics) *Model Code of Pre-Arraignment Procedure* (1975), there ought to be a bright-line rule controlling the length of stops. Here's the model duration rule:

SECTION 110.2. STOPPING OF PERSONS

A law enforcement officer, lawfully present in any place, may . . . order a person to remain in the officer's presence . . . for such period as is reasonably necessary  . but in no case for more than twenty minutes . . . if such action is reasonably necessary to obtain or verify the identification of such person, to obtain or verify an account of such person's presence or conduct, or to determine whether to arrest such person.

The U.S. Supreme Court has so far declined to adopt this rule. Why? Because the Court prefers to keep its options open and to give officers plenty of room for discretionary decision making. That way neither the Court nor officers are confined to a bright-line rule that may hamper crime control. You can see the Court's hesitation to limit reasonable duration to an exact number of minutes by rejecting it in *U.S. v. Sharpe and Savage* (1985), the leading case dealing with the duration element of the scope of reasonable stops.

# CASE    *Was the Duration "Brief"?*

## U.S. v. Sharpe and Savage
### 470 U.S. 675 (1985)

### HISTORY

William Sharpe and Donald Savage were convicted in the U.S. District Court for the District of South Carolina, of possession of a controlled substance with intent to distribute, and they appealed. The U.S. Fourth Circuit Court reversed the convictions, and the Government petitioned for certiorari. The Supreme Court granted the petition, and vacated and remanded the case for further consideration. On remand, the Court of Appeals again reversed the convictions, and the Government petitioned for certiorari. The Supreme Court reversed and remanded again.

BURGER, C.J.

### FACTS

On the morning of June 9, 1978, Agent Cooke of the Drug Enforcement Administration (DEA) was on patrol in an unmarked vehicle on a coastal road near Sunset Beach, North Carolina, an area under surveillance for suspected drug trafficking. At approximately 6:30 A.M., Cooke noticed a blue pickup truck with an attached camper shell traveling on the highway in tandem with a blue Pontiac Bonneville. Donald Savage was driving the pickup, and William Sharpe was driving the Pontiac. The Pontiac also carried a passenger, Davis, the charges against whom were later dropped. Observing that the truck was riding low in the rear and that the camper did not bounce or sway appreciably when the truck drove over bumps or around curves, Agent Cooke concluded that it was heavily loaded. A quilted material covered the rear and side windows of the camper.

Cooke's suspicions were sufficiently aroused to follow the two vehicles for approximately 20 miles as they proceeded south into South Carolina. He then decided to make an "investigative stop" and radioed the State Highway Patrol for assistance. Officer Thrasher, driving a marked patrol car, responded to the call. Almost immediately after Thrasher caught up with the procession, the Pontiac and the pickup turned off the highway and onto a campground road. Cooke and Thrasher followed the two vehicles as the latter drove along the road at 55 to 60 miles an hour, exceeding the speed limit of 35 miles an hour. The road eventually looped back to the highway, onto which Savage and Sharpe turned and continued to drive south.

At this point, all four vehicles were in the middle lane of the three right-hand lanes of the highway. Agent Cooke asked Officer Thrasher to signal both vehicles to stop. Thrasher pulled alongside the Pontiac, which was in the lead, turned on his flashing light, and motioned for the driver of the Pontiac to stop. As Sharpe moved the Pontiac into the right lane, the pickup truck cut between the Pontiac and Thrasher's patrol car, nearly hitting the patrol car, and continued down the highway. Thrasher pursued the truck while Cooke pulled up behind the Pontiac.

Cooke approached the Pontiac and identified himself. He requested identification, and Sharpe produced a Georgia driver's license bearing the name of Raymond J. Pavlovich. Cooke then attempted to radio Thrasher to determine whether he had been successful in stopping the pickup truck, but he was unable to make contact for several minutes, apparently because Thrasher was not in his patrol car. Cooke radioed the local police for assistance, and two officers from the Myrtle Beach Police Department arrived about 10 minutes later. Asking the two officers to "maintain the situation," Cooke left to join Thrasher.

In the meantime, Thrasher had stopped the pickup truck about one-half mile down the road. After stopping the truck, Thrasher had approached it with his revolver drawn, ordered the driver, Savage, to get out and assume a "spread eagled" position against the side of the truck, and patted him down. Thrasher then holstered his gun and asked Savage for his driver's license and the truck's vehicle registration. Savage produced his own Florida driver's license and a bill of sale for the truck bearing the name of

Pavlovich. In response to questions from Thrasher concerning the ownership of the truck, Savage said that the truck belonged to a friend and that he was taking it to have its shock absorbers repaired.

When Thrasher told Savage that he would be held until the arrival of Cooke, whom Thrasher identified as a DEA agent, Savage became nervous, said that he wanted to leave, and requested the return of his driver's license. Thrasher replied that Savage was not free to leave at that time.

Agent Cooke arrived at the scene approximately 15 minutes after the truck had been stopped. Thrasher handed Cooke Savage's license and the bill of sale for the truck; Cooke noted that the bill of sale bore the same name as Sharpe's license. Cooke identified himself to Savage as a DEA agent and said that he thought the truck was loaded with marihuana.

Cooke twice sought permission to search the camper, but Savage declined to give it, explaining that he was not the owner of the truck. Cooke then stepped on the rear of the truck and, observing that it did not sink any lower, confirmed his suspicion that it was probably overloaded. He put his nose against the rear window, which was covered from the inside, and reported that he could smell marihuana. Without seeking Savage's permission, Cooke removed the keys from the ignition, opened the rear of the camper, and observed a large number of burlap-wrapped bales resembling bales of marihuana that Cooke had seen in previous investigations.

Agent Cooke then placed Savage under arrest and left him with Thrasher. Cooke returned to the Pontiac and arrested Sharpe and Davis. Approximately 30 to 40 minutes had elapsed between the time Cooke stopped the Pontiac and the time he returned to arrest Sharpe and Davis. Cooke assembled the various parties and vehicles and led them to the Myrtle Beach police station. That evening, DEA agents took the truck to the Federal Building in Charleston, South Carolina.

Several days later, Cooke supervised the unloading of the truck, which contained 43 bales weighing a total of 2,629 pounds. Acting without a search warrant, Cooke had eight randomly selected bales opened and sampled. Chemical tests showed that the samples were marihuana.

Sharpe and Savage were charged with possession of a controlled substance with intent to distribute it in violation of 21 U.S.C. § 841(a)(1) and 18 U.S.C. § 2. The U.S. District Court for the District of South Carolina denied (Sharpe's and Savage's motion to suppress the contraband), and they were convicted.

## OPINION

The Fourth Amendment is not a guarantee against all searches and seizures, but only against unreasonable searches and seizures. . . . The Court of Appeals . . . concluded that the 30- to 40-minute detention of Sharpe and the 20-minute detention of Savage "failed to meet the [Fourth Amendment's] requirement of brevity." . . . The Court of Appeals' decision would effectively establish a per se rule that a 20-minute detention is too long to be justified under the *Terry* doctrine [excerpted on p. 88]. Such a result is clearly and fundamentally at odds with our approach in this area.

In assessing whether a detention is too long in duration to be justified as an investigative stop, we consider it appropriate to examine whether the police diligently pursued a means of investigation that was likely to confirm or dispel their suspicions quickly, during which time it was necessary to detain the defendant. A court making this assessment should take care to consider whether the police are acting in a swiftly developing situation, and in such cases the court should not indulge in unrealistic second-guessing.

A creative judge engaged in [after the fact] evaluation of police conduct can almost always imagine some alternative means by which the objectives of the police might have been accomplished. But "the fact that the protection of the public might, in the abstract, have been accomplished by 'less intrusive' means does not, itself, render the search unreasonable." The question is not simply whether some other alternative was available, but whether the police acted unreasonably in failing to recognize or to pursue it.

We readily conclude that, given the circumstances facing him, Agent Cooke pursued his investigation in a diligent and reasonable manner. During most of Savage's 20-minute detention, Cooke was attempting to contact Thrasher and enlisting the help of the local police who remained with Sharpe while Cooke left to pursue Officer Thrasher and the pickup. Once Cooke reached Officer Thrasher and Savage, he proceeded expeditiously: within the space of a few minutes, he examined Savage's driver's license and the truck's bill of sale, requested (and was denied) permission to search the truck, stepped on the rear bumper and noted that the truck did not move, confirming his suspicion that it was probably overloaded. He then detected the odor of marihuana. . . .

We reject the contention that a 20-minute stop is unreasonable when the police have acted diligently and a suspect's actions contribute to the added delay about which he complains. The judgment of the Court of Appeals is reversed, and the case is remanded for further proceedings consistent with this opinion.

## DISSENT

BRENNAN, J.

. . . The Framers did not enact the Fourth Amendment to further the investigative powers of the authorities, however, but to curtail them: *Terry*'s exception to the probable-cause safeguard must not be expanded to the point where the constitutionality of a citizen's detention turns only on whether the individual officers were coping as best they could given inadequate training, marginal resources, negligent supervision, or botched communications. Our precedents require more—the demonstration by the Government that it was infeasible to conduct the training, ensure the smooth communications, and commit the sort of resources that would have minimized the intrusions.

The Court today has evaded these requirements, failed even to acknowledge the evidence of bungling, miscommunication, and reasonable investigative alternatives, and pronounced simply that the individual officers "acted diligently." Thus the Court has moved a step or two further in what appears to be "an emerging tendency on the part of the Court to convert the *Terry* decision into a general statement that the Fourth Amendment requires only that any seizure be reasonable," a balancing process in which the judicial thumb apparently will be planted firmly on the law enforcement side of the scales.

Justice Douglas, the lone dissenter in *Terry*, warned that "there have been powerful hydraulic pressures throughout our history that bear heavily on the Court to water down constitutional guarantees and give the police the upper hand." Those hydraulic pressures are readily apparent in the outcome of this case. The Court's . . . breed of decision making breaches faith with our high constitutional duty "to prevent wholesale intrusions upon the personal security of our citizenry." . . .

## Questions

1. Describe what happened during the 30 to 40 minutes the officers detained Sharpe.

2. Explain the court's reasons for concluding the detention satisfied the "brevity" requirement of reasonable stops.

3. According to the dissent, why did the 30- to 40-minute detention not satisfy the brevity requirement?

4. Compare the length of the detention in this case with that of Officer McFadden's detention of Terry in *Terry v. Ohio* (excerpted earlier). In your opinion, was the 30- to 40-minute detention reasonable based on *Terry*? Back up your answer with facts and arguments from the opinions in *Terry* and in this case.

5. Should there be a bright-line 20-minute duration rule? Defend your answer.

***"On the Spot" Investigation*** Before *Terry v. Ohio* (1968), whenever a law enforcement officer moved a suspect to another place, it was an "arrest," requiring probable cause to back it up. For example, the court in one case ruled that taking the suspect to a police call box less than a block away was an arrest (*U.S. v. Mitchell* 1959). But today officers are allowed some leeway. According to search and seizure expert, Professor Wayne R. LaFave (2004), often quoted in criminal procedure cases, "*some* movement of the suspect in the *vicinity* of the stop is permissible without converting what would otherwise be a . . . [stop] into an arrest" (4:348). Recall that Officer McFadden moved Terry, Chilton, and Katz into the nearest store, and the Court didn't question this move. According to the court in *People v. Courtney* (1970):

> No exact formula exists for determining reasonableness; each case must be decided on the facts and circumstances presented to the officers at the time they were required to act. We note that an otherwise permissible detention of a person for investigation is clearly not restricted to the precise point of accostation. It is proper in such a case for the police to require one to step out of an automobile, or to "step back to the police vehicle." It is common and, so far as we know, accepted practice to continue questioning of a suspect in a nearby police car. And it has been held not per se unreasonable to take a person under investigation "to the police station . . . for further investigation."

However, it's *not* reasonable to take someone down to the station (*Hayes v. Florida* 1985) for further investigation, unless there's an emergency, as the California Court of Appeals concluded there was in our next case excerpt, *People v. Courtney* (1970).

**Is Taking a Suspect to a Police Station for Questioning a Reasonable Stop?**

## People v. Courtney
90 Cal.Rptr. 370 (Cal.App.3d 1970)

### HISTORY

Jack Courtney, Defendant, was convicted in the Superior Court, Santa Clara County, John S. McInerny, J., of possession of marijuana, and he appealed from an order placing him on probation. The Court of Appeal affirmed.

ELKINGTON, J.

### FACTS

George Bruschi was employed as a police officer by Stanford University, a private educational institution. During midafternoon of December 1, 1968, he was on mobile patrol in a residential area which was the private property of the university. There had been an alarming number of crimes in the area. The officer had had an "extreme" amount of trouble there, including burglaries and indecent exposures.

The home of the university's president was nearby and he had personally been threatened. His office had been fire bombed and gasoline had been found in his garage. There had been other threats of bombings and actual bombings on the university grounds. Another problem was "a run of people stealing women's underclothing" from clotheslines. The university's police were advised to "be cautious."

Officer Bruschi observed defendant Jack Courtney walking through the area. He was dressed in unusual garb and when he saw the uniformed officer he turned his head away "kind of like to avoid me." Courtney appeared to be a stranger to the neighborhood so the officer pulled up to "ascertain if he had business" and identification. Courtney showed a draft card in his name and said he was going to a certain residence. The occupant of the residence to which he said he was going was known by the officer to have a police record.

The officer "felt it was necessary" to investigate further so he told Courtney "that I was going to run a check through police radio to further his identification." The officer testified, "And at that time before I even had a chance—I just had my hand on the receiver of the police radio—he stated he had no driver's license because it was revoked for hit and run; (that he had been) busted for dope, whatever that meant and also carrying a concealed .38 weapon on his person."

At that point the officer observed an unusual "bulge" under Courtney's jacket, and felt concern for his safety. He called for assistance over the police radio. Asked what the bulge was, Courtney replied that it was none of the officer's business because he was not under arrest. Officer Bruschi then reached out toward the bulge "to possibly identify by the feel if it could be a weapon." But Courtney pulled back; the officer couldn't "get a good enough feel of the thing" except that it felt firm—"rather hard." At one time Courtney pulled out the object briefly and said, "Here it is" and quickly replaced it in his pocket. The object was a bag but its contents could not be seen.

In the meantime another officer arrived and a crowd of 18 to 20 people had gathered. Further inquiry as to the nature of the bulge was futile, Courtney insisting, "he was not under arrest, and he did not have to reveal what was in his pocket." Since other officers had had trouble with crowds while making "investigations on the campus," Officer Bruschi told Courtney he "was going to hold him for further investigation because there was a crowd gathering on the corner. For both our welfare—"; he felt "it was common sense to get us both off the street." He further testified: "I told him that I would have to transport him to the Stanford Police Station for further interrogation because there was a crowd gathering, and I felt it wasn't common sense to stay out there at that intersection any longer than we had already been."

Officer Sanguinetti who had responded to the radio call testified: "I arrived there, and I got out of my vehicle, and Officer Bruschi came to me and said, 'I have a problem here that I'd like you to stand by with me for a few minutes.' " I said, "All right." I said, "What seems to be the trouble?" He said, "Well, this fellow has got something concealed under his coat." I stated, "Did you ask him what it was?" And he said, "Yes, but he won't tell me." And I said—well, I believe I addressed the defendant then—I said, "Son, what do you have under your coat?" And he said, "You will have to arrest me before I show you. . . ."

I was standing behind the defendant off to the side where I could watch him because we thought he had a dangerous weapon or something on him, which Officer Bruschi said that he told him that he had been in trouble before. And also hit run with something to do with narcotics. And so with this bulge under this pea coat, we presumed it could be possibly a dangerous weapon. . . . We had to keep watching him, make sure he wasn't going to produce a weapon. . . .

We finally decided we weren't getting anywhere with the young fellow; so Officer Bruschi said, "We are going to have to take you to the Stanford Police Department and continue this," because there was a crowd of people gathering, and on Stanford a crowd of people can sometimes be hostile to police; let's face it. . . .

Both officers testified that Courtney was not under arrest at this point.

## OPINION

It is now established law "that circumstances short of probable cause to make an arrest may still justify an officer's stopping pedestrians or motorists on the streets for questioning. . . ." Because of the stranger's paucity of identification and his statement that he was headed for the home of one known to have a police record, the officer's decision to detain him while he ran a radio check was proper. . . . In the meantime a large and apparently hostile crowd had gathered.

The issue seems to narrow to whether an adjournment of the investigation and weapon search to the university police station would have been unreasonable and therefore violative of Fourth Amendment standards. If so, then any evidence resulting from a threat to do so would be constitutionally inadmissible.

No exact formula exists for determining reasonableness; each case must be decided on the facts and circumstances presented to the officers at the time they were required to act. We note that an otherwise permissible detention of a person for investigation is clearly not restricted to the precise point of accostation. It is proper in such a case for the police to require one to step out of an automobile, or to "step back to the police vehicle." It is common and, so far as we know, accepted practice to continue questioning of a suspect in a nearby police car. And it has been held not per se unreasonable to take a person under investigation "to the police station . . . for further investigation."

A recapitulation of the totality of "facts and circumstances" here presented to the officers is helpful. They observed a person in a private (university) community who apparently had no business there. The area had been the scene of much crime and violence including bombing and threats of bombing. Without constitutional infringement they learned that the person had a police record for "hit and run" driving, narcotics violation, and carrying a concealed

.38 caliber weapon. They were refused an opportunity to determine the contents of a bag which caused a bulge in the suspect's clothing.

Under the circumstances the police could reasonably suspect that it contained a weapon, or even explosives which today may take a wide variety of shapes and consistencies. Further investigation would obviously require some force which if used on the street would probably antagonize a growing and apparently hostile crowd of bystanders.

Certainly there was no Fourth Amendment compulsion on the police to choose between an on-the-spot continuation of their investigation at the probable cost of their own safety, or abandoning the investigation, thus allowing the suspect to continue his mission, whatever it might be, without further inquiry. We recognize that it is only in a rare case where, absent probable cause for arrest, the removal of a suspect to a police station for further investigation is constitutionally permissible. Nevertheless we are constrained to hold, and we do hold, that under the totality of facts and circumstances here known to the police, it was reasonable for them to remove Courtney to the university police station for that purpose. The Fourth Amendment test of reasonableness has been met. . . .

AFFIRMED.

## Questions

1. State the facts and circumstances that backed up Officers Sanguinetti and Bruschi's decision to take Jack Courtney to the station for further investigation.

2. State the court's test for deciding whether the officers' decision was consistent with the on-the-spot rule.

3. Summarize the court's reasons for ruling the decision didn't violate the Fourth Amendment.

4. Do you agree with the court's decision? Defend your answer.

# FRISKS AND THE FOURTH AMENDMENT

*Protective search*

The U.S. Supreme Court in *Minnesota v. Dickerson* (1993) summarized the power to frisk this way:

> *Terry* . . . held that "when an officer is justified in believing that the individual whose suspicious behavior he is investigating at close range is armed and presently dangerous to the officer or to others," the officer may conduct a patdown search to determine whether the person is in fact carrying a weapon.
>
> The purpose of this limited search is not to discover evidence of crime, but to allow the officer to pursue his investigation without fear of violence. . . . A protective search—permitted without a warrant and on the basis of reasonable suspicion less than probable

| TABLE 4.5 | Elements of a Lawful Frisk |

1. Officers must have a reasonable suspicion a crime may be afoot *before* stopping a suspect.
2. Officers must have reasonable suspicion the suspect may be armed.
3. Officers may do a once-over-lightly pat down to detect weapons only (not contraband or evidence).

cause—must be strictly limited to that which is necessary for the discovery of weapons which might be used to harm the officer or others nearby. If the protective search goes beyond what is necessary to determine if the suspect is armed, it is no longer valid under *Terry* and its fruits will be suppressed. (373)

Frisks are the least invasive searches; body-cavity searches stand at the other extreme (Chapter 7). However, to say that frisks are the least invasive doesn't mean they're not invasions of privacy. After all, even a slight touch, when it's not wanted, can be highly offensive, not to mention the crime of battery. So it's not surprising that, since *Terry*, the U.S. Supreme Court has never wavered from calling frisks Fourth Amendment searches. Table 4.5 summarizes the elements of a lawful frisk.

Whether a frisk is reasonable depends on balancing the government's interest in criminal law enforcement against the individual's privacy right not to be touched by an officer. The basic idea is that we shouldn't expect police officers to risk their lives unnecessarily to investigate suspicious persons and circumstances. At the same time, we have to obey the Fourth Amendment command to keep people "secure in their persons" against unreasonable searches.

The U.S. Sixth Circuit Court of Appeals in our next excerpt, *U.S. v. McCargo* (2006), struck the balance in favor of protecting officers over the invasion of Dustin McCargo's privacy in a frisk based on a Buffalo, New York, police department rule requiring officers to "pat down all persons before placing them in the back of a police car" (196).

C A S E    *Did Officer Safety Trump Dustin McCargo's Privacy?*

### U.S. v. McCargo
464 F.3d 192 (CA2 N.Y. 2006)

### HISTORY

Dustin McCargo, Defendant, was charged with possession of a firearm by a convicted felon. The United States District Court for the Western District of New York, John T. Elfvin, J., adopting recommendations of H. Kenneth Schroeder, Jr., United States Magistrate Judge, held that initial stop and detention of defendant was constitutional, but granted defendant's motion to exclude gun found during pat-down of defendant. Defendant and government appealed. Reversed and remanded.

WALKER, C.J.

Defendant-appellee-cross-appellant Dustin L. McCargo ("defendant" or "McCargo") was stopped by the Buffalo

Police on July 28, 2003, blocks from a reported attempted burglary. The officers decided to take McCargo back to the scene of the alleged crime to see if the victim could identify him. Because the officers planned to transport him in the back of their patrol car, they frisked him for weapons in accordance with a departmental policy. During the frisk, the officers discovered a handgun. McCargo was arrested and later charged in federal court with possession of a firearm by a convicted felon. See 18 U.S.C. §§ 922(g)(1), 924(a)(2).

McCargo moved to suppress the gun. He argued that the frisk of his person, without a reasonable suspicion that he was armed, violated his Fourth Amendment rights. The district court agreed and suppressed the gun. It held that the initial stop and detention of McCargo was constitutional but that the officers were not permitted to frisk him unless they had a reasonable suspicion that he was armed. The government appealed, and McCargo, claiming error in the district court's holding that the initial stop was constitutional, cross-appealed.

## FACTS

At 12:53 A.M. on July 28, 2003, the 911 operator for the Buffalo Police Department was told by a caller from 501 Berkshire Avenue that someone was attempting to break into his residence. The only additional details the caller provided were that more than one person was trying to enter the house and that some of the perpetrators had gone around to the back of the house. Based on this 911 call, a Buffalo Police dispatcher transmitted a radio message to patrol cars in the area of 501 Berkshire Avenue.

Buffalo Police officers Sterlace and White were in a patrol car less than two blocks from 501 Berkshire when they received the radio transmission. They then proceeded eastbound on Berkshire. As they came to the intersection of Berkshire and Suffolk Street, the officers saw McCargo crossing Berkshire and continuing to walk north on the east side of Suffolk. The residence at 501 Berkshire is located on the south side of Berkshire, approximately 200 feet to the east of the intersection. The officers testified that as McCargo was walking north he was staring intently to his right at another patrol car that had already arrived at 501 Berkshire, so intently in fact that he did not notice Sterlace and White's car as the officers approached him.

The officers turned left onto Suffolk, drew along side the defendant, and told him to stop and approach the car. Sterlace testified that he wanted to detain McCargo to take him back to 501 Berkshire for possible identification by the victim. Both officers then left their car, and Sterlace patted down the defendant. White testified that it was departmental policy to pat down all persons before placing them in the back of a police car to protect the officers' safety.

While patting down McCargo, Sterlace felt a gun in McCargo's waistband. McCargo jumped away from Sterlace, and the gun became lodged in McCargo's sweatshirt and eventually fell to the ground. McCargo was placed under arrest and taken to police headquarters. A total of two minutes and thirty-eight seconds elapsed between the time the officers advised dispatch that they were proceeding to the scene and the time of the arrest. Because the officers responded to the dispatch call at most three minutes after the initial 911 call, less than six minutes elapsed between the time the 911 call was placed and the time of McCargo's arrest.

A federal grand jury indicted McCargo for the possession of a firearm by a convicted felon. (18 U.S.C. §§ 922(g)(1), 924(a)(2)). After McCargo moved to suppress the gun as the product of an unconstitutional search, the motion was referred to a magistrate judge who found that the police had reasonable suspicion to stop McCargo, based on his location near the scene of the crime in a high-crime area very soon after the 911 call. The magistrate judge determined, however, that the pat-down was unconstitutional because the officers had no suspicion that McCargo was armed and recommended that the gun be suppressed. The U.S. District Court adopted the magistrate judge's recommendations. The government appealed pursuant to 18 U.S.C. § 3731, and McCargo filed a cross-appeal.

## OPINION

. . . This case requires us to deal with three Fourth Amendment questions: (1) whether the initial stop and brief detention of McCargo by the police was constitutional under *Terry*; (2) whether the police were entitled, as part of the *Terry* stop, to transport McCargo to the scene of the crime to see if an identification could be made by the victim; and (3) whether the police were entitled to pat down McCargo before transporting him to the crime scene in a police car. We review de novo each of these legal questions. For the weapon to be admissible against McCargo, each question must be answered in the affirmative.

### II. The Initial *Terry* Stop

[*The court held that the stop was lawful.*]

### III. Transportation to the Scene of the Crime

[*The court ruled that putting McCargo in the police car in order to transport to the scene of the crime didn't exceed the reasonable scope of the stop.*]

### IV. The Frisk

The officers patted down McCargo preparatory to placing him in the police car to transport him to the crime scene and, in so doing, found the handgun that formed the basis for the charges against him and that McCargo wants suppressed. *Terry* itself specifically authorized a pat-down where, following a stop, the officers believed that the person detained was armed.

The pat-down here, however, was pursuant to a policy of the Buffalo Police Department that required pat-downs before transporting any person in a police car to ensure officer safety. Thus, the question we must answer is whether a suspect may be frisked in certain circumstances as part of a *Terry* stop without officers' relying on a reasonable suspicion that he is armed. The answer requires an examination of *Terry* and its progeny as well as those cases in which the Fourth Amendment permits suspicionless searches or seizures. The fundamental command of the Fourth Amendment is that governmental intrusions on persons be reasonable, and, as *Terry* explained, the "limitations [on protective searches and seizures] will have to be developed in the concrete factual circumstances of individual cases." . . .

An interest in officer safety has been the justification for *Terry* stops from their inception. Our examination of *Terry*'s progeny reaffirms this conclusion. The lesson we take from these cases is that the strictures of the Fourth Amendment must not be so burdensome as to impose unreasonable and avoidable risks on police officers during their investigations.

In the typical *Terry* stop, we have no doubt that the powers the police possess over the suspect, including the power to order the suspect to move to a more convenient or safer location, adequately protect the important state interest in the safety of police officers and others. There are important differences, however, between the typical *Terry* stop where the suspect is detained on the street and this case where the suspect is to be transported in the back of a patrol car. In the typical case on the street, the officers have the ability to terminate the stop or arrest the suspect at any moment and to control the location of the stop to minimize the danger the suspect poses to the police and others.

The transportation of the suspect in the back of a police car as part of the *Terry* stop is markedly different. The officers are less able to protect themselves from the possibility of violence. The officers cannot depart or remove themselves temporarily from the situation and call in additional officers as backup. The suspect and the officers are in close proximity to each other for the duration of the transportation; the suspect sits behind them, a few feet away in the rear of the car, frequently separated by only a wire grate. And the suspect is not subject to the officers' immediate physical control or restraint: if the suspect turns out to be armed, the police are at his mercy.

In sum, we think the dangers posed to police officers in situations where a suspect, who may be armed, is placed in the rear of a police car are substantially different and greater than those posed in the typical *Terry* stop. The increased threat to police safety informs the balance to be struck between the safety interests of the police and the privacy interests of individuals. For what the Constitution forbids is not all searches and seizures, but unreasonable searches and seizures.

Permitting a limited frisk for weapons before placing a suspect in a police car, pursuant to an established policy, reflects an appropriate balancing of the interests at stake. Because the suspect is placed in the rear of the car—a location where, were he armed, he would expose the officers to peril—we think the most reasonable, and least intrusive, solution is to permit a pat-down for weapons. The possibility of danger to the officers can be eliminated simply by ensuring that the suspect does not have a weapon that can be used against them.

The justification for the pat-down is not that the suspect is reasonably suspected of being armed; it is rather a matter of sound police administration: police officers should be certain before transporting members of the public, whom they do not know, that none of them is armed. The administrative nature of the search is evidenced by the existence of the Buffalo Police's department-wide policy that requires the pat-down whenever a person is transported in a police car. The fact that the policy is administrative and

universally applied to all who are transported eliminates any selective-use concern.

Courts have long upheld suspicionless searches conducted under an official policy as not violative of the Fourth Amendment. Although the reasonableness balance differs following an arrest, permitting greater intrusion, post-arrest administrative searches are justified, not by probable cause or suspicion, but by the same safety rationale applicable in this case.

Arrested persons have also been known to injure themselves—or others—with belts, knives, drugs or other dangerous items on their person while being detained. Dangerous instrumentalities—such as razor blades, bombs, or weapons—can be concealed in innocent-looking articles taken from the arrestee's possession. The bare recital of these mundane realities justifies reasonable measures by police to limit these risks. . . .

Our holding in this case is a narrow one. We are not holding that the police are entitled to pat down a person, absent reasonable suspicion that he is armed, simply because they have stopped that person pursuant to a lawful *Terry* stop. However, in cases where the police may lawfully transport a suspect to the scene of the crime in the rear of a police car, the police may carry out a departmental policy, imposed for reasons of officer safety, by patting down that person. Because the police must have a legitimate law-enforcement reason to transport a suspect, we see little danger that policies such as these might be used as a pretext for a suspicionless frisk.

Applying these rules to this case is now straightforward. We have already said that McCargo was lawfully stopped and that the police were entitled to transport McCargo to the scene of the crime. The officers testified, and the district court found, that the officers frisked McCargo pursuant to a generally applicable police policy that required all persons placed in patrol cars to be frisked. There are no allegations, much less proof, of bad faith or pretext on the part of the police. Therefore, the frisk of McCargo was constitutional, and the judgment of the district court should be REVERSED.

## Questions

1. List the invasions of Dustin McCargo's privacy revealed in the facts of the case.

2. Summarize the court's description of the government's interest in the case.

3. Summarize how the court weighed the balance between the government's interest in protecting the Buffalo officers' safety and McCargo's privacy.

4. State the court's holding, and explain how, according to the court, the holding was narrow.

5. How would you balance the interests in the case? Explain your answer.

Let's turn from the important question of balancing to the answers to two other critical questions regarding frisks: (1) What's reasonable suspicion to frisk? and (2) What's the scope of lawful frisks? (See Table 4.5 for the elements of lawful frisks.)

## Reasonable Suspicion to Back Up Frisks

*Terry v. Ohio* established that facts that back up a stop don't *automatically* also back up a frisk—with one major exception, when suspects are stopped for crimes of violence. The facts of *Terry* are an excellent example of the **violent crime–automatic frisk exception**. Officer McFadden reasonably suspected that Terry and Chilton might be about to commit armed robbery. If it was reasonable to suspect that they might be about to commit armed robbery, it was also reasonable to suspect they might use weapons to commit it. So it was reasonable to frisk Terry and his companions for weapons.

In nonviolent crimes, the rule is that the circumstances must add up to a reasonable suspicion that stopped suspects may be armed. In practice, however, police frequently are told to assume that "every person encountered may be armed" (LaFave 2004, 624). And lower courts take the position that the power to frisk in a wide variety of situations and circumstances is automatic

> whenever the suspect has been stopped on suspicion . . . [of] a crime for which the suspect may be armed, whether the weapon would be used to actually commit the crime, to escape if the scheme went awry, or for protection against the victim or others involved. (625)

Courts have held that automatic frisks are reasonable in such crimes as robbery in *Terry*, burglary, rape, assault with weapons, and dealing in large quantities of illegal drugs (625–26). Other offenses require specific facts suggesting suspects are armed. Table 4.6 lists some of the offenses courts have held don't justify automatic frisks.

Table 4.7 lists some of the many circumstances that courts have ruled justify frisks in crimes that don't qualify for automatic frisks.

Some critics claim that the lower courts have weakened the reasonable suspicion requirement so much that, in practice, the power to frisk is left almost entirely to law enforcement officers' discretion. In other words, the power to frisk, in practice, requires no separate reasonable suspicion that suspects may be armed and dangerous. Instead, it follows automatically from the lawful stop. According to Professor David Harris (1998),

| TABLE 4.6 | Examples of Circumstances That Don't Justify Automatic Frisks |
|---|---|

| | |
|---|---|
| • Trafficking in small amounts of illegal drugs | • Passing bad checks |
| • Possession of marijuana | • Underage drinking |
| • Illegal possession of alcohol | • Driving under the influence |
| • Prostitution | • Minor assault without a weapon |
| • Bookmaking | • Curfew violation |
| • Shoplifting | • Vagrancy |

Source: LaFave 2004, 626–27.

| TABLE 4.7 | Circumstances That Justify Frisks |

| | |
|---|---|
| • Sudden inexplicable movement toward a pocket | • Awareness of suspect's previous serious criminal conduct |
| • Inexplicable failure to remove a hand from a pocket | • Awareness suspect had been armed previously |
| • Awkward movement in an apparent effort to conceal something | • Awareness of suspect's recent aggressive behavior |
| • Backing away from an officer | • Discovery suspect possessed another weapon |
| • Bulge in clothing | • Discovery suspect is wearing a bulletproof vest |

*Source:* LaFave 2004, 628–30.

one of the leading critics of the automatic power to frisk, his reading of the cases indicates that:

> Lower courts have consistently expanded the *types of offenses* always considered violent regardless of the individual circumstances. . . . When confronted with these offenses . . . , police may *automatically* frisk, whether or not any individualized circumstances point to danger. Soon, *anyone* stopped by police may have to undergo a physical search at the officer's discretion, however benign the circumstances of the encounter or the conduct of the "suspect." (5)

## The Scope of Reasonable Frisks

The same day the Supreme Court decided *Terry v. Ohio*, it decided *Sibron v. New York* (1968), another important but less-publicized case. In *Sibron*, the Court emphatically rejected New York's argument that after a lawful stop an automatic frisk for evidence and contraband was lawful. Why? Because, according to the Court, frisks are so intrusive that only the enormous interest in saving officers from "armed and dangerous" suspects who might wound or kill them justifies the invasion of a frisk during the brief "freeze" of a stop to investigate suspicious people and circumstances.

No matter how compelling the government's interest in protecting officers from armed and dangerous suspects is, they're allowed to use only the amount of bodily contact necessary to detect weapons. In most cases, this means officers may lightly touch suspects' outer clothing to locate and seize concealed weapons. Courts are vague about how much further police officers may lawfully go. Table 4.8 cites examples of when it may be permissible for officers to go further than pat downs of outer clothing.

In our next case excerpt, *Minnesota v. Dickerson*, the U.S. Supreme Court held that a Minneapolis police officer went too far when during a lawful frisk for weapons he rolled around a lump between his fingers to determine whether it was a rock of crack cocaine.

| TABLE 4.8 | Examples That Justify a Scope of Frisk of More Than an Outer-Clothing Pat-Down |

- Feeling a hard object inside a coat pocket that could be a weapon authorizes reaching inside the coat.
- Encountering unusually bulky winter clothing may require feeling underneath the outer clothing.
- Suspecting the contents of a closed handbag may be illegal can justify opening the handbag.

# Was the Discovery of Crack Cocaine within the Lawful Scope of the Frisk?

## Minnesota v. Dickerson
### 508 U.S. 366 (1993)

### HISTORY

After the Hennepin County District Court in Minnesota denied his motion to suppress the seizure of crack cocaine, Timothy Dickerson, Respondent, was convicted of possession of crack cocaine and sentenced to two years probation. He appealed. The Minnesota Court of Appeals reversed. The State appealed. The Minnesota Supreme Court affirmed. The U.S. Supreme Court granted the State's petition for certiorari, and affirmed the Minnesota Supreme Court.

WHITE, J.

In this case, we consider whether the Fourth Amendment permits the seizure of contraband detected through a police officer's sense of touch during a protective patdown search.

### FACTS

On the evening of November 9, 1989, two Minneapolis police officers were patrolling an area on the city's north side in a marked squad car. At about 8:15 P.M., one of the officers observed respondent leaving a 12-unit apartment building on Morgan Avenue North. The officer, having previously responded to complaints of drug sales in the building's hallways and having executed several search warrants on the premises, considered the building to be a notorious "crack house."

According to testimony credited by the trial court, respondent began walking toward the police but, upon spotting the squad car and making eye contact with one of the officers, abruptly halted and began walking in the opposite direction. His suspicion aroused, this officer watched as respondent turned and entered an alley on the other side of the apartment building. Based upon respondent's seemingly evasive actions and the fact that he had just left a building known for cocaine traffic, the officers decided to stop respondent and investigate further.

The officers pulled their squad car into the alley and ordered respondent to stop and submit to a patdown search. The search revealed no weapons, but the officer conducting the search did take an interest in a small lump in respondent's nylon jacket. The officer later testified:

> As I pat-searched the front of his body, I felt a lump, a small lump, in the front pocket. I examined it with my fingers and it slid and it felt to be a lump of crack cocaine in cellophane.

The officer then reached into respondent's pocket and retrieved a small plastic bag containing one fifth of one gram of crack cocaine. Respondent was arrested and charged in Hennepin County District Court with possession of a controlled substance.

Before trial, respondent moved to suppress the cocaine. The trial court first concluded that the officers were justified under *Terry v. Ohio* (1968), in stopping respondent to investigate whether he might be engaged in criminal activity. The court further found that the officers were justified in frisking respondent to ensure that he was not carrying a weapon.

Finally, analogizing to the "plain-view" doctrine [discussed in Chapter 3], under which officers may make a warrantless seizure of contraband found in plain view during a lawful search for other items, the trial court ruled that the officers' seizure of the cocaine did not violate the Fourth Amendment . . .

His suppression motion having failed, respondent proceeded to trial and was found guilty. On appeal, the Minnesota Court of Appeals reversed. The court agreed with the trial court that the investigative stop and protective patdown search of respondent were lawful under *Terry* because the officers had a reasonable belief based on specific and articulable facts that respondent was engaged in criminal behavior and that he might be armed and dangerous. The court concluded, however, that the officers had overstepped the bounds allowed by *Terry* in seizing the cocaine. In doing so, the Court of Appeals "declined to adopt the plain feel exception" to the warrant requirement.

The Minnesota Supreme Court affirmed. Like the Court of Appeals, the State Supreme Court held that both the stop and the frisk of respondent were valid under *Terry*, but found the seizure of the cocaine to be unconstitutional. The court expressly refused "to extend the plain view doctrine to the sense of touch" on the grounds that "the sense of touch is inherently less immediate and less reliable than the sense of sight" and that "the sense of touch is far more intrusive into the personal privacy that is at the core of the Fourth Amendment." The court thus appeared to adopt a categorical rule barring the seizure of any contraband detected by an officer through the sense of touch during a patdown search for weapons. The court further noted that "even if we recognized a 'plain feel' exception, the search in this case would not qualify" because "the pat search of the defendant went far beyond what is permissible under *Terry*." As the State Supreme Court read the record, the officer conducting the search ascertained that the lump in respondent's jacket was contraband only after probing and investigating what he certainly knew was not a weapon.

We granted certiorari to resolve a conflict among the state and federal courts over whether contraband detected through the sense of touch during a patdown search may be admitted into evidence. We now AFFIRM.

## OPINION

. . . *Terry* . . . held that "when an officer is justified in believing that the individual whose suspicious behavior he is investigating at close range is armed and presently dangerous to the officer or to others," the officer may conduct a patdown search to determine whether the person is in fact carrying a weapon. The purpose of this limited search is not to discover evidence of crime, but to allow the officer to pursue his investigation without fear of violence. . . . A protective search—permitted without a warrant and on the basis of reasonable suspicion less than probable cause—must be strictly "limited to that which is necessary for the discovery of weapons which might be used to harm the officer or others nearby. If the protective search goes beyond what is necessary to determine if the suspect is armed, it is no longer valid under *Terry* and its fruits will be suppressed.

. . . The question presented today is whether police officers may seize nonthreatening contraband detected during a protective patdown search of the sort permitted by *Terry*. We think the answer is clearly that they may, so long as the officers' search stays within the bounds marked by *Terry*. . . .

[*The Court held that "touch" is part of the "plain view" doctrine discussed in Chapter 3.*]

It remains to apply these principles to the facts of this case. Respondent has not challenged the finding made by the trial court and affirmed by both the Court of Appeals and the State Supreme Court that the police were justified under *Terry* in stopping him and frisking him for weapons. Thus, the dispositive question before this Court is whether the officer who conducted the search was acting within the lawful bounds marked by *Terry* at the time he gained probable cause to believe that the lump in respondent's jacket was contraband.

The State District Court did not make precise findings on this point, instead finding simply that the officer, after feeling "a small, hard object wrapped in plastic" in respondent's pocket, "formed the opinion that the object . . . was crack . . . cocaine." The District Court also noted that the officer made "no claim that he suspected this object to be a weapon," a finding affirmed on appeal (the officer "never thought the lump was a weapon"). The Minnesota Supreme Court, after "a close examination of the record," held that the officer's own testimony "belies any notion that he 'immediately' " recognized the lump as crack cocaine. Rather, the court concluded, the officer determined that the lump was contraband only after "squeezing, sliding and otherwise manipulating the contents of the defendant's pocket"— a pocket which the officer already knew contained no weapon.

Under the State Supreme Court's interpretation of the record before it, it is clear that the court was correct in holding that the police officer in this case overstepped the bounds of the "strictly circumscribed" search for weapons allowed under *Terry*. . . . Here, the officer's continued exploration of respondent's pocket after having concluded that it contained no weapon was unrelated to "the sole justification of the search [under *Terry*:] . . . the protection of the police officer and others nearby." It therefore amounted to the sort of evidentiary search that *Terry* expressly refused to authorize, and that we have condemned in subsequent cases.

. . . In *Arizona v. Hicks*, this Court held invalid the seizure of stolen stereo equipment found by police while executing a valid search for other evidence. Although the police were lawfully on the premises, they obtained probable cause to believe that the stereo equipment was contraband only after moving the equipment to permit officers to read its serial numbers. The subsequent seizure of the equipment could not be justified by the plain-view doctrine, this Court explained, because the incriminating character of the stereo equipment was not immediately apparent; rather, probable cause to believe that the equipment was stolen arose only as a result of a further search—the moving of the equipment—that was not authorized by a search warrant or by any exception to the warrant requirement.

The facts of this case are very similar. Although the officer was lawfully in a position to feel the lump in respondent's pocket, because *Terry* entitled him to place his hands upon respondent's jacket, the court below determined that the incriminating character of the object was not immediately apparent to him. Rather, the officer determined that the item was contraband only after conducting a further search, one not authorized by *Terry* or by any other exception to the warrant requirement. Because this further search of respondent's pocket was constitutionally invalid, the seizure of the cocaine that followed is likewise unconstitutional.

For these reasons, the judgment of the Minnesota Supreme Court is AFFIRMED.

## CONCURRING OPINION

### SCALIA, J.

I take it to be a fundamental principle of constitutional adjudication that the terms in the Constitution must be given the meaning ascribed to them at the time of their ratification. . . . Thus, when the Fourth Amendment provides that "the right of the people to be secure in their persons, houses, papers, and effects, against *unreasonable searches and seizures*, shall not be violated" [emphasis added], it is to be construed in the light of what was deemed an unreasonable search and seizure when it was adopted. The purpose of the provision, in other words, is to preserve that degree of respect for the privacy of persons and the inviolability of their property that existed when the provision was adopted—even if a later, less virtuous age should become accustomed to considering all sorts of intrusion "reasonable."

My problem with the present case is that I am not entirely sure that the physical search—the "frisk"—that produced the evidence at issue here complied with that constitutional standard. . . .

I am unaware . . . of any precedent for a physical search of a person . . . temporarily detained for questioning. . . . I frankly doubt, moreover, whether the fiercely proud men who adopted our Fourth Amendment would have allowed themselves to be subjected, on mere *suspicion* of being armed and dangerous, to such indignity—which is described as follows in a police manual:

Check the subject's neck and collar. A check should be made under the subject's arm. Next a check should be made of the upper back. The lower back should also be checked.

A check should be made of the upper part of the man's chest and the lower region around the stomach. The belt, a favorite concealment spot, should be checked. The inside thigh and crotch area also should be searched. The legs should be checked for possible weapons. The last items to be checked are the shoes and cuffs of the subject. . . .

### Questions

1. Describe exactly the frisk of Dickerson conducted by the Minneapolis police officer.
2. State the test the U.S. Supreme Court applied to determine whether the frisk was within the scope of a lawful frisk.
3. Summarize Justice White's reasons for deciding the frisk exceeded its lawful scope.
4. Summarize Justice Scalia's reasons for agreeing with the Court's conclusion that the scope of the frisk was unreasonable.
5. In your opinion, should the frisk be considered reasonable?
6. Even if the frisk exceeded the permissible scope, should it be legal to seize the crack?

Still, the Court has made it clear that it's not *always* unreasonable to seize evidence and contraband during a frisk. Suppose an officer is patting down a suspect who was stopped lawfully and is reasonably suspected of being armed. She pats down the suspect and comes upon marijuana. Can she seize it? Yes, as long as the frisk for weapons isn't a pretext for looking for marijuana.

# SPECIAL SITUATION STOPS AND FRISKS

In this last section, we'll look at the power of officers to freeze situations briefly to check out their suspicions that a crime "may be afoot." They include (1) removing passengers from stopped vehicles; (2) detaining suspects at international borders; and (3) setting up checkpoints and roadblocks.

## Removing Passengers from Stopped Vehicles

What happens if an officer lawfully stops an individual but lacks reason to suspect the stopped person is armed? Is she banned from taking any action to protect herself? No, at least not when the stop involves vehicles. In *Pennsylvania v. Mimms* (1977), the Supreme Court ruled that when an officer lawfully stops a vehicle, without any reason to suspect the driver is armed, the officer can demand that the driver get out of the car to reduce "the possibility, otherwise substantial that the driver can make unobserved movements" (111). Removing the driver from the car is a "trivial invasion" because the driver is already stopped. Balancing the possible danger to the officer clearly outweighs the trivial invasion of removing the driver from the car.

But is it a trivial invasion to order *passengers* (who officers don't suspect of any wrongdoing) out of the car while officers sort out their suspicions of the driver? Yes, said the U.S. Supreme Court in our next case excerpt, *Maryland v. Wilson* (1997).

# CASE

## *Was the Order to Get Out of the Car Reasonable?*

### Maryland v. Wilson
### 519 U.S. 408 (1997)

### HISTORY

Jerry Lee Wilson, Respondent, moved to suppress crack cocaine seized by a police officer during a traffic stop. The trial court granted the motion. The State appealed. The Maryland Court of Special Appeals affirmed. The Maryland Court of Appeals denied certiorari. The U.S. Supreme Court granted certiorari and reversed and remanded the case.

REHNQUIST, C.J., JOINED BY O'CONNOR, SCALIA, SOUTER, THOMAS, GINSBURG, AND BREYER, JJ.

### FACTS

At about 7:30 P.M. on a June evening, Maryland state trooper David Hughes observed a passenger car driving southbound on I-95 in Baltimore County at a speed of 64 miles per hour. The posted speed limit was 55 miles per hour, and the car had no regular license tag; there was a torn piece of paper reading "Enterprise Rent-A-Car" dangling from its rear. Hughes activated his lights and sirens, signaling the car to pull over, but it continued driving for another mile and a half until it finally did so.

During the pursuit, Hughes noticed there were three occupants in the car and that the two passengers turned to look at him several times, repeatedly ducking below sight level and then reappearing. As Hughes approached the car on foot, the driver alighted and met him halfway. The driver was trembling and appeared extremely nervous, but nonetheless produced a valid Connecticut driver's license.

Hughes instructed him to return to the car and retrieve the rental documents, and he complied. During this encounter, Hughes noticed that the front-seat passenger, Jerry Lee Wilson (the respondent), was sweating and also appeared extremely nervous. While the driver was sitting in the driver's seat looking for the rental papers, Hughes ordered Wilson out of the car.

When Wilson exited the car, a quantity of crack cocaine fell to the ground. Wilson was then arrested and charged with possession of cocaine with intent to distribute. Before trial, Wilson moved to suppress the evidence, arguing that Hughes' ordering him out of the car constituted an unreasonable seizure under the Fourth Amendment. The Circuit Court for Baltimore County agreed, and granted respondent's motion to suppress. On appeal, the Court of Special Appeals of Maryland affirmed, ruling that *Pennsylvania v. Mimms* does not apply to passengers. The Court of Appeals of Maryland denied certiorari. We granted certiorari, and now reverse.

### OPINION

In *Mimms*, we considered a traffic stop much like the one before us today. There, Mimms had been stopped for driving with an expired license plate, and the officer asked him to step out of his car. When Mimms did so, the officer noticed a bulge in his jacket that proved to be a .38-caliber revolver, whereupon Mimms was arrested for carrying a concealed deadly weapon.

Mimms, like Wilson, urged the suppression of the evidence on the ground that the officer's ordering him out of the car was an unreasonable seizure, and the Pennsylvania Supreme Court, like the Court of Special Appeals of Maryland, agreed.

We reversed, explaining that "the touchstone of our analysis under the Fourth Amendment is always 'the reasonableness in all the circumstances of the particular governmental invasion of a citizen's personal security,'" and that reasonableness "depends 'on a balance between the public interest and the individual's right to personal security free from arbitrary interference by law officers.'"

On the public interest side of the balance, we noted that the State "freely conceded" that there had been nothing unusual or suspicious to justify ordering Mimms out of the car, but that it was the officer's "practice to order all drivers [stopped in traffic stops] out of their vehicles as a matter of course" as a "precautionary measure" to protect the officer's safety. We thought it "too plain for argument" that this justification—officer safety—was "both legitimate and weighty." In addition, we observed that the danger to the officer of standing by the driver's door and in the path of oncoming traffic might also be "appreciable."

On the other side of the balance, we considered the intrusion into the driver's liberty occasioned by the officer's ordering him out of the car. Noting that the driver's car was already validly stopped for a traffic infraction, we deemed the additional intrusion of asking him to step outside his car "de minimis" [*trivial*]. Accordingly, we concluded that "once a motor vehicle has been lawfully detained for a traffic violation, the police officers may order the driver to get out of the vehicle without violating the Fourth Amendment's proscription of unreasonable seizures." Wilson urges, and the lower courts agreed, that this *per se* rule does not apply to Wilson because he was a passenger, not the driver. . . .

We must therefore now decide whether the rule of *Mimms* applies to passengers as well as to drivers. On the public interest side of the balance, the same weighty interest in officer safety is present regardless of whether the occupant of the stopped car is a driver or passenger. Regrettably, traffic stops may be dangerous encounters. In 1994 alone, there were 5,762 officer assaults and 11 officers killed during traffic pursuits and stops. Federal Bureau of

Investigation, Uniform Crime Reports: Law Enforcement Officers Killed and Assaulted 71, 33 (1994).

In the case of passengers, the danger of the officer's standing in the path of oncoming traffic would not be present except in the case of a passenger in the left rear seat, but the fact that there is more than one occupant of the vehicle increases the possible sources of harm to the officer.

On the personal liberty side of the balance, the case for the passengers is in one sense stronger than that for the driver. There is probable cause to believe that the driver has committed a minor vehicular offense, but there is no such reason to stop or detain the passengers. But as a practical matter, the passengers are already stopped by virtue of the stop of the vehicle. The only change in their circumstances which will result from ordering them out of the car is that they will be outside of, rather than inside of, the stopped car.

Outside the car, the passengers will be denied access to any possible weapon that might be concealed in the interior of the passenger compartment. It would seem that the possibility of a violent encounter stems not from the ordinary reaction of a motorist stopped for a speeding violation, but from the fact that evidence of a more serious crime might be uncovered during the stop. And the motivation of a passenger to employ violence to prevent apprehension of such a crime is every bit as great as that of the driver. . . .

In summary, danger to an officer from a traffic stop is likely to be greater when there are passengers in addition to the driver in the stopped car. While there is not the same basis for ordering the passengers out of the car as there is for ordering the driver out, the additional intrusion on the passenger is minimal. We therefore hold that an officer making a traffic stop may order passengers to get out of the car pending completion of the stop.

The judgment of the Court of Special Appeals of Maryland is reversed, and the case is remanded for proceedings not inconsistent with this opinion. It is so ordered.

## DISSENT

STEVENS, J., JOINED BY KENNEDY, J.

. . . My concern is not with the ultimate disposition of this particular case, but rather with the literally millions of other cases that will be affected by the rule the Court announces.

Though the question is not before us, I am satisfied that—under the rationale of *Terry v. Ohio*—if a police officer conducting a traffic stop has an articulable suspicion of possible danger, the officer may order passengers to exit the vehicle as a defensive tactic without running afoul of the Fourth Amendment. Accordingly, I assume that the facts recited in the majority's opinion provided a valid justification for this officer's order commanding the passengers to get out of this vehicle. But the Court's ruling goes much farther. It applies equally to traffic stops in which there is not even a scintilla of evidence of any potential risk to the police officer. In those cases, I firmly believe that the Fourth Amendment prohibits routine and arbitrary seizures of obviously innocent citizens.

The majority suggests that the personal liberty interest at stake here . . . is outweighed by the need to ensure officer safety. The Court correctly observes that "traffic stops may be dangerous encounters." The magnitude of the danger to police officers is reflected in the statistic that, in 1994 alone, "there were 5,762 officer assaults and 11 officers killed during traffic pursuits and stops." There is, unquestionably, a strong public interest in minimizing the number of such assaults and fatalities. The Court's statistics, however, provide no support for the conclusion that its ruling will have any such effect.

Those statistics do not tell us how many of the incidents involved passengers. Assuming that many of the assaults were committed by passengers, we do not know how many occurred after the passenger got out of the vehicle, how many took place while the passenger remained in the vehicle, or indeed, whether any of them could have been prevented by an order commanding the passengers to exit.

There is no indication that the number of assaults was smaller in jurisdictions where officers may order passengers to exit the vehicle without any suspicion than in jurisdictions where they were then prohibited from doing so.

Indeed, there is no indication that any of the assaults occurred when there was a complete absence of any articulable basis for concern about the officer's safety—the only condition under which I would hold that the Fourth Amendment prohibits an order commanding passengers to exit a vehicle. In short, the statistics are as consistent with the hypothesis that ordering passengers to get out of a vehicle increases the danger of assault as with the hypothesis that it reduces that risk.

Furthermore, any limited additional risk to police officers must be weighed against the unnecessary invasion that will be imposed on innocent citizens under the majority's rule in the tremendous number of routine stops that occur each day. We have long recognized that "because of the extensive regulation of motor vehicles and traffic . . . the extent of police–citizen contact involving automobiles will be substantially greater than police–citizen contact in a home or office." Most traffic stops involve otherwise law abiding citizens who have committed minor traffic offenses. A strong interest in arriving at a destination—to deliver a patient to a hospital, to witness a kick-off, or to get to work on time—will often explain a traffic violation without justifying it. In the aggregate, these stops amount to significant law enforcement activity.

Indeed, the number of stops in which an officer is actually at risk is dwarfed by the far greater number of routine stops. If Maryland's share of the national total is about average, the State probably experiences about 100 officer assaults each year during traffic stops and pursuits. Making the unlikely assumption that passengers are responsible for one-fourth of the total assaults, it appears that the Court's new rule would provide a potential benefit to

Maryland officers in only roughly 25 stops a year. These stops represent a minuscule portion of the total. In Maryland alone, there are something on the order of one million traffic stops each year. Assuming that there are passengers in about half of the cars stopped, the majority's rule is of some possible advantage to police in only about one out of every twenty thousand traffic stops in which there is a passenger in the car. And, any benefit is extremely marginal. In the overwhelming majority of cases posing a real threat, the officer would almost certainly have some ground to suspect danger that would justify ordering passengers out of the car.

In contrast, the potential daily burden on thousands of innocent citizens is obvious. That burden may well be "minimal" in individual cases. But countless citizens who cherish individual liberty and are offended, embarrassed, and sometimes provoked by arbitrary official commands may well consider the burden to be significant. In all events, the aggregation of thousands upon thousands of petty indignities has an impact on freedom that I would characterize as substantial, and which in my view clearly outweighs the evanescent safety concerns pressed by the majority. . . .

To order passengers about during the course of a traffic stop, insisting that they exit and remain outside the car, can hardly be classified as a de minimis intrusion. The traffic violation sufficiently justifies subjecting the driver to detention and some police control for the time necessary to conclude the business of the stop. The restraint on the liberty of blameless passengers that the majority permits is, in contrast, entirely arbitrary.

In my view, wholly innocent passengers in a taxi, bus, or private car have a constitutionally protected right to decide whether to remain comfortably seated within the vehicle rather than exposing themselves to the elements and the observation of curious bystanders. The Constitution should not be read to permit law enforcement officers to order innocent passengers about simply because they have the misfortune to be seated in a car whose driver has committed a minor traffic offense.

Unfortunately, the effect of the Court's new rule on the law may turn out to be far more significant than its immediate impact on individual liberty. Throughout most of our history the Fourth Amendment embodied a general rule requiring that official searches and seizures be authorized by a warrant, issued "upon probable cause, supported by Oath or affirmation, and particularly describing the place to be searched, and the persons or things to be seized." During the prohibition era, the exceptions for warrantless searches supported by probable cause started to replace the general rule.

In 1968, in the landmark "stop and frisk" case *Terry v. Ohio*, the Court placed its stamp of approval on seizures supported by specific and articulable facts that did not establish probable cause. The Court crafted *Terry* as a narrow exception to the general rule that "the police must, whenever practicable, obtain advance judicial approval of searches and seizures through the warrant procedure." The intended scope of the Court's major departure from prior practice was reflected in its statement that the "demand for specificity in the information upon which police action is predicated is the central teaching of this Court's Fourth Amendment jurisprudence."

In the 1970s, the Court twice rejected attempts to justify suspicionless seizures that caused only "modest" intrusions on the liberty of passengers in automobiles. Today, however, the Court takes the unprecedented step of authorizing seizures that are unsupported by any individualized suspicion whatsoever.

The Court's conclusion seems to rest on the assumption that the constitutional protection against "unreasonable" seizures requires nothing more than a hypothetically rational basis for intrusions on individual liberty. How far this ground-breaking decision will take us, I do not venture to predict. I fear, however, that it may pose a more serious threat to individual liberty than the Court realizes.

I respectfully DISSENT.

#### KENNEDY, J.

Traffic stops, even for minor violations, can take upwards of 30 minutes. When an officer commands passengers innocent of any violation to leave the vehicle and stand by the side of the road in full view of the public, the seizure is serious, not trivial. As Justice Stevens concludes, the command to exit ought not to be given unless there are objective circumstances making it reasonable for the officer to issue the order. (We do not have before us the separate question whether passengers, who, after all are in the car by choice, can be ordered to remain there for a reasonable time while the police conduct their business.) . . .

Coupled with *Whren v. U.S.* [excerpted in Chapter 6] the Court puts tens of millions of passengers at risk of arbitrary control by the police. If the command to exit were to become commonplace, the Constitution would be diminished in a most public way. As the standards suggested in dissent are adequate to protect the safety of the police, we ought not to suffer so great a loss. . . .

Most officers, it might be said, will exercise their new power with discretion and restraint; and no doubt this often will be the case. It might also be said that if some jurisdictions use today's ruling to require passengers to exit as a matter of routine in every stop, citizen complaints and political intervention will call for an end to the practice.

These arguments, however, would miss the point. Liberty comes not from officials by grace but from the Constitution by right. For these reasons, and with all respect for the opinion of the Court, I DISSENT.

## Questions

1. List the specific invasions Jerry Lee Wilson experienced after the vehicle he was a passenger in was stopped.

2. Identify the government's interest that was furthered by ordering Wilson out of the car.

3. In your opinion, did the government's interest outweigh the degree of invasion against Wilson? In your answer, consider both the majority and dissenting opinions.

4. State specifically the objective basis for ordering Wilson out of the car.

5. State the Court's "bright-line rule" governing officers' power to order passengers out of cars they've stopped.

6. Summarize the arguments the majority gave to back up its bright-line rule.

7. Describe the empirical evidence the majority's opinion was based on. In view of the dissenting justices' criticism of the statistics, how much weight do they carry in your opinion?

8. How do the dissenting justices answer the majority's arguments in (7)? Which side has the better arguments? Defend your answer.

 Go to Exercise 4.3 on the Samaha Criminal Procedure website 7e to learn more about *Maryland v. Wilson*: academic.cengage.com/criminaljustice/samaha.

## Detentions at International Borders

The strong government interest in controlling who and what comes into the United States substantially reduces the liberty and privacy of individuals at the Mexican and Canadian land boundaries, at the seaports along the East and West Coasts, and at all airports on flights coming from foreign countries. Routine detentions don't require reasonable suspicion to back up lengthy detentions or frisks, which include examining purses, wallets, and pockets (*Henderson v. U.S.* 1967) and up-close dog sniffs (*U.S. v. Kelly* 2002).

The strong government interest extends to many kinds of people and to many things that demand preventive measures, but here we'll use as our example preventing illegal drug smuggling, particularly the difficulty for law enforcement created by balloon swallowers. (We'll take up preventing terrorist attacks and apprehending terrorist suspects in Chapter 15.) These are smugglers who bring illegal drugs into the country hidden in their alimentary canal or vaginas.

The U.S. Supreme Court upheld a 16-hour detention of Rosa Elvira Montoya de Hernandez, a suspected "balloon swallower," in close confinement under constant surveillance and a strip search at Los Angeles International Airport in *U.S. v. Montoya de Hernandez* (1985).

---

## CASE    *Is the 16-Hour Detention of a Suspected "Balloon-Swallower" a Reasonable Stop?*

### U.S. v. Montoya de Hernandez
473 U.S. 531 381 (1985)

### HISTORY

Rosa Elvira Montoya de Hernandez was charged with narcotics violations. She moved to suppress the narcotics. The U.S. District Court denied the motion and admitted the cocaine in evidence. Montoya de Hernandez was convicted of possessing cocaine with intent to distribute and unlawful importation of cocaine. A divided U.S. Court of Appeals for the 9th Circuit reversed the conviction. The government appealed to the U.S. Supreme Court. The Supreme Court reversed.

REHNQUIST, J., JOINED BY BURGER, C.J., AND WHITE, BLACKMUN, POWELL, AND O'CONNOR, JJ.

### FACTS

Montoya de Hernandez arrived at Los Angeles International Airport shortly after midnight, March 5, 1983, on Avianca Flight 080, a direct 10-hour flight from Bogotá, Colombia. Her visa was in order so she was passed through

Immigration and proceeded to the customs desk. At the customs desk she encountered Customs Inspector Talamantes, who reviewed her documents and noticed from her passport that she had made at least eight recent trips to either Miami or Los Angeles.

Talamantes referred respondent to a secondary customs desk for further questioning. At this desk Talamantes and another inspector asked Montoya de Hernandez general questions concerning herself and the purpose of her trip. Montoya de Hernandez revealed that she spoke no English and had no family or friends in the United States. She explained in Spanish that she had come to the United States to purchase goods for her husband's store in Bogotá.

The customs inspectors recognized Bogotá as a "source city" for narcotics. Montoya de Hernandez possessed $5,000 in cash, mostly $50 bills, but had no billfold. She indicated to the inspectors that she had no appointments with merchandise vendors, but planned to ride around Los Angeles in taxicabs visiting retail stores such as J.C. Penney and K-Mart in order to buy goods for her husband's store with the $5,000.

Montoya de Hernandez admitted she had no hotel reservations, but said she planned to stay at a Holiday Inn. Montoya de Hernandez could not recall how her airline ticket was purchased. When the inspectors opened Montoya de Hernandez's one small valise they found about four changes of "cold weather" clothing. Montoya de Hernandez had no shoes other than the high-heeled pair she was wearing. Although Montoya de Hernandez possessed no checks, waybills, credit cards, or letters of credit, she did produce a Colombian business card and a number of old receipts, waybills, and fabric swatches displayed in a photo album. At this point Talamantes and the other inspector suspected that Montoya de Hernandez was a "balloon swallower," one who attempts to smuggle narcotics into this country hidden in her alimentary canal. Over the years Inspector Talamantes had apprehended dozens of alimentary canal smugglers arriving on Avianca Flight 080. . . .

The inspectors requested a female customs inspector to take Montoya de Hernandez to a private area and conduct a pat down and strip search. During the search the female inspector felt Montoya de Hernandez's abdomen area and noticed a firm fullness, as if Montoya de Hernandez were wearing a girdle. The search revealed no contraband, but the inspector noticed that Montoya de Hernandez was wearing two pairs of elastic underpants with a paper towel lining the crotch area.

When Montoya de Hernandez returned to the customs area and the female inspector reported her discoveries, the inspector in charge told Montoya de Hernandez that he suspected she was smuggling drugs in her alimentary canal. . . . The inspector then gave Montoya de Hernandez the option of returning to Colombia on the next available flight, agreeing to an x-ray, or remaining in detention until she produced a monitored bowel movement that would confirm or rebut the inspectors' suspicions.

Montoya de Hernandez chose the first option and was placed in a customs office under observation. She was told that if she went to the toilet she would have to use a wastebasket in the women's restroom, in order that female inspectors could inspect her stool for balloons or capsules carrying narcotics. The inspectors refused Montoya de Hernandez's request to place a telephone call. . . .

Montoya de Hernandez sat in the customs office, under observation, for the remainder of the night. . . . She remained detained in the customs office under observation, for most of the time curled up in a chair leaning to one side. She refused all offers of food and drink, and refused to use the toilet facilities. The Court of Appeals noted that she exhibited symptoms of discomfort with "heroic efforts to resist the usual calls of nature." . . .

At the shift change at 4:00 . . . the next afternoon, almost 16 hours after her flight had landed, Montoya de Hernandez still had not defecated or urinated or partaken of food or drink. At that time customs officials sought a court order authorizing . . . an x-ray, and a rectal examination. The Federal Magistrate issued an order just before midnight that evening, which authorized a rectal examination and involuntary x-ray. . . . A physician conducted a rectal examination and removed from Montoya de Hernandez's rectum a balloon containing a foreign substance. Montoya de Hernandez was then placed formally under arrest. By 4:10 A.M. Montoya de Hernandez had passed 6 similar balloons; over the next four days she passed 88 balloons containing a total of 528 grams of 80% pure cocaine hydrochloride.

After a suppression hearing, the District Court admitted the cocaine in evidence against Montoya de Hernandez. She was convicted of possession of cocaine with intent to distribute . . . [a]nd unlawful importation of cocaine. . . . A divided panel of the United States Court of Appeals for the Ninth Circuit reversed Montoya de Hernandez's convictions. . . .

## OPINION

The Fourth Amendment commands that searches and seizures be reasonable. What is reasonable depends upon all of the circumstances surrounding the search or seizure itself. . . . The permissibility of a particular law enforcement practice is judged by "balancing its intrusion on the individual's Fourth Amendment interest against its promotion of legitimate governmental interests." . . .

Here the seizure of Montoya de Hernandez took place at the international border. Since the founding of our Republic, Congress has granted the Executive plenary authority to conduct routine searches and seizures at the border, without probable cause or a warrant, in order to regulate the collection of duties and to prevent the introduction of contraband into this country. . . . The Fourth Amendment's balance of reasonableness is qualitatively different at the international border than in the interior. Routine searches of the persons and effects of entrants are not subject to any requirement of reasonable suspicion, probable cause, or warrant, and first-class mail may be opened without a warrant on less than probable cause. . . .

These cases reflect long-standing concern for the protection of the integrity of the border. This concern is, if anything, heightened by the veritable national crisis in law enforcement caused by smuggling of illicit narcotics . . . and in particular by the increasing utilization of alimentary canal smuggling. This desperate practice appears to be a relatively recent addition to the smugglers' repertoire of deceptive practices, and it also appears to be exceedingly difficult to detect. . . .

Balanced against the sovereign's interests at the border are the Fourth Amendment rights of Montoya de Hernandez. Having presented herself at the border for admission, and having subjected herself to the criminal enforcement powers of the Federal Government . . . she was entitled to be free from unreasonable search and seizure. ·

But not only is this expectation of privacy less at the border than in the interior . . . the Fourth Amendment balance between the interests of the Government and the privacy right of the individual is also struck much more favorably to the Government at the border. . . .

We have not previously decided what level of suspicion would justify a seizure of an incoming traveler for purposes other than a routine border search. . . . The Court of Appeals viewed "clear indication" as an intermediate standard between "reasonable suspicion" and "probable cause." . . . No other court, including this one, has ever adopted . . . "clear indication" language as a Fourth Amendment standard. . . . We do not think that the Fourth Amendment's emphasis upon reasonableness is consistent with the creation of a third verbal standard in addition to "reasonable suspicion" and "probable cause." . . .

We hold that detention of a traveler at the border, beyond the scope of a routine customs search and inspection, is justified at its inception if customs agents, considering all the facts surrounding the traveler and her trip, reasonably suspect that the traveler is smuggling contraband in her alimentary canal. . . . The facts, and their rational inferences, known to customs inspectors in this case clearly supported a reasonable suspicion that Montoya de Hernandez was an alimentary canal smuggler. . . .

The trained customs inspectors had encountered many alimentary canal smugglers and certainly had more than an "inchoate and unparticularized suspicion or 'hunch,'" . . . that Montoya de Hernandez was smuggling narcotics in her alimentary canal. The inspectors' suspicion was a "'common-sense conclusion about human behavior' upon which 'practical people,' . . . including government officials, are entitled to rely." . . .

The final issue in this case is whether the detention of Montoya de Hernandez was reasonably related in scope to the circumstances which justified it initially. In this regard we have cautioned that courts should not indulge in "unrealistic second-guessing," . . . and we have noted that "creative judges, engaged in [after the fact] evaluations of police conduct can almost always imagine some alternative means by which the objectives of the police might have been accomplished." . . .

The rudimentary knowledge of the human body which judges possess in common with the rest of humankind tells us that alimentary canal smuggling cannot be detected in the amount of time in which other illegal activity may be investigated through brief *Terry*-type stops. It presents few, if any external signs; a quick frisk will not do, nor will even a strip search.

In the case of Montoya de Hernandez the inspectors had available, as an alternative to simply awaiting her bowel movement, an x-ray. They offered her the alternative of submitting herself to that procedure. But when she refused that alternative, the customs inspectors were left with only two practical alternatives: detain her for such a time as necessary to confirm their suspicions, a detention which would last much longer than the typical *Terry* stop, or turn her loose into the interior carrying the reasonably suspected contraband drugs. . . .

The inspectors in this case followed this former procedure. They no doubt expected that Montoya de Hernandez, having recently disembarked from a 10-hour direct flight with a full and stiff abdomen, would produce a bowel movement without extended delay. But her visible efforts to resist the call of nature, which the court below labeled "heroic," disappointed this expectation and in turn caused her humiliation and discomfort.

Our prior cases have refused to charge police with delays in investigatory detention attributable to the suspect's evasive actions. . . . Montoya de Hernandez alone was responsible for much of the duration and discomfort of the seizure. Under these circumstances, we conclude that the detention was not unreasonably long. It occurred at the international border, where the Fourth Amendment balance of interests leans heavily to the Government. . . . Montoya de Hernandez's detention was long, uncomfortable indeed, humiliating; but both its length and its discomfort resulted solely from the method by which she chose to smuggle illicit drugs into this country. . . .

## CONCURRING OPINION

### STEVENS, J.

If a seizure and search of the person of the kind disclosed by this record may be made on the basis of reasonable suspicion, we must assume that a significant number of innocent persons will be required to undergo similar procedures.

The rule announced in this case cannot, therefore, be supported on the ground that Montoya de Hernandez's prolonged and humiliating detention "resulted solely from the method by which she chose to smuggle illicit drugs into this country." . . .

The prolonged detention of Montoya de Hernandez was, however, justified by a different choice that Montoya de Hernandez made; she withdrew her consent to an x-ray examination that would have easily determined whether the reasonable suspicion that she was concealing contraband was justified. . . .

## DISSENT

BRENNAN, J., JOINED BY MARSHALL, J.

We confront a "disgusting and saddening episode" at our Nation's border. . . . "That Montoya de Hernandez so degraded herself as to offend the sensibilities of any decent citizen is not questioned." That is not what we face. For "it is a fair summary of history to say that the safeguards of liberty have frequently been forged in controversies involving not very nice people." . . .

The standards we fashion to govern the ferreting out of the guilty apply equally to the detention of the innocent, and "may be exercised by the most unfit and ruthless officers as well as by the fit and reasonable." . . . Nor is the issue whether there is a "veritable national crisis in law enforcement caused by smuggling illicit narcotics." . . . "In our democracy such enforcement presupposes a moral atmosphere and a reliance upon intelligence whereby the effective administration of justice can be achieved with due regard for those civilized standards in the use of the criminal law which are formulated in our Bill of Rights."

The issue, instead, is simply this: Does the Fourth Amendment permit an international traveler, citizen or alien, to be subjected to the sort of treatment that occurred in this case without the sanction of a judicial officer and based on nothing more than the "reasonable suspicion" of low ranking investigative officers that something might be amiss? The Court today concludes that the Fourth Amendment grants such sweeping and unmonitored authority to customs officials. . . . I dissent.

Indefinite involuntary incommunicado detentions "for investigation" are the hallmark of a police state, not a free society. . . . In my opinion, Government officials may no more confine a person at the border under such circumstances for purposes of criminal investigation than they may within the interior of the country. The nature and duration of the detention here may well have been tolerable for spoiled meat or diseased animals, but not for human beings held on simple suspicion of criminal activity.

. . . Finally, I believe that the warrant and probable cause safeguards equally govern Justice STEVENS' proffered alternative of exposure to x-irradiation for criminal investigative purposes. . . . The available evidence suggests that the number of highly intrusive border searches of suspicious-looking but ultimately innocent travelers may be very high. One physician who at the request of customs officials conducted many "internal searches"—rectal and vaginal examinations and stomach pumping—estimated that he had found contraband in 15 to 20 percent of the persons he had examined. It has similarly been estimated that only 16 percent of women subjected to body cavity searches at the border were in fact found to be carrying contraband. It is precisely to minimize the risk of harassing so many innocent people that the Fourth Amendment requires the intervention of a judicial officer. . . .

The Court argues, however, that the length and "discomfort" of de Hernandez' detention "resulted solely from the method by which she chose to smuggle illicit drugs into this country," and it speculates that only her "heroic" efforts prevented the detention from being brief and to the point. . . . Although we now know that de Hernandez was indeed guilty of smuggling drugs internally, such post hoc [after the fact] rationalizations have no place in our Fourth Amendment jurisprudence, which demands that we "prevent hindsight from coloring the evaluation of the reasonableness of a search or seizure." . . . At the time the authorities simply had, at most, a reasonable suspicion that de Hernandez might be engaged in such smuggling.

Neither the law of the land nor the law of nature supports the notion that petty government officials can require people to excrete on command; indeed, the Court relies elsewhere on "the rudimentary knowledge of the human body" in sanctioning the "much longer than . . . typical" duration of detentions such as this. And, with all respect to the Court, it is not "unrealistic second-guessing," to predict that an innocent traveler, locked away in incommunicado detention in unfamiliar surroundings in a foreign land, might well be frightened and exhausted as to be unable so to "cooperate" with the authorities. . . .

It is tempting, of course, to look the other way in a case that so graphically illustrates the "veritable national crisis" caused by narcotics trafficking. But if there is one enduring lesson to be learned in the long struggle to balance individual rights against society's need to defend itself against lawlessness, it is that it is easy to make light of insistence on scrupulous regard for the safeguards of civil liberties when invoked on behalf of the unworthy. It is too easy. History bears testimony that by such disregard are the rights of liberty extinguished, heedlessly at first, then stealthily, and brazenly in the end.

## Questions

1. Identify the government interests the invasions of Montoya de Hernandez's liberty and privacy were intended to protect.

2. Compare the duration, location, and subjective invasiveness of Montoya de Hernandez's detention with that of John Terry in *Terry v. Ohio*.

3. Assume first you're a prosecutor and then a defense lawyer. Relying on the facts and opinion in *Terry v. Ohio*, argue, first, that the detention and searches of Montoya de Hernandez pass the reasonableness test

and, then, that they fail the reasonableness test. Make sure you include all of the elements of reasonableness we've discussed in this chapter.

4. Now, assume you're a judge. Based on your view of the law, write an opinion supporting your decision whether the government actions in this case were reasonable under the Fourth Amendment.

 Go to Exercise 4.4 on the Samaha Criminal Procedure 7e website to learn more about *U.S. v. Montoya de Hernandez:* academic.cengage.com/criminaljustice/samaha.

## Checkpoints and Roadblocks

The government sets up *roadblocks*—barricades for stopping vehicles and questioning their occupants—that invade drivers' and passengers' liberty and privacy to protect a number of legitimate public interests. So we see many kinds of roadblocks for checking vehicles and their occupants, including:

- Driver's license and vehicle safety checks

- Weigh stations for trucks

- Game warden road checks

- Agricultural inspection stops

- Criminal investigation stops (to solve a specific crime)

- Border stops (to check for smuggled goods, contraband, and/or illegal aliens)

- Sobriety checkpoints

- Drug stops (to check for the possession and transport of illegal drugs)

Roadblocks to apprehend fleeing felons, to check vehicle safety requirements, and to prevent illegal aliens from entering the country are all legal. Amid a lot of controversy, a number of states have created roadblocks to prevent drunk driving and apprehend and prosecute drunk drivers (Hickey and Axline 1992; Weiner and Royster 1991). Are DWI roadblocks unreasonable stops? As you might expect by this point in reading the book, the U.S. Supreme Court answered, "It all depends . . . ," in our next case excerpt, *Michigan v. Sitz* (1990).

---

C A S E | *Was the DWI Roadblock an Unreasonable Seizure?*

### *Michigan v. Sitz*
496 U.S. 444 (1990)

### HISTORY

Rick Sitz and other drivers (respondents) brought an action to challenge the constitutionality of a highway sobriety checkpoint program. The Circuit Court of Wayne County, Michigan, invalidated the program, and the Michigan Department of State Police (petitioners) appealed. The Court of Appeals of Michigan affirmed. The U.S. Supreme

Court granted certiorari. The Supreme Court reversed and remanded the case.

REHNQUIST, C.J., JOINED BY WHITE, O'CONNOR, SCALIA, AND KENNEDY, JJ.

### FACTS

The Michigan Department of State Police and its Director (petitioners), established a sobriety checkpoint pilot program in early 1986. . . . [Under the plan] checkpoints would be set up at selected sites along state roads. All vehicles passing through a checkpoint would be stopped and their drivers briefly examined for signs of intoxication. In cases where a checkpoint officer detected signs of intoxication, the motorist would be directed to a location out of the traffic flow where an officer would check the motorist's driver's license and car registration and, if warranted, conduct further sobriety tests. Should the field tests and the officer's observations suggest that the driver was intoxicated, an arrest would be made. All other drivers would be permitted to resume their journey immediately.

The first—and to date the only—sobriety checkpoint operated under the program was conducted in Saginaw County with the assistance of the Saginaw County Sheriff's Department. During the hour-and-fifteen-minute duration of the checkpoint's operation, 126 vehicles passed through the checkpoint. The average delay for each vehicle was approximately 25 seconds. Two drivers were detained for field sobriety testing, and one of the two was arrested for driving under the influence of alcohol. A third driver who drove through without stopping was pulled over by an officer in an observation vehicle and arrested for driving under the influence.

On the day before the operation of the Saginaw County checkpoint, Sitz and the other drivers (respondents) filed a complaint in the Circuit Court of Wayne County seeking declaratory and injunctive relief from potential subjection to the checkpoints. Sitz and each of the other drivers "is a licensed driver in the State of Michigan . . . who regularly travels throughout the State in his automobile." During pretrial proceedings, the Michigan Department of State Police (petitioners) agreed to delay further implementation of the checkpoint program pending the outcome of this litigation.

After the trial, at which the court heard extensive testimony concerning . . . the "effectiveness" of highway sobriety checkpoint programs, the court ruled that the Michigan program violated the Fourth Amendment and Art. 1, § 11, of the Michigan Constitution. On appeal, the Michigan Court of Appeals affirmed the holding that the program violated the Fourth Amendment and, for that reason, did not consider whether the program violated the Michigan Constitution. After the Michigan Supreme Court denied Department of State Police's application for leave to appeal, we granted certiorari.

To decide this case the trial court performed a balancing test derived from our opinion in *Brown v. Texas* (1979). As described by the Court of Appeals, the test involved

1. "balancing the state's interest in preventing accidents caused by drunk drivers,

2. the effectiveness of sobriety checkpoints in achieving that goal, and

3. the level of intrusion on an individual's privacy caused by the checkpoints."

The Court of Appeals agreed that "the Brown three-prong balancing test was the correct test to be used to determine the constitutionality of the sobriety checkpoint plan." As characterized by the Court of Appeals, the trial court's findings with respect to the balancing factors were that the State has "a grave and legitimate" interest in curbing drunken driving; that sobriety checkpoint programs are generally "ineffective" and, therefore, do not significantly further that interest; and that the checkpoints' "subjective intrusion" on individual liberties is substantial. According to the court, the record disclosed no basis for disturbing the trial court's findings, which were made within the context of an analytical framework prescribed by this Court for determining the constitutionality of seizures less intrusive than traditional arrests.

## OPINION

The Department of State police (petitioners) concede, correctly in our view, that a Fourth Amendment "seizure" occurs when a vehicle is stopped at a checkpoint. . . . The question thus becomes whether such seizures are "reasonable" under the Fourth Amendment. . . . We address only the initial stop of each motorist passing through a checkpoint and the associated preliminary questioning and observation by checkpoint officers.

Detention of particular motorists for more extensive field sobriety testing may require satisfaction of an individualized suspicion standard. No one can seriously dispute the magnitude of the drunken driving problem or the States' interest in eradicating it. . . . "Drunk drivers cause an annual death toll of over 25,000 and in the same time span cause nearly one million personal injuries and more than five billion dollars in property damage." For decades, this Court has "repeatedly lamented the tragedy." Conversely, the weight bearing on the other scale—the measure of the intrusion on motorists stopped briefly at sobriety checkpoints—is slight. . . . The trial court and the Court of Appeals, thus, accurately gauged the "objective" intrusion, measured by the duration of the seizure and the intensity of the investigation, as minimal.

With respect to what it perceived to be the "subjective" intrusion on motorists, however, the Court of Appeals found such intrusion substantial. The court first affirmed the trial court's finding that the guidelines governing checkpoint operation minimize the discretion of the officers on the scene. But the court also agreed with the trial court's conclusion that the checkpoints have the potential to generate fear and surprise in motorists. This was so because the record failed to demonstrate that approaching motorists would be aware of their option to make U-turns or turnoffs to avoid the checkpoints. On that basis, the court deemed the subjective intrusion from the checkpoints unreasonable.

We believe the Michigan courts misread our cases concerning the degree of "subjective intrusion" and the potential for generating fear and surprise. The "fear and surprise" to be considered are not the natural fear of one who has been drinking over the prospect of being stopped at a sobriety checkpoint but, rather, the fear and surprise engendered in law-abiding motorists by the nature of the stop. . . .

The Court of Appeals went on to consider as part of the balancing analysis of the "effectiveness" of the proposed checkpoint program. Based on extensive testimony in the trial record, the court concluded that the checkpoint program failed the "effectiveness" part of the test, and that this failure materially discounted petitioners' strong interest in implementing the program. We think the Court of Appeals was wrong on this point as well. . . . Experts in police science might disagree over which of several methods of apprehending drunken drivers is preferable as an ideal. But for purposes of Fourth Amendment analysis, the choice among such reasonable alternatives remains with the governmental officials who have a unique understanding of, and a responsibility for, limited public resources, including a finite number of police officers.

. . . This case involves neither a complete absence of empirical data nor a challenge of random highway stops. During the operation of the Saginaw County checkpoint, the detention of each of the 126 vehicles that entered the checkpoint resulted in the arrest of two drunken drivers. Stated as a percentage, approximately 1.5 percent of the drivers passing through the checkpoint were arrested for alcohol impairment.

In addition, an expert witness testified at the trial that experience in other states demonstrated that, on the whole, sobriety checkpoints resulted in drunken driving arrests of around 1 percent of all motorists stopped. . . .

In sum, the balance of the state's interest in preventing drunken driving, the extent to which this system can reasonably be said to advance that interest, and the degree of intrusion upon individual motorists who are briefly stopped, weighs in favor of the state program. We therefore hold that it is consistent with the Fourth Amendment. The judgment of the Michigan Court of Appeals is accordingly reversed, and the case is remanded for further proceedings not inconsistent with this opinion.

REVERSED.

# DISSENT

### BRENNAN, J., JOINED BY MARSHALL, J.

. . . Some level of individualized suspicion is a core component of the protection the Fourth Amendment provides against arbitrary government action. By holding that no level of suspicion is necessary before the police may stop a car for the purpose of preventing drunken driving, the Court potentially subjects the general public to arbitrary or harassing conduct by the police. . . .

I do not dispute the immense social cost caused by drunken drivers, nor do I slight the government's efforts to prevent such tragic losses. Indeed, I would hazard a guess that today's opinion will be received favorably by a majority of our society, who would willingly suffer the minimal intrusion of a sobriety checkpoint stop in order to prevent drunken driving. But consensus that a particular law enforcement technique serves a laudable purpose has never been the touchstone of constitutional analysis.

The Fourth Amendment was designed not merely to protect against official intrusions whose social utility was less as measured by some "balancing test" than its intrusion on individual privacy; it was designed in addition to grant the individual a zone of privacy whose protections could be breached only where the "reasonable" requirements of the probable cause standard were met. Moved by whatever momentary evil has aroused their fears, officials—perhaps even supported by a majority of citizens—may be tempted to conduct searches that sacrifice the liberty of each citizen to assuage the perceived evil. But the Fourth Amendment rests on the principle that a true balance between the individual and society depends on the recognition of "the right to be let alone—the most comprehensive of rights and the right most valued by civilized men." *Olmstead v. U. S.* (1928) (Brandeis, J., dissenting).

In the face of the "momentary evil" of drunken driving, the Court today abdicates its role as the protector of that fundamental right. I respectfully DISSENT.

### STEVENS, J., JOINED BY BRENNAN AND MARSHALL, JJ.

. . . The record in this case makes clear that a decision holding these suspicionless seizures unconstitutional would not impede the law enforcement community's remarkable progress in reducing the death toll on our highways. Because the Michigan program was patterned after an older program in Maryland, the trial judge gave special attention to that state's experience. Over a period of several years, Maryland operated 125 checkpoints; of the 41,000 motorists passing through those checkpoints, only 143 persons (0.3%) were arrested. The number of man-hours devoted to these operations is not in the record, but it seems inconceivable that a higher arrest rate could not have been achieved by more conventional means.

. . . Any relationship between sobriety checkpoints and an actual reduction in highway fatalities is even less substantial than the minimal impact on arrest rates. As the Michigan Court of Appeals pointed out, Maryland had conducted a study comparing traffic statistics between a county using checkpoints and a control county. The results of the study showed that alcohol-related accidents in the checkpoint county decreased by ten percent, whereas the control county saw an eleven percent decrease; and while fatal accidents in the control county fell from sixteen to three, fatal accidents in the checkpoint county actually doubled from the prior year.

In light of these considerations, it seems evident that the Court today . . . overvalues the law enforcement interest in using sobriety checkpoints [and] undervalues the citizen's interest in freedom from random, unannounced investigatory seizures. . . .

. . . A Michigan officer who questions a motorist at a sobriety checkpoint has virtually unlimited discretion to detain the driver on the basis of the slightest suspicion. A ruddy complexion, an unbuttoned shirt, bloodshot eyes or a speech impediment may suffice to prolong the detention.

Any driver who had just consumed a glass of beer, or even a sip of wine, would almost certainly have the burden of demonstrating to the officer that her driving ability was not impaired.

. . . These fears are not, as the Court would have it, solely the lot of the guilty. To be law abiding is not necessarily to be spotless, and even the most virtuous can be unlucky. Unwanted attention from the local police need not be less discomforting simply because one's secrets are not the stuff of criminal prosecutions. Moreover, those who have found—by reason of prejudice or misfortune—that encounters with the police may become adversarial or unpleasant without good cause will have grounds for worrying at any stop designed to elicit signs of suspicious behavior. Being stopped by the police is distressing even when it should not be terrifying, and what begins mildly may by happenstance turn severe. . . .

. . . In my opinion, unannounced investigatory seizures are, particularly when they take place at night, the hallmark of regimes far different from ours; the surprise intrusion upon individual liberty is not minimal. On that issue, my difference with the Court may amount to nothing less than a difference in our respective evaluations of the importance of individual liberty, a serious albeit inevitable source of constitutional disagreement. On the degree to which the sobriety checkpoint seizures advance the public interest, however, the Court's position is wholly indefensible. . . .

. . . The evidence in this case indicates that sobriety checkpoints result in the arrest of a fraction of one percent of the drivers who are stopped, but there is absolutely no evidence that this figure represents an increase over the number of arrests that would have been made by using the same law enforcement resources in conventional patrols. Thus, although the gross number of arrests is more than zero, there is a complete failure of proof on the question whether the wholesale seizures have produced any net advance in the public interest in arresting intoxicated drivers. . . .

The most disturbing aspect of the Court's decision today is that it appears to give no weight to the citizen's interest in freedom from suspicionless unannounced investigatory seizures. . . . On the other hand, the Court places a heavy thumb on the law enforcement. . . . Perhaps this tampering with the scales of justice can be explained by the Court's

obvious concern about the slaughter on our highways, and a resultant tolerance for policies designed to alleviate the problem by "setting an example" of a few motorists. . . .

This is a case that is driven by nothing more than symbolic state action—an insufficient justification for an otherwise unreasonable program of random seizures. Unfortunately, the Court is transfixed by the wrong symbol—the illusory prospect of punishing countless intoxicated motorists—when it should keep its eyes on the road plainly marked by the Constitution.

I respectfully DISSENT.

## Questions

1. According to the Court, why are DWI checkpoints Fourth Amendment seizures?

2. Why, according to the Court, are they reasonable seizures?

3. What interests does the Court balance in reaching its result?

4. What does Justice Stevens mean when he says that he and the majority disagree over the meaning of freedom?

5. What does he have to say about the need for and effectiveness of DWI checkpoints?

6. What does Justice Brennan mean when he says that the degree of the intrusion begins, not ends, the inquiry about whether DWI checkpoints are reasonable seizures?

7. How would you identify and balance the interests at stake in the DWI checkpoints? Are the checkpoints effective? Explain.

8. According to the American Civil Liberties Union (ACLU), "highly publicized local law enforcement efforts such as random roadblocks" are "Orwellian intrusions into individual privacy." What does the ACLU mean? Do you agree? Explain.

To learn more about State Constitutional Law, read *Sitz v. Michigan* (1993) and find out what happened after the case was remanded to the lower court on the Samaha Criminal Procedure 7e website: academic. cengage.com/criminaljustice/samaha.

# SUMMARY

### I. Stops, Frisks, and the Fourth Amendment

A. The power to stop and question suspicious persons is ancient.

B. This power was never questioned until the 1960s during the due process revolution. People argued that "outsiders" needed protection from police and their right to stop and arrest.

C. Police argued that until they made an arrest, their good judgment, based on their professional experience, was good enough.

D. Fourth Amendment stops are brief detentions that allow law enforcement officers to freeze suspicious situations briefly, so they can investigate them.

E. Fourth Amendment frisks are once-over-lightly pat downs of outer clothing to protect officers by taking away suspects' weapons.

F. Law enforcement officers need to prove fewer suspicious facts and circumstances to back up stops and frisks than they do for arrest and full-blown searches.

G. Since stops and frisks take place in public, the display of police power is for all to see, and this ultimately shapes the public's opinion of police power more than the greater invasions by arrest and searches that we never see.

H. Facts surrounding stops and frisks:
1. Officers stop many people who haven't done anything wrong, and they frisk many unarmed people.
2. Most of these same people want police protection and need it more than people who live in safe neighborhoods.
3. Both lawbreakers and law abiders in high-street-crime neighborhoods form lasting opinions about the police from street encounters they've watched or experienced.
4. Stops and frisks aren't distributed evenly; they fall most heavily on Black and Latino young men in poor urban neighborhoods.

## II. Stop-and-Frisk Law

A. Stop-and-frisk law follows a slight alteration of the three-step analysis of a search:
1. Was the officer's action a stop or a frisk?
2. If the government action was a stop or a frisk, was it reasonable?
3. If the stop or frisk was unreasonable, should evidence obtained during the stop and/or frisk be excluded from legal proceedings against the defendants?

B. The Fourth Amendment consists of two clauses:
1. Reasonableness clause. This states that people have a right to be secure in their persons, houses, papers, and effects against unreasonable searches and seizures.
2. Warrant clause. This allows warrants to issue only upon probable cause, supported by oath or affirmation, and particularly describing the place to be searched and the persons or things to be seized.

C. Until the 1960s, the U.S. Supreme Court followed the conventional Fourth Amendment approach, which says that the reasonableness and warrant clauses are firmly connected.

D. In the 1960s, the Supreme Court shifted from the conventional approach to the reasonableness Fourth Amendment approach, which says that the two clauses are separate, and they address separate problems.

E. We cannot read the Fourth Amendment to mean searches and seizures without warrants and probable clause are *always* unreasonable.

F. When the Supreme Court decided there were more reasonable searches and seizures without warrants than with them, it created two problems:
1. When does the Fourth Amendment require warrants?

2. What does "unreasonable" mean?
   a. One type of reasonable search and seizure is based on warrants and probable cause.
   b. The other type—which in practice includes the vast majority of searches—has to pass the reasonableness test.

## III. The Reasonableness Test

A. The reasonableness test consists of two elements the government has to prove:
   1. Balancing element. The need to search and/or seize outweighs the invasion of liberty and privacy rights of the individuals.
   2. Objective basis. There are facts to back up the search and/or seizure.
      a. Reasonable suspicion is required to back up stops and frisks.
      b. Probable cause is required for arrests and full-blown searches.
      c. Both require individualized suspicion.
B. Courts have to decide whether searches and seizures are reasonable on a case-by-case basis. To do this, they look at the totality of circumstances surrounding the specific searches and seizures in individual cases.

## IV. *Terry v. Ohio* and Stop and Frisk

A. Today's stop-and-frisk law grew out of the practical problems police officers face in preventing and investigating crime on the streets and other public places in our largest cities.
B. The answer to the Fourth Amendment issues surrounding suspicious circumstances in light of an officer's professional training, depend on three possible interpretations:
   1. The Fourth Amendment applies only to full searches and arrests, so what officers do is left to their discretion.
   2. Even brief street detentions are arrests, and pat downs are searches, so the police can't do anything unless they've got probable cause.
   3. Stops and frisks are searches and seizures, but they're "minor" ones, so officers have to back them up with facts. But they need fewer facts than they need to arrest and search.
C. By choosing the third interpretation, the Supreme Court says that it gives police enough power to "freeze" suspicious events and people briefly to check out criminal activity that "may be afoot."
D. The Fourth Amendment also gives officers the power to protect themselves by frisking the people they stop. However:
   1. Police stops and frisks have to be reasonable:
      a. The need to control crime outweighs the intrusions against the individual's rights.
      b. Officers cannot stop and frisk people on a hunch; they need facts to back them up.
   2. Courts can later review their stops and frisks to make sure they were reasonable.

## V. Stops and the Fourth Amendment

A. The framework for analyzing police encounters with individuals can be divided into three categories:
   1. Voluntary encounters. These fall outside the Fourth Amendment if there's no coercion or detention.

2. Stops. These are brief "seizures" that require reasonable suspicion to back them up.
3. Arrests. These are longer detentions in police stations that require probable cause to justify them.

B. If the police action is a stop, it has to be reasonable in the totality of circumstances surrounding the stop:
1. Does the objective basis for the stop add up to reasonable suspicion?
2. Are the requirements of the "scope of the stop" met?
   a. The duration is short.
   b. The location of the investigation is at the scene of the stop.

## VI. Reasonable Suspicion to Back Up Stops

A. The U.S. Supreme Court called the objective basis for a stop "articulable facts"—facts we can name—that lead an officer in light of her training and experience to *suspect* that "criminal activity *may* be afoot."

B. Officers can rely on two sources of information to build reasonable suspicion:
1. Direct information. This is information officers learn firsthand.
2. Hearsay information. This is information officers learn secondhand.

C. Officers can rely on two other sources of information to back up reasonable suspicion:
1. Individualized suspicion. This consists of "facts that would tell both the officer on the street and a court deciding a suppression motion whether or not there was reasonable suspicion."
2. Categorical suspicion. This refers to suspects who fall into broad categories. The broad categories include:
   a. "High crime" and "known for drug trafficking" neighborhoods.
   b. Characterizing a neighborhood in this way is often crucial to the finding of reasonable suspicion.
   c. Race and ethnicity:
      (1). The U.S. Supreme Court has made it clear that race and ethnicity by themselves can never amount to reasonable suspicion.
      (2). But the Court also found that race and ethnicity are part of reality and can be used as *part* of reasonable suspicion.
   d. Profiles. These consist of lists of circumstances that might, or might not, be linked to certain types of behaviors, such as terrorism and drug couriers.

## VII. The Scope of Reasonable Stops

A. The scope of a reasonable stop has two elements: a short duration and an on-the-spot investigation requirement.

B. Short duration. The U.S. Supreme Court has declined to adopt a specific time limit on stops, giving officers plenty of room for discretionary decision making.

C. "On the spot" investigation requirement:
1. The brief freeze of a stop has to take place where the officers stop the suspect.
2. Officers have some leeway to move suspects a short distance.

## VIII. Frisks and the Fourth Amendment

A. The purpose of a frisk isn't to discover evidence of crime but to allow the officer to pursue her investigation without fear of injury.

B. A lawful frisk has three elements:
   1. A lawful stop
   2. Reasonable suspicion the suspect is armed
   3. A once-over-lightly pat down of outer clothing to detect weapons
C. The reasonableness of frisks depends on balancing the government's interest in criminal law enforcement against the individual's privacy right not to be touched by an officer.
D. Frisks are the least invasive Fourth Amendment searches; body-cavity searches stand at the other extreme.
E. Facts that back up a stop don't automatically also back up a frisk, except for when suspects are stopped for crimes of violence.
F. Some frisks need to go further than just a once-over-lightly pat down:
   1. Feeling a hard object inside a coat pocket that could be a weapon authorizes reaching inside the coat.
   2. Encountering unusually bulky winter clothing may require feeling underneath the outer clothing.
G. Suspecting the contents of a closed handbag may be illegal can justify opening the handbag.
H. If contraband is discovered during a frisk, it can be seized as long as the frisk for weapons isn't a pretext for looking for contraband.

## IX. Special Situation Stops and Frisks
A. In *Pennsylvania v. Mimms,* the Supreme Court ruled that it's lawful for officers to order drivers out of vehicles they legally stop because of the possibility that drivers can make unobserved movements.
B. Because of the government's interest in protecting national security, detentions at international borders, which substantially reduce the liberty and privacy of individuals who come into the United States, are lawful.
C. Such detentions don't require reasonable suspicion to back up lengthy detentions or frisks.
D. Inspections such as roadblocks can be conducted without individualized suspicion, as long as they include all vehicles or all vehicles of a specific type.

## REVIEW QUESTIONS

1. Describe the history behind the power of police to stop and question suspicious persons. Why did the power change?

2. How do stops differ from arrests?

3. How do frisks differ from searches?

4. Why do stops and frisks have a greater impact on opinions of police power than arrests and searches?

5. What's the ratio of stops to arrests?

6. Identify four realities of stop and frisk.

7. Identify the three steps in the analysis used to decide whether stops and frisks are reasonable Fourth Amendment search and seizures.

8. Identify the two parts of the Fourth Amendment and the role they play in the conventional and reasonableness approach to the Fourth Amendment.

9. Describe the two clauses that make up the reasonableness Fourth Amendment approach.

10. Identify the two prongs to the reasonableness test.

11. Explain how the "totality of circumstances" test works in practice.

12. Describe the background and summarize the significance of *Terry v. Ohio*.

13. Identify three possible interpretations of the Fourth Amendment and which interpretation the Supreme Court has settled on.

14. Identify three categories for analyzing police encounters with individuals.

15. Reasonable stops depend on two elements. Identify and describe each.

16. Identify four sources of information officers can rely on to build reasonable suspicion. Give an example of each.

17. Does unprovoked flight + high-crime area = reasonable suspicion? Explain.

18. Can race be used in building reasonable suspicion? Explain.

19. What's the difference between individualized suspicion and a profile?

20. Identify seven primary characteristics and four secondary characteristics of drug couriers.

21. Identify the two necessary elements that meet the scope of a reasonable stop.

22. Identify three elements of a lawful frisk.

23. What's reasonable suspicion to frisk?

24. What's the scope of a lawful frisk?

25. Why is it reasonable to remove passengers from a stopped vehicle even when there's no suspicion that they may be involved in a crime?

26. Why are the liberty and the privacy of individuals severely restricted at international borders?

27. Identify the legitimate purposes for roadblocks, and explain the objective basis that makes roadblocks reasonable Fourth Amendment seizures.

## KEY TERMS

# Seizure of Persons: Arrest

## MAIN POINTS

- Arrests are a vital tool that can help law enforcement catch the guilty and free the innocent.
- Arrests are Fourth Amendment seizures but are more invasive than stops.
- Probable cause and the manner of arrest are both required elements of a reasonable arrest.
- The probable cause requirement balances the societal interest in crime control and the individual right to free movement.
- Officers can use both direct information and hearsay to build probable cause.
- Arrest warrants are required to enter homes to arrest.
- Officers may only use the amount of force necessary to get and maintain control of suspects they have probable cause to arrest.
- After an arrest, felony suspects usually are taken to the police station for further processing; misdemeanor suspects usually are released.
- It's constitutionally reasonable, but not necessarily wise, for officers to make full custodial arrests for fine-only offenses.

At about 10:45 P.M. Memphis Police Officers Elton Hymon and Leslie Wright were dispatched to answer a "prowler inside call." Upon arriving at the scene they saw a woman standing on her porch gesturing toward the adjacent house. She told them she had heard glass breaking and that "they" or "someone" was breaking in next door. While Wright radioed the dispatcher to say that they were on the scene, Hymon went behind the house. He heard a door slam and saw someone run across the backyard. The fleeing suspect, 15-year-old Edward Garner, stopped at a 6-feet-high chain link fence at the edge of the yard. With the aid of a flashlight, Hymon was able to see Garner's face and hands. He saw no sign of a weapon, and though not certain, was "reasonably sure" and "figured" that Garner was unarmed. He thought Garner was 17 or 18 years old and about 5'5" or 5'7" tall.

While Garner was crouched at the base of the fence, Hymon called out "police, halt" and took a few steps toward him. Garner began to climb over the fence. Convinced that if Garner made it over the fence he would elude capture, Hymon shot him. The bullet hit Garner in the back of the head. Garner was taken by ambulance to a hospital, where he died on the operating table. Ten dollars and a purse taken from the house were found on his body.

*Tennessee v. Garner* (1985), U.S. Supreme Court

A rrests are a vital tool that can help law enforcement catch the guilty and free the innocent. But the officers' arrests have to meet the requirements of the U.S. Constitution. The noble end of crime control doesn't justify unreasonable arrests to attain that end.

Arrests, like the *stops* you learned about in Chapter 4, are Fourth Amendment seizures. But they're more invasive than stops, and they require a higher objective basis to make them reasonable. Stops are measured in minutes; arrests can last hours, sometimes even days. The duration of the seizure is one difference. Stops begin and end on streets and in other public places with other people around; arrested people are taken to the isolated and intimidating surroundings of the local police department and jail where they're held against their will for hours, sometimes even days. A change in location is a second distinction.

Third, whereas most stops don't get "written up," arrests produce written documents that become part of a person's record, or "rap sheet." Fourth, stops (unless accompanied by frisks) don't involve body searches. Full-body searches (usually) and strip and body-cavity searches (sometimes) accompany arrests (Chapter 7). Interrogations (Chapter 8) and lineups (Chapter 9) can also accompany arrests (Table 5.1).

In this chapter, you'll learn the definition of arrest; the objective basis for arrests, which is probable cause to arrest; how courts decide whether the actions taken by officers before and during arrests—namely, entering homes to make arrests and using force to get and maintain control of suspects—were reasonable; and, finally, the criteria for determining whether actions officers took after the arrests were reasonable.

**TABLE 5.1**    **Characteristics of a Custodial Arrest**

- The police officer says to the suspect, "You're under arrest."
- The suspect is put into a squad car.
- The suspect is taken to the police station.
- The suspect is photographed, booked, and fingerprinted.
- The suspect is searched.
- The suspect is locked up either at the police station or in a jail cell.
- The suspect is interrogated.
- The suspect may be put into a lineup.

# THE DEFINITION OF ARREST

Arrests can produce fear, anxiety, and loss of liberty. They can also cause loss of income and even the loss of a job. Furthermore, these losses don't just affect arrested suspects; they also embarrass and cause economic hardship to their families. These embarrassments and hardships rarely accompany a Fourth Amendment stop.

| TABLE 5.2 | Deprivations of Liberty from Stops to Imprisonment | | | |
|---|---|---|---|---|
| Deprivation | Objective Basis | Duration | Location | Degree of Invasion |
| Voluntary contact | None | Brief | On the spot | Moral and psychological pressure |
| Stop | Reasonable suspicion | Minutes | At or near the stop on the street or in another public place | Reveal identification and explain whereabouts |
| Arrest | Probable cause | Hours to a few days | Usually removal to a police station | Fingerprints, booking, photograph, interrogation, identification procedures |
| Detention | Probable cause | Days to months | Jail | Inventory, full-body, strip, and body-cavity searches; restricted contact with the outside |
| Imprisonment | Proof beyond a reasonable doubt | Years to life | Prison | Same as detention with heightened invasions of privacy, liberty, andproperty |

These are the characteristics of **custodial arrests**, defined as an official taking a person into custody and holding her to answer criminal charges. But considerably less invasive seizures can also be arrests. Think of arrest as a zone, not a point, within a spectrum of invasions between investigatory stops at one end and imprisonment at the other end (see Table 5.2). That zone begins when stops end and continues through full custodial arrests (detention) that involve all the invasions listed in Table 5.1.

Within that zone, arrests may contain only some of the characteristics in Table 5.1. The duration and location also may vary significantly from the characteristics in the tables. How long does a seizure have to last to turn a stop into an arrest? How far do officers have to move an individual to turn a stop into an arrest? No "bright line" separates stops from arrests. But it does matter where we draw the line because of one element common to all arrests within the zone: The Fourth Amendment requires probable cause to make them reasonable.

# A REASONABLE ARREST

There are two elements in a reasonable arrest:

1. *Objective basis*. The arrest was backed up by probable cause.

2. *Manner of arrest*. The way the arrest was made was reasonable.

In this section, we'll look at the first of these elements. Then, we'll turn to the manner of arrest in the next section.

# Probable Cause

**Probable cause to arrest** requires that an officer, in the light of her training and experience, knows enough facts and circumstances to reasonably believe that:

1. A crime has been, is being, or is about to be committed, *and*

2. The person arrested has committed, is committing, or is about to commit the crime

(Contrast this definition with the reasonable-grounds-to-suspect standard for stops discussed in Chapter 4.) Probable cause lies on a continuum between reasonable suspicion on one end and proof beyond a reasonable doubt on the other. Table 5.2 shows how the requirement for an objective basis increases as the level of invasiveness increases in criminal procedure.

The probable cause requirement balances the societal interest in crime control and the individual right of *locomotion*—the freedom to come and go as we please. According to the classic probable cause case *Brinegar v. U.S.* (1949):

> These long prevailing standards [of probable cause] seek to safeguard citizens from rash and unreasonable interferences with privacy and from unfounded charges of crime. They also seek to give fair leeway for enforcing the law in the community's protection. Because many situations which confront officers in the course of executing their duties are more or less ambiguous, room must be allowed for some mistakes on their part.
>
> But the mistakes must be those of reasonable men, acting on facts leading sensibly to their conclusions of probability. The rule of probable cause is a practical, nontechnical conception affording the best compromise that has been found for accommodating these often opposing interests. Requiring more would unduly hamper law enforcement. To allow less would be to leave law-abiding citizens at the mercy of the officers' whim or caprice. (176)

The day-to-day application of finding probable cause rests mainly with officers on the street who have to make quick decisions. They don't have the luxury that professors in their studies, judges in their chambers, and you wherever you're reading this chapter have to think deeply about technical matters. According to the Court in *Brinegar* (1949), "In dealing with probable cause . . . as the very name implies, we deal with probabilities. These are not technical; they are the factual and practical considerations of everyday life on which reasonable and prudent men, not legal technicians, act." So, although officers can't arrest on a hunch, a whim, or mere suspicion, and judges have the final say on whether the officers had probable cause, courts tend to accept the facts as police see them. According to one judge:

> Police officers patrolling the streets do not prearrange the setting within which they operate. They do not schedule their steps in the calm reflective atmosphere of some remote law library. Events occur without warning and policemen are required as a matter of duty to act as a reasonably prudent policeman would under the circumstances as those circumstances unfold before him. (*People v. Brown* 1969, 869)

The basis for reasonable belief can be either direct information or hearsay. Let's look at these two kinds of information.

## Direct Information

*Direct information* is firsthand information known to arresting officers through what they see, hear, feel, taste, and smell. Direct information doesn't automatically make the case for probable cause. The courts look for patterns, or a totality of circumstances, that build the case for probable cause. Table 5.3 lists some of the facts and circumstances officers usually acquire firsthand, and which either alone or in combination a judge may rule amounts to probable cause.

| TABLE 5.3 | Probable Cause Information Officers Know Firsthand | |
| --- | --- | --- |
| • Fleeing ("flight") | | • Attempting to destroy evidence |
| • Resisting officers | | • Matching fingerprints |
| • Making furtive movements | | • Matching hair samples |
| • Hiding | | • Matching blood samples |
| • Giving evasive answers | | • Matching |
| • Giving contradictory explanations | | • DNA profile |

## Hearsay

Officers don't have to rely on direct information to make their case for probable cause. They can (and often do) rely on *hearsay*, information they get secondhand from victims, witnesses, other police officers, and professional informants. According to the **hearsay rule**, courts don't admit secondhand evidence to prove guilt, but, if it's reliable and truthful, they'll accept it to show probable cause to arrest. Why? Because arrests aren't trials.

Of course, arrests can still cost suspects their liberty—but only long enough to decide whether there's enough evidence to charge them with a crime (Chapter 12) and put them on trial (Chapter 13). At trial, there are legal experts in the courtroom to testify and plenty of time to weigh the evidence. However, police officers on the street—and at the precinct station—aren't lawyers, and they aren't supposed to be. They don't have the leisure to sort out the evidence they've acquired. As you learned earlier, officers either have to act immediately or forever lose their chance to arrest suspects. So allowing hearsay to show probable cause reflects the deference that courts concede to the realities of police work.

Not all hearsay carries equal weight; some informants are more trustworthy than others. In determining probable cause, magistrates weigh both the trustworthiness and the source of the information. So, according to the court in *Allison v. State* (1974), "If the citizen or victim informant is an eyewitness this will be enough to support probable cause even without specific corroboration of reliability." But this isn't true if victims or witnesses refuse to identify themselves. So anonymous tips alone never are enough to establish probable cause to arrest (see *Draper v. U.S.* [1958], the case excerpt on the next page).

There's another problem. Bystander eyewitnesses aren't the source of most hearsay information; professional informants (almost always) are. And snitches create greater problems with credibility than victims and nonprofessional eyewitnesses. In *Jones v. U.S.* (1959), the U.S. Court of Appeals for the District of Columbia wrote:

> It is notorious that the narcotics informer is often himself involved in the narcotics traffic and is often paid for his information in cash, narcotics, immunity from prosecution, or lenient punishment. . . . The reliability of such persons is obviously suspect. . . . The present informer practice amounts to condoning felonies on condition that the confessed or suspected felon brings about the conviction of others. Under such stimulation it is to be expected that the informer will not infrequently reach for shadowy leads, or even seek to incriminate the innocent. The practice of paying fees to the informer for the cases he makes may also be expected from time to time, to induce him to lure no-users into the drug habit and then entrap them into law violations. (928)

(We'll discuss informants further and the test for evaluating their information in Chapter 6 when we get to probable cause to search.)

One of the best discussions of probable cause, and one of the clearest explanations of its application to the facts of an arrest based on a combination of direct and hearsay information (hearsay corroborated by an officer's direct observations), appears in our first case excerpt, *Draper v. U.S.* (1959).

---

## CASE — *Does an Informant's Corroborated Information Amount to Probable Cause to Arrest?*

### Draper v. U.S.
358 U.S. 307 (1959)

#### HISTORY

James Alonzo Draper was prosecuted for knowingly concealing and transporting heroin in violation of federal narcotics laws. The U.S. District Court for the District of Colorado denied Draper's motion to suppress the heroin, and Draper was convicted. Draper appealed. The U.S. Court of Appeals affirmed the conviction. The U.S. Supreme Court granted certiorari and affirmed.

WHITTAKER, J.

#### FACTS

The evidence offered at the hearing on the motion to suppress . . . established that . . . Marsh, a federal narcotic agent with 29 years' experience, was stationed at Denver; that . . . Hereford had been engaged as a "special employee" of the Bureau of Narcotics at Denver for about six months, and from time to time gave information to Marsh regarding violations of the narcotics laws, for which Hereford was paid small sums of money, and that Marsh had always found the information given by Hereford to be accurate and reliable.

On September 3, 1956, Hereford told Marsh that James Draper (petitioner) recently had taken up abode at a stated address in Denver and "was peddling narcotics to several addicts" in that city. Four days later, on September 7, Hereford told Marsh "that Draper had gone to Chicago the day before (September 6) by train and that he was going to bring back three ounces of heroin and that he would return to Denver either on the morning of the 8th of September or the morning of the 9th of September also by train." Hereford also gave Marsh a detailed physical description of Draper and of the clothing he was wearing. Hereford told Marsh that Draper was a Negro of light brown complexion, 27 years of age, 5 feet 8 inches tall, weighed about 160 pounds, and that he was wearing a light colored raincoat, brown slacks, and black shoes.

He said that he would be carrying "a tan zipper bag," and that he habitually "walked real fast."

On the morning of September 8, Marsh and a Denver police officer went to the Denver Union Station and kept watch over all incoming trains from Chicago, but they did not see anyone fitting the description that Hereford had given. Repeating the process on the morning of September 9, they saw a person, having the exact physical attributes and wearing the precise clothing described by Hereford, alight from an incoming Chicago train and start walking "fast" toward the exit. He was carrying a tan zipper bag in his right hand and the left was thrust in his raincoat pocket.

Marsh, accompanied by the police officer, overtook, stopped and arrested him. They then searched him and found the two "envelopes containing heroin" clutched in his left hand in his raincoat pocket, and found the syringe in the tan zipper bag. Marsh then took him (petitioner) into custody. Hereford died four days after the arrest and therefore did not testify at the hearing on the motion.

#### OPINION

The Narcotic Control Act of 1956, provides, in pertinent part: The Commissioner . . . and agents, of the Bureau of Narcotics . . . may—(2) make arrests without warrant for violations of any law of the United States relating to narcotic drugs . . . where the violation is committed in the presence of the person making the arrest or where such person has reasonable grounds to believe that the person to be arrested has committed or is committing such violation.

The crucial question for us then is whether knowledge of the related facts and circumstances gave Marsh "probable cause" within the meaning of the Fourth Amendment, and "reasonable grounds" within the meaning of § 104(a) to believe that petitioner had committed or was committing a violation of the narcotics laws. The terms probable cause as used in the Fourth Amendment and reasonable grounds as used in § 104 (a) of the Narcotic Control Act, 70 Stat. 570, are substantial equivalents of the same meaning.

If it did, the arrest, though without a warrant, was lawful and the subsequent search of petitioner's person and the seizure of the found heroin were validly made incident to a lawful arrest, and therefore the motion to suppress was properly overruled and the heroin was competently received in evidence at the trial.

Petitioner contends (1) that the information given by Hereford to Marsh was "hearsay" and, because hearsay is not legally competent evidence in a criminal trial, could not legally have been considered, but should have been put out of mind, by Marsh in assessing whether he had "probable cause" and "reasonable grounds" to arrest petitioner without a warrant, and (2) that, even if hearsay could lawfully have been considered, Marsh's information should be held insufficient to show "probable cause" and "reasonable grounds" to believe that petitioner had violated or was violating the narcotic laws and to justify his arrest without a warrant.

Considering the first contention, we find petitioner entirely in error. The criterion of admissibility in evidence, to prove the accused's guilt, of the facts relied upon to show probable cause goes much too far in confusing and disregarding the difference between what is required to prove guilt in a criminal case and what is required to show probable cause for arrest or search. It approaches requiring (if it does not in practical effect require) proof sufficient to establish guilt in order to substantiate the existence of probable cause. There is a large difference between the two things to be proved (guilt and probable cause), as well as between the tribunals which determine them, and therefore a like difference in the quanta and modes of proof required to establish them. . . .

Nor can we agree with petitioner's second contention that Marsh's information was insufficient to show probable cause and reasonable grounds to believe that petitioner had violated or was violating the narcotic laws and to justify his arrest without a warrant. The information given to narcotic agent Marsh by "special employee" Hereford may have been hearsay to Marsh, but coming from one employed for that purpose and whose information had always been found accurate and reliable, it is clear that Marsh would have been derelict in his duties had he not pursued it.

And when, in pursuing that information, he saw a man, having the exact physical attributes and wearing the precise clothing and carrying the tan zipper bag that Hereford had described, alight from one of the very trains from the very place stated by Hereford and start to walk at a "fast" pace toward the station exit, Marsh had personally verified every facet of the information given him by Hereford except whether petitioner had accomplished his mission and had the three ounces of heroin on his person or in his bag. And surely, with every other bit of Hereford's information being thus personally verified, Marsh had "reasonable grounds" to believe that the remaining unverified bit of Hereford's information—that Draper would have the heroin with him—was likewise true.

In dealing with probable cause . . . as the very name implies, we deal with probabilities. These are not technical; they are the factual and practical considerations of everyday life on which reasonable and prudent men, not legal technicians, act. Probable cause exists where "the facts and circumstances within their (the arresting officers') knowledge and of which they had reasonably trustworthy information are sufficient in themselves to warrant a man of reasonable caution in the belief that" an offense has been or is being committed.

We believe that, under the facts and circumstances here, Marsh had probable cause and reasonable grounds to believe that petitioner was committing a violation of the laws of the United States relating to narcotic drugs at the time he arrested him. The arrest was therefore lawful, and the subsequent search and seizure, having been made incident to that lawful arrest, were likewise valid. It follows that petitioner's motion to suppress was properly denied and that the seized heroin was competent evidence lawfully received at the trial.

AFFIRMED.

## DISSENT

### DOUGLAS, J.

Decisions under the Fourth Amendment, taken in the long view, have not given the protection to the citizen which the letter and spirit of the Amendment would seem to require. One reason, I think, is that wherever a culprit is caught redhanded, as in leading Fourth Amendment cases, it is difficult to adopt and enforce a rule that would turn him loose. A rule protective of law-abiding citizens is not apt to flourish where its advocates are usually criminals. Yet the rule we fashion is for the innocent and guilty alike. If the word of the informer on which the present arrest was made is sufficient to make the arrest legal, his word would also protect the police who, acting on it, hauled the innocent citizen off to jail.

Of course, the education we receive from mystery stories and television shows teaches that what happened in this case is efficient police work. The police are tipped off that a man carrying narcotics will step off the morning train. A man meeting the precise description does alight from the train. No warrant for his arrest has been—or, as I see it, could then be—obtained. Yet he is arrested; and narcotics are found in his pocket and a syringe in the bag he carried. This is the familiar pattern of crime detection which has been dinned into public consciousness as the correct and efficient one. It is, however, a distorted reflection of the constitutional system under which we are supposed to live. . . .

The Court is quite correct in saying that proof of "reasonable grounds" for believing a crime was being committed need not be proof admissible at the trial. It could be inferences from suspicious acts, e.g., consort with known peddlers, the surreptitious passing of a package, an intercepted message suggesting criminal activities, or any number of such events coming to the knowledge of the officer. But, if he takes the law into his own hands and does not seek the protection of a warrant, he must act on some evidence known to him.

The law goes far to protect the citizen. Even suspicious acts observed by the officers may be as consistent with innocence as with guilt. That is not enough, for even the guilty may not be implicated on suspicion alone. The reason is, as I have said, that the standard set by the Constitution and by the statute is one that will protect both the officer and the citizen. For if the officer acts with "probable cause" or on "reasonable grounds," he is protected even though the citizen is innocent.

This important requirement should be strictly enforced, lest the whole process of arrest revert once more to whispered accusations by people. When we lower the guards as we do today, we risk making the role of the informer—odious in our history—once more supreme. I think the correct rule was stated in *Poldo v. U.S.* "Mere suspicion is not enough; there must be circumstances represented to the officers through the testimony of their senses sufficient to justify them in a good-faith belief that the defendant had violated the law."

Here the officers had no evidence—apart from the mere word of an informer—that petitioner was committing a crime. The fact that petitioner walked fast and carried a tan zipper bag was not evidence of any crime. The officers knew nothing except what they had been told by the informer.

If they went to a magistrate to get a warrant of arrest and relied solely on the report of the informer, it is not conceivable to me that one would be granted. For they could not present to the magistrate any of the facts which the informer may have had. They could swear only to the fact that the informer had made the accusation. They could swear to no evidence that lay in their own knowledge. They could present, on information and belief, no facts which the informer disclosed. No magistrate could issue a warrant on the mere word of an officer, without more. We are not justified in lowering the standard when an arrest is made without a warrant and allowing the officers more leeway than we grant the magistrate.

With all deference I think we break with tradition when we sustain this arrest. We said in *U.S. v. Di Re*, "A search is not to be made legal by what it turns up. In law it is good or bad when it starts and does not change character from its success." In this case it was only after the arrest and search were made that there was a shred of evidence known to the officers that a crime was in the process of being committed.

## Questions

1. List all the facts and circumstances supporting the conclusion there was probable cause to arrest Draper.

2. Identify which were firsthand, hearsay, or a combination of the two.

3. Do you think Justice Douglas is overreacting to the decision in this case? Or does he have a point that the hearsay provided by the informant amounts to nothing of substance that would lead a reasonable person to conclude that a crime was committed or in progress and that James Draper committed it?

4. Does the majority ruling favor crime control at the expense of procedural regularity and controlling government?

5. Does the Court give clear guidelines in regard to what constitutes probable cause to arrest? Explain.

 Go to Exercise 5.1 on the Samaha Criminal Procedure 7e website to learn more about probable cause: academic.cengage.com/criminaljustice/samaha.

## EXPLORING FURTHER

# *Probable Cause*

## 1. Did They Have Probable Cause?

*State v. Bumpus*, 459 N.W.2d 619 (Iowa 1990)

*FACTS* Des Moines police officers Gary Bryan and Michael Stueckrath were patrolling the vicinity of the Another World Lounge at about 11:00 P.M. They noticed Claude Bumpus, Marvin Taylor, and another man they didn't recognize in the parking lot of the lounge crouching behind a car. The officers observed that the men were exchanging something, but they couldn't see what it was. The Another World Lounge was a notorious site for drug transactions.

Based on their past experience with the location, the nature and furtiveness of the three men's actions, the notoriety of the location, and the lateness of the hour, the officers pulled their patrol car into the parking lot. Bumpus ran away from them into the bar. Once inside, Bumpus tried to conceal a black pouch from the officer who pursued him.

Officer Bryan grabbed Bumpus's arm and asked him to step outside. Once outside, Bumpus threw the pouch over a fence and tried to flee. After a brief struggle, Bryan seized and arrested Bumpus. The trial court decided that Officer Bryan arrested Bumpus not when he said, "You're under arrest," but when he grabbed his arm inside the bar and escorted him outside. Did Bryan have probable cause at the moment of the arrest?

*DECISION* The Iowa Supreme Court said yes: "While flight alone does not give rise to probable cause . . . in this case not only did Bumpus flee from officers but he also attempted to conceal the pouch." Therefore, when he grabbed Bumpus's arm, Officer Bryan had probable cause to arrest him.

## 2. Was There Probable Cause to Believe a Drug Deal Had Taken Place?

*People v. Brown*, 248 N.E.2d 867 (N.Y. 1969)

*FACTS* Detective Odesto, the arresting officer, testified at a suppression hearing that at 11:45 P.M., in a high-crime area in Manhattan, he observed Nathaniel Brown, in the "company of someone he suspected of being a narcotics addict." The suspected addict walked away from Brown and entered a building, returning shortly to Brown. The two came "close together," Detective Odesto said, adding: "I observed what appeared to be a movement of hand. At that time I started to go across the street and intercepted the two persons when Mr. Brown walked in my direction with 'a fast shuffling gait' and the other person walked in the opposite direction."

Detective Odesto arrested Brown for possession of a narcotic drug. At the suppression hearing, Detective Odesto explained that this was typical behavior for drug transactions in that neighborhood:

> Most of its persons engaged in the selling of narcotics do not carry narcotics on them. They usually have a place where it is stored in or carried by someone else. . . . [U]sually the person would have a conversation with the potential seller, give him his money . . . and then . . . the potential seller will go to his place where he stores the narcotics and bring it back, give it to that person, and they'll go in opposite directions.

Did Detective Odesto have probable cause to arrest Brown?

DECISION  The trial judge said yes; the appellate court reversed:

> Although the observed acts of the defendant and the suspected narcotic addict were not inconsistent with a culpable narcotics transaction, they were also susceptible of many innocent interpretations, even between persons with a narcotics background. The behavior, at most "equivocal and suspicious," was not supplemented by any additional behavior raising "the level of inference from suspicion to probable cause." Thus, for example only, there was no recurring pattern of conduct sufficient to negate inferences of innocent activity, no overheard conversation between the suspects that might clarify the acts observed, no flight at the approach of the officer, and no misstatements when questioned about observed activity.
>
> The logical and practical problem is that even accepting ungrudgingly, as one should, the police officer's expertness in detecting a pattern of conduct characteristic of a particular criminal activity, the detected pattern, being only the superficial part of a sequence, does not provide probable cause for arrest if some sketchy pattern occurs just as frequently or even more frequently in innocent transactions. The point is that the pattern is equivocal and is neither uniquely nor generally associated with criminal conduct, and unless it is there is no probable cause. Thus, for example, the observation of a known or obvious prostitute talking to a man she meets (or accosts) on the street does not establish probable cause. More of a pattern

must be shown, either by proof of the conversation or ensuing culpable conduct.

## 3. Was "Flight" Enough to Amount to Probable Cause?

*People v. Washington,* 236 Cal.Rptr. 840 (Cal.App. 1987)

FACTS  Officers Lewis and Griffin were in the vicinity of 1232 Buchanan Street. They observed Michael Washington, the defendant, along with four other individuals in a courtyard area between 1133 Laguna and 1232 Buchanan. Washington and the others were observed talking in a "huddle" formation with "a lot of hand movement" inside the huddle, but the officers could not see what was in the hands of any member of the group.

The officers then walked toward the group, at which point everyone looked in the officers' direction, whispered, and quickly dispersed. When Washington saw the officers, he immediately turned around and started walking at a fast pace through the lobby of 1232 Buchanan.

The officers followed him for a quarter of a block when Officer Griffin called out to Washington. He replied, "Who, me?" Officer Griffin answered, "Yes," and Washington immediately ran away. The officers chased him. Two minutes later, while still chasing Washington, Officer Lewis saw him discard a plastic bag containing five white bundles. Officer Lewis scooped up the bag as he continued to give chase. Shortly thereafter, the officers apprehended Washington.

Officer Lewis testified that during the four years he had been a patrolman he had made at least one hundred arrests concerning cocaine in the area frequented by the defendant that night. On cross-examination, Officer Lewis answered yes when asked if most of the black men he saw in the area usually had something to hide if they ran from police.

The officer stated that prior to the chase he saw no contraband, nor was anything about the group's dispersal significant. Nor did the officer explain why they singled out the defendant to follow. The trial court denied the defendant's motion to suppress.

Did Officers Lewis and Griffin have probable cause to arrest Washington?

DECISION  The court said no:

> Prior to defendant's abandonment of the cocaine, the police lacked the "articulable suspicion that a person has committed or is about to commit a crime." The officers spotted the group of men in an open courtyard at 6:15 P.M.; the men made no attempt to conceal themselves and did not exhibit any furtive behavior. The hand gestures were, on the police officer's own testimony, inconclusive and unrevealing. Furthermore, the time at which the detention occurred is not the "late or unusual hour . . . from which any inference of criminality may be drawn." The fact that defendant was seen in what was a high crime area also does not elevate the facts into a

reasonable suspicion of criminality. Courts have been reluctant to conclude that a location's crime rate transforms otherwise innocent-appearing circumstances into circumstances justifying the seizure of an individual.

Once the officers made their approach visible, they gave no justification for their decision to follow defendant apart from the others in the group. Neither officer knew defendant or knew of defendant's past criminal record, nor did Officer Lewis testify that defendant appeared to be a principal or a leader in the group.

Further, the defendant had the right to walk away from the officers. He had no legal duty to submit to the attention of the officers; he had the freedom to "go on his way," free of stopping even momentarily for the officers. By walking at a brisk rate away from the officers, defendant could have been exercising his right to avoid the officers or avoid any other person, or could have simply walked rapidly through sheer nervousness at the sight of a police officer.

We see no change in the analysis when defendant decided to run from the officers. Flight alone does not trigger an investigative detention; rather, it must be combined with other objective factors that give rise to an articulable suspicion of criminal activity.

No such factors existed, nor does Officer Lewis's assertion that the "black men [they] see in the project usually have something to hide when they run" justify a detention. Mere subjective speculation as to the [person's] purported motives . . . carries no weight. Thus, prior to defendant's abandonment of the contraband, the circumstances of defendant's actions were not reasonably consistent with criminal activity.

Here, the officers conceded they had no objective factors upon which to base any suspicions that the group was involved in illegal activity, and the officers offered no explanation why they singled out defendant to follow. Indeed, the only justification for engaging in pursuit was that defendant was a Black male, and that it was the officer's subjective belief that Black men run from police when they have something to hide. Thus, a single factor—the defendant's race—triggered the detention. . . .

 To read the full text of the Exploring Further excerpts, go to the Samaha Criminal Procedure 7e website: academic.cengage.com/criminaljustice/samaha.

# THE MANNER OF ARREST

Probable cause by itself isn't enough to make an arrest a reasonable Fourth Amendment seizure; there's also a **reasonable manner of arrest requirement**. This means the *way* officers conduct the arrest also has to be reasonable. What's a reasonable manner? Two points are clear from the cases: First, officers have to get warrants, based on the totality of the circumstances, before they enter homes to arrest suspects. Second, officers can't use excessive force to arrest suspects, wherever they're arrested. Let's look at each of these requirements.

## The Warrant Requirement

For centuries, under the English and American common law, before the Fourth Amendment was adopted, warrants weren't required to make arrests for *felonies* outside the home lawful; probable cause was enough. In misdemeanors, warrants were required unless the offense took place in the officer's presence.

The rule that probable cause is enough to make a felony arrest outside the home lawful, even if there's time to go to a judge and get one, is followed in nearly all jurisdictions (LaFave 2004, 175). Surprisingly, it wasn't until 1976 that the U.S. Supreme Court settled the important question of whether the rule satisfied the requirements of the Fourth Amendment. In our next case excerpt, *U.S. v. Watson*, the Court ruled that it did.

## U.S. v. Watson
423 U.S. 411 (1976)

### HISTORY

Henry Watson, Defendant, was convicted before the U.S. District Court for the Central District of California, of possessing stolen mail, and he appealed. The Court of Appeals for the Ninth Circuit reversed, holding that defendant's arrest was unconstitutional because the postal inspector failed to secure an arrest warrant though he had time to do so. The Supreme Court granted certiorari. The Supreme Court reversed.

WHITE, J.

### FACTS

The relevant events began on August 17, 1972, when an informant, one Khoury, telephoned a postal inspector informing him that respondent Watson was in possession of a stolen credit card and had asked Khoury to cooperate in using the card to their mutual advantage. On five to 10 previous occasions Khoury had provided the inspector with reliable information on postal inspection matters, some involving Watson. Later that day Khoury delivered the card to the inspector.

On learning that Watson had agreed to furnish additional cards, the inspector asked Khoury to arrange to meet with Watson. Khoury did so, a meeting being scheduled for August 22. In the meantime the inspector had verified that the card was stolen. Watson canceled that engagement, but at noon on August 23, Khoury met with Watson at a restaurant designated by the latter.

Khoury had been instructed that if Watson had additional stolen credit cards, Khoury was to give a designated signal [*light a cigarette*]. The signal was given, the officers closed in, and Watson was forthwith arrested. He was removed from the restaurant to the street where he was given the warnings required by *Miranda v. Arizona* (1966). A search having revealed that Watson had no credit cards on his person, the inspector asked if he could look inside Watson's car, which was standing within view. Watson said, "Go ahead," and repeated these words when the inspector cautioned that "if I find anything, it is going to go against you."

Using keys furnished by Watson, the inspector entered the car and found under the floor mat an envelope containing two credit cards in the names of other persons. These cards were the basis for two counts of a four-count indictment charging Watson with possessing stolen mail in violation of 18 U.S.C. § 1708. Title 18 U.S.C. § 1708 punishes the theft of mail as well as the possession of stolen mail. The punishment is a fine of not more than $2,000 or imprisonment for not more than five years, or both.

Prior to trial, Watson moved to suppress the cards, claiming that his arrest was illegal for want of probable cause and an arrest warrant and that his consent to search the car was involuntary and ineffective because he had not been told that he could withhold consent.

[*The part of the Court's opinion dealing with the consent to search is omitted. See "Consent Searches" in Chapter 6.*]

The motion was denied, and Watson was convicted of illegally possessing the two cards seized from his car. Watson was acquitted on the second count. The fourth was dismissed prior to trial.

A divided panel of the Court of Appeals for the Ninth Circuit reversed, ruling that the admission in evidence of the two credit cards found in the car was prohibited by the Fourth Amendment. In reaching this judgment, the court decided two issues in Watson's favor. First, notwithstanding its agreement with the District Court that Khoury was reliable and that there was probable cause for arresting Watson, the court held the arrest unconstitutional because the postal inspector had failed to secure an arrest warrant although he concededly had time to do so. Second, based on the totality of the circumstances, one of which was the illegality of the arrest, the court held Watson's consent to search had been coerced and hence was not a valid ground for the warrantless search of the automobile. We granted certiorari.

### OPINION

. . . Contrary to the Court of Appeals' view, Watson's arrest was not invalid because executed without a warrant. Title 18 U.S.C. § 3061(a)(3) expressly empowers the Board of Governors of the Postal Service to authorize Postal Service officers and employees "performing duties related to the inspection of postal matters" to

> make arrests without warrant for felonies cognizable under the laws of the United States if they have reasonable grounds to believe that the person to be arrested has committed or is committing such a felony.

By regulation, 39 CFR § 232.5(a)(3) (1975), and in identical language, the Board of Governors has exercised that power and authorized warrantless arrests. Because there was probable cause in this case to believe that Watson had violated § 1708, the inspector and his subordinates, in arresting Watson, were acting strictly in accordance with the governing statute and regulations. . . .

Section 3061 represents a judgment by Congress that it is not unreasonable under the Fourth Amendment for postal inspectors to arrest without a warrant provided they have probable cause to do so. This was not an isolated or quixotic judgment of the legislative branch. Other federal law enforcement officers have been expressly authorized by statute for many years to make felony arrests on probable cause but without a warrant. This is true of United States marshals, and of agents of the Federal Bureau of Investigation; the Drug Enforcement Administration; the Secret Service; and the Customs Service.

Because there is a "strong presumption of constitutionality due to an Act of Congress, especially when it turns on what is reasonable, obviously the Court should be reluctant to decide that a search thus authorized by Congress was unreasonable and that the Act was therefore unconstitutional. Moreover, there is nothing in the Court's prior cases indicating that under the Fourth Amendment a warrant is required to make a valid arrest for a felony. Indeed, the relevant prior decisions are uniformly to the contrary. . . .

. . . The necessary inquiry, therefore, was not whether there was a warrant or whether there was time to get one, but whether there was probable cause for the arrest. . . . The crucial question in *Draper v. U.S.* (1959) was whether there was probable cause for the warrantless arrest. If there was, the Court said, "the arrest, though without a warrant, was lawful. . . ."

[*The Court here discussed more cases upholding the same rule.*]

The cases construing the Fourth Amendment thus reflect the ancient common-law rule that a peace officer was permitted to arrest without a warrant for a misdemeanor or felony committed in his presence as well as for a felony not committed in his presence if there was reasonable ground for making the arrest. This has also been the prevailing rule under state constitutions and statutes. The rule of the common law, that a peace officer or a private citizen may arrest a felon without a warrant, has been generally held by the courts of the several States to be in force in cases of felony punishable by the civil tribunals. . . .

The balance struck by the common law in generally authorizing felony arrests on probable cause, but without a warrant, has survived substantially intact. It appears in almost all of the States in the form of express statutory authorization. In 1963, the American Law Institute undertook the task of formulating a model statute governing police powers and practice in criminal law enforcement and related aspects of pretrial procedure. In 1975, after years of discussion, A Model Code of Pre-arraignment Procedure was proposed. Among its provisions was § 120.1, which authorizes an officer to take a person into custody if the officer has reasonable cause to believe that the person to be arrested has committed a felony, or has committed a misdemeanor or petty misdemeanor in his presence. The commentary to this section said: "The Code thus adopts the traditional and almost universal standard for arrest without a warrant."

This is the rule Congress has long directed its principal law enforcement officers to follow. Congress has plainly decided against conditioning warrantless arrest power on proof of exigent circumstances. Law enforcement officers may find it wise to seek arrest warrants where practicable to do so, and their judgments about probable cause may be more readily accepted where backed by a warrant issued by a magistrate. But we decline to transform this judicial preference into a constitutional rule when the judgment of the Nation and Congress has for so long been to authorize warrantless public arrests on probable cause rather than to encumber criminal prosecutions with endless litigation with respect to the existence of exigent circumstances, whether it was practicable to get a warrant, whether the suspect was about to flee, and the like.

Watson's arrest did not violate the Fourth Amendment, and the Court of Appeals erred in holding to the contrary. In consequence, we reverse the judgment of the Court of Appeals.

So ordered.

REVERSED.

## DISSENT

MARSHALL, J., JOINED BY BRENNAN, J.

. . . One of the few absolutes of our law is the requirement that, absent the presence of one of a few jealously and carefully drawn exceptions, a warrant be obtained prior to any search. . . .

The rule the Court announces today for arrests is the reverse of this approach. . . . The . . . approach simply does not provide adequate protection for the important personal privacy interests codified in the Fourth Amendment. Given the history of the use, and not infrequent abuse, of the power to arrest, *and the fact that arrests are, in terms, as fully governed by the Fourth Amendment as searches, the logical presumption is that arrests and searches should be treated equally under the Fourth Amendment. Analysis of the interests involved confirms this supposition.*

The Court has typically engaged in a two-part analysis in deciding whether the presumption favoring a warrant should be given effect in situations where a warrant has not previously been clearly required. Utilizing that approach we must now consider (1) whether the privacy of our citizens will be better protected by ordinarily requiring a warrant to be issued before they may be arrested; and (2) whether a warrant requirement would unduly burden legitimate governmental interests.

The first question is easily answered. Of course, the privacy of our citizens will be better protected by a warrant requirement. We have recognized that "the Fourth Amendment protects people, not places." *Katz v. U.S.* [excerpted in Chapter 3]. Indeed, the privacy guaranteed by the Fourth Amendment is quintessentially personal. Thus a warrant is required in search situations not because of some high regard for property, but because of our regard for the individual, and his interest in his possessions and person. . . .

Being arrested and held by the police, even if for a few hours, is for most persons, awesome and frightening.

Unlike other occasions on which one may be authoritatively required to be somewhere or do something, an arrest abruptly subjects a person to constraint, and removes him to unfamiliar and threatening surroundings. Moreover, this exercise of control over the person depends not just on his willingness to comply with an impersonal directive, such as a summons or subpoena, but on an order which a policeman issues on the spot and stands ready then and there to back up with force. The security of the individual requires that so abrupt and intrusive an authority be granted to public officials only on a guarded basis.

A warrant requirement for arrests would, of course, minimize the possibility that such an intrusion into the individual's sacred sphere of personal privacy would occur on less than probable cause. Primarily for this reason, a warrant is required for searches. Surely there is no reason to place greater trust in the partisan assessment of a police officer that there is probable cause for an arrest than in his determination that probable cause exists for a search. . . . Maximum protection of individual rights can only be realized by requiring a magistrate's review of the factual justification prior to any arrest. . . . We come then to the second part of the warrant test: whether a warrant requirement would unduly burden legitimate law enforcement interests. . . . I believe . . . the argument that a warrant requirement for arrests would be an onerous chore for the police seems somewhat anomalous in light of the Government's concession that it is the standard practice of the Federal Bureau of Investigation (FBI) to present its evidence to the United States Attorney, and to obtain a warrant, before making an arrest. In the past, the practice and experience of the FBI have been taken as a substantial indication that no intolerable burden would be presented by a proposed rule of procedure. There is no reason to accord less deference to the FBI practice here. . . .

. . . It is always disheartening when the Court ignores a relevant body of precedent and eschews any considered analysis. It is more so when the result of such an approach is a rule that leaves law-abiding citizens at the mercy of the officers' whim or caprice, and renders the constitutional protection of our "persons" a nullity. . . .

### Questions

1. State the rule regarding the warrant requirement for arrests that the Court majority adopted.
2. Summarize the arguments the majority makes to support the rule.
3. State the rule the dissent would adopt regarding the warrant requirement for arrest.
4. Summarize the arguments the dissent makes to support its rule.
5. In your opinion, which is the better rule, and which are the most persuasive arguments to support it? Explain your answer.

Probable cause is enough when officers want to make an arrest outside the home, but what about when they want to enter a home to make the arrest? We'll look next at what officers need to make arrests inside the home, the effect of exigent circumstances on what is "reasonable" entry and arrest, and reasons officers might secure a warrant even when it's not required.

***Arrests in Homes*** Police enter homes for a variety of reasons, but the major purpose seems to be expecting, or at least hoping, they'll find a suspect they want to arrest (LaFave, Israel, and King 2004, 3:262). Whether the entry to arrest is lawful most often becomes important not because of the arrest but because of evidence obtained as a result of the entry (262).

The evidence may come to light while the officers are searching for the person named in the arrest warrant (262). But officers also discover evidence during searches inside the house *after* the arrest, including during movements of the arrested person while she changes clothes before leaving with the officer (363–69); while searching for possible accomplices (370–73); or during "protective sweeps" for the protection of the officer (373–87).

*Ordinarily*, to enter a home to arrest a suspect requires an arrest warrant. In our next excerpt, *Payton v. New York*, the U.S. Supreme Court explains why officers have to get warrants and also discusses some extraordinary circumstances when they don't have to get warrants.

## *Payton v. New York*
### 445 U.S. 573 (1980)

## HISTORY

Theodore PAYTON and Obie RIDDICK, defendants, were convicted in the Courts of New York, and the convictions were affirmed by the Supreme Court, Appellate Division, First Department, and by the Supreme Court, Appellate Division, Second Department. The convictions were again affirmed by the Court of Appeals of New York. The U.S. Supreme Court reversed the judgments and remanded the cases.

STEVENS, J.

## FACTS

### Theodore Payton's Arrest

On January 14, 1970, after two days of intensive investigation, New York detectives had assembled evidence sufficient to establish probable cause to believe that Theodore Payton had murdered the manager of a gas station two days earlier. At about 7:30 A.M. on January 15, six officers went to Payton's apartment in the Bronx, intending to arrest him. They had not obtained a warrant. Although light and music emanated from the apartment, there was no response to their knock on the metal door. They summoned emergency assistance and, about 30 minutes later, used crowbars to break open the door and enter the apartment. No one was there. In plain view, however, was a .30-caliber shell casing that was seized and later admitted into evidence at Payton's murder trial.

A thorough search of the apartment resulted in the seizure of additional evidence tending to prove Payton's guilt, but the prosecutor stipulated that the officers' warrantless search of the apartment was illegal and that all the seized evidence except the shell casing should be suppressed.

*Mr. Jacobs:* There's no question that the evidence that was found in bureau drawers and in the closet was illegally obtained. I'm perfectly willing to concede that, and I do so in my memorandum of law. There's no question about that.

In due course Payton surrendered to the police, was indicted for murder, and moved to suppress the evidence taken from his apartment. The trial judge held that the warrantless and forcible entry was authorized by the New York Code of Criminal Procedure, and that the evidence in plain view was properly seized. He found that exigent circumstances justified the officers' failure to announce their purpose before entering the apartment as required by the statute. He had no occasion, however, to decide whether those circumstances also would have justified the failure to obtain a warrant, because he concluded that the warrantless entry was adequately supported by the statute without regard to the circumstances. The Appellate Division, First Department, summarily affirmed.

### Obie Riddick's Arrest

On March 14, 1974, Obie Riddick was arrested for the commission of two armed robberies that had occurred in 1971. He had been identified by the victims in June 1973, and in January 1974 the police had learned his address. They did not obtain a warrant for his arrest. At about noon on March 14, a detective, accompanied by three other officers, knocked on the door of the Queens house where Riddick was living. When his young son opened the door, they could see Riddick sitting in bed covered by a sheet.

They entered the house and placed him under arrest. Before permitting him to dress, they opened a chest of drawers two feet from the bed in search of weapons and found narcotics and related paraphernalia. Riddick was subsequently indicted on narcotics charges. At a suppression hearing, the trial judge held that the warrantless entry into his home was authorized by the revised New York statute, and that the search of the immediate area was reasonable under *Chimel v. California* (1969) [excerpted in Chapter 6]. The Appellate Division, Second Department, affirmed the denial of the suppression motion. The New York Court of Appeals, in a single opinion, affirmed the convictions of both Payton and Riddick.

## OPINION

. . . To be arrested in the home involves not only the invasion attendant to all arrests but also an invasion of the sanctity of the home. This is simply too substantial an invasion to allow without a warrant, at least in the absence of exigent circumstances, even when it is accomplished under statutory authority and when probable cause is clearly present. We find this reasoning to be persuasive and in accord with this Court's Fourth Amendment decisions.

The majority of the New York Court of Appeals, however, suggested that there is a substantial difference in the relative intrusiveness of an entry to search for property and an entry to search for a person. It is true that the area that may legally be searched is broader when executing a search warrant than when executing an arrest warrant in the home. This difference may be more theoretical than real, however, because the police may need to check the entire premises for safety reasons, and sometimes they ignore the restrictions on searches incident to arrest.

But the critical point is that any differences in the intrusiveness of entries to search and entries to arrest are merely ones of degree rather than kind. The two intrusions share this fundamental characteristic: the breach of the entrance to an individual's home. The Fourth Amendment protects the individual's privacy in a variety of settings. In none is the zone of privacy more clearly defined than when bounded by the unambiguous physical dimensions of an individual's home—a zone that finds its roots in clear and specific constitutional terms: "The right of the people to be secure in their . . . houses . . . shall not be violated." That language unequivocally establishes the proposition that at the very core of the Fourth Amendment stands the right of a man to retreat into his own home and there be free from unreasonable governmental intrusion. In terms that apply equally to seizures of property and to seizures of persons, the Fourth Amendment has drawn a firm line at the entrance to the house. Absent exigent circumstances, that threshold may not reasonably be crossed without a warrant.

## Common Law Understanding

. . . The common-law rules of arrest developed in legal contexts that substantially differ from the cases now before us. In these cases, which involve application of the exclusionary rule, the issue is whether certain evidence is admissible at trial. At common law, the question whether an arrest was authorized typically arose in civil damages actions for trespass or false arrest, in which a constable's authority to make the arrest was a defense. . . .

A study of the common law on the question whether a constable had the authority to make warrantless arrests in the home . . . reveals a surprising lack of judicial decisions and a deep divergence among scholars. . . . The common-law commentators disagreed sharply on the subject. Three distinct views were expressed. Lord Coke, widely recognized by the American colonists "as the greatest authority of his time on the laws of England," clearly viewed a warrantless entry for the purpose of arrest to be illegal. . . . Blackstone, Chitty, and Stephen took the opposite view, that entry to arrest without a warrant was legal. . . . It is obvious that the common-law rule on warrantless home arrests was not as clear as the rule on arrests in public places. . . . The common-law sources display a sensitivity to privacy interests that could not have been lost on the Framers. The zealous and frequent repetition of the adage that a "man's house is his castle," made it abundantly clear that both in England and in the Colonies "the freedom of one's house" was one of the most vital elements of English liberty. . . .

. . . We have found no direct authority supporting forcible entries into a home to make a routine arrest and the weight of the scholarly opinion is somewhat to the contrary. Indeed, the absence of any 17th- or 18th-century English cases directly in point, together with the unequivocal endorsement of the tenet that "a man's house is his castle," strongly suggests that the prevailing practice was not to make such arrests except in hot pursuit or when authorized by a warrant. In all events, the issue is not one that can be said to have been definitively settled by the common law at the time the Fourth Amendment was adopted.

## Majority of States' Law

A majority of the States that have taken a position on the question permit warrantless entry into the home to arrest even in the absence of exigent circumstances. At this time, 24 States permit such warrantless entries; 15 States clearly prohibit them, though 3 States do so on federal constitutional grounds alone; and 11 States have apparently taken no position on the question.

A number of courts in these States, though not directly deciding the issue, have recognized that the constitutionality of such entries is open to question. But these current figures reflect a significant decline during the last decade in the number of States permitting warrantless entries for arrest. Recent dicta in this Court raising questions about the practice, and Federal Courts of Appeals' decisions on point, have led state courts to focus on the issue. Virtually all of the state courts that have had to confront the constitutional issue directly have held warrantless entries into the home to arrest to be invalid in the absence of exigent circumstances.

Three state courts have relied on Fourth Amendment grounds alone, while seven have squarely placed their decisions on both federal and state constitutional grounds. A number of other state courts, though not having had to confront the issue directly, have recognized the serious nature of the constitutional question. Apparently, only the Supreme Court of Florida and the New York Court of Appeals in this case have expressly upheld warrantless entries to arrest in the face of a constitutional challenge.

A longstanding, widespread practice is not immune from constitutional scrutiny. But neither is it to be lightly brushed aside. This is particularly so when the constitutional standard is as amorphous as the word "reasonable," and when custom and contemporary norms necessarily play such a large role in the constitutional analysis. In this case, although the weight of state-law authority is clear, there is by no means the kind of virtual unanimity on this question that was present in *U.S. v. Watson*, with regard to warrantless arrests in public places. [*See the excerpt earlier in this section.*]

Only 24 of the 50 States currently sanction warrantless entries into the home to arrest, and there is an obvious declining trend. Further, the strength of the trend is greater than the numbers alone indicate. Seven state courts have recently held that warrantless home arrests violate their respective *State* Constitutions. That is significant because by invoking a state constitutional provision, a state court immunizes its decision from review by this Court. This heightened degree of immutability underscores the depth of the principle underlying the result.

## Congressional Authority

No congressional determination that warrantless entries into the home are "reasonable" has been called to our attention. None of the federal statutes cited in the *Watson* opinion reflects any such legislative judgment. Thus, that support for the *Watson* holding finds no counterpart in this case. . . .

## Practical Consequences of Warrant Requirement

The parties have argued at some length about the practical consequences of a warrant requirement as a precondition to a felony arrest in the home. In the absence of any evidence that effective law enforcement has suffered in those States that already have such a requirement, we are inclined to view such arguments with skepticism. More fundamentally, however, such arguments of policy must give way to a constitutional command that we consider to be unequivocal.

## Conclusion

Because no arrest warrant was obtained in either of these cases, the judgments must be reversed and the cases remanded to the New York Court of Appeals for further proceedings not inconsistent with this opinion.

IT IS SO ORDERED.

## DISSENT

WHITE, J., JOINED BY BURGER, C.J.,
AND REHNQUIST, J.

. . . As early as the 15th century, the common law had limited the Crown's power to invade a private dwelling in order to arrest. A *Year Book* case of 1455 held that in civil cases the sheriff could not break doors to arrest for debt or trespass, for the arrest was then only in the private interests of a party. The holdings of these cases were condensed in the maxim that "every man's house is his castle."

However, this limitation on the Crown's power applied only to private civil actions. In cases directly involving the Crown, the rule was that "the king's keys unlock all doors." The Year Book case cited above stated a different rule for criminal cases: for a felony, or suspicion of felony, one may break into the dwelling house to take the felon, for it is the common weal and to the interest of the King to take him. Likewise, *Semayne's Case* stated in dictum:

In all cases when the King is party, the Sheriff (if the doors be not open) may break the party's house, either to arrest him, or to do other execution of the King's process, if otherwise he cannot enter. . . .

As the Court notes, commentators have differed as to the scope of the constable's inherent authority, when not acting under a warrant, to break doors in order to arrest. Probably the majority of commentators would permit arrest entries on probable suspicion even if the person arrested were not in fact guilty. . . . [*Justice White reviews the views of the leading English writers on this interpretation.*] These authors . . . would have permitted the type of home arrest entries that occurred in the present cases. The inclusion of Blackstone in this list is particularly significant in light of his profound impact on the minds of the colonists at the time of the framing of the Constitution and the ratification of the Bill of Rights.

A second school of thought, on which the Court relies, held that the constable could not break doors on mere "bare suspicion." Although this doctrine imposed somewhat greater limitations on the constable's inherent power, it does not support the Court's hard-and-fast rule against warrantless nonexigent home entries upon probable cause. . . . [*Justice White reviews the views of the leading English writers on this interpretation.*] These authorities can be read as imposing a somewhat more stringent requirement of probable cause for arrests in the home than for arrests elsewhere. But they would not bar nonexigent, warrantless home arrests in all circumstances, as the Court does today. . . .

The history of the Fourth Amendment does not support the rule announced today. At the time that Amendment was adopted the constable possessed broad inherent powers to arrest. . . . Far from restricting the constable's arrest power, the institution of the warrant was used to expand that authority by giving the constable delegated powers of a superior officer such as a justice of the peace. Hence at the time of the Bill of Rights, the warrant functioned as a powerful tool of law enforcement rather than as a protection for the rights of criminal suspects. . . .

The Court cites Pitt's March 1763 oration in the House of Commons as indicating an "overriding respect for the sanctity of the home." But this speech was in opposition to a proposed excise tax on cider. Nothing in it remotely suggests that Pitt objected to the constable's traditional power of warrantless entry into dwellings to arrest for felony.

. . . [According to] the important early [American] case of *Rohan v. Sawin*, (1851):

It has been sometimes contended, that an arrest of this character, without a warrant, was a violation of the great fundamental principles of our national and state constitutions, forbidding unreasonable searches and arrests, except by warrant founded upon a complaint made under oath. Those provisions doubtless had another and different purpose, . . . to arrest without warrant those who have committed felonies. The public safety, and the due apprehension of criminals, charged with heinous offences, imperiously require that such arrests should be made without warrant by officers of the law." . . .

This Court apparently first questioned the reasonableness of warrantless nonexigent entries to arrest in *Jones v. U.S.* (1958), noting in dictum that such entries would pose a "grave constitutional question" if carried out at night. . . . . Despite . . . *Jones* . . . a majority of the States that have taken a position on the question permit warrantless entry into the home to arrest even in the absence of exigent circumstances. At this time, 24 States permit such warrantless entries; 15 States clearly prohibited them, though 3 States do so on federal constitutional grounds alone; and 11 States have apparently taken no position on the question." *Ante*, at 1386 (footnotes omitted).

This consensus, in the face of seemingly contrary dicta from this Court, is entitled to more deference than the Court today provides.

Today's decision ignores the carefully crafted restrictions on the common-law power of arrest entry and thereby overestimates the dangers inherent in that practice. At common law, absent exigent circumstances, entries to arrest could be made only for felony. Even in cases of felony, the officers were required to announce their presence, demand admission, and be refused entry before they were entitled to break doors. Further, it seems generally accepted that entries could be made only during daylight hours. And, in my view, the officer entering to arrest must have reasonable grounds to believe, not only that the arrestee has committed a crime, but also that the person suspected is present in the house at the time of the entry.

These four restrictions on home arrests—felony, knock and announce, daytime, and stringent probable cause—constitute powerful and complementary protections for the privacy interests associated with the home. The felony requirement guards against abusive or arbitrary enforcement and ensures that invasions of the home occur only in case of the most serious crimes. The knock-and-announce and daytime requirements protect individuals against the fear, humiliation, and embarrassment of being aroused from their beds in states of partial or complete undress. And these requirements allow the arrestee to surrender at his front door, thereby maintaining his dignity and preventing the officers from entering other rooms of the dwelling. The stringent probable-cause requirement would help ensure against the possibility that the police would enter when the suspect was not home, and, in searching for him, frighten members of the family or ransack parts of the house, seizing items in plain view.

In short, these requirements, taken together, permit an individual suspected of a serious crime to surrender at the front door of his dwelling and thereby avoid most of the humiliation and indignity that the Court seems to believe necessarily accompany a house arrest entry. Such a front-door arrest, in my view, is no more intrusive on personal privacy than the public warrantless arrests which we found to pass constitutional muster in *U.S. v. Watson* [excerpted earlier in this section].

All of these limitations on warrantless arrest entries are satisfied on the facts of the present cases. The arrests here were for serious felonies—murder and armed robbery—and both occurred during daylight hours. The authorizing statutes required that the police announce their business and demand entry; neither Payton nor Riddick makes any contention that these statutory requirements were not fulfilled. And it is not argued that the police had no probable cause to believe that both Payton and Riddick were in their dwellings at the time of the entries.

Today's decision, therefore, sweeps away any possibility that warrantless home entries might be permitted in some limited situations other than those in which exigent circumstances are present. The Court substitutes, in one sweeping decision, a rigid constitutional rule in place of the common-law approach, evolved over hundreds of years, which achieved a flexible accommodation between the demands of personal privacy and the legitimate needs of law enforcement. . . .

While exaggerating the invasion of personal privacy involved in home arrests, the Court fails to account for the danger that its rule will "severely hamper effective law enforcement." The policeman on his beat must now make subtle discriminations that perplex even judges in their chambers. . . . Police will sometimes delay making an arrest, even after probable cause is established, in order to be sure that they have enough evidence to convict. Then, if they suddenly have to arrest, they run the risk that the subsequent exigency will not excuse their prior failure to obtain a warrant. This problem cannot effectively be cured by obtaining a warrant as soon as probable cause is established because of the chance that the warrant will go stale before the arrest is made. . . .

Our cases establish that the ultimate test under the Fourth Amendment is one of "reasonableness." I cannot join the Court in declaring unreasonable a practice which has been thought entirely reasonable by so many for so long. It would be far preferable to adopt a clear and simple rule: after knocking and announcing their presence, police may enter the home to make a daytime arrest without a warrant when there is probable cause to believe that the person to be arrested committed a felony and is present in the house. This rule would best comport with the common-law background, with the traditional practice in the States, and with the history and policies of the Fourth Amendment. Accordingly, I respectfully DISSENT.

## Questions

1. Summarize the details of the arrests of Theodore Payton and Obie Riddick.

2. State the elements of the test the Court applied to determine whether the arrests required a warrant to make them reasonable.

3. Summarize the arguments of the majority for holding that the arrests required a warrant.

4. Summarize the arguments of the dissent for concluding that the arrests didn't require a warrant.

5. In your opinion, how important, if at all, is the Court's discussion of history? Should it be important? Explain your answer.

6. In your opinion, which arguments are more persuasive, those of the majority or those of the dissent? Defend your answer.

# Entering Homes to Arrest

## 1. Was the Arrest Made *in* His Home?

*State v. Holeman*, 693 P.2d 89 (Wash. 1985)

*FACTS* Two uniformed police officers went to David Holeman's home to question him about the theft of a bicycle. David's father, Clarence Holeman, met the officers at the door and called David to the doorway. The officers, while remaining outside, questioned David as he was standing in the doorway. David denied any involvement in the theft. During the discussion, Clarence Holeman became angry and told the police they had no right to arrest David without a warrant. At this point, the officers read David his *Miranda* rights and decided to question him at the police station despite the fact that they did not have a warrant. Both parties agree that at this point David was under arrest.

*DECISION* Was the arrest without a warrant reasonable? No, according to the court:

> David was under arrest at this point in time despite the fact that the officers never told David that he was under arrest. A person is under arrest for constitutional purposes when, by a show of authority, his freedom of movement is restrained. Here, when the police began reading David his *Miranda* rights, he was not free to leave and, as such, was under arrest for Fourth Amendment purposes.
>
> This arrest of David was unlawful because, without a warrant and absent exigent circumstances, the police are prohibited from arresting a suspect while the suspect is standing in the doorway of his house.
>
> The Fourth Amendment has drawn a firm line at the entrance to the house. Absent exigent circumstances, that threshold may not reasonably be crossed without a warrant. It is no argument to say that the police never crossed the threshold of David's house. It is not the location of the arresting officer that is important in determining whether an arrest occurred in the home for Fourth Amendment purposes.
>
> A person does not forfeit his Fourth Amendment privacy interests by opening his door to police officers. A person's home can be invaded to the same extent when the police remain outside the house and call a person to the door as when the police physically enter the household itself. . . . Here the police did not have the proper authority of law; *i.e.*, a warrant. Consequently, this . . . arrest of David was unlawful.

## 2. Did He Voluntarily Expose Himself to the Police?

*U.S. v. Vaneaton*, 49 F.3d 1423 (CA9 Ore., 1995)

*FACTS* Armed with . . . ample probable cause to arrest Jack Vaneaton for receiving stolen property . . . officers . . . went . . . to his motel room to see if he was there and to arrest him if he was. Wearing their uniforms and with their guns in their holsters, Portland police officers knocked on the door to Vaneaton's motel room. They made no demands; in fact, they said nothing. Vaneaton opened the curtains of a window, saw the officers, and opened the door. Detective Carpenter asked him if he was Jack Vaneaton, and when he said he was, he was arrested.

At the moment of his arrest, Vaneaton was standing at the doorway but just inside the threshold. The arresting officer was immediately outside the threshold of the room and did not enter before advising Vaneaton he was under arrest. Vaneaton was then handcuffed. . . .

*OPINION* Did the arrest require a warrant? No. According to the court:

> . . . The question presented in this case is not decided only on the basis of whether Vaneaton was standing inside or outside the threshold of his room, but whether he "voluntarily exposed himself to warrantless arrest" by freely opening the door of his motel room to the police. If he so exposed himself, the presumption created by *Payton* is overcome.
>
> . . . The arrest in the instant case involves factors that distinguish it from the arrests made in *Payton* and its consolidated companion case, *Riddick v. New York*. In *Payton*, the police who entered Payton's apartment broke through a closed door with crowbars. . . . In *Riddick*, the closed door of Riddick's house on which the police knocked was opened by Riddick's young son. Riddick could be seen sitting inside the apartment on a bed. He was covered by a sheet. Without any behavior on Riddick's part that could be construed as consent, the police entered and arrested him on the spot. In both cases, the entries preceded the arrests.
>
> By contrast, in Vaneaton's case the uniformed police used no force or threats, and . . . they did not resort to a subterfuge or a ruse, or draw weapons. When Vaneaton saw them through the window, he voluntarily opened the door and exposed both himself and the immediate area to them. No threats or force were used by the police to get him to open the door, and his actions were not taken in response to a claim of lawful authority. The police did not enter the house until they formally placed Vaneaton under arrest. . . . Accordingly, by opening the door as he did, Vaneaton exposed himself in a public place. His warrantless arrest, therefore, does not offend the Fourth Amendment.

*DISSENT* The majority holds that police officers, acting with probable cause, but without a warrant, may arrest a citizen inside his or her home, merely because that citizen opens the door in response to their knock. This result is flatly contrary to *Payton v. New York* (1980), in which the Supreme Court held that the Fourth Amendment "prohibits the police from making a warrantless and nonconsensual entry into a suspect's home in order to make a routine felony arrest."

. . . The majority's opinion is also bad policy. It will have the effect of discouraging private citizens from answering knocks on the door by uniformed police officers, by subjecting citizens to warrantless arrests inside their own homes, stemming from nothing more than the exercise of common courtesy in answering a police officer's knock on the door. Indeed, it provides a justification for refusing to answer a police officer's knock. The result is bound to make routine police investigation more difficult and further to strain relations between the citizenry and police.

While making police work more difficult, the majority's decision simultaneously erodes the privacy interests protected by the Fourth Amendment. The majority has,

quite literally, opened the door to warrantless invasions of the home, ignoring the Supreme Court's warning that "the 'physical entry of the home is the chief evil against which the wording of the Fourth Amendment is directed.' "

Because the police crossed *Payton's* bright line and, in doing so, violated Vaneaton's Fourth Amendment rights, I would vacate Vaneaton's conviction and reverse the district court's order denying his motion to suppress the evidence obtained as the fruit of this unconstitutional conduct.

 To read the full text of the Exploring Further excerpts, go to the Samaha Criminal Procedure 7e website: academic.cengage.com/criminaljustice/samaha.

*Exigent Circumstances*  The U.S. Supreme Court in *Payton v. New York* accepted the lower court's finding that the arrests of Payton and Riddick were

> routine arrests in which there was ample time to obtain a warrant. Accordingly, we have no occasion to consider the sort of emergency or dangerous situation, described in our cases as "**exigent circumstances**," that would justify a warrantless entry into a home for the purpose of either arrest or search. (583)

The courts have held that a variety of exigent circumstances don't require officers to get arrest warrants before they enter homes to make arrests. One you might have heard of is "hot pursuit," first recognized by the U.S. Supreme Court in *Warden v. Hayden* (1967). In that case, the police were informed that an armed robbery had taken place, and that Bennie Joe Hayden had entered 2111 Cocoa Lane less than five minutes before the officers had arrived. According to the Court:

> [T]hey acted reasonably when they entered the house and began to search for a man of the description they had been given and for weapons which he had used in the robbery or might use against them.
>
> The Fourth Amendment does not require police officers to delay in the course of an investigation if to do so would gravely endanger their lives or the lives of others. Speed here was essential, and only a thorough search of the house for persons and weapons could have insured that Hayden was the only man present and that the police had control of all weapons which could be used against them or to effect an escape. (298–99)

Table 5.4 lists the major exigent circumstances that allow officers to enter homes to arrest without a warrant.

### TABLE 5.4 — Exigent Circumstances that May Make Entering Homes to Arrest without Arrest Warrants Reasonable

- A serious offense, particularly violent crime
- Reasonable belief the suspect is armed
- More than the amount of probable cause needed to get a warrant
- A strong reason to believe the suspect is inside
- A likelihood the suspect will escape if not swiftly apprehended
- Nonforcible entry

*Source: Dorman v. U.S. (1974).*

*Arrest Warrants*   As the previous sections have shown, the vast majority of arrests don't require officers to get arrest warrants to make the arrest reasonable. Even though the Fourth Amendment doesn't demand that officers get arrest warrants to arrest felony suspects outside their homes, it may still be a good idea to do so. Why? Because a judge's approval before making an arrest means officers don't have to worry about the lawfulness of arrests.

If officers need a warrant to make an arrest in a home, or if they want to get a warrant to ensure an arrest is reasonable, the Fourth Amendment requires that arrest warrants include three elements:

1. *A neutral magistrate.* A disinterested judge to decide whether there is probable cause before officers arrest suspects.

2. *An **affidavit** (sworn statement).* This is made by someone (nearly always a law enforcement officer) who swears under oath to the facts and circumstances amounting to probable cause.

3. *The name of the person to be arrested.* The warrant has to identify specifically the person(s) the officers are going to arrest.

Let's look more closely at each of these requirements.

- *A neutral magistrate.* The requirement that officers get approval from a neutral magistrate (one who will fairly and adequately review the warrant) before they arrest assumes that magistrates carefully review the information that law enforcement officers supply them. However, both the outcomes of cases and social science research suggest otherwise:

  There is little reason to be reassured by what we know about magistrates in operation. The magistrate can know there are factual issues to be explored only if he looks behind the particulars presented. Yet it is rare for such initiatives to be taken. Most magistrates devote very little time to appraising the affidavit's sufficiency. They assume that the affiant is being honest.

  . . . They tend to ask no questions and to issue warrants in routine fashion. Over the years the police have adapted their practice not only to the law's requirements but also to the opportunities presented by the manner in which the law is administered. They have often relied on the magistrate's passivity to insulate from review affidavits that are only apparently sufficient—sometimes purposely presenting them through officers who are "ignorant of the circumstances" and, therefore, less likely to provide awkward details in the unlikely event that questions are asked. . . . (Goldstein 1987, 1182)

  Summarizing the results of a study of probable cause determination, Professor Abraham S. Goldstein (1987) found:

  Proceedings before magistrates generally lasted only two to three minutes and the magistrate rarely asked any questions to penetrate the boilerplate language or the hearsay in the warrant. Witnesses other than the police applicant were never called. And the police often engaged in "magistrate shopping" for judges who would give only minimal scrutiny to the application. (1183)

  Whether a judge is, in fact, neutral can become an issue, when the validity of a warrant is challenged because it's charged that the magistrate failed to properly determine whether the requirements for showing probable cause had been met before issuing the warrant. This happened in *Barnes v. State* (1975):

  At the hearing held by the trial court (challenging the issuance of a warrant) in the absence of the jury, Justice of the Peace Matthews testified that, although he did not read all of the three-page, single-spaced affidavit presented him by Officers Blaisdale and Bridges, but only "touched the high parts," he did question the officers in detail about its contents and about the necessity of issuing the warrant. Further, he was acquainted with the requirements for showing probable cause, and it was only after satisfying himself that probable cause existed for the search of the premises described that he issued the warrant.

According to the court, the charge that J. P. Matthews wasn't a "neutral and detached magistrate" had no merit (401).

- *An affidavit.* The Fourth Amendment requires that magistrates base their probable cause determination on information sworn to under oath. The pain of *perjury* (the crime of lying under oath) charges encourages truthfulness. If the affidavit establishes probable cause, the magistrate issues the warrant.

  The written statement isn't always enough to establish probable cause; sometimes it's purposely vague. For example, police officers who want to preserve the anonymity of undercover agents may make only vague references to the circumstances surrounding the information (*Fraizer v. Roberts* 1971). In these cases, supplemental oral information can satisfy the requirement in some jurisdictions. However, other courts require that all information be in writing (*Orr v. State* 1980).

  Officers usually appear before magistrates with the written affidavit, but not all jurisdictions require officers to appear in person. For example, the *Federal Rules of Criminal Procedure* (2002, 41[d][3]), authorize officers to phone or radio their information to a federal magistrate. The magistrate records the information verbatim. If the information satisfies the probable cause requirement, the magistrate authorizes the officer to sign the magistrate's name to a warrant.

  Some argue that modern electronic advances should eliminate the need for most warrantless arrests. According to this argument, officers can always obtain advance judicial approval for arrests, except in emergencies, without hindering effective law enforcement. According to Professor Craig Bradley (1985), a former clerk to Chief Justice Rehnquist, if courts adopted this practice:

  > The Supreme Court could actually enforce the warrant doctrine to which it has paid lip service for so many years. That is, a warrant is always required for every search and seizure when it is practicable to obtain one. However, in order that this requirement be workable and not be swallowed by its exception, the warrant need not be in writing but rather may be phoned or radioed into a magistrate (where it will be tape recorded and the recording preserved) who will authorize or forbid the search orally. By making the procedure for obtaining a warrant less difficult (while only marginally reducing the safeguards it provides), the number of cases where "emergencies" justify an exception to the warrant requirement should be very small. (1471)

- *The name of the person to be arrested.* The Fourth Amendment requires specific identification of the person to be arrested. To satisfy this particularity requirement, the *Federal Rules of Criminal Procedure* provide that an arrest warrant "must contain the defendant's name or, if it is unknown, a name or description by which the defendant can be identified with reasonable certainty" (4[b][1][A]).

## Arrest by Force

Whether the manner of an arrest was reasonable is affected by whether the level of force applied (if any) was reasonable. Usually, when we hear about the use of force to make an arrest, it's when the officers have killed a suspect. This tends to distort the public's view of the frequency of the use of **deadly force**—restraint capable of producing death. In reality, there are far more forcible arrests using nondeadly force than deadly force. And the vast majority of all arrests are made without the use of any force at all. Keeping these facts in mind, let's look at the use of deadly and nondeadly force to arrest suspects.

*Deadly Force* Throughout most of our history, states have followed the ancient common-law rule that allowed officers to use deadly force when it was necessary to apprehend fleeing felons. By the 1960s, many police departments had adopted rules that restricted this common-law rule. The gist of these rules is that officers can use deadly force only under two conditions: (1) it's necessary to apprehend "dangerous" suspects, *and* (2) it doesn't put innocent people in danger.

In *Tennessee v. Garner* (1985), the U.S. Supreme Court adopted these two rules as Fourth Amendment requirements in using deadly force to make arrests. Here's how it applied the rules to the facts of the case.

---

CASE | *Is Shooting a Fleeing Suspected Felon an Unreasonable Seizure?*

### *Tennessee v. Garner*
### 471 U.S. 1 (1985)

#### HISTORY

Fifteen-year-old Edward Garner was killed by the Memphis Police Department when he fled the scene of a suspected burglary. His father, Cleamtree Garner, sued the Department under U.S.C.A. § 1983 [discussed in Chapter 11] for violating his son's Fourth Amendment right against unreasonable seizures. The U.S. District Court ruled that the shooting was not an unreasonable seizure. The U.S. Court of Appeals reversed. The U.S. Supreme Court affirmed.

WHITE, J., JOINED BY BRENNAN, MARSHALL, BLACKMUN, POWELL, AND STEVENS, JJ.

#### FACTS

At about 10:45 P.M. on October 3, 1974, Memphis Police Officers Elton Hymon and Leslie Wright were dispatched to answer a "prowler inside call." Upon arriving at the scene they saw a woman standing on her porch gesturing toward the adjacent house. She told them she had heard glass breaking and that "they" or "someone" was breaking in next door. While Wright radioed the dispatcher to say that they were on the scene, Hymon went behind the house. He heard a door slam and saw someone run across the backyard.

The fleeing suspect, who was appellee–respondent's decedent, Edward Garner, stopped at a 6-feet-high chain link fence at the edge of the yard. With the aid of a flashlight, Hymon was able to see Garner's face and hands. He saw no sign of a weapon, and though not certain, was "reasonably sure" and "figured" that Garner was unarmed. He thought Garner was 17 or 18 years old and about 5'5" or 5'7" tall. While Garner was crouched at the base of the fence, Hymon called out "police, halt" and took a few steps toward him.

Garner began to climb over the fence. Convinced that if Garner made it over the fence he would elude capture, Hymon shot him. The bullet hit Garner in the back of the head. Garner was taken by ambulance to a hospital, where he died on the operating table. Ten dollars and a purse taken from the house were found on his body.

In using deadly force to prevent escape, Hymon was acting under the authority of a Tennessee statute and pursuant to Police Department policy. The statute provides that "if, after notice of the intention to arrest the defendant, he either flee or forcibly resist, the officer may use all the necessary means to effect the arrest." Tenn. Code Ann. § 40-7-108 (1982). The Department policy was slightly more restrictive than the statute, but still allowed the use of deadly force in cases of burglary. The incident was reviewed by the Memphis Police Firearm's Review Board and presented to a grand jury. Neither took any action.

Garner's father then brought this action in the Federal District Court for the Western District of Tennessee, seeking damages under 42 U.S.C. § 1983 for asserted violations of Garner's constitutional rights. The complaint alleged that the shooting violated the Fourth, Fifth, Sixth, Eighth, and Fourteenth Amendments of the United States Constitution. It named as defendants Officer Hymon, the Police Department, its Director, and the Mayor and City of Memphis.

After a 3-day bench trial, the District Court entered judgment for all defendants. It dismissed the claims against the Mayor and the Director for lack of evidence. It then concluded that Hymon's actions were authorized by the Tennessee statute, which in turn was constitutional. Hymon had employed the only reasonable and practicable means of preventing Garner's escape. Garner had "recklessly and heedlessly attempted to vault over the fence to escape, thereby assuming the risk of being fired upon."

The District Court . . . found that the statute, and Hymon's actions, were constitutional. The Court of Appeals reversed and remanded. . . .

# OPINION

. . . Whenever an officer restrains the freedom of a person to walk away, he has seized that person. . . . There can be no question that apprehension by the use of deadly force is a seizure subject to the reasonableness requirement of the Fourth Amendment.

A police officer may arrest a person if he has probable cause to believe that person committed a crime. Petitioners and appellant argue that if this requirement is satisfied the Fourth Amendment has nothing to say about how that seizure is made. The submission ignores the many cases in which this Court, by balancing the extent of the intrusion against the need for it, has examined the reasonableness of the manner in which a search or seizure is conducted. . . .

The use of deadly force to prevent the escape of all felony suspects, whatever the circumstances, is constitutionally unreasonable. It is not better that all felony suspects die than that they escape. Where the suspect poses no immediate threat to the officer and no threat to others, the harm resulting from failing to apprehend him does not justify the use of deadly force to do so. It is no doubt unfortunate when a suspect who is in sight escapes, but the fact the police arrive a little late or are a little slower afoot does not always justify killing the suspect. A police officer may not seize an unarmed, nondangerous suspect by shooting him dead. The Tennessee statute is unconstitutional insofar as it authorizes the use of deadly force against such fleeing suspects. . . .

Officer Hymon could not reasonably have believed that Garner—young, slight, and unarmed—posed any threat. Indeed, Hymon never attempted to justify his actions on any basis other than the need to prevent escape. . . . The fact that Garner was a suspected burglar could not, without regard to the other circumstances, automatically justify the use of deadly force. Hymon did not have probable cause to believe that Garner, whom he correctly believed to be unarmed, posed any physical danger to himself or to others.

# DISSENT

O'CONNOR, J., JOINED BY BURGER, C.J.,
AND REHNQUIST, J.

For purposes of Fourth Amendment analysis, I agree with the Court that Officer Hymon "seized" Garner by shooting him. Whether that seizure was reasonable and therefore permitted by the Fourth Amendment requires a careful balancing of the important public interest in crime prevention and detection and the nature and quality of the intrusion upon legitimate interests of the individual. In striking this balance here, it is crucial to acknowledge that police use of deadly force to apprehend a fleeing criminal suspect falls within the "rubric of police conduct . . . necessarily [invoking] swift action predicated upon the on-the-spot observations of the officer on the beat." . . .

The public interest involved in the use of deadly force as a last resort to apprehend a fleeing burglary suspect relates primarily to the serious nature of the crime. Household burglaries represent not only the illegal entry into a person's home, but also "pose a real risk of serious harm to others." According to recent Department of Justice statistics, "Three-fifths of all rapes in the home, three-fifths of all home robberies, and about a third of home aggravated and simple assaults are committed by burglars." . . .

Against the strong public interests justifying the conduct at issue here must be weighed the individual interests implicated in the use of deadly force by police officers.

The majority declares that "the suspect's fundamental interest in his own life need not be elaborated upon." This blithe assertion hardly provides an adequate substitute for the majority's failure to acknowledge the distinctive manner in which the suspect's interest in his life is even exposed to risk. For purposes of this case, we must recall that the police officer, in the course of . . . investigating a nighttime burglary, had reasonable cause to arrest the suspect and ordered him to halt. The officer's use of force resulted because the suspected burglar refused to heed this command and the officer reasonably believed that there was no means short of firing his weapon to apprehend the suspect.

. . . The policeman's hands should not be tied merely because of the possibility that the suspect will fail to cooperate with legitimate actions by law enforcement personnel. . . .

## Questions

1. Should the Fourth Amendment apply to the manner of arrest? Defend your answer.

2. Professor H. Richard Uviller (1986), a longtime student of police power and the Constitution, commented on the decision in *Tennessee v. Garner*:

   > It is embarrassing for a law professor to be blind-sided in his own territory. But the truth is, I didn't see it coming. It had never occurred to me that a police officer shooting to kill a fleeing felon might be engaging in an unconstitutional search and seizure. Of course, I can see the connection now that it has been explained to me, but I did not spontaneously equate a deadly shot with an arrest. And I have had some prior acquaintance not only with the fourth amendment, but specifically with the issue of the bullet aimed at the back of a retreating felon. (706)

   Is shooting a suspect a "seizure"?

3. Professor Uviller asks the following questions: Would the rule in this case permit an officer to shoot a drunk driver swerving erratically down the road headed toward a town? A person wanted for a series of violent crimes but not presently armed who flees from the police? How would you answer Professor Uviller's questions? Defend your answers.

4. Will this rule embolden criminals? Did the Court tilt the balance too far toward process and societal interests and too far away from the interest in results? Defend your answer.

*Nondeadly Force* Shooting is the most dramatic and publicized use of force to arrest suspects, but, in practice, officers are far more likely to use nondeadly force. In *Graham v. Connor* (1989), our next case excerpt, the Supreme Court applied the **objective standard of reasonable force** that it adopted in *Tennessee v. Garner*. According to the standard, the Fourth Amendment permits officers to use the amount of force necessary to apprehend and bring suspects under control. The standard is objective because it doesn't depend on the officer's intent or motives. So, as long as an officer uses a reasonable amount of force, it doesn't matter that he might have used it out of malice or prejudice; as long as there's probable cause and the amount of force used is reasonable, the arrest is reasonable. By the same token, no amount of good intentions and noble motive will make the use of excessive force reasonable.

The Court in *Graham* didn't decide whether the force used to bring Dethorne Graham under control was excessive, but it did establish the criteria that lower courts have to use to decide the question (Table 5.5).

**TABLE 5.5** **Lower Courts' Applications of "Objective Standard of Reasonable Force" Test**

| Type of Force | Case |
| --- | --- |
| Police dog to bite and hold | 1. *Kuha v. City of Minnetonka* (see excerpt on page 176) |
| | 2. *Miller v. Clark County*, 340 F. 3d 959 (CA9 2003). A deputy's use of a police dog to bite and hold a plaintiff's arm until backup arrived a minute later was objectively reasonable. |
| Pepper spray | 1. *Isom v. Town of Warren*, 360 F.3d 7 (CA1 2004). An officer's use of pepper spray to disarm a suspect armed with an axe was objectively reasonable. |
| | 2. *McCormick v. City of Fort Lauderdale*, 333 F.3d 1234 (CA11 2003). It was objectively reasonable to use pepper spray against a suspect who had recently assaulted another person; "pepper spray ordinarily causes only temporary discomfort." |
| | 3. *Vinyard v. Wilson*, 311 F.3d 1340 (CA11 2002). Using pepper spray in a minor crime, when the suspect is secured, is not acting violently, and "there is no threat to officers or anyone else," is objectively unreasonable but *is* objectively reasonable when the "plaintiff was either resisting arrest or refusing police requests, such as requests to enter a patrol car or go to the hospital." |
| Fire lead-filled bean bag rounds from shotgun | 1. *Bell v. Irwin*, 321 F.3d 637 (CA7 2003). Firing bean bag rounds from a shotgun when a suspect threatened to blow up a home with propane and kerosene and then "leaned toward a tank with what appeared to be a cigarette lighter" was objectively reasonable. |
| | 2. *Deorle v. Rutherford*, 272 F.3d 1272 (CA9 2001). Use of lead-filled bean bag rounds is objectively reasonable only when a strong government interest compels its use, because it can cause serious injury. |

| **TABLE 5.5** | **Continued** |
| --- | --- |
| **Type of Force** | **Case** |
| Hog tying | *Cruz v. City of Laramie*, 239 F.3d 1183 (CA10 2001). Binding the ankles to the wrists behind a suspect's back is "forbidden when an individual's diminished capacity is apparent" because of the high risk of suffocation. When permissible "such restraint should be used with great care and continual observation of the well-being of the subject." |
| Tight handcuffing | 1. *Payne v. Pauley*, 337 F.3d 767 (CA7 2003). Handcuffing a suspect tightly was objectively reasonable when the suspect "resisted arrest, failed to obey orders, [and] was accused of a more serious or violent crime." <br><br> 2. *Kopec v. Tate*, 361 F.3d 772 (CA3 2004). Placing excessively tight handcuffs on a suspect and needlessly failing to respond for 10 minutes to pleas to loosen them, causing permanent damage, was objectively unreasonable. |
| Taser (stun gun) | *Draper v. Reynolds*, 369 F.3d 1270 (CA11 2004). A deputy's use of a Taser to bring a motorist under control in a difficult, tense situation where a "single use of the taser gun may well have prevented a physical struggle and serious harm to either" the driver or the officer was objectively reasonable. |

# C A S E   *What Determines Whether the Force Was Excessive?*

## *Graham v. Connor*
### 490 U.S. 386 (1989)

### HISTORY

Dethorne Graham, a diabetic, brought a § 1983 action to recover damages for injuries sustained when law enforcement officers used physical force against him during an investigatory stop. The U.S. District Court directed a verdict for the defendant police officers. The court of appeals affirmed. The U.S. Supreme Court granted certiorari and reversed.

REHNQUIST, C.J., JOINED BY WHITE, STEVENS, O'CONNOR, SCALIA, AND KENNEDY, JJ.

### FACTS

On November 12, 1984, Dethorne Graham, a diabetic, felt the onset of an insulin reaction. He asked a friend, William Berry, to drive him to a nearby convenience store so he could purchase some orange juice to counteract the reaction. Berry agreed, but when Graham entered the store, he saw a number of people ahead of him in the checkout line. Concerned about the delay, he hurried out of the store and asked Berry to drive him to a friend's house instead.

Respondent Connor, an officer of the Charlotte, North Carolina, Police Department, saw Graham hastily enter and leave the store. The officer became suspicious that something was amiss and followed Berry's car. About one-half mile from the store, he made an investigative stop. Although Berry told Connor that Graham was simply suffering from a "sugar reaction," the officer ordered Berry and Graham to wait while he found out what, if anything, had happened at the convenience store. When Officer Connor returned to his patrol car to call for backup assistance, Graham got out of the car, ran around it twice, and finally sat down on the curb, where he passed out briefly.

In the ensuing confusion, a number of other Charlotte police officers arrived on the scene in response to Officer Connor's request for backup. One of the officers rolled Graham over on the sidewalk and cuffed his hands tightly behind his back, ignoring Berry's pleas to get him some sugar. Another officer said: "I've seen a lot of people with sugar diabetes that never acted like this. Ain't nothing wrong with the M. F. but drunk. Lock the S. B. up." Several officers then lifted Graham up from behind, carried him over to Berry's car, and placed him face down on its hood.

Regaining consciousness, Graham asked the officers to check in his wallet for a diabetic decal that he carried. In response, one of the officers told him to "shut up" and shoved his face down against the hood of the car. Four officers grabbed Graham and threw him headfirst into the police car. A friend of Graham's brought some orange juice to the car, but the officers refused to let him have it. Finally, Officer Connor received a report that Graham had done nothing wrong at the convenience store, and the officers drove him home and released him.

At some point during his encounter with the police, Graham sustained a broken foot, cuts on his wrists, a bruised forehead, and an injured shoulder; he also claims to have developed a loud ringing in his right ear that continues to this day. He commenced this action under 42 U.S.C. § 1983 against the individual officers involved in the incident, all of whom are respondents here, alleging that they had used excessive force in making the investigatory stop, in violation of "rights secured to him under the Fourteenth Amendment to the United States Constitution and 42 U.S.C. § 1983."

The case was tried before a jury. At the close of petitioner's evidence, respondents moved for a directed verdict. In ruling on that motion, the District Court considered the following four factors, which it identified as "the factors to be considered in determining when the excessive use of force gives rise to a cause of action under § 1983":

1. the need for the application of force;

2. the relationship between that need and the amount of force that was used;

3. the extent of the injury inflicted; and

4. whether the force was applied in a good faith effort to maintain and restore discipline or maliciously and sadistically for the very purpose of causing harm.

Finding that the amount of force used by the officers was "appropriate under the circumstances," that "there was no discernable injury inflicted," and that the force used "was not applied maliciously or sadistically for the very purpose of causing harm," but in "a good faith effort to maintain or restore order in the face of a potentially explosive situation," the District Court granted respondents' motion for a directed verdict.

A divided panel of the Court of Appeals for the Fourth Circuit affirmed. . . . We granted certiorari, and now REVERSE.

## OPINION

Fifteen years ago, in *Johnson v. Glick* 1974, the Court of Appeals for the Second Circuit addressed a § 1983 damages claim filed by a pretrial detainee who claimed that a guard had assaulted him without justification. In evaluating the detainee's claim, Judge Friendly applied neither the Fourth Amendment nor the Eighth, the two most textually obvious sources of constitutional protection against physically abusive governmental conduct. Instead, he looked to "substantive due process," holding that "quite apart from any 'specific' of the Bill of Rights, application of undue force by law enforcement officers deprives a suspect of liberty without due process of law." As support for this proposition, he relied upon our decision in *Rochin v. California* (1952) [excerpted in Chapter 2], which used the Due Process Clause to void a state criminal conviction based on evidence obtained by pumping the defendant's stomach. If a police officer's use of force which "shocks the conscience" could justify setting aside a criminal conviction, Judge Friendly reasoned, a correctional officer's use of similarly excessive force must give rise to a due process violation actionable under § 1983.

Judge Friendly went on to set forth four factors to guide courts in determining "whether the constitutional line has been crossed" by a particular use of force—the same four factors relied upon by the courts below in this case.

In the years following *Johnson v. Glick*, the vast majority of lower federal courts have applied its four-part "substantive due process" test indiscriminately to all excessive force claims lodged against law enforcement and prison officials under § 1983, without considering whether the particular application of force might implicate a more specific constitutional right governed by a different standard. Indeed, many courts have seemed to assume, as did the courts . . . in this case, that there is a generic "right" to be free from excessive force, grounded not in any particular constitutional provision but rather in "basic principles of § 1983 jurisprudence." We reject this notion that all excessive force claims brought under § 1983 are governed by a single generic standard.

As we have said many times, § 1983 "is not itself a source of substantive rights," but merely provides "a method for vindicating federal rights elsewhere conferred." In addressing an excessive force claim brought under § 1983, analysis begins by identifying the specific constitutional right allegedly infringed by the challenged application of force. . . . In most instances, that will be either the Fourth Amendment's prohibition against unreasonable seizures of the person, or the Eighth Amendment's ban on cruel and unusual punishments, which are the two primary sources of constitutional protection against physically abusive governmental conduct. The validity of the claim must then be judged by reference to the specific constitutional standard which governs that right, rather than to some generalized "excessive force" standard.

Where, as here, the excessive force claim arises in the context of an arrest or investigatory stop of a free citizen, it is most properly characterized as one invoking the protections of the Fourth Amendment, which guarantees citizens the right "to be secure in their persons . . . against unreasonable . . . seizures" of the person. . . . Today we . . . hold that all claims that law enforcement officers have used excessive force—deadly or not—in the course of an arrest, investigatory stop, or other "seizure" of a free citizen should be analyzed under the Fourth Amendment and its "reasonableness" standard, rather than under a "substantive due process" approach. Because the Fourth Amendment provides an explicit textual source of constitutional protection against this sort of physically intrusive governmental conduct, that Amendment, not the more generalized notion of "substantive due process," must be the guide for analyzing these claims. . . .

Determining whether the force used to effect a particular seizure is "reasonable" under the Fourth Amendment requires a careful balancing of "the nature and quality of the intrusion on the individual's Fourth Amendment interests" against the countervailing governmental interests at stake. Our Fourth Amendment jurisprudence has long recognized that the right to make an arrest or investigatory stop necessarily carries with it the right to use some degree of physical coercion or threat thereof to effect it. . . .

With respect to a claim of excessive force, the . . . standard of reasonableness at the moment applies: Not every push or shove, even if it may later seem unnecessary in the peace of a judge's chambers, violates the Fourth Amendment. The calculus of reasonableness must embody allowance for the fact that police officers are often forced to make split-second judgments—in circumstances that are tense, uncertain, and rapidly evolving—about the amount of force that is necessary in a particular situation.

As in other Fourth Amendment contexts, however, the "reasonableness" inquiry in an excessive force case is an objective one: the question is whether the officers' actions are "objectively reasonable" in light of the facts and circumstances confronting them, without regard to their underlying intent or motivation. An officer's evil intentions will not make a Fourth Amendment violation out of an objectively reasonable use of force; nor will an officer's good intentions make an objectively unreasonable use of force constitutional.

Because petitioner's excessive force claim is one arising under the Fourth Amendment, the Court of Appeals erred in analyzing it under the four-part *Johnson v. Glick* test. That test, which requires consideration of whether the individual officers acted in "good faith" or "maliciously and sadistically for the very purpose of causing harm," is incompatible with a proper Fourth Amendment analysis. We do not agree with the Court of Appeals' suggestion, that the "malicious and sadistic" inquiry is merely another way of describing conduct that is objectively unreasonable under the circumstances. Whatever the empirical correlations between "malicious and sadistic" behavior and objective unreasonableness may be, the fact remains that the "malicious and sadistic" factor puts in issue the subjective motivations of the individual officers, which our prior cases make clear has no bearing on whether a particular seizure is "unreasonable" under the Fourth Amendment.

Nor do we agree with the Court of Appeals' conclusion, that because the subjective motivations of the individual officers are of central importance in deciding whether force used against a convicted prisoner violates the Eighth Amendment, it cannot be reversible error to inquire into them in deciding whether force used against a suspect or arrestee violates the Fourth Amendment. Differing standards under the Fourth and Eighth Amendments are hardly surprising: the terms "cruel" and "punishment" clearly suggest some inquiry into subjective state of mind, whereas the term "unreasonable" does not. Moreover, the less protective Eighth Amendment standard applies only after the State has complied with the constitutional guarantees traditionally associated with criminal prosecutions.

The Fourth Amendment inquiry is one of "objective reasonableness" under the circumstances, and subjective concepts like "malice" and "sadism" have no proper place in that inquiry.

Because the Court of Appeals reviewed the District Court's ruling on the motion for directed verdict under an erroneous view of the governing substantive law, its judgment must be vacated and the case REMANDED to that court for reconsideration of that issue under the proper Fourth Amendment standard.

## Questions

1. List all the specific uses of force by the officers.

2. State the standard that the Court adopted for determining whether the use of force violated the Fourth Amendment.

3. How does the Court's standard differ from the test that the Court of Appeals applied in the case?

4. Why did the Court change the standard? Which test do you favor? Explain your answer.

5. If you were applying the tests to the facts of this case, what decision would you reach? Defend your answer.

 Go to Exercise 5.2 on the Samaha Criminal Procedure 7e website to learn more about the manner of arrest: academic.cengage.com/criminaljustice/samaha.

As noted in the text introducing *Graham v. Connor*, the Supreme Court left it to lower courts to apply the criteria of the objective-standard-of-reasonable-force test to a variety of types of force officers use to take and maintain control over arrested suspects. The major ones are listed in Table 5.5. Let's use another excerpt to show how one court applied the test, holding that the use of a dog trained in the bite-and-hold technique met the requirements of the test. According to the technique used in the excerpt, "if given a 'find' command, Arco [the dog] will find, 'bite' and 'hold' a suspect until commanded to release."

## C A S E — *Was the Bite-Hold Method Excessive Force?*

### Kuha v. City of Minnetonka
365 F.3d 590 (CA8 Minn., 2003)

### HISTORY

Jeff Kuha, Arrestee, who was bitten by a police dog, brought an action against the city of Minnetonka, Minnesota, and police officers, alleging the use of excessive force in violation of his civil rights under § 1983. . . . and asserting state law claims of assault and battery and negligence. The U.S. District Court for the District of Minnesota, granted summary judgment in favor of the defendants. Kuha appealed. The Court of Appeals affirmed in part and reversed in part, and rehearing was granted.

MELLOY, J.

### FACTS

On the evening of September 22, 1999, Kuha went to a bar with friends. He had four or five beers at the bar and then drove to a friend's house. Kuha claims he left his friend's home at approximately 1:00 A.M., intending to drive home. Shortly after leaving, he drove his car into a roadside curb, damaging the car and flattening the tire. Kuha walked back to his friend's house to get help. He and his friend changed the tire and placed the damaged tire on the front seat of the car. Kuha then continued on his way home.

At approximately 5:30 A.M., Kuha encountered Officer Roth, a Minnetonka police officer, who was driving in the opposite direction. Kuha failed to dim his lights when he approached the oncoming police car. Officer Roth made a U-turn and pulled Kuha over. Officer Roth called in the vehicle's license plate information and started to get out of the car for what appeared to be a routine traffic stop.

At this point, Kuha opened his door, got out, looked at the officer, and ran from his car, heading for a ditch and swamp abutting the road. Officer Roth attempted to follow Kuha but Kuha disappeared into the swamp. Beyond the swamp was a hilly area with high grass and dense brush and foliage. Beyond that were apartment and office buildings. Officer Roth returned to his police car and called for back-up. While waiting for back-up, Officer Roth inspected Kuha's car, noting its damage and the flat tire on the front seat. He also found Kuha's wallet and concluded that the picture on the license matched that of the person who had fled from the scene.

Within minutes, Officers Warosh and Anderson arrived. They were accompanied by Officer Anderson's K-9 partner, "Arco." Arco is trained under a "bite and hold" method; thus, if given a "find" command, Arco will find, "bite" and "hold" a suspect until commanded to release. While tracking Kuha, Officer Anderson held Arco's leash in one hand and a flashlight in the other. Officer Warosh provided cover for the K-9 team. Arco remained on his leash as they tracked plaintiff up a steep, woody hill and toward a grassy field.

Approximately thirty minutes after the initial stop, and as the K-9 team reached the top of a hill, Arco alerted, indicating that plaintiff was relatively nearby. At this point, Arco was around ten feet out on his lead. Arco bounded into the three-foot-high grass and "seized" Kuha. Arco is trained to bite and hold the first body part that he reaches. In this instance, Arco bit Kuha's upper leg. Kuha was naked except for his boxer shorts. He claims that he took off his clothes after swimming through the swamp because they were wet and cold.

Kuha states that he held his hands up to surrender as the officers approached and before Arco bit him, but concedes that the officers may not have seen him because of the high grass. The officers aver that they did not see the seizure but instead heard Kuha scream and arrived on the scene immediately thereafter. Prior to calling off Arco, Officers Anderson and Warosh inspected the area around and under Kuha to ensure he was unarmed. During this time, Kuha gripped Arco's head trying to free his hold. Officer Anderson repeatedly told Kuha he would not call off the dog until Kuha let go of the dog and put his hands up. Kuha eventually complied and Officer Anderson called off the dog. It is undisputed that the entire apprehension, from bite to release, took no more than ten to fifteen seconds.

The officers then handcuffed Kuha and noticed that Kuha was bleeding from the site where Arco bit him. They applied pressure to the wound and called for an ambulance. A subsequent medical examination revealed that Arco's bite had pierced plaintiff's femoral artery, causing substantial blood loss.

On May 25, 2000, Kuha pled guilty to the charge of disobeying a police officer. According to Kuha, he ran from Officer Roth because he feared he may have been over the legal alcohol consumption limit. Kuha claims he was afraid of being convicted for driving under the influence which would have severely hindered his prospects for a career as a commercial pilot. A sample of Kuha's blood was taken at the hospital when he was treated for the dog bite. The sample placed Kuha's blood alcohol level above the legal limit. He was not charged with driving under the influence, however, because of concerns that his blood loss may have altered the results of the test.

## OPINION

Kuha asserts that Officers Anderson and Warosh used excessive force in violation of the Fourth and Fourteenth Amendments in: (1) using a dog trained in the "bite and hold" method under the circumstances of the case—where Kuha had fled from a minor traffic violation and there was no legitimate concern that he was armed or dangerous; (2) allowing the dog to attack Kuha without warning; and (3) refusing to call off the dog when it was clear that Kuha was unarmed and not dangerous. Kuha alleges municipal liability based on the City's failure to properly formulate a police dog policy that contemplates less dangerous methods—e.g., the "find and bark" method. . . .

Kuha's excessive force claim is analyzed under the Fourth Amendment's "objective reasonableness" standard. (See *Graham v. Connor*, 1989, clarifying that *"all* claims that law enforcement officers have used excessive force—deadly or not—in the course of an arrest, investigatory stop, or other 'seizure' of a free citizen should be analyzed under the Fourth Amendment and its 'reasonableness' standard.") The test of reasonableness under the Fourth Amendment is not capable of precise definition or mechanical application. However, its proper application requires careful attention to the facts and circumstances of each particular case, including the severity of the crime at issue, whether the suspect poses an immediate threat to the safety of the officers or others, and whether he is actively resisting arrest or attempting to evade arrest by flight. In sum, the nature and quality of the intrusion on the individual's Fourth Amendment interests must be balanced against the importance of the governmental interests alleged to justify the intrusion.

The reasonableness of a particular use of force must be judged from the perspective of a reasonable officer on the scene, rather than with the 20/20 vision of hindsight. The calculus of reasonableness must embody allowance for the fact that police officers are often forced to make split-second judgments—in circumstances that are tense, uncertain, and rapidly evolving—about the amount of force that is necessary in a particular situation. The question is whether the officers' actions are "objectively reasonable" in light of the facts and circumstances confronting them, without regard to their underlying intent or motivation. An officer's evil intentions will not make a Fourth Amendment violation out of an objectively reasonable use of force; nor will an officer's good intentions make an objectively unreasonable use of force constitutional.

In reviewing Kuha's claims, . . . the relevant inquiry is whether Kuha presented enough proof in support of his claim that a jury could properly find that the degree of force used against him was not objectively reasonable. We conclude that he did. . . .

. . . We conclude that a jury could properly find it objectively unreasonable to use a police dog trained in the bite and hold method without first giving the suspect a warning and opportunity for peaceful surrender. . . . The presence or absence of a warning is a critical fact in virtually every excessive force case involving a police dog.

The district court held that the officers were not required to put themselves in danger by giving away their location to a hiding suspect whom they did not know for certain was unarmed. We agree that officer safety is paramount but disagree that the district court properly decided as a matter of law that requiring a verbal warning will put officers at increased risk. To the contrary, such a practice would likely diminish the risk of confrontation by increasing the likelihood that a suspect will surrender. While there may be exceptional cases where a warning is not feasible, we see no reason why, in this case, a rational jury would be precluded from finding that the officers could have placed themselves out of harm's way—e.g., at the top of the hill where they had a good vantage point, or behind one of the nearby apartment buildings—and given a loud verbal warning that a police dog was present and trained to seize by force. Although a verbal warning will not always result in a peaceful surrender, it may be, as argued by plaintiff, that, without such a warning, seizure by force is a nearly foregone conclusion.

. . . Kuha contends that the use of a police dog trained only in the bite and hold method was objectively unreasonable. In essence, Kuha argues that the governmental interest in apprehending a fleeing misdemeanant will never outweigh the potential harm inherent in canine assisted apprehensions. We disagree. Police dogs serve important law enforcement functions, and their use is not inherently dangerous.

There are innumerable situations where the use of a properly trained and utilized police dog, even one trained only in the bite and hold technique, will not result in physical interaction with the suspect, most obviously because the dog remains on a leash until his handler releases him.

Police are trained, and constitutionally obligated, to use only that amount of force reasonably necessary to effect a seizure. We will not presume that officers will abuse their discretion in this respect. And, as discussed above, we believe it will be the rare case where a verbal warning prior to releasing the dog would not facilitate a peaceful resolution of the situation.

In sum, the mere use of a police dog trained to bite and hold does not rise to the level of a constitutional violation. And in this particular case, we agree that, given the odd turn of events initiated by Kuha, the initial decision to use Arco to assist in Kuha's apprehension was objectively reasonable as a matter of law.

Kuha's claim of excessive force by the officers in the moments following his apprehension by Arco is a closer question. We must decide whether, construing the facts in the light most favorable to Kuha, a jury could properly conclude that it was objectively unreasonable for the officers to require Kuha to release Arco prior to calling off the dog. As Arco was biting Kuha's upper leg, Kuha's hands gripped the dog's head in an attempt to minimize the damage and pain. Officer Anderson repeatedly told Kuha that he would not call off the dog until Kuha raised his hands in the air. Kuha states that he tried to comply but his hands would instinctively return to the dog's head. Eventually Kuha did comply with Officer Anderson's order and the dog was called off. Kuha emphasizes that he was nearly naked during the attack, that he was clearly unarmed, and that the officers had no indication that he was dangerous.

Kuha's argument is compelling. It does not, however, end our analysis. *Graham* requires "careful attention to the facts and circumstances of each particular case," and cautions against hindsight. Here, the officers were confronted with an inexplicable flight from a minor traffic stop in the early hours of the morning. They knew the suspect had chosen to swim through a swamp rather than encounter a police officer. The area they were searching was difficult to traverse. The officers knew there were inhabited apartment buildings nearby and that residents would soon be leaving for work. They knew that Officer Roth had not seen a gun in the brief moments before Kuha fled, but, given the totality of the circumstances, they were reasonably wary of what they might encounter when they found Kuha, and reasonably concerned for their safety.

Turning to the actual seizure, it is undisputed that the entire incident lasted only ten to fifteen seconds. Moreover, we note that this is not a case where the officers are accused of siccing a police dog on a manifestly unarmed and compliant suspect. It appears uncontested that the officers did not see the initial seizure since Arco was ten feet ahead on his lead. They heard the scream and arrived immediately thereafter. On arrival, the officers were confronted with Arco "holding" a nearly naked suspect who had been hiding in three-feet-high grass. During the ten seconds or so that ensued, the officers were searching the area under and around Kuha to ensure that he was not hiding a weapon which could be used against the officers or the dog. At the same time, Officer Anderson was ordering Kuha to release the dog's head.

In light of the short time frame at issue and the conditions under which Kuha fled and was found, we conclude that as a matter of law the officers' actions after Kuha was bitten were not objectively unreasonable. We are mindful that we must construe the facts in the light most favorable to Kuha, and we do so. But we cannot ignore the undisputed facts that are equally relevant to our analysis. To do otherwise would vitiate *Graham*'s explicit recognition of, and allowance for, a measure of deference to officer judgment given the "tense, uncertain, and rapidly evolving" circumstances that officers often confront. . . .

With respect to Kuha's § 1983 claim, we REVERSE the district court's judgment in favor of the City and REMAND for further proceedings consistent with this opinion. . . .

# AFTER ARREST

Immediately after an arrest, as we've just seen, police officers may use force to subdue unruly suspects; to prevent escape; and to protect suspects, officers, other people, or property. When they arrest suspects for felonies, officers almost always take the following actions:

1. Search suspects (see Chapter 6)
2. Take suspects to the police station and then "book" them, by putting their name and address, the time the crime was committed, and other information into the police blotter

3. Photograph and fingerprint them

4. Interrogate them (Chapter 8)

5. Put them into lineups (Chapter 9)

6. Turn the results of the initial investigations over to prosecutors (Chapter 12)

7. Present prisoners to a magistrate (Chapter 12)

Misdemeanor suspects are not usually arrested; they're issued a citation. But not always. Sometimes, officers make a custodial arrest and take some or all of the seven actions in the list above. Are these full custodial arrests reasonable Fourth Amendment seizures? A sharply divided U.S. Supreme Court answered yes in the next case excerpt, *Atwater v. City of Lago Vista*.

---

C A S E  **Was the Custodial Arrest for Violating the Fine-Only Seat Belt Law Reasonable?**

### *Atwater v. City of Lago Vista*
532 U.S. 318 (2001)

### HISTORY

Gail Atwater was charged with driving without her seatbelt fastened, failing to secure her children in seatbelts, driving without a license, and failing to provide proof of insurance. She pleaded no contest to the misdemeanor seatbelt offenses and paid a $50 fine; the other charges were dismissed. Atwater and her husband, Michael Haas, sued Officer Bart Turek, the City of Lago Vista, and the Lago Vista Chief of Police Frank Miller. The City removed the suit to the U.S. District Court for the Western District of Texas. The District Court granted the City's summary judgment motion. A panel of the U.S. Court of Appeals for the Fifth Circuit reversed. Sitting en banc, the Court of Appeals vacated the panel's decision and affirmed the District Court's summary judgment for the City. The U.S. Supreme Court affirmed.

SOUTER, J., JOINED BY REHNQUIST, C.J., AND SCALIA, KENNEDY, THOMAS, JJ.

### FACTS

In Texas, if a car is equipped with safety belts, a front-seat passenger must wear one, Tex. Tran. Code Ann. §545.413 (a) (1999), and the driver must secure any small child riding in front, §545.413(b). Violation of either provision is "a misdemeanor punishable by a fine not less than $25 or more than $50." §545.413(d). Texas law expressly authorizes "[a]ny peace officer [to] arrest without warrant a person found committing a violation" of these seatbelt laws, §543.001, although it permits police to issue citations in lieu of arrest, §§543.003–543.005.

In March 1997, Gail Atwater was driving her pickup truck in Lago Vista, Texas, with her 3-year-old son and 5-year-old daughter in the front seat. None of them was wearing a seatbelt. Bart Turek, a Lago Vista police officer at the time, observed the seatbelt violations and pulled Atwater over.

According to Atwater's complaint (the allegations of which we assume to be true for present purposes), Turek approached the truck and "yelled" something to the effect of "we've met before" and "you're going to jail." (Turek had previously stopped Atwater for what he had thought was a seatbelt violation, but had realized that Atwater's son, although seated on the vehicle's armrest, was in fact belted in.) Atwater acknowledged that her son's seating position was unsafe, and Turek issued a verbal warning. He then called for backup and asked to see Atwater's driver's license and insurance documentation, which state law required her to carry. Tex. Tran. Code Ann. §§521.025, 601.053 (1999). When Atwater told Turek that she did not have the papers because her purse had been stolen the day before, Turek said that he had "heard that story two hundred times."

Atwater asked to take her "frightened, upset, and crying" children to a friend's house nearby, but Turek told her, "you're not going anywhere." As it turned out, Atwater's friend learned what was going on and soon arrived to take charge of the children.

Turek then handcuffed Atwater, placed her in his squad car, and drove her to the local police station, where booking officers had her remove her shoes, jewelry, and eyeglasses, and empty her pockets. Officers took Atwater's "mug shot" and placed her, alone, in a jail cell for about one hour, after which she was taken before a magistrate and released on $310 bond.

### OPINION

The question is whether the Fourth Amendment forbids a warrantless arrest for a minor criminal offense, such as a misdemeanor seatbelt violation punishable only by a fine. We hold that it does not.

The Fourth Amendment safeguards "the right of the people to be secure in their persons, houses, papers, and effects, against unreasonable searches and seizures." . . . If we were to derive a rule exclusively to address the uncontested facts of this case, Atwater might well prevail. She was a known and established resident of Lago Vista with no place to hide and no incentive to flee, and common sense says she would almost certainly have buckled up as a condition of driving off with a citation. In her case, the physical incidents of arrest were merely gratuitous humiliations imposed by a police officer who was (at best) exercising extremely poor judgment. Atwater's claim to live free of pointless indignity and confinement clearly outweighs anything the City can raise against it specific to her case. [Atwater argues for a new] . . . arrest rule . . . forbidding custodial arrest, even upon probable cause, when conviction could not ultimately carry any jail time and when the government shows no compelling need for immediate detention.

But we have traditionally recognized that a responsible Fourth Amendment balance is not well served by standards requiring sensitive, case-by-case determinations of government need, lest every discretionary judgment in the field be converted into an occasion for constitutional review. Often enough, the Fourth Amendment has to be applied on the spur (and in the heat) of the moment, and the object in implementing its command of reasonableness is to draw standards sufficiently clear and simple to be applied with a fair prospect of surviving judicial second-guessing months and years after an arrest or search is made.

Courts attempting to strike a reasonable Fourth Amendment balance thus credit the government's side with an essential interest in readily administrable rules. See *New York v. Belton* [excerpted in Chapter 6] (Fourth Amendment rules "ought to be expressed in terms that are readily applicable by the police in the context of the law enforcement activities in which they are necessarily engaged" and not "qualified by all sorts of ifs, ands, and buts"). . . .

. . . Atwater's . . . rule . . . promises very little in the way of administrability. It is no answer that the police routinely make judgments on grounds like risk of immediate repetition; they surely do and should. But there is a world of difference between making that judgment in choosing between the discretionary leniency of a summons in place of a clearly lawful arrest, and making the same judgment when the question is the lawfulness of the warrantless arrest itself. It is the difference between no basis for legal action challenging the discretionary judgment, on the one hand, and the prospect of evidentiary exclusion or (as here) personal § 1983 liability for the misapplication of a constitutional standard, on the other.

Atwater's rule therefore would not only place police in an almost impossible spot but would guarantee increased litigation over many of the arrests that would occur. For all these reasons, Atwater's various distinctions between permissible and impermissible arrests for minor crimes strike us as "very unsatisfactory lines" to require police officers to draw on a moment's notice.

One may ask, of course, why these difficulties may not be answered by a simple tie breaker for the police to follow in the field: if in doubt, do not arrest. . . . Whatever help the tie breaker might give would come at the price of a systematic disincentive to arrest in situations where . . . arresting would serve an important societal interest. [For example,] an officer not quite sure that drugs weighed enough to warrant jail time or not quite certain about a suspect's risk of flight would not arrest, even though it could perfectly well turn out that, in fact, the offense called for incarceration and the defendant was long gone on the day of trial. Multiplied many times over, the costs to society of such under enforcement could easily outweigh the costs to defendants of being needlessly arrested and booked, as Atwater herself acknowledges.

Just how easily the costs could outweigh the benefits may be shown by asking, as one Member of this Court did at oral argument, "how bad the problem is out there." The very fact that the law has never jelled the way Atwater would have it leads one to wonder whether warrantless misdemeanor arrests need constitutional attention, and there is cause to think the answer is no. So far as such arrests might be thought to pose a threat to the probable cause requirement, anyone arrested for a crime without formal process, whether for felony or misdemeanor, is entitled to a magistrate's review of probable cause within 48 hours, and there is no reason to think the procedure in this case atypical in giving the suspect a prompt opportunity to request release, see Tex. Tran. Code Ann. §543.002 (1999) (persons arrested for traffic offenses to be taken "immediately" before a magistrate).

Many jurisdictions, moreover, have chosen to impose more restrictive safeguards through statutes limiting warrantless arrests for minor offenses. . . . It is, in fact, only natural that States should resort to this sort of legislative regulation, for . . . it is in the interest of the police to limit petty-offense arrests, which carry costs that are simply too great to incur without good reason.

Finally, . . . the preference for categorical treatment of Fourth Amendment claims gives way to individualized review when a defendant makes a colorable argument that an arrest, with or without a warrant, was "conducted in an extraordinary manner, unusually harmful to [his] privacy or even physical interests."

The upshot of all these influences, combined with the good sense (and, failing that, the political accountability) of most local lawmakers and law-enforcement officials, is a dearth of horribles demanding redress. Indeed, when Atwater's counsel was asked at oral argument for any indications of comparably foolish, warrantless misdemeanor arrests, he could offer only one. We are sure that there are others, but just as surely the country is not confronting anything like an epidemic of unnecessary minor-offense arrests. That fact caps the reasons for rejecting Atwater's request for the development of a new and distinct body of constitutional law.

Accordingly, we confirm today what our prior cases have intimated: the standard of probable cause "applies to all arrests, without the need to 'balance' the interests and circumstances involved in particular situations." If an officer has probable cause to believe that an individual has committed even a very minor criminal offense in his presence, he may, without violating the Fourth Amendment, arrest the offender.

Atwater's arrest satisfied constitutional requirements. There is no dispute that Officer Turek had probable cause to believe that Atwater had committed a crime in his presence. She admits that neither she nor her children were wearing seat belts, as required by Tex. Tran. Code Ann. §545.413 (1999). Turek was accordingly *authorized* (not *required*, but authorized) to make a *custodial* [italics added] arrest without balancing costs and benefits or determining whether or not Atwater's arrest was in some sense necessary. Nor was the arrest made in an "extraordinary manner, unusually harmful to her privacy or . . . physical interests." . . .

The question whether a search or seizure is "extraordinary" turns, above all else, on the manner in which the search or seizure is executed. *Tennessee v. Garner* (1985) ("seizure by means of deadly force") [excerpted earlier on p. 170], *Wilson v. Arkansas* (1995) ("unannounced entry into a home") [excerpted in Chapter 6], *Welsh v. Wisconsin* (1984) ("entry into a home without a warrant"), and *Winston v. Lee* (1985) ("physical penetration of the body").

Atwater's arrest was surely "humiliating," as she says in her brief, but it was no more "harmful to . . . privacy or . . . physical interests" than the normal custodial arrest. She was handcuffed, placed in a squad car, and taken to the local police station, where officers asked her to remove her shoes, jewelry, and glasses, and to empty her pockets. They then took her photograph and placed her in a cell, alone, for about an hour, after which she was taken before a magistrate, and released on $310 bond. The arrest and booking were inconvenient and embarrassing to Atwater, but not so extraordinary as to violate the Fourth Amendment.

The Court of Appeals' en banc judgment is AFFIRMED. . . .

## DISSENT

O'CONNOR, J., JOINED BY STEVENS, GINSBURG, AND BREYER, JJ.

. . . The Court recognizes that the arrest of Gail Atwater was a "pointless indignity" that served no discernible state interest, and yet holds that her arrest was constitutionally permissible. Because the Court's position is inconsistent with the explicit guarantee of the Fourth Amendment, I dissent. A full custodial arrest, such as the one to which Ms. Atwater was subjected, is the quintessential seizure.

When a full custodial arrest is effected without a warrant, the plain language of the Fourth Amendment requires that the arrest be reasonable. . . . "The touchstone of our analysis under the Fourth Amendment is always the reasonableness in all the circumstances of the particular governmental invasion of a citizen's personal security." . . .

. . . [We] "evaluate the search or seizure under traditional standards of reasonableness by assessing, on the one hand, the degree to which it intrudes upon an individual's privacy and, on the other, the degree to which it is needed for the promotion of legitimate governmental interests." In other words, in determining reasonableness, "each case is to be decided on its own facts and circumstances." . . .

A custodial arrest exacts an obvious toll on an individual's liberty and privacy, even when the period of custody is relatively brief. The arrestee is subject to a full search of her person and confiscation of her possessions. If the arrestee is the occupant of a car, the entire passenger compartment of the car, including packages therein, is subject to search as well. The arrestee may be detained for up to 48 hours without having a magistrate determine whether there in fact was probable cause for the arrest. Because people arrested for all types of violent and nonviolent offenses may be housed together awaiting such review, this detention period is potentially dangerous. And once the period of custody is over, the fact of the arrest is a permanent part of the public record.

. . . If the State has decided that a fine, and not imprisonment, is the appropriate punishment for an offense, the State's interest in taking a person suspected of committing that offense into custody is surely limited, at best. This is not to say that the State will never have such an interest. A full custodial arrest may on occasion vindicate legitimate state interests, even if the crime is punishable only by fine.

Arrest is the surest way to abate criminal conduct. It may also allow the police to verify the offender's identity and, if the offender poses a flight risk, to ensure her appearance at trial. But when such considerations are not present, a citation or summons may serve the State's remaining law enforcement interests every bit as effectively as an arrest. . . .

Because a full custodial arrest is such a severe intrusion on an individual's liberty, its reasonableness hinges on "the degree to which it is needed for the promotion of legitimate governmental interests." In light of the availability of citations to promote a State's interests when a fine-only offense has been committed, I cannot concur in a rule which deems a full custodial arrest to be reasonable in every circumstance. Giving police officers constitutional carte blanche to effect an arrest whenever there is probable cause to believe a fine-only misdemeanor has been committed is irreconcilable with the Fourth Amendment's command that seizures be reasonable.

Instead, I would require that when there is probable cause to believe that a fine-only offense has been committed, the police officer should issue a citation unless the officer is "able to point to specific and articulable facts which, taken together with rational inferences from those facts, reasonably warrant [the additional] intrusion" of a full custodial arrest. . . .

The majority insists that a bright-line rule focused on probable cause is necessary to vindicate the State's interest in easily administrable law enforcement rules. . . . While clarity is certainly a value worthy of consideration in our Fourth Amendment jurisprudence, it by no means trumps the values of liberty and privacy at the heart of the Amendment's protections. . . .

The record in this case makes it abundantly clear that Ms. Atwater's arrest was constitutionally unreasonable. Atwater readily admits—as she did when Officer Turek pulled her over—that she violated Texas' seatbelt law. While Turek was justified in stopping Atwater, neither law nor reason supports his decision to arrest her instead of simply giving her a citation. The officer's actions cannot sensibly be viewed as a permissible means of balancing Atwater's Fourth Amendment interests with the State's own legitimate interests.

There is no question that Officer Turek's actions severely infringed Atwater's liberty and privacy. Turek was loud and accusatory from the moment he approached Atwater's car. Atwater's young children were terrified and hysterical. Yet when Atwater asked Turek to lower his voice because he was scaring the children, he responded by jabbing his finger in Atwater's face and saying, "You're going to jail." Having made the decision to arrest, Turek did not inform Atwater of her right to remain silent. He instead asked for her license and insurance information.

Atwater asked if she could at least take her children to a friend's house down the street before going to the police station. But Turek—who had just castigated Atwater for not caring for her children—refused and said he would take the children into custody as well. Only the intervention of neighborhood children who had witnessed the scene and summoned one of Atwater's friends saved the children from being hauled to jail with their mother.

With the children gone, Officer Turek handcuffed Ms. Atwater with her hands behind her back, placed her in the police car, and drove her to the police station. Ironically, Turek did not secure Atwater in a seat belt for the drive. At the station, Atwater was forced to remove her shoes, relinquish her possessions, and wait in a holding cell for about an hour. A judge finally informed Atwater of her rights and the charges against her, and released her when she posted bond. Atwater returned to the scene of the arrest, only to find that her car had been towed.

Ms. Atwater ultimately pleaded no contest to violating the seatbelt law and was fined $50. Even though that fine was the maximum penalty for her crime, and even though Officer Turek has never articulated any justification for his actions, the city contends that arresting Atwater was constitutionally reasonable because it advanced two legitimate interests: "the enforcement of child safety laws and encouraging [Atwater] to appear for trial." It is difficult to see how arresting Atwater served either of these goals any more effectively than the issuance of a citation. With respect to the goal of law enforcement generally, Atwater did not pose a great danger to the community.

She had been driving very slowly—approximately 15 miles per hour—in broad daylight on a residential street that had no other traffic. Nor was she a repeat offender; until that day, she had received one traffic citation in her life—a ticket, more than 10 years earlier, for failure to signal a lane change. Although Officer Turek had stopped Atwater approximately three months earlier because he thought that Atwater's son was not wearing a seatbelt, Turek had been mistaken. Moreover, Atwater immediately accepted responsibility and apologized for her conduct.

Thus, there was every indication that Atwater would have buckled herself and her children in had she been cited and allowed to leave. With respect to the related goal of child welfare, the decision to arrest Atwater was nothing short of counterproductive.

Atwater's children witnessed Officer Turek yell at their mother and threaten to take them all into custody. Ultimately, they were forced to leave her behind with Turek, knowing that she was being taken to jail. Understandably, the 3-year-old boy was "very, very, very traumatized." After the incident, he had to see a child psychologist regularly, who reported that the boy "felt very guilty that he couldn't stop this horrible thing . . . he was powerless to help his mother or sister."

Both of Atwater's children are now terrified at the sight of any police car. According to Atwater, the arrest "just never leaves us. It's a conversation we have every other day, once a week, and it's—it raises its head constantly in our lives." Citing Atwater surely would have served the children's interests well. It would have taught Atwater to ensure that her children were buckled up in the future. It also would have taught the children an important lesson in accepting responsibility and obeying the law. Arresting Atwater, though, taught the children an entirely different lesson: that "the bad person could just as easily be the policeman as it could be the most horrible person they could imagine."

The City also contends that the arrest was necessary to ensure Atwater's appearance in court. Atwater, however, was far from a flight risk. A 16-year resident of Lago Vista, population 2,486, Atwater was not likely to abscond. Although she was unable to produce her driver's license because it had been stolen, she gave Officer Turek her license number and address. In addition, Officer Turek knew from their previous encounter that Atwater was a local resident.

The city's justifications fall far short of rationalizing the extraordinary intrusion on Gail Atwater and her children. Measuring "the degree to which [Atwater's custodial arrest was] needed for the promotion of legitimate governmental interests," against "the degree to which it intruded upon her privacy," it can hardly be doubted that Turek's actions were disproportionate to Atwater's crime. The majority's assessment that "Atwater's claim to live free of pointless indignity and confinement clearly outweighs anything the City can raise against it specific to her case," is quite correct. In my view, the Fourth Amendment inquiry ends there.

The Court's error, however, does not merely affect the disposition of this case. The per se rule that the Court creates has potentially serious consequences for the everyday lives of Americans. A broad range of conduct falls into the category of fine-only misdemeanors. In Texas alone, for example, disobeying any sort of traffic warning sign is a misdemeanor punishable only by fine, as is failing to pay a highway toll, and driving with expired license plates. Nor are fine-only crimes limited to the traffic context. In several States, for example, littering is a criminal offense punishable only by fine.

To be sure, such laws are valid and wise exercises of the States' power to protect the public health and welfare. My concern lies not with the decision to enact or enforce these laws, but rather with the manner in which they may be enforced.

Under today's holding, when a police officer has probable cause to believe that a fine-only misdemeanor offense has occurred, that officer may stop the suspect, issue a citation, and let the person continue on her way. Or, if a traffic violation, the officer may stop the car, arrest the driver, search the driver, search the entire passenger compartment of the car including any purse or package inside, and impound the car and inventory all of its contents. Although the Fourth Amendment expressly requires that the latter course be a reasonable and proportional response to the circumstances of the offense, the majority gives officers unfettered discretion to choose that course without articulating a single reason why such action is appropriate.

Such unbounded discretion carries with it grave potential for abuse. The majority takes comfort in the lack of evidence of "an epidemic of unnecessary minor-offense arrests." But the relatively small number of published cases dealing with such arrests proves little and should provide little solace. Indeed, as the recent debate over racial profiling demonstrates all too clearly, a relatively minor traffic infraction may often serve as an excuse for stopping and harassing an individual. After today, the arsenal available to any officer extends to a full arrest and the searches permissible concomitant to that arrest. An officer's subjective motivations for making a traffic stop are not relevant considerations in determining the reasonableness of the stop. But it is precisely because these motivations are beyond our purview that we must vigilantly ensure that officers' poststop actions—which are properly within our reach—comport with the Fourth Amendment's guarantee of reasonableness.

The Court neglects the Fourth Amendment's express command in the name of administrative ease. In so doing, it cloaks the pointless indignity that Gail Atwater suffered with the mantle of reasonableness. I respectfully dissent.

## Questions

1. List all of Officer Turek's actions leading up to, during, and following Gail Atwater's arrest.

2. List all the actions taken by booking officers after Officer Turek turned her over to them.

3. According to the majority opinion, what is the bright-line rule regarding arrests for fine-only offenses?

4. Summarize the majority's arguments supporting the bright-line rule.

5. According to the majority, what are the exceptions to the bright-line rule?

6. Summarize the dissent's arguments against the bright-line rule.

7. State the rule the dissent recommends for fine-only offenses.

8. Summarize the dissent's arguments in favor of the rule it recommends.

9. List the exceptions the dissent recommends should apply to its rule.

 Go to Exercise 5.3 on the Samaha Criminal Procedure 7e website to learn more about *Atwater v. Lago Vista:* academic.cengage.com/criminaljustice/samaha.

## EXPLORING FURTHER

### *After Arrest*

#### Was the Custodial Arrest Reasonable?

*Hedgepeth v. Washington Metro Area Transit and others,* 284 F.Supp.2nd 145 (D.C.C. 2003)

*FACTS*  It was the start of another school year and the Washington Metropolitan Area Transit Authority (WMATA) was once again getting complaints about bad behavior by students using the Tenleytown/American University Metrorail station. In response WMATA embarked on a week-long undercover operation to enforce a "zero-tolerance" policy with respect to violations of certain ordinances, including one that makes it unlawful for any person to eat or drink in a Metrorail station.

"Zero tolerance" had more fateful consequences for children than for adults. Adults who violate § 35-251(b) typically receive a citation subjecting them to a fine of $10 to $50. *Id.* § 35-253. District of Columbia law, however, does not provide for the issuance of citations for non-traffic offenses to those under eighteen years of age. Instead, a minor who has committed what an officer has reasonable grounds to believe is a "delinquent act" "may be taken into custody."

Committing an offense under District of Columbia law, such as eating in a Metrorail station, constitutes a "delinquent act." The upshot of all this is that zero-tolerance enforcement of § 35-251(b) entailed the arrest of every offending minor but not every offending adult.

The undercover operation was in effect on October 23, 2000, when twelve-year-old Ansche Hedgepeth and a classmate entered the Tenleytown/AU station on their way home from school. Ansche had stopped at a fast-food restaurant on the way and ordered a bag of french fries—to go. While waiting for her companion to purchase a fare-card, Ansche removed and ate a french fry from the take-out bag she was holding.

After proceeding through the fare-gate, Ansche was stopped by a plain-clothed Metro Transit Police officer, who identified himself and informed her that he was arresting her for eating in the Metrorail station. The officer then handcuffed Ansche behind her back while another officer searched her and her backpack. Pursuant to established procedure, her shoelaces were removed.

Upset and crying, Ansche was transported to the District of Columbia's Juvenile Processing Center some distance away, where she was fingerprinted and processed before being released into the custody of her mother three hours later.

The no-citation policy was not, it turned out, carved in stone. The negative publicity surrounding Ansche's arrest prompted WMATA to adopt a new policy effective January 31, 2001, allowing WMATA officers to issue citations to juveniles violating § 35-251(b). Zero tolerance was also not a policy for the ages. Effective May 8, 2001, WMATA adopted a new Written Warning Notice Program, under which juveniles eating in the Metro are neither arrested nor issued citations, but instead given written warnings, with a letter notifying their parents and school. Only after the third infraction over the course of a year may a juvenile be formally prosecuted.

On April 9, 2001, Ansche's mother Tracey Hedgepeth brought this action as Ansche's next friend in the United States District Court for the District of Columbia. The complaint was filed under 42 U.S.C. § 1983 and named WMATA, its General Manager, the arresting officer, and the District of Columbia as defendants. . . . It alleged that Ansche's arrest . . . was an unreasonable seizure under the Fourth Amendment. The complaint sought declaratory and injunctive relief against the enforcement policies leading to Ansche's arrest, and expungement of Ansche's arrest record. . . .

OPINION . . . The law of this land does not recognize a fundamental right to freedom of movement when there is probable cause for arrest. That is true even with respect to minor offenses. . . . Ansche has made no effort to establish that there is a fundamental right, "deeply rooted in this Nation's history and tradition," to free movement when there is probable cause for arrest. The fact that the Fourth Amendment specifically addresses when freedom of movement may be restrained, and permits such restraint upon probable cause, makes any such effort exceedingly difficult. . . .

Ansche . . . challenges her arrest on the ground that it was an unreasonable seizure in violation of the Fourth Amendment. This claim quickly runs into the Supreme Court's recent holding in *Atwater*. . . . The Court in *Atwater* undertook a two-step inquiry in addressing the plaintiff's argument that a warrantless arrest for a fine-only offense was unreasonable under the Fourth Amendment. It first concluded that Atwater's argument that such arrests were not supported by the common law at the Founding, "while by no means insubstantial," ultimately failed.

The Court then declined the plaintiff's invitation "to mint a new rule of constitutional law" based on a balancing of competing interests and an assessment according to "traditional standards of reasonableness." Reasoning that "the standard of probable cause 'applies to all arrests, without the need to balance the interests and circumstances involved in particular situations,'" the Court concluded that "if an officer has probable cause to believe that an individual has committed even a very minor criminal offense in his presence, he may, without violating the Fourth Amendment, arrest the offender."

On the basis of this passage, the defendants argue that Ansche's arrest does not violate the Fourth Amendment, for it is undisputed that the arresting officer had probable cause to believe Ansche had committed a criminal offense, however minor. No balancing or inquiry into whether Ansche's probable cause arrest was otherwise reasonable is permitted. . . . The Court acknowledged that "if we were to derive a rule exclusively to address the uncontested facts of this case, Atwater might well prevail." But because a rule allowing ad hoc reasonableness review of an arrest decision, even when there is probable cause, would hobble the officer's discretion, the Court declined to engage in any inquiry beyond probable cause. . . .

In addition, the "very fact that [Fourth Amendment] law has never jelled the way Atwater would have it" led the Court to doubt "whether warrantless misdemeanor arrests need constitutional attention." The Court enumerated a number of protections, both constitutional and practical, that it thought obviated the need for reasonableness scrutiny above and beyond probable cause. The Court concluded that "the upshot of all these influences, combined with the good sense (and, failing that, political accountability) of most *local lawmakers* and law-enforcement officials, is a dearth of horribles demanding redress." The *Atwater* Court even cited WMATA's decision in this case to change its policy, and to provide for citations in lieu of arrest for "subway snackers," as an example of the efficacy of the "practical and political considerations" supporting the absence of a need for a reasonableness balancing beyond probable cause.

While we can inquire into the reasonableness of the manner in which an arrest is conducted, the only cases in which we have found it necessary actually to perform the balancing analysis involved searches and seizures conducted in an extraordinary manner, unusually harmful to an individual's privacy or even physical interests. *Graham v. Connor* [excerpted earlier on p. 173]; *Tennessee v. Garner* [excerpted earlier on p. 170]. The most natural reading of *Atwater* is that we cannot inquire further into the reasonableness of a decision to arrest when it is supported by probable cause. That is true whether the decision to arrest upon probable cause is made by the officer on the beat or at a more removed policy level. . . .

 To read the full text of the Exploring Further excerpt, go to the Samaha Criminal Procedure 7e website: academic.cengage.com/criminaljustice/samaha.

# SUMMARY

## I. The Definition of Arrest

A. Arrests are a vital tool that help law enforcement officers catch the guilty and free the innocent, but arrests have to square with the U.S. Constitution.

B. Arrests, in which one is seized and detained for a period, are more invasive than stops in five ways:
1. Stops are measured in minutes; arrests can last for hours or even days.
2. Stops begin and end in public places; arrested people are taken to isolated and intimidating surroundings, such as the police department or jail.
3. Stops don't produce written documentation unlike arrests, which produce a "rap sheet."
4. Stops don't involve full-body searches such as strip or body-cavity searches.
5. Stops aren't accompanied by interrogations or lineups.

C. Arrest is a zone, not a point, within a spectrum of invasions.

D. The Fourth Amendment requires that probable cause accompany an arrest to make it reasonable.

## II. A Reasonable Arrest

A. There are two elements in a reasonable arrest:
1. *Objective basis.* The arrest was backed up by probable cause.
2. *Manner of arrest.* The way the arrest was made was reasonable.

B. Probable cause is required for an arrest to be reasonable.
1. Probable cause to arrest a suspicious person requires that an officer must know enough facts and circumstances to reasonably believe two things:
   a. A crime has been, is being, or is about to be committed.
   b. The person arrested has committed, is committing, or is about to commit the crime.
2. Probable cause lies on a continuum between reasonable suspicion and proof beyond a reasonable doubt.
3. The probable cause requirement balances the societal interest in crime control and the individual right of locomotion.
4. In its day-to-day application, probable cause rests mainly with officers on the street, who have to make quick decisions.
5. Reasonable suspicion can be based on either direct information or hearsay.
   a. Direct information is information known to officers personally.
   b. Hearsay is information officers receive from someone.
   c. Courts won't admit hearsay evidence to prove guilt, but if it's reliable and truthful, they will accept it to show probable cause to arrest. After all, arrests aren't trials.

## III. The Manner of Arrest

A. Probable cause by itself isn't enough to make an arrest a reasonable Fourth Amendment seizure. There are two reasonable manner of arrest stipulations:
1. Officers have to get warrants before they enter homes to arrest suspects.
2. Officers can use only reasonable force to gain and maintain control over arrested suspects.

B. The warrant requirement depends on where the arrest takes place and the degree of urgency involved.
1. Warrants aren't required to make arrests reasonable, except when officers want to arrest someone in a home.
2. The courts have held that a variety of exigent circumstances don't require officers to get arrest warrants before they enter homes to make an arrest.
3. Obtaining a warrant before making an arrest ensures that an officer knows in advance she has enough probable cause to back up the arrest.
4. Arrest warrants include three elements:
   a. A neutral magistrate must decide whether there's probable cause before officers are allowed to arrest suspects.
   b. A sworn statement (affidavit) by a law enforcement officer has to attest to the facts and circumstances amounting to probable cause.
   c. The warrant has to identify specifically the person to be arrested.
C. Arrest by force is a factor in evaluating the manner of arrest requirement.
1. Whether the manner of an arrest was reasonable is affected by whether the level of force applied was reasonable.
2. Two types of force are applied to arrest suspects:
   a. *Deadly force.* Restraint capable of producing death is reasonable to use only if:
      (1) It's necessary to apprehend "dangerous" suspects.
      (2) It doesn't put innocent people in danger.
   b. *Nondeadly force.* Officers are more likely to use nondeadly force to subdue suspects than deadly force.
3. The Fourth Amendment permits officers to use the amount of force necessary to apprehend and bring suspects under control.

## IV. After Arrest
A. When arrested for felonies, suspects are taken to the police station for further processing.
B. When arrested for misdemeanors, suspects usually are released.

## REVIEW QUESTIONS

1. Compare and contrast Fourth Amendment stops with full custodial arrests on four criteria.

2. Identify the characteristics of a full custodial arrest.

3. Identify two elements that make an arrest reasonable.

4. Identify two facts and circumstances that amount to probable cause to arrest.

5. Contrast the definition of *probable cause* with that of *reasonable suspicion*.

6. What two societal interests does the probable cause requirement balance?

7. Identify and give an example of each of the two sources law enforcement officers can rely on to build reasonable suspicion.

8. Describe the trustworthiness aspect of hearsay information.

9. Identify and describe the two elements that satisfy the manner of arrest requirement.

10. Why do officers need to obtain warrants to arrest a suspect in a home?

11. Identify and give an example of the exceptions to the arrest warrant requirement to enter homes.

12. Describe and give an example of an exigent circumstance.

13. Identify three elements that make up an arrest warrant.

14. List a positive and a negative aspect to the neutral magistrate requirement.

15. Why are some affidavits purposely vague?

16. According to Professor Craig Bradley, what should the U.S. Supreme Court do regarding arrest warrants?

17. Contrast deadly force with nondeadly force. Which one is used more to subdue suspects?

18. What two conditions have to be satisfied to use deadly force?

19. Why is the standard of reasonable force to arrest an objective standard?

20. Identify the actions taken after an arrest for a felony.

21. Why is it lawful for officers to arrest suspects for a misdemeanor?

## KEY TERMS

# Searches for Evidence

## MAIN POINTS

- Crime control couldn't survive without searches, but the power to search comes at a price: It tempts those who hold it to abuse it.
- Searches incident to arrest without warrants are reasonable constitutionally, because they protect officers, prevent escape, and preserve evidence.
- Pretext arrests are powerful investigative tools in the "drug war."
- Consent searches allow officers to search without warrants or probable cause.
- The scope of consent extends as far as the officer conducting the search reasonably believes it to be.
- Consent can be withdrawn at any time during a search.
- The legality of a consent to search given by a third person depends on the officer's reasonable belief that the consenting party had the authority to give consent.
- Searches of vehicles without warrants are reasonable, constitutionally, because of their mobility and the reduced expectation of privacy in vehicles.
- Searches of containers and persons within the vehicles without warrants are reasonable, constitutionally, as long as officers have probable cause.
- Emergency searches are based on the idea that it's sometimes impractical to require officers to obtain warrants before they search.

6

Dylan Rodney stepped off a bus in Washington, D.C., arriving from New York City. As Rodney left the bus station, Detective Vance Beard, dressed in plainclothes and carrying a concealed weapon, approached him from behind. A second officer waited nearby. Beard displayed identification and asked if Rodney would talk to him. Rodney agreed. Beard asked Rodney whether he was carrying drugs in his travel bag. After Rodney said no, Beard obtained permission to search the bag. As he did so, the other officer advanced to within about five feet of Rodney. The search failed to turn up any contraband.

Beard then asked Rodney whether he was carrying drugs on his person. After Rodney again said no, Beard requested permission to conduct a body search. Rodney said "Sure" and raised his arms above his head. Beard placed his hands on Rodney's ankles and, in one sweeping motion, ran them up the inside of Rodney's legs. As he passed over the crotch area, Beard felt small, rock-like objects.

Rodney exclaimed: "That's me!" Detecting otherwise, Beard placed Rodney under arrest. 

*U.S. v. Rodney, 956 F.2d 295 (CADC 1992)*

Crime control couldn't survive without searches, but, like all good things, the power to search comes at a price. Searches invade the privacy of individuals, their homes, and their "stuff." But the power to search, like all power, tempts those who hold it to abuse it. No one appreciated the price and the temptation to abuse the power to search more than U.S. Supreme Court Justice Robert H. Jackson. At the end of World War II, President Truman appointed Justice Jackson chief prosecutor at the Nazi war crimes trials in Nuremberg, Germany. There, Justice Jackson learned details of the Nazis' atrocities against the German people's "persons, houses, papers and effects" (Hockett 1991, 257–99).

These discoveries were a defining moment for Justice Jackson, and when he returned to the Supreme Court, he spoke eloquently of the right against unreasonable searches and seizures. Worried that Americans didn't fully appreciate the importance of the Fourth Amendment, Justice Jackson disapproved of what he believed was the Supreme Court's tendency to treat the rights against unreasonable searches and seizures as "second-class rights":

> I protest, [the rights against unreasonable searches and seizures] are not mere second-class rights but belong in the catalog of indispensable freedoms. Among deprivations of rights, none is so effective in cowing a population, crushing the spirit of the individual and putting terror in every heart.
>
> Uncontrolled search and seizure is one of the first and most effective weapons in the arsenal of every arbitrary government. And one need only briefly to have dwelt and worked among a people possessed of many admirable qualities but deprived of these rights to know that the human personality deteriorates and dignity and self-reliance disappear where homes, persons and possessions are subject at any hour to unheralded search and seizure by the police.
>
> But the right against searches and seizures is one of the most difficult to protect. Since the officers are themselves the chief invaders, there is no enforcement outside of court.
> *Brinegar v. U.S.* 1949, 180–81

Notice that Justice Jackson didn't condemn all searches, only "uncontrolled" searches." That's because he knew very well how important searches are in controlling crime. (Jackson was an aggressive prosecutor at one point in his life.) But he also knew the Fourth Amendment doesn't just confer the power on good officers searching bad people, their homes, and stuff; it bestows the same power on bad officers searching good people. So, Jackson urged, courts had to balance the need for searches against the privacies they invade.

The three-step analysis we used to examine the government actions in Chapter 3, the stops and frisks in Chapter 4, and the arrests in Chapter 5 also applies to the searches we'll examine in this chapter:

1. Was the government action a search? (Chapter 3)
2. If it was a search, was it reasonable?
3. If it was unreasonable, then should the evidence be excluded? (Chapter 10)

But we won't repeat the first step in the analysis (the definition of search) because we already examined it in Chapter 3. To consider the issues affecting the reasonableness of searches, we'll divide our discussion into searches for evidence of crime (this chapter) and special-needs searches that go beyond crime control (Chapter 7). Let's look first at searches with warrants and then searches without warrants.

# SEARCHES WITH WARRANTS

The Fourth Amendment commands that "no warrants shall issue, but upon probable cause, supported by oath or affirmation, and particularly describing the place to be searched, and the persons or things to be seized." (See the discussion on neutral magistrates in the Arrest Warrants section of Chapter 5.) According to the distinguished U.S. Supreme Court Justice Felix Frankfurter:

> With minor and severely confined exceptions . . . every search . . . is unreasonable when made without a magistrate's authority expressed through a validly issued warrant. (*Harris v. U.S.* 1947, 162)

That may be true, but there are a lot of exceptions to the warrant requirement (up to 30, depending on how you count them).

Three elements are required to meet the Fourth Amendment's warrant requirement:

1. Particularity
2. An affidavit supporting probable cause
3. The "knock and announce" rule

Let's look at each.

## The Particularity Requirement

To comply with the Fourth Amendment, search warrants have to "particularly describe the place to be searched"; this is known as the **particularity requirement**. The address of a single-dwelling house, "404 Blake Road," particularly describes the place to be searched; a warrant to search "1135 Stone Street," a 16-floor apartment complex, doesn't. Warrants also have to "particularly describe the things to be seized." A warrant to search for and seize "one book entitled *Criminal Procedure*, 7th edition, by Joel Samaha" is good enough. So are warrants naming whole classes of items, such as "address books, diaries, business records, documents, receipts, warranty books, guns, stereo equipment, and a color television" in a list of stolen property. Catchall categories might also meet the requirement. For example, a search warrant that named "records, notes, and documents indicating involvement in and control of prostitution activity" was particular enough in one case, because the officers were directed to seize only items related to prostitution.

## The Probable Cause Affidavit

This is the same as the requirement for arrest warrants (Chapter 5), so we won't repeat the details here, except to point out that the probable cause in search warrant affidavits has to include evidence to support the claim that the items or classes of items named in the warrant will be found in the place to be searched.

## The "Knock-and-Announce" Rule

Most states and the U.S. government have many specific requirements for how search warrants are supposed to be executed. One of these rules, the **knock-and-announce rule**, has 700 years of English and U.S. history behind it; it also has centuries of controversy surrounding it. According to the rule, officers have to knock and announce they're officers with a search warrant before they enter the places they're about to search.

But does the Fourth Amendment require this knock-and-announce rule or is a no-knock entry reasonable, too? Oddly enough, for all the history behind the rule, and the controversy surrounding it, the U.S. Supreme Court didn't answer this important question until 1995, when it decided that it did. It did so in *Wilson v. Arkansas*, our first case excerpt.

---

C A S E   *Was the "No-Knock" Entry an Unreasonable Search?*

### Wilson v. Arkansas
514 U.S. 927, 115 S.Ct. 1914 (1995)

### HISTORY

Sharlene Wilson was charged with illegal possession of marijuana and methamphetamine. The Circuit Court, Hot Springs County, Arkansas, denied Wilson's motion to suppress marijuana, amphetamines, and other evidence seized during a "no knock" search of her house. She was convicted and sentenced to 32 years in prison. She appealed and the Arkansas Supreme Court affirmed. The U.S. Supreme Court granted certiorari and reversed and remanded.

THOMAS, J. FOR A UNANIMOUS COURT.

### FACTS

During November and December 1992, Sharlene Wilson made a series of narcotics sales to a Joann Potts, an informant acting at the direction of the Arkansas State Police. In late November, Potts purchased marijuana and methamphetamine at the home that Wilson shared with Bryson Jacobs. On December 30, Potts telephoned Wilson at her home and arranged to meet her at a local store to buy some marijuana. According to testimony presented below, Wilson produced a semiautomatic pistol at this meeting and waved it in Potts's face, threatening to kill her if she turned out to be working for the police. Wilson then sold Potts a bag of marijuana.

The next day, police officers applied for and obtained warrants to search Wilson's home and to arrest both Wilson and Jacobs. Affidavits filed in support of the warrants set forth the details of the narcotics transactions and stated that Jacobs had previously been convicted of arson and firebombing. The search was conducted later that afternoon.

Police officers found the main door to Wilson's home open. While opening an unlocked screen door and entering the residence, they identified themselves as police officers and stated that they had a warrant. Once inside the home, the officers seized marijuana, methamphetamine, valium, narcotics paraphernalia, a gun, and ammunition. They also found Wilson in the bathroom, flushing marijuana down the toilet.

Wilson and Jacobs were arrested and charged with delivery of marijuana, delivery of methamphetamine, possession of drug paraphernalia, and possession of marijuana.

Before trial, Wilson filed a motion to suppress the evidence seized during the search. Wilson asserted that the search was invalid on various grounds, including that the officers had failed to "knock and announce" before entering her home. The trial court summarily denied the suppression motion. After a jury trial, Wilson was convicted of all charges and sentenced to 32 years in prison.

The Arkansas Supreme Court affirmed Wilson's conviction on appeal. The court noted that "the officers entered the home while they were identifying themselves," but it rejected Wilson's argument that "the Fourth Amendment requires officers to knock and announce prior to entering the residence." Finding "no authority for [Wilson's] theory that the knock and announce principle is required by the Fourth Amendment," the court concluded that neither Arkansas law nor the Fourth Amendment required suppression of the evidence.

We granted certiorari to resolve the conflict among the lower courts as to whether the common-law knock-and-announce principle forms a part of the Fourth Amendment reasonableness inquiry. We hold that it does, and accordingly reverse and remand.

## OPINION

Although the common law generally protected a man's house as "his castle of defense and asylum," common-law courts long have held that "when the King is party, the sheriff (if the doors be not open) may break the party's house, either to arrest him, or to do other execution of the King's process, if otherwise he cannot enter." *Semayne's Case*, 5 Co. Rep. 91a, 91b, 77 Eng.Rep. 194, 195 (K.B.1603).

To this rule, however, common-law courts appended an important qualification: But before he breaks it, he ought to signify the cause of his coming, and to make request to open doors . . . , for the law without a default in the owner abhors the destruction or breaking of any house (which is for the habitation and safety of man) by which great damage and inconvenience might ensue to the party, when no default is in him; for perhaps he did not know of the process, of which, if he had notice, it is to be presumed that he would obey it. . . .

Several prominent founding-era commentators agreed on this basic principle. According to Sir Matthew Hale, the "constant practice" at common law was that "the officer may break open the door, if he be sure the offender is there, if after acquainting them of the business, and demanding the prisoner, he refuses to open the door." William Hawkins propounded a similar principle: "the law doth never allow" an officer to break open the door of a dwelling "but in cases of necessity," that is, unless he "first signify to those in the house the cause of his coming, and request them to give him admittance." Sir William Blackstone stated simply that the sheriff may "justify breaking open doors, if the possession be not quietly delivered."

The common-law knock-and-announce principle was woven quickly into the fabric of early American law. Most of the States that ratified the Fourth Amendment had enacted constitutional provisions or statutes generally incorporating English common law. . . . Our own cases have acknowledged that the common law principle of announcement is "embedded in Anglo-American law," but we have never squarely held that this principle is an element of the reasonableness inquiry under the Fourth Amendment.

We now so hold. Given the long-standing common-law endorsement of the practice of announcement, we have little doubt that the Framers of the Fourth Amendment thought that the method of an officer's entry into a dwelling was among the factors to be considered in assessing the reasonableness of a search or seizure. Contrary to the decision below, we hold that in some circumstances an officer's unannounced entry into a home might be unreasonable under the Fourth Amendment.

This is not to say, of course, that every entry must be preceded by an announcement. The Fourth Amendment's flexible requirement of reasonableness should not be read to mandate a rigid rule of announcement that ignores countervailing law enforcement interests. As even Wilson concedes, the common-law principle of announcement was never stated as an inflexible rule requiring announcement under all circumstances. . . .

Thus, because the common-law rule was justified in part by the belief that announcement generally would avoid "the destruction or breaking of any house . . . by which great damage and inconvenience might ensue," courts acknowledged that the presumption in favor of announcement would yield under circumstances presenting a threat of physical violence. See for example, *Mahomed v. The Queen* (1843): "While he was firing pistols at them, were they to knock at the door, and to ask him to be pleased to open it for them? The law in its wisdom only requires this ceremony to be observed when it possibly may be attended with some advantage, and may render the breaking open of the outer door unnecessary."

Similarly, courts held that an officer may dispense with announcement in cases where a prisoner escapes from him and retreats to his dwelling. Proof of "demand and refusal" was deemed unnecessary in such cases because it would be a "senseless ceremony" to require an officer in pursuit of a recently escaped arrestee to make an announcement prior to breaking the door to retake him.

Finally, courts have indicated that unannounced entry may be justified where police officers have reason to believe that evidence would likely be destroyed if advance notice were given.

We need not attempt a comprehensive catalog of the relevant countervailing factors here. For now, we leave to the lower courts the task of determining the circumstances under which an unannounced entry is reasonable under the Fourth Amendment. We simply hold that although a search or seizure of a dwelling might be constitutionally defective if police officers enter without prior announcement, law enforcement interests may also establish the reasonableness of an unannounced entry.

Arkansas contends that the judgment below should be affirmed because the unannounced entry in this case was justified for two reasons. First, Arkansas argues that police officers reasonably believed that a prior announcement would have placed them in peril, given their knowledge that Wilson had threatened a government informant with a semiautomatic weapon and that Mr. Jacobs had previously been convicted of arson and firebombing. Second, Arkansas suggests that prior announcement would have produced an unreasonable risk that Wilson would destroy easily disposable narcotics evidence.

These considerations may well provide the necessary justification for the unannounced entry in this case. Because the Arkansas Supreme Court did not address their sufficiency, however, we remand to allow the state courts to make any necessary findings of fact and to make the determination of reasonableness in the first instance.

The judgment of the Arkansas Supreme Court is REVERSED, and the case is REMANDED for further proceedings not inconsistent with this opinion. It is so ordered.

## Questions

1. What does the history Justice Thomas relates have to do with whether the Fourth Amendment requires officers to "knock and announce"?

2. Did the officers satisfy the knock-and-announce rule? List the facts that might indicate that the officers satisfied the requirement.

3. Identify the three exceptions to the knock-and-announce rule Justice Thomas referred to in the excerpt from the Court's opinion. What do they all have in common? Do you agree that they should be exceptions? Explain.

4. Assume you're the prosecutor when the case is remanded. Argue that the facts of the case fit into one or more of the exceptions.

5. Assume you're the judge on remand. Decide the case and give your reasons.

## EXPLORING FURTHER

# The Knock-and-Announce Rule

### Were the Officers' Actions After an Announced Entry Reasonable?

*State v. Ross*, 639 N.W.2d 225 (Wisc.App. 2001)

FACTS At approximately 6:15 P.M., on June 27, 2000, West Allis, Wisconsin, police officers executed a search warrant for Ryan Ross's house. Detective Jeffrey Nohelty testified that on arrival at Ross's residence, police officers got out of their vehicles with guns drawn and ordered Ross, who was outside mowing his lawn, to the ground. Police then knocked on his front door, identified themselves, and announced that they had a search warrant.

No one responded, but the officers heard dogs barking inside the house. They knocked and announced their presence a second time and then tried the door but found it locked. Detective Nohelty asked Ross if anyone was inside, and Ross answered no. The officers then used a battering ram to open the door. Inside, the officers found four or five pit bulls and approximately 25 grams of marijuana. Following his arrest, Ross moved to suppress the evidence recovered in the search of his home. He argued that *Wilson v. Arkansas* (1995) and *Richards v. Wisconsin* (1997) support his claim that the officers' actions were unreasonable. The State contended that *Wilson* and *Richards* didn't apply to this case, because they involved unannounced entries and Ross's case involved an announced entry. Who was right, the state or Ross?

OPINION The state was right, according to the Wisconsin Court of Appeals:

This court concludes that, clearly, under the circumstances presented to the officers at the time they executed the warrant, their entry was reasonable.

Detective Nohelty testified that the officers knocked and announced their presence two times before trying to enter the residence, thereby putting any occupant on notice of their presence and intent. By knocking and announcing twice and waiting a reasonable time before entering, police gave any occupants the opportunity to open the door. At the time of entry, police only had Ross's word that the house was unoccupied. The dogs were barking, thus making it difficult to discern whether anyone was in the house or to determine what the police might face on entry.

Ross contends that the police officers should have asked for his keys rather than entering by force. He fails, however, to present any legal authority to support his contention.

Moreover, as the State notes, "There is no indication in the record that [Ross] had been removed from the immediate vicinity nor is there any indication that Ross made any attempt to assist the police by indicating he had the keys to open the door. . . ." Further, Detective Nohelty clarified that asking Ross for his keys would have delayed the entry, thus increasing the potential for destruction of evidence. And finally, Detective Nohelty added, forcibly entering the residence, while leaving Ross on the ground outside, prevented Ross from commanding the dogs to attack.

 To read the full text of the Exploring Further excerpt, go to the Samaha Criminal Procedure 7e website: academic.cengage.com/criminaljustice/samaha.

Let's look more closely at exceptions to the knock-and-announce rule and at what happens when occupants fail to respond to officers' announcement before entering.

***Exceptions to the Knock-and-Announce Rule*** With the *Wilson v. Arkansas* decision, we now know the "knock and announce rule" is part of the Fourth Amendment. We also know there are three major exceptions to the rule: to prevent violence, the destruction of evidence, and the escape of suspects. And there may be more to come. In the following excerpt from *Wilson v. Arkansas*, Justice Thomas sent a not-too-subtle invitation to lower courts to come up with more exceptions to the knock-and-announce rule:

> We need not attempt a comprehensive catalog of the relevant countervailing factors here. For now, we leave to the lower courts the task of determining the circumstances under which an unannounced entry is reasonable under the Fourth Amendment. We simply hold that although a search or seizure of a dwelling might be constitutionally defective if police officers enter without prior announcement, law enforcement interests may also establish the reasonableness of an unannounced entry. (936)

The Wisconsin Supreme Court wasted no time in accepting Justice Thomas's invitation in *State v. Richards* (1996) when it approved a blanket "drug house" exception to the knock-and-announce rule. Steiney Richards, the defendant, argued that, "The blanket 'drug house' exception to the 'knock and announce' rule violates the Fourth Amendment's reasonableness requirement" (219). The Wisconsin Supreme Court disagreed:

> The issue is simply stated: whether the Fourth Amendment allows a blanket exception to the general requirement of "knock and announce" (the rule of announcement) for entries into premises pursuant to a search warrant for evidence of felonious drug delivery.
>
> We conclude that exigent circumstances are always present in the execution of search warrants involving felonious drug delivery: an extremely high risk of serious if not deadly injury to the police as well as the potential for the disposal of drugs by the occupants prior to entry by the police. The public interests inherent in these circumstances far outweigh the minimal privacy interests of the occupants of the dwelling for which a search warrant has already been issued. . . . [We] conclude that police are not required to adhere to the rule of announcement when executing a search warrant involving felonious drug delivery. (219)

Richards appealed to the U.S. Supreme Court. In *Richards v. Wisconsin* (1997), the Court rejected the blanket "drug house" exception to the knock-and-announce rule. According to Justice Stevens, writing for a unanimous Court:

> In *Wilson v. Arkansas* (1995), we held that the Fourth Amendment incorporates the common law requirement that police officers entering a dwelling must knock on the door and announce their identity and purpose before attempting forcible entry. At the same time, we recognized that the "flexible requirement of reasonableness should not be read to mandate a rigid rule of announcement that ignores countervailing law enforcement interests," and left "to the lower courts the task of determining the circumstances under which an unannounced entry is reasonable under the Fourth Amendment."
>
> In this case, the Wisconsin Supreme Court concluded that police officers are never required to knock and announce their presence when executing a search warrant in a felony drug investigation. . . . We disagree with the court's conclusion that the Fourth Amendment permits a blanket exception to the knock-and-announce requirement for this entire category of criminal activity. (387–88)

Go to Exercise 6.1 on the Samaha Criminal Procedure 7e website to learn more about the knock-and-announce rule: academic.cengage.com/criminaljustice/samaha.

Nevertheless, the Court upheld the Wisconsin Supreme Court's decision ". . . because the evidence presented to support the officers' actions in this case establishes that the decision not to knock and announce was a reasonable one under the circumstances . . ." (388).

*Occupants' Failure to Respond to Officers' Announcement* Announcing their presence doesn't automatically authorize officers to break and enter. They have to "wait a reasonable amount of time" before they break and enter, unless occupants refuse to allow them to come in (LaFave 2004, 2:672–73; *U.S. v. Spikes* 1998, 925). How long do they have to wait? There's no **bright-line rule**—that is, no rule that applies to all cases. The test is reasonableness, which depends on the totality of the circumstances in each individual case. The Sixth Circuit U.S. Court of Appeals put it this way:

> The Fourth Amendment's "knock and announce" principle, given its fact-sensitive nature, cannot be distilled into a constitutional stop-watch where a fraction of a second assumes controlling significance. (*U.S. v. Spikes* 1998, 926)

The totality of circumstances hardly ever makes very brief waits, say 2 to 4 seconds, reasonable; 10 to 20 seconds usually are (LaFave 2004, 673–74). Professor LaFave, frequently cited by the U.S. Supreme Court and other courts, concludes that courts are "unduly lenient" to officers on the time requirement (674). Consider *U.S. v. Knapp* (1993). According to the court:

> The officers were aware that Mr. Knapp was an amputee, and suspected that he was home since lights were on in the house. Additionally, the officers knew Mr. Knapp could not readily dispose of the marijuana and did not believe Mr. Knapp was dangerous. The agents heard nothing as they approached the door. Agent Olachea knocked three times and announced, "DEA. We've got a warrant. Open the door." After hearing no sounds from within for ten to twelve seconds, the officers broke the door down with a battering ram. (1030)

The Court of Appeals held that the officers waited a reasonable amount of time before they battered down the door and entered Knapp's house.

Professor LaFave concludes that *Knapp* and cases like it are "clearly incorrect":

> Because whether there has yet occurred a "constructive refusal" should be determined only by taking into account the circumstances of the particular case, as they reasonably appear to the police at the time of the entry. More understandable is the view that such brief periods will suffice when "a reasonable inference may be drawn that the inhabitants of the house had observed the arrival of the police and were well aware of the officers' authority and purpose," as well as the conclusion that no wait is necessary when the officer has given the notice to an occupant face-to-face through an open door. (675–76)

In our next case excerpt, *U.S. v. Banks* (2003), the U.S. Supreme Court ruled that it was reasonable for officers to use the "ultimate 'master key,' a battering ram," to break down Lashawn Banks's front door after calling out "police search warrant" and waiting 10 seconds (33).

CASE    ***Was the 10-Second Wait Reasonable?***

### U.S. v. Banks
540 U.S. 31 (2003)

### HISTORY

Lashawn Lowell Banks, Defendant, was convicted on a conditional guilty plea in the U.S. District Court for the District of Nevada, of narcotics trafficking and weapons charges, and he appealed. The U.S. Court of Appeals for the Ninth Circuit reversed. Certiorari was granted. The U.S. Supreme Court reversed.

SOUTER, J. FOR A UNANIMOUS COURT

### FACTS

With information that Lashawn Banks was selling cocaine at home, North Las Vegas Police Department officers and Federal Bureau of Investigation agents got a warrant to search his two-bedroom apartment. As soon as they arrived there, about 2 o'clock on a Wednesday afternoon, officers posted in front called out "police search warrant" and rapped hard enough on the door to be heard by officers at the back door.

There was no indication whether anyone was home, and after waiting for 15 to 20 seconds with no answer, the officers broke open the front door with a battering ram. Banks was in the shower and testified that he heard nothing until the crash of the door, which brought him out dripping to confront the police. The search produced weapons, crack cocaine, and other evidence of drug dealing.

In response to drug and firearms charges, Banks moved to suppress evidence, arguing that the officers executing the search warrant waited an unreasonably short time before forcing entry, and so violated both the Fourth Amendment and 18 U.S.C. § 3109. The statute provides:

> The officer may break open any outer or inner door or window of a house, or any part of a house, or anything therein, to execute a search warrant, if, after notice of his authority and purpose, he is refused admittance or when necessary to liberate himself or a person aiding him in the execution of the warrant.

The District Court denied the motion, and Banks pleaded guilty, reserving his right to challenge the search on appeal.

A divided panel of the Ninth Circuit reversed and ordered suppression of the evidence found. In assessing the reasonableness of the execution of the warrant, the panel majority set out a nonexhaustive list of "factors that an officer reasonably should consider" in deciding when to enter premises identified in a warrant, after knocking and announcing their presence but receiving no express acknowledgment:

(a) size of the residence;

(b) location of the residence;

(c) location of the officers in relation to the main living or sleeping areas of the residence;

(d) time of day;

(e) nature of the suspected offense;

(f) evidence demonstrating the suspect's guilt;

(g) suspect's prior convictions and, if any, the type of offense for which he was convicted; and

(h) any other observations triggering the senses of the officers that reasonably would lead one to believe that immediate entry was necessary.

The majority also defined four categories of intrusion after knock and announcement, saying that the classification "aids in the resolution of the essential question whether the entry made herein was reasonable under the circumstances":

(1) entries in which exigent circumstances exist and non-forcible entry is possible, permitting entry to be made simultaneously with or shortly after announcement;

(2) entries in which exigent circumstances exist and forced entry by destruction of property is required, necessitating more specific inferences of exigency;

(3) entries in which no exigent circumstances exist and non-forcible entry is possible, requiring an explicit refusal of admittance or a lapse of a significant amount of time; and

(4) entries in which no exigent circumstances exist and forced entry by destruction of property is required, mandating an explicit refusal of admittance or a lapse of an even more substantial amount of time.

The panel majority put the action of the officers here in the last category, on the understanding that they destroyed the door without hearing anything to suggest a refusal to admit even though sound traveled easily through the small apartment. The majority held the 15- to-20-second delay after knocking and announcing to be "insufficient . . . to satisfy the constitutional safeguards."

Judge Fisher dissented, saying that the majority ought to come out the other way based on the very grounds it stressed: Banks's small apartment, the loud knock and announcement, the suspected offense of dealing in cocaine, and the time of the day. Judge Fisher thought the lapse of 15 to 20 seconds was enough to support a reasonable inference that admittance had been constructively denied.

We granted certiorari to consider how to go about applying the standard of reasonableness to the length of time police with a warrant must wait before entering without permission after knocking and announcing their intent in a felony case. We now reverse.

## OPINION

There has never been a dispute that these officers were obliged to knock and announce their intentions when executing the search warrant, an obligation they concededly honored. Despite this agreement, we start with a word about standards for requiring or dispensing with a knock and announcement, since the same criteria bear on when the officers could legitimately enter after knocking.

The Fourth Amendment says nothing specific about formalities in exercising a warrant's authorization, speaking to the manner of searching as well as to the legitimacy of searching at all simply in terms of the right to be "secure . . . against unreasonable searches and seizures." Although the notion of reasonable execution must therefore be fleshed out, we have done that case by case, largely avoiding categories and protocols for searches. Instead, we have treated reasonableness as a function of the facts of cases so various that no template is likely to produce sounder results than examining the totality of circumstances in a given case; it is too hard to invent categories without giving short shrift to details that turn out to be important in a given instance, and without inflating marginal ones. We have, however, pointed out factual considerations of unusual, albeit not dispositive, significance.

In *Wilson v. Arkansas* (1995), we held that the common law knock-and-announce principle is one focus of the reasonableness enquiry; and we subsequently decided that although the standard generally requires the police to announce their intent to search before entering closed premises, the obligation gives way when officers have a reasonable suspicion that knocking and announcing their presence, under the particular circumstances, would be dangerous or futile, or . . . would inhibit the effective investigation of the crime by, for example, allowing the destruction of evidence. When a warrant applicant gives reasonable grounds to expect futility or to suspect that one or another such exigency already exists or will arise instantly upon knocking, a magistrate judge is acting within the Constitution to authorize a "no-knock" entry. And even when executing a warrant silent about that, if circumstances support a reasonable suspicion of exigency when the officers arrive at the door, they may go straight in.

Since most people keep their doors locked, entering without knocking will normally do some damage, a circumstance too common to require a heightened justification when a reasonable suspicion of exigency already justifies an unwarned entry. We have accordingly held that police in exigent circumstances may damage premises so far as necessary for a no-knock entrance without demonstrating the suspected risk in any more detail than the law demands for an unannounced intrusion simply by lifting the latch. Either way, it is enough that the officers had a reasonable suspicion of exigent circumstances. The standard for a no-knock entry . . . applies on reasonable suspicion of exigency or futility. Because the facts here go to exigency, not futility, we speak of that alone.

. . . This case turns on the significance of exigency revealed by circumstances known to the officers . . . [at] the time . . . the officers reasonably anticipated some danger calling for action without delay. . . . The Government claims that a risk of losing evidence arose shortly after knocking and announcing. Although the police concededly arrived at Banks's door without reasonable suspicion of facts justifying a no-knock entry, they argue that announcing their presence started the clock running toward the moment of apprehension that Banks would flush away the easily disposable cocaine, prompted by knowing the police would soon be coming in. . . . The Government argues it was . . . reasonable for the officers to go in with force here as soon as the danger of disposal had ripened.

Banks does not . . . deny that exigency may develop in the period beginning when officers with a warrant knock to be admitted, and the issue comes down to whether it was reasonable to suspect imminent loss of evidence after the 15 to 20 seconds the officers waited prior to forcing their way. Though . . . this call is a close one, we think that after 15 or 20 seconds without a response, police could fairly suspect that cocaine would be gone if they were reticent any longer. Courts of Appeals have, indeed, routinely held similar wait times to be reasonable in drug cases with similar facts including easily disposable evidence (and some courts have found even shorter ones to be reasonable enough).

A look at Banks's counterarguments shows why these courts reached sensible results, for each of his reasons for saying that 15 to 20 seconds was too brief rests on a mistake about the relevant enquiry: the fact that he was actually in the shower and did not hear the officers is not to the point, and the same is true of the claim that it might have taken him longer than 20 seconds if he had heard the knock and headed straight for the door. As for the shower, it is enough to say that the facts known to the police are what count in judging reasonable waiting time, and there is no indication that the police knew that Banks was in the shower and thus unaware of an impending search that he would otherwise have tried to frustrate. Compare *Graham v. Connor* [excerpted in Chapter 5]. ("The 'reasonableness' of a particular use of force must be judged from the perspective of a reasonable officer on the scene, rather than with the 20/20 vision of hindsight.")

And the argument that 15 to 20 seconds was too short for Banks to have come to the door ignores the very risk that justified prompt entry. True, if the officers were to justify their timing here by claiming that Banks's failure to admit them fairly suggested a refusal to let them in, Banks could at least argue that no such suspicion can arise until an occupant has had time to get to the door, a time that will vary with the size of the establishment, perhaps five seconds to open a motel room door, or several minutes to move through a townhouse.

In this case, however, the police claim exigent need to enter, and the crucial fact in examining their actions is not time to reach the door but the particular exigency claimed. On the record here, what matters is the opportunity to get rid of cocaine, which a prudent dealer will keep near a commode or kitchen sink. The significant circumstances include the arrival of the police during the day, when anyone inside would probably have been up and around, and the sufficiency of 15 to 20 seconds for getting to the bathroom or the kitchen to start flushing cocaine down the drain.

That is, when circumstances are exigent because a pusher may be near the point of putting his drugs beyond reach, it is imminent disposal, not travel time to the entrance, that governs when the police may reasonably enter; since the bathroom and kitchen are usually in the interior of a dwelling, not the front hall, there is no reason generally to peg the travel time to the location of the door, and no reliable basis for giving the proprietor of a mansion a longer wait than the resident of a bungalow, or an apartment like Banks's. And 15 to 20 seconds does not seem an unrealistic guess about the time someone would need to get in a position to rid his quarters of cocaine.

Our emphasis on totality analysis necessarily rejects positions taken on each side of this case. *Ramirez*, for example, cannot be read with the breadth the Government espouses, as "reflect[ing] a general principle that the need to damage property in order to effectuate an entry to execute a search warrant should not be part of the analysis of whether the entry itself was reasonable." At common law, the knock-and-announce rule was traditionally "justified in part by the belief that announcement generally would avoid 'the destruction or breaking of any house . . . by which great damage and inconvenience might ensue.'" *Semayne's Case*, 5 Co. Rep. 91a, 91b, 77 Eng. Rep. 194, 196 (K.B.1603). One point in making an officer knock and announce, then, is to give a person inside the chance to save his door. That is why, in the case with no reason to suspect an immediate risk of frustration or futility in waiting at all, the reasonable wait time may well be longer when police make a forced entry, since they ought to be more certain the occupant has had time to answer the door. It is hard to be more definite than that, without turning the notion of a reasonable time under all the circumstances into a set of sub-rules as the Ninth Circuit has been inclined to do. Suffice it to say that the need to damage property in the course of getting in is a good reason to require more patience than it would be reasonable to expect if the door were open. Police seeking a stolen piano may be able to spend more time to make sure they really need the battering ram.

On the other side, we disapprove of the Court of Appeals's four-part scheme for vetting knock-and-announce entries. To begin with, the demand for enhanced evidence of exigency before a door can reasonably be damaged by a warranted no-knock intrusion was already bad law before the Court of Appeals decided this case. In *Ramirez* (a case from the Ninth Circuit), we rejected an attempt to subdivide felony cases by accepting "mild exigency" for entry without property damage, but requiring "more specific inferences of exigency" before damage would be reasonable.

. . . The Court of Appeals's overlay of a categorical scheme on the general reasonableness analysis threatens to distort the "totality of the circumstances" principle, by replacing a stress on revealing facts with resort to pigeonholes. Attention to cocaine rocks and pianos tells a lot about the chances of their respective disposal and its bearing on reasonable time. Instructions couched in terms like "significant amount of time," and "an even more substantial amount of time," tell very little. . . .

The judgment of the Court of Appeals is REVERSED. *So ordered.*

## Questions

1. Summarize the facts and circumstances of obtaining the warrant, the announcement, and the entry of Lashawn Banks's home by North Las Vegas Police Department officers and FBI agents.

2. State the elements of the test used by the U.S. Court of Appeals to determine whether the officers waited a reasonable amount of time before they broke down the door and entered Banks's home. Summarize the reasons why the Court of Appeals found the officers' actions unreasonable.

3. Summarize the U.S. Supreme Court's arguments for rejecting the Court of Appeals' test.

4. Summarize the Supreme Court's reasons for its decision that the police officers' actions you summarized in your answer to question 1 satisfy the Court's totality-of-circumstances test of reasonableness.

5. In your opinion, which test do you prefer? Defend your answer.

# SEARCHES WITHOUT WARRANTS

The U.S. Supreme Court has repeatedly said the Fourth Amendment expresses a strong preference for search warrants with only a few well-defined exceptions. That's the *law*, but what's the *practice*? The vast number of searches are made without warrants, because the exceptions are interpreted broadly to satisfy the strong preference of law enforcement officers and the clear practical need for searches without warrants (Haddad 1977, 198–225; Sutton 1986, 411).

One former Washington, D.C., assistant U.S. attorney said of this practical element in searches without warrants:

> As anyone who has worked in the criminal justice system knows, searches conducted pursuant to these exceptions, particularly searches incident to arrest, automobile and "stop and frisk" searches, far exceed searches performed pursuant to warrants. (Bradley 1985, 1475)

According to this attorney, the reason "is simple: the clear rule that warrants are required is unworkable and to enforce it would lead to exclusion of evidence in many cases where the police activity was essentially reasonable" (1475).

Law enforcement officers frequently express frustration with the delay in getting search warrants. One police officer said it takes four hours from the time he decides he wants a warrant until the time he has one in his hand:

> And that's if everything goes right. You find people and . . . get 'em typed and you can find the judges when they are sitting at the bench—because a lot of judges won't see people in their offices. [If you miss them there,] they leave and go to lunch and you have to wait until they come back for the afternoon dockets, and if they are already into the afternoon dockets, they are not going to interrupt the procedures [for a warrant]. So you sit and wait through three or four docket sessions. . . . It can take all day. (Sutton 1986, 411)

Frustration tempts officers to "get around" the Fourth Amendment. One detective explained how he gets around the warrant requirement by "shamming" consent:

> You tell the guy, "Let me come in and take a look at your house." And he says, "No, I don't want to." And then you tell him, "Then I'm going to leave Sam here, and he's going to live with you until we come back. Now we can do it either way." And very rarely do the people say, "Go get your search warrant, then." (Sutton 1986, 415)

Let's look at the five major exceptions to the warrant requirement approved by the U.S. Supreme Court:

1. Searches incident to arrest
2. Consent searches
3. Vehicle searches
4. Container searches
5. Emergency searches (also called "exigent circumstances searches")

## Searches Incident to (at the Time of) Arrest

The brilliant constitutional lawyer and historian Telford Taylor concluded from his research that "There is little reason to doubt that search of an arrested person and premises [without warrants or probable cause] is as old as the institution of arrest itself" (28). **Searches incident to arrest** are old, but are they reasonable Fourth Amendment searches? Yes, says the U.S. Supreme Court. Why? Three reasons:

1. They protect officers from suspects who might injure or kill them.
2. They prevent arrested suspects from escaping.
3. They preserve evidence that suspects might destroy or damage.

Forty years ago, Associate Justice Hugo Black put the case for the reasonableness of searches incident to arrest this way:

> One thing is clear. . . . Search of an arrested man and of the items within his immediate reach must in almost every case be reasonable. There is always a danger that the suspect will try to escape, seizing concealed weapons with which to overpower and injure the arresting officers, and there is a danger that he may destroy evidence vital to the prosecution. Circumstances in which these justifications would not apply are sufficiently rare that inquiry is not made into searches of this scope, which have been considered reasonable throughout. (*Chimel v. California* 1969, 773)

There's some debate about Professor Taylor's history (Davies 1999), but as to searches of arrested *persons* without warrants, there's no doubt about their constitutionality.

The same certainty doesn't extend to searching the *place* where arrests take place. In fact, an analysis of decisions by the U.S. Supreme Court, the lower federal courts, and the state courts and commentators reveal zigging and zagging, creating enormous confusion.

As early as 1969, the U.S. Supreme Court tried to clear up the confusion over how far beyond the arrested person an officer can search. In *Chimel v. California* (1969), our next case excerpt, the Court decided that officers who arrested Ted Chimel in his home could search only as far as Chimel could reach either to grab a weapon or to destroy evidence. Before we get to the case, you should be aware of one critical fact the cases hardly ever mention about what officers do in practice when they arrest suspects. According to available evidence, after officers arrest suspects, they immediately handcuff them. That's what department rules prescribe; it's what police cadets are trained to do; it's what most officers do (Moskovitz 2002). Keep this in mind as you read *Chimel* and all the materials in this section on searches incident to arrest.

## C A S E     *Was the Search Incident to the Arrest?*

### Chimel v. California
395 U.S. 752 (1969)

### HISTORY

Ted Chimel was prosecuted for the burglary of a coin shop. He was convicted in the Superior Court, Orange County, California, and appealed. The California Supreme Court affirmed, and Chimel petitioned the U.S. Supreme Court for a writ of certiorari. The Supreme Court granted the writ and reversed the California Supreme Court's judgment.

STEWART, J.

### FACTS

. . . Late in the afternoon of September 13, 1965, three police officers arrived at the Santa Ana, California, home of Ted Chimel with a warrant authorizing his arrest for the burglary of a coin shop. The officers knocked on the door, identified themselves to Chimel's wife, and asked if they might come inside. She ushered them into the house, where they waited 10 or 15 minutes until Chimel returned home from work.

When Chimel entered the house, one of the officers handed him the arrest warrant and asked for permission to "look around." Chimel objected, but was advised that "on the basis of the lawful arrest," the officers would nonetheless conduct a search. No search warrant had been issued.

Accompanied by Chimel's wife, the officers then looked through the entire three-bedroom house, including the attic, the garage, and a small workshop. In some rooms the search was relatively cursory. In the master bedroom and sewing room, however, the officers directed Mrs. Chimel to open drawers and "to physically move contents of the drawers from side to side so that (they) might view any items that would have come from (the) burglary." After completing the search, they seized numerous items—primarily coins, but also several medals, tokens, and a few other objects. The entire search took between 45 minutes and an hour.

At Chimel's subsequent state trial on two charges of burglary, the items taken from his house were admitted into evidence against him, over his objection that they had been unconstitutionally seized. He was convicted, and the judgments of conviction were affirmed by both the California Court of Appeal, and the California Supreme Court. . . . We granted certiorari in order to consider Chimel's substantial constitutional claims.

### OPINION

. . . When an arrest is made, it is reasonable for the arresting officer to search the person arrested in order to remove any weapons that the latter might seek to use in order to resist arrest or effect his escape. Otherwise, the officer's safety might well be endangered, and the arrest itself frustrated.

In addition, it is entirely reasonable for the arresting officer to search for and seize any evidence on the arrestee's person in order to prevent its concealment or destruction.

And the area into which an arrestee might reach in order to grab a weapon or evidentiary items must, of course, be governed by a like rule. A gun on a table or in a drawer in front of one who is arrested can be as dangerous to the arresting officer as one concealed in the clothing of the person arrested.

There is ample justification, therefore, for a search of the arrestee's person and the area "within his immediate control"—construing that phrase to mean the area from within which he might gain possession of a weapon or destructible evidence. There is no comparable justification, however, for routinely searching any room other than that in which an arrest occurs—or, for that matter, for searching through all the desk drawers or other closed or concealed areas in that room itself. Such searches, in the absence of well-recognized exceptions, may be made only under the authority of a search warrant. The "adherence to judicial processes" mandated by the Fourth Amendment requires no less. . . .

It is argued in the present case that it is "reasonable" to search a man's house when he is arrested in it. But that argument is founded on little more than a subjective view regarding the acceptability of certain sorts of police conduct, and not on consideration relevant to Fourth Amendment interests. Under such an unconfined analysis, Fourth Amendment protection in this area would approach the evaporation point. . . .

After arresting a man in his house, to rummage at will among his papers in search of whatever will convict him, appears to us to be indistinguishable from what might be done under a general warrant; indeed, the warrant would give more protection, for presumably it must be issued by a magistrate. . . . Application of sound Fourth Amendment principles to the facts of this case produces a clear result.

The search here went far beyond the petitioner's person and the area from within which he might have obtained either a weapon or something that could have been used as evidence against him. There was no constitutional justification, in the absence of a search warrant, for extending the search beyond that area. The scope of the search was, therefore, "unreasonable" under the Fourth and Fourteenth Amendments and the petitioner's conviction cannot stand. . . .

REVERSED. . . .

## DISSENT

### WHITE, J., JOINED BY BLACK, J.

. . . The Fourth Amendment does not proscribe "warrantless searches" but instead it proscribes "unreasonable searches" and this Court has never held nor does the majority today assert that warrantless searches are necessarily unreasonable. . . . This case provides a good illustration . . . that it is unreasonable to require police to leave the scene of an arrest in order to obtain a search warrant when they already have probable cause to search and there is a clear danger that the items for which they may reasonably search will be removed before they return with a warrant.

Chimel was arrested in his home. . . . There was doubtless probable cause not only to arrest Chimel, but also to search his house. He had obliquely admitted, both to a neighbor and to the owner of the burglarized store, that he had committed the burglary. In light of this, and the fact that the neighbor had seen other admittedly stolen property in petitioner's house, there was surely probable cause on which a warrant could have issued to search the house for the stolen coins.

Moreover, had the police simply arrested Chimel, taken him off to the station house, and later returned with a warrant, it seems very likely that Chimel's wife, who in view of Chimel's generally garrulous nature must have known of the burglary, would have removed the coins. For the police to search the house while the evidence they had probable cause to search out and seize was still there cannot be considered unreasonable.

## Questions

1. Describe the search that followed Chimel's arrest.

2. How does the Court define the area "within [a suspect's] immediate control"?

3. If you were defining the phrase, would you have included the whole house within the scope of the rule? Explain your answer, including what interests you consider paramount in formulating your definition.

4. Does Justice White, in his dissent, have the better argument in the case? Summarize his argument and then evaluate it.

---

Now, let's look at other issues raised by searches incident to arrests, including how the courts define the "grabbable"—or searchable—area and whether it extends to vehicles; the time frame officers have to conduct a search before it is no longer considered incident to the arrest; and searches incident to misdemeanors and pretext arrests.

**The Grabbable Area** According to *Chimel v. California*, law enforcement officers can only search the **grabbable area**—namely, the arrested person and the area under her or his immediate physical control. The rule seems clear enough, but confusion arose when police were faced with applying the rule to arrests of suspects in vehicles. The courts were divided over whether the grabbable area rule even applied to searches of vehicles. Some courts quickly said it did; others were reluctant.

The case history of our next case excerpt, *New York v. Belton* (1981), is a good example of this division. The trial court said the "grabbable area" rule applied even when the arrested person was outside the car and under the control of the police and so highly unlikely to escape, grab a weapon, or destroy evidence inside the vehicle. The intermediate appeals court agreed, but a divided Court of Appeals, New York's highest court, said the rule didn't include a search of the car when the arrested suspects were outside the car. The U.S. Supreme Court resolved the problem, not only for New York but for the country, when it upheld the car search incident to Roger Belton's arrest in *New York v. Belton* (1981).

# CASE    *Is Searching a Jacket on a Car's Back Seat Incident to Arrest?*

## *New York v. Belton*
### 453 U.S. 454 (1981)

### HISTORY

Roger Belton was convicted in the Ontario County Court, of attempted criminal possession of a small amount of cocaine, and he appealed. The New York Supreme Court, Appellate Division, affirmed. The New York Court of Appeals reversed. The U.S. Supreme Court granted certiorari and reversed.

STEWART, J.

### FACTS

On April 9, 1978, Trooper Douglas Nicot, a New York State policeman driving an unmarked car on the New York Thruway, was passed by another automobile traveling at an excessive rate of speed. Nicot gave chase, overtook the speeding vehicle, and ordered its driver to pull it over to the side of the road and stop. There were four men in the car, one of whom was Roger Belton. The policeman asked to see the driver's license and automobile registration, and discovered that none of the men owned the vehicle or were related to its owner.

Meanwhile, the policeman had smelled burnt marijuana and had seen on the floor of the car an envelope marked "Supergold" that he associated with marijuana. He therefore directed the men to get out the car, and placed them under arrest for the unlawful possession of marijuana.

He patted down each of the men and "split them up into four separate areas of the Thruway at this time so they would not be in physical touching area of each other." He then picked up the envelope marked "Supergold" and found that it contained marijuana.

After giving the arrestees the warnings required by *Miranda v. Arizona* [excerpted and discussed in Chapter 8], the state policeman searched each one of them. He then searched the passenger compartment of the car. On the back seat he found a black leather jacket belonging to Belton. He unzipped one of the pockets of the jacket and discovered cocaine. Placing the jacket in his automobile, he drove the four arrestees to a nearby police station.

Belton was subsequently indicted for criminal possession of a controlled substance. In the trial court he moved that the cocaine the trooper had seized from the jacket pocket be suppressed. The court denied the motion. Belton then pleaded guilty to a lesser included offense, but preserved his claim that the cocaine had been seized in violation of the Fourth and Fourteenth Amendments.

The Appellant Division of the New York Supreme Court upheld the constitutionality of the search and seizure, reasoning that "once defendant was validly arrested for possession of marijuana, the officer was justified in searching the immediate area for other contraband."

The New York Court of Appeals reversed, holding that "a warrantless search of the zippered pockets of an unaccessible jacket may not be upheld as a search incident to a lawful arrest where there is no longer any danger that the arrestee or a confederate might gain access to the article." Two judges dissented. They pointed out that the "search was conducted by a lone peace officer who was in the process of arresting four unknown individuals whom he had stopped in a speeding car owned by none of them and apparently containing an uncertain quantity of a controlled substance. The suspects were standing by the side of the car as the officer gave it a quick check to confirm his suspicions before attempting to transport them to police headquarters. . . ."

We granted certiorari to consider the constitutionally permissible scope of a search in circumstances such as these.

## OPINION

It is a first principle of Fourth Amendment jurisprudence that the police may not conduct a search unless they first convince a neutral magistrate that there is probable cause to do so. This Court has recognized, however, that "the exigencies of the situation" may sometimes make exemption from the warrant requirement "imperative." Specifically, the Court held in *Chimel v. California* [the case excerpted on page 201] that a lawful custodial arrest creates a situation which justifies the contemporaneous search without a warrant of the person arrested and of the immediately surrounding area. Such searches have long been considered valid because of the need "to remove any weapons that [the arrestee] might seek to use in order to resist arrest or effect his escape" and the need to prevent the concealment or destruction of evidence.

The Court's opinion in *Chimel* emphasized the principle that, as the Court had said in *Terry v. Ohio* (1968) [excerpted and discussed in Chapter 4], "the scope of a search must be 'strictly tied to and justified by' the circumstances which rendered its initiation permissible."

Thus while the Court in *Chimel* found "ample justification" for a search of "the area from within which [an arrestee] might gain possession of a weapon or destructible evidence," the Court found "no comparable justification . . . for routinely searching any room other than that in which an arrest occurs—or, for that matter, for searching through all the desk drawers or other closed or concealed areas in that room itself." Although the principle that limits a search incident to a lawful custodial arrest may be stated clearly enough, courts have discovered the principle difficult to apply in specific cases.

Yet, as one commentator has pointed out, the protection of the Fourth and Fourteenth Amendments "can only be realized if the police are acting under a set of rules which, in most instances, makes it possible to reach a correct determination beforehand as to whether an invasion of privacy is justified in the interest of law enforcement." In short, "a single, familiar standard is essential to guide police officers, who have only limited time and expertise to reflect on and balance the social and individual interests involved in the specific circumstances they confront." . . .

But no straightforward rule has emerged . . . respecting the question involved here—the question of the proper scope of a search of the interior of an automobile incident to a lawful custodial arrest of its occupants. . . . When a person cannot know how a court will apply a settled principle to a recurring factual situation, that person cannot know the scope of his constitutional protection, nor can a policeman know the scope of his authority.

While the *Chimel* case established that a search incident to an arrest may not stray beyond the area within the immediate control of the arrestee, courts have found no workable definition of "the area within the immediate control of the arrestee" when that area arguably includes the interior of an automobile and the arrestee is its recent occupant.

Our reading of the cases suggests the generalization that articles inside the relatively narrow compass of the passenger compartment of an automobile are in fact generally, even if not inevitably, within "the area into which an arrestee might reach in order to grab a weapon or evidentiary item." In order to establish the workable rule this category of cases requires, we read *Chimel's* definition of the limits of the area that may be searched in light of that generalization.

Accordingly, we hold that when a policeman has made a lawful custodial arrest of the occupant of an automobile, he may, as a contemporaneous incident of that arrest, search the passenger compartment of that automobile. It follows from this conclusion that the police may also examine the contents of any containers found within the passenger compartment, for if the passenger compartment is within reach of the arrestee, so also will containers in it be within his reach.

Such a container may . . . be searched whether it is open or closed, since the justification for the search is not that the arrestee has no privacy interest in the container, but that the lawful custodial arrest justifies the infringement of any privacy interest the arrestee may have. "Container" here denotes any object capable of holding another object. It thus includes closed or open glove compartments, consoles, or other receptacles located anywhere within the passenger compartment, as well as luggage, boxes, bags, clothing, and the like. Our holding encompasses only the interior of the passenger compartment of an automobile and does not encompass the trunk.

Thus, while the Court in *Chimel* held that the police could not search all the drawers in an arrestee's house simply because the police had arrested him at home, the Court noted that drawers within an arrestee's reach could be searched because of the danger their contents might pose to the police.

It is true . . . that these containers will sometimes be such that they could hold neither a weapon nor evidence of the criminal conduct for which the suspect was arrested. However, in *U.S. v. Robinson*, the Court rejected the argument that such a container—there a "crumpled up cigarette package"—located during a search of Robinson incident to his arrest could not be searched:

The authority to search the person incident to a lawful custodial arrest, while based upon the need to disarm and to discover evidence, does not depend on what a court may later decide was the probability in a particular arrest situation that weapons or evidence would in fact be found upon the person of the suspect. A custodial arrest of a suspect based on probable cause is a reasonable intrusion under the Fourth Amendment; that intrusion being lawful, a search incident to the arrest requires no additional justification. . . .

It is not questioned that Belton was the subject of a lawful custodial arrest on a charge of possessing marijuana. The search of Belton's jacket followed immediately upon that arrest. The jacket was located inside the passenger compartment of the car in which Belton had been a passenger just before he was arrested. The jacket was thus within the area which we have concluded was "within the arrestee's immediate control" within the meaning of the *Chimel* case. The search of the jacket, therefore, was a search incident to a lawful custodial arrest, and it did not violate the Fourth and Fourteenth Amendments.

Accordingly, the judgment is REVERSED.

## DISSENT

### BRENNAN, J., JOINED BY MARSHALL, J.

. . . As the facts of this case make clear, the Court today substantially expands the permissible scope of searches incident to arrest by permitting police officers to search areas and containers the arrestee could not possibly reach at the time of arrest. These facts demonstrate that at the time Belton and his three companions were placed under custodial arrest—which was after they had been removed from the car, patted down, and separated—none of them could have reached the jackets that had been left on the back seat of the car. . . .

By approving the constitutionality of the warrantless search in this case, the Court carves out a dangerous precedent that is not justified by the concerns underlying *Chimel*. . . . The Court for the first time grants police officers authority to conduct a warrantless "area" search under circumstances where there is no chance that the arrestee "might gain possession of a weapon or destructible evidence." Under the approach taken today, the result would presumably be the same even if Officer Nicot had handcuffed Belton and his companions in the patrol car before placing them under arrest, and even if his search had extended to locked luggage or other inaccessible containers located in the back seat of the car. . . .

The Court seeks to justify its departure from the principles underlying *Chimel* by proclaiming the need for a new "bright-line" rule to guide the officer in the field. . . . However, "the mere fact that law enforcement may be made more efficient can never by itself justify disregard of the Fourth Amendment." . . . Because the Court's new rule abandons the justifications underlying *Chimel*, it offers no guidance to the police officer seeking to work out these answers for himself.

As we warned in *Chimel*:

No consideration relevant to the Fourth Amendment suggests any point of rational limitation, once the search is allowed to go beyond the area from which the person arrested might obtain weapons or evidentiary items.

By failing to heed this warning, the Court has undermined rather than furthered the goal of consistent law enforcement: it has failed to offer any principles to guide the police and the courts in their application of the new rule to nonroutine situations.

The standard announced in *Chimel* is not nearly as difficult to apply as the Court suggests. To the contrary, I continue to believe that *Chimel* provides a sound, workable rule for determining the constitutionality of a warrantless search incident to arrest. Under *Chimel*, searches incident to arrest may be conducted without a warrant only if limited to the person of the arrestee, or to the area within the arrestee's "immediate control."

While it may be difficult in some cases to measure the exact scope of the arrestee's immediate control, relevant factors would surely include the relative number of police officers and arrestees, the manner of restraint placed on the arrestee, and the ability of the arrestee to gain access to a particular area or container.

Certainly there will be some close cases, but when in doubt the police can always turn to the rationale underlying *Chimel*—the need to prevent the arrestee from reaching weapons or contraband—before exercising their judgment. A rule based on that rationale should provide more guidance than the rule announced by the Court today. Moreover, unlike the Court's rule, it would be faithful to the Fourth Amendment.

## Questions

1. Describe the details of the searches Officer Nicot conducted following his arrests of Belton and the other occupants in the car.

2. State the Court's definition of a grabbable area in this case, and compare it with the definition in *Chimel v. California* (p. 201). Are the definitions consistent? Explain.

3. In your opinion, which definition best balances the government's interest in controlling illegal drugs and Belton's right against unreasonable seizure? Defend your answer.

4. Do you prefer the bright-line rule that the Court adopted or the case-by-case approach that the dissent favors? Why?

5. Should the officer have been permitted to search not only the interior of the car but also the trunk? under the hood? a locked glove compartment?

6. Should the officer have been restricted to patting down the outer part of Belton's jacket? Is the Court's expansion of the grabbable area applicable only to vehicle cases, or should it apply to houses, too?

7. After the case was decided one commentator (Hancock 1982) noted:

Ten years ago most state court judges might have welcomed the Supreme Court's . . . decision. The new automobile search rule for arrested motorists [that deems the interior of an automobile always to be within the grabbable area] . . . certainly makes it easier for courts to apply the law of searches incident to arrest in such cases. . . . This new rule not only allows police to be more certain about the precise scope of their search powers, it also frees lower courts from the burden of case-by-case adjudication of the frequently disputed factual issue of actual grabbing area. (1085)

Do you agree? Do you favor the rule per se for that reason? Why or why not?

8. Consider the concerns expressed by Professor Wayne LaFave (1993), an expert on the law of search and seizure:

There is good reason to be . . . concerned with the Court's . . . holding in *New York v. Belton* that in every instance in which "a policeman has made a lawful custodial arrest of the occupant of an automobile, he may, as a contemporaneous incident of that arrest, search the passenger compartment of that automobile." In all such instances . . . "there is always the possibility that a police officer, lacking probable cause to obtain a search warrant, will use a traffic arrest as a pretext to conduct a search." Given that very few drivers can traverse any appreciable distance without violating some traffic regulation, this is indeed a frightening possibility. It is apparent that virtually anyone who ventures out onto the public streets and highways may then, with little effort by the police, be placed in a position where his or her person and vehicle are subject to search. (243)

Do you agree with Professor LaFave's contention that the ruling in *New York v. Belton* has created a "frightening possibility"?

 Go to Exercise 6.2 on the Samaha Criminal Procedure 7e website to learn more about *New York v. Belton*: academic.cengage.com/criminaljustice/samaha.

## EXPLORING FURTHER

# Search Incident to Arrest

## 1. Was the Search of the Suitcase on the Road Next to the Suspect Reasonable?

*People v. Brooks,* 257 Cal.Rptr. 840 (Cal.App. 1989)

FACTS A California police officer discovered a pistol and drugs on a hitchhiker during a lawful pat down, arrested and handcuffed him, and put him in a police vehicle. Only then did a second officer open an unlocked suitcase that had been sitting on the road next to the suspect at the time of the arrest; inside the suitcase were more drugs. Was the search of the suitcase incident to the arrest?

DECISION The California Court of Appeals said it was, holding that if a container is close enough that the arrested suspect could have reached it at the moment of arrest, it's reasonable to search it:

[A] search does not become unlawful because the police first separate the arrestee from the reach of the article, or handcuff or otherwise restrain the arrestee, so long as the search is made immediately thereafter, while the arrestee is still nearby at the scene of the arrest and before the arresting officers have turned their attention to tasks unrelated to securing the safety of persons and property involved in the arrest.

## 2. Was the Search of the Suspect's Jacket While He Was Held at the Other End of the Room Reasonable?

*State v. Ricks,* 771 P.2d 1364 (Alaska.App. 1989)

FACTS Alaska police officers entered a tavern and arrested the bartender for selling drugs moments earlier to an informer. Fifteen minutes later, while the suspect was being held at the other end of the room, an officer searched the jacket from which the suspect had gotten the drugs, which had been hanging all along on a coatrack some 10 to 15 feet from the bar. Was the search of the jacket incident to the arrest?

DECISION The Alaska Supreme Court ruled that it wasn't because the jacket wasn't accessible to the suspect at the moment of the arrest:

Physical proximity at the time of the arrest—with the consequent threat to safety and risk of destruction—is the basic requirement upon which the search incident to arrest exception is predicated.

The majority held that the exigencies of the situation at the point of the suspect's arrest didn't call for a search of the jacket.

## 3. Was the Area of the Search "Conceivably Accessible" to the Suspect?

*In re Sealed Case 96-3167,* 153 F.3d 759 (CADC 1998)

FACTS Officer William Riddle saw the defendant running up a flight of steps. The officer chased the defendant up the stairs and into a large, darkened bedroom. Once there, Officer Riddle saw the defendant "standing sideways" to the door, and facing "an extremely dark corner of the bedroom." Repeatedly calling out his identity as a police officer but receiving no answer, Officer Riddle pointed his weapon at the defendant and instructed him to show his hands. Before ultimately complying, the defendant's "hands came away from his body around his waist area, went into a dark corner of the bedroom, then came back toward the middle of his body, and at that point he showed Riddle his hands." Amidst his shouted instructions, Riddle did not hear anything hit the floor.

Officer Riddle then led the defendant into the hallway, patted him down for weapons, took him downstairs to the first floor, and handed him off to other officers who had just arrived. The defendant was not handcuffed. Riddle immediately returned upstairs to the large bedroom. Unable to turn the light on, Riddle used his flashlight. In the darkened corner, "where [defendant] was standing next to, and then his arms and hands had went into," Riddle discovered "laying in a chair, a plastic bag, which appeared to have busted open, or come open in some manner, and several large white rocks," later identified as crack cocaine. On the floor beside the chair was a semiautomatic handgun. The gun was lying "on top of a pair of shoes, and I believe a handbag, or some type of soft object."

Upon finding this evidence, Riddle went directly back downstairs and handcuffed the defendant. . . . The defendant moved to suppress the evidence seized from his house. . . . The district court . . . held that . . . the items recovered from that large bedroom were lawfully "seized incident to the arrest." . . . Accordingly, the district court denied the defendant's motion to suppress. After the denial of his motion to suppress, the defendant entered a conditional plea of guilty to the cocaine and firearm charge. . . .

Was the search incident to the arrest? The Court of Appeals said yes.

OPINION In Chimel v. U.S., the Supreme Court held that, incident to a lawful arrest, the police may properly search the area within the arrestee's "immediate control." A search of that area is permissible, regardless whether in the circumstances of a particular case it is probable that "weapons or evidence would in fact be found" there.

In this case, it is clear that the guns and drugs Officer Riddle found in the large bedroom were located in an area under the defendant's "immediate control." The defendant was arrested while standing next to a chair in the bedroom. The drugs were found on that chair, and the gun was found beside it.

The defendant contends that Chimel is inapplicable here. "Although the larger bedroom was the room in which [he] had been arrested," the defendant emphasizes that he was at the bottom of the stairs by the time the bedroom was searched. By that time, the large bedroom was no longer under his "immediate control." The critical time for analysis, however, is the time of the arrest and not the time of the search. In New York v. Belton, the Supreme Court held that when the police lawfully arrest the occupant of an automobile, they may "as a contemporaneous incident of that arrest, search the passenger compartment," even if the occupant has been removed and is no longer in the car at the time of the search.

We have since rejected the argument that Belton applies only to automobiles, and affirmed that the area under a defendant's "immediate control" for Chimel purposes must be examined as of the time the arrest occurs. . . . As long as a search is "contemporaneous with" and an "integral part of" a lawful arrest, we held, the police may search a container that was within reach "when the arrest occurs, even if the officer has since seized it and gained exclusive control over it." . . .

The "determination of immediate control must be made when the arrest occurs." . . . Making the test turn exclusively on the time of the search "might create a perverse incentive for an arresting officer to prolong the period during which the arrestee is kept in an area where he could pose a danger to the officer." . . . However, . . . a search is incident to arrest only so long as it is an "integral part" of the arrest process. The relevant distinction turns upon "whether the arrest and search are so separated in time or by intervening events that the latter cannot fairly be said to have been incident to the former." Such a temporal separation did not occur in this case: Officer Riddle searched the large bedroom immediately after arresting and removing the defendant.

. . . Not only must the area searched be under the defendant's "immediate control" at the time of the arrest, it must also be "conceivably accessible" to the defendant at the time of the search. Whether or not this added requirement is consistent with the reasoning of Belton . . . , it is satisfied in this case. . . . Showing that the area searched was conceivably accessible at the time of the search was not meant to be difficult. . . .

The case at bar satisfies the "conceivably accessible" test. . . . The defendant was not handcuffed or otherwise immobilized at the time of the search of the large bedroom. He did not suffer any physical infirmity; to the contrary, the officers had just watched him move through the neighborhood at a rapid pace. . . . The defendant both had specifically sought access to the room being searched and had demonstrated the capacity and desire to avoid arrest: he had fled from Officer Riddle into the very bedroom at issue. . . . The defendant had a motive for going back to the room—he knew there was a weapon there. Finally, although the defendant was at the bottom of the stairs at the time of the search, only minutes before he had raced up those very stairs in an effort to evade Riddle. Under these circumstances, the bedroom here was . . . conceivably accessible to the defendant. . . .

 To read the full text versions of the Exploring Further excerpts, go to the Samaha Criminal Procedure 7e website: academic.cengage.com/criminaljustice/samaha.

***The Time Frame of "Incident To"*** What's the time frame of "incident to arrest," or as it's often called, "contemporaneous with the arrest"? According to the U.S. Supreme Court, "incident to" includes the time before, during, and after arrest. For example, in *Cupp v. Murphy* (1973), right before Portland, Oregon, police officers arrested Daniel Murphy, they scraped his fingernails for blood residue to see if it matched his strangled wife's. The U.S. Supreme Court held that because the officers *could* have arrested Murphy before they searched him (they had probable cause), the search was incident to the arrest.

In *U.S. v. Edwards* (1974), Eugene Edwards was arrested shortly after 11:00 P.M. and put in jail. The next morning, officers took his clothing and searched it for paint chips that would link Edwards to a burglary. Despite the 10-hour gap between the arrest and the search, and over a strong dissent arguing the officers had plenty of time to present their evidence to a neutral magistrate to get a search warrant, the Supreme Court ruled that the search was incident to the arrest.

***Searches Incident to Misdemeanor Arrests*** Until now, we've looked at the reasonableness of searches incident to felony arrests, but what about the reasonableness of searches incident to arrests for misdemeanors? The U.S. Supreme Court answered the question in *U.S. v. Robinson* (1973). Officer Richard Jenks, a 15-year veteran of the Washington, D.C., Police Department, arrested Willie Robinson for driving without a license (a misdemeanor). Jenks then searched Robinson. During the search, Jenks felt a lump in Robinson's coat pocket. Reaching inside, he found a crumpled-up cigarette package. Jenks took the package out of Robinson's pocket, opened it, and found heroin inside.

Robinson was charged with illegally possessing narcotics. He moved to suppress the evidence, but the court denied his motion and admitted the heroin. The heroin was the main evidence that convicted Robinson. The Supreme Court upheld the conviction and formulated a "bright line" *Robinson* **rule**: Officers can always search anyone they're authorized to take into custody. (Be clear that officers don't have to search; many times they won't, but whether they do is a matter of individual officer discretion.) According to Justice Rehnquist, writing for the majority:

> A police officer's determination as to how and where to search the person of a suspect whom he has arrested is necessarily a quick ad hoc judgment which the Fourth Amendment does not require to be broken down in each instance into an analysis of each step in the search. The authority to search the person incident to a lawful custodial arrest, while based upon the need to disarm and to discover evidence, does not depend upon what a court may later decide was the probability in a particular arrest situation that weapons or evidence would in fact be found upon the person of the suspect. A custodial arrest of a suspect based on probable cause is a reasonable intrusion under the Fourth Amendment; that intrusion being lawful, a search incident to the arrest requires no additional justification. It is the fact of the lawful arrest which establishes the authority to search, and we hold that in the case of a lawful custodial arrest a full search of the person is not only an exception to the warrant requirement of the Fourth Amendment, but is also a "reasonable" search under that Amendment. (234–35)

What's the justification for the "bright line" *Robinson* rule? Two reasons, according to the Court:

1. The possible danger to police officers taking suspects into custody

2. The logical impossibility of the Court's reviewing every police decision

The *Robinson* bright-line rule shows the Court's reluctance to second-guess law enforcement decisions. However, six state courts—Alaska, California, Hawaii, New York,

Oregon, and West Virginia—haven't been so reluctant; they rejected the bright-line *Robinson* rule. Five—Illinois, Michigan, Montana, New Hampshire, and Texas—have adopted it (Latzer 1991, 64).

Are *automatic* searches incident to traffic citations reasonable under the *Robinson* rule? (As most of you probably know, citations are substitutes for arrests.) A unanimous U.S. Supreme Court said no in our next case excerpt, *Knowles v. Iowa* (1998), a case challenging an Iowa statute that created a search-incident-to-citation exception to the warrant requirement.

## CASE | *Was the Automatic Search Incident to Citation Reasonable?*

### Knowles v. Iowa

525 U.S. 113 (1998)

### HISTORY

Patrick Knowles was charged with possession of marijuana and keeping marijuana in a car. After the court denied his motion to suppress the marijuana as evidence, he was convicted of both offenses. The Iowa Supreme Court affirmed.

The U.S. Supreme Court granted certiorari and reversed and remanded the case.

REHNQUIST, C.J.

An Iowa police officer stopped Knowles for speeding, but issued him a citation rather than arresting him. The question presented is whether such a procedure authorizes the officer, consistently with the Fourth Amendment, to conduct a full search of the car. We answer this question "no."

### FACTS

Patrick Knowles was stopped in Newton, Iowa, after having been clocked driving 43 miles per hour on a road where the speed limit was 25 miles per hour. The police officer issued a citation to Knowles, although under Iowa law he might have arrested him. The officer then conducted a full search of the car, and under the driver's seat he found a bag of marijuana and a "pot pipe." Knowles was then arrested and charged with violation of state laws dealing with controlled substances.

Before trial, Knowles moved to suppress the evidence so obtained. He argued that the search could not be sustained under the "search incident to arrest" exception recognized in *U.S. v. Robinson* (1973), because he had not been placed under arrest. At the hearing on the motion to suppress, the police officer conceded that he had neither Knowles' consent nor probable cause to conduct the search. He relied on Iowa law dealing with such searches.

Iowa Code Ann. § 321.485(1)(a) provides that Iowa peace officers having cause to believe that a person has violated any traffic or motor vehicle equipment law may arrest the person and immediately take the person before a magistrate. Iowa law also authorizes the far more usual practice of issuing a citation in lieu of arrest or in lieu of continued custody after an initial arrest.

Section 805.1(4) provides that the issuance of a citation in lieu of an arrest "does not affect the officer's authority to conduct an otherwise lawful search." The Iowa Supreme Court has interpreted this provision as providing authority to officers to conduct a full-blown search of an automobile and driver in those cases where police elect not to make a custodial arrest and instead issue a citation—that is, a search incident to citation.

Based on this authority, the trial court denied the motion to suppress and found Knowles guilty. The Supreme Court of Iowa, sitting en banc, affirmed by a divided vote. Relying on its earlier opinion in *State v. Doran* (Iowa 1997), the Iowa Supreme Court upheld the constitutionality of the search under a bright-line "search incident to citation" exception to the Fourth Amendment's warrant requirement, reasoning that so long as the arresting officer had probable cause to make a custodial arrest, there need not in fact have been a custodial arrest. We granted certiorari, and we now reverse.

### OPINION

In *U.S. v. Robinson*, we noted the two historical rationales for the "search incident to arrest" exception: (1) the need to disarm the suspect in order to take him into custody, and (2) the need to preserve evidence for later use at trial. But neither of these underlying rationales for the search incident to arrest exception is sufficient to justify the search in the present case.

We have recognized that the first rationale—officer safety—is "both legitimate and weighty," *Maryland v. Wilson* [excerpted in Chapter 4]. The threat to officer safety from issuing a traffic citation, however, is a good deal less than in the case of a custodial arrest. In *Robinson*, we stated that a custodial arrest involves "danger to an officer" because of "the extended exposure which follows the taking of a suspect into custody and transporting him to the police station."

We recognized that "the danger to the police officer flows from the fact of the arrest, and its attendant proximity, stress, and uncertainty, and not from the grounds for arrest." A routine traffic stop, on the other hand, is a relatively brief encounter and "is more analogous to a so-called '*Terry* stop' . . . than to a formal arrest." Where there is no formal arrest . . . a person might well be less hostile to the police and less likely to take conspicuous, immediate steps to destroy incriminating evidence.

This is not to say that the concern for officer safety is absent in the case of a routine traffic stop. It plainly is not. But while the concern for officer safety in this context may justify the "minimal" additional intrusion of ordering a driver and passengers out of the car, it does not by itself justify the often considerably greater intrusion attending a full field-type search.

Even without the search authority Iowa urges, officers have other, independent bases to search for weapons and protect themselves from danger. For example, they may order out of a vehicle both the driver; perform a "patdown" of a driver and any passengers upon reasonable suspicion that they may be armed and dangerous, *Terry v. Ohio* (1968); conduct a "*Terry* patdown" of the passenger compartment of a vehicle upon reasonable suspicion that an occupant is dangerous and may gain immediate control of a weapon; and even conduct a full search of the passenger compartment, including any containers therein, pursuant to a custodial arrest, *New York v. Belton* (1981).

Nor has Iowa shown the second justification for the authority to search incident to arrest—the need to discover and preserve evidence. Once Knowles was stopped for speeding and issued a citation, all the evidence necessary to prosecute that offense had been obtained. No further evidence of excessive speed was going to be found either on the person of the offender or in the passenger compartment of the car.

Iowa nevertheless argues that a "search incident to citation" is justified because a suspect who is subject to a routine traffic stop may attempt to hide or destroy evidence related to his identity (e.g., a driver's license or vehicle registration), or destroy evidence of another, as yet undetected crime. As for the destruction of evidence relating to identity, if a police officer is not satisfied with the identification furnished by the driver, this may be a basis for arresting him rather than merely issuing a citation. As for destroying evidence of other crimes, the possibility that an officer would stumble onto evidence wholly unrelated to the speeding offense seems remote.

In *Robinson*, we held that the authority to conduct a full field search as incident to an arrest was a "bright-line rule," which was based on the concern for officer safety and destruction or loss of evidence, but which did not depend in every case upon the existence of either concern. Here we are asked to extend that "bright-line rule" to a situation where the concern for officer safety is not present to the same extent and the concern for destruction or loss of evidence is not present at all. We decline to do so.

The judgment of the Supreme Court of Iowa is REVERSED, and the cause REMANDED for further proceedings not inconsistent with this opinion. It is so ordered.

## Questions

1. Summarize the reasons for Iowa's claim that the search incident to a citation is reasonable. Do you agree? Explain.

2. Summarize the reasons why the U.S. Supreme Court decided that the Iowa statute was unconstitutional. Do you agree? Explain.

3. Do you think the Supreme Court retreated from its sweeping decision in *U.S. v. Robinson*? If so, do you think it's a good idea that it did? Defend your answer.

 Go to Exercise 6.3 on the Samaha Criminal Procedure 7e website to learn how the Iowa Attorney General reacted to *Knowles v. Iowa*: academic.cengage.com/criminaljustice/samaha.

***Searches Incident to Pretext Arrests*** Suppose an officer has only a hunch that a college student has marijuana in her car. The officer sees her make a left turn without signaling. What luck, he thinks, now I've got my chance. He stops her for turning without signaling so that he can search the car for marijuana—the arrest is simply a pretext for the search. **Pretext arrests** (arrests for one offense where probable cause exists, motivated by officers' desire to search for evidence of another unrelated offense where probable cause doesn't exist) are powerful investigative tools in the "drug war." Most people commit traffic offenses, so officers can use this fact of life to act on their hunches that drivers are committing drug crimes.

Critics argue that searches incident to pretext traffic arrests put a heavy thumb on the government side of the balance between government and individuals. According to Professor Daniel S. Jonas (1989):

The conflict between liberty and law enforcement is particularly sharp in the area of pretextual police conduct. Police would have a powerful investigative tool if it were constitutional, for example, to arrest a felony suspect on the basis of a parking ticket that had not been paid, when the facts relating to the felony did not provide probable cause. Precisely because its investigative potential is so great, pretextual police conduct poses an alarming threat to individual freedom from government intrusion. (1792)

In our next case excerpt, *Whren v. U.S.* (1996), a unanimous U.S. Supreme Court decided that police officers' search of Michael Whren's Nissan Pathfinder incident to Whren's arrest for traffic violations was a reasonable Fourth Amendment search.

## CASE   *Was the Search Incident to a Pretext Arrest Reasonable?*

### Whren v. U.S.
517 U.S 806 (1996)

### HISTORY

Michael A. Whren and James L. Brown were convicted in the U.S. District Court for the District of Columbia of drug offenses, and they appealed. The Court of Appeals affirmed. The U.S. Supreme Court granted certiorari. The U.S. Supreme Court affirmed.

SCALIA, J.

### FACTS

On the evening of June 10, 1993, plainclothes vice-squad officers of the District of Columbia Metropolitan Police Department were patrolling a "high drug area" of the city in an unmarked car. Their suspicions were aroused when they passed a dark Nissan Pathfinder with temporary license plates and youthful occupants waiting at a stop sign, the driver looking down into the lap of the passenger at his right. The Pathfinder remained stopped at the intersection for what seemed an unusually long time—more than 20 seconds.

When the police car executed a U-turn in order to head back toward the truck, the Pathfinder turned suddenly to its right, without signaling, and sped off at an "unreasonable" speed. The policemen followed, and in a short while overtook the Pathfinder when it stopped behind other traffic at a red light. They pulled up alongside, and Officer Ephraim Soto stepped out and approached the driver's door, identifying himself as a police officer and directing the driver, James Brown, to put the vehicle in park.

When Soto drew up to the driver's window, he immediately observed two large plastic bags of what appeared to be crack cocaine in James Whren's hands. Brown and Whren were arrested, and quantities of several types of illegal drugs were retrieved from the vehicle.

Brown and Whren were charged in a four-count indictment with violating various federal drug laws, including 21 U.S.C. §§ 844(a) and 860(a). At a pretrial suppression hearing, they challenged the legality of the stop and the resulting seizure of the drugs. They argued that the stop had not been justified by probable cause to believe, or even reasonable suspicion, that they were engaged in illegal drug-dealing activity; and that Officer Soto's asserted ground for approaching the vehicle—to give the driver a warning concerning traffic violations—was pretextual.

The District Court denied the suppression motion, concluding that "the facts of the stop were not controverted," and "there was nothing to really demonstrate that the actions of the officers were contrary to a normal traffic stop." Whren and Brown were convicted. . . . The Court of Appeals affirmed the convictions, holding with respect to the suppression issue that, "regardless of whether a police officer subjectively believes that the occupants of an automobile may be engaging in some other illegal behavior, a traffic stop is permissible as long as a reasonable officer in the same circumstances *could* [emphasis added] have stopped the car for the suspected traffic violation." We granted certiorari.

### OPINION

. . . As a general matter, the decision to stop an automobile is reasonable where the police have probable cause to believe that a traffic violation has occurred. Brown and Whren accept that Officer Soto had probable cause to believe that various provisions of the District of Columbia traffic code had been violated:

1. 18 D.C. Mun. Regs. §§ 2213.4 (1995) An operator shall . . . give full time and attention to the operation of the vehicle;

2. 2204.3 No person shall turn any vehicle . . . without giving an appropriate signal;

3. 2200.3 No person shall drive a vehicle . . . at a speed greater than is reasonable and prudent under the conditions.

They argue, however, that "in the unique context of civil traffic regulations" probable cause is not enough. Since, they contend, the use of automobiles is so heavily and minutely regulated that total compliance with traffic and safety rules is nearly impossible, a police officer will almost invariably be able to catch any given motorist in a technical violation. This creates the temptation to use traffic stops as a means of investigating other law violations, as to which no probable cause or even articulable suspicion exists.

→ Whren and Brown, who are both Black, further contend that police officers might decide which motorists to stop based on decidedly impermissible factors, such as the race of the car's occupants. To avoid this danger, they say, the Fourth Amendment test for traffic stops should be, not the normal one (applied by the Court of Appeals) of whether probable cause existed to justify the stop; but rather, whether a police officer, acting reasonably, *would* [emphasis added] have made the stop for the reason given.

Whren and Brown contend that the standard they propose is consistent with our past cases' disapproval of police attempts to use valid bases of action against citizens as pretexts for pursuing other investigatory agendas. We are reminded that in *Florida v. Wells* (1990), we stated that "an inventory search must not be used as a ruse for a general rummaging in order to discover incriminating evidence"; that in *Colorado v. Bertine* (1987), in approving an inventory search, we apparently thought it significant that there had been "no showing that the police, who were following standard procedures, acted in bad faith or for the sole purpose of investigation"; and that in *New York v. Burger* (1987), we observed, in upholding the constitutionality of a warrantless administrative inspection, that the search did not appear to be a pretext for obtaining evidence of . . . violation of . . . penal laws.

. . . Not only have we never held, outside the context of inventory search [discussed in Chapter 7] or administrative inspection, that an officer's motive invalidates objectively justifiable behavior under the Fourth Amendment, but we have repeatedly held and asserted the contrary. . . . In *U.S. v. Robinson* (1973) [discussed earlier on p. 208], we held that a traffic violation arrest (of the sort here) would not be rendered invalid by the fact that it was "a mere pretext for a narcotics search," and that a lawful post arrest search of the person would not be rendered invalid by the fact that it was not motivated by the officer-safety concern that justifies such searches. . . . *Robinson* . . . established

that "the fact that the officer does not have the state of mind which is hypothecated by the reasons which provide the legal justification for the officer's action does not invalidate the action taken as long as the circumstances, viewed objectively, justify that action." [*The Court discussed other cases not included here.*] We think these cases foreclose any argument that the constitutional reasonableness of traffic stops depends on the actual motivations of the individual officers involved.

We of course agree with Whren and Brown that the Constitution prohibits selective enforcement of the law based on considerations such as race. But the constitutional basis for objecting to intentionally discriminatory application of laws is the Equal Protection Clause, not the Fourth Amendment. Subjective intentions play no role in ordinary, probable-cause Fourth Amendment analysis. . . .

Whren and Brown's claim that a reasonable officer *would not* [emphasis added] have made this stop is based largely on District of Columbia police regulations which permit plainclothes officers in unmarked vehicles to enforce traffic laws "only in the case of a violation that is so grave as to pose an immediate threat to the safety of others." . . . This basis of invalidation would not apply in jurisdictions that had a different practice. And it would not have applied even in the District of Columbia, if Officer Soto had been wearing a uniform or patrolling in a marked police cruiser.

. . . Whren and Brown argue that the balancing inherent in any Fourth Amendment inquiry requires us to weigh the governmental and individual interests implicated in a traffic stop such as we have here. That balancing, they claim, does not support investigation of minor traffic infractions by plainclothes police in unmarked vehicles; such investigation only minimally advances the government's interest in traffic safety, and may indeed retard it by producing motorist confusion and alarm—a view said to be supported by the Metropolitan Police Department's own regulations generally prohibiting this practice. . . .

It is of course true that in principle every Fourth Amendment case, since it turns upon a "reasonableness" determination, involves a balancing of all relevant factors. With rare exceptions not applicable here, however, the result of that balancing is not in doubt where the search or seizure is based upon probable cause. . . . Where probable cause has existed, the only cases in which we have found it necessary actually to perform the "balancing" analysis involved searches or seizures conducted in an extraordinary manner, unusually harmful to an individual's privacy or even physical interests—such as, for example, seizure by means of deadly force, see *Tennessee v. Garner* (1985) [excerpted in Chapter 5], unannounced entry into a home, see *Wilson v. Arkansas* (1995) [excerpted earlier on p. 192], entry into a home without a warrant, see *Welsh v. Wisconsin* (1984), or physical penetration of the body, see *Winston v. Lee* (1985).

The making of a traffic stop out-of-uniform does not remotely qualify as such an extreme practice, and so is governed by the usual rule that probable cause to believe the law has been broken "outbalances" private interest in avoiding police contact.

Whren and Brown urge as an extraordinary factor in this case that the "multitude of applicable traffic and equipment regulations" is so large and so difficult to obey perfectly that virtually everyone is guilty of violation, permitting the police to single out almost whomever they wish for a stop. But we are aware of no principle that would allow us to decide at what point a code of law becomes so expansive and so commonly violated that infraction itself can no longer be the ordinary measure of the lawfulness of enforcement. And even if we could identify such exorbitant codes, we do not know by what standard (or what right) we would decide, as Whren and Brown would have us do, which particular provisions are sufficiently important to merit enforcement.

For the run of the mine case, which this surely is, we think there is no realistic alternative to the traditional common-law rule that probable cause justifies a search and seizure. Here the District Court found that the officers had probable cause to believe that petitioners had violated the traffic code. That rendered the stop reasonable under the Fourth Amendment, the evidence thereby discovered admissible, and the upholding of the convictions by the Court of Appeals for the District of Columbia Circuit correct.

Judgment AFFIRMED.

## Questions

1. List all the actions Officer Soto and his partner took that affected Whren and Brown's liberty and privacy.

2. What's the evidence that Officer Soto and his partner conducted a pretext search?

3. Did Officer Soto and his partner have probable cause to arrest Whren and Brown? List the relevant facts and circumstances relevant to deciding whether they had probable cause.

4. For what "crimes" did the officers have probable cause to arrest Brown and Whren?

5. Explain the "could have" and "would have" tests to determine the reasonableness of the pretext search. What test did the Court adopt? Why?

6. Do you agree with Professor Jonas in the quotation at the opening of this section that pretext searches threaten individual rights too much? That they give the government too much power? Or do you believe that the government needs this power to fight the "war on drugs"?

7. Consider the following excerpt from the Petitioner's Brief (*Whren v. U.S.* 1996a) in *Whren v. U.S.*:

Justice Jackson's observation nearly a half-century ago is no less true today: "I am convinced that there are . . . many unlawful searches of homes and automobiles of innocent people which turn up nothing incriminating, in which no arrest is made, about which courts do nothing, and about which we never hear." *Brinegar v. U.S.*, 338 U.S. 160 (1949) (JACKSON, J., dissenting).

Because police do not generally keep records of traffic stops that turn up nothing and in which no one is ticketed, it is no simple matter to substantiate Justice Jackson's suspicions. However, reporters from the *Orlando Sentinel* had the unique opportunity to document this phenomenon when they obtained 148 hours of videotaped "traffic" stops of 1,084 motorists along Interstate 95 in Florida (Brazil and Berry, "Color of Driver Is Key to Stops in I-95 Videos," *Orlando Sentinel*, Aug. 23, 1992).

Although all of the stops were purportedly based on traffic violations, only nine drivers (less than one percent) were issued citations. Searches were made in almost half the stops, but only 5 percent of all stops resulted in an arrest. Most shocking is how racially disproportionate the stops were. Although blacks and Hispanics made up only 5 percent of the drivers on that stretch of I-95 and only 15 percent of traffic convictions statewide, approximately 70 percent of those stopped were black or Hispanic.

On average, stops of minority drivers lasted more than twice as long as stops of white drivers. For some, the tapes showed it was not the first time they had been singled out: "There is the bewildered black man who stands on the roadside trying to explain to the deputies that it is the seventh time he has been stopped. And the black man who shakes his head in frustration as his car is searched; it is the second time in minutes he has been stopped." This kind of baseless "checking out" of racial minorities generally gets public attention only when someone well-known speaks out.

Materials in a class action involving pretextual traffic stops along Interstate 95 near Philadelphia show a similar pattern. The class representatives alleged that, while returning from a church celebration in 1991, they were stopped and subjected to a sniff by a police dog before being told, "in order to make this a legitimate stop, I'm going to give you a warning for obstruction of your car's rear-view mirror." The only object hanging from the mirror was a thin piece of string on which an air freshener had once been attached. When the driver pointed out that the officer could not have seen the string, the officer stated that they were stopped "because you are young, black and in a high drug-trafficking area, driving a nice car."

Materials and follow-up interviews in the Tinicum Township case showed: First, the interdiction program is based on the power to make a pretextual traffic stop. Numerous vehicles have been stopped, for example, for having small items tied to their rearview mirrors, for outdated inspection stickers, or for other minor violations, all supposedly observed as the car passed the police at sixty miles per hour. Second, the stops are racially disproportionate. Third, claims of consent are rebutted by numerous innocent individuals who give consistent accounts of being told that they would have to wait for a police dog, have their car towed, or suffer other types of roadside detention unless they consented to a search. (24–27)

How does this passage affect your opinion of the reasonableness of pretext searches? Is it more relevant to claims under the equal protection than the due process clause? (Refer to Chapter 2 on due process and equal protection.)

8. Consider the following remarks made by a police officer to researchers Lawrence Tiffany and his colleagues (1967):

You can always get a guy legitimately on a traffic violation if you tail him for a while, and then a search can be made. You don't have to follow a driver very long before he will move to the other side of the yellow line and then you can arrest and search him for driving on the wrong side of the highway. In the event that we see a suspicious automobile or occupant and wish to search the person or the car, or both, we will usually follow the vehicle until the driver makes a technical violation of a traffic law. Then we have a means of making a legitimate search. (131)

What's your reaction to this comment? Do you think things might have changed since the 1950s when the research for this quote was completed? Explain your answer.

9. Present arguments that both defense lawyers and prosecutors might make to support the reasonableness and the unreasonableness of searches incident to pretext traffic arrests. Then, assume the role of judge and decide the reasonableness of pretext traffic arrest searches in light of Fourth Amendment reasonableness.

 Go to Exercise 6.4 on the Samaha Criminal Procedure 7e website to learn more about *Whren v. U.S.* and State Constitutional Law in *State v. Ladson*: academic.cengage.com/criminaljustice/samaha.

## Consent Searches

**Consent searches** are searches in which individuals give officers permission to search them and/or their houses and personal belongings without either warrants or probable cause. It's difficult to estimate the number of consent searches, but they may be the most common of all searches. We do know that "the vast majority of people" who do consent to searches or to allow officers to conduct a pat down are innocent (Nadler 2002, 209–10). We also know that consent searches definitely make law enforcement officers' job easier, because they don't have to go through the hassle of either getting warrants before they search or proving probable cause to a judge later.

Finally, we know that consent searches allow officers to search in instances where they couldn't otherwise because they couldn't get warrants or they lacked probable cause to conduct the searches without warrants.

Lawrence P. Tiffany, Donald M. McIntyre, Jr., and Daniel L. Rotenberg, in their classic *The Detection of Crime* (1967), studied consent searches as part of the distinguished American Bar Foundation's massive research into the day-to-day operations of criminal justice in America. They found that officers prefer to search by consent even when they have probable cause to obtain warrants because consent searches are convenient. "Search warrant procedure is overly technical and time-consuming, and . . . has no corresponding advantages for them or meaningful protections for the individual" (157–61).

But convenience isn't the only reason for consent searches. Necessity also drives police officers to ask individuals to consent to searches. Officers need consent when they don't have probable cause to search. For example, it's well known that drug dealers travel by bus or plane, but officers don't have probable cause to search most passengers. So they approach travelers, ask if they can talk to them, explain the seriousness of the drug problem, and ask them if they mind having officers search them and their belongings. According to the anecdotal evidence supplied by officers, most travelers give their consent, especially when officers are polite and respectful.

In *U.S. v. Blake* (1988), Detective Perry Kendrick, who worked the Fort Lauderdale Airport, testified that people willingly consent even to searches of their crotches in the public part of airports (*U.S. v. Rodney*, excerpted later in this chapter). According to Kendrick, on just one day,

> he talked with 16 to 20 people and most consented, but one or two did not. He testified further that initially some complain after the search, but that after the deputies explain their mission in interdicting narcotics moving from airport to airport within the United States, that the persons understand and many "thank us for the job we're doing." (927)

Many legal issues surround consent, including the test of whether consent was given; the scope of consent; when consent can be withdrawn after it's given; and when one person can consent to searches of other people, their houses, and personal belongings. Let's look at each.

*The Test of Consent*  When police officers ask for consent to search, they're really asking individuals to give up their rights against unreasonable searches and seizures. Because it's a serious matter to give up one of the fundamental rights our ancestors fought the Revolutionary War to protect, the U.S. Supreme Court demands that as a minimum requirement, the government has to prove by a preponderance of the evidence that the consent was voluntary. The **voluntariness test of consent** searches looks at the totality of circumstances in each case to determine if the suspect consented voluntarily. These circumstances can include all of the following:

- Knowledge of constitutional rights in general
- Knowledge of the right to refuse consent
- Sufficient age and maturity to make an independent decision
- Intelligence to understand the significance of consent
- Education in or experience with the workings of the criminal justice system
- Cooperation with officers, such as saying, "Sure, go ahead and search"
- Attitude toward the likelihood that officers will discover contraband
- Length of detention and nature of questioning regarding consent
- Coercive police behavior surrounding the consent

A signed consent form is another example of how officers can demonstrate that a suspect voluntarily consented to a search. The New Jersey "Consent to Search" form, adopted by the New Jersey State Police, is an example. It

> authorizes a trooper to conduct a "complete search" of a motor vehicle or other premises as described by the officer on the face of the form. The form also states:
>
> > I further authorize the above member of the New Jersey State Police to remove and search any letters, documents, papers, materials, or other property which is considered pertinent to the investigation, provided that I am subsequently given a receipt for anything which is removed.
> >
> > I have knowingly and voluntarily given my consent to the search described above.
> >
> > I have been advised by [the investigating officer] and fully understand that I have the right to refuse giving my consent to search.

I have been further advised that I may withdraw my consent at any time during the search.

The form is filled out by the officer to include, among other things, the officer's name and a description of the vehicle to be searched. It then is presented to the consentee for his or her signature. (*State v. Carty* 2002, 907)

In our first consent case excerpt, the leading U.S. Supreme Court consent search case, *Schneckloth v. Bustamonte* (1973), the Court created the totality-of-circumstances test and held that the search of Clyde Bustamonte passed the test.

C A S E    *Did Bustamonte Voluntarily Consent?*

## Schneckloth v. Bustamonte
### 412 U.S. 218 (1973)

### HISTORY

Clyde Bustamonte was tried in a California state court for possessing a check with intent to defraud. The trial judge denied his motion to suppress and Bustamonte was convicted. The California Court of Appeals affirmed. The California Supreme Court denied review. Bustamonte brought a petition for habeas corpus in the U.S. District Court for the Northern District of California. The District Court denied the petition. The U.S. Court of Appeals for the Ninth Circuit vacated the District Court's order, and remanded. The U.S. Supreme Court reversed.

STEWART, J.

### FACTS

While on routine patrol in Sunnyvale, California, at approximately 2:40 in the morning, Police Officer James Rand stopped an automobile when he observed that one headlight and its license plate light were burned out. Six men were in the vehicle. Joe Alcala and Robert Clyde Bustamonte were in the front seat with Joe Gonzales, the driver. Three older men were seated in the rear. When, in response to the policeman's question, Gonzales could not produce a driver's license, Officer Rand asked if any of the other five had any evidence of identification. Only Alcala produced a license, and he explained that the car was his brother's.

After the six occupants had stepped out of the car at the officer's request and after two additional policemen had arrived, Officer Rand asked Alcala if he could search the car. Alcala replied, "Sure, go ahead." Prior to the search no one was threatened with arrest and, according to Officer Rand's uncontradicted testimony, it "was all very congenial at this time." Gonzales testified that Alcala actually helped in the search of the car, by opening the trunk and glove compartment. In Gonzales' words: The police officer asked Joe (Alcala), he goes, "Does the trunk open?" And Joe said, "Yes." He went to the car and got the keys and opened up the trunk. Wadded up under the left rear seat, the police officers found three checks that had previously been stolen from a car wash.

### OPINION

It is well settled under the Fourth Amendment . . . that one of the specifically established exceptions to the requirements of both a warrant and probable cause is a search that is conducted pursuant to consent. . . . The precise question in this case . . . is what must the prosecution prove to demonstrate that a consent was "voluntarily" given. And upon that question there is a square conflict of views between the state and federal courts that have reviewed the search involved in the case before us.

The Court of Appeals for the Ninth Circuit concluded that it is an essential part of the State's initial burden to prove that a person knows he has a right to refuse consent. The California courts have followed the rule that voluntariness is a question of fact to be determined from the totality of all the circumstances, and that the state of a defendant's knowledge is only one factor to be taken into account in assessing the voluntariness of a consent.

The most extensive judicial exposition of the meaning of "voluntariness" has been developed in those cases in which the Court has had to determine the "voluntariness" of a defendant's confession . . . [discussed in Chapter 8]. This Court's decisions reflect a frank recognition that the Constitution requires the sacrifice of neither security nor liberty. The Due Process Clause does not mandate that the police forgo all questioning, or that they be given carte blanche to extract what they can from a suspect. The ultimate test remains . . . [the same] test in Anglo-American courts for two hundred years: the test of voluntariness. Is the confession the product of an essentially free and unconstrained choice by its maker? If it is, if he has willed to confess, it may be used against him. If it is not, if his will has been overborne and his capacity for self-determination critically impaired, the use of his confession offends due process.

In determining whether a defendant's will was overborne in a particular case, the Court has assessed the totality of all the surrounding circumstances—both the characteristics of the accused and the details of the interrogation. Some of the factors taken into account have included the youth of the accused, his lack of education, or his low intelligence, the lack of any advice to the accused of his constitutional rights, the length of detention, the repeated and prolonged nature of the questioning, and the use of physical punishment such as the deprivation of food or sleep. In all of these cases, the Court determined the factual circumstances surrounding the confession, assessed the psychological impact on the accused, and evaluated the legal significance of how the accused reacted.

The significant fact about all of these decisions is that none of them turned on the presence or absence of a single controlling criterion; each reflected a careful scrutiny of all the surrounding circumstances. In none of them did the Court rule that the Due Process Clause required the prosecution to prove as part of its initial burden that the defendant knew he had a right to refuse to answer the questions that were put. While the state of the accused's mind, and the failure of the police to advise the accused of his rights, were certainly factors to be evaluated in assessing the "voluntariness" of an accused's responses, they were not in and of themselves determinative.

Similar considerations lead us to agree with the courts of California that the question whether a consent to a search was in fact "voluntary" or was the product of duress or coercion . . . is a question of fact to be determined from the totality of all the circumstances. While knowledge of the right to refuse consent is one factor to be taken into account, the government need not establish such knowledge as [indispensable to] an effective consent. As with police questioning, two competing concerns must be accommodated in determining the meaning of a voluntary consent—the legitimate need for such searches and the equally important requirement of assuring the absence of coercion.

In situations where the police have some evidence of illicit activity, but lack probable cause to arrest or search, a search authorized by a valid consent may be the only means of obtaining important and reliable evidence. In the present case for example, while the police had reason to stop the car for traffic violations, the State does not contend that there was probable cause to search the vehicle or that the search was incident to a valid arrest of any of the occupants. Yet, the search yielded tangible evidence that served as a basis for a prosecution, and provided some assurance that others, wholly innocent of the crime, were not mistakenly brought to trial. . . . In short, a search pursuant to consent may result in considerably less inconvenience for the subject of the search, and, properly conducted, is a constitutionally permissible and wholly legitimate aspect of effective police activity.

But the Fourth Amendment requires that a consent not be coerced. . . . In examining all the surrounding circumstances to determine if in fact the consent to search was coerced, account must be taken of subtly coercive police questions, as well as the possibly vulnerable subjective state of the person who consents. Those searches that are the product of police coercion can thus be filtered out without undermining the continuing validity of consent searches. . . .

The approach of the Court of Appeals for the Ninth Circuit . . . that the State must affirmatively prove that the subject of the search knew that he had a right to refuse consent, would, in practice, create serious doubt whether consent searches could continue to be conducted. There might be rare cases where it could be proved from the record that a person in fact affirmatively knew of his right to refuse—such as a case where he announced to the police that if he didn't sign the consent form, "you (police) are going to get a search warrant." . . . But more commonly where there was no evidence of any coercion . . . the prosecution would nevertheless be unable to demonstrate that the subject of the search in fact had known of his right to refuse consent. . . .

[Bustamonte also argues] that the Court's decision in the *Miranda* case [excerpted in Chapter 8] requires the conclusion that knowledge of a right to refuse is an indispensable element of a valid consent. . . . In *Miranda* the Court found that the techniques of police questioning and the nature of custodial surroundings produce an inherently coercive situation. . . . The Court noted that "without proper safeguards the process of in-custody interrogation of persons suspected or accused of crime contains inherently compelling pressures which work to undermine the individual's will to resist and to compel him to speak where he would not otherwise do so freely."

In this case, there is no evidence of any inherently coercive tactics—either from the nature of the police questioning or the environment in which it took place. Indeed, since consent searches will normally occur on a person's own familiar territory, the specter of incommunicado police interrogation in some remote station house is simply inapposite. There is no reason to believe, under circumstances such as are present here, that the response to a policeman's question is presumptively coerced; and there is, therefore, no reason to reject the traditional test for determining the voluntariness of a person's response. . . .

It is also argued that the failure to require the Government to establish knowledge as a prerequisite to a valid consent, will relegate the Fourth Amendment to the special province of "the sophisticated, the knowledgeable and the privileged." We cannot agree. The traditional definition of voluntariness we accept today has always taken into account evidence of minimal schooling, low intelligence, and the lack of any effective warnings to a person of his rights; and the voluntariness of any statement taken under those conditions has been carefully scrutinized to determine whether it was in fact voluntarily given. . . .

Our decision today is a narrow one. We hold only that when the subject of a search is not in custody and the State attempts to justify a search on the basis of his consent, the <u>Fourth Amendment requires that it demonstrate that the consent was in fact voluntarily given, and not the result of . . . coercion.</u> . . . Voluntariness is a question of fact to be determined from all the circumstances, and while the subject's knowledge of a right to refuse is a factor to be taken into account, the prosecution is not required to demonstrate such knowledge as a prerequisite to establishing a voluntary consent.

Judgment of Court of Appeals REVERSED.

## DISSENT

MARSHALL, J.

Several years ago, Mr. Justice Stewart reminded us that "the Constitution guarantees . . . a society of free choice. Such a society presupposes the capacity of its members to choose." I would have thought that the capacity to choose necessarily depends upon knowledge that there is a choice to be made. But today the Court reaches the curious result that one can choose to relinquish a constitutional right— the right to be free of unreasonable searches—without knowing that he has the alternative of refusing to accede to a police request to search. . . .

Consent . . . is a mechanism by which substantive requirements . . . are avoided. In the context of the Fourth Amendment, the relevant substantive requirements are that searches be conducted only after evidence justifying them has been submitted to an impartial magistrate for a determination of probable cause. . . .

. . . Consent searches are permitted, not because [of] . . . an exception to the requirements of probable cause and warrant is essential to proper law enforcement, but because we permit our citizens to choose whether or not they wish to exercise their constitutional rights. Our prior decisions do not support the view that a meaningful choice has been made solely because no coercion was brought to bear on the subject. . . .

I am at a loss to understand why consent cannot be taken literally to mean a "knowing choice." In fact, I have difficulty in comprehending how a decision made without knowledge of available alternatives can be treated as a choice at all. . . . I can think of no other situation in which we would say that a person agreed to some course of action if he convinced us that he did not know that there was some other course he might have pursued. . . .

The Court contends that if an officer paused to inform the subject of his rights, the informality of the exchange would be destroyed. I doubt that a simple statement by an officer of an individual's right to refuse consent would do much to alter the informality of the exchange, except to alert the subject to a fact that he surely is entitled to know.

It is not without significance that for many years the agents of the Federal Bureau of Investigation have routinely informed subjects of their right to refuse consent, when they request consent to search. The reported cases in which the police have informed subjects of their right to refuse consent show, also, that the information can be given without disrupting the casual flow of events.

What evidence there is, then, rather strongly suggests that nothing disastrous would happen if the police, before requesting consent, informed the subject that he had a right to refuse consent and that his refusal would be respected.

I must conclude with some reluctance that when the Court speaks of practicality, what it really is talking of is the continued ability of the police to capitalize on the ignorance of citizens so as to accomplish by subterfuge what they could not achieve by relying only on the knowing relinquishment of constitutional rights.

Of course it would be "practical" for the police to ignore the commands of the Fourth Amendment, if by practicality we mean that more criminals will be apprehended, even though the constitutional rights of innocent people also go by the board. But such a practical advantage is achieved only at the cost of permitting the police to disregard the limitations that the Constitution places on their behavior, a cost that a constitutional democracy cannot long absorb.

I find nothing in the opinion of the Court to dispel my belief that . . . under many circumstances a reasonable person might read an officer's "May I" as the courteous expression of a demand backed by force of law. [In] most cases, in my view . . . consent is ordinarily given as acquiescence in an implicit claim of authority to search. Permitting searches in such circumstances, without any assurance at all that the subject of the search knew that, by his consent, he was relinquishing his constitutional rights, is something that I cannot believe is sanctioned by the Constitution.

The proper resolution of this case turns, I believe, on a realistic assessment of the nature of the interchange between citizens and the police. . . . Although the Court says . . . it "cannot agree," the holding today confines the protection of the Fourth Amendment against searches conducted without probable cause to the sophisticated, the knowledgeable, and, I might add, the few.

The Court's half-hearted defense, that lack of knowledge is to be "taken into account," rings rather hollow, in light of the apparent import of the opinion that even a subject who proves his lack of knowledge may nonetheless have consented "voluntarily," under the Court's peculiar definition of voluntariness. In the final analysis, the Court now sanctions a game of blindman's buff, in which the police always have the upper hand, for the sake of nothing more than the convenience of the police.

But the guarantees of the Fourth Amendment were never intended to shrink before such an ephemeral and changeable interest. The Framers of the Fourth Amendment struck the balance against this sort of convenience and in favor of certain basic civil rights. It is not for this Court to restrike that balance because of its own views of the needs of law enforcement officers. I fear that that is the effect of the Court's decision today. . . .

## Questions

1. State the elements of the voluntariness test created by the U.S. Supreme Court.

2. List all the facts and circumstances relevant to deciding whether Clyde Bustamonte consented to the search of the car.

3. Describe the Court's application of the voluntariness test to consent in the case.

4. Explain why the Court says there's a fundamental difference between rights guaranteeing a fair trial and the rights against searches and seizures.

5. According to Justice Marshall, do individuals ever voluntarily consent to police requests, or are all police requests polite orders? Do you agree with Justice Marshall? Defend your answer.

6. State the elements of the waiver test favored by Justice Marshall.

7. Apply the majority's voluntariness test and the dissent's waiver test to the facts of the consent in the case.

8. Consider the consent form used by the St. Paul, Minnesota, Police Department in Figure 6.1. If Bustamonte had signed this form, would his consent have been voluntary? Would it matter if the officer just handed the form to him without explaining its importance? Explain your answer.

## Consent Searches

### 1. Was the Consent Given While Handcuffed, After Promises and Threats, Voluntary?

*U.S. v. Ceballos*, 812 F.2d 42 (2d Cir. 1987)

*FACTS*    Secret Service agents had information that Abraham Ceballos and Efrian Adames were counterfeiting U.S. currency. After a number of agents entered the P & J Printing Company where Ceballos worked, they handcuffed and escorted him out. Later, they advised him of his right to remain silent. Ceballos was taken to the field office and questioned. The agents warned him of the seriousness of a counterfeiting offense and threatened to get a search warrant unless he consented to a search of his apartment. They offered to help Ceballos obtain low bail and retain his job if he cooperated.

After a couple of hours, Ceballos consented to a search of his apartment. At the apartment, Ceballos located counterfeit plates and surrendered them to the agents. He was taken back to the field office, whereupon he and Adames were indicted on counterfeiting and conspiracy charges.

---

WAIVER AND CONSENT TO SEARCH

The undersigned _____

residing at _____

_____ hereby authorizes

the following named St. Paul Police Officers _____

to search the _____

_____

(insert description of place or auto, lic. number, etc.)

owned by/or in possession of the undersigned.
I do hereby waive any and all objections that may be made by me to said search and declare that this waiver and consent is freely and voluntarily given of my own free will and accord.

Signed _____ day of _____ 20___ at _____ PM    AM

     Signed _____

     Witnessed _____

**FIGURE 6.1**  St. Paul, Minnesota, Consent Search Form

Did Ceballos voluntarily consent to the search of his apartment?

*DECISION* Yes, according to the U.S. Second Circuit Court of Appeals:

> . . . Agents forcibly removed Ceballos from his place of work in handcuffs. There is also no question that the agents sought to persuade Ceballos to consent to a search and to confess. They warned him of the disruption to his household of execution of a court-ordered search warrant. They promised him aid in obtaining low bail and retaining his job if he cooperated. Nonetheless, the totality of the circumstances suggest that Ceballos' consent to search . . . was voluntarily given. The record indicates that the only use of force was in connection with the arrest. Thereafter the agents gave Ceballos a *Miranda* warning. They questioned him at their field office for a couple of hours before he consented to the search. . . . We find that the warnings made and promises offered by the agents did not overbear Ceballos' free will.

### 2. Was Consent Voluntary When Given After the Trooper Asked to Search the Stopped Car?

*Ohio v. Robinette*, 117 S.Ct. 417 (1996)

*FACTS* This case arose on a stretch of Interstate 70 north of Dayton, Ohio, where the posted speed limit was 45 miles per hour because of construction. Robert D. Robinette was clocked at 69 miles per hour as he drove his car along this stretch of road, and he was stopped by Deputy Roger Newsome of the Montgomery County Sheriff's office. Newsome asked for and was handed Robinette's driver's license, and he ran a computer check, which indicated that Robinette had no previous violations. Newsome then asked Robinette to step out of his car, turned on his mounted video camera, issued a verbal warning to Robinette, and returned his license.

At this point, Newsome asked, "One question before you get gone: Are you carrying any illegal contraband in your car? Any weapons of any kind, drugs, anything like that?" Robinette answered "no" to these questions, after which Deputy Newsome asked if he could search the car. Robinette consented. In the car, Deputy Newsome discovered a small amount of marijuana and, in a film container, a pill that was later determined to be Ecstasy (MDMA). Robinette was then arrested and charged with knowing possession of a controlled substance (Ohio Rev.Code Ann. § 2925.11(A) (1993)).

Did Robinette voluntarily consent to the search?

*DECISION* Yes, said the U.S. Supreme Court:

> We have long held that the "touchstone of the Fourth Amendment is reasonableness." Reasonableness, in turn, is measured in objective terms by examining the totality of the circumstances. In applying this test we have consistently eschewed bright-line rules, instead emphasizing the fact-specific nature of the reasonableness inquiry. . . . In *Schneckloth v. Bustamonte*, 412 U.S. 218 (1973), it was argued that such a consent could not be valid unless the defendant knew that he had a right to refuse the request. We rejected this argument: "While knowledge of the right to refuse consent is one factor to be taken into account, the government need not establish such knowledge as the sine qua non of an effective consent." And just as it "would be thoroughly impractical to impose on the normal consent search the detailed requirements of an effective warning," so too would it be unrealistic to require police officers to always inform detainees that they are free to go before a consent to search may be deemed voluntary.

 To read the full text of the Exploring Further excerpts, go to the Samaha Criminal Procedure 7e website: academic.cengage.com/criminaljustice/samaha.

*Empirical Research and Consent Searches* The U.S. Supreme Court expressed great confidence that lower courts would carefully scrutinize the "totality of circumstances" in each case to make sure consent searches were voluntary. In practice, available empirical evidence shows that the lower courts find consent was voluntary in all but the most extreme cases. One unpublished study conducted by Georgetown University Law Center student (cited in Cole 1999) examined all consent cases decided by the U.S. D.C. Court of Appeals from January 1989 to April 15, 1995. In every case, the court found the consent was voluntary. In most of the cases, the Court didn't even discuss the circumstances the Supreme Court said in *Schneckloth* were important in determining voluntariness. "When they did mention them, the courts turned a blind eye to factors strongly suggesting a less than voluntary encounter." In one case, the court found the consent given by a 24-year-old defendant with a 10th-grade education, who previously had refused to consent four times and was searched anyway, was voluntary. (Cole 1999, 32).

The majority of justices in *Schneckloth v. Bustamonte* (1973) also claimed that if suspects know they have a right to refuse consent, it "would, in practice, create serious doubt whether consent searches could continue to be conducted . . ." (229–30). Available empirical evidence suggests otherwise. Professor Illya Lichtenberg (2001) examined Ohio State Police data on all highway stops between 1995 and 1997. These years included the year before and after the Ohio Supreme Court ruled that Ohio officers had to warn drivers stopped for traffic violations that they had the right to refuse officers' requests to search (Exploring Further, p. 220). He found no decrease in consent rates after police were required to give the warning.

Lichtenberg interviewed a random sample of a group of drivers from the Ohio data. Of the 54 in the sample, 49 consented; 5 refused (251). Of the 49 who consented, 47 said they consented because they were afraid of what would happen to them if they refused. Here are a few answers:

#15373. I knew *legally* I didn't have to, but I kind of felt I had to. (264)

#3371. It would be very, very inconvenient to be locked up for the night. I didn't know if that was an option, and I didn't want to find out. (261)

#4337. At first I didn't think there was any reason to [consent] and then I realized that if I didn't they would do it anyway. (261)

#16633. To this day I do not know what would have happened if I had said, "No, absolutely not." (263)

Finally, the Supreme Court interprets a consent search as an act of good citizenship; it reinforces the rule of law and should, in the words of Justice Kennedy for the majority in *U.S. v. Drayton* (2002), be "given a weight and dignity of its own" (207). Most of Lichtenberg's sample drivers gave more mixed interpretations. Three were definitely positive:

#01568. I wish they would do it more. (283)

#14735. I'm just glad I had nothing to hide. (284)

#07267. I guess they were just doing their job. (284)

The rest were strongly negative:

#14735. It was embarrassing. It pissed me off. . . . They just treat you like you're nothing. . . . I think about it every time I see a cop. (283)

#15494. I feel really violated. I felt like my rights had been infringed upon. I feel really bitter about the whole thing. (285)

#12731. I don't trust the police anymore. I've lost all trust in them. (288)

Professor Janice Nadler (2002) summed up Lichtenberg's findings in her survey of empirical studies of Fourth Amendment consent searches this way:

> Consent search encounters with police often have a substantial impact on people—they do not forget about the experience quickly, and most people, in this sample at least, had lasting negatives toward the incident (and sometimes toward the police) as a result. Finally, unlike people who are discovered carrying unlawful contraband, innocent citizens who are subjected to coercive consent searches have no practical recourse—it is difficult to prove a constitutional violation even when their privacy interests protected by the Fourth Amendment were violated, and in any event the amount of money damages recovered is likely to be quite small. (212–13; see Chapter 11)

*The Scope of Consent* How far can officers go in searching after they get permission to search? Only as far as the person who gave it consented to. But how far is that? As far as the person who gave it intended the search to be, or as far as the officer believes the consent goes? According to the U.S. Supreme Court, the consent is as broad as the officers reasonably believe it to be. In *Florida v. Jimeno* (1991), officers asked for permission to search Jimeno's "car." He agreed. The police searched not only the car itself but also a brown paper bag found in the trunk of the car. (The officer found drugs in the paper bag.)

The U.S. Supreme Court upheld the reasonableness of the search. According to the Court, "The Fourth Amendment is satisfied when, under the circumstances, it is objectively reasonable for the officer to believe that the scope of the suspect's consent permitted him to open a particular container within the automobile" (248–49).

The scope of consent searches is a major issue in so-called crotch searches, a tactic used in drug law enforcement. Specially trained officers who patrol bus stations, airports, and railway stations approach people with no reasonable suspicion. They get into some light conversation and then ask, "Do you mind if I search you?" If the people agree, the officers immediately pat down their crotch area. The U.S. Supreme Court hasn't decided whether consent to search "you" includes searching the genital area, especially if the search occurs in the public areas of busy airports, bus stations, and railway stations. The U.S. Circuit Courts are divided. Some say consent to search "you" includes the groin area. Others say officers have to ask specifically, "Can I search your genital area?" In the next excerpt, *U.S. v. Rodney* (1992), the D.C. Circuit Court decided that Dylan Rodney's consent to search his person included his groin area.

C A S E  ***Did Dylan Rodney Consent to a Search of His Crotch?***

### U.S. v. Rodney
956 F.2d 295 (CADC 1992)

### HISTORY

Dylan Rodney pleaded guilty to possession with intent to distribute crack cocaine. After the court denied his motion to suppress, Rodney appealed. The court of appeals affirmed.

THOMAS, J.

### FACTS

. . . On February 17, 1990, Dylan Rodney stepped off a bus that had arrived in Washington, D.C., from New York City. As Rodney left the bus station, Detective Vance Beard, dressed in plainclothes and carrying a concealed weapon, approached him from behind. A second officer waited nearby. Beard displayed identification and asked if Rodney would talk to him. Rodney agreed. Beard asked Rodney whether he lived in either Washington or New York. Rodney replied that he lived in Florida, but had come to Washington to try to find his wife. She lived on

Georgia Avenue, Rodney said, although he was unable to identify any more precise location. Beard asked Rodney whether he was carrying drugs in his travel bag. After Rodney said no, Beard obtained permission to search the bag. As he did so, the other officer advanced to within about five feet of Rodney. The search failed to turn up any contraband.

Beard then asked Rodney whether he was carrying drugs on his person. After Rodney again said no, Beard requested permission to conduct a body search. Rodney said "Sure" and raised his arms above his head. Beard placed his hands on Rodney's ankles and, in one sweeping motion, ran them up the inside of Rodney's legs. As he passed over the crotch area, Beard felt small, rock-like objects.

Rodney exclaimed: "That's me!" Detecting otherwise, Beard placed Rodney under arrest. At the police station, Beard unzipped Rodney's pants and retrieved a plastic bag containing a rock-like substance that was identified as cocaine base. Rodney was charged with possession and intent to distribute.

Rodney moved to suppress the crack. Rodney argued . . . that . . . the consent did not include a search of his crotch area. . . . The DC District Court . . . denied the motion, finding that Rodney had "given his consent voluntarily to the search of his person and belongings." Rodney entered a conditional guilty plea, reserving the right to withdraw it if this court [DC Circuit] reversed the denial of his suppression motion.

## OPINION

Rodney first contends that the District Court erred in finding that his consent to the body search was voluntary, and therefore not prohibited by the Fourth Amendment. In determining the voluntariness of a consent, a district court must examine "the totality of all the surrounding circumstances—both the characteristics of the accused and the details of the interrogation." *Schneckloth v. Bustamonte* (1973) [excerpted earlier on p. 216].

Relevant factors include: the youth of the accused; his lack of education; or his low intelligence; the lack of any advice to the accused of his constitutional rights; the length of detention; the repeated and prolonged nature of the questioning; and the use of physical punishment such as the deprivation of food or sleep. We review only for clear error. . . .

Rodney . . . argues that . . . he did not consent to the search of his crotch area. A consensual search cannot exceed the scope of the consent. The scope of the consent is measured by a test of "'objective' reasonableness": it depends on how broadly a reasonable observer would have interpreted the consent under the circumstances. *Florida v. Jimeno* (1991) [discussed earlier on p. 222]. Here, Rodney clearly consented to a search of his body for drugs. We conclude that a reasonable person would have understood that consent to encompass the search undertaken here.

Under *Jimeno*, "the scope of a search is generally defined by its expressed object." In this case, Rodney authorized a search for drugs. Dealers frequently hide drugs near their genitals. Indeed, Beard testified that his colleagues make up to 75 percent of their drug recoveries from around the crotch area. For these reasons, we conclude that a request to conduct a body search for drugs reasonably includes a request to conduct some search of that area.

Although *Jimeno* states the test "generally" used to determine the scope of a consent to search, we doubt that the Supreme Court would have us apply that test unflinchingly in the context of body searches. At some point, we suspect, a body search would become so intrusive that we would not infer consent to it from a generalized consent, regardless of the stated object of the search. For example, although drugs can be hidden virtually anywhere on or in one's person, a generalized consent to a body search for drugs surely does not validate everything up to and including a search of body cavities.

The search undertaken here, however, was not unusually intrusive, at least relative to body searches generally. It involved a continuous sweeping motion over Rodney's outer garments, including the trousers covering the crotch area. In this respect, the search was no more invasive than the typical pat-down frisk for weapons described by the Supreme Court over two decades ago: The officer must feel with sensitive fingers every portion of the [defendant's] body. A thorough search must be made of the defendant's arms and armpits, waistline and back, the groin and area about the testicles, and entire surface of the legs down to the feet. *Terry v. Ohio* (1968) [excerpted in Chapter 4].

We conclude that the frisk of Rodney's fully clothed body involved nothing so intrusive, relative to body searches generally, as to require a separate consent above and beyond the consent to a body search that Rodney had given voluntarily. . . . We hold only that Rodney's generalized consent authorized the kind of "traditional frisk search" undertaken here, and we express no view on questions involving . . . consensual searches of a more intrusive nature. . . . We conclude that Rodney voluntarily consented to a search of his body for drugs, which encompassed the frisk undertaken here. . . .

Accordingly, the judgment of conviction is AFFIRMED.

## DISSENT

WALD, J.

I disagree with the panel ruling that a citizen's consent to a search of his "person" on a public thoroughfare, given in response to a police request made in the absence of probable cause or even "reasonable suspicion" to believe that he has committed a crime, encompasses authority to conduct a palpation of the person's genital area in an effort to detect drugs. Because I believe that in this case such an intimate and intrusive search exceeded the scope of any general permission to search granted, I would find the search nonconsensual and the drugs seized inadmissible. . . .

. . . The issue before us is whether a person against whom there is no articulable suspicion of wrongdoing who is asked to submit to a body search on a public street expects that search to include manual touching of the genital area. I do not believe any such expectation exists at the time a cooperative citizen consents to an on-the-street search. Rather, that citizen anticipates only those kinds of searches that unfortunately have become a part of our urban living, searches ranging from airport security personnel passing a hand-held magnometer over a person's body, to having a person empty his pockets, and subject himself to a patting-down of sides, shoulders, and back. Any search that includes touching genital areas or breasts would not normally be expected to occur in public.

In all aspects of our society, different parts of the body are subject to very different levels of privacy and expectations about intrusions. We readily bare our heads, arms, legs, backs, even midriffs, in public, but, except in the most unusual circumstances, certainly not our breasts or genitals. On the streets, in elevators, and on public transportation, we often touch, inadvertently or even casually, each others' hands, arms, shoulders, and backs, but it is a serious affront, and sometimes even a crime, to intentionally touch another's intimate body parts without explicit permission; and while we feel free to discuss other people's hair, facial features, weight, height, noses or ears, similar discussions about genitals or breasts are not acceptable.

Thus in any consensual encounter, it is not "objectively reasonable" for a citizen desiring to cooperate with the police in a public place to expect that permission to search her body includes feeling, even "fully clothed," the most private areas of her body. Under our social norms that requires "special permission," given with notice of the areas to be searched. . . . The mere fact that drug couriers often hide their stash in the crotch area [can't] justify the search of such area without some elementary form of notice to the citizen that such an offensive procedure is about to take place. The ordinary citizen's expectation of privacy in intimate parts of her body is certainly well enough established to merit a particularized request for consent to such an intimate search in public. . . .

A general consent to a search of a citizen's "person" in a public place does not include consent to touch the genital or breast areas. The majority today upholds a practice that allows police under the rubric of a general consent to conduct intimate body searches, and in so doing defeats the legitimate expectations of privacy that ordinary citizens should retain during cooperative exchanges with the police on the street. I believe the search was impermissible.

## Questions

1. State the specific rule the majority adopted to cover the scope of consent searches of a person.

2. State exactly what the officers asked Rodney to consent to.

3. Assume you're Rodney's lawyer. Relying on the facts as they're outlined in the case, argue that Rodney didn't consent to a search of his crotch.

4. Now assume you're the prosecutor, and argue that Rodney voluntarily consented to the search of his crotch.

5. Now assume you are the judge. Rule on the consent and its scope.

*Withdrawing Consent*  The U.S. Supreme Court hasn't decided if someone who has voluntarily consented to a search may later withdraw the consent. Lower federal courts and state courts have ruled unanimously that people can withdraw their consent but with a major qualification: "any such withdrawal must be supported by unambiguous acts or unequivocal statements" (*U.S. v. Sanders* 2005, 774).

The court applied this **unequivocal acts or statements withdrawal of consent rule** in *U.S. v. Miner* (1973). The facts were:

> On April 28, 1972, at Los Angeles International Airport, Gary Miner approached the counter to check in for a United Air Lines flight from Los Angeles to Portland, Oregon. He was in a hurry, seemed nervous, and was determined by one of the ticket agents on duty to fit the Federal Aviation Administration's "profile" of possible airline highjackers. Two airline employees thereupon escorted Miner to a different area of the airport and asked him to walk through a magnetometer, a gadget designed to detect the presence of metal on boarding passengers. Miner complied, but the machine did not register. A third airline employee joined the group. Miner was then asked to open a small suitcase which he was carrying, but refused saying, "No, it's personal." (1077)

According to the court, "No, it's personal" signaled withdrawal of his consent:

> At that point, the airline employees would have been justified in refusing to permit him to fly, but they could not compel him to submit to further search. Asking Miner to open his suitcase could be justified only if he continued to manifest an intention to board the plane, or if he otherwise consented to the search. (1077)

In our withdrawing consent excerpt, *U.S. v. Gray* (2004), the Court reached the opposite conclusion.

## U.S. v. Gray

369 F.3d 1024 (CA8 Ark., 2004)

### HISTORY

Following a jury trial, Darnell Gray, defendant/appellant was convicted in the United States District Court for the Eastern District of Arkansas, James M. Moody, J., of aiding and abetting possession of more than five kilograms of cocaine with the intent to distribute the substance, and defendant appealed. The U.S. Eighth Circuit Court of Appeals affirmed.

WOLLMAN, J.

### FACTS

. . . Arkansas State Trooper Kyle Drown . . . stopped the 1975 Chevrolet Camaro occupied by Darnell Gray and driven by Denise Lawrence, and "issued a warning citation after observing the Camaro follow a truck too closely and weave in its lane." After Drown issued the warning citation, he secured permission from both occupants to search the vehicle. He didn't find any contraband so he turned to Rudy, his drug detection dog, who alerted to narcotics. A further search revealed 17.5 pounds of cocaine hidden in the Camaro's firewall.

After obtaining consent at approximately 11:09 A.M., Drown searched the vehicle and its contents for some 20 minutes without incident. Shortly after 11:30 A.M., Gray and Lawrence began expressing concern about the length of the search. Gray testified that he stated "this is ridiculous" and asked how long the search was going to take. He admitted, however, that he did not ask to leave during this initial conversation, and it is undisputed that Drown continued looking through the vehicle.

A few minutes later, at approximately 11:33 A.M., Drown received a phone call, following which Gray and Drown had a second conversation, the content of which they recall differently. Drown testified that Gray merely asked that the search be speeded up and did not withdraw consent, whereas Gray testified that he attempted to withdraw consent by again indicating that the length of the search was "ridiculous" and twice saying that he and Lawrence were "ready to go now."

Depending on whose testimony is credited, Drown responded to this second conversation by either asking or telling Gray about using the canine. The district court found that Trooper Drown responded by saying: "Well, I'm going to use the dog and then you can leave or not depending on what the dog does." In any event, Drown moved the luggage that was outside the vehicle away from the vehicle's exterior and then conducted the canine search.

### OPINION

Withdrawal of consent need not be effectuated through particular "magic words," but an intent to withdraw consent must be made by unequivocal act or statement. The district court found that Gray and Lawrence made protests to leave, but concluded that there was no specific request to leave, and under the circumstances, . . . Trooper Drown was reasonable in continuing the search beyond the initial contact at 11:30. The district court further found that when the defendants became more strident about their desire to leave, Trooper Drown decided to use Rudy, and only about nine or ten minutes elapsed between the time Gray first began objecting and the time Rudy alerted.

The district court's finding that Gray did not make a specific request to leave is not clearly erroneous. At most, Gray's first conversation with Drown amounted to an expression of impatience, which is not sufficient to terminate consent. Furthermore, even if we assume that Gray's later statements were enough to withdraw consent (which the district court did not find), the district court did not clearly err in finding that Trooper Drown responded by using Rudy. . . .

The judgment is AFFIRMED.

### Questions

1. List all the facts relevant to deciding whether Darnell Gray withdrew his consent to the search.

2. Do you agree that he didn't make clear that he withdrew his consent?

3. Is the unequivocal rule the correct one? Should the burden be on the citizen to indicate withdrawal clearly? Or should the burden be on the government to make sure officers still have consent after the citizen speaks equivocal words and/or commits equivocal actions? Explain your answer.

**TABLE 6.1**    Examples of Valid Third-Party Consent Searches

- One lover consents to a search of the room shared with the other lover.
- One roommate consents to a search of an entire apartment, including the other roommate's separate bedroom.
- A homeowner consents to a search of the room that a houseguest occupies.
- One joint user of a duffel bag consents to a search of the shared duffel bag.
- A high-school principal consents to a search of high-school students' lockers.
- A college dean permits a search of students' rooms for marijuana.

*Third-Party Consent Searches* Can you consent to a search of your roommate's bedroom? It depends. Sometimes, one person can consent to a search in place of another person; this is called a **third-party consent search**. Authority to search for others usually comes up in common relationships: spouse-spouse, parent-child, roommate-roommate, employer-employee, landlord-tenant, and school administrator–student.

But these relationships don't automatically give one person the authority to consent for the other person. For example, consent to search given out of spite can invalidate the consent. Also, employers can't consent to searches of their employees' desks where employees have a reasonable expectation of privacy. So a principal couldn't consent to searching a guidance counselor's desk that was locked; was located in the counselor's office; and contained psychological profiles and other confidential student records. On the other hand, a factory manager can consent to searching items on top of an employee's workbench. Janitors, clerks, and drivers can't consent to searches of their employers' premises, but managers can. (Table 6.1 lists examples of valid third-party consent searches.)

There is both an objective and a subjective rule to decide whether one person can consent to a search for someone else.

1. *Actual authority (subjective) third-party consent.* Only someone who in fact has the legal authority to consent for someone else can give law enforcement officers permission to search that other person's house or stuff.

2. *Apparent authority (objective) third-party consent.* Consent given by someone who law enforcement officers reasonably believe (but who in fact doesn't) have the authority to consent for another makes the search reasonable.

Federal and state courts were divided over which of these two tests to adopt. In *Illinois v. Rodriguez* (1990), our next excerpt, the U.S. Supreme Court settled the question in the federal system by adopting the apparent-authority objective test as the minimum required by the Fourth Amendment.

C A S E    *Was the Search a Valid Consent Search?*

### Illinois v. Rodriguez
497 U.S. 177 (1990)

### HISTORY

Edward Rodriguez, who was charged with possession of a controlled substance with intent to deliver, moved to suppress seized evidence. The Circuit Court, Cook County, Illinois, granted the motion, and the People appealed. The Appellate Court affirmed. The People petitioned for leave to appeal. The Supreme Court denied the petition without published opinion. The People petitioned for a writ of certiorari. The Supreme Court granted the writ and reversed and remanded.

SCALIA, J., JOINED BY REHNQUIST, C.J., AND WHITE, BLACKMUN, O'CONNOR, AND KENNEDY, JJ.

## FACTS

On July 26, 1985, police were summoned to the residence of Dorothy Jackson on South Wolcott in Chicago. They were met by Ms. Jackson's daughter, Gail Fischer, who showed signs of a severe beating. She told the officers that she had been assaulted by Edward Rodriguez earlier that day in an apartment on South California. Fischer stated that Rodriguez was then asleep in the apartment, and she consented to travel there with the police in order to unlock the door with her key so that the officers could enter and arrest him. During this conversation, Fischer several times referred to the apartment on South California as "our" apartment, and said that she had clothes and furniture there. It is unclear whether she indicated that she currently lived at the apartment, or only that she used to live there.

The police officers drove to the apartment on South California, accompanied by Fischer. They did not obtain an arrest warrant for Rodriguez, nor did they seek a search warrant for the apartment. At the apartment, Fischer unlocked the door with her key and gave the officers permission to enter. They moved through the door into the living room, where they observed in plain view drug paraphernalia and containers filled with white powder that they believed (correctly, as later analysis showed) to be cocaine. They proceeded to the bedroom, where they found Rodriguez asleep and discovered additional containers of white powder in two open attaché cases. The officers arrested Rodriguez and seized the drugs and related paraphernalia.

Rodriguez was charged with possession of a controlled substance with intent to deliver. He moved to suppress all evidence seized at the time of his arrest, claiming that Fischer had vacated the apartment several weeks earlier and had no authority to consent to the entry. The Cook County Circuit Court granted the motion, holding that at the time she consented to the entry Fischer did not have common authority over the apartment.

The Court concluded that Fischer was not a "usual resident" but rather an "infrequent visitor" at the apartment on South California, based upon its findings that Fischer's name was not on the lease, that she did not contribute to the rent, that she was not allowed to invite others to the apartment on her own, that she did not have access to the apartment when Rodriguez was away, and that she had moved some of her possessions from the apartment.

The Circuit Court also rejected the State's contention that, even if Fischer did not possess common authority over the premises, there was no Fourth Amendment violation if the police reasonably believed at the time of their entry that Fischer possessed the authority to consent. The Appellate Court of Illinois affirmed the Circuit Court in all respects. The Illinois Supreme Court denied the State's petition for leave to appeal, and we granted certiorari.

## OPINION

The Fourth Amendment prohibits the warrantless entry of a person's home, whether to make an arrest or to search for specific objects. The prohibition does not apply, however, to situations in which voluntary consent has been obtained, either from the individual whose property is searched, *Schneckloth v. Bustamonte* (1973) [excerpt on p. 216], or from a third party who possesses common authority over the premises, *U.S. v. Matlock* (1974). The State of Illinois contends that that exception applies in the present case.

As we stated in *Matlock*, "common authority" rests "on mutual use of the property by persons having joint access or control. . . ." The burden of establishing that common authority rests upon the State. On the basis of this record, it is clear that burden was not sustained. The evidence showed that although Fischer, with her two small children, had lived with Rodriguez beginning in December 1984, she had moved out on July 1, 1985, almost a month before the search at issue here, and had gone to live with her mother. She took her and her children's clothing with her, though leaving behind some furniture and household effects. During the period after July 1 she sometimes spent the night at Rodriguez's apartment, but never invited her friends there, and never went there herself when he was not home. Her name was not on the lease nor did she contribute to the rent. She had a key to the apartment, which she said at trial she had taken without Rodriguez's knowledge (though she testified at the preliminary hearing that Rodriguez had given her the key). On these facts the State has not established that, with respect to the South California apartment, Fischer had "joint access or control for most purposes." To the contrary, the Appellate Court's determination of no common authority over the apartment was obviously correct.

The State contends that, even if Fischer did not in fact have authority to give consent, it suffices to validate the entry that the law enforcement officers reasonably believed she did. . . . Rodriguez asserts that permitting a reasonable belief of common authority to validate an entry would cause a defendant's Fourth Amendment rights to be "vicariously waived." We disagree.

We have been unyielding in our insistence that a defendant's waiver of his trial rights cannot be given effect unless it is "knowing" and "intelligent." We would assuredly not permit, therefore, evidence seized in violation of the Fourth Amendment to be introduced [at trial] on the basis of a trial court's mere "reasonable belief"—derived from statements by unauthorized persons—that the defendant has waived his objection. But one must make a distinction between, on the one hand, trial rights that derive from the violation of constitutional guarantees and, on the other hand, the nature of those constitutional guarantees themselves.

What Rodriguez is assured by the trial right of the exclusionary rule . . . is that no evidence seized in violation of the Fourth Amendment will be introduced at his trial unless he consents. What he is assured by the Fourth Amendment itself, however, is not that no government search of his house will occur unless he consents; but that no such search will occur that is "unreasonable."

There are various elements that can make a search of a person's house "reasonable"—one of which is the consent of the person or his cotenant. The essence of Rodriguez's argument is that we should impose upon this element a requirement that we have not imposed upon other elements that regularly compel government officers to exercise judgment regarding the facts: namely, the requirement that their judgment be not only responsible but correct.

The fundamental objective that alone validates all unconsented government searches is the seizure of persons who have committed or are about to commit crimes, or of evidence related to crimes. But "reasonableness," with respect to this necessary element, does not demand that the government be factually correct in its assessment that that is what a search will produce. . . . What is demanded . . . is not that [officers] always be correct, but that they always be reasonable. As we put it in *Brinegar v. U.S.* (1949):

> Because many situations which confront officers in the course of executing their duties are more or less ambiguous, room must be allowed for some mistakes on their part. But the mistakes must be those of reasonable men, acting on facts leading sensibly to their conclusions of probability.

We see no reason to depart from this general rule with respect to facts bearing upon the authority to consent to a search. Whether the basis for such authority exists is the sort of recurring factual question to which law enforcement officials must be expected to apply their judgment; and all the Fourth Amendment requires is that they answer it reasonably. The Constitution is no more violated when officers enter without a warrant because they reasonably (though erroneously) believe that the person who has consented to their entry is a resident of the premises, than it is violated when they enter without a warrant because they reasonably (though erroneously) believe they are in pursuit of a violent felon who is about to escape. . . .

What we hold today does not suggest that law enforcement officers may always accept a person's invitation to enter premises. Even when the invitation is accompanied by an explicit assertion that the person lives there, the surrounding circumstances could conceivably be such that a reasonable person would doubt its truth and not act upon it without further inquiry. As with other factual determinations bearing upon search and seizure, determination of consent to enter must be judged against an objective standard: would the facts available to the officer at the moment . . . warrant a man of reasonable caution in the belief that the consenting party had authority over the premises? *Terry v. Ohio* (1968) [excerpted Chapter 4]. If not, then warrantless entry without further inquiry is unlawful unless authority actually exists. But if so, the search is valid.

In the present case, the Appellate Court found it unnecessary to determine whether the officers reasonably believed that Fischer had the authority to consent, because it ruled as a matter of law that a reasonable belief could not validate the entry. Since we find that ruling to be in error, we remand for consideration of that question.

The judgment of the Illinois Appellate Court is REVERSED, and the case is REMANDED for further proceedings not inconsistent with this opinion.

## DISSENT

MARSHALL, J., JOINED BY BRENNAN AND STEVENS, JJ.

Dorothy Jackson summoned police officers to her house to report that her daughter Gail Fischer had been beaten. Fischer told police that Ed Rodriguez, her boyfriend, was her assaulter. During an interview with Fischer, one of the officers asked if Rodriguez dealt in narcotics. Fischer did not respond. Fischer did agree, however, to the officers' request to let them into Rodriguez's apartment so that they could arrest him for battery. The police, without a warrant and despite the absence of an exigency, entered Rodriguez's home to arrest him. As a result of their entry, the police discovered narcotics that the State subsequently sought to introduce in a drug prosecution against Rodriguez.

The Court holds that the warrantless entry into Rodriguez's home was nonetheless valid if the officers reasonably believed that Fischer had authority to consent. The majority's defense of this position rests on a misconception of the basis for third-party consent searches. That such searches do not give rise to claims of constitutional violations rests not on the premise that they are "reasonable" under the Fourth Amendment, but on the premise that a person may voluntarily limit his expectation of privacy by allowing others to exercise authority over his possessions.

Thus, an individual's decision to permit another "joint access [to] or control [over the property] for most purposes," *U.S. v. Matlock* (1974), limits that individual's reasonable expectation of privacy and to that extent limits his Fourth Amendment protections. If an individual has not so limited his expectation of privacy, the police may not dispense with the safeguards established by the Fourth Amendment.

. . . We have recognized that the "physical entry of the home is the chief evil against which the wording of the Fourth Amendment is directed." We have further held that "a search or seizure carried out on a suspect's premises without a warrant is per se unreasonable, unless the police can show that it falls within one of a carefully defined set of exceptions." . . . The Court has often heard, and steadfastly rejected, the invitation to carve out further exceptions to the warrant requirement for searches of the home because of the burdens on police investigation and prosecution of crime.

Our rejection of such claims is not due to a lack of appreciation of the difficulty and importance of effective law enforcement, but rather to our firm commitment to "the view of those who wrote the Bill of Rights that the privacy of a person's home and property may not be totally sacrificed in the name of maximum simplicity in enforcement of the criminal law." The weighty constitutional interest in preventing unauthorized intrusions into the home overrides any law enforcement interest in relying on the reasonable but potentially mistaken belief that a third party has authority to consent to such a search or seizure. . . .

Against this law enforcement interest in expediting arrests is "the right of a man to retreat into his own home and there be free from unreasonable governmental intrusion." To be sure, in some cases in which police officers reasonably rely on a third party's consent, the consent will prove valid, no intrusion will result, and the police will have been spared the inconvenience of securing a warrant. But in other cases, such as this one, the authority claimed by the third party will be false. . . . The concerns of expediting police work and avoiding paperwork are never very convincing reasons and, in these circumstances, certainly are not enough to by-pass the constitutional requirement.

In this case, no suspect was fleeing or likely to take flight. The search was of permanent premises, not of a movable vehicle. No evidence or contraband was threatened with removal or destruction. . . . If the officers in this case were excused from the constitutional duty of presenting their evidence to a magistrate, it is difficult to think of a case in which it should be required.

Unlike searches conducted pursuant to the recognized exceptions to the warrant requirement, third-party consent searches are not based on an exigency and therefore serve no compelling social goal. Police officers, when faced with the choice of relying on consent by a third party or securing a warrant, should secure a warrant and must therefore accept the risk of error should they instead choose to rely on consent.

. . . A search conducted pursuant to an officer's reasonable but mistaken belief that a third party had authority to consent is thus on an entirely different constitutional footing from one based on the consent of a third party who in fact has such authority. Even if the officers reasonably believed that Fischer had authority to consent, she did not, and Rodriguez's expectation of privacy was therefore undiminished.

Rodriguez accordingly can challenge the warrantless intrusion into his home as a violation of the Fourth Amendment. This conclusion flows directly from *Stoner v. California* (1964). There, the Court required the suppression of evidence seized in reliance on a hotel clerk's consent to a warrantless search of a guest's room. The Court reasoned that the guest's right to be free of unwarranted intrusion "was a right . . . which only [he] could waive by word or deed, either directly or through an agent." Accordingly, the Court rejected resort to "unrealistic doctrines of 'apparent authority'" as a means of

upholding the search to which the guest had not consented. . . .

Our cases demonstrate that third-party consent searches are free from constitutional challenge only to the extent that they rest on consent by a party empowered to do so. The majority's conclusion to the contrary ignores the legitimate expectations of privacy on which individuals are entitled to rely. That a person who allows another joint access to his property thereby limits his expectation of privacy does not justify trampling the rights of a person who has not similarly relinquished any of his privacy expectation.

## Questions

1. List all the facts relevant to determining whether the search in this case was a lawful search.

2. How does the majority define third-party consent? How does the dissent define it?

3. Why did the Supreme Court hold that Fischer's consent made the search of Rodriguez's apartment a lawful search?

4. Do you agree that someone can consent for another even when the person giving consent doesn't have the authority to do so?

5. Do you agree that if you share your property with someone else you "assume the risk" that the other person may give the police permission to search the property?

6. What arguments does the dissent make to reject the validity of Fischer's consent to search Rodriguez's apartment?

7. How do the majority and the dissent balance differently Rodriguez's rights and law enforcement's needs for consent searches? How would you balance the interests in the case?

 Go to Exercise 6.5 on the Samaha Criminal Procedure 7e website to learn more about *Illinois v. Rodriguez* and State Constitutional Law on third-party consent: academic. cengage.com/criminaljustice/samaha.

## EXPLORING FURTHER

# *Third-Party Consent*

### Can He Overrule His Estranged Wife's Consent?

*Georgia v. Randolph*, 126 S.Ct. 1515 (2006)

SOUTER, J.

*FACTS* Scott Randolph and his wife, Janet, separated in late May 2001, when she left the marital residence in Americus, Georgia, and went to stay with her parents in Canada, taking their son and some belongings. In July, she returned to the Americus house with the child, though the record does not reveal whether her object was reconciliation or retrieval of remaining possessions.

On the morning of July 6, she complained to the police that after a domestic dispute her husband took their son away, and when officers reached the house she told them that her husband was a cocaine user whose habit had caused financial troubles. Shortly after the police arrived, Scott Randolph returned and explained that he had removed the child to a neighbor's house out of concern that his wife might take the boy out of the country again.

One of the officers, Sergeant Murray, went with Janet Randolph to reclaim the child, and when they returned she not only renewed her complaints about her husband's drug use, but also volunteered that there were "items of drug evidence" in the house. Sergeant Murray asked Scott Randolph for permission to search the house, which he unequivocally refused. The sergeant turned to Janet Randolph for consent to search, which she readily gave. She led the officer upstairs to a bedroom that she identified as Scott's, where the sergeant noticed a section of a drinking straw with a powdery residue he suspected was cocaine.

Could Janet Randolph overrule Scott Randolph's refusal to consent?

*DECISION*   No, said the majority of the U.S. Supreme Court:

> . . . We have . . . lived our whole national history with an understanding of the ancient adage that a man's home is his castle [to the point that t]he poorest man may in his cottage bid defiance to all the forces of the Crown.
>
> Disputed permission is thus no match for this central value of the Fourth Amendment, and the State's other countervailing claims do not add up to outweigh it. Yes, we recognize the consenting tenant's interest as a citizen in bringing criminal activity to light. And we understand a co-tenant's legitimate self-interest in siding with the police to deflect suspicion raised by sharing quarters with a criminal. . . .
>
> This case invites a straightforward application of the rule that a physically present inhabitant's express refusal of consent to a police search is dispositive as to him, regardless of the consent of a fellow occupant. Scott Randolph's refusal is clear, and nothing in the record justifies the search on grounds independent of Janet Randolph's consent.
>
> The State does not argue that she gave any indication to the police of a need for protection inside the house that might have justified entry into the portion of the premises where the police found the powdery

straw (which, if lawfully seized, could have been used when attempting to establish probable cause for the warrant issued later). Nor does the State claim that the entry and search should be upheld under the rubric of exigent circumstances, owing to some apprehension by the police officers that Scott Randolph would destroy evidence of drug use before any warrant could be obtained.

The judgment of the Supreme Court of Georgia is therefore AFFIRMED.

The dissent concluded otherwise. Chief Justice Roberts, joined by Justice Scalia, wrote:

### ROBERTS, C.J., JOINED BY SCALIA, J.

. . . The rule the majority fashions does not implement the high office of the Fourth Amendment to protect privacy, but instead provides protection on a random and happenstance basis, protecting, for example, a co-occupant who happens to be at the front door when the other occupant consents to a search, but not one napping or watching television in the next room. And the cost of affording such random protection is great, as demonstrated by the recurring cases in which abused spouses seek to authorize police entry into a home they share with a nonconsenting abuser.

The correct approach . . . is clearly mapped out in our precedents: The Fourth Amendment protects privacy. If an individual shares information, papers, *or places* with another, he assumes the risk that the other person will in turn share access to that information or those papers *or places* with the government. . . . Just because the individual happens to be present at the time, so too someone who shares a place with another cannot interpose an objection when that person decides to grant access to the police, simply because the objecting individual happens to be present.

A warrantless search is reasonable if police obtain the voluntary consent of a person authorized to give it. Co-occupants have assumed the risk that one of their number might permit a common area to be searched. Just as Mrs. Randolph could walk upstairs, come down, and turn her husband's cocaine straw over to the police, she can consent to police entry and search of what is, after all, her home, too.

### THOMAS, J.

The Court has long recognized that it is an act of responsible citizenship for individuals to give whatever information they may have to aid in law enforcement. . . . No Fourth Amendment search occurs where, as here, the spouse of an accused voluntarily leads the police to potential evidence of wrongdoing by the accused. . . .

 To read the full text of the Exploring Further excerpt, go to the Samaha Criminal Procedure 7e website: academic.cengage.com/criminaljustice/samaha.

# Vehicle Searches

Searching vehicles without warrants began with a 1789 act of Congress. This was the same Congress that had adopted the Fourth Amendment, so the hated British general warrants were fresh in their minds. Despite these bitter memories, the 1789 statute authorized law enforcement officers without a warrant "to enter any ship or vessel, in which they shall have reason to suspect any goods, wares or merchandise subject to duty shall be concealed; and therein to search for, seize, and secure any such goods, wares or merchandise."

Ships were one thing; homes were quite another. Officers who suspected people were hiding taxable stuff in their houses had to get a warrant based on probable cause before they searched. Why the difference between boats and houses? Necessity: "Goods in course of transportation and concealed in a movable vessel . . . readily could be put out of reach of a search warrant." Later, the U.S. Supreme Court added another reason for the vehicle exception—the reduced expectation of privacy in vehicles:

> Throughout the 19th and 20th centuries, Congress continued to enact search and seizure statutes with a vehicle exception. In 1815, Congress authorized officers "not only to board and search vessels within their own and adjoining districts, but also to stop, search, and examine any vehicle, beast, or person on which or whom they should suspect there was merchandise which was subject to duty." In the Indian Appropriation Act of 1917, Congress authorized officers without warrants to seize and forfeit "automobiles used in introducing or attempting to introduce intoxicants into the Indian territory." (*Carroll v. U.S.* 1925, 152–53)

Not a single U.S. Supreme Court case ever challenged this exception until 1925 during Prohibition when the modern history of the vehicle exception began. You've seen the impact of technology on the Fourth Amendment in several cases in Chapter 3 (eavesdropping microphones in *Katz v. U.S.*, radio transmitters in *U.S. v. White* and thermal imaging in *Kyllo v. U.S.*). Their impact, however, can't compare with the single greatest technological advance of the 20th century that affected the Fourth Amendment—the car, and now SUVS and trucks.

As car ownership spread throughout all classes in society, its use as a crime tool advanced and so did Fourth Amendment law. Prohibition, the fear of alcohol-related crimes, and the ubiquity of the car were behind the landmark case that created the vehicle exception, *Carroll v. U.S.* (1925), in the 1920s. (The fear of illegal drugs still drives the interpretation of the Fourth Amendment, as so many cases in Chapters 3 through 6 clearly demonstrate.)

In *Carroll*, federal Prohibition agents Cronenwett, Scully, and Thayer and Michigan state trooper Peterson had probable cause to believe bootleggers George Carroll and John Kiro were illegally carrying liquor from Detroit to Grand Rapids in their Oldsmobile convertible. While on regular duty patrolling the road looking for Prohibition law violations, they stopped the car and searched it without a warrant. They found 68 bottles of blended Scotch whiskey and Gordon gin stuffed in hollowed-out upholstery, which they had to rip open to find. The U.S. Supreme Court upheld the search without a warrant based on the rationale that it was "not practicable to secure a warrant, because the vehicle can be quickly moved out of the locality or jurisdiction in which the warrant must be sought" (153). Chief Justice William Howard Taft, writing for the majority continued:

> Having thus established that contraband goods concealed and illegally transported in an automobile or other vehicle may be searched for without a warrant, we come now to consider under what circumstances such search may be made. It would be intolerable and

unreasonable if a prohibition agent were authorized to stop every automobile on the chance of finding liquor, and thus subject all persons lawfully using the highways to the inconvenience and indignity of such a search. . . . their vehicles are carrying contraband or illegal merchandise. (153–54)

The Court created the vehicle exception according to this rule:

On reason and authority the true rule is that if the search and seizure without a warrant are made upon probable cause, that is, upon a belief, reasonably arising out of circumstances known to the seizing officer, that an automobile or other vehicle contains that which by law is subject to seizure and destruction, the search and seizure are valid. The Fourth Amendment is to be construed in the light of what was deemed an unreasonable search and seizure when it was adopted, and in a manner which will conserve public interests as well as the interests and rights of individual citizens. (149)

The decision was immediately controversial. We were fighting a war on drugs; alcohol was the drug; cars were a new technological weapon used by the enemy and the government. As in our own drug wars, critics complained that we were sacrificing our rights to fight the war. The dissent joined the critics. Justice McReynolds, a staunch conservative wrote:

The damnable character of the "bootlegger's" business should not close our eyes to the mischief which will surely follow any attempt to destroy it by unwarranted methods. To press forward to a great principle by breaking through every other great principle that stands in the way of its establishment; in short, to procure an eminent good by means that are unlawful, is as little consonant to private morality as to public justice. (163)

Following *Carroll*, the Court began a slow, although not steady, expansion of what was soon called the **vehicle exception** to the warrant requirement. One expansion was to add to the mobility of vehicles the rationale that there's a reduced expectation of privacy in vehicles.

In a series of other decisions, the exception came to include all searches of vehicles without warrants, as long as they're based on probable cause to believe they contain contraband or evidence. The exception extended to all integral parts of the automobile, including the passenger compartment, the glove compartment, and the trunk. Then, the Court turned its attention to two other very important related searches: of containers inside the vehicle's integral parts and of occupants and their belongings. Let's look at each of these searches.

*Searches of Containers in Vehicles* Officers with probable cause but without warrants can search containers inside vehicles not integral to the vehicle. Until 1990, officers could only search containers in vehicles if they had separate probable cause to search both the vehicle and the container. If they had probable cause to search the container but not the vehicle, they had to get a warrant.

The Court established the rule governing searches of containers in vehicles in *California v. Acevedo* (1991). Police officers observed Charles Acevedo leave an apartment where officers knew there was marijuana. Acevedo was carrying a brown paper bag the size of marijuana packages the officers had seen earlier. Acevedo put the bag into the trunk of his car. As he drove away, the police stopped his car, opened the trunk, opened the bag, and found marijuana in it. The Court held it was reasonable to search the container without a warrant because they had probable cause to believe the bag contained marijuana.

The Court recognized Acevedo's expectation of privacy in the brown bag but concluded that the risks the car might drive off and the marijuana might disappear trumped Acevedo's expectation of privacy.

*Searches of Vehicle Passengers* Before *Acevedo*, car searches focused on containers, such as luggage, purses, and paper bags, and a debate over the Fourth Amendment allowed officers to open to see what was inside them. *Acevedo* seemed to settle the debate: As long as officers have probable cause to believe they contain contraband, they can search containers in the vehicle. But it didn't. Left unsettled was whether officers could search containers attached to people in the car, such as the wallet in the pocket of the jacket you're wearing, or in the purse hanging over your shoulder, or on the seat beside you.

Recall that one of the reasons for the vehicle exception to the warrant requirement is a reduced expectation of privacy in vehicles. Do passengers as well as drivers have a reduced expectation of privacy? And, if they do, can officers search a passenger's purse when they have no probable cause to suspect her of the crime they arrested the driver for? In our next excerpt, *Wyoming v. Houghton* (1999), a divided U.S. Supreme Court answered, yes.

## CASE    *Was Her Purse Part of the Vehicle Exception?*

### Wyoming v. Houghton
526 U.S. 295 (1999)

### HISTORY

Sandra Houghton was convicted in the District Court, Natrona County, Wyoming, of felony possession of methamphetamine, and she appealed. The Wyoming Supreme Court reversed and remanded. The U.S. Supreme Court granted certiorari and reversed.

SCALIA, J., JOINED BY REHNQUIST, C.J., AND O'CONNOR, KENNEDY, THOMAS, AND BREYER, JJ.

### FACTS

In the early morning hours of July 23, 1995, a Wyoming Highway Patrol officer (Officer Baldwin) stopped an automobile for speeding and driving with a faulty brake light. There were three passengers in the front seat of the car: David Young (the driver), his girlfriend, and Houghton.

While questioning Young, the officer noticed a hypodermic syringe in Young's shirt pocket. He left the occupants under the supervision of two backup officers as he went to get gloves from his patrol car. Upon his return, he instructed Young to step out of the car and place the syringe on the hood. The officer then asked Young why he had a syringe; with refreshing candor, Young replied that he used it to take drugs.

At this point, the backup officers ordered the two female passengers out of the car and asked them for identification. Houghton falsely identified herself as "Sandra James" and stated that she did not have any identification.

Meanwhile, in light of Young's admission, the officer searched the passenger compartment of the car for contraband. On the back seat, he found a purse, which Houghton claimed as hers. He removed from the purse a wallet containing Houghton's driver's license, identifying her properly as Sandra K. Houghton. When the officer asked her why she had lied about her name, she replied: "In case things went bad."

Continuing his search of the purse, the officer found a brown pouch and a black wallet-type container. Houghton denied that the former was hers, and claimed ignorance of how it came to be there; it was found to contain drug paraphernalia and a syringe with 60 cc's of methamphetamine.

Houghton admitted ownership of the black container, which was also found to contain drug paraphernalia, and a syringe (which Houghton acknowledged was hers) with 10 cc's of methamphetamine—an amount insufficient to support the felony conviction at issue in this case. The officer also found fresh needle-track marks on Houghton's arms. He placed her under arrest.

The State of Wyoming charged Houghton with felony possession of methamphetamine in a liquid amount greater than three-tenths of a gram. After a hearing, the trial court denied her motion to suppress all evidence obtained from the purse as the fruit of a violation of the Fourth and Fourteenth Amendments. The court held that the officer had probable cause to search the car for contraband, and, by extension, any containers therein that could hold such contraband. A jury convicted Houghton as charged.

The Wyoming Supreme Court, by divided vote, reversed the conviction and announced the following rule: Generally, once probable cause is established to search a vehicle, an officer is entitled to search all containers therein which may contain the object of the search.

However, if the officer knows or should know that a container is the personal effect of a passenger who is not suspected of criminal activity, then the container is outside the scope of the search unless someone had the opportunity to conceal the contraband within the personal effect to avoid detection.

The court held that the search of Houghton's purse violated the Fourth and Fourteenth Amendments because the officer "knew or should have known that the purse did not belong to the driver, but to one of the passengers," and because "there was no probable cause to search the passengers' personal effects and no reason to believe that contraband had been placed within the purse."

## OPINION

. . . It is uncontested in the present case that the police officers had probable cause to believe there were illegal drugs in the car. *Carroll v. U.S.* (1925) [discussed on p. 231] similarly involved the warrantless search of a car that law enforcement officials had probable cause to believe contained contraband—in that case, bootleg liquor. The Court concluded that the Framers would have regarded such a search as reasonable. . . . Thus, the Court held that "contraband goods concealed and illegally transported in an automobile or other vehicle may be searched for without a warrant" where probable cause exists.

We have furthermore read the historical evidence to show that the Framers would have regarded as reasonable (if there was probable cause) the warrantless search of containers within an automobile. In *U.S. v. Ross* (1982), we upheld as reasonable the warrantless search of a paper bag and leather pouch found in the trunk of Ross's car by officers who had probable cause to believe that the trunk contained drugs. . . .

*Ross* summarized its holding as follows: "If probable cause justifies the search of a lawfully stopped vehicle, it justifies the search of every part of the vehicle and its contents that may conceal the object of the search." And our later cases describing *Ross* have characterized it as applying broadly to all containers within a car, without qualification as to ownership.

To be sure, there was no passenger in *Ross*, and it was not claimed that the package in the trunk belonged to anyone other than the driver. Even so . . . , neither *Ross* itself nor the historical evidence it relied upon admits of a distinction among packages or containers based on ownership. When there is probable cause to search for contraband in a car, it is reasonable for police officers—like customs officials in the Founding era—to examine packages and containers without a showing of individualized probable cause for each one. A passenger's personal belongings, just like the driver's belongings or containers attached to the car like a glove compartment, are "in" the car, and the officer has probable cause to search for contraband in the car.

Even if the historical evidence . . . were thought to be equivocal, we would find that the balancing of the relative interests weighs decidedly in favor of allowing searches of a passenger's belongings. Passengers, no less than drivers, possess a reduced expectation of privacy with regard to the property that they transport in cars. . . .

Whereas the passenger's privacy expectations are . . . considerably diminished, the governmental interests at stake are substantial. Effective law enforcement would be appreciably impaired without the ability to search a passenger's personal belongings when there is reason to believe contraband or evidence of criminal wrongdoing is hidden in the car. As in all car-search cases, the "ready mobility" of an automobile creates a risk that the evidence or contraband will be permanently lost while a warrant is obtained.

In addition, a car passenger . . . will often be engaged in a common enterprise with the driver, and have the same interest in concealing the fruits or the evidence of their wrongdoing. . . .

To be sure, these factors favoring a search will not always be present, but the balancing of interests must be conducted with an eye to the generality of cases. To require that the investigating officer have positive reason to believe that the passenger and driver were engaged in a common enterprise, or positive reason to believe that the driver had time and occasion to conceal the item in the passenger's belongings, surreptitiously or with friendly permission, is to impose requirements so seldom met that a "passenger's property" rule would dramatically reduce the ability to find and seize contraband and evidence of crime.

Of course these requirements would not attach (under the Wyoming Supreme Court's rule) until the police officer knows or has reason to know that the container belongs to a passenger. But once a "passenger's property" exception to car searches became widely known, one would expect passenger-confederates to claim everything as their own. And one would anticipate a bog of litigation—in the form of both civil lawsuits and motions to suppress in criminal trials—involving such questions as whether the officer should have believed a passenger's claim of ownership, whether he should have inferred ownership from various objective factors, whether he had probable cause to believe that the passenger was a confederate, or to believe that the driver might have introduced the contraband into the package with or without the passenger's knowledge.

When balancing the competing interests, our determinations of "reasonableness" under the Fourth Amendment must take account of these practical realities. We think they militate in favor of the needs of law enforcement, and against a personal-privacy interest that is ordinarily weak. . . .

We hold that police officers with probable cause to search a car may inspect passengers' belongings found in the car that are capable of concealing the object of the search.

The judgment of the Wyoming Supreme Court is REVERSED.

## CONCURRING OPINION

### BREYER, J.

. . . I . . . point out certain limitations upon the scope of the bright-line rule that the Court describes. Obviously, the rule applies only to automobile searches. Equally obviously, the rule applies only to containers found within automobiles. And it does not extend to the search of a person found in that automobile. As the Court notes, and as *U.S. v. Di Re*, relied on heavily by Justice STEVENS' dissent, makes clear, the search of a person, including even "a limited search of the outer clothing," is a very different matter in respect to which the law provides "significantly heightened protection."

Less obviously, but in my view also important, is the fact that the container here at issue, a woman's purse, was found at a considerable distance from its owner, who did not claim ownership until the officer discovered her identification while looking through it. Purses are special containers. They are repositories of especially personal items that people generally like to keep with them at all times.

So I am tempted to say that a search of a purse involves an intrusion so similar to a search of one's person that the same rule should govern both. However, given this Court's prior cases, I cannot argue that the fact that the container was a purse automatically makes a legal difference, for the Court has warned against trying to make that kind of distinction.

But I can say that it would matter if a woman's purse, like a man's billfold, were attached to her person. It might then amount to a kind of "outer clothing." In this case, the purse was separate from the person, and no one has claimed that, under those circumstances, the type of container makes a difference. For that reason, I join the Court's opinion.

## DISSENT

### STEVENS, J., JOINED BY SOUTER AND GINSBURG, JJ.

. . . In all of our prior cases applying the automobile exception to the Fourth Amendment's warrant requirement, either the defendant was the operator of the vehicle and in custody of the object of the search, or no question was raised as to the defendant's ownership or custody. In the only automobile case confronting the search of a passenger defendant—*U.S. v. Di Re* (addressing searches of the passenger's pockets and the space between his shirt and underwear, both of which uncovered counterfeit fuel rations)—the Court held that the exception to the warrant requirement did not apply.

In *Di Re*, as here, the information prompting the search directly implicated the driver, not the passenger. Today, instead of adhering to the settled distinction between drivers and passengers, the Court fashions a new rule that is based on a distinction between property contained in clothing worn by a passenger and property contained in a passenger's briefcase or purse. In cases on both sides of the Court's newly minted test, the property is in a "container" (whether a pocket or a pouch) located in the vehicle.

Moreover, unlike the Court, I think it quite plain that the search of a passenger's purse or briefcase involves an intrusion on privacy that may be just as serious as was the intrusion in *Di Re*. . . . I [am not] persuaded that the mere spatial association between a passenger and a driver provides an acceptable basis for presuming that they are partners in crime or for ignoring privacy interests in a purse. Whether or not the Fourth Amendment required a warrant to search Houghton's purse, at the very least the trooper in this case had to have probable cause to believe that her purse contained contraband. The Wyoming Supreme Court concluded that he did not.

Finally, in my view, the State's legitimate interest in effective law enforcement does not outweigh the privacy concerns at issue. I am as confident in a police officer's ability to apply a rule requiring a warrant or individualized probable cause to search belongings that are—as in this case—obviously owned by and in the custody of a passenger as is the Court in a "passenger-confederate's" ability to circumvent the rule. Certainly the ostensible clarity of the Court's rule is attractive. But that virtue is insufficient justification for its adoption. Moreover, a rule requiring a warrant or individualized probable cause to search passenger belongings is every bit as simple as the Court's rule; it simply protects more privacy. . . .

Instead of applying ordinary Fourth Amendment principles to this case, the majority extends the automobile warrant exception to allow searches of passenger belongings based on the driver's misconduct. Thankfully, the Court's automobile-centered analysis limits the scope of its holding. But it does not justify the outcome in this case.

I respectfully dissent.

## Questions

1. State the rule the majority of the Court adopted for searching passengers' "containers."

2. Explain how the majority applied the rule to the search of Sandra Houghton's purse.

3. Summarize the dissent's arguments for concluding the purse search was unreasonable.

4. Summarize Justice Breyer's hesitation about supporting the majority decision.

5. Consider your summaries. Which opinion do you think is the most convincing? Defend your answer.

# Emergency Searches

Emergency searches (also called "exigent circumstance searches") are based on the idea that it's sometimes impractical (even dangerous) to require officers to obtain warrants before they search. The danger might be (1) to officers' safety, justifying frisks or pat downs for weapons (Chapter 4); (2) that suspects or others might destroy evidence during the time it takes to get a search warrant; (3) that fleeing felons might escape while officers are trying to obtain search warrants, or (4) that individuals in the community are in immediate danger. Because we've already examined frisks, in which officers' reasonable suspicion that a lawfully stopped suspect is armed justifies a pat down for weapons (Chapter 4), we won't repeat that discussion here. Let's look at the other three types of emergencies.

*Destruction of Evidence* If police officers have probable cause to search, and they reasonably believe evidence is about to be destroyed now, they can search without a warrant. For example, in *Cupp v. Murphy* (1973), the U.S. Supreme Court held that police officers who had probable cause to believe Daniel Murphy had strangled his wife didn't need a warrant to take scrapings of what looked like blood under his fingernails. Why? Because Murphy knew the officers suspected he was the strangler, so he had a motive to destroy the short-lived bloodstain evidence.

In *Schmerber v. California* (1966; Chapter 8), the Supreme Court held that rapidly declining blood alcohol levels justified giving a blood alcohol test to Schmerber without a warrant. And in *Ker v. California* (1963), the Court held that a warrantless entry into a home was justified by the reasonable fear that Ker was about to destroy or hide marijuana.

*Hot Pursuit* Hot pursuit is another emergency created by the need to apprehend a fleeing suspect. If officers are chasing a suspect whom they have probable cause to arrest, they can follow the suspect into a house without getting a warrant (*U.S. v. Santana* 1976). So officers wouldn't need a warrant to enter a home to search for a fleeing armed robbery suspect and weapons.

But how extensive can the search be? Only as extensive as is necessary to prevent the suspect from escaping or resisting. So officers can't search every nook and cranny of a house just because they got in lawfully during a hot pursuit (*Warden v. Hayden* 1967). For example, they can't search dresser drawers for contraband. Nor can they search every room of a hotel because a robber entered the hotel (*U.S. v. Winsor* 1988).

*Danger to the Community* Police officers can sidestep the warrant requirement if they have probable cause to believe either that a suspect has committed a violent crime or that they or others in the community are in immediate danger. So officers could enter and search a house in a residential area because they reasonably believed guns and bombs were in the house (*U.S. v. Lindsey* 1989). It was also reasonable to enter a house without a warrant to search for a weapon when police found a dead body on the front porch (*U.S. v. Doe* 1985).

Other dangers to the public include fires and explosions. Police officers at the scene of a fire don't need a warrant to stay inside a burned building long enough to look for possible injured victims and to investigate the cause of the fire or explosion. But once they determine the cause of the fire, officers have to get a warrant if they want to search for evidence of a crime (*Michigan v. Clifford* 1984). Furthermore, they can't enter just because a fire or explosion might be in the offing. For example, a court ruled that it wasn't reasonable for officers to enter a house where they knew a man had kept dangerous chemicals in his house for two weeks and wasn't at home (*U.S. v. Warner* 1988).

# SUMMARY

## I. Searches for Evidence

A. Crime control couldn't survive without searches, but the right against unreasonable searches and seizures is one of the most difficult to protect.

B. The Fourth Amendment balances the need for searches against the invasion of individuals' privacy resulting from searches.

C. The three-step analysis used to examine government action is the same applied to stops and frisks and arrests.

D. Searches for evidence of crime include:
   1. Searches with warrants
   2. Searches without warrants

## II. Searches with Warrants

A. The Fourth Amendment commands that officers get search warrants, but in reality there are far more searches without warrants than with warrants.

B. Three elements are required to meet the Fourth Amendment's warrant requirement:
   1. Particularity describes the place to be searched and the things to be seized.
   2. An affidavit supporting probable cause has to include evidence to support the claim that the items or classes of items named in the warrant will be found in the place to be searched.
   3. The "knock and announce" rule requires two elements:
      a. Officers have to knock and announce they are officers with a search warrant before they enter the place they're about to search.
      b. Officers have to wait a "reasonable amount of time" before breaking and entering.

## III. Searches without Warrants

A. The U.S. Supreme Court has repeatedly said the Fourth Amendment expresses a strong preference for search warrants with a few well-defined exceptions.

B. The broad interpretation of the well-defined exceptions satisfies the strong preference of law enforcement officers to search without warrants.

## IV. Searches Incident to Arrest

   1. They don't require warrants or probable cause.
   2. They serve three main functions:
      a. Protect officers
      b. Prevent escape
      c. Preserve evidence

B. The time frame of incident to arrest includes the time before, during, and after arrest.

C. Officers can only search the area under the immediate control of the arrested persons.
   1. This is called the "grabbable area."
   2. The rule extends to vehicles.

D. Under the *Robinson* rule, officers can always search anyone they're authorized to take into custody. Why?
  1. It lessens danger to police officers.
  2. It creates a bright-line rule, because it's impossible for the Court to review every police decision.
E. There's no automatic search incident to citation rule.
F. Pretext arrests are a powerful, but criticized, investigative tool in the war on drugs.

## V. Consent Searches
A. The easiest and most convenient way for officers to search a person, house, or effects is for someone to give up her constitutional right against unreasonable searches and seizures.
B. Consent searches are reasonable only if consent is voluntary.
C. Government has to prove voluntariness by a totality of circumstances, including:
  1. Did the suspect know his or her right to refuse consent?
  2. Has the suspect gained sufficient age and maturity to make an independent decision?
  3. Does the suspect have experience with the workings of the criminal justice system?
  4. Did the suspect cooperate with officers?
  5. What was the suspect's attitude toward the likelihood that officers would discover contraband during the search?
  6. How long was the suspect detained, and what was the nature of the questioning regarding consent?
  7. Was there coercive police behavior surrounding the consent?
D. The scope of the search is as far as the police officer conducting the search reasonably believes it to be (not how the person believes it to be).
E. Once a person gives consent, he or she can withdraw the consent at any time.
F. One person can consent to a search for another person, called a third-party consent search. Relationships—even spouse-spouse, parent-child, roommate-roommate—don't automatically give one person the authority to consent for the other person.
  1. There's both an objective and a subjective rule to decide whether one person can consent to a search for someone else:
     a. Actual authority third-party consent is the objective rule.
     b. Apparent authority third-party consent is the subjective rule.
  2. The U.S. Supreme Court adopted the apparent authority objective test as the minimum requirement.

## VI. Vehicle Searches
A. Searches of vehicles based on probable cause don't require warrants because:
  1. Vehicles are mobile and can leave the area.
  2. There's a reduced expectation of privacy in vehicles.
B. Persons and containers within a vehicle are subject to search.

## VII. Container Searches
A. Officers require probable cause to believe there's evidence of a crime inside the containers.

B. The reasonable expectation of privacy in containers is greater in cars but less than in homes.

## VIII. Emergency (Exigent) Searches

A. Emergency searches are based on the idea that it's sometimes impractical to require officers to obtain warrants before they search.

B. If police officers have probable cause to search, and they reasonably believe evidence is about to be destroyed, they can search without a warrant.

C. If officers are chasing a suspect whom they have probable cause to arrest, they can follow the suspect into a house without getting a warrant.

D. If officers have probable cause to believe either that a suspect has committed a violent crime or that they or others in the community are in immediate danger, they can search without obtaining a warrant.

# REVIEW QUESTIONS

1. Describe Supreme Court Justice Jackson's experience in dealing with search and seizure law. What does he mean by "second class rights"?

2. Identify the three steps in the analysis of whether government actions are searches.

3. Identify and describe each of the three elements required to meet the Fourth Amendment's warrant requirement.

4. According to the "knock and announce" rule, what's a reasonable amount of time to wait before breaking and entering?

5. Compare and contrast the preference and practice regarding searches with warrants and without.

6. Identify five major exceptions to the warrant requirement approved by the U.S. Supreme Court.

7. List three reasons why searches incident to arrest are reasonable.

8. Identify the scope and time frame of "incident" to arrest.

9. Describe the *Robinson* rule and the justification for it.

10. Describe why pretext arrests are a powerful investigative tool.

11. In a consent search, what's the person really consenting to?

12. Identify some characteristics the courts use to determine the voluntariness of consent.

13. Based on empirical research data, give some examples of why people consent to searches.

14. Describe the elements of scope of consent and the withdrawal of consent.

15. Give an example of a third-party consent search.

16. Identify the subjective and objective element in determining whether one person can consent to a search for someone else.

17. Identify the two reasons why vehicle searches are reasonable without warrants.

18. According to *Wyoming v. Houghton,* what's the rule regarding searches of containers in passenger vehicles?

19. Identify three emergency searches and tell why the Supreme Court finds them reasonable searches without warrants.

## KEY TERMS

# Special-Needs Searches

## MAIN POINTS

- The U.S. Supreme Court has applied the Fourth Amendment to a wide range of searches that meet "special needs" in addition to criminal law enforcement.
- Special-needs searches are directed at people generally; can result in criminal prosecution; and don't require warrants or probable cause.
- The reasonableness of special-needs searches depends on balancing special government needs against individual liberties.
- By following routine, department-approved procedures, officers can conduct inventory searches to protect the owners' stuff, to prevent lawsuits from loss or damage, and to protect law enforcement agents.
- The right of the sovereign to control who and what comes into its borders makes international border searches reasonable without warrants or probable cause.
- The special need to maintain security outweighs the minimal invasions of walking through metal detectors and allowing luggage to be observed by X-ray.
- The special needs to maintain safety, security, and discipline over people locked up in jails and prisons, probationers, and parolees outweigh the significantly reduced expectation of privacy that society grants to people in the custody of the criminal justice system.
- Historically, prisoners have had no Fourth Amendment rights; however, the U.S. Supreme Court has repeatedly said that prisoners aren't completely beyond the reach of the Constitution.
- Strip and body-cavity searches are reasonable searches in prisons if the need for security and safety outweighs the prisoners' expectation of privacy.
- With advanced technology, the collecting and storing of incarcerated felons' DNA is reasonable constitutionally.
- Probationers and parolees have diminished Fourth Amendment rights, even though they aren't locked up.
- Searches for employee drug use through drug testing are directed at the special need to reduce danger to public safety.
- Student searches are reasonable if the schools' legitimate need to maintain a healthy learning environment outweighs the students' expectation of privacy.
- Drug testing of students who participate in *any* school activity is a reasonable search.
- College students have greater expectations of privacy than high school students.

Mary Beth G. and Sharon N. were stopped for traffic violations; they were arrested and taken to detention centers because there were outstanding parking tickets against their cars. They were subjected to the strip search policy of the city of Chicago. That policy, as described by the city, required each woman placed in detention facilities of the Chicago Police Department to be searched by female personnel to:

1. Lift her blouse or sweater and unhook and lift her brassiere to allow a visual inspection of the breast area, to replace these articles of clothing

2. Pull up her skirt or dress or lower her pants and pull down any undergarments, to squat two or three times facing the detention aide, and to bend over at the waist to permit visual inspection of the vaginal and anal area.

The city claimed that all searches were conducted in a closed room away from the view of all persons except the person conducting the search. The strip search policy was not applied to males. Men were searched thoroughly by hand. The male detainee would place his hands against the wall and stand normally while the searching officer, with his fingers, would go through the hair, into the ears, down the back, under the armpits, down both arms, down the legs, into the groin area, and up the front. The officer would also search the waistband and require the detainee to remove his shoes and sometimes his socks.

Mary Beth G. v. City of Chicago (1983), U.S. Court of Appeals (7th Cir.)

Until now, we've only discussed searches and seizures conducted for the purpose of gathering evidence of crime, but crime control isn't the only reason for searches. The U.S. Supreme Court has applied the Fourth Amendment to a wide range of searches that go beyond criminal law enforcement to meet "special needs." **Special-needs searches** include:

1.  *Inventory searches.* Documenting inventory searches of persons and containers in government custody to protect the owners from theft and damage, government agencies from lawsuits, and jails from danger
2.  *International border searches.* Conducting international border checks to control who and what comes into and goes out of the country
3.  *Airport searches.* Examining airport passengers and their baggage to protect the safety of travelers
4.  *Custody-related searches.* Searching prisoners, probationers, parolees, and visitors and employees of prisons and jails to control contraband
5.  *Student searches.* Searching students to maintain a thriving learning environment
6.  *Employee drug testing.* Testing employees for drug use to increase workplace safety

Other special-needs searches include "inspecting" businesses, such as restaurants and bars, to make sure they're complying with health and safety codes and conducting vehicle safety checks to make the roads safer.

"Special needs" doesn't mean these searches are totally unrelated to law enforcement. Take the best example, the frisks you learned about in Chapter 4. Their sole purpose is to protect officers, but if evidence of a crime turns up during the frisk, it can be seized and used as evidence in criminal trials. The same is true of all the special-needs searches you'll learn about in this chapter; in fact, many of the cases discussed in the chapter involve evidence of crimes discovered during the special need beyond law enforcement that justified the search in the first place.

The variety of special-needs searches shouldn't hide their four common characteristics:

1.  They're directed at people generally, not criminal suspects and defendants specifically.
2.  They can result in criminal prosecution and conviction.
3.  They don't require warrants or probable cause.
4.  Their reasonableness depends on balancing special government needs against invasions of individual privacy.

We'll look at several of these special-needs searches to gain a greater understanding of how they serve the aims of protecting the public.

# INVENTORY SEARCHES

*Inventory searches* consist of making a list of people's personal property and containers held in government custody. Containers include vehicles, purses, clothing, or anything else where people in custody might put their "stuff." After looking through ("searching") the containers, officials make a list of the items and put them away ("seize") for safekeeping. The reasonableness of an inventory search depends on satisfying two elements (Chapter 4):

1. *Balancing interests.* Searches have to balance the government's special need to inspect against the invasion of individuals' privacy caused by the search. If the government's special need outweighs the individual's right to privacy (courts almost always find that it does), the search is reasonable.

2. *Objective basis.* Routine procedures, not probable cause or even reasonable suspicion, are required in special-needs searches.

Let's look at each element.

## Balancing Interests

Law enforcement officers take inventories to satisfy three government interests that aren't directly connected to searching for evidence of a crime:

1. To protect owners' stuff while it's in police custody

2. To protect law enforcement agencies against lawsuits for the loss, destruction, or theft of owners' stuff

3. To protect law enforcement officers, detained suspects, and offenders from the danger of bombs, weapons, and illegal drugs that might be hidden in owners' "stuff"

## Objective Basis

According to the U.S. Supreme Court, inventories taken by law enforcement officers are Fourth Amendment searches, but they're reasonable without either probable cause or warrants. Why? Because they're not searches for gathering evidence to prosecute crime. This doesn't mean inventory special-needs searches are left entirely to officer discretion. Following routine, department-approved, written procedures takes the place of probable cause and reasonable suspicion in inventory searches. We'll call this requirement that officers follow written, departmental procedures when conducting inventory searches the **routine-procedure limit**.

The requirement still leaves officers plenty of room to exercise discretion, as our next case excerpt, the leading inventory search case, *Colorado v. Bertine* (1987), made clear when the Court approved the inventory search of Steven Lee Bertine's lawfully detained van and his knapsack.

## Colorado v. Bertine
### 479 U.S. 367 (1987)

### HISTORY

Steven Lee Bertine was charged with driving while under the influence of alcohol, unlawful possession of cocaine with intent to dispense, sell, and distribute, and unlawful possession of methaqualone. The People appealed from an order of the District Court, Boulder County, which granted Bertine's motion to suppress evidence seized from defendant's backpack during an inventory search. The Colorado Supreme Court affirmed. Certiorari was granted. The U.S. Supreme Court reversed.

REHNQUIST, C.J., DELIVERED THE OPINION OF THE COURT, IN WHICH WHITE, BLACKMUN, POWELL, STEVENS, O'CONNOR, AND SCALIA, JJ., JOINED.

### FACTS

On February 10, 1984, a police officer in Boulder, Colorado, arrested respondent Steven Lee Bertine for driving while under the influence of alcohol. After Bertine was taken into custody and before the arrival of a tow truck to take Bertine's van to an impoundment lot, a backup officer inventoried the contents of the van. The officer opened a closed backpack in which he found controlled substances, cocaine paraphernalia, and a large amount of cash.

The backup officer inventoried the van in accordance with local police procedures, which require a detailed inspection and inventory of impounded vehicles. He found the backpack directly behind the front seat of the van. Inside the pack, the officer observed a nylon bag containing metal canisters. Opening the canisters, the officer discovered that they contained cocaine, methaqualone tablets, cocaine paraphernalia, and $700 in cash. In an outside zippered pouch of the backpack, he also found $210 in cash in a sealed envelope. After completing the inventory of the van, the officer had the van towed to an impound lot and brought the backpack, money, and contraband to the police station.

After Bertine was charged with the offenses described above, he moved to suppress the evidence found during the inventory search. . . . The Colorado trial court ruled that probable cause supported Bertine's arrest and that the police officers had made the decisions to impound the vehicle and to conduct a thorough inventory search in good faith.

Although noting that the inventory of the vehicle was performed in a "somewhat slipshod" manner, the District Court concluded that "the search of the backpack was done for the purpose of protecting the owner's property,

protection of the police from subsequent claims of loss or stolen property, and the protection of the police from dangerous instrumentalities. The court observed that the standard procedures for impounding vehicles mandated a "detailed inventory involving the opening of containers and the listing of [their] contents."

Based on these findings, the court determined that the inventory search did not violate Bertine's rights under the Fourth Amendment of the United States Constitution. The court, nevertheless, granted Bertine's motion to suppress, holding that the inventory search violated the Colorado Constitution. . . . The Supreme Court of Colorado affirmed. In contrast to the District Court, however, the Colorado Supreme Court premised its ruling on the United States Constitution.

### OPINION

Inventory searches are now a well-defined exception to the warrant requirement of the Fourth Amendment. The policies behind the warrant requirement are not implicated in an inventory search, nor is the related concept of probable cause. The standard of probable cause is peculiarly related to criminal investigations, not routine, noncriminal procedures. . . . The probable-cause approach is unhelpful when analysis centers upon the reasonableness of routine administrative caretaking functions, particularly when no claim is made that the protective procedures are a subterfuge for criminal investigations.

By contrast, an inventory search may be "reasonable" under the Fourth Amendment even though it is not conducted pursuant to a warrant based upon probable cause. . . . [In *Opperman v. South Dakota* (1976), the Court stated that] inventory procedures serve to protect an owner's property while it is in the custody of the police, to insure against claims of lost, stolen, or vandalized property, and to guard the police from danger. In light of these strong governmental interests and the diminished expectation of privacy in an automobile, we upheld the search. In reaching this decision, we observed that our cases accorded deference to police caretaking procedures designed to secure and protect vehicles and their contents within police custody.

In the present case, there was no showing that the police, who were following standardized procedures, acted in bad faith or for the sole purpose of investigation. In addition, the governmental interests justifying the inventory search *Opperman* . . . are nearly the same as those which obtain here. In each case, the police were potentially responsible for the property taken into their custody. By securing the property, the police protected the property from unauthorized interference. Knowledge of the precise nature of the property helped guard against claims of theft, vandalism, or negligence. Such knowledge also helped to avert any danger to police or others that may have been posed by the property. . . .

The Supreme Court of Colorado also expressed the view that the search in this case was unreasonable because . . . Bertine . . . could have been offered the opportunity to make other arrangements for the safekeeping of his property. . . . While giving Bertine an opportunity to make alternative arrangements would undoubtedly have been possible, the real question is not what could have been achieved, but whether the Fourth Amendment *requires* such steps. The reasonableness of any particular governmental activity does not necessarily or invariably turn on the existence of alternative less intrusive means.

We conclude that . . . reasonable police regulations relating to inventory procedures administered in good faith satisfy the Fourth Amendment, even though courts might as a matter of hindsight be able to devise equally reasonable rules requiring a different procedure.

The Supreme Court of Colorado also thought it necessary to require that police, before inventorying a container, weigh the strength of the individual's privacy interest in the container against the possibility that the container might serve as a repository for dangerous or valuable items. . . . When a legitimate search is under way, and when its purpose and its limits have been precisely defined, nice distinctions between closets, drawers, and containers, in the case of a home, or between glove compartments, upholstered seats, trunks, and wrapped packages, in the case of a vehicle, must give way to the interest in the prompt and efficient completion of the task at hand.

. . . A single familiar standard is essential to guide police officers, who have only limited time and expertise to reflect on and balance the social and individual interests involved in the specific circumstances they confront.

Bertine finally argues that the inventory search of his van was unconstitutional because departmental regulations gave the police officers discretion to choose between impounding his van and parking and locking it in a public parking place. . . . Nothing . . . prohibits the exercise of police discretion so long as that discretion is exercised according to standard criteria and on the basis of something other than suspicion of evidence of criminal activity. Here, the discretion afforded the Boulder police was exercised in light of standardized criteria, related to the feasibility and appropriateness of parking and locking a vehicle rather than impounding it. There was no showing that the police chose to impound Bertine's van in order to investigate suspected criminal activity.

. . . The judgment of the Supreme Court of Colorado is therefore REVERSED.

## DISSENT

MARSHALL, J., JOINED BY BRENNAN, J.

. . . In assessing the reasonableness of searches conducted in limited situations such as these, where we do not require probable cause or a warrant, we have consistently emphasized the need for . . . set procedures: standardless and unconstrained discretion is the evil the Court has discerned when in previous cases it has insisted that the discretion of the official in the field be circumscribed. . . .

The Court greatly overstates the justifications for the inventory exception to the Fourth Amendment. Chief Justice BURGER, writing for the majority in *South Dakota v. Opperman* (1976), relied on three governmental interests to justify the inventory search of an unlocked glove compartment in an automobile impounded for overtime parking:

(i) "the protection of the owner's property while it remains in police custody";

(ii) "the protection of the police against claims or disputes over lost or stolen property"; and

(iii) "the protection of the police from potential danger."

. . . Only the first of these interests is actually served by an automobile inventory search.

The protection-against-claims interest did not justify the inventory search . . . in this case. The use of secure impoundment facilities effectively eliminates this concern. . . . Officer Reichenbach's inventory in this case would not have protected the police against claims lodged by respondent, false or otherwise. Indeed, the trial court's characterization of the inventory as "slip-shod" is the height of understatement. For example, Officer Reichenbach failed to list $150 in cash found in respondent's wallet or the contents of a sealed envelope marked "rent," $210, in the relevant section of the property form. His reports make no reference to other items of value, including respondent's credit cards, and a converter, a hydraulic jack, and a set of tire chains, worth a total of $125. The $700 in cash found in respondent's backpack, along with the contraband, appeared only on a property form completed later by someone other than Officer Reichenbach. The interior of the vehicle was left in disarray, and the officer "inadvertently" retained respondent's keys—including his house keys—for two days following his arrest.

The third interest—protecting the police from potential danger—failed to receive the endorsement of a majority of the Court in *Opperman*. After noting that "there is little danger associated with impounding unsearched vehicles," Justice POWELL recognized that "there does not appear to be any effective way of identifying in advance those circumstances or classes of automobile impoundments which represent a greater risk."

. . . Thus, only the government's interest in protecting the owner's property actually justifies an inventory search of an impounded vehicle. While I continue to believe that preservation of property does not outweigh the privacy and security interests protected by the Fourth Amendment, I fail to see how preservation can even be asserted as a justification for the search in this case. . . . The owner was present to make other arrangements for the safekeeping of his belongings, yet the police made no attempt to ascertain whether in fact he wanted them to "safeguard" his property.

Furthermore, since respondent was charged with a traffic offense, he was unlikely to remain in custody for more than a few hours. He might well have been willing to leave his valuables unattended in the locked van for such a short period of time. Had he been given the choice, respondent indicated . . . that he "would have parked the van in the lot across the street and had somebody come and get it."

Thus, the government's interests in this case are weaker than in *Opperman*, but the search here is much more intrusive. *Opperman* did not involve a search of closed containers or other items that touch upon intimate areas of an individual's personal affairs. . . .

Not only are the government's interests weaker here . . . , but respondent's privacy interest is greater. In upholding the search in *Opperman*, the Court emphasized the fact that the defendant had a diminished expectation of privacy in his automobile, due to pervasive and continuing governmental regulation and controls, including periodic inspection and licensing requirements and "the obviously public nature of automobile travel."

. . . Here the Court completely ignores respondent's expectation of privacy in his backpack. Whatever his expectation of privacy in his automobile generally, . . . he retained a reasonable expectation of privacy in the backpack and its contents. Indeed, the Boulder police officer

who conducted the inventory acknowledged that backpacks commonly serve as repositories for personal effects. Thus, even if the governmental interests in this case were the same as those in *Opperman*, they would nonetheless be outweighed by respondent's comparatively greater expectation of privacy in his luggage.

. . . The word "automobile" is not a talisman in whose presence the Fourth Amendment fades away and disappears. By upholding the search in this case, the Court not only ignores that principle, but creates another talisman to overcome the requirements of the Fourth Amendment—the term "inventory." Accordingly, I dissent.

### Questions

1. List the three reasons why inventory searches are reasonable without either warrants or probable cause.

2. Why should the evidence of a crime obtained in an inventory search be admitted to convict a person when the purpose of the search was for one or more of the reasons you listed in question 1?

3. Assume you're the lawyer for the government in this case. Answer the dissent's arguments that the inventory search of Steven Lee Bertine's van and his knapsack was unreasonable.

# INTERNATIONAL BORDER SEARCHES

According to the U.S. Supreme Court in *U.S. v. Ramsey* (1977), searches at international borders are reasonable even without warrants or probable cause. This is known as the **border search exception**. The special need of border searches is the right to control who and what comes into and goes out of the country. In *Ramsey*, a batch of incoming, letter-sized airmail envelopes from Thailand (a known source of narcotics) was bulky and much heavier than normal airmail letters. So a customs inspector opened the envelopes for inspection at the General Post Office in New York City (considered a "border") and found heroin in them. The inspector seized the heroin and used it to convict the recipient. The customs inspector didn't obtain a warrant to search the envelopes, even though he had time to get one.

Still, according to the U.S. Supreme Court, it wasn't an illegal search and seizure:

That searches made at the border, pursuant to the long-standing right of the sovereign to protect itself by stopping and examining persons and property crossing into this country, are reasonable simply by virtue of the fact that they occur at the border, should, by now, require no extended demonstration. The Congress which proposed the Bill of Rights, including the Fourth Amendment, to the state legislatures on September 25, 1789, had, some two months prior to that proposal, enacted the first customs statute. . . . This statute granted customs officials "full power and authority" to enter and search "any ship or vessel, in which they shall have reason to suspect any goods, wares or merchandise subject to duty shall be concealed. . . ." The historical importance of the enactment of this customs statute by the same Congress which proposed the Fourth Amendment is, we think, manifest. (606)

Applying the balancing test to border searches, the U.S. Supreme Court found that the national interest in controlling our international borders outweighs the invasions of individual privacy caused by border searches. So border checks require neither warrants nor individualized suspicion. However, reasonable suspicion is required to back up strip searches for contraband and weapons, because people coming into the country are "forced to disrobe to a state which would be offensive to the average person." Body-cavity searches at the border are reasonable only if they're backed up by probable cause (LaFave and Israel 1984, 1:327–28).

# AIRPORT SEARCHES

Ever since a series of airline hijackings and terrorist bombings in the 1970s, travelers have had to pass through detectors before they can board airplanes. Passengers also must pass their luggage through X-ray machines for examination. Additionally, inspectors sometimes open and look through baggage. If they discover suspicious items, they investigate further.

Applying the balancing test of Fourth Amendment reasonableness, the U.S. Supreme Court has held that airport searches are reasonable even without warrants or probable cause. According to the Court, airport searches serve two extremely important special needs—the security and the safety of air travelers. These special needs clearly outweigh the minimal invasion of privacy caused by having passengers pass through metal detectors and allowing their luggage to be observed by X-ray. Furthermore, these invasions apply equally to all passengers, who are notified in advance that they're subject to them. So passengers are free not to board the airplane if they don't want to subject their person and their luggage to these intrusions (LaFave and Israel 1984, 1:332–33).

Since September 11, 2001, the searches have become more frequent and more intrusive but so has the sense of urgency about security. To date, there have been no court challenges (that I'm aware of) to these security changes. But if a court challenge arises, it's not likely the balance will be struck against the current practice. Of course, if passengers are singled out for more-frequent and more-invasive measures because of their Middle Eastern background and/or their Muslim religion, that's a different matter.

# CUSTODY-RELATED SEARCHES

Prisoners and their cells; prison visitors and employees; prisoners released on parole; probationers who could be but aren't locked up; and even defendants detained *before* they're convicted all can be searched without warrants or probable cause—and sometimes without any individualized suspicion at all. Why? Because the special need to maintain safety, security, and discipline over people locked up in jails and prisons, and probationers and parolees under state supervision in the community, outweighs the significantly reduced expectation of privacy that society grants to people in the custody of the criminal justice system.

Let's examine this balance as it applies to prisoners, probationers, and parolees and prison visitors and employees.

# Prisoners

Historically, prisoners had no Fourth Amendment rights; the Constitution stopped at the prison gate. Referring to convicted prisoners, the Virginia court in *Ruffin v. Commonwealth* (1871) said, "The bill of rights is a declaration of general principles to govern a society of freemen." Prisoners "are the slaves of the State" (1025). As for people detained in jails before they're convicted, in *Lanza v. New York* (1962), the U.S. Supreme Court ruled that "a jail shares none of the attributes of privacy of a home, automobile, an office or hotel room, . . . and official surveillance has traditionally been the order of the day in prisons" (139).

In the 1980s, the Court conceded that prisoners have an expectation of privacy that society recognizes. According to the Court, in *Hudson v. Palmer* (1984), "We have repeatedly held that prisons are not beyond the reach of the Constitution. No 'iron curtain' separates one from the other," *but*, the Court continued, "imprisonment carries with it the circumscription or loss of many significant rights" (523).

The reasonableness of prisoner searches depends on balancing the need to maintain prison and jail security, safety, and discipline against the invasion of prisoners' substantially reduced reasonable expectation of privacy. The Court applied the balancing approach in *Hudson v. Palmer* (1984). According to Russell Thomas Palmer, the prisoner:

> On 9-16-81 around 5:50 P.M., officer Hudson shook down my locker and destroyed a lot of my property, i.e.: legal materials, letters, and other personal property only as a means of harassment.
>
> Officer Hudson has violated my Constitutional rights. The shakedown was no routine shakedown. It was planned and carried out only as harassment. Hudson stated the next time he would really mess my stuff up. I have plenty of witnesses to these facts. (541)

The Court accepted Palmer's version of the facts. Still, Chief Justice Burger, writing for the majority, held that the "shakedown routine"—unannounced searches of prisoners and their cells for weapons and contraband—was not a search at all:

> Notwithstanding our caution in approaching claims that the Fourth Amendment is inapplicable in a given context, we hold that society is not prepared to recognize as legitimate any . . . expectation of privacy that a prisoner might have in his prison cell and that, accordingly, the Fourth Amendment proscription against unreasonable searches does not apply within the confines of the prison cell. The recognition of privacy rights for prisoners in their individual cells simply cannot be reconciled with the concept of incarceration and the needs and objectives of penal institutions. (525–26)

The Court ruled the Fourth Amendment doesn't apply even if the motive behind the shakedown was harassment, as Palmer claimed it was. Four justices disagreed. According to Justice Stevens, writing for the dissenters:

> Measured by the conditions that prevail in a free society, neither the possessions nor the slight residuum of privacy that a prison inmate can retain in his cell, can have more than the most minimal value. From the standpoint of the prisoner, however, that trivial residuum may mark the difference between slavery and humanity (542). . . .
>
> Personal letters, snapshots of family members, a souvenir, a deck of cards, a hobby kit, perhaps a diary or a training manual for an apprentice in a new trade, or even a Bible—a variety of inexpensive items may enable a prisoner to maintain contact with some part of his past and an eye to the possibility of a better future. Are all of these items subject to unrestrained perusal, confiscation, or mutilation at the hands of a possibly hostile guard? Is the Court correct in its perception that "society" is not prepared to recognize any privacy or possessory interest of the prison inmate—no matter how remote the threat to prison security may be (542–43)?

. . . The view once held that an inmate is a mere slave is now totally rejected. The restraints and the punishment which a criminal conviction entails do not place the citizen beyond the ethical tradition that accords respect to the dignity and intrinsic worth of every individual. "Liberty" and "custody" are not mutually exclusive concepts." . . . By telling prisoners that no aspect of their individuality, from a photo of a child to a letter from a wife, is entitled to constitutional protection, the Court breaks with the ethical tradition that I had thought was enshrined forever in our jurisprudence. (557–58)

Let's look at two other Fourth Amendment issues that have been raised by prisoners: conducting strip and body-cavity searches on prisoners and testing their DNA and storing it.

## Strip and Body-Cavity Searches

The U.S. Supreme Court concedes that full-body, strip, and body-cavity searches are Fourth Amendment searches, but they're reasonable without either warrants or probable cause *if*, in the particular situation, the need for security, safety, or discipline outweighs prisoners' reasonable expectation of privacy in the particular circumstances of the case. For example, in *Bell v. Wolfish* (1979; Chapter 12), the U.S. Supreme Court ruled that it was reasonable to require jail inmates awaiting trial to expose their body cavities for visual inspection after every visit with a person from outside the jail. The Court said these body-cavity searches were reasonable to maintain safety and order in the jail.

As broad as the government's power is, the Fourth Amendment doesn't leave prisoners' rights completely up to the discretion of government officials. Sometimes, the balance between the special need and individual privacy weighs in favor of prisoners. Highly intrusive custodial searches when security, safety, and discipline don't require them can violate the rights of prisoners. Also, they require an objective basis of reasonable suspicion to back them up. In our next case excerpt, *Mary Beth G. v. City of Chicago* (1983), the U.S. Seventh Circuit Court of Appeals found Chicago's policy of strip-searching all women confined in the Cook County Jail was unreasonable.

---

C A S E    *Was the Strip Search Reasonable?*

### *Mary Beth G. v. City of Chicago*
723 F.2d 1263 (7th Cir. 1983)

### HISTORY

Mary B. G., Sharon N., Mary Ann Tikalsky, and Hinda Hoffman were arrested for misdemeanor traffic violations. While they were awaiting bail in lockups, jail matrons strip-searched them. The four women challenged the constitutionality of Chicago's strip search policy. The U.S. District Court entered judgment in favor of the women. The U.S. Seventh Circuit Court of Appeals held that the city of Chicago's strip search policy violated the Fourth Amendment, that the jury awards were not excessive, and that plaintiffs were entitled to attorney's fees.

WOOD, J.

### FACTS

Mary Beth G. and Sharon N. were stopped for traffic violations, arrested, and taken to detention centers because there were outstanding parking tickets on their cars. Hinda Hoffman was stopped for making an improper left turn, arrested, and taken to the police station when she failed to produce her driver's license. [*Mary Ann Tikalsky's specific traffic offense is not mentioned.*]

All four women were subjected to the strip search policy of the City of Chicago. That policy, as described by the City, required each woman placed in detention facilities of the Chicago Police Department and searched by female personnel to: 1. lift her blouse or sweater and unhook and lift her brassiere to allow a visual inspection of the breast area, to replace these articles of clothing and then 2. pull up her skirt or dress or to lower her pants and pull down any undergarments, to squat two or three times facing the detention aide and to bend over at the waist to permit visual inspection of the vaginal and anal area. . . .

The strip search policy wasn't applied to males. Male detainees were subject to a strip search only if the arresting officers or detention aides had reason to believe the detainee was concealing weapons or contraband. Otherwise, men were searched thoroughly by hand. The male detainee would place his hands against the wall and stand normally while the searching officer, with his fingers, would go through the hair, into the ears, down the back, under the armpits, down both arms, down the legs, into the groin area, and up the front. The officer would also search the waistband and require the detainee to remove his shoes and sometimes his socks.

Originally, women detainees were also searched in this manner, but in 1952 the City changed its policy and began conducting the strip searches.

## OPINION

. . . The City argues that its strip search policy is valid under two recognized exceptions to the warrant requirement. One exception allows warrantless searches [because the Fourth Amendment] . . . permits warrantless searches incident to the detention of persons lawfully arrested. . . .

Our starting point is the balancing test announced in *Bell v. Wolfish* (1979), beginning with the magnitude of the invasion of personal rights. Strip searches involving the visual inspection of the anal and genital areas are "demeaning, dehumanizing, undignified, humiliating, terrifying, unpleasant, embarrassing, and repulsive, signifying degradation and submission. . . ."

Balanced against this invasion of personal privacy is the governmental interest in conducting the particular searches in question. In these cases, the governmental interest alleged by the City to justify these particular strip searches was the need to maintain the security of the City lockups by preventing misdemeanor offenders from bringing in weapons or contraband; the need was apparently felt to be so great that women misdemeanants were strip searched even when there was no reason to believe they were hiding weapons or contraband on their persons.

The evidence the City offered to demonstrate the need for requiring strip searches of women minor offenders to maintain jail security, however, belies its purported concerns.

The affidavits of the lockup personnel, which lack specificity, suggest that only a few items have been recovered from the body cavities of women arrested on minor charges over the years. In the only analytical survey submitted by the City, conducted over a thirty-five day period in June and July of 1965, all of the items found in the body orifices of the 1,800 women searched during that period were taken from women charged with either prostitution (7 items), assault (1 item), or a narcotics violation (1 item).

These are the kinds of crimes, unlike traffic or other offenses, that might give rise to a reasonable belief that the woman arrestee was concealing an item in a body cavity.

Although a detention center may be a place "fraught with serious security dangers," the evidence does not support the view that those dangers are created by women minor offenders entering the lockups for short periods while awaiting bail. Here, the "need for the particular search," a strip search, is hardly substantial enough, in light of the evidence regarding the incidence of weapons and contraband found in the body cavities of women minor offenders, to justify the severity of the governmental intrusion.

Balancing the citizen's right to be free from substantial government intrusions against the mission of law enforcement personnel to ensure a safer society is often a difficult task. While the need to assure jail security is a legitimate and substantial concern, we believe that, on the facts here, the strip searches bore an insubstantial relationship to security needs so that, when balanced against plaintiffs-appellees' privacy interests, the searches cannot be considered "reasonable."

The reasonableness standard usually requires, "at a minimum, that the facts upon which an intrusion is based be capable of measurement against 'an objective standard,' whether this be probable cause or a less stringent test." The more intrusive the search, the closer governmental authorities must come to demonstrating probable cause for believing that the search will uncover the objects for which the search is being conducted.

Based on these principles, we agree with the District Court that insuring the security needs of the City by strip searching plaintiffs-appellees was unreasonable without a reasonable suspicion by the authorities that either of the twin dangers of concealing weapons or contraband existed. . . .

Accordingly, because the court and jury . . . could reasonably conclude that the strip search policy of the City as applied in these cases was unreasonable under the fourth amendment, we uphold their determinations on this issue.

AFFIRMED.

## Questions

1. Identify the special government need and the searches used to meet the need.

2. How did the court balance the need to maintain jails and the privacy rights of Mary Beth G. and the other

women who sued the city? How would you balance these interests?

3. Identify the objective basis the court decided was necessary to back up the searches, and explain why the court decided on this level of objective basis.

4. Is labeling someone a "prisoner" ever enough to justify the kind of searches used in this case? Or should this kind of search always require individualized suspicion?

5. Would you go further and say that these searches should require probable cause to believe the person searched is concealing weapons or contraband? Why or why not?

6. The jury awarded the plaintiffs $25,000 each, except for Hinda Hoffman, who received $60,000 because male officers had watched and uttered rude remarks during her search. The city of Chicago claimed the awards were excessive. Do you agree? How do you assess how much money these intrusions are worth? Why do you suppose the Chicago policy remained unchallenged for so many years?

 Go to Exercise 7.1 on the Samaha Criminal Procedure 7e website to learn about strip-search liability: academic.cengage.com/criminaljustice/samaha.

## Testing and Storing DNA

Every state and the federal government now has a statute that mandates DNA testing of all incarcerated felons (*State v. Raines* 2004). Courts have defined the testing and storing of DNA as Fourth Amendment searches and seizures. The U.S. Supreme Court hasn't ruled on the reasonableness of the testing, but the Eleventh Circuit U.S. Court of Appeals upheld Georgia's statute (*Padgett v. Donald* 2005). The statute requires convicted, incarcerated felons to provide a sample of their DNA to the Georgia Department of Corrections for analysis and storage in a data bank maintained by the Georgia Bureau of Investigation (1275).

The DNA profiles can be released from the data bank "to federal, state, and local law enforcement officers upon a request made in furtherance of an official investigation of any criminal offense." The statute applies to all persons convicted of a felony and incarcerated on or after July 1, 2000, and all felons incarcerated as of that date (1275):

> In implementing the statute, the Georgia Department of Corrections (DOC) formulated policy dictating that members of the prison staff obtain the samples by swabbing the inside of felons' mouths for saliva. The GDOC then sends the swabs to the GBI for typing and placement in the DNA database. Inmates that refuse to submit to the procedure are subjected to disciplinary reports followed by hearings and possible disciplinary action. If any inmate still refuses to cooperate, the prison staff takes the sample by force. (1275–76)

Roy Padgett and several other imprisoned convicted felons brought a civil suit asking for an injunction against testing them on the ground that it was an illegal search and seizure of their saliva. The U.S. Court of Appeals affirmed the U.S. District's rejection of the prisoners' claim. The court found that the statute was "reasonable under a totality of the circumstances analysis":

> We employ a balancing test, weighing the degree to which the search intrudes on an individual's privacy against the degree to which it promotes a legitimate governmental interest. Because we believe that Georgia's legitimate interest in creating a permanent identification record of convicted felons for law enforcement purposes outweighs the minor intrusion involved in taking prisoners' saliva samples and storing their DNA profiles, given prisoners' reduced expectation of privacy in their identities, we . . . hold that the statute does not violate the Fourth Amendment. (1280)

# Probationers and Parolees

Probationers and parolees also have diminished Fourth Amendment rights, even though they're not locked up (LaFave and Israel 1984, 1:336–38). Their reduced expectation of privacy subjects probationers and parolees to arrest and searches of their persons, their vehicles, and their houses without warrants or probable cause. Why? Some courts say it's because they're still in state custody, and conditional release is a privilege, not a right. After all, they could still be locked up; it's only by the grace of the state they're conditionally released, and one of the conditions for release is to be searched at the discretion of the state. Other courts say they're consent searches and seizures, signed and agreed to in their "contract" of release.

Still other courts adopt a balancing approach to the searches of probationers and parolees. On the "special need" side of the balance is the government's interest in protecting society and reducing recidivism; on the other side is the privacy and right against unreasonable searches and seizures. Let's look more closely at each group.

***Probationers*** The Supreme Court applied the balancing approach in *Griffin v. Wisconsin* (1987), the first and still most widely cited modern case involving the Fourth Amendment rights of probationers. Wisconsin law puts probationers in the custody of the Wisconsin Department of Health and Social Services. One of the department's regulations permits probation officers to search probationers' homes without a warrant as long as the searches are backed up by reasonable suspicion that contraband is in the house (870–71).

Michael Lew, Joseph Griffin's probation officer's supervisor, had reasonable suspicion that "there might be guns in Griffin's house." Lew went to the house without a warrant and searched the house. He found a handgun, a violation of Griffin's probation. Griffin was charged with possession of a firearm by a convicted felon, a felony in Wisconsin. The trial court denied Griffin's motion to suppress the gun, a jury convicted him, and the court sentenced him to two years in prison. The Wisconsin Court of Appeals and the Wisconsin Supreme Court affirmed his conviction (871–72). The U.S. Supreme Court also affirmed. According to the Court:

> A probationer's home, like anyone else's, is protected by the Fourth Amendment's requirement that searches be "reasonable." Although we usually require that a search be undertaken only pursuant to a warrant (and thus supported by probable cause, as the Constitution says warrants must be), we have permitted exceptions when special needs, beyond the normal need for law enforcement, make the warrant and probable-cause requirement impracticable. (873)
>
> To a greater or lesser degree, it is always true of probationers (as we have said it to be true of parolees) that they do not enjoy "the absolute liberty to which every citizen is entitled, but only . . . conditional liberty properly dependent on observance of special [probation] restrictions." (874)
>
> These restrictions are meant to assure that the probation serves as a period of genuine rehabilitation and that the community is not harmed by the probationer's being at large. These same goals require and justify the exercise of supervision to assure that the restrictions are in fact observed. . . . Supervision, then, is a "special need" of the State permitting a degree of impingement upon privacy that would not be constitutional if applied to the public at large. (875)

The matter of balancing seemed settled: *Probation officers* can search probationers' homes without warrants as long as they're backed up by reasonable suspicion. Then, 13 years later, *U.S. v. Knights* (2001) expanded the reasonableness to include searches by *law enforcement officers*. Mark James Knights was convicted of a drug offense and was placed on probation, subject to the condition that he "submit his . . . person, property, place of residence, vehicle, personal effects, to search at anytime, with or without a search warrant, warrant of arrest or reasonable cause by any probation officer or law enforcement officer." Knights signed the probation order, which stated immediately above his signature that "I HAVE RECEIVED A COPY, READ AND UNDERSTAND THE ABOVE TERMS AND CONDITIONS OF PROBATION AND AGREE TO ABIDE BY SAME." (114)

Three days later, Todd Hancock, a sheriff's detective, without Knights' knowledge or participation, searched his apartment without a warrant but with enough information to reasonably suspect there might be "incendiary materials" in the apartment (115–16).

A unanimous U.S. Supreme Court ruled that the search passed the balancing test. Conceding that the search condition "significantly diminished Knights' reasonable expectation of privacy" (120), the Court turned to the "special needs" side of the balance:

> The State has a dual concern with a probationer. On the one hand is the hope that he will successfully complete probation and be integrated back into the community. On the other is the concern, quite justified, that he will be more likely to engage in criminal conduct than an ordinary member of the community. . . .
>
> We hold that . . . when an officer has reasonable suspicion that a probationer subject to a search condition is engaged in criminal activity, there is enough likelihood that criminal conduct is occurring that an intrusion on the probationer's significantly diminished privacy interests is reasonable. (120–21)

To read the full opinion in *U.S. v. Knights* (2001), go to the Samaha Criminal Procedure 7e website: academic.cengage.com/criminaljustice/samaha.

### Parolees

> . . . Parolees, who are on the continuum of state-imposed punishments, have fewer expectations of privacy than probationers, because parole is more akin to imprisonment than probation is to imprisonment. As this Court has pointed out, "parole is an established variation of imprisonment of convicted criminals. . . . The essence of parole is release from prison, before the completion of the sentence, on the condition that the prisoner abides by certain rules during the balance of the sentence." (*Samson v. California* 2006, 2198)

Although the majority of the U.S. Supreme Court justices hold this view as well, there's plenty of controversy over whether the empirical data supports their view. And there's sharp disagreement among the justices over the majority's view.

You'll learn more about the majority and the dissent's views of parole and the empirical data in our next case excerpt, *Samson v. California* (2006). *Samson v. California* expanded the rule in *Knights* (discussed in the last section) as it applies to parolees. Over the strong, even the passionate, dissents of three justices, the Court ruled that law enforcement officers can search parolees' homes without either warrants or individualized reasonable suspicion.

---

**C A S E** | ***Was the Suspicionless Search of the Parolee's Home Reasonable?***

### Samson v. California
126 S.Ct. 2193 (2006)

#### HISTORY

Donald Curtis Samson, Defendant, was convicted in the California Appellate Division of the Superior Court of possession of methamphetamine, and sentenced to seven years in prison. Defendant appealed. The California Court of Appeal, affirmed. Defendant appealed. Certiorari was granted. The U.S. Supreme Court affirmed.

THOMAS, J., JOINED BY ROBERTS, C.J., AND SCALIA, KENNEDY, GINSBURG, AND ALITO, JJ.

California law provides that every prisoner eligible for release on state parole "shall agree in writing to be subject to search or seizure by a parole officer or other peace officer at any time of the day or night, with or without a search warrant and with or without cause." Cal.Penal

Code Ann. § 3067(a). We granted certiorari to decide whether a suspicionless search, conducted under the authority of this statute, violates the Constitution. We hold that it does not.

## FACTS

In September 2002, petitioner Donald Curtis Samson was on state parole in California, following a conviction for being a felon in possession of a firearm. On September 6, 2002, Officer Alex Rohleder of the San Bruno Police Department observed petitioner walking down a street with a woman and a child. Based on a prior contact with petitioner, Officer Rohleder was aware that petitioner was on parole and believed that he was facing an at large warrant. Accordingly, Officer Rohleder stopped petitioner and asked him whether he had an outstanding parole warrant. Petitioner responded that there was no outstanding warrant and that he "was in good standing with his parole agent." Officer Rohleder confirmed, by radio dispatch, that petitioner was on parole and that he did not have an outstanding warrant.

Nevertheless, pursuant to Cal.Penal Code Ann. § 3067(a) and based solely on petitioner's status as a parolee, Officer Rohleder searched petitioner. During the search, Officer Rohleder found a cigarette box in petitioner's left breast pocket. Inside the box he found a plastic baggie containing methamphetamine.

The State charged petitioner with possession of methamphetamine pursuant to Cal. Health & Safety Code Ann. § 11377(a). The trial court denied petitioner's motion to suppress the methamphetamine evidence, finding that Cal.Penal Code Ann. § 3067(a) authorized the search and that the search was not "arbitrary or capricious." A jury convicted petitioner of the possession charge and the trial court sentenced him to seven years' imprisonment.

The California Court of Appeal affirmed. . . . The court held that suspicionless searches of parolees are lawful under California law; "that such a search is reasonable within the meaning of the Fourth Amendment as long as it is not arbitrary, capricious or harassing"; and that the search in this case was not arbitrary, capricious, or harassing.

We granted certiorari, to answer a variation of the question this Court left open in *U.S. v. Knights* (2001)— whether a condition of release can so diminish or eliminate a released prisoner's reasonable expectation of privacy that a suspicionless search by a law enforcement officer would not offend the Fourth Amendment. Answering that question in the affirmative today, we affirm the judgment of the California Court of Appeal.

## OPINION

Under our general Fourth Amendment approach we examine the totality of the circumstances to determine whether a search is reasonable within the meaning of the Fourth Amendment. Whether a search is reasonable is determined by assessing, on the one hand, the degree to which it intrudes upon an individual's privacy and, on the other, the degree to which it is needed for the promotion of legitimate governmental interests.

We recently applied this approach in *U.S. v. Knights*. . . . We noted in *Knights* [that] parolees are on the "continuum" of state-imposed punishments. On this continuum, parolees have fewer expectations of privacy than probationers, because parole is more akin to imprisonment than probation is to imprisonment. . . . In most cases, the State is willing to extend parole only because it is able to condition it upon compliance with certain requirements.

. . . An inmate-turned-parolee remains in the legal custody of the California Department of Corrections through the remainder of his term, § 3056, and must comply with all of the terms and conditions of parole, including mandatory drug tests, restrictions on association with felons or gang members, and mandatory meetings with parole officers. . . . Parolees may also be subject to special conditions, including psychiatric treatment programs, mandatory abstinence from alcohol, residence approval, and "any other condition deemed necessary by the Board [of Parole Hearings] or the Department [of Corrections and Rehabilitation] due to unusual circumstances." § 2513. The extent and reach of these conditions clearly demonstrate that parolees like petitioner have severely diminished expectations of privacy by virtue of their status alone.

Additionally, . . . the parole search condition under California law—requiring inmates who opt for parole to submit to suspicionless searches by a parole officer or other peace officer "at any time" (Cal. Penal Code Ann. § 3067(a)) was "clearly expressed" to petitioner. He signed an order submitting to the condition and thus was "unambiguously" aware of it. . . . Examining the totality of the circumstances pertaining to petitioner's status as a parolee, an established variation on imprisonment, including the plain terms of the parole search condition, we conclude that petitioner did not have an expectation of privacy that society would recognize as legitimate.

The State's interests, by contrast, are substantial. This Court has repeatedly acknowledged that a State has an "overwhelming interest" in supervising parolees because "parolees . . . are more likely to commit future criminal offenses." Similarly, this Court has repeatedly acknowledged that a State's interests in reducing recidivism and thereby promoting reintegration and positive citizenship among probationers and parolees warrant privacy intrusions that would not otherwise be tolerated under the Fourth Amendment.

The empirical evidence presented in this case clearly demonstrates the significance of these interests to the State of California. As of November 30, 2005, California had over 130,000 released parolees. California's parolee population has a 68-to-70 percent recidivism rate. This Court has acknowledged the grave safety concerns that attend recidivism. See *Ewing v. California* (2003).

. . . The Fourth Amendment does not render the States powerless to address these concerns *effectively*. . . . California's ability to conduct suspicionless searches of parolees serves its interest in reducing recidivism, in a manner that aids, rather than hinders, the reintegration of parolees into productive society.

. . . The California Legislature has concluded that, given the number of inmates the State paroles and its high recidivism rate, a requirement that searches be based on individualized suspicion would undermine the State's ability to effectively supervise parolees and protect the public from criminal acts by reoffenders. This conclusion makes eminent sense. Imposing a reasonable suspicion requirement, as urged by petitioner, would give parolees greater opportunity to anticipate searches and conceal criminality. This Court concluded that the incentive-to-conceal concern justified an "intensive" system for supervising probationers in *Griffin*. That concern applies with even greater force to a system of supervising parolees.

The dissent argues that, "once one acknowledges that parolees do have legitimate expectations of privacy beyond those of prisoners, our Fourth Amendment jurisprudence does not permit the conclusion, reached by the Court here for the first time, that a search supported by neither individualized suspicion nor 'special needs' is nonetheless 'reasonable.'"

That simply is not the case. The touchstone of the Fourth Amendment is reasonableness, not individualized suspicion. Thus, while this Court's jurisprudence has often recognized that to accommodate public and private interests some quantum of individualized suspicion is usually a prerequisite to a constitutional search or seizure, we have also recognized that the Fourth Amendment imposes no irreducible requirement of such suspicion.

Therefore, although this Court has only sanctioned suspicionless searches in limited circumstances, namely programmatic and special needs searches, we have never held that these are the only limited circumstances in which searches absent individualized suspicion could be "reasonable" under the Fourth Amendment. In light of California's earnest concerns respecting recidivism, public safety, and reintegration of parolees into productive society, and because the object of the Fourth Amendment is *reasonableness*, our decision today is far from remarkable. Nor, given our prior precedents and caveats, is it "unprecedented."

Nor is there merit to the argument that California's parole search law permits "a blanket grant of discretion untethered by any procedural safeguards." The concern that California's suspicionless search system gives officers unbridled discretion to conduct searches, thereby inflicting dignitary harms that arouse strong resentment in parolees and undermine their ability to reintegrate into productive society, is belied by California's prohibition on "arbitrary, capricious or harassing" searches.

Thus, we conclude that the Fourth Amendment does not prohibit a police officer from conducting a suspicionless search of a parolee. Accordingly, we affirm the judgment of the California Court of Appeal. *It is so ordered.*

# DISSENT

STEVENS, J. JOINED BY SOUTER AND BREYER, JJ.

Our prior cases have consistently assumed that the Fourth Amendment provides some degree of protection for probationers and parolees. The protection is not as robust as that afforded to ordinary citizens; we have held that probationers' lowered expectation of privacy may justify their warrantless search upon reasonable suspicion of wrongdoing. We have also recognized that the supervisory responsibilities of probation officers, who are required to provide individualized counseling and to monitor their charges' progress, *Griffin v. Wisconsin* (1987), and who are in a unique position to judge how close a supervision the probationer requires, may give rise to special needs justifying departures from Fourth Amendment strictures. But neither *Knights* nor *Griffin* supports a regime of suspicionless searches, conducted pursuant to a blanket grant of discretion untethered by any procedural safeguards, by law enforcement personnel who have no special interest in the welfare of the parolee or probationer.

What the Court sanctions today is an unprecedented curtailment of liberty. . . . Our Fourth Amendment jurisprudence does not permit the conclusion, reached by the Court here for the first time, that a search supported by neither individualized suspicion nor "special needs" is nonetheless "reasonable."

The suspicionless search is the very evil the Fourth Amendment was intended to stamp out. While individualized suspicion is not an irreducible component of reasonableness under the Fourth Amendment, the requirement has been dispensed with only when programmatic searches were required to meet a "'special need' divorced from the State's general interest in law enforcement."

Not surprisingly, the majority does not seek to justify the search of petitioner on "special needs" grounds. Although the Court has in the past relied on special needs to uphold warrantless searches of probationers, it has never gone so far as to hold that a probationer or parolee may be subjected to full search at the whim of any law enforcement officer he happens to encounter, whether or not the officer has reason to suspect him of wrongdoing. *Griffin*, after all, involved a search *by a probation officer* that was supported by *reasonable suspicion*. The special role of probation officers was critical to the analysis; "we deal with a situation," the Court explained, "in which there is an ongoing supervisory relationship—and one that is not, or at least not entirely, adversarial—between the object of the search and the decisionmaker." The State's interest or "special need," as articulated in *Griffin*, was an interest in supervising the wayward probationer's reintegration into society—not, or at least not principally, the general law enforcement goal of detecting crime.

. . . None of our special needs precedents has sanctioned the routine inclusion of law enforcement, both in the design of the policy and in using arrests, either threatened or real, to implement the system designed for the special needs objectives. Ignoring just how closely guarded is that category of constitutionally permissible suspicion-less searches, the Court for the first time upholds an entirely suspicionless search unsupported by any special need. And it goes further: In special needs cases we have at least insisted upon programmatic safeguards designed to ensure evenhandedness in application; if individualized suspicion is to be jettisoned, it must be replaced with measures to protect against the state actor's unfettered discretion. Here, by contrast, there are no policies in place—no standards, guidelines, or procedures, to rein in officers and furnish a bulwark against the arbitrary exercise of discretion that is the height of unreasonableness.

The Court is able to make this unprecedented move only by making another. . . . Prisoners have no legitimate expectation of privacy; parolees are like prisoners; therefore, parolees have no legitimate expectation of privacy. The conclusion is remarkable not least because we have long embraced its opposite. . . .

Threaded through the Court's reasoning is the suggestion that deprivation of Fourth Amendment rights is part and parcel of any convict's punishment. If a person may be subject to random and suspicionless searches in prison, the Court seems to assume, then he cannot complain when he is subject to the same invasion outside of prison, so long as the State still *can* imprison him. Punishment, though, is not the basis [for depriving prisoners of their Fourth Amendment rights]. . . .

Nor, to my knowledge, have we ever sanctioned the use of any search as a punitive measure. Instead, the question in every case must be whether the balance of legitimate expectations of privacy, on the one hand, and the State's interests in conducting the relevant search, on the other, justifies dispensing with the warrant and probable-cause requirements that are otherwise dictated by the Fourth Amendment. That balance is not the same in prison as it is out. We held in *Knights*—without recourse to *Hudson*—that the balance favored allowing the State to conduct searches based on reasonable suspicion. Never before have we plunged below that floor absent a demonstration of "special needs."

Had the State imposed as a condition of parole a requirement that petitioner submit to random searches by his parole officer, who is supposed to have in mind the welfare of the parolee and guide the parolee's transition back into society, the condition might have been justified either under the special needs doctrine or because at least part of the requisite "reasonable suspicion" is supplied in this context by the individual-specific knowledge gained through the supervisory relationship.

Likewise, this might have been a different case had a court or parole board imposed the condition at issue based on specific knowledge of the individual's criminal history and projected likelihood of reoffending, or if the State had had in place programmatic safeguards to ensure evenhandedness. See *supra*, at 2197. Under either of those scenarios, the State would at least have gone some way toward averting the greatest mischief wrought by officials'

unfettered discretion. But the search condition here is imposed on *all* parolees—whatever the nature of their crimes, whatever their likelihood of recidivism, and whatever their supervisory needs—without any programmatic procedural protections.

The Court seems to acknowledge that unreasonable searches "inflict dignitary harms that arouse strong resentment in parolees and undermine their ability to reintegrate into productive society." It is satisfied, however, that the California courts' prohibition against "arbitrary, capricious or harassing" searches suffices to avert those harms—which are of course counterproductive to the State's purported aim of rehabilitating former prisoners and reintegrating them into society.

I am unpersuaded. The requirement of individualized suspicion, in all its iterations, is the shield the Framers selected to guard against the evils of arbitrary action, caprice, and harassment. To say that those evils may be averted without that shield is, I fear, to pay lip service to the end while withdrawing the means.

Respectfully, I dissent.

## Questions

1. Identify the government's "special needs" and Donald Curtis Samson's diminished expectations of privacy. How would you balance the needs and this reduction of privacy? Explain your answer.

2. Summarize the arguments of the majority supporting its decision that searches of parolees' homes without either warrants or reasonable suspicion are reasonable.

3. Summarize the arguments of the dissent supporting its argument that searches of parolees' homes without either warrants or reasonable suspicion are unreasonable.

4. Which side has the better arguments? Explain your answer without just repeating the arguments.

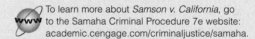 To learn more about *Samson v. California*, go to the Samaha Criminal Procedure 7e website: academic.cengage.com/criminaljustice/samaha.

## EXPLORING FURTHER

# Strip Searches

### Was the Strip Search of the Corrections Officer Reasonable?

*Kennedy v. Hardiman*, 684 F.Supp. 540 (U.S. District Court, N.D. Illinois, Eastern Division 1988)

*FACTS* Some time before noon, Cook County Corrections investigator Leison Linzy received a phone call from a man identifying himself as Agent Gary Miller of the Federal Bureau of Investigation. Agent Miller told Linzy that an Officer Kennedy would be transporting heroin into

Division 5 later that day. He didn't know the officer's first name, nor did he indicate the source of his information. Linzy then called the FBI and confirmed that they employed a man by the name of Gary Miller. Linzy also checked the personnel roster and confirmed that an Officer Kennedy—Alphonso Kennedy—was assigned to work the late shift at Division 5. At this point, Linzy decided he would search Kennedy later that day, and informed Investigators Alfred Brown and Leonard Peterson they'd have to work a little overtime that evening.

As Cook County Corrections Officer Alphonso Kennedy was about to begin his 4:00 P.M.–to-midnight shift, Director of Cook County Department of Corrections Roy Patrick approached Kennedy while he was standing at roll call and ordered him into the nearby men's locker room. Patrick also contacted Linzy, Peterson, and Brown and told them to come to the locker room. Once there, they surrounded Kennedy and searched him, his briefcase, and his locker, forcing him to remove all of his clothes. Then, in plain view of other officers, they examined his body cavities. They found nothing. Was the strip search reasonable?

*DECISION* No. According to the District Court:

> In this case, a reasonable jury could certainly conclude that the extensive search of plaintiff was unreasonable. The search was initiated by Patrick who knew, at most, that an FBI agent had informed Linzy that an Officer Kennedy would be bringing drugs into the prison. He did not know the source of the agent's information, the first name of the accused officer, or the intended recipient of the drugs. Nor does it appear that he, or any of the investigators, had any information regarding the quantity of drugs that the officer would be bringing into the prison.
>
> Nevertheless, he authorized an extensive strip/body cavity search of an officer in a place where the officer's friends and colleagues would be almost certain to witness it. Under these circumstances, this court cannot say that the search was reasonable as a matter of law. . . . A bare anonymous tip does not provide the requisite "reasonable suspicion" for an extensive strip/body cavity search such as the one involved here. The only "corroboration" Patrick had of the anonymous tip was that an Officer Kennedy did indeed work in Division 5, a fact no more indicative that he sold drugs than that he had an inmate who did not like him.
>
> Further, there is no evidence in the record that the officer or officers who conducted the body cavity search had any more information than did Patrick regarding the identity or the reliability of the informant. Thus, this court cannot say as a matter of law that the search was reasonable under clearly established legal principles.

 To read the full text of the Exploring Further excerpt, go to the Samaha Criminal Procedure 7e website: academic.cengage.com/criminaljustice/samaha.

# EMPLOYEE DRUG SEARCHES

Searches to uncover employee drug use through drug testing are directed at the special need to reduce the danger to public safety caused by pilots, bus drivers, railway engineers, and others who work while they're under the influence of alcohol and other drugs. But meeting that need obviously conflicts with these employees' privacy. According to Associate U.S. Supreme Court Justice Sandra Day O'Connor, dissenting in *Vernonia School District v. Acton* (1995, 672): "State-compelled, state-monitored collecting of urine, while perhaps not the most intrusive of searches (visual body cavity searches) is still particularly destructive of privacy and offensive to personal dignity."

The Supreme Court dealt with the problem of balancing the government's need and employees' privacy in the companion cases of *Skinner v. Railway Labor Executive Association* (1989) and *National Treasury Employees Union v. Von Raab* (1989). The Court ruled in both cases that testing the blood, breath, and urine of some public employees, in accordance with administrative regulations, without either warrants or individualized suspicion, is reasonable.

In *Skinner*, the Court upheld Federal Railroad Administration (FRA) regulations mandating drug and alcohol testing of employees following their involvement in major accidents and breath and urine tests for employees who violated safety rules. The

Court stressed the need to "prevent and deter that hazardous conduct" (633) by "those engaged in safety-sensitive tasks" (620). It also stressed "the limited discretion exercised" by the employers during the testing (633).

*Von Raab* approved Treasury regulations that required testing U.S. Customs Service employees whenever they were transferred or promoted to positions directly related to drug interdiction or to positions requiring them to carry firearms. According to the Court, the testing regulations passed the balancing test:

> We think Customs employees who are directly involved in the interdiction of illegal drugs or who are required to carry firearms in the line of duty . . . have a diminished expectation of privacy in respect to the intrusions occasioned by a urine test. Unlike most private citizens or government employees in general, employees involved in drug interdiction reasonably should expect effective inquiry into their fitness and probity.
>
> Much the same is true of employees who are required to carry firearms. Because successful performance of their duties depends uniquely on their judgment and dexterity, these employees cannot reasonably expect to keep from the Service personal information that bears directly on their fitness.
>
> While reasonable tests designed to elicit this information doubtless infringe some privacy expectations, we do not believe these regulations outweigh the Government's compelling interest in preventing the promotion of drug users to positions where they might endanger the integrity of our Nation's borders or the life of the citizenry. (672)

Justices Marshall and Brennan dissented in both cases, reiterating their position opposing any "special needs" exception to the probable cause requirement; protesting the expansion of the exception to include body searches (breath, urine, and blood tests) without even reasonable suspicion; and challenging the majority's tipping the balance in favor of the government.

Justices Stevens and Scalia dissented in *Von Raab*. They argued that whereas the result in *Skinner* was supported by "the demonstrated frequency of drug and alcohol use by the targeted class of employees, and the demonstrated connection between such use and grave harm," in *Von Raab*, the government didn't cite a single instance "in which the cause of bribe-taking, or of poor aim, or of unsympathetic law enforcement, or of compromise of classified information was drug use" (683). According to Justice Scalia, who wrote the dissent:

> . . . I do not believe for a minute that the driving force behind these drug-testing rules was any of the feeble justifications put forward by counsel here and accepted by the Court. The only plausible explanation, in my view, is what the Commissioner himself offered in the concluding sentence of his memorandum to Customs Service employees announcing the program: "Implementation of the drug screening program would set an important example in our country's struggle with this most serious threat to our national health and security." . . . (686)
>
> What better way to show that the Government is serious about its "war on drugs" than to subject its employees on the front line of that war to this invasion of their privacy and affront to their dignity? To be sure, there is only a slight chance that it will prevent some serious public harm resulting from Service employee drug use, but it will show to the world that the Service is "clean," and—most important of all—will demonstrate the determination of the Government to eliminate this scourge of our society! I think it obvious that this justification is unacceptable; that the impairment of individual liberties cannot be the means of making a point; that symbolism, even symbolism for so worthy a cause as the abolition of unlawful drugs, cannot validate an otherwise unreasonable search. (686–87)
>
> Those who lose because of the lack of understanding that begot the present exercise in symbolism are not just the Customs Service employees, whose dignity is thus offended, but all of us—who suffer a coarsening of our national manners that ultimately give the Fourth Amendment its content, and who become subject to the administration of federal officials whose respect for our privacy can hardly be greater than the small respect they have been taught to have for their own. (687)

# STUDENT SEARCHES

For centuries, minors have lacked some fundamental rights enjoyed by adults, including the right to be let alone by the government. This is especially true while they're in school. According to the legal doctrine *in loco parentis*, school administrators are substitute parents while students are in school. Inspections of students and their stuff during school hours and activities are searches. To determine whether they're reasonable searches, courts weigh the special need for schools to maintain an environment where learning can thrive against students' privacy.

The U.S. Supreme Court had to balance the special need of high schools against high-school students' privacy in *New Jersey v. T. L. O.* (1985). A teacher at a New Jersey high school caught T. L. O., a 14-year-old freshman, and a friend smoking cigarettes in the girls' bathroom. The teacher took them to the principal's office. T. L. O. denied she was smoking; in fact, she denied she smoked at all.

The assistant vice-principal demanded to see her purse, opened it, and found a pack of cigarettes; he also noticed a package of cigarette rolling papers commonly used in smoking marijuana. So he searched the purse more thoroughly and found marijuana, a pipe, plastic bags, a fairly substantial amount of money, and two letters that implicated T. L. O. in marijuana dealing.

The state brought delinquency charges, and the case eventually reached the U.S. Supreme Court, where the Court had to decide whether the Fourth Amendment applied to searches by school officials. Two questions confronted the Court: Does the Fourth Amendment apply to school searches? And was this search reasonable? According to the Court, the answer to both questions is yes. The Court held that the Fourth Amendment's ban on unreasonable searches and seizures applies to searches conducted by public school officials. Furthermore, school officials can't escape the commands of the Fourth Amendment because of their authority over schoolchildren. When they search students, they aren't *in loco parentis* (acting as parents); so students have a reasonable expectation of privacy. But that expectation is limited. Striking a balance between students' reasonable expectations of privacy and the school's legitimate need to maintain a healthy learning environment calls for easing the restrictions on searches of students.

Therefore, school officials don't have to get warrants, and they don't need probable cause before they search students. Reasonable suspicion is enough.

Does the right to search high-school students extend to testing some for drugs? And how does the law view searching college students' dorm rooms? Let's look at each of these issues.

## Drug Testing of High-School Students

The most frequent special need that courts have dealt with, and the first case to reach the U.S. Supreme Court, involved student athlete drug testing. In *Vernonia School District v. Acton* (1995), the Court found that random (without individualized suspicion) drug testing of all students voluntarily participating in the school district's athletic programs was reasonable.

School policy required all students wishing to participate in school sports to sign a form consenting to urinalysis testing for drugs. Parental consent was also required. Athletes were tested at the beginning of the season for their sport. Then, once a week, 10 percent of the teams were selected blindly for follow-up testing. An adult of the same sex accompanied an athlete undergoing testing to a restroom. Each fully clothed boy would produce a sample at a urinal with his back to the monitor, who stood 12 to 15 feet behind the boy. The monitor was allowed to (but didn't always) watch while the sample was produced and to listen for "normal sounds of urination" (650). Girls produced their samples in an enclosed bathroom stall, where monitors could hear but not observe the girls.

If athletes tested positive, they had to take a second test. If they tested positive twice, they had the option of participating in a six-week assistance program, including weekly testing or being suspended from athletics for a specific length of time.

To determine reasonableness, the Court balanced the competing interests. On the privacy side, Justice Scalia pointed out that high-school students have a lesser expectation of privacy than adults. Student athletes have even less than students generally because they have to suit up and shower in public locker rooms. Furthermore, the way the testing was done minimized the invasion—boys were observed only from behind; girls were behind closed stall doors.

On the special-need side, the Court called the government's interest in deterring drug use by school kids "important—indeed perhaps compelling" (661). According to the Court:

> As for the immediacy of the District's concerns: We are not inclined to question—indeed, we could not possibly find clearly erroneous—the District Court's conclusion that "a large segment of the student body, particularly those involved in interscholastic athletics, was in a state of rebellion," that "disciplinary actions had reached 'epidemic proportions,'" and that "the rebellion was being fueled by alcohol and drug abuse as well as by the student's misperceptions about the drug culture." (662–63)

The Court concluded that the special need trumped the student athletes' privacy and held that the warrantless searches without individualized suspicion were reasonable.

*Vernonia* wasn't the Court's last word on school drug testing. In our next case excerpt, *Board of Education v. Earls* (2002), the Court expanded the reasonableness of drug testing to include students who participated in *all* school activities.

## C A S E   *Was the Student Urinalysis Testing Reasonable?*

### Board of Education of Independent School District No. 92 of Pottawatomie County v. Earls

535 U.S. 822 (2002)

#### HISTORY

Lindsay Earls and other high school students challenged the constitutionality of their school's suspicionless urinalysis drug testing policy. The U.S. District Court for the Western District of Oklahoma upheld the school's policy, and the students appealed. The U.S. Court of Appeals for the Tenth Circuit reversed. After granting certiorari, the Supreme Court reversed.

THOMAS, J., JOINED BY REHNQUIST, C.J., AND SCALIA, KENNEDY, AND BREYER, JJ.

The Student Activities Drug Testing Policy implemented by the Board of Education of Independent School District

No. 92 of Pottawatomie County (School District) requires all students who participate in competitive extracurricular activities to submit to drug testing. Because this Policy reasonably serves the School District's important interest in detecting and preventing drug use among its students, we hold that it is constitutional.

#### FACTS

The city of Tecumseh, Oklahoma, is a rural community located approximately 40 miles southeast of Oklahoma City. The School District administers all Tecumseh public schools. In the fall of 1998, the School District adopted the Student Activities Drug Testing Policy (Policy), which requires all middle and high school students to consent to drug testing in order to participate in any extracurricular activity.

In practice, the Policy has been applied only to competitive extracurricular activities sanctioned by the Oklahoma Secondary Schools Activities Association, such as the

Academic Team, Future Farmers of America, Future Home-makers of America, band, choir, pom-pom, cheerleading, and athletics. Under the Policy, students are required to take a drug test before participating in an extracurricular activity, must submit to random drug testing while partic-ipating in that activity, and must agree to be tested at any time upon reasonable suspicion. The urinalysis tests are designed to detect only the use of illegal drugs, including amphetamines, marijuana, cocaine, opiates, and barbitu-rates, not medical conditions or the presence of autho-rized prescription medications.

At the time of their suit, both respondents attended Tecumseh High School. Respondent Lindsay Earls was a member of the show choir, the marching band, the Academic Team, and the National Honor Society. Respondent Daniel James sought to participate in the Academic Team. Together with their parents, Earls and James brought a § 1983 action [Chapter 11] against the School District. . . .

## OPINION

. . . Given that the School District's Policy is not in any way related to the conduct of criminal investigations, respon-dents do not contend that the School District requires probable cause before testing students for drug use. Respondents instead argue that drug testing must be based at least on some level of individualized suspicion. It is true that we generally determine the reasonableness of a search by balancing the nature of the intrusion on the individ-ual's privacy against the promotion of legitimate govern-mental interests.

But we have long held that the Fourth Amendment imposes no irreducible requirement of individualized sus-picion. . . . Significantly, this Court has previously held that "special needs" inhere in the public school context. . . . In particular, a finding of individualized suspicion may not be necessary when a school conducts drug testing.

In *Vernonia*, this Court held that the suspicionless drug testing of athletes was constitutional. The Court, however, did not simply authorize all school drug testing, but rather conducted a fact-specific balancing of the intrusion on the children's Fourth Amendment rights against the promotion of legitimate governmental interests. Apply-ing the principles of *Vernonia* to the somewhat different facts of this case, we conclude that Tecumseh's Policy is also constitutional.

We first consider the nature of the privacy interest allegedly compromised by the drug testing. . . . A student's privacy interest is limited in a public school environment where the State is responsible for maintaining discipline, health, and safety. Schoolchildren are routinely required to submit to physical examinations and vaccinations against disease. Securing order in the school environment sometimes requires that students be subjected to greater controls than those appropriate for adults.

. . . Students who participate in competitive extracur-ricular activities voluntarily subject themselves to . . .

intrusions on their privacy. . . . Some of these clubs and activities require occasional off-campus travel and com-munal undress. All of them have their own rules and requirements for participating students that do not apply to the student body as a whole. . . . This regulation of extracurricular activities further diminishes the expecta-tion of privacy among schoolchildren. We therefore con-clude that the students affected by this Policy have a lim-ited expectation of privacy.

Next, we consider the character of the intrusion imposed by the Policy. Urination is "an excretory function traditionally shielded by great privacy." But the "degree of intrusion" on one's privacy caused by collecting a urine sample "depends upon the manner in which production of the urine sample is monitored."

Under the Policy, a faculty monitor waits outside the closed restroom stall for the student to produce a sample and must "listen for the normal sounds of urination in order to guard against tampered specimens and to insure an accurate chain of custody." The monitor then pours the sample into two bottles that are sealed and placed into a mailing pouch along with a consent form signed by the student. This procedure is virtually identical to that reviewed in *Vernonia*, except that it additionally protects privacy by allowing male students to produce their sam-ples behind a closed stall. Given that we considered the method of collection in *Vernonia* a "negligible" intrusion, the method here is even less problematic.

In addition, the Policy clearly requires that the test results be kept in confidential files separate from a stu-dent's other educational records and released to school personnel only on a "need to know" basis. . . .

Moreover, the test results are not turned over to any law enforcement authority. Nor do the test results here lead to the imposition of discipline or have any academic conse-quences. Rather, the only consequence of a failed drug test is to limit the student's privilege of participating in extracur-ricular activities. Indeed, a student may test positive for drugs twice and still be allowed to participate in extracur-ricular activities. . . . Only after a third positive test will the student be suspended from participating in any extracurric-ular activity for the remainder of the school year, or 88 school days, whichever is longer. Given the minimally intrusive nature of the sample collection and the limited uses to which the test results are put, we conclude that the invasion of students' privacy is not significant.

Finally, this Court must consider the nature and imme-diacy of the government's concerns and the efficacy of the Policy in meeting them. This Court has already articulated in detail the importance of the governmental concern in preventing drug use by schoolchildren. . . . The necessity for the State to act is magnified by the fact that this evil is being visited not just upon individuals at large, but upon children for whom it has undertaken a special responsi-bility of care and direction. . . . The nationwide drug epi-demic makes the war against drugs a pressing concern in every school.

. . . The School District in this case has presented specific evidence of drug use at Tecumseh schools. Teachers testified that they had seen students who appeared to be under the influence of drugs and that they had heard students speaking openly about using drugs. A drug dog found marijuana cigarettes near the school parking lot. Police officers once found drugs or drug paraphernalia in a car driven by a Future Farmers of America member. And the school board president reported that people in the community were calling the board to discuss the "drug situation." . . .

Respondents consider the proffered evidence insufficient and argue that there is no "real and immediate interest" to justify a policy of drug testing nonathletes. We have recognized, however, that a demonstrated problem of drug abuse is not in all cases necessary to the validity of a testing regime, but that some showing does "shore up an assertion of special need for a suspicionless general search program." . . .

Given the nationwide epidemic of drug use, and the evidence of increased drug use in Tecumseh schools, it was entirely reasonable for the School District to enact this particular drug testing policy. . . .

We also reject respondents' argument that drug testing must presumptively be based upon an individualized reasonable suspicion of wrongdoing. . . . Such a regime would place an additional burden on public school teachers who are already tasked with the difficult job of maintaining order and discipline. A program of individualized suspicion might unfairly target members of unpopular groups. The fear of lawsuits resulting from such targeted searches may chill enforcement of the program, rendering it ineffective in combating drug use. . . .

Finally, we find that testing students who participate in extracurricular activities is a reasonably effective means of addressing the School District's legitimate concerns in preventing, deterring, and detecting drug use. . . . We conclude that the drug testing of Tecumseh students who participate in extracurricular activities effectively serves the School District's interest in protecting the safety and health of its students.

Within the limits of the Fourth Amendment, local school boards must assess the desirability of drug testing schoolchildren. In upholding the constitutionality of the Policy, we express no opinion as to its wisdom. Rather, we hold only that Tecumseh's Policy is a reasonable means of furthering the School District's important interest in preventing and deterring drug use among its schoolchildren.

Accordingly, we REVERSE the judgment of the Court of Appeals. *It is so ordered.*

## DISSENT

GINSBURG, J., JOINED BY STEVENS, O'CONNOR, AND SOUTER, JJ.

. . . Tecumseh students participating in competitive extracurricular activities other than athletics share two relevant characteristics with the athletes of *Vernonia*. First, both groups attend public schools. . . . Concern for student health and safety is basic to the school's caretaking, and it is undeniable that "drug use carries a variety of health risks for children, including death from overdose."

. . . This case resembles *Vernonia* only in that the School Districts in both cases conditioned engagement in activities outside the obligatory curriculum on random subjection to urinalysis. The defining characteristics of the two programs, however, are entirely dissimilar. The Vernonia district sought to test a subpopulation of students distinguished by their reduced expectation of privacy, their special susceptibility to drug-related injury, and their heavy involvement with drug use. The Tecumseh district seeks to test a much larger population associated with none of these factors. It does so, moreover, without carefully safeguarding student confidentiality and without regard to the program's untoward effects. . . . Its unreasonable reach renders it impermissible under the Fourth Amendment.

In *Chandler v. Miller* (1997), this Court inspected Georgia's requirement that candidates for state office pass a drug test; we held that the requirement did not fit within the closely guarded category of constitutionally permissible suspicionless searches. Georgia's testing prescription, the record showed, responded to no "concrete danger," was supported by no evidence of a particular problem, and targeted a group not involved in "high-risk, safety-sensitive tasks," We concluded:

What is left, after close review of Georgia's scheme, is the image the State seeks to project. By requiring candidates for public office to submit to drug testing, Georgia displays its commitment to the struggle against drug abuse. . . . The need revealed, in short, is symbolic, not "special," as that term draws meaning from our case law.

Close review of Tecumseh's policy compels a similar conclusion. That policy was not shown to advance the special needs existing in the public school context to maintain swift and informal disciplinary procedures and order in the schools. What is left is the School District's undoubted purpose to heighten awareness of its abhorrence of, and strong stand against, drug abuse. But the desire to augment communication of this message does not trump the right of persons—even of children within the schoolhouse gate—to be "secure in their persons . . . against unreasonable searches and seizures." U.S. Const., Amdt. 4.

In *Chandler*, the Court referred to a pathmarking dissenting opinion in which Justice Brandeis recognized the importance of teaching by example: "Our Government is the potent, the omnipresent teacher. For good or for ill, it teaches the whole people by its example." (*Olmstead v. U.S.*, 1928). That wisdom should guide decision makers in the instant case: The government is nowhere more a teacher than when it runs a public school.

It is a sad irony that the petitioning School District seeks to justify its edict here by trumpeting "the schools' custodial and tutelary responsibility for children." In regulating an athletic program or endeavoring to combat an exploding drug epidemic, a school's custodial obligations may permit searches that would otherwise unacceptably abridge students' rights. When custodial duties are not ascendant, however, schools' tutelary obligations to their students require them to "teach by example" by avoiding symbolic measures that diminish constitutional protections. "That [schools] are educating the young for citizenship is reason for scrupulous protection of Constitutional freedoms of the individual, if we are not to strangle the free mind at its source and teach youth to discount important principles of our government as mere platitudes." *West Virginia Bd. of Ed. v. Barnette.*

## Questions

1. Identify the special need and the privacy invasions in the case.

2. How would you balance them? Explain your answer.

3. Summarize the arguments of the majority opinion supporting its decision that the drug testing policy amounts to a reasonable Fourth Amendment search and seizure.

4. Summarize the arguments of the dissenting opinion supporting its conclusion that the drug testing policy is an unreasonable Fourth Amendment search and seizure.

5. Do you see a *constitutional* difference between the group tested in *Vernonia* and in *Earls*? Explain your answer.

6. Would it be reasonable to test all high-school students? Why or why not? Would you favor such a policy?

7. Who should decide the reasonableness of drug testing students: the state legislature, board of education, or the courts? Explain your answer.

## Searches of College Students

What about searches of college students? The rules are different because the setting is different. Most searches are of dormitory rooms, and, more often than not, law enforcement officers (municipal or college police) participate in the searches. Also, college students are older and are entitled to a greater expectation of privacy. Do these differences matter to the Fourth Amendment? The U.S. Supreme Court hasn't answered the question of how much protection the Fourth Amendment guarantees to college students in their dormitory rooms, but federal and state courts have. One decision is our next case excerpt, *Commonwealth v. Neilson* (1996), which upheld the suppression of marijuana evidence in a state drug prosecution. The marijuana was found in a search of Eric Neilson's dorm room.

## CASE *Was the Search of the Dormitory Room Reasonable?*

### Commonwealth v. Neilson
666 N.E.2d 984 (Mass. 1996)

### HISTORY

The defendant, Eric W. Neilson, was charged with illegal possession of marihuana and cultivating and distributing marihuana, in violation of G.L. c. 94C, § § 32C, 34 (1994 ed.). A District Court judge granted Neilson's motion to suppress evidence and contraband obtained in a search of his dormitory room at Fitchburg State College. The Massachusetts Supreme Judicial Court

transferred the case from the Massachusetts Appeals Court, and affirmed the District Court's decision.

LYNCH, J.

### FACTS

At the time of his arrest, Eric Neilson (defendant) was a twenty-three-year-old student living in a dormitory at Fitchburg State College, a public institution. Before moving into the dormitory, the defendant signed a residence hall contract, which stated, in relevant part, that "residence life staff members will enter student rooms to inspect for hazards to health or personal safety."

On the morning of April 30, 1993, a maintenance worker heard a cat inside a dormitory suite containing four bedrooms, including the defendant's. He reported the information to college officials, who visited the suite and informed one of the residents (not the defendant) that any cat must be removed pursuant to the college's health and safety regulations.

That afternoon, a college official posted notices on all four bedroom doors of the suite, informing the students of the possible violation of college policy and alerting them that a "door to door check" would be conducted by 10 P.M. that night to ensure that the cat had been removed.

That night, the officials returned; the defendant was not present. While searching the defendant's bedroom, the officials noticed a light emanating from the closet. The officials, fearing a fire hazard, opened the closet door. There, they discovered two four-foot tall marihuana plants, along with lights, fertilizer, and numerous other materials for marihuana cultivation and use.

The officials stopped their investigation at that point, and requested the assistance of the Fitchburg State College campus police, who have powers of arrest. The police arrived at the suite, entered the bedroom, and observed the marihuana plants and other apparatus. They took photographs of the evidence and then, with the help of the college officials, removed it from the room. At no time did the police seek, obtain, or possess a warrant for the search.

## OPINION

. . . The right to be free from unreasonable searches and seizures as guaranteed by the Fourth Amendment to the United States Constitution applies when the police search a dormitory room in a public college. A dormitory room is a student's home away from home. To be reasonable in the constitutional sense, a search usually must be supported by probable cause and be accompanied by a search warrant, unless there are circumstances excusing the use of a warrant. The probable cause and warrant requirements are relaxed, however, in the case of searches that occur in elementary and secondary public schools. . . .

The Commonwealth urges us to extend the lesser protections afforded to high school students into the collegiate arena. Although the courts that have examined the issue are split on whether the Fourth Amendment requires probable cause and a warrant in college searches, when police are involved and the evidence obtained is to be used in a criminal proceeding, courts generally require probable cause and a warrant, absent express consent or exigent circumstances.

The defendant does not contend (and the District Court judge did not find) that the initial search of the dormitory room by college officials was improper. The defendant consented to reasonable searches to enforce the college's health and safety regulations when he signed the residence contract. The hunt for the elusive feline fit within the scope of that consent. Similarly, when the college officials opened the closet door they were reasonably concerned about health and safety. Thus, the initial search was reasonable because it was intended to enforce a legitimate health and safety rule that related to the college's function as an educational institution.

Instead, the crux of the defendant's argument is that constitutional violation occurred when the campus police searched the room and seized evidence. We agree. The police entered the room without a warrant, consent, or exigent circumstances. This search was unreasonable and violated the defendant's Fourth Amendment rights. The Commonwealth contends that, since the college officials were in the room by consent, and observed the drugs in plain view while pursuing legitimate objectives, the police officers' warrantless entry was proper. Furthermore, the Commonwealth argues, the police action was lawful because it did not exceed the scope of the prior search and seizure by college officials. We disagree.

First, there was no consent to the police entry and search of the room. The defendant's consent was given, not to police officials, but to the University and the latter cannot fragmentize, share or delegate it. While the college officials were entitled to conduct a health and safety inspection, they clearly had no authority to consent to or join in a police search for evidence of crime.

Second, the plain view doctrine does not apply to the police seizure, where the officers were not lawfully present in the dormitory room when they made their plain view observations. While the college officials were legitimately present in the room to enforce a reasonable health and safety regulation, the sole purpose of the warrantless police entry into the dormitory room was to confiscate contraband for purposes of a criminal proceeding. An entry for such a purpose required a warrant where, as here, there was no showing of express consent or exigent circumstances.

We conclude that, when the campus police entered the defendant's dormitory room without a warrant, they violated the defendant's Fourth Amendment rights. All evidence obtained as a result of that illegal search was properly suppressed by the judge below.

Judgment AFFIRMED.

## Questions

1. Explain why the court concluded Neilson gave consent to the officials but not to the campus police to enter and search his room. Do you agree? Defend your answer.

**2.** List the specific invasions on Neilson's privacy.

**3.** Summarize the reasons why the court decided the search by college officials was reasonable and the search by campus police was unreasonable.

**4.** Assume you're Neilson's lawyer and argue that the search by college officials was unreasonable. Back up your answer with facts and arguments made by the state in the case.

**5.** Do you think Neilson's privacy outweighs the college's special needs? Back up your answer.

**6.** Does it matter whether the officials or campus police or city police conduct the search? Defend your answer.

## SUMMARY

**I. Special-Needs Searches**
  A. The U.S. Supreme Court has applied the Fourth Amendment to a wide range of searches to meet "special needs" that go beyond criminal law enforcement.
  B. Special-needs searches include:
    1. Inventory searches
    2. International border searches
    3. Airport searches
    4. Custody-related searches
    5. Student searches
    6. Employee drug testing
  C. "Special-needs searches" doesn't mean they're totally unrelated to law enforcement.
  D. Special-needs searches share four common characteristics:
    1. They're directed at people generally, not just criminal suspects and defendants specifically.
    2. They can result in criminal prosecution and conviction.
    3. They don't require warrants or probable cause.
    4. Their reasonableness depends on balancing the government's special needs against invasions of individual privacy.

**II. Inventory Searches**
  A. Inventory searches consist of examining and making a list of people's personal property and containers held in government custody.
  B. The reasonableness of an inventory search depends on satisfying two elements:
    1. Balancing interests. A search is reasonable if the government's special need outweighs the individual's privacy rights and if it meets at least one of three criteria:
      a. To protect owners' stuff while it's in police custody
      b. To protect law enforcement agencies against lawsuits for the loss, destruction, or theft of owners' stuff
      c. To protect law enforcement officers, detained suspects, and offenders from the danger of bombs, weapons, and illegal drugs that might be hidden in owners' "stuff"

2. Objective basis. Routine procedures, not probable cause or reasonable suspicion, are required:
   a. Following routine, department-approved, written procedures takes the place of probable cause and reasonable suspicion in inventory searches.
   b. This still allows plenty of discretionary decision making by officers.

### III. International Border Searches
A. Searches at international borders without warrants or probable cause are reasonable.
B. The government's special interest in controlling who and what comes into and goes out of the country makes the searches reasonable.
C. Reasonable suspicion is required to back up strip searches for contraband and weapons.
D. Body-cavity searches at the border are only reasonable if they're backed up by probable cause.

### IV. Airport Searches
A. The U.S. Supreme Court has held that airport searches are reasonable without warrants or probable cause.
B. The searches serve two extremely important special needs: the security and safety of air travelers.
C. The special needs clearly outweigh the minimal invasion of privacy, and all invasions apply equally to all passengers who are notified in advance of the searches.

### V. Custody-Related Searches
A. The balance between the special needs to maintain safety, security, and discipline over people locked up in jails and prisons and probationers and parolees outweighs the significantly reduced expectation of privacy that society grants to such people.
B. Prisoners
   1. The reasonableness of searches of prisoners depends on balancing the need to maintain prison and jail security, safety, and discipline against the invasion of prisoners' substantially reduced reasonable expectation of privacy.
   2. Historically, prisoners had no Fourth Amendment rights; the Constitution stopped at the prison gate.
   3. Since *Hudson v. Palmer*, the U.S. Supreme Court has held that prisoners aren't beyond the reach of the Constitution and that no "iron curtain" separates free society from prison society; however, "imprisonment carries with it the loss of many significant rights."
   4. Full-body, strip, and body-cavity searches are Fourth Amendment searches, but they're reasonable without warrants or probable cause if in the particular situation, the need for security, safety, or discipline outweighs prisoners' reasonable expectation of privacy in the particular circumstances of the case.
   5. According to *Padgett v. Donald*, it's reasonable to require incarcerated felons to provide a sample of DNA for analysis and storage in a data bank.
C. Probationers and Parolees
   1. Probationers and parolees have diminished Fourth Amendment rights, even though they're not locked up.
   2. Some courts see conditional release as a privilege, not a right. Other courts have adopted a balancing approach that protects the interest of society by

trying to reduce recidivism while still limiting parolees' and prisoners' right against unreasonable searches and seizures:

    a. Probationers don't enjoy absolute liberty; instead, they get conditional liberty.

    b. Probation and law enforcement officers can search probationers' houses without warrants as long as the searches are backed up by reasonable suspicion.

   3. Parolees have fewer expectations of privacy than probationers, because parole is closer to imprisonment than is probation.

   4. Law enforcement officers can search parolees' homes without either warrants or individualized reasonable suspicion.

## VI. Employee Drug Searches

   A. Searches for employee drug use through drug testing are directed at the special need to reduce danger to the public safety caused by pilots, bus drivers, railway engineers, and others who work while they're under the influence of alcohol or other drugs.

   B. The testing of some public employees without warrants or individualized suspicion, if conducted according to administrative regulations, is reasonable.

## VII. Student Searches

   A. Inspections of students and their stuff during school hours are searches and are weighed against the special needs for schools to maintain an environment where learning can thrive against students' right to privacy.

   B. School officials don't have to get warrants and don't need probable cause to search; reasonable suspicion is enough.

   C. In *Vernonia School District v. Acton,* the U.S. Supreme Court found it reasonable for the school to randomly drug test students who were voluntarily participating in the school district's athletic programs.

   D. In *Board of Education v. Earls,* the Court expanded the ruling to include drug testing for all students involved in all school activities.

   E. College students are entitled to a greater expectation of privacy than high-school students, according to *Commonwealth v. Neilson.*

# REVIEW QUESTIONS

**1.** Identify six special-needs searches that the U.S. Supreme Court recognizes.

**2.** Identify four characteristics that all special-needs searches have in common.

**3.** Identify the two elements that have to be satisfied for an inventory search to be reasonable.

**4.** Under the balancing element, identify the three government interests that make the taking of inventories by law enforcement officers reasonable.

**5.** Identify the objective basis for an inventory search.

**6.** Identify the border exception and the special need the government balances at international borders.

**7.** Identify two extremely important special needs airport searches serve.

8. Why does the court approve of such minimal invasions of privacy during airport searches?

9. Identify the balance in custody-related searches for prisoners, probationers, and parolees.

10. Identify the special need and the objective basis for searches of prisoners.

11. When are strip and body-cavity searches of prisoners reasonable? Explain.

12. Summarize the facts and explain the significance of the Supreme Court's holding in *Hudson v. Palmer*. Summarize the dissent's argument in the case.

13. What, if any significance, does harassment have on prison shakedowns?

14. Explain the significance of testing and storing the DNA of incarcerated felons.

15. Identify two reasons why courts say that probationers and parolees have diminished Fourth Amendment rights.

16. What is the significance of *U.S. v. Knights* in dealing with searches and seizures of probationers?

17. Why do parolees have even more diminished rights against searches and seizures than probationers?

18. Why are employee drug tests reasonable without warrants or probable cause?

19. Identify the special need and the expectation of privacy balanced in searches of high-school students as outlined by the U.S. Supreme Court in *New Jersey v. T. L. O.*

20. Identify the special need and privacy balanced in searches of high-school students.

21. Summarize the facts and the majority and dissenting opinions in *Vernonia School District v. Acton*.

22. Summarize the facts and the majority and dissenting opinions in *Board of Education v. Earls*.

23. How does the setting of searches of college students differ from the setting of searches of high-school students?

24. According to *Commonwealth v. Neilson*, why are searches of college students' dorm rooms reasonable only if backed up by warrants and probable cause?

## KEY TERMS

special-needs searches, p. 244
inventory searches, p. 244
routine-procedure limit, p. 245

border search exception, p. 248
*in loco parentis*, p. 261

# Self-Incrimination

## MAIN POINTS

- Confessions create access to defendants' innermost beliefs, knowledge, and thinking; as such, they're uniquely powerful evidence of guilt *and* remorse.
- Defendants confess their guilt in a variety of settings—to friends, in court, during sentencing, and during interrogations.
- *Miranda* is part of our culture—and our culture wars.
- Interrogation may be unpleasant, but it can help convict the guilty *and* free the innocent.
- Interrogation still takes place in private; privacy results in secrecy, and secrecy depends on an interrogation room where what goes on is hidden.
- Most suspects speak when interrogated.
- Some states require that all interrogations be videotaped to create an objective reviewable record.
- The right to remain silent is tied to the ancient common-law rule that confessions have to be voluntary.
- Modern self-incrimination law grew out of early cases involving White mobs who terrorized and tortured poor, illiterate Blacks until they confessed.
- As soon as the police focus their attention on a single suspect, the suspect's right to counsel attaches.
- *Miranda v. Arizona* established a "bright line" rule (the *Miranda* warnings) to govern custodial interrogation.
- *Miranda* focused on coercive *environments*, not just coercive *places*.
- Whenever a police officer conducts a custodial interrogation, she has to issue the *Miranda* warnings before the interrogation begins.
- Suspects can, and most do, expressly or impliedly waive their right to remain silent and to have a lawyer, but the waiver has to be voluntary and based on knowledge of their rights.
- Confessions are involuntary only if officers engaged in coercive behavior and the coercive conduct caused the suspect to make incriminating statements.

*No person shall be compelled in any criminal case to be a witness against himself.*

U.S. Constitution, Fifth Amendment

*No person would teach such a doctrine to his children; the lessons parents preach is that while a misdeed, even a serious one, will generally be forgiven, a failure to make a clean breast of it will not. Every hour of the day people are being asked to explain their conduct to parents, employers or teachers. Those who are questioned consider themselves to be morally bound to respond, and the questioners believe it to be proper to take action if they do not.* 🔊

Judge Henry Friendly (1968)

"**M**iranda has become embedded in routine police practice to the point where the warnings have become part of our national culture." These are the words of Chief Justice William Rehnquist (2000). What was the occasion for his comment? He was reading the U.S. Supreme Court's decision in *Dickerson v. U.S.* (2000). In that case, the Court ruled that Congress doesn't have the power to overrule *Miranda v. Arizona* (1966), something it had tried to do in 1968. In that year, in a burst of "get tough on criminals" legislation, Congress passed a law saying officers don't have to warn suspects of their rights to a lawyer and against self-incrimination before they interrogate them. Federal and state officials ignored the law until 1997 when a Virginia federal court relied on the 1968 statute to admit Charles Dickerson's confession obtained after FBI agents gave him defective *Miranda* warnings. The 1968 law, the 1997 case relying on it, and the Supreme Court's decision declaring the law unconstitutional reflect a long and emotional debate over the right against self-incrimination.

In this chapter, we'll look at the role of confessions, what the Constitution has to say about self-incrimination, the landmark *Miranda v. Arizona* case and how it has changed the way confessions and interrogations are handled by the law, and what happens when suspects waive their right to remain silent and voluntarily incriminate themselves.

# THE NATURE AND THE ROLE OF CONFESSIONS

Confessions play an ambivalent role in society and law, and that ambivalence is ancient. In many religions, confession is the first step to forgiveness and finally redemption; in the law, they're the proof that justifies blame and punishment. Because confessions create access to defendants' innermost beliefs, knowledge, and thinking, they're uniquely powerful evidence of guilt *and* contrition. But they can also be uniquely dangerous and misleading. "The upshot has been heavy reliance on confessions coupled with extensive regulation of their use" (Seidman 2002, 229).

Defendants confess their guilt, or make incriminating statements, in four different settings. (*Incriminating statements* refers to statements that fall short of full confessions.) First, some confess to their friends and associates, who report the statements to officials. These confessions can be used against those who make them, with a major exception you'll learn about when we look at the right to counsel. Second, anyone who pleads guilty confesses his or her guilt; these are far and away the most common confessions in the criminal justice system (Chapter 13). Third, convicted offenders make incriminating statements during the sentencing process, most often because they want to demonstrate they're sorry.

Fourth, and most important to us in this chapter, suspects confess, or at least make incriminating statements, during police interrogations after they're arrested. These confessions have generated controversy and a complicated set of rules regulating them. We'll devote most of the chapter to confessions made during police interrogation.

But we'll also examine broader questions related to confessions and self-incrimination, including the importance of the constitutional provisions that regulate them.

Let's look first at the settings in which people incriminate themselves. Then, we'll examine the importance of confessions and interrogations and the effect videotaping has on confessions.

## The Self-Incrimination Setting

The chief justice was certainly right in his chapter opening quote—*Miranda* is part of our culture. But what he left out is it's also part of our culture wars. Perhaps no procedure has generated more hostility between social conservatives and social liberals. On the popular TV cop show *NYPD Blue,* the "good cops" Andy Sipowicz and whoever his current partner was (it was a long list) waged a "war on *Miranda.*" In almost every episode, a "scumbag" murderer—or his lawyer—made a "mockery of the system" by taunting the cops with his "rights." Then, Sipowicz and his partner threatened, shoved, and usually wound up beating a confession out of the "worthless animal" called a "suspect." We all knew he was guilty (it was always a man by the way), and we were invited to hate not only the murderer but also the system that provided such scumbags with rights.

But this popular portrayal of saintly cops and satanic criminals hid the complexity of self-incrimination in practice where it most frequently occurs, police interrogation and resulting confessions. The atmosphere in police stations is (and it's supposed to be) strange, intimidating, and hostile to criminal suspects. It's not like being stopped, asked a few questions, and frisked in the familiar surroundings of public places (Chapter 4).

In police stations, suspects are searched thoroughly—sometimes strip-searched and, occasionally, subjected to body-cavity searches (Chapter 6); they have to stand in lineups (Chapter 9); and, they're interrogated incommunicado. (This isn't a criticism; it's a description.) Being taken to police stations isn't supposed to be pleasant for suspects. The atmosphere and the actions are supposed to flush out the truth about suspects' possible criminal behavior or what they know about someone else's criminal behavior.

By the time officers bring arrested suspects to police stations, their investigation has focused on those particular suspects. This period when the police have shifted their attention from a general investigation of a crime to building a case against a named individual is called the **accusatory stage of the criminal process.** During this stage, balancing the needs of law enforcement against the interests of individual privacy and liberty carries higher stakes for both suspects and law enforcement. Defining the proper balance between these competing social interests during the period when the police hold suspects in custody but before prosecutors have charged them with crimes has always generated controversy over how much the U.S. Constitution protects criminal suspects in police custody.

These aren't black-and-white issues. Consider the following hypothetical situations. In which cases can the persons "be compelled to be witnesses" against themselves?

1. A police officer asks a man he has stopped on the street, "What are you doing out at 1:30 A.M.?" The man replies, "I'm trying to buy some crystal meth, as if it's any of your business."

2. An officer hears screams coming from an apartment. He enters without knocking and asks, "What's going on here?" A woman answers, "I just beat up my baby."

3. An elderly woman is beaten when she won't give her purse to three muggers. She is left on the street and dies of exposure. Officers in relays question an 18-year-old suspect for six hours without a break. Some officers get tough, bullying the youth and telling him he's in "big trouble" if he doesn't talk. But they never touch him. One officer befriends him, telling him the officer knows whoever took the purse didn't mean to kill the woman and that, anyway, it was really her fault for resisting. The young man finally weakens and confesses.

4. A police officer, while interrogating a suspect in the police station, promises, "If you'll just tell me the truth about raping the college student, I'll see to it that the prosecutor only charges you with misdemeanor assault." The suspect asks, "You can do that?" The officer replies, "Sure, I wouldn't tell you something I couldn't do." The suspect says, "O.K., I did it." He later puts the confession in writing.

5. An officer tells a suspect brought to the police station for questioning, "You might as well admit you killed your husband, because your neighbor already told us he saw the whole thing." The officer is lying. The suspect replies, "My God, I knew I should've pulled the shades; that nosy bastard's always spying on me."

Reconsider your answers after you've read the rest of the chapter. In the meantime, to better understand the law of self-incrimination, interrogation, and confessions, we'll examine their importance and look at the potential for the abuse of interrogation.

## The Importance of Confessions and Interrogation

Almost a half century ago, U.S. Supreme Court Justice Felix Frankfurter (*Culombe v. Connecticut* 1961) explained why he believed police interrogation and confessions were important:

> Despite modern advances in the technology of crime detection, offenses frequently occur about which things cannot be made to speak. And where there cannot be found innocent human witnesses to such offenses, nothing remains—if police investigation is not to be balked before it has fairly begun—but to seek out possible guilty witnesses and ask them questions, witnesses, that is, who are suspected of knowing something about the offense precisely because they are suspected of implication in it. (571)

Fred Inbau—for 60 years a professor of law, author of the leading manual on police interrogation, and one of the best interrogators of his time—gave three reasons why he supported Justice Frankfurter's position:

1. Police can't solve many crimes unless guilty people confess or suspects give police information that can convict someone else who's guilty.

2. Criminals don't confess unless the police either catch them in the act or interrogate them in private.

3. Police have to use "less refined methods" when they interrogate suspects than are "appropriate for the transaction of ordinary, every-day affairs by and between law-abiding citizens." (Inbau 1961)

We don't know, empirically, how close to the truth Justice Frankfurter and Professor Inbau were about the importance of interrogations and confessions. U.S. Supreme Court Chief Justice Earl Warren—himself an experienced and effective former prosecutor—explained why: "Interrogation still takes place in privacy. Privacy results in secrecy and this in turn results in a gap in our knowledge as to what in fact goes on in the interrogation room" (*Miranda v. Arizona* 1966).

We know very little about the truth today because there's very little empirical research, and it's conflicting. Sociologist Richard Leo's (1996, 1998) research has made a significant start. Professor Leo spent more than five hundred hours inside the interrogation rooms of a major urban police department and also viewed videotaped **custodial interrogations** (police questioning suspects while holding them against their will, usually in a police station but sometimes in other places) from two other departments. His observations produced important findings, including:

1. Interrogators rarely coerce suspects to confess (4 out of 182 cases; none of the four involved *physical* coercion).

2. Almost all interrogations last less than an hour.

3. One in four suspects invokes his *Miranda* rights.

4. Sixty-four percent of suspects interrogated after they waive their rights incriminated themselves. (1998, 65–74) (Paul Cassell [1996] studied a different jurisdiction, the Salt Lake City County Prosecutor's office; he found that 33.3% confessed, gave incriminating statements, or were locked into a false alibi.)

Summing up his findings, Professor Leo (1996) concluded:

Police have successfully adapted their practices to the legal requirements by using conditioning, deemphasizing guilt, and persuasive strategies to orchestrate consent to custodial questioning in most cases. In addition, in response to *Miranda*, police have developed increasingly specialized, sophisticated, and effective interrogation with which they elicit statements from suspects during interrogation. (675)

## False Confessions and Videotaping Interrogations

It is not because a peace officer is more dishonest than the rest of us that we should demand an objective recording of the custodial events. Rather, it is because we are entitled to assume that the police are no less human—and equally inclined to reconstruct and interpret past events in a favorable light—that we should not permit them to be judges of their own cause. (Yale Kamisar in Drizin and Reich 2004, n. 120)

In 1949, U.S. Supreme Court Justice Robert Jackson wrote that he was troubled by three cases the Court decided that day (*Watts v. Indiana* 1949):

In each case police were confronted with one or more brutal murders which the authorities were under the highest duty to solve. Each of these murders was unwitnessed, and the only positive knowledge on which a solution could be based was possessed by the killer. In each there was reasonable ground to suspect an individual but not enough legal evidence to charge him with guilt. In each the police attempted to meet the situation by taking the suspect into custody and interrogating him. This extended over varying periods. In each, confessions were made and received in evidence at the trial.

Checked with external evidence, they are inherently believable, and were not shaken as to truth by anything that occurred at the trial. Each confessor was convicted by a jury and state courts affirmed. This Court sets all three convictions aside. . . . No one suggests that any course held promise of solution of these murders other than to take the suspect into custody for questioning. The alternative was to close the books on the crime and forget it, with the suspect at large. This is a grave choice for a society in which two-thirds of the murders already are closed out as insoluble. (57–58)

I doubt very much if . . . [our Constitution and Bill of Rights] require us to hold that the State may not take into custody and question one suspected reasonably of an unwitnessed murder. *If it does, the people of this country must discipline themselves to seeing their police stand by helplessly while those suspected of murder prowl about unmolested. Is it a necessary price to pay for the fairness which we know as "due process of law"?* [emphasis added] (61–62)

In addition to the danger created by brutal murderers who "prowl about unmolested," Justice Jackson pointed to another danger—false confessions created by police interrogation tactics:

> Of course, no confession that has been obtained by any form of physical violence to the person is reliable and hence no conviction should rest upon one obtained in that manner. *Such treatment not only breaks the will to conceal or lie, but may even break the will to stand by the truth.* [emphasis added] (59–60)

We know there are still false confessions, and we know police still "elicit" them. We *don't* know how often they occur, how often they lead to wrongful convictions, or how much personal and social harm they cause. One reason we don't know is because "most interrogations leading to disputed confessions are not recorded" (Leo and Ofshe 1998, 430–31). This is so despite "numerous authors, from all points on the political spectrum [who] have advocated that police interrogations be taped" (Slobogin 2003, 309). These calls are nothing new. "Calls for recording interrogations are almost as old as the technology itself" (Drizin and Reich 2004, 620). In his classic *Convicting the Innocent* (1932), Edwin Borchard recommended that the solution to protect suspects' right against self-incrimination and to prevent unreliable confessions was to make "phonographic records, which shall alone be introducible as evidence of the prisoner's statements" (370–71).

Many state courts have spoken warmly of recording the whole process of interrogation from *Miranda* warnings, through interrogation, to the confession (*State v. Cook* 2004). However, only two state supreme courts, Alaska (*Stephan v. State* 1985) and Minnesota (*State v. Scales* 1994), require that the police record them. Illinois enacted a statute in 2003 requiring law enforcement departments to record the entire interrogations of murder suspects, not just their confessions (Allen and others 2005, 838).

Before the law went into effect, juries in two cases were shown videotapes of confessions but not interrogations; they acquitted both defendants. Some members of the jury said they could have benefited from the new law. "I wish there had been more videotape of more of the proceedings," one of the jurors said. "We saw 12 minutes, and so it was very hard for me to look at this tape and judge how much of it was truth and how much of it was a lie" (Rozas and Howes 2003, Metro 1).

Other jurors agreed. One, however, didn't. Susanne Sugrue said "showing the video would be too time-consuming and might not convince some jurors, who seem to be predisposed not to trust the police." In the second case, one juror, who didn't want to be identified, offered a third opinion:

> I don't know if that [watching the entire interrogation] would have changed how I voted. I would have to see what was on there before I could say that. But, I definitely think it would be helpful.

Woody Jordan, defense lawyer for one of the acquitted defendants, favors videotaping entire interrogations, but he foresees a problem. Take, for example, his client's case; the interrogation lasted 18 hours. Jordan can see the agencies objecting, "Are you going to tell me you're going to have a jury watch 18 hours of videotape?" Jordan provides his answer, "Well, yeah. It's a murder trial."

The arguments in favor of recording include:

- It creates an objective, reviewable record.

- It enhances jurors' and judges' assessment of credibility by providing a complete record.

- It provides judges and juries with a more accurate picture of what was said; words can convey different meanings, depending on the tone of voice or nuance used.

- It can improve the quality of police work by providing law enforcement officials with the ability to monitor the quality of the interrogation process, and recordings can be used in training courses to demonstrate effective versus ineffective, or legally impermissible, interrogation techniques.

- It preserves judicial resources by discouraging defendants from raising "frivolous" pretrial challenges to confessions. (*State v. Cook* 2004, 556–57)

There are also drawbacks to videotaping:

- The cost, including purchasing the equipment, maintenance, storage, transcription, and remodeling interrogation rooms, can be high.

- It can interfere with interrogation techniques and hamper officers' ability to obtain truthful confessions.

- Suspects may be reluctant to speak candidly in front of cameras. (557–58)

# THE CONSTITUTION AND SELF-INCRIMINATION

The right to remain silent in the face of an accusation has ancient religious and legal origins. The ancient Talmudic law, which put the teachings of Moses into writing, contained an absolute ban on self-incrimination. The ban couldn't ever be waived because self-incrimination violated the natural right of survival.

Jesus was probably exercising this right when he stood before the Roman governor Pontius Pilate, who demanded to know if Jesus was guilty of treason. When Pilate asked,

> "Art thou King of the Jews?"
> Jesus artfully replied, "Thou sayest." Then the chief priests and elders accused Jesus of many crimes. Jesus stood and "answered them nothing."
> Surprised at Jesus' obstinacy, Pilate demanded, "Hearest thou not how many things they witness against thee?" And still Jesus answered him to never a word, insomuch that the governor marveled greatly. (Matthew 27:11–14, Authorized [King James] Version)

The origin of the right to remain silent is also tied to another ancient rule, the common-law rule that confessions had to be voluntary. By the time the right to remain silent appeared in the Fifth Amendment to the U.S. Constitution, it had followed a controversial and complicated history (Levy 1968).

The U.S. Supreme Court has relied on three provisions in the U.S. Constitution to develop rules to control police interrogation and confessions (Table 8.1):

1. *Fourteenth Amendment due process clause.* "No state shall . . . deprive any person of life, liberty, or property without due process of law."

## TABLE 8.1   The U.S. Constitution and Self-Incrimination

| Amendment | Stage of Criminal Process Where It's Applicable |
| --- | --- |
| Fifth and Fourteenth Amendment due process clauses | All stages |
| Sixth Amendment right-to-counsel clause | All stages after formal charges |
| Fifth Amendment self-incrimination clause | Custodial interrogation and all following stages |

2. *Sixth Amendment right-to-counsel clause.* "In all criminal prosecutions, the accused shall . . . have the assistance of counsel for his defense."

3. *Fifth Amendment self-incrimination clause.* "No person . . . shall be compelled in any criminal case to be a witness against himself."

Each of these constitutional provisions has led to a different approach to police interrogation and suspects' confessions. We'll look at all three: the due process approach, the right-to-counsel approach, and the self-incrimination approach.

## The Due Process Approach

The due process, right-to-counsel, and self-incrimination approaches overlap, but they follow a roughly chronological line. In *Brown v. Mississippi* (1936), the U.S. Supreme Court applied the Fourteenth Amendment due process clause to the confessions extracted by torture in that tragic case (Chapter 2). The basic idea behind the **due process approach to confessions** is that confessions must be voluntary. Involuntary confessions violate due process, not because they're "compelled," but because they're not reliable (meaning they might be false). The **reliability rationale for due process** is that admitting unreliable evidence to prove guilt denies defendants the right to their lives (Brown, Stewart, and Ellington were sentenced to death) without due process of law. In *Brown*, the confessions were the only evidence against the defendants. Here's what Chief Justice Hughes wrote for the Court:

> The state is free to regulate the procedure of its courts in accordance with its own conceptions of policy. . . . But the freedom of the state in establishing its policy . . . is limited by the requirement of due process of law. . . . The rack and torture chamber may not be substituted for the witness stand. . . . And the trial . . . is a mere pretense where the state authorities have contrived a conviction resting solely on the confessions obtained by violence. The due process clause requires that state action . . . shall be consistent with the fundamental principles of liberty and justice which lie at the base of all our civil and political institutions. It would be difficult to conceive of methods more revolting to the sense of justice than those taken to procure the confessions of these petitioners, and the use of the confessions thus obtained as the basis for conviction and sentence was a clear denial of due process. (286)

The unreliability of coerced confessions provided the rationale for the reviews of most of the early state confessions cases decided by the U.S. Supreme Court after *Brown v. Mississippi*. After several cases intimated there was a second rationale for reviewing state confession cases, the Court made the **accusatory system rationale** explicit in *Rogers v. Richmond* (1961). According to the accusatory system rationale, forced confessions violate due process even if they're true, because under our system the government alone has the burden of proving guilt beyond a reasonable doubt. In applying the accusatory system rationale in *Rogers*, the Court threw out a confession that the police got after they threatened to bring Rogers's arthritic wife in for questioning. According to Justice Felix Frankfurter:

> Our decisions under . . . [the Fourteenth] Amendment [due process clause] have made clear that convictions following the admission into evidence of confessions which are involuntary, i.e., the product of coercion, either physical or psychological, cannot stand. This is so not because such confessions are unlikely to be true but because the methods used to extract them offend an underlying principle in the enforcement of our criminal law: that ours is an accusatorial and not an inquisitorial system—a system in which the State must establish guilt by evidence independently and freely secured and may not by coercion prove its charge against an accused out of his own mouth.
>
> To be sure, confessions cruelly extorted may be and have been, to an unascertained extent, found to be untrustworthy. But the constitutional principle of excluding confessions

that are not voluntary does not rest on this consideration. Indeed, in many of the cases in which the command of the Due Process Clause has compelled us to reverse state convictions involving the use of confessions obtained by impermissible methods, independent corroborating evidence left little doubt of the truth of what the defendant had confessed. Despite such verification, confessions were found to be the product of constitutionally impermissible methods in their inducement. Since a defendant had been subjected to pressures to which, under our accusatorial system, an accused should not be subjected, we were constrained to find that the procedures leading to his conviction had failed to afford him that due process of law which the Fourteenth Amendment guarantees. (540–41)

The Court relied on a third rationale for reviewing state confessions in *Townsend v. Sain* (1963). Ailing Frank Sain's confession was obtained by questioning him after he received "truth serum"; the interrogating police officers were unaware of the drug's effects. According to the **free will rationale**, involuntary confessions aren't just unreliable and contrary to the accusatory system of justice; they're also coerced if they're not "the product of a rational intellect and a free will" (307). According to Chief Justice Warren:

> Numerous decisions of this Court have established the standards governing the admissibility of confessions into evidence. If an individual's will was overborne or if his confession was not the product of a rational intellect and a free will, his confession is inadmissible because coerced. These standards are applicable whether a confession is the product of physical intimidation or psychological pressure and, of course, are equally applicable to a drug induced statement. It is difficult to imagine a situation in which a confession would be less the product of a free intellect, less voluntary, than when brought about by a drug having the effect of a "truth serum."
>
> It is not significant that the drug may have been administered and the questions asked by persons unfamiliar with hyoscine's properties as a "truth serum," if these properties exist. Any questioning by police officers which in fact produces a confession which is not the product of a free intellect renders that confession inadmissible. . . . If the confession which petitioner made was in fact involuntary, the conviction cannot stand. . . . (307–8)

During the 30 years between *Brown v. Mississippi* (1936) and *Miranda v. Arizona* (1966), the Supreme Court threw out 40 state confessions because they violated due process. Most of the early cases involved southern White mobs who had rounded up poor, illiterate Blacks and tortured them until they confessed. The Court was much more reluctant to overturn the convictions of less "sympathetic criminals" from other parts of the country. In *Lisenba v. California* (1941), for example, Ray Lisenba (an educated White business executive from California) confessed he'd "tied his wife to a chair, subjected her to rattlesnake bites, and then drowned her in a pond." The police grilled Lisenba in several all-night sessions for two weeks, refusing to grant his repeated demands to see a lawyer and to remain silent until he did.

But even in the face of these tactics, the Court refused to overturn Lisenba's conviction by throwing out his confession. According to the Court, his incriminating statements, looked at in the light of his intelligence and business experience, were not caused by police "overbearing his will" but instead were "a calculated attempt to minimize his culpability after carefully considering statements by the accomplice."

In *Stein v. New York* (1953), another case of "unsympathetic criminals"—this time involving clever, experienced White robbers in rural New York State—Justice Jackson impatiently referred to the defendants as criminals who were "convinced their dance was over and the time had come to pay the fiddler."

According to Justice Jackson:

> The limits in any case depend upon a weighing of the circumstances of pressure against the power of resistance of the person confessing. What would be overpowering to the weak of will or mind might be utterly ineffective against an experienced criminal. (184)

## The Right-to-Counsel Approach

At the same time the U.S. Supreme Court was developing the due process approach to the review of state confessions cases, a growing minority of the Court was looking for tougher measures to control police interrogation. They found one of these tougher measures in the Sixth Amendment, which reads: "In all criminal prosecutions, the accused shall . . . have the assistance of counsel for his defense." The problem is the phrase "all criminal prosecutions"; it suggests proceedings in court, not in police stations.

But by 1958, four of nine justices, including Chief Justice Warren and Associate Justices Black, Douglas, and Brennan, were calling custodial interrogation a **critical stage in criminal prosecutions** (the point when suspects' right to a lawyer kicked in). In *Crooker v. California* (1958), John Russell Crooker, Jr. was a former law student working as a houseboy for a woman with whom he was having an affair. She broke off the affair when she found another boyfriend. After 14 hours in police custody, Crooker confessed to stabbing and strangling her. Although the police wouldn't let Crooker call his lawyer, there was no evidence officers had forced him to confess. He was allowed to eat, drink, and smoke, and interrogation sessions lasted only about an hour at a time. The U.S. Supreme Court affirmed Crooker's conviction, but Chief Justice Warren and Justices Black, Douglas, and Brennan dissented.

Justice Douglas explained:

> The mischief and abuse of the third degree will continue as long as an accused can be denied the right to counsel at the most critical period of his ordeal. For what takes place in the secret confines of the police station may be more critical than what takes place at trial. (444–45)

A change in Court membership brought to a slim majority of 5–4 the number of justices who favored the **right-to-counsel approach** to police interrogation. In 1964, in *Escobedo v. Illinois* (1964), the Supreme Court by a 5–4 vote turned to the Sixth Amendment right-to-counsel clause as the basis for reviewing state confessions cases.

Danny Escobedo asked his Chicago police interrogators to let him see his lawyer. They refused. His lawyer came to the station at Escobedo's mother's behest, but the officers repeatedly refused his requests to see Danny. Finally, Escobedo confessed. The Supreme Court threw out the confession because Escobedo had given it without the advice of his lawyer. According to the Court, as soon as a police investigation focuses on a particular suspect (the accusatory stage), criminal prosecution begins and the right to counsel attaches. If defendants don't have a right to a lawyer until they go to trial and they confess before trial without a lawyer, then the trial is "no more than an appeal from the interrogation."

Four dissenting justices argued that allowing lawyers in interrogation rooms would kill the use of confessions. Why? Because, "Any lawyer worth his salt will tell the suspect in no uncertain terms to make no statement to the police under any circumstances" (*Watts v. Indiana* 1949, 59).

According to Justice White, dissenting in *Escobedo*:

> I do not suggest for a moment that law enforcement will be destroyed by the rule announced today. The need for peace and order is too insistent for that. But it will be crippled and its task made a great deal more difficult. (499)

# The Self-Incrimination Approach

In 1966, just two years after adopting the right-to-counsel approach to custodial interrogations, the Court abruptly dropped it. In a 5–4 decision in the landmark *Miranda v. Arizona* (1966) case, the Court majority relied on the Fifth Amendment self-incrimination clause to decide the constitutionality of custodial interrogation.

The due process, right-to-counsel, and self-incrimination doctrines are all still applied in combination to decide cases. To decide whether a police custodial interrogation before formal charges was inherently coercive, the Court relies on the Fifth Amendment self-incrimination clause. To decide whether coercion was used after formal charges, the Court relies on the Sixth Amendment right to counsel. To review whether suspects and defendants have knowingly and voluntarily made incriminating statements whenever they take place, the Court relies on the Fourteenth Amendment due process clause (Table 8.1).

To claim successfully that their Fifth Amendment right against self-incrimination was violated, defendants have to prove three elements:

1. *Compulsion.* "No person . . . shall be compelled . . ."

2. *Incrimination.* " . . . in any criminal case"

3. *Testimony.* "to be a witness against himself"

This is the order the elements appear in within the self-incrimination clause, but we'll begin with the preliminary requirement: testimony. Then, we'll discuss what it means to be "compelled" to be a witness against oneself.

***The Meaning of "Witness against Himself"*** The Fifth Amendment says you can't be compelled to be a "witness" against yourself, but what does this mean? According to the U.S. Supreme Court, it means the government can't force you to give **testimony** (the content of what you say and write) against yourself. But content doesn't include the voice that spoke the words. So the government can compel you to speak particular words that might help a witness identify your voice. Also, drivers involved in accidents don't incriminate themselves when they have to give their names and addresses to the police. And, if some law says you have to turn over information in your personal books, papers, bank accounts, and other records, you aren't being compelled to incriminate yourself. (See Table 8.2 for more examples.)

In *Schmerber v. California* (1966), our next case excerpt, the Supreme Court decided that taking blood alcohol samples from Armando Schmerber didn't compel him to be a witness against himself.

---

**TABLE 8.2**   **Incriminating Evidence Not Protected by the Fifth Amendment**

- Weapons
- Photographs
- Contraband
- Appearance in lineup
- Stolen property
- Bullets removed from the body
- Handwriting samples

- Products of consent searches
- Hair samples
- Books, papers, documents
- Voice samples
- Records required by law to be kept
- Fingerprints

---

## Schmerber v. California
### 384 U.S. 757 (1966)

### HISTORY

Armando Schmerber was convicted in the Los Angeles Municipal Court of driving an automobile while under the influence of intoxicating liquor, and he appealed. The Appellate Department of the California Superior Court affirmed. The U.S. Supreme Court granted certiorari and affirmed.

BRENNAN, J.

### FACTS

Armando Schmerber and a companion had been drinking at a tavern and bowling alley. Schmerber was driving from the bowling alley about midnight November 12, 1964, when the car skidded, crossed the road and struck a tree. Both Schmerber and his companion were injured and taken to a hospital for treatment. At the direction of a police officer, a blood sample was then withdrawn from Schmerber's body by a physician at the hospital.

The chemical analysis of this sample revealed a percent by weight of alcohol in his blood at the time of the offense which indicated intoxication, and the report of this analysis was admitted in evidence at the trial. Schmerber objected to receipt of this evidence of the analysis on the ground that the blood had been withdrawn despite his refusal, on the advice of his counsel, to consent to the test.

He contended that in that circumstance the withdrawal of the blood and the admission of the analysis in evidence denied him due process of law under the Fourteenth Amendment, as well as specific guarantees of the Bill of Rights secured against the States by that Amendment: his privilege against self-incrimination under the Fifth Amendment. . . . [*Schmerber's claim that taking his blood was an unreasonable search and seizure is omitted here.*] The Appellate Department of the California Superior Court rejected these contentions and affirmed the conviction. . . .

We granted certiorari. We AFFIRM.

### OPINION

. . . In *Malloy v. Hogan*, we held that the Fourteenth Amendment secures against state invasion the same privilege that the Fifth Amendment guarantees against federal infringement—the right of a person to remain silent unless he chooses to speak in the unfettered exercise of his own will, and to suffer no penalty for such silence.

We therefore must now decide whether the withdrawal of the blood and admission in evidence of the analysis involved in this case violated petitioner's privilege. We hold that the privilege protects an accused only from being compelled to testify against himself, or otherwise provide the State with evidence of a testimonial or communicative nature, and that the withdrawal of blood and use of the analysis in question in this case did not involve compulsion to these ends.

It could not be denied that in requiring Schmerber to submit to the withdrawal and chemical analysis of his blood the State compelled him to submit to an attempt to discover evidence that might be used to prosecute him for a criminal offence. He submitted only after the police officer rejected his objection and directed the physician to proceed. The officer's direction to the physician to administer the test over Schmerber's objection constituted compulsion for the purposes of the privilege. The critical question, then, is whether petitioner was thus compelled "to be a witness against himself." . . .

The withdrawal of blood necessarily involves puncturing the skin for extraction, and the percent by weight of alcohol in that blood, as established by chemical analysis, is evidence of criminal guilt. Compelled submission fails on one view to respect the "inviolability of the human personality." Moreover, since it enables the State to rely on evidence forced from the accused, the compulsion violates at least one meaning of the requirement that the State procure the evidence against an accused "by its own independent labors." . . .

However, . . . history and a long line of authorities in lower courts have consistently limited [the self-incrimination] protection to situations in which the State seeks to . . . obtain evidence against an accused through "the cruel, simple expedient of compelling it from his own mouth. In sum, the privilege is fulfilled only when the person is guaranteed the right to remain silent unless he chooses to speak in the unfettered exercise of his own will." The leading case in this Court is *Holt v. U.S.* There the question was whether evidence was admissible that the accused, prior to trial and over his protest, put on a blouse that fitted him. It was contended that compelling the accused to submit to the demand that he model the blouse violated the privilege.

Mr. Justice Holmes, speaking for the Court, rejected the argument as "based upon an extravagant extension of the 5th Amendment," and went on to say:

> The prohibition of compelling a man in a criminal court to be witness against himself is a prohibition of the use of physical or moral compulsion to extort communications from him, not an exclusion of his body as evidence when it may be material. The objection in principle would forbid a jury to look at a prisoner and compare his features with a photograph in proof.

. . . Both federal and state courts have usually held that [the privilege against self-incrimination] offers no protection against compulsion to submit to fingerprinting, photographing, or measurements, to write or speak for identification, to appear in court, to stand, to assume a stance, to walk, or to make a particular gesture. The distinction which has emerged, often expressed in different ways, is that the privilege is a bar against compelling "communications" or "testimony," but that compulsion which makes a suspect or accused the source of "real or physical evidence" does not violate it. . . . Not even a shadow of testimonial compulsion upon or enforced communication by the accused was involved either in the extraction or in the chemical analysis. Schmerber's testimonial capacities were in no way implicated; indeed, his participation, except as a donor, was irrelevant to the results of the test, which depend on chemical analysis and on that alone.

Since the blood test evidence, although an incriminating product of compulsion, was neither Schmerber's testimony nor evidence relating to some communicative act or writing by Schmerber, it was admissible. . . .

AFFIRMED.

## DISSENT

BLACK, J., JOINED BY DOUGLAS, J.

. . . It seems to me that the compulsory extraction of petitioner's blood for analysis so that the person who analyzed it could give evidence to convict him had both a "testimonial" and a "communicative nature." The sole purpose of this project which proved to be successful was to obtain "testimony" from some person to prove that Schmerber had alcohol in his blood at the time he was arrested. And the purpose of the project was certainly "communicative" in that the analysis of the blood was to supply information to enable a witness to communicate to the court and jury that petitioner was more or less drunk. . . .

How can it reasonably be doubted that the blood test evidence was not in all respects the actual equivalent of "testimony" taken from Schmerber when the result of the test was offered as testimony, was considered by the jury as testimony, and the jury's verdict of guilt rests in part on that testimony? . . . Believing with the Framers that constitutional safeguards broadly construed by independent tribunals of justice provide our best hope for keeping our people free from governmental oppression, I deeply regret the Court's holding. . . .

## Questions

1. Describe the details of the blood test performed on Schmerber.

2. According to the Court, why doesn't the self-incrimination clause apply to the blood test?

3. Summarize the dissent's arguments presented by Justices Black and Douglas in favor of applying the self-incrimination clause to the blood test. Is the dissent more persuasive than the majority? Why?

*The Meaning of "Compelled"* The due process approach to self-incrimination relied on the voluntariness test to decide whether suspects were "compelled" to be witnesses against themselves. According to the voluntariness test of self-incrimination, confessions and other incriminating statements violate due process if the totality of circumstances surrounding the statements shows that suspects didn't confess voluntarily. In 1966, a combination of three factors produced one of the most famous (and most controversial and hated, too) decisions in U.S. constitutional history—*Miranda v. Arizona:*

1. Uneasiness about tactics used against suspects in the intimidating atmosphere of police stations

2. Dissatisfaction with the vagueness of the totality-of-circumstances approach

3. Impatience with the case-by-case approach to deciding whether confessions were voluntarily given and gotten

Let's turn now to an analysis of this famous case, and it's importance in several key areas: self-incrimination, confessions, police interrogation, and the right to counsel.

# MIRANDA V. ARIZONA

In *Miranda v. Arizona* (1966), a bare 5–4 majority of the U.S. Supreme Court established a "bright line" rule to govern custodial interrogation. According to the Court majority, custodial interrogation is "**inherently coercive**." Why? First, because suspects are held in strange surroundings where they're not free to leave or even to call for emotional support from relatives and friends. Second, skilled police officers use tricks, lies, and psychological pressure to "crack" the will of suspects. These circumstances, according to the Court, require strong measures to prevent involuntary confessions.

Those measures (what we all know as the *Miranda* warnings) mandated by the Court majority in its decision and the reasons for them were hotly debated in our next case excerpt, *Miranda v. Arizona*.

---

## C A S E    *Does the Fifth Amendment Apply to Custodial Interrogation?*

### *Miranda v. Arizona*
#### 384 U.S. 436 (1966)

### HISTORY

Ernesto Miranda was convicted of rape and robbery in the Superior Court, Maricopa County, Arizona, and sentenced to twenty to thirty years in prison for each crime. He appealed. The Arizona Supreme Court affirmed. The U.S. Supreme Court granted certiorari and reversed.

WARREN, C.J.

### FACTS

On March 13, 1963, Ernesto Miranda, was arrested at his home and taken into custody to a Phoenix police station. He was there identified by the complaining witness. The police then took him to "Interrogation Room No. 2" of the detective bureau, where two police officers questioned him. The officers admitted at trial Miranda was not advised he had a right to have an attorney present. . . .

Two hours later, the officers emerged from the interrogation room with a written confession signed by Miranda. At the top of the statement was a typed paragraph stating the confession was made voluntarily, without threats or promises of immunity and "with full knowledge of my legal rights, understanding any statement I make may be used against me." One of the officers testified he read this paragraph to Miranda. Apparently, however, he did not do so until after Miranda had confessed orally.

At his trial before a jury, the written confession was admitted into evidence over the objection of defense counsel, and the officers testified to the prior oral confession made by Miranda during the interrogation. Miranda was found guilty of kidnapping and rape. He was sentenced to 20 to 30 years' imprisonment on each count, the sentences to run concurrently. On appeal, the Supreme Court of Arizona held that Miranda's constitutional rights were not violated in obtaining the confession and affirmed the conviction. In reaching its decision, the court emphasized heavily the fact that Miranda did not specifically request counsel.

### OPINION

The constitutional issue we decide . . . is the admissibility of statements obtained from a defendant questioned while in custody or otherwise deprived of his freedom of action in any significant way. . . . The modern practice of in-custody interrogation is psychologically rather than physically oriented. . . . Interrogation takes place in privacy [and] privacy results in secrecy.

[But] from . . . representative samples of interrogation techniques, found in police manuals and texts on interrogation, the setting . . . becomes clear: To be alone with the subject is essential to prevent distraction and to deprive him of any outside support. The aura of confidence in his guilt undermines his will to resist. He merely confirms the preconceived story the police seek to have him describe.

Patience and persistence, at times relentless questioning, are employed. . . . When normal procedures fail to produce the needed result, the police may resort to deceptive stratagems such as giving false legal advice. It is important to keep the subject off balance, for example, by trading on his insecurity about himself or his surroundings. The police then persuade, trick, or cajole him out of exercising his constitutional rights.

In *Miranda*, we concern ourselves primarily with this interrogation atmosphere and the evils it can bring. The police arrested Miranda and took him to a special interrogation room where they secured a confession. . . . Miranda was thrust into an unfamiliar atmosphere and run through menacing police interrogation procedures. The potentiality for compulsion is forcefully apparent, for example, where the indigent Mexican defendant was a seriously disturbed individual with pronounced sexual fantasies. To be sure, the records do not evince overt physical coercion or patent psychological ploys. . . .

We have concluded that without proper safeguards the process of in-custody interrogation . . . contains inherently compelling pressures which work to undermine the individual's will to resist and to compel him to speak where he would not otherwise do so freely. In order to combat these pressures and to permit a full opportunity to exercise the privilege against self-incrimination, the accused must be adequately and effectively apprised of his rights and the exercise of those rights must be fully honored. . . .

If a person in custody is to be subjected to interrogation, he must first be informed in clear and unequivocal terms that he has the right to remain silent. . . . Such a warning is an absolute prerequisite in overcoming the inherent pressures of the interrogation atmosphere. . . . The Fifth Amendment privilege is so fundamental to our system of constitutional rule and the expedient of giving an adequate warning as to the availability of the privilege so simple, we will not pause to inquire in individual cases whether the defendant was aware of his rights without a warning being given. . . .

The warning of the right to remain silent must be accompanied by the explanation that anything said can and will be used against the individual in court. This warning is needed in order to make him aware not only of the privilege, but also of the consequences of forgoing it. . . . This warning may serve to make the individual more acutely aware that he is faced with a phase of the adversary system—that he is not in the presence of persons acting solely in his interest.

. . . We hold that an individual held for interrogation must be clearly informed that he has the right to consult with a lawyer and to have the lawyer with him during interrogation under the system for protecting the privilege we delineate today. As with the warnings of the right to remain silent and that anything stated can be used in evidence against him, this warning is an absolute prerequisite to interrogation. No amount of circumstantial evidence that the person may have been aware of this right will suffice to stand in its stead. . . .

. . . In order fully to apprise a person interrogated of the extent of his rights under this system, it is necessary to warn him not only that he has the right to consult with an attorney, but also that if he is indigent [poor] a lawyer will be appointed to represent him. Without this additional warning, the admonition of the right to consult with counsel would often be understood as meaning only that he can consult with a lawyer if he has one or has the funds to obtain one. The warning of a right to counsel would be hollow if not couched in terms that would convey to the indigent . . . that he too has a right to have counsel present. . . .

Once warnings have been given, the subsequent procedure is clear. If the individual indicates in any manner, at any time prior to or during questioning, that he wishes to remain silent, the interrogation must cease. . . . If the individual states that he wants an attorney, the interrogation must cease until an attorney is present. . . . If the individual cannot obtain an attorney and he indicates that he wants one before speaking to police, they must respect his decision to remain silent. . . .

If the interrogation continues without the presence of an attorney and a statement is taken, a heavy burden rests on the government to demonstrate that the defendant knowingly and intelligently waived his privilege against self-incrimination and his right to retained or appointed counsel. . . . Since the State is responsible for establishing the isolated circumstances under which the interrogation takes place and has the only means of making available corroborated evidence of warnings given during incommunicado interrogation, the burden is rightly on its shoulders. . . .

In dealing with statements obtained through interrogation, we do not purport to find all confessions inadmissible. Confessions remain a proper element in law enforcement. Any statement given freely and voluntarily without any compelling influences is, of course, admissible in evidence. . . .

A recurrent argument made in these cases is that society's need for interrogation outweighs the privilege. . . . [But] if the individual desires to exercise his privilege, he has the right to do so. This is not for the authorities to decide.

An attorney may advise his client not to talk to police until he has had an opportunity to investigate the case, or he may wish to be present with his client during any police questioning. . . . This is not cause for considering the attorney a menace to law enforcement. He is merely carrying out what he is sworn to do under his oath—to protect to the extent of his ability the rights of his client. In fulfilling this responsibility the attorney plays a vital role in the administration of criminal justice under our Constitution. . . .

Over the years the Federal Bureau of Investigation has compiled an exemplary record of effective law enforcement while advising any suspect or arrested person, at the outset of an interview, that he is not required to make a statement, that any statement may be used against him in court, that the individual may obtain the services of an attorney of his own choice and, more recently, that he has a right to free counsel if he is unable to pay. A letter received from the Solicitor General in response to a question from the Bench makes it clear that the present pattern of warnings and respect for the rights of the individual followed as a practice by the FBI is consistent with the procedure which we delineate today. . . . The practice of the FBI can readily be emulated by state and local enforcement agencies.

The argument that the FBI deals with different crimes than are dealt with by state authorities does not mitigate the significance of the FBI experience.

It is also urged upon us that we withhold decision on this issue until state legislative bodies and advisory groups have had an opportunity to deal with these problems by rule making. . . . The Constitution does not require any specific code of procedures for protecting the privilege against self-incrimination during custodial interrogation. Congress and the States are free to develop their own safeguards for the privilege, so long as they are fully as effective as those described above in informing accused persons of their right of silence and in affording a continuous opportunity to exercise it. [But] the issues presented are of constitutional dimensions and must be determined by the courts. The admissibility of a statement in the face of a claim that it was obtained in violation of the defendant's constitutional rights is an issue the resolution of which has long since been undertaken by this Court. Judicial solutions to problems of constitutional dimension have evolved decade by decade. As courts have been presented with the need to enforce constitutional rights, they have found means of doing so. . . . Where rights secured by the Constitution are involved, there can be no rule making or legislation which would abrogate them. . . .

From the testimony of the officers and by the admission of Arizona, it is clear that Miranda was not in any way apprised of his right to consult with an attorney and to have one present during the interrogation, nor was his right not to be compelled to incriminate himself effectively protected in any other manner. Without these warnings the statements were inadmissible. The mere fact that he signed a statement which contained a typed-in clause stating that he had "full knowledge" of his "legal rights" does not approach the knowing and intelligent waiver required to relinquish constitutional rights.

Judgment of the Supreme Court of Arizona REVERSED.

## DISSENT

### CLARK, J.

It is with regret that I find it necessary to write in this case. However, I am unable to join . . . in the Court's criticism of the present practices of police and investigatory agencies as to custodial interrogation. The materials it refers to as "police manuals" are, as I read them, merely writings in this filed by professors and some police officers. Not one is shown by the record here to be the official manual of any police department, much less in universal use in crime detection. Moreover the examples of police brutality mentioned by the

Court are rare exceptions to the thousands of cases that appear every year in the law reports. The police agencies—all the way from municipal and state forces to the federal bureaus—are responsible for law enforcement and public safety in this country. I am proud of their efforts, which in my view are not fairly characterized by the Court's opinion.

### HARLAN, J., JOINED BY STEWART AND WHITE, JJ.

. . . The new rules are not designed to guard against police brutality or other unmistakably banned forms of coercion.

. . . Rather, the thrust of the new rules is to negate all pressures, to reinforce the nervous or ignorant suspect, and ultimately to discourage any confession at all. The aim in short is toward "voluntariness" in a utopian sense, or to view it from a different angle, voluntariness with a vengeance. . . .

Without at all subscribing to the generally black picture of police conduct painted by the Court, I think it must be frankly recognized at the outset that police questioning . . . may inherently entail some pressure on the suspect and may seek advantage in his ignorance or weaknesses. The atmosphere and questioning techniques, proper and fair though they be, can in themselves exert a tug on the suspect to confess. . . . Until today, the role of the Constitution has been only to sift out undue pressure, not to assure spontaneous confessions. . . .

The Court largely ignores that its rules impair, if they will not eventually serve wholly to frustrate, an instrument of law enforcement that has long and quite reasonably been thought worth the price paid for it. There can be little doubt that the Court's new code would markedly decrease the number of confessions. To warn the suspect that he may remain silent and remind him that his confession may be used in court are minor obstructions. To require also an express waiver by the suspect and an end to questioning whenever he demurs must heavily handicap questioning. And to suggest or provide counsel for the suspect simply invites the end of the interrogation.

How much harm this decision will inflict on law enforcement cannot fairly be predicted with accuracy. Evidence on the role of confessions is notoriously incomplete. . . . [But] we do know that some crimes cannot be solved without confessions, that ample expert testimony attests to their importance in crime control, and that the Court is taking a real risk with society's welfare in imposing its new regime on the country. The social costs of crime are too great to call the new rules anything but a hazardous experimentation. . . .

### WHITE, J., JOINED BY HARLAN AND STEWART, JJ.

Only a tiny minority of our judges who have dealt with the question, including today's majority, have considered in custody interrogation . . . to be a violation of the Fifth Amendment. And this Court, as every member knows, has left standing literally thousands of criminal convictions that rested at least in part on confessions taken in the course of interrogation by the police after arrest.

. . . More than the human dignity of the accused is involved; the human personality of others in the society must also be preserved. Thus the values reflected by the privilege are not the sole desideratum; society's interest in the general security is of equal weight.

The obvious underpinning of the Court's decision is a deep-seated distrust of all confessions. . . . This is the not so subtle overtone of the opinion—that it is inherently wrong for the police to gather evidence from the accused himself.

And this is precisely the nub of this dissent. I see nothing wrong or immoral, and certainly nothing unconstitutional, in the police's asking a suspect whom they have reasonable cause to arrest whether or not he killed his wife or in confronting him with the evidence on which the arrest was based, at least where he has been plainly advised that he may remain completely silent. . . . Moreover, it is by no means certain that the process of confessing is injurious to the accused. To the contrary it may provide psychological relief and enhance the prospects for rehabilitation.

. . . There is, in my view, every reason to believe that a good many criminal defendants who otherwise would have been convicted on what this Court has previously thought to be the most satisfactory kind of evidence will now under this new version of the Fifth Amendment, either not be tried at all or will be acquitted if the State's evidence, minus the confession, is put to the test of litigation. I have no desire whatsoever to share the responsibility for any such impact on the present criminal process. In some unknown number of cases the Court's rule will return a killer, a rapist or other criminal to the streets and to the environment which produced him, to repeat his crime whenever it pleases him. As a consequence, there will not be a gain, but a loss, in human dignity. The real concern is not the unfortunate consequences of this new decision on the criminal law as an abstract, disembodied series of authoritative proscriptions, but the impact on those who rely on the public authority for protection and who without it can only engage in violent self-help with guns, knives and the help of their neighbors similarly inclined. . . .

## Questions

1. According to the Supreme Court, what do the words *custody* and *interrogation* mean?

2. Why is custodial interrogation "inherently coercive," according to the majority?

3. Identify and explain the criteria for waiving the right against self-incrimination in custodial interrogation.

4. On what grounds do the dissenters disagree with the majority's decision? What interests are in conflict, according to the Court?

5. How do the majority and the dissent explain the balance of interests established by the Constitution?

6. Which makes more sense regarding the law of police interrogation, the majority's bright-line rule, requiring warnings, or the dissent's due process test, weighing the totality of circumstances on a case-by-case basis? Defend your answer.

 Go to Exercise 8.1 on the Samaha Criminal Procedure 7e website to learn more about *Miranda v. Arizona* and read the Rest of the Story: academic. cengage.com/criminaljustice/samaha.

Just what impact do the *Miranda* warnings have on interrogation and confessions? To answer this, we'll examine the *Miranda* bright-line rules, the meaning of "custody," the public safety exception to the rules, and the Fifth and Sixth Amendment meanings of "interrogation."

## The *Miranda* "Bright-Line" Rules

The Supreme Court intended the *Miranda* warnings to provide a **bright-line rule**—sometimes called a "per se rule"—to prevent police coercion while still allowing police pressure. The rule is that whenever police officers conduct a custodial interrogation, they have to give suspects the now famous four warnings:

1. You have a right to remain silent.

2. Anything you say can and will be used against you in court.

3. You have a right to a lawyer.

4. If you can't afford a lawyer, one will be appointed for you.

What's the reason for the bright-line rule? To avoid what the Court called the "inherently coercive nature of custodial interrogation."

The Court created five more bright-line rules for the interrogating officer, prosecutors, and judges. But police officers don't have to tell suspects about these rules:

1. Suspects can claim their right to remain silent at any time. If at any time they indicate in any way they don't want to talk, the interrogation has to stop immediately.

2. If, before interrogation begins, suspects indicate in any manner they want a lawyer, interrogation can't start; if it has already started, it has to stop immediately.

3. Any statement obtained without a lawyer present puts a "heavy burden" on the prosecution to prove defendants waived two constitutional rights: the right against self-incrimination and the right to a lawyer. Neither silence nor later confessions count as a waiver.

4. Statements obtained in violation of the rules can't be admitted into evidence.

5. Exercising the right against self-incrimination can't be penalized. So prosecutors can't suggest or even hint at trial that the defendant's refusal to talk is a sign of guilt.

In *Commonwealth v. Zook* (1989), these additional *Miranda* warnings were applied. Robert Zook confessed to two murders. He was charged with the murders, a jury found him guilty, and the trial court sentenced him to death. Zook appealed, claiming his confession was obtained illegally because the police denied his request for a lawyer during the interrogation. During the trial, the assistant district attorney elicited the following on direct examination of Lieutenant Landis (the interrogating officer):

Q: During the interview, did Mr. Zook ever request an attorney?

A: Approximately—I don't know, two-thirds of the way into the interview, something like that, right around the time we got through talking about whether he knew Conard or Wiker, he asked if he could use the phone to call his mother to see if she could get him an attorney. At that point, I said are you saying you want us to stop questioning you until you have an attorney present? And he said no, go ahead and finish with what you are doing. That was the only time that he came close to asking for an attorney, if that's what that was.

Did he waive his right to counsel? No. The Pennsylvania Supreme Court ruled:

We think that the trial court was in error in failing to suppress all statements made by Appellant after he made the request to use the phone to have his mother get an attorney. . . . It is inconsistent with *Miranda* and its progeny for the authorities, at their instance, to reinterrogate an accused in custody if he has clearly asserted his right to counsel. (920)

One final point about the bright-line *Miranda* rule: On TV "cop shows," whenever, wherever, and as soon as police officers arrest anyone, they "mirandize" him immediately or say something like, "Read him his rights." However, *Miranda v. Arizona* doesn't command officers to warn suspects "whenever" they arrest them. Officers have to give the famous warnings only if they intend both to (1) take the suspects into custody *and* (2) interrogate them. These limits still leave the police plenty of leeway for questioning individuals who aren't in custody, including:

1. Questioning people at crime scenes
2. Questioning people before they become suspects
3. Questioning people during Fourth Amendment stops (Chapter 4)

## The Meaning of "Custody"

In *Miranda*, the U.S. Supreme Court defined **custody** as being held by the police in a police station or depriving an individual of "freedom of action in any significant way." According to the Court, deciding whether suspects are in "custody" boils down to "whether there was a formal arrest or restraint on freedom of movement of the degree associated with a formal arrest." The Court used this language to prevent police officers from getting around the *Miranda* requirements by questioning suspects away from a police station. The Court was sending the message that *Miranda* targets coercive atmospheres, not just coercive places.

Whether suspects are in custody depends on a case-by-case evaluation of the totality of circumstances surrounding the interrogation. These circumstances include:

- Whether officers had probable cause to arrest
- Whether officers intended to detain suspects
- Whether suspects believed their freedom was significantly restricted
- Whether the investigation had focused on the suspect
- The language officers used to summon suspects
- The physical surroundings
- The amount of evidence of guilt officers presented to suspects
- How long suspects were detained
- The amounts and kinds of pressure officers used to detain suspects

Three types of detentions don't qualify as being in custody:

- Detaining drivers and passengers during routine traffic stops (*Berkemer v. McCarty* 1984)
- Requiring probationers to attend routine meetings with their probation officers (*Minnesota v. Murphy* 1984)
- Detaining persons during the execution of search warrants (*Michigan v. Summers* 1981)

What about questioning suspects in their homes? It depends on the totality of the circumstances in each case. In *Orozco v. Texas*, four police officers entered Reyes Arias Orozco's bedroom at 4:00 A.M., woke him up, and immediately started questioning him about a shooting. The Court held that even though Orozco was at home in his own bed he was still in custody, because he was "deprived of his liberty in a significant way." The Court relied heavily on the officers' testimony that from the moment Orozco gave them his name, he wasn't free to go anywhere.

On the other hand, the Court ruled that Carl Mathiason (*Oregon v. Mathiason* 1977) and Jerry Beheler (*California v. Beheler* 1983) were not in custody when they went voluntarily to their local police stations and confessed.

In our next case excerpt, *Berkemer v. McCarty* (1984), the U.S. Supreme Court applied the totality-of-circumstances test to Richard McCarty, a suspect questioned about his sobriety while he was stopped for a traffic violation.

## Berkemer, Sheriff of Franklin County, v. McCarty

468 U.S. 420 (1984)

### HISTORY

Richard McCarty was convicted of operating a motor vehicle while under the influence of alcohol and/or drugs. The U.S. District Court for the Southern District of Ohio denied his petition for habeas corpus. The U.S. Court of Appeals reversed. The U.S. Supreme Court granted certiorari and affirmed.

MARSHALL, J.

### FACTS

On the evening of March 31, 1980, Trooper Williams of the Ohio State Highway Patrol observed Richard McCarty's car weaving in and out of a lane on Interstate Highway 270. After following the car for two miles, Williams forced McCarty to stop and asked him to get out of the vehicle.

When McCarty complied, Williams noticed that he was having difficulty standing. At that point, "Williams concluded that McCarty would be charged with a traffic offense and, therefore, his freedom to leave the scene was terminated." However, McCarty was not told he would be taken into custody. Williams then asked McCarty to perform a field sobriety test, commonly known as a "balancing test." McCarty could not do so without falling.

While still at the scene of the traffic stop, Williams asked McCarty whether he had been using intoxicants. McCarty replied "he had consumed two beers and had smoked several joints of marijuana a short time before." McCarty's speech was slurred, and Williams had difficulty understanding him. Williams thereupon formally placed McCarty under arrest and transported him in the patrol car to the Franklin County Jail.

At the jail, McCarty was given an intoxilyzer test to determine the concentration of alcohol in his blood. The test did not detect any alcohol whatsoever in his system.

Williams then resumed questioning McCarty in order to obtain information for inclusion in the State Highway Patrol Alcohol Influence Report. McCarty answered affirmatively a question whether he had been drinking. When then asked if he was under the influence of alcohol, he said, "I guess, barely." Williams next asked McCarty to indicate on the form whether the marihuana he had smoked had been treated with any chemicals. In the section of the report headed "Remarks," McCarty wrote, "No angel dust or PCP in the pot." At no point in this sequence of events did Williams or anyone else tell McCarty that he had a right to remain silent, to consult with an attorney, and to have an attorney appointed for him if he could not afford one.

McCarty was charged with operating a motor vehicle while under the influence of alcohol and/or drugs. Under Ohio law, that offense is a first-degree misdemeanor and is punishable by fine or imprisonment for up to six months. Incarceration for a minimum of three days is mandatory. McCarty moved to exclude the various incriminating statements he had made to Trooper Williams on the ground that introduction into evidence of those statements would violate the Fifth Amendment insofar as he had not been informed of his constitutional rights prior to his interrogation.

When the trial court denied the motion, McCarty pleaded "no contest" and was found guilty. He was sentenced to 90 days in jail, 80 of which were suspended, and was fined $300, $100 of which were suspended. [According to Ohio law,] "The plea of no contest does not preclude a defendant from asserting upon appeal that the trial court prejudicially erred in ruling on a pretrial motion, including a pretrial motion to suppress evidence." . . . We granted certiorari to resolve confusion in the federal and state courts regarding the applicability of our ruling in *Miranda* to . . . questioning of motorists detained pursuant to traffic stops. . . .

### OPINION

. . . In the years since the decision in *Miranda*, we have frequently reaffirmed the central principle established by that case: if the police take a suspect into custody and then ask him questions without informing him of the rights enumerated above, his responses cannot be introduced into evidence to establish his guilt. The one exception to this consistent line of decisions is *New York v. Quarles* (1984) [excerpted in this chapter on page 293]. . . . There can be no question that McCarty was "in custody" at least as of the moment he was formally placed under arrest and instructed to get into the police car. Because he was not informed of his constitutional rights at that juncture, McCarty's subsequent admissions should not have been used against him.

To assess the admissibility of the self-incriminating statements made by McCarty prior to his formal arrest, we are obliged to decide . . . whether the roadside questioning of a motorist detained pursuant to a routine traffic stop should be considered "custodial interrogation." . . . A traffic stop significantly curtails the "freedom of action" of the driver and the passengers of the detained vehicle. . . . Certainly few motorists would feel free either to disobey a directive to pull over or to leave the scene of a traffic stop without being told they might do so. . . . Thus, we must decide whether a traffic stop exerts upon a detained person pressures that sufficiently impair his free exercise of his privilege against self-incrimination to require that he be warned of his constitutional rights.

Two features of an ordinary traffic stop mitigate the danger that a person questioned will be induced "to speak" where he would not otherwise do so freely." First . . . the vast majority of roadside detentions last only a few minutes. A motorist's expectations, when he sees a policeman's light flashing behind him, are that he will be obliged to spend a short period of time answering questions and waiting while the officer checks his license and registration, that he may then be given a citation, but that in the end he most likely will be allowed to continue on his way. In this respect, questioning incident to an ordinary traffic stop is quite different from stationhouse interrogation, which frequently is prolonged, and in which the detainee often is aware that questioning will continue until he provides his interrogators the answers they seek.

Second, circumstances associated with the typical traffic stop are not such that the motorist feels completely at the mercy of the police. To be sure, the aura of authority surrounding an armed, uniformed officer and the knowledge that the officer has some discretion in deciding whether to issue a citation, in combination, exert some pressure on the detainee to respond to questions. But other aspects of the situation substantially offset these forces. Perhaps most importantly, the typical traffic stop is public. . . . Passersby, on foot or in other cars, witness the interaction of officer and motorist. This exposure to public view both reduces the ability of an unscrupulous policeman to use illegitimate means to elicit self-incriminating statements and diminishes the motorist's fear that, if he does not cooperate, he will be subjected to abuse. The fact that the detained motorist typically is confronted by only one or at most two policemen further mutes his sense of vulnerability. In short, the atmosphere surrounding an ordinary traffic stop is substantially less "police dominated" than that surrounding the kinds of interrogation at issue in *Miranda*. . . .

. . . The safeguards prescribed by *Miranda* become applicable as soon as a suspect's freedom of action is curtailed to a "degree associated with formal arrest." If a motorist who has been detained pursuant to a traffic stop thereafter is subjected to treatment that renders him "in custody" for practical purposes, he will be entitled to the full panoply of protections prescribed by *Miranda*. . . .

Turning to the case before us, we find nothing in the record that indicates that McCarty should have been given *Miranda* warnings at any point prior to the time Trooper Williams placed him under arrest. . . . We reject the contention that the initial stop of McCarty's car, by itself, rendered him "in custody." And McCarty has failed to demonstrate that, at any time between the initial stop and the arrest, he was subjected to restraints comparable to those associated with a formal arrest. Only a short period of time elapsed between the stop and the arrest. At no point during that interval was McCarty informed that his detention would not be temporary. . . . Nor do other aspects of the interaction of Williams and McCarty support the contention that McCarty was exposed to "custodial interrogation" at the scene of the stop. . . . A single police officer asked McCarty a modest number of questions and requested him to perform a simple balancing test at a location visible to passing motorists. Treatment of this sort cannot fairly be characterized as the functional equivalent of formal arrest.

We conclude . . . that McCarty was not taken into custody for the purposes of *Miranda* until Williams arrested him. Consequently, the statements McCarty made prior to that point were admissible against him.

AFIRMED.

## Questions

1. List all the facts relevant to deciding whether Richard McCarty's freedom was "limited in any significant way."

2. Summarize the arguments the Court gives for its rule that people stopped for traffic violations aren't typically in custody.

3. List the facts and circumstances in *Miranda* and *McCarty* that differ.

4. According to the Court, when can a noncustodial traffic stop turn into a custodial stop for purposes of *Miranda*?

5. Summarize how the Court applied its definition of "custody" to the stop of Richard McCarty.

## The Public Safety Exception

What if "mirandizing" a suspect before questioning her would endanger an officer or someone nearby? Would officers have to give the warnings anyway? No, said the U.S. Supreme Court in *New York v. Quarles* (1984), a case that created a **public safety exception** to *Miranda*.

In *Quarles*, a woman came up to two NYPD officers and told them she had been raped by a man carrying a gun who had just gone into a supermarket across the street.

Officer Kraft ran to the market and saw Benjamin Quarles, who fit the woman's description. Kraft briefly lost sight of Quarles, then saw him again, pulled his own gun, ordered Quarles to stop and put his hands over his head, frisked him, discovered an empty shoulder holster, and handcuffed him.

Without mirandizing Quarles, Kraft asked him where the gun was. Nodding to some cartons, Quarles said, "The gun's over there." Among the cartons, Kraft found a loaded .38 caliber revolver.

By a 5–4 vote, the Court decided Officer Kraft didn't have to warn Quarles. According to the Court, the cost of *Miranda* is that some guilty people will go free, a cost worth paying in most cases because of the premium we put on the right against coerced self-incrimination. But the cost is too high if giving the warning would endanger public safety:

> We conclude that the need for answers to questions in a situation posing a threat to the public safety outweighs the need for the . . . rule protecting the . . . privilege against self-incrimination. We decline to place officers such as Officer Kraft in the untenable position of having to consider, often in a matter of seconds, whether it best serves society for them to ask the necessary questions without the *Miranda* warnings and render whatever probative evidence they uncover inadmissible, or for them to give the warnings in order to preserve the admissibility of evidence they might uncover but possibly damage or destroy their ability to obtain that evidence and neutralize the volatile situation confronting them. (657–58)

So the Court created the public safety exception to the *Miranda* rule:

> In recognizing a narrow exception to the *Miranda* rule in this case, we acknowledge that to some degree we lessen the desirable clarity of that rule. . . . The exception will not be difficult for police officers to apply because in each case it will be circumscribed by the exigency which justifies it. We think police officers can and will distinguish almost instinctively between questions necessary to secure their own safety or the safety of the public and questions designed solely to elicit testimonial evidence from a suspect. (658)

Justice O'Connor, who agreed the exception made sense, nonetheless, dissented because of the confusion she believed making exceptions to *Miranda's* bright-line rule would cause:

> Since the time *Miranda* was decided, the Court has repeatedly refused to bend the literal terms of that decision. . . . Wherever an accused has been taken into "custody" and subjected to "interrogation" without warnings, the Court has consistently prohibited the use of his responses for prosecutorial purposes at trial. As a consequence, the "meaning of *Miranda* has become reasonably clear and law enforcement practices have adjusted to its strictures." . . .
>
> In my view, a "public safety" exception unnecessarily blurs the edges of the clear line heretofore established and makes *Miranda's* requirements more difficult to understand. . . . The end result will be a fine spun new doctrine on public safety exigencies incident to custodial interrogation, complete with the hair-splitting distinctions that currently plague our Fourth Amendment jurisprudence. (662–64)

Go to Exercise 8.2 on the Samaha Criminal Procedure 7e website to learn more about the public safety exception: academic.cengage.com/criminaljustice/samaha.

## The Meaning of "Interrogation"

The words *interrogation* and *confession* don't appear in the Fifth, Sixth, or Fourteenth Amendment. Their constitutional significance arises out of their relation to

1. The Fifth Amendment guarantee against compelling individuals to be witnesses against themselves

2. The Sixth Amendment right to counsel

3. The Fifth and Fourteenth Amendment guarantees against the denial of life, liberty, and property without due process of law

**Interrogation** means something different in each of these amendments. Fifth Amendment self-incrimination requires the "functional equivalent" of a question to trigger its protection. "Deliberately eliciting a response" is good enough to trigger the Sixth Amendment right to counsel. Due process focuses on coercion and its mirror image, voluntariness. Before formal proceedings start, the Fifth Amendment self-incrimination clause gives more leeway to the police in getting incriminating information from suspects. Why? First, the Fifth Amendment requires coercion; the Sixth Amendment doesn't. Second, the power of the government isn't as focused on suspects in police stations during interrogations as it is on defendants formally charged with crimes. Third, suspects in police stations don't need experts as much as defendants who have to appear in court. A fourth, more practical (but usually not openly admitted), reason for the stricter definition of Fifth Amendment interrogation is that the lawyers interfere with police efforts to get information from suspects.

Let's look more closely at each of the tests.

### The Fifth Amendment "Functional Equivalent of a Question" Test

The Supreme Court adopted and applied the "**functional equivalent of a question**" **test** in *Rhode Island v. Innis* (1980). Thomas Innis, a cab driver, was arrested for robbing and murdering another cab driver, John Mulvaney, with a sawed-off shotgun. Officers immediately, and several times after that, gave Innis the warnings; Innis said he wanted to talk to a lawyer. Three officers put Innis in the squad car to take him to the station. On the way, the officers talked among themselves about finding the shotgun because there was a school for handicapped kids nearby. At that point, Innis said he'd show them where the gun was; he did.

The Rhode Island state court tried and convicted Innis of murder. The Rhode Island supreme court overturned the conviction because the officers got his confession by "subtle coercion" equivalent to *Miranda* interrogation (296). The U.S. Supreme Court was faced with choosing between a narrow view of interrogation—namely, that it includes only direct questions—and a broad view like that adopted by the Rhode Island court. The Court rejected the narrow view, but this didn't mean that "all statements obtained by police after a person has been taken into custody are to be considered the product of interrogation" (299). Interrogation, as *Miranda* conceptualized it, has to "reflect a measure of compulsion above and beyond that inherent in custody itself" (300).

The Court elaborated:

> We conclude that the *Miranda* safeguards come into play whenever a person in custody is subjected to either express questioning or its functional equivalent. That is to say, the term "interrogation" under *Miranda* refers not only to express questioning, but also to any words or actions on the part of the police (other than those normally attendant to arrest and custody) that the police should know are reasonably likely to elicit an incriminating response from the suspect. The latter portion of this definition focuses primarily upon the perceptions of the suspect, rather than the intent of the police. This focus reflects the fact that the *Miranda* safeguards were designed to vest a suspect in custody with an added measure of protection against coercive police practices, without regard to objective proof of the underlying intent of the police. A practice that the police should know is reasonably likely to evoke an incriminating response from a suspect thus amounts to interrogation. But, since the police surely cannot be held accountable for the unforeseeable results of their words or actions, the definition of interrogation can extend only to words or actions on the part of police officers that they should have known were reasonably likely to elicit an incriminating response. (300–3)

***The Sixth Amendment "Deliberately Eliciting a Response" Test*** The *Innis* "functional equivalent" definition is based on the Fifth Amendment right against self-incrimination. As such, the definition of "interrogation" differs from the Sixth Amendment right-to-counsel clause, which applies only to interrogation after formal charges are brought. The test for interrogation after formal charges, called the **"deliberately eliciting a response" standard** (also called "deliberately elicit"), focuses squarely on police intent (it's irrelevant in *Innis*, which as you just learned adopted an objective standard).

The "deliberately elicited" test provides broader protection to interrogated suspects and more restrictions on interrogating officers. Notice that the Sixth Amendment says nothing about coercion; it guarantees the right to counsel in *all* criminal prosecutions (italics added). "Prosecution" means when the government starts formal proceedings (formal charge, preliminary hearing, indictment, information, or arraignment). At that point, the Sixth Amendment kicks in and defendants can always have their lawyers present.

Any incriminating statements suspects make when a lawyer isn't present, *even if they're voluntary*, violate the suspect's right to counsel. For example, in *Massiah v. U.S.* (1964), Winston Massiah was indicted for cocaine dealing and released on bail. The police arranged for Massiah's co-defendant to discuss with him the pair's pending trial in a car while the co-defendant was wired with a radio transmitter hooked up to police officers. The Court held that Massiah's right to counsel was violated even though officers never directly asked him anything. According to the Court, the incriminating words Massiah communicated to his co-defendant resulted from interrogation because they "were deliberately elicited from him" by federal agents.

Why has the Supreme Court interpreted interrogation broadly once the right to counsel kicks in? Two reasons: First, once formal proceedings begin, all the power of the government is aimed at convicting criminal defendants. Second, at this stage, technical knowledge of the law and its procedures becomes critical. Defendants need experts (defense lawyers) to guide them through the maze of highly technical rules and procedures just as the state relies on its own experts (prosecutors) to do the same for the government.

Our next case excerpt, *Brewer v. Williams* (1977), involved the grisly murder of a 10-year-old girl on Christmas Eve. The Court applied the "deliberately elicited" test and threw Robert Williams's confession (although true) out. The majority decision provoked strong dissents from several justices, one of them extremely angry that this horrible crime was going to go unpunished. Not to worry. The case was retried, this time on a different theory; Williams was convicted, and the Court upheld his conviction, in *Nix v. Williams* (1984).

C A S E    ***Did the Officers "Deliberately Elicit" Incriminating Statements?***

### *Brewer v. Williams*
430 U.S. 387 (1977)

#### HISTORY

Robert Williams, a state prisoner convicted of murder, petitioned for a writ of habeas corpus. The U.S. District Court for the Southern District of Iowa granted the petition, and the state appealed. The Court of Appeals affirmed, and certiorari was granted. The Supreme Court affirmed.

STEWART, J.

An Iowa trial jury found the respondent, Robert Williams, guilty of murder. The judgment of conviction was affirmed in the Iowa Supreme Court by a closely divided vote. In a subsequent habeas corpus proceeding a Federal District Court ruled that under the United States Constitution

Williams is entitled to a new trial, and a divided Court of Appeals for the Eighth Circuit agreed. The question before us is whether the District Court and the Court of Appeals were wrong.

## FACTS

On the afternoon of December 24, 1968, a 10-year-old girl named Pamela Powers went with her family to the YMCA in Des Moines, Iowa, to watch a wrestling tournament in which her brother was participating. When she failed to return from a trip to the washroom, a search for her began. The search was unsuccessful.

Robert Williams, who had recently escaped from a mental hospital, was a resident of the YMCA. Soon after the girl's disappearance Williams was seen in the YMCA lobby carrying some clothing and a large bundle wrapped in a blanket. He obtained help from a 14-year-old boy in opening the street door of the YMCA and the door to his automobile parked outside. When Williams placed the bundle in the front seat of his car the boy "saw two legs in it and they were skinny and white." Before anyone could see what was in the bundle Williams drove away. His abandoned car was found the following day in Davenport, Iowa, roughly 160 miles east of Des Moines. A warrant was then issued in Des Moines for his arrest on a charge of abduction.

On the morning of December 26, a Des Moines lawyer named Henry McKnight went to the Des Moines police station and informed the officers present that he had just received a long-distance call from Williams, and that he had advised Williams to turn himself in to the Davenport police. Williams did surrender that morning to the police in Davenport, and they booked him on the charge specified in the arrest warrant and gave him the warnings required by *Miranda v. Arizona*. The Davenport police then telephoned their counterparts in Des Moines to inform them that Williams had surrendered. McKnight, the lawyer, was still at the Des Moines police headquarters, and Williams conversed with McKnight on the telephone.

In the presence of the Des Moines chief of police and a police detective named Leaming, McKnight advised Williams that Des Moines police officers would be driving to Davenport to pick him up, that the officers would not interrogate him or mistreat him, and that Williams was not to talk to the officers about Pamela Powers until after consulting with McKnight upon his return to Des Moines. As a result of these conversations, it was agreed between McKnight and the Des Moines police officials that Detective Leaming and a fellow officer would drive to Davenport to pick up Williams, that they would bring him directly back to Des Moines, and that they would not question him during the trip.

In the meantime Williams was arraigned before a judge in Davenport on the outstanding arrest warrant. The judge advised him of his *Miranda* rights and committed him to jail. Before leaving the courtroom, Williams conferred with a lawyer named Kelly, who advised him not to make any statements until consulting with McKnight back in Des Moines.

Detective Leaming and his fellow officer arrived in Davenport about noon to pick up Williams and return him to Des Moines. Soon after their arrival they met with Williams and Kelly, who, they understood, was acting as Williams' lawyer. Detective Leaming repeated the *Miranda* warnings, and told Williams:

> We both know that you're being represented here by Mr. Kelly and you're being represented by Mr. McKnight in Des Moines, and . . . I want you to remember this because we'll be visiting between here and Des Moines.

Williams then conferred again with Kelly alone, and after this conference Kelly reiterated to Detective Leaming that Williams was not to be questioned about the disappearance of Pamela Powers until after he had consulted with McKnight back in Des Moines. When Leaming expressed some reservations, Kelly firmly stated that the agreement with McKnight was to be carried out that there was to be no interrogation of Williams during the automobile journey to Des Moines. Kelly was denied permission to ride in the police car back to Des Moines with Williams and the two officers.

The two detectives, with Williams in their charge, then set out on the 160-mile drive. At no time during the trip did Williams express a willingness to be interrogated in the absence of an attorney. Instead, he stated several times that "when I get to Des Moines and see Mr. McKnight, I am going to tell you the whole story." Detective Leaming knew that Williams was a former mental patient, and knew also that he was deeply religious.

The detective and his prisoner soon embarked on a wide-ranging conversation covering a variety of topics, including the subject of religion. Then, not long after leaving Davenport and reaching the interstate highway, Detective Leaming delivered what has been referred to in the briefs and oral arguments as the "Christian burial speech." Addressing Williams as "Reverend," the detective said:

> I want to give you something to think about while we're traveling down the road. . . . Number one, I want you to observe the weather conditions, it's raining, it's sleeting, it's freezing, driving is very treacherous, visibility is poor, it's going to be dark early this evening. They are predicting several inches of snow for tonight, and I feel that you yourself are the only person that knows where this little girl's body is, that you yourself have only been there once, and if you get a snow on top of it you yourself may be unable to find it. And, since we will be going right past the area on the way into Des Moines, I feel that we could stop and locate the body, that the parents of this little girl should be entitled to a Christian burial for the little girl who was snatched away from them on Christmas Eve and murdered. And I feel we should stop and locate it on the way in rather than waiting until morning and trying to come back out after a snow storm and possibly not being able to find it at all.

Williams asked Detective Leaming why he thought their route to Des Moines would be taking them past the girl's body, and Leaming responded that he knew the body was in the area of Mitchellville, a town they would be passing on the way to Des Moines. The fact of the matter, of course, was that Detective Leaming possessed no such knowledge. Leaming then stated: "I do not want you to answer me. I don't want to discuss it any further. Just think about it as we're riding down the road."

As the car approached Grinnell, a town approximately 100 miles west of Davenport, Williams asked whether the police had found the victim's shoes. When Detective Leaming replied that he was unsure, Williams directed the officers to a service station where he said he had left the shoes; a search for them proved unsuccessful. As they continued towards Des Moines, Williams asked whether the police had found the blanket, and directed the officers to a rest area where he said he had disposed of the blanket. Nothing was found. The car continued towards Des Moines, and as it approached Mitchellville, Williams said that he would show the officers where the body was. He then directed the police to the body of Pamela Powers.

Williams was indicted for first-degree murder. Before trial, his counsel moved to suppress all evidence relating to or resulting from any statements Williams had made during the automobile ride from Davenport to Des Moines. After an evidentiary hearing the trial judge denied the motion. . . . The evidence in question was introduced over counsel's continuing objection at the subsequent trial. The jury found Williams guilty of murder, and the judgment of conviction was affirmed by the Iowa Supreme Court, a bare majority of whose members agreed with the trial court that Williams had waived his right to the presence of his counsel on the automobile ride from Davenport to Des Moines. . . .

Williams then petitioned for a writ of habeas corpus in the United States District Court for the Southern District of Iowa. Counsel for the State and for Williams stipulated that "the case would be submitted on the record of facts and proceedings in the trial court, without taking of further testimony." The District Court made findings of fact as summarized above, and concluded as a matter of law that the evidence in question had been wrongly admitted at Williams' trial. . . . The Court of Appeals for the Eighth Circuit, with one judge dissenting, affirmed this judgment, and denied a petition for rehearing en banc. We granted certiorari to consider the constitutional issues presented.

## OPINION

. . . The right to counsel granted by the Sixth and Fourteenth Amendments means at least that a person is entitled to the help of a lawyer at or after the time that judicial proceedings have been initiated against him whether by way of formal charge, preliminary hearing, indictment, information, or arraignment. There can be no doubt in the present case that judicial proceedings had been initiated

against Williams before the start of the automobile ride from Davenport to Des Moines. A warrant had been issued for his arrest, he had been arraigned on that warrant before a judge in a Davenport courtroom, and he had been committed by the court to confinement in jail. The State does not contend otherwise.

There can be no serious doubt, either, that Detective Leaming deliberately and designedly set out to elicit information from Williams just as surely as and perhaps more effectively than if he had formally interrogated him. Detective Leaming was fully aware before departing for Des Moines that Williams was being represented in Davenport by Kelly and in Des Moines by McKnight. Yet he purposely sought during Williams' isolation from his lawyers to obtain as much incriminating information as possible. Indeed, Detective Leaming conceded as much when he testified at Williams' trial:

*Q:* In fact, Captain, whether he was a mental patient or not, you were trying to get all the information you could before he got to his lawyer, weren't you?

*A:* I was sure hoping to find out where that little girl was, yes, sir.

*Q:* Well, I'll put it this way: You was [*sic*] hoping to get all the information you could before Williams got back to McKnight, weren't you?

*A:* Yes, sir.

Counsel for petitioner, in the course of oral argument in this Court, acknowledged that the "Christian burial speech" was tantamount to interrogation:

*Q:* But isn't the point, really, Mr. Attorney General, what you indicated earlier, and that is that the officer wanted to elicit information from Williams?

*A:* Yes, sir.

*Q:* By whatever techniques he used, I would suppose a lawyer would consider that he were [*sic*] pursuing interrogation.

*A:* It is, but it was very brief.

The state courts clearly proceeded upon the hypothesis that Detective Leaming's "Christian burial speech" had been tantamount to interrogation. Both courts recognized that Williams had been entitled to the assistance of counsel at the time he made the incriminating statements. Yet no such constitutional protection would have come into play if there had been no interrogation. . . .

The crime of which Williams was convicted was senseless and brutal, calling for swift and energetic action by the police to apprehend the perpetrator and gather evidence with which he could be convicted. No mission of law enforcement officials is more important. Yet disinterested zeal for the public good does not assure either wisdom or right in the methods it pursues. Although we do not lightly affirm the issuance of a writ of habeas corpus in this case, so clear a violation of the Sixth and Fourteenth Amendments as here occurred cannot be condoned. The pressures on state executive and judicial officers charged with the administration of the criminal law are great, especially when the crime is murder and the victim a small child. But it is precisely the predictability of those pressures that makes imperative a resolute loyalty to the guarantees that the Constitution extends to us all.

The judgment of the Court of Appeals is AFFIRMED. *It is so ordered.*

## CONCURRENCES

### MARSHALL, J.

. . . The dissenters have, I believe, lost sight of the fundamental constitutional backbone of our criminal law. They seem to think that Detective Leaming's actions were perfectly proper, indeed laudable, examples of "good police work." In my view, good police work is something far different from catching the criminal at any price. It is equally important that the police, as guardians of the law, fulfill their responsibility to obey its commands scrupulously. For in the end life and liberty can be as much endangered from illegal methods used to convict those thought to be criminals as from the actual criminals themselves. . . .

### POWELL, J.

. . . The record evidence clearly indicates that the police engaged in interrogation of Williams. . . . The District Court quoted extensively from Leaming's testimony, including the following:

*Q:* In fact, Captain, whether [Williams] was a mental patient or not, you were trying to get all the information you could before he got to his lawyer, weren't you?

*A:* I was sure hoping to find out where that little girl was, yes, sir.

*Q:* Well, I'll put it this way: You were hoping to get all the information you could before Williams got back to McKnight, weren't you?

*A:* Yes, sir.

. . . Nothing that we write, no matter how well reasoned or forcefully expressed, can bring back the victim of this tragedy or undo the consequences of the official neglect which led to the respondent's escape from a state mental institution. The emotional aspects of the case make it difficult to decide dispassionately, but do not qualify our obligation to apply the law with an eye to the future as well as with concern for the result in the particular case before us. . . .

## DISSENT

### BURGER, C.J.

The result in this case ought to be intolerable in any society which purports to call itself an organized society. It continues the Court by the narrowest margin on the much-criticized course of punishing the public for the mistakes and misdeeds of law enforcement officers, instead of punishing the officer directly, if in fact he is guilty of wrongdoing. It mechanically and blindly keeps

reliable evidence from juries whether the claimed constitutional violation involves gross police misconduct or honest human error.

Williams is guilty of the savage murder of a small child; no member of the Court contends he is not. While in custody, and after no fewer than five warnings of his rights to silence and to counsel, he led police to the concealed body of his victim. The Court concedes Williams was not threatened or coerced and that he spoke and acted voluntarily and with full awareness of his constitutional rights. In the face of all this, the Court now holds that because Williams was prompted by the detective's statement—not interrogation but a statement—the jury must not be told how the police found the body.

. . . In so ruling the Court regresses to playing a grisly game of "hide and seek," once more exalting the sporting theory of criminal justice which has been experiencing a decline in our jurisprudence. With Justices WHITE, BLACKMUN, and REHNQUIST, I categorically reject the remarkable notion that the police in this case were guilty of unconstitutional misconduct, or any conduct justifying the bizarre result reached by the Court. . . .

In his concurring opinion Mr. Justice POWELL suggests that the result in this case turns on whether Detective Leaming's remarks constituted "interrogation," as he views them, or whether they were "statements" intended to prick the conscience of the accused. I find it most remarkable that a murder case should turn on judicial interpretation that a statement becomes a question simply because it is followed by an incriminating disclosure from the suspect. The Court seems to be saying that since Williams said he would "tell the whole story" at Des Moines, the police should have been content and waited; of course, that would have been the wiser course, especially in light of the nuances of constitutional jurisprudence applied by the Court, but a murder case ought not turn on such tenuous strands.

. . . It is striking that the Court fails even to consider whether the benefits secured by application of the exclusionary rule in this case outweigh its obvious social costs. . . .

### WHITE, J., JOINED BY BLACKMUN AND REHNQUIST, JJ.

The consequence of the majority's decision is, as the majority recognizes, extremely serious. A mentally disturbed killer whose guilt is not in question may be released. Why? The police did nothing wrong, let alone anything unconstitutional. To anyone not lost in the intricacies of the prophylactic rules of *Miranda v. Arizona*, the result in this case seems utterly senseless. . . .

### BLACKMUN, J., JOINED BY WHITE AND REHNQUIST, JJ.

. . . Not every attempt to elicit information should be regarded as "tantamount to interrogation." I am not persuaded that Leaming's observations and comments, made as the police car traversed the snowy and slippery miles between Davenport and Des Moines that winter afternoon, were an interrogation, direct or subtle, of Williams. Contrary to this Court's statement. . . . Williams, after all, was counseled by lawyers, and warned by the arraigning judge in Davenport and by the police, and yet it was he who started the travel conversations and brought up the subject of the criminal investigation. Without further reviewing the circumstances of the trip, I would say it is clear there was no interrogation. . . .

In summary, it seems to me that the Court is holding that [the right to counsel] . . . is violated whenever police engage in any conduct, in the absence of counsel, with the subjective desire to obtain information from a suspect after arraignment. Such a rule is far too broad. Persons in custody frequently volunteer statements in response to stimuli other than interrogation.

. . . One final word: I can understand the discomfiture the Court obviously suffers and expresses. . . . This was a brutal, tragic, and heinous crime inflicted upon a young girl on the afternoon of the day before Christmas. With the exclusionary rule operating as the Court effectuates it, the decision today probably means that, as a practical matter, no new trial will be possible at this date eight years after the crime, and that this respondent necessarily will go free. . . . .

### Questions

1. List all the facts relevant to deciding whether the officers deliberately elicited Williams's incriminating statements.

2. According to the Court's definition, do you agree that the officer "interrogated" Williams? Explain your answer.

3. Summarize each of the opinions excerpted. Which is closest to your view? Explain your answer.

4. Can you understand Chief Justice Burger's emotional response? Does it belong in a Supreme Court opinion? Explain.

# THE WAIVER OF THE RIGHT TO REMAIN SILENT

After *Miranda v. Arizona* was decided there was a lot of talk about "handcuffing the police." The talk was created by a fear that suspects wouldn't talk if officers told them they had a right not to talk to police and to have lawyers with them if they did talk. As it turned out, these fears were greatly exaggerated. Most defendants waived their rights and talked to the police anyway. They still do. Richard Leo (1996) estimates that about 75 percent of suspects routinely waive their *Miranda* rights and talk to the police (653). Based on this reality, the Supreme Court said, "[G]iving the warnings and getting a waiver has generally produced a virtual ticket of admissibility" (*Missouri v. Seibert* 2004, 601). Because so many suspects waive their rights and talk to interrogators with no lawyer in sight, two questions are of great constitutional *and* practical importance:

1. What is a valid waiver of the right against self-incrimination? and

2. What is a voluntary confession?

In *Miranda v. Arizona* (1966), the Court addressed the issue of what constitutes a valid waiver:

> An express statement that the individual is willing to make a statement and does not want an attorney followed closely by a statement could constitute a waiver. But a valid waiver will not be presumed simply from the silence of the accused after warnings are given or simply from the fact that a confession was in fact eventually obtained. (475)

This statement strongly suggests the Court was referring to an **express waiver test**, which means you have to make clear statements that indicate you know your rights, know you're giving them up, and know the consequences of giving them up. But the Court doesn't require express waivers; instead, it has adopted an **implied waiver test**, which says the totality of circumstances in each case has to prove that before suspects talked, they knew they had the rights and knew they were giving them up.

| TABLE 8.3 | Circumstances Relevant to Showing a Knowing Waiver |
| --- | --- |

- Intelligence
- Physical condition
- Education
- Mental condition

- Age
- Ability to understand English
- Familiarity with the criminal justice system

In *North Carolina v. Butler* (1979), officers read Willie Butler his *Miranda* rights. Butler said he knew his rights, but he refused to sign a waiver form. ("I will talk to you but I am not signing any form" [371].) The North Carolina trial court threw out the confession because Butler didn't expressly waive his right to remain silent. The North Carolina supreme court affirmed. The U.S. Supreme Court reversed, adopting instead the implied waiver test.

According to Justice Stewart, writing for the majority:

> An express written or oral statement of waiver of the right to remain silent or of the right to counsel is usually strong proof of the validity of that waiver, but is not inevitably either necessary or sufficient to establish waiver. The question is not one of form, but rather whether the defendant in fact knowingly and voluntarily waived the rights delineated in the *Miranda* case. As was unequivocally said in *Miranda*, mere silence is not enough.
>
> That does not mean that the defendant's silence, coupled with an understanding of his rights and a course of conduct indicating waiver, may never support a conclusion that a defendant has waived his rights. The courts must presume that a defendant did not waive his rights; the prosecution's burden is great; but in at least some cases waiver can be clearly inferred from the actions and words of the person interrogated. (373)
>
> This is not the first criminal case to question whether a defendant waived his constitutional rights. It is an issue with which courts must repeatedly deal. Even when a right so fundamental as that to counsel at trial is involved, the question of waiver must be determined on "the particular facts and circumstances surrounding that case, including the background, experience, and conduct of the accused." (374–75)

Circumstances commonly considered in making the waiver determination are listed in Table 8.3, and examples of cases in which courts ruled there was a knowing waiver appear in Table 8.4.

In our next case excerpt, *Moran v. Burbine* (1986), the Supreme Court ruled that preventing Brian Burbine's lawyer from seeing him didn't invalidate Burbine's waiver of his rights.

| TABLE 8.4 | Cases in Which Courts Found a Knowing Waiver |
| --- | --- |

- No evidence showed the suspect was threatened, tricked, or cajoled. (*Connecticut v. Barrett* 1987)

- The suspect invoked the right to counsel and then, after a five-hour ride in the back of a squad car signed a waiver when police officers asked "if there was anything he would like to tell them." (*Henderson v. Florida* 1985)

- The suspect asked for a lawyer, didn't get one, and then signed a waiver after repeated warnings and "nagging" by police officers. (*Watkins v. Virginia* 1986)

- After refusing to sign an express waiver, the defendant talked to the police. (*U.S. v. Barahona* 1993)

- The defendant said, "I don't got nothing to say" when he was presented with a waiver form but then answered questions during an interview that followed. (*U.S. v. Banks* 1995)

## Moran, Superintendent, Rhode Island Department of Corrections, v. Burbine

### 475 U.S. 412 (1986)

### HISTORY

Following his conviction for murder and the affirmance of that conviction by the Rhode Island Supreme Court, Brian Burbine, the defendant, petitioned for federal habeas corpus relief. The United States District Court for the District of Rhode Island, denied relief, and defendant appealed. The United States Court of Appeals for the First Circuit, reversed. Certiorari was granted. The Supreme Court reversed and remanded.

O'CONNOR, J., JOINED BY BURGER, C.J., AND WHITE, BLACKMUN, POWELL, AND REHNQUIST, JJ.

### FACTS

On the morning of March 3, 1977, Mary Jo Hickey was found unconscious in a factory parking lot in Providence, Rhode Island. Suffering from injuries to her skull apparently inflicted by a metal pipe found at the scene, she was rushed to a nearby hospital. Three weeks later she died from her wounds.

Several months after her death, the Cranston, Rhode Island, police arrested respondent and two others in connection with a local burglary. Shortly before the arrest, Detective Ferranti of the Cranston police force had learned from a confidential informant that the man responsible for Ms. Hickey's death lived at a certain address and went by the name of "Butch." Upon discovering that respondent lived at that address and was known by that name, Detective Ferranti informed respondent of his *Miranda* rights. When respondent refused to execute a written waiver, Detective Ferranti spoke separately with the two other suspects arrested on the breaking and entering charge and obtained statements further implicating respondent in Ms. Hickey's murder. At approximately 6 P.M., Detective Ferranti telephoned the police in Providence to convey the information he had uncovered. An hour later, three officers from that department arrived at the Cranston headquarters for the purpose of questioning respondent about the murder.

That same evening, at about 7:45 P.M., respondent's sister telephoned the Public Defender's Office to obtain legal assistance for her brother. Her sole concern was the breaking and entering charge, as she was unaware that respondent was then under suspicion for murder. She asked for Richard Casparian who had been scheduled to meet with respondent earlier that afternoon to discuss another charge

unrelated to either the break-in or the murder. As soon as the conversation ended, the attorney who took the call attempted to reach Mr. Casparian. When those efforts were unsuccessful, she telephoned Allegra Munson, another Assistant Public Defender, and told her about respondent's arrest and his sister's subsequent request that the office represent him.

At 8:15 P.M., Ms. Munson telephoned the Cranston police station and asked that her call be transferred to the detective division.

A male voice responded with the word "Detectives." Ms. Munson identified herself and asked if Brian Burbine was being held; the person responded affirmatively. Ms. Munson explained to the person that Burbine was represented by attorney Casparian who was not available; she further stated that she would act as Burbine's legal counsel in the event that the police intended to place him in a lineup or question him. The unidentified person told Ms. Munson that the police would not be questioning Burbine or putting him in a lineup and that they were through with him for the night. Ms. Munson was not informed that the Providence Police were at the Cranston police station or that Burbine was a suspect in Mary's murder.

At all relevant times, respondent was unaware of his sister's efforts to retain counsel and of the fact and contents of Ms. Munson's telephone conversation.

Less than an hour later, the police brought respondent to an interrogation room and conducted the first of a series of interviews concerning the murder. Prior to each session, respondent was informed of his *Miranda* rights, and on three separate occasions he signed a written form acknowledging that he understood his right to the presence of an attorney and explicitly indicating that he "did not want an attorney called or appointed for him" before he gave a statement. Uncontradicted evidence at the suppression hearing indicated that at least twice during the course of the evening, respondent was left in a room where he had access to a telephone, which he apparently declined to use. Eventually, respondent signed three written statements fully admitting to the murder.

Prior to trial, respondent moved to suppress the statements. The court denied the motion. . . . The jury found respondent guilty of murder in the first degree. . . . After unsuccessfully petitioning the U.S. District Court for the District of Rhode Island for a writ of habeas corpus, respondent appealed to the Court of Appeals for the First Circuit. That court reversed. . . .

We granted certiorari to decide whether a prearraignment confession preceded by an otherwise valid waiver must be suppressed either because the police misinformed an inquiring attorney about their plans concerning the suspect or because they failed to inform the suspect of the attorney's efforts to reach him. We now reverse.

## OPINION

. . . Respondent does not dispute that the Providence police followed *Miranda* procedures with precision. . . . He contends instead that the confessions must be suppressed because the police's failure to inform him of the attorney's telephone call deprived him of information essential to his ability to knowingly waive his Fifth Amendment rights. In the alternative, he suggests that to fully protect the Fifth Amendment values served by *Miranda*, we should extend that decision to condemn the conduct of the Providence police. We address each contention in turn.

. . . *Miranda* holds that the defendant may waive effectuation of the rights conveyed in the warnings provided the waiver is made voluntarily, knowingly and intelligently. The inquiry has two distinct dimensions. First, the relinquishment of the right must have been voluntary in the sense that it was the product of a free and deliberate choice rather than intimidation, coercion, or deception. Second, the waiver must have been made with a full awareness of both the nature of the right being abandoned and the consequences of the decision to abandon it. Only if the "totality of the circumstances surrounding the interrogation" reveal both an uncoerced choice and the requisite level of comprehension may a court properly conclude that the *Miranda* rights have been waived.

Under this standard, we have no doubt that respondent validly waived his right to remain silent. . . . The voluntariness of the waiver is not at issue. As the Court of Appeals correctly acknowledged, the record is devoid of any suggestion that police resorted to physical or psychological pressure to elicit the statements. Indeed it appears that it was respondent, and not the police, who spontaneously initiated the conversation that led to the first and most damaging confession. Nor is there any question about respondent's comprehension of the full panoply of rights set out in the *Miranda* warnings and of the potential consequences of a decision to relinquish them. Nonetheless, the Court of Appeals believed that the "deliberate or reckless" conduct of the police, in particular their failure to inform respondent of the telephone call, fatally undermined the validity of the otherwise proper waiver. . . .

. . . Whether intentional or inadvertent, the state of mind of the police is irrelevant to the question of the intelligence and voluntariness of respondent's election to abandon his rights. Although highly inappropriate, even deliberate deception of an attorney could not possibly affect a suspect's decision to waive his *Miranda* rights unless he were at least aware of the incident. Nor was the failure to inform respondent of the telephone call the kind of "trick[ery]" that can vitiate the validity of a waiver. Granting that the "deliberate or reckless" withholding of information is objectionable as a matter of ethics, such conduct is only relevant to the constitutional validity of a waiver if it deprives a defendant of knowledge essential to his ability to understand the nature of his rights and the consequences of abandoning them. Because respondent's voluntary decision to speak was made with full awareness and comprehension of all the information *Miranda* requires the police to convey, the waivers were valid.

. . . Finally, respondent contends that the conduct of the police was so offensive as to deprive him of the fundamental fairness guaranteed by the Due Process Clause of the Fourteenth Amendment. Focusing primarily on the impropriety of conveying false information to an attorney, he invites us to declare that such behavior should be condemned as violative of canons fundamental to the "traditions and conscience of our people." We do not question that on facts more egregious than those presented here police deception might rise to a level of a due process violation. . . . We hold only that, on these facts, the challenged conduct falls short of the kind of misbehavior that so shocks the sensibilities of civilized society as to warrant a federal intrusion into the criminal processes of the States. . . .

We hold therefore that the Court of Appeals erred in finding that the Federal Constitution required the exclusion of the three inculpatory statements.

Accordingly, we REVERSE and REMAND for proceedings consistent with this opinion. *So ordered.*

## DISSENT

STEVENS, J., JOINED BY BRENNAN AND MARSHALL, JJ.

This case poses fundamental questions about our system of justice. As this Court has long recognized . . . "ours is an accusatorial and not an inquisitorial system." The Court's opinion today represents a startling departure from that basic insight.

The Court concludes that the police may deceive an attorney by giving her false information about whether her client will be questioned, and that the police may deceive a suspect by failing to inform him of his attorney's communications and efforts to represent him. For the majority, this conclusion, though "distaste[ful]," is not even debatable. The deception of the attorney is irrelevant because the attorney has no right to information, accuracy, honesty, or fairness in the police response to her questions about her client. The deception of the client is acceptable, because, although the information would affect the client's assertion of his rights, the client's actions in ignorance of the availability of his attorney are voluntary, knowing, and intelligent; additionally, society's interest in apprehending, prosecuting, and punishing criminals outweighs the suspect's interest in information regarding his attorney's efforts to communicate with him. Finally, even mendacious police interference in the communications between a suspect and his lawyer does not violate any notion of fundamental fairness because it does not shock the conscience of the majority.

. . . The murder of Mary Jo Hickey was a vicious crime, fully meriting a sense of outrage and a desire to find and prosecute the perpetrator swiftly and effectively. Indeed, by the time Burbine was arrested on an unrelated breaking-and-entering charge, the Hickey murder had been the subject of a local television special. Not surprisingly, Detective Ferranti, the Cranston Detective who "broke" the case, was rewarded with a special commendation for his efforts.

The recognition that ours is an accusatorial, and not an inquisitorial system nevertheless requires that the government's actions, even in responding to this brutal crime, respect those liberties and rights that distinguish this society from most others. As Justice Jackson observed shortly after his return from Nuremberg, cases of this kind present "a real dilemma in a free society . . . for the defendant is shielded by such safeguards as no system of law except the Anglo-American concedes to him." Justice Frankfurter similarly emphasized that it is "a fair summary of history to say that the safeguards of liberty have been forged in controversies involving not very nice people." And, almost a century and a half ago, Macaulay observed that the guilt of Titus Oates could not justify his conviction by improper methods: "That Oates was a bad man is not a sufficient excuse; for the guilty are almost always the first to suffer those hardships which are afterwards used as precedents against the innocent."

The Court's holding focuses on the period after a suspect has been taken into custody and before he has been charged with an offense. The core of the Court's holding is that police interference with an attorney's access to her client during that period is not unconstitutional. The Court reasons that a State has a compelling interest, not simply in custodial interrogation, but in lawyer-free, incommunicado custodial interrogation. Such incommunicado interrogation is so important that a lawyer may be given false information that prevents her presence and representation; it is so important that police may refuse to inform a suspect of his attorney's communications and immediate availability. This conclusion flies in the face of this Court's repeated expressions of deep concern about incommunicado questioning. Until today, incommunicado questioning has been viewed with the strictest scrutiny by this Court; today, incommunicado questioning is embraced as a societal goal of the highest order that justifies police deception of the shabbiest kind.

. . . This case turns on a proper appraisal of the role of the lawyer in our society. If a lawyer is seen as a nettlesome obstacle to the pursuit of wrongdoers—as in an inquisitorial society—then the Court's decision today makes a good deal of sense. If a lawyer is seen as an aid to the understanding and protection of constitutional rights—as in an accusatorial society—then today's decision makes no sense at all.

Like the conduct of the police in the Cranston station on the evening of June 29, 1977, the Court's opinion today serves the goal of insuring that the perpetrator of a vile crime is punished. Like the police on that June night as well, however, the Court has trampled on well-established legal principles and flouted the spirit of our accusatorial system of justice.

I respectfully dissent.

### Questions

1. List all the facts relevant to deciding whether Brian Burbine voluntarily, knowingly, and intelligently waived his right to remain silent.

2. Summarize the majority's arguments in favor of its decision that Burbine waived his rights.

3. Summarize the dissent's arguments that the waiver wasn't valid.

4. How would you characterize the police behavior regarding the public defender Allegra Munson? Explain your answer.

# VOLUNTARY SELF-INCRIMINATION

Great fears and equally great hopes—depending on whether those who voiced them were more afraid of street criminals or of government abuse of power—were expressed that *Miranda v. Arizona* (1966) would kill police interrogation as a tool to collect evidence. But it didn't happen. As we've already learned, Richard Leo found that only 25 percent of suspects invoke their right to remain silent and/or to speak to a lawyer (p. 277). One experienced interrogator, Sergeant James DeConcini (now retired), of the Minneapolis Police Department, suggests the reason is that knowledge is a two-way street. Not only do police officers want to find out what suspects know about crimes they're investigating, but suspects also want to know how much police officers know.

Suspects believe that by cooperating with the police, they might find out if they "have something on them." That most suspects waive their right to remain silent and agree to custodial interrogation brings us back to the due process requirement of voluntariness. Even if officers have warned suspects and have gotten a knowing waiver, they still may not have gotten voluntarily the incriminating statements that follow. To determine whether incriminating statements were made voluntarily, the U.S. Supreme Court adopted another of its totality-of-circumstances tests: Confessions are involuntary only if the totality of the circumstances proves two things:

1. Officers engaged in coercive conduct during the interrogation.

2. The coercive conduct caused the suspect to make incriminating statements.

According to Chief Justice Rehnquist, writing for a majority of the U.S. Supreme Court in *Colorado v. Connelly* (1986):

> . . . The cases considered by this Court over the 50 years since *Brown v. Mississippi* have focused on the crucial element of police overreaching. While each confession case has turned on its own set of factors . . . , all have contained a substantial element of coercive police conduct. Absent police conduct causally related to the confession, there is simply no basis for concluding that any state actor has deprived a criminal defendant of due process of law. . . . As interrogators have turned to more subtle forms of psychological persuasion, courts have found the mental condition of the defendant a more significant factor in the "voluntariness" calculus. But this fact does not justify a conclusion that a defendant's mental condition, by itself apart from its relation to official coercion, should ever dispose of the inquiry into constitutional "voluntariness." (163)

The most common circumstances courts consider in determining whether coercive state action caused people to confess include the following:

- The location where the questioning took place
- Whether the suspect initiated the contact with law enforcement
- Whether the *Miranda* warnings were given
- The number of interrogators
- The length of the questioning
- Whether food, water, and toilet facilities were denied
- Whether the police used threats, promises, lies, or tricks
- Whether the suspect was denied access to a lawyer
- The suspect's characteristics, such as age, gender, race, physical and mental condition, education, drug problems, and experience with the criminal justice system

Courts have ruled that none of the following actions caused suspects to confess (*Twenty-Sixth Annual Review of Criminal Procedure* 1997, 967–68):

- Promises of leniency
- Promises of treatment
- Confronting the accused with other evidence of guilt

- The interrogator's appeal to the defendant's emotions
- False and misleading statements made by the interrogator

In our next case excerpt, *Colorado v. Connelly* (1986), the U.S. Supreme Court ruled that Francis Connelly's confession was voluntary even though his serious mental illness led him to believe God ordered him to "confess or commit suicide."

# C A S E    *Did He Confess Voluntarily?*

## *Colorado v. Connelly*
### 479 U.S. 157 (1986)

## HISTORY

The trial court suppressed statements made by Francis Barry Connelly. The state appealed. The Colorado Supreme Court affirmed. The U.S. Supreme Court granted certiorari, reversed, and remanded the case.

REHNQUIST, C.J., JOINED BY WHITE, POWELL, O'CONNOR, AND SCALIA, JJ. AND, IN ALL BUT PART III-A, BLACKMUN, J.

## FACTS

On August 18, 1983, Officer Patrick Anderson of the Denver Police Department was in uniform, working in an off-duty capacity in downtown Denver. Francis Connelly approached Officer Anderson and, without any prompting, stated he had murdered someone and wanted to talk about it. Anderson immediately advised Connelly he had the right to remain silent, that anything he said could be used against him in court, and that he had the right to an attorney prior to any police questioning. Connelly stated that he understood these rights but he still wanted to talk about the murder. Understandably bewildered by this confession, Officer Anderson asked Connelly several questions.

Connelly denied he had been drinking, denied he had been taking any drugs, and stated that, in the past, he had been a patient in several mental hospitals. Officer Anderson again told Connelly he was under no obligation to say anything. Connelly replied it was "all right," and that he would talk to Officer Anderson because his conscience had been bothering him. To Officer Anderson, Connelly appeared to understand fully the nature of his acts.

Shortly thereafter, Homicide Detective Stephen Antuna arrived. Connelly was again advised of his rights, and Detective Antuna asked him "what he had on his mind." Connelly answered that he had come all the way from Boston to confess to the murder of Mary Ann Junta, a young girl whom he had killed in Denver sometime during November 1982. Connelly was taken to police headquarters, and a search of police records revealed that the body of an unidentified female had been found in April 1983. Connelly

openly detailed his story to Detective Antuna and Sergeant Thomas Haney, and readily agreed to take the officers to the scene of the killing. Under Connelly's sole direction, the two officers and Connelly proceeded in a police vehicle to the location of the crime.

Connelly pointed out the exact location of the murder. Throughout this episode, Detective Antuna perceived no indication whatsoever that Connelly was suffering from any kind of mental illness. Connelly was held overnight.

During an interview with the public defender's office the following morning, he became visibly disoriented. He began giving confused answers to questions, and for the first time, stated "voices" had told him to come to Denver and he had followed the directions of these voices in confessing. Connelly was sent to a state hospital for evaluation. He was initially found incompetent to assist in his own defense. By March 1984, however, the doctors evaluating Connelly determined he was competent to proceed to trial.

At a preliminary hearing, Connelly moved to suppress all of his statements. Dr. Jeffrey Metzner, a psychiatrist employed by the state hospital, testified that Connelly was suffering from chronic schizophrenia and was in a psychotic state at least as of August 17, 1983, the day before he confessed. Metzner's interviews with Connelly revealed that he was following the "voice of God." This voice instructed him to withdraw money from the bank, to buy an airplane ticket, and to fly from Boston to Denver. When he arrived from Boston, God's voice became stronger and told him either to confess to the killing or to commit suicide. Reluctantly following the command of the voices, he approached Officer Anderson and confessed.

Dr. Metzner testified that, in his expert opinion, Connelly was experiencing "command hallucinations." This condition interfered with his "volitional abilities— that is, his ability to make free and rational choices." Dr. Metzner further testified that Connelly's illness did not significantly impair his cognitive abilities. Thus, he understood the rights he had when Officer Anderson and Detective Antuna advised him that he need not speak. Dr. Metzner admitted that the "voices" could in reality be Connelly's interpretation of his own guilt, but explained that in his opinion, Connelly's psychosis motivated his confession.

On the basis of this evidence the Colorado trial court decided that Connelly's statements must be suppressed because they were "involuntary." The court ruled that a confession is admissible only if it is a product of the defendant's rational intellect and "free will." Although the court found that the police had done nothing wrong or coercive in securing Connelly's confession, his illness destroyed his volition and compelled him to confess. The trial court also found that Connelly's mental state vitiated his attempted waiver of the right to counsel and the privilege against compulsory self-incrimination. Accordingly, Connelly's initial statements and his custodial confession were suppressed.

. . . The Colorado Supreme Court affirmed the trial court's decision to suppress all of Connelly's statements.

## OPINION

. . . The cases considered by this Court over the 50 years since *Brown v. Mississippi* have focused upon the crucial element of police overreaching. While each confession case has turned on its own set of factors justifying the conclusion that police conduct was oppressive, all have contained a substantial element of coercive police conduct. Absent police conduct causally related to the confession, there is simply no basis for concluding that any state actor has deprived a criminal defendant of due process of law. Connelly correctly notes that as interrogators have turned to more subtle forms of psychological persuasion, courts have found the mental condition of the defendant a more significant factor in the "voluntariness" calculus. But this fact does not justify a conclusion that a defendant's mental condition, by itself and apart from its relation to official coercion, should ever dispose of the inquiry into constitutional "voluntariness." . . . Our "involuntary confession" jurisprudence is entirely consistent with the settled law requiring some sort of "state action" to support a claim of violation of the Due Process Clause of the Fourteenth Amendment. The Colorado trial court found that the police committed no wrongful acts, and that finding has been neither challenged by Connelly nor disturbed by the Supreme Court of Colorado. The latter court, however, concluded that sufficient state action was present by virtue of the admission of the confession into evidence in a court of the State.

The difficulty with the approach of the Supreme Court of Colorado is that it fails to recognize the essential link between coercive activity of the State, on the one hand, and a resulting confession by a defendant, on the other.

The flaw in Connelly's constitutional argument is that it would expand our previous line of "voluntariness" cases into a far-ranging requirement that courts must divine a defendant's motivation for speaking or acting as he did even though there be no claim that governmental conduct coerced his decision.

. . . We have previously cautioned against expanding "currently applicable exclusionary rules by erecting additional barriers to placing truthful and probative evidence before state juries." . . . We abide by that counsel now. "The central purpose of a criminal trial is to decide the factual question of the defendant's guilt or innocence," and while we have previously held that exclusion of evidence may be necessary to protect constitutional guarantees, both the necessity for the collateral inquiry and the exclusion of evidence deflect a criminal trial from its basic purpose. Connelly would now have us require sweeping inquiries into the state of mind of a criminal defendant who has confessed, inquiries quite divorced from any coercion brought to bear on the defendant by the State. We think the Constitution rightly leaves this sort of inquiry to be resolved by state laws governing the admission of evidence and erects no standard of its own in this area. A statement rendered by one in the condition of Connelly might be proved to be quite unreliable, but this is a matter to be governed by the evidentiary laws of the forum, and not by the Due Process Clause of the Fourteenth Amendment. . . .

We hold that coercive police activity is a necessary predicate to the finding that a confession is not "voluntary" within the meaning of the Due Process Clause of the Fourteenth Amendment. We also conclude that the taking of Connelly's statements, and their admission into evidence, constitute no violation of that Clause.

. . . We think that the Supreme Court of Colorado erred in importing into this area of constitutional law notions of "free will" that have no place there. . . . The sole concern of the Fifth Amendment, on which *Miranda* was based, is governmental coercion. Indeed, the Fifth Amendment privilege is not concerned "with moral and psychological pressures to confess emanating from sources other than official coercion." The voluntariness of a waiver of this privilege has always depended on the absence of police overreaching, not on "free choice" in any broader sense of the word. . . .

Connelly urges this Court to adopt his "free will" rationale, and to find an attempted waiver invalid whenever the defendant feels compelled to waive his rights by reason of any compulsion, even if the compulsion does not flow from the police. But such a treatment of the waiver issue would "cut this Court's holding in [*Miranda*] completely loose from its own explicitly stated rationale." *Miranda* protects defendants against government coercion leading them to surrender rights protected by the Fifth Amendment; it goes no further than that. Connelly's perception of coercion flowing from the "voice of God," however important or significant such a perception may be in other disciplines, is a matter to which the United States Constitution does not speak.

The judgment of the Supreme Court of Colorado is accordingly REVERSED, and the cause is REMANDED for further proceedings not inconsistent with this opinion. . . .

## DISSENT

BRENNAN, J. JOINED BY MARSHALL, J.

Today the Court denies Mr. Connelly his fundamental right to make a vital choice with a sane mind, involving a determination that could allow the State to deprive him of liberty or even life. This holding is unprecedented: "Surely in the present stage of our civilization a most basic sense of justice is affronted by the spectacle of incarcerating a human being upon the basis of a statement he made while insane. . . ." Because I believe that the use of a mentally ill person's involuntary confession is antithetical to the notion of fundamental fairness embodied in the Due Process Clause, I dissent.

Connelly's seriously impaired mental condition is clear on the record of this case. At the time of his confession, Mr. Connelly suffered from a "longstanding severe mental disorder," diagnosed as chronic paranoid schizophrenia. He had been hospitalized for psychiatric reasons five times prior to his confession; his longest hospitalization lasted for seven months. Mr. Connelly heard imaginary voices and saw nonexistent objects. He believed that his father was God, and that he was a reincarnation of Jesus.

. . . The state trial court found that the "overwhelming evidence presented by the Defense" indicated that the prosecution did not meet its burden of demonstrating by a preponderance of the evidence that the initial statement to Officer Anderson was voluntary. While the court found no police misconduct, it held: There's no question that the Defendant did not exercise free will in choosing to talk to the police. He exercised a choice both [sic] of which were mandated by auditory hallucination, had no basis in reality, and were the product of a psychotic break with reality. The Defendant at the time of the confession had absolutely in the Court's estimation no volition or choice to make.

. . . The absence of police wrongdoing should not, by itself, determine the voluntariness of a confession by a mentally ill person. The requirement that a confession be voluntary reflects a recognition of the importance of free will and of reliability in determining the admissibility of a confession, and thus demands an inquiry into the totality of the circumstances surrounding the confession. Today's decision restricts the application of the term "involuntary" to those confessions obtained by police coercion.

Confessions by mentally ill individuals or by persons coerced by parties other than police officers are now considered "voluntary." The Court's failure to recognize all forms of involuntariness or coercion as antithetical to due process reflects a refusal to acknowledge free will as a value of constitutional consequence. But due process derives much of its meaning from a conception of fundamental fairness that emphasizes the right to make vital choices voluntarily: "The Fourteenth Amendment secures against state invasion . . . the right of a person to remain silent unless he chooses to speak in the unfettered exercise of his own will. . . ." This right requires vigilant protection if we are to safeguard the values of private conscience and human dignity. . . .

A true commitment to fundamental fairness requires that the inquiry be not whether the conduct of state officers in obtaining the confession is shocking, but whether the confession was "free and voluntary." . . . Since the Court redefines voluntary confessions to include confessions by mentally ill individuals, the reliability of these confessions becomes a central concern. A concern for reliability is inherent in our criminal justice system, which relies upon accusatorial rather than inquisitorial practices. While an inquisitorial system prefers obtaining confessions from criminal defendants, an accusatorial system must place its faith in determinations of "guilt by evidence independently and freely secured."

In *Escobedo v. Illinois* (1964), we justified our reliance upon accusatorial practices: We have learned the lesson of history, ancient and modern, that a system of criminal law enforcement which comes to depend on the "confession" will, in the long run, be less reliable and more subject to abuses than a system which depends on extrinsic evidence independently secured through skillful investigation.

I dissent.

## Questions

1. List all the facts relevant to deciding whether Francis Connelly's confession was voluntary.

2. What are the two parts of the test that the U.S. Supreme Court announced for determining whether confessions are voluntary?

3. Do you agree with the majority that the confession was voluntary? If yes, what persuaded you? If no, do you agree with the dissent? Explain why.

### EXPLORING FURTHER

# Voluntary Self-Incrimination

### Was He Coerced by a Private Person?

*State v. Bowe*, 881 P.2d 538 (1994)

FACTS On January 21, 1990, a brawl involving a number of individuals occurred at one of the dormitory buildings on the University of Hawai`i-Manoa (UH) campus. During the fight, Steven Oshiro (Victim) was beaten and sustained physical injuries.

On February 9, 1990, Sergeant John Pinero (Sergeant Pinero) of the Honolulu Police Department (HPD) contacted Wallace, head coach of the UH Men's Basketball Team. He requested Wallace's assistance in making arrangements for the police to interview certain members of the basketball team, who were suspected of being involved in the January 21, 1990, fight. Sergeant Pinero provided Wallace with a list of suspects that included Troy Bowe. Wallace later told Bowe that he needed to go to the police station and that he would go with him if he required assistance.

On February 12, 1990, Bowe went to the police station accompanied by Wallace. Bowe was given *Miranda* warnings and subsequently signed an HPD Form 81, waiving his constitutional rights to counsel and to remain silent. After waiving his constitutional rights, an interrogation commenced in which Bowe admitted assaulting the victim.

On September 17, 1991, an Oahu Grand Jury indicted Defendant and Vincent Smalls for Assault in the Second Degree. On November 21, 1991, Bowe filed a Motion to suppress evidence on the grounds that his February 12, 1990, statement to the police was involuntary because it was obtained through the use of official state coercion in violation of Bowe's constitutional right to due process. On May 8, 1992, the circuit court granted Bowe's motion to suppress.

In determining that Defendant's statement was coerced, the circuit court entered the following findings of fact:

1. On or about January or February of 1990, Sergeant John Pinero was an employee of the [HPD], who was at that time working on an investigation of an assault which allegedly involved TROY BOWE.

2. In his capacity as a police officer with the [HPD], Sergeant Pinero called Riley Wallace, at that time basketball coach of the University of Hawaii at Manoa Basketball Team (hereinafter "Basketball Team"), and gave Wallace a list of suspects who were on the Basketball Team that Sergeant Pinero wanted Wallace to bring down to the [HPD] (hereinafter "List").

3. Wallace, as head basketball coach, had the authority to suspend athletes or remove them from the Basketball Team and, in the case of scholarship-athletes, to initiate procedures to withdraw their athletic-scholarships.

4. TROY BOWE was a scholarship-athlete on the Basketball Team.

5. TROY BOWE was on said List.

6. Sergeant Pinero specifically asked Wallace to locate the individuals on the List and have them meet with Sergeant Pinero.

7. Sergeant Pinero, however, did not request that Wallace use force or coercion while attempting to have individuals on the List meet with Sergeant Pinero.

8. Wallace then contacted Defendant TROY BOWE and informed him that he had to go down to the [HPD] to meet with Sergeant Pinero.

9. Wallace informed TROY BOWE that Wallace would accompany him to the [HPD] in place of an attorney and instructed TROY BOWE to make a statement to Sergeant Pinero.

10. Wallace did not inform TROY BOWE that he could or should have an attorney present with him when he went to be interviewed by Sergeant Pinero.

11. TROY BOWE believed that he could not refuse to follow Wallace's directions because if he did so Wallace could suspend him from the Basketball Team or institute procedures to revoke Defendant TROY BOWE's athletic-scholarship.

Was the coercive conduct of Coach Wallace, a private person, sufficient to render Bowe's confession inadmissible? Yes, said the Hawaii supreme court.

*OPINION* While the Supreme Court in *Connelly* stated that, "the sole concern of the Fifth Amendment . . . is governmental coercion," we have recognized that one of the basic considerations underlying the exclusion of confessions obtained through coercion is the "inherent untrustworthiness of involuntary confessions." Accordingly, we reject the Supreme Court's narrow focus on police coercion in *Connelly*. . . . We recognize that an individual's capacity to make a rational and free choice between confessing and remaining silent may be overborne as much by the coercive conduct of a private individual as by the coercive conduct of the police. [Therefore,] we hold that the coercive conduct of a private person may be sufficient to render a confession inadmissible based on article 1, sections 5 and 10 of the Hawaii Constitution. Nevertheless, we acknowledge that some sort of state action is required to support a defendant's claim that his due process rights were violated. . . . Although no state action is involved where an accused is coerced into making a confession by a private individual, we find that the state participates in that violation by allowing the coerced statements to be used as evidence.

 Go to Exercise 8.3 on the Samaha Criminal Procedure 7e website to learn more about voluntary confessions: academic.cengage.com/criminaljustice/samaha.

# SUMMARY

### I. The Nature and the Role of Confessions

A. Confessions play an ambivalent role in society and law, an ambivalence that's ancient.

  1. They provide access to defendants' innermost beliefs, knowledge, and thinking.

  2. They are also powerful evidence of guilt *and* remorse.

B. Defendants confess their guilt or make incriminating statements in four different settings:

  1. They confess to friends and associates, who report these statements to officials.

2. They confess during plea bargaining or while pleading guilty (the most common setting).
3. They confess during sentencing when making incriminating statements to show their remorse.
4. They confess during police interrogations following their arrest.
C. The Self-Incrimination Setting
 1. The atmosphere in police stations is strange and intimidating; suspects are searched thoroughly, have to stand in lineups, and are interrogated nonstop.
 2. As soon as police officers have shifted their search from a general investigation to building a case against an individual—the accusatory stage of the criminal process—the needs of law enforcement versus the interests of individual privacy and liberty carry higher stakes for both suspects and law enforcement.
 3. Defining the proper constitutional balance between law enforcement needs and suspects' privacy has created much controversy.
D. The Importance of Confessions and Interrogation
 1. Fred Inbau—professor of law and author—cited three reasons why he supported interrogations:
  a. Police can't solve many crimes unless guilty people confess or suspects give information that can convict someone else.
  b. Criminals don't confess unless the police either catch them in the act or interrogate them in private.
  c. Police have to use "less refined methods" when they interrogate suspects than are "appropriate for the transaction of ordinary, every-day affairs by and between law-abiding citizens."
 2. Some empirical research suggests that:
  a. Interrogators rarely coerce suspects to confess.
  b. Almost all interrogations last less than one hour.
  c. One in four suspects invokes his *Miranda* rights.
  d. Sixty-four percent of suspects interrogated after they waive their rights incriminated themselves.
E. False Confessions and Recording Interrogations
 1. We know that there are false confessions.
 2. We do *not* know:
  a. How often they occur
  b. How often they lead to wrongful convictions
  c. How much social harm they cause
 3. Interrogations leading to confessions aren't recorded in most cases.
  a. Currently, only two states require officers to videotape interrogations.
  b. Arguments in favor of videotaping include:
   (1) It creates an objective, reviewable record.
   (2) It enhances jurors' and judges' assessment of credibility by providing a complete record.
   (3) It provides judges and juries with a more accurate picture of what was said, because words can convey different meanings depending on the intonation.
   (4) It improves the quality of police work by providing both good and bad examples for training police interrogators.

(5) It preserves judicial resources by discouraging defendants from raising "frivolous" pretrial challenges to confessions.

   c. Arguments against videotaping include:

     (1) The cost is significant.

     (2) It interferes with interrogation techniques.

     (3) Suspects may be reluctant to speak in front of cameras.

## II. The Constitution and Self-Incrimination

  A. The right to remain silent (against self-incrimination) is ancient and controversial.

    1. Jesus invoked it.

    2. Talmudic law commanded it.

  B. The U.S. Supreme Court has relied on three provisions in the U.S. Constitution to develop rules to control police interrogation and confessions:

    1. The Fourteenth Amendment due process clause

    2. The Sixth Amendment right-to-counsel clause

    3. The Fifth Amendment self-incrimination clause

  C. The Due Process Approach

    1. The basic idea behind the due process approach is that all confessions must be voluntary or they're not reliable.

    2. The reliability rationale for due process is that admitting unreliable evidence to prove guilt denies defendants the right to their lives, liberty, and/or property without due process of law.

    3. According to the accusatory system rationale, forced confessions violate due process even if they're true; under our system, the government alone has the burden of proving guilt.

    4. Because involuntary confessions are unreliable and contrary to the accusatory system of justice, all confessions are coerced if they're not "the product of a rational intellect and a free will."

    5. Most early cases that the U.S. Supreme Court threw out involving false confessions dealt with White mobs who had rounded up poor, illiterate Blacks and tortured them until they confessed.

  D. The Right-to-Counsel Approach

    1. In *Escobedo v. Illinois,* the U.S. Supreme Court held that as soon as a police investigation focuses on a particular suspect, criminal prosecution begins and the right to counsel attaches (Sixth Amendment).

    2. The Court soon shifted to the Fifth Amendment self-incrimination approach in *Miranda v. Arizona.*

  E. The Self-Incrimination Approach

    1. To decide whether a police custodial interrogation was inherently coercive before formal charges were filed, the Court relies on the Fifth Amendment.

    2. For defendants to claim their Fifth Amendment rights were violated, they have to prove:

     a. Compulsion

      (1) Whether testimony was "compelled" is measured by the totality of circumstances surrounding the statements.

      (2) According to due process, confessions must be voluntary and knowing.

b. Incrimination

c. Testimony

   (1) Testimony is the content of what you say and write.

   (2) The government can't force defendants to give testimony against themselves—the meaning of "witness against himself."

   (3) The Fifth Amendment protects testimony, not physical evidence (for example blood, hair samples, DNA evidence).

## III. *Miranda v. Arizona*

A. The U.S. Supreme Court established a "bright line" rule to govern custodial interrogation.

B. Custodial interrogation is "inherently coercive" because:

  1. Suspects are held in strange surroundings where they're not free to leave.

  2. Skilled police officers use unrefined methods to "crack" the will of suspects.

C. The *Miranda* "Bright-Line" Rules

  1. The Supreme Court intended the *Miranda* warnings to prevent police *coercion* while still allowing police *pressure*.

  2. Whenever police officers conduct a custodial interrogation, they have to give suspects the four warnings:

    a. You have the right to remain silent.

    b. Any incriminating statements you make will be used in court.

    c. You have the right to a lawyer.

    d. If you can't afford an attorney, one will be appointed for you.

  3. The Court also established five "bright line" rules for the interrogating officer, which officers don't need to tell suspects.

    a. Interrogation has to stop immediately if suspects indicate at any time they don't want to talk further.

    b. Interrogation has to stop immediately if a suspect indicates in any manner she wants a lawyer.

    c. Any statement without a lawyer places a "heavy burden" on the government to prove defendants waived their right to remain silent and their right to a lawyer.

    d. Statements obtained in violation of the rules can't be admitted into evidence.

    e. Suspects can't be punished for asserting their right to remain silent.

  4. *Miranda v. Arizona* doesn't command officers to warn suspects whenever they arrest them. They are required to only if they take suspects into custody and interrogate them.

D. The Meaning of "Custody"

  1. The U.S. Supreme Court defined *custody* as being held by the police in a police station or depriving an individual of "freedom of action in any significant way."

  2. The Court sent the message that *Miranda* targets coercive environments, not just coercive places.

  3. Circumstances that show custody:

    a. Whether officers had probable cause to arrest

    b. Whether officers intended to detain suspects

    c. Whether suspects believed their freedom was significantly restricted

    d. Whether the investigation had focused on the suspect

    e. The language officers use to summon suspects

    f. The physical surroundings

    g. The amount of evidence of guilt officers presented to suspects

    h. How long suspects were detained

    i. The amounts and kinds of pressure officers used to detain suspects

  4. Circumstances that don't show custody:

    a. Detaining drivers and passengers during routine traffic stops

    b. Requiring probationers to attend routine meetings with their probation officers

    c. Detaining persons during the execution of search warrants

E. The Meaning of "Interrogation"

  1. *Interrogation* means something different in the Fifth, Sixth, and Fourteenth Amendments.

  2. The Fifth Amendment requires coercion; the Sixth Amendment doesn't.

  3. The Fifth Amendment "Functional Equivalent of a Question" Test provides less protection to suspects.

  4. *Miranda* safeguards come into play whenever a person in custody is subjected to either express questioning or its functional equivalent.

  5. The Sixth Amendment "Deliberately Eliciting a Response" Test provides broader protection for interrogated suspects and more restrictions on interrogating officers.

  6. As soon as the government starts formal proceedings, the Sixth Amendment right to counsel kicks in.

F. Under the public safety exception, if "mirandizing" a suspect would endanger an officer or someone nearby, officers don't need to read a suspect the warnings.

## IV. The Waiver of the Right to Remain Silent

A. Because so many suspects waive their rights and talk to interrogators with no lawyer in sight, two questions are of great constitutional concern:

  1. What is a valid wavier of the right against self-incrimination?

  2. What is a voluntary confession?

B. There are two waiver tests:

  1. Express waiver test. The suspect makes it clear that he knows his rights, knows he's giving them up, and knows the consequences.

  2. Implied wavier test. The totality of circumstances surrounding each case has to prove that before suspects talked, they knew their rights and knew they were giving them up.

  3. The Supreme Court has adopted the implied waiver test.

C. Circumstances relevant to showing a voluntary and knowing wavier include:

  1. Intelligence

  2. Physical condition

  3. Education

  4. Mental condition

  5. Age

  6. Ability to understand English

  7. Familiarity with the criminal justice system

## V. Voluntary Self-Incrimination

A. Most suspects talk when interrogated because knowledge is a two-way street.

B. Confessions are involuntary only if the totality of circumstances proves two things:

    1. Officers engaged in coercive conduct during the interrogation.

    2. The coercive conduct caused the suspect to make incriminating statements.

C. The most common circumstances courts consider in determining whether coercive action caused people to confess include:

    1. The location of the questioning

    2. The initiator of the contact with the officer

    3. Whether *Miranda* warnings were given

    4. The number of interrogators

    5. The length of questioning

    6. Whether food, water, and toilet facilities were denied

    7. Whether the police used threats, promises, lies, or tricks

    8. Whether the suspect was denied access to a lawyer

    9. The suspects ascribed and achieved status

D. Courts have ruled that none of the following actions caused suspects to confess:

    1. Promises of leniency

    2. Promises of treatment

    3. Confronting the accused with other evidence of guilt

    4. The interrogator's appeal to the defendant's emotions

    5. False and misleading statements made by the interrogator

## REVIEW QUESTIONS

1. Describe the ambivalence surrounding confessions in social and legal history.

2. Identify four different settings where defendants confess their guilt or make incriminating statements.

3. Identify when the accusatory stage of the criminal process triggers the rights afforded to suspects.

4. Identify three reasons why Fred Inbau supported interrogations.

5. List four findings of Richard Leo's research on police interrogation, and describe what his findings are based on.

6. List arguments both in favor of and against videotaping interrogations.

7. What is the meaning and significance of the statement, "Pressure yes; coercion no"?

8. Identify and state the contents of the three provisions in the U.S. Constitution that limit police interrogation and confessions.

9. What is the basic idea behind the due process approach to confessions?

10. What is the significance of *Rogers v. Richmond?*

11. What is the significance of *Townsend v. Sain?*

12. When does the right to counsel kick in during interrogations?

13. What three elements have to be satisfied for defendants to claim that their Fifth Amendment rights were violated?

14. Can physical evidence serve as a witness against a suspect? Explain.

15. Describe the voluntariness test of self-incrimination.

16. Identify three factors behind the decision in *Miranda v. Arizona*.

17. *Miranda v. Arizona* established a "bright line" rule regarding warnings to suspects. State and give the reasons for the rule.

18. State the two circumstances that have to be present before officers have to give the *Miranda* warnings.

19. Identify five circumstances to determine custody.

20. Identify three types of detentions that aren't custodial.

21. State and summarize the reason for the public safety exception to the *Miranda* warnings.

22. Identify and describe the Fifth Amendment test used to determine interrogation.

23. Identify and describe the Sixth Amendment test used to determine when the right to counsel kicks in.

24. Identify the two elements of a valid wavier of the rights to counsel and to remain silent.

25. List some circumstances relevant to showing a knowing wavier.

26. Identify the two elements of involuntary confessions.

27. List some circumstances courts consider in determining whether coercive action caused people to confess.

28. List some circumstances that courts have determined don't cause suspects to confess.

## KEY TERMS

accusatory stage of the criminal process, p. 275
custodial interrogation, p. 277
due process approach to confessions, p. 280
reliability rationale for due process, p. 280
accusatory system rationale, p. 280

free will rationale, p. 281
critical stage in criminal prosecutions, p. 282
right-to-counsel approach, p. 282
testimony, p. 283
inherently coercive, p. 286
bright-line rule, p. 289
custody, p. 291

public safety exception, p. 293
interrogation, p. 295
"functional equivalent of a question" test, p. 295
deliberately eliciting a response standard, p. 296
express waiver test, p. 300
implied waiver test, p. 300

# Identification Procedures

## MAIN POINTS

- Proving a crime was committed is a lot easier than proving who committed it.
- Relying on eyewitness identification of strangers is very risky, because the risk of misidentification is high.
- Most mistaken identifications result from the imperfections of human perception, memory, suggestion, and recall.
- Making simple, inexpensive changes to procedures can reduce some risks of misidentification.
- The U.S. Constitution allows wide latitude in admitting eyewitness identification, leaving it to juries to sort out the reliability.
- Empirical evidence doesn't back up the assumptions on which the U.S. Supreme Court's test for the admissibility of eyewitness identification relies.
- Lineups are the least used and the least unreliable means of eyewitness identification; photo identifications are the most unreliable and the most widely used.
- Most courts admit DNA profile evidence, but they differ widely over the standards of admission.

# 9

Jimmy D. Glover was a trained African American undercover state police officer. Just after sunset, while there was still daylight, Glover and Henry Alton Brown, an informant, went to an apartment building at 201 Westland, in Hartford, to buy narcotics from "Dickie Boy" Cicero, a known narcotics dealer. Glover knocked at the door of one of two apartments at the top of the stairs on the third floor. The door Glover knocked on might not have been to Cicero's apartment and the transaction that followed "was with some other person than" Cicero. Natural light from a window in the hallway illuminated the third floor hallway. Someone opened the door 12 to 18 inches in response to the knock. Glover observed a man standing at the door and, behind him, a woman. Glover asked for "two things" of narcotics. The man at the door held out his hand, and Glover gave him two $10 bills. The door closed. Soon the man returned and handed Glover two glassine bags.

Manson v. Brathwaite (1977), U.S. Supreme Court

Proving a crime was committed is a lot easier than identifying who committed it. Of course, some suspects are caught red-handed; victims and witnesses personally know others; and some confess. Also, technological advances can identify some. Bite-mark evidence helped to convict the notorious serial rapist Ted Bundy, and fiber evidence led to the conviction of Wayne Williams for the murders of two young children in Atlanta.

Many courts now admit DNA (deoxyribonucleic acid) evidence, touted as the "single greatest advance in the search for truth since cross-examination," to prove the defendant is the perpetrator (Coleman and Swenson 1994, 11).

Despite technological advances, eyewitness identification remains the most widely used, and sometimes the only, way to identify and prove the guilt of *strangers* (perpetrators that victims don't know). Law enforcement uses three major procedures to help witnesses identify suspects who are strangers to them: lineups, show-ups, and "mug shot" photo identifications.

In this chapter, we'll first examine the risks and causes of eyewitness misidentification; the important contributions psychologists have made to our understanding of misidentification; and some recommendations for improving the reliability of eyewitness identification.

Then, we'll turn to the U.S. Constitution to examine how the U.S. Supreme Court has relied on it to provide minimum safeguards against misidentification. The dominant theme in the Court's decisions is balancing the need to protect defendants from wrongful convictions without encroaching on the jury's prerogative to decide guilt. According to the Court, identification evidence should be admitted unless identification procedures create a "very substantial likelihood of irreparable misidentification":

> Short of that point, such evidence is for the jury to weigh. We are content to rely upon the good sense and judgment of American juries, for evidence with some element of untrustworthiness is customary grist for the jury mill. Juries are not so susceptible that they cannot measure intelligently the weight of identification testimony that has some questionable feature. (*Manson v. Brathwaite* 1977, 116)

Finally, we'll look at the growing reliance on DNA testing, its reliability, and the standards for admitting it as evidence in criminal trials.

## MISTAKEN EYEWITNESS IDENTIFICATION

Relying on eyewitness identification of *strangers* in criminal cases is a very risky business. The risks of mistaken identification are high, even in ideal settings, and the most common identification procedures—lineups and photo ("mug shot") identifications—don't take place in ideal settings. According to one expert, mistaken identifications of strangers present the "greatest single threat to the achievement of our ideal that no inno-cent person shall be punished." Best guesses (there aren't any reliable exact figures) are that about half of all wrongful convictions resulted from mistaken identifications by eyewitnesses. Take one famous example: Seven eyewitnesses swore that Bernard Pagano, a Roman Catholic priest, robbed them with a small, chrome-plated pistol. In a dramatic moment in the middle of Father Pagano's trial, Ronald Clouser confessed that he—not Father Pagano—had committed the robberies (*National Law Journal* 1979, 1).

## Memory and Mistaken Identification of Strangers

Victims make mistakes when identifying criminals who are strangers to them because of problems with their memory. Psychologists usually separate memory into three phases:

1. *Acquisition of memory.* Information the brain takes in at the time of the crime

2. *Retention of memory.* Information the brain stores between the time of the crime and the lineup, show-up, or picture identification

3. *Retrieval of memory.* Information retrieved from memory at the time of the lineup, show-up, or picture identification

Let's look more closely at each of these.

*Acquisition* Contrary to common belief, the brain isn't a DVR (digital video recorder) that records what witnesses see. For well over a century, psychologists have proven repeatedly that the brain doesn't record exact images sent to it through our eyes. Unlike cameras, people have expectations, and our expectations and our highly developed thought processes heavily influence our acquisition of information. In short, our per-ceptions outweigh reality. Like beauty, the physical characteristics of criminals are in the eye of the beholder.

Attention also shapes our observations. Observers—even trained ones—don't take in everything that happens during a crime. We all pay only selective attention to what's going on around us, and this selective attention leaves wide gaps in our memories.

The degree of accuracy of witnesses' first observation of strangers during a crime depends on the interaction among five circumstances:

1. *Length of time* to observe the stranger

2. *Distractions* during the observation

3. *Focus* of the observation

4. *Stress* on the witness during the observation

5. *Race* of the witness and the stranger (Wells and Olson 2003, 279)

The longer the witness observes the stranger, the more reliable the observation. The problem is, most crimes are over in seconds. Even when they take longer, there are other obstacles to accurate observation. Descriptions witnesses give of obvious (but crucial) details, such as age, height, and weight, are often highly inaccurate. Time estimates are also unreliable, particularly during stressful situations like getting robbed or raped. Witnesses also get distracted from focusing on the physical description to other "details" like the gun the robber waved or the knife a rapist held to his victim's face. Understandable as this focus is, the weapon is obviously not as important as the description of the robber or rapist. Also, crimes aren't always committed under physi-cal conditions ideal for accurately describing details; bad lighting is a good example. Equally important, stress distorts our observations.

It may sound convincing when a witness says, "I was so scared I could never forget that face," but research demonstrates convincingly that accuracy sharply declines during stressful events. According to C. Ronald Huff, an identification expert who conducted one study:

> Many of the cases we have identified involve errors by victims of robbery and rape, where the victim was close enough to the offender to get a look at him—but under conditions of extreme stress. . . . Such stress can significantly affect perception and memory and should give us cause to question the reliability of such eyewitness testimony. (Yant 1991, 99)

Discouraging as the natural limits of observation, distracted focus, poor lighting, and stress are to accurate identification, race complicates matters further. Researchers have demonstrated that identifying strangers of another race clearly raises the risk of mistaken identification. In one famous experiment, researchers showed observers a photo of a White man waving a razor blade in an altercation with a Black man on a subway. When asked immediately afterward to describe what they saw, over half the subjects reported that the Black man was carrying the weapon:

> Considerable evidence indicates that people are poorer at identifying members of another race than of their own. Some studies have found that, in the United States at least, whites have greater difficulty recognizing blacks than vice versa. Moreover, counterintuitively, the ability to perceive the physical characteristics of a person from another racial group apparently does not improve significantly upon increased contact with other members of that race. Because many crimes are cross-racial, these factors may play an important part in reducing the accuracy of eyewitness perception. (Gross 1987, 398–99)

*Retention* Fading memory raises the already high risk of mistake caused by faulty observation. Memory fades most during the first few hours after an event (the very time when it's most important to keep it sharp); after that, it remains stable for several months. Curiously, at the same time witnesses' memory is fading, their confidence in their memory is rising. Unfortunately, courts and juries place enormous weight on witnesses' confidence, even in the face of clear proof that confidence isn't related to accuracy.

*Retrieval* Retrieval consists of two types: recall and recognition. In **recall**, eyewitnesses are given hints, such as a time frame, and then asked to report what they observed. In **recognition**, eyewitnesses are shown persons or objects and then asked to indicate whether they were involved in the crime. Retrieval errors can be either errors of omission (for example, failure to recall some detail or to recognize a perpetrator) or errors of commission (picking an innocent person in a photo array) (Wells 2002, 665).

## The Power of Suggestion

As if faulty observation and fading memory aren't enough, **suggestion** is a powerful contributor to mistaken identification during the retrieval phase of memory. According to the widely accepted findings of psychologists, most mistaken identifications happen because of a combination of the natural imperfections of memory, and the normal susceptibility to innocent (and usually quite subtle) suggestion (Wells and Olson 2003, 277).

Suggestion is particularly powerful (and most threatening to accuracy) during the retention and retrieval phases. Witnesses store in one mental memory storage "bin" everything about the crime acquired by faulty perception at the time of the crime *and* what they learned later. According to psychologist and respected eyewitness expert Elizabeth Loftus (1996), witnesses in her research add to their stories of crimes, and what they add depends on how *she* describes what happened. The power of Loftus's suggestions shapes what witnesses later take out of their memory "bin" and recall during the identification process.

Steven Penrod, a psychologist at the University of Wisconsin, says witnesses (like all of us) embellish their stories: "A witness tells his story to the police, to the family, then to friends, then to the prosecutor." As the story gets retold, it becomes less reality and more legend. Witnesses "feel very confident about what they now think happened and that confidence is communicated to the jury" (Yant 1991, 100).

The procedures used to identify strangers add to the problem created by the power of suggestion. Witnesses think of lineups and photo arrays as multiple-choice tests without a "none of the above" choice. And they think of show-ups and single pictures as true/false tests. So they feel that they have to choose the "best" likeness in the line-ups and the right "true" or "false" likeness in the show-ups. They feel pressured by the possibility they might look foolish if they "don't know the answer." So they're ripe for suggestion, particularly in uncomfortable or threatening situations.

Suggestions by authority figures, such as the police, aggravate these tendencies (not *intentionally*, it should be stressed). For example, the very fact that police have arranged an identification procedure puts pressure on witnesses. They believe the police must have found the culprit or they wouldn't have gone to the trouble of arranging the identification event. So, they tell themselves, the culprit *has to be* in the lineup or the one person in the show-up or photo.

# IDENTIFICATION PROCEDURES

Law enforcement uses three procedures to help witnesses identify suspects:

1. *Lineups*. Witnesses try to pick the suspect out of a group.

2. *Show-ups*. Witnesses try to match the suspect with one person.

3. *Photo arrays*. Witnesses try to pick the suspect from one (photo show-up) or several (photo lineup) mug shots.

Lineups are least often used and the most reliable (more accurately, least unreliable). Show-ups are used more but are more unreliable than lineups. "Mug shot" (photo) identifications are by far the most frequently used *and* the most unreliable. Let's look at each of these procedures.

## Lineups

The reliability of a lineup depends largely upon its makeup *and* the way the police conduct the identification process. The lineup should comprise enough people and participants who resemble one another. The International Association of Chiefs of Police (IACP) recommends the following characteristics:

1. Five to six participants

2. Same race, ethnicity, and skin color

3. Similar age, height, weight, hair color, and body build

4. Similar clothing

Unfortunately, real lineups often fall short of these recommendations. Understand that this gap is hardly ever intentional; it's almost always because the only people available to put in lineups are police officers and jail inmates. But no matter how wide the gap, most courts don't throw out lineup identifications. Why? Courts trust jurors' common sense and daily experience to detect wrong identifications.

Unfortunately, a significant, consistent, and convincing body of empirical research demonstrates that courts' trust in jurors' ability to discern lineup misidentifications is misplaced. Jennifer Davenport and Steven Penrod (1997) surveyed the state of our knowledge on the point and concluded:

> Jurors tend to rely on factors that are not diagnostic of eyewitness accuracy, such as an eyewitness's memory for peripheral details and eyewitness confidence, tend to overestimate eyewitness accuracy, and have difficulty applying their commonsense knowledge of lineup suggestiveness to their verdict decisions. (353)

And, according to one study in their survey, "The numbers for inaccurate eyewitnesses are quite disturbing, because they suggest jurors may believe "three out of four mistaken identifications" (348).

The *way* police conduct lineups is also critical to reducing the risk of picking the wrong person. Most of the difficulties in administering the lineup result from the way police use the power of suggestion. To weaken this influence, researchers recommend police departments follow these rules for conducting lineups (and for photo identifications—discussed later):

1. Tell the witness the offender might or might *not* be in the lineup.

2. Have someone who doesn't know who the suspect is, a **blind administrator**, conduct the lineup.

3. Present members of the lineup one at a time (**sequential presentation**) and require witnesses to answer "yes" or "no" as they're presented. Don't use traditional **simultaneous presentation**, in which members are standing together at the same time. This gives witnesses the opportunity to treat the procedure like a multiple-choice test with a "best," but maybe not "right," answer.

4. If a witness identifies the suspect, immediately ask her how sure she is of the identification *before* other information contaminates her decision. (Wells and Seelau 1995, 765)

Researchers have shown repeatedly that telling witnesses before they view lineups or mug shots that the "culprit might or might *not* be in the group" (the **might-or-might-not-be-present instruction**) improves the ratio of right-to-wrong identifications. Also, *blind administrators*—administrators who don't know who the suspects are and therefore can't influence witnesses' identification by suggestion—should conduct lineups (Wells and Olson 2003, 286–87). *Sequential lineups* reduce the power of suggestion and minimize the multiple-choice test effect—that is, picking the one who most resembles the perpetrator (Wells 2002, 666)

The need to reduce the risk of mistaken identification is crucial because once witnesses have positively identified a stranger, it's difficult to shake their conclusion—even if it's wrong. This fact is extremely important for at least three reasons. First, empirical research refutes the commonsense idea that confidence means accuracy. Second, courts rarely throw out eyewitness identifications, no matter how high the risk of misidentification is.

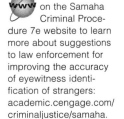

Go to Exercise 9.1 on the Samaha Criminal Procedure 7e website to learn more about suggestions to law enforcement for improving the accuracy of eyewitness identification of strangers: academic.cengage.com/criminaljustice/samaha.

Third, confident eyewitness testimony is particularly damning in front of juries. Jurors repeatedly dismiss even what should be convincing alibi evidence when they're faced with a confident eyewitness (*Stanford Law Review* 1977, 969). Jurors report over and over that they placed great confidence in witnesses who identified their victimizer. These in-court identifications are often given more weight by jurors than physical evidence—and more credibility than their reliability deserves.

## Show-Ups

Show-ups—identifications of a single person—are substantially less reliable than lineups, because presenting only one person to identify is more suggestive than providing a group of people to choose from. Nevertheless, courts usually admit show-up identification evidence.

Here are three common situations in which courts are likely to admit show-up identifications:

1. Witnesses accidentally run into suspects, such as in courthouse corridors.

2. Witnesses identify suspects during emergencies, such as when witnesses are hospitalized (*Stovall v. Denno* 1967, discussed on page 324).

3. Witnesses identify suspects while they're loose and being pursued by police, such as when police cruise crime scenes with witnesses. (*McFadden v. Cabana* 1988)

Table 9.1 summarizes the findings on the contrast between what we assume is true about eyewitness identifications and the reality.

| **TABLE 9.1** | **The Validity of Five Eyewitness Identification Factors** | |
|---|---|---|
| **Factor** | **Assumption** | **Validity** |
| 1. The opportunity the witnesses have to view the criminal at the crime scene | The better the opportunity to view a person, the more accurate a later identification | Some validity |
| 2. The witnesses' degree of attention | The greater the attention paid to a person, the more accurate a later identification | At least 1/2 and perhaps as much as more than 3/4 of the identifications were wrong |
| 3. The accuracy of their prior description of the criminal | The more accurate their description of a person, the more accurate a later identification | At least 1/2 and perhaps as much as more than 3/4 of the identifications were wrong |
| 4. The level of certainty they demonstrated when confronting the accused | The greater the level of certainty of the identification, the more accurate the description | At least 1/2 and perhaps as much or more than 3/4 of the identifications were wrong |
| 5. The length of time between the crime and the identification | The less time between the crime and the identification, the more accurate the identification | At least 1/2 and perhaps as much as more than 3/4 of the identifications were wrong |

*Source:* Gerald F. Uelman (1980), 16:359–68.

The U.S. Supreme Court hasn't hesitated to affirm the use of show-up identifications, despite the strong empirical evidence of their unreliability. The Court applies the same totality-of-circumstances test to show-ups that it applies to lineups.

## "Mug Shot" (Photo) Identification

The least reliable form of eyewitness identification is a picture display (called a "photo lineup" if there's more than one picture or a "photo show-up" if there's only one). The two-dimensional nature of photos distorts their accuracy, so they're inherently unreliable. Also, the fewer the photos, the less reliable the identifications because their suggestiveness grows as their numbers shrink. If the suspect stands out because of unique features, photos are even more suggestive and less reliable. Despite their widely recognized unreliability—and despite the urging of commentators that courts exclude them if lineups and show-ups can be substituted—photographs are the most widely used means of identification.

# THE CONSTITUTION AND IDENTIFICATION PROCEDURES

Until 1967, the courts, including the Supreme Court, adopted a "hands-off" approach to admitting evidence of lineups, show-ups, and photo identification. The reasoning was that it was up to juries to assess their reliability, not courts. Then came *Stovall v. Denno* (1967). Dr. Paul Behrendt was stabbed to death in his kitchen. His wife, also a doctor, followed her husband to the kitchen and jumped the assailant, who knocked her down and stabbed her 11 times. The police found a shirt on the floor with keys in the pocket, which they traced to Ted Stovall. Seven police officers brought Stovall to Dr. Behrendt's hospital room the day after she underwent surgery to save her life. Stovall, handcuffed to one of the seven officers, was the only Black in the room. Dr. Behrendt identified him. At trial, Dr. Behrendt testified to her out-of-court identification and identified Stovall again in the courtroom (295).

The Court recognized, for the first time, that due process was a basis for challenging identification testimony on constitutional grounds. Whether the hospital room show-up was a violation of due process depended on whether it

> was so unnecessarily suggestive and conducive to irreparable mistaken identification that he was denied due process of law. . . . The practice of showing suspects singly to persons for the purpose of identification, and not as part of a lineup, has been widely condemned. However, a claimed violation of due process of law in the conduct of a confrontation depends on the totality of the circumstances surrounding it, and the record in the present case reveals that the showing of Stovall to Mrs. Behrendt in an immediate hospital confrontation was imperative.
>
> Here was the only person in the world who could possibly exonerate Stovall. Her words, and only her words, "He is not the man" could have resulted in freedom for Stovall. The hospital was not far distant from the courthouse and jail. No one knew how long Mrs. Behrendt might live. Faced with the responsibility of identifying the attacker, with the need for immediate action and with the knowledge that Mrs. Behrendt could not visit the jail, the police followed the only feasible procedure and took Stovall to the hospital room. Under these circumstances, the usual police station line-up, which Stovall now argues he should have had, was out of the question. (302)

## Reliability Is the Linchpin

*Stovall* brought the Constitution only a small way into eyewitness identification procedures. For the identification evidence to be thrown out on due process grounds, defendants have to prove two elements by a **preponderance of the evidence** (it's more likely than not):

1. The lineup, show-up, or photographic array was **unnecessarily and impermissibly suggestive**. (*Twenty-Sixth Annual Review of Criminal Procedure* 1997, 944–45)

2. The totality of circumstances proves the unnecessarily and impermissibly suggestive procedures created a **very substantial likelihood of misidentification**. (*Twenty-Sixth Annual Review of Criminal Procedure* 1997, 944–45)

Notice the effect of the two-pronged test: Unnecessarily and impermissibly suggestive identifications are admissible *unless* defendants can prove they create a "very substantial likelihood of misidentification." The two-prong test demonstrates that reliability is the linchpin of the Court's due process approach to eyewitness identification. It shouldn't surprise you to learn that *courts* rarely, if ever, throw out eyewitness identification evidence. Juries, of course, can choose to give it little or no weight, depending on the circumstances.

## "Very Substantial Likelihood of Misidentification"

The Court has identified five factors in the "totality of circumstances" that should weigh heavily in determining whether the "unnecessarily and impermissibly suggestive" procedure created a "very substantial likelihood of misidentification":

1. Witnesses' opportunity to view defendants at the time of the crime

2. Witnesses' degree of attention at the time of the crime

3. Witnesses' accuracy of description of defendants prior to the identification

4. Witnesses' level of certainty when identifying defendants at the time of the identification procedure

5. The length of time between the crime and the identification (*Twenty-Sixth Annual Review of Criminal Procedure* 1997, 945–46)

The Court applies the same test to lineups, show-ups, and photo identification. In our next case excerpt, *Manson v. Brathwaite* (1977), the Court rejected Nowell Brathwaite's claim that State Trooper Jimmy Glover's single photo show-up identification violated due process.

---

**CASE** *Did the Photo Show-Up Create a "Very Great Likelihood of Misidentification"?*

### *Manson v. Brathwaite*
432 U.S. 98 (1977)

#### HISTORY

Nowell Brathwaite was charged with possession and sale of heroin. The jury found him guilty, and the judge sentenced him to not less than six nor more than nine years. The Supreme Court of Connecticut affirmed. Fourteen months later, Brathwaite filed a petition for habeas corpus in the U.S. District Court for the District of Connecticut. The District Court dismissed his petition. On appeal, the U.S. Court of Appeals for the Second Circuit reversed. The U.S. District Court for the District of Connecticut denied relief, and Brathwaite appealed. The Court of Appeals, Second Circuit, reversed. The U.S. Supreme Court granted certiorari and reversed.

BLACKMUN, J.

# FACTS

Jimmy D. Glover, a trained Black undercover state police officer was assigned to the Narcotics Division in 1970. On May 5 of that year, at about 7:45 P.M., EDT, and while there was still daylight, Glover and Henry Alton Brown, an informant, went to an apartment building at 201 Westland, in Hartford, to buy narcotics from "Dickie Boy" Cicero, a known narcotics dealer.

Cicero, it was thought, lived on the third floor of that apartment building. Glover and Brown entered the building, observed by back-up Officers D'Onofrio and Gaffey, and proceeded by stairs to the third floor. Glover knocked at the door of one of the two apartments served by the stairway. It appears that the door on which Glover knocked may not have been that of the Cicero apartment. Petitioner [John Manson, Commissioner of Corrections] concedes that the transaction "was with some other person than had been intended." The area was illuminated by natural light from a window in the third floor hallway.

The door opened 12 to 18 inches. Glover observed a man standing at the door and, behind him, a woman. Brown identified himself. Glover then asked for "two things" of narcotics. The man at the door held out his hand, and Glover gave him two $10 bills. The door closed. Soon the man returned and handed Glover two glassine bags. . . . This was Glover's testimony. Brown later was called as a witness for the prosecution. He testified on direct examination that, due to his then use of heroin, he had no clear recollection of the details of the incident. On cross-examination, as in an interview with defense counsel the preceding day, he said that it was a woman who opened the door, received the money, and thereafter produced the narcotics. On redirect, he acknowledged that he was using heroin daily at the time, that he had had some that day, and that there was "an inability to recall and remember events."

While the door was open, Glover stood within two feet of the person from whom he made the purchase and observed his face. Five to seven minutes elapsed from the time the door first opened until it closed the second time.

Glover and Brown then left the building. This was about eight minutes after their arrival. Glover drove to headquarters where he described the seller to D'Onofrio and Gaffey. Glover at that time did not know the identity of the seller. He described him as being "a colored man, approximately five feet eleven inches tall, dark complexion, black hair, short Afro style, and having high cheekbones, and of heavy build. He was wearing at the time blue pants and a plaid shirt."

D'Onofrio, suspecting from this description that respondent might be the seller, obtained a photograph of Brathwaite from the Records Division of the Hartford Police Department. He left it at Glover's office. D'Onofrio was not acquainted with Brathwaite personally but did know him by sight and had seen him "several times" prior to May 5. Glover, when alone, viewed the photograph for the first time upon his return to headquarters on May 7;

he identified the person shown as the one from whom he had purchased the narcotics.

Brathwaite was arrested on July 27 while visiting at the apartment of a Mrs. Ramsey on the third floor of 201 Westland. This was the apartment where the narcotics sale took place on May 5. Brathwaite testified: "Lots of times I have been there before in that building." He also testified that Mrs. Ramsey was a friend of his wife, that her apartment was the only one in the building he ever visited, and that he and his family, consisting of his wife and five children, did not live there but at 453 Albany Avenue, Hartford.

Brathwaite was charged, in a two-count information, with possession and sale of heroin. At his trial in January 1971, the photograph from which Glover had identified Brathwaite was received in evidence without objection on the part of the defense. Glover also testified that, although he had not seen Brathwaite in the eight months that had elapsed since the sale, "there was no doubt whatsoever" in his mind that the person shown on the photograph was respondent. Glover also made a positive in-court identification without objection. No explanation was offered by the prosecution for the failure to utilize a photographic array or to conduct a lineup.

Brathwaite, who took the stand in his own defense, testified that on May 5, the day in question, he had been ill at his Albany Avenue apartment ("a lot of back pains, muscle spasms . . . a bad heart . . . high blood pressure . . . neuralgia in my face, and sinus") and that at no time on that particular day had he been at 201 Westland. His wife testified that she recalled, after her husband had refreshed her memory, that he was home all day on May 5.

Doctor Wesley M. Vietzke, an internist and assistant professor of medicine at the University of Connecticut, testified that Brathwaite had consulted him on April 15, 1970, and that he took a medical history from him, heard his complaints about his back and facial pain, and discovered that he had high blood pressure. The physician found Brathwaite, subjectively, "in great discomfort." Respondent in fact underwent surgery for a herniated disc at L5 and S1 on August 17.

The jury found Brathwaite guilty on both counts of the information. He received a sentence of not less than six nor more than nine years. His conviction was affirmed . . . by the Supreme Court of Connecticut. That court noted the absence of an objection to Glover's in-court identification and concluded that Brathwaite "has not shown that substantial injustice resulted from the admission of this evidence." Under Connecticut law, substantial injustice must be shown before a claim of error not made or passed on by the trial court will be considered on appeal.

Fourteen months later, Brathwaite filed a petition for habeas corpus in the U.S. District Court for the District of Connecticut. He alleged that the admission of the identification testimony at his state trial deprived him of due process of law to which he was entitled under the Fourteenth Amendment. The District Court dismissed Brathwaite's petition. On appeal, the United States Court of Appeals for the Second Circuit reversed. In brief summary, the court felt that evidence as to the photograph should have been excluded, regardless of reliability, because the examination of the single photograph was unnecessary and suggestive. And, in the court's view, the evidence was unreliable in any event. We granted certiorari.

## OPINION

. . . The petitioner, Connecticut Commissioner of Corrections, acknowledges that "the procedure in the instant case was suggestive (because only one photograph was used) and unnecessary" (because there was no emergency or exigent circumstance). Brathwaite, in agreement with the Court of Appeals, proposes a per se rule of exclusion that he claims is dictated by the demands of the Fourteenth Amendment's guarantee of due process. He rightly observes this is the first case in which this Court has had occasion to rule upon . . . out-of-court identification evidence of the challenged kind.

Since the decision in *Neil v. Biggers,* the Courts of Appeals appear to have developed at least two approaches to such evidence. The first, or **per se approach**, employed by the Second Circuit in the present case, focuses on the procedures employed and requires exclusion of the out-of-court identification evidence, without regard to reliability, whenever it has been obtained through unnecessarily suggestive confrontation procedures. The justifications advanced are the elimination of evidence of uncertain reliability, deterrence of the police and prosecutors, and the stated "fair assurance against the awful risks of misidentification."

The second, or more lenient, approach is one that continues to rely on the **totality of the circumstances [approach]**. It permits the admission of the confrontation evidence if, despite the suggestive aspect, the out-of-court identification possesses certain features of reliability. Its adherents feel that the per se approach is not mandated by the Due Process Clause of the Fourteenth Amendment. This second approach, in contrast to the other, is ad hoc and serves to limit the societal costs imposed by a sanction that excludes relevant evidence from consideration and evaluation by the trier of fact.

Mr. Justice STEVENS, in writing for the Seventh Circuit in *Kirby v. Illinois,* observed: "There is surprising unanimity among scholars in regarding such a rule (the per se approach) as essential to avoid serious risk of miscarriage of justice." He pointed out that well-known federal judges have taken the position that "evidence of, or derived from, a showup identification should be inadmissible unless the prosecutor can justify his failure to use a more reliable identification procedure." Indeed, the ALI *Model Code of Pre-Arraignment Procedure* §§ 160.1 and 160.2 (1975) (hereafter *Model Code*), frowns upon the use of a showup or the display of only a single photograph.

The respondent here stresses the same theme and the need for deterrence of improper identification practice, a factor he regards as pre-eminent. Photographic identification, it is said, continues to be needlessly employed. He

notes that the legislative regulation "the Court had hoped would engender," has not been forthcoming. He argues that a totality rule cannot be expected to have a significant deterrent impact; only a strict rule of exclusion will have direct and immediate impact on law enforcement agents.

Identification evidence is so convincing to the jury that sweeping exclusionary rules are required. Fairness of the trial is threatened by suggestive confrontation evidence, and thus, it is said, an exclusionary rule has an established constitutional predicate.

There are, of course, several interests to be considered and taken into account. The driving force behind *United States v. Wade* (1967), *Gilbert v. California* (1967) (right to counsel at a post-indictment line-up), and *Stovall,* all decided on the same day, was the Court's concern with the problems of eyewitness identification. Usually the witness must testify about an encounter with a total stranger under circumstances of emergency or emotional stress. The witness' recollection of the stranger can be distorted easily by the circumstances or by later actions of the police. Thus, *Wade* and its companion cases reflect the concern that the jury not hear eyewitness testimony unless that evidence has aspects of reliability. It must be observed that both approaches before us are responsive to this concern. The per se rule, however, goes too far since its application automatically and peremptorily, and without consideration of alleviating factors, keeps evidence from the jury that is reliable and relevant.

The second factor is deterrence. Although the per se approach has the more significant deterrent effect, the totality approach also has an influence on police behavior. The police will guard against unnecessarily suggestive procedures under the totality rule, as well as the per se one, for fear that their actions will lead to the exclusion of identifications as unreliable.

The third factor is the effect on the administration of justice. Here the per se approach suffers serious drawbacks. Since it denies the trier reliable evidence, it may result, on occasion, in the guilty going free. Also, because of its rigidity, the per se approach may make error by the trial judge more likely than the totality approach. And in those cases in which the admission of identification evidence is error under the per se approach but not under the totality approach—cases in which the identification is reliable despite an unnecessarily suggestive identification procedure—reversal is a Draconian sanction. Unlike a warrantless search, a suggestive preindictment identification procedure does not in itself intrude upon a constitutionally protected interest.

Thus, considerations urging the exclusion of evidence deriving from a constitutional violation do not bear on the instant problem. Certainly, inflexible rules of exclusion that may frustrate rather than promote justice have not been viewed recently by this Court with unlimited enthusiasm. . . . The standard, after all, is that of fairness as required by the Due Process Clause of the Fourteenth Amendment. . . .

We turn, then, to the facts of this case and apply the analysis:

1. *The opportunity to view.* Glover testified that for two to three minutes he stood at the apartment door, within two feet of the respondent. The door opened twice, and each time the man stood at the door. The moments passed, the conversation took place, and payment was made. Glover looked directly at his vendor. It was near sunset, to be sure, but the sun had not yet set, so it was not dark or even dusk or twilight. Natural light from outside entered the hallway through a window. There was natural light, as well, from inside the apartment.

2. *The degree of attention.* Glover was not a casual or passing observer, as is so often the case with eyewitness identification. Trooper Glover was a trained police officer on duty—and specialized and dangerous duty—when he called at the third floor of 201 Westland in Hartford on May 5, 1970. Glover himself was a Negro and unlikely to perceive only general features of "hundreds of Hartford black males," as the Court of Appeals stated. It is true that Glover's duty was that of ferreting out narcotics offenders and that he would be expected in his work to produce results. But it is also true that, as a specially trained, assigned, and experienced officer, he could be expected to pay scrupulous attention to detail, for he knew that subsequently he would have to find and arrest his vendor. In addition, he knew that his claimed observations would be subject later to close scrutiny and examination at any trial.

3. *The accuracy of the description.* Glover's description was given to D'Onofrio within minutes after the transaction. It included the vendor's race, his height, his build, the color and style of his hair, and the high cheekbone facial feature. It also included clothing the vendor wore.

4. No claim has been made that respondent did not possess the physical characteristics so described. D'Onofrio reacted positively at once. Two days later, when Glover was alone, he viewed the photograph D'Onofrio produced and identified its subject as the narcotics seller.

5. *The witness' level of certainty.* There is no dispute that the photograph in question was that of respondent. Glover, in response to a question whether the photograph was that of the person from whom he made the purchase, testified: "There is no question whatsoever." Tr. 38. This positive assurance was repeated.

6. *The time between the crime and the confrontation.* Glover's description of his vendor was given to D'Onofrio within minutes of the crime. The photographic identification took place only two days later. We do not have here the passage of weeks or months between the crime and the viewing of the photograph.

These indicators of Glover's ability to make an accurate identification are hardly outweighed by the corrupting effect of the challenged identification itself. Although identifications arising from single-photograph displays may be viewed in general with suspicion, we find in the instant case little pressure on the witness to acquiesce in the suggestion that such a display entails. D'Onofrio had left the photograph at Glover's office and was not present when Glover first viewed it two days after the event. There thus was little urgency and Glover could view the photograph at his leisure. And since Glover examined the photograph alone, there was no coercive pressure to make an identification arising from the presence of another. The identification was made in circumstances allowing care and reflection.

Although it plays no part in our analysis, all this assurance as to the reliability of the identification is hardly undermined by the facts that respondent was arrested in the very apartment where the sale had taken place, and that he acknowledged his frequent visits to that apartment. Mrs. Ramsey was not a witness at the trial.

Surely, we cannot say that under all the circumstances of this case there is "a very substantial likelihood of irreparable misidentification." Short of that point, such evidence is for the jury to weigh. We are content to rely upon the good sense and judgment of American juries, for evidence with some element of untrustworthiness is customary grist for the jury mill. Juries are not so susceptible that they cannot measure intelligently the weight of identification testimony that has some questionable feature.

Of course, it would have been better had D'Onofrio presented Glover with a photographic array including "so far as practicable . . . a reasonable number of persons similar to any person then suspected whose likeness is included in the array." Model Code, § 160.2(2). The use of that procedure would have enhanced the force of the identification at trial and would have avoided the risk that the evidence would be excluded as unreliable. But we are not disposed to view D'Onofrio's failure as one of constitutional dimension to be enforced by a rigorous and unbending exclusionary rule. The defect, if there be one, goes to weight and not to substance.

We conclude that the criteria laid down in *Biggers* are to be applied in determining the admissibility of evidence offered by the prosecution concerning a post-*Stovall* identification, and that those criteria are satisfactorily met and complied with here.

The judgment of the Court of Appeals is REVERSED.

# CONCURRING OPINION

### STEVENS, J.

. . . The arguments in favor of fashioning new rules to minimize the danger of convicting the innocent on the basis of unreliable eyewitness testimony carry substantial force.

Nevertheless, . . . I am persuaded that this rulemaking function can be performed more effectively by the legislative process than by a somewhat clumsy judicial fiat and that the Federal Constitution does not foreclose experimentation by the States in the development of such rules. . . .

# DISSENT

## MARSHALL, J., JOINED BY BRENNAN, J.

. . . It is distressing to see the Court virtually ignore the teaching of experience . . . and blindly uphold the conviction of a defendant who may well be innocent. . . . Relying on numerous studies made over many years by such scholars as Professor Wigmore and Mr. Justice Frankfurter, the Court in *U.S. v. Wade* concluded that "the vagaries of eyewitness identification are well-known; the annals of criminal law are rife with instances of mistaken identification." It is, of course, impossible to control one source of such errors—the faulty perceptions and unreliable memories of witnesses—except through vigorously contested trials conducted by diligent counsel and judges. The Court acted, however, to minimize the more preventable threat posed to accurate identification by "the degree of suggestion inherent in the manner in which the prosecution presents the suspect to witnesses for pretrial identification." . . .

Despite my strong disagreement with the Court over the proper standards [totality of circumstances] to be applied in this case, . . . assuming applicability of the totality test, the facts of the present case require [the exclusion of the identification in this case because it raises a very substantial likelihood of misidentification].

I consider first the opportunity that Officer Glover had to view the suspect. Careful review of the record shows he could see the heroin seller only for the time it took to speak three sentences of four or five short words, to hand over some money, and later after the door reopened, to receive the drugs in return. The entire face-to-face transaction could have taken as little as 15 or 20 seconds. But during this time, Glover's attention was not focused exclusively on the seller's face. He observed that the door was opened 12 to 18 inches, that there was a window in the room behind the door, and, most importantly, that there was a woman standing behind the man. Glover was, of course, also concentrating on the details of the transaction—he must have looked away from the seller's face to hand him the money and receive the drugs. The observation during the conversation thus may have been as brief as 5 or 10 seconds.

As the Court notes, Glover was a police officer trained in and attentive to the need for making accurate identifications. Nevertheless, both common sense and scholarly study indicate that while a trained observer such as a police officer "is somewhat less likely to make an erroneous identification than the average untrained observer, the mere fact that he has been so trained is no guarantee that he is correct in a specific case. His identification testimony should be scrutinized just as carefully as that of the normal witness." . . .

Another factor on which the Court relies, the witness' degree of certainty in making the identification, is worthless as an indicator that he is correct. Even if Glover had been unsure initially about his identification of Brathwaite's picture, by the time he was called at trial to present a key piece of evidence for the State that paid his salary, it is impossible to imagine his responding negatively to such questions as "is there any doubt in your mind whatsoever" that the identification was correct. As the Court noted in *Wade*: "'It is a matter of common experience that, once a witness has picked out the accused at the (pretrial confrontation), he is not likely to go back on his word later on.'"

Next, the Court finds that because the identification procedure took place two days after the crime, its reliability is enhanced. While such nearness in time makes the identification more reliable than one occurring months later, the fact is that the greatest memory loss occurs within hours after an event. After that, the dropoff continues much more slowly. Thus, the reliability of an identification is increased only if it was made within several hours of the crime. . . .

Finally, the Court makes much of the fact that Glover gave a description of the seller to D'Onofrio shortly after the incident. Despite the Court's assertion that because "Glover himself was a Negro and unlikely to perceive only general features of 'hundreds of Hartford black males,' as the Court of Appeals stated," the description given by Glover was actually no more than a general summary of the seller's appearance. We may discount entirely the seller's clothing, for that was of no significance later in the proceeding. Indeed, to the extent that Glover noticed clothes, his attention was diverted from the seller's face.

Otherwise, Glover merely described vaguely the seller's height, skin color, hairstyle, and build. He did say that the seller had "high cheekbones," but there is no other mention of facial features, nor even an estimate of age. Conspicuously absent is any indication that the seller was a native of the West Indies, certainly something which a member of the black community could immediately recognize from both appearance and accent. Brathwaite had come to the United States from his native Barbados as an adult. . . .

In contrast, the procedure used to identify Brathwaite was both extraordinarily suggestive and strongly conducive to error. . . . By displaying a single photograph of Brathwaite to the witness Glover under the circumstances in this record almost everything that could have been done wrong was done wrong.

In the first place, there was no need to use a photograph at all. Because photos are static, two-dimensional, and often outdated, they are "clearly inferior in reliability" to live person lineups and showups. While the use of photographs is justifiable and often essential where the police have no knowledge of an offender's identity, the poor reliability of photos makes their use inexcusable where any other means of identification is available.

Here, since Detective D'Onofrio believed he knew the seller's identity, further investigation without resort to a photographic showup was easily possible. With little inconvenience, a live person lineup including Brathwaite might have been arranged. Indeed, the police carefully staged Brathwaite's arrest in the same apartment that was used for the sale, indicating that they were fully capable of keeping track of his whereabouts and using this information in their investigation. . . .

Worse still than the failure to use an easily available live person identification was the display to Glover of only a single picture, rather than a photo array. With good reason, such single-suspect procedures have "been widely condemned." They give no assurance the witness can identify the criminal from among a number of persons of similar appearance, surely the strongest evidence that there was no misidentification. . . .

The danger of error is at its greatest when "the police display to the witness only the picture of a single individual. . . ." The use of a single picture (or the display of a single live suspect, for that matter) is a grave error, of course, because it dramatically suggests to the witness that the person shown must be the culprit. Why else would the police choose the person? And it is deeply ingrained in human nature to agree with the expressed opinions of others—particularly others who should be more knowledgeable—when making a difficult decision.

In this case, moreover, the pressure was not limited to that inherent in the display of a single photograph. Glover, the identifying witness, was a state police officer on special assignment. He knew that D'Onofrio, an experienced Hartford narcotics detective, presumably familiar with local drug operations, believed respondent to be the seller. There was at work, then, both loyalty to another police officer and deference to a better-informed colleague. . . .

While the Court is impressed by D'Onofrio's immediate response to Glover's description . . . the detective, who had not witnessed the transaction, acted on a wild guess that Brathwaite was the seller. D'Onofrio's hunch rested solely on Glover's vague description, yet D'Onofrio had seen respondent only "several times, mostly in his vehicle." There was no evidence that respondent was even a suspected narcotics dealer, and D'Onofrio thought that the drugs had been purchased at a different apartment from the one Glover actually went to. The identification of respondent provides a perfect example of the investigator and the witness bolstering each other's inadequate knowledge to produce a seemingly accurate but actually worthless identification.

The Court discounts this overwhelming evidence of suggestiveness, however. It reasons that because D'Onofrio was not present when Glover viewed the photograph, there was "little pressure on the witness to acquiesce in the suggestion." That conclusion blinks psychological reality. There is no doubt in my mind that even in D'Onofrio's absence, a clear and powerful message was telegraphed to Glover as he looked at respondent's photograph. He was emphatically told that "this is the man," and he responded by identifying respondent then and at trial "whether or not he was in fact 'the man.'"

I must conclude that this record presents compelling evidence that there was "a very substantial likelihood of misidentification" of respondent Brathwaite. The suggestive display of Brathwaite's photograph to the witness Glover likely erased any independent memory Glover had retained of the seller from his barely adequate opportunity to observe the criminal.

Accordingly, I dissent.

## Questions

1. Describe the three approaches to dealing with misidentifications outlined by the majority opinion.

2. Which approach does the Court adopt? Why?

3. List the facts in each of the five factors and the majority opinion's assessment of them.

4. List the facts in the same way and the dissenting opinion's assessment of them.

5. Do you think the circumstances demonstrate "a very substantial likelihood of irreparable misidentification"?

6. Summarize the dissent's argument in favor of the per se test and against the totality test. Is the dissent correct in arguing that the Court wrongfully evaluated the impact of the exclusionary rule and the totality of circumstances? Evaluate those arguments.

7. Is the dissent's stress on Brathwaite's Barbados ancestry important? Explain.

8. Would you side with the dissent or the majority in this case? Defend your answer.

# DNA PROFILE IDENTIFICATION

DNA (deoxyribonucleic acid) testing can *potentially* identify suspects or *absolutely* exclude individuals as suspects in cases where perpetrators have left DNA at the scene of a crime or where victims have left DNA on items traceable to perpetrators. This capacity to use DNA to identify criminal suspects has come about because of rapid advances in molecular biology since DNA was discovered in 1953.

DNA is a long, double-stranded molecule found in everyone's chromosomes. Chromosomes are carried in the nucleus of body cells that have nuclei. These include white blood cells, sperm cells, cells surrounding the hair roots, and saliva cells. DNA testing involves comparing the DNA samples in the nuclei of cells found at crime scenes with either similar DNA samples taken from the nuclei of cells of suspects or DNA samples left by victims on items traceable to perpetrators.

The most widely used test, in which long sections of DNA are broken into fragments, is called **DNA fingerprinting (DNA profiling)**. The test measures the fragments, which tend to vary from person to person. If samples from crime scenes have lengths that differ from those of the suspect, that excludes the suspect. If the sample at the scene and that of the suspect have the same lengths, the samples might have a common source. To reduce the element of chance, laboratories measure six or more distinct fragments. Two commercial laboratories, Cellmark Diagnostics Corporation and Lifecodes Corporation, and the FBI are the major sites for DNA testing in the United States (Kreiling 1993, 449; Thompson 1993, 26–27).

Let's look more closely at the reliability of DNA testing and the legal standards for admitting DNA profiles as evidence.

## The Reliability of DNA Testing

DNA testing quickly entered the legal system, heralded by one court as "the greatest advance in crime fighting technology since fingerprinting." But then a serious scientific controversy broke out; some challenged the theory of DNA itself, and others challenged the testing methods. Most, however, accepted the soundness of the theory and the testing technology, attacking, instead, the admission of the specific tests. According to Professor Edward Imwinkelried of the University of California, Davis, School of Law:

> My reading of the proficiency studies of forensic DNA testing laboratories is that the most common cause of error is not the inherent limitations of the technique, but the way in which the specific test was conducted. What the courts don't understand is that no matter how impressive studies are of the validity of a scientific technique, they are worthless as a guarantee of reliability unless you replicate the variables of the experiment. (Goldberg 1992, 85)

In 1989, in *People v. Castro*, the defense lawyers, who were knowledgeable about DNA testing, obtained the aid of disinterested scientists to challenge DNA evidence successfully. Lifecodes, the laboratory that did the testing, violated its own rules and was charged with scientific fraud. In the face of a unanimity of scientific opinion, including even experts hired by the prosecution, Lifecodes admitted that the testing didn't amount to a match. The wide coverage that the case received in both the popular and scientific press led to a full-scale debate. The controversy got so heated that John Hicks, head of the FBI Laboratory Division, contended "this is no longer a search for the truth; it is a war" (Thompson 1993, 23).

## Legal Standards for Admitting DNA Profile Evidence

Most courts have admitted DNA tests as evidence, but the courts remain divided over the standards for admission. Some courts have adopted the *Frye* **standard**. Named after *Frye v. U.S.* (1923), the *Frye* standard finds DNA evidence is admissible if the technique is "sufficiently established to have gained general acceptance in the particular field in which it belongs." Other courts have adopted a *Frye* **plus standard**, which finds that in addition to gaining general acceptance, admissibility requires showing that "the testing laboratory in the particular case performed the accepted scientific techniques in analyzing forensic samples." A third group of courts has adopted the *Federal Rules of Evidence* standard, which determines whether the relevancy of the evidence outweighs the tendency of the evidence to prejudice the defendant unfairly. A fourth group of courts has adopted a relevancy plus standard, a hybrid that adds the *Frye* standard and other requirements to the *Federal Rules of Evidence* standard (Goldberg 1992, 84).

The correct identification of criminal suspects by means of DNA testing, whatever the standard a particular court adopts, depends on the answers to the following three questions and the inferences that jurors or other fact finders make about them:

1. Is a reported match between the sample at the scene of the crime and the sample from the suspect a true match?

2. Is the suspect the source of the trace of DNA left at the scene of the crime?

3. Is the suspect the perpetrator of the crime?

A *reported* match strongly suggests a *true* match. However, mistakes in DNA processing do occur. Technical errors, such as enzyme failures, salt concentrations, and dirt spots, can produce misleading patterns. Human errors, including contaminations, mislabelings, misrecordings, misrepresentations, case mix-ups, and errors of interpretation, also occur. Assuming that the match is true, it strongly suggests that the suspect is the source of the trace of DNA left at the scene of the crime. Still, the match might be coincidental. The coincidence depends on the frequency of matching traits among the relevant population, usually the ethnic group of the suspect. However, the validity of this reference population isn't foolproof either; it depends on the correct identification of the suspect's ethnic group.

Further, prosecutors, experts, and jurors often exaggerate the weight to give to the match between the trace and the suspect by speaking in terms of odds. According to one trial transcript, after testifying that the blood of a victim matched a sample from a blanket, the following exchange took place:

*Q [Prosecutor]:* And in your profession and in the scientific field when you say match what do you mean?

*A [Expert]:* They are identical.

*Q [Prosecutor]:* So the blood on the blanket can you say it came from [the victim]?

*A [Expert]:* With great certainty I can say that those two DNA samples match and they are identical. And with population statistics we can derive a probability of it being anyone other than the victim.

*Q [Prosecutor]:* What is the probability in this case?

*A [Expert]:* In this case that probability is that it is one in 7 million chances that it could be anyone other than that victim. (Koehler 1995, 21)

But Professor Jonathan Koehler, at the University of Texas at Austin, says the expert's claim that population statistics can show the victim was probably *not* the source is false.

Finally, evidence the suspect is the source of the trace is also evidence the suspect committed the crime. But maybe not! The suspect could have left the trace innocently either before or after the commission of the crime. So the use of the match to prove guilt depends on an inference—perhaps a fair inference but not an automatic, or always correct, inference.

Whatever the problems and criticisms of the use of DNA testing to identify suspects and link them to crimes, the impact of DNA (and other scientific evidence, too, for that matter) is substantial. According to one researcher, about 25 percent of jurors said they would have voted not guilty if scientific evidence had *not* been introduced.

In another survey, 75 percent of judges and lawyers throughout the United States said that they believe judges believe scientific evidence more than other kinds of evidence, and 70 percent said they think jurors do, too (Giannelli 1991, 794).

Go to Exercise 9.2 on the Samaha Criminal Procedure 7e website to learn more about DNA crime labs: academic.cengage.com/criminaljustice/samaha.

## SUMMARY

**I. Mistaken Eyewitness Identification**
    A. Relying on victims' identification of strangers is risky even in ideal circumstances.
    B. Memory problems result in mistaken identifications of strangers.
       1. Memory consists of acquisition, retention, and retrieval.
       2. *Acquisition* of memory is the information the brain takes in at the time of the crime.
          a. The brain isn't a DVR.
          b. Perceptions trump reality.
          c. We all pay selective attention to what's going around us.
          d. The accuracy of witnesses' observations depends on
             (1) Length of time to observe
             (2) Distractions during the observations
             (3) Focus of the observations
             (4) Stress during the observations
          e. Race affects the accuracy of identifications.
       3. *Retention* of memory concerns the information the brain stores between the time of a crime and the lineup, show-up, or picture identification.
          a. Fading memory raises the risk of mistakes.
          b. Memory fades most during the first few hours after the crime.
          c. Then, it remains stable for months.
          d. Confidence in our memory rises as its reliability actually fades.
       4. *Retrieval* of memory refers to the information retrieved from memory at the time of the lineup, show-up, or picture identification.
          a. There are two types of memory: recall and recognition.
          b. Errors of omission result in failure to recall a key detail.
          c. Errors of commission result in picking an innocent person in a photo array.
    C. The power of suggestion can lead to misidentifications of strangers.
       1. Most misidentifications result from a combination of natural memory imperfections and suggestion (usually subtle and innocent).
       2. Suggestion is most powerful during the retention and the retrieval phases.
       3. Loftus's "memory bin" research has provided much of what we know about the power of suggestion on witnesses' memories.
       4. Police identification procedures increase the power of suggestion.

## II. Identification Procedures

 A. Lineups

  1. They're the least often used and the least unreliable.

  2. Their reliability depends on their makeup and the procedures used.

  3. IACP recommendations for their makeup include:

   a. Five or six participants

   b. Similar race, ethnicity, and skin color

   c. Similar age, height, weight, hair color, and body build

   d. Similar clothing

  4. The power of suggestion is one of the biggest threats to proper lineup procedures.

  5. Recommendations to reduce the influence of suggestions include:

   a. Tell witnesses the suspect might not be in the lineup.

   b. Use a blind administrator.

   c. If the witness identifies the suspect, immediately ask the witness how sure she is of her identification.

   d. Use sequential, not simultaneous, presentation.

  6. It's difficult to shake a witness's confidence once he makes an identification, even if it's wrong.

 B. Show-Ups

  1. They're less reliable than lineups but used more frequently.

  2. The three common situations in which courts are most likely to admit show-up evidence include:

   a. Accidental encounters between witnesses and suspects

   b. Emergencies

   c. Suspects on the loose

 C. "Mug Shot" (Photo) Identification

  1. By far, they're the least reliable but also the most widely used.

  2. Their two-dimensional nature enhances the inaccuracy of identifications made from them.

## III. The Constitution and Identification Procedures

 A. Until the 1960s, the Supreme Court adopted a "hands-off" approach to admitting evidence from lineups, show-ups, and photo identifications.

 B. *Stovall v. Denno* (1967) established the due process basis for challenging identifications on constitutional grounds.

 C. Reliability is the linchpin.

  1. Defendants have to prove by a preponderance of the evidence two elements regarding a lineup, show-up, or photo ID:

   a. They were "unnecessarily and impermissibly suggestive."

   b. The procedure used created a "very substantial likelihood of misidentification."

  2. Five factors form the "totality of circumstances" courts use to determine witnesses' reliability:

   a. Witnesses' opportunity to view defendants at the time of the crime

   b. Witnesses' degree of attention at the time of the crime

   c. Witnesses' accuracy of description of suspects prior to the identification

d. Witnesses' level of certainty when identifying suspects at the time of the identification procedure

e. The length of time between the crime and the identification

3. It's questionable to assume that reliability improves if a witness's identification meets the reliability test.

4. There's some validity to the "opportunity to view the suspect during the crime" factor, but none of the other factors improves reliability.

## IV. DNA Profile Identification

A. DNA can potentially identify individuals or absolutely exclude them as suspects.

B. Reliability issues arise not from technology but from DNA testing procedures.

C. The three legal standards for admitting DNA profiles as evidence are:

1. *Frye test*. It's admissible if the technique has gained general scientific acceptance.

2. *Frye plus*. It's admissible if the technique has gained general scientific acceptance and testing in the particular case followed accepted scientific techniques.

3. *Federal Rules of Evidence*. It's admissible if the relevance of the evidence outweighs any tendency to hurt unfairly the defendant's case.

D. Correct identification based on DNA depends on answers to three questions:

1. Is a reported match between the sample at the scene of the crime and the sample from the suspect a true match?

2. Is the suspect the source of the trace of DNA left at the scene of the crime?

3. Is the suspect the perpetrator of the crime?

E. Problems with use of DNA evidence in court include:

1. Mistakes do happen.

2. The match might be coincidental.

3. Prosecutors, experts, and jurors exaggerate the weight of DNA evidence.


# REVIEW QUESTIONS

1. Why is identification of strangers risky in criminal cases?

2. Identify and define three mental processes that account for mistakes in identifying strangers.

3. Identify five circumstances that affect the accuracy of identifying strangers.

4. Describe how memory affects the accuracy of eyewitness identification.

5. Describe how suggestion works based on Elizabeth Loftus's research.

6. Describe how witnesses' descriptions of criminal events change over time.

7. When is the effect of suggestion most powerful and threatening,? Why?

8. Explain why the procedures used to identify strangers add to the problem of misidentification.

9. Identify and describe three ways to reduce the inaccuracy of eyewitness identification by police procedures and legal rules.

10. Identify three constitutional provisions identification procedures can violate and when in the criminal process they kick in.

11. Identify four characteristics of lineups recommended by the International Association of Chiefs of Police.

12. Summarize what empirical research has shown about the reliability of lineups.

13. Describe and give an example of how the power of suggestion works in administering lineups.

14. List three rules Wells and Seelau recommend for reducing misidentification in lineups.

15. Identify the two-steps in the totality-of-circumstances due process test of admissibility of eyewitness identification created by the U.S. Supreme Court.

16. Identify, describe, and give an example of the five circumstances in the totality-of-circumstances due process test you identified in question 15.

17. Why are photo identifications the most unreliable eyewitness identification procedure?

18. Identify and compare the three legal tests for admitting DNA evidence in court.

19. Correct identification based on DNA depends on answers to three questions. Identify the three questions.

20. Summarize the importance jurors, lawyers, and judges attach to scientific evidence as proof of guilt.

## KEY TERMS

# Remedies for Constitutional Violations I: The Exclusionary Rule and Entrapment

## MAIN POINTS

- Individuals have numerous remedies against government misconduct (at least on paper).
- The two remedies discussed in this chapter—the exclusionary rule and the defense of entrapment—aren't constitutional rights.
- The United States is unusual in its adoption of the exclusionary rule, which bans the use of illegally obtained evidence to prove guilt.
- The social cost of the exclusionary rule is that some guilty people go free, because keeping good evidence out of court undermines the prosecution's case.
- Because of the social cost of freeing guilty people, the use of the exclusionary rule is restricted to the government's case-in-chief, where it's most likely to deter unconstitutional conduct by police.
- There's considerable controversy over how high the social costs and how great the deterrent effects of the exclusionary rule are.
- Courts throw out cases where officers encouraged defendants to commit crimes they wouldn't have committed without the encouragement.
- Government encouragement of criminal behavior is an undercover police tactic directed mainly at consensual crimes, such as official corruption, drugs, pornography, and prostitution.

In January 1991, Phoenix police officer Bryan Sargent saw Isaac Evans driving the wrong way on a one-way street in front of the police station. The officer stopped Evans and asked to see his driver's license. After Evans told him that his license had been suspended, the officer entered Evans's name into a computer data terminal located in his patrol car. The computer inquiry confirmed that Evans's license had been suspended and also indicated that there was an outstanding misdemeanor warrant for his arrest. Based upon the outstanding warrant, Officer Sargent arrested Evans. While the police were handcuffing him, Evans dropped a hand-rolled cigarette that the officers determined smelled of marijuana. The officers proceeded to search his car and discovered a bag of marijuana under the passenger's seat.

The State charged Evans with possession of marijuana. When the police notified the Justice Court that they had arrested him, the Justice Court discovered that the arrest warrant previously had been quashed [vacated or voided] and notified the police. Evans argued that because his arrest was based on a warrant that had been quashed 17 days before his arrest, the marijuana seized incident to the arrest should be suppressed as the fruit of an unlawful arrest. ⊚

Arizona v. Evans (1995), U.S. Supreme Court

## CASES COVERED

Mapp v. Ohio,
367 U.S. 643 (1961)

U.S. v. Leon,
468 U.S. 897 (1984)

Arizona v. Evans,
514 U.S. 1 (1995)

Jacobson v. U.S.,
503 U.S. 540 (1992)

When I was a very junior member of a Minneapolis mayor's committee to examine police misconduct, our committee held a neighborhood meeting to educate residents about our work. But I learned a lot more than the residents. One resident that night made a comment and then asked a great question. His comment: "We all know what happens when we break the law—we get arrested and prosecuted." His question: "What I want to know is what happens when the police break the law against us? What recourse do we have?" The answer is, "We have lots of remedies" (at least, on paper).

We'll divide the discussion of the remedies into two types and between this chapter and the next. First, we'll look at remedies that can affect the outcome of the state's criminal case against defendants (the trial stage). They're part of the criminal case against defendants. Two of these remedies are the subject of this chapter:

1. *Exclusionary rule.* The government throws out illegally obtained evidence in the case against the defendant (by far the most frequently used remedy).

2. *Defense of entrapment.* The government dismisses cases against defendants who committed crimes they (or a hypothetical, reasonable person) wouldn't have committed if law enforcement officers hadn't encouraged them to commit them.

"Encouragement" is a widely used undercover police tactic directed mainly at consensual crimes, such as official corruption, and crimes without complaining victims, such as illegal drugs, pornography, and prostitution. Citizens have no constitutional right to either the exclusionary rule or the defense of entrapment. The exclusionary rule is a device created by the U.S. Supreme Court to enforce constitutional rights, but it's not a right itself. The defense of entrapment is a right created by either federal and state statutes or court decisions.

The remedies covered in Chapter 11 require proceedings separate from the criminal case against defendants. Some of these proceedings take place inside, and others outside, the judicial system. They include:

1. *Criminal prosecution* of police officers for their illegal actions
2. *Civil lawsuits* to seek and obtain remedies from individual officers, and/or the administrators of departments and government units responsible for their wrongdoing
3. *Administrative review* of police misconduct to discipline officers who break police rules

# THE EXCLUSIONARY RULE

The U.S. legal system, like all others, excludes the use of some irrelevant or untrustworthy evidence. But the *exclusionary rule*, mandating courts to ban the introduction of "good" evidence obtained by "bad" law enforcement, is more prevalent in the United States than in most other countries' legal systems. In Judge Cardozo's famous words, "The culprit goes free because the constable blundered" (*People v. Defore* 1926, 587). **"Good evidence"** refers to **probative evidence**—evidence that proves (or at least helps to prove) defendants committed the crimes they're charged with. **"Bad methods"** refers to police actions and procedures that violate any of five constitutional rights:

1. The Fourth Amendment ban on unreasonable searches and seizures (Chapters 3–7)

2. The Fifth Amendment ban on coerced incriminating statements (Chapter 8)

3. The Sixth Amendment right to counsel (Chapter 12)

4–5. The Fifth and Fourteenth Amendment guarantees of due process of law in administering identification procedures (Chapter 9)

In this section, we'll trace the history of the exclusionary rule. Then, we'll examine the rationales for and the scope of the rule; what happens when people are brought to court based on illegal arrests; the reasonable, good-faith exception to the exclusionary rule; whether bad methods employed by non–law enforcement government officials should result in the exclusion of evidence obtained based on their mistakes; and the social costs of the exclusionary rule.

## History

The Bill of Rights to the U.S. Constitution doesn't mention the exclusionary rule (or for that matter any other remedies we'll be discussing in this chapter and Chapter 11). James Madison, in an address to Congress in 1789 (*Annals of Congress* 1789), explains this silence:

> If these rights are incorporated into the Constitution, independent tribunals of justice will consider themselves in a peculiar manner the guardians of those rights; they will be an impenetrable bulwark against every assumption of power in the Legislative or Executive; they will naturally be led to resist every encroachment upon rights expressly stipulated for in the Constitution by the declaration of rights. (457)

In other words, the Constitution didn't have to spell out the remedies because judges would create appropriate ones to fit the circumstances of each case.

Until the 20th century, the only remedies for constitutional violations were private lawsuits against officials. All this dramatically changed in 1914, when the U.S. Supreme Court created the exclusionary rule in *Weeks v. U.S.* (1914). In that case, while Fremont Weeks was at work in Union Station, Kansas City, Kansas, police officers broke into his house without a warrant. They searched the house and seized "all of his books, letters, money, papers, notes, evidences of indebtedness, stock certificates, insurance policies, deeds, abstracts of title, bonds, candies, clothes, and other property." Then, the officers arrested Weeks while he was at work. Soon, he was charged with illegal gambling.

The trial court refused Weeks's motion to return the seized evidence, and he was convicted and sentenced to a fine and imprisonment. On appeal, the U.S. Supreme Court reversed the conviction because the letters . . . were taken from the house of the accused by an official of the United States, acting under color of his office, in direct violation of the constitutional rights of the defendant; that having made a seasonable application for their return, which was heard and passed upon by the court, there was involved in the order refusing the application a denial of the constitutional rights of the accused; and that the court should have restored these letters to the accused. In holding them and permitting their use upon the trial, we think prejudicial error was committed. (398)

Notice two points here. First, the rule established in *Weeks* applied only to federal law enforcement; the states could choose any remedy they saw fit to enforce their own citizens' constitutional rights under their state constitutions. Second, the rule applied only to Weeks's private papers and other belongings he legally possessed. The Court said nothing about what it would've decided if Weeks had demanded the return of contraband. The importance of the case is that it started a trend toward the use of the exclusionary rule to enforce law enforcement violations of constitutional rights.

The Court broadened the *Weeks* rule in *Silverthorne Lumber Co. v. U.S.* (1920). After arresting Fred Silverthorne and his father, Justice Department officers and a U.S. marshal "without a shadow of authority" went to the Silverthornes' Lumber Company office and "made a clean sweep of all the books, papers and documents found there." The officers immediately took all the stuff they seized to the office of the U.S. District Attorney's office.

The Silverthornes demanded and got back their illegally seized books and papers, but, by that time, the government had already copied and photographed them. They used the copies and photographs to get a subpoena from the trial court, ordering the Silverthornes to turn over the originals. When the Silverthornes refused to obey the subpoena, the trial court fined and jailed them for contempt.

According to Justice Oliver Wendell Holmes, although the government's search and seizure "was an outrage," the government claims "it may study the papers before it returns them, copy them, and then . . . use the knowledge" to order the owners to turn over the papers. In other words, the Constitution protects the papers themselves from forbidden acts,

> but not any advantages the Government can gain from the forbidden act. . . . In our opinion such is not the law. It reduces the Fourth Amendment to a form of words. . . . The essence of a provision forbidding the acquisition of evidence in a certain way is that not merely evidence so acquired shall not be used before the Court but that it shall not be used at all. (392)

This expansion of the exclusionary rule to ban the use of evidence indirectly based on an illegal government action is called the **fruit-of-the-poisonous-tree doctrine**. The basic idea behind the doctrine is that the government should never be in a better position after violating the Constitution than it was before it broke the law. We'll discuss later the opposite idea: the government shouldn't be in a worse position after violating the Constitution than it was before. (See the "Fruit of the Poisonous Tree" section later.)

*Weeks* and *Silverthorne* still restricted the exclusionary rule to private papers. But in *Agnello v. U.S.* (1925), the Court created "a full-blown rule of exclusion at federal trials." The government had illegally seized cocaine from Frank Agnello's house, and Agnello argued that the court should have suppressed the cocaine at his trial. The Supreme Court agreed, expanding the rule beyond papers to include the contraband cocaine. Years later, Justice Potter Stewart (1983, 1376–77) contended that after the decision in *Agnello* in 1925, "the annexation of the exclusionary rule to the Fourth Amendment was complete."

As we've already noted, *Weeks*, *Silverthorne*, and *Agnello* applied only to federal cases. States still were free to apply the exclusionary rule or not. (Remember, it wasn't until the 1930s that the Court began to apply the Bill of Rights to state criminal proceedings [discussed in Chapter 2].) So the Court would have to decide in future cases whether the Fourteenth Amendment due process clause ("no state shall deny any person of life, liberty, or property without due process of law") applied to state criminal proceedings.

Do unreasonable searches and seizures violate the due process clause of the Fourteenth Amendment? It wasn't until 1949 that the Court took up the question in *Wolf v. Colorado* (1949). In fact, the Court was faced with two questions:

1. Does the Fourteenth Amendment due process clause apply the right against unreasonable searches and seizures to the states at all? and

2. If it does, is the exclusionary rule part of the right?

The Court answered "Yes" to the first question and "No" to the second. In other words, states have to enforce the ban on unreasonable searches and seizures, but the Fourth Amendment leaves it up to the states how to enforce it.

Twelve years later, in *Mapp v. Ohio* (1961), the Court changed its answer to the second question in *Wolf* to yes. The circumstances surrounding the decision to reverse itself were unusual, to put it mildly. The case started out and reached the Court as a free speech case. Dollree Mapp was convicted of possession of pornography in Ohio. The question the Supreme Court was asked to review—and which both the briefs and the oral argument were almost entirely devoted to—was whether Ohio's pornography statute violated Mapp's right to free speech.

Until the first draft of the opinion circulated among the justices, the only mention of *Wolf* was in three sentences in an **amicus curiae brief** (an argument the Court allows to be submitted by someone—or more likely some interest group—who isn't a party but who has an interest in the case) of the American Civil Liberties Union. In fact, when asked about *Wolf v. Colorado* during oral arguments, Mapp's attorney admitted he'd never heard of the case.

Justice Stewart (1983) later recalled:

> I was shocked when Justice [Tom C.] Clark's proposed Court opinion reached my desk. I immediately wrote him a note expressing my surprise and questioning the wisdom of overruling an important doctrine in a case in which the issue was not briefed, argued, or discussed by the state courts, by the parties' counsel, or at our conferences following the oral argument. After my shock subsided, I wrote a brief memorandum concurring in the judgment . . . and agreeing with Justice Harlan's dissent that the issue was not properly before the Court. The *Mapp* majority, however, stood its ground. . . . The case . . . provides significant insight into the judicial process and the evolution of law—a first amendment controversy was transformed into perhaps the most important search-and-seizure case in history. (1367)

## CASE | *Should the Court Exclude the Evidence?*

### *Mapp v. Ohio*
367 U.S. 643 (1961)

### HISTORY

Dollree Mapp was tried and convicted of illegal possession of pornography. Over her objection, the trial court admitted the pornography in evidence against her. On appeal, the Ohio Supreme Court affirmed. The U.S. Supreme Court reversed.

CLARK, J.

### FACTS

On May 23, 1957, three Cleveland police officers arrived at Dollree Mapp's house pursuant to information that "a person was hiding out in the home, who was wanted for questioning in connection with a recent bombing, and that there was a large amount of policy paraphernalia being hidden in the home." Miss Mapp and her daughter by a former marriage lived on the top floor of the two-family dwelling. Upon their arrival at that house, the officers knocked on the door and demanded entrance but Mapp, after telephoning her attorney, refused to admit them without a search warrant. They advised their headquarters of the situation and undertook a surveillance of the house.

The officers again sought entrance some three hours later when four or more additional officers arrived on the scene. When Miss Mapp did not come to the door immediately, at least one of the several doors to the house was forcibly opened and the policemen gained admittance. Officer Carl DeLau testified that "we did pry the screen door to gain entrance"; the attorney on the scene testified that a policeman "tried . . . to kick the door" and then "broke the glass in the door and somebody reached in and opened the door and let them in"; Mapp testified that "The back door was broken."

Meanwhile Miss Mapp's attorney arrived, but the officers, having secured their own entry, and continuing in their defiance of the law, would permit him neither to see Miss Mapp nor to enter the house. It happens that Miss Mapp was halfway down the stairs from the upper floor to the front door when the officers, in this high-handed manner, broke into the hall. She demanded to see the search warrant. A paper, claimed to be a warrant, was held up by one of the officers. She grabbed the "warrant" and placed it in her bosom. A struggle ensued in which the officers recovered the piece of paper as a result of which they handcuffed Mapp because she had been "belligerent" in resisting their official rescue of the "warrant" from her person.

Running roughshod over Mapp, a policeman "grabbed" her, "twisted her hand," and she "yelled and pleaded with him" because "it was hurting." Mapp, in handcuffs, was then forcibly taken upstairs to her bedroom where the officers searched the dresser, a chest of drawers, a closet and some suitcases. They also looked in a photo album and through personal papers belonging to Mapp. The search spread to the rest of the second floor including the child's bedroom, the living room, the kitchen, and a dinette. The basement of the building and a trunk found therein were also searched. The obscene materials for possession of which she was ultimately convicted were discovered in the course of that widespread search.

At the trial no search warrant was produced by the prosecution, nor was the failure to produce one explained or accounted for. At best, "There is, in the record, considerable doubt as to whether there ever was any warrant for the search of defendant's home." The Ohio Supreme Court believed a "reasonable argument" could be made that the conviction should be reversed "because the 'methods' employed to obtain the evidence . . . were such as to 'offend a sense of justice,'" but the court found determinative the fact that the evidence had not been taken "from defendant's person by the use of brutal or offensive physical force against defendant."

## OPINION

In 1949, 35 years after *Weeks v. U.S.* (1914) was announced, this Court, in *Wolf v. Colorado*, . . . for the first time, discussed the effect of the Fourth Amendment upon the States through the operation of the Due Process Clause of the Fourteenth Amendment. . . . The Court decided that the *Weeks* exclusionary rule would not then be imposed upon the States as "an essential ingredient of the right." . . .

The Court in *Wolf* . . . stated that "the contrariety of views of the States" on the adoption of the exclusionary rule . . . was "particularly impressive"; and . . . it could not "brush aside the experience of the States which deem the incidence of such conduct by the police too slight to call for a deterrent remedy . . . by overriding the States' relevant rules of evidence." While in 1949, prior to the *Wolf* case, almost two-thirds of the States were opposed to the use of the exclusionary rule, now . . . more than half . . . have wholly or partly adopted or adhered to the *Weeks* rule.

Significantly, among those now following the rule is California which, according to its highest court, was "compelled to reach that conclusion because other remedies have completely failed to secure compliance with the constitutional provisions. . . ." The second basis elaborated in *Wolf* in support of its failure to enforce the exclusionary doctrine against the States was that "other means of protection" have been afforded "the right of privacy." The experience of California that such other remedies have been worthless and futile is buttressed by the experience of other States. The obvious futility of relegating the Fourth Amendment to the protection of other remedies has, moreover, been recognized by this Court since *Wolf*. . . .

Since the Fourth Amendment's right of privacy has been declared enforceable against the States through the Due Process Clause of the Fourteenth, it is enforceable against them by the same sanction of exclusion as is used against the Federal Government. Were it otherwise, then . . . the assurance against unreasonable federal searches and seizures would be "a form of words," valueless and undeserving of mention in a perpetual charter of inestimable human liberties, so too, without that rule the freedom from state invasions of privacy would be so ephemeral and so neatly severed from its conceptual nexus with the freedom from all brutish means of coercing evidence as not to merit this Court's high regard as a freedom "implicit in the concept of ordered liberty." . . .

There are those who say, as did Justice Cardozo, that under our constitutional exclusionary doctrine "the criminal is to go free because the constable has blundered." In some cases this will undoubtedly be the result. But, there is another consideration—the imperative of judicial integrity. The criminal goes free, if he must, but it is the law that sets him free. Nothing can destroy a government more quickly than its failure to observe its own laws, or worse, its disregard of the charter of its own existence. [As Justice Brandeis, dissenting in *Olmstead v. U.S.* (1928), wrote:]

Our Government is the potent, the omnipresent teacher. For good or for ill, it teaches the whole people by its example. . . . If the Government becomes a lawbreaker, it breeds contempt for law; it invites every man to become a law unto himself; it invites anarchy.

Nor can it lightly be assumed that, as a practical matter, adoption of the exclusionary rule fetters law enforcement. Only last year this Court expressly considered that contention and found that "pragmatic evidence of a sort" to the contrary was not wanting. The Court noted that the federal courts themselves have operated under the exclusionary rule . . . for almost half a century; yet it has not been suggested either that the Federal Bureau of Investigation has thereby been rendered ineffective, or that the administration of criminal justice in the federal courts has thereby been disrupted. Moreover, the experience of the states is impressive. . . . The movement towards the rule of exclusion has been halting but seemingly inexorable.

. . . Our decision, founded on reason and truth, gives to the individual no more than that which the Constitution guarantees him, to the police officer no less than that to which honest law enforcement is entitled, and, to the courts, that judicial integrity so necessary in the true administration of justice.

REVERSED and REMANDED.

### DISSENT

HARLAN, J., JOINED BY FRANKFURTER AND WHITTAKER, JJ.

At the heart of the majority's opinion in this case is the following syllogism:

(1) the rule excluding in federal criminal trial evidence which is the product of an illegal search and seizure is "part and parcel" of the Fourth Amendment;

(2) *Wolf* held that the "privacy" assured against federal action by the Fourth Amendment is also protected against state action by the Fourteenth Amendment; and

(3) it is therefore "logically and constitutionally necessary" that the *Weeks* exclusionary rule should also be enforced against the States.

This reasoning ultimately rests on the unsound premise that because *Wolf* carried into the States, as part of "the concept of ordered liberty" embodied in the Fourteenth Amendment, the principle of "privacy" underlying the Fourth Amendment, it must follow that whatever configurations of the Fourth Amendment have been developed in the . . . federal precedents are likewise to be deemed a part of "ordered liberty," and as such are enforceable against the States. For me, this does not follow at all. . . .

Since there is not the slightest suggestion that Ohio's policy is "affirmatively to sanction . . . police incursion into privacy" what the Court is now doing is to impose upon the States not only federal substantive standards of "search and seizure" but also the basic federal remedy for violation of those standards. For I think it entirely clear that the *Weeks* exclusionary rule is but a remedy which, by penalizing past official misconduct, is aimed at deterring such conduct in the future.

I would not impose upon the States this federal exclusionary remedy.

### Questions

1. List the reasons the Court gave for overruling *Wolf v. Colorado*. Do you agree?

2. Are Justice Stewart's recollections of any importance? Explain.

3. According to the Court majority, why should Dollree Mapp go free? Because the Cleveland police blundered?

4. What remedies are available to Dollree Mapp besides the exclusion of the evidence? Which would you recommend?

 To learn more about *Mapp v. Ohio*, go to the Samaha Criminal Procedure 7e website and read the "Rest of the Story": academic.cengage.com/criminaljustice/samaha.

## Justifications

To put it mildly, the exclusionary rule is controversial. Critics say it sets criminals free on "technicalities." Supporters reply, these "technicalities" are rights for which our ancestors fought and died. Why do we throw good evidence out of court? The U.S. Supreme Court has relied on three justifications:

1. *Constitutional right.* It's part of the constitutional rights against unreasonable seizure and coerced confessions and the rights to a lawyer and due process of law.

2. *Judicial integrity.* It preserves the honor and honesty of the courts.

3. *Deterrence.* It prevents officers from breaking the law.

The **constitutional right justification** stems from an ancient legal saying, "There's no right without a remedy" (Stewart 1983, 1380–83). One commentator summed it up with this great image: "It's like one hand clapping" (Uviller 1988).

In *Weeks v. U.S.* (1914), the case that created the exclusionary rule for the federal system, U.S. Supreme Court Justice William Rufus Day put it this way:

> If letters and private documents can . . . be seized and held and used in evidence against a citizen accused of an offense, the protection of the Fourth Amendment declaring his right to be secure against such searches and seizures is of no value, and . . . may as well be stricken from the Constitution. (393)

The **judicial integrity justification** maintains that the honor and honesty of courts forbid them to participate in unconstitutional conduct. Dissenting in *Olmstead v. U.S.* (1928), a famous case upholding the constitutionality of wiretapping (Chapter 3), Justice Oliver Wendell Holmes spoke to the dilemma of throwing out good evidence because it was obtained by bad official behavior:

> We must consider two objects of desire, both of which we cannot have, and make up our minds which to choose. It is desirable that criminals should be detected, and to that end that all available evidence should be used. It also is desirable that the Government should not itself foster and pay for other crimes, when they are the means by which the evidence is to be obtained. . . . For my part, I think it is less evil that some criminals should escape than that the Government should play an ignoble part. (470)

The **deterrence justification** says throwing out good evidence because it was obtained illegally sends a strong message to law enforcement. Here's how the distinguished Justice Potter Stewart (who probably knew more about the Fourth Amendment than any other U.S. Supreme Court justice in our history) summed up the deterrence justification:

> The rule is calculated to prevent, not to repair. Its purpose is to deter—to compel respect for the constitutional guaranty in the only effective available way—by removing the incentive to disregard it. (*Elkins v. U.S.* 1960, 217)

Since the 1980s, the Court has relied on deterrence as the only justification for excluding valid evidence. The Court has adopted another form of its old friend the balancing test in applying the deterrence justification. This form of the test weighs the social cost of excluding "good" evidence—namely, setting criminals free—against the deterrent effect that excluding good evidence might have on the illegal conduct of law enforcement officers. If the social costs outweigh the deterrent effect, then the evidence comes in.

The constitutional significance of letting evidence seized illegally into court because the social cost of keeping it out is too high is that the exclusionary rule isn't a constitutional right. (See "Social Costs and Deterrence" later for more discussion.) According to the U.S. Supreme Court in *U.S. v. Leon* (1984; excerpted later in this section on page 350), excluding evidence isn't a constitutional right; it's a **prophylactic rule**—a protective procedure against violations of constitutional rights (Schroeder 1981, 1378–86).

The exclusionary rule brings into bold relief the tension between ends and means—namely, between result and process in the law of criminal procedure. By throwing out good evidence because of bad practices, the rule puts the search for truth second to fair procedures. No one has put the case for the exclusionary rule better than Associate Justice Louis D. Brandeis in his famous dissent in *Olmstead v. U.S.* (1928):

Decency, security, and liberty alike demand that government officials shall be subjected to the same rules of conduct that are commands to the citizen. In a government of laws, existence of the government will be imperiled if it fails to observe the law scrupulously. Our government is the potent, the omnipresent teacher. For good or for ill, it teaches the whole people by its example. Crime is contagious. If the government becomes a lawbreaker, it breeds contempt for law; it invites every man to become a law unto himself; it invites anarchy.

To declare that in the administration of the criminal law the end justifies the means—to declare that the government may commit crimes in order to secure the conviction of a private criminal—would bring terrible retribution. Against that pernicious doctrine this court should resolutely set its face. (468)

## Scope

The social cost of the rule—freeing guilty people and undermining the prosecution's case by keeping good evidence out of court—led the U.S. Supreme Court to limit it to cases it believes are most likely to deter police misconduct. The Court has decided that proceedings outside the trial don't deter police misconduct and that even major parts of the trial have no deterrent effect on police misconduct. The Court has created numerous exceptions to the exclusionary rule to cover cases that it believes don't deter police misconduct.

We'll discuss five of the major exceptions:

1. Collateral use

2. Cross-examination

3. Attenuation of the taint of unconstitutional official conduct

4. Independent source

5. Inevitable discovery

Let's look at each of these.

*Collateral Use* The collateral-use exception allows the use of illegally obtained evidence in nontrial proceedings (*U.S. v. Calandra* 1974). What proceedings does this include? The general answer is proceedings related to the case but not the trial. (The term **collateral proceedings** means proceedings "off to the side" of the main case.) Specifically, these include bail hearings (Chapter 12); preliminary hearings (Chapter 12); grand jury proceedings (Chapter 12); and some kinds of habeas corpus proceedings (Chapter 13). So prosecutors can present illegally obtained evidence to deny defendants bail; get grand juries to indict defendants; and get judges in preliminary hearings to send cases on for trial.

*Cross-Examination* The exclusionary rule applies only to one part (an extremely important part) of one very important criminal proceeding: the **government's case-in-chief** in the criminal trial. *Case-in-chief* means the part of the trial where the government presents its evidence to prove the defendant's guilt. The case-in-chief doesn't include cross-examination of defense witnesses.

In *Walder v. U.S.* (1954), Walder was tried for purchasing and possessing heroin. During direct examination, Walder denied he'd ever bought or possessed heroin. The government then introduced heroin capsules seized during an illegal search to prove to the jury that he was a liar. The trial court admitted the capsules but cautioned the jury not to use the heroin capsules to prove Walder's guilt, only to **impeach** (undermine the believability of) his testimony.

The U.S. Supreme Court ruled that the exclusionary rule didn't apply:

> It is one thing to say that the Government cannot make an affirmative use of evidence unlawfully obtained. It is quite another to say that the defendant can turn the illegal method by which evidence in the Government's possession was obtained to his own advantage, and provide himself with a shield against contradiction of his untruths. Such an extension of the *Weeks* doctrine would be a perversion of the Fourth Amendment. (65)

***"Fruit of the Poisonous Tree": Attenuation, Independent Source, and Inevitable Discovery*** The basic idea of the fruit-of-the-poisonous-tree doctrine is that the government shouldn't be in a better position after it breaks the law. But what if the government's position is worse? That's where three complicated exceptions—attenuation, independent source, and inevitable discovery—come in. As you read and try to understand these exceptions, keep in mind that they're exceptions to the poisonous-tree doctrine. So their effect is to let more evidence into court. (Remember the effect of the doctrine is to keep evidence out of court.) Maybe it'll help you to think of the exceptions as antidotes to the poison of illegal government actions. As the U.S. Supreme Court said, not all evidence is "'fruit of the poisonous tree' simply because it would not have come to light but for the illegal actions of the police" (*Wong Sun v. U.S.* 1963, 488).

The noun *attenuation* (according to the dictionary) means "thinning, weakening, or emaciation." The **attenuation exception** says the illegally obtained evidence can come in if the poisonous connection between illegal police actions and the evidence they got illegally from their actions weakens (attenuates) enough.

The U.S. Supreme Court hasn't written a bright-line attenuation rule. Instead, each case has to be decided on its own facts according to the totality of circumstances. One circumstance is the closeness in time between the poisonous tree (illegal government act) and getting its fruit (evidence). For example, in *Wong Sun v. U.S.* (1963, 491), federal narcotics officers in San Francisco illegally broke into James Wah Toy's home and chased him down the hall into his bedroom. Agent Wong pulled his gun, illegally arrested Toy, and handcuffed him. Toy then told the officers Johnny Yee had sold him heroin. The officers immediately went to Yee's home. Yee admitted he had heroin and gave it to the officers. The Court ruled that the time between the illegal arrest and getting the heroin from Yee was too close to dissipate the poison of the arrest.

In the same case, the same narcotics officers arrested another man, Wong Sun, illegally. A few days later, after Wong Sun was charged and released on bail, he went back voluntarily to the Narcotics Bureau, where he told detectives he'd delivered heroin to Johnny Yee and smoked it with him. In his case, the U.S. Supreme Court decided "the connection between the arrest and the statement had become so attenuated as to dissipate the taint."

Another circumstance that might attenuate the poison enough to let the evidence in is an "intervening independent act of free will" after the illegal act. Let's go back to James Wah Toy in his bedroom after the illegal arrest. The government argued that when Toy told the officers that Yee had sold him heroin, he did it of his own free will. But the Court rejected the argument, not because an independent act of free will can't attenuate the poison but because it didn't fit the facts of this case.

According to the Court:

> Six or seven officers had broken the door and followed on Toy's heels into the bedroom where his wife and child were sleeping. He had been almost immediately handcuffed and arrested. Under such circumstances it is unreasonable to infer that Toy's response was sufficiently an act of free will to purge the primary taint of the unlawful invasion. (*Wong Sun v. U.S.* 1963, 416–17)

What if police officers violate the Constitution looking for evidence and, then, in a totally separate action, get the same evidence lawfully? It's admissible under the *independent source exception*. For example, in *U.S. v. Moscatiello* (1985), federal agents entered a South Boston warehouse illegally where they saw marijuana in plain view. They left the warehouse without touching the marijuana and kept the warehouse under surveillance while they went to get a search warrant. In applying for the warrant, the officers didn't build their probable cause on anything they'd learned during the unlawful entry of the warehouse.

In ruling the marijuana was admissible as evidence, the U.S. Circuit Court of Appeals wrote:

> We can be absolutely certain that the warrantless entry in no way contributed in the slightest either to the issuance of a warrant or to the discovery of the evidence during the lawful search that occurred pursuant to the warrant. This is as clear a case as can be imagined where the discovery of the contraband in plain view was totally irrelevant to the later securing of a warrant and the successful search that ensued. As there was no causal link whatever between the illegal entry and the discovery of the challenged evidence, we find no error in the court's refusal to suppress. (*U.S. v. Moscatiello* 1985, 603)

In upholding the U.S. Court of Appeals, the U.S. Supreme Court wrote:

> While the government should not profit from its illegal activity, neither should it be placed in a worse position than it would otherwise have occupied. So long as a later, lawful seizure is genuinely independent of an earlier, tainted [one] . . . there is no reason why the independent source doctrine should not apply. . . . (*Murray v. U.S.* 1988, 542–43)

So, in a nutshell, the **independent source exception** says, even if officers break the law, unless their law-breaking causes the seizure of evidence, the evidence is admissible in court.

But what if official law-breaking is the cause of getting the evidence? Is the evidence banned from use? Not if officers, acting within the Constitution, would eventually find it anyway. And this is the nub of the **inevitable discovery exception**.

The inevitable discovery exception was the issue in *Nix v. Williams* (1984), an appeal from the retrial of Robert Williams, whom you met in Chapter 8 (excerpted on p. 296). Recall that Williams was suspected of brutally murdering 10-year-old Pamela Powers. During an illegal police interrogation, Williams led police officers to the place where he had hidden the body. At the same time, a separate search party was combing the same area near where some of Pamela's clothing had been found. The search party took a break from the search only 2½ miles from where Williams led the officers to the body; the location was within the area they planned to search.

So two searches were converging on the dead body. One search was being lawfully conducted by a search party. The other was the fruit of the poisonous illegal interrogation. The fruit-of-the-poisonous-tree search was the discovery of the body during the legal search party's break. Should the evidence be admitted? Yes, said the U.S. Supreme Court. Why? Because the body would've been discovered anyway by the legal search party.

Emphasizing the purpose of the fruit-of-the-poisonous-tree doctrine, and why the inevitable discovery exception was consistent with that purpose, the Court wrote:

> Exclusion of evidence that would inevitably have been discovered would . . . put the government in a worse position, because the police would have obtained that evidence if no misconduct had taken place. [This] rationale . . . justifies our adoption of the . . . inevitable discovery exception to the exclusionary rule. (444)

## Persons Seized Illegally

The fruit of poisonous illegal government actions is usually either physical evidence or a confession. But what if a person is the "fruit" of an illegal arrest? Does the fruit-of-the-poisonous-tree doctrine apply? How do we "suppress" or "exclude" a person? Specifically, these questions boil down to whether courts can (or should) dismiss a criminal case against individuals who are in court because the police arrested them illegally. In *Ker v. Illinois* (1886), the U.S. Supreme Court answered, "No" (cited in *Frisbie v. Collins* 1952). (Based on my own survey of state cases, the answer in the 1800s was a loud "No!")

Why aren't persons arrested illegally fruit of a poisonous arrest? Because, as my research in the state cases made clear, courts historically have closed their eyes to how defendants got to court; they have opened them only when court proceedings began. The basic idea was (and still is) that how defendants got into court was police business, not court business. The business of courts is to see to it that defendants get a fair trial. The exclusionary rule bans courts from admitting evidence seized illegally to prove defendants' guilt at trial, but there's no parallel rule that bans courts from claiming jurisdiction (power) over persons seized illegally; so they can be tried.

The practice of trying defendants who were brought to court by means of illegal seizures is controversial. The U.S. Supreme Court has repeatedly ruled that an illegal detention doesn't bar either a subsequent prosecution or a conviction (*U.S. v. Crews* 1980).

## The Reasonable, Good-Faith Exception

The **reasonable, good-faith exception** allows the government to use evidence obtained from searches based on unlawful search warrants if officers honestly and reasonably believed they were lawful. Although the good-faith exception is narrow, when the U.S. Supreme Court created it, in *U.S. v. Leon* (1984), a firestorm of controversy broke out. Civil libertarians spun the exception to mean it would strangle the Fourth Amendment and blow a hole in the wall against government invasion of individual privacy.

Law enforcement interest groups spun the exception just as furiously to mean the Court had finally taken the handcuffs off the police so that public safety would be the winner. But when we slow down the spin so we can get a better look at reality, we see the reality hasn't changed much. The number of search warrants hasn't changed, and the number of cases in which judges keep evidence seized illegally out of court hasn't changed either (*Uchida and Bynum* 1991, 1035). Keep this reality in mind as you read our next case excerpt, *U.S. v. Leon*, the case that created the good-faith exception (Ashdown 1983; Kamisar 1984; Schlag 1982).

---

## CASE   *Did They Act in Good Faith?*

### U.S. v. Leon
468 U.S. 897 (1984)

### HISTORY

Police officers obtained a search warrant that led to the seizure of large quantities of methaqualone, heroin, and other evidence. Alberto Leon, "Patsy" Stewart, Ricardo del Castillo, and Armando Sanchez were indicted and moved to suppress the drugs and other evidence. The U.S. District Court granted the motion to suppress. The U.S. Court of Appeals affirmed. The U.S. Supreme Court granted certiorari and reversed.

WHITE, J, JOINED BY BURGER, C.J., AND BLACKMUN, POWELL, REHNQUIST, AND O'CONNOR, JJ.

## FACTS

In August 1981, a confidential informant of unproven reliability informed an officer of the Burbank Police Department that two persons known to him as "Armando" and "Patsy" were selling large quantities of cocaine and methaqualone from their residence at 620 Price Drive in Burbank, Cal. The informant also indicated that he'd witnessed a sale of methaqualone by "Patsy" at the residence approximately five months earlier and had observed at that time a shoebox containing a large amount of cash that belonged to "Patsy." He further declared that "Armando" and "Patsy" generally kept only small quantities of drugs at their residence and stored the rest at another location in Burbank.

On the basis of this information, the Burbank police initiated an extensive investigation focusing first on the Price Drive residence and later on two other residences as well. Cars parked at the Price Drive residence were determined to belong to Armando Sanchez, who had previously been arrested for possession of marihuana, and Patsy Stewart, who had no criminal record. During the course of the investigation, officers observed an automobile belonging to Ricardo Del Castillo (who had previously been arrested for possession of 50 pounds of marihuana) arrive at the Price Drive residence. The driver of that car entered the house, exited shortly thereafter carrying a small paper sack, and drove away.

A check of Del Castillo's probation records led the officers to Alberto Leon, whose telephone number Del Castillo had listed as his employer's. Leon had been arrested in 1980 on drug charges, and a companion had informed the police at that time that Leon was heavily involved in the importation of drugs into this country.

Before the current investigation began, the Burbank officers had learned that an informant had told a Glendale police officer Leon stored a large quantity of methaqualone at his residence in Glendale. During the course of this investigation, the Burbank officers learned that Leon was living at 716 South Sunset Canyon in Burbank.

Subsequently, the officers observed several persons, at least one of whom had prior drug involvement, arriving at the Price Drive residence and leaving with small packages; observed a variety of other material activity at the two residences as well as at a condominium at 7902 Via Magdalena; and witnessed a variety of relevant activity involving respondents' automobiles. The officers also observed Sanchez and Stewart board separate flights for Miami.

The pair later returned to Los Angeles together, consented to a search of their luggage that revealed only a small amount of marihuana, and left the airport. Based on these and other observations summarized in the affidavit, Officer Cyril Rombach of the Burbank Police Department, an experienced and well-trained narcotics investigator, prepared an application for a warrant to search 620 Price Drive, 716 South Sunset Canyon, 7902 Via Magdalena, and automobiles registered to each of the respondents for an extensive list of items believed to be related to respondents'

drug-trafficking activities. Officer Rombach's extensive application was reviewed by several Deputy District Attorneys.

A facially valid search warrant [*the warrant appeared legal*] was issued in September 1981 by a State Superior Court Judge. The ensuing searches produced large quantities of drugs at the Via Magdalena and Sunset Canyon addresses and a small quantity at the Price Drive residence. Other evidence was discovered at each of the residences and in Stewart's and Del Castillo's automobiles.

Alberto Leon, "Patsy" Stewart, Ricardo del Castillo, and Armando Sanchez were indicted by a grand jury in the District Court for the Central District of California and charged with conspiracy to possess and distribute cocaine and a variety of substantive counts. They then filed motions to suppress the evidence seized pursuant to the warrant.

The District Court held an evidentiary hearing and, while recognizing the case was close, granted the motions to suppress. It concluded that the affidavit was insufficient to establish probable cause. . . . The judge said: I just cannot find this warrant sufficient for a showing of probable cause. There is no question of the reliability and credibility of the informant as not being established.

Some details given tended to corroborate, maybe, the reliability of [the informant's] information about the previous transaction, but if it is not a stale transaction, it comes awfully close to it; and all the other material I think is as consistent with innocence as it is with guilt. So I just do not think this affidavit can withstand the test. I find, then, that there is no probable cause in this case for the issuance of the search warrant. . . .

In response to a request from the Government, the court made clear that Officer Rombach had acted in good faith, but it rejected the Government's suggestion that the Fourth Amendment exclusionary rule should not apply where evidence is seized in reasonable, good-faith reliance on a search warrant. [According to the judge:] On the issue of good faith, obviously that is not the law of the Circuit, and I am not going to apply that law. I will say certainly in my view, there is not any question about good faith. [Officer Rombach] went to a Superior Court judge and got a warrant; obviously laid a meticulous trail. Had surveilled for a long period of time, and I believe his testimony—and I think he said he consulted with three Deputy District Attorneys before proceeding himself, and I certainly have no doubt about the fact that that is true.

The District Court denied the Government's motion for reconsideration, and a divided panel of the Court of Appeals for the Ninth Circuit affirmed. . . .

## OPINION

The Government's petition for certiorari . . . presented only the question "whether the Fourth Amendment exclusionary rule should be modified so as not to bar the admission of evidence seized in reasonable, good-faith reliance on a search warrant that is subsequently held to be defective." We granted certiorari to consider the propriety of such a modification. . . . We have concluded that, in the Fourth Amendment context, the exclusionary rule can be modified somewhat without jeopardizing its ability to perform its intended functions. . . .

. . . The Fourth Amendment contains no provision expressly precluding the use of evidence obtained in violation of its commands, and an examination of its origin and purposes makes clear that the use of fruits of a past unlawful search or seizure "works no new Fourth Amendment wrong." The wrong condemned by the Amendment is "fully accomplished" by the unlawful search or seizure itself, and the exclusionary rule is neither intended nor able to "cure the invasion of the defendant's rights which he has already suffered." The rule thus operates as "a judicially created remedy designed to safeguard Fourth Amendment rights generally through its deterrent effect, rather than a personal constitutional right of the party aggrieved."

Whether the exclusionary sanction is appropriately imposed in a particular case, our decisions make clear, is "an issue separate from the question whether the Fourth Amendment rights of the party seeking to invoke the rule were violated by police conduct." Only the former question is currently before us, and it must be resolved by weighing the costs and benefits of preventing the use in the prosecution's case in chief of inherently trustworthy tangible evidence obtained in reliance on a search warrant issued by a detached and neutral magistrate that ultimately is found to be defective.

The substantial social costs exacted by the exclusionary rule for the vindication of Fourth Amendment rights have long been a source of concern. "Our cases have consistently recognized that unbending application of the exclusionary sanction to enforce ideals of governmental rectitude would impede unacceptably the truth-finding functions of judge and jury." An objectionable collateral consequence of this interference with the criminal justice system's truth-finding function is that some guilty defendants may go free or receive reduced sentences as a result of favorable plea bargains.

Researchers have only recently begun to study extensively the effects of the exclusionary rule on the disposition of felony arrests. One study [Thomas Davies. 1983. "A Hard Look at What We Know (and Still Need to Learn) about the 'Social Costs' of the Exclusionary Rule: The NIJ Study and Other Studies of 'Lost' Arrests." *American Bar Foundation Research Journal*, 640] suggests the rule results in the nonprosecution or nonconviction of between 0.6% and 2.35% of individuals arrested for felonies. The estimates are higher for particular crimes the prosecution of which depends heavily on physical evidence. Thus, the cumulative loss due to nonprosecution or nonconviction of individuals arrested on felony drug charges is probably in the range of 2.8% to 7.1%. Davies' analysis of California data suggests that screening by police and prosecutors results in the release because of illegal searches or seizures of as many as 1.4% of all felony arrestees, id., at 650, that 0.9% of felony arrestees are released, because of illegal searches or seizures, at the preliminary hearing or after trial, and that roughly 0.05% of all felony arrestees benefit

from reversals on appeal because of illegal searches. The exclusionary rule also has been found to affect the plea-bargaining process.

Many of these researchers have concluded that the impact of the exclusionary rule is insubstantial, but the small percentages with which they deal mask a large absolute number of felons who are released because the cases against them were based in part on illegal searches or seizures. "'Any rule of evidence that denies the jury access to clearly probative and reliable evidence must bear a heavy burden of justification, and must be carefully limited to the circumstances in which it will pay its way by deterring official unlawlessness." Because we find that the rule can have no substantial deterrent effect in the sorts of situations under consideration in this case, we conclude that it cannot pay its way in those situations.

Particularly when law enforcement officers have acted in objective good faith or their transgressions have been minor, the magnitude of the benefit conferred on such guilty defendants offends basic concepts of the criminal justice system. Indiscriminate application of the exclusionary rule, therefore, may well "generate disrespect for the law and administration of justice." . . .

As yet, we have not recognized any form of good-faith exception to the Fourth Amendment exclusionary rule. But the balancing approach that has evolved during the years of experience with the rule provides strong support for the modification currently urged upon us. . . . Because a search warrant "provides the detached scrutiny of a neutral magistrate" . . . we have expressed a strong preference for warrants . . . concluded that the preference for warrants is most appropriately effectuated by according "great deference" to a magistrate's determination.

Deference to the magistrate, however, is not boundless. It is clear . . . that the deference accorded to a magistrate's finding of probable cause does not preclude inquiry into the knowing or reckless falsity of the affidavit on which that determination was based. . . . To the extent proponents of exclusion rely on its behavioral effects on judges and magistrates . . . their reliance is misplaced. First, the exclusionary rule is designed to deter police misconduct rather than to punish the errors of judges and magistrates.

Second, there exists no evidence suggesting that judges and magistrates are inclined to ignore or subvert the Fourth Amendment or that lawlessness among these actors requires application of the extreme sanction of exclusion.

Third, and most important, we discern no basis, and are offered none, for believing that exclusion of evidence seized pursuant to a warrant will have a significant deterrent effect on the issuing judge or magistrate. . . . Judges and magistrates are not adjuncts to the law enforcement team; as neutral judicial officers, they have no stake in the outcome of particular criminal prosecutions. The threat of exclusion thus cannot be expected significantly to deter them. . . .

We have frequently questioned whether the exclusionary rule can have any deterrent effect when the offending officers acted in the objectively reasonable belief their conduct did not violate the Fourth Amendment. . . . This is particularly true, we believe, when an officer acting with objective good faith has obtained a search warrant from a judge or magistrate and acted within its scope. In most such cases, there is no police illegality and thus nothing to deter. . . . "Once the warrant issues, there is literally nothing more the policeman can do in seeking to comply with the law." Penalizing the officer for the magistrate's error, rather than his own, cannot logically contribute to the deterrence of Fourth Amendment violations.

We conclude that the marginal or nonexistent benefits produced by suppressing evidence obtained in objectively reasonable reliance on a subsequently invalidated search warrant cannot justify the substantial costs of exclusion.

We do not suggest, however, that exclusion is always inappropriate in cases where an officer has obtained a warrant and abided by its terms. . . . The officer's reliance on the magistrate's probable-cause determination and on the technical sufficiency of the warrant he issues must be objectively reasonable, and it is clear that in some circumstances the officer will have no reasonable grounds for believing that the warrant was properly issued. . . . The good-faith exception for searches conducted pursuant to warrants is not intended to signal our unwillingness strictly to enforce the requirements of the Fourth Amendment, and we do not believe it will have this effect. . . .

We have now reexamined the purposes of the exclusionary rule and the propriety of its application in cases where officers have relied on a subsequently invalidated search warrant. Our conclusion is that the rule's purposes will only rarely be served by applying it in such circumstances.

. . . Officer Rombach's application for a warrant clearly was supported by much more than a "bare bones" affidavit. The affidavit related the results of an extensive investigation and . . . provided evidence sufficient to create disagreement among thoughtful and competent judges as to the existence of probable cause. Under these circumstances, the officers' reliance on the magistrate's determination of probable cause was objectively reasonable, and application of the extreme sanction of exclusion is inappropriate.

Accordingly, the judgment of the Court of Appeals is REVERSED.

## CONCURRING OPINION

### BLACKMUN, J.

As the Court's opinion in this case makes clear, the Court has narrowed the scope of the exclusionary rule because of an empirical judgment that the rule has little appreciable effect in cases where officers act in objectively reasonable reliance on search warrants. Because I share the view that the exclusionary rule is not a constitutionally compelled corollary of the Fourth Amendment itself, I see no way to avoid making an empirical judgment of this sort, and I am satisfied the Court has made the correct one on the information before it. Like all courts, we face institutional limitations on our ability to gather information about "legislative facts," and the

exclusionary rule itself has exacerbated the shortage of hard data concerning the behavior of police officers in the absence of such a rule. Nonetheless, we cannot escape the responsibility to decide the question before us, however imperfect our information may be, and I am prepared to join the Court on the information now at hand.

What must be stressed, however, is that any empirical judgment about the effect of the exclusionary rule in a particular class of cases necessarily is a provisional one. By their very nature, the assumptions on which we proceed today cannot be cast in stone. To the contrary, they now will be tested in the real world of state and federal law enforcement, and this Court will attend to the results. If it should emerge from experience that, contrary to our expectations, the good-faith exception to the exclusionary rule results in a material change in police compliance with the Fourth Amendment, we shall have to reconsider what we have undertaken here. The logic of a decision that rests on untested predictions about police conduct demands no less.

## DISSENT

### BRENNAN, J. JOINED BY MARSHALL, J.

Ten years ago, I expressed that the Court's decision "may signal that a majority of my colleagues have positioned themselves to reopen the door [to evidence secured by official lawlessness] still further and abandon altogether the exclusionary rule in search-and-seizure cases." Since then, in case after case, I have witnessed the Court's gradual but determined strangulation of the rule. It now appears that the Court's victory over the Fourth Amendment is complete. . . . Today the Court sanctions the use in the prosecution's case in chief of illegally obtained evidence against the individual whose rights have been violated—a result that had previously been thought to be foreclosed.

The Court seeks to justify this result on the ground that the "costs" of adhering to the exclusionary rule in cases like those before us exceed the "benefits." But the language of deterrence and of cost/benefit analysis, if used indiscriminately, can have a narcotic effect. . . . It suggests that not only constitutional principle but also empirical data support the majority's result. When the Court's analysis is examined carefully, however, it is clear that we have not been treated to an honest assessment of the merits of the exclusionary rule, but have instead been drawn into a curious world where the "costs" of excluding illegally obtained evidence loom to exaggerated heights and where the "benefits" of such exclusion are made to disappear with a mere wave of the hand. . . .

. . . Since the Fourth Amendment became part of the Nation's fundamental law in 1791, what the Framers understood then remains true today—that the task of combating crime and convicting the guilty will in every era seem of such critical and pressing concern that we may be lured by the temptations of expediency into forsaking our commitment to protecting individual liberty and privacy.

It was for that very reason that the Framers of the Bill of Rights insisted that law enforcement efforts be permanently and unambiguously restricted in order to preserve personal freedoms. In the constitutional scheme they ordained, the sometimes unpopular task of ensuring that the government's enforcement efforts remain within the strict boundaries fixed by the Fourth Amendment was entrusted to the courts. . . .

The Court's decisions over the past decade have made plain that the entire enterprise of attempting to assess the benefits and costs of the exclusionary rule in various contexts is a virtually impossible task for the judiciary to perform honestly or accurately. Although the Court's language in those cases suggests that some specific empirical basis may support its analyses, the reality is that the Court's opinions represent inherently unstable compounds of intuition, hunches, and occasional pieces of partial and often inconclusive data. . . .

To the extent empirical data is available regarding the general costs and benefits of the exclusionary rule, it has shown, on the one hand . . . that the costs aren't as substantial as critics have asserted in the past, and, on the other hand, that while the exclusionary rule may well have certain deterrent effects, it is extremely difficult to determine with any degree of precision whether the incident of unlawful conduct by police is now lower than it was prior to *Mapp v. Ohio* (1961).

The Court has sought to turn this uncertainty to its advantage by casting the burden of proof upon proponents of the rule. . . .

. . . A doctrine that is explained as if it were an empirical proposition but for which there is only limited empirical support is both inherently unstable and an easy mark for critics. The extent of this Court's fidelity to Fourth Amendment requirements, however, should not turn on such statistical uncertainties. . . . "Personal liberties are not rooted in the law of averages." Rather than seeking to give effort to the liberties secured by the Fourth Amendment through guesswork about deterrence, the Court should restore to its proper place the principle framed 70 years ago in *Weeks v. U.S.* (1914) that an individual whose privacy has been invaded in violation of the Fourth Amendment has a right grounded in that Amendment to prevent the government from subsequently making use of any evidence so obtained.

## Questions

1. According to the majority, is the exclusionary rule a constitutional right? Explain.

2. State exactly the Court's definition of the reasonable, good-faith exception.

3. What two elements does the Court balance, and how does it weigh the balance to justify the creation of the good-faith exception?

4. List all the facts the Court considers relevant to deciding whether the exception applies to Leon and the other defendants.

5. Summarize the empirical evidence the majority uses to back up its decision.

6. What is Justice Blackmun's main point in his concurring opinion?

7. List and state exactly Justice Brennan's objections to the exception.

8. Based on the majority, concurring, and dissenting opinions, how much do you think we really know about the deterrent effect of the exclusionary rule?

 To learn more about State Constitutional Law and the good-faith exception, go to the Samaha Criminal Procedure 7e website: academic. cengage.com/criminaljustice/samaha.

# "Bad Methods" by Non–Law Enforcement Government Officials

*U.S. v. Leon* made it clear that the good-faith exception was created to deter law enforcement officers—and no other government officials, such as court employees and judges. Why?

1. There's "no evidence suggesting that judges and magistrates are inclined to ignore or subvert the Fourth Amendment or that lawlessness among these actors requires the application of the extreme sanction of exclusion." (*Arizona v. Evans* 1995, 14)

2. There's "no basis for believing that exclusion of evidence seized pursuant to a warrant would have a significant deterrent effect on the issuing judge or magistrate" (14). Because, according to the Court, other officials aren't likely to get carried away with fighting crime, they're not susceptible to fooling around with evidence, and they're not deterred by threats of throwing out evidence if they make mistakes. (15)

But the world of criminal justice began to change rapidly after *Leon* was decided in 1984. One change particularly caused concern that maybe limiting the reasonable, good-faith exception to law enforcement officers should be reconsidered. In *Arizona v. Evans* (1995), Justice Ginsburg summarized the change:

> Widespread reliance on computers to store and convey information generates, along with manifold benefits, new possibilities of error, due to both computer malfunctions and operator mistakes. Most germane to this case, computerization greatly amplifies an error's effect, and correspondingly intensifies the need for prompt correction; for inaccurate data can infect not only one agency, but the many agencies that share access to the database.
>
> The computerized databases of the Federal Bureau of Investigation's National Crime Information Center (NCIC), to take a conspicuous example, contain over 23 million records, identifying, among other things, persons and vehicles sought by law enforcement agencies nationwide. NCIC information is available to approximately 71,000 federal, state, and local agencies. Thus, any mistake entered into the NCIC spreads nationwide in an instant.

Justice Ginsburg told of one horrible example of the effects of this explosion in computerized criminal justice data banks:

> The Los Angeles Police Department, in 1982, had entered into the NCIC computer an arrest warrant for a man suspected of robbery and murder. Because the suspect had been impersonating Terry Dean Rogan, the arrest warrant erroneously named Rogan. Compounding the error, the Los Angeles Police Department had failed to include a description of the suspect's physical characteristics. During the next two years, this incorrect and incomplete information caused Rogan to be arrested four times, three times at gunpoint, after stops for minor traffic infractions in Michigan and Oklahoma. (*Rogan v. Los Angeles* 1987, 1384)

Until 1990, all the Supreme Court exclusionary rule cases dealt with one kind of government behavior—unconstitutional acts by police. But what if some other government official (such as the magistrate who issued the warrant in *Leon*) was guilty of "bad methods"? Does *Leon* mean the exclusionary rule can only apply to police?

In 1995, the U.S. Supreme Court answered the question (sort of). In that year, our next case excerpt, *Arizona v. Evans*, concerned a conviction for using marijuana seized during a contested search. Isaac Evans was arrested and convicted based on an illegal warrant that a justice of the peace court clerk should have removed from the court's database. The Court decided that the good-faith exception applied.

---

## CASE   *Was the Good-Faith Exception Intended Only to Deter Law Enforcement Officers?*

### Arizona v. Evans
514 U.S. 1 (1995)

### HISTORY

Isaac Evans moved to suppress marijuana seized from his car. The motion was granted by the Superior Court, Maricopa County. The Arizona Court of Appeals reversed. The Arizona Supreme Court reversed. The U.S. Supreme Court granted certiorari and reversed and remanded.

REHNQUIST, C.J., JOINED BY O'CONNOR, SCALIA, KENNEDY, SOUTER, THOMAS, AND BREYER, JJ.

### FACTS

In January 1991, Phoenix police officer Bryan Sargent observed Isaac Evans driving the wrong way on a one-way street in front of the police station. The officer stopped Evans and asked to see his driver's license. After Evans told him his license had been suspended, the officer entered Evans's name into a computer data terminal located in his patrol car. The computer inquiry confirmed Evans's license had been suspended and also indicated there was an outstanding misdemeanor warrant for his arrest. Based upon the outstanding warrant, Officer Sargent placed Evans under arrest. While being handcuffed, Evans dropped a hand-rolled cigarette the officers determined smelled of marijuana. Officers proceeded to search his car and discovered a bag of marijuana under the passenger's seat.

The State charged Evans with possession of marijuana. When the police notified the Justice Court they had arrested him, the Justice Court discovered the arrest warrant previously had been quashed and so advised the police. Evans argued that because his arrest was based on a warrant that had been quashed 17 days prior to his arrest, the marijuana seized incident to the arrest should be suppressed as the fruit of an unlawful arrest. Evans also argued that "the 'good faith' exception to the exclusionary rule was inapplicable . . . because it was police error, not judicial error, which caused the invalid arrest."

At the suppression hearing, the Chief Clerk of the Justice Court testified that a Justice of the Peace had issued the arrest warrant on December 13, 1990, because Evans had failed to appear to answer for several traffic violations. On December 19, 1990, Evans appeared before a substitute Justice of the Peace who entered a notation in Evans's file to "quash warrant." The Chief Clerk also testified regarding the standard court procedure for quashing a warrant. Under that procedure:

1. A justice court clerk calls and informs the warrant section of the Sheriff's Office when a warrant has been quashed.

2. The Sheriff's Office then removes the warrant from its computer records.

3. After calling the Sheriff's Office, the clerk makes a note in the individual's file indicating the clerk who made the phone call and the person at the Sheriff's Office to whom the clerk spoke.

The Chief Clerk testified that there was no indication in Evans's file that a clerk had called and notified the Sheriff's Office his arrest warrant had been quashed. A records clerk from the Sheriff's Office also testified that the Sheriff's Office had no record of a telephone call informing it that respondent's arrest warrant had been quashed.

At the close of testimony, Evans argued that the evidence obtained as a result of the arrest should be suppressed because "the purposes of the exclusionary rule would be served here by making the clerks for the court, or the clerk for the Sheriff's office, whoever is responsible for this mistake, to be more careful about making sure that warrants are removed from the records." The trial court granted the motion to suppress because it concluded the State had been at fault for failing to quash the warrant. Presumably because it could find no "distinction between State action, whether it happens to be the police department or not," the trial court made no factual finding as to whether the Justice Court or Sheriff's Office was responsible for the continued presence of the quashed warrant in the police records.

A divided panel of the Arizona Court of Appeals reversed because it believed the exclusionary rule was not intended to deter justice court employees or Sheriff's Office employees who are not directly associated with the arresting officers or the arresting officers' police department. Therefore, "the purpose of the exclusionary rule would not be served by excluding the evidence obtained in this case."

The Arizona Supreme Court reversed. The court rejected the "distinction drawn by the court of appeals . . . between clerical errors committed by law enforcement personnel and similar mistakes by court employees." The court predicted that application of the exclusionary rule would "hopefully serve to improve the efficiency of those who keep records in our criminal justice system." Finally, the court concluded that "even assuming that deterrence is the principal reason for application of the exclusionary rule, we disagree with the court of appeals that such a purpose would not be served where carelessness by a court clerk results in an unlawful arrest."

We granted certiorari to determine whether the exclusionary rule requires suppression of evidence seized incident to an arrest resulting from an inaccurate computer record, regardless of whether police personnel or court personnel were responsible for the record's continued presence in the police computer. We now reverse.

## OPINION

. . . In *Leon* [excerpted on page 350], we . . . determined there was no sound reason to apply the exclusionary rule as a means of deterring misconduct on the part of judicial officers who are responsible for issuing warrants.

First, we noted the exclusionary rule was historically designed "to deter police misconduct rather than to punish the errors of judges and magistrates." Second, there was "no evidence suggesting that judges and magistrates are inclined to ignore or subvert the Fourth Amendment or that lawlessness among these actors requires the application of the extreme sanction of exclusion." Third, and of greatest importance, there was no basis for believing that exclusion of evidence seized pursuant to a warrant would have a significant deterrent effect on the issuing judge or magistrate.

The *Leon* Court then examined whether application of the exclusionary rule could be expected to alter the behavior of the law enforcement officers. We concluded:

Where the officer's conduct is objectively reasonable, "excluding the evidence will not further the ends of the exclusionary rule in any appreciable way; for it is painfully apparent that . . . the officer is acting as a reasonable officer would and should act in similar circumstances. Excluding the evidence can in no way affect his future conduct unless it is to make him less willing to do his duty."

. . . "Suppressing evidence because the judge failed to make all the necessary clerical corrections despite his assurances that such changes would be made will not serve the deterrent function that the exclusionary rule was designed to achieve." Thus, we held that the "marginal or nonexistent benefits produced by suppressing evidence obtained in objectively reasonable reliance on a subsequently invalidated search warrant cannot justify the substantial costs of exclusion." . . .

Applying the reasoning of *Leon* to the facts of this case, we conclude that the decision of the Arizona Supreme Court must be reversed. . . .

[The Arizona Supreme Court's] holding is contrary to the reasoning of *Leon*. If court employees were responsible for the erroneous computer record, the exclusion of evidence at trial would not sufficiently deter future errors so as to warrant such a severe sanction. First, the exclusionary rule was historically designed as a means of deterring police misconduct, not mistakes by court employees. Second, Evans offers no evidence that court employees are inclined to ignore or subvert the Fourth Amendment or that lawlessness among these actors requires application of the extreme sanction of exclusion. To the contrary, the Chief Clerk of the Justice Court testified at the suppression hearing that this type of error occurred once every three or four years.

Finally, and most important, there is no basis for believing that application of the exclusionary rule in these circumstances will have a significant effect on court employees responsible for informing the police that a warrant has been quashed. Because court clerks are not adjuncts to the law enforcement team engaged in the often competitive enterprise of ferreting out crime, they have no stake in the outcome of particular criminal prosecutions. The threat of exclusion of evidence could not be expected to deter such individuals from failing to inform police officials that a warrant had been quashed.

If it were indeed a court clerk who was responsible for the erroneous entry on the police computer, application of the exclusionary rule also could not be expected to alter the behavior of the arresting officer. As the trial court in this case stated: "I think the police officer was bound to arrest. I think he would have been derelict in his duty if he failed to arrest." . . . "Excluding the evidence can in no way affect the officer's future conduct unless it is to make him less willing to do his duty." The Chief Clerk of the Justice Court testified that this type of error occurred "once every three or four years." In fact, once the court clerks discovered the error, they immediately corrected it, and then proceeded to search their files to make sure that no similar mistakes had occurred. There is no indication the arresting officer was not acting objectively reasonably when he relied upon the police computer record. Application of the *Leon* framework supports a categorical exception to the exclusionary rule for clerical errors of court employees.

The judgment of the Supreme Court of Arizona is therefore REVERSED, and the case is REMANDED to that court for proceedings not inconsistent with this opinion.

## CONCURRING OPINIONS

### O'CONNOR, J., JOINED BY SOUTER AND BREYER, JJ.

. . . In recent years, we have witnessed the advent of powerful, computer-based record keeping systems that facilitate arrests in ways that have never before been possible. The police, of course, are entitled to enjoy the substantial advantages this technology confers. They may not, however, rely on it blindly. With the benefits of more efficient law enforcement mechanisms comes the burden of corresponding constitutional responsibilities.

### SOUTER, J., JOINED BY BREYER, J.

In joining the Court's opinion . . . I add . . . that we do not answer another question that may reach us in due course, that is, how far, in dealing with fruits of computerized error, our very concept of deterrence by exclusion of evidence should extend to the government as a whole, not merely the police, on the ground that there would otherwise be no reasonable expectation of keeping the number of resulting false arrests within an acceptable minimum limit.

## DISSENTS

### STEVENS, J.

. . . The Court seems to assume the Fourth Amendment—and particularly the exclusionary rule, which effectuates the Amendment's commands—has the limited purpose of deterring police misconduct. Both the constitutional text and the history of its adoption and interpretation identify a more majestic conception. . . . The Amendment is a constraint on the power of the sovereign, not merely on some of its agents. The remedy for its violation imposes costs on that sovereign, motivating it to train all of its personnel to avoid future violations. . . .

Even if one accepts deterrence as the sole rationale for the exclusionary rule, the Arizona Supreme Court's decision is correct on the merits. The majority's reliance on *U.S. v. Leon* is misplaced. The search in that case had been authorized by a presumptively valid warrant issued by a California Superior Court Judge. In contrast, this case involves a search pursuant to an arrest made when no warrant at all was outstanding against Evans. The holding in *Leon* rested on the majority's doubt "that exclusion of evidence seized pursuant to a warrant will have a significant deterrent effect on the issuing judge or magistrate." The reasoning in *Leon* assumed the existence of a warrant; it was, and remains, wholly inapplicable to warrantless searches and seizures. . . .

The Phoenix Police Department was part of the chain of information that resulted in respondent's unlawful, warrantless arrest. We should reasonably presume that law enforcement officials, who stand in the best position to monitor such errors as occurred here, can influence mundane communication procedures in order to prevent those errors.

That presumption comports with the notion that the exclusionary rule exists to deter future police misconduct *systemically* [emphasis added]. The deterrent purpose extends to law enforcement *as a whole* [emphasis added], not merely to "the arresting officer." Consequently, the Phoenix officers' good faith does not diminish the deterrent value of invalidating their arrest of respondent.

The Court seeks to minimize the impact of its holding on the security of the citizen by referring to the testimony of the Chief Clerk of the East Phoenix Number One Justice Court that in her "particular court" this type of error occurred "maybe once every three or four years."

Q: In your eight years as a chief clerk with the Justice of the Peace, have there been other occasions where a warrant was quashed but the police were not notified?

A: That does happen on rare occasions.

Q: And when you say rare occasions, about how many times in your eight years as chief clerk?

A: In my particular court, they would be like maybe one every three or four years.

Q: When something like this happens, is anything done by your office to correct that problem?

A: Well, when this one happened, we searched all the files to make sure that there were no other ones in there, which there were three other ones on that same day that it happened. Fortunately, they weren't all arrested.

Apart from the fact that the Clerk promptly contradicted herself, this is slim evidence on which to base a conclusion that computer error poses no appreciable threat to Fourth Amendment interests. For support, the Court cites a case from 1948. The Court overlooks the reality that computer technology has changed the nature of threats to citizens' privacy over the past half century. What has not changed is the reality that only that fraction of Fourth Amendment violations held to have resulted in unlawful arrests is ever noted and redressed. As Justice Jackson observed: There may be, and I am convinced that there are, many unlawful searches . . . of innocent people which turn up nothing incriminating, in which no arrest is made, about which courts do nothing, and about which we never hear.

Moreover, even if errors in computer records of warrants were rare, that would merely minimize the cost of enforcing the exclusionary rule in cases like this.

. . . One consequence of the Court's holding seems immediately obvious. Its most serious impact will be on the otherwise innocent citizen who is stopped for a minor traffic infraction and is wrongfully arrested based on erroneous information in a computer data base. I assume the police officer who reasonably relies on the computer information would be immune from liability in a § 1983 action. [*Chapter 11*]

Of course, the Court has held that *respondeat superior* [*employer is liable for employee's misconduct*] is unavailable as a basis for imposing liability on his or her municipality [*Chapter 11*]. Thus, if courts are to have any power to

discourage official error of this kind, it must be through application of the exclusionary rule.

. . . The offense to the dignity of the citizen who is arrested, handcuffed, and searched on a public street simply because some bureaucrat has failed to maintain an accurate computer data base strikes me as . . . outrageous. In this case, of course, such an error led to the fortuitous detection of respondent's unlawful possession of marijuana, and the suppression of the fruit of the error would prevent the prosecution of his crime. That cost, however, must be weighed against the interest in protecting other, wholly innocent citizens from unwarranted indignity. In my judgment, the cost is amply offset by an appropriately "jealous regard for maintaining the integrity of individual rights." For this reason . . . I respectfully dissent.

GINSBURG, J., JOINED BY STEVENS, J.

This case portrays the increasing use of computer technology in law enforcement. . . . Specifically, the Arizona Supreme Court saw the growing use of computerized records in law enforcement as a development presenting new dangers to individual liberty; excluding evidence seized as a result of incorrect computer data, the Arizona court anticipated, would reduce the incidence of uncorrected records. . . .

. . . Widespread reliance on computers to store and convey information generates, along with manifold benefits, new possibilities of error, due to both computer malfunctions and operator mistakes. Most germane to this case, computerization greatly amplifies an error's effect, and correspondingly intensifies the need for prompt correction; for inaccurate data can infect not only one agency, but the many agencies that share access to the database. The computerized data bases of the Federal Bureau of Investigation's National Crime Information Center (NCIC), to take a conspicuous example, contain over 23 million records, identifying, among other things, persons and vehicles sought by law enforcement agencies nationwide. NCIC information is available to approximately 71,000 federal, state, and local agencies. Thus, any mistake entered into the NCIC spreads nationwide in an instant.

Isaac Evans' arrest exemplifies the risks associated with computerization of arrest warrants. Though his arrest was in fact warrantless—the warrant once issued having been quashed over two weeks before the episode in suit—the computer reported otherwise. Evans' case is not idiosyncratic. *Rogan v. Los Angeles*, 668 F.Supp. 1384 (CD Cal. 1987), similarly indicates the problem. There, the Los Angeles Police Department, in 1982, had entered into the NCIC computer an arrest warrant for a man suspected of robbery and murder. Because the suspect had been impersonating Terry Dean Rogan, the arrest warrant erroneously named Rogan. Compounding the error, the Los Angeles Police Department had failed to include a description of the suspect's physical characteristics. During the next two years, this incorrect and incomplete information caused

Rogan to be arrested four times, three times at gunpoint, after stops for minor traffic infractions in Michigan and Oklahoma.

. . . In this electronic age, particularly with respect to record keeping, court personnel and police officers are not neatly compartmentalized actors. Instead, they serve together to carry out the State's information-gathering objectives. Whether particular records are maintained by the police or the courts should not be dispositive where a single computer data base can answer all calls. Not only is it artificial to distinguish between court clerk and police clerk slips; in practice, it may be difficult to pinpoint whether one official, e.g., a court employee, or another, e.g., a police officer, caused the error to exist or to persist.

Applying an exclusionary rule as the Arizona court did may well supply a powerful incentive to the State to promote the prompt updating of computer records. That was the Arizona Supreme Court's hardly unreasonable expectation. The incentive to update promptly would be diminished if court-initiated records were exempt from the rule's sway. . . . The Arizona Supreme Court found it "repugnant to the principles of a free society," to take a person "into police custody because of a computer error precipitated by government carelessness." Few, I believe, would disagree.

Whether, in order to guard against such errors, "the exclusionary rule is a 'cost' we cannot afford to be without," seems to me a question this Court should not rush to decide. . . .

## Questions

1. State the Court's reasons for limiting the deterrence justification to law enforcement officers.

2. Identify the dissenting justices' reasons for arguing that the deterrence justification for the good-faith exception should be applied to all government officials.

3. Which of the opinions do you agree with? Support your answer.

4. How do you explain the differing interpretations of the clerk's testimony about the number of mistakes that the clerks made? Is this disagreement important? Should Chief Justice Rehnquist have included the whole testimony, as Justice Stevens did? Does it make any difference?

## Social Costs and Deterrence

In 1960, in *Mapp v. Ohio*, the U.S. Supreme Court, headed by Chief Justice Earl Warren, applied the exclusionary rule to the states because the Court assumed the rule would deter illegal searches and seizures. But there's a social cost for deterring law enforcement officers from violating individuals' rights: keeping good evidence from juries may set some criminals free. Since the 1970s, in case after case, the majorities of the Burger and then the Rehnquist Courts have decided (on the basis of their assumption) that the social cost is too high a price to pay. Which Court's assumption is right?

Ever since the Court decided *Mapp*, a growing stack of empirical studies has tested the correctness of the two assumptions. What's the answer? According to Professor Christopher Slobogin (1999, 368–69), "No one is going to win the empirical debate over whether the exclusionary rule deters the police from committing a significant number of illegal searches and seizures." It's true, say most of the studies, that police officers pay more attention to the Fourth Amendment than they did in 1960. But many officers don't take the rule into account when they're deciding whether to make a search or a seizure. "In short, we do not know how much the rule deters" (369) either individual officers whose evidence courts throw out (special deterrence) or other officers who might be thinking of illegally searching or seizing (general deterrence).

"We probably never will" (369). Why? Because it's hard to conduct empirical research; so we have to rely on speculation (370). And what's the speculation? Both supporters and opponents of the rule make plausible claims for their positions. It's reasonable for supporters to claim "officers who know illegally seized evidence will be excluded cannot help but try to avoid illegal searches because they will have nothing to gain from them."

Equally reasonable, those who oppose the rule can point out that its most direct consequence is imposed on the prosecutor rather than on the cop, that police know and count on the fact that the rule is rarely applied (for both legal and not-so-legal reasons), and that the rule cannot affect searches and seizures the police believe will not result in prosecution (372).

Despite these limits to the empirical research, some of it provides us with some insights. The social costs of letting guilty criminals go free by excluding credible evidence that would convict them might not be as high as we commonly believe. According to Thomas Y. Davies, who studied the exclusionary rule in California and whose research the Court cited in *U.S. v. Leon*, prosecutors almost never reject cases involving violent crimes because of the exclusionary rule. In California, evidence seized illegally led to dismissals in a mere 0.8 percent of all criminal cases and only 4.8 percent of felonies. Davies found that prosecutors rejected only 0.06 percent of homicide, 0.09 percent of forcible rape, and 0.13 percent of assault cases because of illegal searches and seizures. They rejected less than 0.50 percent of theft cases and only 0.19 percent of burglary cases. The largest number of cases rejected for prosecution because of illegal searches and seizures involved the possession of small amounts of drugs (Davies 1983).

Other studies reached similar conclusions—that is, the exclusionary rule affects only a small portion of cases, and most of those aren't crimes against persons (cited in Davies 1983). Less than one-tenth of 1 percent of all criminal cases will be dismissed because the police seized evidence illegally. The rule leaves violent crimes and serious property offenses virtually unaffected.

Furthermore, not all cases involving illegally obtained evidence that are rejected or lost fail because of the exclusionary rule. Peter F. Nardulli (1987) found, for example, that in some cases of drug possession, the police weren't interested in successful prosecution but rather in getting contraband off the street.

Most criminal justice professionals seem to agree that the exclusionary rule is worth the price. The American Bar Association (1988) gathered information from police officers, prosecutors, defense attorneys, and judges in representative urban and geographically distributed locations on the problems they face in their work. They also conducted a telephone survey of 800 police administrators, prosecutors, judges, and defense attorneys based on a stratified random selection technique to obtain a representative group of small-to-large cities and counties.

The results showed the following:

> Although the prosecutors and police . . . interviewed believe that a few Fourth Amendment restrictions are ambiguous or complex, and thus, present training and field application problems, they do not believe that Fourth Amendment rights or their protection via the exclusionary rule are a significant impediment to crime control. . . . A number of . . . police officials also report that the demands of the exclusionary rule and resulting police training on Fourth Amendment requirements have promoted professionalism in police departments across the country. Thus, the exclusionary rule appears to be providing a significant safeguard of Fourth Amendment protections for individuals at modest cost in terms of either crime control or effective prosecution. This "cost," for the most part, reflects the values expressed in the Fourth Amendment itself, for the Amendment manifests a preference for privacy and freedom over that level of law enforcement efficiency which could be achieved if police were permitted to arrest and search without probable cause or judicial authorization. (11)

In view of its limited application, restrictions on the exclusionary rule hardly seem adequate cause for either critics of the rule to rejoice that these restrictions will make society safer or for supporters to lament that they'll throttle individual liberties.

 Go to Exercise 10.1 on the Samaha Criminal Procedure 7e website to learn more about the reasonable, good-faith exception: academic.cengage.com/criminaljustice/samaha.

Probably the strongest argument for the exclusionary rule is that it helps to ensure judicial integrity. Courts, by excluding illegally obtained evidence, announce publicly and in writing their refusal to participate in or condone illegal police practices. At the end of the day, what the exclusionary rule does is exact the price of setting a few criminals free to maintain the rule of law for everybody; it sacrifices the correct result in an individual case for the general interest in the essential fairness of constitutional government for all people.

One final, very important point about the exclusionary rule: Every year, there are approximately 175,000 motions to exclude evidence obtained by illegal searches and seizures. In contrast, there are only a few thousand lawsuits against police and a few dozen criminal charges based on illegal searches and seizures (Allen, Hoffman, Livingston, and Stuntz (2005, 336). This lopsided distribution may

> have a large effect on the substance of Fourth Amendment law. The exclusionary rule shapes the kinds of Fourth Amendment cases judges see. All exclusionary claims seek to suppress incriminating evidence; if no incriminating evidence is found, there is nothing for the defendant to exclude. *Thus, judges see the cases where the police find cocaine in the car, not the cases where they find nothing* [emphasis added]. Perhaps that affects the way judges think about car searches. (336)

# THE DEFENSE OF ENTRAPMENT

What if law enforcement agents (usually undercover cops) get people to commit crimes they wouldn't have committed if the government hadn't encouraged them? Sometimes, defendants in such cases are entitled to the *defense of entrapment*, meaning courts will dismiss the criminal charges.

For most of our history, U.S. courts didn't recognize entrapment as a defense. In 1864, a New York court explained why:

> Even if inducements to commit crime could be assumed to exist in this case, the allegation of the defendant would be but the repetition of the pleas as ancient as the world, and first interposed in Paradise: "The serpent beguiled me and I did eat." That defense was overruled by the great Lawgiver, and whatever estimate we may form, or whatever judgment pass upon the character or conduct of the tempter, this plea has never since availed to shield crime or give indemnity to the culprit, and it is safe to say that under any code of civilized, not say Christian ethics, it never will. (*Board of Commissioners v. Backus* 1864, 42)

Another court, in 1904, summed up this attitude toward entrapment:

> We are asked to protect the defendant, not because he is innocent, but because a zealous public officer exceeded his powers and held out a bait. The courts do not look to see who held out the bait, but to see who took it. (*People v. Mills* 1904, 791)

These attitudes stemmed from indifference to government enticements to commit crimes. After all, "once the crime is committed, why should it matter what particular incentives were involved and who offered them?" However, attitudes have shifted from indifference to "limited sympathy" toward entrapped defendants and a growing intolerance of government inducements to entrap individuals who are basically law-abiding people (Marcus 1986).

The present law of entrapment attempts to balance criminal predisposition and law enforcement practices; that is, it casts a net for habitual criminals, while trying not to capture law-abiding people in the net. The practice of entrapment wasn't a response to violent crime or other crimes with complaining victims. Rather, the practice arose because of the difficulty in detecting consensual crimes—namely, illegal drug offenses, gambling, pornography, and prostitution—because "victims" don't want to report the crimes to the police.

The use of government encouragement as a law enforcement tool is neither new nor limited to the United States. The practice has been associated with some highly unsavory characters throughout world history. Ancient tyrants and modern dictators alike have relied on government agents to get innocent people to commit crimes (the infamous agents provocateurs), so that these autocrats could silence and destroy their political opponents. From the days of Henry VIII to the era of Hitler, Mussolini, Franco, and Stalin to Manuel Noriega, Slobodan Milosevic, and Saddam Hussein (and too many others to list) in our own time, police states have used government informers to get dissidents to admit their disloyalty.

Unfortunately, inducement isn't a tool used only by dictators to oppress their opponents. In all societies and political systems, it's used in ordinary law enforcement, too, creating the risk that law-abiding people will commit crimes they wouldn't have committed if they hadn't been encouraged. Enticement to commit crimes flies in the face of good government. The great Victorian British Prime Minister William Gladstone admonished government to make it easy to do right and hard to do wrong. And consider the plea in the Christian Lord's Prayer's to "lead us not into temptation, but deliver us from evil" (Carlson 1987).

Encouragement is likely to occur whenever law enforcement officers do any of the following:

- Pretend they're victims
- Intend to entice suspects to commit crimes
- Communicate the enticement to suspects
- Influence the decision to commit crimes

Here's how encouragement works in typical cases: One officer provides an opportunity for targets to commit a crime while other officers witness the event; that way, they have proof of the target's guilt. But it's usually not enough for officers just to present targets an opportunity or even to "ask" them to commit a crime. In most cases, officers have to actively encourage their targets because, like most of us, targets are wary of strangers. Active encouragement usually requires using tactics, such as

- Asking targets over and over to commit a crime
- Developing personal relationships with targets
- Appealing personally to targets
- Supplying or helping targets get contraband (LaFave and Israel 1984, 1:412–13)

The defense of entrapment is not a constitutional right; it's a defense to criminal liability created and defined by statutes and courts. It's what we call an **affirmative defense**. That means defendants have the burden of introducing some evidence they were entrapped. If they meet this burden, then the burden shifts to the government to prove defendants weren't entrapped. The jury—or the judge in trials without juries—decides whether officers, in fact, entrapped defendants. The courts have adopted two types of tests for entrapment: one is subjective, and the other is objective.

## The Subjective Test

Encouragement is entrapment only if it crosses the line from acceptable to unacceptable encouragement. How do we know when officers have crossed that line? Most states and the federal government have adopted a **subjective test of entrapment**, which focuses on whether defendants had the predisposition to commit the crimes. According to the subjective test, defendants are entitled to the defense of entrapment if they can show some evidence of two elements:

1. They had no desire to commit the crime before the government's encouragement.

2. The government's encouragement caused them to commit the crime.

The crucial question in the subjective test is, "Where did criminal intent originate?" If it originated with the defendant, then the government didn't entrap the defendant. If it originated with the government, then the government did entrap the defendant. Put another way, if the defendant was predisposed to commit the crime and the government only provided her with the opportunity to commit it, then she wasn't entrapped.

According to the Minnesota Court of Appeals, government encouragement has to "go beyond mere solicitation . . . ; it requires something in the nature of persuasion, badgering or pressure by the state" (*State v. Fitiwi* 2003). The legal encyclopedia *Corpus Juris Secundum* (2003, § 61) says the government has to use "trickery, persuasion, or fraud."

In a leading U.S. Supreme Court case, *Sherman v. U.S.* (1958), government informant and undercover agent Kalchinian and drug addict Joe Sherman met in a treatment center. Kalchinian struck up a friendship with Sherman and eventually asked Sherman to get him some heroin. At first, Sherman refused. However, after Kalchinian begged and pleaded for several weeks, Sherman finally gave in and got Kalchinian the heroin. The police promptly arrested Sherman. The Court understandably found that the intent originated with the government. According to the Court, given that Sherman was in treatment for his addiction he was hardly predisposed to commit a drug offense.

Once defendants have produced some evidence that the government agent persuaded the defendant to commit the crime, the government then has to prove the defendant was predisposed to commit it. The circumstances the government can use vary somewhat from state to state, but they usually boil down to either the defendants' character or their behavior. Minnesota's list is typical:

1. Active solicitation of the crime

2. Prior criminal convictions

3. Prior criminal activity not resulting in conviction

4. Defendant's criminal reputation

5. By any other adequate means (*State v. Wright* 2001)

In our next case excerpt, *Jacobson v. U.S.* (1992), the U.S. Supreme Court held that Keith Jacobson was not predisposed to possess child pornography.

## Jacobson v. U.S.

503 U.S. 540 (1992)

### HISTORY

Keith Jacobson was convicted in the U.S. District Court for the District of Nebraska of receiving child pornography through the mail. A panel (3 members) of the Court of Appeals for the Eighth Circuit reversed. On rehearing en banc (the full court) affirmed. The U.S. Supreme Court reversed.

WHITE, J., JOINED BY BLACKMUN, STEVENS, SOUTER, AND THOMAS, JJ.

### FACTS

In February 1984, Keith Jacobson, a 56-year-old Korean War veteran-turned-farmer who supported his elderly father in Nebraska, ordered two magazines and a brochure from a California adult bookstore. The magazines, entitled *Bare Boys I* and *Bare Boys II*, contained photographs of nude preteen and teenage boys. The contents of the magazines startled petitioner, who testified that he had expected to receive photographs of "young men 18 years or older." On cross-examination, he explained his response to the magazines:

[Prosecutor]: You were shocked and surprised that there were pictures of very young boys without clothes on, is that correct?

[Jacobson]: Yes, I was.

[Prosecutor]: Were you offended?

[Jacobson]: I was not offended because I thought these were a nudist type publication. Many of the pictures were out in a rural or outdoor setting. There was—I didn't draw any sexual connotation or connection with that.

The young men depicted in the magazines were not engaged in sexual activity, and Jacobson's receipt of the magazines was legal under both federal and Nebraska law.

Within three months, the law with respect to child pornography changed; Congress passed the Act illegalizing the receipt through the mails of sexually explicit depictions of children. In the very month the new provision became law, postal inspectors found Jacobson's name on the mailing list of the California bookstore that had mailed him *Bare Boys I* and *II*. There followed over the next $2^{1}/_{2}$ years repeated efforts by two Government agencies, through five fictitious organizations and a bogus pen pal, to explore Jacobson's willingness to break the new law by ordering sexually explicit photographs of children through the mail.

The Government began its efforts in January 1985 when a postal inspector sent Jacobson a letter supposedly from the American Hedonist Society, which in fact was a fictitious organization. The letter included a membership application and stated the Society's doctrine: that members had the "right to read what we desire, the right to discuss similar interests with those who share our philosophy, and finally that we have the right to seek pleasure without restrictions being placed on us by outdated puritan morality." Jacobson enrolled in the organization and returned a sexual attitude questionnaire that asked him to rank on a scale of one to four his enjoyment of various sexual materials, with one being "really enjoy," two being "enjoy," three being "somewhat enjoy," and four being "do not enjoy." Jacobson ranked the entry "pre-teen sex" as a two, but indicated that he was opposed to pedophilia.

For a time, the Government left Jacobson alone. But then a new "prohibited mailing specialist" in the Postal Service found Jacobson's name in a file, and in May 1986, Jacobson received a solicitation from a second fictitious consumer research company, "Midlands Data Research," seeking a response from those who "believe in the joys of sex and the complete awareness of those lusty and youthful lads and lasses of the neophite [sic] age."

The letter never explained whether "neophite" referred to minors or young adults. Jacobson responded: "Please feel free to send me more information, I am interested in teenage sexuality. Please keep my name confidential." Jacobson then heard from yet another Government creation, "Heartland Institute for a New Tomorrow" (HINT), which proclaimed it was

> an organization founded to protect and promote sexual freedom and freedom of choice. We believe that arbitrarily imposed legislative sanctions restricting your sexual freedom should be rescinded through the legislative process.

The letter also enclosed a second survey. Jacobson indicated that his interest in "preteen sex–homosexual" material was above average, but not high. In response to another question, Jacobson wrote:

> Not only sexual expression but freedom of the press is under attack. We must be ever vigilant to counter attack right wing fundamentalists who are determined to curtail our freedoms.

HINT replied, portraying itself as a lobbying organization seeking to repeal "all statutes which regulate sexual activities, except those laws which deal with violent behavior, such as rape. HINT is also lobbying to eliminate any legal definition of 'the age of consent.'" These lobbying efforts were to be funded by sales from a catalog to be published in the future "offering the sale of various items which we believe you will find to be both interesting and stimulating." HINT also provided computer matching of group members with similar survey responses; and, although petitioner was supplied with a list of potential "pen pals," he did not initiate any correspondence.

Nevertheless, the Government's "prohibited mailing specialist" began writing to Jacobson, using the pseudonym "Carl Long." The letters employed a tactic known as "mirroring," which the inspector described as "reflecting whatever the interests are of the person we are writing to." Jacobson responded at first, indicating that his interest was primarily in "male-male items." Inspector "Long" wrote back:

> My interests too are primarily male-male items. Are you satisfied with the type of VCR tapes available? Personally, I like the amateur stuff better if it's well produced as it can get more kinky and also seems more real. I think the actors enjoy it more.

Jacobson responded:

> As far as my likes are concerned, I like good looking young guys (in their late teens and early 20's) doing their thing together.

Jacobson's letters to "Long" made no reference to child pornography. After writing two letters, petitioner discontinued the correspondence.

By March 1987, 34 months had passed since the Government obtained Jacobson's name from the mailing list of the California bookstore, and 26 months had passed since the Postal Service had commenced its mailings to petitioner. Although Jacobson had responded to surveys and letters, the Government had no evidence that petitioner had ever intentionally possessed or been exposed to child pornography. The Postal Service had not checked Jacobson's mail to determine whether he was receiving questionable mailings from persons—other than the Government—involved in the child pornography industry.

At this point, a second Government agency, the Customs Service, included Jacobson in its own child pornography sting, "Operation Borderline," after receiving his name on lists submitted by the Postal Service. Using the name of a fictitious Canadian company called "Produit Outaouais," the Customs Service mailed petitioner a brochure advertising photographs of young boys engaging in sex. Jacobson placed an order that was never filled.

The Postal Service also continued its efforts in the Jacobson case, writing to petitioner as the "Far Eastern Trading Company Ltd." The letter began:

> As many of you know, much hysterical nonsense has appeared in the American media concerning "pornography" and what must be done to stop it from coming across your borders. This brief letter does not allow us to give much comments; however, why is your government spending millions of dollars to exercise international censorship while tons of drugs, which makes yours the world's most crime ridden country are passed through easily.

The letter went on to say:

> We have devised a method of getting these to you without prying eyes of U.S. Customs seizing your mail. . . . After consultations with American solicitors, we have been advised that once we have posted our material through your system, it cannot be opened for any inspection without authorization of a judge.

The letter invited Jacobson to send for more information. It also asked Jacobson to sign an affirmation that he was "not a law enforcement officer or agent of the U.S. Government acting in an undercover capacity for the purpose of entrapping Far Eastern Trading Company, its agents or customers." Jacobson responded. A catalog was sent, and Jacobson ordered *Boys Who Love Boys*, a pornographic magazine depicting young boys engaged in various sexual activities. Jacobson was arrested after a controlled delivery of a photocopy of the magazine.

When Jacobson was asked at trial why he placed such an order, he explained the Government had succeeded in piquing his curiosity: "Well, the statement was made of all the trouble and the hysteria over pornography and I wanted to see what the material was. It didn't describe the—I didn't know for sure what kind of sexual action they were referring to in the Canadian letter."

In Jacobson's home, the Government found the *Bare Boys* magazines and materials that the Government had sent to him in the course of its protracted investigation, but no other materials that would indicate Jacobson collected, or was actively interested in, child pornography.

Jacobson was indicted for violating 18 U.S.C. § 2252 (a)(2)(A). The trial court instructed the jury on Jacobson's entrapment defense. The jury was instructed: As mentioned, one of the issues in this case is whether the defendant was entrapped. If the defendant was entrapped he must be found not guilty. The government has the burden of proving beyond a reasonable doubt that the defendant was not entrapped.

If the defendant before contact with law-enforcement officers or their agents did not have any intent or disposition to commit the crime charged and was induced or persuaded by law-enforcement officers or their agents to commit that crime, then he was entrapped.

On the other hand, if the defendant before contact with law-enforcement officers or their agents did have an intent or disposition to commit the crime charged, then he was not entrapped even though law-enforcement officers or their agents provided a favorable opportunity to commit the crime or made committing the crime easier or even participated in acts essential to the crime.

Jacobson was convicted, and a divided Court of Appeals for the Eighth Circuit, sitting en banc, affirmed, concluding "Jacobson was not entrapped as a matter of law." We granted certiorari.

# OPINION

There can be no dispute about the evils of child pornography or the difficulties that laws and law enforcement have encountered in eliminating it. Likewise, there can be no dispute that the Government may use undercover agents to enforce the law. . . . In their zeal to enforce the law, however, Government agents may not originate a criminal design, implant in an innocent person's mind the disposition to commit a criminal act, and then induce commission of the crime so that the Government may prosecute. Where the Government has induced an individual to break the law and the defense of entrapment is at issue, as it was in this case, the prosecution must prove beyond reasonable doubt that the defendant was disposed to commit the criminal act prior to first being approached by Government agents.

Inducement is not at issue in this case. The Government does not dispute that it induced Jacobson to commit the crime. The sole issue is whether the Government carried its burden of proving that Jacobson was predisposed to violate the law before the Government intervened. . . . The Government's internal guidelines for undercover operations provide that an inducement to commit a crime should not be offered unless:

(a) There is a reasonable indication, based on information developed through informants or other means, that the subject is engaging, has engaged, or is likely to engage in illegal activity of a similar type; or

(b) The opportunity for illegal activity has been structured so that there is reason for believing that persons drawn to the opportunity, or brought to it, are predisposed to engage in the contemplated illegal activity.

Thus, an agent deployed to stop the traffic in illegal drugs may offer the opportunity to buy or sell drugs and, if the offer is accepted, make an arrest on the spot or later. In such a typical case, or in a more elaborate "sting" operation involving government-sponsored fencing where the defendant is simply provided with the opportunity to commit a crime, the entrapment defense is of little use because the ready commission of the criminal act amply demonstrates the defendant's predisposition. Had the agents . . . simply offered Jacobson the opportunity to order child pornography through the mails, and Jacobson . . . had promptly availed himself of this criminal opportunity, it is unlikely his entrapment defense would have warranted a jury instruction.

But that is not what happened here. By the time Jacobson finally placed his order, he had already been the target of 26 months of repeated mailings and communications from Government agents and fictitious organizations. Therefore, although he had become predisposed to break the law by May 1987, it is our view that the Government did not prove this predisposition was independent and not the product of the attention the Government had directed at Jacobson since January 1985.

The prosecution's evidence of predisposition falls into two categories: evidence developed prior to the Postal Service's mail campaign, and that developed during the course of the investigation. The sole piece of preinvestigation evidence is Jacobson's 1984 order and receipt of the *Bare Boys* magazines. But this is scant if any proof of Jacobson's predisposition to commit an illegal act. . . . It may indicate a predisposition to view sexually oriented photographs that are responsive to his sexual tastes; but evidence that merely indicates a generic inclination to act within a broad range, not all of which is criminal, is of little probative value in establishing predisposition.

Furthermore, Jacobson was acting within the law at the time he received these magazines. Receipt through the mails of sexually explicit depictions of children for non-commercial use did not become illegal under federal law until May 1984, and Nebraska had no law that forbade his possession of such material until 1988. Evidence of predisposition to do what once was lawful is not, by itself, sufficient to show predisposition to do what is now illegal, for there is a common understanding that most people obey the law even when they disapprove of it. . . . Hence, the fact that Jacobson legally ordered and received the *Bare Boys* magazines does little to further the Government's burden of proving he was predisposed to commit a criminal act. This is particularly true given Jacobson's unchallenged testimony that he did not know until they arrived that the magazines would depict minors.

The prosecution's evidence gathered during the investigation also fails to carry the Government's burden. Jacobson's responses to the many communications prior to the ultimate criminal act were at most indicative of certain personal inclinations, including a predisposition to view photographs of preteen sex and a willingness to promote a given agenda by supporting lobbying organizations. Even so, his responses hardly support an inference that he would commit the crime of receiving child pornography through the mails. Furthermore, a person's inclinations and "fantasies . . . are his own and beyond the reach of government. . . ."

On the other hand, the strong arguable inference is that, by waving the banner of individual rights and disparaging the legitimacy and constitutionality of efforts to restrict the availability of sexually explicit materials, the Government not only excited Jacobson's interest in sexually explicit materials banned by law but also exerted substantial pressure on Jacobson to obtain and read such material as part of a fight against censorship and the infringement of individual rights.

For instance, HINT described itself as "an organization founded to protect and promote sexual freedom and freedom of choice" and stated that "the most appropriate means to accomplish its objectives is to promote honest dialogue among concerned individuals and to continue its lobbying efforts with State Legislators." These lobbying efforts were to be financed through catalog sales. Ibid. Mailings from the equally fictitious American Hedonist Society, and the correspondence from the nonexistent Carl Long, endorsed these themes.

Similarly, the two solicitations in the spring of 1987 raised the specter of censorship while suggesting Jacobson ought to be allowed to do what he had been solicited to do.

The mailing from the Customs Service referred to "the worldwide ban and intense enforcement on this type of material," observed that "what was legal and commonplace is now an 'underground' and secretive service," and emphasized that "this environment forces us to take extreme measures" to ensure delivery. The Postal Service solicitation described the concern about child pornography as "hysterical nonsense," decried "international censorship," and assured petitioner, based on consultation with "American solicitors," that an order that had been posted could not be opened for inspection without authorization of a judge. It further asked petitioner to affirm he was not a Government agent attempting to entrap the mail order company or its customers. In these particulars, both Government solicitations suggested receiving this material was something Jacobson ought to be allowed to do.

Jacobson's ready response to these solicitations cannot be enough to establish beyond reasonable doubt he was predisposed, prior to the Government acts intended to create predisposition, to commit the crime of receiving child pornography through the mails. The evidence that he was ready and willing to commit the offense came only after the Government had devoted $2^1/_2$ years to convincing him he had or should have the right to engage in the very behavior proscribed by law.

Rational jurors could not say beyond a reasonable doubt that Jacobson possessed the requisite predisposition prior to the Government's investigation and that it existed independent of the Government's many and varied approaches to him. . . . The Government may not play on the weaknesses of an innocent party and beguile him into committing crimes which he otherwise would not have attempted. Law enforcement officials go too far when they implant in the mind of an innocent person the disposition to commit the alleged offense and induce its commission in order that they may prosecute. . . .

When the Government's quest for convictions leads to the apprehension of an otherwise law-abiding citizen who, if left to his own devices, likely would have never run afoul of the law, the courts should intervene. Because we conclude this is such a case and the prosecution failed . . . to adduce evidence to support the jury verdict Jacobson was predisposed, independent of the Government's acts and beyond a reasonable doubt, to violate the law by receiving child pornography through the mails, we REVERSE the Court of Appeals' judgment affirming the conviction of Keith Jacobson.

## DISSENT

O'CONNOR, J., JOINS WITH REHNQUIST, C.J.,
AND KENNEDY AND SCALIA, JJ.

Keith Jacobson was offered only two opportunities to buy child pornography through the mail. Both times, he ordered. Both times, he asked for opportunities to buy more.

He needed no Government agent to coax, threaten, or persuade him; no one played on his sympathies, friendship, or suggested that his committing the crime would further a greater good. In fact, no Government agent even contacted him face to face. The Government contends that from the enthusiasm with which Mr. Jacobson responded to the chance to commit a crime, a reasonable jury could permissibly infer beyond a reasonable doubt that he was predisposed to commit the crime. I agree. . . .

Today, the Court holds that Government conduct may be considered to create a predisposition to commit a crime, even before any Government action to induce the commission of the crime. In my view, this holding changes entrapment doctrine. Generally, the inquiry is whether a suspect is predisposed before the Government induces the commission of the crime, not before the Government makes initial contact with him. There is no dispute here that the Government's questionnaires and letters were not sufficient to establish inducement; they did not even suggest that Mr. Jacobson should engage in any illegal activity. . . . Yet the Court holds that the Government must prove not only that a suspect was predisposed to commit the crime before the opportunity to commit it arose, but also before the Government came on the scene.

. . . While the Court states that the Government "exerted substantial pressure on petitioner to obtain and read such material as part of a fight against censorship and the infringement of individual rights," one looks at the record in vain for evidence of such "substantial pressure." The most one finds is letters advocating legislative action to liberalize obscenity laws, letters which could easily be ignored or thrown away. Much later, the Government sent separate mailings of catalogs of illegal materials. Nowhere did the Government suggest that the proceeds of the sale of the illegal materials would be used to support legislative reforms.

. . . In sum, . . . [i]t was surely reasonable for the jury to infer that Mr. Jacobson was predisposed beyond a reasonable doubt, even if other inferences from the evidence were also possible. . . . Because I believe there was sufficient evidence to uphold the jury's verdict, I respectfully dissent.

## Questions

1. What specific facts demonstrate that the government induced Keith Jacobson to order the child pornography?

2. What evidence demonstrates that Keith Jacobson was predisposed to commit the crime?

3. Why did the Court reverse the conviction even though the jury convicted him?

4. What does the dissent mean when it says that the majority has changed the law of entrapment?

5. Commentary following the Court's decision claimed the decision "ties the hands of law enforcement officers." Do you agree? Defend your answer.

# The Objective Test

A minority (but growing number) of courts has adopted an **objective test of entrapment**, also called the "hypothetical person" test (*State v. Wilkins* 1983). The objective test of entrapment doesn't focus on the predisposition of the specific defendant in the case. Instead, it focuses on whether the actions of government officers would get a hypothetical, "reasonable person" to commit a crime. According to the objective test, if the actions of the officer would induce an "ordinarily law-abiding" person to commit the crime, the court should dismiss the case. This test is a prophylactic rule aimed to deter "unsavory police methods." Courts (not juries) decide whether police methods would cause a hypothetical, reasonable person to commit a crime they wouldn't commit otherwise.

U.S. Supreme Court Justice Felix Frankfurter, concurring in *Sherman v. U.S.* (1958, discussed earlier) about the core idea behind the objective test, wrote:

> No matter what the defendant's past record and present inclinations to criminality, or the depths to which he has sunk in the estimation of society, certain police conduct to ensnare him into further crime is not to be tolerated by an advanced society. (382–83)

# SUMMARY

### I. Remedies against Officer Misconduct
    A. Two types of remedies are aimed at officer misconduct:
        1. The exclusionary rule and the defense of entrapment are remedies affecting the outcome of the state's criminal case against defendants.
        2. Three types of remedies may be sought in separate proceedings:
            a. Criminal prosecution of officers
            b. Civil lawsuits to sue officers, departments, and/or municipalities
            c. Administrative review of police misconduct
    B. Remedies aren't mutually exclusive (plaintiffs don't have to choose among them).
    C. Citizens have no constitutional right to the exclusionary rule or the defense of entrapment.

### II. The Exclusionary Rule
    A. The United States has the only criminal justice system in the world in which courts throw out "good evidence" because the government used "bad methods" to get it.
        1. "Good evidence" means evidence that can help prove the defendant's guilt.
        2. "Bad methods" means conduct that violates the:
            a. Fourth Amendment ban on unreasonable searches and seizures
            b. Fifth Amendment right against self-incrimination
            c. Sixth Amendment right to counsel
            d. Fifth and Fourteenth Amendment rights to due process of law
    B. History
        1. There's no mention of the exclusionary rule in the Constitution; but James Madison believed it was implied in judicial power.
        2. 1914, *Weeks v. U.S.* The U.S. Supreme Court created the exclusionary rule.
            a. It applied only to federal courts.
            b. It covered only private papers and belongings.

3. 1920, *Silverthorne Lumber Co. v. U.S.* The Court expanded the rule to cover evidence that was indirectly based on illegal government action ("fruit of the poisonous tree").

4. 1925, *Agnello v. U.S.* The Court expanded the rule to cover contraband.

5. 1949, *Wolf v. Colorado.* The Court applied the Fourth Amendment, but not the exclusionary rule, to state proceedings; states could decide the remedy for themselves.

6. 1961, *Mapp v. Ohio.* The Court applied the exclusionary rule to state criminal proceedings.

7. 1984, *U.S. v. Leon.* The exclusionary rule isn't a constitutional right; it's a device to protect constitutional rights.

C. Justifications

1. *Constitutional right.* The Fourth, Fifth, Sixth, and Fourteenth Amendment rights wouldn't mean anything without the exclusion.

2. *Judicial integrity.* The courts shouldn't participate in unconstitutional behavior by approving it.

3. *Deterrence.* Prevent unconstitutional conduct by government officers.

D. Scope

1. The scope of the rule is restricted because of the belief that the social costs of freeing guilty people and of undermining the prosecution's case are too high and keep good evidence out of court.

2. The rule is restricted to the government's case-in-chief at trial.

3. The Court created five main exceptions to the exclusionary rule:

   a. *Collateral use.* Illegally obtained evidence is admissible in all nontrial settings (bail hearings, preliminary hearings, grand jury proceedings, habeas corpus proceedings).

   b. *Cross-examination.* The prosecution can use illegally obtained evidence to undermine defense witnesses' (including the defendant's) credibility.

   c. *Fruit of the poisonous tree.* The basic idea is that government shouldn't be in a worse position after illegal conduct. It consists of the remaining three exceptions:

      (1) *Attenuation.* Tainted evidence is admissible if the totality of circumstances in the case proves that the poisonous connection between police illegality and the evidence has weakened enough.

      (2) *Independent source.* Tainted evidence is admissible if after violating the Constitution, officers get the same evidence in a totally separate lawful action.

      (3) *Inevitable discovery.* Tainted evidence is admissible if police law-breaking produced the evidence but the evidence would've been discovered eventually anyway.

E. Persons seized illegally (arrested)

1. Persons arrested illegally aren't fruit of the poisonous tree, so they can be produced, tried, and convicted in court.

2. Courts don't ask how individuals got to court (that's a police matter).

F. Reasonable, good-faith exception

1. This exception applies only to evidence obtained by search warrants that later turn out to be illegal.

2. Evidence obtained during execution of an illegal search warrant is admissible only if the government can prove:
   a. Officers honestly relied on the legality of the warrants.
   b. It was reasonable for officers to believe the warrants were legal.
3. The reason is there's no deterrent effect if officers honestly and reasonably believed the warrants were lawful.
G. Non–law enforcement government officials
   1. Prevention of government unconstitutional behavior is the only justification for the exclusionary rule.
   2. The rule applies to police because they're deterred by exclusion.
   3. The rule doesn't apply to judges and other court personnel (such as clerks), because there's no evidence exclusion would deter their misconduct.

## III. The Defense of Entrapment
A. Criminal cases are dismissed if the government pressured defendants to commit crimes they wouldn't have committed without pressure.
B. Encouragement isn't entrapment.
C. Two tests determine the line between entrapment and encouragement:
   1. The subjective test focuses on defendants' predisposition to commit the crime.
      a. Defendants have the burden of presenting some evidence of two elements:
         (1) They had no predisposition to commit the crime.
         (2) Government pressure caused them to commit the crimes.
      b. If defendants meet their burden, the government has to prove the defendants were predisposed.
      c. The government can prove disposition by any of a variety of circumstances related to the following:
         (1) The defendants' past conduct, such as prior criminal activity, suggests they could be predisposed to commit the crime.
         (2) The defendants' character, such as their reputation, is questionable.
   2. The objective test focuses on the behavior of law enforcement.
   3. If the government's actions would induce an ordinarily law-abiding person to commit the crime, the case should be dismissed.

# REVIEW QUESTIONS

1. Identify two types of remedies against government wrongdoing and the differences between them, and give examples of each.

2. Is there a constitutional right to the exclusionary rule and the defense of entrapment? Explain your answer.

3. Briefly trace the history of the exclusionary rule through the leading U.S. Supreme Court cases that created and expanded it.

4. Identify and explain the rationales behind the three justifications for the exclusionary rule. Which justification does the U.S. Supreme Court use today?

5. Explain the balancing test the U.S. Supreme Court adopted to apply the deterrence justification.

6. Summarize U.S. Supreme Court Justice Louis Brandeis's arguments in favor of the exclusionary rule.

7. List and explain five exceptions to the exclusionary rule.

8. Identify the rationale for the attenuation, independent source, and inevitable discovery exceptions to the exclusionary rule.

9. Why aren't persons who are arrested illegally "fruit of a poisonous tree"?

10. State the narrow scope of the reasonable, good-faith exception to the exclusionary rule.

11. Identify the assumptions of the Warren and Rehnquist Courts regarding the exclusionary rule.

12. According to Professor Christopher Slobogin, why is no one likely to win the empirical debate over the accuracy of the assumptions you identified in question 11?

13. Describe and explain the U.S. Supreme Court's attitude toward the defense of entrapment throughout most of our history.

14. Identify four examples of active law enforcement encouragement.

15. Identify the difference between the subjective and the objective tests of entrapment.

16. Identify two elements in the subjective test of entrapment.

17. What's the crucial question in the subjective test of entrapment?

18. Describe how the U.S. Supreme Court applied the subjective case to the facts of *Sherman v. U.S.*

19. Identify the two kinds of circumstances the government can use to prove defendants' predisposition to commit crimes. Give an example of each.

20. According to U.S. Supreme Court Justice Felix Frankfurter, what's the core idea behind the objective test of entrapment?

## KEY TERMS

# Constitutional Violations II: Other Remedies Against Official Misconduct

## OUTLINE

## MAIN POINTS

- A wide range of remedies exists to hold officers, departments, and governments accountable for illegal acts.
- Most illegal police conduct is also a crime, but it's difficult (and should be) to prove criminal intent beyond a reasonable doubt.
- Most people who seek compensation for official wrongdoing don't succeed.
- Law enforcement officers and the governments responsible for them aren't liable for injuries if officers acted reasonably, in good faith, and without malice.
- Individual law enforcement officers and the governments responsible for them have no affirmative duty to protect individuals from other individuals who violate their constitutional rights.
- Judges are absolutely immune and prosecutors are nearly absolutely immune from damage suits.
- Internal department disciplinary procedures are based on the idea that the police can best enforce measures to deal with police misconduct.
- External civilian review of police misconduct is based on the idea that the police shouldn't police themselves.

> *A State's failure to protect an individual against private violence simply doesn't constitute a violation of the Due Process Clause.*
>
> *Pinder v. Johnson* (1995)

## CASES COVERED

*Anderson v. Creighton,*
  483 U.S. 635 (1987)

*Pinder v. Johnson,*
  54 F.3d 1169 (CA4 1995)

W̶e talked about remedies that affect the determination of guilt (trial stage) in criminal cases against defendants (the exclusionary rule and the defense of entrapment) in Chapter 10. In this chapter, you'll learn about remedies against officers that aren't available in the criminal trial case against defendants. They result from three separate actions:

1. *Criminal law.* Prosecuting the officer
2. *Civil law.* Suing the officer, the police department, or the government
3. *Internal departmental review.* Disciplining the officer outside the judicial system

Let's look at these three types of actions and the remedies that flow from them.

# CRIMINAL ACTIONS

Most police misconduct can be a crime. So a police officer who illegally shoots and kills a person might have committed criminal homicide. Illegal arrests can be false imprisonment. Illegal searches can be trespasses—and maybe breaking and entering, too.

How likely is it that police officers will be charged with crimes, convicted, and punished when they break the law? Not very. Why? Judges and juries don't see police misconduct as a crime. And with good reason. In our criminal justice system, the government has to prove criminal intent beyond a reasonable doubt. If police officers honestly believe they were enforcing the law and not committing a crime (which in most cases is either true or difficult to prove beyond a reasonable doubt), they're not guilty. And this is the way it should be. The standard of proof has to be the same for officers as for everybody else.

There's a second reason. Even if officers are guilty of criminal misconduct, prosecutors hesitate to prosecute, and juries are unwilling to convict, police officers who are "only trying to do their job." This is true especially when the "victims" might be criminals (or at least people who associate with criminals).

# CIVIL ACTIONS

Most individuals seeking a remedy for official lawbreaking (**plaintiffs**) want compensation (technically called **damages**) for the injuries caused by police misconduct. How do they get damages? The only way is by becoming plaintiffs in court in a **civil action** (meaning it's not a criminal case).

Who can plaintiffs sue for money damages? Any or all of the following:

- Individual law enforcement officers
- Officers' superiors (such as police chiefs and sheriffs)

- Departments
- Government units in charge of officers and departments

Where do they sue? In state and federal courts. We'll look separately at civil actions for damages against federal officers and the federal government; state officers and departments; state and local government units; and other government employees, because they're controlled by different statutes, court decisions, and governments. We'll also examine what happens when law enforcement officers fail to protect individuals and some of the hurdles to suing the government.

## Suing U.S. Officers and the U.S. Government

Lawsuits against individual federal law enforcement officers are called **constitutional tort (*Bivens*) actions**. Lawsuits against the federal government for their officers' constitutional torts are called **Federal Tort Claims Act (FTCA) actions**. Let's look at each.

***Suing U.S. Officers*** Until 1971, individuals were banned from suing federal officers for violations of their constitutional rights. All that changed after the U.S. Supreme Court decided *Bivens v. Six Unnamed FBI Agents* (1971). In that case, six FBI agents entered Webster Bivens's apartment without a search or arrest warrant. After they searched his apartment "from stem to stern," the agents arrested Bivens for violating federal drug laws and handcuffed him in the presence of his wife and children.

The agents took Bivens first to the Brooklyn Federal Courthouse and then to the Federal Bureau of Narcotics, "where he was interrogated, fingerprinted, photographed, subjected to search of his person, and booked." Bivens claimed these events caused him "great humiliation, embarrassment, and mental suffering" and would "continue to do so." He sought damages of $15,000 from each of the six officers (390).

In *Bivens*, the Court created a *constitutional tort*, a private right to sue federal officers for violations of plaintiffs' constitutional rights. Called "*Bivens* actions," plaintiffs have to prove two elements:

1. Officers were acting "under color of authority" or the appearance of power. (Garner 1987, 123–24)

2. Officers' actions deprived the plaintiff of a constitutional right.

Even if plaintiffs prove these two elements, they don't automatically "win" their case. Law enforcement officers have a defense called **qualified immunity** (also called the **"good faith" defense**). According to this complex defense, individual officers can't be held personally liable for official action if

1. Their action meets the test of "objective legal reasonableness."

2. Reasonableness is measured by legal rules "clearly established" at the time the officers acted.

The reason for creating this easy test was to protect officers' broad discretion to do their job and keep them (and the courts) from being bombarded with frivolous lawsuits.

The U.S. Supreme Court created and explained why it created the qualified immunity defense against constitutional torts in *Anderson v. Creighton* (1987).

## Anderson v. Creighton
### 483 U.S. 635 (1987)

### HISTORY

Robert E. Creighton Jr., his wife, and others sued FBI Agent Russell Anderson in the U.S. District Court for the District of Minnesota. The U.S. District Court granted **summary judgment** [*a motion that the court enter a judgment without a trial because there's not enough evidence to support the plaintiff's claim*] in favor of the agent. The Court of Appeals for the Eighth Circuit reversed and remanded. The U.S. Supreme Court granted certiorari, vacated the Circuit Court's judgment and remanded the case.

SCALIA, J., JOINED BY REHNQUIST, C.J., AND WHITE, BLACKMUN, POWELL, AND O'CONNOR JJ.

### FACTS

Russell Anderson is an agent of the Federal Bureau of Investigation. On November 11, 1983, Anderson and other state and federal law enforcement officers conducted a warrantless search of the Creighton family's home. The search was conducted because Anderson believed that Vadaain Dixon, a man suspected of a bank robbery committed earlier that day, might be found there. He was not.

. . . On the night of November 11, 1983, Sarisse and Robert Creighton and their three young daughters were spending a quiet evening at their home when a spotlight suddenly flashed through their front window. Mr. Creighton opened the door and was confronted by several uniformed and plainclothes officers, many of them brandishing shotguns. All of the officers were white; the Creightons are black. Mr. Creighton claims that none of the officers responded when he asked what they wanted.

Instead, by his account (as verified by a St. Paul police report), one of the officers told him to "keep his hands in sight" while the other officers rushed through the door. When Mr. Creighton asked if they had a search warrant, one of the officers told him, "We don't have a search warrant and don't need one; you watch too much TV." Mr. Creighton asked the officers to put their guns away because his children were frightened, but the officers refused.

Mrs. Creighton awoke to the shrieking of her children, and was confronted by an officer who pointed a shotgun at her. She allegedly observed the officers yelling at her three daughters to "sit their damn asses down and stop screaming." She asked the officer, "What the hell is going on?" The officer allegedly did not explain the situation and simply said to her, "Why don't you make your damn kids sit on the couch and make them shut up."

One of the officers asked Mr. Creighton if he had a red and silver car. As Mr. Creighton led the officers downstairs to his garage, where his maroon Oldsmobile was parked, one of the officers punched him in the face, knocking him to the ground, and causing him to bleed from the mouth and the forehead. Mr. Creighton alleges that he was attempting to move past the officer to open the garage door when the officer panicked and hit him. The officer claims that Mr. Creighton attempted to grab his shotgun, even though Mr. Creighton was not a suspect in any crime and had no contraband in his home or on his person. Shaunda, the Creighton's ten-year-old daughter, witnessed the assault and screamed for her mother to come help. She claims that one of the officers then hit her.

Mrs. Creighton phoned her mother, but an officer allegedly kicked and grabbed the phone and told her to "hang up that damn phone." She told her children to run to their neighbor's house for safety. The children ran out and a plainclothes officer chased them. The Creightons' neighbor allegedly told Mrs. Creighton that the officer ran into her house and grabbed Shaunda by the shoulders and shook her. The neighbor allegedly told the officer, "Can't you see she's in shock; leave her alone and get out of my house." Mrs. Creighton's mother later brought Shaunda to the emergency room at Children's Hospital for an arm injury caused by the officer's rough handling.

During the melee, family members and friends began arriving at the Creightons' home. Mrs. Creighton claims that she was embarrassed in front of her family and friends by the invasion of their home and their rough treatment as if they were suspects in a major crime. At this time, she again asked Anderson for a search warrant. He allegedly replied, "I don't need a damn search warrant when I'm looking for a fugitive." The officers did not discover the allegedly unspecified "fugitive" at the Creightons' home or any evidence whatsoever that he had been there or that the Creightons were involved in any type of criminal activity.

Nonetheless, the officers then arrested and handcuffed Mr. Creighton for obstruction of justice and brought him to the police station where he was jailed overnight, then released without being charged.

The Creightons later filed suit against Anderson in a Minnesota state court, asserting among other things a claim for money damages under the Fourth Amendment. (*Bivens v. Six Unknown Fed. Narcotics Agents*, 1971). After removing the suit to Federal District Court, Anderson filed a motion to dismiss or for summary judgment, arguing that the *Bivens* claim was barred by Anderson's qualified immunity from civil damages liability. Before any discovery took place, the District Court granted summary judgment on the ground that the search was lawful, holding that the undisputed facts revealed that Anderson had had probable cause to search the Creightons' home and that his failure to obtain a warrant was justified by the presence of exigent circumstances.

The Creightons appealed to the Court of Appeals for the Eighth Circuit, which reversed. The Court of Appeals held . . . Anderson was not entitled to summary judgment on qualified immunity grounds, since the right Anderson was alleged to have violated—the right of persons to be protected from warrantless searches of their home unless the searching officers have probable cause and there are exigent circumstances—was clearly established.

Anderson filed a petition for certiorari, arguing that the Court of Appeals erred by refusing to consider his argument that he was entitled to summary judgment on qualified immunity grounds if he could establish as a matter of law that a reasonable officer could have believed the search to be lawful. We granted the petition, to consider that important question.

## OPINION

When government officials abuse their offices, actions for damages may offer the only realistic avenue for vindication of constitutional guarantees. On the other hand, permitting damages suits against government officials can entail substantial social costs, including the risk that fear of personal monetary liability and harassing litigation will unduly inhibit officials in the discharge of their duties.

Our cases have accommodated these conflicting concerns by generally providing government officials performing discretionary functions with a qualified immunity, shielding them from civil damages liability as long as their actions could reasonably have been thought consistent with the rights they are alleged to have violated.

Somewhat more concretely, whether an official protected by qualified immunity may be held personally liable for an allegedly unlawful official action generally turns on the "objective legal reasonableness" of the action, assessed in light of the legal rules that were "clearly established" at the time it was taken. . . .

The contours of the right must be sufficiently clear that a reasonable official would understand that what he is doing violates that right. This is not to say that an official action is protected by qualified immunity unless the very action in question has previously been held unlawful, but it is to say that in the light of pre-existing law the unlawfulness must be apparent. . . .

The Creightons [argue] . . . that even if Anderson is entitled to qualified immunity under the usual principles of qualified immunity . . . an exception should be made to those principles in the circumstances of this case. . . . We reject the Creightons' . . . proposal that no immunity should be provided to police officers who conduct unlawful warrantless searches of innocent third parties' homes in search of fugitives. They rest this proposal on the assertion that officers conducting such searches were strictly liable at

English common law if the fugitive was not present. Although it is true that we have observed that our determinations as to the scope of official immunity are made in the light of the "common-law tradition," we have never suggested that the precise contours of official immunity can and should be slavishly derived from the often arcane rules of the common law. . . .

The general rule of qualified immunity is intended to provide government officials with the ability reasonably to anticipate when their conduct may give rise to liability for damages. Where that rule is applicable, officials can know that they will not be held personally liable as long as their actions are reasonable in light of current American law. That security would be utterly defeated if officials were unable to determine whether they were protected by the rule without entangling themselves in the vagaries of the English and American common law. . . . We therefore decline to make an exception to the general rule of qualified immunity for cases involving allegedly unlawful warrantless searches of innocent third parties' homes in search of fugitives.

For the reasons stated, we vacate the judgment of the Court of Appeals and REMAND the case for further proceedings consistent with this opinion.

## DISSENT

STEVENS, J., JOINED BY BRENNAN AND MARSHALL, JJ.

. . . The Court . . . announces a new rule of law that protects federal agents who make forcible nighttime entries into the homes of innocent citizens without probable cause, without a warrant, and without any valid emergency justification for their warrantless search. . . . The Court of Appeals understood the principle of qualified immunity . . . to shield government officials performing discretionary functions from exposure to damages liability unless their conduct violated clearly established statutory or constitutional rights of which a reasonable person would have known.

Applying this principle, the Court of Appeals held that the Creightons' Fourth Amendment rights and the exigent circumstances doctrine were clearly established at the time of the search. Moreover, apparently referring to the "extraordinary circumstances" defense . . . for a defendant who "can prove that he neither knew nor should have known of the relevant legal standard," the Court determined that Anderson could not reasonably have been unaware of these clearly established principles of law.

. . . The Court of Appeals' judgment rejecting Anderson's claim to immunity . . . raises the question whether this Court should approve a double standard of reasonableness—the constitutional standard already embodied in the Fourth Amendment and an even more generous standard that protects any officer who reasonably could have believed that his conduct was constitutionally reasonable. . . . Accepting for the moment the Court's double standard of reasonableness, I would affirm the judgment of the Court of Appeals because it correctly concluded that Anderson has not satisfied the . . . standard for immunity. . . .

In this Court, Anderson has not argued that any relevant rule of law—whether the probable-cause requirement or the exigent-circumstances exception to the warrant requirement—was not "clearly established" in November 1983. Rather, he argues that a competent officer might have concluded that the particular set of facts he faced did constitute "probable cause" and "exigent circumstances," and that his own reasonable belief that the conduct engaged in was within the law suffices to establish immunity. . . .

The Court's decision today represents a departure from the view we expressed two years ago in *Mitchell v. Forsyth* (1985). We held that petitioner was entitled to qualified immunity for authorizing an unconstitutional wiretap because it was not clearly established that warrantless domestic security wiretapping violated the Fourth Amendment. We added in a footnote:

> We do not intend to suggest that an official is always immune from liability or suit for a warrantless search merely because the warrant requirement has never explicitly been held to apply to a search conducted in identical circumstances. But in cases where there is a legitimate question whether an exception to the warrant requirement exists, it cannot be said that a warrantless search violates clearly established law.

Of course, the probable-cause requirement for an officer who faces the situation Anderson did was clearly established.

In addition, an officer's belief that his particular warrantless search was justified (by exigent circumstances, in this case) is analytically no different from a situation in which the warrant requirement has not been explicitly held to apply to the particular search undertaken by the officer. . . .

Although the question does not appear to have been argued in, or decided by, the Court of Appeals, this Court has decided to apply a double standard of reasonableness in damages actions against federal agents who are alleged to have violated an innocent citizen's Fourth Amendment rights. By double standard I mean a standard that affords a law enforcement official two layers of insulation from liability or other adverse consequence, such as suppression of evidence.

Having already adopted such a double standard in applying the exclusionary rule to searches authorized by an invalid warrant, *U.S. v. Leon*, (1984) [excerpted Chapter 10], the Court seems prepared and even anxious in this case to remove any requirement that the officer must obey the Fourth Amendment when entering a private home. I remain convinced that in a suit for damages as well as in a hearing on a motion to suppress evidence, an official search and seizure cannot be both unreasonable and reasonable at the same time. A federal official may not with impunity ignore the limitations which the controlling law has placed on his powers.

The effect of the Court's (literally unwarranted) extension of qualified immunity, I fear, is that it allows federal agents to ignore the limitations of the probable-cause and warrant requirements with impunity. The Court does so in the name of avoiding interference with legitimate law enforcement activities even though the probable-cause requirement, which limits the police's exercise of coercive authority, is itself a form of immunity that frees them to exercise that power without fear of strict liability. . . .

The argument that police officers need special immunity to encourage them to take vigorous enforcement action when they are uncertain about their right to make a forcible entry into a private home has already been accepted in our jurisprudence. We have held that the police act reasonably in entering a house when they have probable cause to believe a fugitive is in the house and exigent circumstances make it impracticable to obtain a warrant. This interpretation of the Fourth Amendment allows room for police intrusion, without a warrant, on the privacy of even innocent citizens.

In *Pierson v. Ray*, we held that police officers would not be liable in an action brought under 42 U.S.C. § 1983 "if they acted in good faith and with probable cause. . . ." We explained:

> Under the prevailing view in this country a peace officer who arrests someone with probable cause is not liable for false arrest simply because the innocence of the suspect is later proved. A policeman's lot is not so unhappy that he must choose between being charged with dereliction of duty if he does not arrest when he has probable cause, and being mulcted in damages if he does.

Thus, until now the Court has not found intolerable the use of a probable-cause standard to protect the police officer from exposure to liability simply because his reasonable conduct is subsequently shown to have been mistaken.

Today, however, the Court counts the law enforcement interest twice and the individual's privacy interest only once. The Court's double-counting approach reflects understandable sympathy for the plight of the officer and an overriding interest in unfettered law enforcement. It ascribes a far lesser importance to the privacy interest of innocent citizens than did the Framers of the Fourth Amendment.

The importance of that interest and the possible magnitude of its invasion are both illustrated by the facts of this case. The home of an innocent family was invaded by several officers without a warrant, without the owner's consent, with a substantial show of force, and with blunt expressions of disrespect for the law and for the rights of the family members.

. . . I see no reason why the family's interest in the security of its own home should be accorded a lesser weight than the Government's interest in carrying out an invasion that was unlawful. Arguably, if the Government considers it important not to discourage such conduct, it should provide indemnity to its officers. Preferably, however, it should furnish the kind of training for its law enforcement agents that would entirely eliminate the necessity for the Court to distinguish between the conduct that a competent officer considers reasonable and the conduct that the Constitution deems reasonable. . . . On the other hand, surely an innocent family should not bear the entire risk that a trial court, with the benefit of hindsight, will find that a federal agent reasonably believed that he could break into their home equipped with force and arms but without probable cause or a warrant. . . .

The Fourth Amendment protects the individual's privacy in a variety of settings. In none is the zone of privacy more clearly defined than when bounded by the unambiguous physical dimensions of an individual's home—a zone that finds its roots in clear and specific constitutional terms: "The right of the people to be secure in their houses . . . shall not be violated." That language unequivocally establishes the proposition that at the very core of the Fourth Amendment stands the right of a man to retreat into his own home and there be free from unreasonable governmental intrusion. In terms that apply equally to seizures of property and to seizures of persons, the Fourth Amendment has drawn a firm line at the entrance to the house. Absent exigent circumstances, that threshold may not reasonably be crossed without a warrant.

The warrant requirement safeguards this bedrock principle of the Fourth Amendment, while the immunity bestowed on a police officer who acts with probable cause permits him to do his job free of constant fear of monetary liability. The Court rests its doctrinally flawed opinion upon a double standard of reasonableness which unjustifiably and unnecessarily upsets the delicate balance between respect for individual privacy and protection of the public servants who enforce our laws.

I respectfully dissent.

### Questions

1. State the test for qualified immunity adopted by the majority.
2. List the reasons the Court gives for defining "qualified immunity" the way it does.
3. Summarize the dissent's objections to the majority's definition of "qualified immunity."
4. Which of the opinions do you agree with?
5. Do you believe the Robert and Sarisse Creighton and their children should receive damages for what happened? Defend your answer, relying on the facts and the arguments of the majority and the dissent.

---

**Suing the U.S. Government** *Bivens* didn't decide whether Webster Bivens could also sue the U.S. government for the six FBI officers' constitutional torts. According to the **doctrine of sovereign immunity** (a holdover from the days when kings didn't have to appear in court), governments can't be sued without their consent. The U.S. and most state governments have laws waiving their sovereign immunity (at least to some degree).

That's what Congress did in the Federal Tort Claims Act (FTCA). After *Bivens*, Congress permitted FTCA suits against the U.S. government for the constitutional torts of federal law enforcement agents "empowered by law to execute searches, to seize evidence, or to make arrests for violations of Federal law." The U.S. government's "deep pockets" make FTCA actions attractive to plaintiffs—probably more attractive than *Bivens* actions against individual officers. But both remedies are available to plaintiffs. According to Professors Whitebread and Slobogin (2000):

> [T]he plaintiff whose constitutional rights have been violated by a federal police officer in bad faith can be assured of monetary compensation [in an FTCA action] at the same time he can expect direct "revenge" [in a *Bivens* action] against the official to the extent the official can afford it. (51–52)

## Suing State Officers

Plaintiffs can sue individual state officers in two kinds of actions: state tort lawsuits and federal U.S. Civil Rights Act lawsuits. Let's look at each.

**State Tort Actions** Most illegal acts by state police, county sheriffs' and their deputies, and local police officers and their chiefs are also **torts**, meaning plaintiffs can sue individual officers for damages for acts such as assault, false arrest or false imprisonment, and trespass or breaking and entering. But the right to recover damages for injuries caused by officials' torts has to be balanced against law enforcement's job of protecting the public. So, although individual officers are liable for their own torts, there's a huge difference between suing an ordinary person and a cop.

The **defense of official immunity** limits officers' liability for their torts. This defense says that "a public official charged by law with duties which call for the exercise of his judgment or discretion is not personally liable to an individual unless he is guilty of a willful or malicious wrong." Why? Because "to encourage responsible law enforcement, . . . police are afforded a wide degree of discretion precisely because a more stringent standard could inhibit action."

In *Pletan v. Gaines et al.* (1992), the Minnesota Supreme Court balanced the rights of injured individuals and the needs of law enforcement when the court decided a police officer wasn't liable for the death of a small boy he killed during a high-speed chase to catch a fleeing shoplifter. If the officer were held liable, the court said, officers in the future might shy away from vigorously enforcing the law.

### U.S. Civil Rights Act (§ 1983) Actions

**U.S. Civil Rights Act (§ 1983) Actions** Civil Rights Act actions (called § 1983 actions because they're brought under Title 42, Section 1983, of the Civil Rights Act of 1871, passed just after the Civil War) allow plaintiffs to go into federal courts to sue state police officers and their agency heads; county sheriffs and their deputies; and municipal police officers and their chiefs for violating plaintiffs' federal constitutional rights.

Section 1983 provides:

> Every person who, under color of any statute, ordinance, regulation, custom, or usage, of any State or Territory, subjects, or causes to be subjected, any citizen of the United States or other person within the jurisdiction thereof to the deprivation of any rights, privileges, or immunities secured by the Constitution and laws, shall be liable to the party injured. U.S. Code 2002, Title 42, § 1983

As interpreted by the U.S. Supreme Court, plaintiffs have to prove two elements similar to those in *Bivens* constitutional tort actions:

1. Officers acted "under color of state law," which includes all acts done within the scope of their employment.

2. Officers' actions caused a deprivation of plaintiffs' rights guaranteed by the U.S. Constitution.

Section 1983 doesn't mean officers are liable every time they violate individuals' constitutional rights. Far from it. The U.S. Supreme Court has read several limits into the statutory protection. First, plaintiffs can't recover for accidental or even negligent violations; violations have to be deliberate. Second, state and local officers are protected by the same qualified immunity under § 1983 that federal officers have under *Bivens* and the Federal Tort Claims Act.

## Suing State and Local Governments

Plaintiffs have two options in deciding to sue state and local governments instead of (or in addition to) suing individual officers. They can sue governments in state courts for the torts of their officers, or they can sue them under the U.S. Civil Rights Act (see the "Suing State Officers" section). Let's look at each of these complicated routes to recovering damages from governments instead of individuals.

**State Tort Actions** What if the boy's parents in the Minnesota high-speed chase case (discussed above) had sued the police department or the city instead of the individual officer? Under the **doctrine of *respondeat superior***, state and local governments and their agencies are liable for the torts of their employees but only if the employees committed the torts during the course of their employment.

There's another catch; not all states have adopted the doctrine. In these states, government units enjoy the **defense of vicarious official immunity**, which means police departments and local governments can claim the official immunity of its employees. To determine whether government units are entitled to the defense of vicarious official immunity, courts apply a balancing test of local government liability. This test balances two elements: (1) the need for effective law enforcement and (2) the need to avoid putting the public at risk.

In the Minnesota Supreme Court's application of the balancing test in *Pletan v. Gaines et al.* (1992), the high-speed chase case, the court found the need to enforce the criminal law outweighed the risk to the public created by the high-speed chase. So, the court held, the municipality wasn't liable for the boy's death (42–43).

### U.S. Civil Rights Act (§ 1983) Actions

As you learned from *Anderson v. Creighton* (excerpted earlier on p. 376), suing individual officers for violating constitutional rights is a complicated business. Suing a department or a city under § 1983 is even more complicated. In fact, until the Court decided to undertake "a fresh analysis of debate on the Civil Rights Act of 1871" in *Monell v. New York City Department of Social Services* (1978), the Court had interpreted § 1983 to mean Congress didn't intend to allow individuals to sue municipalities and counties at all. But in *Monell*, the Court changed its mind, deciding the legislative history of the act "compels the conclusion that Congress did intend municipalities and other local government units to be included among those persons to whom § 1983 applies."

According to the *Monell* Court, individuals could sue local government units if they could prove two elements:

1. Officers either acted according to written policies, statements, ordinances, regulations, or decisions approved by authorized official bodies; or acted according to unwritten custom even though the custom wasn't formally approved through official decision-making channels.

2. The action caused the violation of the plaintiff's constitutional right(s).

So according to the Supreme Court in the *Monell* case:

> A local government cannot be sued for an injury inflicted solely by its employees or agents. Instead, it is when execution of a government's policy or custom, whether made by its lawmakers or by those whose edicts or acts may fairly be said to represent official policy, inflicts the injury that the government as an entity is responsible for it under § 1983. (695)

 Go to Exercise 11.1 on the Samaha Criminal Procedure 7e website to learn more about suing local governments: academic.cengage.com/ criminaljustice/samaha.

## Law Enforcement Failure to Protect

Until now, we've talked only about remedies that protect individuals from government violations of their rights, but what about failure by the government to protect people from each other? Most police departments conceive their mission broadly: "To protect and serve." But is their mission "to protect" a constitutional command? In other words, do governments and their officers have a constitutional duty to protect individuals from other private individuals who violate their rights? No. (At least not most of the time.)

According to the U.S. Supreme Court, neither the language of the due process clauses nor the history of the Fifth and Fourteenth Amendments (which contain the due process clauses) imposes an affirmative duty on law enforcement to protect individuals from other private individuals who would deprive them of their right to life, liberty, or property (*DeShaney v. Winnegabo County* 1989). Nor does it bestow an affirmative right on individuals to be protected from those individuals. So, according to what we'll call the Supreme Court's **no-affirmative-duty-to-protect rule**, plaintiffs can't sue individual officers or government units for failing to stop private people from violating their rights by inflicting injuries on them.

But there's at least one exception to the no-duty-to-protect rule—the **special-relationship exception**. The special relationship is custody. When the government takes it upon itself to put people in jail, prison, or mental institutions against their will and keeps them there, it's cruel and unusual punishment (in violation of the Eighth Amendment to the U.S. Constitution) to fail to protect them when they can't protect themselves (*DeShaney*, 199).

Some of the U.S. Courts of Appeals have created a **state-created-danger exception** (*Robinson v. Township of Redford* 2002, 929). This is a narrow exception, and, to qualify for it and collect damages under § 1983, plaintiffs have to prove three elements:

1. An officer's actions created a special danger of violent harm to the plaintiff (not to the general public).

2. The officer knows or should have known her actions would encourage this plaintiff to rely on her actions.

3. The danger created by the officer's actions either caused harm from the violence itself or increased the plaintiff's vulnerability to harm from violence.

Other U.S. Courts of Appeals have soundly rejected the state-created-danger exception.

The Fourth Circuit Court of Appeals stuck to the special-relationship exception created by custody as the only exception to the no-affirmative-duty-to-protect rule. The court explained why in our next case excerpt, *Pinder v. Johnson* (1995).

---

CASE    *Did the Police Have a Constitutional Duty to Protect Her and Her Children?*

## Pinder v. Johnson
54 F.3d 1169 (CA4 1995)

### HISTORY

Carol Pinder filed suit individually and as the survivor of her minor children against the municipality of Cambridge, Maryland, and Donald Johnson PFC, a police officer in the municipality of Cambridge. The U.S. District Court for the District of Maryland denied Johnson's motion for summary judgment. A three-judge panel of the Fourth Circuit Court of Appeals affirmed. An **en banc review** [*review by the whole circuit*] reversed.

WILKINSON, J. JOINED BY HALL, WILKINS, NIEMEYER, AND WILLIAMS, JJ. WIDENER, MOTZ, HAMILTON, AND LUTTIG, JJ. CONCURRED IN PART, AND CONCURRED IN THE JUDGMENT.

### FACTS

The facts of this case are genuinely tragic. On the evening of March 10, 1989, Officer Donald Johnson responded to a call reporting a domestic disturbance at the home of Carol Pinder. When he arrived at the scene, Johnson discovered that Pinder's former boyfriend, Don Pittman, had broken into her home. Pinder told Officer Johnson that when Pittman broke in, he was abusive and violent. He pushed her, punched her, and threw various objects at her.

Pittman was also screaming and threatening both Pinder and her children, saying he would murder them all. A neighbor, Darnell Taylor, managed to subdue Pittman and restrain him until the police arrived.

Officer Johnson questioned Pittman, who was hostile and unresponsive. Johnson then placed Pittman under arrest. After confining Pittman in the squad car, Johnson returned to the house to speak with Pinder again. Pinder explained to Officer Johnson that Pittman had threatened her in the past, and that he had just been released from prison after being convicted of attempted arson at Pinder's residence some ten months earlier. She was naturally afraid for herself and her children, and wanted to know whether it would be safe for her to return to work that evening.

Officer Johnson assured her that Pittman would be locked up overnight. He further indicated that Pinder had to wait until the next day to swear out a warrant against Pittman because a county commissioner would not be available to hear the charges before morning. Based on these assurances, Pinder returned to work.

That same evening, Johnson brought Pittman before Dorchester County Commissioner George Ames, Jr. for an initial appearance. Johnson only charged Pittman with trespassing and malicious destruction of property having a value of less than three hundred dollars, both of which are misdemeanor offenses. Consequently, Ames simply released Pittman on his own recognizance and warned him to stay away from Pinder's home.

Pittman did not heed this warning. Upon his release, he returned to Pinder's house and set fire to it. Pinder was still at work, but her three children were home asleep and died of smoke inhalation. Pittman was later arrested and charged with first degree murder. He was convicted and is currently serving three life sentences without possibility of parole.

Pinder brought this action for herself and for the estates of her three children, seeking damages under 42 U.S.C. § 1983, as well as state law theories, against the Commissioners of Cambridge and Officer Johnson. She alleged that defendants had violated their affirmative duty to protect her and her children, thereby depriving them of their constitutional right to due process under the Fourteenth Amendment.

Johnson moved for summary judgment, arguing that he had no constitutionally imposed affirmative duty to protect the Pinders and that he was shielded from liability by the doctrine of qualified immunity. The district court, however, refused to dismiss plaintiff's due process claim, finding that Officer Johnson was not entitled to qualified immunity. Johnson brought an interlocutory appeal [*an appeal that takes place before the trial court rules on the case*].

. . . A divided panel of this court affirmed, finding that Pinder had stated a cognizable substantive due process claim and that Johnson did not have a valid immunity defense. We granted rehearing en banc, and now reverse the judgment of the district court.

## OPINION

. . . Qualified immunity under § 1983 shields officials from civil liability unless their actions violated "clearly established statutory or constitutional rights of which a reasonable person would have known." The linchpin of qualified immunity is objective reasonableness. . . . Important to this reasonableness inquiry is whether the rights alleged to have been violated were clearly established at the time of the challenged actions. If the law supporting the allegedly violated rights was not clearly established, then immunity must lie. Where the law is clearly established, and where no reasonable officer could believe he was acting in accordance with it, qualified immunity will not attach.

The purpose of this doctrine is to ensure that police officers and other government actors have notice of the extent of constitutional restrictions on their behavior. Thus, qualified immunity prevents officials from being blindsided by liability derived from newly invented rights or new, unforeseen applications of pre-existing rights. In short, officials cannot be held to have violated rights of which they could not have known.

Here, the question is simply whether the due process right Pinder claims was clearly established at the time of her dealings with Johnson. This inquiry depends upon an assessment of the settled law at the time, not the law as it currently exists. Also, the rights Pinder asserts must have been clearly established in a particularized and relevant sense, not merely as an overarching entitlement to due process. . . .

Pinder can point to no clearly established law supporting her claim at the time of the alleged violation. Pinder's claim is that Officer Johnson deprived her and her children of their due process rights by failing to protect them from the violent actions of Pittman. Eighteen days before the events giving rise to this action, the Supreme Court handed down its decision in *DeShaney v. Winnebago County Department of Social Services* (1989) which squarely rejected liability under 42 U.S.C. § 1983 based on an affirmative duty theory.

The facts in *DeShaney* were as poignant as those in this case. There, the Winnebago County Department of Social Services (DSS) received a number of reports that a young boy, Joshua DeShaney, was being abused by his father. As this abuse went on, several DSS workers personally observed the injuries that had been inflicted on Joshua. They knew firsthand of the threat to the boy's safety, yet they failed to remove him from his father's custody or otherwise protect him from abuse. Ultimately, Joshua's father beat him so violently that the boy suffered serious brain damage. Joshua's mother brought a § 1983 action on his behalf, arguing that the County and its employees had deprived Joshua of his liberty interests without due process by failing to provide adequate protection against his father's violent acts.

Despite natural sympathy for the plaintiff, the Court held that there was no § 1983 liability under these circumstances. It noted that the Due Process Clause of the Fourteenth Amendment does not require governmental actors to affirmatively protect life, liberty, or property against intrusion by private third parties. Instead, the Due Process Clause works only as a negative prohibition on state action. "Its purpose was to protect the people from the State, not to ensure that the State protected them from each other." This view is consistent with our general conception of the Constitution as a document of negative restraints, not positive entitlements.

The *DeShaney* Court concluded that:

if the Due Process Clause does not require the State to provide its citizens with particular protective services, it follows that the State cannot be held liable under the Clause for injuries that could have been averted had it chosen to provide them. As a general matter, then, we conclude that a State's failure to protect an individual against private violence simply does not constitute a violation of the Due Process Clause.

The affirmative duty of protection that the Supreme Court rejected in *DeShaney* is precisely the duty Pinder relies on in this case. Joshua's mother wanted the state to be held liable for its lack of action, for merely standing by when it could have acted to prevent a tragedy. Likewise, Pinder argues Johnson could have, and thus should have, acted to prevent Pittman's crimes. *DeShaney* makes clear, however, that no affirmative duty was clearly established in these circumstances.

The *DeShaney* Court did indicate that an affirmative duty to protect may arise when the state restrains persons from acting on their own behalf. The Court explained that

when the State by the affirmative exercise of its power so restrains an individual's liberty that it renders him unable to care for himself, and at the same time fails to provide for his basic human needs . . . it transgresses the substantive limits on state action set by the Eighth Amendment and the Due Process Clause.

The specific source of an affirmative duty to protect, the Court emphasized, is the custodial nature of a "special relationship."

*DeShaney* reasoned that "the affirmative duty to protect arises not from the State's knowledge of the individual's predicament or from its expressions of intent to help him, but from the limitation which it has imposed on his freedom to act on his own behalf." Some sort of confinement of the injured party—incarceration, institutionalization, or the like—is needed to trigger the affirmative duty. This Court has consistently read *DeShaney* to require a custodial context before any affirmative duty can arise under the Due Process Clause.

There was no custodial relationship with Carol Pinder and her children in this case. Neither Johnson nor any other state official had restrained Pinder's freedom to act on her own behalf. Pinder was never incarcerated, arrested, or otherwise restricted in any way. Without any such limitation imposed on her liberty, *DeShaney* indicates Pinder was due no affirmative constitutional duty of protection from the state, and Johnson would not be charged with liability for the criminal acts of a third party.

Pinder argues, however, that Johnson's explicit promises that Pittman would be incarcerated overnight created the requisite "special relationship." We do not agree. By requiring a custodial context as the condition for an affirmative duty, *DeShaney* rejected the idea that such a duty can arise solely from an official's awareness of a specific risk or from promises of aid. There, as here, plaintiff alleged that the state knew of the special risk of harm at the hands of a third party. There, as here, plaintiff alleged that the state had "specifically proclaimed, by word and by deed, its intention to protect" the victim. Neither allegation was sufficient to support the existence of an affirmative duty in *DeShaney*, and the same holds true in this case.

Promises do not create a special relationship—custody does. Unlike custody, a promise of aid does not actually place a person in a dangerous position and then cut off all outside sources of assistance. Promises from state officials can be ignored if the situation seems dire enough, whereas custody cannot be ignored or changed by the persons it affects. It is for this reason that the Supreme Court made custody the crux of the special relationship rule. Lacking the slightest hint of a true "special relationship," Pinder's claim in this case boils down to an insufficient allegation of a failure to act.

We also cannot accept Pinder's attempt to escape the import of *DeShaney* by characterizing her claim as one of affirmative misconduct by the state in "creating or enhancing" the danger, instead of an omission. She emphasizes the "actions" that Johnson took in making assurances, and in deciding not to charge Pittman with any serious offense. By this measure, every representation by the police and every failure to incarcerate would constitute "affirmative actions," giving rise to civil liability. . . .

No amount of semantics can disguise the fact that the real "affirmative act" here was committed by Pittman, not by Officer Johnson. . . . The most that can be said of the state functionaries . . . is that they stood by and did nothing when suspicious circumstances dictated a more active role for them.

Given the principles laid down by *DeShaney*, it can hardly be said that Johnson was faced with a clearly established duty to protect Pinder or her children in March of 1989. Indeed, it can be argued that *DeShaney* established exactly the opposite, i.e., that no such affirmative duty existed because neither Pinder nor her children were confined by the state. . . .

It is true, as the district court noted, that some cases [have] found an "affirmative duty" arising outside the traditional custodial context. None of these cases, however, clearly establish the existence of the right Pinder alleges was violated. First, none of these cases found a particularized due process right to affirmative protection based solely on an official's assurances that the danger posed by a third party will be eliminated. All involved some circumstance wherein the state took a much larger and more direct role in "creating" the danger itself.

These cases involve a wholly different paradigm than that presented here. When the state itself creates the dangerous situation that resulted in a victim's injury . . . the state is not merely accused of a failure to act; it becomes much more akin to an actor itself directly causing harm to the injured party. See, e.g., *Cornelius v. Town of Highland Lake*, (11th Cir. 1989) (duty when state brought inmates into victim's workplace); *Wells v. Walker*, (8th Cir. 1988) (duty when state brought dangerous prisoners to victim's store); *Nishiyama v. Dickson County*, (6th Cir. 1987) (duty when state provided unsupervised parolee with squad car). At most, these cases stand for the proposition that state actors may not disclaim liability when they themselves throw others to the lions. They do not, by contrast, entitle persons who rely on promises of aid to some greater degree of protection from lions at large. . . .

The extensive debate provoked by this case should be proof enough that the law in this area was anything but clearly established at the time Officer Johnson gave assurances to Pinder. To impose liability in the absence of a clearly established constitutional duty is to invite litigation over a limitless array of official acts. . . . There are good reasons why the constitutional right to protection sought by Pinder was not clearly established by the courts. As the First Circuit noted in a similar case, "enormous economic consequences could follow from the reading of the Fourteenth Amendment that plaintiff here urges." The consequences, however, are not just economic, and their gravity indicates why the right Pinder asserts was never clearly established.

The recognition of a broad constitutional right to affirmative protection from the state would be the first step down the slippery slope of liability. Such a right potentially would be implicated in nearly every instance where a private actor inflicts injuries that the state could have prevented. Every time a police officer incorrectly decided it was not necessary to intervene in a domestic dispute, the victims of the ensuing violence could bring a § 1983 action. Every time a parolee committed a criminal act, the victims could argue the state had an affirmative duty to keep the prisoner incarcerated. Indeed, victims of virtually every crime could plausibly argue that if the authorities had done their job, they would not have suffered their loss. Broad affirmative duties thus provide a fertile bed for § 1983 litigation, and the resultant governmental liability would wholly defeat the purposes of qualified immunity.

If the right Pinder asserts were ever clearly established, it would entail other significant consequences. A general obligation of the state to protect private citizens . . . makes law enforcement officials constitutional guarantors of the conduct of others. . . . It is no solution to say that such a right to affirmative protection has its inherent limitations. It is no answer to contend that the duty here was created only by Johnson's promise and Pinder's reliance on that promise, and is limited by Johnson's awareness of the risk. Such "limitations" are no barrier to increased lawsuits.

There are endless opportunities for disagreements over the exact nature of an official's promise, the intent behind it, the degree of the reliance, the causal link between the promise and the injury, and so on. Similarly, the extent of the state's affirmative duty to protect and the degree of the state's awareness of the risk are also subjects that would tie up state and local officials in endless federal litigation. . . .

In cases like this, it is always easy to second-guess. Tragic circumstances only sharpen our hindsight, and it is tempting to express our sense of outrage at the failure of Officer Johnson to protect Pinder's children from Pittman's villainy. The Supreme Court in *DeShaney* specifically rejected the "shocks the conscience" test of *Rochin v. California* (1952) [Chapter 2] as a basis for imposing § 1983 liability in the affirmative duty context, however. We cannot simply ignore the lack of any clearly established constitutional duty to protect and the concomitant immunity from civil liability. Hard cases can make bad law, and it is to protect against that possibility that police officers possess the defense of qualified immunity.

For the foregoing reasons, the judgment of the district court denying qualified immunity to Officer Johnson is REVERSED.

## DISSENT

RUSSELL, J., JOINED BY ERVIN, C.J., AND MURNAGHAN AND MICHAEL, JJ.

. . . Because I believe the Court casually disregards the very real ways in which Officer Johnson's conduct placed Pinder and her children in a position of danger, I respectfully dissent. In March 1989, the time of the fire, the law "clearly established" that the state has a duty to protect an individual where the state, by its affirmative action, creates a dangerous situation or renders an individual more vulnerable to danger. As the Seventh Circuit stated in *Bowers v. DeVito* (1982):

> If the state puts a man in a position of danger from private persons and then fails to protect him, it will not be heard to say that its role was merely passive; it is as much an active tort feasor [*wrong doer*] as if it had thrown him into a snake pit.

The Seventh Circuit and other circuits, including our own, have reaffirmed this duty. The Supreme Court's decision in *DeShaney* did not reject the state's clearly established duty to protect an individual where the state, through its affirmative action, has created a dangerous situation or rendered the individual more vulnerable to danger. The Supreme Court held only that the state has no duty to protect an individual from the actions of third parties where the state was aware of the dangers but played no part in their creation. The fact that the state did not create the danger was central to the Court's holding.

In this case, Officer Johnson was not merely aware of the danger; he placed Pinder and her children in a position of danger. Officer Johnson knew Pittman had broken into Pinder's home and had been abusive and violent. Pittman had punched Pinder and thrown objects at her. When the officers arrived at the scene, Pittman was screaming and threatening that he "wasn't going to jail for nothing this time; this time it would be for murder." After the officers restrained Pittman, Pinder explained to Officer Johnson that Pittman had threatened Pinder before, that he had attempted to set fire to her house ten months earlier, and that he had just finished serving his sentence for the attempted arson.

Given Pittman's threats and violent behavior, Pinder was understandably concerned about the safety of herself and her children. She explained to Officer Johnson that she needed to return to work and specifically asked him whether it was safe to do so. Officer Johnson assured Pinder several times that Pittman would remain in police custody until morning. Officer Johnson indicated to Pinder that Pittman could not be released that night because a county commissioner would not be available until the morning.

Instead of remaining home with her children or making other arrangements for their safety, Pinder, relying on Officer Johnson's assurances, returned to work, leaving her children alone at home. At the police station, Officer Johnson charged Pittman only with two minor offenses, trespassing and malicious destruction of property having a value of less than three hundred dollars. Despite his previous representation to Pinder that no county commissioner would be available before the morning, Officer Johnson brought Pittman before a county commissioner that evening.

Because Officer Johnson charged Pittman only with two misdemeanors, the county commissioner released Pittman on his own recognizance. Upon his release, Pittman went directly to Pinder's house and burned it down, killing the three children in the conflagration.

I cannot understand how the majority can recount these same events in its own opinion and not conclude that Officer Johnson placed Pinder and her children in a position of danger. Officer Johnson made assurances to Pinder that Pittman would remain in police custody overnight and falsely represented that no county commissioner would be available until morning. He induced Pinder to return to work and leave her children vulnerable to Pittman's violence. After witnessing Pittman's violent behavior and murderous threats, he charged Pittman with only minor offenses, assuring his release. Officer Johnson had a duty to protect Pinder and her children from Pittman, at least to an extent necessary to dispel the false sense of security that his actions created.

Unlike the majority, I believe that the law at the time of the incident clearly established that Officer Johnson had a duty to protect Pinder and her children upon Pittman's release.

The Court finds it significant that no case before March 1989 contained the precise holding that due process creates a duty of affirmative protection based on an official's assurances that the danger posed by a third party will be eliminated. Such a particular holding, however, is not required in order to conclude that a right was clearly established.

In *Anderson v. Creighton* (1987) [excerpted on p. 376], the Supreme Court . . . explained that "the contours of the right must be sufficiently clear that a reasonable official would understand that what he is doing violated that right." On the other hand, the Court also rejected the view that "an official action is protected by qualified immunity unless the very action in question has previously been held unlawful. . . ." Requiring such a level of specificity would transform the defense of qualified immunity into a defense of absolute immunity. Instead, the Court held that the preexisting law had to be only specific enough that the unlawfulness of the official's conduct would be apparent to a reasonable person.

I believe that a reasonable officer in Officer Johnson's position would have recognized that, given his assurances to Pinder that Pittman would remain in police custody until morning and his failure to charge Pittman with an offense serious enough to ensure that he remained in custody overnight, he placed Pinder and her children in a dangerous position. He induced Pinder to let her guard down, dissuading her from taking actions to protect herself and her children from Pittman. Certainly, a reasonable officer would have recognized that he had a duty at least to phone Pinder and warn her that Pittman had been released from police custody.

Pinder's children were left alone at home, vulnerable to the rampage of a violent, intemperate man, and deprived of their mother's protection because of the hollow word of an irresponsible, thoughtless police officer. Today the Court holds that this police officer, who took no action to correct a dangerous situation of his own creation, did not violate Pinder's due process rights and is otherwise immune from prosecution because he did not violate a clearly established right. I disagree.

## Questions

1. List the facts relevant to deciding whether Donald Johnson is liable for damages to Carol Pinder.

2. Apply the facts you listed in (1) to the no-affirmative-duty-to-protect rule, the special-relationship exception, and the state-created-danger exception.

3. Summarize the court's majority and dissenting opinions' arguments in favor of or against the rule and exceptions in (3).

4. Which rule do you favor, and why?

# Suing Judges and Prosecutors

Most plaintiffs in civil actions sue law enforcement officers, who enjoy qualified immunity from being sued for damages. But what about prosecutors and judges? Can individuals sue them? The answer is "no" to suing a judge, and it's "hardly ever" to suing prosecutors Why? Because judges enjoy **absolute immunity** from civil suits, meaning they can't be sued even if they acted maliciously and in bad faith. The only remedy against misbehaving judges is either impeachment or, if they're elected, voting them out of office.

Prosecutors enjoy what's called **functional immunity**. This means their immunity depends on the function they're performing at the time of the misconduct. When they act as advocates, they're absolutely immune from civil liability even when plaintiffs prove they acted in bad faith and with malice. When they act as administrators or investigators, they're entitled to qualified immunity; that is, they're immune unless their misconduct violated clearly established law that a reasonable prosecutor would have known.

Before we examine the law regarding prosecutors' functional immunity, be aware of this widely documented observation about prosecutors:

> While certainly the vast majority of prosecutors are ethical lawyers engaged in vital public service, the undeniable fact is that many innocent people have been convicted of crimes as a result of prosecutorial misconduct, and the victims of this misconduct are generally denied any civil remedy because of prosecutorial immunities. (Johns 2005, 53, citing and summarizing many empirical studies, pp. 59–64)

Furthermore, prosecutors rarely suffer for their misconduct (Johns 2005, 70). According to the Center for Public Integrity, since 1970 there were more than two thousand cases of prosecutorial misconduct, but only 44 disciplinary actions and two disbarments (70). Another study found only 100 disciplinary proceedings against prosecutors between the years 1886 and 2000 (70).

In theory, prosecutors are criminally liable for their nonadvocacy functions. But since the Civil Rights Act, § 242, in 1866, created criminal liability for public officials who violate constitutional rights, only one prosecutor has ever been convicted (70–71).

The U.S. Supreme Court developed the functional immunity doctrine in four cases. Here's a brief summary of each:

1. *Imbler v. Pachtman* (1976). Paul Imbler was convicted of felony murder and sentenced to death following a trial in which District Attorney Richard Pachtman knowingly used false evidence and suppressed exculpatory evidence. Imbler was freed after he served nine years in prison. He sued Pachtman for § 1983 money damages. The Supreme Court ruled that Pachtman was absolutely immune from civil damages, because his misconduct occurred while he was performing his advocacy function.

2. *Burns v. Reed* (1990). Speculating that Kathy Burns had multiple personalities, one of which was responsible for shooting her two sons, Indiana police officers Paul Cox and Donald Scroggins decided to interview Burns under hypnosis. They were concerned that hypnosis "might be an unacceptable investigative technique" and sought Chief Deputy Prosecutor Rick Reed's advice. He told them they could question Burns under hypnosis.

While she was hypnotized, she referred to both herself and the shooter as "Katie." Interpreting this as support for their multiple personality theory, the police detained her and consulted Reed again, who told them they "probably had probable cause" to arrest her (482).

At a probable cause hearing the next day, in response to Reed's questioning, an officer testified that Burns confessed, but neither the officer nor Reed informed the judge about the hypnosis or that Burns had otherwise consistently denied guilt. The judge issued the warrant on the basis of this misleading presentation. When this came to light, the trial judge ordered the confession suppressed, and the prosecutor dropped the charges.

Burns sued the prosecutor, Reed, for damages under § 1983. The trial court dismissed the case, ruling that Reed was entitled to absolute immunity. The Supreme Court agreed, partly. The Court ruled that absolute immunity extended to initiation and presentation of the case, which included the probable cause hearing, but it didn't extend to the advice the prosecutor gave to the officers regarding the confession under hypnosis.

3. *Buckley v. Fitzsimmons* (1993). Stephen Buckley had been incarcerated for three years in the DuPage County jail on rape and murder charges, growing out of the highly publicized murder of 11-year-old Jeanine Nicarico. When he was finally released, he sued DuPage County State's Attorney Michael Fitzsimmons for damages under § 1983 for fabricating evidence during the preliminary investigation.

The fabricated evidence related to a boot print on the door of the Nicarico home, apparently left by the killer when he kicked in the door. Three separate studies by experts from the DuPage County Crime Lab, the Illinois Department of Law Enforcement, and the Kansas Bureau of Identification all failed to make a reliable connection between the print and a pair of boots that Buckley had voluntarily supplied. The respondents (including Fitzsimmons and sheriff's deputies) then obtained a "positive identification" from Louise Robbins, an anthropologist in North Carolina. She was allegedly well known for her willingness to fabricate unreliable expert testimony.

They obtained her opinion during the early stages of the investigation, which was being conducted under the joint supervision and direction of the sheriff and Fitzsimmons, whose police officers and assistant prosecutors were performing essentially the same investigatory functions (262–63).

Was Fitzsimmons acting as an advocate or an investigator when Robbins faked the boot print on the victim's door? The Supreme Court ruled that he was acting as an investigator, because the fabrication took place before there was probable cause to arrest; prior to probable cause to arrest, a prosecutor can't be an advocate.

4. *Kalina v. Fletcher* (1997). Lynne Kalina, a deputy prosecutor in King County, Washington, followed standard practice when she filed three documents to begin second-degree burglary proceedings against Rodney Fletcher based on alleged computer theft from a school. One was an information and the second was a motion for an arrest warrant that required "sworn testimony establishing the grounds for issuing the warrant" (121). To satisfy this requirement, Kalina issued a third document that summarized the evidence supporting the charge. In this "Certification for Determination of Probable Cause" (the equivalent of an affidavit), Kalina "personally vouched for the truth of the facts set forth in the certification under penalty of perjury" (121).

There were two false statements in the affidavit. First, it stated that Fletcher had "never been associated with the school in any manner and did not have permission to enter the school." In fact, he worked in the school and was authorized to enter. She also stated that an electronics store employee identified Fletcher in a mug shot lineup as the person who asked for an appraisal of a computer stolen from the school. The employee didn't identify him.

Based on the affidavit, the trial court found probable cause and issued the warrant. Fletcher was arrested and spent a day in jail. A month later, the charges were dropped on Kalina's motion. Fletcher sued under § 1983 seeking damages from Kalina based on her alleged violations of his constitutional rights (122).

The U.S. Supreme Court ruled that the *preparation* of the three documents, including the preparation of the motion for an arrest warrant was covered by the functional immunity doctrine; Kalina was acting as an advocate and therefore absolutely immune from liability (129). But the Court went on to rule that in *executing* the certification on her own, she was acting as the complaining witness, which any nonlawyer was qualified to do, and which police officers routinely do. Therefore, in executing the certification, she wasn't immune from prosecution (131).

## Hurdles to Suing Officers and Governments

People who sue the government or its officers (even in the most brutal cases) rarely win. Why? According to Allison Patton (1993):

> There are three major weaknesses to section 1983 suits. First, these actions are difficult and expensive to pursue. Since most victims of misconduct are minorities without financial resources, only a small percentage of police brutality incidents become lawsuits. Those victims who are able to get legal representation face a long and arduous litigation process, because police departments rarely settle section 1983 suits. Second, the Supreme Court has severely limited the ability of plaintiffs to enjoin a particular police technique, even one that frequently results in the use of excessive force. Third, juries are more likely to believe the police officer's version of the incident than the plaintiff's. Often there are no witnesses, or each side has an equal number of supporting witnesses. For a variety of sociological and psychological reasons, juries do not want to believe that their police officers are bad people or liars. Thus, plaintiffs rarely win absent help from independent corroborative witnesses or physical evidence. (753–54)

There are other reasons. First, qualified immunity and absolute immunity present legal hurdles. Anthony Amsterdam (1974), defense attorney and constitutional law professor, adds several more:

> Where are the lawyers going to come from to handle these cases for the plaintiffs? . . . What on earth would possess a lawyer to file a claim for damages . . . in an ordinary search-and-seizure case? The prospect of a share in the substantial damages to be expected? The chance to earn a reputation as a police-hating lawyer, so that he can no longer count on straight testimony concerning the length of skid marks in his personal injury cases? The gratitude of his client when his filing of the claim causes the prosecutor to refuse a lesser-included offense plea or to charge priors or pile on "cover" charges? The opportunity to represent his client without fee in these resulting criminal matters?
>
> Police cases are an unadulterated investigative and litigate nightmare. Taking on the police in any tribunal involves a commitment to the most frustrating and thankless legal work I know. And the idea that an unrepresented, inarticulate, prosecution-vulnerable citizen can make a case against a team of professional investigators and testifiers in any tribunal begs belief. Even in a tribunal having recognized responsibilities and some resources to conduct independent investigations, a plaintiff without assiduous counsel devoted to developing his side of the case would be utterly outmastered by the police. No, I think we shall have airings of police searches and seizures on suppression motions or not at all. (430)

Further, the no-affirmative-duty-to-protect rule protects most officials from being sued successfully. Finally, some plaintiffs shouldn't get damages, because their cases are frivolous (Slobogin 1998, 561).

# ADMINISTRATIVE REMEDIES

Until now, we've dealt with court cases aimed at making police and other public officials accountable for their violations of individuals' constitutional rights, but accountability for official misconduct isn't limited to lawsuits. In fact, the most common accountability procedure for all kinds of police misconduct (not just violations of constitutional rights) is administrative review and discipline outside the courts.

There are two types of administrative review:

1. *Internal affairs units (IAU)*. Review of police misconduct by special officers inside police departments

2. *External civilian review*. Review of complaints against police officers with participation by individuals who aren't sworn police officers

## Internal Review

Most large and mid-sized police departments have special internal affairs units (IAU) that review police misconduct. According to Professor Douglas W. Perez (1994, 88–89), a former deputy sheriff, "most cops do not like internal affairs." They don't trust IAU, and some even think IAU investigators are traitors. Still, most officers believe IAU operations are a necessary evil. For one thing, they're a good defense against external review. As the famed Chicago chief of police O. W. Wilson said, "It is clearly apparent that if the police do not take a vigorous stand on the matter of internal investigation, outside groups—such as review boards consisting of laymen and other persons outside the police service—will step into the void" (Griswold 1994, 215–21).

Internal review consists of four successive stages:

1. Intake

2. Investigation

3. Deliberation

4. Disposition

The Internal Affairs Section of the Oakland, California, Police Department is considered an excellent unit, so we'll use it as an example of how internal review proceeds through these four stages. The unit is housed inside the department building. The department intake policy is "anyone anywhere should accept a complaint if a citizen wishes it taken." All complaints alleging excessive force, police corruption, and racial discrimination are followed up (Perez 1994, 92–93).

Then, someone besides the intake officer investigates complaints. The investigator gathers evidence, usually interviewing the officer involved last. If officers refuse to cooperate, they're subject to discipline, such as dismissal for refusing to obey an order of the chief.

Completed investigations go to the IAU supervisor. If the supervisor approves, complaints go to the decision-making, or deliberation, stage. Four possible decisions can be made in the deliberation stage (Figure 11.1):

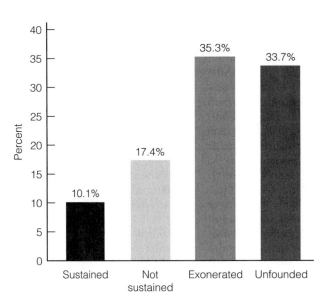

**FIGURE 11.1** Disposition of Excessive Force Complaints

**Source:** Pate and Fridell 1993, 116.

1. *Unfounded*. The investigation proved that the act didn't take place.

2. *Exonerated*. The acts took place, but the investigation proved that they were justified, lawful, and proper.

3. *Not sustained*. The investigation failed to gather enough evidence to clearly prove the allegations in the complaint.

4. *Sustained*. The investigation disclosed enough evidence to clearly prove the allegations in the complaint. (Perez 1994, 96)

If the decision is "unfounded," "exonerated," or "not sustained," the case is disposed of by closing it. If the decision is "sustained," the supervisor recommends disciplinary action. Recommended disciplinary actions ranked from least to most severe include:

1. Reprimand

2. Written reprimand

3. Transfer

4. Retraining

5. Counseling

6. Suspension

7. Demotion

8. Fine

9. Dismissal

After the initial disposition, the case goes up the chain of command inside the department until it finally reaches the chief. In about half the cases, there's a discrepancy between the chief's recommendations and those of the immediate supervisor. These discrepancies are important because the immediate supervisor, usually a sergeant of patrol, works on the street with other patrol officers. The supervisors of sergeants usually go along with the recommendations of sergeants. Chiefs of police, on the other hand, are removed from the day-to-day street operations of patrol officers and their immediate supervisors. They have departmentwide perspectives and are responsible to "local political elites" for their department's performance. So chiefs may find the disciplinary penalty too light and make it heavier. Figure 11.2 shows the distribution of disciplinary measures taken in a national sample of city police departments.

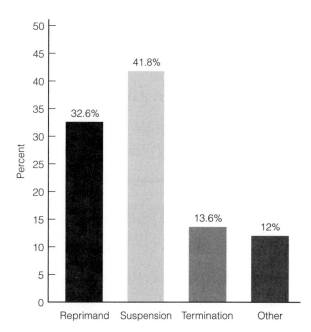

**FIGURE 11.2** Distribution of Disciplinary Actions
**Source:** Pate and Fridell 1993, 116.

## External Review

The basic objection to internal review is police shouldn't police themselves. To the question, "Who will watch the watchmen?" the answer is, "Not the watchmen!" So external review has grown. In **external review**, individuals who aren't sworn police officers participate in the review of complaints against the police. Usually called "civilian review," it has sparked controversy for nearly half a century.

Police oppose external review because it interferes with their independence; they have no confidence outsiders know enough about police work to review it; and they know outside scrutiny could pierce the **blue curtain**, the wall of protection that hides their "real" work from public view.

Strong police unions, chiefs who opposed external review, and the creation of internal review procedures (discussed in the last section) successfully prevented external review during the 1960s, when it became a popular proposal among some liberal reformers and citizen groups. However, by the early 1990s, 72 percent of the 50 largest cities had created some form of civilian review procedures (Walker and Bumpus 1992, 1, 3–4). Let's look at the types of external review and how well review by civilians has worked.

***The Types of External Review*** The differences among civilian review procedures all turn on the point in the process when nonofficers participate. The possible entry points are:

1. The initial investigation to collect the facts

2. The review of the investigation reports

3. The recommendation for disposition to the chief

4. The review of decisions made by the chief

No matter at what point nonofficers participate, civilian review boards can only recommend disciplinary action to police chiefs, because under civil service laws only police chiefs can decide on disciplinary action against police officers (Walker and Bumpus 1992, 3–4).

***The Effectiveness of Civilian Review*** Does civilian review work? The answer depends on the definition and the measures of effectiveness. "Effectiveness" can mean at least four things, all of which are important in determining the value of civilian review procedures:

1. Maintaining effective control of police misconduct

2. Providing resolutions to complaints that satisfy individual complainants

3. Preserving public confidence in the police

4. Influencing police management by providing "feedback from consumers" (Walker and Bumpus 1992, 8)

It's difficult to measure the effectiveness of civilian review because official data are ambiguous. Take the number of complaints, for example. A large number of complaints might mean a large volume of police misconduct, but it can also indicate confidence in the review procedures. Following the Rodney King incident in Los Angeles, observers noted that San Francisco, a city known for its strong review procedures, received more complaints than the much larger city of Los Angeles.

In Los Angeles, the Independent Commission heard a number of citizen complaints that the LAPD created "significant hurdles" to filing complaints, that they were afraid of the process, and that the complaint process was "unnecessarily difficult or impossible." Further, the ACLU collected evidence suggesting that the LAPD "actively discouraged the filing of complaints." The beating of Rodney King, in fact, would never have come to public attention without the video, according to the Independent Commission. This is because, according to the commission, the efforts of Rodney King's brother Paul to file a complaint following the beating were "frustrated" by the LAPD (Pate and Fridell 1993, 39).

The numbers and rates of complaints are also difficult to assess because we don't know the numbers of incidents where people don't file complaints. In one national survey, of all the people who said the police mistreated them, only 30 percent said they filed complaints. One thing, however, is clear. Misconduct isn't distributed evenly among individuals and neighborhoods. In one survey, only 40 percent of the addresses in one city had any contact with the police in a year. Most contacts between private individuals and the police occur in poor neighborhoods. In New York City, the rate of complaints ranges from 1 to 5 for every 10,000 people, depending on the neighborhood.

Official data have consistently indicated racial minority males are disproportionately represented among complainants. So the perception of a pattern of police harassment is a major factor in conflict between the police and racial minority communities (Walker and Bumpus 1992, 10).

Whatever the ambiguity of numbers and rates in the official statistics, observers have noted civilian review procedures rarely sustain complaints. Furthermore, the rates of complaints sustained in civilian review are about the same as the rates in internal affairs units (Walker and Bumpus 1992, 16–17).

# SUMMARY

## I. Remedies against Official Misconduct
   A. Remedies for official law-breaking are separate from trials of criminal defendants (discussed in Chapter 10).
   B. Two kinds of actions hold officers and government accountable for misconduct:
      1. *Criminal actions.* Officers are prosecuted for criminal acts.
      2. *Civil actions.* Officers, departments, and governments are sued for damages and/or injunctions.
   C. Remedies aren't mutually exclusive; all can be pursued at the same time.

## II. Criminal Actions
   A. Most police misconduct can be a crime.
   B. Most police officers aren't charged with, convicted of, or punished for criminal actions because:
      1. Criminal intent doesn't exist, or it's difficult to prove beyond a reasonable doubt.
      2. Officers who "honestly believe" their acts are lawful don't have criminal intent.
      3. Prosecutors and juries are unwilling to convict officers for "doing their job."
      4. There's a lack of sympathy for possible criminals and/or those they associate with.

### III. Civil Actions

A. Most plaintiffs who sue officers and governments want compensation for injuries caused by police misconduct.

B. Plaintiffs can sue any or all of the following:
1. Individual officers and their superiors (chiefs and sheriffs)
2. Departments (police and sheriff's)
3. Governments responsible for officers and departments (municipalities, counties, states, and the U.S. government)

C. They can sue in U.S. courts and state courts.

D. Laws governing damages vary, depending on whether defendants are
1. Individuals or departments and governments
2. Federal or state, county, and municipal officers, departments, and governments

E. Plaintiffs can sue federal officers and the U.S. government.
1. Suing individual officers is a private right, called a "constitutional tort," or "*Bivens*, action."
   a. Individual federal officers are liable for their acts that violate plaintiffs' constitutional rights if plaintiffs can prove:
      (1) Officers acted with apparent legal authority.
      (2) Their actions deprived plaintiffs of their constitutional rights.
   b. It's difficult to win *Bivens* cases because of the defense of qualified immunity.
      (1) Officers acted with objective reasonableness.
      (2) Reasonableness is measured by legal rules clearly established at the time the officers acted.
      (3) Courts want to preserve officers' discretion to do their job.
      (4) Courts also want to prevent frivolous lawsuits.
2. Plaintiffs can pursue FTCA actions to sue the U.S. government.
   a. Sovereign immunity is waived in Federal Tort Claims Act (FTCA).
   b. The U.S. government's "deep pockets" make FTCA actions attractive.
   c. Plaintiffs can pursue both FTCA and *Bivens* actions.

F. Plaintiffs can pursue both state and U.S. Civil Rights actions against state officers.
1. State tort actions
   a. Most illegal police acts are also state torts.
   b. Tort law gives injured plaintiffs the right to recover damages.
   c. State tort actions balance the need for officer discretion and protecting officers.
   d. Officers are liable only for "willful or deliberate wrong" (defense of official immunity).
2. U.S. Civil Rights actions (§ 1983 actions)
   a. Plaintiffs can go into federal courts to sue state, county, and municipal officers for violations of their constitutional rights.
   b. Elements of § 1983 include:
      (1) Officers acted within the scope of their employment ("under color of law")
      (2) Officers' actions caused deprivation of a constitutional right.
   c. Liability is for deliberate (not negligent or accidental) acts of officers.

        d. Liability may be limited by the qualified immunity defense (same as *Bivens* and FTCA).

   G. Suing state and local governments

     1. State tort actions against state and local governments

       a. State and local governments are liable for their employees' torts (*respondeat superior*).

       b. Not all states have adopted *respondeat superior*. Those governments have the same defense as individual officers (vicarious official immunity).

       c. Liability extends only to acts within the scope of employment.

     2. U.S. Civil Rights actions against state and local government

       a. Elements of state and local government liability include:

         (1) Officers acted according to either officially approved written policies or unwritten customs.

         (2) Officers' actions violated the plaintiff's constitutional right.

       b. It's more complicated to prove government liability than an individual's (even though proving individual liability is also complicated).

   H. Law enforcement has no affirmative constitutional duty to protect individuals from each other.

     1. This is known as the "no-affirmative-duty-to-protect rule."

     2. Only individuals in custody have a constitutional right to protection (special-relationship exception).

     3. Some U.S. Courts of Appeals have adopted a state-created-danger exception to the no-affirmative-duty-to-protect rule.

     4. Elements of this narrow exception include:

       a. Officers created a danger of violent harm to the plaintiff (not to the general public).

       b. Officers knew or should have known their actions encouraged this plaintiff to rely on their actions.

       c. The danger created by the officers caused actual harm from violence or increased the plaintiff's vulnerability to harm from violence.

   I. Suing judges and prosecutors

     1. Judges have absolute immunity from lawsuits.

     2. The only remedy is either impeaching or voting them out of office.

     3. Prosecutors have absolute immunity when acting as advocates for the state in criminal prosecutions.

     4. They have limited liability when acting as administrators or investigators.

   J. Hurdles to suing officers and the government

     1. People who sue the government or its officers rarely win.

     2. Reasons for failure include:

       a. It's expensive.

       b. It takes a long time.

       c. Juries are more likely to believe police officers than plaintiffs.

       d. Officials have absolute, qualified, and/or official immunity.

       e. Officers have no affirmative duty to protect.

       f. Some cases are frivolous.

**IV. Administrative Remedies**

   A. There are two types of administrative remedies: internal review and external civilian review.

B. Internal review is by internal affairs units (IAU) made up of department officers.
   1. Internal review has four stages:
      a. *Intake.* Intake officers accept complaints.
      b. *Investigation.* Other officers gather evidence and interview witnesses.
      c. *Deliberation.* Other officers weigh evidence.
      d. *Disposition.* Making a decision involves three stages.
         (1) *First stage.* The deliberating officers decide among four dispositions:
             (a) *Unfounded.* The act didn't take place.
             (b) *Exonerated.* The act took place but was justified, lawful, and proper.
             (c) *Not sustained.* There's not enough evidence to prove the allegations in the complaint.
             (d) *Sustained.* The evidence proved the allegations.
         (2) *Next stage.* The officers recommend disciplinary action for sustained complaints.
             (a) Oral reprimand
             (b) Written reprimand
             (c) Transfer
             (d) Retraining
             (e) Counseling
             (f) Suspension
             (g) Demotion
             (h) Fine
             (i) Dismissal
         (3) *Final stage.* The recommendations are forwarded and moved up the chain of command to the chief for final disposition.
   2. Internal review has its critics.
      a. Police can't police themselves.
      b. Some parts of the public don't accept the legitimacy of self-supervision.
C. External review was set up to overcome criticism of internal review: "Who will watch the watchman?"
   1. Civilians outside the department review (or participate in reviewing) complaints.
   2. Police don't like civilian review.
      a. It interferes with police independence.
      b. Outsiders don't understand police work.
      c. It pierces the "blue curtain" that hides "real" police work from view.
   3. The point in reviews when civilians (nonofficers) participate varies.
      a. Collect facts
      b. Review investigation report
      c. Recommend disciplinary action to chief
      d. Review chief's disposition
   4. Civil service laws require that only chiefs have the legal authority to order disciplinary action.
   5. How effective is civilian review?
      a. The definition of "effectiveness" varies.
         (1) Controlling police misconduct
         (2) Resolving complaints to satisfy complainants

(3) Preserving public confidence in police

(4) Influencing police management by providing "feedback" from citizens

b. Civilian review rarely sustains complaints.

c. Sustained rates are similar to those in internal review.

d. The increased volume of complaints can mean either the level of misconduct or the level of confidence in the review process has risen (San Francisco, for example).

e. The number of incidents not reported isn't known.

# REVIEW QUESTIONS

1. How likely is it that police officers will be charged and convicted of criminal conduct? Why?

2. Summarize the *Bivens v. Six Unnamed FBI Agents* case, and explain its significance.

3. Identify the two elements of the qualified immunity defense, and explain why the test is so easy for officers to pass.

4. What specific remedy does the Federal Tort Claims Act (FTCA) provide plaintiffs, and why is it attractive to plaintiffs?

5. Identify and describe the differences between two kinds of state civil lawsuits against individual state officers.

6. Describe the balance that has to be struck in state cases against state officers.

7. Identify two elements plaintiffs in § 1983 actions against state and local law enforcement officers have to prove.

8. Identify and describe two limits the U.S. Supreme Court placed on § 1983 actions against state and local officers.

9. Describe the extent and limits of state tort actions against state and local governments.

10. Identify the elements in the balancing test used to decide whether to grant the defense of vicarious official immunity.

11. According to the U.S. Supreme Court in *Monell v. New York City Department of Social Services,* what two elements do plaintiffs have to prove to succeed in suing local government units?

12. According to the U.S. Supreme Court, what (if any) constitutional duty do law enforcement officers have to protect private individuals from each other?

13. Identify and explain the three elements in the state-created-danger exception to the no-affirmative-duty-to-protect rule.

14. Can you sue a judge for damages? A prosecutor? Explain.

15. Identify and explain the reasons for the hurdles plaintiffs have to overcome when they sue officers and the governments in charge of them.

16. Identify and briefly describe the two types of administrative remedies against police misconduct.

17. Identify and describe the stages, possible dispositions, and disciplinary actions in internal review procedures.

18. Identify the basic objection to internal review. How is external review supposed to overcome the objection?

19. Identify three reasons why police oppose civilian review.

20. Does civilian review work? Explain.

## KEY TERMS

# Court Proceedings I: Before Trial

## MAIN POINTS

- After arrest, interrogation, and identification procedures at police stations, responsibility for criminal procedure changes hands from police to lawyers in courts.
- The power of prosecutors to transform suspects into defendants by charging them with crimes is the starting point of court proceedings.
- The "unreasonable seizure" ban in the Fourth Amendment commands that suspects detained after arrest be taken "quickly" before a magistrate to decide whether there's probable cause to back up their detention.
- The decision to bail or release defendants balances the needs to guarantee the appearance of defendants in court and protect public safety against the rights of defendants who haven't been convicted of crimes.
- The U.S. Supreme Court has interpreted the right to counsel to include the right to *effective* counsel for all defendants charged with all crimes with penalties of actual incarceration.
- Before cases go to trial, the strength of the government's case is tested to make sure the public's resources and the hardships on defendants and their families are based on enough evidence.
- If the government passes the test of having enough evidence to go to trial, defendants have to come to court to hear and answer the charges against them.
- Before the trial begins, decisions that don't require a trial are disposed of in pretrial motions.

12

*The prosecutor's power to charge gives her more control over life, liberty, and reputation than any other person in America.*

U.S. Supreme Court Justice Robert Jackson (1940, 3)

*In all criminal prosecutions, the accused shall enjoy the right . . . to have the assistance of counsel for his defense.*

U.S. Constitution, Amendment VI

*Excessive bail shall not be required.*

U.S. Constitution, Amendment VIII

*In all criminal prosecutions, the accused shall enjoy the right to a speedy and public trial [in] the state and district wherein the crime shall have been committed.*

U.S. Constitution, Amendment VI

After arrest, interrogation, and identification procedures, the action moves first from the police station to prosecutors' and defense attorneys' offices and then to the courts. In the interval between arrest and the first time defendants appear in court, both the police and the prosecutor have to make critical decisions.

First, the police decide if the case should go forward or be dropped. Police take the strong cases they want prosecuted to the prosecutor's office. Prosecutors then make their own judgments about how to dispose of these cases. If they decide to prosecute, they start formal court proceedings by filing a complaint, information, or indictment.

All three proceedings have a single goal: to test the objective basis for the decision to charge. In these proceedings, either judges or grand juries consider the evidence the government has collected to prove its case. If the government has enough evidence, defendants have to appear and answer the criminal charges against them (called **arraignment**).

The decision to start criminal court proceedings is not just a technicality. According to the U.S. Supreme Court in *Kirby v. Illinois* (1972):

> The initiation of judicial criminal proceedings is far from a mere formalism. It is the starting point of our whole system of adversary criminal justice. For it is only then that the Government has committed itself to prosecute, and only then that the adverse positions of Government and defendant have solidified. It is then that a defendant finds himself faced with the prosecutorial forces of organized society, and immersed in the intricacies of substantive and procedural criminal law. It is this point, therefore, that marks the commencement of the "criminal prosecutions." (689)

In this chapter, we'll look at the decision to charge; the rules regulating probable cause to detain; what happens during defendants' first appearance in court after being charged; bail and pretrial detention; the right to counsel; testing the government's case in grand jury and preliminary hearings; bringing defendants to court to hear and answer the charges against them (arraignment); and pretrial motions: double jeopardy, a speedy trial, a change of venue, and the suppression of illegally obtained evidence.

# THE DECISION TO CHARGE

Once the police bring a case to the prosecutor, lawyers take over the management of the criminal process. Although the police fade into the background, they don't disappear. Lawyers need them to clarify, investigate further, and perhaps testify in court. Prosecutors are likely to take at face value the recommendations from officers with a reputation for establishing "good" cases. They're just as likely to discount cases from officers with poor track records.

Prosecutors drop some cases without further action. If they don't think they can prove the case, they drop it and release the suspect outright. Even if they think they can prove their case, prosecutors don't automatically charge suspects. Why? Prosecutors have dual roles in our justice system. They represent the public in prosecuting criminal cases, but they're also officers of the court. In that capacity, their mission is to "do justice"—and doing justice doesn't always mean charging and prosecuting suspects.

In *People v. Camargo* (1986), the defendant was charged with the criminal sale and possession of cocaine. By the time he was indicted, the defendant was in an advanced stage of AIDS and related complicating illnesses. He had Pneumocystis carinii pneumonia. The virus had invaded his brain and his stomach, and peripheral nerve damage caused him pain and suffering to the extent that doctors ordered him to limit his physical exercise to sitting in a chair for one hour a day. His doctors' prognosis was death within three to four months.

The government dropped the case, because "it did not appear that the interest of justice would be substantially served by the defendant's continued prosecution under this indictment." According to the court:

> The uncompromising rampage of the multiple disease processes have condemned this defendant to a painful, imminent death. When the rationale for incarceration becomes unjustifiable because of . . . a deadly disease, it becomes imperative to allow the sufferer to live his last days in the best circumstances possible and with dignity and compassion. (1007)

In the interests of justice, prosecutors also can divert suspects into a program for community service, restitution, substance abuse, or family violence treatment. In these **diversion cases**, prosecutors agree to drop the case before formal judicial proceedings begin if suspects participate in and complete these programs. The number of cases prosecutors decide not to pursue ranges from a few in some jurisdictions to nearly half of all cases in others (Boland and others 1988).

Several reasons determine the **decision to charge**—to start formal court proceedings by filing a complaint, information, or indictment. Most important is the strength of the case against defendants. For example, if prosecutors don't have enough evidence to prosecute—no witnesses or weak witnesses, poor physical evidence, and no confessions or other admissions by suspects—they won't charge.

Witnesses might be neither reliable nor convincing. Witness problems increase if victims know their assailants in violent crimes. In over half of these cases, witnesses and victims refuse to cooperate because they're either afraid or have a change of heart over prosecuting people they know (and often care about).

Sometimes, prosecutors can't use evidence because the police seized it illegally (see Chapter 10). But contrary to the popular belief that many guilty criminals go unpunished because of the exclusionary rule, fewer than 2 percent of all cases (and practically no violent crime cases) are dropped because of it (Davies 1983, n. 89; Nardulli 1983).

Selective prosecution is another reason behind the decision to charge. Lack of resources makes it impossible to prosecute every case, even when prosecutors have enough evidence and it's in the interests of justice to prosecute. Time and money make prosecutors set priorities: suspects guilty of petty thefts go to restitution to allow prosecutions for armed robbery; prosecuting violent sex offenses takes precedence over prostitution; and charging a few well-known tax evaders serves as examples to deter tax evasion.

According to some critics, selective prosecution cuts into the legislature's power to make the laws. Others argue that selectively prosecuting only some individuals in a category—for example, "fat cats" or notorious tax evaders—undermines impartial law enforcement.

Which (if any) of the following suspects should a prosecutor selectively charge?

1. A student stole a cassette recorder to record his criminal procedure class because the professor talks too fast. He works part time to pay for school, and, although he could've paid for the recorder, it would've been difficult. He has never been in trouble with the law before and says he'll pay for the recorder.

2. A woman who works only occasionally stole a cordless phone for a friend who agreed to pay $35, half the phone's value. The woman has taken compact discs, tape cassettes, and an answering machine from the same store within the past six months.

3. A 50-year-old woman slipped a pair of stereo earphones into her purse. The woman is wealthy and indignantly denied that she intended to steal the earphones. She told the detective she put the device in her bag because she wanted to pick up some film, batteries, and other small items and simply forgot she had put it there.

You might want to review your decisions after completing this chapter.

Despite criticisms of the extent of prosecutorial power, U.S. Supreme Court Justice Robert Jackson's words in 1940 are still true: The prosecutor's power to charge gives her "more control over life, liberty, and reputation than any other person in America" (3). So except for violating due process by vindictively prosecuting individuals or violating equal protection by selectively prosecuting members of groups (Chapter 2)—violations rarely charged and hardly ever successfully when they are—the prosecutor's discretionary power to charge is practically unlimited.

# PROBABLE CAUSE TO DETAIN SUSPECTS

An urgent situation arises when the following circumstances combine: defendants are arrested without warrants; they have no lawyers because they're too poor to hire one; they haven't been charged with any crime; and they're locked up in jail. The U.S. Constitution and state laws command that independent magistrates (not police officers whose zeal to root out crime might color their objectivity) have to decide *soon* whether there's probable cause to back up this severe deprivation of liberty.

Of course, protecting public safety requires that police have the power to arrest suspects before a judge has decided there was probable cause for the arrest. Otherwise, suspects who turn out to be criminals might escape, commit further crimes, or destroy evidence. But once suspects are in jail, these dangers evaporate. Now, the guarantees of due process and protection of innocent people take over. In *County of Riverside v. McLaughlin* (1991), the U.S. Supreme Court spoke about "reconciling these competing interests":

> On the one hand, States have a strong interest in protecting public safety by taking into custody those persons who are reasonably suspected of having engaged in criminal activity, even where there has been no opportunity for a prior judicial determination of probable cause. On the other hand, prolonged detention based on incorrect or unfounded suspicion may unjustly "imperil a suspect's job, interrupt his source of income, and impair his family relationships." We sought to balance these competing concerns by holding that States "must provide a fair and reliable determination of probable cause as a condition for any significant pretrial restraint of liberty, and this determination must be made by a judicial officer either before or promptly after arrest." (52)

Before we go on, let's clear up something that might confuse you—there are two kinds of probable cause. **Probable cause to detain a suspect** is decided at a court proceeding called the **first appearance** (sometimes the "probable cause hearing"). **Probable cause to go to trial** is decided in preliminary hearings or grand jury proceedings. Probable cause to detain (Chapter 5) requires fewer facts than probable cause to go to trial.

In *Gerstein v. Pugh* (1975), the U.S. Supreme Court decided that the Fourth Amendment ban on "unreasonable seizure" demands that suspects locked up in jail be taken "promptly" to a magistrate to decide whether there are enough facts to back up the detention.

The question is, How prompt is fast enough to satisfy the Fourth Amendment? Lower federal courts and state courts for a long time said the Fourth Amendment gives the police enough time to complete the "administrative steps incident to arrest." This usually means the police can do all of the following before they take suspects to court (*Sanders v. City of Houston* 1982, 700):

1. Complete paperwork

2. Search the suspect

3. Conduct an inventory search

4. Inventory property found

5. Fingerprint the suspect

6. Photograph the suspect

7. Check for a possible prior criminal record

8. Test laboratory samples

9. Interrogate the suspect

10. Check an alibi

11. Conduct a lineup

12. Compare the crime with similar crimes

Some jurisdictions are more specific; they spell out exactly how much time the police get to finish the administrative steps. Depending on the jurisdiction, times range from 24 to 36 hours (Brandes 1989). The U.S. Supreme Court prescribed a flexible definition of "promptly" in our next case excerpt, *County of Riverside v. McLaughlin* (1991).

---

## CASE  *Was Judicial Determination of Probable Cause "Prompt"?*

### *County of Riverside v. McLaughlin*
500 U.S. 44 (1991)

### HISTORY

Donald Lee McLaughlin and others brought a **class action** [*an action in which one person or a small group of people represents the interests of a larger group*] under 42 U.S.C. § 1983,

challenging how the County of Riverside, California, handles probable cause determinations for individuals arrested without a warrant. The U.S. District court granted a preliminary injunction. The Ninth Circuit U.S. Court of Appeals affirmed. The U.S. Supreme Court granted certiorari, vacated the judgment of the Court of Appeals, and remanded the case.

O'CONNOR, J., JOINED BY REHNQUIST, C.J., AND WHITE, KENNEDY, AND SOUTER, JJ.

# FACTS

In August 1987, Donald Lee McLaughlin filed a complaint in the U.S. District Court for the Central District of California. The complaint alleged that McLaughlin was then currently incarcerated in the Riverside County Jail and had not received a probable cause determination. He requested "an order and judgment requiring that the defendants and the County of Riverside provide in-custody arrestees, arrested without warrants, prompt probable cause, bail and arraignment hearings." A second complaint named three additional plaintiffs—Johnny E. James, Diana Ray Simon, and Michael Scott Hyde. . . . The complaint alleged that each of the named plaintiffs had been arrested without a warrant, had received neither prompt probable cause nor bail hearings, and was still in custody. . . .

In March 1989, plaintiffs asked the District Court to issue a preliminary injunction requiring the County to provide all persons arrested without a warrant a judicial determination of probable cause within 36 hours of arrest. The District Court issued the injunction, holding that the County's existing practice violated this Court's decision in *Gerstein*. Without discussion, the District Court adopted a rule that the County provide probable cause determinations within 36 hours of arrest, except in exigent circumstances.

The court "retained jurisdiction indefinitely" to ensure that the County established new procedures that complied with the injunction. The U.S. Court of Appeals for the Ninth Circuit consolidated this case with another challenging an identical preliminary injunction issued against the County of San Bernardino. On November 8, 1989, the Court of Appeals affirmed the order granting the preliminary injunction against Riverside County. . . .

The Court of Appeals . . . determined that the County's policy of providing probable cause determinations at arraignment within 48 hours was "not in accord with *Gerstein*'s requirement of a determination 'promptly after arrest'" because no more than 36 hours were needed "to complete the administrative steps incident to arrest." The Ninth Circuit thus joined the Fourth and Seventh Circuits in interpreting *Gerstein* as requiring a probable cause determination immediately following completion of the administrative procedures incident to arrest. By contrast, the Second Circuit understands *Gerstein* to "stress the need for flexibility" and to permit States to combine probable cause determinations with other pretrial proceedings. We granted certiorari to resolve this conflict among the Circuits as to what constitutes a "prompt" probable cause determination under *Gerstein*.

# OPINION

. . . In *Gerstein v. Pugh* (1975), this Court held unconstitutional Florida procedures under which persons arrested without a warrant could remain in police custody for 30 days or more without a judicial determination of probable cause. In reaching this conclusion we attempted to reconcile important competing interests. On the one hand, States have a strong interest in protecting public safety by taking into custody those persons who are reasonably suspected of having engaged in criminal activity, even where there has been no opportunity for a prior judicial determination of probable cause.

On the other hand, prolonged detention based on incorrect or unfounded suspicion may unjustly "imperil a suspect's job, interrupt his source of income, and impair his family relationships." We sought to balance these competing concerns by holding that States "must provide a fair and reliable determination of probable cause as a condition for any significant pretrial restraint of liberty, and this determination must be made by a judicial officer either before or promptly after arrest." The Court thus established a "practical compromise" between the rights of individuals and the realities of law enforcement. . . . We left it to the individual States to integrate prompt probable cause determinations into their differing systems of pretrial procedures. . . .

Inherent in *Gerstein*'s invitation to the States to experiment and adapt was the recognition that the Fourth Amendment does not compel an immediate determination of probable cause upon completing the administrative steps incident to arrest. Plainly, if a probable cause hearing is constitutionally compelled the moment a suspect is finished being "booked," there is no room whatsoever for "flexibility and experimentation by the States."

Incorporating probable cause determinations "into the procedure for setting bail or fixing other conditions of pretrial release"—which *Gerstein* explicitly contemplated—would be impossible. Waiting even a few hours so that a bail hearing or arraignment could take place at the same time as the probable cause determination would amount to a constitutional violation. *Clearly*, Gerstein is not that inflexible. . . .

But flexibility has its limits; *Gerstein* is not a blank check. A State has no legitimate interest in detaining for extended periods individuals who have been arrested without probable cause. The Court recognized in *Gerstein* that a person arrested without a warrant is entitled to a fair and reliable determination of probable cause and that this determination must be made promptly. Unfortunately, as lower court decisions applying *Gerstein* have demonstrated, it is not enough to say that probable cause determinations must be "prompt." This vague standard simply has not provided sufficient guidance. Instead, it has led to a flurry of systemic challenges to city and county practices, putting federal judges in the role of making legislative judgments and overseeing local jail house operations.

Our task in this case is to articulate more clearly the boundaries of what is permissible under the Fourth Amendment. Although we hesitate to announce that the Constitution compels a specific time limit, it is important to provide some degree of certainty so that States and counties may establish procedures with confidence that they fall within constitutional bounds. Taking into account the competing interests articulated in *Gerstein*, we believe that a jurisdiction that provides judicial determinations of probable cause within 48 hours of arrest will, as a general matter, comply with the promptness requirement of *Gerstein*. For this reason, such jurisdictions will be immune from systemic challenges.

This is not to say that the probable cause determination in a particular case passes constitutional muster simply because it is provided within 48 hours. Such a hearing may nonetheless violate *Gerstein* if the arrested individual can prove that his or her probable cause determination was delayed unreasonably. Examples of unreasonable delay are delays for the purpose of gathering additional evidence to justify the arrest, a delay motivated by ill will against the arrested individual, or delay for delay's sake. In evaluating whether the delay in a particular case is unreasonable, however, courts must allow a substantial degree of flexibility. Courts cannot ignore the often unavoidable delays in transporting arrested persons from one facility to another, handling late-night bookings where no magistrate is readily available, obtaining the presence of an arresting officer who may be busy processing other suspects or securing the premises of an arrest, and other practical realities.

Where an arrested individual does not receive a probable cause determination within 48 hours, the calculus changes. In such a case, the arrested individual does not bear the burden of proving an unreasonable delay. Rather, the burden shifts to the government to demonstrate the existence of a bona fide emergency or other extraordinary circumstance. The fact that in a particular case it may take longer than 48 hours to consolidate pretrial proceedings does not qualify as an extraordinary circumstance. Nor, for that matter, do intervening weekends. A jurisdiction that chooses to offer combined proceedings must do so as soon as is reasonably feasible, but in no event later than 48 hours after arrest. . . .

For the reasons we have articulated, we conclude that Riverside County is entitled to combine probable cause determinations with arraignments. The record indicates, however, that the County's current policy and practice do not comport fully with the principles we have outlined. The County's current policy is to offer combined proceedings within two days, exclusive of Saturdays, Sundays, or holidays. As a result, persons arrested on Thursdays may have to wait until the following Monday before they receive a probable cause determination. The delay is even longer if there is an intervening holiday. Thus, the County's regular practice exceeds the 48-hour period we deem constitutionally permissible, meaning that the County is not immune from systemic challenges, such as this class action.

As to arrests that occur early in the week, the County's practice is that "arraignments usually take place on the last day" possible. There may well be legitimate reasons for this practice; alternatively, this may constitute delay for delay's sake. We leave it to the Court of Appeals and the District Court, on remand, to make this determination.

The judgment of the Court of Appeals is vacated and the case is REMANDED for further proceedings consistent with this opinion.

# DISSENT

## SCALIA, J.

. . . "The Fourth Amendment requires a judicial determination of probable cause as a prerequisite to extended restraint of liberty," "either before or promptly after arrest." Though how "promptly" we did not say, it was plain enough that the requirement left no room for intentional delay unrelated to the completion of "the administrative steps incident to arrest." Plain enough, at least, that all but one federal court considering the question understood *Gerstein* that way.

Today, however, the Court discerns something quite different in *Gerstein*. It finds that the plain statements set forth above (not to mention the common law tradition of liberty upon which they were based) were trumped by the implication of a later dictum in the case which, according to the Court, manifests a "recognition that the Fourth Amendment does not compel an immediate determination of probable cause upon completing the administrative steps incident to arrest." . . .

Determining the outer boundary of reasonableness is an . . . objective and . . . manageable task. We were asked to undertake it in *Gerstein*, but declined—wisely, I think, since we had before us little data to support any figure we might choose. . . . The data available are enough to convince me, however, that certainly no more than 24 hours is needed.

With one exception, no federal court considering the question has regarded 24 hours as an inadequate amount of time to complete arrest procedures, and with the same exception every court actually setting a limit for probable cause determination based on those procedures has selected 24 hours. (The exception would not count Sunday within the 24-hour limit.) . . . And state courts have similarly applied a 24-hour limit under state statutes requiring presentment without "unreasonable delay." . . .

. . . A few weeks before issuance of today's opinion there appeared in the *Washington Post* the story of protracted litigation arising from the arrest of a student who entered a restaurant in Charlottesville, Virginia, one evening to look for some friends. Failing to find them, he tried to leave—but refused to pay a $5 fee (required by the restaurant's posted rules) for failing to return a red tab he had been issued to keep track of his orders. According to the story, he "was taken by police to the Charlottesville jail" at the restaurant's request. "There, a magistrate refused to issue an arrest warrant," and he was released.

That is how it used to be; but not, according to today's decision, how it must be in the future. If the Fourth Amendment meant then what the Court says it does now, the student could lawfully have been held for as long as it would have taken to arrange for his arraignment, up to a maximum of 48 hours.

Justice Story wrote that the Fourth Amendment "is little more than the affirmance of a great constitutional doctrine of the common law." It should not become less than that. One hears the complaint, nowadays, that the Fourth Amendment has become constitutional law for the guilty; that it benefits the career criminal (through the exclusionary rule) often and directly, but the ordinary citizen remotely if at all.

By failing to protect the innocent arrestee, today's opinion reinforces that view. The common law rule of prompt hearing had as its primary beneficiaries the innocent—not those whose fully justified convictions must be overturned to scold the police; nor those who avoid conviction because the evidence, while convincing, does not establish guilt beyond a reasonable doubt; but those so blameless that there was not even good reason to arrest them. While in recent years we have invented novel applications of the Fourth Amendment to release the unquestionably guilty, we today repudiate one of its core applications so that the presumptively innocent may be left in jail.

Hereafter, a law-abiding citizen wrongfully arrested may be compelled to await the grace of a Dickensian bureaucratic machine, as it churns its cycle for up to two days—never once given the opportunity to show a judge that there is absolutely no reason to hold him, that a mistake has been made. In my view, this is the image of a system of justice that has lost its ancient sense of priority, a system that few Americans would recognize as our own.

### Questions

1. What reasons does the Court give for deciding that under ordinary circumstances, 48 hours is a reasonable time to satisfy the Fourth Amendment interest in providing a prompt determination of probable cause?

2. What interests did the Court balance in making its decision?

3. What administrative steps and specific circumstances did the Court consider in balancing these interests?

4. What does the history of the common law have to do with a decision made in 1991?

5. What rule would you adopt? Why?

## THE FIRST APPEARANCE

The **criminal complaint** (the document that formally charges defendants with specific crimes) authorizes magistrates to conduct the first appearance. Magistrates complete four tasks at the first appearance:

1. Inform defendants of the charges against them

2. Inform defendants of their constitutional rights

3. Set bail or detain suspects

4. Appoint attorneys for indigent defendants

Felony defendants rarely enter a plea at their first appearance; they wait until their *arraignment* (a proceeding that orders defendants to come to court and plead to the charges against them). Misdemeanor defendants usually plead (almost always guilty) at their first appearance, especially if the penalty is a small fine.

When suspects—now called "defendants"—first appear in court, magistrates tell them the charges against them. If defendants don't have a lawyer present, the court gives them copies of the complaint, the police report, and other papers supporting the complaint. The court also informs defendants of their constitutional rights.

Informing defendants of their constitutional rights follows this typical court rule in Minnesota's Rules of Criminal Procedure (Minnesota Rules of Criminal Procedure 2006, Rule 5.01):

The judge, judicial officer, or other duly authorized personnel shall advise the defendant substantially as follows:

(a) That the defendant is not required to say anything or submit to interrogation and that anything the defendant says may be used against the defendant in this or any subsequent proceeding;

(b) That the defendant has a right to counsel in all subsequent proceedings, including police line-ups and interrogations, and if the defendant appears without counsel and is financially unable to afford counsel, that counsel will forthwith be appointed without cost to the defendant charged with an offense punishable upon conviction by incarceration;

(c) That the defendant has a right to communicate with defense counsel and that a continuance will be granted if necessary to enable defendant to obtain or speak to counsel;

(d) That the defendant has a right to a jury trial or a trial to the court;

(e) That if the offense is a misdemeanor, the defendant may either plead guilty or not guilty, or demand a complaint prior to entering a plea;

(f) That if the offense is a designated gross misdemeanor as defined in Rule 1.04(b) and a complaint has not yet been made and filed, a complaint must be issued within 10 days if the defendant is not in custody or within 48 hours if the defendant is in custody.

The judge, judicial officer, or other duly authorized personnel may advise a number of defendants at once of these rights, but each defendant shall be asked individually before arraignment whether the defendant heard and understood these rights as explained earlier.

# BAIL AND PRETRIAL DETENTION

Most defendants (in some places more than 90 percent) are released on bail while they wait for trial or the results of a plea bargain (see Chapter 13). Still, locking up even 10 percent of defendants adds to the never-ending problem of crowded jails.

Pretrial detention can last for quite a while (more than 30 days for 33 percent of detainees; more than 90 days for 20 percent), and detention costs money ($30+ a day for every defendant). About 20 percent of defendants, charged with petty offenses, are released without even appearing before judges. These defendants receive a citation release (like a traffic ticket), or they're released after posting bond according to bail schedules that list amounts for specific offenses (Toborg 1981).

Judges can attach a variety of conditions to release. Sometimes, defendants are **released on recognizance (ROR)**—their promise to appear in court on their court date. Some judges release defendants on the condition that they either report at scheduled times to a pretrial release program or promise not to leave town before their trial. Sometimes, judges impose supervised release—for example, requiring defendants to report to relatives or their local police department; to participate in a treatment program for illegal drugs, alcohol abuse, or mental illness; or to attend employment programs (Toborg 1981).

Money bonds, in which defendants are released as soon as money is put up, come in several forms. With the unsecured bond, defendants have to pay only if they don't appear for their court date. With the court-administered deposit bond, defendants have to post 10 percent of the amount of the bond; if they appear, the court returns their deposit. Under privately administered bail bonds, bail bondsmen (most are men) or bondswomen charge 10 percent of the amount of the bond they turn over to the courts. Defendants forfeit the 10 percent fee even if they appear (Feeley 1979, Chapter 4).

Obviously, being locked up before trial is a major loss of freedom, but it's more than that. Temporary loss of wages and even permanent loss of a job, separation from family and friends, restrictions on aiding in their own defense, and loss of reputation are also possible for detained defendants. And—all of these take place before defendants are convicted.

But pretrial release is also a risk for society. Defendants on bail can escape the jurisdiction of the court by fleeing; commit new crimes; and expose the community to anxiety, fear, and outrage over the threats to public safety. Clearly, the decision of whether to release or detain defendants before they're found guilty demands that courts strike the right balance between the right of defendants to be free until they're proved guilty and the need of the community to feel safe from crime and bring criminals to justice. Striking that balance boils down to two issues:

1. What are the constitutional rights of bailed and detained defendants?

2. What are the legitimate community interests in bailed and detained defendants?

To examine these issues, we'll look at how bail was viewed in the Constitution, whether preventive detention denies suspects their constitutional rights, and what rights defendants retain during pretrial detention.

## Bail and the Constitution

There's no absolute constitutional right to bail, only a right against excessive bail. The Eighth Amendment to the U.S. Constitution provides that "Excessive bail shall not be required," but the word "excessive" is subject to interpretation. So legislatures and courts are left to spell out the precise constitutional limit. In a controversial case from the Cold War era, *Stack v. Boyle* (1951), U.S. Chief Justice Fred M. Vinson wrote for the majority:

> From the passage of the Judiciary Act of 1789, to the present . . . federal law has unequivocally provided that a person arrested for a non-capital offense shall be admitted to bail.
>
> This traditional right to freedom permits the unhampered preparation of a defense, and serves to prevent the infliction of punishment prior to conviction. . . . Unless this right to bail before trial is preserved, the presumption of innocence, secured only after centuries of struggle, would lose its meaning. (4)

In *Stack*, 12 people were charged with conspiring to violate the Smith Act, which made it a crime to advocate the violent overthrow of the government. The case arose at the height of the Cold War, when anticommunism and fear of radicalism gripped the nation. The trial court fixed bail at $50,000 apiece. The U.S. Supreme Court ruled that amounts that are more than necessary to ensure that petitioners come to court for their trials are "excessive." The Court held that magistrates have to calculate how much money it will take to guarantee that defendants will appear.

Naturally, the amount will vary according to the circumstances of each case, but the main concerns include:

1. The seriousness of the offense

2. The amount of evidence against the defendant

3. The defendant's family ties, employment, financial resources, character, and mental condition

4. The length of the defendant's residence in the community

5. The defendant's criminal history

6. The defendant's prior record for appearing and/or "jumping" bail

Sometimes, no amount of money is enough to guarantee that rich defendants will come to court. In *U.S. v. Abrahams* (1978), Herbert Abrahams had three previous convictions;

was an escaped prisoner from another state; had given false information at a prior bail hearing; had failed to appear on a former bail of $100,000; had failed to appear on a previous charge in California from which he was a fugitive; had several aliases; and had recently transferred $1.5 million to Bermuda! The U.S. First Circuit Court of Appeals upheld the U.S. District Court's conclusion that no condition "or any combination . . . will reasonably assure the appearance of defendant for trial if admitted to bail."

In the 1980s, former U.S. Attorney General William French Smith maintained that the problem of rich defendants jumping bail is especially serious among major drug dealers, who can easily post bail in amounts of $1 million: "Some of these people net $250,000 to $500,000 a month from their drug sales. Paying bail of $100,000 is like getting rid of pocket money to these people."

At the other extreme (and a lot more common), any amount is too much for poor defendants to pay. Noted bail scholar Professor Caleb Foote (1965) believes our bail system violates the Constitution in three ways when it comes to poor defendants. It denies them:

1. *Due process* of law, because defendants can't help with their own defense if they're locked up

2. *Equal protection* of the law, because they're jailed because they're poor

3. The *right against excessive bail*, because they can't raise any amount required

The U.S. Fifth Circuit Court of Appeals dealt with the problem of indigent defendants' bail in *Pugh v. Rainwater* (1977). Florida's bail system set up a range of release conditions. However, the system didn't create either a presumption in favor of release on recognizance or a priority for nonfinancial conditions. According to the Court:

> Because it gives the judge essentially unreviewable discretion to impose money bail, the rule is . . . discriminatory . . . : When a judge decides to set money bail, the indigent will be forced to remain in jail. We hold that equal protection standards are not satisfied unless the judge is required to consider less financially onerous forms of release before he imposes money bail. Requiring a presumption in favor of non-money bail accommodates the State's interest in assuring the defendant's appearance at trial as well as the defendant's right to be free pending trial, regardless of his financial status.

So, as the court put it later on rehearing the case, for

> an indigent, whose appearance at trial could reasonably be assured by one of the alternative forms of release, pretrial confinement for inability to post money bail would constitute imposition of an excessive restraint.

Pretrial detention is an obstacle to defendants trying to prepare their defense. They can't help investigators find witnesses and physical evidence. Cramped jail quarters and short visiting hours inhibit conferences with their lawyers. Jailing also affects defendants' appearance and demeanor; they can't conceal rumpled clothes and a pale complexion. Free defendants, on the other hand, can help their defense and show the court that they're working and otherwise responsible for themselves and their families.

## Preventive Detention

Commentators, lawyers, judges, and criminal justice personnel have hotly debated whether the only acceptable purpose for bail and pretrial detention is to make sure defendants come to court. Can courts also deny bail and use pretrial detention to lock up "dangerous" defendants? Yes. **Preventive detention** allows judges to deny bail to defendants who might intimidate, hurt, and terrorize victims and witnesses or who might commit new crimes.

To reduce these dangers, the U.S. Congress enacted the **Bail Reform Act of 1984**, which authorizes federal courts to jail arrested defendants when a judge determines, after a hearing, that no condition of release would "reasonably" guarantee the appearance of the defendant and the safety of the community.

At preventive detention hearings, the Bail Reform Act guarantees defendants' rights:

1. To have an appointed lawyer

2. To testify at the hearing

3. To present evidence

4. To cross-examine witnesses

If the judge decides there's clear and convincing evidence (more than probable cause but less than proof beyond a reasonable doubt) that the defendant either won't appear or is a threat to public safety, she can order the defendant to be "preventively detained" (jailed).

Preventive detention gives rise to both empirical and constitutional questions. The major empirical question is, Does probable cause to believe a person has committed a crime predict future dangerous behavior? The question is hard to answer because the word "dangerous" is vague, and because behavior, especially violent behavior, is hard to predict (Moore and others 1984, 1).

The constitutional questions are:

1. Does preventive detention violate the Eighth Amendment ban on "cruel and unusual punishment"?

2. Does preventive detention violate the Fifth and Fourteenth Amendments and deny defendants liberty without due process of law?

In our next case excerpt, *U.S. v. Salerno* (1987), the U.S. Supreme Court answered "no" to both questions.

---

C A S E     *Were Their Pretrial Detentions "Punishment"?*

### U.S. v. Salerno

481 U.S. 739 (1987)

### HISTORY

Anthony Salerno and Vincent Cafaro were committed for pretrial detention pursuant to the Bail Reform Act by the U.S. District Court, Southern District of New York. The U.S. Court of Appeals, Second Circuit, vacated the commitment and remanded the case. On writ of certiorari, the U.S. Supreme Court reversed.

REHNQUIST, C.J., JOINED BY WHITE, BLACKMUN, POWELL, O'CONNOR, AND SCALIA, JJ.

### FACTS

Anthony Salerno and Vincent Cafaro were arrested on March 21, 1986, after being charged in a 29-count indictment alleging various Racketeer Influenced and Corrupt Organizations Act (RICO) violations, mail and wire fraud offenses, extortion, and various criminal gambling violations. The RICO counts alleged 35 acts of racketeering activity, including fraud, extortion, gambling, and conspiracy to commit murder. At their arraignment, the Government moved to have Salerno and Cafaro detained pursuant to § 3142(e) of the Bail Reform Act of 1984 on the ground that no condition of release would assure the safety of the community or any person. The District Court held a hearing at which the Government made a detailed proffer (offer) of evidence.

The Government's case showed that Salerno was the "boss" of the Genovese Crime Family of La Cosa Nostra and that Cafaro was a "captain" in the Genovese Family. According to the Government's proffer, based in large part on conversations intercepted by a court-ordered wiretap, the two respondents had participated in wide-ranging conspiracies to aid their illegitimate enterprises through violent means. The Government also offered the testimony of two of its trial witnesses, who would assert that Salerno personally participated in two murder conspiracies. Salerno opposed the motion for detention, challenging the credibility of the Government's witnesses. He offered the testimony of several character witnesses as well as a letter from his doctor stating that he was suffering from a serious medical condition. Cafaro presented no evidence at the hearing, but instead characterized the wiretap conversations as merely "tough talk."

## OPINION

The Bail Reform Act of 1984 allows a federal court to detain an arrestee pending trial if the government demonstrates by clear and convincing evidence after an adversary hearing that no release conditions "will reasonably assure . . . the safety of any other person and the community." The United States Court of Appeals for the Second Circuit struck down this provision of the Act as facially unconstitutional, because, in that court's words, this type of pretrial detention violates "substantive due process." We granted certiorari because of a conflict among the Courts of Appeals regarding the validity of the Act. We hold that . . . the Act fully comports with constitutional requirements. We therefore reverse.

Responding to "the alarming problems of crimes committed by persons on release," Congress formulated the Bail Reform Act of 1984. . . . To this end, § 3141(a) of the Act requires a judicial officer to determine whether an arrestee shall be detained. § 3142(e) provides:

> If, after a hearing pursuant to the provisions of subsection (f), the judicial officer finds that no condition or combination of conditions will reasonably assure the appearance of the person as required and the safety of any other person and the community, he shall order the detention of the person prior to trial. . . .

The judicial officer is not given unbridled discretion in making the detention determination. Congress has specified the consideration relevant to that decision. These factors include the nature and seriousness of the charges, the substantiality of the government's evidence against the arrestee, the arrestee's background and characteristics, and the nature and seriousness of the danger posed by the suspect's release. Should a judicial officer order detention, the detainee is entitled to expedited appellate review of the detention order. . . .

Respondents present two grounds for invalidating the Bail Reform Act's provisions permitting pretrial detention on the basis of future dangerousness.

1. They rely upon the Court of Appeals' conclusion that the Act exceeds the limitations placed upon the Federal Government by the Due Process Clause of the Fifth Amendment.

2. They contend that the Act contravenes the Eighth Amendment's proscription against excessive bail.

We treat those contentions in turn. . . . Respondents first argue that the Act violates substantive due process because the pretrial detention it authorizes constitutes impermissible punishment before trial. The Government, however, has never argued that pretrial detention could be upheld if it were "punishment." . . . Pretrial detention under the Bail Reform Act is regulatory, not penal. . . .

The government's interest in preventing crime by arrestees is both legitimate and compelling. . . . On the other side of the scale, of course, is the individual's strong interest in liberty. We do not minimize the importance and fundamental nature of this right. But, as our cases hold, this right may, in circumstances where the government's interest is sufficiently weighty, be subordinated to the greater needs of society. . . .

Respondents also contend that the Bail Reform Act violates the Excessive Bail Clause of the Eighth Amendment. . . . We think that the Act survives a challenge founded upon the Eighth Amendment. . . . While we agree that a primary function of bail is to safeguard the courts' role in adjudicating the guilt or innocence of defendants, we reject the proposition that the Eighth Amendment categorically prohibits the government from pursuing other admittedly compelling interests through regulation of pretrial release. . . . Nothing in the text of the Bail Clause limits permissible government considerations solely to questions of flight. . . .

We believe that when Congress has mandated detention on the basis of a compelling interest other than prevention of flight, as it has here, the Eighth Amendment does not require release on bail. . . .

In our society liberty is the norm, and detention prior to trial or without trial is the carefully limited exception. We hold that the provisions for pretrial detention in the Bail Reform Act of 1984 fall within that carefully limited exception. The Act authorizes the detention prior to trial of arrestees charged with serious felonies who are found after an adversary hearing to pose a threat to the safety of individuals or to the community which no condition of release can dispel. . . . We are unwilling to say that this congressional determination, based as it is upon that primary concern of every government—a concern for the safety and indeed the lives of its citizens—on its face violates either the Due Process Clause of the Fifth Amendment or the Excessive Bail Clause of the Eighth Amendment.

The judgment of the Court of Appeals is therefore REVERSED.

## DISSENT

MARSHALL, J., JOINED BY BRENNAN, J.

The statute now before us declares that persons who have been indicted may be detained if a judicial officer finds clear and convincing evidence that they pose a danger to individuals or to the community. . . . The conclusion is inescapable that the indictment has been turned into evidence, if not that the defendant is guilty of the crime charged, then that left to his own devices he will soon be guilty of something else. "If it suffices to accuse, what will become of the innocent?" . . .

"It is a fair summary of history to say that the safeguards of liberty have frequently been forged in controversies involving not very nice people." Honoring the presumption of innocence is often difficult; sometimes we must pay substantial social costs as a result of our commitment to the values we espouse. But at the end of the day the presumption of innocence protects the innocent; the shortcuts we take with those whom we believe to be guilty injure only those wrongfully accused and, ultimately, ourselves.

Throughout the world today there are men, women, and children interned indefinitely, awaiting trials which may never come or which may be a mockery of the word, because their governments believe them to be "dangerous." Our Constitution, whose construction began two centuries ago, can shelter us forever from the evils of such unchecked power. Over two hundred years it has slowly, through our efforts, grown more durable, more expansive, and more just. But it cannot protect us if we lack the courage, and the self-restraint, to protect ourselves. Today, a majority of the Court applies itself to an ominous exercise in demolition. Theirs is truly a decision which will go forth without authority, and come back without respect.

### Questions

1. In your opinion, is pretrial detention punishment or a "regulatory device"? What criteria do you use to answer this question?
2. What did Chief Justice John Marshall mean when he said, "If it suffices to accuse, what will become of the innocent?"
3. Does pretrial detention undermine the presumption of innocence?
4. What, in your opinion, is the proper purpose(s) of bail? Defend your answer.

## Conditions of Pretrial Confinement

Detention prior to trial, whether to secure defendants' appearance or to protect public safety, is still confinement. Jailed defendants aren't free to leave; they're locked up in cells and subject to jail discipline. They also have to follow rules designed to maintain safety and order. But jailed defendants are legally innocent; they don't forfeit their constitutional rights just because they're in jail. A jail administrator was asked if surveillance in cells through two-way mirrors (prisoners didn't know they were two-way mirrors) violated the prisoners' right to privacy. The administrator replied, "They have no rights." The administrator was wrong. Jailed defendants do have rights, but they're watered down in jail. That's what the U.S. Supreme Court decided in our next case excerpt, *Bell v. Wolfish* (1979).

## CASE    *Were They "Punished" Before Conviction?*

### *Bell v. Wolfish*
441 U.S. 520 (1979)

### HISTORY

Jailed defendants sued in U.S. District Court, Southern District of New York, challenging the constitutionality of numerous conditions of confinement and practices in the Metropolitan Correctional Center, a federally operated, short-term custodial facility for pretrial detainees in New York City. The U.S. District Court enjoined various practices in the facility. The U.S. Court of Appeals, Second Circuit, affirmed. On writ of certiorari, the U.S. Supreme Court reversed.

REHNQUIST, J., JOINED BY BURGER, C.J., AND STEWART, WHITE, AND BLACKMUN, JJ.

## FACTS

The MCC (Metropolitan Correctional Center) differs markedly from the familiar image of a jail; there are no barred cells, dank, colorless corridors, or clanging steel gates. It was intended to include the most advanced and innovative features of modern design of detention facilities. "It represented the architectural embodiment of the best and most progressive penological planning." The key design element of the 12-story structure is the "modular" or "unit" concept, whereby each floor designed to house inmates has one or two largely self-contained residential units that replace the traditional cellblock jail construction.

Each unit in turn has several clusters or corridors of private rooms or dormitories radiating from a central 2-story "multipurpose" or common room, to which each inmate has free access approximately 16 hours a day. Because our analysis does not turn on the particulars of the MCC concept design, we need not discuss them further.

When the MCC opened in August 1975, the planned capacity was 449 inmates, an increase of 50% over the former West Street facility. Despite some dormitory accommodations, the MCC was designed primarily to house these inmates in 389 rooms, which originally were intended for single occupancy. While the MCC was under construction, however, the number of persons committed to pretrial detention began to rise at an "unprecedented" rate. The Bureau of Prisons took several steps to accommodate this unexpected flow of persons assigned to the facility, but despite these efforts, the inmate population at the MCC rose above its planned capacity within a short time after its opening.

To provide sleeping space for this increased population, the MCC replaced the single bunks in many of the individual rooms and dormitories with double bunks. Also, each week some newly arrived inmates had to sleep on cots in the common areas until they could be transferred to residential rooms as space became available.

On November 28, 1975, less than four months after the MCC had opened, the named respondents initiated this action by filing in the District Court a petition for writ of habeas corpus. . . . The petition served up a veritable potpourri of complaints that implicated virtually every facet of the institution's conditions and practices. Respondents charged they had been deprived of their statutory and constitutional rights because of overcrowded conditions, undue length of confinement, improper searches, inadequate recreational, educational, and employment opportunities, insufficient staff, and objectionable restrictions on the purchase and receipt of personal items and books.

The District Court, in the words of the Court of Appeals for the Second Circuit, "intervened broadly into almost every facet of the institution" and enjoined no fewer than 20 MCC practices on constitutional and statutory grounds. The Court of Appeals largely affirmed the District Court's constitutional rulings and in the process held that under the Due Process Clause of the Fifth Amendment, pretrial detainees may "be subjected to only those 'restrictions and privations' which 'inhere in their confinement itself or which are justified by compelling necessities of jail administration.'" We granted certiorari to consider the important constitutional questions raised by these decisions and to resolve an apparent conflict among the Circuits. We now reverse.

## OPINION

. . . Not every disability imposed during pretrial detention amounts to "punishment" in the constitutional sense. . . . Once the Government has exercised its conceded authority to detain a person pending trial, it obviously is entitled to employ devices that are calculated to effectuate this detention. Traditionally, this has meant confinement in a facility which, no matter how modern or antiquated, results in restricting the movement of a detainee in a manner in which he would not be restricted if he simply were free to walk the streets pending trial. Whether it be called a jail, a prison, or a custodial center, the purpose of the facility is to detain.

Loss of freedom of choice and privacy are inherent incidents of confinement in such a facility. And the fact that such detention interferes with the detainee's understandable desire to live as comfortably as possible and with as little restraint as possible during confinement does not convert the conditions or restrictions of detention into "punishment." . . .

Judged by this analysis, respondents' claim that "double-bunking" violated their due process rights fails. . . . On this record, we are convinced as a matter of law that "double-bunking" as practiced at the MCC did not amount to punishment and did not, therefore, violate respondents' rights under the Due Process Clause of the Fifth Amendment.

Each of the rooms at the MCC that house pretrial detainees has a total floor space of approximately 75 square feet. Each of them designated for "double-bunking" contains a double bunkbed, certain other items of furniture, a wash basin, and an uncovered toilet. Inmates are generally locked into their rooms from 11 P.M. to 6:30 A.M. and for brief periods during the afternoon and evening head counts. During the rest of the day, they may move about freely between their rooms and the common areas. . . .

We disagree with both the District Court and the Court of Appeals that there is some sort of "one man, one cell" principle lurking in the Due Process Clause of the Fifth Amendment. While confining a given number of people in a given amount of space in such a manner as to cause them to endure genuine privations and hardships over an extended period of time might raise serious questions under the Due Process Clause as to whether those conditions amounted to punishment, nothing even approaching such hardship is shown by this record.

Detainees are required to spend only seven or eight hours each day in their rooms, during most or all of which they presumably are sleeping. During the remainder of the time, the detainees are free to move between their rooms and the common area. While "double-bunking" may have taxed some of the equipment or particular facilities in certain of the common areas, this does not mean that the conditions at the MCC failed to meet the standards required by the Constitution. Our conclusion in this regard is further buttressed by the detainees' length of stay at the MCC. Nearly all of the detainees are released within 60 days. We simply do not believe that requiring a detainee to share toilet facilities and this admittedly small sleeping space with another person for generally a maximum period of 60 days violates the Constitution. . . .

. . . Maintaining institutional security and preserving internal order and discipline are essential goals that may require limitation or retraction of the retained constitutional rights of both convicted prisoners and pretrial detainees. "Central to all other corrections goals is the institutional consideration of internal security within the corrections facilities themselves." . . .

Finally, . . . the problems that arise in the day-to-day operations of the corrections facility are not susceptible to easy solutions. Prison administrators therefore should be accorded wide-ranging deference in the adoption and execution of policies and practices that in their judgment are needed to preserve internal order and discipline and to maintain institutional security. . . .

Inmates at all Bureau of Prison facilities, including the MCC, are required to expose their body cavities for visual inspection as part of a strip search conducted after every contact visit with a person from outside the institution. Corrections officials testified that visual cavity searches were necessary not only to discover but also to deter the smuggling of weapons, drugs, and other contraband into the institution. The District Court upheld the strip-search procedure but prohibited the body-cavity searches, absent probable cause to believe that the inmate is concealing contraband.

Because petitioners proved only one instance in the MCC's short history where contraband was found during a body-cavity search, the Court of Appeals affirmed. In its view, the "gross violation of personal privacy inherent in such a search cannot be outweighed by the government's security interest in maintaining a practice of so little actual utility." Admittedly, this practice instinctively gives us the most pause.

However, assuming for present purposes that inmates, both convicted prisoners and pretrial detainees, retain some Fourth Amendment rights upon commitment to a corrections facility, we nonetheless conclude that these searches do not violate that Amendment. The Fourth Amendment prohibits only unreasonable searches, and under the circumstances, we do not believe that these searches are unreasonable. . . .

A detention facility is a unique place fraught with serious security dangers. Smuggling of money, drugs, weapons, and other contraband is all too common an occurrence. And inmate attempts to secrete these items into the facility by concealing them in body cavities is documented in this record. That there has been only one instance where an MCC inmate was discovered attempting to smuggle contraband into the institution on his person may be more a testament to the effectiveness of this search technique as a deterrent than to any lack of interest on the part of the inmates to secrete and import such items when the opportunity arises. . . .

There was a time not too long ago when the federal judiciary took a completely "hands-off" approach to the problem of prison administration. In recent years, however, these courts largely have discarded this "hands-off" attitude and have waded into this complex arena. . . . But many of these same courts have, in the name of the Constitution, become increasingly enmeshed in the minutiae of prison operations. Judges, after all, are human. They, no less than others in our society, have a natural tendency to believe that their individual solutions to often intractable problems are better and more workable than those of the persons who are actually charged with and trained in the running of the particular institution under examination.

But under the Constitution, the first question to be answered is not whose plan is best, but in what branch of the Government is lodged the authority to initially devise the plan. . . . The wide range of "judgment calls" that meet constitutional and statutory requirements are confided to officials outside of the Judicial Branch of Government.

## DISSENT

STEVENS, J., JOINED BY BRENNAN, J.

This is not an equal protection case. An empirical judgment that most persons formally accused of criminal conduct are probably guilty would provide a rational basis for a set of rules that treat them like convicts until they establish their innocence. No matter how rational such an approach might be—no matter how acceptable in a community where equality of status is the dominant goal—it is obnoxious to the concept of individual freedom protected by the Due Process Clause. If ever accepted in this country, it would work a fundamental change in the character of our free society.

Nor is this an Eighth Amendment case. That provision of the Constitution protects individuals convicted of crimes from punishment that is cruel and unusual. The pretrial detainees whose rights are at stake in this case, however, are innocent men and women who have been convicted of no crimes. Their claim is not that they have been subjected to cruel and unusual punishment in violation of the Eighth Amendment, but that to subject them to any form of punishment at all is an unconstitutional deprivation of their liberty.

This is a due process case. The most significant—and I venture to suggest the most enduring—part of the Court's opinion today is its recognition of this initial constitutional premise. The Court squarely holds that "under the Due Process Clause, a detainee may not be punished prior to an adjudication of guilt in accordance with due process of law." . . .

Prior to conviction every individual is entitled to the benefit of a presumption both that he is innocent of prior criminal conduct and that he has no present intention to commit any offense in the immediate future. . . . It is not always easy to determine whether a particular restraint serves the legitimate, regulatory goal of ensuring a detainee's presence at trial and his safety and security in the meantime, or the unlawful end of punishment. . . .

[*Double-bunking and searches of mail and cells are omitted from this excerpt.*]

The body-cavity search—clearly the greatest personal indignity—may be the least justifiable measure of all. After every contact visit a body-cavity search is mandated by the rule. The District Court's finding that searches have failed in practice to produce any demonstrable improvement in security is hardly surprising. Detainees and their visitors are in full view during all visits, and are fully clad. To insert contraband into one's private body cavities during such a visit would indeed be "an imposing challenge to nerves and agility." There is no reason to expect, and the petitioners have established none, that many pretrial detainees would attempt, let alone succeed, in surmounting this challenge absent the challenged rule.

Moreover, as the District Court explicitly found, less severe alternatives are available to ensure that contraband is not transferred during visits. Weapons and other dangerous instruments, the items of greatest legitimate concern, may be discovered by the use of metal detecting devices or other equipment commonly used for airline security. In addition, inmates are required, even apart from the body-cavity searches, to disrobe, to have their clothing inspected, and to present open hands and arms to reveal the absence of any concealed objects. These alternative procedures "amply satisfy" the demands of security. In my judgment, there is no basis in this regard to disagree.

It may well be, as the Court finds, that the rules at issue here were not adopted by administrators eager to punish those detained at MCC. The rules can be explained as the easiest way for administrators to ensure security in the jail. But the easiest course for jail officials is not always one that our Constitution allows them to take. If fundamental rights are withdrawn and severe harms are indiscriminately inflicted on detainees merely to secure minimal savings in time and effort for administrators, the guarantee of due process is violated.

## Questions

1. Summarize the arguments of the majority and the dissent. Which is better? Defend your answer, relying on the facts and arguments made in the case.

2. Distinguish between *detention* and *punishment*.

3. One critic said that it was all well and good for Supreme Court justices to say this case involved detention, not punishment, but it probably would be little comfort for the detainees to know that. Do you agree? Explain your answer.

4. Does it matter that most pretrial detainees are subject to confinement because they can't afford bail?

5. What interests are at stake in this case? How would you balance them?

# THE RIGHT TO COUNSEL

Lawyers are everywhere in the criminal justice system today, but that wasn't always true. During colonial times and for some time afterward, victims had to find and hire their own private prosecutors. Defendants in felony cases didn't even have the right to a lawyer to defend them during their trials.

Until the 1960s due process revolution (Chapter 2), a lawyer's job was to represent people once they got to court, not before they were charged or after they were convicted. Since the due process revolution, even police departments and corrections agencies have to hire lawyers, because the Constitution protects people on the street, in police stations, and when they're locked up before trial.

The remaining chapters will show that the right to a lawyer reaches even into prison cells and until the death penalty is carried out. This extension of constitutional protection (and the complex, technical legal rules accompanying it) has created the need for lawyers, not just for suspects, defendants, and convicts but also for police and corrections officers and departments. Here, we'll concentrate on counsel for suspects, defendants, and appellants.

The Sixth Amendment to the U.S. Constitution provides that "In all criminal prosecutions, the accused shall enjoy the right . . . to have the assistance of counsel for his defense."

Courts have always recognized criminal defendants' Sixth Amendment right to **retained counsel** (a lawyer paid for by the client). But they didn't recognize the right to **appointed counsel** (lawyers for people who can't afford to hire lawyers) until well into the 1900s. **Indigent defendants** (defendants too poor to hire their own lawyers) had to rely on **counsel pro bono** (lawyers willing to represent clients at no charge). Even today, many jurisdictions rely on lawyers who donate their services to represent poor defendants.

But most counties with large populations, and the U.S. government, have permanent defenders (called **public defenders**) paid by the public to defend poor clients. As we saw in *Powell v. Alabama* (1932; Chapter 2), the U.S. Supreme Court ruled that "fundamental fairness" requires courts to appoint lawyers for indigent defendants.

In *Johnson v. Zerbst* (1938), the Supreme Court elaborated the reasons for the right to counsel:

> [The right to counsel is] necessary to insure fundamental human rights of life and liberty. Omitted from the Constitution as originally adopted, provisions of this and other Amendments were submitted by the first Congress . . . as essential barriers against arbitrary or unjust deprivation of human rights. The Sixth Amendment stands as a constant admonition that if the constitutional safeguards it provides be lost, justice will not "still be done." It embodies a realistic recognition of the obvious truth that the average defendant doesn't have the necessary professional legal skills to protect himself when brought before a tribunal with power to take his life or liberty, wherein the prosecution is represented by experienced and learned counsel. That which is simple, orderly, and necessary to the lawyer—to the untrained layman—may appear intricate, complex, and mysterious. (462)

*Zerbst*, however, recognized only a narrow right to counsel: The Sixth Amendment guarantees poor defendants a right to a lawyer at their trial in federal courts. It says nothing about a right to counsel either before trial in federal courts or to any proceedings at all in state courts. The U.S. Supreme Court confronted the right to counsel in state courts in *Betts v. Brady* (1942).

Betts was convicted of robbery and sentenced to prison. At his trial, he asked for a lawyer, claiming that he was too poor to afford one. The judge denied his request because Carroll County, Maryland, the site of the trial, provided counsel only in murder and rape cases. Hearings on Betts's petition for habeas corpus eventually reached the Supreme Court. The Court, adopting the fundamental fairness approach, decided the due process clause didn't incorporate the Sixth Amendment right to counsel.

The Court went further to hold that, except in "special circumstances," denial of counsel doesn't deprive a defendant of a fair trial. In other words, the right to counsel was not "inherent in the concept of ordered liberty" (Chapter 2). The Court reviewed the history of representation by counsel, noting that English courts didn't allow defendants— even if they could afford to hire one—to have a lawyer in felony cases until 1843.

The Court concluded that the Sixth Amendment right to counsel allowed defendants to have a lawyer but it didn't compel the state to provide one. The Court interpreted parallel state provisions of the right to counsel similarly:

> This material demonstrates that, in the great majority of the states, it has been the considered judgment of the people, their representatives and their courts that appointment of

counsel is not a fundamental right, essential to a fair trial. . . . In the light of this evidence we are unable to say that the concept of due process incorporated in the Fourteenth Amendment obligates the states, whatever may be their own views, to furnish counsel in every such case. (471)

In our next case excerpt, *Gideon v. Wainwright* (1963), the Supreme Court accepted Clarence Gideon's petition for certiorari. The Court agreed to review the Florida Supreme Court's dismissal of Gideon's petition for habeas corpus based on a claim similar to that of Betts. The Court ordered the parties to argue the question of whether it should overrule *Betts v. Brady*.

# CASE    *Did He Have a Right to a Lawyer?*

## Gideon v. Wainwright
### 372 U.S. 335 (1963)

### HISTORY

Clarence Gideon brought habeas corpus proceedings against the director of the Division of Corrections. The Florida Supreme Court denied all relief. The U.S. Supreme Court granted certiorari. The Court reversed and remanded the case to the Florida Supreme Court for further action.

BLACK, J., FOR A UNANIMOUS COURT.

### FACTS

Clarence Gideon was charged in a Florida state court with having broken and entered a poolroom with intent to commit a misdemeanor. This offense is a felony under Florida law. Appearing in court without funds and without a lawyer, Gideon asked the court to appoint counsel for him, whereupon the following colloquy took place:

*The Court:* Mr. Gideon, I am sorry, but I cannot appoint Counsel to represent you in this case. Under the laws of the State of Florida, the only time the Court can appoint Counsel to represent a Defendant is when that person is charged with a capital offense. I am sorry, but I will have to deny your request to appoint Counsel to defend you in this case.

*The Defendant:* The United States Supreme Court says I am entitled to be represented by Counsel.

Put to trial before a jury, Gideon conducted his defense about as well as could be expected from a layman. He made an opening statement to the jury, cross-examined the State's witnesses, presented witnesses in his own defense, declined to testify himself, and made a short argument "emphasizing his innocence to the charge contained in the Information filed in this case."

The jury returned a verdict of guilty, and petitioner was sentenced to serve five years in the state prison.

Later, petitioner filed in the Florida Supreme Court this habeas corpus petition attacking his conviction and sentence on the ground that the trial court's refusal to appoint counsel for him denied him rights "guaranteed by the Constitution and the Bill of Rights by the United States Government."

Later in the petition for habeas corpus, signed and apparently prepared by Gideon himself, he stated, "I, Clarence Earl Gideon, claim that I was denied the rights of the 4th, 5th and 14th Amendments of the Bill of Rights." Treating the petition for habeas corpus as properly before it, the State Supreme Court, "upon consideration thereof" but without an opinion, denied all relief. Since 1942, when *Betts v. Brady* was decided by a divided Court, the problem of a defendant's federal constitutional right to counsel in a state court has been a continuing source of controversy and litigation in both state and federal courts.

To give this problem another review here, we granted certiorari. Since Gideon was proceeding in forma pauperis [*As a poor person who can't afford a lawyer*], we appointed counsel to represent him and requested both sides to discuss in their briefs and oral arguments the following: "Should this Court's holding in *Betts v. Brady* be overruled?"

### OPINION

Treating due process as "a concept less rigid and more fluid than those envisaged in other specific and particular provisions of the Bill of Rights," the Court held that refusal to appoint counsel under the particular facts and circumstances in the *Betts* case was not so "offensive to the common and fundamental ideas of fairness" as to amount to a denial of due process. Since the facts and circumstances of the two cases are so nearly indistinguishable, we think the *Betts v. Brady* holding if left standing would require us to reject Gideon's claim that the Constitution guarantees him the assistance of counsel.

Upon full consideration we conclude that *Betts v. Brady* should be overruled. The Sixth Amendment provides, "In all criminal prosecutions, the accused shall enjoy the right . . . to have the Assistance of Counsel for his defence." . . . In our adversary system of criminal justice, any person haled into court, who is too poor to hire a lawyer, cannot be assured a fair trial unless counsel is provided for him. This seems to us to be an obvious truth.

Governments, both state and federal, quite properly spend vast sums of money to establish machinery to try defendants accused of crime. Lawyers to prosecute are everywhere deemed essential to protect the public's interest in an orderly society. Similarly, there are few defendants charged with crime, few indeed, who fail to hire the best lawyers they can get to prepare and present their defenses. That government hires lawyers to prosecute and defendants who have the money hire lawyers to defend are the strongest indications of the widespread belief that lawyers in criminal courts are necessities, not luxuries.

The right of one charged with crime to counsel may not be deemed fundamental and essential to fair trials in some countries, but it is in ours. From the very beginning, our state and national constitutions and laws have laid great emphasis on procedural and substantive safeguards designed to assure fair trials before impartial tribunals in which every defendant stands equal before the law. This noble ideal cannot be realized if the poor man charged with crime has to face his accusers without a lawyer to assist him. A defendant's need for a lawyer is nowhere better stated than in the moving words of Mr. Justice Sutherland in *Powell v. Alabama:*

> The right to be heard would be, in many cases, of little avail if it did not comprehend the right to be heard by counsel. Even the intelligent and educated layman . . . requires the guiding hand of counsel at every step in the proceedings against him. Without it, though he be not guilty, he faces the danger of

conviction because he does not know how to establish his innocence.

The Court in *Betts v. Brady* departed from the sound wisdom upon which the Court's holding in *Powell v. Alabama* rested. Florida, supported by two other States, has asked that *Betts v. Brady* be left intact. Twenty-two States, as friends of the Court, argue that *Betts* was "an anachronism when handed down" and that it should now be overruled.

We agree. The judgment is reversed and the cause is remanded to the Supreme Court of Florida for further action not inconsistent with this opinion.

REVERSED.

### *Questions*

1. What exactly did the Court decide that the "right to counsel" means?

2. On what theory did it apply the right to counsel to state proceedings?

3. Why did the Court take the unusual step of overruling its decision in *Betts v. Brady?*

4. Do you agree that the right to counsel should apply to state proceedings, or should states decide for themselves whether poor criminal defendants in their jurisdictions have a right to a lawyer assigned by the court?

5. Does the Court apply the right to counsel to state proceedings to further the interest in correct result? to further the interest in process? as a matter of efficiency? Explain your answer.

 To learn more about Clarence Gideon, go to the Samaha Criminal Procedure 7e website and read the Rest of the Story: academic.cengage.com/criminaljustice/samaha.

At what point does the right to counsel kick in? We'll look at this issue next. Then, we'll examine what the Court meant when it said that the right to counsel applied to "all criminal prosecutions." And just how poor does a person have to be before the court has to appoint defense counsel? What does the right to "effective counsel" mean? Let's look at each of these issues.

## When the Right to Counsel Attaches

The Sixth Amendment guarantees the right to counsel in all criminal "prosecutions," but what proceedings does prosecution include? Clearly, it includes the trial and appeal, when defendants most need special legal expertise. But what about before trial?

The U.S. Supreme Court has ruled that the right to counsel attaches to all *critical stages of criminal proceedings.* Table 12.1 shows the stages in the criminal process and indicates the ones the U.S. Supreme Court has declared critical stages. It's clear from the table that defendants have the right to counsel to represent them at all procedures after the first appearance.

| TABLE 12.1 | Critical Stages and the Right to Counsel |
|---|---|
| **Stage of Criminal Process** | **Right to Counsel?** |
| Investigative stop | No |
| Frisk for weapons | No |
| Arrest | No |
| Search following arrest | No |
| Custodial interrogation | Yes |
| Lineup before formal charges | No |
| Lineup after formal charges | Yes |
| First appearance | No |
| Grand jury review/Preliminary hearing | Yes |
| Arraignment | Yes |
| Pretrial hearings | Yes |
| Trial (Chapter 13) | Yes |
| Appeal/Collateral attack (Chapter 14) | Yes |

But what about the stages at the police station before the first appearance? Specifically, do you have a right to a lawyer during police interrogation and identification procedures (lineups, show-ups, and photo identification (Chapters 8 and 9))? The U.S. Supreme Court first applied the right to a lawyer in police stations in 1964, in *Escobedo v. Illinois* (1964). The Court held that the right to counsel attached at the accusatory stage of a criminal case—namely, when a general investigation focused on a specific suspect.

According to the Court, that point was reached in *Escobedo* when the police made up their minds that Danny Escobedo had committed the murder they were investigating. After they made up their minds he was the murderer, Chicago police officers tried to get him to confess by interrogating him. During the interrogation, Escobedo asked to see his lawyer, who was in the police station. The officers refused. Eventually, he confessed and was tried and convicted with the help of the confession. The U.S. Supreme Court said the confession was not admissible because it was obtained during the accusatory stage without the help of Escobedo's lawyer.

Just two years later, in *Miranda v. Arizona*, the Court decided that police officers have to tell suspects that they have a right to a lawyer during custodial interrogation (Chapter 8). As for identification procedures, those conducted *after* indictment are a critical stage; those conducted *before* indictment aren't (Chapter 9).

## The Meaning of "All Criminal Prosecutions"

In 1932, *Powell v. Alabama* (Chapter 2) established the rule that due process commands that appointed counsel represent poor defendants in capital cases. In *Gideon v. Wainwright* (1963), the Court extended the right to counsel to poor defendants prosecuted for felonies against property. In 1972, the Court went further; all poor defendants prosecuted for misdemeanors punishable by jail terms have a right to an appointed lawyer.

In *Argersinger v. Hamlin* (1972), Jon Richard Argersinger, a Florida indigent, was convicted of carrying a concealed weapon, a misdemeanor punishable by up to six months' imprisonment, a $1,000 fine, or both. A Florida rule limited assigned counsel

## TABLE 12.2 The Leading Right-to-Counsel Cases

| Case | Year | Right Upheld |
|------|------|--------------|
| *Powell v. Alabama* | 1932 | Appointed counsel for poor, illiterate, ignorant, isolated defendants in state capital cases |
| *Johnson v. Zerbst* | 1938 | Appointed counsel in federal cases at trial (not before or after) |
| *Betts v. Brady* | 1942 | Appointed counsel in state cases under "special circumstances" |
| *Chandler v. Fretag* | 1954 | Retained (paid for) counsel in all criminal cases |
| *Gideon v. Wainwright* | 1963 | Appointed counsel in state felony cases (overruled *Betts v. Brady*) |
| *Argersinger v. Hamlin* | 1972 | Appointed counsel in any offense punishable by incarceration |
| *Scott v. Illinois* | 1979 | No right to counsel for sentences that don't result in actual jail time |

to "non-petty offenses punishable by more than six months imprisonment." The Court struck down the rule, holding that states have to provide a lawyer for defendants charged with any offense punishable by incarceration no matter what the state's criminal code calls it (misdemeanor, petty misdemeanor, or felony).

Notice what the Court didn't say in *Argersinger*: Poor people have a right to a lawyer paid for by the government in all criminal cases. Why? Because the Court was well aware of a practical problem: There isn't enough money to pay for everyone to have a lawyer. Of course, strictly speaking, constitutional rights can't depend on money; but as a practical matter, money definitely affects how many people get their rights in real life. We know many poor people who have a right to a lawyer don't get one because counties and other local governments simply don't have the money to pay for them. Why? Because taxpayers don't want their tax dollars spent on lawyers for "criminals." Table 12.2 summarizes the leading cases on the right to counsel.

This mix of practical reality and constitutional rights surfaced in *Scott v. Illinois* (1979). The Court specifically addressed the question of whether the right to assigned counsel extends to offenses that don't actually result in prison sentences. Aubrey Scott was convicted of shoplifting merchandise valued at less than $150. An Illinois statute set the maximum penalty at a $500 fine or one year in jail, or both. Scott argued that a line of this Court's cases, culminating in *Argersinger*, required state-paid counsel whenever imprisonment is an authorized penalty.

The U.S. Supreme Court rejected that argument. Instead, it agreed with the Supreme Court of Illinois, which was "not inclined to extend *Argersinger*" to a case in which the defendant wasn't facing jail time. The statutory offense that Scott was charged with authorized imprisonment upon conviction but courts didn't impose it. The Court held that " . . . the Federal Constitution does not require a state trial court to appoint counsel for a criminal defendant such as [Scott]" . . . (369).

In their dissent, Justices Brennan, Marshall, and Stevens pointed to the importance of the cost in the majority's decision:

> The apparent reason for the Court's adoption of the "actual imprisonment" standard for all misdemeanors is concern for the economic burden that an "authorized imprisonment" standard might place on the States. But, with all respect, that concern is both irrelevant and

speculative. This Court's role in enforcing constitutional guarantees for criminal defendants cannot be made dependent on the budgetary decisions of state governments. . . . The invidiousness of the discrimination that exists when criminal procedures are made available only to those who can pay is not erased by any differences in the sentences that may be imposed. The State's fiscal interest is, therefore, irrelevant.

In any event, the extent of the alleged burden on the States is, as the Court admits, speculative. . . . Public defender systems have proved economically feasible, and the establishment of such systems to replace appointment of private attorneys can keep costs at acceptable levels even when the number of cases requiring appointment of counsel increases dramatically. The public defender system alternative also answers the argument that an authorized imprisonment standard would clog the courts with inexperienced appointed counsel. . . .

Perhaps the strongest refutation of . . . alarmist prophecies that an authorized imprisonment standard would wreak havoc on the States is that the standard has not produced that result in the substantial number of States that already provide counsel in all cases where imprisonment is authorized—States that include a large majority of the country's population and a great diversity of urban and rural environments. (384–88)

## The Standard of Indigence

The U.S. Supreme Court has never defined indigence. However, U.S. Courts of Appeals have established some general guidelines on how to determine whether defendants are poor enough to qualify for a lawyer paid for by the government:

1. Poor defendants don't have to be completely destitute.

2. Earnings and assets count; help from friends and relatives doesn't.

3. Actual, not potential, earnings are the measure.

4. The state can tap defendants' future earnings to get reimbursement for the costs of counsel, transcripts, and fees for expert witnesses and investigators.

Some states have set up detailed standards for determining indigence. Minnesota's rules (1987, Rule 5, 112–15) to help judges determine indigency at the first appearance are typical. They provide:

STANDARD OF INDIGENCE.

A defendant is financially unable to obtain counsel if he is financially unable to obtain adequate representation without substantial hardship for himself or his family.

(1). A defendant will be presumed to be financially unable to afford counsel if:
    a. his cash assets are less than $300.00 when entitled to only a court trial; or
    b. his current weekly net income does not exceed $500.00 when entitled to a jury trial; and
    c. his current weekly net income does not exceed forty times the federal minimum hourly wage . . . if he is unmarried and without dependents; or,
    d. his current weekly net income and that of his spouse do not exceed sixty times the federal minimum hourly wage . . . if he is married and without dependents.
In determining the amounts under either section (c) or section (d), for each dependent the amount shall be increased by $25.00 per week.

(2). A defendant who has cash assets or income exceeding the amounts in paragraph (1) shall not be presumed to be financially able to obtain counsel. The determination shall be made by the court as a practical matter, taking into account such other factors as the defendant's length of employment or unemployment, prior income, the value and nature of his assets, number of children and other family responsibilities, number and nature of debts arising from any source, the amount customarily charged by members of the practicing bar for representation of the type in question, and any other relevant factor.

(3). In determining whether a defendant is financially able to obtain adequate representation without substantial hardship to himself or his family:

    a. cash assets include those assets which may be readily converted to cash . . . without jeopardizing the defendant's ability to maintain his home or employment. A single family automobile shall not be considered an asset.

    b. the fact that defendant has posted or can post bail is irrelevant. . . .

    c. the fact that the defendant is employable but unemployed shall not be in itself proof that he is financially able to obtain counsel without substantial hardship to himself or his family.

    d. the fact that parents or other relatives of the defendant have the financial ability to obtain counsel for the defendant is irrelevant, except under the following circumstances:

        i. where the defendant is unemancipated, under the age of 21 years, living with his parent or other relatives, and such parents or other relatives have the clear ability to obtain counsel; or

        ii. where the parents or other relatives of the defendant have the financial ability to obtain counsel for the defendant but are unwilling to do so only because of the relatively minor nature of the charge.

(4). Financial Inquiry. An inquiry to determine financial eligibility of a defendant for the appointment of counsel shall be made whenever possible prior to the court appearance and by such persons as the court may direct.

## The Right to "Effective" Counsel

In 1932, the U.S. Supreme Court said due process requires not just counsel but *effective counsel*, but the Court didn't say much to clarify what "effective" means. So lower federal courts and state courts stepped in and adopted the **mockery of justice standard**. Under this standard, only lawyers whose behavior is so "shocking" that it turns the trial into a "joke" are constitutionally ineffective. One lawyer called it the "mirror test." (Put a mirror under the lawyer's nose; if it steams up he passes.) What prompted this professional criticism?

In actual cases, appellate courts ruled that lawyers who slept through trials; came to court drunk; couldn't name a single precedent related to the case they were arguing; or were released from jail to represent their clients hadn't turned the proceedings into a joke and met the mockery of justice standard. When one defendant claimed he got ineffective representation because his lawyer slept through the trial, the judge said, "You have a right to a lawyer; that doesn't mean you have a right to one who's awake." That decision was affirmed by the reviewing court. Courts and commentators have criticized the mockery of justice standard for being too subjective, vague, and narrow. The standard's focus on the trial excludes many serious errors that lawyers make in preparing for trial. Furthermore, in the overwhelming majority of cases disposed of by guilty pleas, the standard is totally irrelevant.

Judge David Bazelon (1973), an experienced and respected federal judge, said the test requires "such a minimal level of performance from counsel that it is itself a mockery of the Sixth Amendment" (28). "I have often been told that if my court were to reverse in every case in which there was inadequate counsel, we would have to send back half the convictions in my jurisdiction" (22–23).

Courts resist getting involved in the touchy question of judging the performance of defense attorneys. Why? For one thing, too much interference can damage not only professional relationships but also the professional independence of defense lawyers and even the adversary system itself. Furthermore, judges who criticize defense lawyers are criticizing fellow professionals, lawyers who appear in their courts regularly.

Most jurisdictions have abandoned the mockery of justice standard, replacing it with the **reasonably competent attorney standard**. According to this standard, judges measure lawyers' performance against the "customary skills and diligence that a reasonably competent attorney would perform under similar circumstances." Attorneys have to be more diligent under the reasonably competent attorney standard than under the mockery of justice standard. Nevertheless, both the mockery of justice and the reasonably competent attorney standards are "vague to some appreciable degree and . . . susceptible to greatly varying subjective impressions" (LaFave and Israel 1984, 2:99–102).

The U.S. Supreme Court has tried to increase the clarity of the reasonably competent attorney test by announcing a new **two-pronged effective counsel test** to evaluate effectiveness of counsel. The test was announced in *Strickland v. Washington* (1984). In 1976, David Leroy Washington went on a 10-day crime spree that ended in three murders. After his lawyer, William Tunkey, was appointed, Washington confessed; he also pleaded guilty at his trial. Washington waived his right to an advisory jury to decide whether he should get the death penalty.

During the sentencing phase of the proceedings, Tunkey didn't present any character evidence, didn't present any medical or psychiatric evidence, and only cross-examined some of the state's witnesses. The judge sentenced Washington to death. Washington went through the state and then the federal courts claiming ineffectiveness of counsel. The U.S. Court of Appeals for the Eleventh Circuit ruled in his favor and the state appealed.

The U.S. Supreme Court reversed, applying its new two-pronged test of ineffective counsel. Under the first prong, called the **reasonableness prong**, defendants have to prove that their lawyer's performance wasn't reasonably competent, meaning that the lawyer was so deficient that she "was not functioning as the 'counsel' guaranteed the defendant by the Sixth Amendment."

Under the reasonableness prong, reviewing courts have to look at the totality of the facts and circumstances to decide whether the defense lawyer's performance was reasonably competent. Reviewing courts have to start with a presumption in favor of the defense lawyer's competence, meaning they have lots of leeway to make tactical and strategic decisions that fall within the wide range of available professional judgment. So as long as defense counsel's choices fall within that wide range, representation is presumed reasonable.

If the defendant proves his lawyer's performance was unreasonable, he still has to prove the second-prong of the test, called the **prejudice prong** of the reasonable competence test. Under the prejudice prong, defendants have to prove that their lawyer's incompetence was probably responsible for their conviction.

Go to Exercise 12.1 on the Samaha Criminal Procedure 7e website to learn more about the rejection of the two-pronged test by some states: academic.cengage.com/criminaljustice/samaha.

# TESTING THE GOVERNMENT'S CASE

After the decision to charge, the action moves from the prosecutor's office into court. At this point, decisions inside the courtroom are based more on formal rules than informal discretion. These rules govern the pretrial proceedings to test the government's case and hear motions. Testing the government's case means deciding whether there's enough evidence to go to trial. Still more complex rules control the centerpiece of formal criminal justice, the criminal trial.

But don't be deceived by these public formal proceedings. Discretionary decision making hasn't disappeared; it has just moved out of the courtroom and into the corridors in and around the courthouse. Here's where plea bargaining takes place—or, where defendants decide they just want to plead guilty without bargaining, hoping to get a lighter sentence by admitting their guilt and saving the court and lawyers time. In these cases (the vast majority by all counts), courtroom proceedings only ratify what was worked out by informal negotiations.

We saw earlier that the decision to charge (pp. 402–404) demonstrates the government's commitment to criminal prosecution and that the first appearance (pp. 408–409) prepares defendants for the consequences of this decision. But the government's commitment and the first appearance aren't enough by themselves to start a criminal trial.

First, one of two procedures has to test the strength of the government's case against the defendant. There are good reasons for this test. According to the Seventh Circuit U.S. Court of Appeals in *U.S. v. Udziela* (1982):

> While in theory a trial provides a defendant with a full opportunity to contest and disprove charges against him, in practice, the handing up of an indictment will often have a devastating personal and professional impact that a later dismissal or acquittal can never undo. (1001)

Two procedures test the government's case against defendants: (1) preliminary hearings and (2) grand jury review. A **preliminary hearing** is an adversarial proceeding that tests the government's case; a **grand jury review** is a secret proceeding to test the government's case.

When prosecutors draw up a criminal *information* (a written formal charge made by prosecutors without a grand jury indictment), they test their case at a preliminary hearing before a judge. When they seek an **indictment**, they test the government's case by presenting it to a grand jury for grand jury review. If the government passes the test of the grand jury review, the grand jury returns the indictment as a **true bill**, which records the number of **grand jurors** (citizens selected to serve a term) voting for indictment. If the government passes the test in the preliminary hearing, the judge **binds over** the defendant; that is, he sends the case on for trial.

Both preliminary hearings and grand jury review test the government's case, but they differ in several important respects (see Table 12.3). Preliminary hearings are public; grand jury proceedings are secret. Preliminary hearings are adversarial proceedings, in which the defense can challenge the prosecution's case; grand juries hear only the prosecution's case without the defense's participation. Judges preside over preliminary hearings; prosecutors manage grand jury proceedings without judicial participation. In preliminary hearings, magistrates determine whether there's enough evidence to go to trial; grand jury review relies on grand jurors selected to decide whether there's enough evidence. Finally, defendants and their lawyers attend preliminary hearings; defendants and their lawyers are banned from grand jury review (ex parte proceedings).

---

**TABLE 12.3**    **Contrasts between the Preliminary Hearing and Grand Jury Review**

| Preliminary Hearing | Grand Jury Review |
|---|---|
| Held in public | Secret proceeding |
| Adversarial hearing | Only the government's case is presented |
| Judge presides | Prosecutor presides |
| Judge determines the facts | Grand jurors decide the facts |

The differences between preliminary hearings and grand jury proceedings reflect different values in the criminal process. The preliminary hearing stresses adversarial, open, accusatory values and control by experts. Grand jury review, on the other hand, underscores the value of the democratic dimension of the criminal process: lay participation in criminal proceedings. But their goal is the same: deciding whether there's enough evidence to bring defendants to trial.

## The Preliminary Hearing

Preliminary hearings are held after the first appearance. In most states, all judges are authorized to conduct preliminary hearings, but, in practice, they're conducted by magistrates, justices of the peace, municipal court judges, or other members of the lower court judiciary. There's no constitutional right to a preliminary hearing. But if states do provide for preliminary hearings, the Sixth Amendment guarantees defendants the right to have a lawyer represent them at the hearing (*Gerstein v. Pugh* 1975).

Preliminary hearings are adversarial proceedings. The prosecution presents evidence, and then the defense can challenge it and even present its own evidence. Preliminary hearings are also public. This may sound like a trial, but it's not.

First, the rigid rules of evidence followed during trials are relaxed during preliminary hearings. In some states, preliminary hearing judges even admit illegally seized evidence and hearsay (LaFave and Israel 1984, 2:263–64). Prosecutors reveal only enough of the state's evidence (for example, a witness or two and minimal physical evidence) to satisfy the **bind-over standard** (there's enough evidence for the judge to decide to go to trial). Why? Because it takes time and, probably more important, prosecutors don't want to give away any more of their case than they have to. The defense typically introduces no evidence, because they don't want to give away their case either; instead, defense attorneys limit their participation to cross-examining the state's witnesses.

The objective basis for going to trial is probable cause, but don't confuse this with probable cause to arrest (Chapter 6). Most courts hold that it takes more probable cause to bind over someone for trial than it does to arrest the person. Why? Because the consequences of going to trial are graver. Defendants are detained longer, and the ordeals of criminal prosecution, conviction, and punishment are greater. Even if they aren't convicted, defendants have to pay their lawyers; suffer the stigma of prosecution; and subject their families to hardships. As one prominent exonerated defendant asked, "How do I get my reputation back?" The consequences fall not only on defendants but also on the government. The state has to spend scarce resources to prove guilt, and that takes away resources for other services, such as education and road repairs.

The bind-over standard reflects the idea that the greater the invasions and deprivations against individuals, the more facts that are needed to back them up. Just how many facts does it take to move a case to trial? Some courts have adopted a **prima facie case rule**. According to this standard, the judge can bind over a defendant if the prosecution presents evidence that could convict if the defense doesn't rebut it at trial. Others have adopted a **directed verdict rule**. According to this rule, preliminary hearing judges should look at the case as if it's a trial and they're deciding whether there's enough believable evidence to send the case to the jury. If there isn't enough, then the judge should dismiss the case. The minimum amount of evidence required to bind over under the directed verdict rule is more than enough to add up to probable cause to arrest but less than enough to "prove the defendant's guilt beyond a reasonable doubt" (*Myers v. Commonwealth* 1973, 824).

# Grand Jury Review

Grand jury review is ancient. Originating in medieval England as a council of local residents that helped the king look into matters of royal concern (crime, revenues, and official misconduct), the grand jury was an investigating body. However, by the time of the American Revolution, the grand jury had another duty: it screened criminal cases to protect individuals from malicious and unfounded prosecution. So the grand jury had two functions: to act as a sword to root out crime and corruption and as a shield to protect innocent people from unwarranted state intrusion.

Colonists warmly approved of the grand jury shield function, because it "shielded" them from prosecution for their antiroyalist sentiments. For that reason, the Fifth Amendment to the U.S. Constitution provides that "no person shall be held to answer for a capital, or otherwise infamous crime, unless on a presentment or indictment by a Grand Jury. . . ." But grand jury indictment is one of the very few provisions in the Bill of Rights that doesn't apply to state court proceedings under the incorporation doctrine (Chapter 2).

Grand juries vary from state to state both in their membership and in the procedures they follow. Let's look at grand jury membership, grand jury proceedings, and the debate over grand juries.

*The Members of the Grand Jury* We'll use as an example of choosing grand jury members the operation of the federal grand jury in the Southern District of New York, a jurisdiction that includes Manhattan, the Bronx, and several New York counties as far north as Albany (Frankel and Naftalis 1977, Chapter 4). Federal grand juries consist of not fewer than 16 or more than 23 jurors. To qualify, prospective grand jurors have to

1. Be U.S. citizens
2. Be 18 or over
3. Reside in the jurisdiction
4. Have no felony convictions
5. Speak, write, and read English
6. Suffer from no physical impairments that might hamper their participation, such as impaired hearing or vision

The jurisdiction sometimes summons nearly 200 citizens for jury service—many more than are needed. The process of narrowing down the number of potential jurors and selecting the final 16 to 23 is called "purging" the grand jury. The process does eliminate prospective grand jurors with compelling reasons not to serve—business, family, and health obligations—but it often hinders the selection of a representative grand jury. The resulting composition of federal grand juries overrepresents retired persons and those not burdened with other responsibilities.

*Grand Jury Proceedings* After swearing in the grand jurors, judges **charge the grand jury**. Some charges are calls to action against specific dangers. Others resemble stump speeches for law and order or constitutional rights. Almost all include a history and outline of grand jury duties and responsibilities, warnings about the secrecy of grand jury proceedings, and admonitions to protect the innocent and condemn the guilty. Following the charge, judges turn grand jurors over to prosecutors to conduct grand jury proceedings. Unlike preliminary hearings, grand jury proceedings don't require a judge's participation.

Grand jury secrecy severely restricts who's allowed to attend proceedings. In addition to the grand jurors themselves, only the prosecutor, witnesses called to testify, and stenographers appear in the grand jury room. Defendants are banned. So are witnesses' attorneys, even though these witnesses are often themselves grand jury *targets* (individuals who themselves are under suspicion and investigation). But witnesses may (and often do) bring their lawyers to the courthouse for consultation outside the grand jury room.

After all witnesses have testified and prosecutors have introduced any other evidence, prosecutors draw up an indictment and present it to the grand jury for consideration. Prosecutors then sum up the reasons the evidence amounts to a crime and leave during grand jury deliberations, which ordinarily take only a few minutes. Grand juries rarely disagree with prosecutors' recommendations. Forepersons sign both the indictment and the true bill, which records the number of jurors who voted to indict. Federal grand jury proceedings require 12 jurors' concurrence to indict.

The entire grand jury, accompanied by the prosecutor, then proceeds to a designated courtroom to hand up the indictment, an action that amounts to the formal filing of charges, requiring defendants to answer in court. After judges check to ensure all documents are in order, they accept the indictment, which becomes a matter of public record. They also accept the true bill, but it doesn't become a public record. The judges' acceptance initiates the criminal prosecution by indictment.

***The Debate over the Grand Jury*** Since the 16th century, observers have found a lot to criticize about the grand jury. The Elizabethan justice of the peace William Lambarde's charges to the Kent grand juries have preserved these early criticisms (Read 1962). Justice Lambarde praised the grand juries' capacity to aid in law enforcement but scorned their conduct in carrying out their responsibilities. Mainly, Lambarde attacked their sword function, berating them for being too timid in rooting out crimes. But he also criticized their shield function, too, attacking their weakness in screening cases.

In modern times, the debate has focused almost entirely on the grand jury's screening function. From the early 1900s, confidence in science and experts led many reformers to call for banning nonexperts from participating in criminal justice decision making. Those at the extreme wanted to abolish grand and trial juries and replace them with panels of "trained experts" to weigh evidence. However, two prestigious presidential commissions, the Wickersham Commission, appointed by President Herbert Hoover, and the National Advisory Commission, appointed by President Richard Nixon, were more in the mainstream. Both urged the abolition only of mandatory grand jury review.

Since the early 1980s, most legal commentary has condemned the grand jury. Critics make several arguments against grand jury screening. One line of attack is that grand juries are prosecutors' rubber stamps. According to one former prosecutor, "A [prosecutor] can indict anybody, at any time, for almost anything before a grand jury." Statistics bear out this claim. Grand juries issue no-bills (refusals to indict) in only a tiny percentage of cases. Even the no-bills don't necessarily show grand jury independence.

In sensitive or controversial cases, prosecutors choose grand jury review over preliminary hearings to put the burden for deciding whether or not to charge on the grand jury (LaFave and Israel 1984, 2:282–83). Critics also condemn the nonadversarial nature of grand jury review, charging it prevents either effectively screening cases or adequately protecting citizens against unwarranted prosecutions. Also, the secrecy of grand jury proceedings creates doubts and suspicion. That defendants and their lawyers can't attend grand jury sessions provides further ammunition for critics' charges that this exclusion is both unfair and results in inadequate screening. Critics also argue grand jury review is inefficient, expensive, and time-consuming.

Impaneling and servicing a grand jury is costly in terms of space, human resources, and money. The members have to be selected, notified, sworn, housed, fed, and provided other services. Finally, grand jury screening takes more time than preliminary hearings. The law surrounding grand jury proceedings is complex and technical, creating delays in the proceedings themselves and, later, in successful challenges to grand jury proceedings. In several jurisdictions, the intricacies and complexities of impaneling a grand jury guarantee attack by a skilled defense attorney and frequently result in dismissal of charges for minor discrepancies in the impaneling procedure.

On the other side, supporters of grand jury review have their arguments, too. First, they maintain grand juries cost no more than preliminary hearings. Preliminary hearings, they charge, have turned into needless "minitrials," elaborate affairs to which lawyers, judges, other court personnel, and witnesses devote a great deal of court time. Furthermore, the number of requests that defense attorneys make for continuances leads to a greater delay in, and a better chance of successful challenges to, preliminary hearings than grand jury proceedings.

Grand jury supporters also reject the contention that the grand jury doesn't effectively screen cases. They cite prosecutors who believe that grand juries are valuable sounding boards and that grand jurors definitely have minds of their own. The high percentage of indictments grand juries return is not the important figure, according to supporters. Rather, the percentage of convictions—as high as 98 percent—based on indictments demonstrates that grand juries effectively screen out cases that shouldn't go to trial (Younger 1963).

Go to Exercise 12.2 on the Samaha Criminal Procedure 7e website to learn more about testing the government's case: academic.cengage.com/criminaljustice/samaha.

Finally, grand jury review shows democracy at work. Supporters maintain that what grand jury review loses in secret and nonadversarial proceedings it more than recaptures in community participation in screening criminal cases. Citizen participation enhances public confidence in the criminal justice system. In a system where most cases don't go to trial, grand jury proceedings provide private citizens with their only opportunity to participate actively on the "front lines" of the criminal process. But, in fact, grand jurors aren't as representative of the community as trial jurors—who aren't all that representative either. Grand jury duty spans a long period of time, usually a year, and requires service at least two or three days a week. Only citizens with a lot of free time can devote such extended service in the criminal process (Graham and Letwin 1971, 681).

# ARRAIGNMENT

If defendants are indicted or bound over, the next step in the criminal process is arraignment. *Arraignment* means to bring defendants to court to hear and to answer (plead to) the charges against them. Don't confuse arraignment with the first appearance. The first appearance takes place within days of the arrest, and defendants don't have to answer the charges; arraignment happens sometimes months after the arrest, and defendants have to answer something.

There are four possible pleas (answers) to the charges:

1. Not guilty

2. Not guilty by reason of insanity

3. Nolo contendere

4. Guilty (Chapter 13)

"Nolo contendere" means defendants don't contest the issue of guilt or innocence.

There's no right to plead nolo contendere; the court has to consent to it. Why do defendants plead nolo contendere? Because it might help them in civil lawsuits, a complicated matter we don't need to explore in a criminal procedure course. Also, if a defendant pleads guilty, the court has to decide whether the plea is knowing and voluntary (later in this chapter).

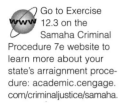

# PRETRIAL MOTIONS

**Pretrial motions** are written or oral requests asking the court to decide questions that don't require a trial to be ruled on. They're an important part of both prosecutors' and defense counsel's work. They definitely spend a lot more time on "motion practice" than they spend trying cases—and probably more time than they do on plea bargaining.

Let's look briefly at the main pretrial motions:

1. Double jeopardy

2. Speedy trial

3. Change of venue

4. Suppression of evidence

## Double Jeopardy

The Fifth Amendment to the U.S. Constitution guarantees that, "No person . . . shall . . . be subject for the same offence to be twice put in jeopardy of life or limb. . . ." Although the words "life or limb" suggest only death and corporal punishment, this guarantee against double jeopardy applies to all crimes, including decisions in juvenile proceedings.

The ban on **double jeopardy** protects several interests both of the state and defendants (Table 12.4). It's supposed to allow the government "one fair shot" at convicting criminals. At the same time, it bans the government's use of its greater share of power and resources to subject less-powerful citizens accused of crimes to repeated attempts to

**TABLE 12.4**  **Interests Protected by a Ban on Double Jeopardy**

| Interest | State | Defendant |
|---|---|---|
| Allows one fair shot at convicting defendants | Yes | |
| Limits the government's advantage of greater resources | | Yes |
| Reduces prolonged stress that multiple trials would lead to | | Yes |
| Promotes finality (closure) in criminal cases | Yes | Yes |
| Reduces the costs that multiple trials would lead to | Yes | Yes |

convict them. Furthermore, it protects individuals from the embarrassment, expense, and ordeal—and the anxiety and insecurity—that repeated prosecutions generate.

Defendants also have an interest in completing their trials under one tribunal and jury. In addition, both the state and defendants have an interest in the finality and integrity of judgments that aren't susceptible to repeated reconsideration. Finally, the prohibition against double jeopardy reduces costs both to defendants and to the state. Retrials consume time and impede the efficient and economical disposition of other cases on crowded criminal court calendars.

The Fifth Amendment prohibition against double jeopardy kicks in as soon as the state "puts defendants to trial." In jury trials, this happens when the jury is impaneled and sworn in. The U.S. Supreme Court referred to the history of this definition of jury trials in *Crist v. Bretz* (1978), when it struck down Montana's rule that despite swearing in the jury, jeopardy didn't attach until the first witness commenced testifying:

> The reason for holding that jeopardy attaches when the jury is empaneled and sworn lies in the need to protect the interest of an accused in retaining a chosen jury. . . . It is an interest with roots deep in the historic development of trial by jury in the Anglo-American system of criminal justice. Throughout that history there ran a strong tradition that once banded together a jury should not be discharged until it had completed its solemn task of announcing a verdict. (36)

In **bench trials**—trials without juries, in which judges find the facts—jeopardy kicks in when the court begins to hear evidence. Why? Because until the court begins to hear evidence, the trial hasn't started. The point when jeopardy kicks in, or attaches, has been called the "linchpin" of the double jeopardy inquiry, but the Fifth Amendment prohibits only double jeopardy. So the attachment of jeopardy is necessary but not enough to kick in double jeopardy; it's only enough when defendants are exposed to double jeopardy.

What actions are protected by the ban on double jeopardy? According to the U.S. Supreme Court, the double jeopardy prohibition bans these three actions:

1. A second prosecution for the same offense after conviction
2. A second prosecution for the same offense after acquittal
3. Multiple punishments for the same offense

In cases in which jeopardy has kicked in but the proceedings end before conviction or acquittal, the double jeopardy clause doesn't prevent a second prosecution for the same offense. This can happen in two types of cases. First, if the defendant moves to dismiss the case (or asks for or accepts a mistrial), and the judge rules in the defendant's favor, the prosecution can reprosecute. Second, even where defendants object to dismissal or a mistrial, the government can reprosecute for the same offense if the judge dismissed the case or ordered a mistrial because dismissal "serves the ends of justice" (**manifest necessity doctrine**).

The classic example of manifest necessity is the **hung jury**—a jury unable to reach a verdict. Why? According to the U.S. Supreme Court (*U.S. v. Perez* 1824):

> We think that in cases of this nature, the law has invested Courts of justice with the authority to discharge a jury from giving any verdict, whenever, in their opinion, taking all the circumstances into consideration, there is a manifest necessity for the act, or the ends of public justice would otherwise be defeated. They are to exercise a sound discretion on the subject; and it is impossible to define all the circumstances, which would render it proper to interfere. To be sure, the power ought to be used with the greatest of caution, under urgent circumstances. (580)

The manifest necessity doctrine isn't limited to hung juries. It also applies to a range of situations in which the prosecution is in a no-win situation. For example, when a court declared a mistrial because a defective indictment would have been enough to overturn a conviction, the U.S. Supreme Court (*Illinois v. Somerville* 1973) ruled that prosecuting the case again didn't violate the double jeopardy clause. The Court balanced two interests in reaching its decision, saying "a defendant's valued right to have his trial completed by a particular tribunal must in some instances be subordinated to the public's interests in fair trials designed to end in just judgments."

According to the Court:

A trial judge properly exercises his discretion to declare a mistrial . . . if a verdict of conviction could be reached but would have to be reversed on appeal due to an obvious procedural error in the trial. If an error would make reversal on appeal a certainty, it would not serve "the ends of public justice" to require that the Government proceed with its proof, when, if it succeeded before the jury, it would automatically be stripped of that success by an appellate court. (464)

The double jeopardy clause bans both multiple punishments and multiple prosecutions. The main purpose of the double jeopardy clause is to restrain prosecutors and judges. Although legislatures are free to define crimes and prescribe punishments, once they act "courts may not impose more than one punishment for the same offense and prosecutors ordinarily may not attempt to secure that punishment in more than one trial."

Still, it's not double jeopardy to prosecute and punish a defendant for the same acts in separate jurisdictions. According to the **dual sovereignty doctrine**, a crime arising out of the same facts in one state is not the same crime in another state. (In other words, "same offense" doesn't mean "identical offense.") The dual sovereignty doctrine arises most often when the same conduct is a crime under both state and federal law.

In *Heath v. Alabama* (1985), Larry Heath hired Charles Owens and Gregory Lumpkin for $2,000 to kill his wife, who was then nine months' pregnant. The killers fulfilled their part of the deal. Heath was sentenced to life imprisonment in a Georgia court after he pleaded guilty. However, part of the crime was committed in Alabama, so Alabama prosecuted Heath, too. He was convicted in Alabama of murder committed during a kidnapping and sentenced to death. He appealed the conviction on the grounds of double jeopardy. The U.S. Supreme Court affirmed the conviction, holding that successive prosecutions for the same crime in two different states didn't put him in jeopardy twice.

According to Justice O'Connor, writing for the majority of the Court:

To deny a State its power to enforce its criminal laws because another State has won the race to the courthouse "would be a shocking and untoward deprivation of the historic right and obligation of the States to maintain peace and order within their confines." Such a deprivation of a State's sovereign powers cannot be justified by the assertion that under "interest analysis" the State's legitimate penal interests will be satisfied through a prosecution conducted by another State. A State's interest in vindicating its sovereign authority through enforcement of its laws by definition can never be satisfied by another State's enforcement of its own laws. The Court has always understood the words of the Double Jeopardy Clause to reflect this fundamental principle, and we see no reason why we should reconsider that understanding today. (93)

Also, it doesn't put defendants in double jeopardy to prosecute them in multiple trials for separate offenses arising out of the same incident. The U.S. Supreme Court decided this in the horrible multiple-murder case, *Ciucci v. Illinois* (1958). Vincent Ciucci was married and had three children. When he fell in love with a 21-year-old woman he wanted to marry, his wife wouldn't give him a divorce. So he shot her and all three of his children in the head one by one while they slept. Illinois used the same evidence to convict Ciucci in three separate murder trials. The Court decided that the multiple trials, even if they stemmed from the same incident, didn't put Ciucci in jeopardy more than once.

## A Speedy Trial

According to the Sixth Amendment, "In all criminal trials, the accused shall enjoy the right to a speedy . . . trial." The idea of speedy justice is more than 900 years older than the Bill of Rights. In 1187, King Henry II provided for "speedy justice" in the Assizes of Clarendon. King John promised in the Magna Carta in 1215 that "every subject of this realme . . . may . . . have justice . . . speedily without delay." In his *Institutes*—called by Thomas Jefferson, "the universal elementary book of law students" (*Klopfer v. North Carolina* 1967, 225)—Sir Edward Coke wrote that the English itinerant justices in 1600 "have not suffered the prisoner to be long detained, but at their next coming have given the prisoner full and speedy justice . . . without detaining him long in prison" ([Coke 1797 in] *Klopfer v. North Carolina* 1967). The Virginia Declaration of Rights in 1776 (the state's "bills of rights") and the speedy trial clause of the Sixth Amendment reflect this history. And even though the state constitutions guarantee a speedy trial, the U.S. Supreme Court has extended the federal speedy trial protection of the Sixth Amendment to the states (225).

The speedy trial clause promotes and balances several interests. For the accused, it prevents prolonged detention before trial; reduces the anxiety and uncertainty surrounding criminal prosecution; and guards against weakening the defense's case through loss of alibi witnesses and other evidence. And because most detained defendants are poor, both the process interest in ensuring equal protection of the laws and the societal interest in protecting the poor and less powerful are at stake in speedy trial decisions (*Report to the Nation on Crime and Justice* 1988, 123).

The speedy trial provision also promotes the interest in obtaining the correct result. Delay means lost evidence and lost witnesses—or at least the loss of their memory—not only for the defense but also for the prosecution. The clause also promotes process goals, particularly that decisions should be made in a timely fashion. Organizational interests are at stake as well. Failure to provide prompt trials contributes to large case backlogs, particularly in urban areas. Furthermore, long pretrial detention is costly to taxpayers. In addition to feeding and housing detained defendants, lost wages and greater welfare burdens result from incarceration.

According to the U.S. Supreme Court, the Sixth Amendment "speedy trial clock" doesn't start ticking until suspects are formally charged with crimes. Before they're charged, defendants have to depend on either statutes spelling out the length of time allowed between the commission of crimes and the filing of charges (statutes of limitations) or the due process clauses. So in rejecting a speedy trial violation in a delay of three years between the commission of the crime and an indictment, the Court said:

> The due process clause of the Fifth Amendment would require dismissal of the indictment if it were shown at trial that the pre-indictment delay . . . caused substantial prejudice to appellants' rights to a fair trial and that the delay was an intentional device to gain tactical advantage over the accused. (*U.S. v. Marion* 1971, 324)

The speedy trial clause bans only *undue* delays. According to the U.S. Supreme Court, flexibility governs whether delays are undue enough to violate the speedy trial clause. The Court has adopted another one of its balancing tests to decide whether delays hurt ("prejudice," if you want the technical term) defendants' cases. Four elements make up the balance:

1. The length of the delay
2. The reason for the delay
3. The defendant's assertion of his or her right to a speedy trial
4. The prejudice (harm) the delay causes to the defendant's case

What are the consequences of violating the speedy trial guarantee? According to the Court, there are only two remedies for the violation of the speedy trial clause:

1. ***Dismissal without prejudice.*** Allows a new prosecution for the same offense
2. ***Dismissal with prejudice.*** Terminates the case with the provision that it can't be prosecuted again

According to a unanimous U.S. Supreme Court, even though there's enough evidence for conviction, undue delay subjects defendants to "emotional stress" that requires dismissal as "the only possible remedy." The Court's ruling has raised the strong objection that the high price of dismissal will make courts "extremely hesitant" to find speedy trial violations because judges don't want to be responsible for freeing criminals (*Strunk v. U.S.* 1973).

Although the Sixth Amendment doesn't require it, several states have enacted statutes or court rules that set time limits for bringing cases to trial. These limits vary widely among the states. The Federal Speedy Trial Act provides definite time periods for bringing defendants to trial. The government has to start prosecution within 30 days after arrest (60 days if there's no grand jury in session); arraign defendants within 10 days after filing indictments or informations; and bring defendants to trial within 60 days following arraignment.

According to the act, the following delays don't count in computing days:

1. Delays needed to determine the defendant's competency to stand trial
2. Delays due to other trials of the defendant
3. Delays due to hearings on pretrial motions
4. Delays because of *interlocutory appeals*—provisional appeals that interrupt the proceedings, such as an appeal from a ruling on a pretrial motion

## A Change of Venue

The Sixth Amendment provides that "in all criminal prosecutions, the accused shall enjoy the right to a . . . public trial, by an impartial jury of the State and district wherein the crime shall have been committed." A defendant's pretrial motion to change the venue (the place where the trial is held) waives the Sixth Amendment right to have a trial in the state and district where the crime was committed. Only defendants, not the prosecution, may move to change the venue, and changes of venue aren't automatic.

According to Rule 21(a) of the *Federal Rules of Criminal Procedure* (2002):

> The court upon motion of the defendant shall transfer the proceeding as to that defendant to another district . . . if the court is satisfied that there exists in the district where the prosecution is pending so great a prejudice against the defendant that the defendant cannot obtain a fair and impartial trial at any place fixed for holding court in that district.

Why do defendants give up their right to a trial in the place where the crime was committed? Because they believe they can't get an impartial public trial in that location. When courts rule on the motion, they balance the right to a public trial in the place where the crime was committed against the right to an impartial trial. In that respect, changing venue reflects the interest in obtaining a proper result in the individual case—prejudiced jurors can't find the truth. Process values are also at stake: the integrity of the judicial process requires a calm, dignified, reflective atmosphere; due process demands unbiased fact-finding; the equal protection clause prohibits trying defendants who are the object of public outrage differently from other defendants.

In *Sheppard v. Maxwell* (1966), the U.S. Supreme Court held that "where there is a reasonable likelihood that the prejudicial news prior to trial will prevent a fair trial, the judge should continue the case until the threat abates, or transfer it to another county not so permeated with publicity" (363). In this case, Ohio tried Dr. Sam Sheppard for the bludgeoning murder of his pregnant wife, Marilyn, a Cleveland socialite.

The case dominated the news and gripped the public's attention before, during, and after the trial. Lurid headlines and long stories appeared regularly, detailing the brutality of the murder and Sheppard's failure to cooperate with authorities. The editorials accused Sheppard of the murder. One charged on the front page that "somebody is getting away with murder," alleging that Sheppard's wealth and prominent social position protected him from a full-fledged investigation by police. Finally, the papers printed detailed analyses of evidence that came to light during the investigation, editorializing about its credibility, relevance, and materiality to the case.

As for the trial itself, the press, the public, and other observers packed the courtroom every day. One local radio station set up broadcasting facilities on the third floor of the courthouse. Television and newsreel cameras waiting outside on the courthouse steps filmed jurors, lawyers, witnesses, and other participants in the trial. All the jurors were exposed to the heavy publicity prior to the trial. Referring to the "carnival atmosphere" at the trial, the Supreme Court concluded that Sheppard was entitled to a new trial without showing actual prejudice—a reasonable likelihood of prejudice was sufficient.

Fascination with the case didn't stop even after Sheppard's appeal to the U.S. Supreme Court. The popular 1960s television drama *The Fugitive* was based on the case. So was the 1990s movie with the same title. (The fascination continued for television viewers who watched a short-lived 2001 version of *The Fugitive*.)

In granting Sheppard a new trial, the U.S. Supreme Court ruled that the proceedings should have been postponed or the trial venue moved because of a reasonable likelihood of prejudice. The **reasonable-likelihood-of-prejudice test** requires courts to balance four elements in each change-of-venue case:

1. The kind and amount of community bias that endangers a fair trial

2. The size of the community where jury panels are selected

3. The details and seriousness of the offense

4. The status of the victim and the accused

These elements may vary in intensity, and they don't all have to be present in each case; they're guidelines for judges when they measure the likelihood the defendant will receive a fair trial.

Most courts don't grant changes of venue even if defendants show there's a reasonable likelihood of prejudice. Instead, they adopt an **actual prejudice test** to determine whether to either change the venue or take less drastic measures. Under the actual

| TABLE 12.5 | Factors Considered in Change-of-Venue Motions |
| --- | --- |

- Trials at distant locations burden witnesses.
- Communities have a substantial interest in the trial taking place where the crime was committed.
- Changing prosecutors disrupts the state's case.
- Courts can't decide the partiality question until the jury has been impaneled.
- Courts don't want to transfer a case after all the time spent in picking a jury.

prejudice test courts have to decide whether jurors were in fact prejudiced by harmful publicity. In *Swindler v. State* (1979), for example, John Edward Swindler proved that three jurors had read and heard about the case and that over 80 percent of prospective jurors were excused for cause. This didn't stop the Arkansas Supreme Court from rejecting Swindler's claim that the trial court's refusal to grant his motion for change of venue denied him a fair trial and upholding Swindler's death sentence. Swindler's experience is an example of how rare change of venue is.

In deciding whether the venue should be changed, courts consider a number of issues (Table 12.5). Moving proceedings to jurisdictions farther away, providing for witnesses to appear, and working in unfamiliar court surroundings hinder smooth, efficient, economical resolution of criminal cases. Furthermore, society has a strong interest in maintaining public confidence in the criminal justice system and providing an outlet for community reaction to crime. Citizens resent moving trials both because they want to follow the proceedings, and they feel insulted by a ruling that their own jurisdiction can't guarantee a fair trial.

## The Suppression of Evidence

As you've already learned, almost every case excerpt dealing with police work is about a struggle between defendants who want to keep evidence out of court and prosecutors who want to get it in. And you've also learned the reason for this struggle is the exclusionary rule (Chapter 11). Whether the exclusionary rule applies is decided in a pretrial hearing triggered by a defense motion to suppress evidence that law enforcement officers obtained by searches, seizures, confessions, or identification procedures (Chapters 4–9). The decision whether to let evidence in or keep it out is a legal question, meaning judges, not juries, decide whether to exclude evidence.

## SUMMARY

**I. Starting Court Proceedings**
   A. Police have to make decisions after the arrest, interrogation, and identification procedures are completed.
       1. Police decide whether to drop the case or take it to the prosecutor.
       2. Police focus on two elements to make their decisions.
           a. Is the suspect guilty?
           b. Can they give prosecutors enough evidence to prove it?
   B. Prosecutors have three options after receiving the case from police.
       1. They can dispose of the case.
       2. They can divert the suspect to an alternative program.
       3. They can charge the suspect with a crime.

## II. The Decision to Charge

A. Prosecutors perform dual roles.
1. They represent the public in prosecuting defendants.
2. They represent the court in doing justice to individual defendants—which can mean diverting suspects into restitution, treatment, or community service.

B. The decision to charge starts the adversarial criminal justice process.

C. Prosecutors' decision to charge focuses on two elements.
1. Is the case against the suspect strong enough to convict?
2. Is prosecuting this suspect a wise use of limited resources (selective prosecution)?

## III. Probable Cause to Detain Suspects

A. The Fourth Amendment commands against "unreasonable seizure."
1. Detained suspects have to be brought promptly before a neutral magistrate.
2. Magistrates decide whether there's probable cause to detain suspects.

B. The Fourth Amendment allows detention long enough (usually no longer than 48 hours) for police to complete "administrative steps" before taking suspects to magistrates.

## IV. The First Appearance

A. The purpose is to inform suspects of the charges against them.

B. Judges inform suspects of their constitutional rights:
1. They have a right to remain silent.
2. They have a right to counsel.
3. They have a right to a jury trial.

## V. Bail and Pretrial Detention

A. In deciding whether to permit bail or require pretrial detention, the judge balances public safety and the need to bring defendants to justice against the rights of defendants not yet convicted of crimes.

B. Conditions judges attach to release on bail include:
1. *Release on recognizance (ROR).* The defendant promises to appear in court.
2. *Money bond.* The defendant pays usually 10% of the bond amount.
3. *Supervised release.* For example, the defendant may be required to report to the local police department.

C. Detention has consequences for defendants.
1. They may lose their wages and/or job.
2. It affects defendants and their families.
3. It restricts defendants' ability to aid lawyers with their own defense.

D. The U.S. Constitution, Eighth Amendment bans "excessive," not all, bail.
1. The amount of bail depends on:
   a. The seriousness of the offense
   b. The amount of the evidence against the defendant
   c. The defendant's family ties, employment, financial resources, character, and mental condition
   d. The length of the defendant's residence in the community
   e. The defendant's criminal history
   f. The defendant's prior record for appearing and/or "jumping" bail
2. The Constitution permits detaining suspects who threaten public safety.
3. Preventive detention doesn't violate the due process rights of defendants even though they're presumed innocent.

4. Preventive detention isn't punishment, so the Eighth Amendment cruel and unusual punishment ban doesn't apply to it.

## VI. The Right to Counsel

A. The right attaches to all "critical stages" in criminal proceedings.
   1. This includes all proceedings after the first appearance.
   2. It doesn't include police interrogations before the first appearance. (Chapter 8)
B. The right applies to "all criminal prosecutions."
   1. This includes all felonies.
   2. It includes all misdemeanors in which the punishment is jail time.
C. Indigent (poor) defendants have a right to appointed counsel.
   1. Poor defendants don't have to be completely destitute.
   2. Earnings and assets count; help from friends and relatives doesn't.
   3. Actual, not potential, earnings are the measure.
   4. The state can tap defendants' future earnings to get reimbursement for the costs of counsel, transcripts, and fees for expert witnesses and investigators.
   5. Defendants have a right to "effective" counsel.
      a. In *Strickland v. Washington*, the Court developed a two-pronged test of whether a defense counsel was effective.
      b. Defendants have to prove both the reasonableness and the prejudice prongs.
         (1) *Reasonableness prong.* Defendants have to prove their lawyer's performance wasn't reasonably competent. There's a presumption that lawyers are competent, and the courts give them lots of leeway in tactics and strategy.
         (2) *Prejudice prong.* Defendants have to prove their lawyer's incompetence was probably responsible for their conviction.

## VII. Testing the Government's Case

A. After the decision to charge, the case moves from the prosecutor's office to the court.
B. Two procedures test the government's case (determine whether there's enough evidence to go to trial).
   1. A preliminary hearing is public.
      a. It tests both government and defense cases (it's not a minitrial).
      b. A judge presides.
      c. The judge decides whether the government's case passes the test (meets the bind-over standard).
   2. A grand jury review is secret.
      a. The grand jury hears only the government's case.
      b. A prosecutor presides.
      c. Grand jurors decide whether the government's case passes the test (indictment).
      d. Grand jurors have to meet membership requirements.
         (1) They have to be U.S. citizens over 18.
         (2) They have to reside in the jurisdiction.
         (3) They can't have any felony convictions.
         (4) They have to speak, read, and write English.
         (5) They can't have any physical impairments that would hinder their participation (hearing, vision).

## VIII. Arraignment

A. Arraignment brings defendants to court to hear and answer (plead to) charges.

B. Defendants can enter four possible pleas (answers):

1. Not guilty
2. Not guilty by reason of insanity
3. Nolo contendere (no contest)
4. Guilty

## IX. Pretrial motions

A. Pretrial motions decide questions before trial that don't require a trial to answer.

B. The Fifth Amendment bans double jeopardy.

1. This protects the interests of both governments and defendants.
   a. For governments, it:
      (1) Allows one fair shot to convict
      (2) Promotes closure because it's final
      (3) Reduces costs that multiple trials would lead to
   b. For defendants, it:
      (1) Limits the government's advantage of greater resources
      (2) Reduces prolonged stress that multiple trials would lead to
      (3) Provides finality, because acquittals can't be overturned
      (4) Reduces costs that multiple trials would lead to

2. Jeopardy begins:
   a. In a jury trial when the jury is sworn in
   b. In a bench trial (by the judge without a jury) when the judge begins to hear evidence

3. Double jeopardy doesn't prevent a second prosecution if
   a. The judge grants the defendant's motion to dismiss
   b. The judge dismisses or orders a mistrial to "serve the ends of justice"— (hung jury)

C. The Sixth Amendment requires a speedy trial.

1. The requirement begins when the government formally charges suspects.
2. The ban is only on undue delays.
3. The balancing test looks at several factors:
   a. The length of the delay
   b. The reason for the delay
   c. The defendant's assertion of the right to a speedy trial
   d. Prejudice (harm) the delay causes to the defendant's case
4. There are two consequences for undue delay:
   a. Dismissal without prejudice allows new prosecution.
   b. Dismissal with prejudice bars new prosecution.
5. The Federal Speedy Trial Act provides definite time periods for bringing defendants to trial.
   a. Prosecution has to begin within 30 days after the arrest (60 if no grand jury is in session).
   b. Arraignment has to take place within 10 days after the indictment or the information is filed.
   c. The trial has to begin within 60 days of the arraignment.

D. The change-of-venue motion seeks to move the case to another community.

1. This motion waives the defendant's Sixth Amendment right to trial in the district where the crime was committed.
2. Only defendants can file a motion to change the venue.
3. Trying the case in the community where the crime was committed protects the interests of both the defendant and the community.
   a. It protects the defendant's right to a fair and impartial trial.
   b. It protects the community's interest in administering justice where the crime was committed.
4. Courts use two tests for granting motions to change the venue because of harmful publicity.
   a. The reasonable-likelihood-of-prejudice test, used by a minority of courts, balances:
      (1) The kind and amount of bias
      (2) The size of the community where juries are selected
      (3) The details and seriousness of the offense
      (4) The status of the victim and the accused
   b. The actual prejudice test, used by the majority of courts, requires proof that jurors were in fact (not just reasonably likely to have been) prejudiced by harmful publicity.
E. The motion to suppress evidence tries to let defendants keep out damaging information.
   1. An inquiry regarding the exclusionary rule (Chapter 10) triggers the motion.
   2. Exclusion is a legal question decided by judges.

# REVIEW QUESTIONS

1. Describe what occurs following arrest, interrogation, and identification procedures.

2. List the reasons that affect whether police drop cases or take them to prosecutors.

3. Identify the two roles of prosecutors and how the roles affect their decisions.

4. According to the U.S. Supreme Court, why is the initiation of judicial proceedings not just a "mere formalism"?

5. List and explain the importance of the reasons behind the decision of prosecutors to charge, divert, or drop criminal cases.

6. Why and when do police officers have to take arrested suspects to a magistrate?

7. Explain the difference between probable cause to detain a suspect and probable cause to go to trial.

8. What's the significance of the U.S. Supreme Court case *Gerstein v. Pugh*?

9. List the "administrative steps" police officers can complete before they take detained suspects to magistrates.

10. Identify and describe the consequences of detention before trial.

11. Describe the balance struck in the decision to bail or detain defendants.

12. Exactly what does the constitutional right to bail consist of?

13. Identify three constitutional rights our bail system denies to poor defendants, and explain how each is denied.

14. Describe the obstacles pretrial detention creates for defendants trying to prepare their defense.

15. According to the 1984 Bail Reform Act, when can judges preventively detain defendants?

16. What constitutional rights do pretrial detainees have regarding the conditions of their confinement?

17. List the "critical stages" of criminal prosecutions.

18. Summarize the facts of the U.S. Supreme Court decision in *Argersinger v. Hamlin*.

19. List four guidelines for defining indigence developed by the U.S. Courts of Appeals, and summarize the detailed definition of indigence adopted in Minnesota.

20. Identify, define, and explain the two-prongs of the U.S. Supreme Court's test of "effective" counsel adopted in *Strickland v. Washington*.

21. List and describe the differences between testing the government's case by grand jury review and by preliminary hearing.

22. Identify the four possible pleas defendants can enter at their arraignment.

23. Describe and explain the significance of the U.S. Supreme Court decisions in *Heath v. Alabama* and *Ciucci v. Illinois*.

24. According to the Federal Speedy Trial Act, when does the government have to begin prosecution? arraign defendants? bring defendants to trial?

25. Summarize the arguments against changes of venue.

26. Describe and summarize the significance of the U.S. Supreme Court decision in *Sheppard v. Maxwell*.

27. What kind of question is answered by the motion to suppress evidence?

## *KEY TERMS*

arraignment, p. 402
diversion cases, p. 403
decision to charge, p. 403
probable cause to detain suspects, p. 405
first appearance, p. 405
probable cause to go to trial, p. 405
class action, p. 405
criminal complaint, p. 408
release on recognizance (ROR), p. 409
preventive detention, p. 412
Bail Reform Act of 1984, p. 412
retained counsel, p. 418
appointed counsel, p. 418
indigent defendants, p. 418

counsel pro bono, p. 418
public defender, p. 418
mockery of justice standard, p. 424
reasonably competent attorney standard, p. 425
two-pronged effective counsel test, p. 425
reasonableness prong, p. 425
prejudice prong, p. 425
preliminary hearing p. 426
grand jury review, p. 426
indictment, p. 426
true bill, p. 426
grand jurors, p. 426
bind over, p. 426

bind-over standard, p. 427
prima facie case rule, p. 427
directed verdict rule, p. 427
charge the grand jury, p. 428
pretrial motions, p. 431
double jeopardy, p. 431
bench trials, p. 432
manifest necessity doctrine, p. 432
hung jury, p. 432
dual sovereignty doctrine, p. 433
dismissal without prejudice, p. 435
dismissal with prejudice, p. 435
reasonable-likelihood-of-prejudice test, p. 436
actual prejudice test, p. 436

# Court Proceedings II: Trial and Conviction

## MAIN POINTS

- Court proceedings are sharply divided into adversarial proceedings inside the courtroom and informal negotiations outside the courtroom.
- Most cases are decided by guilty pleas, not by trial.
- Defendants have a constitutional right to a jury trial in all but "petty" offenses.
- There's no constitutional right to a 12-member jury *or* to a unanimous verdict.
- The government has the whole burden of proving defendants are guilty beyond a reasonable doubt; defendants have no burden at all to prove they're not guilty.
- There's no empirical data to resolve the ongoing debate over the benefits and costs of plea bargaining.
- Courts' acceptance of guilty pleas and plea bargaining is constitutional, even when defendants maintain they're innocent.

Claude Ballew was charged with "distributing obscene materials" in violation of the Georgia Code by knowingly showing the film "Behind the Green Door" that "contained obscene and indecent scenes." After a jury of 5 persons had been selected and sworn, Ballew moved to have the court impanel a jury of 12 persons. That court, however, tried its misdemeanor cases before juries of five persons pursuant to Ga. Const., Art. 6, paragraph 16, § 1. Ballew contended that for an obscenity trial, a jury of only five was constitutionally inadequate to assess the contemporary standards of the community. He also argued that the Sixth and Fourteenth Amendments required a jury of at least six members in criminal cases. 🌀

Ballew v. Georgia (1978), U.S. Supreme Court

## CASES COVERED

*Ballew v. Georgia,*
435 U.S. 223 (1978)

*Lockhart v. McCree,*
476 U.S. 162 (1986)

*North Carolina v. Alford,*
400 U.S. 25 (1970)

Court proceedings are sharply divided into adversarial proceedings inside the courtroom and informal negotiations outside the courtroom. Three constitutional commands lie behind the trial and conviction of defendants in criminal cases:

> ARTICLE III, § 2 The Trial of all Crimes, except in Cases of Impeachment, shall be by Jury; and such Trial shall be held in the State where the Crimes shall have been committed.

> THE FIFTH AMENDMENT No person shall be . . . compelled in any criminal case to be a witness against himself. . . .

> THE SIXTH AMENDMENT In all criminal prosecutions, the accused shall enjoy the right to a speedy and public trial, by an impartial jury of the State and District wherein the crime shall have been committed . . . to be confronted with the witnesses against him, . . . and to have the assistance of Counsel for his defense.

These constitutional commands set high standards because conviction for a crime can result in the greatest deprivations (loss of property, liberty, privacy, and perhaps even life itself) in the criminal process. These commands are directed almost exclusively at criminal trials, but, in practice, only about 10 percent of criminal cases are decided in trials. Although trials receive most of the attention in the news, and of course in movies and television, they account for only about 10 out of every 100 convictions. The other 90 result from guilty pleas. Some of these guilty pleas result from plea bargaining, but many are **straight guilty pleas** (pleas of guilty without negotiation).

Trials and guilty pleas promote different interests. The trial promotes fact-finding by the adversarial process, procedural regularity, and public participation in criminal proceedings. The guilty plea promotes efficiency, economy, harmony, and speed. Plea negotiations also promote fact-finding by informal discussion and the give-and-take that occur in reaching an agreement over the plea.

In this chapter, we'll examine the constitutionally mandated trial by jury, the stages and rules of jury trials, and conviction by guilty pleas.

# TRIAL BY JURY

Trial by jury is ancient, with roots in the societies of the Teutonic tribes in Germany and the Normans before their conquest of England. The Assizes of Clarendon in 1187 and the Magna Carta in 1215 also contain traces of its origins. The jury trial was provided for specifically in the English Bill of Rights in 1689, and, from that time, it became common practice in the British American colonies.

From the start, the colonists resented royal interference with the right to a jury trial. Complaints regarding that interference appear in the Stamp Act, Congress's resolutions, the First Continental Congress's resolves, and the Declaration of Independence.

Article III, § 2, in the body of the U.S. Constitution, and the Sixth Amendment reflect the new nation's commitment to jury trial. Every state constitution guarantees it, and the U.S. Supreme Court has interpreted the due process clause of the Fourteenth Amendment to require states to provide it (*Duncan v. Louisiana* 1968).

Trial by jury promotes several interests. It checks and balances government power by putting an independent community-dominated body between the state with all its resources and a single individual. Jury trial also balances official power with citizen participation in criminal law enforcement. In addition, it guarantees that accused citizens who prefer that other citizens decide their innocence or guilt will have that preference honored.

In extending the Sixth Amendment's jury trial right to the states, Justice Byron R. White wrote the following:

> The guarantees of jury trial . . . reflect a profound judgment about the way in which law should be enforced and justice administered. . . . Providing an accused with the right to be tried by a jury of his peers gave him an inestimable safeguard against the corrupt or overzealous prosecutor and against the compliant, biased, or eccentric judge. . . . Beyond this, the jury trial . . . reflects a . . . reluctance to entrust plenary powers over the life and liberty of the citizen to one judge or to a group of judges. Fear of unchecked power, so typical of our State and Federal Governments in other respects, found expression in the criminal law in this insistence upon community participation in the determination of guilt or innocence. (*Duncan v. Louisiana* 1968, 156)

Let's explore more fully the meaning of the right to a trial by jury by examining how this right is affected by the moral seriousness standard, the issue of how many citizens are required to sit on a jury, the jury selection process, and the right to a public trial.

## The Moral Seriousness Standard

According to the U.S. Supreme Court, there's one major exception to the right to a jury trial for "all crimes," in Article III, § 2, and "all criminal prosecutions," in the Sixth Amendment. That exception is for "petty offenses" (*Duncan v. Louisiana* 1968, 160). In jurisdictions where there's no specific law drawing a line between petty and other offenses, the Court has used six months' imprisonment as the dividing line (*Baldwin v. New York* 1970). But, by taking the "moral quality" of offenses into account, courts have declared some offenses serious even if the penalty is less than six months' imprisonment.

So, under this **moral seriousness standard**, courts have decided defendants had a right to a jury trial when charged with conspiring to deceive immigration officials (*U.S. v. Sanchez-Meza* 1976), driving while intoxicated (*U.S. v. Craner* 1981), and shoplifting (*State v. Superior Court* 1978), even though the penalty for these offenses was less than six months in jail.

## The 12-Member Jury Requirement

The 12-member jury at one time was regarded by the U.S. Supreme Court as essential to the right to a jury trial (*Thompson v. Utah* 1898). The Court has since retreated from that position. Justice Byron R. White spelled out the reasons in *Williams v. Florida* (1970):

1. We can't "pretend" to know the Framers' intent.

2. The number 12 is based on superstition about the number (12 apostles, 12 tribes).

3. History doesn't give good enough reasons to stick to 12 members in today's world.

So, according to the Court in *Williams v. Florida* (1970), the Sixth Amendment only demands enough jurors to achieve the goals of a jury trial: to find the truth and allow for community participation in criminal justice decision making. And that number isn't necessarily 12:

> That the jury at common law was composed of precisely 12 is a historical accident, unnecessary to effect the purposes of the jury system and wholly without significance "except to mystics." To read the Sixth Amendment as forever codifying a feature so incidental to the real purpose of the Amendment is to ascribe a blind formalism to the Framers which would require considerably more evidence than we have been able to discover in the history and language of the Constitution or in the reasoning of our past decisions. (102)

The 12-member jury has strong supporters, despite the Court's dismissal of it as superstitious. Justice John Marshall Harlan called the accident of superstition argument "much too thin." If the number 12 was merely an accident, it was one that "has recurred without interruption since the 14th century." Also, according to Justice Harlan:

> If 12 jurors are not essential, why are six? Can it be doubted that a unanimous jury of 12 provides a greater safeguard than a majority vote of six? The uncertainty that will henceforth plague the meaning of trial by jury is itself a further reason for not hoisting the anchor of history. . . . The [Court's] circumvention of history is compounded by the cavalier disregard of numerous pronouncements of this Court that reflect the understanding of the jury as one of twelve members and have fixed expectations accordingly. (*Baldwin v. New York* 1970, 126)

Judges aren't the only ones who support the 12-member jury. Social scientists have found that juries with 12 members are right more often, and they represent the community better than juries with fewer than 12 members. Hans Zeisel, a major authority on the jury, had this to say about the 12-member jury:

> Suppose that in a given community, 90 percent of the people share one viewpoint and the remaining 10 percent have a different viewpoint. Suppose further that we draw 100 twelve-member and 100 six-member juries. Using standard statistical methods, it can be predicted that approximately 72 of the twelve-member juries will contain a representative of the 10 percent minority, as compared to only 47 juries composed of six persons. This difference is by no means negligible. (LaFave and Israel 1984, 2:696, n. 57)

Six-member juries are enough to satisfy the Sixth Amendment but what about five? The Supreme Court answered "no" in our next case excerpt, *Ballew v. Georgia* (1978).

---

# C A S E  —  *Does a Five-Member Jury Guarantee a Jury Trial?*

### *Ballew v. Georgia*
435 U.S. 223 (1978)

### HISTORY

Claude Ballew was charged with "distributing obscene matter" (a misdemeanor), tried by a five-member jury, convicted, and sentenced to a one-year incarceration and a fine of $1,000, the term of incarceration to be suspended upon payment of the fine. The Georgia Supreme Court denied certiorari. The U.S. Supreme Court granted certiorari, reversed

the judgment, and remanded the case for proceedings consistent with the decision excerpted here.

BLACKMUN, J., JOINED BY STEVENS, J.

### FACTS

In November 1973, Claude Davis Ballew was the manager of the Paris Adult Theatre at 320 Peachtree Street, Atlanta, Ga. On November 9, two investigators from the Fulton County Solicitor General's office viewed at the theater a motion picture film entitled "Behind the Green Door."

On September 14, 1974, Ballew was charged with "distributing obscene materials" in violation of the Georgia Code by knowingly showing the film "Behind the Green Door" that "contained obscene and indecent scenes." Ballew was brought to trial in the Criminal Court of Fulton County. After a jury of 5 persons had been selected and sworn, Ballew moved to have the court impanel a jury of 12 persons. That court, however, tried its misdemeanor cases before juries of five persons pursuant to Ga. Const., Art. 6, paragraph 16, § 1. Ballew contended that for an obscenity trial, a jury of only five was constitutionally inadequate to assess the contemporary standards of the community.

He also argued that the Sixth and Fourteenth Amendments required a jury of at least six members in criminal cases.

The motion for a 12-person jury was overruled, and the trial went on to its conclusion before the 5-person jury that had been impaneled. At the conclusion of the trial, the jury deliberated for 38 minutes and returned a verdict of guilty on both counts of the accusation. The court imposed a sentence of one year and a $1,000 fine on each count, the periods of incarceration to run concurrently and to be suspended upon payment of the fines.

The Supreme Court of Georgia denied certiorari and the U.S. Supreme Court granted certiorari.

## OPINION

The Fourteenth Amendment guarantees the right of trial by jury in all state nonpetty criminal cases. The purpose of the jury trial is to prevent oppression by the Government. This purpose is attained by the participation of the community in determinations of guilt and by the application of the common sense of laymen who, as jurors, consider the case.

Rather than requiring 12 members . . . the Sixth Amendment mandates a jury only of sufficient size to promote group deliberation, to insulate members from outside intimidation, and to provide a representative cross-section of the community.

When the Court in *Williams v. Florida* (1970) . . . held that a jury of six was not unconstitutional—it expressly reserved ruling on the issue whether a number smaller than six passed constitutional scrutiny. The Court refused to speculate when this so-called "slippery slope" would become too steep. We face now, however, the two-fold question whether a further reduction in the size of the state criminal trial jury does make the grade too dangerous, that is, whether it inhibits the functioning of the jury as an institution to a significant degree, and, if so, whether any state interest counterbalances and justifies the disruption so as to preserve its constitutionality.

First, recent empirical data suggest that progressively smaller juries are less likely to foster effective group deliberation. At some point, this decline leads to inaccurate fact-finding and incorrect application of the common sense of the community to the facts. The smaller the group, the less likely are members to make critical contributions necessary for the solution of a given problem. As juries decrease in size, then, they are less likely to have members who remember each of the important pieces of evidence or argument. Furthermore, the smaller the group, the less likely it is to overcome the biases of its members to obtain an accurate result. When individual and group decision making were compared, it was seen that groups performed better because prejudices of individuals were frequently counterbalanced, and objectivity resulted.

Second, the data now raise doubts about the accuracy of the results achieved by smaller and smaller panels. Statistical studies suggest that the risk of convicting an innocent person rises as the size of the jury diminishes. Third, the data suggest that the verdicts of jury deliberation in criminal cases will vary as juries become smaller, and that the variance amounts to an imbalance to the detriment of one side, the defense. Fourth, a jury's decrease in size foretells problems not only for jury decision making, but also for the representation of minority groups in the community.

The Court repeatedly has held that meaningful community participation cannot be attained with the exclusion of minorities or other identifiable groups from jury service. While we adhere to, and reaffirm our holding in *Williams v. Florida*, these studies, most of which have been made since *Williams* was decided in 1970, lead us to conclude that the purpose and functioning of the jury in a criminal trial is seriously impaired, and to a constitutional degree, by a reduction in size to below six members. With the reduction in the number of jurors below six creating a substantial threat to Sixth and Fourteenth Amendment guarantees, we must consider whether any interest of the State justifies the reduction. We find no significant state advantage in reducing the number of jurors from six to five.

The States utilize juries of less than 12 primarily for administrative reasons. Savings in court time and in financial costs are claimed to justify the reductions. A reduction in size from six to five or four or even three would save the States little. They could reduce slightly the daily allowances, but with a reduction from six to five the saving would be minimal.

The judgment of the Court of Appeals is REVERSED, and the case is REMANDED for further proceedings not inconsistent with this opinion. It is so ordered.

### Questions

1. Why does a six-member jury satisfy the Constitution but not a five-member jury, according to the Court?

2. How does the Court arrive at its conclusion?

3. Does social science research provide a better guide to how many jurors should constitute a jury than does history? Explain your answer.

## Jury Selection

According to the U.S. Supreme Court, the Sixth Amendment right to an "impartial jury" requires that juries represent a "fair cross section" of the community. Furthermore, the equal protection clause of the Fourteenth Amendment prohibits the systematic exclusion of members of defendants' racial, gender, ethnic, or religious group. The Federal Jury Selection and Service Act meets these constitutional requirements by requiring that juries be

1. "Selected at random from a fair cross section of the community in the district or division wherein the court convenes," and

2. "No citizen shall be excluded from service as a grand or petit juror in the district courts of the United States on account of race, color, religion, sex, national origin, or economic status."

Most states have similar provisions. To implement them, jurisdictions select jurors at random from the following sources: local census reports, tax rolls, city directories, telephone books, and driver's license lists. Some states, mainly in New England and the South, use the **key-man system**, in which civic and political leaders recommend people from these lists that they know personally or by reputation. Understandably, the key-man system faces repeated challenges that it doesn't represent a fair cross section of the community and that it discriminates against various segments in the community (LaFave and Israel 1984, 2:708).

Jury service isn't popular; most prospective jurors ask to be excused (Table 13.1). Courts rarely refuse their requests because it's "easier, administratively and financially, to excuse unwilling people" (LaFave and Israel 1984, 2:708). Some groups are ordinarily exempt from jury service: persons below voting age, convicted felons, and persons who can't write and read English.

Some occupations are also exempt in some states: doctors, pharmacists, teachers, clergy, lawyers, judges, criminal justice professionals, and some other public employees (LaFave and Israel 1984, 2:708–9).

From the **jury panel** (the potential jurors drawn from the list of eligible citizens not excused), the attorneys for the government and the defendant pick the jurors who will actually serve. The process of picking the actual jurors from the pool of potential jurors by questioning them is called the **voir dire**—literally, "to speak the truth." Both prosecutors and defense attorneys can remove jurors during the voir dire. There are two ways of removing (usually called "striking") potential jurors, **peremptory challenges** (striking without having to give a reason) and **challenges for cause** (striking by showing the juror is biased). Lawyers almost always use their peremptory challenges to strike potential jurors who look like they're going to sympathize with the other side. Attorneys use challenges for cause only when they can convince judges of juror bias.

The number of peremptory challenges depends on the jurisdiction; the number of challenges for cause is unlimited. In the federal courts, both the prosecution and the

---

**TABLE 13.1**    **Common Excuses for Exemption from Jury Service**

| | |
|---|---|
| • Economic hardship | • Need to care for small children |
| • Advanced age | • Distance between home and the courthouse is too far |
| • Illness | |

defense have 20 peremptories in capital offenses and 3 in misdemeanors. In felony cases, defendants have 10, and the government has 6. Both sides rarely exercise their right to challenges for cause—usually one to three times to assemble a jury of 12 (Van Dyke 1977, 14).

Inquiring into racial prejudice during voir dire is sensitive. In *Dukes v. Waitkevitch* (1976), for example, the First Circuit U.S. Court of Appeals ruled that the trial court didn't commit a constitutional error when it refused to inquire into racial prejudice in a case in which the Black defendant was charged with participating in a gang rape of White women. In capital cases, however, the U.S. Supreme Court has ruled otherwise:

> The risk of racial prejudice infecting capital sentencing proceedings is especially serious in light of the complete finality of the death sentence. . . . We hold that a capital defendant accused of an interracial crime is entitled to have prospective jurors informed of the race of the victim and questioned on the issue of racial bias. (*Turner v. Murray* 1986, 35)

The problem of the bias—if not outright prejudice—of death-qualified juries has troubled courts. A **death-qualified jury** is made up of jurors who aren't categorically opposed to the death penalty in cases where death is a possible sentence. Supporters of the death penalty believe that jurors who are opposed to the death penalty can't be impartial in death penalty cases. Opponents of the death penalty believe that jurors who support the death penalty are always biased toward conviction. The U.S. Supreme Court held that death-qualified jurors can be impartial in our next case excerpt, *Lockhart v. McCree* (1986).

---

### C A S E      *Can Death-Qualified Juries Be Impartial?*

#### Lockhart v. McCree
476 U.S. 162 (1986)

#### HISTORY

Ardia McCree was convicted of capital murder. The Arkansas supreme court affirmed. McCree filed a habeas corpus petition. The U.S. District Court for the Eastern District of Arkansas granted the petition. The U.S. Circuit Court for the Eighth Circuit affirmed. On writ of certiorari, the U.S. Supreme Court reversed.

REHNQUIST, J., JOINED BY BURGER, C.J., AND WHITE, POWELL, AND O'CONNOR, JJ.

#### FACTS

McCree was charged with capital felony murder. In accordance with Arkansas law, the trial judge at voir dire removed for cause, over McCree's objections, those prospective jurors who stated that they could not under any circumstances vote the imposition of the death penalty. Eight prospective jurors were excluded for this reason. The jury convicted McCree of capital felony murder, but rejected the State's request for the death penalty, instead setting McCree's punishment at life imprisonment without parole.

The District Court held a hearing on the "death qualification" issue in July 1981, receiving in evidence numerous social science studies concerning the attitudes and beliefs of "*Witherspoon-excludables*" [*jurors opposed to the death penalty*], along with the potential effects of excluding them from the jury prior to the guilt phase of a bifurcated capital trial. In August 1983, the court concluded, based on the social science evidence, that "death qualification" produced juries that "were more prone to convict" capital defendants than "non-death-qualified" juries.

The Eighth Circuit found "substantial evidentiary support" for the District Court's conclusion and affirmed the grant of habeas relief on the ground that such removal for cause violated McCree's constitutional right to a jury selected from a fair cross-section of the community.

#### OPINION

In the case we address the question, Does the Constitution prohibit the removal for cause, prior to the guilt phase of a bifurcated capital trial, of prospective jurors whose opposition to the death penalty is so strong that it would prevent or substantially impair the performance of their duties as jurors at the sentencing phase of the trial? We hold that it does not.

Of the six studies introduced by McCree that at least purported to deal with the central issue in this case, namely, the potential effects on the determination of guilt or innocence of excluding "*Witherspoon*-excludables" from the jury, three were also before this Court when it decided *Witherspoon*. There, this Court reviewed the studies and concluded: The data adduced by the petitioner . . . are too tentative and fragmentary to establish that jurors not opposed to the death penalty tend to favor the prosecution in the determination of guilt. We simply cannot conclude, either on the basis of the record now before us or as a matter of judicial notice, that the exclusion of jurors opposed to capital punishment results in an unrepresentative jury on the issue of guilt or substantially increases the risk of conviction. In the light of the presently available information, we are not prepared to announce a per se constitutional rule requiring the reversal of every conviction returned by a jury selected as this one was.

It goes almost without saying that if these studies were "too tentative and fragmentary" to make out a claim of constitutional error in 1968, the same studies, unchanged but for having aged some eighteen years, are still not sufficient to make out such a claim in this case.

Nor do the three post–*Witherspoon* studies introduced by McCree on the "death qualification" issue provide substantial support for the "per se constitutional rule" McCree asks this Court to adopt. All three of the "new" studies were based on the responses of individuals randomly selected from some segment of the population, but who were not actual jurors sworn under oath to apply the law to the facts of an actual case involving the fate of an actual capital defendant. We have serious doubts about the value of these studies in predicting the behavior of actual jurors.

In addition, two of the three "new" studies did not even attempt to simulate the process of jury deliberation, and none of the "new" studies was able to predict to what extent, if any, the presence of one or more "*Witherspoon*-excludables" on a guilt-phase jury would have altered the outcome of the guilt determination.

Finally, and most importantly, only one of the six "death qualification" studies introduced by McCree even attempted to identify and account for the presence of so-called "nullifiers," or individuals who, because of their deep-seated opposition to the death penalty, would be unable to decide a capital defendant's guilt or innocence fairly and impartially.

Having identified some of the more serious problems with McCree's studies, however, we will assume for purposes of this opinion that the studies are both methodologically valid and adequate to establish that "death qualification" in fact produces juries somewhat more "conviction-prone" than "non-death-qualified" juries. We hold, nonetheless, that the Constitution does not prohibit the States from "death qualifying" juries in capital cases. We have never invoked the fair cross-section principle to invalidate the use of either for-cause or peremptory challenges to prospective jurors, or to require petit juries, as opposed to jury panels or venires, to reflect the composition of the community at large. We remain convinced that an extension of the fair cross-section requirement to petit juries would be unworkable and unsound, and we decline McCree's invitation to adopt such an extension.

The essence of a "fair cross-section" claim is the systematic exclusion of "a 'distinctive' group in the community." In our view, groups defined solely in terms of shared attitudes that would prevent or substantially impair members of the group from performing one of their duties as jurors, such as the "*Witherspoon*-excludables" at issue here, are not "distinctive groups" for fair cross-section purposes.

Our prior jury-representativeness cases have involved such groups as blacks, women, and Mexican-Americans. The wholesale exclusion of these large groups from jury service clearly contravened the fair cross-section requirement. The exclusion from jury service of large groups of individuals not on the basis of their inability to serve as jurors, but on the basis of some immutable characteristic such as race, gender, or ethnic background, undeniably gave rise to an "appearance of unfairness."

The group of "*Witherspoon*-excludables" involved in the case at bar differs significantly from the groups we have previously recognized as "distinctive." "Death qualification," unlike the wholesale exclusion of blacks, women, or Mexican-Americans from jury service, is carefully designed to serve the State's concededly legitimate interest in obtaining a single jury that can properly and impartially apply the law to the facts of the case at both the guilt and sentencing phases of a capital trial.

Furthermore, unlike blacks, women, and Mexican-Americans, "*Witherspoon*-excludables" are singled out for exclusion in capital cases on the basis of an attribute that is within the individual's control. It is important to remember that not all who oppose the death penalty are subject to removal for cause in capital cases; those who firmly believe that the death penalty is unjust may nevertheless serve as jurors in capital cases so long as they state clearly that they are willing to temporarily set aside their own beliefs in deference to the rule of law.

McCree argues that, even if we reject the Eighth Circuit's fair cross-section holding, we should affirm the judgment below on the alternative ground, adopted by the District Court, that "death qualification" violated his constitutional right to an impartial jury. We do not agree. According to McCree, when the State "tips the scales" by excluding prospective jurors with a particular viewpoint, an impermissibly partial jury results. We have consistently rejected this view of jury impartiality, including as recently as last Term when we squarely held that an impartial jury consists of nothing more than "jurors who will conscientiously apply the law and find the facts."

## DISSENT

MARSHALL, J., JOINED BY BRENNAN AND STEVENS, JJ.

The data strongly suggest that death qualification excludes a significantly large subset—at least 11% to 17%—of potential jurors who could be impartial during the guilt phase of trial. Among the members of this excludable class are a disproportionate number of blacks and women.

The perspectives on the criminal justice system of jurors who survive death qualification are systematically different from those of the excluded jurors. Death-qualified jurors are, for example, more likely to believe that a defendant's failure to testify is indicative of his guilt, more hostile to the insanity defense, more distrustful of defense attorneys, and less concerned about the danger of erroneous convictions.

This pro-prosecution bias is reflected in the greater readiness of death-qualified jurors to convict or to convict on more serious charges. And, finally, the very process of death qualification—which focuses attention on the death penalty before the trial has even begun—has been found to predispose the jurors that survive it to believe that the defendant is guilty.

The evidence thus confirms, and is itself corroborated by, the more intuitive judgments of scholars and of so many of the participants in capital trials—judges, defense attorneys, and prosecutors. The chief strength of respondent's evidence lies in the essential unanimity of the results obtained by researchers using diverse subjects and varied methodologies. Even the Court's haphazard jabs cannot obscure the power of the array. Faced with the near unanimity of authority supporting respondent's claim that death qualification gives the prosecution a particular advantage in the guilt phase of capital trials, the majority here makes but a weak effort to contest that proposition.

### Questions

1. Do death-qualified juries deny defendants fair trials?
2. Is the majority or the dissent "right" in interpreting the statistics?
3. Should juries represent a fair cross section of attitudes in the community? Why? or Why not?
4. Why are attitudes different from race, ethnicity, and gender, according to the Court? Should they be? Explain.
5. How would you have decided this case? Defend your decision.

## The Right to a Public Trial

Three constitutional amendments guarantee defendants the right to a public trial:

1. The Sixth Amendment right to confront witnesses
2. The Fifth Amendment due process right
3. The Fourteenth Amendment due process right

Public trials protect two distinct rights:

1. *Public access.* The right of the public to attend the proceedings
2. *Defendants' rights.* The right of defendants to attend their own trials

The right to a public trial extends to "every stage of the trial," including jury selection, communications between the judge and the jury, jury instructions (judges' explanations of the law to the jury), and in-chamber conversations between the judge and jurors. It doesn't include brief conferences at the bench outside the defendant's hearing or other brief conferences involving only questions of law.

Public trials support defendants' interests in avoiding persecution through secret proceedings, enhance community participation in law enforcement, and aid in the search for truth by encouraging witnesses to come forward who otherwise might not.

These interests aren't absolute. Courtroom size limits public access. Furthermore, the need to protect threatened witnesses even justifies closing the courtroom. Protecting undercover agents also authorizes exclusion of the public during their testimony. Moreover, public trials may discourage shy and introverted witnesses from coming forward. Finally, judges can limit public access during sensitive proceedings.

For example, it's justifiable to exclude spectators while alleged rape victims are testifying about the "lurid details" of the crime (*U.S. ex rel Latimore v. Sielaff* 1977).

Defendants don't have an absolute right to attend their own trials; they can forfeit that right by their disruptive behavior. For example, in *Illinois v. Allen* (1970), William Allen, while being tried for armed robbery, repeatedly interrupted the judge in a "most abusive and disrespectful manner." He also threatened him, "When I go out for lunchtime, you're going to be a corpse here." When the judge warned Allen that he could attend only as long as he behaved himself, Allen answered, "There is going to be no proceeding. I'm going to start talking all through the trial. There's not going to be no trial like this." According to the U.S. Supreme Court, the judge properly removed Allen from the courtroom:

> It is essential to the proper administration of criminal justice that dignity, order, and decorum be the hallmarks of all court proceedings in our country. The flagrant disregard in the courtroom of elementary standards of proper conduct should not and cannot be tolerated. We believe that trial judges confronted with disruptive, contumacious, stubbornly defiant defendants must be given sufficient discretion to meet the circumstances of each case. We think there are at least three constitutionally permissible ways for a trial judge to handle an obstreperous defendant like Allen: (1) bind and gag him, thereby keeping him present; (2) cite him for contempt; (3) take him out of the courtroom until he promises to conduct himself properly. (343)

Judges can also exclude defendants during the questioning of child witnesses in sexual abuse cases. For example, in *Kentucky v. Stincer* (1987), Sergio Stincer was on trial for sodomizing two children, ages 7 and 8. The trial court conducted an in-chambers hearing to determine whether the children could remember certain details and whether they understood the significance of telling the truth in court. The judge permitted his lawyer to attend but refused Stincer's request to do so. The U.S. Supreme Court upheld the judge's ruling because Stincer had an adequate opportunity to "confront" the children during the trial.

Courts can also require dangerous defendants to appear under guard to protect the public, witnesses, and court officials from harm and to prevent defendants from escaping. However, defendants ordinarily have the right not just to be at their trial but also to be presented in a way that doesn't prejudice their case. For example, the government can't bring defendants to court in jail dress (*Estelle v. Williams* 1976) or make defense witnesses testify in shackles, because their dress prejudices the jury, furthers no state policy, and mainly hurts poor defendants (*Holbrook v. Flynn* 1986).

# THE STAGES AND RULES OF JURY TRIALS

The adversarial process reaches its high point in the jury trial. Strict, technical rules control trials. The main stages in the criminal trial include:

1. Opening statements, with the prosecution first, followed by the defense
2. Presenting the evidence—the state's and the defendants' cases
3. Closing arguments
4. Instructions to the jury
5. Jury deliberations

Let's look at each of these stages. Then, we'll examine the issues of whether the law requires unanimous verdicts and jury nullification.

# Opening Statements

Prosecutors and defense counsel can make **opening statements**—address the jury before they present their evidence. Prosecutors make their opening statements first; defense counsel address the jury either immediately after the prosecutor's opening statement or, in a few jurisdictions, following the presentation of the state's case.

The opening statements have a narrow scope: to outline the case that the two sides hope to prove, not to prove the case. Proving the case takes place during the presentation-of-evidence phase of the criminal trial. In fact, it's unprofessional for either side to refer to any evidence they don't honestly believe will be admissible in court. Although it's rare for them to do so, appeals courts sometimes reverse cases in which prosecutors have referred to points they intend to prove with evidence they know is inadmissible, incompetent, or both (LaFave and Israel 1984, 3:12).

# Presenting Evidence

The prosecution presents its case first because of its burden to prove defendants' guilt. In presenting its case, the rules of evidence restrict what evidence the state may use, mainly excluding illegally obtained testimony and physical evidence and most hearsay. The prosecution has to prove every element in the case, but the defense frequently "stipulates" (agrees not to contest) some facts, particularly those that might prejudice the defendant's case—detailed photographs and descriptions of a brutally murdered victim, for example. The prosecution can decline a stipulation. Most courts don't compel the prosecution to accept stipulations, because it might weaken the state's case (*People v. McClellan* 1969).

The state ordinarily presents all the available eyewitnesses to the crime. In some instances, if the prosecution doesn't call a material witness, particularly a victim, the defense can ask for a "missing witness instruction"—an instruction that jurors can infer that the witness's testimony would have been unfavorable to the prosecution. The prosecution can ask the court to inform the jury that a key witness is unavailable and not to draw negative inferences from his failure to testify. Prosecutors also may decide not to call witnesses—such as spouses, priests, and doctors—that they know will claim a valid privilege; doing so may result in reversible error (*Bowles v. U.S.* 1970).

Issues that affect the presenting of evidence include cross-examination, the admission of hearsay evidence, compelling witnesses to testify, the prosecutor's burden to prove all elements of a crime, and proof beyond a reasonable doubt. Let's look at each.

***Cross-Examination*** The **Sixth Amendment confrontation clause** includes the right to cross-examine the prosecution's witnesses. In *Smith v. Illinois* (1968), when the prosecution's key witness, an informant, testified that he bought heroin from Smith, the trial court allowed him to use an alias, concealing his real name and address. The U.S. Supreme Court ruled that this violated Smith's right to confrontation:

> When the credibility of a witness is at issue, the very starting point in "exposing falsehood and bringing out the truth" through cross-examination must necessarily be to ask the witness who he is and where he lives. The witness's name and address open countless avenues of in-court examination and out-of-doors investigation. . . . It is of the essence of a fair trial that reasonable latitude be given to the cross-examiner, even though he is unable to state to the court what facts a reasonable cross-examination might develop. . . . To say that prejudice can be established only by showing that the cross-examination, if pursued, would necessarily have brought out facts tending to discredit testimony in chief, is to deny a substantial right and withdraw one of the safeguards essential to a fair trial. (132)

*Hearsay Evidence* The confrontation clause also restricts the prosecution's use of **hearsay testimony**—out-of-court statements offered to prove the truth of the statements. Hearsay violates the confrontation clause because defendants can't ferret the truth through the adversarial process unless the defense can cross-examine the witnesses against them. Therefore, the jury can't have an adequate basis for fact-finding.

However, the confrontation clause doesn't bar hearsay testimony absolutely. The prosecution can introduce hearsay if it meets two tests:

1. It demonstrates the witness's unavailability and, hence, the necessity to use out-of-court statements.

2. It shows that the state obtained the evidence under circumstances that clearly establish its reliability.

In *Ohio v. Roberts* (1980), the majority of the Supreme Court found that the state satisfied the tests under these circumstances:

- The witness's mother said the witness, her daughter, had left home, saying she was going to Tucson, two years earlier.

- Shortly thereafter, a San Francisco social worker contacted the mother concerning a welfare claim her daughter had filed there.

- The mother was able to reach her daughter only once, by phone.

- When the daughter called a few months prior to the trial, she told her mother she was traveling but didn't reveal her whereabouts.

The dissent argued that relying solely on the parents wasn't sufficient; the prosecution had the burden to go out and find the witness. The Court disagreed.

*Compulsory Process* The Sixth Amendment guarantees the defendant's right "to have **compulsory process** for obtaining witnesses in [his or her] . . . favor." This means defendants can compel witnesses to come to court to testify for them. Most states pay for poor defendants' process, but they don't pay for process to get evidence that only corroborates (adds to) evidence already available. And most states make defendants spell out exactly why they need the evidence.

*The Burden of Proof* The Fifth Amendment provides that "no person . . . shall be compelled in any criminal case to be a witness against himself. . . ." This means the state can't call defendants to the witness stand in criminal trials. It also prohibits the prosecution from commenting on defendants' refusal to testify; it even entitles defendants to ask judges to instruct juries not to infer guilt from their silence. However, if defendants decide to take the stand to tell their side of the story, the prosecution can cross-examine them as they would any other witness.

The defense doesn't have to present a case; cross-examining the prosecution's witnesses by itself can raise a reasonable doubt about the proof against the defendant. Or defendants may call their own witnesses for the sole purpose of rebutting the prosecution's witnesses. Of course, they may also call witnesses to create a reasonable doubt about their guilt—to establish alibis, for example.

Defendants may also have affirmative defenses that justify or excuse what would otherwise be criminal conduct (self-defense, insanity, duress, and entrapment). Or maybe they have evidence that reduces the grade of the offense, such as provocation to reduce murder to manslaughter or diminished capacity to reduce first-degree murder to second-degree murder. The prosecution, of course, has the right to cross-examine defense witnesses.

| TABLE 13.2 | Sample of Trial Court Definitions of Proof beyond a Reasonable Doubt |
|---|---|

- A doubt that would cause prudent people to hesitate before acting in a matter of importance to themselves
- A doubt based on reason and common sense
- A doubt that is neither frivolous nor fanciful and that can't be easily explained away
- Substantial doubt
- Persuasion to a reasonable or moral certainty
- Doubt beyond that which is reasonable; about "7½ on a scale of 10" (rejected by the appellate court)
- When the "scales of justice are substantially out of equipoise" (rejected by the appellate court)

*Proof beyond a Reasonable Doubt* Defendants don't have to prove their innocence or help the government prove their guilt. The right against self-incrimination gives defendants an absolute right to say nothing at all and not have it count against them. So trials can proceed, and some do, where neither defendants nor their lawyers present a case. Sometimes, no defense is the best defense. The government, on the other hand, carries the whole burden to prove defendants are guilty beyond a reasonable doubt.

The U.S. Supreme Court ruled, in *In re Winship* (1970), that due process requires both federal and state prosecutors to prove every element of a crime beyond a reasonable doubt:

> The **reasonable doubt standard** is bottomed on a fundamental value determination of our society that it is far worse to convict an innocent man than to let a guilty man go free. [Two propositions cannot be disputed:] First, in a judicial proceeding in which there is a dispute about the facts of some earlier event, the fact finder cannot acquire unassailably accurate knowledge of what happened. Instead, all the fact finder can acquire is a belief of what probably happened. The intensity of this belief—the degree to which a fact finder is convinced that a given act actually occurred—can, of course, vary. In this regard, a standard of proof represents an attempt to instruct the fact finder concerning the degree of confidence our society thinks he should have in the correctness of factual conclusions for a particular type of adjudication. Although the phrases "preponderance of the evidence" and "proof beyond a reasonable doubt" are quantitatively imprecise, they do communicate to the finder of fact different notions concerning the degree of confidence he is expected to have in the correctness of his factual conclusions. (373)

Despite the constitutional requirement of proof beyond a reasonable doubt, the U.S. Supreme Court hasn't decided that due process requires judges to define proof beyond a reasonable doubt. Nevertheless, courts struggle to tell jurors what reasonable doubt means. Table 13.2 provides some examples of court definitions.

## Closing Arguments

After they've presented their evidence, both the state and the defense make their closing arguments. Prosecutors close first, the defense follows, and then the prosecution rebuts. Prosecutors can't waive their right to make a closing argument and save their remarks for rebuttal. If they waive their right to make a closing argument, they're barred automatically from making a rebuttal. Prosecutors can't raise "new" matters in rebuttal either; they can only rebut what either they or the defense counsel brought up during closing arguments. Why? It's only fair that the defense should hear all the arguments in favor of conviction before responding to them.

Formally, prosecutors have the duty not only to convict criminals but also to seek justice. The American Bar Association's *Standard for Criminal Justice* (1980, § 3.5) includes the following guidelines for prosecutors. It's improper to

- Misstate intentionally the evidence or mislead the jury
- Refer to evidence excluded or not introduced at trial
- Express personal beliefs or opinions about the truth or falsity of the evidence or the defendant's guilt
- Engage in arguments that divert jurors' attention by injecting issues beyond the case or predicting consequences of the jury's verdict
- Make arguments calculated to inflame jurors' passions and prejudices

However, violating these standards rarely results in reversal:

If every remark made by counsel outside of the testimony were grounds for a reversal, comparatively few verdicts would stand, since in the ardor of advocacy, and in the excitement of the trial, even the most experienced counsel are occasionally carried away by this temptation. (*Dunlop v. U.S.* 1897)

When determining whether to reverse convictions based on improper closing arguments, appellate courts consider whether:

1. Defense counsel invited or provoked the remarks.
2. Defense counsel made timely objection to the remarks.
3. The trial judge took corrective action, such as instructing the jury to disregard the remarks.
4. The comments were brief and isolated in an otherwise proper argument.
5. Other errors occurred during the trial.
6. The evidence of guilt was overwhelming. (LaFave and Israel 1984, 3:15)

Although appellate courts rarely reverse convictions for these abuses, they frequently express their displeasure with prosecutors' improper remarks made during closing arguments. In *Bowen v. Kemp* (1985), Charlie Bowen was convicted of raping and murdering a 12-year-old girl. The prosecutor, in the course of the closing statement, made several comments focusing on the accused:

And now we come up here with this idea that a man . . . is subject to be rehabilitated and released back into society. Yeah, I guess he can be rehabilitated. Hitler could have been. I believe in about six or eight months if I'd had him chained to a wall and talked to him and beat him on one side of the head for a while with a stick telling him you believe this don't you then beat him on the other side with a stick telling him you believe that don't you I believe I could have rehabilitated Hitler. (678)

The prosecutor went on to call Bowen "a product of the devil" and a "liar" who was "no better than a beast."

And, you know for a criminal to go without proper punishment is a disgrace to the society we live in and it's shown to us every day by the fruits that we reap from day to day in our society when we have the bloody deeds such as this occur. (680)

Bowen appealed his conviction on the basis that the prosecutor's remarks affected the jury's verdict. While conceding that the remarks were improper, the circuit court of appeals affirmed the conviction. It found "no reasonable probability that, absent the improper statements of opinion, Bowen would not have been sentenced to death" (682).

## Jury Instructions

Before jurors begin their deliberations, judges "instruct" them on what the law is and how they should apply it. **Jury instructions** usually inform the jury about the following subjects:

1. The respective roles of the judge to decide the law and the jury to decide the facts

2. The principle that defendants are presumed innocent until proven guilty

3. The principle that the state bears the burden of proving guilt beyond a reasonable doubt

4. The definition of all the elements of the crime with which the defendant is charged

5. Jury room procedures

Both the prosecution and the defense can ask the judge to provide the jury with specific instructions. And they can object if the judge refuses to give the requested instruction and frequently do base appeals on such refusals. A number of jurisdictions use *pattern instructions*—published boilerplate instructions that fit most cases. Supporters praise the clarity, accuracy, impartiality, and efficiency of pattern instructions; critics say they're too general to help jurors. However, most empirical evaluations show that jurors understand only about half of judges' instructions, whether patterned or individually crafted (LaFave and Israel 1984, 3:39–40).

## Jury Deliberations

After the judge instructs the jury, she orders them to retire to a separate room under supervision and without interruption to deliberate together until they reach a verdict.

The jurors take the instructions, any exhibits received in evidence, and a list of the charges against the defendant with them into the jury room. During the course of their deliberations, they may ask the court for further instruction or information concerning the evidence or any other matter. The court can discharge *hung juries*—juries unable to reach a verdict after protracted deliberations.

Juries can return one of three verdicts:

1. Guilty

2. Not guilty

3. Special, mainly related to insanity or capital punishment

If the jury acquits, or issues the not guilty verdict, the defendants' ordeal with the criminal process stops immediately; they're free to go. If the jury convicts, the case continues to **judgment**—the court's final decision on the legal outcome of the case. Juries can't pass legal judgment; their word is final only as to the facts. Following the court's judgment of guilt or acquittal, the criminal trial ends.

## The "Unanimous Verdict" Requirement

Like 12-member juries (discussed earlier), unanimous verdicts are an ancient requirement and still enjoy strong support (Table 13.3). In 1900, the U.S. Supreme Court held that the Sixth Amendment demanded conviction by unanimous jury verdicts. The Court changed its mind in 1972 when it ruled, in *Apodaca v. Oregon*, that verdicts of 11–1 and 10–2 didn't violate two convicted felons' right to a jury trial:

TABLE 13.3    Arguments for Unanimous Verdicts

- They instill confidence in the criminal justice process.
- They guarantee that the jury carefully reviews the evidence.
- They ensure the hearing and consideration of minority viewpoints.
- They prevent government oppression.
- They support the principle that convicting innocent defendants is worse than freeing guilty ones.
- They fulfill the proof-beyond-a-reasonable-doubt requirement.

Source: LaFave and Israel 1984, 698.

> A requirement of unanimity. . . does not materially contribute to . . . [the jury's] common-sense judgment. . . . A jury will come to such a verdict as long as it consists of a group of laymen representative of a cross section of the community who have the duty and the opportunity to deliberate, free from outside attempts at intimidation, on the question of a defendant's guilt. In terms of this function we perceive no difference between juries required to act unanimously and those permitted to convict or acquit by votes of 10 to two or 11 to one. Requiring unanimity would obviously produce hung juries in some situations where nonunanimous juries will convict or acquit. But in either case, the interest of the defendant in having the judgment of his peers interposed between himself and the officers of the state who prosecute and judge him is equally well served. (411)

In *Johnson v. Louisiana* (1972), in upholding a robbery conviction based on a 9–3 verdict, Justice Byron R. White wrote:

> Nine jurors—a substantial majority of the jury—were convinced by the evidence. Disagreement of the three jurors does not alone establish reasonable doubt, particularly when such a heavy majority of the jury, after having considered the dissenters' views, remains convinced of guilt. (362)

Still, the Supreme Court hasn't answered the question of how many votes short of unanimity are required to satisfy the Sixth Amendment. What about less than unanimous verdicts by fewer than 12-member juries? A unanimous U.S. Supreme Court in *Burch v. Louisiana* (1979) struck down a Louisiana statute providing that misdemeanors punishable by more than six months "shall be tried before a jury of six persons, five of whom must concur to render a verdict." According to the Court, to preserve the right to jury trial, it had to draw a line at nonunanimous verdicts of six-member juries—a line supported by the "near-uniform judgment of the nation" (only two other states had permitted these verdicts).

## Jury Nullification

The jury's function is to decide the facts in a case and apply them to the law as the judge has defined the law. Nevertheless, juries have the power to acquit even when the facts clearly fit the law. Jury acquittals are final, meaning the prosecution can't appeal them. The practice of acquitting in the face of proof beyond a reasonable doubt is called **jury nullification**. Why do juries nullify? Usually, it's because either they sympathize with particular defendants (for example, in a mercy killing) or because the state has prosecuted defendants for breaking unpopular laws (for example, possession of small amounts of marijuana for personal use).

Jury nullification has an ancient lineage. The "pages of history shine on instances of the jury's exercise of its prerogative to disregard uncontradicted evidence and instructions of the judge." In the famous John Peter Zenger case (*New York v. Zenger* 1735), the jury ignored the facts and the judge's instructions and acquitted Zenger of the charge of sedition (LaFave and Israel 1984, 3:700).

The U.S. Supreme Court has indirectly approved jury nullification. Although the Court obviously didn't like the jury's power, it conceded in *Sparf and Hansen v. U.S.* (1895):

> If a jury may rightfully disregard the direction of the court in matters of law and determine for themselves what the law is in the particular case before them, it is difficult to perceive any legal ground upon which a verdict of conviction can be set aside by the court as being against law. (101)

Probably more than any other doctrine in criminal procedure we've studied, nullification promotes community participation in criminal law enforcement. As community representatives, juries act as safety valves in exceptional cases by allowing "informal communication from the total culture" to override the strict legal bonds of their instructions from the judge (*U.S. v. Dougherty* 1972).

 Go to Exercise 13.1 on the Samaha Criminal Procedure 7e website to learn more about your state's trial procedures: academic.cengage.com/ criminaljustice/samaha.

# CONVICTION BY GUILTY PLEA

There are two types of guilty plea: (1) straight pleas and (2) negotiated pleas. *Straight guilty pleas* (pleading guilty without negotiation) are ordinarily made in what are called "dead bang" cases, meaning proof of guilt is overwhelming. **Negotiated guilty pleas** (pleading guilty in exchange for concessions by the state) appear mainly in large urban courts. They arise when the state's case is weak, defendants have a strong defense, and/or they can gain the jury's sympathy.

Although widely used for more than a century, negotiated pleas weren't recognized formally by courts until 1970. In that year, in *Brady v. U.S.*, the U.S. Supreme Court ruled that bargained pleas are constitutional. According to the Court, "the chief virtues of the plea system are speed, economy, and finality." Whatever might be the situation in an ideal world, plea bargaining and guilty pleas are important (and can be beneficial) parts of our criminal justice system:

> The defendant avoids lengthy incarceration and the anxieties and uncertainties of a trial; he gains a speedy disposition of his case, the chance to acknowledge his guilt, and a prompt start in realizing whatever potential there may be for rehabilitation. Judges and prosecutors conserve vital and scarce resources. The public is protected from the risks posed by those charged with criminal offense who are at large on bail while awaiting completion of criminal proceedings. (*Blackledge v. Allison* 1977, 71)

Let's look further at the debate over plea bargaining and how guilty pleas impact defendants' Constitutional rights.

## The Debate over Conviction by Guilty Plea

The arguments for and against conviction by guilty plea are heated, complex, and by no means empirically resolved. Some say negotiation better serves the search for truth; others argue that the adversarial process best serves the ends of justice. Some maintain guilty pleas save time; others contend plea negotiations more than make up for the time it takes to go to trial. Some insist the criminal justice system would collapse under its own weight if only a few of the now vast majority of defendants who plead guilty asserted their right to trial; others contend banning plea bargaining would make little difference in how many defendants plead guilty. Some maintain the guilty plea intimidates the innocent and emboldens the guilty; others say outcomes between jury trials and guilty pleas don't differ much at all. The public and police officers oppose plea bargaining, because they believe it "lets criminals off"; however, the available empirical data don't resolve these questions.

## The Constitution and Guilty Pleas

The social scientists and policy makers may not have resolved the empirical and policy questions surrounding conviction by plea, but the U.S. Supreme Court has settled the question of its constitutionality. When they plead guilty, defendants *waive* (give up) three constitutional rights:

1. The Fifth Amendment right to remain silent
2. The Sixth Amendment right to a trial by jury
3. The Sixth Amendment right to confront the witnesses against them

To give up these constitutional rights, defendants have to do so knowingly (also called "intelligently") and voluntarily. According to the Court:

> The criminal justice system enforces a minimum requirement that [a defendant's] plea be the voluntary expression of his own choice. But the plea is more than an admission of past conduct; it is the defendant's consent that judgment of conviction may be entered without a trial—a waiver of his right to trial before a jury or a judge. Waivers of constitutional rights not only must be voluntary but must be knowing, intelligent acts done with sufficient awareness of the relevant circumstances and likely consequences. (*Brady v. U.S.* 1970, 748)

It's up to trial judges to make sure defendants' pleas are voluntary and knowing. The Supreme Court has established the following standard for trial judges' inquiries:

> A plea of guilty entered by one fully aware of the direct consequences, including the actual value of any commitments made to him by the court, prosecutor, or his own counsel, must stand unless induced by threats (or promises to discontinue improper harassment), misrepresentation (including unfulfilled or unfulfillable promises), or perhaps by promises that are by their nature improper as having no prior relationship to the prosecutor's business (e.g., bribes). (*Brady v. U.S.* 1970, 756)

The Supreme Court has held that a trial judge's failure to ask defendants questions concerning their plea is **reversible error**—grounds to reverse the trial court's judgment of guilt. Why? Because the trial court accepted the plea "without an affirmative showing that it was intelligent and voluntary" (*Boykin v. Alabama* 1969). A court can't presume that defendants give up fundamental rights by pleading guilty "from a silent record." Judges have to make clear to defendants when they plead guilty that they're giving up their rights to trial (Sixth Amendment), to confrontation (Sixth Amendment), and not to incriminate themselves (Fifth Amendment).

According to the Court, defendants have to know "the true nature of the charges" against them. For example, in one case, the defendant pleaded guilty to second-degree murder without knowing the elements of the crime. Neither his lawyer nor the trial judge had explained to him that second-degree murder required an intent to kill and that his version of what he did negated intent. The U.S. Supreme Court ruled that the record didn't establish a knowing plea. Most jurisdictions now require that judges determine that there's a factual basis for guilty pleas. To determine the factual basis, for example, judges might ask defendants to describe the conduct that led to the charges, ask the prosecutor and defense attorney similar questions, and consult presentence reports (*North Carolina v. Alford* 1970).

*Brady v. U.S.* (1970) established that guilty pleas aren't automatically voluntary; the Court left it to lower courts to decide on a case-by-case basis whether the totality of circumstances shows that defendants voluntarily and knowingly pleaded guilty.

What about defendants who are **factually innocent** (they didn't commit the crime) but **legally guilty** (the government has enough evidence to convict them) who plead guilty because they don't want to take the chance that by going to trial they'll get a harsher sentence than they can get by pleading guilty? Is their plea voluntary and knowing? "Yes," the U.S. Supreme Court answered in our next case excerpt, *North Carolina v. Alford* (1970).

# C A S E    *Was His Guilty Plea Voluntary?*

## North Carolina v. Alford
### 400 U.S. 25 (1970)

### HISTORY

Henry Alford was indicted for the capital offense of first-degree murder. North Carolina law provided for three possible punishments for murder: (1) life imprisonment when a plea of guilty was accepted for first-degree murder; (2) death following a jury verdict of guilty of first-degree murder unless the jury recommended life imprisonment; (3) two to thirty years' imprisonment for second-degree murder. Alford's attorney recommended that Alford plead guilty to second-degree murder, which the prosecutor accepted. Alford pleaded guilty and was sentenced to 30 years in prison. On writ of habeas corpus, the U.S. Court of Appeals found Alford's plea involuntary. On writ of certiorari, the U.S. Supreme Court reversed.

WHITE, J., JOINED BY BURGER, C.J., AND HARLAN, STEWART, AND BLACKMUN, JJ.

### FACTS

On December 2, 1963, Alford was indicted for first-degree murder, a capital offense under North Carolina law. The court appointed an attorney to represent him, and this attorney questioned all but one of the various witnesses who appellee said would substantiate his claim of innocence. The witnesses, however, did not support Alford's story but gave statements that strongly indicated his guilt. Faced with strong evidence of guilt and no substantial evidentiary support for the claim of innocence, Alford's attorney recommended that he plead guilty, but left the ultimate decision to Alford himself. The prosecutor agreed to accept a plea of guilty to a charge of second-degree murder, and on December 10, 1963, Alford pleaded guilty to the reduced charge.

Before the plea was finally accepted by the trial court, the court heard the sworn testimony of a police officer who summarized the State's case. Two other witnesses besides Alford were also heard. Although there was no eyewitness to the crime, the testimony indicated that shortly before the killing Alford took his gun from his house, stated his intention to kill the victim and returned home with the declaration that he had carried out the killing.

After the summary presentation of the State's case, Alford took the stand and testified that he had not committed the murder but that he was pleading guilty because he faced the threat of the death penalty if he did not do so. In response to the questions of his counsel, he acknowledged that his counsel had informed him of the difference between second- and first-degree murder and of his rights in case he chose to go to trial.

The trial court then asked Alford if, in light of his denial of guilt, he still desired to plead guilty to second-degree murder and appellee answered, "Yes, sir. I plead guilty on—from the circumstances that he [Alford's attorney] told me." After eliciting information about Alford's prior criminal record, which was a long one, the trial court sentenced him to 30 years' imprisonment, the maximum penalty for second-degree murder.

After giving his version of the events of the night of the murder, Alford stated: "I pleaded guilty on second degree murder because they said there is too much evidence, but I ain't shot no man, but I take the fault for the other man. We never had an argument in our life and I just pleaded guilty because they said if I didn't they would gas me for it, and that is all." In response to questions from his attorney, Alford affirmed that he had consulted several times with his attorney and with members of his family and had been informed of his rights if he chose to plead not guilty.

Alford then reaffirmed his decision to plead guilty to second-degree murder:

Q: [by Alford's attorney] And you authorized me to tender a plea of guilty to second degree murder before the court?

A: Yes, sir.

Q: And in doing that, you have again affirmed your decision on that point?

A: Well, I'm still pleading that you all got me to plead guilty. I plead the other way, circumstantial evidence; that the jury will prosecute me on—on the second. You told me to plead guilty, right. I don't—I'm not guilty but I plead guilty.

On appeal, a divided panel of the Court of Appeals for the Fourth Circuit reversed on the ground that Alford's guilty plea was made involuntarily.

## OPINION

The standard [for determining the validity of a quality plea is] whether the plea represents a voluntary and intelligent choice among the alternative courses of action open to the defendant. Ordinarily, a judgment of conviction resting on a plea of guilty is justified by the defendant's admission that he committed the crime charged against him and his consent that judgment be entered without a trial of any kind. The plea usually subsumes both elements, and justifiably so, even though there is no separate, express admission by the defendant that he committed the particular acts claimed to constitute the crime charged in the indictment.

Here Alford entered his plea but accompanied it with the statement that he had not shot the victim. . . . While most pleas of guilty consist of both a waiver of trial and an express admission of guilt, the latter element is not a constitutional requisite to the imposition of criminal penalty. An individual accused of crime may voluntarily, knowingly, and understandably consent to the imposition of a prison sentence even if he is unwilling or unable to admit his participation in the acts constituting the crime.

Nor can we perceive any material difference between a plea that refuses to admit commission of the criminal act and a plea containing a protestation of innocence when, as in the instant case, a defendant intelligently concludes that his interests require entry of a guilty plea and the record before the judge contains strong evidence of actual guilt.

Here the State had a strong case of first-degree murder against Alford. Whether he realized or disbelieved his guilt, he insisted on his plea because in his view he had absolutely nothing to gain by a trial and much to gain by pleading. Because of the overwhelming evidence against him, a trial was precisely what neither Alford nor his attorney desired.

Confronted with the choice between a trial for first-degree murder, on the one hand, and a plea of guilty to second-degree murder, on the other, Alford quite reasonably chose the latter and thereby limited the maximum penalty to a 30-year term. When his plea is viewed in light of the evidence against him, which substantially negated his claim of innocence and which further provided a means by which the judge could test whether the plea was being intelligently entered, its validity cannot be seriously questioned. In view of the strong factual basis for the plea demonstrated by the State and Alford's clearly expressed desire to enter it despite his professed belief in his innocence, we hold that the trial judge did not commit constitutional error in accepting it.

Alford now argues in effect that the State should not have allowed him this choice but should have insisted on proving him guilty of murder in the first degree. The States in their wisdom may take this course by statute or otherwise and may prohibit the practice of accepting pleas to lesser included offenses under any circumstances. But this is not the mandate of the Fourteenth Amendment and the Bill of Rights. The prohibitions against involuntary or unintelligent pleas should not be relaxed, but neither should an exercise in arid logic render those constitutional guarantees counterproductive and put in jeopardy the very human values they were meant to preserve.

The Court of Appeals judgment directing the issuance of the writ of habeas corpus is vacated and the case is REMANDED to the Court of Appeals for further proceedings consistent with this opinion. It is so ordered.

## DISSENT

BRENNAN, J., JOINED BY DOUGLAS AND MARSHALL, JJ.

Last Term, this Court held, over my dissent, that a plea of guilty may validly be induced by an unconstitutional threat to subject the defendant to the risk to death, so long as the plea is entered in open court and the defendant is represented by competent counsel who is aware of the threat, albeit not of its unconstitutionality. *Brady v. U.S.* (1970). Today the Court makes clear that its previous holding was intended to apply even when the record demonstrates that the actual effect of the unconstitutional threat was to induce a guilty plea from a defendant who was unwilling to admit his guilt.

I adhere to the view that, in any given case, the influence of such an unconstitutional threat must necessarily be given weight in determining the voluntariness of a plea. . . . I believe that at the very least such a denial of guilt is . . . a relevant factor in determining whether the plea was voluntarily and intelligently made. With these factors in mind, it is sufficient in my view to state that the facts set out in the majority opinion demonstrate that Alford was "so gripped by fear of the death penalty" that his decision to plead guilty was not voluntary but was "the product of duress as much so as choice reflecting physical constraint."

## Questions

**1.** Did Henry Alford knowingly and voluntarily plead guilty?

**2.** Consider the dissent's comment that Henry Alford was "so gripped by fear of the death penalty" that his decision was "the product of duress." Should defendants ever be allowed to plead guilty if they believe they're innocent? Why? or Why not? Back up your answer with arguments from the majority and dissenting opinions.

 Go to Exercise 13.2 on the Samaha Criminal Procedure 7e website to learn more about standards for pleading guilty: academic.cengage.com/criminaljustice/samaha.

# SUMMARY

### I. After the Decision to Charge
    A. After the decision to charge, court proceedings divide into two forms.
    B. Adversarial proceedings take place inside the courtroom.
    C. Informal negotiations take place outside the courtroom.

### II. Conviction by Jury Trial
    A. The Constitution creates a right to trial by jury.
        1. It protects the right in all crimes.
        2. The exception is in trials for "petty offenses"—moral seriousness standard.
    B. There's no constitutional right to a 12-member jury.
        1. The constitutional test consists of two elements;
            a. Are there enough jurors to find the truth?
            b. Are there enough to allow community participation in decision making?
        2. The U.S. Supreme Court ruled that five jurors aren't enough. (*Ballew v. Georgia* 1978)
    C. Jury selection: The Federal Jury Selection Act is followed in most states.
        1. It requires a random selection from a "fair cross section of the community."
        2. No exclusions can be based on "race, color, religion, sex, national origin, or economic status."
        3. Jury list sources include local census reports, tax rolls, city directories, telephone books, and driver's license lists.
        4. Prosecutors and defense counsel use voir dire to select jurors from the jury panel.
            a. Peremptory challenges (striking without having to give a reason) are limited by statute.
            b. Prosecutors and defense counsel have an unlimited number of challenges for cause (striking biased jurors).
            c. Prospective jurors in death penalty cases can be struck for cause if they're opposed to the death penalty.
    D. The Right to a Public Trial
        1. Public trials support the right of public access.
        2. Defendants have a right to attend their own trials.
        3. Defendants' rights aren't absolute.
            a. Their appearance has to comport with the dignity of the proceedings.
            b. They can't be disruptive.
        4. The right applies to all stages of a trial.

## III. The Stages and Rules of Jury Trials

A. Opening statements let the prosecutor and defense counsel outline their cases to the jury.

B. *Presenting evidence.* The state presents first, then the defendant.

   1. The state presents admissible evidence to prove guilt beyond a reasonable doubt.

   2. The defendant raises a reasonable doubt of guilt.

C. Closing arguments let the prosecution and defense counsel highlight the salient points of their cases.

   1. Prosecutors present first, then the defense, and finally the prosecution rebuts.

   2. Appellate courts frequently express disapproval of prosecutors' "improper" remarks but rarely reverse because of them.

D. Instructing the Jury

   1. Judges "instruct" juries on what the law is and how they should apply it.

   2. Juries decide facts; the judge decides the law.

   3. Principles juries are instructed to follow include:

      a. Defendants are innocent until proven guilty.

      b. The state has the burden to prove guilt beyond a reasonable doubt.

   4. The judge defines all the elements of the crime the prosecution has to prove.

   5. The judge explains jury room procedures.

E. Jury Deliberations

   1. Juries can return one of three verdicts:

      a. Guilty

      b. Not guilty

      c. Special, mainly related to insanity or capital punishment

   2. If the jury acquits, the defendant is free to go.

   3. If the jury convicts, the case continues to judgment—the court's final decision on the legal outcome of the case.

   4. Juries can't pass legal judgment; they can only decide the facts.

   5. After the court's judgment of guilt or acquittal, the criminal trial ends.

F. Unanimous Verdicts

   1. There's no constitutional requirement for a unanimous verdict.

   2. Verdicts of 11–1, 10–2, and 9–3 are all OK.

   3. Verdicts in six-member juries have to be unanimous.

G. Jury Nullification

   1. Juries nullify the law when they acquit defendants even though they believe they're guilty beyond a reasonable doubt.

   2. Jury nullification reflects a community role as a safety valve to relax the law's rigidity and provide justice in individual cases.

## IV. Conviction by Guilty Plea

A. There are two types of guilty pleas:

   1. *Straight guilty pleas.* Defendants plead guilty without concessions.

   2. *Negotiated guilty pleas.* Defendants plead guilty after getting concessions through negotiation.

B. There's a debate over guilty pleas.

   1. Empirical studies don't answer questions of accuracy, need, and the fairness of pleas.

2. The U.S. Supreme Court decided guilty pleas and plea bargaining are constitutional.
    C. Constitutional requirements of plea bargains include:
        1. Pleas must be voluntary and knowing.
        2. Judges must determine there's a factual basis for the plea.
    D. Courts can accept guilty pleas from defendants even if they maintain their innocence.

## REVIEW QUESTIONS

1. Contrast conviction by trial with conviction by guilty plea.

2. Identify five sources most jurisdictions use to draw up jury lists, and list six reasons jurors give to be excused from jury service. Why do most courts accept their excuses?

3. Explain the difference between peremptory challenges and challenges for cause.

4. Summarize the controversy over death-qualified jurors.

5. List and briefly summarize the stages in the criminal trial.

6. Describe and explain the significance of the U.S. Supreme Court case of *In re Winship*.

7. What's the difference between the jury's verdict and the judgment of the court?

8. Describe and explain the significance of the U.S. Supreme Court decisions in *Apodaca v. Oregon* and *Johnson v. Louisiana*.

9. Explain the difference between straight and negotiated guilty pleas.

10. Summarize the arguments for and against plea bargaining.

11. List three constitutional rights defendants waive when they plead guilty.

12. Explain how a defendant can be factually innocent but legally guilty.

13. Describe and explain the significance of the U.S. Supreme Court decision in *Brady v. U.S.*

## KEY TERMS

straight guilty pleas, p. 446
moral seriousness standard, p. 447
key-man system, p. 450
jury panel, p. 450
voir dire, p. 450
peremptory challenges, p. 450
challenges for cause, p. 450
death-qualified jury, p. 451

*Witherspoon*-excludables, p. 451
opening statements, p. 455
Sixth Amendment confrontation clause, p. 455
hearsay testimony, p. 456
compulsory process, p. 456
reasonable doubt standard, p. 457

jury instructions, p. 459
judgment, p. 459
jury nullification, p. 460
negotiated guilty pleas, p. 461
reversible error, p. 462
factually innocent, p. 463
legally guilty, p. 463

# After Conviction

## MAIN POINTS

- After conviction, the presumption of innocence enjoyed by defendants shifts to a strong presumption of guilt against offenders.
- Retribution aims at punishing past crimes; deterrence looks ahead to preventing future crimes.
- The history of sentencing is a pendulum swing between fitting sentences to punish crimes and tailoring sentences to suit offenders.
- Empirical evaluations suggest that mandatory minimum sentences, in practice, aren't as effective as their supporters hoped they would be.
- The U.S. Supreme Court applies a *narrow* proportionality requirement to the constitutional ban on cruel and unusual punishment.
- The Supreme Court has recently shifted from a hands-off approach to sentencing procedures to an application of constitutional trial rights.
- The U.S. Supreme Court has ruled that death sentences aren't "cruel and unusual punishment."
- There's no *constitutional* right to appeal a conviction, but there's a *statutory* right to appeal.
- There's an extremely limited right to attack a conviction indirectly by habeas corpus.

Trial determines a defendant's guilt; sentencing prescribes an offender's fate. . . .

Berman and Bibas 2006, 37

The jury-trial right attaches to offense conduct and not offender characteristics *because the state defines "crimes," accuses, and prosecutes based on what people do and not who they are. When the law ties punishment to specific conduct, such as the amount of money or drugs, weapon use, or injury, the state has defined particular behavior that merits criminal punishment and stigma. A defendant has a right to demand that before he is punished, a jury find each and every one of the facts central to offense conduct.*

*Once a jury trial or guilty plea has established offense conduct, a judge may consider whether offender characteristics call for more or less punishment of that conduct. When the law ties punishment to a defendant's past and character, such as his criminal history, employment record, or age, the state is not defining criminal conduct. States should be able to structure judicial consideration of these offender characteristics through statutes or guidelines without involving juries.*

*. . . This offense/offender distinction, in addition to being suggested by the text of the Constitution, reflects juries' and judges' distinctive institutional competences. Juries can sensibly determine all offense conduct at trial, and the state can prove to a jury at trial all the specific offense conduct for which the state seeks to punish. Judges, however, are better positioned to consider potentially prejudicial information concerning an offender's life and circumstances at sentencing.*

Berman and Bibas 2006, 56

## CASES COVERED

*Ewing v. California,* 538 U.S. 11 (2003)

*Blakely v. Washington,* 542 U.S. 296 (2004)

After conviction defendants become "offenders." You might think this is just a change of words. But you would be wrong. It's a dramatic shift in status with grave consequences. In court before conviction, the shield of constitutional rights protects defendants by the presumption of innocence and all that goes with it (Chapters 12 and 13). But in the three main procedures following conviction—sentencing, appeal, and habeas corpus—a tough-to-overcome **presumption of guilt** rules the day. The significance of this presumption is the reduction or even absence of rights for convicted offenders during sentencing and appeal. They also face growing restrictions on the **right of habeas corpus,** a civil action to determine if the offender is being lawfully detained.

There's a powerful assumption (not necessarily backed up by empirical evidence) that by the time defendants are convicted, the state and defendants have had one fair shot at justice and that's enough. Lots of time, energy, and money are devoted to deciding guilt. For their part, prosecutors have enormous resources at their command—the whole law enforcement machinery—to help them make their case. To offset the state's advantage, defendants are shielded by an array of constitutional rights (we've examined them in previous chapters).

After that fair shot, there's a strong consensus that we're wasting time, money, and energy to allow defendants to climb up, first, the ladder of appeals and then up a second ladder of **collateral attack** (habeas corpus review of convictions by offenders in a separate civil action) to decide if they're being lawfully detained. As in all things (even the pursuit of justice), there comes a time to call it quits and move on—for the state to fight other crimes, and for offenders to pay for their crimes, put their lives together, and get back into society as productive members of their community.

Before 2000, the answer to the question "Which constitutional rights apply to convicted defendants during sentencing?" would have been simple. Hardly any. Since then, a series of U.S. Supreme Court decisions has applied the constitutional rights of trial by jury and proof beyond a reasonable doubt to sentencing.

We'll devote most of the chapter to sentencing, because it's where most activity after conviction occurs. Then, we'll study the extent to which the constitutional rights that protect defendants before conviction apply to convicted defendants during sentencing. Finally, we'll look at the appeals process and habeas corpus proceedings.

Let's turn now to the three proceedings after conviction: sentencing, appeal, and habeas corpus.

# SENTENCING

For more than a thousand years, policy makers have debated whether to fit sentences to the crime or to tailor sentences to suit the criminal. As early as 700 C.E., the Roman Catholic Church's penitential books revealed a tension between prescribing penance strictly according to the sin and tailoring it to suit individual sinners (Samaha 1978). **Determinate**, or **fixed**, **sentencing** (fitting punishment to the crime) puts sentencing authority in the hands of legislators. **Indeterminate sentencing** (tailoring punishment to suit the criminal) puts the power to sentence in the hands of judges and parole boards.

Like the ancient tension between fixed and indeterminate sentencing, there's an ancient debate about judicial discretion in sentencing. Arguments over who should impose sentences indelibly mark the history of sentencing (Samaha 1989). There's also an ancient debate over what sentences to impose—about capital and corporal punishment, the length of imprisonment, what kinds of prisons to put prisoners in, and how to treat them while they're there. The early arguments regarding sinners and penance, judges and punishment, and the aims and kinds of punishment all sound a lot like current debates over the proper authority, aims, kinds, and amounts of punishment sentences ought to reflect.

In this section, we'll concentrate on fixed and indeterminate sentencing. We'll begin by looking at the history of sentencing, examine more closely the division of sentencing authority, and then look at sentencing guidelines.

## The History of Sentencing

*Fixed sentencing*, tailored to fit the crime, prevailed in the United States from the 1600s to the late 1800s. Then, a shift toward *indeterminate sentencing*, tailored to fit individual criminals, began. However, neither fixed nor indeterminate sentences has ever totally dominated criminal sentencing. The tension between the need for certainty and flexibility in sentencing decisions has always required both a measure of predictability (fixed sentences) and a degree of flexibility (indeterminate sentences). Shifting ideological commitments and other informed influences on sentencing ensure that neither fixed nor indeterminate sentences will ever exclusively prevail in sentencing policies and practices.

Following the American Revolution, fixed but relatively moderate penalties became the rule. States abolished the death penalty for many offenses. The rarity of the use of corporal punishment (whipping), mutilation (cutting off ears and slitting tongues), and shaming (the ducking stool) led to their extinction. Imprisonment, which up to that time had been used mainly to detain accused people while they waited for their trial, by 1850, had become the dominant form of criminal punishment after conviction.

Statutes fixed prison terms for most felonies. In practice, liberal use of pardons, early release for "good time," and other devices permitted judges to use informal discretionary judgment in altering formally fixed sentences (Rothman 1971).

The modern history of sentencing began around 1870. Ironically, demands for reform at that time were the opposite of those today; they grew out of deep dissatisfaction with legislatively fixed harsh prison sentences. Reformers complained that prisons were nothing more than warehouses for the poor and the undesirable, and that harsh prison punishment didn't work. Proof of that, the reformers maintained, were the crime rates that continued to grow at unacceptable rates despite harsh, fixed prison sentences. Furthermore, the reformers documented that the prisons were full of recent immigrants and others on the lower rungs of society. Many public officials and concerned citizens agreed. Particularly instrumental in demanding reform were prison administrators and other criminal justice officials. By 1922, all but four states had adopted some form of indeterminate sentencing law.

When the indeterminate sentence became the prevailing practice, administrative sentencing by parole boards and prison officials took precedence over legislative and judicial sentence fixing. At its extreme, judges set no time on sentencing, leaving it wholly to parole boards and correctional officers to determine informally the length of a prisoner's incarceration. More commonly, judges were free to grant probation, suspend sentences in favor of alternatives to incarceration such as community service, or pick confinement times within minimums and maximums prescribed by statutes. Then, parole boards and corrections officers determined the exact release date.

Indeterminate sentencing remained dominant until the 1970s, when several forces coalesced to oppose it. Prison uprisings, especially at Attica and the Tombs in New York in the late 1960s, dramatically portrayed rehabilitation as little more than rhetoric and prisoners as deeply and dangerously discontented. Advocates for individuals' rights challenged the widespread and unreviewable informal discretionary powers exercised by criminal justice officials in general and judges in particular. Demands for increased formal accountability spread throughout the criminal justice system. Courts required public officials to justify their decisions in writing and empowered defendants to dispute allegations against them at sentencing. The courts required even prisons to publish their rules and grant prisoners the right to challenge rules that they were accused of breaking.

Several statistical and experimental studies showed a pernicious discrimination in sentencing. In particular, some research strongly suggested that the poor and Blacks were sentenced more harshly than Whites and middle- and upper-class Americans. Finally, official reports showed steeply rising street crime rates. The National Research Council created a distinguished panel to review sentencing. It concluded that by the early 1970s, a "remarkable consensus emerged along left and right, law enforcement officials and prisoners groups, reformers and bureaucrats that the indeterminate sentencing era was at its end" (Blumstein et al. 1983, 48–52).

By the late 1970s, the emphasis in crime policy had shifted from fairness to crime prevention. Crime prevention was based on incarceration, general deterrence, and retribution; prevention by rehabilitation was definitely losing ground. Civil libertarians and "law and order" supporters alike called for sentencing practices that would advance swift and certain punishment. They differed only on the length of sentences. To civil libertarians, determinate sentencing meant short, fixed sentences; to conservatives, it meant long, fixed sentences.

Three ideas came to dominate thinking about sentencing:

1. Many offenders deserve severe punishment, because they have committed serious crimes.

2. Repeat career offenders require severe punishment to incapacitate them.

3. All crimes deserve some punishment to retain the deterrent potency of the criminal law.

According to the National Council on Crime and Delinquency (1992):

> By 1990, the shift in goals of sentencing reform was complete. Virtually all new sentencing law was designed to increase the certainty and length of prison sentences to incapacitate the active criminal and deter the rest. (6)

Harsher penalties accompanied the shift in the philosophy of punishment. Public support for the death penalty grew; the U.S. Supreme Court ruled that the death penalty was not cruel and unusual punishment; courts sentenced more people to death; and the states began to execute criminals. Judges sentenced more people to prison and to longer prison terms; by 2006, the United States was sentencing more people to prison than any other country in the world (Hartney 2006, 1).

## The Division of Sentencing Authority

Throughout U.S. history, three institutions—legislatures, courts, and administrative agencies—have exercised sentencing power. In the **legislative sentencing model**, legislatures prescribe specific penalties for crimes without regard to the persons who committed them. The punishment fits the crime, not the criminal, and judges and parole boards can't alter these penalties. Removing discretion from judges and parole boards doesn't eliminate evils arising from prejudicial laws that criminalize conduct peculiar to certain groups in society, but it does limit the making of criminal law to legislatures.

In the **judicial sentencing model**, judges prescribe sentences within broad formal contours set by legislative acts. Typically, a statute prescribes a range, such as 1 to 10 years, 0 to 5 years, or 20 years to life. Judges then fix the exact time that convicted criminals serve.

In the **administrative sentencing model**, both the legislature and the judge prescribe a wide range of allowable prison times for particular crimes. Administrative agencies, typically parole boards and prison administrators, determine the exact release date. Under this model, administrative agencies have broad discretion to determine how long prisoners serve and under what conditions they can be released.

As models, these sentencing schemes never operate in pure form. At all times in U.S. history, all three sentencing institutions have overlapped considerably; all have included the exercise of wide discretion. For example, plea bargaining (Chapter 13) has prevented fixing sentencing authority in any of these three. Charge bargaining gets around legislatively fixed sentences, sentence bargaining avoids judicially fixed sentencing, and both alter administratively fixed sentences. But until sentencing reforms in the 1970s began to change policy and practice, legislatures set the general range of penalties, judges picked a specific penalty within that range, and parole boards released offenders after some time spent in prison. Under this practice, judges, parole boards, and prison authorities had considerable discretion in sentencing criminal defendants.

## Sentencing Guidelines and Mandatory Minimum Sentences

The indeterminate sentence, parole boards, and good time still remain a part of the sentencing structure of many states. But some form of fixed sentence is growing. Fixed sentencing has taken two primary forms—sentencing guidelines and mandatory minimum prison sentences. The federal government and most states have adopted both forms.

Both are based, at least in theory, on limiting or even eliminating discretion in sentencing. Both respond to three demands from experts and the public:

1. *Uniformity.* Similar offenses should receive similar punishment.

2. *Certainty and truth in sentencing.* Convicted offenders, victims, and the public should know that the sentence imposed is similar to the sentence actually served. ("Do the crime; do the time.")

3. *Retribution, deterrence, and incapacitation.* The rehabilitation of individual offenders isn't the primary aim of punishment.

Let's look more closely at sentencing guidelines and mandatory minimum prison sentences.

*Sentencing Guidelines* In **sentencing guidelines**, a commission establishes a relatively narrow range of penalties, and judges are supposed to choose a specific sentence within that range. The guideline sentence depends on a combination of the seriousness of the crime and the offender's criminal history. Sentences are either presumptively incarceration or presumptively probation. Judges can depart from the range set in the guidelines, but usually they have to give written reasons for their departure. Letting judges choose within a range without departing from the guidelines builds a flexibility into the system that allows for differences in individual cases. Characteristics such as the amount of money stolen, the extent of personal injury inflicted, and the criminal history of the offender can affect the sentence that judges impose without undermining the basic goals of uniformity and equity.

 Go to Exercise 14.1 on the Samaha Criminal Procedure 7e website to apply U.S. sentencing guidelines to a real case: academic.cengage.com/criminaljustice/samaha.

*Mandatory Minimum Sentences* The other type of fixed sentence, **mandatory minimum sentences**, requires judges to impose a nondiscretionary minimum amount of prison time that all offenders convicted of the offense have to serve. Judges can sentence offenders to more than the minimum but not less. Mandatory minimum sentence laws promise that "If you do the crime, you will do the time." Mandatory penalties are very old. The "eye for an eye" and "tooth for a tooth" in the Old Testament were mandatory penalties. The Anglo-Saxon king Alfred prescribed a detailed mandatory penal code, including such provisions as "If one knocks out another's eye, he shall pay 66 shillings, 6 1/3 pence. If the eye is still in the head, but the injured man can see nothing with it, one-third of the payment shall be withheld" (Lee n.d.).

As early as 1790 in the United States, most states had established mandatory penalties for capital crimes. Throughout the 19th century, Congress enacted mandatory penalties—usually short prison sentences—for a long list of crimes, including refusal to testify before Congress, failure to report seaboard saloon purchases, or causing a ship to run aground by use of a false light (Wallace 1993, 9).

From 1900 to the 1950s, the use of mandatory minimum penalties fell into disuse. The Boggs Act (1951), named after its sponsor, Alabama Representative Hale Boggs, signaled a shift to mandatory minimum sentences. It set minimum sentences for those convicted of importing drugs or distributing marijuana. In the 1950s, fear that crime and drug problems were caused by a Communist plot to get Americans "hooked" on especially potent "pure Communist heroin" from China led Congress to enact the Narcotic Control Act of 1956 (U.S. Congress 1954, 7). It further increased the penalties set in the Boggs Act.

In 1956, the Senate Judiciary explained why Congress needed a mandatory minimum sentence drug law:

There is a need for the continuation of the policy of punishment of a severe character as a deterrent to narcotic law violations. [The Committee] therefore recommends an increase in maximum sentences for first as well as subsequent offenses. With respect to the mandatory minimum features of such penalties, and prohibition of suspended sentences or probation, the Committee recognizes objections in principle. It feels, however, that, in order to define the gravity of this class of crime and the assured penalty to follow, these features of the law must be regarded as essential elements of the desired deterrents, although some differences of opinion still exist regarding their application to first offenses of certain types. (U.S. Sentencing Commission 1991, 5–7)

The 1956 statute imposed stiff mandatory minimum sentences for narcotics offenses, requiring judges to pick within a range of penalties. Judges couldn't suspend sentences or put convicted offenders on probation. In addition, offenders weren't eligible for parole if they were convicted under the act. For example, the act punished the first conviction for selling heroin by a term of from 5 to 10 years of imprisonment. Judges had to sentence offenders to at least 5 years in prison, judges couldn't suspend the sentence or put offenders on probation, and offenders weren't eligible for parole for at least the minimum period of the sentence. For second offenders, the mandatory minimum was raised to 10 years. The penalty for the sale of narcotics to persons under 18 ranged from a mandatory minimum of 10 years to a maximum of life imprisonment or death (U.S. Sentencing Commission 1991, 6).

In 1970, Congress retreated from the mandatory minimum sentence approach. In the Comprehensive Drug Abuse Prevention and Control Act of 1970, Congress repealed virtually all of the mandatory minimum provisions adopted in the 1956 act, because the increased sentence lengths "had not shown the expected overall reduction in drug law violations." Among the reasons for the repeal of mandatory minimum penalties for drug law offenses were that they

- Alienated youths from the general society

- Hampered the rehabilitation of drug offenders

- Infringed on judicial authority by drastically reducing discretion in sentencing

- Reduced the deterrent effect of drug laws because even prosecutors thought the laws were too severe

According to the House committee that considered the repeal of the bill:

The severity of existing penalties, involving in many instances minimum sentences, have [sic] led in many instances to reluctance on the part of prosecutors to prosecute some violations, where the penalties seem to be out of line with the seriousness of the offenses. In addition, severe penalties, which do not take into account individual circumstances, and which treat casual violators as severely as they treat hardened criminals, tend to make conviction more difficult to obtain. (U.S. Congress 1970, 11)

The retreat from mandatory minimum sentences was short-lived, because public concern about violence and drugs again rose to the top of the national agenda. The public and legislatures blamed rising crime rates on the uncertainty and "leniency" of indeterminate sentences. Beginning in the early 1970s, the states and the federal government enacted more and longer mandatory minimum prison sentences. By 1991, 46 states and the federal government had enacted mandatory minimum sentencing laws. Although the list of mandatory minimum laws is long (the U.S. Criminal Code contains at least one hundred), the main targets of mandatory minimum sentences are drug offenses, violent crimes, and crimes committed with a weapon (Wallace 1993, 11).

Mandatory minimum sentences are supposed to satisfy three basic aims of criminal punishment: retribution, incapacitation, and deterrence. According to supporters, mandatory minimum sentence laws mean those committing serious crimes will receive severe punishment. Furthermore, violent criminals, criminals who use weapons, and drug offenders can't harm the public if they're in prison. And the knowledge that committing mandatory minimum crimes will bring certain, swift, and severe punishment should deter these types of crimes.

Several evaluations, however, suggest that, in practice, mandatory minimum penalties don't always achieve the goals their supporters hoped they would. In 1990, Congress ordered the U.S. Sentencing Commission to evaluate the rapidly increasing number of mandatory minimum sentencing provisions in the federal system. The results of the commission's study provided little empirical support for the success of mandatory sentencing laws, as these findings demonstrate:

1. Only a few of the mandatory minimum sentencing provisions are ever used. Nearly all those used relate to drug and weapons offenses.

2. Only 41 percent of defendants whose characteristics and behavior qualify them for mandatory minimum sentences actually receive them.

3. Mandatory minimum sentences actually introduce disparity in sentencing. For example, the commission found that race influences disparity in a number of ways. Whites are less likely than Blacks and Hispanics to be indicted or convicted at the mandatory minimum. Whites are also more likely than Blacks and Hispanics to receive reductions for "substantial assistance" in aiding in the prosecution of other offenders.

The mandatory minimum sentence laws allow an exception for offenders who provide "substantial assistance" in investigating other offenders. But judges can reduce the minimum for substantial assistance only on the motion of the prosecutors.

4. Substantial assistance also leads to disparities quite apart from race. It tends to favor the very people the law was intended to reach—those higher up in the chain of drug dealing, because underlings have less to offer the government. In one case, for example, Stanley Marshall, who sold less than one gram of LSD, got a 20-year mandatory prison sentence. Jose Cabrera, on the other hand, who the government estimated made more than $40 million from importing cocaine and who would have qualified for life plus 200 years, received a prison term of 8 years for providing "substantial assistance" in the case of Manuel Noriega. According to Judge Terry J. Hatter, Jr., "The people at the very bottom who can't provide substantial assistance end up getting [punished] more severely than those at the top" (*Criminal Justice Newsletter* 1993, 5; Wallace 1993, 11).

5. Mandatory minimum sentences don't eliminate discretion; they just shift it from judges to prosecutors. Prosecutors can use their discretion in a number of ways, including manipulating the "substantial assistance" exception and deciding not to charge defendants with crimes carrying mandatory minimum sentences or to charge them with mandatory minimum crimes of lesser degree.

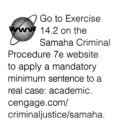 Go to Exercise 14.2 on the Samaha Criminal Procedure 7e website to apply a mandatory minimum sentence to a real case: academic. cengage.com/ criminaljustice/samaha.

The U.S. Sentencing Commission recommended further study before making any final conclusions about the effectiveness of mandatory penalties. But their findings, along with other research on federal and state mandatory minimum sentences, suggest that mandatory minimum penalties aren't the easy answer to the crime problem that politicians promise and the public hopes for (Campaign for an Effective Crime Policy 1993; Schulhofer 1993, 199).

## The Constitution and Sentencing

There are two kinds of constitutional questions regarding sentencing. One has to do with the sentence itself—namely, whether it's banned by the Eighth Amendment "cruel and unusual punishment" clause. Whether it's cruel and unusual depends on the answer to another question, "Does the Eighth Amendment embody a proportionality requirement?" The **proportionality principle** states that a punishment is cruel and unusual if its harshness is "grossly disproportionate" to the "gravity of the offense" (*Harmelin v. Michigan* 1991, 997). In other words, does the punishment fit the crime?

The other constitutional question has to do with the procedures used to determine the sentence. That question is, What, if any, rights that defendants enjoyed *before* conviction during trial and plea bargaining do they enjoy *after* conviction during sentencing? Let's look at each of these questions. We'll also examine the rights offenders have related to procedures surrounding the death penalty.

*The Proportionality Principle* We need to distinguish proportionality in death sentence cases from sentences to prison. A solid majority of the U.S. Supreme Court has made it clear that the proportionality principle applies to death sentences. Two justices on the present Court have concluded that the Eighth Amendment includes no proportionality requirement. (We don't know the position of the two newest members of the Court, Chief Justice Roberts and Justice Alito.) As of 2007, the Court has ruled that the sentence of death fits only the crime of murder (*Gregg v. Georgia* 1976) but not if the killer was retarded (*Atkins v. Virginia* 2002) or under 18 (*Roper v. Simmons* 2005). We also know that a death sentence for raping an adult woman is "grossly disproportionate" (*Coker v. Georgia* 1977, 592). A death sentence for a felony murderer who didn't do the actual killing and lacked the intent to kill (*Enmund v. Florida* 1982) is also disproportionate.

When it comes to sentences of imprisonment, the Court is deeply divided. Some justices have concluded that proportionality never applies to sentences of imprisonment. A narrow and shifting majority have concluded that there's a "narrow proportionality principle" regarding prison sentences (*Harmelin v. Michigan* 1991, 997). For example, it would be cruel and unusual punishment to sentence someone to life in prison for failing to pay a parking ticket (*Rummell v. Estelle* 1980, 274, n. 11).

By a slim majority and over strong dissents, the Supreme Court held that it was not cruel and unusual punishment to sentence first-time offender Ronald Allen Harmelin to life in prison with no chance of parole for possessing 672 grams of cocaine (*Harmelin v. Michigan* 1991). The majority, however, couldn't agree as to why. Justice Scalia and Chief Justice Rehnquist's reason was because there's no proportionality requirement in the Eighth Amendment. Justices O'Connor, Kennedy, and Souter concluded that the sentence wasn't grossly disproportionate to the crime. Four justices dissented because the sentence was grossly disproportionate to the crime.

In our next case excerpt, *Ewing v. California* (2003), the Supreme Court, again narrowly, held that it wasn't cruel and unusual punishment to sentence Gary Ewing to 25 years to life for shoplifting three golf clubs under California's "three strikes" law.

# Is 25 Years to Life for Third-Strike Shoplifting Cruel and Unusual?

## Ewing v. California
538 U.S. 11 (2003)

### HISTORY

Gary Ewing, Defendant, was convicted in a California state court of felony grand theft, and sentenced to 25 years to life under that state's three strikes law. The California Court of Appeal, Second Appellate District, affirmed sentence, and the State Supreme Court denied review. Certiorari was granted. The Supreme Court affirmed.

O'CONNOR, J. ANNOUNCED THE JUDGMENT OF THE COURT AND DELIVERED AN OPINION, JOINED BY REHNQUIST, C.J. AND KENNEDY, J.

California's current three strikes law consists of two virtually identical statutory schemes designed to increase the prison terms of repeat felons. When a defendant is convicted of a felony, and he has previously been convicted of one or more prior felonies defined as "serious" or "violent" in Cal.Penal Code Ann. §§ 667.5 and 1192.7, sentencing is conducted pursuant to the three strikes law. Prior convictions must be alleged in the charging document, and the defendant has a right to a jury determination that the prosecution has proved the prior convictions beyond a reasonable doubt. § 1025; § 1158.

If the defendant has one prior "serious" or "violent" felony conviction, he must be sentenced to "twice the term otherwise provided as punishment for the current felony conviction." § 667(e)(1) (West 1999); § 1170.12(c)(1). If the defendant has two or more prior "serious" or "violent" felony convictions, he must receive "an indeterminate term of life imprisonment." § 667(e)(2)(A); § 1170.12(c)(2)(A). Defendants sentenced to life under the three strikes law become eligible for parole on a date calculated by reference to a "minimum term," which is the greater of (a) three times the term otherwise provided for the current conviction, (b) 25 years, or (c) the term determined by the court pursuant to § 1170 for the underlying conviction, including any enhancements. §§ 667(e)(2)(A)(i)–(iii) (West 1999); §§ 1170.12(c)(2)(A)(i)–(iii).

Under California law, certain offenses may be classified as either felonies or misdemeanors. These crimes are known as "wobblers." Some crimes that would otherwise be misdemeanors become "wobblers" because of the defendant's prior record. For example, petty theft, a misdemeanor, becomes a "wobbler" when the defendant has previously served a prison term for committing specified theft-related crimes. § 490 (West 1999); § 666. Other crimes, such as grand theft, are "wobblers" regardless of the defendant's prior record. See § 489(b). Both types of "wobblers" are triggering offenses under the three strikes law only when they are treated as felonies. Under California law, a "wobbler" is presumptively a felony and "remains a felony except when the discretion is actually exercised" to make the crime a misdemeanor.

In California, prosecutors may exercise their discretion to charge a "wobbler" as either a felony or a misdemeanor. Likewise, California trial courts have discretion to reduce a "wobbler" charged as a felony to a misdemeanor either before preliminary examination or at sentencing to avoid imposing a three strikes sentence. Cal.Penal Code Ann. §§ 17(b)(5), 17(b)(1). In exercising this discretion, the court may consider "those factors that direct similar sentencing decisions," such as "the nature and circumstances of the offense, the defendant's appreciation of and attitude toward the offense, . . . [and] the general objectives of sentencing."

California trial courts can also vacate allegations of prior "serious" or "violent" felony convictions, either on motion by the prosecution or *sua sponte* [*on their own*]. In ruling whether to vacate allegations of prior felony convictions, courts consider whether, "in light of the nature and circumstances of [the defendant's] present felonies and prior serious and/or violent felony convictions, and the particulars of his background, character, and prospects, the defendant may be deemed outside the [three strikes'] scheme's spirit, in whole or in part." *People v. Williams*, 948 P.2d 429, 437 (1998). Thus, trial courts may avoid imposing a three strikes sentence in two ways: first, by reducing "wobblers" to misdemeanors (which do not qualify as triggering offenses), and second, by vacating allegations of prior "serious" or "violent" felony convictions.

### FACTS

On parole from a 9-year prison term, petitioner Gary Ewing walked into the pro shop of the El Segundo Golf Course in Los Angeles County on March 12, 2000. He walked out with three golf clubs, priced at $399 apiece, concealed in his pants leg. A shop employee, whose suspicions were aroused when he observed Ewing limp out of the pro shop, telephoned the police. The police apprehended Ewing in the parking lot.

Ewing is no stranger to the criminal justice system. . . . [*Justice O'Connor here summarizes 9 prior convictions between 1984 and the offenses counting toward the three-strikes conviction in 1993.*] In October and November 1993, Ewing committed three burglaries and one robbery at a Long Beach, California, apartment complex over a 5-week period. He awakened one of his victims, asleep on her living room sofa, as he tried to disconnect her video cassette recorder from the television in that room. When she screamed, Ewing ran out the front door. On another occasion, Ewing accosted a victim in the mailroom of the apartment complex. Ewing claimed to have a gun and ordered the victim to hand over his wallet. When the victim resisted, Ewing produced a knife and forced the victim back to the apartment itself. While Ewing rifled through the bedroom, the victim fled the apartment screaming for help. Ewing absconded with the victim's money and credit cards.

On December 9, 1993, Ewing was arrested on the premises of the apartment complex for trespassing and lying to a police officer. The knife used in the robbery and a glass cocaine pipe were later found in the back seat of the patrol car used to transport Ewing to the police station. A jury convicted Ewing of first-degree robbery and three counts of residential burglary. Sentenced to nine years and eight months in prison, Ewing was paroled in 1999.

Only 10 months later, Ewing stole the golf clubs at issue in this case. He was charged with, and ultimately convicted of, one count of felony grand theft of personal property in excess of $400. See Cal.Penal Code Ann. § 484; § 489. As required by the three strikes law, the prosecutor formally alleged, and the trial court later found, that Ewing had been convicted previously of four serious or violent felonies for the three burglaries and the robbery in the Long Beach apartment complex.

At the sentencing hearing, Ewing asked the court to reduce the conviction for grand theft, a "wobbler" under California law, to a misdemeanor so as to avoid a three strikes sentence. Ewing also asked the trial court to exercise its discretion to dismiss the allegations of some or all of his prior serious or violent felony convictions, again for purposes of avoiding a three strikes sentence. Before sentencing Ewing, the trial court took note of his entire criminal history, including the fact that he was on parole when he committed his latest offense. The court also heard arguments from defense counsel and a plea from Ewing himself.

In the end, the trial judge determined that the grand theft should remain a felony. The court also ruled that the four prior strikes for the three burglaries and the robbery in Long Beach should stand. As a newly convicted felon with two or more "serious" or "violent" felony convictions in his past, Ewing was sentenced under the three strikes law to 25 years to life.

## OPINION

The Eighth Amendment, which forbids cruel and unusual punishments, contains a "narrow proportionality principle" that "applies to noncapital sentences." . . .

For many years, most States have had laws providing for enhanced sentencing of repeat offenders. Yet between 1993 and 1995, three strikes laws effected a sea change in criminal sentencing throughout the Nation. These laws responded to widespread public concerns about crime by targeting the class of offenders who pose the greatest threat to public safety: career criminals. As one of the chief architects of California's three strikes law has explained: "Three Strikes was intended to go beyond simply making sentences tougher. It was intended to be a focused effort to create a sentencing policy that would use the judicial system to reduce serious and violent crime."

Throughout the States, legislatures enacting three strikes laws made a deliberate policy choice that individuals who have repeatedly engaged in serious or violent criminal behavior, and whose conduct has not been deterred by more conventional approaches to punishment, must be isolated from society in order to protect the public safety. Though three strikes laws may be relatively new, our tradition of deferring to state legislatures in making and implementing such important policy decisions is longstanding.

Our traditional deference to legislative policy choices finds a corollary in the principle that the Constitution does not mandate adoption of any one penological theory. A sentence can have a variety of justifications, such as incapacitation, deterrence, retribution, or rehabilitation. Some or all of these justifications may play a role in a State's sentencing scheme. Selecting the sentencing rationales is generally a policy choice to be made by state legislatures, not federal courts.

When the California Legislature enacted the three strikes law, it made a judgment that protecting the public safety requires incapacitating criminals who have already been convicted of at least one serious or violent crime. Nothing in the Eighth Amendment prohibits California from making that choice. To the contrary, our cases establish that States have a valid interest in deterring and segregating habitual criminals. . . .

To be sure, California's three strikes law has sparked controversy. Critics have doubted the law's wisdom, cost-efficiency, and effectiveness in reaching its goals. This criticism is appropriately directed at the legislature, which has primary responsibility for making the difficult policy choices that underlie any criminal sentencing scheme. We do not sit as a "superlegislature" to second-guess these policy choices. It is enough that the State of California has a reasonable basis for believing that dramatically enhanced sentences for habitual felons "advance[s] the goals of [its] criminal justice system in any substantial way." See *Solem*, 463 U.S., at 297, n. 22, 103 S.Ct. 3001.

Against this backdrop, we consider Ewing's claim that his three strikes sentence of 25 years to life is unconstitutionally disproportionate to his offense of "shoplifting three golf clubs." We first address the gravity of the offense compared to the harshness of the penalty. At the threshold, we note that Ewing incorrectly frames the issue. The gravity of his offense was not merely "shoplifting three golf clubs." Rather, Ewing was convicted of felony grand theft for stealing nearly $1,200 worth of merchandise after previously having been convicted of at least two "violent" or "serious" felonies. Even standing alone, Ewing's theft should not be taken lightly. His crime was certainly not "one of the most passive felonies a person could commit." . . .

In weighing the gravity of Ewing's offense, we must place on the scales not only his current felony, but also his long history of felony recidivism. Any other approach would fail to accord proper deference to the policy judgments that find expression in the legislature's choice of sanctions. In imposing a three strikes sentence, the State's interest is not merely punishing the offense of conviction, or the "triggering" offense: "It is in addition the interest . . . in dealing in a harsher manner with those who by repeated criminal acts have shown that they are simply incapable of conforming to the norms of society as established by its criminal law." To give full effect to the State's choice of this legitimate penological goal, our proportionality review of Ewing's sentence must take that goal into account.

Ewing's sentence is justified by the State's public-safety interest in incapacitating and deterring recidivist felons, and amply supported by his own long, serious criminal record. Ewing has been convicted of numerous misdemeanor and felony offenses, served nine separate terms of incarceration, and committed most of his crimes while on probation or parole. His prior "strikes" were serious felonies including robbery and three residential burglaries. To be sure, Ewing's sentence is a long one. But it reflects a rational legislative judgment, entitled to deference, that offenders who have committed serious or violent felonies and who continue to commit felonies must be incapacitated. The State of California was entitled to place upon [Ewing] the onus of one who is simply unable to bring his conduct within the social norms prescribed by the criminal law of the State. Ewing's is not the rare case in which a threshold comparison of the crime committed and the sentence imposed leads to an inference of gross disproportionality.

We hold that Ewing's sentence of 25 years to life in prison, imposed for the offense of felony grand theft under the three strikes law, is not grossly disproportionate and therefore does not violate the Eighth Amendment's prohibition on cruel and unusual punishments.

The judgment of the California Court of Appeal is AFFIRMED. *It is so ordered.*

## CONCURRING OPINION

SCALIA, J.

In my opinion in *Harmelin v. Michigan* (1991), I concluded that the Eighth Amendment's prohibition of "cruel and unusual punishments" was aimed at excluding only certain *modes* of punishment, and was not a "guarantee against disproportionate sentences." Out of respect for the principle of stare decisis, I might nonetheless accept the contrary holding of *Solem v. Helm* (1983)—that the Eighth Amendment contains a narrow proportionality principle—if I felt I could intelligently apply it. This case demonstrates why I cannot.

Proportionality—the notion that the punishment should fit the crime—is inherently a concept tied to the penological goal of retribution. It becomes difficult even to speak intelligently of "proportionality," once deterrence and rehabilitation are given significant weight—not to mention giving weight to the purpose of California's three strikes law: incapacitation. In the present case, the game is up once the plurality has acknowledged that "the Constitution does not mandate adoption of any one penological theory," and that a "sentence can have a variety of justifications, such as incapacitation, deterrence, retribution, or rehabilitation." That acknowledgment having been made, it no longer suffices merely to assess "the gravity of the offense compared to the harshness of the penalty"; that classic description of the proportionality principle (alone and in itself quite resistant to policy-free, legal analysis) now becomes merely the "first" step of the inquiry. Having completed that step (by a discussion which, in all fairness, does not convincingly establish that 25-years-to-life is a "proportionate" punishment for stealing three golf clubs), the plurality must then add an analysis to show that "Ewing's sentence is justified by the State's public-safety interest in incapacitating and deterring recidivist felons."

Which indeed it is—though why that has anything to do with the principle of proportionality is a mystery. Perhaps the plurality should revise its terminology, so that what it reads into the Eighth Amendment is not the unstated proposition that all punishment should be reasonably proportionate to the gravity of the offense, but rather the unstated proposition that all punishment should reasonably pursue the multiple purposes of the criminal law. That formulation would make it clearer than ever, of course, that the plurality is not applying law but evaluating policy.

Because I agree that petitioner's sentence does not violate the Eighth Amendment's prohibition against cruel and unusual punishments, I concur in the judgment.

THOMAS, J.

. . . In my view, the Cruel and Unusual Punishments Clause of the Eighth Amendment contains no proportionality principle. Because the plurality concludes that petitioner's sentence does not violate the Eighth Amendment's prohibition on cruel and unusual punishments, I concur in the judgment.

## DISSENT

STEVENS, J., JOINED BY SOUTER, GINSBURG, AND BREYER, JJ.
. . . Proportionality review is not only capable of judicial application but also required by the Eighth Amendment. . . . This Court has held that the Constitution directs judges to apply their best judgment in determining the proportionality of fines, bail, and other forms of punishment, including the imposition of a death sentence. It would be anomalous indeed to suggest that the Eighth Amendment makes proportionality review applicable in the context of bail and fines but not in the context of other forms of punishment, such as imprisonment. Rather, by broadly prohibiting excessive sanctions, the Eighth Amendment directs judges to exercise their wise judgment in assessing the proportionality of all forms of punishment.

. . . From the beginning of the Republic, federal judges were entrusted with wide sentencing discretion. It was not unheard of for a statute to authorize a sentence ranging from one year to life, for example. In exercising their discretion, sentencing judges wisely employed a proportionality principle that took into account all of the justifications for punishment—namely, deterrence, incapacitation, retribution, and rehabilitation. Likewise, I think it clear that the Eighth Amendment's prohibition of "cruel and unusual punishments" expresses a broad and basic proportionality principle that takes into account all of the justifications for penal sanctions. It is this broad proportionality principle that would preclude reliance on any of the justifications for punishment to support, for example, a life sentence for overtime parking.

Accordingly, I respectfully DISSENT.

BREYER, J., JOINED BY STEVENS, SOUTER, AND GINSBURG, JJ.

. . . A comparison of Ewing's sentence with other sentences requires answers to two questions. First, how would other jurisdictions (or California at other times, *i.e.*, without the three strikes penalty) punish the *same offense conduct?* Second, upon what other conduct would other jurisdictions (or California) impose the *same prison term?* Moreover, since hypothetical punishment is beside the point, the relevant prison time, for comparative purposes, is *real* prison time, *i.e.*, the time that an offender must *actually serve.* . . .

As to California itself, we know the following: First, between the end of World War II and 1994 (when California enacted the three strikes law), no one like Ewing could have served more than *10* years in prison. . . . From 1976 to 1994 (and currently, absent application of the three strikes penalty), a Ewing-type offender would have received a maximum sentence of four years. And we know that California's "habitual offender" laws did not apply to grand theft. We also know that the time that any offender actually served was likely far less than 10 years. This is because statistical data show that the median time actually served for grand theft (other than auto theft) was about two years, and 90 percent of all those convicted of that crime served less than three or four years.

Second, statistics suggest that recidivists *of all sorts* convicted during that same time period in California served a small fraction of Ewing's real-time sentence. On average, recidivists served three to four additional (recidivist-related) years in prison, with 90 percent serving less than an additional real seven to eight years.

Third, we know that California has reserved, and still reserves, Ewing-type prison time, *i.e.*, at least 25 real years in prison, for criminals convicted of crimes far worse than was Ewing's. Statistics for the years 1945 to 1981, for example, indicate that typical (nonrecidivist) male first-degree murderers served between 10 and 15 real years in prison, with 90 percent of all such murderers serving less than 20 real years. Moreover, California, which has moved toward a real-time sentencing system (where the statutory punishment approximates the time served), still punishes far less harshly those who have engaged in far more serious conduct. It imposes, for example, upon nonrecidivists guilty of arson causing great bodily injury a maximum sentence of nine years in prison (prison term of 5, 7, or 9 years for arson that causes great bodily injury); it imposes upon those guilty of voluntary manslaughter a maximum sentence of 11 years (prison term of 3, 6, or 11 years for voluntary manslaughter). It reserves the sentence that it here imposes upon (former-burglar-now-golf-club-thief) Ewing for nonrecidivist, first-degree murderers.

As to other jurisdictions, we know the following: The United States, bound by the federal Sentencing Guidelines, would impose upon a recidivist, such as Ewing, a sentence that, in any ordinary case, would not exceed 18 months in prison. . . . Ewing also would not have been subject to the federal "three strikes" law, for which grand theft is not a triggering offense. . . .

. . . Given the information available . . . we can assume for constitutional purposes that the following statement is true: Outside the California three strikes context, Ewing's recidivist sentence is virtually unique in its harshness for his offense of conviction, and by a considerable degree. . . .

Justice Scalia and Justice Thomas argue that we should not review for gross disproportionality a sentence to a term of years. Otherwise, we make it too difficult for legislators and sentencing judges to determine just when their sentencing laws and practices pass constitutional muster. I concede that a bright-line rule would give legislators and sentencing judges more guidance. But application of the Eighth Amendment to a sentence of a term of years requires a case-by-case approach. And, in my view, like that of the plurality, meaningful enforcement of the Eighth Amendment demands that application—even if only at sentencing's outer bounds.

A case-by-case approach can nonetheless offer guidance through example. Ewing's sentence is, at a minimum, 2 to 3 times the length of sentences that other jurisdictions would impose in similar circumstances. That sentence itself is sufficiently long to require a typical offender to spend virtually all the remainder of his active life in prison. These and the other factors that I have discussed [*not all included in this excerpt*] . . . should help to identify "gross disproportionality" in a fairly objective way—at the outer bounds of sentencing. In sum, even if I accept for present purposes the plurality's analytical framework, Ewing's sentence (life imprisonment with a minimum term of 25 years) is grossly disproportionate to the triggering offense conduct—stealing three golf clubs—Ewing's recidivism notwithstanding.

## Questions

1. List California's reasons for adopting their "three strikes" law.

2. How does the plurality know that the three-strikes law isn't cruel and unusual?

3. How does the dissent know that it *is* cruel and unusual?

4. Are their opinions purely subjective or are they based on some standards? If so, what are the standards?

5. Should the California legislature or the U.S. Supreme Court decide whether punishments are cruel and unusual? Explain your answer.

6. Do you believe 25 years to life is "grossly disproportionate" to Gary Ewing's crime? How do *you* know whether it is or isn't?

***Trial Rights at Sentencing*** Until the present era of sentencing guidelines and mandatory minimum sentencing, the U.S. Supreme Court adopted a **hands-off approach to sentencing proceedings**, leaving the way sentences were determined to trial judges. Put another way, the Constitution places few, if any, limits on judicial discretionary decision making.

In the leading case applying the hands-off sentencing procedures, *Williams v. New York* (1949), Samuel Titto Williams was sentenced to death by the trial judge even though the jury recommended life imprisonment:

> In giving his reasons for imposing the death sentence the judge discussed in open court the evidence upon which the jury had convicted stating that this evidence had been considered in the light of additional information obtained through the court's Probation Department, and through other sources. [The additional information] revealed many material facts concerning appellant's background which though relevant to the question of punishment could not properly have been brought to the attention of the jury in its consideration of the question of guilt.
>
> He referred to the experience appellant "had had on thirty other burglaries in and about the same vicinity" where the murder had been committed. The appellant had not been convicted of these burglaries although the judge had information that he had confessed to some and had been identified as the perpetrator of some of the others.
>
> The judge also referred to certain activities of appellant as shown by the probation report that indicated appellant possessed "a morbid sexuality" and classified him as a "menace to society." The accuracy of the statements made by the judge as to appellant's background and past practices were not challenged by appellant or his counsel, nor was the judge asked to disregard any of them or to afford appellant a chance to refute or discredit any of them by cross-examination or otherwise. (242–44)

Williams contended that sentencing him to death based on the additional information would deny him life without due process of law. The Court rejected his contention:

> Tribunals passing on the guilt of a defendant always have been hedged in by strict evidentiary procedural limitations. But both before and since the American colonies became a nation, courts in this country and in England practiced a policy under which a sentencing judge could exercise a wide discretion in the sources and types of evidence used to assist him in determining the kind and extent of punishment to be imposed within limits fixed by law. Out-of-court affidavits have been used frequently, and of course in the smaller communities sentencing judges naturally have in mind their knowledge of the personalities and backgrounds of convicted offenders. (246)

In addition to history, the Court continued, there are "sound practical reasons" for different rules governing trials and sentencing procedures:

> In a trial before verdict the issue is whether a defendant is guilty of having engaged in certain criminal conduct of which he has been specifically accused. Rules of evidence have been fashioned for criminal trials which narrowly confine the trial contest to evidence that is strictly relevant to the particular offense charged. These rules rest in part on a necessity to prevent a time consuming and confusing trial of collateral issues. They were also designed to prevent tribunals concerned solely with the issue of guilt of a particular offense from being influenced to convict for that offense by evidence that the defendant had habitually engaged in other misconduct.
>
> A sentencing judge, however, is not confined to the narrow issue of guilt. His task within fixed statutory or constitutional limits is to determine the type and extent of punishment after the issue of guilt has been determined. Highly relevant—if not essential—to his selection of an appropriate sentence is the possession of the fullest information possible concerning the defendant's life and characteristics.

And modern concepts individualizing punishment have made it all the more necessary that a sentencing judge not be denied an opportunity to obtain pertinent information by a requirement of rigid adherence to restrictive rules of evidence properly applicable to the trial. (246–47)

That was 1949, when the rehabilitative ideal and judicial discretion was in full favor. Then came the history briefly related at the beginning of this section. The period saw the adoption of sentencing guidelines and mandatory minimum sentencing laws based on retribution, deterrence, and incapacitation and the accompanying curbs on judicial discretion. All this history came to a head in 2000 when the U.S. Supreme Court, to the surprise of many, dropped the hands-off approach and brought the Constitution into sentencing proceedings in *Apprendi v. New Jersey*.

Charles Apprendi, Jr., was convicted of possessing a firearm with an unlawful purpose, a felony in New Jersey normally punishable by 5 to 10 years in prison. New Jersey also had a hate crime statute providing for an extended punishment of 10 to 20 years if the judge found by a preponderance of the evidence that the defendant committed the crime with a "purpose to intimidate an individual or group of individuals because of race, color, gender, handicap, religion, sexual orientation or ethnicity" (469).

Apprendi argued that "racial purpose" was an element of the crime that required proof beyond a reasonable doubt. New Jersey argued that the choice of elements of offenses is for legislatures to make, and that New Jersey's legislature chose to make "racial purpose" a "sentencing factor." The 5-member majority agreed with Apprendi and adopted the *Apprendi* **bright-line rule**:

> Other than the fact of prior conviction, any fact that increases the penalty for a crime beyond the prescribed statutory maximum must be submitted to a jury, and proved beyond a reasonable doubt. (490)

Four justices dissented. According to Justice O'Connor, the

> Court has long recognized that not every fact that bears on a defendant's punishment need be charged in an indictment, submitted to a jury, and proved by the government beyond a reasonable doubt. . . . We have proceeded with caution before deciding that a certain fact must be treated as an offense element despite the legislature's choice not to characterize it as such. We have therefore declined to establish any bright-line rule for making such judgments and have instead approached each case individually, sifting through the considerations most relevant to determining whether the legislature has acted properly within its broad power to define crimes and their punishments or has sought to evade the constitutional requirements associated with the characterization of a fact as an offense element. (524)
>
> In one bold stroke the Court today casts aside our traditional cautious approach and instead embraces a universal and seemingly bright-line rule limiting the power of Congress and state legislatures to define criminal offenses and the sentences that follow from convictions thereunder. The Court states: "Other than the fact of a prior conviction, any fact that increases the penalty for a crime beyond the prescribed statutory maximum must be submitted to a jury, and proved beyond a reasonable doubt." In its opinion, the Court marshals virtually no authority to support its extraordinary rule. Indeed, it is remarkable that the Court cannot identify a *single instance,* in the over 200 years since the ratification of the Bill of Rights, that our Court has applied, as a constitutional requirement, the rule it announces today. (525)

The Court followed *Apprendi* with four other decisions, made up of shifting 5–4 majorities (Table 14.1) and several concurring opinions—overall displaying a badly splintered Court. The two newest justices, Chief Justice Roberts and Justice Alito, haven't

## TABLE 14.1 Major U.S. Supreme Court Sentencing Rights Cases

| Case | Sentencing Rights Affected |
|---|---|
| 1. *Apprendi v. New Jersey*, 530 U.S. 466 (2000), 5–4 | Struck down a New Jersey statute empowering judges to raise *maximum* sentences based on facts judges found to be true by a preponderance of evidence but not found by juries beyond a reasonable doubt or confessed to by defendants |
| 2. *Apprendi v. New Jersey*, 530 U.S. 466 (2000), 5–4 | Affirmed judges' power to increase maximum sentence based on prior convictions without juries finding there were prior convictions or defendants confessing to them |
| 3. *Harris v. U.S.*, 536 U.S. 545 (2002), 5–4 | Upheld a statute permitting judges to raise *mandatory minimum* sentences based on facts found by judges, not juries |
| 4. *Blakely v. Washington*, 542 U.S. 296 (2004), 5–4 | Struck down a Washington State statute that empowered judges to *increase* the length of prison time beyond the "standard range" prescribed by Washington's sentencing guidelines based on facts not found by juries beyond a reasonable doubt |
| 5. *U.S. v. Booker*, 543 U.S. 220 (2005), 5–4 | • Struck down provisions in the U.S. sentencing guidelines that allowed judges to increase individual sentences beyond the standard range based on facts not found by juries beyond a reasonable doubt<br><br>• Ruled that guidelines are advisory, but they enjoy the presumption of reasonableness |

yet participated in any decisions on the point, so we don't know how they might vote on this issue.

You can get some idea of the various views of the Court in our next case excerpt, *Blakely v. Washington*, applying the *Apprendi* bright-line rule to strike down Washington State's respected sentencing guidelines procedures for increasing maximum sentences.

---

## CASE  Are Washington State's Sentencing Guidelines Constitutional?

### *Blakely v. Washington*
542 U.S. 296 (2004)

### HISTORY

After Ralph Blakely, Jr., Defendant, pled guilty in the Superior Court, Grant County, to second-degree kidnapping involving domestic violence and use of a firearm, and the trial judge sentenced him to more than three years above the 53-month statutory maximum of the standard range for his offense, Blakely appealed his exceptional sentence. The Court of Appeals of Washington, affirmed. The Washington Supreme Court denied discretionary review. The U.S. Supreme Court granted certiorari, and reversed and remanded.

SCALIA, J.

Petitioner Ralph Howard Blakely, Jr., pleaded guilty to the kidnapping of his estranged wife. The facts admitted in his

plea, standing alone, supported a maximum sentence of 53 months. Pursuant to state law, the court imposed an "exceptional" sentence of 90 months after making a judicial determination that he had acted with "deliberate cruelty." We consider whether this violated petitioner's Sixth Amendment right to trial by jury.

### FACTS

Petitioner married his wife Yolanda in 1973. He was evidently a difficult man to live with, having been diagnosed at various times with psychological and personality disorders including paranoid schizophrenia. His wife ultimately filed for divorce. In 1998, he abducted her from their orchard home in Grant County, Washington, binding her with duct tape and forcing her at knifepoint into a wooden box in the bed of his pickup truck. In the process, he implored her to dismiss the divorce suit and related trust proceedings.

When the couple's 13-year-old son Ralphy returned home from school, petitioner ordered him to follow in another car, threatening to harm Yolanda with a shotgun if he did not do so. Ralphy escaped and sought help when they stopped at a gas station, but petitioner continued on with Yolanda to a friend's house in Montana. He was finally arrested after the friend called the police.

The State charged petitioner with first-degree kidnapping. Upon reaching a plea agreement, however, it reduced the charge to second-degree kidnapping involving domestic violence and use of a firearm. Petitioner entered a guilty plea admitting the elements of second-degree kidnapping and the domestic-violence and firearm allegations, but no other relevant facts.

The case then proceeded to sentencing. In Washington, second-degree kidnapping is a class B felony. State law provides that "no person convicted of a [class B] felony shall be punished by confinement . . . exceeding . . . a term of ten years." § 9A.20.021(1)(b). Other provisions of state law, however, further limit the range of sentences a judge may impose. Washington's Sentencing Reform Act specifies, for petitioner's offense of second-degree kidnapping with a firearm, a "standard range" of 49 to 53 months. See § 9.94A.320 (seriousness level V for second-degree kidnapping).

A judge may impose a sentence above the standard range if he finds "substantial and compelling reasons justifying an exceptional sentence." § 9.94A.120(2). The Act lists aggravating factors that justify such a departure, which it recites to be illustrative rather than exhaustive. Nevertheless, "a reason offered to justify an exceptional sentence can be considered only if it takes into account factors other than those which are used in computing the standard range sentence for the offense." When a judge imposes an exceptional sentence, he must set forth findings of fact and conclusions of law supporting it. § 9.94A.120(3). A reviewing court will reverse the sentence if it finds that "under a clearly erroneous standard there is insufficient evidence in the record to support the reasons for imposing an exceptional sentence."

Pursuant to the plea agreement, the State recommended a sentence within the standard range of 49 to 53 months. After hearing Yolanda's description of the kidnapping, however, the judge rejected the State's recommendation and imposed an exceptional sentence of 90 months—37 months beyond the standard maximum. He justified the sentence on the ground that petitioner had acted with "deliberate cruelty," a statutorily enumerated ground for departure in domestic-violence cases. § 9.94A. 390(2)(h)(iii).

Faced with an unexpected increase of more than three years in his sentence, petitioner objected. The judge accordingly conducted a 3-day bench hearing featuring testimony from petitioner, Yolanda, Ralphy, a police officer, and medical experts. After the hearing, he issued 32 findings of fact, concluding:

The defendant's motivation to commit kidnapping was complex, contributed to by his mental condition and personality disorders, the pressures of the divorce litigation, the impending trust litigation trial and

anger over his troubled interpersonal relationships with his spouse and children. While he misguidedly intended to forcefully reunite his family, his attempt to do so was subservient to his desire to terminate lawsuits and modify title ownerships to his benefit.

The defendant's methods were more homogeneous than his motive. He used stealth and surprise, and took advantage of the victim's isolation. He immediately employed physical violence, restrained the victim with tape, and threatened her with injury and death to herself and others. He immediately coerced the victim into providing information by the threatening application of a knife. He violated a subsisting restraining order.

The judge adhered to his initial determination of deliberate cruelty.

Petitioner appealed, arguing that this sentencing procedure deprived him of his federal constitutional right to have a jury determine beyond a reasonable doubt all facts legally essential to his sentence. The State Court of Appeals affirmed. . . . The Washington Supreme Court denied discretionary review.

## OPINION

This case requires us to apply the rule we expressed in *Apprendi v. New Jersey* (2000):

Other than the fact of a prior conviction, any fact that increases the penalty for a crime beyond the prescribed statutory maximum must be submitted to a jury, and proved beyond a reasonable doubt.

This rule reflects two longstanding tenets of common-law criminal jurisprudence: that the "truth of every accusation" against a defendant "should afterwards be confirmed by the unanimous suffrage of twelve of his equals and neighbours," 4 W. Blackstone, Commentaries on the Laws of England 343 (1769), and that "an accusation which lacks any particular fact which the law makes essential to the punishment is . . . no accusation within the requirements of the common law, and it is no accusation in reason," 1 J. Bishop, Criminal Procedure § 87, p. 55 (2d ed. 1872). These principles have been acknowledged by courts and treatises since the earliest days of graduated sentencing. . . .

In this case, petitioner was sentenced to more than three years above the 53-month statutory maximum of the standard range because he had acted with "deliberate cruelty." The facts supporting that finding were neither admitted by petitioner nor found by a jury. The State nevertheless contends that there was no *Apprendi* violation because the relevant "statutory maximum" is not 53 months, but the 10-year maximum for class B felonies in § 9A.20.021 (1)(b). It observes that no exceptional sentence may exceed that limit. Our precedents make clear, however, that the "statutory maximum" for *Apprendi* purposes is the maximum sentence a judge may impose *solely on the basis of the facts reflected in the jury verdict or admitted by the defendant.* In other words, the relevant "statutory maximum" is not the maximum sentence a judge may impose after finding additional facts, but the maximum he may impose *without* any additional findings. When a judge inflicts punishment that the jury's verdict alone does not allow, the jury has not found all the facts "which the law makes essential to the punishment," and the judge exceeds his proper authority.

The judge in this case could not have imposed the exceptional 90-month sentence solely on the basis of the facts admitted in the guilty plea. Those facts alone were insufficient because, as the Washington Supreme Court has explained, "a reason offered to justify an exceptional sentence can be considered only if it takes into account factors other than those which are used in computing the standard range sentence for the offense," which in this case included the elements of second-degree kidnapping and the use of a firearm. Had the judge imposed the 90-month sentence solely on the basis of the plea, he would have been reversed. . . .

The State tries to distinguish *Apprendi* . . . by pointing out that the enumerated grounds for departure in its regime are illustrative rather than exhaustive. This distinction is immaterial. Whether the judge's authority to impose an enhanced sentence depends on finding a specified fact, one of several specified facts, or *any* aggravating fact (as here), it remains the case that the jury's verdict alone does not authorize the sentence. The judge acquires that authority only upon finding some additional fact. Because the State's sentencing procedure did not comply with the Sixth Amendment, petitioner's sentence is invalid.

Our commitment to *Apprendi* in this context reflects not just respect for longstanding precedent, but the need to give intelligible content to the right of jury trial. That right is no mere procedural formality, but a fundamental reservation of power in our constitutional structure. Just as suffrage ensures the people's ultimate control in the legislative and executive branches, jury trial is meant to ensure their control in the judiciary. *Apprendi* carries out this design by ensuring that the judge's authority to sentence derives wholly from the jury's verdict. Without that restriction, the jury would not exercise the control that the Framers intended. . . .

. . . By reversing the judgment below, we are not . . . finding determinate sentencing schemes unconstitutional. This case is not about whether determinate sentencing is constitutional, only about how it can be implemented in a way that respects the Sixth Amendment. Several policies prompted Washington's adoption of determinate sentencing, including proportionality to the gravity of the offense and parity among defendants. Nothing we have said impugns those salutary objectives.

. . . Ultimately, our decision cannot turn on whether or to what degree trial by jury impairs the efficiency or fairness of criminal justice. One can certainly argue that both these values would be better served by leaving justice entirely in the hands of professionals; many nations of the world, particularly those following civil-law traditions, take just that course. There is not one shred of doubt, however, about the

Framers' paradigm for criminal justice: not the civil-law ideal of administrative perfection, but the common-law ideal of limited state power accomplished by strict division of authority between judge and jury. As *Apprendi* held, every defendant has the *right* to insist that the prosecutor prove to a jury all facts legally essential to the punishment. Under the dissenters' alternative, he has no such right. That should be the end of the matter.

Petitioner was sentenced to prison for more than three years beyond what the law allowed for the crime to which he confessed, on the basis of a disputed finding that he had acted with "deliberate cruelty." The Framers would not have thought it too much to demand that, before depriving a man of three more years of his liberty, the State should suffer the modest inconvenience of submitting its accusation to "the unanimous suffrage of twelve of his equals and neighbours," 4 Blackstone, at 343, rather than a lone employee of the State.

The judgment of the Washington Court of Appeals is REVERSED, and the case is REMANDED for further proceedings not inconsistent with this opinion. *It is so ordered.*

## DISSENT

O'CONNOR, J., JOINED BY REHNQUIST, C.J., BREYER, AND KENNEDY, JJ.

The legacy of today's opinion, whether intended or not, will be the consolidation of sentencing power in the State and Federal Judiciaries. The Court says to Congress and state legislatures: If you want to constrain the sentencing discretion of judges and bring some uniformity to sentencing, it will cost you—dearly. Congress and States, faced with the burdens imposed by the extension of *Apprendi v. New Jersey* (2000), to the present context, will either trim or eliminate altogether their sentencing guidelines schemes and, with them, 20 years of sentencing reform.

It is thus of little moment that the majority does not expressly declare guidelines schemes unconstitutional; for, as residents of "*Apprendi*-land" are fond of saying, "the relevant inquiry is one not of form, but of effect." The "effect" of today's decision will be greater judicial discretion and less uniformity in sentencing. Because I find it implausible that the Framers would have considered such a result to be required by the Due Process Clause or the Sixth Amendment, and because the practical consequences of today's decision may be disastrous, I respectfully dissent.

One need look no further than the history leading up to and following the enactment of Washington's guidelines scheme to appreciate the damage that today's decision will cause. Prior to 1981, Washington, like most other States and the Federal Government, employed an indeterminate sentencing scheme. . . . Sentencing judges, in conjunction with parole boards, had virtually unfettered discretion to sentence defendants to prison terms falling anywhere within the statutory range, including probation—*i.e.*, no jail sentence at all.

This system of unguided discretion inevitably resulted in severe disparities in sentences received and served by defendants committing the same offense and having similar criminal histories. Indeed, rather than reflect legally relevant criteria, these disparities too often were correlated with constitutionally suspect variables such as race.

To counteract these trends, the state legislature passed the Sentencing Reform Act of 1981. . . . Far from disregarding principles of due process and the jury trial right, as the majority today suggests, Washington's reform has served them. Before passage of the Act, a defendant charged with second degree kidnapping, like petitioner, had no idea whether he would receive a 10-year sentence or probation. The ultimate sentencing determination could turn as much on the idiosyncrasies of a particular judge as on the specifics of the defendant's crime or background. . . .

Washington's move to a system of guided discretion has served equal protection principles as well. Over the past 20 years, there has been a substantial reduction in racial disparity in sentencing across the State. The reduction is directly traceable to the constraining effects of the guidelines—namely, their "presumptive range[s]" and limits on the imposition of "exceptional sentences" outside of those ranges.

. . . The extension of *Apprendi* to the present context . . . exacts a substantial constitutional tax. The costs are substantial and real. Under the majority's approach, any fact that increases the upper bound on a judge's sentencing discretion is an element of the offense. Thus, facts that historically have been taken into account by sentencing judges to assess a sentence within a broad range—such as drug quantity, role in the offense, risk of bodily harm—all must now be charged in an indictment and submitted to a jury simply because it is the legislature, rather than the judge, that constrains the extent to which such facts may be used to impose a sentence within a pre-existing statutory range.

. . . The majority may be correct that States and the Federal Government will be willing to bear some of these costs. But simple economics dictate that they will not, and cannot, bear them all. To the extent that they do not, there will be an inevitable increase in judicial discretion with all of its attendant failings.

The majority claims the mantle of history and original intent. But . . . , a handful of state decisions in the mid-19th century and a criminal procedure treatise have little if any persuasive value as evidence of what the Framers of the Federal Constitution intended in the late 18th century. Because broad judicial sentencing discretion was foreign to the Framers, they were never faced with the constitutional choice between submitting every fact that increases a sentence to the jury or vesting the sentencing judge with broad discretionary authority to account for differences in offenses and offenders.

. . . The consequences of today's decision will be as far reaching as they are disturbing. Washington's sentencing system is by no means unique. Numerous other States have enacted guidelines systems, as has the Federal Government. Today's decision casts constitutional doubt over them all and, in so doing, threatens an untold number of criminal judgments. Every sentence imposed under such guidelines in cases currently pending on direct appeal is in jeopardy. . . .

The practical consequences for trial courts, starting today, will be equally unsettling: How are courts to mete out guidelines sentences? Do courts apply the guidelines as to mitigating factors, but not as to aggravating factors? Do they jettison the guidelines altogether? The Court ignores the havoc it is about to wreak on trial courts across the country. . . . What I have feared most has now come to pass: Over 20 years of sentencing reform are all but lost, and tens of thousands of criminal judgments are in jeopardy.

## Questions

1. Summarize the majority's reasons for striking down Washington's sentencing guidelines.

2. Specifically, what kinds of sentences does the decision hold unconstitutional?

3. Identify the specific constitutional provisions the kinds of sentences you identified in question 2 violate.

4. Summarize the arguments of the dissent against the majority opinion.

5. In your opinion, who has the better arguments for its opinion? Explain your answer.

***Death Sentence Procedure Rights*** According to the Supreme Court, "Death is different" from all other punishments, which means death sentences are different, too. So the cruel-and-unusual-punishment clause applies to the death penalty and to death sentences. The U.S. Supreme Court has made it clear that the penalty of death isn't cruel and unusual punishment, at least when it's administered to murderers.

The Court has held that capital punishment for murder isn't cruel and unusual punishment, if the sentencing process allows the judge or jury to consider—and

| TABLE 14.2 | Aggravating and Mitigating Circumstances in Death Penalty Cases | |
| --- | --- | --- |
| **Aggravating Circumstances** | **Mitigating Circumstances** | |
| Prior record of violent felony | No significant prior criminal record | |
| Felony murder | Extreme mental or emotional disturbance | |
| Murder of more than one person | Minor participant in the murder | |
| Murder of police officer or other public official | Youth at the time of the murder | |
| Torture or other heinous killing | | |
| Killing to avoid arrest | | |
| Killing during escape from lawful custody | | |

offers adequate guidance in weighing—mitigating and aggravating circumstances (see Table 14.2) and provides for a review procedure to ensure against discriminatory application of the death penalty (*Lockett v. Ohio* 1978). According to the Supreme Court, the rationale for this is that "it is of vital importance to the defendant and to the community that any decision to impose the death sentence be, and appear to be, based on reason rather than caprice or emotion" (*Gardner v. Florida* 1977).

Statistics indicate there's a pronounced racial disparity in death sentences. Blacks and Whites who kill Whites are more likely to receive the death sentence than either Blacks who kill Blacks or Whites who kill Blacks (Baldus and Woodworth 1998, 399–400). The U.S. Supreme Court has held that these numbers may well prove that race infects death sentencing decisions in general, but that it's not enough to prove cruel and unusual punishment in individual cases. To overturn a death sentence, individual defendants have to prove the death sentencing decision in their case was infected by racial views. Specifically, they have to prove the prosecutor, the jury, or their lawyer's decisions were motivated by race (*McCleskey v. Kemp* 1987).

 APPEALS

It may surprise you to learn (as it surprises most of my students) that convicted offenders don't have a constitutional right to appeal their convictions. According to the U.S. Supreme Court in *Ross v. Moffitt* (1974), "It is clear that the State need not provide any appeal at all." According to that principle, the Court upheld a state court decision that denied a poor defendant a right to a lawyer for his appeal to the state supreme court. According to the Court:

> There are significant differences between the trial and appellate stages of a criminal proceeding. The purpose of the trial stage from the State's point of view is to convert a criminal defendant from a person presumed innocent to one found guilty beyond a reasonable doubt. To accomplish this purpose, the State employs a prosecuting attorney who presents evidence to the court, challenges any witnesses offered by the defendant, argues rulings of the court, and makes direct arguments to the court and jury seeking to persuade them of the defendant's guilt. Under these circumstances reason and reflection require us to recognize that in our adversary system of criminal justice, any person haled into court, who is too poor to hire a lawyer, cannot be assured a fair trial unless counsel is provided for him.
>
> By contrast, it is ordinarily the defendant, rather than the state, who initiates the appellate process, seeking not to fend off the efforts of the state's prosecutor but rather

to overturn a finding of guilty made by a judge or a jury below. The defendant needs an attorney on appeal not as a shield to protect him against being "haled into court" by the state and stripped of his presumption of innocence, but rather as a sword to upset the prior determination of guilt. This difference is significant for, while no one would agree that the state may simply dispense with the trial stage of proceedings without a criminal defendant's consent, it is clear that the state need not provide any appeal at all. (609)

Even though there's no *constitutional* right to appeal, every jurisdiction has created a **statutory right to appeal**. To understand this statutory right, refer to Figure 1.2 in Chapter 1, which depicts our three-tiered judicial system: trial courts, intermediate appeals courts, and supreme courts of appeal. The statutory right to appeal applies only to the intermediate appellate courts (and in capital cases, to the supreme courts).

On the other hand, appeals to the supreme courts are discretionary. Most of the cases in this book, for example, appeals to the U.S. Supreme Court, are **discretionary appeal** cases. The writ of *certiorari* is a discretionary writ, allowing appeals only in cases the U.S. Supreme Court or the state supreme courts decide are of significance beyond the interests of the particular defendants appealing them (Chapter 1, "Appellate Cases").

Since the late 1980s, the U.S. Supreme Court has sharply reduced the number of cases it accepts by means of *certiorari*. By this reduction, the Court has reaffirmed the principle that final appeal isn't a right; it's a matter of discretionary judgment.

Three principal doctrines define the scope of appellate review of criminal cases in state courts:

1. Mootness

2. Raise or waive

3. Plain error

Traditionally, the **mootness doctrine** banned appeals by offenders who had finished their prison sentences or who had paid their fines. Some jurisdictions have retained this traditional definition of mootness. Several others have gone to the other extreme, holding that criminal cases are never moot, because defendants always have an interest in removing the "stigma of guilt." Most jurisdictions have taken a middle ground, retaining the mootness doctrine but carving out exceptions to it.

The **collateral consequences exception** says that if defendants might suffer legal consequences from a criminal conviction, then even if they have fully served their sentence the case isn't moot. These consequences include the possibility of the loss of a professional license, rejection for admission to a professional school, or loss of employment.

The **raise-or-waive doctrine** says defendants have to raise their objections at trial; if they don't, they give up their right to appeal. Why? The **doctrine of judicial economy** says we shouldn't spend time and money on appeals defendants could have avoided by objecting during the trial.

However, defendants don't always waive their right to appeal when they fail to object at trial. When procedural requirements don't provide adequate time for a defendant to object to a trial court error, the defendant doesn't waive the right to appeal the error. Also, circumstances can make it impossible for a defendant to comply with the raise-or-waive rule. And obviously, incompetent lawyers don't object to their own ineffectiveness (LaFave and Israel 1984, 3:252–54).

A major exception to the raise-or-waive rule is the **plain-error rule**, which applies even if defendants don't object to the errors at trial. The plain-error rule applies when "plain errors affecting substantial rights" cause "manifest injustice or miscarriage of justice." Most courts apply the rule "sparingly." Plain error doesn't require or justify a review "of every alleged trial error that has not been properly preserved for appellate review." Furthermore, in most jurisdictions, the "defendant bears the burden of proving that an alleged error is of such magnitude that it constitutes plain error." According to one commentator, "'Plain error' is a concept appellate courts find impossible to define, save that they know it when they see it."

# HABEAS CORPUS (COLLATERAL ATTACK)

Appeals are called **direct attacks**, because they attack the decisions made by the trial court and/or the jury's guilty verdict as part of the same case, the defendants' criminal trial. **Habeas corpus proceedings** are called "collateral attacks," because they indirectly attack the judgment in a new noncriminal (civil) lawsuit. In that new case, the defendant in the criminal case (now the petitioner or plaintiff in the habeas case) asks (petitions the court) for the writ on the ground that the plaintiff is being unlawfully detained.

If the court issues the writ, the writ orders the person (usually a prison warden) to bring the plaintiff before the judge and "show cause" for the detention. The object is to find out if the court in the criminal case had the authority (jurisdiction) to enter the judgment that put the plaintiff in prison and, if so, whether the judgment was reached properly. Depending on the evidence produced, the plaintiff is either set free, bailed, tried, or sent back to prison (Fisher 1888, 454).

Habeas corpus has a long and distinguished history. It's called the "great writ of liberty" because it originated as a bulwark against tyrannical English kings. According to the 19th-century historian of habeas corpus, Sydney George Fisher (1888):

> These rulers of men often want to rid themselves quickly of their personal enemies or of those whom they choose to consider enemies of their country, and of the easiest methods is to arrest on any sort of charge or suspicion, and keep the victim in confinement simply by not allowing him to be brought to trial. And it has often been said,—and the Bastille and the Tower of London will warrant the assertion—that the power to secretly hurry a man to jail, where his sufferings will be unknown or soon forgotten, is more dangerous than all the engines of tyranny. (454)

Fisher contrasted this abuse of the English kings' power with President Lincoln's suspension of the writ of habeas corpus during the Civil War. Fisher vigorously defended Lincoln and scoffed at Lincoln's critics who called him a dictator because, Fisher argued, it was right to take extreme measures to save the Union.

Of course, we're a long way from tyrannical kings and even from Lincoln's use of the writ. Today, most habeas corpus proceedings begin only after criminal cases run through their full course of direct attack in state trial and appellate courts. After all this long and involved process, habeas corpus proceedings start in U.S. District Court, proceed through the U.S. Court of Appeals, and can eventually reach the U.S. Supreme Court for final review.

According to the U.S. Constitution Article I: "The privilege of the Writ of Habeas Corpus shall not be suspended, unless when in Cases of Rebellion or Invasion the public Safety may require it." Two U.S. statutes elaborated on Article I by granting power to U.S. courts to hear petitions of habeas corpus and issue writs of habeas corpus.

The U.S. Judiciary Act of 1789 authorized U.S. courts to deal with the petitions of federal prisoners. The Habeas Corpus Act of 1867 (LaFave and Israel 1984, 292) extended the power of U.S. Courts to deal with habeas corpus petitions of state prisoners. According to the 1867 act:

> The several courts of the United States . . . within their respective jurisdictions, in addition to the authority already conferred by law, shall have power to grant writs of habeas corpus in all cases where any person may be restrained of his or her liberty in violation of the Constitution, or of any treaty or law of the United States. (292)

The language of the 1867 act lends itself to both a narrow interpretation and a broad interpretation of the power of the federal courts to review the imprisonment of state prisoners. According to the **narrow interpretation**, the act authorizes the courts only to review the jurisdiction of the court—that is, its authority over the person and the subject matter of the case. The review asks only whether the court has the power to hear criminal cases and whether it can decide criminal cases involving the prisoner. According to the **broad interpretation**, the act empowers the federal courts to review the whole state proceeding to determine possible violations of federal law and constitutional provisions (LaFave and Israel 1984, 3:292–94).

During the years of the Warren Court (Chief Justice Earl Warren, 1953–1969), when federal rights were expanding through the incorporation doctrine (Chapter 2), the Court opted for a broad view of habeas corpus. The leader of the broad view, Associate Justice William Brennan, argued that the broader view fulfilled the historical purpose of habeas corpus, "providing relief against the detention of persons in violation of their fundamental liberties." As to objections that such expansive review of lower court proceedings threatened the interest in finality, he argued that "conventional notions of finality of litigation" should "have no place where life or liberty is at stake and infringement of constitutional rights is alleged."

In addition to preserving fundamental liberties, the broader view, according to its supporters, furthers the interest in correct results. The more chances to review, the greater the accuracy of the final decision. According to one judge:

> We would not send two astronauts to the moon without providing them with at least three or four back-up systems. Should we send literally thousands of men to prison with even less reserves? . . . With knowledge of our fallibility and a realization of past errors, we can hardly insure our confidence by creating an irrevocable end to the guilt determining process. (LaFave and Israel 1984, 3:298–99)

Justice Brennan's and the Warren Court majority's view have received harsh criticism from judges and commentators. Most of the criticism focuses on the threat to finality and the costs of "endless" reviews of legal issues, which sometimes go on for years. No one has put the argument for finality better than the great advocate John W. Davis in his last argument before the U.S. Supreme Court:

> Somewhere, sometime to every principle comes a moment of repose when it has been so often announced, so confidently relied upon, so long continued, that it passes the limits of judicial discretion and disturbance. (*Brown v. Board of Education* 1954)

Others doubt that the broad view really protects prisoners' fundamental rights. Associate Supreme Court Justice Robert H. Jackson, in *Brown v. Allen* (1953), argued that we have no reason to expect more accuracy in a second review than in the initial decision:

> Reversal by a higher court is not proof that justice is thereby better done. There is no doubt that if there were a super–Supreme Court, a substantial proportion of our reversals of state courts would also be reversed. We are not final because we are infallible, but we are infallible only because we are final. (540)

Justice Jackson attributed the controversy over habeas corpus to three causes:

1. The Supreme Court's use of the due process clause of the Fourteenth Amendment to "subject state courts to increasing federal control"

2. The determination of what due process means by "personal notions of justice instead of by known rules of law"

3. The "breakdown of procedural safeguards against abuse of the writ"

The Burger (Chief Justice Warren Burger, 1969–1986) and Rehnquist (Chief Justice William Rehnquist, 1986–2005) Courts adopted the narrow view of habeas corpus—the power to review only the jurisdiction of the court over the person and the subject matter of the case.

The Rehnquist Court emphasized the balance of interests that habeas corpus proceedings require. On one side of the balance are the constitutional rights of individuals and the need to control government misconduct. On the other side are the following interests:

• The finality of decisions

• Reliability, or obtaining the correct result

• Certainty in decisions, or promoting reliance on decisions

• The stability of decisions, or promoting the permanence of decisions

• Federalism, or respect for state criminal court decisions

• The burden on federal judicial resources in hearing repeated challenges

• Contempt for the system from repeated and long-drawn-out proceedings

• The impediment that many frivolous claims are to the success of meritorious claims

To the Rehnquist Court, the main problem in habeas corpus was an "endless succession of writs." Historically, an English subject could take a petition to every judge in England. The rule of **res judicata**—that once a matter is decided it cannot be reopened—didn't apply to habeas corpus. The remnants of that rule linger in the rule that denial of a first petition for habeas corpus doesn't prohibit filing a second petition.

But, according to the Court in *McCleskey v. Zant* (1991), just because the rule of res judicata doesn't apply doesn't mean that prisoners can file an unlimited number of petitions. Courts have the discretion to deny successive petitions, especially if petitioners try to raise issues they failed to raise in their first petition.

The **abuse-of-the-writ rule** requires petitioners to prove they didn't fail deliberately or negligently to raise an issue in their first petition. Tactical decisions by attorneys and the accidental failure of competent counsel to raise claims aren't enough to avoid the abuse-of-the-writ rule. However, the rule doesn't apply to a failure to raise a claim of ineffective counsel.

According to the **cause-and-prejudice rule**, in addition to proving they didn't fail deliberately or negligently to raise an issue in the first petition (cause), petitioners have to prove the failure to raise the issue probably affected the outcome of the case. Placing this burden of proof on habeas petitioners discourages baseless petitions while at the same time, according to the Court, it keeps the system open for genuine claims for relief.

The cause-and-prejudice rule isn't hard and fast. It permits, but doesn't require, courts to deny petitions if defendants fail to satisfy its requirements. For example, cases of manifest injustice, those in which the petitioner is probably innocent, are an exception to the rule. The word "innocent" refers to *factual innocence*—that is, a case in which the petitioner didn't commit the crime. It doesn't refer to cases where the petitioner may be entitled to an acquittal because of either procedural irregularities or to the government's inability to prove legal guilt beyond a reasonable doubt.

Other obstacles stand in the way of state prisoners' hopes to get federal habeas relief. According to the **exhaustion-of-remedies rule**, when a state prisoner files a petition in a federal court containing any claim for which a state remedy remains available, the court has to dismiss the petition. In such a case, the state prisoner may either strike the unexhausted state claim and file again in federal court or exhaust the claim by filing in state court. Furthermore, the claim has to violate a federal right. Errors in state proceedings that don't violate a federal right have to be pursued in state courts.

Also, federal courts have to respect state court findings of fact. For example, federal courts, in reviewing petitions of state court convictions, can't review the credibility of witnesses (*Marshall v. Lonberger* 1983; *Rose v. Lundy* 1982). The Supreme Court placed perhaps the most significant limit on federal review of state habeas corpus petitions in *Stone v. Powell* (1976). In Stone, the Court held that a state prisoner can't raise a Fourth Amendment illegal-search-and-seizure claim in a federal habeas corpus proceeding if the state has already provided an opportunity for the petitioner to raise the issue in state court. The Court held that the interests in finality and economy outweighed the costs of the exclusionary rule.

## SUMMARY

### I. Procedures after Conviction
A. The defendant's status changes to offender.
  1. Defendants enjoy a presumption of innocence.
  2. Offenders carry a presumption of guilt.
  3. The government and defendants get one fair shot at justice.
B. Three main procedures follow conviction:
  1. Sentencing
  2. Appeals
  3. Habeas corpus, or collateral attack

### II. Sentencing
A. Sentencing has had two contrasting aims:
  1. Fit the sentence to the crime—look back to the crime.
  2. Tailor the sentence to suit the offender—look forward to prevention.
B. The history of sentencing has seen the pendulum swing from fixed to indeterminate sentencing.
C. There's a historical division of sentencing authority among legislature, judges, and administrative agencies.
D. Fixed sentences are determinate.
  1. The goals include uniformity, certainty, retribution, deterrence, and incapacitation.
  2. Guidelines tell judges what they're permitted to do.
    a. The guidelines weigh both the seriousness of the crime and the criminal history of the offender.
    b. Judges choose the sentence within a specified range.

     c. Departures from the range are permitted if backed up with written reasons.

     d. Prosecutors can appeal downward departures, and defendants can appeal upward departures.

  3. Mandatory minimums try to ensure that those who commit the crime do the time.

     a. They prescribe a nondiscretionary minimum amount of prison time.

     b. Empirical support for their effectiveness is weak.

E. The Constitution's view of sentencing is debated by the Court.

  1. The proportionality principle asks, Does the sentence fit the crime?

  2. *Narrow proportionality principle.* The Court looks at whether the prison sentence was "grossly disproportionate" to the gravity of the offense.

  3. Trial rights at sentencing have largely been left up to judges.

     a. Until 2000, the Court took a hands-off approach to criminal sentencing, leaving it to judicial discretion.

     b. *Apprendi v. New Jersey* (2000) created a bright-line rule.

       (1) Defendants have a right to a jury determination of all facts that increase their sentence beyond the guideline's maximum.

       (2) Juries decide whether there's proof beyond a reasonable doubt of the facts in (1).

       (3) Proof of the fact of prior crimes doesn't need to go to juries.

     c. *Harris v. U.S.* The *Apprendi* rule doesn't apply to increasing the mandatory minimum sentence.

     d. *Blakely v. Washington.* The *Apprendi* rule applies to and invalidates sentencing guidelines that increase the standard range of sentences by judges without juries.

     e. *U.S. v. Booker:*

       (1) The *Apprendi* rule invalidates upward departures from the standard range of sentences without a jury determination of facts beyond a reasonable doubt.

       (2) Guidelines are advisory and are presumptively reasonable.

F. Death sentences aren't "cruel and unusual punishment" (Eighth Amendment).

  1. The sentencing process has to allow judges and/or juries to consider mitigating and aggravating circumstances.

  2. Racial disparity in death sentences generally doesn't prove discrimination against specific defendants.

## III. Appeals

A. Convictions are reviewed for errors in the criminal case.

B. There's no constitutional right to appeal convictions.

C. All states and the U.S. government have a statutory right to appeal.

  1. The right applies only to intermediate appellate courts.

  2. Appeals to supreme courts are wholly discretionary.

  3. The U.S. Supreme Court sharply limits discretionary appeals through writs of certiorari.

  4. State supreme court discretionary appeals are limited by:

     a. *Mootness.* The sentence has been served or the fine paid.

     b. *Raise or waive.* The offender failed to raise objections during the trial.

     c. *Plain error.* An error was made that could have led to a miscarriage of justice.

**IV. Collateral attacks (habeas corpus) sue officials (warden or jailer) to challenge the lawfulness of detention.**
   A. *Broad view (Warren Court in 1960s)*. Review the whole state court proceeding to decide whether federal law and the Constitution were violated.
   B. *Narrow view (Burger and Rehnquist Courts)*. Review only whether the state court had jurisdiction (authority over the person and the subject matter) to hear the case.
   C. Finality and efficiency objectives resulted in severe limitations being placed on collateral attack.
   D. There are two review processes—first appeal and then habeas corpus.

## REVIEW QUESTIONS

1. Why is the change of status from defendant to offender more than "just a change of words"?

2. Describe the reasons for the assumption that one shot of justice is enough.

3. In the debate over sentencing, identify the two sides that have characterized its history for more than a thousand years.

4. Trace the history of sentencing from 700 A.D. to the present.

5. List three ideas that came to dominate thinking about sentencing in the 1970s.

6. Identify and describe the three divisions of sentencing authority.

7. Identify three aims of both sentencing guidelines and mandatory minimum sentences.

8. Compare and contrast sentencing guidelines and mandatory minimum sentences.

9. What two elements are balanced in sentencing guidelines?

10. List the reasons for the revival of mandatory minimum sentences in the 1950s.

11. List the reasons for the abandonment of mandatory minimum sentences in the 1970s.

12. Identify the two main targets of current mandatory minimum sentences.

13. Identify the three aims of criminal punishment that mandatory minimum sentences are supposed to satisfy.

14. List and summarize the five main findings of empirical research on the effectiveness of mandatory minimum sentences.

15. Explain how the proportionality principle affects challenges to the constitutional ban on cruel and unusual punishments.

16. Identify and summarize the procedure rights convicted offenders enjoy during sentencing procedures.

17. Summarize the significance of *Williams v. New York* (1949); *Apprendi v. New Jersey* (2000); *Harris v. U.S.* (2002); *Blakely v. Washington* (2004); and *U.S. v. Booker* (2005).

18. When is the sentence of death not cruel and unusual punishment?

19. Identify the nature and circumstances of the right to appeal a conviction.

**20.** What's the difference between an *appeal* and a *collateral attack*?

**21.** Describe appellate review of criminal convictions by direct appeal and collateral attack.

**22.** Summarize the difference between the broad and narrow views of habeas corpus review.

**23.** List the three causes of the controversy over habeas corpus identified by U.S. Supreme Court Justice Robert Jackson.

**24.** Identify eight interests furthered by limits to habeas corpus review.

**25.** According to the Rehnquist Court, what's the main problem in habeas corpus review?

**26.** What's the significance of the U.S. Supreme Court decision in *Stone v. Powell?*

## KEY TERMS

presumption of guilt, p. 470

right of habeas corpus, p. 470

collateral attack, p. 470

fixed (determinate) sentencing, p. 471

indeterminate sentencing, p. 471

legislative sentencing model, p. 473

judicial sentencing model, p. 473

administrative sentencing model, p. 473

sentencing guidelines, p. 474

mandatory minimum sentences, p. 474

proportionality principle, p. 477

hands-off approach to sentencing procedures, p. 482

*Apprendi* bright-line rule, p. 483

statutory right to appeal, p. 489

discretionary appeal, p. 489

mootness doctrine, p. 489

collateral consequences exception, p. 489

raise-or-waive doctrine, p. 489

doctrine of judicial economy, p. 489

plain-error rule, p. 489

direct attack, p. 490

habeas corpus proceedings (collateral attack), p. 490

narrow interpretation (of habeas corpus), p. 491

broad interpretation (of habeas corpus), p. 491

res judicata, p. 492

abuse-of-the-writ rule, p. 492

cause-and-prejudice rule, p. 492

exhaustion-of-remedies rule, p. 493

# Criminal Procedure in Crisis Times

## MAIN POINTS

- The balance between government power and individual liberty and privacy always tips toward more government power during national emergencies.
- Since 9/11, the government has shifted its primary goal from gathering evidence to prosecute terrorists for their crimes to gathering intelligence to prevent their future attacks.
- The USA Patriot Act modifies in the government's favor (but doesn't eliminate) the constitutional balance between government power and individual privacy and liberty.
- The USA Patriot Act adds terrorist crimes to the list of "serious crimes" Congress has made eligible for electronic surveillance and "sneak and peek" searches.
- The president's power to detain suspected terrorists is clear. Decisions defining how long and under what conditions they can be detained and whether there are different rules for citizens and noncitizens are making their way through the courts right now.
- Decisions about the extent of suspects' right to a lawyer, under what conditions and for what purposes the right exists, and whether the rules are different for citizens and noncitizens are making their way through the courts right now, too.
- Suspected terrorists can be tried either for crimes in ordinary courts or for war crimes in special military courts.
- Presidents are authorized to establish military courts to try anyone suspected of war crimes. President G. W. Bush's order creating military courts after 9/11 limits their jurisdiction to trials of noncitizens.
- Trials in military courts aren't bound by the constitutional requirements that apply to criminal trials in ordinary courts, but the U.S. Department of Defense has guaranteed defendants in 9/11 military court proceedings several rights defendants enjoy in ordinary criminal trials.

15

*As terrible as 9/11 was, it didn't repeal the Constitution.*

Judge Rosemary Pooler, November 17, 2003 (Hamblett 2003, 12)

*A strict observance of the written laws is doubtless one of the high duties of a good citizen, but it is not the highest. The laws of necessity, of self-preservation, of saving our country when in danger, are of higher obligation. To lose our country by a scrupulous adherence to written law, would be to lose the law itself, with life, liberty, property and all those who are enjoying them with us; thus absurdly sacrificing the ends to the means.*

Thomas Jefferson, September 20, 1810 (1904, I:146)

*The law is not dead, but sleepeth; the Constitution is eclipsed, but the dark . . . which intercepted its light . . . will soon pass away, and we shall again behold the glorious luminary shining forth in all its original splendor.*

Edward Livingston, 1815 (Gayarré 1903, 601)

*The Constitution of the United States is a law for rulers and people, equally in war and in peace, and covers with the shield of its protection all classes of men, at all times, and under all circumstances.*

Ex Parte Milligan (1866)

$W$e end our journey through the criminal process the way we began—by looking at the balance between government power and individual liberty and privacy. But this time, we'll examine the balance when it's most stressed—during emergencies. You're probably familiar with governors who declare state emergencies during storms, floods, and fires and call out the state National Guard to enforce government orders to evacuate and stay out of the danger areas. Even local governments can declare emergencies and take extraordinary measures. For example, for those of us who live in Minnesota, the city or town government infringes on our freedom by ordering us not to park on the streets during "snow emergencies."

The simple lesson of these examples is that emergency times call for recalibrating the balance between government power and individual liberty and privacy. The balance tips to expanding government power and limiting individual liberty and privacy. But emergency powers are limited by two conditions:

1. *Necessity.* Government can exercise extraordinary power only when and to the extent that it's absolutely needed to protect the people from the dangers created by the emergency.

2. *Temporary nature.* Government has to give up its extraordinary power as soon as the emergency's over.

In this chapter, we'll examine how emergencies affect criminal procedure by looking at the history of criminal procedure during wartime; how terrorism has impacted surveillance laws; "sneak and peek" searches in terrorist cases; the detention of terrorist suspects; and trials for those suspected of terrorism.

## THE HISTORY OF CRIMINAL PROCEDURE IN WARTIME

In fires, floods, and storms, it's easy to apply the conditions that limit emergency powers, because the emergencies are easy to define (our senses clearly tell us the fires, floods, and snowstorms are here); the responses to them are widely known and followed (build firewalls and levies; plow the snow); and it's easy to tell when they're over (we can see the fires and floods have stopped and the snow's gone, or at least they're under control).

All these things used to be true of the subject of this chapter—wartime emergencies. Wars began when governments of one country declared war on another country. They were fought according to long-standing **laws of war**—rules written, understood, and agreed to by almost all the countries fighting the wars (Avalon Project 2003). And they ended when the countries signed peace treaties.

Not all nations always followed the laws of war, and even if they did, there was plenty of play in the joints for interpreting many of the rules. Also, some argue that the "new" wars, those fought since World War I, differ from those fought when the rules were made. In World Wars I and II, the difference was that these were "total wars," meaning the whole people, the governments, and the countries' resources were mobilized for fighting and winning the war. The rules had to change to meet the changes brought about by total war. But even in total wars, most of the basics were the same as they'd always been. The enemies were identifiable foreign nations. Wars began with declarations of war (even if the declaration was by a "sneak attack" like the Japanese attack on Pearl Harbor). Wars ended when treaties were signed between the warring nations.

Then came the Cold War. International communism crossed national boundaries. Communist spies came to the United States. They looked and acted like non-Communists. They got jobs in strategic industries and government for the purpose of "boring from within" to learn secrets and pass them on to Communist governments. They became the feared "invisible enemy within." Waging the Cold War required great emphasis on an old feature of war—**intelligence** (information about the enemy).

The government took strong measures to respond to the Communist "hidden enemy within." These measures were of two types. First, the government sought to get evidence either to prosecute and convict them of crimes or to find and deport them. Second, but far more important, law enforcement focused on gathering intelligence to prevent further Communist infiltration and activity in the United States. The emphasis on intelligence gathering for the purpose of prevention was very different from what we've studied throughout this book—balancing the need for getting evidence for criminal prosecution against the rights of individuals to fair proceedings.

This shift in emphasis from prosecuting terrorists for crimes to preventing them from committing more terrorist attacks continues to be reflected in most of the measures being used (with some modifications) to respond to domestic and international terrorism today. We'll examine both the terrorism prevention and criminal prosecution elements of antiterrorism laws, court decisions, and procedures before September 11, 2001; look at modifications made after September 11 by the 2001 USA Patriot Act (short for Uniting and Strengthening America by Providing Appropriate Tools Required to Intercept and Obstruct Terrorism); and then see how the efforts have fared in three U.S. Supreme Court cases since 2001: *Hamdi v. Rumsfeld* (2004); *Rasul v. Bush* (2004); and *Hamdan v. Rumsfeld* (2006).

Former U.S. Attorney General John Ashcroft (2002) stated clearly the shift in the FBI's role brought about by the September 11 attacks:

> The FBI . . . plays a central role in the enforcement of federal laws and in the proper administration of justice in the United States. In discharging this function, the highest priority is to protect the security of the nation and the safety of the American people against . . . terrorists and foreign aggressors. Investigations by the FBI are premised on the fundamental duty of government to protect the public against . . . those who would threaten the fabric of society through terrorism or mass destruction. (2)

In studying this important subject of balancing government power and individual autonomy since 9/11, we're faced with two limits. First, there's the need for secrecy. The government can't tell us things that might tip off terrorists—things that might help us learn more about the laws but also help terrorists plan future attacks. Second, September 11, 2001, is too recent to have produced more than a few officially reported court cases to analyze. In other words, we have to face a problem (aggravated by current necessity) that social scientists have recognized for nearly two centuries: there's a gap between the "law in books" (the way laws are supposed to work) and the "law in action" (the way the law really works).

With these limits in mind, let's look at what the antiterrorism laws say and (as much as possible) how they're operating regarding four issues you've learned about outside the area of national security:

1. Surveillance (Chapter 3)

2. Search and seizure (Chapters 4–7)

3. Detention (Chapters 4–6, 12)

4. Trial rights (Chapters 13–14)

As you read about these four issues, remember that just as in ordinary criminal procedure, federal antiterrorism procedures are based on the requirement in a constitutional democracy to balance the need for enough government power to prevent and prosecute terrorist acts and the rights of individuals guaranteed by the U.S. Constitution. Comments from Charles Doyle (2002), senior specialist at the Congressional Research Center, on the intelligence gathering provisions of the Patriot Act underscore this emphasis:

> [The Patriot Act was] erected for the dual purpose of protecting the confidentiality of private telephone, face-to-face, and computer communications while enabling authorities to identify and intercept criminal communications. (2)

One last point before we begin our journey through the national security law and its application to antiterrorism. There's a lot of chatter about the dramatic changes in the balance between power and liberty brought about by the USA Patriot Act and actions by the executive branch of the U.S. government and its intelligence and law enforcement agencies. On one side, we're warned that with the expanded government powers authorized by the Patriot Act and actions taken by the executive branch, we'll lose our liberty and privacy to our own government. On the other side, we're warned that without the expanded powers established in the act and taken by the executive branch, we'll lose our liberty and privacy to foreign terrorist organizations. You'll have to decide for yourself whether these extreme positions on the antiterrorism laws are correct or whether the changes in the law are less extreme adjustments to existing laws.

# SURVEILLANCE AND TERRORISM

You're already familiar with law enforcement's use of surveillance to gather evidence in criminal cases, especially in illegal drug cases. You learned in Chapter 3 that, according to the U.S. Supreme Court, the Fourth Amendment ban on unreasonable searches and seizures doesn't protect any of the following highly personal information from law enforcement officers who intercept communications and capture it without warrants or probable cause:

1. Conversations of private individuals secretly listened to after wiring informants for sound (*U.S. v. White*, case excerpt Chapter 3)

2. Telephone company lists of the phone numbers of outgoing calls (**pen registers**) (*Smith v. Maryland*, Chapter 3) and incoming calls (**trap and trace**) to a specific telephone

3. Bank records of individuals' financial dealings (*U.S. v. Miller*, Chapter 3)

**TABLE 15.1** Three Tiers of Federal Law Balancing Government Power and Individual Privacy

| Tier 1 | Tier 2 | Tier 3 |
|---|---|---|
| Least government power/ Most privacy protection | More government power/ Less privacy protection | Most government power/ Least privacy protection |
| 1. General ban on electronic surveillance, interception, and capture | 1. Stored communications and transactions subject to surveillance, interception, and capture of information | 1. Pen registers and trap and trace devices allowed for surveillance, interception, and capture of information |
| 2. Exception: serious crime | 2. Applies to all crimes, not just "serious" crimes | 2. Applies to all crimes, not just "serious" crimes |
| 3. Safeguards: detailed and approved by courts | 3. Safeguards: court order, warrant, or subpoena | 3. Safeguard: certification by law enforcement agency supervisory officer without the need for approval by court order |

The rationale for the Court's decisions in these cases goes like this: The Fourth Amendment bans "unreasonable searches and seizures" by the government, but not all government actions are searches and seizures. If a government action isn't a search or seizure, the ban doesn't apply at all. In other words, it's left to government discretionary judgment whether to act. Here's another "but": Legislatures can control this discretion. And Congress has decided to control government's discretion not just in ordinary criminal cases but in antiterrorism cases, too. Congress passed legislation balancing government power to use electronic surveillance and individual privacy. The USA Patriot Act modified this general legislation.

Federal law has established a three-tiered system to balance government power and individual privacy in government surveillance (see Table 15.1). Tier 1 restricts government power and protects privacy most. Tier 2 authorizes more government power and provides less protection for individual privacy. Tier 3 authorizes the most government power and provides the least protection for individual privacy. The tiers are nothing new; they've been around since the 1960s. We'll look at how terrorism has affected surveillance procedures for each of the three tiers.

## Tier 1: "Real Time" Electronic Surveillance

The first tier was established in 1968 by the **Crime Control and Safe Streets Act** (U.S. Code 2003, Title 18, Chapter 119, §§ 2510–22). This act provides the most protection for individual privacy by placing a general ban on the interception of "wire, oral, or electronic communications" while they're taking place (§ 2511). However, the ban contains a **serious crime exception**. *Serious crimes* are defined as crimes punishable by death or more than one year in prison (§ 2516). The exception contains specific conditions aimed at protecting individual privacy. Here are a few of the more important conditions:

1. The U.S. Attorney General or other senior Department of Justice officials have to approve a law enforcement officer's application for a court order from a federal judge to allow the officer to secretly intercept and capture conversations.

2. The judge may issue the order if the interception "may provide or has provided evidence of any offense punishable by death or imprisonment for more than one year."

| TABLE 15.2 | Terrorist Crimes not Subject to a Ban on Electronic Surveillance |
|---|---|

- Chemical weapons offenses (18 U.S. Code 229)
- Terrorist acts of violence against Americans overseas (§ 2332)
- Use of weapons of mass destruction (§ 2332(a))
- Financial transactions with countries that support terrorists (§ 2332(d))
- Providing material support for terrorists (§ 2339A)
- Providing material support for terrorist organizations (§ 2339B)

3. The application includes
   a. A "full and complete statement of the facts and circumstances relied upon by the applicant, to justify the belief that an order should be issued"
   b. "A full and complete statement as to whether other investigative procedures have been tried and failed or why they reasonably appear to be unlikely to succeed if tried or to be too dangerous"
   c. A statement of how long the interception is going to last

The Patriot Act adds several terrorist crimes to the list of serious crimes excepted from the ban on electronic surveillance (Table 15.2).

## Tier 2: Surveilling Stored Electronic Communications

Tier 2 legislation (the **USA Patriot Act**) tips the balance somewhat in favor of government power and guarantees somewhat less protection for individual privacy. The Patriot Act has significantly expanded government surveillance power beyond the Crime Control and Safe Streets Act of 1968. First, it allows the government to access stored "wire and electronic communications," such as voice mail and e-mail. Second, the power applies to "any criminal investigation," not just to the serious crimes in Tier 1.

The Patriot Act does include definite limits to the government's Tier 2 power. The decision to intercept and capture stored information isn't left to law enforcement's discretionary judgment. If the e-mail and voice mail messages have been stored less than six months, officers have to get a warrant based on probable cause (U.S. Code 2003, Title 18 § 2703; see Chapter 6, "Search," on search warrants). For communications stored for more than six months, the government still needs a warrant to access the information. But they don't have to tell subscribers about the warrant for 90 days, "if the court determines" there's "reason to believe" this "may have an adverse result" on the investigation (§ 2705(a)(1)(A)). "Adverse results" include endangering life, flight from prosecution, destruction of evidence, intimidating potential witnesses, or "otherwise seriously jeopardizing an investigation or unduly delaying a trial" (§ 2705(a)(2)).

## Tier 3: Secret "Caller ID"

Government power in Tier 3 legislation is broader than in Tiers 1 and 2 but doesn't invade individual privacy as deeply as they do. Tier 3 grants the power to capture a record of all telephone numbers (not conversations) from a subscriber's phone, using pen registers and trap-and-trace devices (U.S. Code 2003, Title 18, §§ 3121–27). This **secret "caller ID"** is available to investigate "any crime," without court approval, and without officers' ever notifying subscribers they have it or what they learned from it. Officers are limited in getting and using the secret caller IDs only by having to get the approval of a department senior official.

The Patriot Act expands pen register and trap and trace in two ways (§§ 3121, 3123). First, it allows the use of pen registers and trap-and-trace devices to capture e-mail headers (not messages). Before the act, pen registers and trap and trace were authorized only to capture telephone numbers. Second, it expands the geographical area the pen register and trap-and-trace order covers. Before the act, the court's power was limited to issuing orders only within its own district; the act empowers the court to issue orders to "anywhere in the United States" (§ 3123(b)(1)(C)).

To address objections that e-mail headers reveal more information than telephone numbers, the act (§ 3123(a)(3)) requires any agency getting the court order to submit a detailed report to the court showing:

1. The name of the officer who installed and/or accessed the device

2. The date and time the device was installed, accessed, and uninstalled

3. The configuration of the device when it was installed and any modifications made after installation

4. Information captured by the device

## Controversial Government Surveillance

The surveillance activities of the government's investigation of terrorist activities are understandably hidden, and of the few that have come to light, we know extremely little. What we know and don't know are surrounded by growing controversy because, whether justified or not, fears of another terrorist attack have diminished as we move farther away from 9/11. These diminishing security fears have led to some demands for more privacy.

Some expanded intelligence activities have aroused particularly strong interest, leading to calls by some to recalibrate, or at least clarify and define better, the balance between security and liberty struck immediately after 9/11. Most of the controversy relates to government data mining and collecting of personal information stored in organizations' databases. These databases include information that individuals have turned over without knowing the government might have access to it.

We'll look at two programs that have generated the most public controversy: (1) actions taken pursuant to the so-called libraries provision, section 215 of the Patriot Act, and (2) the National Security Agency's (NSA) Terrorist Surveillance Program (TSP).

**The USA Patriot Act "Libraries Provision"** Section 215 of the Patriot Act, as amended in March 2006, authorizes the FBI to demand books, papers, records, and other items from individuals and organizations (U.S. Code 2007, Title 50 § 1861) "if there are reasonable grounds to believe that the records contain information relevant to a national security investigation" (Posner 2006, 138). Notice that the provision doesn't specifically mention libraries; in fact the government has served "only a few dozen 215 demands" on libraries. Nonetheless, it's widely referred to as the **libraries provision** (139).

The application of § 215 to libraries has generated enormous controversy and opposition by civil libertarians. Civil libertarians contend that spreading the net of FBI demands to include "information relevant to a national security investigation" is too broad. They recommend that the government be allowed to demand only records of individuals the government reasonably believes are "involved in terrorist activity" (138).

Supporters of § 215, such as the distinguished U.S. Circuit Court of Appeals Judge Richard Posner, respond that the terrorist activity requirement is too restrictive:

> To impose it would be either to misunderstand the needs of intelligence or to underestimate the value of intelligence in the struggle against terrorism (or perhaps to underestimate the terrorist threat). Information about an individual who is *not* part of a terrorist ring may nevertheless be highly germane to an investigation of the ring or, what may be as important, to an investigation aimed at the discovery of such rings. The information might concern an imam who, though not himself involved in terrorism, was preaching holy war. It might concern family members of a terrorist, who might have information about his whereabouts. It might contain sales invoices for materials that could be used to create weapons of mass destruction, or of books and articles that expressed admiration of suicide bombers. (138–39)

Despite dissatisfaction and opposition from some civil libertarians, the "libraries provision" and most of the rest of the Patriot Act were, with only a few minor amendments, extended and signed into law by the president in March 2006.

***The National Security Agency "Terrorist Surveillance Program"*** Before we get to the Terrorist Surveillance Program (TSP), you need a little background information. In the wake of the abuses by the National Security Agency during and after the Vietnam War, Congress passed and President Carter signed the **Foreign Intelligence Surveillance Act (FISA)** in 1979. FISA authorizes a secret court, the **Foreign Intelligence Surveillance Court (FISC)**, made up of judges on the U.S. Courts of Appeals, to issue eavesdropping warrants whenever the U.S. Attorney General certifies that the purpose of the surveillance is to acquire *foreign* intelligence information.

The FISC can issue intelligence-gathering warrants only when the government reasonably believes that one party to a telephone conversation or e-mail is affiliated with al Qaeda. In emergency circumstances, FISA specifically authorizes the attorney general to initiate surveillance without a FISA warrant, as long as the National Security Agency (NSA) submits a warrant application within 72 hours.

Within months of 9/11, the president made a major shift in domestic spying operations by permitting some eavesdropping on American citizens inside the United States. Under a presidential order signed in 2002, the president authorized the NSA to eavesdrop on Americans and others inside the United States to search for evidence of terrorist activity. According to the order, intelligence agents could approve telephone and e-mail intercepts without the approval of the secret court ordinarily required for *domestic* phone and e-mail surveillance. Pursuant to that order,

> the intelligence agency has monitored the international telephone calls and international e-mail messages of hundreds, perhaps thousands, of people inside the United States without warrants over the past three years in an effort to track possible "dirty numbers" linked to Al Qaeda, the officials said. The agency, they said, still seeks warrants to monitor entirely domestic communications. (Risen and Lichtblau 2005)

Bush administration officials believe this domestic spying operation, called the **Terrorist Surveillance Program (TSP)**, is necessary. According to officials, it allows the agency to "move quickly to monitor communications that may disclose threats to the United States." Officials are "confident that existing safeguards are sufficient to protect the privacy and civil liberties of Americans. Several officials said that the TSP helped uncover a plot by Iyman Faris, an Ohio trucker who pleaded guilty in 2003 to supporting al Qaeda by planning to bring down the Brooklyn Bridge by blowtorching it. Officials concede that most people targeted by the TSP have never been charged with a crime. This includes an Iranian-American doctor in the South, suspected of "dubious ties" with Osama bin Laden (Risen and Lichtblau 2005).

Despite claims that the TSP was effective, even indispensable, to fighting terrorism by monitoring phone calls and e-mails (President Bush frequently said, "If someone in the United States is talking to al Qaeda, I want to know about it"), the administration abruptly disbanded the program on January 18, 2007. Attorney General Alberto Gonzalez announced that the secret court that administers the Foreign Surveillance Act (FISA) will soon begin to oversee telephone and e-mail eavesdropping to and from the United States. The court will approve these intercepts only when "there is probable cause to believe" that one of the parties to the communications is a member of al Qaeda or an associated terrorist group (Eggan 2007, A1).

At the time of this writing (three days after Attorney General Gonzalez's announcement), there's a lot of chatter about the reasons for this abrupt shift in policy and what difference it will make in discovering terrorists and thwarting their plots. Maybe, by the time you read this, we'll have more answers.

# "SNEAK AND PEEK" SEARCHES

You've already learned that searches of private places are "unreasonable searches." They're banned by the Fourth Amendment unless officers are backed up by warrants based on probable cause and they "knock and announce" their presence before they enter and search (Chapter 6). But you also learned that there's a "no knock" emergency exception to the knock-and-announce rule. "Sneak and peek" searches are a variation of no-knock entries. **Sneak-and-peek search warrants** allow officers to enter private places without the owner or (occupant) consenting or even knowing about it. They're not new.

During the 1980s, the FBI and DEA (Drug Enforcement Agency) asked for, and judges issued, at least thirty-five sneak-and-peek warrants ("Sneak and Peek Warrants," 2002, 1). Here's a description of these warrants from the 1980s:

> Under those warrants the search occurred only when the occupants were absent from the premises. The entry and the search were conducted in such a way as to keep them secret. The warrants prohibited seizures of anything except intangible evidence, i.e., information concerning what had been going on, or now was located, inside the premises. No tangible evidence was seized. The searching officers usually took photographs inside the premises searched. No copy of the warrant or receipt was left on the premises. The time for giving notice of the covert entry might be postponed by the court one or more times. The same premises might be subjected to repeated covert entries under successive warrants. At the end of the criminal investigation the premises previously searched under a sneak and peek warrant were usually searched under a conventional search warrant and tangible evidence was then seized. Generally, it was not until after the police made an arrest or returned with a conventional search warrant that the existence of any covert entries was disclosed. Sometimes this was weeks or even months after the surreptitious search or searches. (1)

Both the Second and Ninth Circuit U.S. Courts of Appeals have upheld the admission of evidence obtained during sneak-and-peek searches. The Second Circuit said they were reasonable searches (*U.S. v. Villegas* 1990; Chapter 6); the Ninth Circuit said the evidence was admissible under the "good faith" exception to the exclusionary rule (*U.S. v. Freitas* 1988; Chapter 11).

The Patriot Act was the first time that sneak-and-peek warrants became part of a statute (§ 213). Section 213 authorizes judges to issue sneak-and-peek warrants if:

1. The court finds reasonable cause to believe that providing immediate notification of the execution of the warrant may have an adverse effect ["adverse effect" includes: "endangering life; flight from prosecution; destruction of evidence; intimidating potential witnesses; or otherwise seriously jeopardizing an investigation or unduly delaying a trial"];

2. The warrant prohibits the seizure of any tangible [personal] property . . . except where the court finds reasonable necessity for the seizure; and

3. The warrant provides for the giving of such notice within a reasonable time of its execution, which period may be extended by the court for good cause shown.

Section 213 set off a storm of protest from politicians from both the Democratic and Republican parties, defense lawyers, and civil libertarians. Here's what the *Georgia Defender* ("Sneak and Peek Warrants" 2002), the publication of the Georgia defense bar, wrote:

> It is obvious that these restrictions [reasonable cause, property seizure, and notice] on issuing sneak and peek search warrants border on the meaningless, especially in light of the somber reality that search warrants are issued secretly and *ex parte* [in the defendant's absence from the proceeding], that they are typically issued on the basis of recurring, generalized, boilerplate allegations, and that the judicial officials who issue them tend to be rubber stamps for law enforcement.
>
> Take, for example, the "adverse result" requirement. The statutory definition of adverse result is so all-encompassing that it is difficult to imagine many criminal investigations where at least one form of such a result is not going to be arguably applicable; furthermore, to satisfy the requirement the court need not have reasonable cause to believe that there will be an adverse result, only that there "may" be an adverse result.
>
> The second requirement, that the warrant prohibit the seizure of tangible property, is drained of significance by the gigantic exception allowing seizure of such property "where the court finds reasonable necessity for the seizure." It will be a rare case indeed where such necessity, if alleged, will not be determined to exist by the issuing court; and it may be confidently predicted that, with the passage of time, requests for seizure of tangible evidence will become the rule rather than the exception in connection with sneak and peek warrants.
>
> The final requirement, that the warrant provide for the giving of notice within a reasonable period, involves merely a question of the wording of a sneak and peek warrant, and the provision permitting the court (acting ex parte) to extend the period (one or more times) "for good cause shown," a standard easily met, makes it likely that such extensions will become routine and pro forma. (1)

On the other side, Massachusetts U.S. Attorney Michael Sullivan told the Boston Anti-Terrorism Task Force that sneak and peek is part of the Patriot Act's "series of necessary, measured, and limited tools without which we would be greatly hampered in the struggle against terrorism" (Murphy 2003). We can't settle this debate here, but keep in mind that all Section 213 did was write into a statute combating terrorism what law enforcement had been doing in enforcing drug laws for 20 years (and off the record probably a lot longer). Further, courts also previously admitted evidence obtained from these searches either because they were "reasonable" Fourth Amendment "searches" or qualified as a "good faith" exception to the exclusionary rule.

# DETAINING TERRORIST SUSPECTS

In Chapter 4, you learned that in ordinary times, under ordinary circumstances, detaining someone on the street for just a few minutes is an "unreasonable" Fourth Amendment seizure (a stop) unless it's backed up by enough facts to amount to reasonable suspicion. You know from Chapter 5 that arresting and detaining someone for hours (and maybe a few days) at a police station is an "unreasonable seizure" if it's not backed up by more facts (probable cause). And, in Chapter 12, you learned that both the Fourth Amendment and the Sixth Amendment "speedy trial" clause require officers to take detained suspects before a judge promptly (usually within 48 hours), so the judge can (1) decide whether there's probable cause to detain them; (2) inform them of their rights; (3) set or deny them bail; and (4) provide them with a lawyer if they can't afford one.

But we aren't living in ordinary times under ordinary circumstances anymore. September 11 changed all that. Three official acts document the changes in the balance between preserving national security and the right of individuals to come and go as they please:

1. Presidential Proclamation 7463

2. Congressional "Authorization for Use of Military Force" (Joint Resolution)

3. The president's Military Order of November 13, 2001, "Detention, Treatment, and Trial of Certain Non-Citizens in the War against Terrorism"

Let's look more closely at these acts, which are the basis for detaining terrorist suspects.

## The Sources Authorizing Terrorist Suspect Detention

On September 14, 2001, President George W. Bush declared a "national emergency by reason of certain terrorist attacks" in **Presidential Proclamation 7463** (Presidential Documents 2001 [Sept. 18], 48199). On that same day, Congress threw its weight behind the president's war power in a Joint Resolution, **Authorization for Use of Military Force (AUMF)**. Section 2 of the AUMF provides:

> That the President is authorized to use all necessary and appropriate force against those nations, organizations, or persons he determines planned, authorized, committed, or aided the terrorist attacks that occurred on September 11, 2001, or harbored such organizations or persons, in order to prevent any future acts of international terrorism against the United States by such nations, organizations or persons. (U.S. Senate 2001)

Third, President George W. Bush issued the **Military Order of November 13, 2001,** "Detention, Treatment, and Trial of Certain Non-Citizens in the War against Terrorism" (Presidential Documents 2001 [Nov. 16], 57831–36). According to the order, "certain non-citizens" included "any individual who is not a U.S. citizen . . . that there is reason to believe:

1. Is or was a member of . . . al Qaida

2. Has engaged in, aided or abetted, or conspired to commit, acts of international terrorism, or acts in preparation therefore, that have caused, threaten to cause, or have as their aim to cause, injury to or adverse effects on the U.S., its citizens, national security, foreign policy, or economy, or

3. Has knowingly harbored one or more individuals described in 1 or 2 . . .

shall be detained by the secretary of defense."

The Military Order of November 13, 2001, applies only to noncitizens. But can citizens be detained under the same circumstances as those outlined in the order? The U.S. Supreme Court spelled out the rights of citizen detainees in *Hamdi v. Rumsfeld* (2004).

Yaser Hamdi was born in Baton Rouge, Louisiana, in 1980, to wealthy Saudi Arabian parents. At 3, his parents returned to Saudi Arabia. In the summer of 2000, when he was a sophomore in college majoring in marketing, he went to Afghanistan. According to a friend, "his agenda was to take a sabbatical from school and try to get his head straight, to live in a strict Islamic environment with other young men like himself"

(Brinkley 2004, 4). He was captured (with a Kalashnikov rifle in hand) by forces of the Northern Alliance, who were fighting the Taliban.

The Northern Alliance turned him over to the U.S. Army, which initially detained and interrogated him in Afghanistan and then, in January 2002, transferred Hamdi to the U.S. Naval Base at Guantanamo Bay, Cuba. In April 2002, when they discovered he was a U.S. citizen, authorities transferred him first to a Virginia naval brig (prison ship) in Norfolk, Virginia, and then to a brig in Charleston, South Carolina. There, he was held incommunicado until early 2004, with no access to a lawyer (Dworkin 2004, 26). The government asserted that Hamdi was an "enemy combatant," which "justifies holding him in the U.S. indefinitely—without formal charges or proceedings—unless and until it makes the determination that access to counsel or further process is warranted" (*Hamdi v. Rumsfeld* 2004, 510–11).

In June 2002, Hamdi's father petitioned the U.S. District Court, Eastern District of Virginia, for a writ of habeas corpus, alleging that Hamdi wasn't fighting on the side of the Taliban but had gone to Afghanistan as a volunteer and relief worker (Dworkin 2004, 26). He argued that

> "as an American citizen . . . Hamdi enjoys the full protections of the Constitution," and that Hamdi's detention in the U.S. without charges, access to an impartial tribunal, or assistance of counsel "violated and continues to violate the [due process clauses of] the Fifth and Fourteenth Amendments to the U.S. Constitution." (*Hamdi v. Rumsfeld* 2004, 511)

The Army responded with the memorandum signed by Michael Mobbs, a minor Defense Department official, declaring without supporting evidence, that Hamdi received weapons training from a Taliban unit he was affiliated with and that he was captured while in possession of a Kalashnikov rifle, when the Taliban unit surrendered to the Northern Alliance. Hamdi's father then filed a new petition, asking that the government either release Hamdi or produce evidence to back up the allegations in Mobbs's memo.

The District Court agreed that the Mobbs memo wasn't sufficient to justify holding Hamdi and ordered the government to produce "elaborate records of the kind that would be required in an ordinary criminal prosecution" (Dworkin 2004, 26). The Fourth Circuit Court of Appeals reversed the District Court, declaring that

> the President as commander in chief has the constitutional power to declare any person captured in any theater of military operations to be an enemy combatant, and that no court has any power to review that presidential designation. (26)

The case went to the U.S. Supreme Court with these two stark positions facing the Court. The defense argued that this is a criminal case and that Hamdi is entitled to all the procedures you've learned about in Chapters 1–12. The government argued that in the emergency created by 9/11, the government has a "blank check" in its authority to protect the country from another attack as long as the danger continues.

It shouldn't surprise you that the Supreme Court took a position between the two extremes. The Court reversed the Fourth Circuit and remanded the case to the U.S. District Court, Eastern District of Virginia. Justice O'Connor wrote that Congress's joint resolution, Authorization for Use of Military Force (AUMF) gave President Bush authority to detain enemy forces captured in battle. Furthermore, the law of war (discussed earlier) granted the president the same power to detain until the end of hostilities to prevent captured enemies from returning to the battlefield.

However, the question before the Court wasn't the power to detain but its extent. The answer to that depends on balancing the grave harm to a person mistakenly and indefinitely detained against the dangers to our security and burdens placed on the military from allowing prisoners to claim judicial review of their detentions. According to Justice O'Connor, the District Court granted too much protection to Hamdi, and the Court of Appeals granted him too little:

> In sum, while the full protections that accompany challenges to detentions in other settings may prove unworkable and inappropriate in the enemy-combatant setting, the threats to military operations posed by a basic system of independent review are not so weighty as to trump a citizen's core rights to challenge meaningfully the Government's case and to be heard by an impartial adjudicator.
>
> In so holding, we necessarily reject the Government's assertion that separation of powers principles mandate a heavily circumscribed role for the courts in such circumstances. . . . We have long since made clear that a state of war is not a blank check for the President when it comes to the rights of the Nation's citizens. (536–37)

With that, Justice O'Connor concluded:

> We therefore hold that a citizen-detainee seeking to challenge his classification as an enemy combatant must receive notice of the factual basis for his classification, and a fair opportunity to rebut the Government's factual assertions before a neutral decision maker. (533)

Furthermore, Hamdi "unquestionably has the right to access to counsel" during all proceedings regarding his detention (539). Finally, because the only purpose of detention without trial is to prevent enemy combatants from returning to the battlefield, citizen detainees can't be detained after hostilities cease in the area where they were fighting.

Justice O'Connor included more detailed suggestions, making it clear that the Court's ruling leaves the government plenty of power. First, the "neutral decision maker" that citizen detainees have a right of access to doesn't have to be an ordinary court; it can be a court-martial, or even a military commission. Second, the rules of evidence might heavily favor the government. Hearsay evidence might be admitted; even the weak hearsay of the Mobbs memo might be enough. Third, the normal burden of proof might be shifted from the government to prove the detainee was an enemy combatant to the detainee to prove she wasn't.

Hamdi's case illustrates just how heavy the burden of proving innocence might be. Take the Mobbs memo. If the government has to reveal only that much evidence, how is Hamdi to rebut even that little bit successfully?

> If there were friendly witnesses to his seizure by the Northern Alliance, he might be able to persuade them to testify before a military commission and to persuade the commissioners to believe them rather than the Mobbs memorandum. But if there were no friendly witnesses willing to testify, he might be forced to find a Northern Alliance warlord somewhere in the Afghan desert who is willing to submit to deposition and cross-examination. (Dworkin 2004, 27)

In fact, Hamdi never needed his day in court; the government ended the case by releasing Hamdi in October 2004. According to the terms of the release, the United States agreed to return Hamdi to Saudi Arabia in civilian clothes. Among the conditions Hamdi agreed to were the following:

1. To remain in Saudi Arabia for 5 years

2. To be banished from the United States for 10 years

3. To renounce his U.S. citizenship

4. Not to participate in any terrorist activity (Smith 2004)

On that same day, a majority of six justices, in *Rasul v. Bush* (2004), held that non-citizen detainees can petition for habeas corpus in federal courts if they're in areas that are in effective and permanent control of the United States, such as Guantanamo Bay.

## Conditions of Detention

Now that you know the government can detain terrorist suspects, let's look at what the government can do with suspects while they're detained. The Military Order of November 13, 2001, spells out the conditions of detention and the treatment of detainees. Persons detained "shall be:

    a. Treated humanely, without any adverse distinction based on race, color, religion, gender, birth, wealth, or any similar criteria;

    b. Afforded adequate food, drinking water, shelter, clothing, and medical treatment;

    c. Allowed the free exercise of religion consistent with the requirements of such detention; and

    d. Detained in accordance with such other conditions as the secretary of defense shall prescribe." (Presidential Document 2001 [Nov. 16], 57834)

## Torture during Detention

> The President has repeatedly reaffirmed the longstanding policy that the United States will neither commit nor condone torture. . . . The United States has assumed an obligation under Article 15 of the Convention against Torture and Other Cruel, Inhuman, or Degrading Treatment or Punishment to "ensure that any statement which is established to have been made as a result of torture shall not be invoked as evidence in any proceedings, except against a person accused of torture as evidence that the statement was made." (Military Instruction No. 10 2006, 1)

Civil libertarians are skeptical about whether the interrogators' actions will match their words when it comes to using torture to get information from suspects. They point to the well-publicized examples of abuse at Abu Ghraib and stories by former suspects *and* interrogators and their superiors about abuses they experienced or practiced (Ross and Esposito 2005).

This highly emotional subject has many dimensions—and little or no agreement about any of them. These include the definition of "torture"; the number and kinds of abuses (Table 15.3 describes some of the tactics reported by CIA interrogators and their superiors); whether torture "works"; and whether it violates the U.S. Constitution.

---

**TABLE 15.3**   **CIA Interrogation Tactics**

- *The Attention Grab.* The interrogator forcefully grabs the shirt front of the prisoner and shakes him.
- *Attention Slap.* An open-handed slap aimed at causing pain and triggering fear.
- *The Belly Slap.* A hard open-handed slap to the stomach. The aim is to cause pain but not internal injury. Doctors consulted advised against using a punch, which could cause lasting internal damage.
- *Long Time Standing.* This technique is described as among the most effective. Prisoners are forced to stand, handcuffed and with their feet shackled to an eye bolt in the floor, for more than forty hours. Exhaustion and sleep deprivation are effective in yielding confessions.
- *The Cold Cell.* The prisoner is left to stand naked in a cell kept near 50 degrees. Throughout the time in the cell, the prisoner is doused with cold water.
- *Water Boarding.* The prisoner is bound to an inclined board, feet raised and head slightly below the feet. Cellophane is wrapped over the prisoner's face and water is poured over him. Unavoidably, the gag reflex kicks in and a terrifying fear of drowning leads to almost instant pleas to bring the treatment to a halt.

---

Source: Ross and Esposito 2005.

We can't begin to answer these questions here, but we can at least touch on the constitutionality of tactics that exceed what's acceptable in the interrogation of suspects in ordinary criminal cases that you learned about in Chapter 8. Recall that in ordinary interrogation, officers can use pressure and some unsavory tactics without violating the bar on coerced confessions. Recall also that in our first case excerpt in Chapter 2, *Rochin v. California* (1952), the Supreme Court ruled that officers' actions to retrieve heroin capsules from Antonin Rochin denied him due process:

> We are compelled to conclude that the proceedings by which this conviction was obtained do more than offend some fastidious squeamishness or private sentimentalism about combating crime too energetically. This is conduct that shocks the conscience. Illegally breaking into the privacy of Rochin, the struggle to open his mouth and remove what was there, the forcible extraction of his stomach's contents—this course of proceeding by agents of government to obtain evidence is bound to offend even hardened sensibilities. They are methods too close to the rack and the screw to permit of constitutional differentiation. (172–73)

There's a significant and relevant difference between *Rochin* and the interrogation of terrorist suspects. The constitutional question in ordinary criminal cases is whether confessions are admissible against suspects to prove their guilt at trial. The interest in getting information from terrorist suspects is not only or even mainly to prove their guilt but to prevent another terrorist attack. (Of course, information gained from terrorists may be used for prosecution in military trials, where self-incrimination is clearly relevant and banned; the point here is that it's not the *main* reason.)

When, if ever, do interrogation tactics "shock the conscience"; that is, do they ever violate the Constitution when their object isn't to prosecute but to discover and prevent terrorist attacks? Judge Posner (2006) poses the constitutional question clearly:

> What process is due a person who refuses to divulge information of utmost importance to the welfare of society? Can the "conscience shocking" effect of a stomach pump be divorced from the circumstances in which the government officers resort to that method of obtaining information, so that the greater the necessity of getting the information the less will forcible methods of getting it shock the conscience? All these are open questions. (81)

And that's where we'll leave these extremely important questions—open—until the courts, and especially the U.S. Supreme Court, give us more guidance.

# TRIALS OF SUSPECTED TERRORISTS

Suspected terrorists can be tried either for crimes (such as treason and murder) in the ordinary courts (called **Article III courts** because their authority comes from Article III of the U.S. Constitution, which created the judiciary) or for war crimes (such as fighting for a terrorist organization) in special military courts called **military commissions** (sometimes called **military tribunals**). If they're tried for ordinary crimes in ordinary courts, all that you've learned in Chapters 10 through 14 applies, so we don't need to go over it again. If they're tried by courts-martial, almost all of what you learned in Chapters 10 through 14 also applies.

Here, we'll examine the relaxed rules of procedure and proof and the diminished rights for defendants that apply to military commissions. A military commission consists of a panel of military officers acting under military authority to try enemy combatants for **war crimes**—acts committed during wartime that inflict "needless and disproportionate suffering and damages" in pursuit of a "military objective." (Don't confuse military commissions with military **courts-martial**, which are also made up of military officers, but they try members of U.S. armed forces for violating the Uniform Code of Military Justice) (Elsea 2001, 7, 16).

The Military Order of November 13, 2001 (Presidential Documents 2001 [Nov. 16], 57831–36), spells out the rules governing military commissions to try suspected terrorists. Let's look at the main points in the Military Order that are relevant to military commissions: the source and the jurisdiction of their authority and the trial proceedings before them.

## The Sources of Military Commission Authority

The president bases his authority to establish military commissions on three sources. First, the U.S. Constitution, Article II, Section 2, makes the president the "commander in chief" of the armed forces. As commander in chief, he's responsible for trying terrorists. Second, Article II, Section 2, also imposes responsibility on the president to "take care that the laws shall be faithfully executed." In this case, according to the Military Order, the laws include trying war crimes under the Articles of War and the Authorization for Use of Military Force, passed by a joint resolution of Congress on September 14, 2001. Third, the joint resolution authorized the president to use "all necessary and appropriate force against those nations, organizations, or persons he determines planned, authorized, committed, or aided" or "harbored" them.

## The Jurisdiction of Military Commissions

The provisions of the order apply only to "certain non-citizens in the war against terrorism" (Presidential Documents 2001 [Nov. 16], 57833). This means the military commission's authority only applies to noncitizens. Here's how Section 2 of the order defines noncitizens and outlines restrictions on their rights, including taking away the power (jurisdiction) of ordinary courts to review military commission decisions regarding them:

> (a) . . . any individual who is not a United States citizen with respect to whom I determine from time to time in writing that:
> (1) there is reason to believe that such individual, at the relevant times,
>    (i) is or was a member of the organization known as al Qaida;
>    (ii) has engaged in, aided or abetted, or conspired to commit, acts of international terrorism, or acts in preparation therefor, that have caused, threaten to cause, or have as their aim to cause, injury to or adverse effects on the United States, its citizens, national security, foreign policy, or economy; or
>    (iii) has knowingly harbored one or more individuals described in subparagraphs (i) or (ii) of subsection 2(a)(1) of this order; and
> (2) it is in the interest of the United States that such individual be subject to this order. (57834)

As noncitizens, the individuals the order applies to don't "necessarily enjoy the same constitutional rights as citizens" even if they're legally in the country. During wartime, aliens of enemy nations can be detained and deported, and their property can be confiscated. "They may also be denied access to the courts of the United States if they would use the courts to the advantage of the enemy or to impede the U.S. prosecution of a war" (Elsea 2001, 28–29).

The order takes away the jurisdiction of all courts inside and outside the United States to try any cases covered by the order. (This jurisdiction-stripping provision was included with some modifications in the Detainee Treatment Act passed by Congress in 2005.)

According to Order Section 7(b)(1), "military tribunals shall have exclusive jurisdiction with respect to offenses by the individual . . ." (57835).

The order also strips individuals of the right to have their cases reviewed by any other courts. According to Sections 7(b)(2) and (c):

> The individual shall not be privileged to seek any remedy or maintain any proceeding, directly or indirectly, or to have any such remedy or proceeding sought on the individual's behalf, in
>> (i) any court of the United States, or any State thereof,
>> (ii) any court of any foreign nation, or
>> (iii) any international tribunal.
>
> (c) This order is not intended to and does not create any right, benefit, or privilege, substantive or procedural, enforceable . . . by any party against the United States, its departments, agencies, or other entities, its officers or employees, or any other person. (57836)

## Trial Proceedings of Military Commissions

Military commissions aren't bound by the constitutional requirements that apply to ordinary (Article III) courts. So defendants may not have traditional constitutional trial rights, such as the right to a speedy trial, to trial by jury, to counsel, to remain silent, or to proof beyond a reasonable doubt.

In our final case excerpt, *Hamdan v. Rumsfeld* (2006), filed by Salim Ahmed Hamdan, the U.S. Supreme Court reviewed the *statutory* basis for challenging the procedures of the first military commissions since World War II. The case involved the first trial by military commission of prisoners at Guantanamo Bay. Hamdan, who admits he's Osama bin Laden's former personal chauffeur, is accused of helping bin Laden ferry weapons and then flee after the 1998 bombings of U.S. embassies in East Africa. He is also accused of having collaborated in the September 11, 2001, terrorist attacks.

The U.S. Supreme Court rejected the government's claim that the power of the president to create military tribunals and to try, convict, and sentence suspected enemy combatants is beyond the reach of the courts until the military commissions complete their proceedings. Then, according to the terms of the Detainee Treatment Act (2005), detainees have a limited right of review in the U.S. District Court for the District of Columbia and then a limited right of appeal to the U.S. D.C. Court of Appeals.

CASE    *Can a Guantanamo Bay Noncitizen Detainee Challenge His Detention in a U.S. Court?*

*Hamdan v. Rumsfeld*
126 S.Ct. 2749 (2006)

Certiorari was granted. The U.S. Supreme Court reversed and remanded.

STEVENS, J.

### HISTORY

Salim Ahmed HAMDAN, Petitioner, an alien, who was detained at Guantanamo Bay, Cuba, and charged with various terrorism-related offenses, was designated for trial before a military commission. He petitioned for habeas relief. The U.S. States District Court for the District of Columbia granted his petition. The Government appealed. The U.S. Court of Appeals for the District of Columbia, reversed.

### FACTS

On September 11, 2001, agents of the al Qaeda terrorist organization hijacked commercial airplanes and attacked the World Trade Center in New York City and the national headquarters of the Department of Defense in Arlington, Virginia. Americans will never forget the devastation wrought by these acts. Nearly 3,000 civilians were killed.

Congress responded by adopting a Joint Resolution authorizing the President to "use all necessary and appropriate force against those nations, organizations, or persons he determines planned, authorized, committed, or aided the terrorist attacks . . . in order to prevent any future acts of international terrorism against the United States by such nations, organizations or persons." Authorization for Use of Military Force (AUMF). . . . On November 13, 2001, while the United States was still engaged in active combat with the Taliban, the President issued a comprehensive military order intended to govern the "Detention, Treatment, and Trial of Certain Non-Citizens in the War against Terrorism" (hereinafter November 13 Order or Order). . . . The November 13 Order vested in the Secretary of Defense the power to appoint military commissions to try individuals subject to the Order, but that power has since been delegated to John D. Altenberg, Jr., a retired Army major general and longtime military lawyer who has been designated "Appointing Authority for Military Commissions."

On July 3, 2003, the President announced his determination that Hamdan and five other detainees at Guantanamo Bay were subject to the November 13 Order and thus triable by military commission. In December 2003, military counsel was appointed to represent Hamdan. Two months later, counsel filed demands for charges and for a speedy trial pursuant to Article 10 of the UCMJ, 10 U.S.C. § 810. On February 23, 2004, the legal adviser to the Appointing Authority denied the applications, ruling that Hamdan was not entitled to any of the protections of the UCMJ. Not until July 13, 2004, after Hamdan had commenced this action in the United States District Court for the Western District of Washington, did the Government finally charge him with the offense for which, a year earlier, he had been deemed eligible for trial by military commission. . . .

. . . Paragraph 12 charges that "from on or about February 1996 to on or about November 24, 2001," Hamdan "willfully and knowingly joined an enterprise of persons who shared a common criminal purpose and conspired and agreed with [named members of al Qaeda] to commit the following offenses triable by military commission: attacking civilians; attacking civilian objects; murder by an unprivileged belligerent; and terrorism." There is no allegation that Hamdan had any command responsibilities, played a leadership role, or participated in the planning of any activity.

Paragraph 13 lists four "overt acts" that Hamdan is alleged to have committed sometime between 1996 and November 2001 in furtherance of the "enterprise and conspiracy": (1) he acted as Osama bin Laden's "bodyguard and personal driver," "believ[ing]" all the while that bin Laden "and his associates were involved in" terrorist acts prior to and including the attacks of September 11, 2001; (2) he arranged for transportation of, and actually transported, weapons used by al Qaeda members and by bin Laden's bodyguards (Hamdan among them); (3) he "drove or accompanied [O]sama bin Laden to various al Qaida-sponsored training camps, press conferences, or lectures,"

at which bin Laden encouraged attacks against Americans; and (4) he received weapons training at al Qaeda-sponsored camps.

. . . On November 7, 2005, we granted certiorari to decide whether the military commission convened to try Hamdan has authority to do so, and whether Hamdan may rely on the Geneva Conventions in these proceedings.

## OPINION

The Constitution makes the President the "Commander in Chief" of the Armed Forces, but vests in Congress the powers to "declare War . . . and make Rules concerning Captures on Land and Water," to "raise and support Armies," to "define and punish . . . Offences against the Law of Nations," and "To make Rules for the Government and Regulation of the land and naval Forces." The interplay between these powers was described by Chief Justice Chase in the seminal case of *Ex parte Milligan:*

> Congress cannot direct the conduct of campaigns, nor can the President, or any commander under him, without the sanction of Congress, institute tribunals for the trial and punishment of offences, either of soldiers or civilians, unless in cases of a controlling necessity, which justifies what it compels, or at least insures acts of indemnity from the justice of the legislature.

. . .

Hamdan raises both general and particular objections to the procedures set forth in Commission Order No. 1. . . . Chief among his particular objections are that he may, under the Commission Order, be convicted based on evidence he has not seen or heard, and that any evidence admitted against him need not comply with the admissibility or relevance rules typically applicable in criminal trials and court-martial proceedings.

The Government objects to our consideration of any procedural challenge at this stage on the grounds that (1) the abstention doctrine . . . [*that regular courts not act until military commissions have reached a final decision*] precludes pre-enforcement review of procedural rules, (2) Hamdan will be able to raise any such challenge following a "final decision" under the DTA [Detainee Treatment Act], and (3) "there is . . . no basis to presume, before the trial has even commenced, that the trial will not be conducted in good faith and according to law." The first of these contentions was disposed of [*omitted from this excerpt*] . . . , and neither of the latter two is sound.

First . . . he has no automatic right to review of the commission's "final decision" before a federal court under the DTA. Second, contrary to the Government's assertion, there *is* a "basis to presume" that the procedures employed during Hamdan's trial will violate the law: The procedures are described with particularity in Commission Order No. 1, and implementation of some of them has already occurred. One of Hamdan's complaints is that he will be, and *indeed already has been,* excluded from his own trial. Under these circumstances, review of the procedures in advance of a "final decision"—the timing of which is left entirely to the discretion of the President under the DTA—is appropriate. We turn, then, to consider the merits of Hamdan's procedural challenge.

. . . Historically [the procedures governing military commissions] have been the same as those governing courts-martial. . . . The uniformity principle is not an inflexible one; it does not preclude all departures from the procedures dictated for use by courts-martial. But any departure must be tailored to the exigency that necessitates it. That understanding is reflected in Article 36 of the UCMJ, which provides:

(a) The procedure, including modes of proof, in cases before courts-martial, courts of inquiry, military commissions, and other military tribunals may be prescribed by the President by regulations which shall, so far as he considers practicable, apply the principles of law and the rules of evidence generally recognized in the trial of criminal cases in the United States district courts, but which may not be contrary to or inconsistent with this chapter.

(b) All rules and regulations made under this article shall be uniform insofar as practicable and shall be reported to Congress.

. . . The Government contends [that] military commissions would be of no use if the President were hamstrung by those provisions of the UCMJ that govern courts-martial. [The Government also contends that] . . . the President's determination that "the danger to the safety of the United States and the nature of international terrorism" renders it impracticable "to apply in military commissions . . . the principles of law and rules of evidence generally recognized in the trial of criminal cases in the United States district courts," is, in the Government's view, explanation enough for any deviation from court-martial procedures.

. . . Without reaching the question whether any provision of Commission Order No. 1 is strictly "contrary to or inconsistent with" other provisions of the UCMJ, we conclude that the "practicability" determination the President has made is insufficient to justify variances from the procedures governing courts-martial. . . . The President here has determined . . . that it is impracticable to apply the rules and principles of law that govern "the trial of criminal cases in the United States district courts" to Hamdan's commission. . . .

Nothing in the record before us demonstrates that it would be impracticable to apply court-martial rules in this case. . . . The only reason offered in support of [impracticability] . . . is the danger posed by international terrorism. Without for one moment underestimating that danger, it is not evident to us why it should require, in the case of Hamdan's trial, any variance from the rules that govern courts-martial.

The absence of any showing of impracticability is particularly disturbing when considered in light of the clear and admitted failure to apply one of the most fundamental protections afforded not just by the Manual for Courts-Martial but also by the UCMJ itself: the right to be present. Whether

or not that departure technically is "contrary to or inconsistent with" the terms of the UCMJ, the jettisoning of so basic a right cannot lightly be excused as "practicable."

Under the circumstances, then, the rules applicable in courts-martial must apply. Since it is undisputed that Commission Order No. 1 deviates in many significant respects from those rules, it necessarily violates Article 36(b).

The Government's objection that requiring compliance with the courts-martial rules imposes an undue burden both ignores the plain meaning of Article 36(b) and misunderstands the purpose and the history of military commissions. The military commission was not born of a desire to dispense a more summary form of justice than is afforded by courts-martial; it developed, rather, as a tribunal of necessity to be employed when courts-martial lacked jurisdiction over either the accused or the subject matter. Exigency lent the commission its legitimacy, but did not further justify the wholesale jettisoning of procedural protections. That history explains why the military commission's procedures typically have been the ones used by courts-martial. That the jurisdiction of the two tribunals today may sometimes overlap . . . does not detract from the force of this history; Article 21 did not transform the military commission from a tribunal of true exigency into a more convenient adjudicatory tool. Article 36, confirming as much, strikes a careful balance between uniform procedure and the need to accommodate exigencies that may sometimes arise in a theater of war. That Article not having been complied with here, the rules specified for Hamdan's trial are illegal.

The procedures adopted to try Hamdan also violate the Geneva Conventions. . . . Article 3, often referred to as Common Article 3 because . . . it appears in all four Geneva Conventions, provides that in a "conflict not of an international character occurring in the territory of one of the High Contracting Parties, each Party to the conflict shall be bound to apply, as a minimum," certain provisions protecting "persons taking no active part in the hostilities, including members of armed forces who have laid down their arms and those placed outside of combat by . . . detention." One such provision prohibits "the passing of sentences and the carrying out of executions without previous judgment pronounced by a regularly constituted court affording all the judicial guarantees which are recognized as indispensable by civilized peoples." . . .

Common Article 3, then, is applicable here and, as indicated above, requires that Hamdan be tried by a "regularly constituted court affording all the judicial guarantees which are recognized as indispensable by civilized peoples." . . . At a minimum, a military commission can be regularly constituted by the standards of our military justice system only if some practical need explains deviations from court-martial practice." . . . No such need has been demonstrated here.

Inextricably intertwined with the question of regular constitution is the evaluation of the procedures governing the tribunal and whether they afford "all the judicial guarantees which are recognized as indispensable by civilized peoples." Like the phrase "regularly constituted court," this phrase is not defined in the text of the Geneva Conventions.

But it must be understood to incorporate at least the barest of those trial protections that have been recognized by customary international law. . . . Common Article 3 obviously tolerates a great degree of flexibility in trying individuals captured during armed conflict; its requirements are general ones, crafted to accommodate a wide variety of legal systems. But *requirements* they are nonetheless. The commission that the President has convened to try Hamdan does not meet those requirements.

We have assumed, as we must, that the allegations made in the Government's charge against Hamdan are true. We have assumed, moreover, the truth of the message implicit in that charge, namely, that Hamdan is a dangerous individual whose beliefs, if acted upon, would cause great harm and even death to innocent civilians, and who would act upon those beliefs if given the opportunity. It bears emphasizing that Hamdan does not challenge, and we do not today address, the Government's power to detain him for the duration of active hostilities in order to prevent such harm. But in undertaking to try Hamdan and subject him to criminal punishment, the Executive is bound to comply with the Rule of Law that prevails in this jurisdiction.

The judgment of the Court of Appeals is REVERSED, and the case is REMANDED for further proceedings. *It is so ordered.*

THE CHIEF JUSTICE TOOK NO PART IN
THE CONSIDERATION OR DECISION OF THIS CASE.

## CONCURRING OPINIONS

BREYER, J., JOINED BY KENNEDY, SOUTER,
AND GINSBURG, JJ.

The dissenters say that today's decision would "sorely hamper the President's ability to confront and defeat a new and deadly enemy." They suggest that it undermines our Nation's ability to "prevent future attacks" of the grievous sort that we have already suffered. That claim leads me to state briefly what I believe the majority sets forth both explicitly and implicitly at greater length. The Court's conclusion ultimately rests upon a single ground: Congress has not issued the Executive a "blank check." Indeed, Congress has denied the President the legislative authority to create military commissions of the kind at issue here. Nothing prevents the President from returning to Congress to seek the authority he believes necessary.

Where, as here, no emergency prevents consultation with Congress, judicial insistence upon that consultation does not weaken our Nation's ability to deal with danger. To the contrary, that insistence strengthens the Nation's ability to determine—through democratic means—how best to do so. The Constitution places its faith in those democratic means. Our Court today simply does the same.

KENNEDY, J., JOINED BY SOUTER, GINSBURG,
AND BREYER, JJ.

Military Commission Order No. 1, which governs the military commission established to try petitioner Salim Hamdan for war crimes, exceeds limits that certain statutes, duly enacted by Congress, have placed on the President's authority to convene military courts. This is not a case, then, where the Executive can assert some unilateral authority to fill a void left by congressional inaction. It is a case where Congress, in the proper exercise of its powers as an independent branch of government, and as part of a long tradition of legislative involvement in matters of military justice, has considered the subject of military tribunals and set limits on the President's authority.

Where a statute provides the conditions for the exercise of governmental power, its requirements are the result of a deliberative and reflective process engaging both of the political branches. Respect for laws derived from the customary operation of the Executive and Legislative Branches gives some assurance of stability in time of crisis. The Constitution is best preserved by reliance on standards tested over time and insulated from the pressures of the moment. These principles seem vindicated here, for a case that may be of extraordinary importance is resolved by ordinary rules. The rules of most relevance here are those pertaining to the authority of Congress and the interpretation of its enactments.

It seems appropriate to recite these rather fundamental points because the Court refers, as it should in its exposition of the case, to the requirement of the Geneva Conventions of 1949 that military tribunals be "regularly constituted"— a requirement that controls here, if for no other reason, because Congress requires that military commissions like the ones at issue conform to the "law of war." Whatever the substance and content of the term "regularly constituted" as interpreted in this and any later cases, there seems little doubt that it relies upon the importance of standards deliberated upon and chosen in advance of crisis, under a system where the single power of the Executive is checked by other constitutional mechanisms. All of which returns us to the point of beginning—that domestic statutes control this case. If Congress, after due consideration, deems it appropriate to change the controlling statutes, in conformance with the Constitution and other laws, it has the power and prerogative to do so.

In assessing the validity of Hamdan's military commission the precise circumstances of this case bear emphasis. The allegations against Hamdan are undoubtedly serious. Captured in Afghanistan during our Nation's armed conflict with the Taliban and al Qaeda—a conflict that continues as we speak—Hamdan stands accused of overt acts in furtherance of a conspiracy to commit terrorism: delivering weapons and ammunition to al Qaeda, acquiring trucks for use by Osama bin Laden's bodyguards, providing security services to bin Laden, and receiving weapons training at a terrorist camp.

Nevertheless, the circumstances of Hamdan's trial present no exigency requiring special speed or precluding careful consideration of evidence. For roughly four years, Hamdan has been detained at a permanent United States military base in Guantanamo Bay, Cuba. And regardless of the outcome of the criminal proceedings at issue, the Government claims authority to continue to detain him based on his status as an enemy combatant. Against this background, the Court is correct to conclude that the military commission the President has convened to try Hamdan is unauthorized. . . .

## DISSENT

### SCALIA, J., JOINED BY THOMAS AND ALITO, JJ.

. . . The principal opinion . . . makes clear that it does not believe that the trials by military commission involve any "military necessity" *at all*. . . . This is quite at odds with the views on this subject expressed by our political branches. Because of "military necessity," a joint session of Congress authorized the President to "use all necessary and appropriate force," including military commissions, "against those nations, organizations, or persons [such as petitioner] he determines planned, authorized, committed, or aided the terrorist attacks that occurred on September 11, 2001." In keeping with this authority, the President has determined that "to protect the United States and its citizens, and for the effective conduct of military operations and prevention of terrorist attacks, it is necessary for individuals subject to this order . . . to be detained, and, when tried, to be tried for violations of the laws of war and other applicable laws by military tribunals." It is not clear where the Court derives the authority—or the audacity—to contradict this determination. . . .

### THOMAS, J., JOINED BY SCALIA AND ALITO JJ.

. . . The President's decision to try Hamdan before a military commission for his involvement with al Qaeda is entitled to a heavy measure of deference. . . . On the same day that the President issued Military Commission Order No. 1, the Secretary of Defense explained that "the president decided to establish military commissions because he wanted the option of a process that is different from those processes which we already have, namely the federal court system . . . and the military court system." . . . The President reached this conclusion because

> we're in the middle of a war, and . . . had to design a procedure that would allow us to pursue justice for these individuals while at the same time prosecuting the war most effectively. And that means setting rules that would allow us to preserve our intelligence secrets, develop more information about terrorist

activities that might be planned for the future so that we can take action to prevent terrorist attacks against the United States. . . . There was a constant balancing of the requirements of our war policy and the importance of providing justice for individuals . . . and *each* deviation from the standard kinds of rules that we have in our criminal courts was motivated by the desire to strike the balance between individual justice and the broader war policy. . . .

### ALITO, JOINED BY SCALIA AND THOMAS, JJ.

I see no basis for the Court's holding that a military commission cannot be regarded as "a regularly constituted court" unless it is similar in structure and composition to a regular military court or unless there is an "evident practical need" for the divergence. There is no reason why a court that differs in structure or composition from an ordinary military court must be viewed as having been improperly constituted. Tribunals that vary significantly in structure, composition, and procedures may all be "regularly" or "properly" constituted. Consider, for example, a municipal court, a state trial court of general jurisdiction, an Article I federal trial court, a federal district court, and an international court, such as the International Criminal Tribunal for the Former Yugoslavia. Although these courts are "differently constituted" and differ substantially in many other respects, they are all "regularly constituted."

## Questions

1. List the specific shortcomings in Salim Hamdan's military commission, according to Justice Stevens.

2. What arguments do Justices Stevens, Breyer, and Kennedy make to support their conclusion that the commission was unlawful?

3. According to Justices Breyer and Kennedy, how can the commissions be changed, and *who* can make the changes to make the commissions lawful?

4. Why, according to Justices Scalia, Thomas, and Alito, is the commission lawful as it is?

5. Identify the interests being balanced in the case. How would you balance the interests? Back up your answer with details in the opinions.

---

*Hamdan v. Rumsfeld* (2006) caused a great stir among lawyers and politicians. As we've seen so often before, the extremists were alternately elated (civil libertarians who thought the Court had smacked down once and for all the imperial president) or angry or depressed (that the imperial Court had exposed us to sure destruction by those who want to kill Americans). The celebrations and lamentations were too early—much too early. Congress and the White House took the advice of four justices in *Hamdan* that "'nothing prevents the President from returning to Congress to seek the authority he believes necessary' to try enemy combatants" (*Hamdan v. Rumsfeld* 2006, [U.S. District Court], 2).

Within four months, Congress had passed, and on October 16, President Bush signed, the Military Commissions Act (MCA) of 2006. On December 12, 2006, the same judge who granted Salim Hamdan the petition for habeas corpus that led to the Supreme Court's decision in *Hamdan v. Rumsfeld* (2006) denied Hamdan's habeas corpus petition *Hamdan v. Rumsfeld* (2006 [U.S.D.C.]) in the U.S. District Court for Washington, D.C. The reason: the Military Commissions Act of 2006 took away the District Court's authority to hear the petition (4).

On January 18, 2007, the Pentagon released its new *Military Commissions Manual*, which will govern the military trials of suspected terrorists. The manual closely tracks the Military Commissions Act. Highlights from the manual include:

- Discretion and deference to independent military judges, who will serve as presiding officials and ensure fairness;
- An independent defense function to represent defendants and protect against the appearance of influence or conflict of interest;
- The presumption of innocence and requirement for the prosecution to prove its case beyond a reasonable doubt;
- A jury system comparable to that used in general courts-martial;
- Requirement that the accused be provided, in advance, evidence to be introduced against him at trial;
- Prohibition against admitting classified evidence outside the presence of the accused;
- A reasonable opportunity for the accused to obtain evidence and witnesses;
- Safeguards to protect the rights of confrontation, protection from self-incrimination, and most common law evidentiary privileges;
- An exclusionary rule allowing the judge to suppress statements obtained by torture or in violation of the Detainee Treatment Act of 2005;
- A requirement for the prosecution to provide exculpatory evidence to an accused consistent with federal and courts-martial practice;
- Requirement for a unanimous verdict by 12 members in cases involving the death penalty; and
- A thorough, comprehensive and independent appellate system. An accused will have access to the Court of Military Commission Review, the Circuit Court for the District of Columbia, and the Supreme Court of the United States. (U.S. Department of Defense 2007)

 Go to Exercise 15.1 on the Samaha Criminal Procedure 7e website to learn more about the Military Commissions Act of 2006: academic.cengage.com/ criminaljustice/samaha.

But the story of military commissions (and for that matter the story of spying, sneak and peek, and detention of terrorist suspects) is far from over. On December 5, 2006, Senators Arlen Specter (R-Pennsylvania) and Patrick Leahy (D-Vermont) introduced the Habeas Corpus Restoration Act of 2006, "which would grant statutory habeas rights to those whose rights were repealed by the MCA" (*Hamdan v. Rumsfeld* 2006, U.S.D.C., 10, n. 4). Other civil libertarian complaints also have entered the court system. So remember that the story of criminal procedure in wartime is tentative and incomplete.

# SUMMARY

**I. Balancing Rights and Security during Emergencies**
   A. Balancing is most challenging during emergencies.
   B. The balance tips toward government power over individual liberty and privacy during emergencies.

C. Government power during emergencies is limited by two things:
1. *Necessity*. Emergency power is available only when and to the extent necessary.
2. *Temporary*. Extraordinary power ends as soon as the emergency ends.

## II. The History of Criminal Procedure in Wartime

A. Clear principles once applied to wars fought between two nations:
1. Declarations of war defined the beginning.
2. Laws of war controlled fighting.
3. Peace treaties defined the end.
B. Total wars (World Wars I and II) required the commitment of the whole government, the nation's resources, and all the people.
C. The Cold War changed everything.
1. International communism crossed national borders.
2. Spies came to U.S. soil and looked and acted like non-Communists.
3. A hidden enemy "bored from within" to learn our secrets and pass them on to Communist governments.
4. Fighting them required not military combat but intelligence gathering about Communists, their actions, and their plans.
5. The goal sometimes was to prosecute but more often to deport them and prevent further infiltration into the United States.
D. The war on terror is a major shift from prosecution to prevention.
1. There's been a primary mission shift in law enforcement from gathering evidence to prosecute terrorists for past attacks to gathering intelligence to prevent future attacks.
2. Prosecution is still a mission.
3. Our knowledge of the USA Patriot Act and other laws is limited to what they say and not how they're operating.
   a. The government argues there's a need for secrecy to guard against future attacks.
   b. The changes are too recent to have produced more than a few court cases.
   c. Questions are based on a constitutional requirement to balance the need for government power to prevent and prosecute terrorist acts and the rights of individuals guaranteed by the U.S. Constitution.

## III. Surveillance and Terrorism

A. The Fourth Amendment (Chapter 3) doesn't protect against:
1. Wiring informants for sound (*U.S. v. White*)
2. Retrieving lists of telephone numbers of outgoing (pen registers, *Smith v. Maryland*) and incoming (trap and trace) calls
3. Obtaining bank records of individuals' financial dealings (*U.S. v. Miller*)
B. Congress created a three-tiered system of balancing government power and individual privacy:
1. Tier 1: "Real-time" electronic surveillance was established in 1968 by the Crime Control and Safe Streets Act.
   a. It protects individual privacy the most.
   b. It bans the interception of "wire, oral, or electronic communications" while they're taking place.
   c. It contains a "serious crime" exception.
      (1) The application for the ban has to be approved by high official.
      (2) A judge has to approve it as well.

(3) The application includes:
   (a) A statement of the facts and circumstances
   (b) A statement about whether other investigative procedures have been tried and failed
   (c) A statement about the projected length of the interception
d. The Patriot Act adds terrorist crimes to the list of "serious crimes."

2. Tier 2: Surveillance of stored electronic communications allows government access to stored communications—voice mail and e-mail messages, not just telephone numbers and e-mail addresses.
   a. The Patriot Act significantly expands government electronic surveillance power.
   b. The surveillance applies to "any criminal investigation."
   c. There are two limits to the government's Tier 2 surveillance power:
      (1) Messages stored less than 6 months require a warrant and probable cause.
      (2) Messages stored more than 6 months require a warrant, but a 90-day delay in notifying the subscriber is allowed if the court determines notification "may have an adverse result."

3. Tier 3: Secret "caller ID" allows the government to access pen registers and trap and trace telephone numbers.
   a. It offers the least protection because it can be used to investigate any crime without court approval and without ever notifying subscribers.
   b. The government's power is broader than in Tier 2 but it invades individual privacy less.
   c. It requires the approval of a department superior.
   d. The Patriot Act:
      (1) Creates the power to seek a court order to retrieve e-mail headers, not messages
      (2) Applies the orders to "anywhere in the U.S.," not just the district where the order is approved
      (3) Requires the government to submit a report to the court showing
         (a) The name of the officer who installed and/or accessed the device
         (b) The date and time of the device installation, access, and disconnection
         (c) The device configuration and modification
         (d) Information captured

## IV. "Sneak and Peek" Searches
A. They're a variation of "no knock" entries. (Chapter 6)
B. They allow officers to enter private places without the owner consenting or knowing about the entry.
C. Until 9/11, they were used mainly in drug cases with court approval but no statute.
D. The Patriot Act included the use of sneak-and-peek warrants if the court finds reasonable cause to believe notification might have an "adverse effect."
   1. The warrant prohibits seizure of any property except where the court finds a reasonable necessity for seizure.
   2. The warrant provides for giving notice within a reasonable time of execution.

3. There's controversy over the Patriot Act provision.
   a. Those against it say it gives the government too much power.
   b. Those in favor say it reasonably balances government need and individual privacy in the fight against terrorism.

**V. Detaining Terrorist Suspects**

A. In ordinary times, even brief detentions are unreasonable Fourth Amendment seizures without an objective basis to back them up. (Chapters 4, 5, 12)

B. Balancing security and rights after 9/11 resulted in new official acts:
   1. Presidential Proclamation 7463 (September 14, 2001) declared a "national emergency."
   2. Congressional joint resolution "Authorization for Use of Military Force (September 14, 2001)" authorized military force to catch the 9/11 attackers and their supporters and to prevent future terrorist attacks.
   3. President Bush's Military Order of November 13, 2001, provided rules for detention, treatment, and trial of "certain non-citizens" in the "war against terrorism."
      a. Its broad definition of "non-citizens" includes any person who there's reason to believe:
         (1) Is a past or present al Qaeda member
         (2) Has acted in some connection with acts of international terrorism or
         (3) Has knowingly harbored one or more individuals described in 1 or 2
      b. The conditions of confinement and treatment of detainees should
         (1) Provide humane and nondiscriminatory treatment
         (2) Afford adequate food, water, shelter, clothing, and medical treatment
         (3) Allow free exercise of religion
      c. The Secretary of Defense may prescribe other conditions.

C. *Hamdi v. Rumsfeld* (2004) raised questions about detaining citizens after 9/11.
   1. The Court's decision affirms the government's right to detain citizens.
   2. The War on Terror isn't a "blank check."
      a. The government has no right to detain citizens indefinitely.
      b. Detained citizens have a right to challenge their detention.
      c. Detainees have a right to counsel. (Chapter 12)

**VI. Trials of Terrorist by Military Courts after 9/11**

A. Suspected terrorists can be tried either for crimes in ordinary (Article III) courts or for war crimes (acts during wartime that inflict "needless and disproportionate suffering and damages" in pursuit of a "military objective") by military commissions (courts).

B. Ordinary rules govern trials in Article III courts. (Chapters 10–14)

C. Special rules with fewer rights and more relaxed procedures and standards of proof govern military commissions.

D. According to the Military Order of November 13, 2001, the sources of military commission authority include:
   1. U.S. Constitution, Article II, Section 2, which:
      a. Makes the president commander-in-chief
      b. Makes the president responsible for trying terrorists

    c. Requires the president to "faithfully" execute the laws, which include (according to the president):
      (1) The Articles of War
      (2) The Authorization for Use of Military Force
  2. The Authorization for Use of Military Force, which authorized the president to use all necessary force against terrorists and their supporters
  3. The law of war (Geneva Conventions)
E. The jurisdiction of military commissions, according to the Military Order of November 13, 2001, applies only to noncitizens as defined in the order.
  1. Individuals subject to the order don't "necessarily enjoy the same constitutional rights as citizens."
  2. The order strips Article III courts of jurisdiction either to hear or review military commission cases (this may not survive constitutional challenges).
F. *Hamdan v. Rumsfeld* (2006) ruled on trial proceedings of suspected enemy-combatant detainees.
  1. They are governed by the
    a. Uniform Code of Military Justice (UCMJ)
    b. Law of war (Geneva Conventions, especially General Article 3)
  2. The Geneva Convention, General Article 3, says:
    a. Detainees have a right to be tried by a "regularly constituted court affording all the judicial guarantees which are recognized as indispensable by civilized peoples."
    b. They have a right to "all the judicial guarantees which are recognized as indispensable by civilized peoples."
  3. Common Article 3 obviously tolerates a great degree of flexibility in trying individuals captured during armed conflict.

## REVIEW QUESTIONS

1. Identify and describe two limits on government's emergency powers.

2. Summarize the history of criminal procedure in wartime.

3. Identify the difference between the responses to ordinary crime we've studied in previous chapters and the responses to domestic and international terrorism.

4. Describe how our study of antiterrorism laws is limited, and give two reasons for this limitation.

5. What requirement of a constitutional democracy are all federal antiterrorism procedure laws based on?

6. Describe both sides of the argument about the changes in the balance between power and liberty brought about by the September 11, 2001, attacks.

7. Identify three types of personal information not protected from electronic surveillance by the Fourth Amendment.

8. According to the U.S. Supreme Court, why aren't they protected?

9. Identify and describe the three tiers of the surveillance system designed to balance government power and individual privacy. Include in your description both government powers and the limits on that power in each tier.

10. How, if at all, has the Patriot Act modified this balance?

11. What were "sneak and peek" searches originally used for, and how has their legal status and definition changed since 9/11?

12. List and describe the three conditions under which the Patriot Act authorizes judges to issue sneak-and-peek warrants.

13. Summarize the two sides of the argument over sneak-and-peek warrants that followed passage of the Patriot Act.

14. Identify and describe the significance of the three sources that have affected the balance between security and rights in the detention of terrorist suspects since 9/11.

15. Explain the difference between how the Sixth Amendment right to counsel works in ordinary criminal cases and terrorist cases where the object isn't to prosecute suspects.

16. Identify and describe two sources for the right to counsel other than the Sixth Amendment.

17. Identify and describe the two kinds of proceedings for the trial of suspected terrorists.

18. Identify the sources of authority for the Military Order of November 13, 2001, and describe the jurisdiction of military commissions created by the order.

19. How do the constitutional requirements that apply to Article III (ordinary) criminal courts differ from those of military commissions?

20. List and summarize the major provisions in the Military Commissions Act of 2006. Sort them according to the power of the government and the rights of the accused. In your opinion, is the power balanced? Too much in favor of the accused? Too much in favor of the government? Explain your answer.

## KEY TERMS

laws of war, p. 500
intelligence, p. 501
pen registers, p. 502
trap and trace, p. 502
Crime Control and Safe Streets Act, p. 503
serious crime exception, p. 503
USA Patriot Act, p. 504
secret "caller ID," p. 504
libraries provision, p. 505

Foreign Intelligence Surveillance Act (FISA), p. 506
Foreign Intelligence Surveillance Court (FISC), p. 506
Terrorist Surveillance Program (TSP), p. 506
sneak-and-peek search warrants, p. 507
Presidential Proclamation 7463, p. 509

Authorization for Use of Military Force (AUMF), p. 509
Military Order of November 13, 2001, p. 509
Article III courts, p. 513
military commissions, p. 513
military tribunals, p. 513
war crimes, p. 513
courts-martial, p. 514

# APPENDIX
# Selected Amendments of the Constitution of the United States

## Amendment IV [1791]

The right of the people to be secure in their persons, houses, papers, and effects, against unreasonable searches and seizures, shall not be violated, and no Warrants shall issue, but upon probable cause, supported by Oath or affirmation, and particularly describing the place to be searched, and the persons or things to be seized.

## Amendment V [1791]

No person shall be held to answer for a capital, or otherwise infamous crime, unless on a presentment or indictment of a Grand Jury, except in cases arising in the land or naval forces, or in the Militia, when in actual service in time of War or public danger; nor shall any person be subject for the same offence to be twice put in jeopardy of life or limb; nor shall be compelled in any criminal case to be a witness against himself, nor be deprived of life, liberty, or property, without due process of law; nor shall private property be taken for public use, without just compensation.

## Amendment VI [1791]

In all criminal prosecutions, the accused shall enjoy the right to a speedy and public trial, by an impartial jury of the State and district wherein the crime shall have been committed, which district shall have been previously ascertained by law, and to be informed of the nature and cause of the accusation; to be confronted with the witnesses against him; to have compulsory process for obtaining witnesses in his favor, and to have the Assistance of Counsel for his defence.

## Amendment VIII [1791]

Excessive bail shall not be required, nor excessive fines imposed, nor cruel and unusual punishments inflicted.

## Amendment XIV [1868]

*Section 1* All persons born or naturalized in the United States, and subject to the jurisdiction thereof, are citizens of the United States and of the State wherein they reside. No State shall make or enforce any law which shall abridge the privileges or immunities of citizens of the United States; nor shall any State deprive any person of life, liberty, or property, without due process of law; nor deny to any person within its jurisdiction the equal protection of the laws.

*Section 2* Representatives shall be apportioned among the several States according to their respective numbers, counting the whole number of persons in each State, excluding Indians not taxed. But when the right to vote at any election for the choice of electors for President and Vice President of the United States, Representatives in Congress, the Executive and Judicial officers of a State, or the members of the Legislature thereof, is denied to any of the male inhabitants of such State, being twenty-one years of age, and citizens of the United States, or in any way abridged, except for participation in rebellion, or other crime, the basis of representation therein shall be reduced in the proportion which the number of such male citizens shall bear to the whole number of male citizens twenty-one years of age in such State.

***Section 3*** No person shall be a Senator or Representative in Congress, or elector of President and Vice-President, or hold any office, civil or military, under the United States, or under any State, who having previously taken an oath, as a member of Congress, or as an officer of the United States, or as a member of any State legislature, or as an executive or judicial officer of any State, to support the Constitution of the United States, shall have engaged in insurrection or rebellion against the same, or given aid or comfort to the enemies thereof. But Congress may by a vote of two thirds of each House, remove such disability.

***Section 4*** The validity of the public debt of the United States, authorized by law, including debts incurred for payment of pensions and bounties for services in suppressing insurrection or rebellion, shall not be questioned. But neither the United States nor any State shall assume or pay any debt or obligation incurred in aid of insurrection or rebellion against the United States, or any claim for the loss or emancipation of any slave; but all such debts, obligations and claims shall be held illegal and void.

***Section 5*** The Congress shall have power to enforce, by appropriate legislation, the provisions of this article.

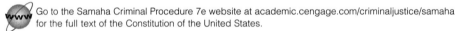

Go to the Samaha Criminal Procedure 7e website at academic.cengage.com/criminaljustice/samaha for the full text of the Constitution of the United States.

# Glossary

**absolute immunity** the absence of liability for actions within the scope of duties; judges have it.

**abuse-of-the-writ rule** habeas corpus petitioners must demonstrate that they neither deliberately nor negligently failed to raise an issue in a prior habeas petition.

**accusatory stage of the criminal process** the point at which the criminal process focuses on a specific suspect.

**accusatory system rationale** a system in which the government bears the burden of proof.

**acquisition of memory** information the brain takes in at the time of the crime.

**actual authority (objective) third-party consent** third-party consent searches aren't valid unless the person consenting had actual authority to consent for another person.

**actual prejudice test** courts have to decide whether jurors were in fact prejudiced by harmful publicity.

**actual seizures** when officers physically grab individuals with the intent to keep them from leaving.

**administrative sentencing model** a sentencing structure in which parole boards and prison administrators determine the exact release date within sentences prescribed by legislatures and judges.

**affidavit** a sworn statement under oath to the facts and circumstances amounting to probable cause.

**affirmative defense** a defense, such as self-defense or insanity, that requires defendants to present facts that support their innocence in addition to denying the charge.

**affirmed** an appellate court decision upholding the decision of a lower court.

**amicus curiae brief** brief filed in court by someone interested in, but not a party to, the case.

**apparent authority (subjective) third-party consent** individuals who it's reasonable to believe (but in fact don't) have authority to consent to a search.

**appellant** the party appealing in an appellate court case.

**appellate court case** case in which a lower court has already taken some action and one of the parties has asked a higher court to review the lower court's action.

**appellee** the party appealed against in an appellate court case.

**appointed counsel** lawyers for people who can't afford to hire lawyers.

***Apprendi* bright-line rule** other than a prior conviction, any fact that increases the penalty for a crime beyond the prescribed statutory maximum must be submitted to a jury, and proved beyond a reasonable doubt.

**arraignment** to bring defendants to court to answer the criminal charges against them.

**arrest** officers took suspects to the police station and kept them there against their will.

**Article III courts** regular federal courts whose authority comes from Article III of the U.S. Constitution, which created the judiciary.

**articulable facts** facts officers can name to back up their stops of citizens.

**attenuation exception** illegally seized evidence is admissible in court if the poisonous connection between illegal police actions and the evidence they illegally got from their actions weakens enough.

**Authorization for Use of Military Force (AUMF)** joint resolution of Congress passed following the September 11 attacks, supporting the president's war power to use "all necessary and appropriate force."

**"bad methods"** using unconstitutional means to obtain evidence.

**Bail Reform Act of 1984** authorizes federal courts to jail arrested defendants when a judge determines, after a hearing, that no condition of release would "reasonably" guarantee the appearance of the defendant and the safety of the community.

**balancing element** the need to search and/or seize outweighs the invasion of individual liberty and/or privacy.

**bench trial** trials without juries, in which judges find the facts.

**bind over** to decide to send a case to trial.

**bind-over standard** enough evidence exists for the judge in a preliminary hearing to decide to send the case to trial.

**blind administrator** a person conducting a lineup who doesn't know which person in the lineup is the suspect.

**blue curtain** wall of protection that hides "real" police work from public view.

**border search exception** searches at international borders are reasonable without probable cause or warrants, because the government interest in what and who enters the country outweighs the invasion of privacy of persons entering.

**bright-line rule** rule that spells out officers' power and applies to all cases rather than assessing the totality of circumstances on a case-by-case basis.

**broad interpretation (of habeas corpus)** view that courts should review all claims that persons are being detained in violation of their fundamental liberties.

**case-by-case basis** deciding whether constitutional requirements were satisfied in each case.

**categorical suspicion** refers to suspicion that falls on suspects because they fit into a broad category of people, such as being in a particular location, being members of a particular race or ethnicity, or fitting a profile.

**cause-and-prejudice rule** permits but doesn't require courts to deny habeas petitions if defendants fail to show cause and prejudice; petitioners must show they didn't deliberately or negligently fail to raise issues and that the prejudice probably changed the outcome of their trials.

**certiorari** Latin for "to be certified," it's a discretionary order of the Supreme Court to review a lower court decision.

**challenges for cause** removal of prospective jurors upon showing their partiality.

**charge the grand jury** the address of the judge to the grand jury.

**citation** tells where you can find the published report of a case.

**civil action** a noncriminal case.

**Civil Rights Act actions** lawsuits initiated by private individuals in federal court against state officers for violating the individuals' constitutional rights; also called § 1983 actions.

**class action** an action in which one person or a small group of people represent the interests of a larger group.

**collateral attack** a proceeding to review the constitutionality of detention or imprisonment.

**collateral consequences exception** the principle that cases aren't moot if conviction can still cause legal consequences despite completion of the sentence.

**collateral proceedings** proceedings "off to the side" of the main case (for example, grand jury proceedings and bail hearings).

**compulsory process** Sixth Amendment guarantee of defendants' right to compel the appearance of witnesses in their favor.

**concurring opinion** statements in which justices agree with the decision but not the reasoning of a court's opinion.

**consent searches** searches the government can prove by the totality of the circumstances suspects consented to don't require probable cause or warrants.

**constitutional democracy** the balance between the power of government and the rights of individuals.

**constitutionalism** refers to the idea that constitutions adopted by the whole people are a higher form of law than ordinary laws passed by legislatures.

**constitutional right justification** the idea that the exclusionary rule is an essential part of constitutional rights.

**constitutional tort (*Bivens*) actions** lawsuits against individual federal law enforcement officers.

**conventional Fourth Amendment approach** the warrant and reasonableness clauses are firmly connected, according to the U.S. Supreme Court when ruling on stop-and-frisk law cases.

**counsel pro bono** lawyers willing to represent clients at no charge.

**court judgment (decision)** how the court disposes of the case.

**court opinions** written explanation for a court's decision.

**courts-martial** military courts made up of military officers to try members of the U.S. armed forces for violating the Uniform Code of Military Justice.

**Crime Control and Safe Streets Act** provides for a general ban on the interception of "wire, oral, or electronic communications" while they're taking place.

**criminal complaint** the formal charging document.

**critical stages in criminal prosecutions** includes all those stages that occur after the government files formal charges; the view that custodial interrogation is so important in criminal prosecutions that during it suspects have a right to a lawyer.

**curtilage** the area immediately surrounding a house that's not part of the open fields doctrine.

**custodial arrest** an official taking a person into custody and holding her to answer criminal charges.

**custodial interrogation** the questioning that occurs after the police have taken suspects into custody.

**custody** depriving people of their "freedom of action in any significant way."

**damages** a remedy in private lawsuits in the form of money for injuries.

**deadly force** constraint capable of producing death.

**death-qualified jury** jurors who aren't opposed to the death penalty.

**decision to charge** the prosecutor's decision to begin formal proceedings against a suspect.

**defense of entrapment** defense to criminal liability based on proof that the government induced the defendant to commit a crime she wouldn't have otherwise committed.

**defense of official immunity** a public official charged by law with duties calling for discretionary decision making isn't personally liable to an individual except for willful or malicious wrongdoing.

**defense of vicarious official immunity** police departments and local governments can claim the official immunity of their employees.

**"deliberately eliciting a response" standard** the test for interrogation focuses on police intent.

**determinate sentencing** see *fixed sentencing.*

**deterrence justification** the justification that excluding evidence obtained in violation of the Constitution prevents illegal law enforcement.

**direct attacks** appeals attacking directly decisions made by trial courts.

**directed verdict rule** enough evidence exists to decide a case without submitting it to the jury.

**direct information** information that officers know firsthand, acquired directly through their physical senses.

**discretionary appeal** allowing appeals only in cases the U.S. Supreme Court or the state supreme courts decide are of significance beyond the interests of the particular defendants appealing them.

**discretionary decision making** informal decision making by professionals based on their training and experience and unwritten rules.

**discriminatory effect** proving that race or some other illegal group characteristic (not a legitimate criterion, such as seriousness of the offense or criminal record) accounts for the official decision.

**discriminatory purpose** a named official in the case at hand intended to discriminate against a named individual because of race or other illegal criteria.

**dismissal without prejudice** the termination of a case with the provision that it can be prosecuted again.

**dismissal with prejudice** the termination of a case with the provision that it can't be prosecuted again.

**dissenting opinion** part of an appellate court case in which justices write opinions disagreeing with the decision and reasoning of a court.

**distinguishing cases** a court decides that a prior decision doesn't apply to the current case because the facts are different.

**diversion cases** prosecutors agree to drop a case before formal judicial proceedings begin if suspects participate in specified programs (for example, community service, restitution, substance abuse, or family violence treatment).

**DNA** deoxyribonucleic acid is a long, double-stranded molecule found in everyone's chromosomes that can potentially identify suspects or absolutely exclude individuals as suspects in cases where perpetrators have left DNA at the scene of a crime or where victims have left DNA on items traceable to perpetrators.

**DNA fingerprinting** the most widely used DNA test, in which long sections of DNA are broken into fragments to measure and compare the lengths of selected strands of DNA in chromosomes; also called "DNA profiling."

**DNA profiling** a special type of DNA pattern that distinguishes one individual from all others.

**doctrine of judicial economy** rule that says that time and money shouldn't be spent on appeals defendants could've avoided by objecting during the trial.

**doctrine of *respondeat superior*** employers are legally liable for their employees' illegal acts.

**doctrine of sovereign immunity** governments can't be sued by individuals without the consent of the government.

**double jeopardy** constitutional protection against being subject to liability for the same offense more than once.

**drug courier profile** lists of characteristics that drug traffickers are supposed to possess.

**dual sovereignty doctrine** the principle that holds that a crime arising out of the same facts in one state isn't the same crime in another state.

**due process** a broad and vague guarantee of fair procedures in deciding cases; the Fifth and Fourteenth Amendment provisions prohibiting the federal government and the states, respectively, from depriving citizens of life, liberty, or property without due process of law.

**due process approach to confessions** confessions must be voluntary; involuntary confessions violate due process, not because they're compelled but because they might not be true.

**due process revolution** U.S. Supreme Court application of the Bill of Rights to state criminal proceedings.

**en banc** see *en banc review*.

**en banc review** a hearing by all the judges on the Court.

**equal protection** state officials can't investigate, apprehend, convict, and punish people for unacceptable reasons.

**exclusionary rule** the rule that illegally seized evidence can't be admitted in criminal trials.

**exhaustion-of-remedies rule** when a state prisoner files a petition containing any claim for which a state remedy remains available, the court has to dismiss the petition.

**exigent circumstances** circumstances requiring prompt action, which eliminates the warrant requirement for a search.

**express waiver test** the suspect specifically says or writes that she knows her rights, knows she's giving them up, and knows the consequences of giving them up.

**external civilian review** review of complaints against police officers with participation by individuals who aren't sworn police officers.

**factually innocent** defendants who didn't commit the crime.

***Federal Rules of Evidence* standard** the test of admissibility of DNA testing by considering whether the relevancy of the evidence outweighs the tendency of the evidence to unfairly prejudice jurors against the defendant.

**Federal Tort Claims Act (FTCA) actions** lawsuits against the federal government for their officers' constitutional torts.

**first appearance** the appearance of a defendant in court for determination of probable cause, determination of bail, assignment of an attorney, and notification of rights; also called a "probable cause hearing."

**fixed (determinate) sentencing** sentences that fit the punishment to the crime.

**Foreign Intelligence Surveillance Act (FISA)** FISA authorizes a secret court (FISC), made up of judges on the U.S. Courts of Appeals, to issue eavesdropping warrants whenever the U.S. Attorney General certifies that the purpose of the surveillance is to acquire *foreign* intelligence information.

**Foreign Intelligence Surveillance Court (FISC)** secret court created by FISA, and made up of judges on the U.S. Courts of Appeals, to issue eavesdropping warrants whenever the U.S. Attorney General certifies that the purpose of the surveillance is to acquire *foreign* intelligence information.

**Fourth Amendment frisks** once-over-lightly pat downs of outer clothing by officers to protect themselves by taking away suspects' weapons.

**Fourth Amendment stops** brief, on-the-spot detentions that freeze suspicious situations so that law enforcement officers can determine whether to arrest, investigate further, or terminate further action.

**free will rationale** involuntary confessions aren't just unreliable and contrary to the accusatory system of justice; they're also coerced if they're not "the product of a rational intellect and a free will."

**fruit-of-the-poisonous-tree doctrine** the principle that evidence derived from illegally obtained sources isn't admissible.

***Frye* plus standard** the test of DNA admissibility that requires showing not only general acceptance of DNA theory but also that "the testing laboratory in the particular case performed the accepted scientific techniques in analyzing forensic samples."

***Frye* standard** the rule that DNA evidence is admissible if the technique is "sufficiently established to have gained general acceptance in the particular field in which it belongs."

**"functional equivalent of a question" test** interrogation refers not only to express questioning but also to any words or actions that the police should know are reasonably likely to elicit an incriminating response from the suspect.

**functional immunity** whether prosecutors have immunity depends on the function they're performing at the time of their misconduct.

**fundamental fairness doctrine** due process is a command to the states to provide two basics of a fair trial: notice and a hearing.

**"good" evidence** probative evidence, or proof of guilt.

**"good faith" defense** officers can't be held personally liable for their actions if they acted according to rules clearly established at the time of their actions; also called "qualified immunity."

**government's case-in-chief** the part of the trial where the government presents its evidence to prove the defendants' guilt.

**grabbable area** the arrestee's person and area within his reach.

**graduated objective basis requirement** the greater the government invasion, the more facts required to back it up.

**grand jurors** members of the grand jury.

**grand jury review** a secret proceeding to test a government case.

**habeas corpus** Latin for "you have the body," it's an action that asks those who hold defendants to justify their detention.

**habeas corpus proceedings** civil action, also called "collateral attack," brought by defendants attacking the lawfulness of their detention.

**hands-off approach to sentencing procedures** U.S. Supreme Court policy of leaving how sentences were determined to trial judges.

**hearsay information** facts and circumstances officers learn secondhand from victims, witnesses, other police officers, and anonymous, professional, or paid informants.

**hearsay rule** courts don't admit secondhand evidence to prove guilt, but, if it's reliable and truthful, they'll accept it to show probable cause to arrest.

**hearsay testimony** evidence not coming from the personal knowledge of witnesses but from repeating what they have heard others say.

**hot pursuit** the exigent circumstance constituting the need to apprehend a fleeing suspect.

**hung jury** a jury that's unable to reach a verdict after protracted deliberations.

**impeach** to show that a witness's credibility is suspect.

**implied waiver test** the totality of circumstances in each case adds up to proof that before suspects talked they knew they had the right to remain silent and knew they were giving up the right.

**incorporation doctrine** the principle that the Fourteenth Amendment due process clause incorporates the provisions of the Bill of Rights and applies them to state criminal procedure.

**independent source exception** evidence is admissible even if police officers violate the Constitution to obtain it if then in a totally separate action, they lawfully get the same evidence.

**indeterminate sentencing** tailoring punishment to suit the criminal; sentencing that relies heavily on the discretion of judges and parole boards in exercising sentencing authority.

**indictment** a formal criminal charge issued by a grand jury.

**indigent defendants** defendants too poor to hire their own lawyers.

**individualized suspicion** suspicion that points to specific individuals and consists of "facts that would tell both the officer on the street and a court ruling on a suppression motion whether or not there was reasonable suspicion."

**inevitable discovery exception** evidence illegally obtained is admissible if officers would've legally discovered it eventually.

**information** prosecutors charge defendants directly without needing a grand jury indictment.

**inherently coercive** custodial interrogation is coercive because police hold suspects in strange surroundings while trying to crack their will, and suspects don't have anyone there to support them.

***in loco parentis*** the principle by which the government stands in place of parents; school administrators are substitute parents while students are in school and have the legal authority to search students and their stuff during school hours and activities.

**intelligence** gathering all kinds of information (not just criminal evidence) about enemies.

**internal affairs units (IAU)** review of police misconduct by special officers inside police departments.

**interrogation** police questioning suspects while holding them against their will, usually in a police station but sometimes in other places; has constitutional significance in the Fourth, Fifth, and Fourteenth Amendments; in each eliciting a response from a suspect can invoke rights under the amendment.

**inventory searches** searches conducted without probable cause or warrants to protect property and the safety of police and to prevent claims against police.

**judgment** the final outcome of a case.

**judicial integrity justification** the idea that the honor and honesty of the courts justify the exclusionary rule.

**judicial review** courts, and ultimately the U.S. Supreme Court, *not* the Congress and *not* the president, have the final word on what the Constitution means.

**judicial sentencing model** a structure in which judges prescribe sentences within broad contours set by legislative acts.

**jurisdiction** the power to hear and decide cases in a specific geographical area (such as a county, a state, or a federal district) or the subject matter (for example, criminal appeals) the court controls.

**jury instructions** instructions from the judge to the jury on what the law is and how they should apply it.

**jury nullification** the jury's authority to reach a not guilty verdict despite proof of guilt.

**jury panel** potential jurors drawn from the list of eligible citizens not excused.

**key-man system** jury lists are made up by civic and political leaders selected from individuals they know personally or by reputation.

**knock-and-announce rule** the practice of law enforcement officers knocking and announcing their presence before entering a home to search it.

**laws of war** rules written, understood, and agreed to by almost all the countries fighting the wars.

**legally guilty** cases in which the government has proved beyond a reasonable doubt the guilt of defendants.

**legislative sentencing model** a structure in which legislatures exercise sentencing authority.

**liberty** the right of citizens to come and go as they please (locomotion) without government interference.

**libraries provision** provision of the Patriot Act that authorizes the FBI to demand books, papers, records, and other items from individuals and organizations.

**lineup** an identification procedure in which the suspect stands in a line with other individuals.

**majority opinion** a decision rendered by five or more Supreme Court justices, which becomes the law.

**mandatory minimum sentences** the legislatively prescribed, nondiscretionary amount of prison time that all offenders convicted of the offense must serve.

**manifest necessity doctrine (in double jeopardy)** the government can reprosecute a defendant for the same offense if the judge dismissed the case or ordered a mistrial because dismissal "served the ends of justice."

**might-or-might-not-be-present instruction** one of the ways to improve the reliability of eyewitness identification of strangers is to tell witnesses the suspect might or might not be among the photos or members of a lineup.

**military commissions** non–Article III courts, consisting of a panel of military officers acting under military authority to try enemy-combatants for war crimes.

**Military Order of November 13, 2001** president's order defining who could be detained following September 11, 2001, and prescribing the conditions of their detention.

**military tribunal** see *military commissions.*

**mockery of justice standard** the standard under which counsel is deemed ineffective only if circumstances reduced the trial to a farce.

***Model Code of Pre-Arraignment Procedure*** American Law Institute's (group of distinguished judges, lawyers, criminal justice professionals, law enforcement professionals, and scholars) model of criminal procedure law in federal court cases.

**mootness doctrine** ban on appeals by offenders who have finished their prison sentences or paid their fines.

**moral seriousness standard** the principle that the Sixth Amendment right to a jury trial extends to morally serious misdemeanors.

**motion for discovery** a legal action asking for a court order to compel one side to turn over information that might help the other side.

**narrow interpretation (of habeas corpus)** power to review only the jurisdiction of the court over the person and the subject matter of the case.

**negotiated guilty plea** a plea of guilty in exchange for a concession to the defendant by the government.

**no-affirmative-duty-to-protect rule** plaintiffs can't sue individual officers or government units for failing to stop private people from violating their rights.

**nonsearch-related plain view** refers to plain view that doesn't involve a Fourth Amendment intrusion at all.

**objective basis** the factual justification for government invasions of individual privacy, liberty, and property.

**objective basis requirement** facts, not hunches, have to back up government invasions of individual liberty and privacy.

**objective privacy** whether the subjective expectation of privacy is "one that society is prepared to recognize as 'reasonable.'"

**objective standard of reasonable force** the Fourth Amendment permits officers to use the amount of force necessary to apprehend and bring suspects under control.

**objective test of entrapment** focuses on whether the actions of government agents would induce a hypothetical reasonable person to commit crimes.

**open fields doctrine** the rule that the Fourth Amendment doesn't prevent government officials from gathering and using information they see, hear, smell, or touch in open fields.

**opening statements** addresses to the jury by the prosecution and defense counsel before they present their evidence.

**parallel rights** state-granted rights similar to those in the U.S. Constitution and Bill of Rights.

**particularity requirement** the requirement that a warrant must identify the person or place to be searched and the items or persons to be seized.

**pen register** telephone company lists of the phone numbers of outgoing calls from a particular telephone number.

**peremptory challenges** removals of jurors without showing cause.

**per se approach** looking at the totality of circumstances to determine whether an identification should be admitted into evidence.

**petitioner** a defendant in a noncriminal case who asks a higher court to review a decision made either by a lower court or some other official.

**photo array** witnesses try to pick the suspect from one (photo show-up) or several (photo lineup) mug shots.

**plain-error rule** review of convictions should take place only when "plain errors affecting substantial rights" cause "manifest injustice or miscarriage of justice."

**plaintiffs** the party who brings a civil action.

**plain view doctrine** doctrine that it's not a "search" to discover evidence inadvertently obtained through ordinary senses if the officers are where they have a right to be and are doing what they have a right to do.

**plurality opinion** a statement in which the greatest number, but not a majority, of the justices favor a court's decision.

**precedent** a prior decision that's binding on a similar present case.

**prejudice prong** the second of a two-prong test of reasonable competence, in which defendants have to show that bad "lawyering" deprived them of a fair trial with a reliable result.

**preliminary hearing** the adversary proceeding that tests the government's case.

**preponderance of the evidence** more evidence than not supports a conclusion.

**Presidential Proclamation 7463** proclamation declaring a national emergency by reason of the terrorist attacks of September 11, 2001.

**presumption of guilt** the reduction of rights of convicted offenders during sentencing, appeal, and habeas corpus processes.

**presumption of regularity** presumes government actions are lawful in the absence of "clear evidence to the contrary."

**pretext arrests** arrests made only for the purpose of conducting a search there's no probable cause to search for.

**pretrial motions** written or oral requests asking the court to decide questions that don't require a trial to be ruled on.

**preventive detention** confining defendants to jail before conviction because they're a threat to public safety.

**prima facie case rule** enough evidence exists to make a decision unless the evidence is contradicted.

**privacy** the value that's sometimes referred to as "the right to be let alone from government invasions."

**privacy doctrine** the doctrine that holds that the Fourth Amendment protects persons, not places, when persons have an expectation of privacy that society is prepared to recognize.

**probable cause to arrest** requires that an officer, in the light of her training and experience, knows enough facts and circumstances to reasonably believe that a crime has been, is being, or is about to be committed and the person arrested has committed, is committing, or is about to commit the crime.

**probable cause to detain suspects** the objective basis for detaining a suspect following arrest.

**probable cause to go to trial** requires a higher objective basis than probable cause to detain and is tested by a preliminary hearing or grand jury review.

**probative evidence** evidence that proves (or at least helps to prove) defendants committed the crimes they're charged with.

**procedural due process** guarantee of fair procedures for deciding cases.

**procedural history** a brief description of the procedural steps and judgments (decisions) made by each court that has heard the case.

**prophylatic rule** mechanisms that aren't themselves constitutional rights but are used to guarantee those rights.

**proportionality principle** a punishment is cruel and unusual if its harshness is "grossly disproportionate" to the "gravity of the offense."

**public defenders** permanently employed defense lawyers paid for at public expense.

**public safety exception** the rule that *Miranda* warnings need not be administered if doing so would endanger the public.

**qualified immunity** grants immunity from tort actions if the party was acting reasonably within the scope of his or her duties; also called the "good faith" defense.

**quantum of proof** the amount of evidence backing up a government invasion.

**raise-or-waive doctrine** the rule that defendants must raise and preserve objections to errors at trial or waive their right to appeal the errors.

**reasonable doubt standard** due process requires both federal and state prosecutors to prove every element of a crime beyond a reasonable doubt.

**reasonable, good-faith exception** searches conducted by officers with warrants they honestly and reasonably believe satisfy the Fourth Amendment requirements.

**reasonable-likelihood-of-prejudice test** the determination that circumstances may prevent a fair trial.

**reasonable manner of arrest requirement** to satisfy the Fourth Amendment, arrests have to be executed in a way that's reasonable.

**reasonableness clause** the clause in the Fourth Amendment that bans "unreasonable searches and seizures" as opposed to the "warrant clause," which outlines the requirements for obtaining arrest and search warrants.

**reasonableness Fourth Amendment approach** the warrant and the reasonableness parts of the Fourth Amendment are separate elements that address separate problems.

**reasonableness prong** defendants have to prove that their lawyer's performance wasn't reasonably competent, meaning that the lawyer was so deficient that she "was not functioning as the 'counsel' guaranteed the defendant by the Sixth Amendment."

**reasonableness test (Fourth Amendment)** the reasonableness of searches and seizures depends on balancing government and individual interests and the objective basis of the searches and seizures.

**"reasonable person would not feel free to leave" definition of seizure** standard used by most courts to determine whether a person was "seized" by law enforcement.

**reasonable suspicion** the totality of articulable facts and circumstances that would lead an officer, in the light of her training and experience, to *suspect* that crime *may* be afoot.

**reasonably competent attorney standard** performance measured by customary skills and diligence.

**recall** information retrieved from memory at the time of the lineup, show-up, or picture identification; eyewitnesses are given hints, such as a time frame, and then asked to report what they observed.

**recognition** information retrieved from memory at the time of the lineup, show-up, or picture identification; eyewitnesses are shown persons or objects and then asked to indicate whether they were involved in the crime.

**release on recognizance (ROR)** release from custody on a mere promise to appear.

**reliability rationale for due process** the justification for reviewing state confessions based on their untrustworthiness.

**remanded** the appellate court sent the case back to the lower court for further action.

**res judicata** once a matter is decided it cannot be reopened.

**retained counsel** a lawyer paid for by the client.

**retention of memory** information the brain stores between the time of the crime and the lineup, show-up, or picture identification.

**retrieval of memory** information retrieved from memory at the time of the lineup, show-up, or picture identification.

**reversed** the appellate court set aside, or nullified, the lower court's judgment.

**reversible error** an error that requires an appellate court to reverse the trial court's judgment in the case.

**right of habeas corpus** the right to a civil action to determine if the offender is being lawfully detained.

**right-to-counsel approach** relies on the clause in the Sixth Amendment that guarantees the right to a lawyer in "all criminal prosecutions."

*Robinson* **rule (searches incident to arrest)** bright-line rule that officers can always search anyone they're authorized to take into custody.

**routine-procedure limit** inventory searches are reasonable if officers follow department guidelines in conducting them.

**rule of four** the requirement that four Supreme Court justices must vote to review a case for its appeal to be heard by the Supreme Court.

**searches incident to arrest** a search made of a lawfully arrested suspect without probable cause or warrant.

**search-related plain view** refers to items in plain view that officers discover while they're searching for items for which they're specifically authorized to search.

**secret "caller ID"** the power of government to capture a record of all telephone *numbers* (not *conversations*) from a subscriber's phone in the investigation of "any crime."

**§ 1983 actions** lawsuits brought by private individuals against law enforcement officers under § 1983 of the U.S. Civil Rights Act.

**sentencing guidelines** a narrow range of penalties established by a commission within which judges are supposed to choose a specific sentence.

**sequential presentation** present members of a lineup one at a time and require witnesses to answer yes/no as they're presented.

**serious crime exception** provides for an exception for serious crimes to the Crime Control and Safe Streets Act's general ban on the interception of "wire, oral, or electronic communications" while they're taking place.

**show-of-authority seizures** submissions to the display of official force.

**show-up** a procedure in which the witness identifies the suspect without other possible suspects present.

**simultaneous presentation** a traditional lineup, in which members are standing together at the same time, giving witnesses the opportunity to treat the procedure like a multiple-choice test with a "best," but maybe not "right," answer.

**Sixth Amendment confrontation clause** the right to cross-examine the prosecution's witnesses.

**sneak-and-peek search warrants** warrants that allow officers to enter private places without the owner or (occupant) consenting or knowing about it.

**special-needs searches** government inspections and other regulatory measures not conducted to gather criminal evidence.

**special-relationship exception** (to the no-affirmative-duty-to-protect rule) governments have a duty to protect individuals they hold in custody.

**stare decisis** the doctrine in which a prior decision binds a present case with similar facts.

**state-created-danger exception** (to the no-affirmative-duty-to-protect rule) the officer's actions created a special danger of violent harm to the plaintiff in the lawsuit; the officer knows or should have known her actions would encourage this plaintiff to rely on her actions; and the danger created by the officer's actions caused either harm or vulnerability to harm.

**statutory right to appeal** nonconstitutional right to appeal a criminal conviction.

**stops** see *First Amendment stops.*

**straight guilty pleas** plea of guilty not based on negotiation, usually when the proof of guilt is overwhelming.

**subjective privacy** whether a "person exhibited an actual [personal] expectation of privacy."

**subjective test of entrapment** the test of entrapment that focuses on whether defendants had the predisposition to commit the crimes.

**suggestion** (in eyewitness identification) interpretation of events shaped by other people's suggestions.

**summary judgment** a motion that the court enter a judgment without a trial because there's not enough evidence to support the plaintiff's claim.

**supervisory power** the power of the U.S. Supreme Court to make rules to manage how lower federal courts conduct their business.

**Terrorist Surveillance Program (TSP)** domestic spying operation.

**testimony** the content of what you say and write against yourself.

**thermal imagers** devices that detect, measure, and record infrared radiation not visible to the naked eye.

**third-party consent searches** one person can consent for another person to a search.

**torts** civil lawsuits for damages over private wrongs.

**totality-of-circumstances approach** weighing all the facts surrounding the government's establishing identification of the suspect to determine if it's reliable enough to be admitted; also called the "per se approach."

**totality-of-circumstances test** the conditions used to determine both the voluntariness of a waiver of rights and of incriminating statements.

**totality-of-facts-and-circumstances test** usually called the "totality-of-circumstances test," it's a favorite standard the Court applies to decide whether official actions are constitutional.

**trap and trace** telephone company lists of the phone numbers of incoming calls to a particular phone number.

**trespass doctrine** the Fourth Amendment doctrine that requires physical intrusions into a "constitutionally protected area" to qualify as a search.

**true bill** the record of the number of grand jurors voting for indictment.

**two-pronged effective counsel test** U.S. Supreme Court test of "effectiveness of counsel," which requires the defense to prove a lawyer's performance wasn't reasonably competent and that the incompetence affected the outcome of the case in favor of conviction.

**unequivocal acts or statements withdrawal of consent rule** people can withdraw their consent, but it must be with actions or statements that are unambiguously clear.

**unnecessarily and impermissibly suggestive** one of the requirements a defendant must prove to have a lineup, show-up, or photo array identification thrown out on due process grounds.

**USA Patriot Act** short for Uniting and Strengthening America by Providing Appropriate Tools Required to Intercept and Obstruct Terrorism, the bill was passed after 9/11 to give the government more powers.

**vehicle exception** exception to the Fourth Amendment that says that if officers have probable cause to believe that a vehicle contains that which by law is subject to seizure, then search and seizure are valid.

**very substantial likelihood of misidentification** one of two requirements to have identification evidence thrown out based on due process grounds; the totality of circumstances must prove that "unnecessarily and impermissibly suggestive" procedures probably led to a misidentification.

**voir dire** the examination of prospective jurors.

**voluntariness test of consent searches** a test in which the totality of circumstances is used to determine whether a consent to search was obtained without coercion, deception, or promises.

**war crimes** crimes committed during wartime that inflict "needless and disproportionate suffering and damages" in pursuit of a "military objective."

**warrant clause** the part of the Fourth Amendment that outlines the requirements for obtaining arrest and search warrants.

**whole picture test** looking at all the facts and circumstances in each case to determine the constitutionality of government actions.

***Witherspoon*-excludables** potential jurors opposed to the death penalty.

**writ of certiorari** discretionary proceeding to review a lower court decision.

# Bibliography

*Abel v. U.S.* 1960. 362 U.S. 217.

*Adams v. Williams.* 1972. 407 U.S. 143.

*Adamson v. California.* 1947. 332 U.S. 46.

*Agnello v. U.S.* 1925. 269 U.S. 20.

*Alabama v. White.* 1990. 496 U.S. 325.

Allen, Francis A. 1978. "The Law as a Path to the World." *Michigan Law Review* 77.

Allen, Ronald J., Joseph L. Hoffman, Debra A. Livingston, and William J. Stuntz. 2005. *Comprehensive Criminal Procedure.* New York: Aspen Publishers.

*Allison v. State.* 1974. 214 N.W.2d 437 (Wisc.).

American Bar Association. 1980. *Standards for Criminal Justice.* 2nd ed. Chicago: ABA.

———. 1988. *Criminal Justice in Crisis.* Chicago: ABA.

American Law Institute. 1975. *Model Code of Pre-Arraignment Procedure.* Philadelphia: ALI.

Amsterdam, Anthony. 1970. "The Supreme Court and the Rights of Suspects in Criminal Cases." *New York University Law Review* 45:785.

———. 1974. "Perspectives on the Fourth Amendment." *Minnesota Law Review* 58:430.

*Anderson v. Creighton.* 1987. 483 U.S. 635.

*Annals of Congress.* 1789. House of Representatives, 1st Cong., 1st sess. http://lcweb2.loc.gov/cgi-bin/ampage?collId=llac&fileName=001/llac001.db&recNum=51.

*Apodaca v. Oregon.* 1972. 406 U.S. 404.

*Apprendi v. New Jersey.* 2000. 530 U.S. 466.

*Argersinger v. Hamlin.* 1972. 407 U.S. 25.

*Arizona v. Evans.* 1995. 514 U.S. 1.

Ashcroft, John. 2002 (May 30). *The Attorney General's Guidelines on General Crimes, Racketeering Enterprise and Terrorism Enterprise Investigations.* Washington, D.C.: U.S. Department of Justice.

Ashdown, Sue. 1983. "Good Faith, the Exclusionary Remedy, and Rule-Oriented Adjudication in the Criminal Process." *William and Mary Law Review* 24:335.

*Atkins v. Virginia.* 2002. 536 U.S. 304.

*Atwater v. City of Lago Vista.* 2001. 532 U.S. 318.

Avalon Project at the Yale Law School. 2003. *The Laws of War.* http://www.yale.edu/lawweb/avalon/lawofwar/lawwar.htm.

Baldus, David C., and George Woodworth. 1998. "Race Discrimination and the Death Penalty: An Empirical and Legal Overview." In James R. Acker, Robert S. Bohm, and Charles S. Lanier, eds., *America's Experiment with Capital Punishment.* Durham, N.C.: Carolina Academic Press.

*Baldwin v. New York.* 1970. 399 U.S. 66.

*Ballew v. Georgia.* 1978. 435 U.S. 223.

*Barnes v. State.* 1975. 520 S.W.2d 401 (Tex.Crim.App.).

*Barron v. Baltimore.* 1833. 32 U.S. (7 Pet.) 243.

Bazelon, David. 1973. "Defective Assistance of Counsel." *University of Cincinnati Law Review* 42:1.

*Bell v. Irwin.* 2003. 321 F.3d 637 (CA7).

*Bell v. Wolfish.* 1979. 441 U.S. 520.

*Berkemer v. McCarty.* 1984. 468 U.S. 420.

Berman, Douglas A., and Stephanos Bibas. 2006. "Making Sentences Sensible." *Ohio State Journal of Criminal Law* 4:37.

*Betts v. Brady.* 1942. 316 U.S. 455.

*Bivens v. Six Unnamed FBI Agents.* 1971. 403 U.S. 388.

*Blackledge v. Allison.* 1977. 431 U.S. 63.

Blumstein, Alfred et al. 1983. *Research on Sentencing: The Search for Reform.* Washington, D.C.: National Academy Press.

*Board of Commissioners v. Backus.* 1864. 29 How. Pr. 33.

*Board of Education of Independent School District No. 92 of Pottawatomie County v. Earls.* 2002. 535 U.S. 822.

Boland, Barbara et al. 1988 (May). *The Prosecution of Felony Arrests, 1982.* Washington, D.C.: National Institute of Justice.

Borchard, Edwin. 1932. *Convicting the Innocent.* Garden City, N.J.: Garden City Publishing Company.

*Bowen v. Kemp.* 1985. 769 F.2d 672 (11th Cir., Ga.).

*Bowles v. U.S.* 1970. 439 F.2d 536 (CADC).

*Boykin v. Alabama.* 1969. 395 U.S. 238.

Bradley, Craig M. 1985. "Two Models of the Fourth Amendment." *Michigan Law Review* 83:1471.

*Brady v. U.S.* 1970. 397 U.S. 742.

Brandes, Wendy. 1989. "Post-Arrest Detention and the Fourth Amendment: Refining the Standard of *Gerstein v. Pugh.*" *Columbia Journal of Law and Contemporary Problems* 22:445–88.

Brazil, Jeff, and Steve Berry. 1992. "Color of Driver Is Key to Stops in I-95 Videos." *Orlando Sentinel,* 23 August.

Brennan, William J. 1977. "State Constitutions and the Protection of Individual Rights." *Harvard Law Review* 90:489–504.

Brewer v. Williams. 1977. 430 U.S. 387.

Brinegar v. United States. 1949. 338 U.S. 160.

Brinkley, Joel. 2004. "From Afghanistan to Saudi Arabia, via Guantanamo." *New York Times,* 16 November.

Brown v. Allen. 1953. 344 U.S. 443.

Brown v. Board of Education. 1954. 347 U.S. 483. Oral Argument.

Brown v. Mississippi. 1936. 297 U.S. 278.

Brown v. Texas. 1979. 443 U.S. 47.

Buckley v. Fitzsimmons. 1993. 509 U.S. 259.

Burch v. Louisiana. 1979. 441 U.S. 130.

Burns v. Reed. 1991. 500 U.S. 478.

California v. Acevedo. 1991. 500 U.S. 565.

California v. Beheler. 1983. 463 U.S. 1121.

California v. Ciraolo. 1986. 476 U.S. 207.

California v. Greenwood. 1988. 486 U.S. 35.

California v. Hodari D. 1991. 499 U.S. 621.

Campaign for an Effective Crime Policy. 1993 (October). "Evaluating Mandatory Minimum Sentences." Washington, D.C.: Campaign for an Effective Crime Policy (unpublished manuscript).

Cardozo, Benjamin. 1921. *The Nature of the Judicial Process.* New Haven, Conn.: Yale University Press.

Carlson, Jonathan. 1987. "The Act Requirement and the Foundations of the Entrapment Defense." *Virginia Law Review* 73:1011.

Carroll v. U.S. 1925. 267 U.S. 132.

Cassell, Paul. 1996. "*Miranda's* Social Costs: An Empirical Reassessment." *Northwestern University Law Review* 90:387.

Chandler v. Florida. 1981. 499 U.S. 560.

Chandler v. Fretag. 1954. 348 U.S. 3.

Chimel v. California. 1969. 395 U.S. 752.

Ciucci v. Illinois. 1958. 356 U.S. 571.

Cloud, Morgan. 1985. "Search and Seizure by the Numbers: The Drug Courier Profile and Judicial Review of Investigative Formulas." *Boston University Law Review* 65:843.

Coke, Edward. 1797. *The Second Part of the Institutes of the Laws of England.* 5th ed. London: Brooke.

Coker v. Georgia. 1977. 433 U.S. 584.

Cole, David. 1999. *No Equal Justice.* New York: New Press.

Coleman, Howard, and Eric Swenson. 1994. *DNA in the Courtroom: A Trial Watcher's Guide.* Seattle: Genelex Corp.

Colorado v. Bertine. 1987. 479 U.S. 367.

Colorado v. Connelly. 1986. 479 U.S. 157.

Commonwealth v. Neilson. 1996. 666 N.E.2d 984 (Mass.).

Commonwealth v. Zook. 1989. 553 A.2d 920 (Pa.).

Connecticut v. Barrett. 1987. 479 U.S. 523.

Copacino, John M. 1994. "Suspicionless Criminal Seizures After *Michigan Department of State Police v. Sitz.*" *American Criminal Law Review* 31:215.

Corpus Juris Secundum. 2003. St Paul, Minn.: West, § 61.

Cortner, Richard C. 1981. *The Supreme Court and the Second Bill of Rights.* Madison: University of Wisconsin Press.

County of Riverside v. McLaughlin. 1991. 500 U.S. 44.

Criminal Justice Newsletter. 1993 (November 15). Washington, D.C.: Pace Publications.

Crist v. Bretz. 1978. 437 U.S. 28.

Cronin, Thomas E. et al. 1981. *U.S. v. Crime in the Streets.* Bloomington: Indiana University Press.

Crooker v. California. 1958. 357 U.S. 433.

Cruz v. City of Laramie. 2001. 239 F.3d 1183 (CA10 Wyo.).

Culombe v. Connecticut. 1961. 367 U.S. 568.

Cupp v. Murphy. 1973. 412 U.S. 291.

Davenport, Jennifer L., and Steven Penrod. 1997. "Eyewitness Identification Evidence: Evaluating Commonsense Evaluations." *Psychology, Public Policy, and Law* 3:338–61.

Davies, Thomas Y. 1983. "A Hard Look at What We Know (and Still Need to Learn) about the 'Social Costs' of the Exclusionary Rule: The NIJ Study and Other Studies of 'Lost' Arrests." *American Bar Foundation Research Journal* 640.

_____. 1999. "Recovering the Original Fourth Amendment." *Michigan Law Review* 98:547.

Deorle v. Rutherford. 2001. 272 F.3d 1272 (CA9 Calif.).

DeShaney v. Winnebago County. 1989. 489 U.S. 189.

Dickerson v. U.S. 2000. 530 U.S. 428.

Dix, George E. 1985. "Nonarrest Investigatory Detentions in Search and Seizure Law." *Duke Law Journal* 849.

Dorman v. U.S. 1974. 419 U.S. 945.

Dow Chemical Co. v. U.S. 1986. 476 U.S. 227.

Doyle, Charles. 2002. *The USA Patriot Act: A Legal Analysis.* Congressional Research Service.

Draper v. Reynolds. 2004. 369 F.3d 1270 (CA11 Ga.).

Draper v. U.S. 1959. 358 U.S. 307.

Drizin, Steven A., and Marissa J. Reich. 2004. "Heeding the Lessons of History: The Need for Mandatory Recording of Police Interrogations to Accurately Assess the Reliability and Voluntariness of Confessions." *Drake Law Review* 52:619.

Dukes v. Waitkevitch. 1976. 536 F.2d 469 (CA1 Mass.).

Duncan v. Louisiana. 1968. 391 U.S. 145.

Dunlop v. U.S. 1897. 165 U.S. 486.

Dworkin, Ronald. 2004. "What the Court Really Said." *New York Review of Books*, August 12.

Eggan, Dan. 2007. "Court Will Oversee Wiretap Program; Change Does Not Settle Qualms about Privacy." *Washington Post*, 19 January.

Elkins v. U.S. 1960. 364 U.S. 206.

Elsea, Jennifer. 2001. *Terrorism and the Law of War: Trying Terrorists as War Criminals before Military Commissions.* Washington, D.C.: Congressional Research Service.

Enmund v. Florida. 1982. 458 U.S. 782.

Ervin, Sam J., Jr. 1983. "The Exclusionary Rule: An Essential Ingredient of the Fourth Amendment." *Supreme Court Review.* Chicago: University of Chicago Press.

Escobedo v. Illinois. 1964. 378 U.S. 478.

Estelle v. Williams. 1976. 425 U.S. 501.

Ewing v. California. 2003. 538 U.S. 11.

Ex Parte Milligan. 1866. 71 U.S. 2.

*Federalist Papers.* 1961. [1788]. Middletown, Conn.: Wesleyan University Press.

*Federal Rules of Criminal Procedure.* 2002. 41(d)(3). http://www.law.cornell.edu/rules/frcrmp/Rule4.htm.

Feeley, Malcolm M. 1979. *The Process Is the Punishment: Handling Cases in a Lower Criminal Court.* New York: Russell Sage Foundation.

Fisher, Sydney George F. 1888. "The Suspension of Habeas Corpus during the War of Rebellion." *Political Science Quarterly* 3.

*Florida v. Bostick.* 1991. 501 U.S. 429.

*Florida v. Jimeno.* 1991. 500 U.S. 248.

*Florida v. J. L.* 2000. 529 U.S. 266.

*Florida v. Royer.* 1983. 460 U.S. 491.

Foote, Caleb. 1965. "The Coming Constitutional Crisis in Bail." *University of Pennsylvania Law Review* 113:959–1185.

*Fraizer v. Roberts.* 1971. 441 F.2d 1224 (CA8 Ark.).

Frankel, Marvin E., and Gary F. Naftalis. 1977. *The Grand Jury: An Institution on Trial.* New York: Hill and Wang.

Friendly, Henry J. 1965. "The Bill of Rights as a Code of Criminal Procedure." *California Law Review* 53:929.

———. 1968. "The Fifth Amendment Tomorrow: The Case for Constitutional Change." *University of Cincinnati Law Review* 37:671.

*Frisbie v. Collins.* 1952. 342 U.S. 519.

*Frye v. U.S.* 1923. 293 F. 1013 (CADC).

*Gardner v. Florida.* 1977. 430 U.S. 349.

Gardner, James A. 1991. "The Failed Discourse of State Constitutionalism." *Michigan Law Review* 90:761.

Garner, Bryan A. 1987. *Dictionary of Modern Legal Usage.* New York: Oxford University Press.

Gayarré, Charles. 1903. *History of Louisiana,* Vol. IV. New Orleans: F.F. Hansell & Bro.

*Georgia v. Randolph.* 2006. 126 S.Ct. 1515.

*Gerstein v. Pugh.* 1975. 420 U.S. 103.

Giannelli, Paul C. 1991. "Criminal Discovery, Scientific Evidence, and DNA." *Vanderbilt Law Review* 44.

*Gideon v. Wainwright.* 1963. 372 U.S. 335.

Goldberg, Stephanie. 1992 (April). "A New Day for DNA?" *American Bar Association Journal* 78.

Goldstein, Abraham S. 1987. "The Search Warrant, the Magistrate, and Judicial Review." *New York University Law Review* 62:1173.

Goldstein, Joseph. 1960. "The State and the Accused: Balance and Advantage in Criminal Procedure." *Yale Law Journal* 69.

*Graham v. Connor.* 1989. 490 U.S. 386.

Graham, Fred. 1970. *The Self-Inflicted Wound.* New York: Macmillan.

Graham, Kenneth, and Leon Letwin. 1971. "The Preliminary Hearing in Los Angeles: Some Field Findings and Legal-Policy Questions." *UCLA Law Review* 18:636.

*Gregg v. Georgia.* 1976. 428 U.S. 153.

*Griffin v. Wisconsin.* 1987. 483 U.S. 868.

Griswold, David B. 1994. "Complaints against the Police: Predicting Dispositions." *Journal of Criminal Justice* 22.

Gross, Samuel R. 1987. "Loss of Innocence: Eyewitness Identification and Proof of Guilt." *Journal of Legal Studies* 16.

Haddad, James B. 1977. "Well-Delineated Exceptions, Claims of Sham, and Fourfold Probable Cause." *Journal of Criminal Law and Criminology* 68:198–225.

Hall, Jerome. 1942. "Objectives of Federal Criminal Rules Revision." *Yale Law Journal* 725.

Hall, John Wesley, Jr. 1993. *Search and Seizure.* 2nd ed. New York: Clark, Boardman, Callaghan.

Hamblett, Mark. 2003. "Tough Questions for U.S. on Detention." *Legal Times,* 24 November.

*Hamdan v. Rumsfeld.* 2006. 126 S.Ct. 2749.

*Hamdan v. Rumsfeld.* 2006. U.S. District Court for the District of Columbia. Civil Action 04-1519-JR.

*Hamdi v. Rumsfeld.* 2004. 542 U.S. 507.

Hamilton, Alexander. 1788. "The Federalist No. 78: The Judiciary Department."

Hancock, Catherine. 1982. "State Court Activism and Searches Incident to Arrest." *Virginia Law Review* 68:1085.

Hand, Learned. 1922. *U.S. v. Garsson.* 291 Fed. 646 (S.D.N.Y.).

*Harmelin v. Michigan.* 1991. 501 U.S. 957.

*Harris v. U.S.* 1947. 331 U.S. 145.

*Harris v. U.S.* 2002. 536 U.S. 545.

Harris, David A. 1998. "Particularized Suspicion, Categorical Judgments: Supreme Court Rhetoric versus Lower Court Reality under *Terry v. Ohio.*" *St. John's Law Review* 72:975.

Hartney, Christopher. 2006 (November). *Fact Sheet.* San Francisco: National Council on Crime and Delinquency.

*Hayes v. Florida.* 1985. 470 U.S. 811.

*Heath v. Alabama.* 1985. 474 U.S. 82.

*Hedgepeth v. Washington Metro Area Transit and others.* 2003. 284 F.Supp.2nd 145 (D.C.C.).

*Henderson v. Florida.* 1985. 473 U.S. 916.

*Henderson v. U.S.* 1967. 390 F.2d 805 (CA9 Calif.).

*Hester v. U.S.* 1924. 265 U.S. 57.

Hickey, Thomas, and Michael Axline. 1992. "Drunk-Driving Roadblocks under State Constitutions: A Reasonable Alternative to *Michigan v. Sitz.*" *Criminal Law Bulletin* 28.

Hockett, Jeffrey D. 1991. "Justice Robert H. Jackson, the Supreme Court, and the Nuremberg Trial." *Supreme Court Review.* Chicago: University of Chicago Press.

*Holbrook v. Flynn.* 1986. 475 U.S. 560.

*Holy Bible, King James Version.* 1990. Nashville: Thomas Nelson.

*Horton v. California.* 1990. 496 U.S. 128.

*Hudson v. Palmer.* 1984. 468 U.S. 523.

*Hurtado v. California.* 1884. 110 U.S. 516.

*Illinois v. Allen.* 1970. 397 U.S. 337.

*Illinois v. Caballes.* 2005. 543 U.S. 405.

*Illinois v. Rodriquez.* 1990. 497 U.S. 177.

*Illinois v. Somerville.* 1973. 410 U.S. 458.

*Illinois v. Wardlow.* 2000. 528 U.S. 119.

*Imbler v. Pachtman.* 1976. 424 U.S. 409.

Inbau, Fred E. 1961. "Police Interrogation and Limitations." *Journal of Criminal Law, Criminology, and Police Science* 52:19.

Inbau, Fred E., James R. Thompson, James B. Zagel, and James P. Manak. 1984. *Criminal Law and Its Administration,* 4th ed. Mineola, N.Y.: Foundation Press.

*In re Sealed Case 96-3167.* 1998. 153 F.3d 759 (CADC).

*In re Winship.* 1970. 397 U.S. 358.

*INS v. Delgado.* 1984. 466 U.S. 210.

*Isom v. Town of Warren.* 2004. 360 F.3d 7 (CA1 R.I.).

Israel, Jerold H. 1982. "Selective Incorporation: Revisited." *Georgetown Law Journal* 71:274.

Jackson, Robert. 1940. "The Federal Prosecutor." *Journal of Criminal Law and Criminology* 31:3.

*Jacobson v. U.S.* 1992. 503 U.S. 540.

Jefferson, Thomas. 1904. *Works.* London: Putnam and Sons.

Johns, Margaret Z. 2005. "Reconsidering Absolute Prosecutorial Immunity. 2005." *Brigham University Law Review* 53.

*Johnson v. Louisiana.* 1972. 406 U.S. 356.

*Johnson v. Zerbst.* 1938. 304 U.S. 458.

Jonas, Daniel S. 1989. "Comment, Pretextual Searches, and the Fourth Amendment: Unconstitutional Abuses of Power." *University of Pennsylvania Law Review* 137:1791.

*Jones v. U.S.* 1959. 266 F.2d 924 (CADC).

Juvelir, Hon. Michael R. 1998. "A Prosecutor's Perspective." *St. John's Law Review* 72:741.

*Kalina v. Fletcher.* 1997. 522 U.S. 118.

Kamisar, Yale. 1984. "*Gates,* 'Probable Cause,' 'Good Faith,' and Beyond." *Iowa Law Review* 69:551.

*Katz v. U.S.* 1967. 389 U.S. 347, 88 S.Ct. 507, 19 L.Ed.2d 576.

Katz, Lewis. 2004. "*Terry v. Ohio* at Thirty-Five: A Revisionist View." *Mississippi Law Journal* 74:423.

*Kennedy v. Hardiman.* 1988. 684 F.Supp. 540 (U.S. District Court, N.D. Illinois, Eastern Division).

Kennedy, Randall. 1997. *Race, Crime, and the Law.* New York: Random House.

*Kentucky v. Stincer.* 1987. 107 S.Ct. 2658.

*Ker v. California.* 1963. 374 U.S. 23.

*Ker v. Illinois.* 1886. 119 U.S. 436.

*Kirby v. Illinois.* 1972. 406 U.S. 682.

*Klopfer v. North Carolina.* 1967. 386 U.S. 213.

*Knowles v. Iowa.* 1998. 525 U.S. 113.

Koehler, Jonathan J. 1995. "Error and Exaggeration in the Presentation of DNA Evidence at Trial." *Jurimetrics Journal* 34.

*Kopec v. Tate.* 2004. 361 F.3d 772 (CA3 Penn.).

Kreiling, Kenneth R. 1993. "DNA Technology in Forensic Science." *Jurimetrics Journal* 33.

*Kuha v. City of Minnetonka.* 2003. 365 F.3d 590 (CA8 Minn.).

Kurland, Philip B., and Gerhard Casper, eds. 1975. "Brief for the NAACP Legal Defense and Educational Fund, Inc., as Amicus Curiae." In the case of *Terry v. Ohio,* *Landmark Briefs and Arguments of the Supreme Court of the United States.* Washington, D.C.: University Publications of America.

*Kyllo v. U.S.* 2001. 533 U.S. 27.

LaFave, Wayne R. 1993. "Police Rule Making and the Fourth Amendment." In *Discretion in Criminal Justice,* edited by Lloyd Ohlin and Frank Remington. Albany, N.Y.: State University of New York Press.

———. 2004. *Search and Seizure.* 4th ed. St. Paul, Minn.: Thomson West.

LaFave, Wayne R., and Jerold H. Israel. 1984. *Criminal Procedure.* St. Paul, Minn.: West.

LaFave, Wayne R., Jerold H. Israel, and Nancy J. King. 2004. *Criminal Procedure.* 4th ed. St. Paul, Minn.: Thomson West.

*Lanza v. New York.* 1962. 370 U.S. 139.

Latzer, Barry. 1991. *State Constitutions and Criminal Justice.* Westport, Conn.: Greenwood.

Lee, F. N. n.d. *King Alfred the Great and Our Common Law.* http://www.dr-fnlee.org/docs6/alfred/alfred.pdf.

Leo, Richard A. 1996. "The Impact of *Miranda* Revisited." *Journal of Criminal Law and Criminology* 86:621.

———. 1998. "From Coercion to Deception: The Changing Nature of Police Interrogation in America." In *The Miranda Debate: Law, Justice and Policing,* edited by Richard Leo and George C. Thomas III. Boston: Northeastern University, 2002.

Leo, Richard A., and Richard J. Ofshe. 1998. "The Consequences of False Confessions: Deprivations of Liberty and Miscarriages of Justice in the Age of Psychological Interrogation." *Journal of Criminal Law and Criminology* 88:429.

Levy, Leonard. 1968. *The Origins of the Fifth Amendment.* New York: Oxford University Press.

Lewis, Anthony. 1994. "The Blackmun Legacy." *New York Times,* 8 April.

Lichtenberg, Illya. 2001. "*Miranda* in Ohio: The Effects of 'Voluntary' Waiver of Fourth Amendment Rights." *Howard Law Journal* 44:349.

*Lisenba v. California.* 1941. 314 U.S. 219.

*Llaguno v. Mingey.* 1985. 763 F.2d 1560 (CA7 Ill.).

*Lockett v. Ohio.* 1978. 438 U.S. 586.

*Lockhart v. McCree.* 1986. 476 U.S. 162.

Loftus, Elizabeth. 1996. *Eyewitness Identification.* Rev. ed. Cambridge: Harvard University Press.

Madison, James. 1787. "The Federalist No. 51." In *The Federalist,* edited by Jacob E. Cooke. Middletown, Conn.: Wesleyan University Press, 1961, 349.

*Malloy v. Hogan.* 1964. 378 U.S. 1.

*Manson v. Brathwaite.* 1977. 432 U.S. 98.

*Mapp v. Ohio.* 1961. 367 U.S. 643.

*Marbury v. Madison.* 1803. 5 U.S. 137.

Marcus, Paul. 1986. "The Development of Entrapment Law." *Wayne Law Review* 336:5.

*Marshall v. Lonberger.* 1983. 459 U.S. 422.

*Mary Beth G. v. City of Chicago.* 1983. 723 F.2d 1262 (7th Cir., Ill.).

*Maryland v. Wilson.* 1997. 519 U.S. 408.

*Massiah v. U.S.* 1964. 377 U.S. 201.

*McCleskey v. Kemp.* 1987. 481 U.S. 279.

*McCleskey v. Zant.* 1991. 499 U.S. 467.

*McCormick v. City of Fort Lauderdale.* 2003. 333 F.3d 1234 (CA11 Fla.).

*McCulloch v. Maryland.* 1819. 17 U.S. 316.

*McFadden v. Cabana.* 1988. 851 F.2d 784 (CA5 Miss.).

*Michigan v. Clifford.* 1984. 464 U.S. 287.

*Michigan v. Sitz.* 1993. 506 N.W.2d 209.

*Michigan v. Summers.* 1981. 452 U.S. 692.

Military Instruction No. 10. 2006. "Certain Evidentiary Determinations." U.S. Department of Defense. http://www.defenselink.mil/news/Mar2006/d20060327MCI10.pdf.

*Miller v. Clark County.* 2003. 340 F. 3d 959 (CA9 Wash.).

*Minnesota v. Dickerson.* 1993. 508 U.S. 366.

*Minnesota v. Murphy.* 1984. 465 U.S. 420.

Minnesota Rules of Criminal Procedure. 2006. http://www.courts.state.mn.us/rules/criminal/RCRP.htm#cr501 (visited December 27, 2006).

*Miranda v. Arizona.* 1966. 384 U.S. 436, 86 S.Ct. 1602.

*Missouri v. Seibert.* 2004. 542 U.S. 600.

*Monell v. New York City Department of Social Services.* 1978. 436 U.S. 658.

Moore, Mark H. et al. 1984. *Dangerous Offenders: The Elusive Target of Justice.* Cambridge, Mass.: Harvard University Press.

*Moran v. Burbine.* 1986. 475 U.S. 412.

Moskovitz, Myron. 2002. "A Rule in Search of a Reason: An Empirical Reexamination of *Chimel* and *Belton*." *Michigan Law Review* 2002:657–97.

Moylan, Charles E., Jr. 1977. "The Fourth Amendment Inapplicable vs. The Fourth Amendment Satisfied: The Neglected Threshold of 'So What.'" *Southern Illinois University Law Journal* 75.

Murphy, Shelley. 2003. "Prosecutors Defend 'Sneak and Peek' Warrant." *Boston Globe,* 20 October.

*Murray v. U.S.* 1988. 487 U.S. 533.

*Myers v. Commonwealth.* 1973. 298 N.E.2d 819 (Mass.).

Nadler, Janice. 2002. "No Need to Shout: Bus Sweeps and the Psychology of Coercion." *Supreme Court Review.* Chicago: University of Chicago Press.

Nardulli, Peter F. 1983 (Summer). "The Societal Cost of the Exclusionary Rule: An Empirical Assessment." *American Bar Foundation Research Journal* 585–609.

_____. 1987. "The Societal Cost of the Exclusionary Rule: Revisited." *University of Illinois Law Review* 585–609.

National Council on Crime and Delinquency. 1992. *Criminal Justice Sentencing Policy Statement.* San Francisco: NCCD.

*National Law Journal.* 1979 (September 10). "Pagano Case Points Finger at Lineups."

*National Treasury Employees Union v. Von Raab.* 1989. 489 U.S. 656.

Nelson, William E. 1988. *The Fourteenth Amendment: From Political Principle to Judicial Doctrine.* Cambridge, Mass.: Harvard University Press.

*New Jersey v. T. L. O.* 1985. 469 U.S. 325.

*New York v. Belton.* 1981. 453 U.S. 454.

*New York v. Quarles.* 1984. 467 U.S. 649.

*New York v. Zenger.* 1735. 17 Howell's St. Tr. 675, 721–22.

*Nix v. Williams.* 1984. 467 U.S. 431.

*North Carolina v. Alford.* 1970. 400 U.S. 25.

*North Carolina v. Butler.* 1979. 441 U.S. 369.

*Ohio v. Roberts.* 1980. 448 U.S. 56.

*Ohio v. Robinette.* 1996. 117 S.Ct. 417.

*Oliver v. U.S.* 1984. 466 U.S. 170.

*Olmstead v. U.S.* 1928. 277 U.S. 438.

*Oregon v. Mathiason.* 1977. 429 U.S. 492.

*Orozco v. Texas.* 1969. 394 U.S. 324.

*Orr v. State.* 1980. 382 So.2d 860 (Fla.App.).

*Padgett v. Donald.* 2005. 401 F.3d 1273 (CA11 Ga.).

*Palko v. Connecticut.* 1937. 302 U.S. 319.

Pate, Anthony M., and Lorie A Fridell. 1993. *Police Use of Force: Official Reports, Citizen Complaints, and Legal Consequences.* Washington, D.C.: Police Foundation.

Patton, Allison. 1993. "The Endless Cycle of Abuse: Why 42 U.S.C. § 1983 Is Ineffective in Deterring Police Brutality." *Hastings Law Journal* 44:753.

*Payne v. Pauley.* 2003. 337 F.3d 767 (CA7 Ill.).

*Payton v. New York.* 1980. 445 U.S. 573.

*Pearce v. Pearce.* 1846. 63 E.R. 950.

*Pennsylvania v. Mimms.* 1977. 434 U.S. 106.

*People v. Brooks.* 1989. 257 Cal.Rptr. 840 (Cal.App.).

*People v. Brown.* 1969. 248 N.E.2d 867 (N.Y.).

*People v. Camargo.* 1986. 516 N.Y.S.2d 1004 (N.Y.).

*People v. Castro.* 1989. 545 N.Y.S.2d 985 (Bronx Cty.).

*People v. Courtney.* 1970. 90 Cal.Rptr. 370. (Cal.App.3d).

*People v. Defore.* 1926. 150 N.E.2d 585 (Ill.).

*People v. McClellan.* 1969. 457 P.2d 871 (Calif.).

*People v. Mills.* 1904. 70 N.E. 786 (N.Y.).

*People v. Washington.* 1987. 236 Cal.Rptr. 840 (Cal.App.).

Perez, Douglas W. 1994. *Common Sense about Police Review.* Philadelphia: Temple University Press.

*Pinder v. Johnson.* 1995. 54 F.3d 1169 (CA4 Md.).

*Pletan v. Gaines et al.* 1992. 494 N.W.2d 38 (Minn.).

*Pointer v. Texas.* 1965. 380 U.S. 400.

Posner, Richard. 2006. *Not a Suicide Pact: The Constitution in a Time of National Emergency.* New York: Oxford University Press.

Pound, Roscoe. 1921. "The Future of the Criminal Law." *Columbia Law Review* 21.

*Powell v. Alabama.* 1932. 287 U.S. 45.

Presidential Documents. 2001 (September 18). "Declaration of National Emergency by Reason of Certain Terrorist Attacks, Proclamation 7463 of September 14, 2001." *Federal Register* 66, no. 181:48199. http:// frwebgate.access.gpo.gov/cgi-bin/getdoc .cgi?dbname= 2001_register&docid=01-23358-filed.

_____. 2001 (November 16). "Military Tribunals for Non-Citizens Involved in Terrorism Activities; Authorization (Military Order of November 13, 2001), Administrative Orders." *Federal Register* 66,

no. 222: 57831–36 [01–28904]. http://frwebgate
.access.gpo.gov/cgi-bin/getdoc.cgi?dbname=2001_
register&docid=01-28904-filed.

*Pugh v. Rainwater.* 1977. 557 F.2d 1189 (CA5 Fla.).

*Rasul v. Bush.* 2004. 542 U.S. 466.

Raymond, Margaret. 1999. "Down on the Corner, Out on
the Street: Considering the Character of the Neighborhood in Evaluating Reasonable Suspicion." *Ohio
State Law Journal* 90:99.

Read, Conyers, ed. 1962. *William Lambarde and Local Government.* Ithaca, N.Y.: Cornell University Press.

Rehnquist, William H. 1974. "Is an Expanded Right of
Privacy Consistent with Fair and Effective Law Enforce-
ment? Or: Privacy, You've Come a Long Way Baby."
*Kansas Law Review* 23.

*Reid v. Georgia.* 1980. 448 U.S. 438.

Remington, Frank. 1960. "The Law Relating to 'On the
Street' Detention, Questioning, and Frisking of
Suspected Persons and Police Arrest Privileges in
General." *Journal of Criminal Law, Criminology, and
Police Science* 50.

Rehnquist, William. 2000. *Dickerson v. U.S.* http://www
.oyez.org/ media/item?type=audio&id=opinion&
parent=cases/1990-1999/1999/1999_99_5525.

*Report to the Nation on Crime and Justice.* 1988. 2nd ed.
Washington, D.C.: Bureau of Justice Statistics.

*Rhode Island v. Innis.* 1980. 446 U.S. 291.

*Richards v. Wisconsin.* 1997. 520 U.S. 385.

Risen, James, and Eric Lichtblau. 2005. "Bush Lets U.S.
Spy on Callers without Courts." *New York Times,*
16 December.

*Rivera v. Murphy.* 1992. 979 F.2d 259 (1st Cir., Mass.).

*Robinson v. California.* 1962. 370 U.S. 660.

*Robinson v. Township of Redford.* 2002. 48 Fed. Appx. 925
(CA6 Mich., not published).

*Rochin v. California.* 1952. 342 U.S. 165.

*Rogan v. Los Angeles.* 1987. 668 F.Supp. 1384 (CD Cal.).

*Rogers v. Richmond.* 1961. 365 U.S. 534.

*Roper v. Simmons.* 2005. 543 U.S. 551.

*Rose v. Lundy.* 1982. 455 U.S. 509.

*Ross v. Moffitt.* 1974. 417 U.S. 600.

Ross, Brian, and Richard Esposito. 2005 (November 18).
"CIA's Harsh Interrogation Techniques Lead to
Questionable Confessions, Sometimes to Death."
ABC News. http://abcnews.go.com/WNT/
Investigation/story?id=1322866.

Rossiter, Clinton. 1948. *Constitutional Dictatorship.*
Princeton, N.J.: Princeton University Press.

Rothman, David. 1971. *The Discovery of the Asylum.*
Boston: Little, Brown.

Rozas, Angela, and Joshua Howes. 2003. "2 Juries
Dubious over Confession Tapes' Merits; They
Wanted More Interrogations Included." *Chicago
Tribune,* 17 August.

Rudstein, David S. 1990/1991. "White on White: Anonymous Tips, Reasonable Suspicion, and the Constitution." *Kentucky Law Journal* 79:661.

*Ruffin v. Commonwealth.* 1871. 62 Va. 1025.

*Rummell v. Estelle.* 1980. 445 U.S. 263.

*Rumsfeld v. Padilla.* 2004. 542 U.S. 426.

Samaha, Joel. 1978. "Discretion and Law in the Early Penitential Books." In *Social Psychology and Discretionary
Law,* edited by Richard Abt. New York: Norton.

———. 1989. "Fixed Sentences and Judicial Discretion in
Historical Perspective." *William Mitchell Law Review*
15:217.

*Samson v. California.* 2006. 126 S.Ct. 2193.

*Sanders v. City of Houston.* 1982. 543 F.Supp. 694 (S.D.
Texas).

Schauer, Frederick. 1987. "Precedent." *Stanford Law
Review* 39.

Schlag, Pierre. 1982. "Assaults on the Exclusionary Rule:
Good Faith, Limitations, and Damage Remedies."
*Journal of Criminal Law and Criminology* 73:875.

*Schmerber v. California.* 1966. 384 U.S. 757.

*Schneckloth v. Bustamonte.* 1973. 412 U.S. 218.

Schroeder, William A. 1981. "Deterring Fourth Amendment Violations." *Georgetown Law Journal* 69:1361.

Schulhofer, Stephen J. 1993. "Rethinking Mandatory
Minimums." *Wake Forest Law Review* 28.

*Scott v. Illinois.* 1979. 440 U.S. 367.

Seidman, Louis. 2002. "Confessions." *Encyclopedia of Crime
and Justice.* 2nd ed. New York: Macmillan Reference.

*Sheppard v Maxwell.* 1966. 384 U.S. 333.

*Sherman v. U.S.* 1958. 356 U.S. 369.

*Sibron v. New York.* 1968. 392 U.S. 40.

*Silverthorne Lumber Company v. U.S.* 1920. 251 U.S. 385.

*Sitz v. Michigan.* 1993. 506 N.W.2d 219 (Mich.).

*Skinner v. Railway Labor Executive Association.* 1989. 489
U.S. 602.

Skolnick, Jerome. 1998. "*Terry* and Community Policing."
*St. Johns Law Review* 72:1265.

Slobogin, Christopher. 1998. *Criminal Procedure: Regulation of Police Investigation.* Charlottesville, Va.: LEXIS
Law Publishing.

———. 1999. "Why Liberals Should Chuck the Exclusionary Rule." *University of Illinois Law Review* 363.

———. 2003. "Toward Taping." *Ohio State Journal of
Criminal Law* 1:309.

*Smith v. Illinois.* 1968. 390 U.S. 129.

*Smith v. Maryland.* 1979. 442 U.S. 745.

Smith, Brandon. 2004. "Hamdi Release Delayed by Negotiation Dispute with Saudi Arabia." *Jurist Legal News
and Research.* http://jurist.law.pitt.edu/paperchase/
2004/09/hamdi-release-delayed-by-negotiation.php
(visited January 6, 2007).

Smith, Page. 1962. *John Adams.* New York: Doubleday.

"Sneak and Peek Warrants and the USA Patriot Act." 2002
(September). *Georgia Defender.* http://www.law.uga
.edu/academics/profiles/dwilkes_more/37patriot.html
(visited May 8, 2007).

*Sparf and Hansen v. U.S.* 1895. 156 U.S. 51.

Spitzer, Eliot. 1999. *The New York City Police Department's
"Stop & Frisk" Practices: A Report to the People of the
State of New York from the Attorney General.* New York:
Civil Rights Bureau.

*Stack v. Boyle.* 1951. 342 U.S. 1.

*Stanford Law Review.* 1977. "Notes: Did Your Eyes Deceive You? Expert Psychological Testimony on the Unreliability of Eyewitness Identification." *Stanford Law Review* 29.

*State v. Bowe.* 1994. 881 P.2d 538.

*State v. Bumpus.* 1990. 459 N.W.2d 619 (Iowa).

*State v. Carty.* 2002. 790 A.2d 903 (N.J.).

*State v. Cook.* 2004. 847 A.2d 530 (N.J.).

*State v. Fitiwi.* 2003. Minnesota Court of Appeals (not reported).

*State v. Holeman.* 1985. 693 P.2d 89 (Wash.).

*State v. Ladson.* 1999. 979 P.2d 833 (Wash.).

*State v. Raines.* 2004. 857 A.2d 19 (Md.).

*State v. Richards.* 1996. 549 N.W.2d 218 (Wisc.).

*State v. Ricks.* 1989. 771 P.2d 1364 (Alaska.App.).

*State v. Ross.* 2001. 639 N.W.2d 225 (Wisc.App.).

*State v. Scales.* 1994. 518 N.W.2d 587 (Minn.).

*State v. Superior Court.* 1978. 589 P.2d 48 (Ariz.App.).

*State v. Wilkins.* 1983. 473 A.2d 295 (Vt.).

*State v. Wright.* 2001. WL 96203 (Minn.App.).

*Stein v. New York.* 1953. 346 U.S. 156.

*Stephan v. State.* 1985. 711 P.2d 1156 (Alaska).

Stern, Loren G. 1967. "Stop and Frisk: An Historical Answer to a Modern Problem." *Journal of Criminal Law, Criminology, and Police Science* 58.

Stewart, Potter. 1983. "The Road to *Mapp v. Ohio* and Beyond: The Origins, Development, and Future of the Exclusionary Rule in Search-and-Seizure Cases." *Columbia Law Review* 83.

*Stone v. Powell.* 1976. 428 U.S. 465.

*Stovall v. Denno.* 1967. 388 U.S. 293.

*Strickland v. Washington.* 1984. 104 S.Ct. 2052.

*Strunk v. U.S.* 1973. 412 U.S. 434.

Stuntz, William. 2002. "Search and Seizure." In *Encyclopedia of Crime and Justice,* 2nd ed., edited by Joshua Dressler. New York: Thomson Learning.

Sutton, Paul. 1986. "The Fourth Amendment in Action: An Empirical View of the Search Warrant Process." *Criminal Law Bulletin* 22:405.

*Swindler v. State.* 1979. 592 S.W.2d 91 (Ark.).

Taylor, Telford. 1969. *Two Studies in Constitutional Interpretation.* Columbus: Ohio State University Press.

*Tennessee v. Garner.* 1985. 471 U.S. 1.

*Terry v. Ohio.* 1968. 392 U.S. 1.

*Thompson v. Utah.* 1898. 170 U.S. 343.

Thompson, William C. 1993. "Evaluating the Admissibility of New Genetic Identification Tests: Lessons from the 'DNA War.'" *Journal of Criminal Law and Criminology* 84.

Tiffany, Lawrence P., Donald M. McIntyre, Jr., and Daniel L. Rotenberg. 1967. *Detection of Crime: Stopping and Questioning, Search and Seizure, Encouragement, and Entrapment.* Boston: Little, Brown.

Toborg, Mary A. 1981. *Pretrial Release: A National Evaluation of Practices and Outcomes.* Washington, D.C.: National Institute of Justice.

*Townsend v. Sain.* 1963. 372 U.S. 293.

*Turner v. Murray.* 1986. 476 U.S. 28.

*Twenty-Sixth Annual Review of Criminal Procedure.* 1997. *Georgetown Law Journal* 85.

Uchida, Craig, and Timothy Bynum. 1991. "Criminology: Search Warrants, Motions to Suppress and 'Lost Cases': The Effects of the Exclusionary Rule in Seven Jurisdictions." *Journal of Criminal Law and Criminology* 81:103.

Uelman, Gerald F. 1980. "Testing the Assumptions of *Neil v. Biggers*: An Experiment in Eyewitness Identification." *Criminal Law Bulletin* 16:359–68.

*U.S. v. Abrahams.* 1978. 575 F.2d 3 (CA1 Mass.).

*U.S. v. Armstrong.* 1996. 517 U.S. 456.

*U.S. v. Banks.* 1995. 78 F.3d 1190 (CA7 Ill.).

*U.S. v. Banks.* 2003. 540 U.S. 31.

*U.S. v. Barahona.* 1993. 990 F.2d 412 (CA8 Mo.).

*U.S. v. Blake.* 1988. 718 F.Supp. (S.D.Fla.).

*U.S. v. Booker.* 2005. 543 U.S. 220.

*U.S. v. Brigoni-Ponce.* 1975. 422 U.S. 873.

*U.S. v. Caicedo.* 1996. 85 F.3d 1184 (6th Cir., Ohio).

*U.S. v. Calandra.* 1974. 414 U.S. 338.

*U.S. v. Ceballos.* 1987. 812 F.2d 42 (2nd Cir., N.Y.).

*U.S. v. Cortez.* 1979. 595 F.2d 505 (CA9 Ariz.).

*U.S. v. Cortez.* 1981. 449 U.S. 411.

*U.S. v. Craner.* 1981. 652 F.2d 23 (CA9 Calif.).

*U.S. v. Crews.* 1980. 445 U.S. 463.

*U.S. v. Doe.* 1985. 819 F.2d 206 (CA9 Ariz.).

*U.S. v. Dougherty.* 1972. 473 F.2d 1113 (CADC).

*U.S. v. Drayton.* 2002. 536 U.S. 194.

*U.S. v. Dunn.* 1987. 480 U.S. 294.

*U.S. v. Edwards.* 1974. 415 U.S. 800.

*U.S. v. Elmore.* 1979. 595 F.2d 1036 (CA5 Ga.).

*U.S. v. Freitas.* 1988. 800 F.2d 1451 (CA9 Calif.).

*U.S. v. Garcia-Camacho.* 1995. 53 F.3d 244 (9th Cir., Calif.).

*U.S. v. Gray.* 2004. 369 F.3d 1024 (CA8 Ark.).

*U.S. v. Halls.* 1995. 40 F.3d 275 (8th Cir., Iowa).

*U.S. v. Jaramillo.* 1994. 25 F.3d 1146 (2nd Cir., N.Y.).

*U.S. v. Kelly.* 2002. 302 F.3d 291 (CA5 Texas).

*U.S. v. Kim.* 1976. 415 F.Supp. 1252 (D.Hawaii).

*U.S. v. Knapp.* 1993. 1 F.3d 1026 (CA10 Colo.).

*U.S. v. Knights.* 2001. 524 U.S. 112.

*U.S. v. Lambert.* 1995. 46 F.3d 1064 (10th Cir., Kans.).

*U.S. v. Leon.* 1984. 468 U.S. 897.

*U.S. v. Lindsey.* 1989. 877 F.2d 777 (CA9 Calif.).

*U.S. v. Marion.* 1971. 404 U.S. 307.

*U.S. v. McCargo.* 2006. 464 F.3d 192 (CA2 N.Y.).

*U.S. v. Mendenhall.* 1980. 446 U.S. 544, 100 S.Ct. 1870, 64 L.Ed.2d 497.

*U.S. v. Miller.* 1976. 425 U.S. 435.

*U.S. v. Miner.* 1973. 484 F.2d 1075 (CA9 Calif.).

*U.S. v. Mitchell.* 1959. 179 F.Supp. 636 (CADC).

*U.S. v. Montoya de Hernandez.* 1985. 473 U.S. 531.

*U.S. v. Moscatiello.* 1985. 771 F.2d 589 (CA1 Mass.).

*U.S. v. Perez.* 1824. 22 U.S. (9 Wheat.) 579.

*U.S. v. Ramsey.* 1977. 431 U.S. 606.

*U.S. v. Robinson.* 1973. 414 U.S. 218.

*U.S. v. Rodney.* 1992. 956 F.2d 295 (CADC).

*U.S. v. Salerno.* 1987. 481 U.S. 739.

*U.S. v. Sanchez-Meza.* 1976. 547 F.2d 461 (CA9 Calif.).

*U.S. v. Sanders.* 2005. 424 F.3d 768 (CA8 Iowa).

*U.S. v. Santana.* 1976. 427 U.S. 38.

*U.S. v. Sharpe and Savage.* 1985. 470 U.S. 675.

*U.S. v. Smith.* 1986. 799 F.2d 704 (11th Cir., Fla.).

*U.S. v. Sokolow.* 1989. 490 U.S. 1.

*U.S. v. Spikes.* 1998. 158 F.3d 913 (CA6 Ohio).

*U.S. v. Tapia.* 1990. 912 F.2d 1367 (11th Cir., Ala.).

*U.S. v. Udziela.* 1982. 671 F.2d 995 (CA7 Ill.).

*U.S. v. Vaneaton.* 1995. 49 F.3d 1423 (CA9 Ore.).

*U.S. v. Villegas.* 1990. 899 F.2d 1324 (CA2 N.Y.).

*U.S. v. Warner.* 1988. 843 F.2d 401 (CA9 Calif.).

*U.S. v. Watson.* 1976. 423 U.S. 411.

*U.S. v. Weaver.* 1992. 966 F.2d 391 (CA8 Mo.).

*U.S. v. White.* 1971. 401 U.S. 745.

*U.S. v. Winsor.* 1988. 846 F.2d 1569 (CA9 Calif.).

USA Patriot Act. 2001. P.L. 107-156, 115 Stat. 272.

U.S. Code. 2002. Title 42. http://uscode.house.gov/ uscode-cgi/fastweb.exe?search.

_____. 2003. Chapter 119, Wire and Electronic Communications Interceptions and Interceptions of Oral Communications. http://www4.law.cornell.edu/ uscode/18/pIch119.html.

_____. 2007. § 1861. "Access to Certain Business Records for Foreign Intelligence and International Terrorism Investigations. Title 50, Chapter 36, Subchapter IV, § 1861. http://www.law.cornell.edu/ uscode/search/display.html?terms=1861(a)(1)&url=/ uscode/html/uscode50/usc_sec_50_00001861- - - -000- .html (visited January 21, 2007).

U.S. Congress. 1954. Senate, Committee on the Judiciary, Hearing before the Subcommittee to Investigate Juvenile Delinquency, Miami, Florida, 83d Cong., 2d sess. Washington, D.C.: Government Printing Office.

U.S. Congress. 1970. H. Rep. No. 1444, 91st Cong., 2nd sess. Washington, D.C.: Government Printing Office.

U.S. Department of Defense. 2007. "Military Commissions." http://www.defenselink.mil/news/commissionsmanual .html (visited May 8, 2007).

*U.S. ex rel. Latimore v. Sielaff.* 1977. 561 F.2d 691 (CA7 Ill.).

U.S. Senate. 2001 (September 14). Authorization for the Use of Military Force. S.J. Res. 23. 107th Cong., 1st sess. http://news.findlaw.com/hdocs/docs/terrorism/ sjres23.enr.html.

U.S. Sentencing Commission. 1991. *Mandatory Minimum Penalties in the Federal Criminal Justice System.* Washington, D.C.: U.S. Sentencing Commission.

Uviller, H. Richard. 1986. "Seizure by Gunshot: The Riddle of the Fleeing Felon." *New York University Review of Law of Social Change* 14:705.

_____. 1988. *Tempered Zeal.* Chicago/New York: Contemporary Books.

Van Dyke, Jon. 1977. *Jury Selection Procedures.* Cambridge, Mass.: Ballinger.

*Vernonia School District v. Acton.* 1995. 515 U.S. 646.

*Vinyard v. Wilson.* 2002. 311 F.3d 1340 (CA11 Ga.).

*Walder v. U.S.* 1954. 347 U.S. 62.

Walker, Samuel, and Vic W. Bumpus. 1992. "The Effectiveness of Civilian Review." *American Journal of Police* 11.

Wallace, Henry Scott. 1993 (September). "Mandatory Minimums and the Betrayal of Sentencing Reform: A Legislative Dr. Jekyll and Mr. Hyde." *Federal Probation.*

*Warden v. Hayden.* 1967. 387 U.S. 294.

*Washington v. Texas.* 1967. 388 U.S. 14.

*Watkins v. Virginia.* 1986. 475 U.S. 1099.

*Watts v. Indiana.* 1949. 338 U.S. 49.

*Weeks v. U.S.* 1914. 232 U.S. 383.

Weiner, William P., and Larry S. Royster. 1991. "Sobriety Checkpoints in Michigan: The *Sitz* Case and Its Aftermath." *T. M. Cooley Law Review* 8:243.

Wells, Gary L. 2002. "Eyewitness Identification: Psychological Aspects." In *Encyclopedia of Crime and Justice,* 2nd ed., edited by Joshua Dressler. New York: Thomson Learning.

Wells, Gary L., and Eric Seelau. 1995. "Eyewitness Identification: Psychological Research and Legal Policy on Lineups." *Psychology, Public Policy, and Law* 1:765.

Wells, Gary L., and Elizabeth A. Olson. 2003. "Eyewitness Testimony." *Annual Review of Psychology* 54: 277–95.

Whitebread, Charles H., and Christopher Slobogin. 2000. *Criminal Procedure.* New York: Foundation Press.

*Whren v. U.S.* 1996. 517 U.S. 806.

*Whren v. U.S.* 1996a. "Petitioners' Brief." http://www .soc.umn.edu/~samaha/cases/whren_v_us_petitioner .htm.

*Williams v. Florida.* 1970. 399 U.S. 78.

*Williams v. New York.* 1949. 337 U.S. 241.

*Wilson v. Arkansas.* 1995. 514 U.S. 927.

*Wolf v. Colorado.* 1949. 338 U.S. 25.

*Wong Sun v. U.S.* 1963. 371 U.S. 471.

*Wyoming v. Houghton.* 1999. 526 U.S. 295.

Yant, Martin. 1991. *Presumed Guilty: When Innocent People Are Wrongly Convicted.* Buffalo: Prometheus Books.

*Ybarra v. Illinois.* 1979. 44 U.S. 85.

Younger, Richard D. 1963. *The People's Panel.* Providence, R.I.: Brown University Press.

# Case Index

# Index